PENGUIN BOOKS

THE PENGUIN BOOK OF HINDU NAMES FOR BOYS

Gandhi was born on 26 August 1956 and was educated at School, Sanawar. She was a magazine editor and columnist before sh ... rked on a career in politics. She is currently a Member of Parliament. Sh ... been Minister of State for Environment and Forests, a post she h ... 1991, and was later appointed Minister of State for Social Justice a ... owerment in 1998.

M ... Gandhi has authored *Sanjay Gandhi*, *Brahma's Hair* (a book on th ... ology of Indian plants) and *Rainbow and Other Stories*, and co-au ... d *The Complete Book of Muslim and Parsi Names* with Ozair H ... Her special interests include Indian mythology, animal welfare (s ... the Managing Trustee of the Ruth Cowell Foundation, which runs th ... ay Gandhi Animal Welfare Centre, India's largest animal hospital ar ... er) and issues related to environmental conservation.

S ... in Delhi with her son, Feroze Varun.

The Penguin Book of Hindu Names for Boys

MANEKA GANDHI

PENGUIN BOOKS

PENGUIN BOOKS
Published by the Penguin Group
Penguin Books India Pvt Ltd, 11 Community Centre, Panchsheel Park, New Delhi 110 017, India
Penguin Group (USA) Inc., 375 Hudson Street, New York, New York 10014, USA
Penguin Group (Canada), 90 Eglinton Avenue East, Suite 700, Toronto, Ontario, M4P 2Y3, Canada (a division of Pearson Penguin Canada Inc.)
Penguin Books Ltd, 80 Strand, London WC2R 0RL, England
Penguin Ireland, 25 St Stephen's Green, Dublin 2, Ireland (a division of Penguin Books Ltd)
Penguin Group (Australia), 250 Camberwell Road, Camberwell, Victoria 3124, Australia (a division of Pearson Australia Group Pty Ltd)
Penguin Group (NZ), cnr Airborne and Rosedale Road, Albany, Auckland 1310, New Zealand (a division of Pearson New Zealand Ltd)
Penguin Group (South Africa) (Pty) Ltd, 24 Sturdee Avenue, Rosebank, Johannesburg 2196, South Africa

Penguin Books Ltd, Registered Offices: 80 Strand, London WC2R 0RL, England

First published by Penguin Books India 2004

10 9 8 7 6 5 4

Typeset by Vans International Limited, Mumbai
Printed at Baba Barkhanath Printers, New Delhi

To Aaryaman, the reason for this book

Introduction

This book started with the realization that I did not know the meaning of my name. All I knew was that Menaka (I spell it Maneka) was the name of an apsara in the court of Indra. No one I had encountered knew the meaning of their names either. Like me, they had been named after historical or mythological people. I hunted for a book, but while the libraries are full of information about the gods, I did not come across one book in India which gave the meaning of the name. What does Sarasvati mean? No, not 'learning' even though she is the goddess of that, but 'full of water'. Chandrashekhar does not mean Shiva but one who bears the moon on his forehead. I waited for someone to write a book but the two that emerged listed 'Menaka' as 'apsara'. When my sister announced that a baby was on the way, I decided to compile the dictionary myself.

The Vedic rishis believed that the name defined the child's character—its face, figure, temper, morals, tastes and profession. The name Anamika or 'without a name' for instance, would ensure that the child's future was what she wanted to make it—since she was not hedged in by any preordained limitations. Most of us look for phonetically pleasing names without realizing their significance. But Minna means 'fat' and Ambika means 'little mother', Sita means 'furrow', Mina means 'fish' and Draupadi has no meaning other than 'daughter of Drupada'. A number of names which are very common do not have any meaning at all. Anita, Lina, Rina and Tina for instance, come from languages other than Indian. If Roma is of Indian origin it means 'hairy'! The Phul, Sona and Pyar family (Phulvati, Phulrani, Sonalika, Soriam, Pyari) have no roots in Sanskrit, Pali or any of the classical Indian languages. Rishma and Rashmini simply do not exist. Malvika is a combination name that has no meaning. (There is however a plant of the Ipomoea family called Malvika.) My mother's name Amteshwar is a corruption of, I think, Amritesvara or lord of the amrita. Alternatively it has no meaning at all Names like Bina are distortions of Vina (the musical instrument), Bihari is not from Bihar, for instance, but from Vihari or roamer. I have left out the local versions of the classical name (Poonam comes from Purnima, Rakhi from Rakshaka, for instance) or the local diminutives or corruptions (e.g. Lacchman or Lakha for Lakshman, Upinder for Upendra, Vanti for Vati). The only exception I have made is for Rima which is a corruption of Hrim—since this happened to be my copy editor's name!

A lot of the names in India are combination names. Two primary names (usually of two gods or of a god and goddess) taken and made into one. For instance Ramakrishna or Radheshyam and in some cases, the conjoining of two gods produces an entirely new deity. I have tried to give as many combinations as possible, especially where there is a historical or mythological person with that compound. However the compounds can be infinite—and a lot of distortion of the primary names takes place in the mixture. Punjab is full of Gurveens, Tarveens, Harleens, Hargurbirinders and Harkirats. Some combinations are unique to certain regions in the country. The suffixes of Jit, Mita and Inder/Indra to the main name are usually from Punjab, Haryana and Rajasthan. Swamy, Appa, Amma show Tamil Nadu and Karnataka. The nagas or serpents who formed such an integral part of pre-Vedic and Vedic mythology are now confined to south and east India—e.g. Seshan, Nagabhushan, Phenamani. Even Manasa, the goddess of serpents, is a name far more common in Bengal than anywhere else in India.

The entries in this dictionary have been designed so that each entry is divided into three categories:

1. The exact or literal meaning. For instance Menaka means 'daughter of Mena'.

2. The intended meaning or rather, the meaning of the meaning. Menaka's intended meaning is 'of the mountains' because, in Indian mythology, Mena is the consort of Himavan who is the lord of the Himalayas.

3. This is divided into two sub-categories. The first is the locating of the name in mythology, history, literature, botany or ornithology. If the name denotes a person out of mythology, history or literature I have tried to give the name of the mythological consort, the children and the name of the dynasty, as well as the names of Sanskrit Vedic commentators, grammarians and playwrights. I have included the names that come from plants, trees, birds and animals along with their Latin and English names.

The last sub-category is 'another name for—'. In Menaka's case, it is 'another name for Parvati' as Parvati was born a daughter of Himavan in her incarnation as Uma. (The name Parvati also means of the mountains.)

I have read the *Mahabharata*, the *Ramayana*, the *Kathasaritsagara*, the *Panchatantra*, the listings of all the Vedas and Upanishads, books on Sanskrit plants and birds, the catalogues that list the thousand names of each major god, Vedic and Puranic encyclopaedias and the Buddhist and Jaina mythologies and histories and, of course, Sanskrit dictionaries to unearth the meanings of the names in this book. Very often the meaning of the name sounds bizarre unless one knows the context. Aparna which is another name for Parvati in her incarnation as Himavan's daughter means 'leafless'. This is explained by the legend of Parvati fasting to marry Shiva.

One result of this search has been new and unexpected perceptions into the traditional Indian way of life. For instance, what is truth? Or again, what is right and what is wrong? Jaya and Vijaya were the two door-keepers of Vishnu's palace in Vaikuntha. One day they were cursed by Lakshmi to be reborn on the earth as mortals. Vishnu modified the curse on his two devoted servants by saying that if they were killed thrice by him, they could come back to Vaikuntha. Jaya and Vijaya chose to be reborn as the most evil (or what we define as evil within the parameters of morality set by our religion) asuras or anti-gods Hiranyaksha and Hiranyakashipu, Ravana and Kumbhakarna, Shisupala and Dantavaktra so that their deaths at the hands of Vishnu—in his incarnation of Narasimha, Rama and Krishna—became quick and inevitable. So were these asuras good or bad? It was inevitable that Sita be separated from Rama for she had imprisoned a pregnant female parrot and had been cursed by the consort of the parrot to suffer the same fate. So, is Rama to be blamed for listening to the jibes of a washerman or was his action inevitable? Krishna means dark or black and Arjuna fair or white. They are reborn from Nara and Narayana or man and superman/god. Do they represent people or the Eastern philosophy of yin and yang, two opposites that fuse to complete? I find my attitude towards people and current affairs, goals and achievements, and even the pursuit of happiness or rather the diminishing of pain has changed with the unfolding of the history of each mythological character.

I would like to thank all the people who helped me in the preparation of this book. The friends who brought in the odd name in the beginning, those who pitched in to type the manuscript over and over again, the pandits and Sanskrit teachers who corrected my mistakes, the editors at Penguin who put the work into order and spent hours proof-reading and inserting new words till the last minute. I have used the Sanskrit classical style of spelling with diacritical marks, to help in the correct pronunciation of the names.

New Delhi — *Maneka Gandhi*

Guide to the Use of the Book

How to Read an Entry

1. All Sanskrit words are marked (S).
2. Genders are differentiated as follows—(M) denotes male.
3. The definition of each name is listed in a numbered sequence in the following order: the subdivision marked '1' gives the literal meaning; '2' is the implied or intended meaning and '3' places the name in its specific mythological/literary/botanical context. Some entries do not feature all the subdivisions as these are not required.
4. All books and scriptures referred to in abbreviated form in the entries are expanded in full at the end of the book.

Pronunciation

ā	—	*fa*ther
ī	—	eagle/pol*i*ce
ū	—	r*u*de
ṛ	—	mer*r*ily
ṅ	—	ki*ng*
ć	—	*ch*ick
ćh	—	*ch*hota
ñ	—	si*ng*e
ṭ	—	*t*omato
ṭh	—	an*th*ill
ḍ	—	*d*rum
ḍh	—	re*dh*aied
ṇ	—	no*ne*
ś	—	*s*ure
ş	—	*sh*un
ṇ or ṁ	—	nasal sound

A

Abādhya (S) (M) **1.** not to be opposed. 2. invincible; ever victorious.

Abala (S) (M) **1.** powerless. 2. weak. 3. a son of Pāńcajañya (*M. Bh.*).

Abālendu (S) (M) **1.** not the nascent moon. 2. the full moon.

Abdhiśayana (S) (M) **1.** sleeping on the ocean. 2. another name for Viṣṇu.

Ābhāsa (S) (M) splendour; light; colour; reflection.

Ābhāsvara (S) (M) **1.** shining one. 3. a class of 64 minor deities who are attendants of Śiva (*Ś. Purāṇa*).

Ābhāta (S) (M) **1.** shining; blazing. 2. appearing; visible.

Abhaya (S) (M) **1.** without fear. 2. undaunted. 3. a son of Bimbisāra (*M. Bh.*); a son of Idhmajīhva (*Bh. Purāṇa*); a son of Dhṛtarāṣṭra (*M. Bh.*); another name for Śiva; the Black Myrobalan tree (*Terminalia chebula*); Khuskhus grass (*Vetiveria zizanioides*).

Abhayada (S) (M) **1.** giving safety. 3. a Jaina Arhat; a son of Manasyu and father of Sudhanvan.

Abhayānanda (S) (M) delighting in fearlessness.

Abhayaṇkara (S) (M) one who causes safety.

Abhayaprada (S) (M) 1. bestower of safety. 3. an Arhat of the Jainas (*J.S. Koṣa*); another name for Viṣṇu.

Abhayasinha (S) (M) fearless lion.

Abhi (S) (M) fearless.

Abhibhava (S) (M) overpowering; powerful; victorious.

Abhibhū (S) (M) **1.** to overcome; predominate; surpass; conquer. 3. a king of the nāgas (*M. Bh.*); the son of the king of Kāśī (*M. Bh.*).

Abhićandra (S) (M) **1.** with a moon-like face. 3. one of the 7 Manus of the Śvetāmbara Jaina sect (*J.S. Koṣa*).

Abhidī (S) (M) radiant.

Abhidīpa (S) (M) illuminated.

Abhidyu (S) (M) heavenly; bright.

Abhigīta (S) (M) praised in song.

Abhihita (S) (M) **1.** expression. 2. word; name.

Abhijana (S) (M) **1.** of noble descent. 2. ornament of a family.

Abhijāta (S) (M) **1.** well-born. 2. fit; proper; wise; learned; handsome; noble.

Abhijaya (S) (M) conquest; complete victory.

Abhiji (S) (M) to conquer completely.

Abhijit (S) (M) **1.** one who has been conquered; one who has conquered. 2. victorious; conquering completely; born under the constellation Abhijit. 3. a son of Punarvasu (*A. Veda*); a star or 22nd constellation (*J. Śāstra*); another name for Viṣṇu.

Abhijñāna (S) (M) recollection; remembrance; a sign or token of remembrance.

Abhijvala (S) (M) blazing forth.

Abhīka (S) (M) **1.** fearless. 2. a passionate lover.

Abhikāma (S) (M) affection; desire.

Abhikāṅkṣa (S) (M) wish; desire; longing.

Abhikhyāna (S) (M) fame; glory.

Abhilāṣin (S) (M) one who desires.

Abhīma (S) (M) **1.** one who causes no fear. 2. one who destroys fear. 3. another name for Viṣṇu.

Abhimand (S) (M) gladdening.

Abhimānī (S) (M) **1.** full of pride. 3. another name for Agni as the eldest son of Brahmā.

Abhimanyu (S) (M) **1.** with self-respect; heroic; fiery. 3. the son of Arjuna and Subhadrā (*M. Bh.*); son of Manu Ćākṣuṣa and Nadvalā (*R. Taraṅgiṇī*).

Abhimanyusuta (S) (M) **1.** son of Abhimanyu. 3. another name for Parīkṣit.

Abhimatijit (S) (M) **1.** one who conquers the ego. 2. subduing enemies.

Abhimoda (S) (M) joy; delight.

Abhinabhas (S) (M) **1.** one whose glory has reached the heavens. **2.** renowned; famous; sagacious.

Abhināmin (S) (M) **1.** one who has a famous name. **2.** renowned. **3.** a ṛṣi of the 6th Manvantara (*V. Purāṇa*).

Abhinanda (S) (M) **1.** to rejoice; to celebrate. **2.** to praise; to bless; to be glad; delight; pleasure; wish; desire. **3.** the first month; another name for the Supreme Being.

Abhinandana (S) (M) **1.** felicitous. **2.** one who pleases; delighting; pleasing all; welcoming. **3.** the 4th Jaina Arhat of the present Avasarpinī who was the son of King Nābhi and Marudevī of Ayodhyā (*J. S. Koṣa*); a prince mentioned in the *Skanda* and *Maudgala Purāṇa*.

Abhinandin (S) (M) **1.** wishing. **2.** rejoicing.

Abhinandita (S) (M) delighted; made happy; saluted; applauded.

Abhinātha (S) (M) **1.** lord of desires. **3.** another name for Kāma.

Abhinava (S) (M) **1.** new; young; fresh; modern. **3.** a Śākta notable for his great learning and spiritual attainment (7th century) (*R.Taraṅgiṇī*).

Abhinavan (S) (M) innovation.

Abhinīta (S) (M) **1.** well carried. **2.** well performed; highly ornamented; proper; suitable; patient; forgiving; evenminded; kind; friendly.

Abhiniveśa (S) (M) **1.** study. **2.** affection; devotion; determination.

Abhipāda (S) (M) **1.** one who steps fearlessly. **3.** a ṛṣi (*Ṛg. Veda*).

Abhipāla (S) (M) protector.

Abhipuṣpa (S) (M) covered with flowers.

Ābhīra (S) (M) cowherd.

Abhirāja (S) (M) **1.** supreme king. **2.** one who reigns everywhere; to shine; one who is brilliant.

Abhirakṣa (S) (M) one who protects.

Abhirakṣita (S) (M) one who is protected.

Abhirāma (S) (M) **1.** pleasing; delightful; agreeable; beautiful. **3.** another name for Śiva.

Abhiramaṇa (S) (M) one who delights.

Abhirāṣṭra (S) (M) one who conquers kingdoms.

Abhirata (S) (M) **1.** immersed. **2.** one who is immersed in worldly affairs.

Abhīru (S) (M) **1.** not a coward. **2.** one who is fearless; strong and powerful. **3.** a rājaṛṣi (*M. Bh.*); another name for Śiva and Bhairava; *Asparagus racemosa.*

Abhiruċa (S) (M) to be bright; to please.

Abhiruċira (S) (M) extremely beautiful; splendid; pleasant; agreeable.

Abhirūpa (S) (M) **1.** pleasing form. **2.** handsome; charming; well-formed; delightful; beloved; favourite; learned; wise; beautiful. **3.** another name for Śiva, Viṣṇu, Kāma and the moon.

Abhisala (S) (M) convergence.

Abhisāra (S) (M) to spread brightness; companion.

Abhiṣeka (S) (M) **1.** anointing or consecrating. **2.** the installation of a king.

Abhiṣikta (S) (M) **1.** anointed. **2.** enthroned.

Abhisneha (S) (M) affection; desire.

Abhiśoka (S) (M) passionate; loving.

Abhiśri (S) (M) to spread brightness.

Abhīṣu (S) (M) ray of light.

Abhīṣumat (S) (M) **1.** radiant. **3.** another name for the sun.

Abhiśyanta (S) (M) **1.** splendid. **3.** a son of Kuru and Vāhinī (*M. Bh.*).

Abhīta (S) (M) fearless.

Abhivāda (S) (M) reverential salutation.

Abhivīra (S) (M) **1.** surrounded by heroes. **2.** a commander.

Abhivirāja (S) (M) full of brightness.

Abhiyuktākṣika (S) (M)**1.** watchful eyed. **2.** observant. **3.** one of the 49 maruts in the *Brahmāṇḍa Purāṇa.*

Abhra (S) (M) **1.** water bearing; clouds. **2.** the sky.

Abhrakāśin (S) (M) **1.** with clouds for shelter. **2.** that which is open to the sky; an ascetic.

Abhrama (S) (M) one who has no illusions; one who does not blunder; steady; clear.

Abhramūpriya (S) (M) **1.** lover of the steady. **3.** another name for Airāvata, the elephant of the east.

Abhranāga (S) (M) **1.** celestial elephant. **3.** one of the 8 elephants of the quarters (*A. Koṣa*).

Abhrānta (S) (M) **1.** unperplexed. **2.** clear; composed.

Abhraroha (S) (M) **1.** borne by the clouds. **2.** Lapis lazuli.

Abhrottha (S) (M) **1.** cloud born. **3.** Indra's thunderbolt (*A. Koṣa*).

Abhū (S) (M) **1.** unborn; not earthly. **3.** another name for Viṣṇu.

Abhyagni (S) (M) **1.** towards the fire. **3.** a son of Aitaśa (*A. Brāhmaṇa*).

Abhyāvarśini (S) (M) **1.** coming repeatedly. **2.** returning. **3.** a king who was a descendant of Pṛthu (*M. Bh.*).

Abhyudaya (S) (M) **1.** sunrise. **2.** elevation; increase; prosperity; happiness; good result.

Abhyudita (S) (M) elevated; risen; prosperous.

Abīr (S) (M) red powder; the red colour used in Holi festival.

Abja (S) (M) **1.** born in water. **2.** a conch; a lotus (*Nelumbium speciosum*). **3.** a son of Viśāla; another name for Dhanvantari and the moon.

Abjayoni (S) (M) **1.** born of the lotus. **3.** another name for Brahmā.

Abjinipati (S) (M) **1.** lord of lotuses. **3.** another name for Sūrya.

Abjit (S) (M) conquering water.

Aćala (S) (M) **1.** immovable. **2.** mountain; rock. **3.** the son of King Subala of Gāndhāra and brother of Śakuni (*M. Bh.*); a bull who was an attendant of Skanda (*M. Bh.*); one of the 9 deities of the Jainas.

Aćalapati (S) (M) **1.** lord of the immovable. **2.** lord of the mountains.

Aćalendra (S) (M) **1.** lord of the immovable. **2.** lord of the mountains. **3.** the Himālayas.

Aćaleśvara (S) (M) **1.** god of the immovable. **3.** another name for Śiva.

Aćaṇḍa (S) (M) **1.** not of a hot temper; without anger. **2.** gentle; mild.

Āćārya (S) (M) **1.** teacher. **3.** another name for Droṇa, Aśvaghoṣa and Kṛpa.

Āćāryanandana (S) (M) **1.** son of the teacher. **3.** another name for Aśvatthāman.

Āćāryaputra (S) (M) **1.** son of the teacher. **3.** another name for Aśvatthāman.

Āćāryasuta (S) (M) **1.** son of the teacher. **3.** another name for Aśvatthāman.

Āćāryatanaya (S) (M) **1.** son of the teacher. **3.** another name for Aśvatthāman.

Aććhindra (S) (M) flawless; uninterrupted; perfect.

Aććhoda (S) (M) **1.** with clear water. **2.** transparent.

Aćintya (S) (M) **1.** surpassing thought. **2.** incogitable; one who cannot be understood easily. **3.** another name for Śiva.

Aćyuta (S) (M) **1.** immovable. **2.** firm; solid; imperishable; neverfailing. **3.** one of the 24 incarnations of Viṣṇu and Kṛṣṇa (*V. Purāṇa*).

Aćyutāgraja (S) (M) **1.** elder brother. **2.** never failing; more perfect. **3.** another name for Balarāma and Indra.

Aćyutānuja (S) (M) **1.** younger brother of Kṛṣṇa. **3.** another name for Bhīma.

Aćyutarāya (S) (M) worshipper of the infallible; a devotee of Viṣṇu.

Aćyutāyu (S) (M) **1.** with an imperishable life. **3.** a warrior on the Kaurava side (*M. Bh.*).

Āḍambara (S) (M) **1.** a great noise; a drum; the roaring of an elephant. **2.** the highest degree. **3.** an attendant of Skanda given to him by Brahmā (*M. Bh.*).

Adambha (S) (M) **1.** free from deceit. **2.** straightforward. **3.** another name for Śiva.

Ādarśa (S) (M) **1.** principle; ideal; perfection. **2.** that which reveals completely; a mirror; a copy; the day of the new moon; mythology. **3.** the son of the 11th Manu (*H. Purāṇa*).

Aḍḍana (S) (M) shield.

Ādelika (S) (M) **1.** approaching the target; successful. **2.** full of concentration.

Ādeśa (S) (M) command; order; advice; instruction; declaration; precept.

Ādeśvara (S) (M) **1.** lord of command. **3.** another name for Skanda.

Adharma (S) (M) **1.** injustice; unrighteousness. **3.** a prajāpati son of Brahmā who was the husband of Hiṁsā or Mṛṣā; an attendant of the sun.

Adhasaśiras (S) (M) **1.** with the head downward. **3.** a sage (*M. Bh.*).

Adhibhū (S) (M) **1.** superior among beings. **2.** a king.

Adhideva (S) (M) **1.** presiding or tutelary deity. **3.** another name for Kṛṣṇa.

Adhiguṇa (S) (M) with superior qualities.

Adhija (S) (M) superior by birth.

Adhikara (S) (M) **1.** principal. **2.** chief; controller. **3.** another name for Śiva.

Adhikṣita (S) (M) lord; ruler.

Adhilokanātha (S) (M) **1.** lord of the lords of the universe. **2.** that which is divine; a deity.

Adhimuhya (S) (M) **1.** above attraction. **3.** Śākyamuni in one of his 34 births (*V's B. Samhitā*).

Adhinātha (S) (M) supreme lord; a chieftain.

Adhipa (S) (M) one who protects; a ruler; a king.

Adhīra (S) (M) **1.** impatient. **3.** a king who became an attendant of Śiva (*P. Purāṇa*).

Adhirāja (S) (M) supreme leader; an emperor.

Adhiratha (S) (M) **1.** charioteer. **3.** a prince of Aṅga who was the son of Satyakarmā and the foster father of Karṇa (*M. Bh.*).

Ādhirathī (S) (M) **1.** one who is on a chariot. **3.** son of Adhiratha; another name for Karṇa.

Adhirohaṇa (S) (M) ascending.

Adhirukma (S) (M) wearing gold.

Adhīśa (S) (M) lord; master.

Adhīśvara (S) (M) supreme lord; an emperor.

Ādhīta (S) (M) **1.** learned; reflected or meditated upon. **2.** a scholar.

Adhivāhana (S) (M) **1.** beyond motion; one who is on a vehicle. **2.** very fast. **3.** a son of Aṅga.

Adhivirāja (S) (M) surpassing in brightness.

Adhokṣaja (S) (M) **1.** son of the lower regions. **2.** universe. **3.** another name for Viṣṇu and Kṛṣṇa.

Adhokṣaya (S) (M) **1.** resting on the lower regions. **3.** Viṣṇu in his 18th incarnation (*V. Purāṇa*).

Adhṛgu (S) (M) **1.** knower of the inconsistent. **3.** a Ṛg Vedic sage who was a protégé of the aśvins and Indra.

Adhṛṣya (S) (M) **1.** unassailable; invincible. **2.** proud.

Adhṛta (S) (M) **1.** unrestrained; uncontrolled. **3.** another name for Viṣṇu.

Adhvara (S) (M) **1.** not causing any injury. **2.** a sacrifice. **3.** a vasu (*A. Koṣa*).

Adhvaryu (S) (M) **1.** best among the priests. **2.** one who knows how to perform yajñas; Ṛg Vedic priests who represent the 5 planets; the priest who performs the ritual.

Adhyapāyana (S) (M) **1.** divider; distributor. **3.** a disciple of Sumantu who divided the *Atharva Veda* into two parts (*Bhā. Purāṇa*).

Ādi (S) (M) **1.** beginning. **2.** firstborn. **3.** a son of the asura Andhaka killed by Śiva (*P. Purāṇa*).

Ādibuddha (S) (M) **1.** the first seer; the primal Buddha. **2.** perceived in the beginning. **3.** the chief deity of the northern Buddhists (*A. Koṣa*).

Ādidaitya (S) (M) **1.** the first demon. **3.** another name for Hiraṇyakaśipu.

Ādideva (S) (M) **1.** the first god. **3.** another name for Brahmā, Viṣṇu, Śiva, Gaṇeśa and the sun.

Ādigadādhara (S) (M) **1.** he who first handled the mace. **3.** another name for Viṣṇu.

Ādikara (S) (M) **1.** the first creator. **3.** another name for Brahmā.

Ādikavi (S) (M) **1.** the first poet. **3.** another name for Brahmā and Vālmīki.

Ādikūrma (S) (M) **1.** the original tortoise. **3.** the incarnation of Viṣṇu as the tortoise who lifted the Mandāra mountain from the Ocean of Milk (*M. Bh.*).

Ādilakṣmaṇa (S) (M) the primal or only Lakṣmaṇa.

Ādima (S) (M) beginning; root; original.

Ādimūla (S) (M) the primal root.

Ādimūrti (S) (M) **1.** the primal idol. **3.** another name for Viṣṇu.

Adīna (S) (M) noble minded.

Ādinārāyaṇa (S) (M) **1.** the first protector of beings. **3.** the primal Viṣṇu.

Ādinātha (S) (M) **1.** the first lord; the Supreme Lord. **3.** a Jina.

Ādīpa (S) (M) kindled; illuminating.

Ādirāja (S) (M) **1.** the first king. **3.** a son of King Kuru of the Purū dynasty (*M. Bh.*); another name for Manu and Pṛthu.

Ādiratha (S) (M) the first chariot.

Ādiśa (S) (M) ordered; directed; commanded; pointed out.

Ādiśankara (S) (M) **1.** the primal god of welfare. **3.** another name for Śiva.

Ādiśeṣan (S) (M) **1.** the primal residue. **2.** the primal serpent, and supporter of the earth.

Ādisiṁha (S) (M) **1.** the primal lion. **3.** a king of Magadha (*H. Koṣa*).

Ādisiśira (S) (M) **1.** the primal head of religious sacrifice. **3.** a disciple of Śākalya, the son of Vyāsa (*Bhā. Purāṇa*).

Ādīśvara (S) (M) the original god; the Absolute Reality.

Ādit (S) (M) first.

Ādita (S) (M) the sun.

Āditeya (S) (M) **1.** son of Aditī. **3.** another name for the sun.

Āditya (S) (M) **1.** belonging to Aditī. **3.** patronymics of 33 of sage Kaśyapa and Aditī's children of whom the most prominent are Dhātā, Mitra, Aryamā, Rudra, Varuṇa, Sūrya, Bhaga, Vivasvān, Pūṣā, Dakṣa, Śakra, Aṅśa, Savitā, Tvaṣṭā and Viṣṇu and these 33 are the fathers of the 33 crore devatās of whom the eldest is Indra and the youngest Vāmana (*M. Bh.*).

Ādityabandhu (S) (M) **1.** friend of the sun. **3.** another name for Sākyamuni.

Ādityabhakta (S) (M) **1.** devotee of the sun. **3.** the plant *Cleome viscosa.*

Ādityagarbha (S) (M) **1.** with the sun as his matrix. **3.** a Bodhisattva (*A. Koṣa*).

Ādityakeśava (S) (M) **1.** the sun and Viṣṇu conjoined. **2.** with long shining hair. **3.** an idol of Viṣṇu (*M. Bh.*).

Ādityaketu (S) (M) **1.** sun bannered. **3.** a son of Dhṛtarāṣṭra (*M. Bh.*).

Ādityaprabhā (S) (M) with the splendour of the sun.

Ādityanandana (S) (M) **1.** son of the sun. **3.** another name for Karṇa.

Ādityasenā (S) (M) **1.** with a glorious army. **2.** one who has a powerful army; one who is well protected; a commander. **3.** a king of the Gupta dynasty of Magadha (*M. Ćarita*).

Ādityasena (S) (M) **1.** with the sun as master. **2.** Sūrya, lord of the ādityas. **3.** a Magadha king (*M. Ćarita*).

Ādityasūnu (S) (M) **1.** son of the sun. **3.** another name for Sugrīva, Yama and Manu.

Ādityavardhana (S) (M) **1.** one who increases glory. **2.** augmented by the sun. **3.** the grandfather of Harṣavardhana (*K. Sāgara*).

Ādityavarman (S) (M) protected by the ādityas.

Ādityavarṇa (S) (M) with the colour of the sun.

Ādityeśa (S) (M) **1.** lord of the ādityas. **3.** another name for the sun.

Ādivaki (S) (M) **1.** the first seer. **3.** another name for Brahmā.

Ādivarāha (S) (M) **1.** the first boar. **3.** Viṣṇu in his boar incarnation.

Admaṇi (S) (M) fire.

Adra (S) (M) **1.** hard; rock. **3.** a solar dynasty king (*M. Bh.*).

Adri (S) (M) **1.** hard; rock; mountain; thunderbolt; cloud; the sun; the number 7 (according to the Hindu scriptures, there are 7 main sacred mountains in the universe and the term Adri, apart from meaning a mountain, is also the name of the 7th mountain of the universe — hence, number 7 is one of the construed meanings). **3.** a king who was the son of Viśvagāśva and the father of Yuvanāśva (*M. Bh.*); a grandson of Pṛthu (*M. Bh.*); the thunderbolt of Indra (*M. Bh.*).

Adrigu (S) (M) **1.** one who goes to the mountains. **3.** a protégé of the aśvins and Indra (*Ṛg Veda*).

Adrīndra (S) (M) **1.** lord of the mountains. **3.** the Himālaya.

Adripati (S) (M) **1.** master of the mountains. **3.** the Himālaya.

Adrīśa (S) (M) lord of the mountains.

Adrupa (S) (M) **1.** consuming the earth. **3.** a son of Bali.

Adūra (S) (M) **1.** not far; near; omnipresent. **2.** soul.

Adūṣita (S) (M) **1.** unspotted; irreproachable. **2.** without guile.

Advaita (S) (M) **1.** with no duplicate; sole; unique. **3.** an Upaniṣad; another name for Viṣṇu and Brahmā.

Advaya (S) (M) **1.** without a second; unique. **2.** one who does not believe in duality. **3.** a Buddha (*A. Koṣa*).

Advayānanda (S) (M) **1.** absolute bliss. **3.** a 15th century founder of a Vaiṣṇava sect in Bengal.

Advika (S) (M) unique.

Advitīya (S) (M) without a second; unique; matchless.

Ādyaśaraṇa (S) (M) protected by the Absolute; taking shelter in the Absolute.

Ādyota (S) (M) **1.** surrounded by light. **2.** brilliant.

Agādhi (S) (M) deep; incogitable; indescribable; unfathomable.

Āgama (S) (M) **1.** coming forth; birth. **2.** knowledge; wisdom.

Agarva (S) (M) free from pride.

Agasti (S) (M) **1.** thrower of mountains. **3.** another name for Agastya; the *Sesbania grandiflora* tree.

Agastya (S) (M) **1.** thrower of mountains. **2.** one who humbles even the mountain. **3.** a great sage who, once while travelling south, had found the Vindhya Mountains in his way and, in order to proceed further, had commanded them to lie down, this sage is believed to have been born in a water jar, is considered the son of Pulastya and Havirbhū — a daughter of sage Kardama according to the Purāṇas, the son of Mitra and Varuṇa by Urvaśī, the husband of Lopāmudrā, the father of Idhmavāha, the preceptor of Droṇa, the presenter of Viṣṇu's bow to Rāma, (*V. Rāmāyaṇa*) and is regarded as the first teacher of science to the Dravidian tribes in South India and is believed to have been immortalized as the star Canopus; the *Sesbania grandiflora* tree; another name for Śiva and the star Canopus.

Agavāha (S) (M) **1.** borne by fire; borne by a mountain; the lord of all the yajñas. **2.** all the oblations poured into the fire. **3.** a son of Vasudeva (*Bhā. Purāṇa*).

Agendra (S) (M) king of the mountains.

Agha (S) (M) **1.** sinful. **3.** an asura follower of Kaṇsa who was the brother of Pūtanā (*Bhā. Parāṇa*).

Aghaghna (S) (M) **1.** destroyer of sin. **2.** one who is virtuous; pious. **3.** another name for Viṣṇu.

Aghamarṣaṇa (S) (M) **1.** destroying sin. **3.** a Vedic ṛṣi who was the author of the doctrine of time (*M. Bh.*).

Aghora (S) (M) **1.** not terrible. **3.** a worshipper of Śiva and Durgā (*Ś. Parāṇa*); another name for Śiva.

Āghrikā (S) (M) **1.** one who sprinkles the fat in the oblation. **2.** one who participates in religious activities. **3.** a son of Viśvāmitra (*M. Bh.*).

Āghṛṇi (S) (M) **1.** glowing with heat. **3.** another name for Pūṣan.

Āghṛṇīvasu (S) (M) **1.** rich with heat. **3.** another name for Agni.

Agira (S) (M) **1.** the sun. **2.** fire. **3.** a rākṣasa (*A. Koṣa*).

Āgneya (S) (M) **1.** son of Agni. **3.** another name for Kārttikeya and Agastya.

Agni (S) (M) **1.** fire. **2.** gold: one of the 5 elements of the universe. **3.** a prominent deity of the *Ṛg Veda,* represented as the eldest son of Brahmā in the post Vedic age, the son of sage Aṅgiras as a marut, as also the son of Saṁyu and Satyā, the grandson of Śāṇḍilya who is appointed by Brahmā as the sovereign of the Quarter between the East and the South, represented as also the grandson of Bṛhaspati the twin brother of Indra, the husband of Sudarśanā and Svāhā, the father of Dakṣiṇam, Gārhapatyam, Āhavanīyam (*D. Bhāgavata*), Pāvaka, Pavamāna, Śući, Dhṛṣṭadyumna, Subrahmaṇya. Bhṛgu and Nīla the monkey, the preceptor of the gods, protector of ceremonies, men, the head, the summit of the sky, the centre of the earth and the conferer of immortality (*A. Purāṇa*).

Agnibāhu (S) (M) **1.** the arms of fire. **2.** smoke. **3.** a son of the first Manu (*H. Purāṇa*); a son of Priyavrata and Kāmyā (*V. Purāṇa*); a seer of the 14th Manvantara (*V. Purāṇa*).

Agnibha (S) (M) **1.** shining like fire. **2.** gold.

Agnibhaṭṭa (S) (M) **1.** as noble as fire. **3.** another name for Agni and the maruts.

Agnibhū (S) (M) **1.** born of fire. **3.** another name for Skanda.

Agnibhūti (S) (M) **1.** produced from fire. **2.** with the lustre of fire. **3.** one of the main disciples of Mahāvīra (*J. literature*).

Agnibīja (S) (M) **1.** the seed of fire. **2.** gold.

Agnidatta (S) (M) **1.** given by fire. **2.** given to the fire. **3.** one who is born as a result of yajña.

Āgnīdhra (S) (M) **1.** descendant of fire. **3.** a son of Priyavrata and Barhiṣmatī, the husband of Pūrvaćittī and the father of Kuru, Nābhi, Kiṁpuruṣa, Hari, Ilāvrata, Ramyaka, Hirañćaya, Bhadrāśva, Ketumāla (*Bhā. Purāṇa*); a seer of the 14th Manvantara (*M. Ćarita*); a son of Manu Svāyambhuva (*Bhā. Purāṇa*).

Āgnidhraka (S) (M) **1.** descendant of fire. **2.** fire like; shining; glowing. **3.** a ṛṣi of the 12th Manvantara (*M. Ćarita*).

Agnija (S) (M) **1.** born of fire. **2.** gold. **3.** another name for Kārttikeya and Viṣṇu.

Agnijvāla (S) (M) **1.** flame of fire. **3.** another name for Śiva; the *Woodfordia fruticosa* shrub.

Āgnika (S) (M) **1.** born of fire. **3.** the Common Marking Nut tree (*Semecarpus anacardium*).

Agnikaṇa (S) (M) particle of fire; spark.

Agniketu (S) (M) **1.** fire bannered. **2.** with fire as the characteristic feature. **3.** a rākṣasa friend of Rāvaṇa (*V. Rāmāyaṇa*).

Agnikumāra (S) (M) **1.** son of Agni. **3.** another name for Subrahmaṇya.

Agnima (S) (M) **1.** torch bearer. **2.** leader; elder brother.

Agnimaśa (S) (M) **1.** stinging like fire. **3.** the Intellect tree (*Celastrus paniculata*).

Agnimitra (S) (M) **1.** friend of fire. **3.** a king of the Śuṅga dynasty (150 B.C.) who was the son of Puṣyamitra and a contemporary of Patañjali (*M. Bh.*).

Agnimukha (S) (M) **1.** fire-faced. **3.** an asura who was the son of Śurapadma and Maya's daughter and the grandson of Kaśyapa (*Bhā. Purāṇa*); *Plumbago zeylanica.*

Agnipā (S) (M) **1.** one who drinks fire. **2.** one who protects the fire. **3.** the son of the Brāhmin Vedanidhi and the husband of 5 gandharva maidens (*P. Purāṇa*).

Agnipūrṇa (S) (M) **1.** full of fire. **2.** extremely powerful. **3.** a solar dynasty king who was the grandson of Dhruva; the son of Sudarśana and the father of Śīghra and Maru (*Bhā. Purāṇa*).

Agnirājan (S) (M) **1.** glorified by fire. **2.** with Agni as king. **3.** another name for the vasus.

Agniruha (S) (M) **1.** fire tree. **3.** the Indian Redwood tree (*Soymida febrifuga*).

Agnisambhava (S) (M) **1.** born of fire. **3.** a solar dynasty king who was the son of Upagupta (*V. Rāmāyaṇa*).

Agniśikha (S) (M) **1.** fire crested. **2.** flame of fire; pointed; arrow; lamp. **3.** Vararuci's father (*K. Sāgara*); saffron (*Crocus sativus*).

Agnisiṇha (S) (M) **1.** fiery lion. **3.** the father of the 7th Black Vasudeva (*J. Literature*).

Agnisoma (S) (M) **1.** fire and nectar conjoined. **3.** a deity born of the conjunction of Agni and Soma (*Ṛg Veda*).

Agniśrī (S) (M) with the brightness of fire.

Agniṣṭu (S) (M) **1.** devotee of fire. **3.** a son of Manu Ćākṣuṣa and Nadvalā (*A. Purāṇa*).

Agniṣṭuta (S) (M) **1.** devotee of fire. **2.** praised by fire; glorious; illuminating; enlightening; all-consuming. **3.** a son of Manu Ćākṣuṣa and Nadvalā (*A. Purāṇa*).

Agnisvāmin (S) (M) lord of fire.

Agnitejas (S) (M) **1.** with the energy and lustre of fire. **3.** a ṛṣi of the 11th Mavantara.

Agnivallabha (S) (M) **1.** beloved of fire. **3.** the Indian Dammer tree (*Shorea robusta*).

Agnivarṅa (S) (M) **1.** fire coloured. **2.** red faced; hot; fiery. **3.** a character in Kalidāsa's poem *Raghuvaṁśa*; a son of Sudarśana (*Bhā. Purāṇa*).

Agniveśa (S) (M) **1.** fire clad. **2.** one who is as glorious as the fire. **3.** a sage who was the disciple of Agastya and the preceptor of Droṇa and Drupada (*M. Bh.*); an authority of medicine in ancient India (*M. Bh.*).

Agniveśya (S) (M) **1.** surrounded by fire. **2.** one who offers an oblation. **3.** a sage who was the preceptor of Droṇa and the most learned in Dhanurveda (*M. Bh.*).

Agnivīrya (S) (M) **1.** with the power of fire. **2.** gold.

Agraha (S) (M) **1.** which cannot be held. **2.** an Agni who was the son of the Agni Bhānu and Suprajā (*M. Bh.*).

Agraja (S) (M) born first; eldest.

Agrasena (S) (M) **1.** chief warrior. **3.** a son of Janamejaya.

Āgrayaṅa (S) (M) **1.** leader; oblation of first fruit. **2.** a form of fire; the first *soma* libation. **3.** a son of the agni Bhānu (*M. Bh.*).

Agrayaṇi (S) (M) **1.** leader. **3.** a son of Dhṛtarāṣṭra (*M. Bh.*).

Agreṇī (S) (M) **1.** first; preceding; leader. **3.** an agni who was a son of the Agni Bhānu and Niśādevī (*M. Bh.*).

Agrima (S) (M) first; foremost; best; excellent; eldest.

Aha (S) (M) **1.** affirmation. **2.** ascertainment. **3.** a vasu who was the son of Dharma and Ratidevī (*M. Bh.*); an asura (*M. Bh.*); a sacred pond (*M. Bh.*).

Ahaṁyāti (S) (M) **1.** egoless. **3.** a son of Saṁyāti (*M. Bh.*).

Ahan (S) (M) dawn; morning.

Ahankāra (S) (M) **1.** that which causes the day. **3.** another name for the sun.

Ahanmaṇi (S) (M) **1.** jewel of the day. **2.** the sun.

Ahannātha (S) (M) **1.** lord of the day. **2.** the sun.

Ahanpati (S) (M) **1.** lord of the day. **3.** another name for Śiva and the sun.

Ahanti (S) (M) indestructible.

Ahar (S) (M) **1.** defender. **3.** day personified as a vasu (*M. Bh.*).

Ahara (S) (M) **1.** tormentor. **3.** a son of Kaśyapa and Danu (*M. Bh.*); a Manu (*H. Purāṇa*).

Aharbāndhava (S) (M) **1.** friend of the defenders. **2.** friend of the day. **3.** another name for the sun.

Aharmaṇi (S) (M) **1.** jewel of the day. **3.** another name for the sun.

Aharpati (S) (M) **1.** lord of the day. **3.** another name for the sun and Śiva.

Ahaskara (S) (M) **1.** producing the day. **3.** another name for Sūrya.

Āhavanīya (S) (M) **1.** to be offered as oblation. **2.** perpetual fire; receiver of oblations. **3.** an agni (*M. Bh.*).

Āhavanīyam (S) (M) **1.** offered as an oblation. **3.** a son of Agni.

Ahi (S) (M) **1.** serpent; cloud; water; sun; the number 8. **3.** a ṛṣi; another name for Rāhu.

Ahijīt (S) (M) **1.** conquerer of the serpent. **3.** another name for Kṛṣṇa and Indra.

Ahīkā (S) (M) of heaven and earth; the Silk Cotton tree (*Salmalica malabarica*).

Ahilocana (S) (M) **1.** serpent eyed. **3.** a servant of Śiva (*Ś. Purāṇa*).

Ahima (S) (M) **1.** not cold; hot. **2.** cloud; water; traveller.

Ahimakara (S) (M) **1.** hot rayed. **3.** another name for the sun.

Ahīna (S) (M) **1.** whole; entire; all. **2.** serpent. **3.** another name for Vāsuki the lord of the serpents.

Ahīnagu (S) (M) **1.** excellent ray. **3.** son of Devānika (*H. Purāṇa*).

Ahīndra (S) (M) **1.** lord of serpents. **3.** another name for Vāsuki and Indra.

Ahiratha (S) (M) **1.** having a snake chariot. **3.** a Purū dynasty king (*M. Bh.*).

Ahirbudhnya (S) (M) **1.** one who knows about serpents. **3.** a son of Viśvakarman and Surabhī (*V. Purāṇa*); one of the 11 maruts in the Mahābhārata; a rudra (*M. Bh.*).

Ahīśvara (S) (M) **1.** lord of serpents. **3.** another name for Śeṣa.

Āhlād (S) (M) causing delight; refreshing.

Āhobala (S) (M) very powerful.

Āhovīra (S) (M) **1.** very strong. **3.** a sage (*M. Bh.*).

Āhuka (S) (M) **1.** offerer; sacrificer. **3.** a Yadu king who was the father of Ugrasena and 99 other sons, the grandfather of Kaṇsa (*M. Bh.*) and great grandfather of Kṛṣṇa (*Bhā. Purāṇa*).

Ahupathi (S) (M) **1.** follower of prayer. **2.** a devotee.

Āhuta (S) (M) **1.** invoked; invited. **2.** called; summoned.

Āhuti (S) (M) **1.** invoking; calling; offering oblations. **3.** a king of Jaruthi (*M. Bh.*); a son of Babhru (*M. Bh.*).

Āhvāna (S) (M) invocation.

Aila (S) (M) **1.** born of intellect; the son of Ilā. **3.** a member of the court of Yama (*M. Bh.*); another name for Purūravas.

Aindradyumni (S) (M) **1.** descendant of Indradyumna. **3.** another name for Janaka.

Airāvata (S) (M) **1.** as fast as the wind. **3.** the lord of elephants, the son of Irāvatī, a descendant of Kaśyapa, the steed of Indra and considered to be one of the 8 elephants guarding the universe (*M. Bh.*); a serpent son of Kaśyapa and Kadru whose descendant Ulūpi married Arjuna (*M. Bh.*); an asura killed by Kṛṣṇa (*M. Bh.*).

Aitareya (S) (M) **1.** unique. **3.** a son of sage Māṇḍuki and Itarā and a great scholar of the Vedas (*Sk. Parāṇa*).

Aiteśvara (S) (M) **1.** lord of the agitated; lord of the fighters. **3.** another name for Indra.

Aiyenar (Tamil) (M) **1.** lord or abode of the mountains. **3.** a tutelary deity said to be a son of Viṣṇu or Śiva (*V. Purāṇa*).

Aja (S) (M) **1.** eternal; driver; mover; instigator; leader of a flock; ram. **3.** a solar dynasty king, father of Daśaratha (*M. Bh.*); a son of King Jahnu and father of Uśika (*M. Bh.*); a son of Surabhī (*A. Purāṇa*); a son of Manu Uttama (*V. Purāṇa*); one of the 11 maruts in the *Bhāgavata Purāṇa*; the vehicle of Agni (*A. Purāṇa*); the zodiac sign of Aries; another name for Brahmā, Viṣṇu, Rudra, Indra, Śiva, Kāma, Sūrya and Agni.

Ajagara (S) (M) **1.** python; a large serpent. **3.** a sage (*M. Bh.*); an asura.

Ajagāva (S) (M) **1.** looking after cattle; that which protects cattle. **3.** the bow of Māndhāta and Pṛthu and the Gāṇḍīva of Arjuna (*V. Purāṇa*); a nāga priest.

Ajaikapāda (S) (M) **1.** herdsman. **3.** one of the 11 maruts in the Mahābhārata; another name for Viṣṇu.

Ajaikapāla (S) (M) **1.** herdsman; protector of cattle. **2.** lord of animals, or one of the 11 rudras born to Sthāṇu (*M. Bh.*); a son of Viśvakarman in charge of protecting all the gold in the world (*M. Bh.*); another name for Viṣṇu.

Ajaka (S) (M) **1.** a young goat; a kid. **3.** an asura son of Kaśyapa and Danu (*M. Bh.*); a descendant of Purūravas; a king of Magadha.

Ājakāra (S) (M) **1.** protector of cattle. **3.** the bull of Śiva (*Ś. Purāṇa*).

Ajakāśva (S) (M) **1.** horse of the unborn; horse of a god. **3.** a Purū king who was the son of Jahnu (*M. Bh.*).

Ajakāva (S) (M) **1.** bow of the unborn. **3.** the bow of Śiva (*A. Koṣa*).

Ajamīdha (S) (M) **1.** one who offers goats as a sacrifice. **2.** a devotee of the absolute. **3.** Purū dynasty king who was the son of Hasti, the husband of Dhūminī, Nīlī and Keśinī and the father of Ṛkṣa, Duṣyanta, Jahnu, Praja and Rūpiṇa (*M. Bh.*); a lunar dynasty king who was the father of Saṁvaraṇa and husband of Sudevā (*M. Bh.*); a son of Suhotra (*M. Bh.*); another name for Yudhiṣṭhira and Dhṛtarāṣṭra.

Ajāmila (S) (M) **1.** indisciplined. **3.** a devotee of Viṣṇu (*Bhā. Purāṇa*).

Ajamukha (S) (M) **1.** goatfaced. **3.** a soldier in Skanda's army (*M. Bh.*).

Ajana (S) (M) **1.** instigator. **3.** another name for Brahmā.

Ajānadeva (S) (M) a god by birth.

Ajānidha (S) (M) **1.** treasure or ocean of instigation. **3.** a seer referred to in a hymn of the *Ṛg Veda*.

Ajapa (S) (M) protector of cattle; one who possesses goats; the sacred Barna or the Garlic Pear tree (which provides nourishment to the cattle apart from giving shade) (*Crataeva nurvala*).

Ajapāla (S) (M) **1.** goatherd. **3.** father of Daśaratha.

Ajapārśva (S) (M) **1.** with sides like a goat; one who possesses many goats. **3.** a son of Śvetakarṇa (*M. Bh.*).

Ajasra (S) (M) not to be obstructed.

Ajāta (S) (M) unborn; a god.

Ajātari (S) (M) **1.** having no enemy. **3.** another name for Yudhiṣṭhira.

Ajātaśatru (S) (M) **1.** with no enemy. **2.** with no equal adversary. **3.** a son of Śamīka; a son of Bimbisāra; father of Arbhaka and grandfather of Udayana (*V. Purāṇa*); a king of Kāśi (*K. Upaniṣad*); a son of the earth (*V. Purāṇa*); a son of Vidhisāra (*V. Purāṇa*); another name for Śiva and Yudhiṣṭhira.

Ajavindu (S) (M) **1.** one who has the knowledge of eternity. **3.** a Suvīra king (*M. Bh.*).

Ajaya (S) (M) **1.** one who cannot be conquered. **2.** invincible. **3.** a king of the Bharata dynasty known for his generosity and kindness (*M. Bh.*); another name for Viṣṇu and Agni.

Ajīgarta (S) (M) **1.** one who has nothing to swallow. **3.** a ṛṣi and Śunahśepa's father (*M. Bh.*).

Ajina (S) (M) **1.** skin of a goat; tiger skin. **3.** a son of Havirdhāna and Dhīṣaṇa (*V. Purāṇa*).

Ajinkya (S) (M) invincible.

Ajira (S) (M) **1.** not slow. **2.** agile; rapid. **3.** the Subramaṇyā priest at the snake festival of the Pānćavaṁśa Brāhmaṇa.

Ajīṣa (S) (M) **1.** lord of goats. **3.** another name for Śiva.

Ajita (S) (M) **1.** invincible; irresistible. **3.** the ṛṣis of the 14th Manvantara (*A. Koṣa*); the 2nd Arhat of the present

Avasarpiṇī (*J. Literature*); a future Buddha (*B. Literature*); another name for Viṣṇu and Śiva.

Ajitābha (S) (M) unconquerable brilliance.

Ajitanātha (S) (M) **1.** lord of the invincible. **3.** the 2nd Jaina Tīrthānkara who was the son of King Jitaśatru and Bijoyā of Ayodhyā (*J. Literature*).

Ajitapāla (S) (M) protector of the invincible.

Ajitātman (S) (M) **1.** one whose soul can never be conquered. **2.** pious; chaste; pure.

Ajodara (S) (M) **1.** goat bellied. **3.** a soldier in Skanda's army (*M. Bh.*).

Ājyapa (S) (M) **1.** drinking clarified butter. **3.** sons of Pulastya or Kardama and ancestors of the Vaiśya caste.

Akalaṅka (S) (M) **1.** without stains. **2.** unblemished; flawless.

Akalmāṣa (S) (M) **1.** sinless; pure. **3.** a son of the 4th Manu (*H. Purāṇa*).

Akalpa (S) (M) ornament; decoration.

Akaluṣa (S) (M) unblemished.

Akāma (S) (M) **1.** without lust. **2.** pious; chaste; virtuous.

Ākampana (S) (M) **1.** unshaken. **2.** calm; resolute. **3.** a rākṣasa son of Sumāli and Ketumatī (*V. Rāmāyaṇa*).

Akampita (S) (M) **1.** unshaken. **2.** calm; resolute; a Jaina or Buddhist saint. **3.** chief pupil of Mahāvīra (*J. S. Koṣa*).

Akaniṣṭha (S) (M) **1.** not young. **2.** elder; superior. **3.** a class of Buddhist deities (*He. Koṣa*).

Akaṅṭaka (S) (M) free from thorns; troubles, enemies.

Akapīvata (S) (M) **1.** unshaken. **2.** firm; tranquil; resolute. **3.** a ṛṣi (*M. Bh.*).

Ākara (S) (M) mine; a collection; a treasure; best.

Akarkkara (S) (M) **1.** handless. **3.** a serpent son of Kadru (*M. Bh.*).

Ākarṣaṇa (S) (M) attraction; handsome; charming.

Ākarṣita (S) (M) attracted; an admirer of beauty.

Ākaṣa (S) (M) a touchstone.

Ākāśa (S) (M) **1.** free or open space. **2.** ether; sky, atmosphere; with an open mind; one whose thoughts pervade the sky.

Ākāśaćamasa (S) (M) **1.** a cup of ether. **2.** the moon which is depicted as a cup of nectar in the sky.

Ākāśagarbhī (S) (M) **1.** one whose womb is the sky. **2.** boundless; limitless; divine. **3.** a bodhisattva (*B. Ćarita*).

Akatha (S) (M) **1.** boisterous. **3.** a son of Maṅkaṇa and devotee of Śiva (*P. Purāṇa*).

Akhaṇḍa (S) (M) **1.** without parts. **2.** indestructible; divine.

Ākhaṇḍala (S) (M) **1.** that which cannot be broken. **3.** another name for Indra and Śiva.

Akhila (S) (M) complete; whole.

Akhilātman (S) (M) the universal soul or Brahman.

Akhilendra (S) (M) lord of the universe.

Akhileśa (S) (M) all pervading god.

Akhileśvara (S) (M) lord of all.

Ākhuga (S) (M) **1.** riding on a rat. **3.** another name for Gaṇeṣa.

Akīla (S) (M) **1.** not fixed; not nailed. **2.** wavering.

Akopa (S) (M) **1.** without anger. **3.** a minister of Daśaratha (*V. Rāmāyaṇa*).

Akra (S) (M) banner; wall; fence.

Akrānta (S) (M) **1.** unsurpassed. **2.** unconquered.

Ākrīḍa (S) (M) **1.** pleasure grove; garden. **3.** a son of Kurūtthāma.

Akṛṣaśāśva (S) (M) **1.** with strong horses. **3.** a king of Ayodhyā (*V. Rāmāyaṇa*).

Akṛṣṇa (S) (M) **1.** not black. **2.** spotless; white; pure. **3.** another name for the moon.

Akṛṣṇakarman (S) (M) free from sins; guiltless.

Akṛtavraṇa (S) (M) **1.** without a wound. **2.** cannot be hurt.

3. a commentator of Purāṇas (*V. Purāṇa*); a companion of Rāma Jāmdagnya (*M. Bh.*).

Ākṛti (S) (M) **1.** form; shape. **3.** a king of Saurāṣṭra (*M. Bh.*).

Ākrodhana (S) (M) **1.** free from anger. **3.** a Purū king who was the son of Ayutanāyi and Kāmā (*M. Bh.*).

Ākroṣa (S) (M) **1.** wild anger. **3.** a king of Mahottha (*M. Bh.*).

Akrūra (S) (M) **1.** not cruel. **2.** gentle. **3.** a son of Śvaphalka and Nandinī, the husband of Sutanu, the father of Devaka and Upadevaka and an advisor and uncle of Kṛṣṇa (*Bhā. Purāṇa*).

Akṣa (S) (M) **1.** the soul; knowledge; senses; sky; earth; the *Eleocarpus ganitrus* or Rudrākṣa which is strung to make rosaries; the Bedda Nut tree (*Terminalia belerica*); cube; dice; axle; the beam of a balance; the number 5; snake. **3.** son of Rāvaṇa (*V. Rāmāyaṇa*); a son of Nara (*Bhā. Purāṇa*); another name for Garuḍa.

Akṣaja (S) (M) **1.** direct knowledge or cognition; thunderbolt; diamond. **3.** another name for Viṣṇu.

Akṣaka (S) (M) **1.** sensual. **3.** the Chariot tree (*Ougeinia oojeinensis*).

Akṣakumāra (S) (M) **1.** eternal prince. **3.** a son of Rāvaṇa and Mandodarī (*V. Rāmāyaṇa*); a soldier of Skanda's army (*M. Bh.*).

Akṣalā (S) (M) **1.** unbroken; whole. **3.** another name for Śiva.

Akṣamālin (S) (M) **1.** wearing a rosary of Rudrākṣa seeds (*Eleocarpus ganitrus*). **3.** another name for Śiva.

Akṣamata (S) (M) **1.** rosary. **2.** a string of beads which include the Rudrākṣa (*Eleocarpus ganitrus*) the coral, the crystal and the ruby.

Akṣapāda (S) (M) **1.** follower of knowledge; pursuer of knowledge. **2.** learned; wise; enlightened. **3.** another name for sage Gautama the founder of the Nyāya philosophy or for a follower of that system.

Akṣara (S) (M) **1.** imperishable. **2.** unalterable. 3. another name for Brahmā, Viṣṇu, Śiva the syllable 'Om', and the final beatitude.

Akṣata (S) (M) **1.** unbroken. **2.** whole; Barley (*Hordeum vulgure*) **3.** another name for Śiva.

Akṣaya (S) (M) **1.** undecaying; imperishable; a day which confers undying religious merit. **3.** the Supreme Spirit.

Akṣīna (S) (M) **1.** not failing. **3.** a son of Viśvamitra (*M. Bh.*).

Akṣīṇa (S) (M) **1.** not perishing; not waning; not diminishing. **3.** a son of Viṣvamitra (*M. Bh.*).

Akṣita (S) (M) **1.** undecaying. **2.** permanent; unfailing.

Akṣitāvasu (S) (M) **1.** possessing undecaying wealth. **3.** another name for Indra (*Ṛg. Veda*).

Akṣitoti (S) (M) **1.** one who abounds in unending wealth. **3.** another name for Indra (*Ṛg Veda*).

Akṣobhya (S) (M) **1.** immovable. **2.** imperturbable; unassailable. **3.** a Buddha (*B. Ćaritā*); a sage (*B. Ćarita*).

Akṣudra (S) (M) **1.** not small or insignificant. **2.** big or important. **3.** another name for Śiva.

Akṣuṇṇa (S) (M) **1.** unconquered. **2.** successful.

Aktu (S) (M) tinge; ray; light.

Akula (S) (M) **1.** transcendental. **2.** casteless; familyless. **3.** another name for Śiva.

Akuṇṭha (S) (M) vigorous; everfresh; eternal.

Akūpāra (S) (M) **1.** unbounded. **2.** free; independent; the ocean. **3.** the tortoise in the Indradyumna lake, regarded as the 2nd incarnation of Viṣṇu (*M. Bh.*) on which the earth is supposed to rest; an āditya (*A. Koṣa*).

Akupya (S) (M) **1.** not base. **2.** gold; silver.

Ākūrća (S) (M) **1.** the guileless one. 3. a Buddha (*B. Literature*).

Akutaśćala (S) (M) **1.** not moveable from a cause. **3.** another name for Śiva.

Alageśa (S) (M) lord of individuals.

Alaghu (S) (M) **1.** not light. **2.** heavy; weighty; serious; solemn. **3.** a son of Vasiṣṭha and Ūrjā (*A. Purāṇa*).

Alakādhipa (S) (M) **1.** lord of Alakā. **3.** another name for Kubera.

Alakaprabhā (S) (M) a glorious girl.

Ālakṣya (S) (M) visible; apparent.

Alakīśvara (S) (M) **1.** lord of Alakā. **3.** another name for Kubera.

Ālamba (S) (M) **1.** support; receptacle; asylum. **3.** a sage in Yudhiṣṭhira's court (*M. Bh.*).

Alambala (S) (M) **1.** with immeasurable power. **3.** an asura son of Jaṭāsura (*M. Bh.*); another name for Śiva.

Ālambāyana (S) (M) **1.** one who supports. **3.** a comrade of Indra (*M. Bh.*).

Ālambi (S) (M) **1.** dependable. **3.** a son of Kaśyapa (*M. Bh.*).

Alambuśa (S) (M) **1.** a line not to be crossed; the palm of the hand with the fingers extended (as once the fingers are extended, the boundary of the palm cannot be stretched any further). **3.** son of the rākṣasa Ṛṣyaśṛṅga (*M. Bh.*); a king on the Kaurava side (*M. Bh.*); king of the rākṣasas (*M. Bh.*); a son of Jaṭāsura (*M. Bh.*).

Alaṅkāra (S) (M) ornament.

Alaṅkṛta (S) (M) **1.** decorated. **2.** adorned.

Alaṅkṛtī (S) (M) ornament.

Alarka (S) (M) **1.** furious. **2.** a mad dog; an unusual animal; the plant *Calotopis gigantea*. **3.** a king of Kāśī and Karuṣā who was a member of Yama's court (*M. Bh.*).

Alāyudha (S) (M) **1.** one whose weapon is a scorpion sting. **3.** brother of Bakāsura (*M. Bh.*).

Alayya (S) (M) **1.** assailant. **3.** another name for Indra.

Aleśa (S) (M) **1.** not little. **2.** much; large.

Alia (S) (M) forehead.

Ālinda (S) (M) the balcony in front of a house.

Alipriya (S) (M) **1.** beloved of the black bee. **2.** the red lotus (*Nymphaea rubra*).

Alobhin (S) (M) **1.** not wanting or desiring anything. **2.** free from greed.

Āloka (S) (M) vision; sight; aspect; light; lustre; splendour.

Alola (S) (M) **1.** unagitated. **2.** firm; steady.

Alolupa (S) (M) **1.** free from desire; unagitated. **2.** firm; steady. **3.** a son of Dhṛtarāṣṭra (*M. Bh.*).

Ālopa (S) (M) a small morsel.

Alpasāras (S) (M) a little jewel.

Alpeśa (S) (M) **1.** the subtle god. **3.** another name for Kṛṣṇa.

Ālūgu (S) (M) **1.** that which divides; that which cuts. **2.** blade.

Āluka (S) (M) **1.** ebony. **3.** another name for Śeṣa.

Amad (S) (M) **1.** without intoxication. **2.** sober; grave; serious.

Amadana (S) (M) **1.** opposed to Kāma. **2.** sexless; free of sexual desires. **3.** another name for Śiva.

Amadhya (S) (M) **1.** not indifferent. **2.** compassionate; humane; loving. **3.** another name for Kṛṣṇa.

Amahatha (S) (M) **1.** wanting a house. **3.** a nāga (*M. Bh.*).

Amahīyu (S) (M) **1.** not of the earth. **2.** celestial; divine. **3.** a ṛṣi and part author of *Ṛg Veda* (ix).

Amala (S) (M) **1.** spotless. **2.** clean; pure; shining; crystal; the tree (*Emblica officianalis*). **3.** another name for Nārāyaṇa.

Amalagarbha (S) (M) **1.** born of purity. **2.** unblemished; flawless; pure; chaste; virtuous. **3.** a Bodhisattva (*B. Carita*).

Amalamaṇi (S) (M) **1.** pure jewel. **2.** crystal.

Amalātman (S) (M) **1.** pure minded. **2.** pure; chaste; virtuous.

Amama (S) (M) **1.** without ego. **3.** the 12th Jaina arhat of a future Utsarpiṇī.

Āmana (S) (M) friendly disposition; kindness; affection.

Amanath (S) (M) **1.** property; treasure. **2.** extremely wealthy.

Amanda (S) (M) not slow; active; merry; bright.

Amandīpa (S) (M) sharp witted; the light of peace; the lamp of peace.

Amanthu (S) (M) **1.** not slow. **2.** sharpwitted; one who lakes decisions instantly. **3.** a king who was the son of Vīravrata of the family of Priyavrata (*Bhā. Purāṇa*).

Amānuṣa (S) (M) **1.** non-human. **2.** divine; celestial; demonic.

Amara (S) (M) **1.** immortal; a god; the number 33 (as there are 33 main deities); imperishable. **3.** a marut (*H. Purāṇa*); the Rudraksha tree (*Elaeocarpus ganitrus*); the Adamant creeper (*Vitis quadrangularis*).

Amarabhartṛ (S) (M) **1.** supporter of the gods. **3.** another name for Indra.

Amaraćandra (S) (M) **1.** moon among the gods; immortal moon. **3.** a poet of Gujarat (13th century) (*B. Bhārata*).

Amarāćārya (S) (M) **1.** teacher of the gods. **3.** another name for Bṛhaspati.

Amaradatta (S) (M) given by the gods.

Amarādhipa (S) (M) **1.** lord of the gods. **3.** another name for Śiva.

Amaraguru (S) (M) **1.** teacher of the gods. **3.** another name for Bṛhaspati.

Amaraja (S) (M) **1.** eternally born. **2.** of an eternal existence. **3.** another name for Bṛhaspati.

Amarajīta (S) (M) conquering the gods.

Amarajota (S) (M) light of the gods.

Amarajyotī (S) (M) eternal light.

Amaranātha (S) (M) **1.** lord of the gods. **3.** another name for Śiva.

Amarañjaya (S) (M) conquering the gods.

Amarapā (S) (M) **1.** lord of the gods. 3. another name for Indra.

Amarapati (S) (M) **1.** master of the gods. **3.** another name for Indra.

Amaraprabhu (S) (M) **1.** lord of the immortals. 3. one of the 1000 names of Viṣṇu.

Amaraprīta (S) (M) immortal love.

Amararāja (S) (M) **1.** king of the gods. **3.** another name for Indra.

Amararatna (S) (M) **1.** jewel of the gods. **2.** crystal.

Amarasinha (S) (M) **1.** lion of the gods. **3.** a 6th century Buddhist lexicographer considered to have been one of the 9 gems of Vikramāditya's court (*B. Literature*).

Amaraśrī (S) (M) **1.** eternally divine. **3.** another name for Indra, Viṣṇu and Śiva.

Amardita (S) (M) unsubdued.

Amarejya (S) (M) **1.** preceptor of the gods. **3.** another name for Bṛhaspati.

Amarendra (S) (M) **1.** lord of the gods. **2.** immortal Indra.

Amareśa (S) (M) **1.** lord of the gods. 3. another name for Rudra-Śiva.

Amareśvara (S) (M) **1.** lord of the gods. **3.** another name for Viṣṇu.

Amarika (S) (M) **1.** one who is deathless. **2.** immortal; divine; a god.

Amarīndra (S) (M) eternal Indra.

Amarīśa (S) (M) lord of the gods.

Amariṣṇu (S) (M) desirous of immortality.

Amarīśvara (S) (M) **1.** lord of the immortals. **3.** another name for Viṣṇu, Śiva and Indra.

Amaropama (S) (M) like a god.

Amarottama (S) (M) **1.** the best among gods. **3.** another name for Indra.

Amarṣa (S) (M) **1.** anger; passion; impatience. **3.** a prince (*V. Purāṇa*).

Amartya (S) (M) **1.** immortal. **2.** divine; a god.

Amaru (S) (M) **1.** immortal. **3.** a king who was the author of *Amaruśataka.*

Amaruka (S) (M) son of an immortal.

Amarūpam (S) (M) god-like.

Amarūttama (S) (M) the best of the gods.

Āmas (S) (M) **1.** fine; soft; tender; raw. **2.** not dark; not hard; not gross. **3.** a son of Kṛṣṇa (*Bhāgavata*); a son of Ghṛtapṛṣṭha (*Bh. Purāṇa*).

Amava (S) (M) **1.** one who cannot be humbled. **2.** violent; strong; powerful.

Amāvasu (S) (M) **1.** deity of the house. **3.** a king who was the son of Purūravas and Urvaśī (*M. Bh.*).

Amāya (S) (M) not cunning; guileless.

Amaya (S) (M) **1.** immeasurable; boundless. **2.** the Costus shrub (*Saussurea lappa*).

Amayātman (S) (M) **1.** with immense powers of the mind. **3.** another name for Viṣṇu.

Ambaka (S) (M) eye.

Ambara (S) (M) **1.** circumference; sky; atmosphere; ether. **2.** saffron (*Crocus sativus*). **3.** a kind of perfume.

Ambaramaṇi (S) (M) **1.** jewel of the sky. **3.** another name for the sun.

Ambarīṣa (S) (M) **1.** lord of the sky. **2.** the atmosphere. **3.** a rājarṣi son of King Vṛṣāgir and the part author of *Ṛg Veda* (i); son of Nābhāga and descendant of Manu Vaivasvata (*M. Bh.*); an Ikṣvāku king the son of Māndhātā and is regarded as one of the 16 great kings of Bhārata (*M. Bh.*); a nāga who received Balarāma's soul (*M. Bh.*); a son of Pulaha (*V. Purāṇa*); another name for Viṣṇu, Śiva and Gaṇeśa; the Indian Hog Plum (*Spondias pinnata*).

Ambastha (S) (M) **1.** devotee of the sky; devotee of goddess Ambā; one who resides in water. **3.** a warrior on the Pāṇḍava side (*M. Bh.*).

Āmbasthya (S) (M) **1.** devotee of the mother. **3.** an *Aitareya Brāhmaṇa* king whose consecration priest was Nārada.

Ambava (S) (M) **1.** water like. **2.** making a sound like running water.

Ambhaspati (S) (M) **1.** lord of the waters. **3.** another name for Varuṇa.

Ambhassāra (S) (M) **1.** the essence of water. **2.** pearl.

Ambhoja (S) (M) **1.** born of water. **2.** the day lotus (*Nelumbium speciosum*).

Ambhoruha (S) (M) **1.** born of water. **3.** a son of Viśvāmitra (*M. Bh.*).

Ambhṛṅa (S) (M) **1.** full of water. **2.** powerful. **3.** a ṛṣi father of Vāća (*Ṛg Veda*).

Ambikāpati (S) (M) **1.** lord of Ambikā. **3.** another name for Śiva and Rudra.

Ambikāsuta (S) (M) **1.** son of Ambikā. **3.** another name for Dhṛtarāṣṭra.

Āmbikeya (S) (M) **1.** of Ambikā. **3.** a mountain (*M. Bh.*); another name for Gaṇeśa, Kārttikeya and Dhṛtarāṣṭra.

Ambu (S) (M) water.

Āmbuda (S) (M) **1.** one who gives water. **2.** a cloud.

Ambudeśvara (S) (M) **1.** lord of the clouds. **3.** another name for Indra.

Ambudhara (S) (M) **1.** water bearer. **2.** a cloud.

Ambuja (S) (M) **1.** produced in water. **2.** the thunderbolt of Indra, the Lotus (*Nelumbo speciosum*); the Sārasa bird (*Ardea nivea*); a conch. **3.** another name for the moon; the Indian Oak tree (*Barringtonia acutangula*).

Ambujabhū (S) (M) **1.** being in a lotus. **3.** another name for Brahmā.

Ambumaṇi (S) (M) **1.** jewel of water. **2.** lotus (*Nelumbo speciosum*); the pearl.

Ambunātha (S) (M) **1.** lord of the waters. **2.** the ocean. **3.** another name for Varuṇa.

Ambunidhi (S) (M) **1.** store of water. **2.** the ocean.

Ambupa (S) (M) **1.** protector of the water. **3.** another name for Varuṇa.

Āmbupati (S) (M) **1.** lord of the waters. **2.** the ocean.

Amburāja (S) (M) **1.** lord of the waters. **2.** the ocean. **3.** another name for Varuṇa.

Amburuha (S) (M) **1.** born in the water. **2.** the Indian lotus (*Nelumbo nucifera*).

Ambuvića (S) (M) **1.** living in water. **3.** king of Magadha (*M. Bh.*).

Amini (S) (M) bailiff; rigid; unalterable.

Āmiṣa (S) (M) an object of enjoyment; a pleasing object; a gift.

Amita (S) (M) unmeasured; unlimited; boundless; great; immense; infinite.

Amitābha (S) (M) **1.** of unmeasured splendour. **3.** deities of the 8th Manvantara.

Amitadhvaja (S) (M) **1.** with an immeasurable flag. **2.** reigns over a huge territory. **3.** a ćakravartin; son of Dharmadhvaja (*V. Purāṇa*); a rākṣasa (*M. Bh.*).

Amitadyuti (S) (M) of infinite splendour.

Amitagati (S) (M) **1.** extremely fast. **3.** a vidyādhara (*H. Purāṇa*).

Amitakratu (S) (M) of unbounded energy.

Amitarući (S) (M) **1.** very glorious. **3.** a Buddhist deity.

Amitāsan (S) (M) **1.** with sacred marks. **2.** omnipresent. **3.** another name for Viṣṇu.

Amitātman (S) (M) with an immense mind.

Amitaujas (S) (M) **1.** with unbounded energy. **2.** the almighty. **3.** a Pāñćāla king who was part incarnation of Ketumān and an ally of the Pāṇḍavas (*M. Bh.*).

Amitavikrama (S) (M) **1.** of unbounded valour. **3.** another name for Viṣṇu.

Amitaya (S) (M) boundless.

Amitāyuṣ (S) (M) **1.** of infinite age. **2.** immortal; divine; a god. **3.** a Dhyāni Buddha (*B. Literature*).

Amiteśa (S) (M) **1.** lord of the infinite. **3.** another name for Viṣṇu.

Amitojas (S) (M) of unbounded energy.

Amitoṣa (S) (M) ever happy.

Amitraghāta (S) (M) **1.** slayer of enemies. **3.** another name for Bindusāra.

Amitrajit (S) (M) **1.** conqueror of enemies. **3.** a son of Suvarṇa; a king who was the husband of Malayagandhinī and the father of Vīra (*Sk. Purāṇa*).

Amitrasāha (S) (M) **1.** one who overcomes enemies. **3.** another name for Indra.

Amlāna (S) (M) **1.** unwithered. **2.** fresh; clean; clear; bright; unclouded.

Āmoda (S) (M) amusement; gladdening; cheering; joy; serenity; pleasure; strong perfume.

Āmodin (S) (M) fragrant; famous.

Amogha (S) (M) **1.** unerring; unfailing; productive; fruitful. **3.** a yakṣa companion of Śiva (*M. Bh.*); a river (*A. Koṣa*); another name for Viṣṇu, Śiva and Skanda.

Amoghadaṅḍa (S) (M) **1.** unerring in punishing. **2.** an unerring judge. **3.** another name for Śiva.

Amoghadarśana (S) (M) **1.** with an unerring eye. **3.** a nāga.

Amoghadarśin (S) (M) **1.** perceiving faultlessly; with unerring perception; a Bodhisattva (*B. Literature*).

Amoghasiddhi (S) (M) **1.** with unfailing success. **3.** the 5th Dhyāni Buddha (*B. Literature*).

Amoghavajra (S) (M) **1.** the unerring thunderbolt. **3.** Buddhist scholar (6th century A.D.) (*B. Literature*).

Amoghavarṣa (S) (M) **1.** productive year; productive reign. **3.** a Ćālukya king.

Amoghavikrama (S) (M) **1.** of unerring valour. **3.** another name for Śiva.

Amoha (S) (M) **1.** without delusion. **2.** that which is errorless; clear; straight.

Amola (S) (M) priceless.

Amolaka (S) (M) priceless.

Ampṛthu (S) (M) strong and healthy.

Āmrapāli (S) (M) guardian of the Mango tree (*Mangifera indica*).

Amṛta (S) (M) **1.** immortal nectar. **2.** nectar of immortality; ambrosia; the Supreme Spirit; god; splendour; light; beautiful; anything sweet; gold; the number 4; a ray of the sun. **3.** another name for Viṣṇu, Śiva, Dhanvantari, Prajāpati, Indra, the sun and the soul; the Dew Bean (*Phaseolus aconilifolius*); *Aconitum heterophyllum*; Couch grass (*Cynodon dactylon*); the *Gloriosa superba* creeper.

Amṛtadrava (S) (M) **1.** that which emits nectar. **3.** another name for the moon.

Amṛtadyuti (S) (M) 1. with immortal rays; nectar rayed. 3. another name for the moon.

Amṛtāharaṇa (S) (M) 1. nectar stealer. 3. another name for Garuḍa as incarnation of Viṣṇu.

Amṛtaka (S) (M) the nectar of immortality.

Amṛtakara (S) (M) 1. nectar rayed. 3. another name for the moon.

Amṛtākṣara (S) (M) imperishable.

Amṛtam (S) (M) ambrosia produced by the churning of the Ocean of Milk; the collective body of immortals; eternity; heaven; a ray of light; milk; butter; sweetmeat; water; gold; the number 4.

Amṛtamaya (S) (M) 1. full of nectar. 2. immortal.

Amṛtānanda (S) (M) the delight of immortals.

Amṛtāṅśu (S) (M) 1. nectar rayed. 3. another name for the moon.

Amṛtapā (S) (M) 1. drinking nectar. 3. a dānava (*M. Bh.*); another name for Viṣṇu.

Amṛtaprabha (S) (M) 1. with eternal glory. 3. a vidyādhara (*K. Sāgara*).

Amṛtāśa (S) (M) 1. whose soul is immortal; one who drinks nectar. 2. a deity. 3. another name for Viṣṇu.

Amṛtasū (S) (M) 1. distilling nectar. 3. another name for the moon.

Amṛtatejas (S) (M) 1. with eternal power. 3. a vidyādhara prince (*K. Sāgara*).

Amṛtavapus (S) (M) 1. of immortal form. 3. another name for Viṣṇu.

Amṛteśa (S) (M) 1. lord of the immortals. 3. another name for Śiva.

Amṛteśaya (S) (M) 1. sleeping in nectar. 3. another name for Viṣṇu.

Amṛteśvara (S) (M) 1. lord of the immortals. 3. another name for Śiva.

Amṛtodana (S) (M) 1. cloud of nectar. 3. a son of Siṇhahanu the uncle of Śākyāmuni (*B. Literature*).

Amteśvara (S) (M) 1. eternal god. 2. virtuous; immortal.

Amūl (S) (M) 1. without a beginning; without roots. 2. one who does not have anyone to follow; without a superior.

Amūlya (S) (M) invaluable.

Amūrā (S) (M) wise; intelligent; sharpsighted.

Amūrta (S) (M) 1. formless. 3. another name for Śiva.

Amūrtarajas (S) (M) 1. with a formless emotion; heavenly emotion; with an indescribable emotion; whose emotions are like those of a god; lofty; universally beneficient. 3. a son of Kuśa and Vaidarbhī.

Amūrtarayas (S) (M) 1. with formless power. 2. whose limits of power are indescribable; one who has divine power. 3. a king of Bharata and the father of King Gaya (*M. Bh.*).

Amūrti (S) (M) 1. formless. 2. incorporeal; all pervading; omnipresent; a god. 3. another name for Viṣṇu.

Anā (Malayalam) (M) elephant.

Anābhayin (S) (M) 1. fearless. 3. another name for Indra.

Anabhiśasta (S) (M) 1. blameless. 2. one who is faultless; pure.

Anabhra (S) (M) cloudless.

Anādṛṣṭi (S) (M) 1. perfect; beyond check. 3. a Purū dynasty king who was the son of Raudrāśva and Miśrakeśī (*M. Bh.*); one of the 7 great Yādava warriors and son of King Vṛddhasena (*M. Bh.*); a son of Śūra; a son of Ugrasena (*Bhā. Purāṇa*).

Anādhṛṣya (S) (M) 1. unchecked; unimpaired. 2. of a free will; without flaw. 3. a Kaurava (*M. Bh.*).

Anādi (S) (M) 1. eternal. 2. immortal; divine. 3. another name for Śiva and Kṛṣṇa.

Anādimadhyaparyanta (S) (M) 1. extending without beginning, middle or end. 3. another name for Kṛṣṇa.

Anādinava (S) (M) faultless; without a beginning; forever new.

Anadīnidhana (S) (M) 1. with no beginning or end. 2. eternal. 3. another name for Kṛṣṇa.

Anādya (S) (M) **1.** existing from eternity. **3.** another name for Kṛṣṇa.

Anādyanta (S) (M) **1.** without beginning or end. **2.** that which is eternal; immortal and divine. **3.** another name for Śiva.

Anagha (S) (M) **1.** without sin. **2.** innocent; pure; above reproach; perfect. **3.** a son of Vasiṣṭha and Ūrjā who became a ṛṣi of the 3rd Manvantara (*V. Rāmāyaṇa*); a gandharva (*M. Bh.*); a child of Garuḍa (*M. Bh.*); another name for Viṣṇu, Śiva and Skanda.

Anaghādru (S) (M) **1.** injuring the sinless. **3.** son of Bali.

Anaka (S) (M) **1.** without weakness; thundercloud. **3.** a warrior of the Yādava dynasty (*Bhā. Purāṇa*).

Anakadundubha (S) (M) **1.** at whose birth drums are beaten; whose birth is eagerly awaited. **3.** Kṛṣṇa's grandfather (*M. Bh.*).

Anakadundubhi (S) (M) **1.** son of Anakadundubha; praised all over; kettledrum; like a thundercloud; very powerful. **3.** another name for Kṛṣṇa's father, Vasudeva.

Anākrānta (S) (M) **1.** unassailable. **2.** invincible; strong; victorious.

Anala (S) (M) **1.** fire; wind; the number 3. **3.** one of the 8 vasus; another name for Agni and Vāyu.

Analajit (S) (M) **1.** conqueror of fire. **2.** pure, blameless and invincible.

Anama (S) (M) **1.** who returns salutations with a blessing. **3.** Jaina Tīrthaṅkara (*J. S. Koṣa*).

Anāmaya (S) (M) **1.** free from disease. **2.** healthy. **3.** another name for Śiva.

Anamitra (S) (M) **1.** without an enemy. **2.** liked by all. **3.** a solar dynasty king who was a son of Nighna (*M. Bh.*); Yādava king who was a son of Dhṛṣṭa (*M. Purāṇa*); a son of King Kroṣṭa and Mādrī (*M. Bh.*); father of Manu Ćākṣuṣa (*Br. Purāṇa*); a son of Vṛṣṇi and father of Sini (*M. Bh.*).

Anamiva (S) (M) **1.** free from disease. **2.** well; happy.

Anamol (S) (M) **1.** priceless. **2.** precious; rare.

Ānana (S) (M) **1.** face. **2.** appearance; visage.

Anānata (S) (M) **1.** not bent. **2.** arrogant; proud; upright; undefeated. **3.** a sage (*Ṛg Veda*).

Ānanda (S) (M) **1.** bliss; happiness; joy; enjoyment; pleasure. **3.** forest on the top of mount Mahāmeru inhabited by devas, gandharvas, apsarās and mahāṛṣis (*P. Purāṇa*); the previous incarnation of Manu Ćākṣuṣa (*Mā. Purāṇa*); another name for Śiva.

Ānandabhairava (S) (M) **1.** causing both bliss and fear. **3.** a form of Śiva.

Ānandabhuj (S) (M) **1.** enjoying happiness. **2.** fortunate.

Ānandaghana (S) (M) **1.** cloud of joy. **2.** consisting of pure joy.

Ānandagiri (S) (M) **1.** the peak of joy. **2.** one who is full of joy and brings happiness to others.

Ānandamohana (S) (M) **1.** delightful. **3.** another name for Kṛṣṇa.

Ānandāmṛta (S) (M) the nectar of joy.

Ānandaprada (S) (M) bestower of pleasure.

Ānandasāgara (S) (M) sea of joy.

Ānandātman (S) (M) **1.** whose essence is happiness; whose soul has attained bliss. **2.** one who is always happy and whose soul has attained Mokṣa or salvation.

Ānandavardhana (S) (M) **1.** increasing joy. **2.** one who augments joy. **3.** a Sanskṛt critic (9th century A.D.) (*R. Taraṅgiṇī*).

Ānadhika (S) (M) having no superior.

Ānandin (S) (M) blissful; happy; cheerful.

Ānandita (S) (M) delighted; happy; blissful.

Anaṅga (S) (M) **1.** limbless; formless. **2.** incorporeal; divine. **3.** a king who was the son of Prajāpati Kardama, the father of Atibala and known for his integrity (*M. Bh.*); another name for Kāma; Arabian Jasmine (*Jasminum sambac*).

Anaṅgada (S) (M) **1.** inspired by Anaṅga. **2.** who inspires love.

Anaṅgam (S) (M) **1.** not of the body. **2.** one who is beyond the body; beyond passion; beyond destruction; divine; immortal; the mind; sky; ether; air.

Anaṅgāṅgahara (S) (M) **1.** destroying the body of Kāma. **3.** another name for Śiva.

Anaṅgapāla (S) (M) **1.** protector of the limbless. **2.** protector of the gods; religious spiritual; immortal; divine. **3.** the founder of Delhi.

Anaṅgapīḍa (S) (M) **1.** self-restrained. **2.** balanced; mature. **3.** a king of Kāśmira.

Anaṅgasuhṛd (S) (M) **1.** friend of Kāma. **2.** vasanta or the season of spring; enemy of Anaṅga. **3.** another name for Śiva.

Ananjan (S) (M) **1.** without collyrium. **2.** faultless; taintless; the sky; the Supreme Spirit. **3.** another name for Viṣṇu.

Ananmaya (S) (M) **1.** one who cannot be broken. **2.** healthy. **3.** another name for Viṣṇu.

Ananta (S) (M) **1.** endless (sky, cloud). **2.** one who is beyond death; immortal; divine; eternal. **3.** a nāga also known as Ādiśeṣa, described as a Prajāpati son of Brahmā (*V. Rāmāyaṇa*) but in reality born of Kaśyapa and Kadru, dwelling in Pātāla wearing the earth as a crown for his 1000 heads and partially incarnated as Balarāma (*M. Bh.*) and Lakṣmaṇa (*Rāmāyaṇa*); a captain of Skanda (*M. Bh.*); a viśvadeva; the Śravaṇa asterism; the 14th Jaina Arhat; another name for Brahmā, Viṣṇu, Śiva, Kṛṣṇa, Balarāma, Śeṣa, Vāsuki and the Supreme Spirit; the Arabian Manna plant (*Alhagi camelorum*); the *Gloriosa Superba* creeper; Couch grass (*Cynodon dactylon*); the *Ichnocarpus frutescens* shrub.

Anantaćāritra (S) (M) **1.** with eternal character. **2.** one who is all pervading, eternal, divine. **3.** a Bodhisattva (*B. Literature*).

Anantadeva (S) (M) **1.** immortal deity. **3.** a king of Kāśmira (*R. Taraṅgiṇī*).

Anantaguṇa (S) (M) with infinite virtues.

Anantajīt (S) (M) **1.** always victorious. **3.** a Jaina Arhat (*J. S. Koṣa*).

Anantamati (S) (M) **1.** with an infinite mind; one whose mind is boundless; all pervading. **2.** a god. **3.** a Bodhisattva.

Anantanāga (S) (M) **1.** infinite mountain. **2.** a very tall mountain. **3.** one of the 8 cobras worn by Śiva (*Ś. Purāṇa*).

Anantanātha (S) (M) **1.** eternal lord; lord of Ananta or Śeṣa the 1000 headed serpent; eternal; divine. **3.** the 14th Jaina Tīrthaṅkara who was the son of King Siṅhasena and Sujaśā of Ayodhyā (*J.S. Koṣa*); another name for Viṣṇu.

Anantarāma (S) (M) ever pleasing.

Anantarūpa (S) (M) **1.** innumerable forms. **3.** another name for Viṣṇu.

Anantaśakti (S) (M) **1.** of boundless power. **3.** another name for the Supreme Spirit.

Anantaśayan (S) (M) **1.** one who sleeps on the serpent Śeṣa. **3.** another name for Viṣṇu.

Anantaśrī (S) (M) **1.** of boundless magnificence. **3.** another name for the Supreme Being.

Anantavarman (S) (M) **1.** possessed with supreme power. **3.** another name for the Supreme Spirit.

Anantavatān (S) (M) **1.** an endless stretch. **3.** one of Brahmā's 4 feet.

Anantavijaya (S) (M) **1.** endless victory. **2.** never defeated. **3.** Yudhiṣṭhira's conchshell (*M. Bh.*).

Anantavikrama (S) (M) **1.** with eternal valour. **3.** a Bodhisattva.

Anantavīrya (S) (M) **1.** with infinite energy. **3.** the 23rd Jaina Arhat of a future age (*J. S. Koṣa*).

Ānantya (S) (M) **1.** endless. **2.** eternal; divine; a god.

Ananyaja (S) (M) **1.** unique son. **3.** another name for Kāma.

Anāpāna (S) (M) **1.** unattained; cannot be competed with. **3.** a son of Aṅga (*M. Bh.*).

Anapāya (S) (M) **1.** without obstacle. **2.** prosperous. **3.** another name for Śiva.

Anapāyaćola (S) (M) **1.** prosperous; Ćola king. **3.** a king of Ćola (11th century A.D.) (*Bhā. Purāṇa*).

Anaraṇya (S) (M) **1.** possessor of eternal power. **3.** a king of Ayodhyā and the father of Pṛthu who cursed Rāvaṇa to die at the hands of Rāma (*Br. Purāṇa*).

Anargha (S) (M) priceless.

Anari (S) (M) enemyless.

Anarśani (S) (M) **1.** injuring. **3.** an asura killed by Indra (*Ṛg Veda*).

Ānarta (S) (M) **1.** stage; theatre. **2.** a king **3.** the son of Śaryāti and the grandson of Vaivasvata Manu (*Br. Purāṇa*).

Anarva (S) (M) irresistible.

Anarvaṇa (S) (M) **1.** uncovering; manifesting. **3.** another name for Pūṣan, the lord of endowment and enlightenment.

Anāśa (S) (M) **1.** indestructible; undivided; sky; the Supreme Being. **3.** a brother of Akrūra (*Bhā. Purāṇa*).

Anāśaya (S) (M) **1.** without any self interest. **2.** selfless.

Anāśin (S) (M) indestructible; imperishable.

Anāśu (S) (M) imperishable; indestructible.

Anasūri (S) (M) **1.** not unwise. **2.** active; alert; energetic; intelligent.

Anaśvan (S) (M) **1.** without any horses. **3.** father of Parīkṣit (*M. Bh.*).

Anaśvara (S) (M) imperishable.

Anaśya (S) (M) **1.** indestructible. **3.** husband of Amṛtā (*M. Bh.*).

Anāthapiṇḍa (S) (M) **1.** one who feeds the poor. **3.** merchant in whose garden Śākyamunī instructed his disciples (*B. Literature*).

Anava (S) (M) **1.** humane. **2.** kind to men. **3.** a seer of the 3rd Manvantara (*Br. Purāṇa*).

Anavaratha (S) (M) **1.** with an eternal chariot. **3.** a son of Madhu and father of Kuruvatsa (*V. Purāṇa*).

Anavatapta (S) (M) **1.** without heat; without jealousy; without disease; without agony. **3.** a nāga king (*B. Literature*); a lake (*V. Rāmāyaṇa*).

Añćala (S) (M) part; valley; hamlet; the pallu of a sari.

Aṇḍaja (S) (M) **1.** born of the egg. **3.** another name for Brahmā.

Aṇḍajeśvara (S) (M) **1.** lord of the eggborn. **3.** another name for Garuḍa the king of birds and the vehicle of lord Viṣṇu.

Āṇḍaka (S) (M) **1.** egg; of an egg. **3.** a daitya.

Andha (S) (M) **1.** blind; dark. **3.** a son of Kaśyapa and Kadru (*M. Bh.*).

Andhaka (S) (M) **1.** blind; lawless. **3.** an asura son of Kaśyapa and Diti (*M. Bh.*); a king of the Yadu dynasty and ancestor of Kṛṣṇa (*Bhāgavatā*); an asura son of Śiva and foster son of Hiraṇyākṣa later incarnated as Bhṛṅgī the head of the asura army (*Vām. Purāṇa*).

Andhakāghātī (S) (M) **1.** destroyer of Andhaka. **3.** another name for Śiva.

Andhakanipātī (S) (M) **1.** descending on Andhaka. **3.** another name for Śiva.

Andhakāri (S) (M) **1.** enemy of Andhaka. **2.** who fights against injustice; ignorance; who stands for all that is fair; correct and just; who is for knowledge and enlightenment. **3.** another name for Śiva.

Andhakaripu (S) (M) **1.** slayer of the asura Andhaka. **3.** another name for Śiva.

Andhakavṛṣṇinātha (S) (M) **1.** lord of the descendants of Andhaka and Vṛṣṇi. **3.** another name for Kṛṣṇa.

Āndhraka (S) (M) **1.** belonging to Āndhra. **3.** an Āndhra king who was a member of the Indraprastha court (*M. Bh.*).

Androṣa (S) (M) introverted.

Anekaloćana (S) (M) **1.** with several eyes. **2.** all-seeing; at all times. **3.** another name for Śiva.

Anekakṛta (S) (M) **1.** doing much. **2.** creating things. **3.** another name for Śiva.

Anenas (S) (M) **1.** blameless; sinless. **3.** a lunar dynasty king who was the son of Āyus and father of Śuddha (*Ṛg Veda*); an Ikṣvāku king who was the son of Kakutstha (*Bhā. Purāṇa*).

Anenasya (S) (M) **1.** freedom from sin. **2.** chaste; pious; pure.

Aṅga (S) (M) **1.** limb. **3.** a son of Ulmuka and husband of Sunīthā (*M. Bh.*); a lunar dynasty king who was the son of Bali and Sudeṣṇā and father of Veṇa (*Bhā. Purāṇa*).

Aṅgabhū (S) (M) **1.** born of the limbs. **2.** a son.

Aṅgada (S) (M) **1.** bestower of limbs; with beautiful limbs. **2.** armlet. **3.** a monkey son of Tārā and Vāli considered to have been the reincarnation of Bṛhaspati and appointed by Rāma as king of Kiṣkindhā (*U. Rāmāyaṇa*); a son of Lakṣmaṇa and Ūrmilā (*V. Rāmāyaṇa*); an elephant of the south;a warrior etc.

Aṅgaja (S) (M) **1.** produced from the body. **2.** a son; ornamental love. **3.** another name for Kāma.

Aṅgama (S) (M) **1.** that which cannot be pierced. **2.** strong; with high integrity.

Aṅganemi (S) (M) follower of the scriptures.

Aṅgāra (S) (M) **1.** burning charcoal. **3.** a king of the maruts (*H. Purāṇa*); another name for the planet Mars (*M. Bh.*).

Aṇgarāja (S) (M) **1.** best among beings with a form; king of Aṅga. **2.** most handsome. **3.** another name for Karṇa.

Aṅgārakā (S) (M) **1.** charcoal; the planet Mars. **3.** an asura who was the father of Aṅgāravatī (*K. Sāgara*); a descendant of King Jayadratha of Sauvīra (*M. Bh.*); one of the 108 sons of the sun (*M. Bh.*); a rudra (*Ś. Purāṇa*).

Aṅgāraparṇa (S) (M) **1.** with charcoal wings. **2.** *Chlerodendron siphonanthus*. **3.** another name for the gandharva king Ćitraratha.

Aṅgāras (S) (M) **1.** charcoal. **3.** a marut; another name for Mars.

Aṅgārasetu (S) (M) **1.** destroyer of fire; one who destroys the invincible. **3.** the father of Gāndhāra (*M. Bh.*).

Āṅgāriṣṭha (S) (M) **1.** one who exists in burning charcoal; knower of the word; with a delicate body. **3.** a king of Bhārata (*M. Bh.*).

Aṅgasvāmi (S) (M) **1.** lord of limbs. **2.** who has mastered his body; strong and powerful.

Aṅgati (S) (M) **1.** one who maintains the sacred fire. **3.** another name for Brahmā and Viṣṇu.

Aṅgavāha (S) (M) **1.** bearer of scriptures. **3.** a Vṛṣṇi dynasty king (*M. Bh.*).

Aṅgeśvara (S) (M) **1.** lord of Aṅga. **3.** another name for Karṇa.

Aṅghāri (S) (M) **1.** enemy of sin. **3.** a celestial guard of the Soma.

Aṅgiras (S) (M) **1.** knows the essence of the parts. **2.** a knower of Vedāṅgas or parts of the Vedas; knower of the scriptures. **3.** a ṛṣi who was one of the 10 prajāpati sons of Brahmā, born from his mouth, considered a Saptaṛṣi of the 1st Manvantara, he had several wives of which the more prominent, were Śubhā, Smṛtī, Śraddhā, Devasenā and Vasudhā, his prominent sons included Agni, Saṁvarta, Bṛhaspati, Utathya, Sudhanvā and Savya who was an incarnation of Indra, notable among his daughters were Sinīvālī, Kuhū, Rākā, Anumatī, Rāgā, Bhānumatī, Arćiṣmatī, Haviṣmatī, Mahiṣmatī and Mahāmatī and in astronomy he is a star in Ursa major (*M. Bh.*).

Āṅgirasa (S) (M) **1.** of Aṅgiras. **3.** another name for Ćyavana and Bṛhaspati.

Aṅgoṣin (S) (M) **1.** resonant; praiseworthy. **3.** Soma.

Aṅgśu (S) (M) with beautiful limbs.

Aṅgula (S) (M) **1.** finger; thumb; a finger's breadth. **3.** another name for Ćāṇakya.

Āṅgūṣa (S) (M) **1.** praising. **2.** a hymn.

Anhu (S) (M) **1.** imperishable, invincible. **3.** an asura killed by Indra (*Ṛg Veda*).

Aniha (S) (M) **1.** indifferent. **3.** a king of Ayodhyā (*M. Bh.*).

Anīka (S) (M) army; front; head, face; splendour, brilliance; form.

Anīkavidāraṇa (S) (M) **1.** slayer of the army. **2.** a warrior. **3.** a brother of King Jayadratha of Sindhu (*M. Bh.*).

Aniketa (S) (M) **1.** homeless. **2.** to whom the entire world is home. **3.** a yakṣa who became king of the Aṅga dynasty (*A. Purāṇa*).

Anīla (S) (M) **1.** not blue, fair. **3.** a serpent mentioned in the *Ādi Parva*.

Anila (S) (M) **1.** wind; the god of wind. **3.** one of the 8 vasus and son of Dharma and Śvasā, (*Vā. Purāṇa*) the husband of Śivā and father of Manojava and Avijña (*M. Bh.*); a son of Garuḍa (*M. Bh.*); the lunar asterism of Svāti (*P. Samhitā*); another name for Viṣṇu and Śiva.

Anīlābha (S) (M) not of blue hue; zephyr; fair; bright; white; shining.

Anilātmaja (S) (M) **1.** son of the wind. **2.** strong; swift. **3.** another name for Hanumān and Bhīma.

Anīlavājin (S) (M) **1.** with white horses. **3.** another name for Arjuna.

Ānili (S) (M) **1.** descendant of Anila. **3.** another name for Hanumān and Bhīma.

Animān (S) (M) **1.** immense; unbounded. **2.** beyond any boundary; limitless; all pervading; divine.

Animeṣa (S) (M) **1.** unwinking. **2.** vigilant; never tired; all seeing; a god.

Animiṣa (S) (M) **1.** unwinking. **2.** a god. **3.** a son of Garuḍa (*M. Bh.*); another name for Śiva and Viṣṇu.

Animiṣāćārya (S) (M) **1.** preceptor of the gods. **3.** another name for Bṛhaspati.

Anina (S) (M) small.

Anindata (S) (M) who does not speak ill of others; who is not spoken ill of.

Anirbāṇa (S) (M) **1.** unextinguished. **2.** never dies; immortal; a god.

Anirjita (S) (M) unconquered.

Aniruddha (S) (M) **1.** unobstructed; unopposed. **3.** son of Pradyumna and grandson of Kṛṣṇa, the husband of Ūṣā and father of Vajra, a part incarnation of Brahmā and Viṣṇu (*Bhāgavata*); an Arhat and contemporary of Śākyamunī (*J. S. Koṣa*); a Vṛṣṇi (*M. Bh.*).

Anirviṇa (S) (M) **1.** not weary; not downcast. **2.** active; energetic; progressive. **3.** another name for Viṣṇu.

Anīśa (S) (M) **1.** without a superior; paramount; supreme. **3.** another name for Viṣṇu.

Anīśvara (S) (M) **1.** without a superior; paramount. **3.** the Supreme Spirit.

Anita (S) (M) **1.** without guile; not driven. **2.** a leader.

Anitābhā (S) (P) **1.** with guileless charm. **3.** a *Ṛg Veda* river.

Aniteja (S) (M) of immeasurable splendour.

Anivartin (S) (M) **1.** does not retreat. **2.** brave. **3.** another name for Viṣṇu and the Supreme Being.

Aṅjaka (S) (M) **1.** decorated; anointed. **3.** a son of Vipracitti (*V. Purāṇa*).

Añjalī (S) (M) **1.** anointed; polished. **2.** honoured; received respectfully. **3.** a sage and colleague of Śaunaka (*Bhāgavata*).

Añjali (S) (M) **1.** cupped palms. **2.** one who reveres, offers salutations, respects, is humble, modest; mark of respect; the folding of hands to make a hollow for offering oblations to a god, a deity.

Añjalika (S) (M) **1.** bearer of cupped arrows. **3.** one of Arjuna's arrows (*M. Bh.*).

Añjami (S) (M) **1.** not black. **2.** nightless; glorious; bright, illuminating.

Añjana (S) (M) **1.** collyrium. **2.** grey in complexion. **3.** a fabulous serpent (*Bhāgavata*); elephant of the southwest quarter (*Br. Purāṇa*); a mountain; son of Kṛti and father of Kurujit (*V. Purāṇa*).

Añjanaparvan (S) (M) **1.** part of night; part of fire; bearer of power. **3.** a son of Ghaṭotkaća and grandson of Bhīma (*M. Bh.*).

Añjanavatī (S) (M) **1.** one who has applied collyrium to her eyes. **3.** female elephant of the northeast quarter.

Āñjaneya (S) (M) **1.** of Añjana; son of Añjanā. **2.** powerful; fiery. **3.** another name for Hanumān.

Anjañi (S) (M) **1.** son of Anjañā. **3.** another name for Hanumān; the Ironwood tree (*Memecylon umbellatum*).

Añjanīnandana (S) (M) **1.** son of Añjanā. **3.** another name for Hanumān.

Añjasa (S) (M) **1.** not dark. **2.** guileless; deceitless; straightforward; honest.

Añjika (S) (M) **1.** blessed; collyrium coloured. **2.** black; dark. **3.** a son of Yadu (*Bhāgavata*); son of Vipraćittī (*V. Purāṇa*).

Añjiṣṇu (S) (M) **1.** who eats up darkness. **2.** removes darkness; one who shines; is brilliant; illuminating; highly brilliant. **3.** another name for the sun.

Añjiṣṭha (S) (M) **1.** highly brilliant. **3.** another name for the sun.

Añjuli (S) (M) revered; worshipped.

Aṅkati (S) (M) **1.** wind; fire. **2.** a Brahmin who maintains the sacred fire. **3.** another name for Brahmā.

Aṅkolita (S) (M) who has been embraced; loved; accepted; respected.

Aṅkura (S) (M) sprout; shoot; blade; new-born.

Anna (S) (M) **1.** grain. **3.** grain which in a mystical sense is considered the coarsest envelope of Viṣṇu, the Supreme Spirit; earth and water.

Annabhuj (S) (M) **1.** who eats grain. **3.** Śiva to whom edible grain is offered as an oblation.

Annabrahman (S) (M) Brahmā as represented by food.

Annada (S) (M) **1.** one who grants food. **3.** another name for Śiva.

Annadeva (S) (M) lord of food.

Annāmallai (S) (M) **1.** lord of the mountains. **3.** another name for Śiva.

Annamaya (S) (M) **1.** full of food. **2.** free from disease; healthy; prosperous.

Annapati (S) (M) **1.** lord of food. **3.** another name for Savitṛ, Agni and Śiva.

Anogopta (S) (M) **1.** not hidden. **2.** wellknown. **3.** a viśvadeva (*M. Bh.*).

Anṛta (S) (M) **1.** lie; falsehood. **3.** a son of Adharma and Hiṁsā (*V. Purāṇa*).

Aṅśa (S) (M) **1.** a share; a part; a day. **3.** a sage who was the son of Aditi, one of the 12 ādityas who represents luck in gaining wealth (*M. Bh.*); a king of the Manu dynasty (*M. Bh.*).

Aṅśaka (S) (M) **1.** has a share in the property. **2.** an heir.

Ansala (S) (M) lusty; strong.

Aṅśala (S) (M) **1.** has a share in the property. **2.** an heir.

Aṅśānśa (S) (M) **1.** part of a part. **2.** a minute part; that which is subtle; part incarnation of a deity.

Aṅśarin (S) (M) **1.** has a share in the property. **2.** an heir.

Aṅśin (S) (M) **1.** has a share in the property. **2.** an heir.

Aṅśrutas (S) (M) **1.** not famous. **3.** a son of Kṛṣṇa (*Bhāgavata*); a son of Dyutimat (*M. Bh.*).

Aṅśu (S) (M) **1.** a ray; filament of the Soma plant; a minute particle; a sunbeam; beam of light; lustre; splendour; brilliance; embellishment; speed. **3.** a sage; a protégé of the aśvins in the *Ṛg Veda*.

Aṅśubāṇa (S) (M) **1.** with rays for arrows. **2.** the sun.

Aṅśudhara (S) (M) **1.** bearer of rays. **3.** another name for the sun.

Aṅśujala (S) (M) **1.** a collection of rays. **2.** a blaze of light; brilliant; illuminating; enlightening.

Aṅśuka (S) (M) **1.** leaf; ray. **2.** tender; bright; illuminating; enlightening.

Aṅśula (S) (M) **1.** radiant; luminous. **2.** enlightening; bright. **3.** another name for Ćāṇakya.

Aṅśumālin (S) (M) **1.** garlanded with rays. **2.** the sun.

Aṅśumān (S) (M) **1.** bearer of rays. **2.** the sun; the moon; radiant; illuminating; enlightening. **3.** a solar dynasty king who was the son of Asamañjas and father of Bhagīratha and Dilīpa (*V. Rāmāyaṇa*); a king of Bhoja who fought on the side of the Pāṇḍavas (*M. Bh.*).

Aṅśumat (S) (M) **1.** bearer of rays. **2.** luminous; radiant. **3.** son of Asamañjas and grandson of Sagara; another name for the sun and moon.

Aṅśupati (S) (M) **1.** lord of rays. **2.** the sun.

Aṅśusvāmi (S) (M) **1.** lord of rays. **2.** the sun.

Aṅśuvāṇa (S) (M) **1.** with rays for arrows. **3.** another name for the sun.

Āntaka (S) (M) **1.** one who causes the end. **2.** Yama (lord of death). **3.** a rajaṛṣi (*Ṛg Veda*).

Antakaripu (S) (M) **1.** enemy of Antaka. **3.** another name for Śiva.

Antama (S) (M) **1.** without darkness; next. **2.** nearest; intimate.

Antara (S) (M) **1.** near; related; intimate; interior; soul; heart; surety; guarantee. **3.** father of Suyajña (*H. Purāṇa*).

Antardhāna (S) (M) **1.** with divine insight. **3.** a son of King Aṅśa of the Manu dynasty and father of Havirdhāna (*M. Bh.*); a son of Pṛthu (*V. Purāṇa*); a weapon of Kubera (*M. Bh.*).

Antardhī (S) (M) **1.** with inner perception. **3.** a son of Emperor Pṛthu (*A. Purāṇa*).

Antarhitātman (S) (M) **1.** with a concealed mind; whose mind is deeply concerned for the general welfare; whose soul cannot be read. **3.** another name for Śiva.

Antarikṣa (S) (M) **1.** space; outer space; sky. **3.** a son of Murāsura killed by Kṛṣṇa (*Bhāgavata*); a king the son of Ṛṣabha and grandson of Nābhi (*Bhāgavata*).

Antarjyotiṣ (S) (M) with an illuminated soul.

Antarvedi (S) (M) **1.** dwelling in an area that lies between 2 rivers. **2.** dwelling in the sacred area between the Gaṅgā and Yamunā rivers.

Anti (S) (M) nearness; living in a sacred area; living in a hermitage.

Antideva (S) (M) **1.** near the gods. **2.** spiritual; virtuous.

Āntya (S) (M) who accomplishes (personified as Bhauvana).

Ānu (S) (M) living; human.

Anu (S) (M) **1.** follower. **3.** a son of Yayāti and Śarmiṣṭhā.

Aṇu (S) (M) **1.** minute; an atom. **2.** subtle; divine. **3.** a son of Digbhraja and husband of Kīrti the daughter of Śuka and Pīvarī (*D. Bhāgavata*); another name for Śiva.

Anubhaj (S) (M) **1.** one who follows worship. **2.** spiritual.

Anubhava (S) (M) experience; perception.

Anubhāvya (S) (M) **1.** known through experience. **2.** divine truth.

Anubodha (S) (M) **1.** afterthought; reviving the scent of an old perfume. **2.** recollection.

Anućakra (S) (M) **1.** who works according to schedule. **2.** organized; punctual; planned. **3.** an attendant given to Skanda by Prajāpati Tvaṣṭā (*M. Bh.*).

Anūćāna (S) (M) well versed in the Vedas; devoted to learning.

Anudāra (S) (M) **1.** mean; dishonest. **3.** a son of Dhṛtarāṣṭra (*M. Bh.*).

Anudātta (S) (M) **1.** not raised; not elevated; neutral. **3.** a son created by Pāñćajanya (*M. Bh.*).

Anudeśya (S) (M) **1.** obedient. **2.** one who proceeds towards the goal.

Anudruhyu (S) (M) **1.** follower of motion. **3.** a son of Yayāti and Śarmiṣṭhā (*A. Purāṇa*).

Aṇudrutta (S) (M) **1.** with subtle movement. **2.** swift; all pervading; divine.

Anudvega (S) (M) free from anxiety.

Anugāyas (S) (M) praised in hymns.

Anugra (S) (M) **1.** not violent. **2.** gentle; mild; peace loving; pacifist.

Anugraha (S) (M) **1.** favour; kindness. **3.** the 5th incarnation of Viṣṇu (*V. Purāṇa*).

Anugya (S) (M) authority.

Anuha (S) (M) **1.** without desire. **2.** satisfied; contented; tranquil; at peace. **3.** a son of Vibhrāja and father of Brahmadatta (*M. Bh.*) (*K. Sāgara*).

Anuhlāda (S) (M) **1.** who seeks pleasure. **3.** a son of Hiraṇyakaṣipu and brother of Prahlāda (*V. Purāṇa*).

Anuhrāda (S) (M) **1.** following the heart. **3.** a son of Hiraṇyakaṣipu (*H. Purāṇa*).

Anūhu (S) (M) **1.** without desire. **3.** an ancient king (*M. Bh.*).

Anujā (S) (M) **1.** the later born. **2.** younger sister.

Anuja (S) (M) **1.** born later. **2.** younger brother.

Anujyeṣṭha (S) (M) next to the eldest.

Ānūka (S) (M) **1.** lying close to. **2.** ornament; jewel.

Anukarman (S) (M) **1.** a subsequent action. **3.** a viśvadeva (*M. Bh.*).

Anukarṣa (S) (M) invoking; summoning by incantation.

Anūkāśa (S) (M) reflection of light.

Anukroṣa (S) (M) **1.** not harsh. **2.** tenderness; compassion.

Anukūla (S) (M) agreeable; favourably disposed.

Anumita (S) (M) **1.** logically established. **2.** analytical; precise.

Anumodana (S) (M) approbation; pleasing; causing pleasure.

Anūna (S) (M) **1.** not inferior. **2.** not less; superior; whole; entire.

Anūnavarćas (S) (M) full of splendour.

Anūpa (S) (M) **1.** unequalled; abounding in water. **2.** unique. **3.** a pond; bank of river; a ṛṣi.

Anupama (S) (M) **1.** incomparable. **2.** matchless; rare; precious; ginger (*Zingiber officinale*).

Aṇupatī (S) (M) **1.** lord of the atom; lord of the subtle. **3.** another name for Kārtavīrya (*M. Bh.*).

Anupradāna (S) (M) gift; donation.

Anuprakha (S) (M) that which pierces.

Anupriyā (S) (M) beloved; very dear.

Anūpya (S) (M) matchless; incomparable.

Anūrādha (S) (M) who bestows happiness and welfare; born under the Anurādhā asterism.

Anurāga (S) (M) attachment; affection; love; passion; red colour.

Anurāgin (S) (M) inducing love.

Anuraj (S) (M) **1.** devoted. **2.** beloved; attracted.

Anurāj (S) (M) **1.** to be brilliant. **2.** illuminating; enlightening.

Anurañjana (S) (M) **1.** satisfying. **2.** who pleases; who induces attachment; who is loved.

Anurañjita (S) (M) pacified; reconciled; satisfied.

Anuratha (S) (M) **1.** following the chariot. **2.** a soldier. **3.** a son of Kuruvatsa and father of Puruhotra (*V. Purāṇa*).

Anurodha (S) (M) request.

Anūrū (S) (M) **1.** thighless. **3.** the dawn that precedes Sūrya and is personified as Aruṇa, the charioteer of the sun who is visualized without legs.

Anuruć (S) (M) **1.** to one's taste. **2.** who is liked; interesting; chosen; preferred.

Anuruddha (S) (M) **1.** soothed; pacified. **3.** a cousin of Śākyamunī (*B. Literature*).

Anurudha (S) (M) who obeys.

Anurūpa (S) (M) **1.** one that follows the form. **2.** in shape; compatible; agreeable; suitable.

Anuśā (S) (M) **1.** following desires. **2.** seeks desires.

Anuśikha (S) (M) **1.** crested. **2.** decorated, embellished; respected.

3. the priest at the snake festival (*P. Brāhmaṇa*).

Anuśobhin (S) (M) 1. shining; follows grace. 2. graceful; glorious; dignified; illuminating; enlightening.

Anuśruta (S) (M) well-known; much heard of; handed down by Vedic tradition.

Anuśrutaśravas (S) (M) 1. with Vedic fame, with unparalleled fame. 3. a son of Somāli (*V. Purāṇa*).

Anuṣtup (S) (M) 1. metre; hymn; invocation; praise. 3. an 8 syllabic metre; one of the 7 horses of Sūrya (*V. Purāṇa*).

Anutoṣa (S) (M) gratification; relief.

Anutta (S) (M) invincible.

Anuttama (S) (M) 1. having no superior. 2. unsurpassed; highest; best. 3. another name for Viṣṇu and Śiva.

Anuvāha (S) (M) 1. following; carrying. 3. one of the 7 tongues of fire.

Anuvās (S) (M) to make fragrant.

Anuvinda (S) (M) 1. one who discovers or obtains; one who strives for success. 3. a king of Ujjain (*K. Sāgara*); a son of Dhṛtarāṣṭra (*M. Bh.*); a prince of Avantī, the brother of Kṛṣṇa's wife Mitravindā who fought on the side of the Kauravas (*Bhāgavata*); a Kekaya prince who fought on the side of the Kauravas (*M. Bh.*).

Anuvitta (S) (M) found; obtained.

Aṇuvrata (S) (M) 1. devoted; faithful; attached. 3. son of Satyakarman.

Anuyātri (S) (M) follower; a companion.

Anuyāyin (S) (M) 1. follower. 3. a son of Dhṛtarāṣṭra (*M. Bh.*).

Anvāgabhānu (S) (M) 1. following the sun. 3. a Purū king who was the son of Manasyu and Misrakeśī (*M. Bh.*).

Anyaṅga (S) (M) 1. spotless. 2. flawless; pure; virtuous; divine.

Anyūna (S) (M) 1. not defective. 2. healthy; whole; entire; complete.

Āpa (S) (M) 1. water. 3. one of the 8 vasus and father of Vaitanda, Śrama, Śānta and Svāni (*V. Purāṇa*); a seer of the 10th Manvantara (*Vā. Purāṇa*).

Apaćita (S) (M) honoured; respected.

Apādeva (S) (M) 1. god of water. 3. another name for Varuṇa.

Āpagāsuta (S) (M) 1. son of the river. 3. another name for Bhīṣma.

Āpageya (S) (M) 1. originating from the river; son of the river. 3. another name for Bhīṣma, the son of the sacred Gaṅgā.

Apaghana (S) (M) 1. cloudless. 2. a limb of the body.

Apan (S) (M) 1. sun. 2. glorious; brilliant; illuminating; enlightening.

Apakuñja (S) (M) 1. not hidden. 3. a younger brother of Śeṣanāga.

Apālāla (S) (M) 1. fleshless; strawless; huskless. 3. a rākṣasa (*V. Rāmāyaṇa*).

Apalāśin (S) (M) free from desire.

Apālaṣuka (S) (M) free from desire.

Apamanyu (S) (M) free from grief.

Apāmpati (S) (M) 1. lord of the waters. 3. another name for the ocean and Varuṇa.

Apāntaratamas (S) (M) 1. completely free of darkness. 2. brilliant; enlightening. 3. a sage born of the sound 'bhu' uttered by Viṣṇu and reincarnated as sage Vyāsa (*Ṛg Veda*).

Āpapati (S) (M) 1. lord of the waters. 2. the ocean. 3. another name for Varuṇa.

Aparāditya (S) (M) 1. not unlike the sun. 2. brilliant; enlightening.

Aparāhṇaka (S) (M) 1. born in the afternoon. 2. as brilliant as the afternoon sun.

Aparājiṣṇu (S) (M) unconquerable; invincible.

Aparājita (S) (M) 1. undefeated; unsurpassed. 3. a nāga son of Kaśyapa and Kadru (*M. Bh.*); a son of Dhṛtarāṣṭra (*M. Bh.*); a Kuru dynasty king (*M. Bh.*); one of the 11 rudras (*A. Purāṇa*); a son of Kṛṣṇa; a class of Jaina divinities (*J. S. Koṣa*); a mythical sword (*Bhāgavata*); another name for Viṣṇu and Śiva (*M. Bh.*).

Aparimāṇa (S) (M) **1.** immeasurable. **2.** immense; unlimited.

Aparimeya (S) (M) **1.** immeasurable. **2.** immense; unbounded; unlimited.

Aparimita (S) (M) **1.** unlimited. **2.** immense; unbounded.

Aparīta (S) (M) irresistible.

Āparīta (S) (M) **1.** gladdened. **2.** joyous.

Aparṇeśa (S) (M) **1.** lord of Pārvatī. **3.** another name for Śiva.

Aparokṣa (S) (M) **1.** not beyond sight. **2.** visible; manifest.

Apārthiva (S) (M) **1.** not earthly. **2.** subtle; immortal; divine.

Aparuṣa (S) (M) free from anger.

Apaśaṅka (S) (M) fearless.

Apaspati (S) (M) **1.** skilful; active. **3.** a son of Uttānapāda (*V. Purāṇa*).

Āpastamba (S) (M) **1.** one who stills water. **3.** a sage who was the husband of Akṣasūtrā and the father of Gārgī (*Ā. Samhitā*).

Apasyu (S) (M) skilful; active.

Āpava (S) (M) **1.** sheltered from wind. **2.** a grove. **3.** another name for Vasiṣṭha (*M. Bh.*).

Āpi (S) (M) friend; ally; acquaintance.

Apiguṅa (S) (M) **1.** one with attributes. **2.** excellent; virtuous.

Apija (S) (M) **1.** born after or in addition to. **2.** a brother.

Apīndra (S) (M) **1.** resembling Indra. **2.** handsome; virtuous; divine.

Apnavāna (S) (M) **1.** the arm. **2.** one who provides support. **3.** a ṛṣi of the line of Bhṛgu (*Ṛg Veda*).

Āpomūrti (S) (M) **1.** with a water-like form. **2.** adaptable; flexible. **3.** an idol of the god of water (*A. Veda*); a son of Manu Svāroćiṣa (*H. Purāṇa*); a ṛṣi of the 10th Manvantara (*H. Purāṇa*).

Āponāptṛ (S) (M) **1.** grandson of the waters. **3.** another name for Agni.

Appayyadīkṣita (S) (M) **1.** with thoughts like water or milk. **2.** one who is clear; clean; pure; without vice. **3.** a reputed Sanskṛt rhetorician (16th century A.D.).

Appitta (S) (M) **1.** fire. **3.** another name for Agni.

Aprakarṣita (S) (M) **1.** undiminished. **2.** irresistible; unequalled.

Apramaya (S) (M) imperishable.

Aprati (S) (M) **1.** without opponents. **2.** irresistible; unequalled.

Apratima (S) (M) **1.** without comparison. **2.** unequalled; irresistible; without opponents.

Apratīpa (S) (M) **1.** not obstinate. **2.** flexible; compromising. **3.** a king of Magadha (*V. Purāṇa*).

Apratiratha (S) (M) **1.** a chariot borne warrior who has no rival. **2.** a matchless warrior. **3.** a ṛṣi considered to be the son of Indra (*Ṛg Veda*); a son of Rantināra (*V. Purāṇa*).

Apratirūpa (S) (M) with matchless beauty.

Apratīvīrya (S) (M) of irresistible power.

Apratiyodhin (S) (M) **1.** not having an adversary. **2.** irresistible.

Apratula (S) (M) **1.** cannot be compared. **2.** unparalleled.

Āprītapā (S) (M) **1.** guarding the joyous. **3.** another name for Viṣṇu.

Apriya (S) (M) **1.** not liked. **2.** unpopular. **3.** a yakṣa (*B. Literature*).

Apsavya (S) (M) **1.** being in the water. **3.** another name for Varuṇa.

Apsuhomya (S) (M) **1.** one who subsists on water alone during the period of offering penance or sacrifice. **3.** a sage in the assembly of Yudhiṣṭhira (*M. Bh.*).

Āpta (S) (M) **1.** achieved the goal. **2.** logical; organized; reliable. **3.** a serpent of the Kaśyapa dynasty (*M. Bh.*).

Aptu (S) (M) small; tender.

Āpu (S) (M) **1.** to be pure. **2.** flawless; virtuous; divine.

Apūpa (S) (M) little; honeycomb; cake.

Apūrva (S) (M) **1.** unprecedented; singular. **2.** Supreme Soul.

Āpyas (S) (M) **1.** belonging to water. **3.** a vasu (*Ṛg Veda*).

Ara (S) (M) **1.** swift. **2.** speedy; the spoke of an altar. **3.** an ocean in Brahmā's world (*Brah. Purāṇa*); the 18th Jaina Arhat of the present Avasarpiṇī (*J. S. Koṣa*).

Arabhaṭa (S) (M) enterprising; courageous.

Ārādhaka (S) (M) worshipper.

Arāga (S) (M) **1.** without passion. **2.** cool; calm.

Ārāgam (S) (M) **1.** assisting; helpful. **3.** another name for Kārttikeya.

Arāli (S) (M) **1.** crooked. **3.** a son of Viśvāmitra (*M. Bh.*).

Aramanas (S) (M) **1.** desire. **2.** pleasure; delight; enjoyment; ready to serve; obedient.

Araṇa (S) (M) **1.** distant. **2.** heaven.

Aranātha (S) (M) **1.** controller of time. **2.** a god. **3.** the 18th Jaina Tīrthaṅkara and the son of King Sudarśana of Hastināpura (*J. S. Koṣa*).

Araṇis (S) (M) **1.** turning round. **3.** another name for the sun.

Araṇya (S) (M) **1.** forest. **2.** a foreign place; a desert. **3.** a son of Manu Raivata (*H. Purāṇa*); an Ikṣvāku king (*Bhāgavata*).

Araṇyakumāra (S) (M) prince of the forest.

Arapaćana (S) (M) **1.** to surrender oneself. **3.** a mystical collective name of the 5 Dhyāni Buddhas (*B. Literature*).

Arāru (S) (M) **1.** without mercy. **2.** cruel. **3.** an asura (*Ṛg Veda*).

Arati (S) (M) moving quickly; delighted; drowned in love.

Aravinda (S) (M) **1.** lotus (*Nelumbium speciosum*). **2.** fragrant; beautiful; auspicious; dear to the gods.

Aravindanābha (S) (M) **1.** the lotus navelled. **3.** another name for Viṣṇu.

Arāvinī (S) (M) **1.** making a tinkling sound. **3.** a son of Jayasena (*V. Purāṇa*).

Arayannam (S) (M) **1.** lover of nature. **2.** living in the forest. **3.** the celestial hansa or swan regarded as the son of Dhṛtarāṣṭra and Kaśyapa (*V. Rāmāyaṇa*).

Arbuda (S) (M) **1.** tumour; 10 million; mountain; foetus. **3.** an asura killed by Indra (*Ṛg Veda*); a nāga (*M. Bh.*); another name for Mount Abu (*M. Bh.*).

Arbudī (S) (M) **1.** born of a tumour. **3.** a Vedic ṛṣi (*Ṛg Veda*).

Arćā (S) (M) **1.** shining; brilliant; worship. **2.** one who is adored; venerated.

Arćanānas (S) (M) **1.** having a rattling carriage. **2.** whose arrival and departure is announced. **3.** a sage in the Atri family who married Rathavīti and became the father of Mahāṛṣi Śyāvāśva (*Ṛg Veda*).

Arćat (S) (M) **1.** shining; praising. **2.** brilliant; glorious; praised. **3.** a ṛṣi and son of Hiraṇyastūpa (*Nirukta*).

Arći (S) (M) **1.** ray; flame; one who offers prayers; to whom the prayers are offered. **3.** one of the 12 ādityas (*K. Brāhmaṇa*).

Ārćika (S) (M) **1.** one who prays. **3.** a descendant of a ṛṣi (*M. Bh.*); another name for Jamadagni.

Arćin (S) (M) **1.** shining; devout. **3.** Varuṇa's feet.

Arćiśmat (S) (M) **1.** flaming. **2.** brilliant; resplendant. **3.** another name for Agni, Viṣṇu and the sun.

Arćita (S) (M) worshipped.

Ardana (S) (M) **1.** moving restlessly. **3.** another name for Śiva.

Ardhaćakrin (S) (M) **1.** half a ćakravartin. **3.** one of the 9 Black vasudevas of the Jainas (*J. S. Koṣa*).

Ardhakāla (S) (M) **1.** half destroyer. **3.** Śiva who when conjoined with Śakti — the female form of energy— brings about complete destruction.

Ardhaketu (S) (M) **1.** half bannered. **3.** the half or crescent moon that adorns the locks of Śiva and is identified with him; a rudra (*Vā. Purāṇa*).

Ardhalakṣmīhari (S) (M) **1.** half Lakṣmī and half Viṣṇu. **3.** a form of Viṣṇu (*V. Purāṇa*).

Ardhanārīśvara (S) (M) **1.** lord who is half female. **3.** form of Śiva where he is conjoined with Śakti — the female form of energy.

Ardhendra (S) (M) one whose half belongs to Indra.

Ardhendu (S) (M) crescent moon.

Ardhendumauli (S) (M) **1.** one whose diadem is the crescent moon. **3.** another name for Śiva.

Ārdra (S) (M) **1.** moist; succulent; green; soft; tender; warm; young. **3.** a grandson of Pṛthu (*H. Purāṇa*).

Areṅu (S) (M) **1.** without dust. **2.** pure; not earthly; celestial; a god.

Argañjan (S) (M) **1.** act of offering. **2.** sacred; venerated; devoted.

Argheśvara (S) (M) **1.** lord of offering. **3.** another name for Śiva.

Arghya (S) (M) **1.** valuable. **2.** the act of offering sacred water to propitiate the deities; an oblation; valuable; one who deserves a respectful reception.

Arha (S) (M) **1.** deserving. **3.** another name for Śiva and Indra.

Arhaṇa (S) (M) **1.** worshipped. **3.** an attendant of Viṣṇu (*V. Purāṇa*).

Arhant (S) (M) **1.** worthy; praised worshipper; without violence. **2.** peaceful; mild; gentle; humane; kind; a Buddha. **3.** another name for Śiva.

Arhat (S) (M) **1.** deserving. **2.** worthy; respectable. **3.** a superior divinity of the Jainas (*J. S. Koṣa*); a Buddhist aspiring for Nirvāṇa (*B. Literature*).

Arhattama (S) (M) most deserving.

Aridamana (S) (M) suppressor of foes.

Ariha (S) (M) **1.** killing enemies. **3.** a lunar dynasty king who was a son of Arvaćina and Maryādā and the father of Mahābhauma (*M. Bh.*); a son of Devātithi.

Arijit (S) (M) **1.** conquering enemies. **3.** a son of Kṛṣṇa and Subhadrā (*Bhāgavata*).

Arimardana (S) (M) **1.** destroying enemies. **3.** a king of owls (*Panćatantra*); a son of Śvaphalka (*H. Purāṇa*).

Ariṁejaya (S) (M) **1.** conqueror of enemies. **3.** a Purū king (*A. Purāṇa*).

Ariṁjaya (S) (M) **1.** shaking enemies. **3.** a son of Śvaphalka; a nāga priest; another name for Kuru.

Ariṁdama (S) (M) **1.** suppresses foes. **3.** the father of Sanaśruta (*A. Brāhmaṇa*); another name for Śiva.

Arin (S) (M) **1.** with spokes. **2.** discus.

Ariṣṭa (S) (M) **1.** unhurt; secure; safe. **3.** an asura son of Bali killed by Kṛṣṇa (*H. Purāṇa*); a son of Manu aivasvata (*V. Purāṇa*); an asura servant of Kaṇsa (*Bhāgavata*); the Neem tree (*Azadirachta indica*).

Ariṣṭahan (S) (M) **1.** slayer of Ariṣṭa. **3.** another name for Viṣṇu.

Ariṣṭamathana (S) (M) **1.** slayer of Ariṣṭa. **3.** another name for Viṣṇu.

Ariṣṭanemi (S) (M) **1.** unbroken felly. **2.** felly whose wheel is intact; smooth and uninter-rupted journey. **3.** a son of Vinatā who was the father of Sumati (*M. Bh.*); the wife of King Sagara (*Rāmāyaṇa*); a son of Kaśyapa (*M. Bh.*); a king in the council of Yama (*M. Bh.*); name assumed by Sahadeva in the Virāta kingdom (*M. Bh.*); the 22 Jaina Tīrthaṅkaras of the present Avasarpiṇī (*A. Koṣa*); a prajāpati who married 4 of Dakṣa's daughters (*Ś. Purāṇa*); a yakṣa who dwells in the chariot of the sun (*Ṛg Veda*); a gandharva (*V. Samhitā*); another name for Kṛṣṇa.

Ariṣṭuta (S) (M) **1.** praised with zeal. **3.** another name for Indra.

Arisūdana (S) (M) killing enemies.

Ārita (S) (M) praised.

Ariyappā (S) (M) eliminating the enemy.

Arjana (S) (M) conqueror of the enemy.

Ārjava (S) (M) **1.** straight. **2.** upright; sincere; honest. **3.** son of Subala and brother of Śakuni (*M. Bh.*).

Arjita (S) (M) **1.** acquired. **2.** gained; earned. **3.** a son of Kṛṣṇa (*Bhāgavata*).

Arjuna (S) (M) **1.** made of silver; peacock; the tree *Tenninalia arjuna*; the White Murdah tree (*Terminalia citrina*); the tree (*Lagerstroemia flos-reginae*); white; clear; bright; the colour of day; lightning; milk; dawn.

2. fair in visage and mind; pure; glorious; illuminating; enlightening. 3. the third Pāṇḍava who was the son of Indra and Kuntī, whose accepted father was Pāṇḍu, regarded as the reincarnation of the sage Nara, equal to Śiva in prowess and as unconquerable as Indra, husband of Draupadī, Ulūpikā, Ćitrāṅgadā and Subhadrā, father of Śrutakīrti (from Draupadī), Irāvān (from Ulūpikā), Babhruvāhana (from Ćitrāṅgadā) and Abhimanyu (from Subhadrā) (*M. Bh.*); a son of Emperor Nimi (*M. Bh.*); a member of Yama's assembly (*M. Bh.*); a son of Kṛtavīrya (*M. Bh.*).

Arjunāgraja (S) (M) 1. elder brother of Arjuna. 3. another name for Bhīma.

Arjunapāla (S) (M) 1. protector of the Arjuna tree; protector of Arjuna. 3. son of Śamīka who guarded the Arjuna tree (*Terminalia arjuna*) (*Bhāgavata*); another name for Kṛṣṇa.

Arjunapūrvaja (S) (M) 1. preceding Arjuna. 3. another name for Bhīma.

Arjunasakhi (S) (M) 1. friend of Arjuna. 2. with Arjuna as companion. 3. another name for Kṛṣṇa.

Arjunātmaja (S) (M) 1. son of Arjuna. 3. another name for Abhimanyu.

Ārjuni (S) (M) 1. son of Arjuna. 3. another name for Abhimanyu.

Arjuni (S) (M) 1. of fair complexion. 2. shining; glorious; illuminating; enlightening. 3. the Phālguni Nakṣatra considered to be very bright (*Ṛg Veda*).

Arka (S) (M) 1. ray; flash of lightning; the sun; fire. 2. crystal; praise; hymn; song; a learned man; an elder brother. 3. another name for Indra; the Red Sandalwood tree (*Pterocarpus satalinus*).

Arkaja (S) (M) 1. born of the sun. 3. another name for Karṇa, Yama, Sugrīva and Saturn.

Arkakara (S) (M) 1. hand of the sun. 2. a sunbeam.

Arkanandana (S) (M) 1. son of the sun. 3. another name of Karṇa and Saturn.

Arkanayana (S) (M) 1. sun eyed. 3. an asura (*H. Purāṇa*).

Arkaprakāśa (S) (M) light of the sun; as bright as the sun.

Arkapriya (S) (M) 1. beloved of the sun. 3. Shoeflower (*Hibiscus rosa chinensis*).

Arkaputra (S) (M) 1. son of the sun. 3. another name for Karṇa, Saturn, Yama and Sugrīva.

Arkaśa (S) (M) 1. illuminated by the sun. 2. visible; manifest.

Arkāśmaṇi (S) (M) 1. jewel of the sun. 2. heliotrope; crystal; sunstone; ruby.

Arkatanaya (S) (M) 1. son of the sun. 3. another name for Saturn, Karṇa, Manu Sāvarṇa and Manu Vaivasvata.

Ārki (S) (M) 1. descendant of the sun. 3. another name for Saturn, Yama, Manu, Sugrīva and Karṇa.

Arkin (S) (M) 1. radiant with light. 2. shining; bright; praised; worshipped.

Arkka (S) (M) 1. the substance; the essence. 2. subtle; divine. 3. an asura reborn as sage Ṛṣika (*M. Bh.*); the plant (*Calotropis gigantea*); another name for the sun.

Arkkaparṇa (S) (M) 1. a leaf of the Arkka plant (*Calotropis gigantea*). 3. a gandharva son of Kaśyapa and Muni (*M. Bh.*).

Ārkṣa (S) (M) 1. stellar; belonging to the stars; descendant of Ṛkṣa. 3. another name for Saṁvaraṇa.

Armugam (S) (M) 1. one who grants emancipation speedily. 3. another name for Kārttikeya.

Arṇava (S) (M) ocean; sea; sun; air; stream; flood; wave.

Ārоćana (S) (M) 1. shining. 2. bright; glorious.

Āroga (S) (M) 1. destroyer; shatterer. 3. one of the 7 suns at the end of a period of the world which in Hindu mythology is termed as Pralaya.

Arokya (S) (M) very pious.

Arśa (S) (M) 1. sky; heaven; celestial; of sacred descent. 2. heavenly; venerated; divine.

Ārṣabhi (S) (M) 1. like a bull. 3. the first Ćakravartin of Bharata.

Ārṣṭiṣena (S) (M) **1.** protected by swords. **2.** a commander. **3.** a sage visited by the Pāṇḍavas (*M. Bh.*).

Arśya (S) (M) **1.** celestial; of sacred descent. **2.** belonging to hermits.

Ārtaparṇa (S) (M) **1.** son of Ṛtaparṇa. **3.** another name for Sudāsa (*H. Purāṇa*).

Arthadarśin (S) (M) **1.** one who knows the meaning; knower of the essence; attained salvation or mokṣa. **2.** a Buddha.

Artham (S) (M) **1.** fortune. **3.** the golden lotus on the forehead of Viṣṇu from which the goddess Śrī originated.

Arthapati (S) (M) **1.** lord of wealth. **3.** the grandfather of the poet Bāṇa; another name for Kubera (*Kad*).

Arthasiddhi (S) (M) **1.** acquisition of wealth. **3.** a son of Puṣya (*H. Purāṇa*).

Arthasādhaka (S) (M) **1.** promoting an aim. **2.** useful; profitable. **3.** a minister of Daśaratha (*V. Rāmāyaṇa*).

Arthvāna (S) (M) with a purpose; wealth; full of sense and meaning.

Ārtimān (S) (M) **1.** suffering from pain; begs for divine mercy for being relieved from suffering. **3.** a mantra that eliminates all fear (*M. Bh.*).

Aru (S) (M) **1.** tawny. **3.** the red blossomed Khadira tree (*Acacia catechu*); another name for the sun.

Arudra (S) (M) **1.** not cruel. **2.** soft; gentle; tender; calm.

Arujas (S) (M) **1.** free from disease. **2.** brisk; gay. **3.** a rākṣasa attendant of Rāvaṇa (*V. Rāmāyaṇa*); Indian Laburnum (*Cassia Fistula*).

Arula (S) (M) **1.** shining as the sun. **2.** brilliant; glorious; enlightening.

Arulamaṇi (S) (M) jewel of the sun.

Arumakham (S) (M) **1.** as vigorous as the sun. **3.** another name for ārttikeya.

Aruṇa (S) (M) **1.** red; gold; saffron; tawny; ruddy. **3.** dawn personified as the charioteer of the sun (*M. Smṛti*); one of the 12 ādityas (*Sk. Purāṇa*); a son of Kaśyapa and Vinatā, brother of Garuḍa, husband of Śyenī, the father of Sampāti and Jaṭāyu (*V. Rāmāyaṇa*), and who became the charioteer of the sun (*M. Bh.*); a solar dynasty king who was the father of Triśaṅku (*D. Bh. Purāṇa*); a ṛṣi born from the flesh of Brahmā (*T. Āraṇyaka*); a dānava born in the dynasty of Vipraćitti (*D. Bh. Purāṇa*); a son of Narakāsura killed by Kṛṣṇa; a son of Kṛṣṇa (*Bhāgavata*); a serpent (*M. Bh.*).

Aruṇāditya (S) (M) **1.** the crimson sun. **3.** one of the 12 forms of the sun (*Sk. Purāṇa*).

Aruṇāgraja (S) (M) **1.** the 1st born of Aruṇa. **3.** another name for Garuḍa.

Aruṇajyotiṣ (S) (M) **1.** as bright as the sun. **3.** another name for Śiva.

Aruṇakamala (S) (M) **1.** the Red lotus (*Nymphaea rubra*). **2.** passionate; fecund; fragrant; famous; dear to the gods.

Aruṇākara (S) (M) **1.** red rayed. **3.** another name for the sun.

Aruṇānśu (S) (M) with red rays.

Aruṇānuja (S) (M) **1.** younger brother of Aruṇa. **3.** another name for Garuḍa.

Aruṇapriya (S) (M) **1.** beloved of the *Nymphaea rubra*. **3.** another name for the sun.

Aruṇarćis (S) (M) the rising sun; with a red glow.

Aruṇasārathī (S) (M) **1.** one whose charioteer is Aruṇa. **3.** another name for the sun.

Aruṇāśva (S) (M) **1.** driving with red horses. **3.** another name for the maruts.

Aruṇāva (S) (M) **1.** the red flavour. **2.** immensely protected; well-preserved.

Arundhatīnātha (S) (M) **1.** lord of Arundhatī. **3.** another name for Vasiṣṭha.

Aruṇeśa (S) (M) **1.** lord of Aruṇa. **3.** another name for Sūrya.

Āruṇi (S) (M) **1.** reddish in complexion. **3.** another name for Uddālaka the disciple of Ayodhyadhaumya (*Bhāgavata*); a serpent of the Dhṛtarāṣṭra family (*M. Bh.*); a soldier of the Kaurava army (*M. Bh.*).

Aruṇodaya (S) (M) **1.** dawn. **2.** blooming; awakened.

Aruṇopala (S) (M) **1.** the stone of the sun. **2.** the ruby.

Arunśu (S) (M) heals wounds.

Aruṣa (S) (M) **1.** without anger; calm; shining; bright; red. **2.** another name for the sun.

Arva (S) (M) **1.** horse. **2.** agile; swift. **3.** a son of Ṛpunjaya (*V. Parāṇa*); a seer of the 2nd Manvantara (*Ś. Brāhmaṇa*).

Arvācīna (S) (M) **1.** turned towards; favouring. **3.** husband of Maryādā (*M. Bh.*).

Arvana (S) (M) **1.** running like a horse. **2.** swift; quick; agile. **3.** a horse of the moon (*A. Koṣa*); another name for Indra.

Arvavasan (S) (M) **1.** borne by horses. **2.** that which is swift. **3.** one of the 7 principal rays of the sun (*Ṛg Veda*).

Arvāvasu (S) (M) **1.** priest of the gods. **2.** immersed in religious and spiritual pursuits; venerated. **3.** a Brāhmaṇa of the gods (*Kau. Upaniṣad*); a son of Raibhya (*M. Bh.*); an ascetic in the court of Yudhiṣṭhira (*M. Bh.*).

Arvīndra (S) (M) lord of horses; lord of wheels; lord of priests.

Arvuda (S) (M) **1.** priest of hymns. **3.** the priest described in the *Kauṣītakī Brāhmaṇa* as a creator of mantras.

Ārya (S) (M) **1.** honoured; noble; master. **2.** kind; auspicious; attached; devoted; dear; excellent; respectable; faithful; worthy; wise and masterly.

Āryabhaṭā (S) (M) **1.** enterprising; best among the masters; courageous. **3.** a famous Indian mathematician and astronomer (5th century A.D.) (*Aryabhatīya*).

Āryaćetas (S) (M) of a noble mind.

Āryadeva (S) (M) **1.** lord of the honoured; noblest. **2.** considered the best among Aryans. **3.** a Buddhist philosopher and foster son of the king of Siṁhala who succeeded Nāgārjuna as the head of the Mādhyamika school in Nālandā and was the author of the *Ćatuḥśataka*.

Āryaka (S) (M) **1.** like an Ārya. **2.** a person who has all the virtues of an Ārya; honourable; respectable. **3.** a serpent advisor of Vāsuki (*M. Bh.*).

Āryakumāra (S) (M) **1.** noble prince. **2.** noble; virtuous; meritorious.

Aryaman (S) (M) **1.** companion; playfellow; the sun. **3.** an āditya or sovereign principle of the *Ṛg Veda,* represented as a son of Kaśyapa and Aditi, standing for honour, nobility, chivalry and the rules of society, considered the original aristocrat and the source of blue blood, the protector of the family, a main Vedic deity that rules over the cosmic body, considered the embodiment of the sun which is the cosmic eye, supposed to be the chief of the manes and whose path is the Milky Way (*T. Brāhmāṇa*); son of Atri and Anasūya and the brother of Anatā, he presides over the Nakṣatra Uttarāphālgunī (*V.'s B. Samhitā*).

Āryaman (S) (M) **1.** surrounded by nobles; of noble lineage. **2.** belonging to the sun.

Āryamik (S) (M) **1.** as meritorious as an Ārya. **2.** noble; virtuous.

Āryamiśra (S) (M) distinguished among nobles.

Āryaśūra (S) (M) **1.** brave among the Āryas. **2.** honourable. **3.** a Buddhist poet and philosopher (*B. Literature*).

Āryāśva (S) (M) **1.** with devoted horses. **3.** a solar dynasty king (*V. Rāmāyaṇa*).

Āryāvarta (S) (M) **1.** land of the worshipped. **3.** a king of the dynasty of Viśvakarmā who was the son of Ṛṣabha and Jayantī (*M. Bh.*); ancient India in the Aryan period (*M. Smrti*).

Āryendra (S) (M) lord of the masters.

Āryika (S) (M) masterly; honoured.

Āṣāḍha (S) (M) **1.** brings hope (hope for the rains that provide a respite from the sweltering heat of the month of Jyeṣṭha [May-June] the hottest month in the Indian Calendar, thus this hope is provided in the form of the moon of Āṣāḍha [June-July] which heralds the monsoons in India).

2. a sacred staff. 3. a king who was a partial incarnation of the rākṣasa Krodhavaśa (*M. Bh.*); another name for Śiva.

Asamañjasa (S) (M) 1. unfit; unbecoming. 2. vascillating. 3. a solar dynasty king who was the son of Sagara and Keśinī and father of Aṅśumān (*V. Rāmāyaṇa*).

Asamātī (S) (M) 1. unequalled. 2. unparalleled; supreme; divine.

Asamabāṇa (S) (M) 1. with an odd number of arrows. 3. another name for Kāma, who releases arrows in odd numbers.

Aśan (S) (M) 1. rock. 2. the firmament; one who is strong yet subtle.

Āsaṅga (S) (M) 1. attachment; devotion. 2. attached; devoted; of a loving nature. 3. a son of Śvaphalka (*Bhāgavata*).

Asaṅgas (S) (M) 1. not attached. 2. free from worldly ties; a flag; a vessel; not blunt; not obstructed; soul; independant. 3. a son of Yuyudhāna (*H. Purāṇa*); another name for Vasubandhu (*B. Ćarita*).

Aśaniprabha (S) (M) 1. as illuminating as a flash of lightning. 3. a rākṣasa (*V. Rāmāyaṇa*).

Aśanis (S) (M) 1. flash of lightning. 2. Indra's thunderbolt; missile; fire. 3. a hermit (*M. Bh.*); one of the 9 names of Rudra; another name for Indra.

Aśaṅka (S) (M) 1. without doubt. 2. fearless; certain.

Aśankita (S) (M) 1. without doubt; without fear. 2. clear; hopeful; fearless. 3. a king of the Bhoja family of Gujarat (*K. Sāgara*).

Āśāpūrṇa (S) (M) 1. whose desire is fulfilled. 2. fulfilling desires.

Aśatrus (S) (M) 1. with no adversaries. 3. another name for the moon.

Aśavijaya (S) (M) conquering the world; heaven and space.

Aśavāha (S) (M) 1. borne by space; the heavens; the world. 2. celestial; heavenly; divine. 3. a son of Kaśyapa and Aditi (*M. Bh.*); a Vṛṣni prince (*M. Bh.*).

Asećana (S) (M) charming; lovely.

Aśeṣa (S) (M) 1. without any remainder. 2. whole; entire; complete; perfect; divine.

Aśiddhārtha (S) (M) 1. one who has mastered archery. 3. a minister of King Daśaratha (*V. Rāmāyaṇa*).

Asikṛṣṇa (S) (M) 1. as sharp as a sword. 3. son of solar dynasty King Aśvamedhas (*Bhāgavata*).

Asiloman (S) (M) 1. with hair as sharp as the points of swords. 3. a minister of Mahiṣāsura (*D. Bh. Purāṇa*).

Asīma (S) (M) endless; limitless.

Asīman (S) (M) 1. unlimited. 2. boundless; immense; divine.

Āśira (S) (M) 1. eating everything. 2. a fragrant root; fire; sun; wind; diamond. 3. a rākṣasa (*A. Koṣa*).

Asīra (S) (M) 1. milk mixed with Soma. 2. pious; energetic.

Āśīṣa (S) (M) 1. a blessing. 2. blessed; venerated; highly sought; rare.

Aśiśira (S) (M) 1. not cool. 2. hot.

Āśīṣṭha (S) (M) 1. very quick. 2. fast; swift; agile; active.

Āsita (S) (M) 1. seated; at rest. 2. tranquil; at peace; poised.

Asita (S) (M) 1. not white; unbounded. 2. dark coloured; blue; black. 3. the planet Saturn (*V's B. Samhitā*); a son of Bharata (*V. Rāmāyaṇa*); a prominent sage and father of Devala who spread the story of Mahābhārata to the public (*R. Aṅkuramaṇkā*); a mountain; Common Indigo (*Indigofera tinctoria*); another name for Kṛṣṇa.

Aśīta (S) (M) 1. not cold. 2. warm; hot.

Asītābha (S) (M) with unrestrained glory; surrounded by light.

Asitadhanvā (S) (M) 1. with an unbound bow; with a blue bow. 2. never had to bind his bow and therefore to fight, conquered his enemy without lifting his bow. 3. a Vedic king who wrote the *Veda* of *Asuravidyā*.

Asītadhvaja (S) (M) 1. with an unbound flag. 2. has a glorious reign. 3. a son of Kaśyapa and Vinatā (*M. Bh.*).

Asitāṅga (S) (M) **1.** blue limbed. **3.** a form of Śiva.

Asitāśman (S) (M) **1.** blue stone. **2.** the Lapis lazuli.

Asitotpala (S) (M) the blue lotus (*Nymphaea stellata*).

Asjita (S) (M) **1.** bearing victory. **2.** always victorious.

Asketa (S) (M) master of will; master of the house; destroyer of apparition.

Askhala (S) (M) **1.** not shaking or slipping. **2.** firm; steady. **3.** an Agni (*A. Purāṇa*).

Askol (S) (M) **1.** painted. **3.** the painted Spurfowl (*Galloperdix lunulatus*).

Askran (S) (M) attacking enemies.

Āśleṣā (S) (M) **1.** an embrace. **3.** the 7th lunar mansion of whose 5 stars are grouped together as if in an embrace (*V's B. Saṃhitā*).

Aśma (S) (M) **1.** hard as stone; a cloud. **2.** the firmament; strong yet subtle. **3.** a sage (*Ṛg Veda*).

Aśmaka (S) (M) **1.** stone; thunderbolt; cloud. **2.** rock; precious stone; the firmament. **3.** a son of Vasiṣṭha and the wife of King Kalmāṣapāda of Ayodhyā (*M. Bh.*); a king on the Pāṇḍava side (*M. Bh.*); a sage (*M. Bh.*).

Aśmakadāyāda (S) (M) **1.** stone thrower; attacking with a thunderbolt. **3.** a son of King Aśmaka who fought on the side of the Kauravas (*M. Bh.*); another name for Indra.

Āśmana (S) (M) **1.** stone; gem; rock; thunderbolt; cloud; mountain; pervading. **3.** another name for Aruṇa.

Aśmanta (S) (M) **1.** a fireplace. **3.** a marutvat (*Vā. Purāṇa*).

Asmi (S) (M) am.

Aśmita (S) (M) **1.** rock born. **2.** very hard; tough; strong.

Aśmuṇḍ (S) (M) existing; shining.

Aśoka (S) (M) **1.** without sorrow; blossom of the Aśoka tree (*Saraca indica*). **3.** a king of Pāṭaliputra (*M. Bh.*); charioteer of Bhīma (*M. Bh.*); a minister of King Daśaratha (*V. Rāmāyaṇa*); a Kalinga king of the family of the asura Aśva (*M. Bh.*); an emperor of the Maurya dynasty who was the son of Bimbisāra and went on to become a Buddhist monk (269 B.C.) (*B. Literature*).

Aśokadatta (S) (M) **1.** given without sorrow. **2.** happily given. **3.** incarnation, of the vidyādhara Aśokavega (*K. Sāgara*).

Aśokakara (S) (M) **1.** eliminating sorrows. **3.** a vidyādhara (*K. Sāgara*).

Aśokavardhana (S) (M) **1.** increasing grieflessness. **3.** a king (*Bh. Purāṇa*).

Aśokavega (S) (M) **1.** whose emotions are without sorrow or suffering. **2.** calm; tranquil; blissful. **3.** a vidyādhara (*K. Sāgara*).

Āspada (S) (M) **1.** seat; dignity; authority; power. **3.** the 10th lunar mansion.

Aśpan (S) (M) **1.** an efficient horse rider. **3.** another name for the Supreme Spirit who controls time which is personified as a horse.

Aśrapa (S) (M) **1.** drinking blood. **3.** a rākṣasa presiding over the 19th lunar mansion.

Aśrava (S) (M) listening to; obedient; compliant.

Āśravya (S) (M) **1.** much heard of; whom people listen to attentatively. **3.** a sage in Indra's assembly (*M. Bh.*).

Āśrayāśa (S) (M) **1.** consuming that which comes in contact. **3.** another name for Agni.

Āśrita (S) (M) dependant.

Āśruta (S) (M) **1.** heard. **2.** well known.

Āśrutavrana (S) (M) **1.** with a well-known injury. **3.** a son of Dyutimat (*V. Purāṇa*).

Aṣṭajīhva (S) (M) **1.** 8 tongued. **3.** a soldier of Skanda's army (*M. Bh.*).

Aṣṭaka (S) (M) **1.** with 8 parts. **2.** an octrahedron. **3.** 8th day after full moon; a Purū dynasty king who was the son of Ajamīdha and brother of Śunahśepa; a son of Viśvāmitra and Mādhavī the wife of Yayāti (*A. Brāhmaṇa*).

Aṣṭakarṇa (S) (M) **1.** 8 eared. **3.** another name for the 4 headed Brahmā.

Aṣṭamūrti (S) (M) **1.** 8 faced. **3.** a form of Śiva.

Aṣṭaratha (S) (M) **1.** with 8 chariots. **3.** a son of Bhīmaratha (*H. Purāṇa*).

Aṣṭāvakra (S) (M) **1.** with 8 bends. **3.** a great sage born with 8 physical deformities, who was the son of Kāhodara and Sujātā or Uddālaka, the husband of Suprabhā and who cursed the apsarās who had made fun of his physical crookedness and because of this they were reborn as the wives of Kṛṣṇa (*A. Purāṇa*).

Aṣṭika (S) (M) **1.** 8th child. **3.** the 8th son of sage Jaratkaru and Manasādevī.

Āstīka (S) (M) **1.** believing in existence and god. **3.** a sage and son of Jaratkaru (*H. Purāṇa*).

Astrita (S) (M) invincible; gold.

Āśu (S) (M) **1.** fast. **2.** quick; agile; active.

Āśuga (S) (M) **1.** swift; fleet. **2.** wind; sun; arrow. **3.** one of the first five followers of Śākyamunī.

Aśūla (S) (M) **1.** without thorns. **2.** without obstacles; peaceful; tranquil; ever happy. **3.** the tree *Vitex alata.*

Āśumat (S) (M) **1.** mentally agile. **2.** quick witted.

Asura (S) (M) **1.** incorporeal. **2.** spiritual; divine; spirit; demon; ghost. **3.** opponents of the gods regarded as children of Diti by Kaśyapa (*Ṛg Veda*/*A. Veda*).

Asurādhipa (S) (M) **1.** lord of the asuras. **3.** another name for Bali.

Asuratarajasa (S) (M) **1.** frightening the asuras. **3.** a son of King Kuśa and Vaidarbhī (*V. Rāmāyaṇa*).

Asurāyana (S) (M) **1.** devoted to demons. **3.** a son of Viśvāmitra (*M. Bh.*).

Asurendra (S) (M) **1.** lord of the asuras. **3.** another name for Vṛtra.

Āsurī (S) (M) **1.** demonlike; very powerful. **3.** a sage and preceptor of sage Panćaśikha and the husband of Kapilā (*M. Bh.*).

Asūrtarajasa (S) (M) **1.** sphere of darkness; mist or gloom of the unknown; living in darkness; remote. **3.** a son of Kuśa (*H. Purāṇa*).

Āśuśukṣaṇi (S) (M) **1.** shining forth. **3.** another name for Agni.

Āśutoṣa (S) (M) **1.** easily pleased. **3.** another name for Śiva.

Aśva (S) (M) **1.** horse; the number 7. **2.** strong; swift; materially successful. **3.** a son of Ćitraka (*H. Purāṇa*); a demon reborn as King Aśoka of Kalinga (*M. Bh.*); a sage and father of Vaśa (*Ṛg Veda*); a dānava (*M. Bh.*).

Aśvadāvan (S) (M) **1.** acceptor of the horse sacrifice. **3.** another name for Indra.

Aśvaghoṣa (S) (M) **1.** neighing. **2.** horse voiced. **3.** a Sanskṛta poet; a Buddhist patriarch (*B. Literature*).

Aśvagrīva (S) (M) **1.** horse necked. **3.** with a long and strong neck. **3.** an asura; a son of Ćitraka; an incarnation of Viṣṇu in horse form; a son of aśyapa and Danu (*M. Bh.*).

Aśvajit (S) (M) horses by conquest gaining.

Aśvaketu (S) (M) **1.** horse bannered. **3.** a king who had performed the Aśvamedha Yajña and was therefore a ćakravartin; a son of King Gāndhāra who fought on the side of the Kauravas (*M. Bh.*).

Aśvala (S) (M) **1.** one who brings horses. **2.** a stableboy. **3.** the priest of King Janaka who led the horse for the Aśvamedha Yajña (*Br. Upaniṣhad*).

Aśvalāvana (S) (M) **1.** causes breath. **2.** revives; a god. **3.** a son of Viśvāmitra (*M. Bh.*).

Aśvamedhas (S) (M) **1.** horse sacrifice. **3.** a descendant of Bharata (*Ṛg Veda*); a son of King Sahasrānīka *Bhāgavata*).

Aśvamedhadatta (S) (M) **1.** obtained from the horse sacrifice. **3.** a son of Śatānīka (*M. Bh.*).

Aśvapati (S) (M) **1.** lord of horses. **3.** king of Madra and father of Sāvitrī (*M. Bh.*); a son of Kaśyapa and Danu (*M. Bh.*); a brother-in-law of Daśaratha (*Rāmāyaṇa*); an asura; another name for Indra.

Aśvarāja (S) (M) **1.** king of horses. **3.** another name for the horse Uććaihśravas.

Aśvarya (S) (M) not ordinary; marvellous; extraordinary; miraculous; surprising; prodigal.

Aśvaśanku (S) (M) **1.** phallus of the horse; possesses ten billion horses. **3.** a son of Kaśyapa and Danu (*M. Bh.*).

Aśvasena (S) (M) **1.** one who has an army of horses. **2.** commander of an army of horse-men. **3.** a son of Kṛṣṇa (*Bhāgavata*); the father of the 23rd Arhat of the present Avasarpinī (*J. S. Koṣa*); a serpent (*M. Bh.*).

Aśvaśiras (S) (M) **1.** horse headed. **3.** a son of Kaśyapa and Danu (*M. Bh.*).

Aśvaśīrṣa (S) (M) **1.** horse headed. **3.** a form of Viṣṇu (*M. Bh.*).

Aśvatara (S) (M) **1.** a better horse. **2.** a swifter, stronger horse chief of the nāgas (*S. Purāṇa*); a sacred pond in Prayāga (*M. Bh.*). **3.** a gandharva (*H. Purāṇa*).

Aśvattha (S) (M) the Aśvattha tree (*Ficus religiosa*); lord of the place where the horses rest; holy tree under which the gods sit.

Aśvatthāman (S) (M) **1.** having the strength of a horse. **3.** son of Droṇa and Kṛpī (*M. Bh.*); an elephant of the king of Mālavā killed by Bhīma (*M. Bh.*); a ṛṣi in the period of Manu Sāvarṇi (*H. Purāṇa*).

Aśvatthanārāyaṇa (S) (M) lord of the Aśvattha tree (*Ficus religiosa*); lord of the place where horses rest.

Aśvatthi (S) (M) the Aśvattha tree (*Ficus religiosa*) under which horses are kept.

Aśvatyama (S) (M) **1.** sees beyond 7 (the number 7 is of tāntric significance and one who sees beyond it is supposed to have attained salvation or mokṣa). **3.** a seer of the 8th Manvantara (*H. Purāṇa*).

Aśvavān (S) (M) **1.** rich in horses. **3.** a son of King Kuru and Vāhinī (*M. Bh.*).

Aśvin (S) (M) **1.** mounted on horseback; with horses; cavalier. **3.** the collective name of the divine physicians — the twin sons of Sūrya and Sañjña, Satya and Dasra, and parents of Nakula and Sahadeva (*M. Bh.*); the zodiac sign of Gemini (*N. Samhitā*); the Vedic god of agriculture (*Ṛg Veda*).

Āśvineya (S) (M) **1.** son of the aśvins. **3.** another name for Sahadeva.

Aśvini (S) (M) **1.** possessing horses. **2.** wealthy; moves swiftly. **3.** the divine physicians (*Ṛg Veda*); the number two (*Ṛg Veda*); a constellation (*V's B. Samhitā*).

Aśvinīkumāra (S) (M) **1.** the son of Aśvinī. **3.** the 2 sons of Vivasvan and Saṇjña in her horse form, named Satya and Dasra, who are the physicians of the gods and the fathers of Nakula and Sahadeva (*Br. Purāṇa*).

Aśvinīsuta (S) (M) **1.** son of Aśvinī. **3.** a son of Sūrya and wife of Sutapas (*Br. Purāṇa*).

Āṭaka (S) (M) **1.** wanderer. **2.** homeless; a sadhu. **3.** a serpent of the Kaurava dynasty (*M. Bh.*).

Aṭala (S) (M) firm; immoveable; stable; steady.

Atalas (S) (M) **1.** bottomless. **2.** depth cannot be gauged. **3.** another name for Śiva.

Atamas (S) (M) **1.** without darkness. **2.** flawless; of a clear mind; virtuous; sinless.

Atandra (S) (M) **1.** free from lassitude. **2.** alert; unwearied.

Atanu (S) (M) **1.** without body. **2.** incorporeal; divine. **3.** another name for Kāma.

Ātapana (S) (M) **1.** causing heat. **3.** another name for Śiva.

Ātāpin (S) (M) **1.** radiating heat. **3.** a daitya (*K. Sāgara*).

Atasa (S) (M) **1.** not gross; air; the soul. **2.** subtle; divine.

Atharvaṇa (S) (M) **1.** place where oblations are made; worshipped by the priests. **2.** an attar. **3.** a sage born from Brahmā's face who rediscovered Agni from the sea and the husband of Śānti and Ćitti (*A. Veda*); a son of Vasiṣṭha (*Bhāgavata*); the 3rd Veda; another name for Śiva.

Athileśa (S) (M) lord of intelligence.

Āti (S) (M) the Aśoka tree (*Saraca indica*); swan (*Turdus ginginianus*).

Atibāhu (S) (M) **1.** long armed. **2.** according to *Sāmudrika Śāstra* which classifies individuals by studying their physical features, people with long arms were considered to be virtuous leaders and warriors. **3.** a ṛṣi of the 14th Manvantara (*H. Purāṇa*); a gandharva son of Kaśyapa and Prādhā and brother of Hāhā, Hūhū and Tumburu (*M. Bh.*).

Atibala (S) (M) **1.** excessive power. **2.** immensely powerful; very strong. **3.** a sage responsible for the death of Rāma and Lakṣmaṇa (*U. Rāmāyaṇa*); an attendant given to Skanda by Vāyu (*M. Bh.*).

Atibhāva (S) (M) **1.** superiority. **2.** superior; one who overcomes people; situations; emotions.

Atibhīma (S) (M) **1.** very strong. **3.** a son of the Agni Tapa (*M. Bh.*).

Atićaṇḍa (S) (M) very fiery.

Atidatta (S) (M) **1.** to whom much has been given. **2.** on whom love and gifts are showered; fortunate. **3.** son of Rājādhideva and brother of Datta (*M. Bh.*).

Atideva (S) (M) surpassing the gods.

Atidhańvan (S) (M) **1.** runs very fast. **3.** a ṛṣi who was a descendant of Śunaka (*V. Brāhmaṇa*).

Atihata (S) (M) firmly fixed.

Atikāya (S) (M) **1.** with a gigantic body;. **3.** a rākṣasa son of Rāvaṇa and gandharvī Ćitrāṇgī (*K. Rāmāyaṇa*).

Atiloma (S) (M) **1.** very hairy. **3.** an asura killed by Kṛṣṇa (*M. Bh.*).

Atima (S) (M) proud.

Atimānita (S) (M) highly honoured.

Atimānuṣa (S) (M) **1.** more than human. **2.** celestial; divine.

Atimanyu (S) (M) **1.** extremely zealous. **3.** a son of Manu (*H. Purāṇa*).

Atimāya (S) (M) **1.** emancipated from illusion. **2.** beyond illusion; attained salvation or mokṣa.

Atināman (S) (M) **1.** renowned. **3.** a ṛṣi of the 6th Manvantara (*H. Purāṇa*).

Atīndra (S) (M) **1.** beyond the senses. **2.** incogitable; control over the senses; shuns sensuous pleasures; pious; chaste; more powerful; meritorious and virtuous than an average king.

Atiratha (S) (M) **1.** with many chariots. **2.** wealthy; great with assets; means. **3.** a son of the Purū King Matināra (*M. Bh.*).

Atirātra (S) (M) **1.** made overnight. **3.** a son of Manu Ćākṣuṣa and Nadvalā (*V. Purāṇa*).

Atirūpa (S) (M) **1.** very beautiful. **3.** another name for the Supreme Being.

Ātiṣa (S) (M) **1.** fire. **2.** sacred; glows; is resplendent; all consuming; purifying.

Atiśakra (S) (M) superior to Indra.

Atiṣaṇḍa (S) (M) **1.** very pushy; extremely impotent. **3.** a serpent among those who received Balarāma's soul (*M. Bh.*).

Atiśaya (S) (M) **1.** excellence. **2.** meritorious; superior; pre-eminent.

Atisena (S) (M) **1.** with large army. **2.** a king; a commander.

Atiśī (S) (M) **1.** surpasses. **2.** excels; full of fire.

Atiśṛṅga (S) (M) **1.** surpasses the peak. **2.** surpassed perfection; divine. **3.** an attendant given to Skanda by Vindhyā (*M. Bh.*).

Atisthira (S) (M) **1.** very stable. **3.** an attendant given to Skanda by Mahāmeru (*M. Bh.*).

Atisvārya (S) (M) **1.** beyond notes. **3.** the 7th note in music which is beyond the 6 notes.

Atithi (S) (M) **1.** arriving without appointment. **2.** a guest. **3.** an attendant of Soma; another name for Agni and Suhotra the grandson of Rāma.

Atithigva (S) (M) **1.** to whom guests should go. **2.** guesthouse. **3.** another name for King Divodāsa who was a helper of Indra (*Ṛg Veda*).

Ativarćas (S) (M) **1.** very glorious. **3.** an attendant given to Skanda by Himavān (*M. Bh.*).

Ativiśva (S) (M) **1.** superior to the universe. **2.** divine; celestial. **3.** a muni (*M. Bh.*).

Atiyā (S) (M) to surpass.

Atiyāma (S) (M) **1.** very black. **2.** very dark. **3.** an attendant given to Skanda by Varuṇa (*M. Bh.*).

Atkīla (S) (M) **1.** solidly fixed. **2.** an ascetic or hermit who is unwavering in his meditation. **3.** a female ṛṣi who was a descendant of Viśvāmitra and author of some Vedic hymns (*Ṛg Veda*).

Ātmabhava (S) (M) **1.** mind born. **2.** created from the mind. **3.** another name for Kāma.

Ātmabhū (S) (M) **1.** creates oneself; self made. **3.** another name for Brahmā, Viṣṇu, Śiva and Kāma.

Ātmājñāna (S) (M) **1.** self knowledge. **2.** attained self realization, salvation or mokṣa.

Ātmajyoti (S) (M) **1.** the light of the soul. **3.** another name for the Supreme Spirit.

Ātman (S) (M) **1.** soul, principle of life. **3.** another name for Kṛṣṇa.

Ātmananda (S) (M) rejoicing in the soul.

Ātmārāma (S) (M) **1.** pervading the soul. **2.** omnipresent; the Supreme Spirit.

Ātmavīra (S) (M) **1.** with a mighty soul. **2.** attained mokṣa or salvation.

Ātmaya (S) (M) blessed with a long life.

Ātmodbhava (S) (M) **1.** born of the soul. **2.** a son. **3.** another name for Kāma.

Atnu (S) (M) the sun.

Ātreya (S) (M) **1.** receptacle of glory; crosses the 3 worlds. **3.** a sage who was a composer of hymns and had the power to cross planets (*Brahma Purāṇa*).

Atri (S) (M) **1.** who devours; overcomes; progresses; prosperous and glorified. **3.** a mind-born son of Brahmā, a great ṛṣi and the author of a number of Vedic hymns who was the husband of Anasūyā, the father of Dattātreya, Durvāsas and Ćandra (or Soma), the moon, who were the incarnations of Viṣṇu, Brahmā and Śiva, as also the father of Prāćinabarhis; according to the Vedas, repre-sents one of the stars in the Great Bear, and according to the Purāṇas is said to have produced the moon from his eye (*A. Purāṇa*); a son of Śukrāćārya (*M. Bh.*); another name for Śiva.

Aṭṭahāsa (S) (M) **1.** with loud laughter. **3.** a Yakṣa; another name for Śiva.

Aṭṭana (S) (M) discus.

Atula (S) (M) unequalled.

Atulavikrama (S) (M) of unequalled valour.

Atulya (S) (M) unequalled.

Atyadbhūta (S) (M) **1.** extremely unique. **3.** Indra in the 9th Manvantara (*H. Purāṇa*).

Atyāditya (S) (M) **1.** surpassing the sun. **2.** surpasses the lustre of the sun; glorious; renowned; enlightened.

Ātyantika (S) (M) **1.** infinite; endless; universal. **2.** continual; uninterrupted; whole; flawless.

Atyarāti (S) (M) **1.** exceedingly envious; maligns. **3.** a son of Janatapa (*M. Bh.*).

Au (S) (M) Śiva.

Audambara (S) (M) **1.** surrounded by water. **2.** cloud. **3.** the king of Udambara and an ally of Yudhiṣṭhira (*M. Bh.*).

Aukthya (S) (M) **1.** belonging to praise. **2.** much praised. **3.** a glorifying prayer of the *Sāma Veda*.

Aurasa (S) (M) produced by oneself; son.

Aurddhva (S) (M) **1.** belonging to the upper world; belonging to the stars. **2.** celestial being; one who travels the star path. **3.** a rāga.

Aurjitya (S) (M) energy; vigour; strength.

Aurva (S) (M) **1.** born of the thigh. **3.** a sage of the Bhṛgu family who was the son of Cyavana and Āruśī and the grandfather of Jamadagni (*M. Bh.*); a son of Vasiṣṭha (*H. Purāṇa*); another name for Agni.

Aurvaseya (S) (M) **1.** son of Urvaśī. **3.** another name for Agastya (*Ṛg Veda*).

Auśija (S) (M) **1.** born of the dawn. **2.** bright as the dawn; renowned; glorious; desirous; zealous. **3.** a king who equalled Indra in strength (*M. Bh.*); a sage who was a son of Aṅgiras and a member of Yudhiṣṭhira's court (*M. Bh.*).

Autathya (S) (M) **1.** knower of the substance. **2.** knows the truth; a philosopher; wise; illumined; enlightened. **3.** son of Utathya (*M. Bh.*).

Auttamikā (S) (M) related to the pious; related to the gods of the sky.

Auttānapadi (S) (M) **1.** descendant of Uttānapāda. **3.** the Dhruva star (*Bhā. Purāṇa*).

Avabhāsita (S) (M) shining; bright.

Avabodha (S) (M) **1.** perception; knowledge; awakening. **2.** wise; enlightened; a preceptor.

Avacūḍa (S) (M) **1.** a pendant. **2.** ornaments; embellishes; the pendant crest or streamer of a standard.

Avadāta (S) (M) clean; clear; pure; blameless; excellent; of white splendour.

Avadha (S) (M) inviolable; invulnerable.

Avadhūteśvara (S) (M) **1.** lord of ascetics. **2.** very pious; very chaste. **3.** an incarnation of Śiva (*S. Purāṇa*).

Avagāha (S) (M) **1.** to plunge into; to be absorbed in. **3.** a warrior of the Vṛṣṇi dynasty (*M. Bh.*).

Āvaha (S) (M) **1.** bearer; conveyor. **2.** a mediator. **3.** a vāyu (*M. Bh.*); one of the 7 tongues of fire.

Āvāha (S) (M) **1.** invitation; a guest of honour. **3.** a son of Śvaphalka (*H. Purāṇa*).

Avajaya (S) (M) overcoming; winning by conquest.

Avajita (S) (M) won by conquest.

Avajyuta (S) (M) **1.** illumining. **2.** illuminates others; enlightened.

Avakāśa (S) (M) visible; manifest; shining. **2.** space; opportunity; room. **3.** certain verses in the Kātyāyana Śrauta-Sūtra.

Avalokiteśvara (S) (M) **1.** watchful lord. **3.** a Bodhisattva (*B. Literature*).

Avanibhūṣaṇa (S) (M) jewel of the earth; ornament of the world.

Avanija (S) (M) **1.** son of the earth. **2.** a king.

Avanikānta (S) (M) beloved of the earth; a king.

Avanimohana (S) (M) attracting the world.

Avanīndra (S) (M) lord of the earth.

Avanipāla (S) (M) protector of the earth.

Avanīśa (S) (M) **1.** lord of the earth. **2.** a king.

Avanīśvara (S) (M) **1.** god of the earth. **2.** a king.

Avantas (S) (M) **1.** crest. **2.** the ornament worn on the head; ornaments; embellishes. **3.** a son of Dhṛṣṭa.

Avantivarman (S) (M) **1.** defending Avanti. **3.** a king (*R. Taraṅgiṇī*).

Āvapāka (S) (M) sinless; spotless; a bracelet of gold.

Avaraja (S) (M) younger brother.

Āvaraṇa (S) (M) **1.** cover; shelter. **3.** a king of the dynasty of Viśvakarman who was the son of Bharata and Pañcajanī (*Bhā. Purāṇa*).

Avarīyas (S) (M) **1.** not better. **2.** belongs to common; to the common masses. **3.** a son of Manu Sāvarṇa (*H. Purāṇa*).

Avarodha (S) (M) **1.** obstacle. **2.** an obstacle for the enemies. **3.** a king of the Bharata dynasty (*A. Brāhmaṇa*).

Avarokin (S) (M) shining; brilliant.

Avas (S) (M) favour; protection; assistance; pleasure.

Avaśa (S) (M) independent; free.

Āvasathya (S) (M) **1.** being in a house; domestic fire. **3.** son of Pavamāna and Saṅśatī (*M. Purāṇa*).

Avasthya (S) (M) **1.** adaptable; suitable. **3.** an Agni (*M. Bh.*).

Avasyu (S) (M) **1.** desirous of helping. **3.** another name for Indra.

Avatāra (S) (M) descent from heaven or a complete incarnation of a god (usually Viṣṇu).

Avatsāra (S) (M) **1.** presentation. **3.** a descendant of Kaśyapa and Praśravaṇa (*M. Bh.*); a seer mentioned in the *Ṛg Veda.*

Avi (S) (M) **1.** favourable; kindly disposed; protector; lord; air, wind; the wooden Soma strainer; favourite; mountain. **3.** another name for the sun.

Avicala (S) (M) immovable; steady; firm.

Avidānta (S) (M) **1.** unsubdued. **3.** a son of Śatadhanvan (*H. Purāṇa*).

Avidoṣa (S) (M) faultless.

Avijita (S) (M) one who cannot be conquered.

Avijña (S) (M) **1.** ignorant. **3.** son of Anila (*M. Bh.*).

Avijñāta (S) (M) **1.** not known; incogitable. **3.** a son of Anala (*H. Purāṇa*).

Avijñātagati (S) (M) **1.** with unknown speed. **2.** very swift. **3.** a son of the vasu Anila; another name for Śiva (*Bhāgavata*).

Avika (S) (M) lives in a group; as hard as the earth; sheep; tough and strong; diamond.

Avikala (S) (M) unimpaired; entire; perfect; whole; all.

Aviklava (S) (M) not confused; not unsteady.

Avikśipa (S) (M) **1.** unable to distribute. **2.** cannot discern between the good and the bad. **3.** a son of Śvaphalka (*H. Purāṇa*).

Avīkṣit (S) (M) **1.** undeveloped; not seen before. **3.** a king who was the son of Karaṅdhama, the father of Marutta and was considered the equal of Indra (*Ṛg Veda*); a son of King Kuru and Vāhinī (*M. Bh.*).

Avilasa (S) (M) free from whims; faithful; constant.

Avimukta (S) (M) **1.** not loosened; not unharnessed. **3.** a Tīrtha near Benaras (*M. Bh.*).

Avimukteśa (S) (M) **1.** firm; resolute; a god. 3. a form of Śiva (*Ś. Purāṇa*).

Avināśa (S) (M) indestructible.

Avindhya (S) (M) **1.** unmoving; firm; solid. **3.** a minister of Rāvaṇa who prevented him from killing Sītā (*V. Rāmāyaṇa*).

Avinīdevas (S) (M) **1.** not showing respect to the gods. **3.** father of Mainda.

Āvinna (S) (M) existing; being.

Avipriya (S) (M) very dear; very favourable; favourite.

Avirāga (S) (M) **1.** unceasing. a Prākṛta poet.

Avirāma (S) (M) **1.** uninterrupted. **2.** in succession; continuous.

Aviratha (S) (M) **1.** continuous. **3.** a hermit of the Kardama family who was the son of Ketuman (*H. Purāṇa*).

Āvirhotra (S) (M) **1.** performing the oblation. **3.** a king of the dynasty of Viśvakarmā and the son of Ṛṣabha and Jayantī (*Ṛg Veda*).

Aviṣa (S) (M) **1.** not poisonous; sky; ocean; king. **3.** nectar-like; life giving.

Avita (S) (M) protected.

Avitṛ (S) (M) protector.

Āvṛta (S) (M) path; direction; order; method.

Avyakta (S) (M) **1.** invisible; imperceptible; the universal spirit. **3.** another name for Viṣṇu, Śiva, Kāma.

Avyaya (S) (M) **1.** not liable to change; imperishable; undecaying. **3.** a serpent of the family of Dhṛtarāṣṭra (*M. Bh.*); a seer of the 13th Manvantara (*H. Purāṇa*).

Avyayas (S) (M) **1.** imperishable; undecaying. **3.** a son of Manu Raivata (*H. Purāṇa*); a nāga demon (*M. Bh.*); another name for Viṣṇu and Śiva.

Ayahkāya (S) (M) **1.** iron bodied. **2.** very strong. **3.** a daitya (*K. Sāgara*).

Ayahśaṅku (S) (M) **1.** an iron bolt. **3.** an asura reborn as a Kekaya prince (*H. Purāṇa*).

Ayahśiras (S) (M) **1.** iron headed. **3.** an asura (*H. Purāṇa*).

Ayahsthūṇa (S) (M) **1.** with iron pillars. **3.** a ṛṣi (*Ś. Brāhmaṇa*).

Ayāsmaya (S) (M) **1.** made of iron. **3.** a son of Manu Svāroćiṣa (*H. Purāṇa*).

Ayāsya (S) (M) indefatigable; valiant; agile.

Ayati (S) (M) **1.** no ascetic; spacious; majestic; dignity. **3.** a son of King Nahuṣa and brother of Yati and Yayāti (*M. Bh.*).

Āyatī (S) (M) coming near; arrival.

Ayobāhu (S) (M) **1.** iron armed. **2.** very strong. **3.** a son of Dhṛtarāṣṭra (*M. Bh.*).

Āyoda (S) (M) **1.** giver of life. **3.** a ṛṣi (*Ṛg Veda*).

Ayodhyā (S) (M) **1.** not to be fought against. **2.** irresistible. **3.** the city of Rāma on the river Śarayū (*V. Rāmāyaṇa*).

Ayodhyadhaumya (S) (M) **1.** the irresistible ascetic. **2.** an ascetic who cannot be defeated in the field of knowledge. **3.** a great sage who was the preceptor of Uddālaka, Upamanyu and Veda (*Ṛg Veda*).

Ayuddha (S) (M) irresistible; unconquerable.

Ayudha (S) (M) does not fight; peace-loving.

Ayugmanetra (S) (M) **1.** with odd numbered eyes. **3.** another name for Śiva who has 3 eyes.

Ayuja (S) (M) without a companion; without an equal.

Āyus (S) (M) **1.** age; duration of life; man; son; family; lineage; a divine personification presiding over life. **3.** fire personified as a son of Purūravas and Urvaśī and father of Nahuṣa by Svarbhāvanavī (*M. Bh.*); the king of frogs whose daughter Suśobhanā married King Parīkṣit (*M. Bh.*).

Āyuṣmān (M) **1.** one blessed with a long life. **3.** a brother of Dhruva (*V. Purāṇa*); a son of Saṁhrāda and grandson of Hiraṇyakaśipū (*A. Parāṣa*); a son of Uttanapāda.

Āyustejas (S) (M) **1.** energy of life. **3.** a Buddha (*B. Literature*).

Ayuta (S) (M) **1.** unimpeded; unbound; myriad. **3.** a son of Rādhikā (*Bhāgavata*).

Ayutājit (S) (M) **1.** conquerer of many. **3. a** king who was the son of Sindhudvīpa and father of Ṛtuparṇa (*Brahma Purāṇa*); a son of Bhajamāna (*V. Purāṇa*).

Ayutanāyi (S) (M) **1.** judge of many. **2.** the head of a province; the leader of a group; a king. **3.** a Purū king who was the son of King Bhauma and Suyajña, the husband of Kāmā and father of Akrodhana (*M. Bh.*).

Ayutāśva (S) (M) **1.** having many horses. **2.** the commander of the cavalries. **3.** a son of Sindhudvīpa (*V. Purāṇa*).

Ayutāyu (S) (M) **1.** with an unlimited age. **3.** a son of Jayasena Ārvin (*V. Purāṇa*); a son of Śrutavat (*V. Purāṇa*); a king who was the son of Śrutaśravas and who ruled for 1000 years (*V. Purāṇa*); the father of King Ṛtuparṇa (*Bhā. Purāṇa*).

Azhagar (Tamil) (M) **1.** the beautiful one. **3.** the god of the Azhagirisami temple of Madurai.

B

Babhri (S) (M) victorious; carrying away.

Babhru (S) (M) **1.** fire. **2.** fierce; brown; tawny; with tawny hair. **3.** a descendant of Atri and an author of *Ṛg Veda*; a son of Viśvāmitra (*M. Bh.*); a son of Viśvagarbha (*H. Purāṇa*); a son of Lomapāda (*V. Rāmāyaṇa*); a gandharva (*V. Purāṇa*); a dis-ciple of Śaunaka (*V. Rāmāyaṇa*); a Yādava of the Vṛṣṇi dynasty who was a friend of Kṛṣṇa (*M. Bh.*); a king of Kāśi (*M. Bh.*); *a* son of King Virāṭa (*M. Bh.*); a son of Druhyu; a constellation (*V's B. Samhitā*); another name for Viṣṇu, Kṛṣṇa and Śiva.

Babhrudaivavṛdha (S) (M) **1.** oldest among the fierce gods. **3.** a Yādava king who was a disciple of Nārada (*Bhāgavata*).

Babhrukeśa (S) (M) brown haired.

Babhruloman (S) (M) brown haired.

Babhrumālin (S) (M) **1.** fire keeper. **3.** a sage who was a prominent member of the court of Yudhiṣṭhira (*M. Bh.*).

Babhrusetu (S) (M) **1.** a bridge of fire. **3.** a Gāndhāra king who was the brother of Druhyu and father of Purovasu (*A. Purāṇa*).

Babhruvāhana (S) (M) **1.** chariot of fire; carrying fire; the brown chariot. **3.** the son of Arjuna and Chitrāṅgadā and king of Mahodaya (*M. Bh.*).

Babila (S) (M) a house; swift.

Bābul (S) (M) father.

Bachharāja (S) (M) **1.** king among the calves. **2.** very strong.

Bachil (S) (M) **1.** one who speaks much. **2.** an orator.

Bādal (S) (M) cloud.

Badara (S) (M) the Jujube tree (*Zizyphus jujuba*).

Bādarāyaṇa (S) (M) **1.** belonging to the Jujube tree (*Zizyphus jujuba*); a descendant of Viṣṇu. **3.** the first teacher to formulate the system of Vedāntic philosophy between 200-450 A.D. (*D. Śāstra*); another name for sage Vyāsa.

Bādarāyaṇi (S) (M) **1.** dwelling on the Jujube tree (*Zizyphus jujuba*). **3.** another name for Śuka.

Badarīdāsa (S) (M) devotee of Viṣṇu.

Badarīnātha (S) (M) **1.** lord of Badarī. **3.** a temple at Badarī (*H. Purāṇa*); another name for Viṣṇu.

Badarīśaila (M) **1.** the rock of Badarī. **2.** the mountain where the badarī or Jujube tree grows.

Baḍavāgni (S) (M) **1.** mare's fire. **3.** another name for Agni in the form of submarine fire.

Baḍavānala (S) (M) **1.** pepper powder. **3.** another name for Agni.

Baddhānanda **1.** bound by pleasure; having pleasure. **2.** attached; joyful.

Baddhānurāga (S) (M) **1.** bound by love. **2.** feeling affection.

Baddharājya (S) (M) **1.** bound to the throne. **2.** succeeding to the throne.

Badhira (S) (M) **1.** deaf. **3.** a serpent who was a son of Kaśyapa (*M. Bh.*).

Bāduli (S) (M) **1.** logician. **2.** argumentative. **3.** a son of Viśvāmitra (*M. Bh.*).

Bāhu (S) (M) **1.** arm. **2.** the shadow of the sundial; the constellation Ārdrā. **3.** a son of Vṛka (*H. Purāṇa*); a son of Vajra (*V. Purāṇa*); a daitya (*M. Bh.*).

Bahubala (S) (M) **1.** with great strength. **2.** a lion.

Bāhubhedin (S) (M) **1.** arm breaker. **3.** another name for Viṣṇu.

Bahudama (S) (M) **1.** suppressor of many. **2.** strong and powerful. **3.** an attendant of Skanda (*M. Bh.*).

Bahudhana (S) (M) having much wealth.

Bahudhara (S) (M) **1.** bearer of many. **2.** supporting many; a king.

Bahudhāra (S) (M) **1.** many edged. **2.** a diamond. **3.** Indra's thunderbolt.

Bahugava (S) (M) **1.** owning many cattle. **3.** a king of the family of Yayāti (*Bhā. Purāṇa*).

Bahugraha (S) (M) **1.** holding much; receiving much. **2.** a water jar; a minister.

Bahuguṇa (S) (M) **1.** with many good qualities; many threaded. **2.** rope. **3.** a gandharva (*M. Bh.*).

Bahujñāna (S) (M) **1.** possessed with great knowledge. **2.** a scholar; a philosopher.

Bahuhiraṇya (S) (M) rich in gold.

Bāhuka (S) (M) **1.** dependant; servile. **2.** the arm. **3.** name assumed by Nala as the charioteer to King Ṛtuparṇa (*Nalopākhyāna*); a son of Vṛka (*Purāṇas*); a serpent of the Kaurava family (*M. Bh.*); a hero of the Vṛṣṇis (*M. Bh.*).

Bahukalyāṇa (S) (M) well-wisher of many; extremely illustrious; noble.

Bahuketu (S) (M) **1.** many peaked. **2.** a mountain.

Bahukṣaṇa (S) (M) **1.** enduring much. **3.** another name for a Buddha or a Jaina saint.

Bahula (S) (M) **1.** thick; dense; broad; spacious; ample; large; abundant. **3.** a Jina born under the Pleiades; the dark half of the month; the month of Kārttika when the moon is near the Pleiades (*A. Koṣa*); a prajāpati (*V. Purāṇa*).

Bahulāśvan (S) (M) **1.** many horses; a strong horse. **3.** a king of the family of Rāma (*Bhā. Purāṇa*).

Bahuli (S) (M) **1.** manifold; magnified; multiplied. **2.** a versatile person. **3.** a son of Viśvāmitra (*H. Purāṇa*).

Bahumānya (S) (M) esteemed and honoured by many.

Bahumārgī (S) (M) follower of many paths; a place where many roads meet.

Bahumitra (S) (M) **1.** friend of many; with many friends. **2.** popular; famous.

Bahumūlaka (S) (M) **1.** with many origins; with many roots. **2.** obtained virtues from many sources. **3.** a serpent who was the son of Kaśyapa and Kadru (*M. Bh.*).

Bahumūlya (S) (M) **1.** high priced. **2.** anxiously sought after; precious; rare.

Bahumurdhan (S) (M) **1.** many headed. **3.** another name for Viṣṇu.

Bahupatu (S) (M) very clever.

Bahuprada (S) (M) one who donates much; liberal.

Bahupriya (S) (M) dear to many.

Bahuputra (S) (M) **1.** with many sons; the devil's tree (*Alstonia scholaris*). **3.** a prajāpati who was one of the spiritual sons of Brahmā (*Vā. Purāṇa*).

Bahurai (S) (M) with great riches.

Bahuratha (S) (M) **1.** one who has many chariots. **2.** a king. **3.** a king belonging to the Bharata family (*Bhā. Purāṇa*).

Bahūrja (S) (M) **1.** full of energy. **2.** energetic; strong; powerful.

Bahurūpa (S) (M) **1.** with many forms. **2.** variegated. **3.** a son of Medhātithi (*Ṛg Veda*); a rudra who was the son of Kaśyapa and Surabhī (*Purāṇas*); another name for Brahmā, Viṣṇu, Śiva, Kāma, Rudra, the Sun and a Buddha.

Bahuśakti (S) (M) very powerful.

Bāhuśakti (S) (M) strong armed.

Bāhuśālin (S) (M) **1.** strong armed. **3.** a son of Dhṛtarāṣṭra (*M. Bh.*); a dānava; another name for Śiva.

Bāhusambhava (S) (M) **1.** born from the arm. **3.** another name for a Kṣatriya—a member of the military class which is supposed to have been born from the arm of Brahmā.

Bahuśasta (S) (M) excellent; right; happy.

Bahuśruta (S) (M) **1.** extremely learned; much heard of. **2.** well versed in the Vedas.

Bahusūkta (S) (M) **1.** made of many hymns. **2.** a stotra.

Bahusuvarṇa (S) (M) rich in gold.

Bahuvāśin (S) (M) **1.** controller of many. **3.** a son of Dhṛtarāṣṭra (*M. Bh.*).

Bāhuvata (S) (M) strong armed.

Bahuvida (S) (M) **1.** very learned. **2.** wise; sagacious; enlightened.

Bahuvidha (S) (M) **1.** very intelligent; knows many arts. **2.** versatile; many faceted; talented. 3. a king of Aṅga (*A. Purāṇa*).

Bahuvikrama (S) (M) very powerful.

Bahuvīrya (S) (M) very powerful.

Bāhuvṛkta (S) (M) 1. surrounded by arms; hailed by arms. 2. a commander; a leader; a preceptor. 3. a sage and descendant of Atri (*V. Rāmāyaṇa*).

Bahuyojanā (S) (M) 1. great planner; a vast area of land. 3. a mother of Skanda's retinue (*M. Bh.*).

Bāhyakarṇa (S) (M) 1. listener; with protruding ears. 2. observer; one with many ambassadors. 3. a serpent son of Kaśyapa and Kadru (*M. Bh.*).

Bāhyakuṇḍa (S) (M) 1. out of its hole. 2. emancipated; progressive; enlightened. 3. a serpent son of Kaśyapa (*M. Bh.*).

Bāhyāśvana (S) (M) 1. protecting from outside troubles. 3. a king of the Purū dynasty who was the son of King Purujit (*M. Bh.*).

Baidaujas (S) (M) 1. without a rhyme. 2. irregular; unbound; free. 3. a son of Viṣṇu and Aditi (*P. Purāṇa*).

Baijanātha (S) (M) 1. descendant of the lord of creation. 3. descendant of Bījanātha or Śiva.

Baira (S) (M) brave.

Bajaraṅga (S) (M) 1. rock-bodied. 2. mighty; powerful. 3. another name for Hanumān.

Bajraṅgabali (S) (M) 1. with a rock-like body. 3. another name for Hanumān.

Baka (S) (M) 1. heron; crane (in Hindu mythology, the crane is represented as a bird of great cunning and circumspection); *Sesbania grandiflora*. 3. a rākṣasa killed by Bhīma (*M. Bh.*); a sage (*M. Bh.*); another name for Kubera.

Bakajita (S) (M) 1. conqueror of Baka. 3. another name for Bhīma.

Bakanakha (S) (M) 1. with nails as sharp as that of a crane. 3. a son of Viśvāmitra (*M. Bh.*).

Bakarāja (S) (M) 1. king of the cranes. 3. another name for Rājadharman the son of Kaśyapa.

Bakaripu (S) (M) 1. enemy of Baka. 3. another name for Bhīma.

Bakasahavāsin (S) (M) 1. fellow lodger of the heron; living with the cranes. 3. another name for the lotus.

Bakavata (S) (M) 1. with the qualities of a heron. 2. very attentive patient; watchful; circumspect.

Bakula (S) (M) 1. resembling a crane; the blossom of the Bakula tree — the flowers of this tree are said to blossom when kissed by women. 3. another name for Śiva.

Bakuleśa (S) (M) lord of blossoms.

Bakura (S) (M) 1. horn; thunderbolt; lightening; trumpet used in battle. 2. illuminates; glorifies.

Bāla (S) (M) 1. young; newly risen. 2. simple; pure. 3. another name for the sun.

Bala (S) (M) 1. power. 2. strength; energy. 3. force personified as a viśvadeva; a son of Kṛṣṇa (*M. Bh.*); a horse of the moon (*V. Purāṇa*); a Jaina elder brother of Vāsudeva; a demon who was the son of Kaśyapa and Danu (*M. Bh.*); a deva born to Varuṇa from his elder brothers's wife (*M. Bh.*); a son of King Parīkṣit of the Ikṣvāku dynasty (*M. Bh.*); a monkey warrior of Rāma (*M. Bh.*); one of the 2 attendants given to Skanda by Vāyu; a sage and son of Aṅgiras (*M. Bh.*); a viśvadeva (*M. Bh.*); a demon killed by Indra and subsequently turned into a diamond mine (*Ṛg Veda*).

Balabandhu (S) (M) 1. having power as a friend. 2. always helped by power; associated with strength. 3. a son of Manu Raivata (*Mā. Purāṇa*); a son of Bhṛgu (*Vā. Purāṇa*).

Balabhadra (S) (M) 1. one with power. 2. strong; powerful. 3. another name for Balarāma or of Ananta the serpent identified with him (*Purāṇas*); a descendant of Bharata (*Bhāgavata*).

Balabhṛt (S) (M) 1. carrying a lot of strength. 2. powerful; mighty; strong.

Balaćakravartin (S) (M) a powerful monarch.

Bālaćandra (S) (M) **1.** the crescent moon. **2.** the young or waxing moon.

Bālaćarya (S) (M) **1.** behaves like a child. **2.** innocent; curious. **3.** another name for Skanda.

Balada (S) (M) **1.** bestower of strength. **3.** the 1st son of the Agni named Bhānu (*M. Bh.*).

Bāladeva (S) (M) a young god.

Baladeva (S) (M) **1.** lord of strength. **2.** the wind. **3.** the elder brother of Kṛṣṇa regarded as a nāga (*M. Bh.*).

Baladeya (S) (M) bestower of strength.

Baladhara (S) (M) bearer of strength.

Baladhī (S) (M) **1.** with a powerful intellect. **2.** deep insight; is perceptive. **3.** an ancient hermit and father of Medhāvin (*M. Bh.*).

Balādhika (S) (M) surpassing all in strength.

Balāḍhya (S) (M) **1.** rich in strength. **2.** a bean.

Bālāditya (S) (M) the newly risen sun.

Baladviṣa (S) (M) **1.** jealous of strength; enemy of the strong; enemy of Bala. **3.** another name for Indra.

Bālagaṅgādhara (S) (M) **1.** the young bearer of the Gaṅgā. **3.** young Śiva.

Bālagopāla (S) (M) **1.** the young cowherd. **3.** young Kṛṣṇa.

Bālagovinda (S) (M) **1.** the young cowherd. **3.** the boy Kṛṣṇa.

Balāgra (S) (M) **1.** first in strength. **2.** best among the powerful.

Balagupta (S) (M) protected by strength.

Balāhaka (S) (M) **1.** cloud; thundercloud. **3.** a serpent famous in the Purāṇas and a member of Varuṇa's court (*M. Bh.*); a brother of King Jayadratha of Sindhu (*M. Bh.*); a horse of Kṛṣṇa (*M. Bh.*); a daitya; a mountain.

Balahantṛ (S) (M) **1.** killer of the powerful; slayer of Bala. **3.** another name for Indra.

Balaja (S) (M) **1.** produced by strength. **2.** grain.

Balāji (S) (M) **1.** strong. **3.** another name for Viṣṇu.

Balajyeṣṭha (S) (M) whose superiority is based on his strength.

Balāka (S) (M) **1.** a mixture of treacle and milk; a kind of crane. **3.** a pupil of Śākyamunī; a son of Purū and grandson of Jahnu (*Bhā. Purāṇa*); a rākṣasa (*V. Purāṇa*); a son of Vatsapri (*Mā. Purāṇa*).

Balakara (S) (M) **1.** bestower of strength. **2.** a strong supporter.

Balakāśva (S) (M) **1.** as strong as a horse. **3.** the grandson of Jahnu, son of Aja and the father of Kuśika (*M. Bh.*).

Bālāki (S) (M) **1.** as innocent as a child. **3.** a hermit who was a son of Gārgya (*Bhāgavata*).

Balaki (S) (M) **1.** of strength. **2.** powerful; strong. **3.** a son of Dhṛtarāṣṭra (*M. Bh.*).

Balākin (S) (M) **1.** abounding in cranes. **3.** a son of Dhṛtarāṣṭra (*M. Bh.*).

Bālakṛṣṇa (S) (M) the boy Kṛṣṇa; young Kṛṣṇa.

Balakṛt (S) (M) obtained by power.

Balākṣa (S) (M) strong eyed.

Balakṣa (S) (M) **1.** the light half of the month. **2.** blameless; innocent; of white hue.

Balakṣagu (S) (M) **1.** white rayed. **3.** another name for the moon.

Bālakunda (S) (M) **1.** a young flower. **2.** the jasmine (*Jasminum pubescens*).

Balamada (S) (M) proud of one's power.

Bālamaṇi (S) (M) a small jewel.

Balamitra (S) (M) **1.** a strong friend; a friend of the strong. **3.** a king who fought with Śatrughna during the horse yajña (*V. Rāmāyaṇa*).

Bālamodaka (S) (M) **1.** favourite of children. **3.** the son of King Suratha of Kuṇḍalanagari (*P. Purāṇa*).

Bālamohana (S) (M) **1.** attracting children; the youth who attracts. **3.** young Kṛṣṇa.

Balamukhya (S) (M) **1.** the chief of an army. **2.** a commander.

Bālamukunda (S) (M) **1.** young blossom. **2.** as tender and soft as a young blossom; a child. **3.** young Kṛṣṇa.

Balar (S) (M) strength; power; might; army.

Balanātha (S) (M) lord of strength.

Balāṅgaka (S) (M) **1.** strong limbed. **2.** the spring season.

Balānīka (S) (M) **1.** with a powerful army. **3.** a son of King Drupada (*M. Bh.*).

Bālānuja (S) (M) **1.** the younger brother of Balarāma. **3.** another name for Kṛṣṇa.

Balapati (S) (M) **1.** commander of an army; lord of strength. **3.** another name for Indra.

Balaprada (S) (M) bestower of strength.

Balaprāṇa (S) (M) **1.** strength and spirit conjoined. **2.** powerful and intelligent.

Balaprasū (S) (M) **1.** creator of strength. **3.** mother of Baladeva; another name for Rohiṇī.

Bālarāja (S) (M) **1.** lord of the rising sun. **2.** the Lapiz lazuli.

Balarāma (S) (M) **1.** abode of strength. **3.** the son of Vasudeva and Rohiṇī, the elder brother of Kṛṣṇa, 3rd of the Rāmas, considered the 8th incarnation of Viṣṇu and sometimes as an incarnation of Ananta (*V. Purāṇa*).

Bālaravi (S) (M) the morning sun.

Bālārka (S) (M) the rising sun.

Bālāruṇa (S) (M) early dawn.

Balaśālin (S) (M) **1.** possessing a great army. **2.** powerful.

Balasena (S) (M) a strong leader.

Bālasinha (S) (M) a young lion.

Balastha (S) (M) abode of strength.

Balasthala (S) (M) **1.** abode of strength. **3.** a son of Parijāta (*Bhāgavata*).

Balasūdana (S) (M) **1.** destroyer of large armies; destroyer of Bala. **3.** another name for Indra.

Bālasūrya (S) (M) **1.** the rising sun. **2.** the purple light of dawn. **3.** the Lapiz lazuli.

Balasvāmi (S) (M) **1.** master of power. **3.** a warrior of Skanda (*M. Bh.*).

Balavala (S) (M) **1.** very powerful. **3.** an asura killed by Balarāma (*M. Bh.*).

Balavāna (S) (M) strong; powerful.

Balavardhana (S) (M) **1.** increasing strength. **3.** a son of Dhṛtarāṣṭra (*M. Bh.*).

Balavarṇin (S) (M) strong and looking well.

Balavata (S) (M) **1.** powerful. **2.** intense; prevailing; dense.

Bālavinaṣṭaka (S) (M) **1.** destroyer of childhood. **2.** wisdom; adulthood.

Balavīra (S) (M) **1.** brave and powerful. **2.** a hero.

Balavīrya (S) (M) **1.** strength and heroism conjoined. **3.** a descendant of Bharata (*Ś. Mahātmya*).

Bālavrata (S) (M) **1.** worshipping the rising sun. **3.** another name for the Buddhist saint Manjuśrī (*B. Literature*).

Bālayani (S) (M) **1.** one liked by the pupil. **3.** a teacher mentioned in the *Bhāgavata.*

Bālayogi (S) (M) **1.** young ascetic. **3.** a king of the Aṅga dynasty who was the son of Bali (*A. Purāṇa*).

Balayukta (S) (M) endowed with strength.

Balāyuṣ (S) (M) **1.** living on his own strength. **3.** a son of Purūravas and Urvaśī (*P. Purāṇa*).

Bālendra (S) (M) Indra in his childlike form.

Bālendu (S) (M) **1.** the crescent moon. **2.** the new or waxing moon.

Baleśa (S) (M) the commander of an army; lord of power.

Bāleśvara (S) (M) **1.** lord of children. **3.** another name for Kṛṣṇa.

Bālhīka (S) (M) **1.** powerful; energetic; a country. **3.** a king who was an incarnation of the asura Krodhāvaśa (*H. Purāṇa*); a king of the Ahara dynasty (*M. Bh.*); the 3rd son of King Janamejaya and the grandson of King Kuru (*M. Bh.*); a son of King Pratīpa of the Kuru dynasty and Sunandā of Śibi (*M. Bh.*); the charioteer of Yudhiṣṭhira (*M. Bh.*); the father of Rohiṇī the wife of Vasudeva (*H. Purāṇa*); a gandharva (*A. Koṣa*).

Balhīkapuṅgava (S) (M) **1.** bull of the Balhīkas. **3.** another name for Śalya.

Bāli (S) (M) **1.** powerful. **3.** a mighty monkey king of Kiṣkindhā who was the son of Indra, half brother of Sugrīva, the husband of Tārā, father of Aṅgada, and was slain by Rāma (*V. Rāmāyaṇa*).

Bali (S) (M) **1.** offering; powerful. **2.** gift; tribute; oblation. **3.** an emperor of the asuras who was the son of Viroćana, the grandson of Prahlāda and was defeated by Viṣṇu in his Vāmana or dwarf incarnation (*M. Bh.*); Indra in the 8th Manvantara (*Purāṇas*); a hermit of Hastināpura (*M. Bh.*); an incarnation of Śiva as a hermit (*Ś. Parāṇa*); a king of the Yādavas who was the son of Kṛtavarman and the husband of Ćārumatī the daughter of Kṛṣṇa (*Bhāgavata*); the monkey king of Aṇava who was the son of Sutapas and the husband of Sudeṣṇā (*Bhāgavata*).

Balibandhana (S) (M) **1.** binder of Bali. **3.** another name for Viṣṇu.

Balibhuja (S) (M) **1.** devouring offerings. **2.** a deity.

Balidhvansī (S) (M) **1.** destroying Bali. **3.** another name for Kṛṣṇa.

Balidhvanśin (S) (M) **1.** destroyer of Bali. **3.** another name for Viṣṇu.

Baliman (S) (M) powerful.

Balin (S) (M) **1.** powerful. **2.** strong; mighty; robust.

Baliśikhā (S) (M) **1.** the best oblation. **3.** a serpent son of Kaśyapa and Kadru (*M. Bh.*).

Baliṣṭha (S) (M) **1.** very powerful. **2.** mighty.

Balivāka (S) (M) **1.** praying at the oblation. **2.** an orator; a preacher. **3.** a hermit who was a member of Yudhiṣṭhira's court (*M. Bh.*).

Ballava (S) (M) **1.** cowherd; bull-keeper. **3.** name assumed by Bhīma at the court of Virāṭa (*M. Bh.*).

Balūla (S) (M) **1.** powerful. **2.** strong.

Balya (S) (M) **1.** powerful. **2.** strong; mighty.

Bālya (S) (M) child-like; the crescent moon.

Bambhāri (S) (M) **1.** lowes like a cow. **3.** one of the 7 tutelary deities of the Soma plant (*Ṛg Veda*).

Bāṇa (S) (M) **1.** arrow; number 5. **2.** a sharp intellect. **3.** an asura who was the son of Bali (*V. Purāṇa*); a poet in the court of Harṣavardhana who was the author of *Kādambarī* and *Harśa Ćarita* (7th century A.D.); a 1000 armed asura considered the son of Pārvatī, who attacked the gods and was killed by Kṛṣṇa (*Bhā. Purāṇa*); a warrior of Skanda (*M. Bh.*); an asura killed by Lakṣmaṇa (*V. Rāmāyaṇa*).

Bāṇajita (S) (M) **1.** conqueror of Bāṇa; conquering with arrows. **3.** another name for Viṣṇu.

Bāṇaliṅga (S) (M) **1.** an arrow shaped phallus; a pointed stone; knowing the secrets of archery. **3.** a white stone found in the river Narmadā and worshipped as the Liṅga of Śiva.

Banamālin (S) (M) **1.** gardener of the forest. **3.** another name for Kṛṣṇa.

Banārasi (S) (M) **1.** belonging to Benaras. **2.** sacred.

Bāṇaśankara (S) (M) **1.** arrow of Śiva. **2.** reaching his target of peace, tranquility and welfare.

Banavāri (S) (M) **1.** dweller of the forest. **3.** another name for Kṛṣṇa.

Bandana (S) (M) **1.** prayer; chant. **2.** sacred; illumined; enlightened; beyond wordly bonds.

Bandhitra (S) (M) **1.** binder. **3.** another name for Kāma, the god of love.

Bandhujīvin (S) (M) lives on friends; on whom the friends live; deep red like the blossom of the *Pentapetes phoenicea*; a ruby.

Bandhumān (S) (M) **1.** with many brothers. **2.** protected. **3.** a king of Videha (*Br. Purāṇa*).

Bandhupāla (S) (M) protecting his kin.

Bandhuprabha (S) (M) **1.** light of the family. **3.** a vidyādhara.

Bandin (S) (M) praiser; a bard; herald.

Baneśvara (S) (M) the Bāṇaliṅga stone; lord of the forest.

Banhimān (S) (M) has plenty.

Banhiṣṭha (S) (M) found in abundance.

Bāṇi (S) (M) **1.** speech. **2.** articulate; an orator.

Bāṇibrata (S) (M) **1.** controller of speech; devoted to speech. **2.** eloquent; an orator.

Baṇkimćandra (S) (M) **1.** crooked moon; half moon. **2.** charming as well as shrewd. **3.** another name for Kṛṣṇa.

Banśi (S) (M) **1.** flute. **2.** sweet-voiced; melodious.

Banśidhara (S) (M) **1.** bearer of flute. **3.** another name for Kṛṣṇa.

Banśika (S) (M) **1.** king of the forest. **2.** the lion.

Banśivinoda (S) (M) **1.** amuses with his flute. **3.** another name for Kṛṣṇa.

Bapannabhaṭṭa (S) (M) scholar of agriculture.

Bappā (S) (M) **1.** universal father. **3.** the Rāṇā of Mewar who was considered the direct descendant of Rāma.

Bappaka (S) (M) **1.** good cook. **3.** a prince.

Bapū (Marathi) (M) the middle child.

Bapudeva (S) (M) lord of the body.

Barayi (S) (M) **1.** lover of the great. **2.** admirer; respect; idolizing great things and people.

Barbarīka (S) (M) **1.** curly haired; wild. **2.** savage. **3.** the son of Ghaṭotkaća and Maurvī (*M. Bh.*); a form of Śiva.

Baren (S) (M) **1.** the lust. **3.** another name for Indra.

Barendra (S) (M) Indra, the best.

Barhaćandra (S) (M) **1.** the eye of a peacock's tail; the moon of peacock feather. **2.** beautiful.

Barhaketu (S) (M) **1.** with the banner of a peacock's tail. **2.** as bright as peacock's feathers. **3.** a son of Sagara (*Bhāgavata*); a son of the 9th Manu (*Mā. Purāṇa*).

Barhaṇa (S) (M) **1.** strong. **2.** vigorous; powerful; energetic; active; agile; dazzling the eyes.

Barhaṇāśva (S) (M) **1.** owner of strong horses; a strong horse. **2.** wealthy; swift; strong. **3.** a son of King Nikumbha of the Pṛthu dynasty (*Bhāgavata*).

Barhanetra (S) (M) **1.** the eye of a peacock's tail. **2.** beautiful.

Barhapīḍa (S) (M) **1.** decorated with peacock-feathers; wearing a wreath of peacock-feathers on the head. **2.** crested; titled; decorated.

Barhidhvaja (S) (M) **1.** peacock-bannered. **2.** symbolized by a peacock; surrounded by peacocks. **3.** another name for Skanda whose mount is the peacock.

Barhin (S) (M) **1.** peacock; a kind of the perfume. **3.** a gandharva (*A. Koṣa*).

Barhis (S) (M) **1.** that which is plucked up. **2.** sacrificial grass; fire; light; splendour. **3.** another name for Agni.

Barhiṣada (S) (M) **1.** seated on sacred grass. **3.** a son of Havirdhana (*Brah. Purāṇa*); a ṛṣi (*V. Rāmāyaṇa*).

Barhiṣakeśa (S) (M) **1.** grass-haired. **2.** fire-haired; blazing. **3.** another name for Agni.

Barhiṣapāla (S) (M) **1.** protector of fire; blazing. **2.** worshipped; sacred; venerated; illuminated; enlightening.

Barhismukha (S) (M) **1.** with fire for a mouth. **2.** a deity to whom sacrifices are offered in fire.

Barhiṣṭha (S) (M) **1.** dwelling in fire. **2.** mightiest; strongest; highest; loudest.

Barhiyāna (S) (M) **1.** whose mount is the peacock. **3.** another name for Skanda.

Barkhā (S) (M) **1.** rain. **2.** moistens; soothes; cools; life giving.

Bāroṭa (S) (M) speech.

Barsāti (S) (M) **1.** protecting from the rain. **2.** a shelter; providing shelter and protect.

Barū (S) (M) **1.** noble. **3.** a descendant of Aṅgiras and an author of Ṛg Veda (x).

Baruṇ (S) (M) **1.** lord of water. **2.** found in water; the sacred barṇa tree (*Crataeva nurvala*).

Basabi (S) (M) resident.

Basantā (S) (M) spring.

Bāsava (S) (M) **1.** bull. **2.** strong; virile. **3.** a minister of a Jaina king who developed the Vīra-Śaiva system (12th century A.D.) (*J.S. Koṣa*).

Bāsavarāja (S) (M) **1.** lord of the bulls. **2.** decorated with many bulls; extremely strong and virile.

Bāṣkala (S) (M) **1.** preceptor; teacher; knower of substance. **2.** well read; wise; illumined; enlightened. **3.** a king of asuras, son of Samhrāda of the Kaśyapa line, a minister of Mahīṣasura and slain by Devī (*D. Bhāgavata*); a disciple of Vyāsa (*M. Bh.*).

Bāṣpa (S) (M) **1.** tears; steam; vapour. **3.** a disciple of Gautama Buddha (*B. Ćarita*).

Basū (S) (M) **1.** wealth. **2.** wealthy.

Baṭer (S) (M) the grey quail (*Telrao coturnix*).

Battu (S) (M) **1.** boy; lad; stripling; youth; a Brāhmin who reads the scriptures daily. **3.** a form of Śiva (*Ś. Purāṇa*).

Baṭuka (S) (M) Brāhmin youth.

Baṭukanātha (S) (M) **1.** lord of boys. **3.** a form of Śiva (*A. Koṣa*).

Bāyabhaṭṭa (S) (M) **1.** knowing the age; an astrologer. **3.** a son of Kṛṣṇna and father of Advaita (*Bhāgavata*).

Beanta (S) (M) **1.** endless. **2.** eternal.

Bekurā (S) (M) **1.** voice; sound; a musical instrument. **2.** melodious; harmonious.

Beman (S) (M) **1.** without interest. **2.** disinterested; detached.

Beṇi (S) (M) plait of hair.

Beṇiprasāda (S) (M) **1.** gift of a wreath of flowers. **2.** flowers sacred enough to be offered to the lord.

Bhābāgrahi (S) (M) **1.** perceiving another's emotions. **2.** understanding; sensitive; considerate.

Bhabeśa (S) (M) lord of existence; lord of the universe; lord of emotions.

Bhadanta (S) (M) **1.** term of respect applied to a Buddhist mendicant. **3.** another name for the poet Aśvaghoṣa.

Bhadra (S) (M) **1.** blessed; auspicious; gracious; good. **2.** fair; happy; prosperous; handsome; fortunate; gentlemanly; excellent. **3.** one of the 12 sons of Viṣṇu (*Bhāgavata*); a son of Upaćārumat (*B. Literature*); the sages of the 3rd Manvantara (*Bhāgavata*); a king of Ćedi who fought on the side of the Pāṇḍavas (*M. Bh.*); one of the 4 elephants that support the world (*V. Rāmāyaṇa*); a son of Śraddha and grandson of Svāyambhuva Manu (*Bhāgavata*); a yakṣa who was a minister of Kubera (*M. Bh.*); a sage who was the son of Pramati and father of Upamanyu (*M. Bh*); a son of Kṛṣṇa and Kālindī (*Bhāgavata*); a son of Vasudeva and Devakī (*Bh. Purāṇa*); another name for Śiva and Mount Meru.

Bhadrabāhu (S) (M) **1.** auspicious armed. **2.** performing ambitious acts. **3.** a son of Vasudeva and Rohiṇī (*Bhāgavata*); a king of Magadha (*M. Bh.*); a celebrated Jaina author (*J.S. Koṣa*); a king of the line of Purū (*M. Bh.*).

Bhadrabalana (S) (M) **1.** strengthening good. **3.** another name for Balarāma.

Bhadrabhuja (S) (M) **1.** whose arms confer prosperity. **2.** a god.

Bhadraćāru (S) (M) **1.** gentle and beautiful. **3.** a son of Kṛṣṇa (*Mā. Purāṇa*); a son of Pradyumna (*Bhā. Purāṇa*).

Bhadradeha (S) (M) **1.** with an auspicious body. **2.** beautiful; handsome. **3.** a son of Vasudeva and Devakī (*Bhāgavata*).

Bhadragupta (S) (M) **1.** collector of good things. **2.** knows the secrets of the good; meritorious; virtuous. **3.** a Jaina saint (*J. Literature*).

Bhadrajātika (S) (M) of noble birth.

Bhadraka (S) (M) **1.** good; handsome. **2.** brave; beautiful; meritorious; virtuous. **3.** an Aṅga king (*A. Purāṇa*).

Bhadrakāra (S) (M) **1.** doer of good. **2.** meritorious; virtuous. **3.** a son of Śiva (*Mā. Purāṇa*); a son of Kṛṣṇa.

Bhadrakāya (S) (M) **1.** with a beautiful body. **3.** a son of Kṛṣṇa (*Bhāgavata*).

Bhadrakṛt (S) (M) **1.** causing prosperity. **3.** 24th arhat of the future Utsarpiṇī.

Bhadrākṣa (S) (M) whose eyes reflect auspiciousness.

Bhadrakumbha (S) (M) **1.** auspicious jar. **2.** a golden jar filled with water from the Gaṅgā.

Bhadramanda (S) (M) **1.** gentle and good. **3.** a son of Kṛṣṇa (*V. Purāṇa*).

Bhadramukha (S) (M) with a handsome face; whose look confers prosperity.

Bhadrāṅga (S) (M) **1.** a beautiful body. **3.** another name for Balarāma.

Bhadranidhi (S) (M) **1.** treasure of goodness. **3.** a vessel offered to Viṣṇu.

Bhadrapāla (S) (M) **1.** protector of goodness. **2.** meritorious; virtuous. **3.** a Bodhisattva.

Bhadraśākha (S) (M) **1.** connoisseur of tasty food. **3.** the goat form of Subrahmaṇya (*M. Bh.*).

Bhadrasāra (S) (M) **1.** essence of goodness; ocean of goodness. **3.** a king of Kāśmira and father of Sudharman (*R. Taraṅgiṇī*).

Bhadrasena (S) (M) **1.** with an army of good people. **2.** good; virtuous. **3.** a son of Vasudeva and Devakī (*Bhāgavata*); a son of Ṛṣabha (*Bhāgavata*); a son of Mahiṣmat (*Bhāgavata*).

Bhadraśīla (S) (M) noble in behaviour.

Bhadraśravas (S) (M) **1.** listening to good things; one about whom good things are said. **3.** a king of Saurāṣṭra mentioned in the Purāṇas; a son of Dharma (*Bhā. Purāṇa*).

Bhadrāśraya (S) (M) abode of auspiciousness; sandalwood which is used in religious ceremonies and therefore considered sacred.

Bhadraśreṇya (S) (M) **1.** belonging to a noble family. **3.** a Hehaya king (*H. Purāṇa*).

Bhadraśreṇya (S) (M) **1.** noble horse; owner of good horses. **3.** a king of the Purū dynasty who was the son of Rahovādi and the husband of Kāntimatī (*M. Bh.*); a son of Āgnīdhra and Pūrvaćitti (*M. Bh.*); a son of Vasudeva and Rohiṇī (*Bhāgavata*); a son of Dhundhumāra (*Bhā. Purāṇa*).

Bhadratanu (S) (M) with a beautiful body.

Bhadrātmaja (S) (M) **1.** son of a noble. **2.** meritorious; virtuous.

Bhadravadana (S) (M) **1.** auspicious faced. **3.** another name for Balarāma.

Bhadravāha (S) (M) bearer of prosperity.

Bhadravarman (S) (M) **1.** a gentle warrior. **2.** overpowering gently and subtly; the Arabian jasmine (*Jasminum sambac*).

Bhadravinda (S) (M) **1.** achieving good. **3.** a son of Kṛṣṇa (*Bhāgavata*).

Bhadrāyu (S) (M) leads a good life.

Bhadreśa (S) (M) **1.** lord of nobles; husband of a noble family; husband of Durgā. **3.** another name for Śiva.

Bhadrika (S) (M) **1.** noble. **3.** a king of the Śākyas.

Bhaga (S) (M) **1.** disperser; lord; patron; happiness; fortune; wealth. **3.** an āditya who bestowes wealth and presides over love and marriage, the brother of dawn and the regent of the Nakṣatra Uttarā Phālgunī (*V.'s B. Samhitā*); a son of Kaśyapa and Aditi (*Bhāgavata*); the sun in the month of Puṣya (*V.'s B. Samhitā*); the celestial dispenser of boons, husband of Siddhi, the father of Vibhu, Prabhu and Mahimān and a member of Indra's assembly (*M. Bh.*); a rudra (*Ṛg Veda*); another name for the sun and the moon.

Bhagadatta (S) (M) **1.** given by good fortune; given by the creator. **3.** a king of Prāgjyotiṣapura who was born from a limb of the demon Bāṣkala and fought on the side of the Kauravas (*M. Bh.*); a king of Kāmrup.

Bhagāditya (S) (M) **1.** the sun which bestows wealth; the sun in the month of Puṣya. **3.** a Rāṇa of Mewar.

Bhagaghna (S) (M) **1.** destroying Bhaga. **3.** another name for Śiva.

Bhagālin (S) (M) **1.** bedecked with skulls. **3.** another name for Śiva.

Bhagana (S) (M) **1.** next; of the nature of happiness. **2.** happy; joyful.

Bhagaratha (S) (M) **1.** with a lucky chariot. **2.** a fortunate warrior who always wins.

Bhagata (S) (M) devotee.

Bhagavāna (S) (M) **1.** with a great fortune. **2.** lord; god.

Bhāgavant (S) (M) **1.** has a fortune. **2.** fortunate; shareholder.

Bhāgavata (S) (M) **1.** spiritual being; a follower of Viṣṇu. **2.** with great fortune; glorious; illustrious; divine; happy; adorable; holy. **3.** a king in the 5th lunar dynasty of Magadha (*Bhāgavata*); a Buddha; another name for Viṣṇu, Kṛṣṇa and Śiva.

Bhagavatīprasāda (S) (M) born from the blessings of goddess Durgā.

Bhagīratha (S) (M) **1.** with a glorious chariot. **3.** the son of Dilīpa (*M. Bh.*) or Anśumān (*Purāṇas*) he brought down the Gaṅgā river to earth and is now a member of Yama's assembly.

Bhāgīrathīputra (S) (M) **1.** son of Bhagīrathī. **2.** another name for Bhīsma.

Bhagnaratha (S) (M) **1.** devoid of chariots. **3.** another name for Ćitraratha.

Bhāguri (S) (M) thinks himself lucky; desiring happiness.

Bhāgyanandana (S) (M) controller of destiny.

Bhaimaseni (S) (M) **1.** son of Bhīmasena. **3.** another name for Ghaṭotkaća and Divodāsa.

Bhaimi (S) (M) **1.** son of Bhīma. **3.** another name for Ghaṭotkaća.

Bhairava (S) (M) **1.** destroyer of fear; making a terrible sound. **2.** formidable; frightening. **3.** a nāga of the Kaurava dynasty (*M. Bh.*); a terrible form of Śiva (*Ś. Purāṇa*); a rāga; a chief of Śiva's host (*K. Purāṇa*); a son of Śiva by Tārāvatī the wife of King Ćandraśekhara of Karavirapura (*M. Bh.*); a rāga.

Bhairavasin (S) (M) **1.** terrible lion. **3.** a son of Narasiṁha and the patron of Rućipati (*V. Purāṇa*).

Bhairavesa (S) (M) **1.** lord of terror. **3.** another name for Śiva.

Bhairika (S) (M) **1.** terrible. **3.** a son of Kṛṣṇa and Satyabhāmā.

Bhairon (S) (M) **1.** terrible. **2.** fear inducing; awesome; formidable. **3.** a village field spirit now identified with Śiva.

Bhajālaṅka (S) (M) **1.** with auspicious marks on the forehead. **3.** another name for Śiva.

Bhajamana (S) (M) **1.** praying through heart. **2.** praying deeply, sincerely, fervently and with a lot of feeling. **3.** a Yādava king who was the son of Satvata and Kauśalyā and the husband of Bāhyakā and Upabāhyakā, the 2 daughters of Sanjaya (*Bhāgavata*).

Bhajana (S) (M) **1.** devotional song. **2.** sacred; venerated.

Bhākoṣa (S) (M) **1.** treasure of light. **3.** another name for the sun.

Bhakta (S) (M) devotee; loyal; honouring; worshipping.

Bhaktarāja (S) (M) **1.** prince among devotees; king of devotees. **2.** best devotee.

Bhālaćandra (S) (M) **1.** with the moon on his forehead. **3.** another name for Śiva and Gaṇeśa.

Bhālandana (S) (M) **1.** with a pleasing forehead. **3.** a king who was the son of Nābhāga (*M. Bh.*).

Bhālanetra (S) (M) **1.** with an eye on his forehead. **3.** another name for Śiva.

Bhālendra (S) (M) **1.** lord of fortune. **3.** another name for Śiva.

Bhalla (S) (M) **1.** auspicious; arrow; spear. **2.** sharp; piercing and reaching its mark. **3.** another name for Śiva.

Bhallāṭa (S) (M) **1.** with a large forehead. **2.** a bear; one who is fortunate; virtuous; learned. **3.** a king of the line of Bharata who was the son of Viśvakṣeṇa and the father of Bṛhadāśva.

Bhaluki (S) (M) **1.** with a large forehead. **2.** a bear. **3.** a sage who was a member of Yudhiṣṭhira's court (*M. Bh.*); a sage who was a disciple of Lāṅgali.

Bhāma (S) (M) light; brightness; splendour.

Bhāmaha (S) (M) **1.** bright. **2.** illuminating; enlightening. **3.** an important Sanskṛta critic (6th century A.D.).

Bhāmaṇḍala (S) (M) **1.** sphere of light; garland of rays. **2.** illuminating; enlightening; renowned. **3.** the sun.

Bhānavīya (S) (M) **1.** belonging to the sun. **2.** sacred; glorious; enlightening.

Bhaṇḍāyanī (S) (M) **1.** praising highly. **3.** a sage of Indra's court (*M. Bh.*).

Bhandila (S) (M) fortune.

Bhānemi (S) (M) **1.** girdle of light. **3.** another name for the sun.

Bhaṅga (S) (M) **1.** to break; to destroy. **2.** destroyer. **3.** a serpent of the Takṣaka dynasty (*Bhā. Purāṇa*).

Bhangakara (S) (M) **1.** destroyer. **3.** a son of Avikṣit and grandson of King Kuru (*M. Bh.*).

Bhānu (S) (M) **1.** appearance. **2.** light; glory; fame; king; master; lord. **3.** an āditya (*Rā. Upaniṣad*); a son of Prativyoma (*Bhāgavata*); a son of Viśvadhara and father of Harinātha (*Rāmāyaṇa*); a son of Kṛṣṇa and Satyabhāmā (*Bhāgavata*); a son of Dyau and the preceptor of Sūrya (*M. Bh.*); a gandharva who was the son of Kaśyapa and Pṛthā (*M. Bh.*); an ancient king who witnessed the battle between Arjuna and Droṇa in Indra's chariot (*M. Bh.*); a Yādava whose daughter married Sahadeva (*M. Bh.*); the king of Ratnapuri and father of Jaina Tīrthaṅkara Dharmanātha (*J.S. Koṣa*); another name for an agni called Pāñćajanya, Śiva and the sun.

Bhānućandra (S) (M) **1.** shining moon; sun and moon conjoined. **2.** can be fierce as well as soothing.

Bhānudatta (S) (M) **1.** given by the sun. **2.** bright; enlightening; sacred. **3.** a brother of Śakuni (*M. Bh.*).

Bhānudeva (S) (M) **1.** lord of glory; sun, the lord. **3.** a Pāñćāla warrior (*M. Bh.*); another name for Sūrya.

Bhānuja (S) (M) **1.** son of the sun. **3.** another name for Karṇa and the planet Saturn.

Bhānukesara (S) (M) **1.** maned with rays; the lion of light. **3.** another name for the sun.

Bhānukopa (S) (M) **1.** with a blazing anger; as angry as the sun. **3.** an asura who fought against Skanda (*M. Bh.*).

Bhānumān (S) (M) **1.** as bright as the sun. **3.** a king belonging to Rāma's dynasty and the father of King Śakradyumna; a son of Kṛṣṇa and Satyabhāmā (*Bhā. Purāṇa*); a prince of Kaliṅga who fought on the side of the Kauravas (*M. Bh.*).

Bhānumata (S) (M) **1.** luminous. **2.** glorious; splendid; handsome. **3.** a son of Kuśadhvaja (*M Bh.*); a son of Bṛhadaśva (*Bhā. Purāṇa*).

Bhānunātha (S) (M) **1.** lord of brightness. **3.** another name for Sūrya.

Bhānuratha (S) (M) **1.** with a glorious chariot. **3.** a son of Bṛhadaśva.

Bhānusena (S) (M) **1.** splendid leader. **2.** with a glorious army. **3.** a son of Karṇa (*M. Bh.*).

Bhānuvarman (S) (M) **1.** sun armoured. **2.** safeguarded; protected by the sun.

Bhāradvāja (S) (M) **1.** son of Bharadvāja. **3.** another name for Droṇa.

Bharadvāja (S) (M) **1.** speed and strength; a skylark. **3.** a Purāṇic sage considered Saptarṣi, the son of Atri, father of Droṇa, the grandfather of Kubera and considered to sit in the council of Brahmā (*Purāṇas*); the eldest son of the Agni Śaṁyu (*M. Bh.*); a renowned sage and the son of King Bharata of the Purū line (*M. Bh.*); a sage born in the Aṅgiras family and the father of Yavakṛta (*V. Rāmāyaṇa*); an Arhat.

Bharadvājasuta (S) (M) **1.** son of Bharadvāja. **3.** another name for Droṇa.

Bharadvājātmaja (S) (M) **1.** son of Bharadvāja. **3.** another name for Droṇa.

Bharanda (S) (M) **1.** one who fulfils. **2.** master; lord.

Bharaṇyu (S) (M) **1.** striving to fulfil. **2.** protector; master; friend; fire. **3.** another name for the moon and the sun.

Bharata (S) (M) **1.** fulfils all desires; well-maintained. **3.** a son of Duṣyanta and Śakuntalā, a partial reincarnation of Viṣṇu, the 1st of the 12 akravartins, and who ruled the land for 27,000 years; a Manu whom this country is named after (*M. Bh.*); an āditya; a son of Daśaratha and Kaikeyī and the husband of Māṇḍavī (*V. Rāmāyaṇa*); a son of Ṛṣabha and the husband of Pañćajanī the daughter of Viśvarūpa (*Bhā. Purāṇa*); a sage and author of *Nāṭyaśāstra* (4th century B.C.); a son of Dhruvasaṇdhi and the father of Asita; various agnis (*V. Rāmāyaṇa*); (*Mā. Purāṇa*); a son of Manu Bhautya (*Mā. Purāṇa*); another name for Rudra.

Bhārata (S) (M) **1.** descended from Bharata. **3.** India; another name for Bhīṣma and Yudhiṣṭhira.

Bhāratabhūṣaṇa (S) (M) ornament of India.

Bharatāćārya (S) (M) **1.** teacher of the Bharatas. **3.** another name for Kṛpa and Droṇa.

Bhāratāćāryaputra (S) (M) **1.** son of the teacher. **3.** another name for Aśvatthāman.

Bhāratāgrya (S) (M) **1.** best of the Bharatas. **3.** another name for Duryodhana.

Bhāratapravara (S) (M) **1.** chief of the Bharatas. **3.** another name for Yudhiṣṭhira.

Bhāratarāma (S) (M) **1.** lover of India; enjoyer of India; pervader of India. **2.** an Indian patriot.

Bharatarāma (S) (M) Rāma and his brother Bharata conjoined.

Bhārataṛṣabha (S) (M) **1.** bull of the Bharatas. **3.** another name for Bhīṣma, Yudhiṣṭhira and Dhṛtarāṣṭra.

Bhārataśardula (S) (M) **1.** tiger of the Bharatas; noblest of the Bharatas. **3.** another name for Yudhiṣṭhira and Dhṛtarāṣṭra.

Bhāratasattama (S) (M) **1.** best of the Bharatas. **3.** another name for Bhīṣma, Dhṛtarāṣṭra and Yudhiṣṭhira.

Bhāratasiṁha (S) (M) **1.** lion of the Bharatas. **3.** another name for Yudhiṣṭhira.

Bhārataśreṣṭha (S) (M) **1.** first of the Bharatas. **3.** another name for Dhṛtarāṣṭra.

Bhāratendu (S) (M) moon of India.

Bharatha (S) (M) **1.** protector of the world. **2.** taking up the responsibilities; a king.

Bhārava (S) (M) a bowstring.

Bhāravi (S) (M) **1.** shining sun. **3.** a Sanskṛt poet and author of *Kirātārjunīya* (6th century A.D.).

Bharga (S) (M) **1.** with fulfilled desires; the number 11. **2.** radiance; splendour; effulgence. **3.** the grandson of Divodāsa, son of Pratardana (*A. Purāṇa*); a son of Veṇuhotra (*H. Purāṇa*); one of Vītihotra's sons (*Bhāgavata*); a son of Vahni (*M. Bh.*); another name for Rudra-Śiva and Brahmā.

Bhārgabhūmi (S) (M) **1.** radiant object. **3.** a king (*V. Purāṇa*).

Bhārgava (S) (M) **1.** attaining radiance; related to Bhṛgu. **2.** archer; preceptor. **3.** another name for Śukra regent of the planet Venus and preceptor of the daityas, Paraśurāma, Jamadagni, Mārkaṇḍeya and Śiva.

Bhārgavaka (S) (M) **1.** radiant. **2.** a diamond.

Bhārgavanandana (S) (M) **1.** son of Bhārgava. **3.** another name for Jamadagni.

Bhārgavapriya (S) (M) **1.** dear to Śukra. **2.** a diamond.

Bhārgavendu (S) (M) **1.** moon of the Bhṛgu family; Venus and moon conjoined. **2.** beautiful; aesthetic; passionate; soothing.

Bhāri (S) (M) **1.** lion; one who supports. **2.** that which nourishes.

Bhārimān (S) (M) **1.** supporting; nourishing. **3.** another name for Viṣṇu.

Bharmyaśva (S) (M) **1.** wandering horse. **3.** a king of Pāñćāla and father of Mudgala (*Bhāgavata*).

Bharosā (S) (M) faith; trust.

Bhartṛhari (S) (M) **1.** protected by god. **2.** a worshipper of god. **3.** a famous Sanskṛta poet of the 7th century (*N. Śataka*).

Bharu (S) (M) **1.** bearing the load. **2.** lord; master; gold; sea. **3.** a son of Kṛṣṇa (*Bhāgavata*); another name for Viṣṇu and Śiva.

Bharuka (S) (M) **1.** responsible. **2.** lifting the load. **3.** a solar dynasty king who was the son of Sudeva and the father of Bāhuka (*Bhāgavata*).

Bhārūpa (S) (M) **1.** with a glorious form. **2.** resplendent; shining; brilliant.

Bhāravi (S) (M) **1.** protected by God. **2.** the shining sun. **3.** the author of *Kirātārjunīya.*

Bhāsakarṇa (S) (M) **1.** with shining ears. **3.** a captain of Rāvaṇa killed by Hanumān (*V. Rāmāyaṇa*).

Bhāsanta (S) (M) **1.** illuminating; shining; radiant. **2.** splendid; beautiful; a star. **3.** another name for the sun and the moon.

Bhāsin (S) (M) shining; brilliant.

Bhāskara (S) (M) **1.** sun; that which radiates; that which emits light; that which illumines. **2.** fire; hero; gold. **3.** a son of Kaśyapa and Aditī (*H. Purāṇa*); an astrologer (10th century) (*J. Śāstra*); another name for Śiva.

Bhāskarāćārya (S) (M) **1.** a teacher as glorious as the sun. **2.** illuminating; enlightening; venerated. **3.** a master astronomer of ancient India who declared in ancient times that the world was round (*J. Śāstra*).

Bhāskarapriya (S) (M) **1.** beloved of the sun. **2.** the ruby.

Bhāskari (S) (M) **1.** son of the sun; one who brings glory. **3.** a sage (*M. Bh.*); another name for Sugrīva and Saturn.

Bhasma (S) (M) **1.** ashes. **3.** another name for Agni.

Bhasmapriya (S) (M) **1.** fond of ashes. **3.** another name for Śiva.

Bhasmaśāyin (S) (M) **1.** lying on ashes. **3.** another name for Śiva.

Bhasmāsura (S) (M) **1.** a demon; the burnt demon; one who can burn others; born of ashes. **3.** an asura who was born of the ashes of Śiva's body.

Bhāsu (S) (M) **1.** creator of light; born of light. **2.** the sun.

Bhāsura (S) (M) **1.** the shining god; crystal; hero. **2.** bright; radiant; splendid; glorious; illuminating; enlightening; sacred; venerated; divine.

Bhāsvān (S) (M) **1.** full of brightness. **3.** another name for Sūrya.

Bhāsvara (S) (M) **1.** luminous; resplendent. **2.** shining; glorious; brilliant; enlightening. **3.** one of the 2 attendants given to Skanda by Sūrya (*M. Bh.*); a Buddhist deity (*B. Literature*).

Bhaṭṭaprayāga (S) (M) **1.** a noble confluence. **2.** one in whom all virtues conjoin. **3.** the spot where the Yamunā joins the Gaṅgā.

Bhaṭṭara (S) (M) **1.** noble lord. **2.** meritorious; virtuous; venerated.

Bhaṭṭāraka (S) (M) **1.** great lord. **2.** sacred; venerable; illuminating; enlightening. **3.** another name for the sun.

Bhaṭṭi (S) (M) **1.** noble. **2.** meritorious; virtuous. **3.** a Sanskṛt poet in the court of Valabhi (7th century A.D.).

Bhaṭṭika (S) (M) **1.** noble. **3.** the son of Ćitragupta, grandson of Brahmā and the mythical progenitor of copyists (*A. Koṣa*).

Bhātu (S) (M) **1.** light. **2.** the sun.

Bhauma (S) (M) **1.** of the earth; son of the earth; the planet Mars. **3.** the 14th Manu (*V. Purāṇa*); a rākṣasa who was the son of Siṅhikā and Vipraćitti and was killed by Paraśurāma (*Br. Purāṇa*); Tuesday the day of the planet Mars (*V. Pañćaviṅśatikā*); another name for Narakāsura.

Bhaumana (S) (M) **1.** creating the earth by a will (to create). **2.** belongs to the earth. **3.** another name for

Viśvakarman, the architect of the universe.

Bhaumendra (S) (M) lord of the earth.

Bhaumika (S) (M) being on the earth.

Bhaumiratna (S) (M) **1.** jewel of the earth. **2.** the coral.

Bhautika (S) (M) **1.** physical; elemental; material; corporeal; the shining one. **2.** the pearl. **3.** another name for Śiva who is fair in visage.

Bhautya (S) (M) **1.** made of elements; composed of the earth. **3.** a Manu (*H. Purāṇa*).

Bhauvana (S) (M) **1.** belonging to the world. **3.** a deity.

Bhava (S) (M) **1.** existing; of the nature of existence. **2.** feeling; sentiment. **3.** one of the 12 sons of Bhṛguvaruṇi and Divyā (*V. Purāṇa*); one of the 11 rudras who was the son of Sthāṇu and grandson of Brahmā (*M. Bh.*); a viśvadeva (*M. Bh.*); a son of Viloman (*V. Parāṇa*); a son of Pratihartṛ (*V. Purāṇa*); a son of Kaśyapa and Surabhī (*M. Bh.*); another name for Śiva and Agni.

Bhavabhūti (S) (M) **1.** the ashes of Śiva; made of existence. **2.** whose existence is felt; welfare; prosperity. **3.** a Sanskṛt poet of the Kaśyapa gotra (8th century A.D.).

Bhavada (S) (M) **1.** giving life; cause of existence. **3.** a follower of Skanda (*M. Bh.*).

Bhavadatta (S) (M) given by Śiva.

Bhavadeva (S) (M) **1.** lord of existence. **3.** another name for Śiva.

Bhāvaja (S) (M) **1.** born of the heart. **3.** another name for Kāma.

Bhavamoćana (S) (M) **1.** one who releases from a worldly existence. **3.** another name for Kṛṣṇa.

Bhāvana (S) (M) **1.** creator; promoter of welfare; pleasing to the heart; forest of rays. **2.** manifesting; causing to be; illuminating; imagining. **3.** another name for Kṛṣṇa.

Bhavanāga (S) (M) **1.** serpent of Śiva. **2.** serpent of existence. **3.** the Kuṇḍalinī which is personified as a 1000 headed serpent and which when uncoiled results in spiritual enlightenment.

Bhavānanda (S) (M) that which delights Śiva; pleasure of life; existence and bliss conjoined.

Bhavanātha (S) (M) lord of creation.

Bhavānīkānta (S) (M) **1.** beloved of Bhavānī. **3.** another name for Śiva.

Bhavānīprasāda (S) (M) given by Bhavānī; blessed by Bhavānī.

Bhavānīśaṇkara (S) (M) Śiva and Pārvatī conjoined.

Bhavamanyu (S) (M) **1.** creator of the universe; universally accepted. **3.** a Purū king (*V. Purāṇa*).

Bhavarudra (S) (M) **1.** Śiva and Rudra conjoined; existence and fear conjoined. **2.** striving to survive by safeguarding himself from fear; pro-life.

Bhavasāgara (S) (M) the ocean of worldly existence.

Bhavaśekhara (S) (M) **1.** Śiva's crest. **3.** another name for the moon.

Bhavatiga (S) (M) **1.** overcoming worldly existence. **2.** attaining salvation or mokṣa.

Bhavātmaja (S) (M) **1.** the son of Śiva. **3.** another name for Gaṇeśa and Kārttikeya.

Bhavayavya (S) (M) **1.** living in glory. **2.** renowned; glorious; respected. **3.** a sage of the *Ṛg Veda* who married Romaṣā the daughter of Bṛhaspati.

Bhaveśa (S) (M) **1.** lord of worldly existence. **3.** another name for Śiva.

Bhavika (S) (M) **1.** well-meaning. **2.** righteous; pious; happy.

Bhavila (S) (M) good.

Bhavin (S) (M) living being; man.

Bhaviṣa (S) (M) **1.** striving to exist; lord of existence. **3.** another name for Śiva.

Bhaviṣṇu (S) (M) **1.** knowing the future. **2.** faring well; thriving.

Bhavitra (S) (M) the 3 worlds.

Bhāvuka (S) (M) **1.** sensitive; sentimental; productive; happy; well. **3.** a king of the solar dynasty who was a son of Ravīya and father of Ćakroddhata (*Bhāgavata*).

Bhavya (S) (M) **1.** magnificent. **2.** existing suitable; fit; proper; handsome; beautiful; excellent; pious; true. **3.** a ṛṣi of the 9th Manvantara (*V. Purāṇa*); a son of Priyavrata (*H. Purāna*); a son of Dhruva and the husband of Śambhu (*V. Purāṇa*); a sage of the Dakṣasāvarṇi Manvantara (*V. Purāṇa*); *Averrhoa carambola.*

Bhayaṅkara (S) (M) **1.** terrible; horrible. **3.** a prince of Sauvīra who was a dependent of Jayadratha (*M. Bh.*); a viśvadeva (*M. Bh.*).

Bhena (S) (M) **1.** the lord of stars. **3.** another name for the sun and the moon.

Bherunda (S) (M) **1.** formidable; terrible. **3.** an intense, fear inducing form of Śiva.

Bhettṛ (S) (M) **1.** pierces. **2.** breaking; splitting; a conqueror. **3.** another name for Skanda.

Bhikṣita (S) (M) obtained as alms.

Bhikṣu (S) (M) **1.** beggar; mendicant; Buddhist monk. **3.** a son of Bhoja (*K. Sāgara*).

Bhīma (S) (M) **1.** terrible; formidable; tremendous. **3.** a gandharva who was the son of Kaśyapa and Munī (*M. Bh.*); the grandson of King Avikṣit, son of Parikṣit and Suyaśā, brother of Janamejaya, husband of Kumārī and the father of Pratiśravas (*M. Bh.*); father of King Divodāsa of Kāśi (*M. Bh.*); father of Damayantī (*Nalopākhyāna*); a son of Dhṛtarāṣṭra (*M. Bh.*); the son of King Īlīna and Rathāntarī (*M. Bh.*); one of the 5 attendants given to Subrahmaṇya by the god called Anśa (*M. Bh.*); a 100 kings in Yama's assembly (*M. Bh.*); a Yādava king who was the father of Andhaka and conqueror of Madhurapuri (*Bhāgavata*); friend of Rāvaṇa (*V. Rāmāyaṇa*); one of the 8 forms of Śiva (*Ś. Purāṇa*); one of the 11 rudras (*Ś. Purāṇa*); the 2nd Pāṇḍava who was the son of Kuntī and Vāyu and noted for his strength and size (*M. Bh.*); a son of Kumbhakarṇa (*V. Rāmāyaṇa*); a vidyādhara (*H. Purāṇa*); a dānava (*V. Rāmāyaṇa*); another name for Śiva.

Bhīmabala (S) (M) **1.** with enormous strength. **3.** a son of Dhṛtarāṣṭra (*M. Bh.*).

Bhīmabhaṭa (S) (M) **1.** great warrior. **3.** a gandharva (*K. Sāgara*).

Bhīmaćandra (S) (M) moon of strength.

Bhīmadhanvā (S) (M) **1.** with a formidable bow. **3.** another name for Bhīma.

Bhīmagupta (S) (M) protected by Bhīma.

Bhīmajānu (S) (M) **1.** strong thighed. **3.** a king in the assembly of Yama (*M. Bh.*).

Bhīmaka (S) (M) **1.** terrible. **3.** an attendant of Śiva.

Bhīmākṣa (S) (M) **1.** terrible-eyed. **3.** a rākṣasa killed by King Haryaśvan (*H. Purāṇa*).

Bhīmanātha (S) (M) lord of strength.

Bhīmāṅgada (S) (M) strong bodied.

Bhīmapāla (S) (M) protected by Bhīma, protected by the powerful.

Bhīmapūrvaja (S) (M) **1.** elder brother of Bhīma. **3.** another name for Yudhiṣṭhira.

Bhīmaratha (S) (M) **1.** with a formidable chariot. **2.** with a powerful chariot. **3.** a king of Viśvāmitra's family who was the son of Ketumān and the father of Divodāsa (*Bhāgavata*); a son of Dhṛtarāṣṭra (*M. Bh.*); a hero on the Kaurava side (*M. Bh.*).

Bhīmaśara (S) (M) **1.** with terrible arrows. **3.** a son of Dhṛtarāṣṭra (*M. Bh.*).

Bhīmasena (S) (M) **1.** having a formidable army. **2.** commander of a formidable army. **3.** the second Pāṇḍava and the son of Vāyu and Kuntī (*M. Bh.*); a yakṣa; a gandharva (*M. Bh.*).

Bhīmasenasuta (S) (M) **1.** son of Bhīma. **3.** another name for Ghaṭotkaća.

Bhīmasenātmaja (S) (M) **1.** son of Bhīma. **3.** another name for Ghaṭotkaća.

Bhīmaśaṅkara (S) (M) **1.** Śiva in his terrible form. **3.** Śiva in his intense, fearful and destructive form; a liṅga.

Bhīmaśastra (S) (M) **1.** with formidable weapons. **2.** highly skilled in the use of weapons. **3.** a son of Dhṛtarāṣṭra (*M. Bh.*).

Bhīmasūnu (S) (M) **1.** son of Bhīma. **3.** another name for Ghaṭotkaća.

Bhīmavega (S) (M) **1.** with a very high speed. **2.** quick; swift; active. **3.** a son of Dhṛtarāṣṭra (*M. Bh.*).

Bhīmavegarava (S) (M) **1.** of terrific velocity and sound. **2.** moving very fast while pounding his feet. **3.** a son of Dhṛtarāṣṭra (*M. Bh.*).

Bhīmrāja (S) (M) **1.** the king of the powerful. **2.** the Racket tailed Drongo (*Dicrurus paradiseus*).

Bhīru (S) (M) **1.** coward. **3.** a son of Maṇībhadra and Puṅyajānī (*H. Purāṇa*).

Bhīṣaṇa (S) (M) **1.** gruesome. **2.** awful. **3.** a son of the demon Baka killed by Arjuna; a form of Bhairava.

Bhiṣaj (S) (M) **1.** medicine; healer; physician. **2.** heals; cures. **3.** a son of Śatadhanvan (*M. Bh.*).

Bhīṣma (S) (M) **1.** dreadful. **2.** terrible; fear-inducing; forbidding. **3.** a son of Śāntanu and Gaṅgā who was renowned for his wisdom, bravery and fidelity to his word and who, after death, lived in heaven as Dyau, one of the 8 vasus (*M. Bh.*) a rākṣasa. (*H. Koṣa*); another name for Śiva.

Bhīṣmahanta (S) (M) **1.** killing Bhīṣma. **3.** another name for Śikhaṇḍī.

Bhīṣmaka (S) (M) **1.** dreadful. **2.** terrifying; fear-inducing; forbidding. **3.** the king of Vidarbha and father of Rukmiṇī (*M. Bh.*).

Bhīṣmasvarāja (S) (M) **1.** king of terrible sounds. **2.** not affected by noise around. **3.** a Buddha (*B. Literature*).

Bhoganātha (S) (M) lord of worldly pleasures.

Bhogīndra (S) (M) **1.** lord of the curved ones, lord of serpents. **3.** another name for Ananta and Patañjali.

Bhogīśa (S) (M) **1.** lord of serpents. **3.** another name for Ananta and Śeṣa.

Bhoja (S) (M) **1.** bestowing enjoyment: bountiful; liberal. **2.** a king with uncommon qualities. **3.** a king of the country of Bhoja near the Vindhya mountains (*H. Purāṇa*); a king of Mālvā (*M. Bh.*); an ancient king of Marttikātava who fought on the side of the Kauravas (*M. Bh.*); a Yadu dynasty king who founded the Bhoja dynasty (*M. Bh.*); a renowned king and a Sanskṛt scholar (11th century A.D.) (*B. Ćarita*); a follower of Sudāsa who once helped sage Viśvāmitra (*M. Bh.*); a king of Kānyakubja (*R. Taraṅgiṇī*).

Bhojadeva (S) (M) **1.** fulfiller of desires. **3.** a celebrated king of Dhārā who was a patron of learning and an author himself (11th century A.D.) (*M Smṛti*).

Bhojanarendra (S) (M) **1.** best among the Bhoja kings. **3.** another name for King Bhojadeva of Dhārā.

Bhojarāja (S) (M) **1.** lord of the generous. **3.** another name for King Bhojadeva of Dhārā.

Bhojarājanyavardhana (S) (M) **1.** increasing the Bhoja dynasty. **3.** another name for Kṛṣṇa.

Bhoktṛ (S) (M) **1.** enjoyer. **2.** consumer; eater; possessor; ruler.

Bholānātha (S) (M) **1.** lord of the innocent. **3.** another name for Śiva.

Bhoneśa (S) (M) lord of the universe.

Bhrāja (S) (M) **1.** shining; glittering. **2.** sacred; illuminating; enlightening. **3.** a gandharva who protects the Soma; an agni; one of the 7 suns.

Bhrājasvata (S) (M) **1.** sparkling; glittering. **2.** illuminates; enlightens; sacred.

Bhrājata (S) (M) **1.** shining; glittering. **2.** gleaming; glorious; enlightening.

Bhrājathu (S) (M) **1.** brilliance. **2.** splendour; glory; fame; enlightenment.

Bhrājiṣṇu (S) (M) **1.** desirous of splendour. **2.** striving for glory; achievement; renown; shining; splendid; radiant. **3.** another name for Viṣṇu and Śiva.

Bhrājiṣṭha (S) (M) **1.** residing in splendour. **2.** splendid; glorious; renowned; enlightened; shining very brightly. **3.** a son of Ghṛtapṛṣṭha (*Ṛg Veda*).

Bhramara (S) (M) **1.** large black bee. **2.** wanderer. **3.** a Sauvīra prince who was a dependant of Jayadratha (*M. Bh.*).

Bhrāsakarṇa (S) (M) **1.** one possessed with dancing ears. **2.** a rapt, attentive listener. **3.** a rākṣasa who was the son of Sumāli and Ketumatī (*Bhāgavata*).

Bhṛgu (S) (M) **1.** born of fire. **3.** a prajāpati son of Brahmā, the founder of the Bhārgava line of sages, considered to have been born twice — first from Brahmā's skin and the second time from the Brahmāyajña the fire of Varuṇa, in the first birth was the husband of Khyāti and fathered Lakṣmī, Dhātā, Vidhātā and Kavi, in the second was the husband of Pulomā and Bhūtā from whom he had the 11 rudras, Bhūta, Ćyavana, Śućihi, Śukra, Sāvana and Vajraśīrṣa, was a member of Brahmā's assembly, his race is said to have brought fire to the earth (*Ṛg Veda*); one of the Saptarṣis or Seven Sages (*H. Purāṇa*); the father of Dhātṛ and Māndhātṛ (*Purāṇa*); a son of Arthapati and uncle of the poet Bāṇa.

Bhṛgunandana (S) (M) **1.** son of Bhṛgu. **3.** another name for the planet Śukra or Venus.

Bhṛgunātha (S) (M) **1.** lord of fire. **3.** another name for Śiva.

Bhṛguśārdūla (S) (M) **1.** tiger of the Bhṛgus; noblest of the Bhṛgus. **3.** another name for Mārkaṇḍeya and Jamadagni.

Bhṛguśreṣṭha (S) (M) **1.** the best among Bhṛgus. **3.** another name for sage Jamadagni and Paraśurāma.

Bhṛguttama (S) (M) **1.** best of the Bhṛgus. **3.** another name for Jamadagni.

Bhṛguvāruṇi (S) (M) **1.** of Varuṇa. **3.** a ṛṣi regarded as the ancestor of the Bhṛgus and part author of *Ṛg Veda* (ix).

Bhṛṅgāra (S) (M) **1.** a vessel of fire; a golden vase of 8 different substances and forms. **2.** meritorious; virtuous; venerated.

Bhṛṅgarāja (S) (M) **1.** king of black bees. **2.** the large black bee. **3.** a tutelary deity (*H. Ć. Ćintāmaṇi*); a kind of oblation or sacrifice (*He. Koṣa*); an ayurvedic herb used for darkening the hair (*S. Samhitā*).

Bhṛṅgarīta (S) (M) **1.** the Indian fig tree (*Ficus indica*) **3.** an attendant of Śiva (*Ś. Purāṇa*).

Bhṛṅgī (S) (M) **1.** 6 footed insect. **3.** a 3 footed sage who was a devotee of Śiva (*V. Purāṇa*).

Bhṛṅgin (S) (M) **1.** the Indian fig tree (*Ficus indica*) **3.** one of Śiva's attendants (*Ś. Purāṇa*).

Bhūbhṛta (S) (M) **1.** supporter of the earth; supported by the earth. **2.** a mountain. **3.** another name for Viṣṇu.

Bhūbhuja (S) (M) **1.** possessor of the earth; enjoyer of the earth. **2.** a king.

Bhūdeva (S) (M) **1.** lord of earth. **2.** a divinity on earth.

Bhūdhana (S) (M) **1.** whose property is the earth. **2.** a king.

Bhūdhara (S) (M) **1.** supporter of the earth. **2.** mountain; the number 7. **3.** another name for Kṛṣṇa, Śiva and Śeṣa.

Bhūgandhapati (S) (M) **1.** lord of the essence of the earth. **3.** another name for Śiva.

Bhūgarbha (S) (M) **1.** womb of the earth. **2.** a tunnel; an underground establishment; who keeps secrets; who is secretive; protects; protected.

Bhujabalin (S) (M) strong armed.

Bhujagarāja (S) (M) **1.** king of serpents. **3.** another name for Śeṣa.

Bhujagāri (S) (M) **1.** enemy of serpents. **2.** a peacock. **3.** another name for Garuḍa.

Bhujageśvara (S) (M) **1.** lord of serpents. **3.** another name for Śeṣa.

Bhujaketu (S) (M) **1.** holding a banner; with a victorious arm. **3.** a king who fought on the side of the Kauravas (*M. Bh.*).

Bhujaṅga (S) (M) **1.** black snake. **2.** lord; the constellation Āśleṣā; the number 8. **3.** a serpent son of Kadru and Kaśyapa (*M. Bh.*); another name for Rāhu.

Bhujaṅgahan (S) (M) **1.** slayer of serpents. **3.** another name for Garuḍa.

Bhujavīrya (S) (M) strong armed.

Bhuji (S) (M) **1.** granting favours. **2.** protector; patron. **3.** another name for the as aśvins and Agni.

Bhujyu (S) (M) **1.** with a desire to enjoy; can be eaten; a connoisseur; an epicurean. **2.** wealthy; rich; edible. **3.** a son of Tugra protected by the aśvins (*Ṛg Veda*).

Bhūkaśyapa (S) (M) **1.** drinker of the earth; tortoise of the earth. **2.** above earthly attachments; supporting the earth. **3.** the father of Vasudeva and the grandfather of Kṛṣṇa (*Bhāgavata*).

Bhūman (S) (M) **1.** consisting of all existing things; consisting of existence. **2.** the earth.

Bhūmanyu (S) (M) **1.** universally accepted; devotee of the earth. **3.** a son of Bharata and Sunandā, grandson of Duṣyanta and the husband of Puṣkariṇī (*M. Bh.*); a grandson of King Kuru and son of Dhṛtarāṣṭra (*M. Bh.*); a gandharva (*M. Bh.*).

Bhūmat (S) (M) **1.** possessing the earth. **2.** a king.

Bhūmija (S) (M) **1.** born of the earth. **2.** produced from the earth.

Bhūmimitra (S) (M) **1.** friend of the earth. **2.** wellwisher of all that exists, of people.

Bhūminātha (S) (M) **1.** controller of the earth. **2.** a king.

Bhūmīndra (S) (M) **1.** lord of the earth. **2.** a king.

Bhūmiñjaya (S) (M) **1.** conqueror of the earth. **3.** a son of Virāṭa; a warrior of the Kaurava side (*M. Bh.*).

Bhūmipāla (S) (M) **1.** guardian of the earth; protector of the earth. **2.** a king. **3.** a king who was a partial incarnation of the asura Krodhavaśa (*M. Bh.*).

Bhūmipati (S) (M) **1.** lord of the earth; master of the earth. **3.** a king mentioned in the (*M. Bh.*).

Bhūmiputra (S) (M) **1.** son of the earth. **3.** another name for the planet Mars.

Bhūmiśaya (S) (M) **1.** sleeping on the earth. **2.** an ascetic; forsaker of earthly pleasures. **3.** a king who gifted a sword to Bharata the son of Duṣyanta (*M. Bh.*).

Bhūmisena (S) (M) **1.** commander of the earth. **2.** an extremely powerful, renowned king. **3.** a son of the 10th Manu (*M. Purāṇa*).

Bhūmīśvara (S) (M) sovereign of the earth.

Bhūmitra (S) (M) **1.** friend of the earth. **2.** a king.

Bhūmya (S) (M) **1.** belonging to the earth. **2.** terrestrial.

Bhūnandana (S) (M) **1.** delighting the earth; son of earth. **2.** a virtuous person.

Bhūnāyaka (S) (M) leader of the earth.

Bhūnetri (S) (M) **1.** leader of the earth; eye of the earth. **2.** a king.

Bhūpa (S) (M) **1.** protector of the earth. **2.** a king.

Bhūpada (S) (M) **1.** fixed on earth. **2.** stable; firm; a tree.

Bhūpāla (S) (M) **1.** guardian of the earth. **2.** a king.

Bhūpat (S) (M) **1.** lord of the earth. **2.** a king. **3.** a king of the lunar dynasty of Indraprastha (*M. Bh.*).

Bhūpati (S) (M) **1.** lord of the earth. **3.** a viśvadeva (*M. Bh.*); another name for Rudra and Śiva; a class of gods under Manu Raivata (*Mā. Purāṇa*).

Bhūpen (S) (M) **1.** lord of the world. **2.** a king.

Bhūpendra (S) (M) **1.** king of kings. **3.** an apsarā; another name for Indra.

Bhūputra (S) (M) **1.** son of the earth. **3.** another name for Mars.

Bhūraṇyu (S) (M) **1.** worshipped by the world. **2.** quick; eager; restless; active. **3.** another name for Viṣṇu and the sun.

Bhūrbhuva (S) (M) **1.** born of the earth; father of the earth. **3.** a mind-born son of Brahmā (*Brah. Purāṇa*); another name for the sun.

Bhūri (S) (M) **1.** much, abundant. **2.** important; mighty; great; boundless; infinite; divine; gold. **3.** a son of King Somadatta of the Bālhikas (*M. Bh.*); a king of the Kuru dynasty who btained a place among the viśvadevas (*M. Bh.*); a son of sage Śuka and Pīvarī (*V. Purāṇa*); another name for Brahmā, Viṣṇu, Śiva and gold.

Bhūribala (S) (M) **1.** very strong. **3.** a son of Dhṛtarāṣṭra (*M. Bh.*).

Bhūrida (S) (M) one who donates in abundance.

Bhūridakṣiṇa (S) (M) **1.** bestowing rich presents; liberal. **3.** another name for Bhūriśravas.

Bhūridhāman (S) (M) **1.** possessing great might. **3.** a son of the 9th Manu (*H. Purāṇa*).

Bhūridyumna (S) (M) **1.** possessing great glory. **3.** a son of Vīradyumna (*M. Upaniṣad*).

Bhuridyumna (S) (M) **1.** killer of many; as glorious as fire. **2.** a warrior; pious; sacred. **3.** a king in the assembly of Yama (*M. Bh.*); a sage and contemporaneous devotee of Kṛṣṇa (*Bhāgavata*); son of Vīradyumna (*M. Bh.*).

Bhūrihan (S) (M) **1.** slayer of many. **3.** a rākṣasa (*M. Bh.*).

Bhūrijyeṣṭha (S) (M) **1.** eldest among all. **2.** greatest; the best. **3.** a son of King Vićakṣus (*V. Purāṇa*).

Bhūrikīrti (S) (M) **1.** very famous; very learned. **3.** a king whose 2 daughters Ćampikā and Sumatī married Lava and Kuśa (*A. Rāmāyaṇa*).

Bhūriṣeṇa (S) (M) **1.** with many armies. **3.** a son of the 10th Manu (*H. Purāṇa*); another name for King Śaryāti (*Bhāgavata*).

Bhūriśravas (S) (M) **1.** about whom much is heard. **3.** a son of King Somadatta of the Bālhikas; the son of King Somada of the Kuru dynasty who helped the Kaurava side (*M. Bh.*); another name for Indra.

Bhūritejas (S) (M) **1.** very glorious. **3.** an ancient king who was a partial incarnation of the asura Krodhavaśa (*M. Bh.*).

Bhūrivasu (S) (M) one who has a lot of wealth.

Bhūśakra (S) (M) **1.** Indra of the earth. **2.** much renowned; powerful; venerated; meritorious king.

Bhūṣaṇa (S) (M) **1.** ornament; embellishment. **2.** that which decorates; adorns.

Bhūṣṇu (S) (M) growing; thriving.

Bhūsura (S) (M) **1.** earth; god. **2.** a cow; a Brahmin.

Bhūta (S) (M) **1.** existent; essence of the material substance. **2.** past; son; a devotee; an ascetic. **3.** a son of Vasudeva and Pauravī (*Bhāgavata*); a priest of the gods (*A. Koṣa*); a son-in-law of Dakṣa and the father of various rudras (*Bhāgavata*); name of a yakṣa (*Bhāgavata*).

Bhutabhāvana (S) (M) **1.** causing the welfare of living beings. **3.** another name for Brahmā, Viṣṇu and Śiva.

Bhūtadhāman (S) (M) **1.** one who dwells in substance. **2.** all pervading; omnipresent. **3.** a son of Indra.

Bhūtādi (S) (M) **1.** originator of all beings. **2.** the Supreme Spirit.

Bhūtajyoti (S) (M) **1.** light of living beings; flame of the 5 essences. **3.** the father of Vasu and son of Sumati.

Bhūtakarman (S) (M) **1.** who acts in accordance with the past; who performs rites to invoke the evil spirits. **3.** a warrior on the side of the Kauravas (*M. Bh.*).

Bhūtaketu (S) (M) **1.** who bears the banner of ascetics; saviour of the ascetics. **3.** a son of Manu Dakṣasāvarṇi.

Bhūtanātha (S) (M) **1.** lord of ascetics; lord of ghosts; lord of essences; lord of existence. **3.** another name for Śiva.

Bhūtānśa (S) (M) **1.** part of existence. **3.** a sage and descendant of Kaśyapa who was an author of *Ṛg Veda* (x).

Bhūtapāla (S) (M) protector of living beings; protector of spirits; protector of existence.

Bhūtapati (S) (M) **1.** lord of beings. **3.** another name for Kṛṣṇa.

Bhūtarāja (S) (M) **1.** lord of living beings. **3.** another name for Viṣṇu.

Bhūtasantāpana (S) (M) **1.** tortures living beings; tortures evil spirits. **3.** a son of Hiraṇyākṣa (*Bhā. Purāṇā*).

Bhūtaśarman (S) (M) **1.** protector of spirits. protector of the existence. **3.** a warrior of the Kauravas (*M. Bh.*).

Bhūtātman (S) (M) **1.** soul of all beings; the Supreme Self; the Universal Self. **3.** another name for Brahmā and Viṣṇu.

Bhūteśa (S) (M) **1.** lord of living beings. **3.** another name for Brahmā, Viṣṇu, Śiva and the sun.

Bhūteśvara (S) (M) **1.** lord of beings. **3.** another name for Kṛṣṇa.

Bhūtibhūṣaṇa (S) (M) **1.** adorned with ashes; ornament among the living beings. **3.** another name for Śiva.

Bhūtigaurī (S) (M) **1.** pervades life. **2.** omnipresent. **3.** another name for Pārvatī the consort of Śiva.

Bhūtikṛt (S) (M) **1.** causing welfare. **3.** another name for Śiva.

Bhūtinanda (S) (M) bestower of pleasure.

Bhūtirāja (S) (M) lord of existence.

Bhūtivardhana (S) (M) **1.** increases welfare. **2.** a king; a eader; a saint.

Bhuva (S) (M) **1.** atmosphere. **3.** a son of Pratihartṛ (*V. Purāṇa*); another name for Agni.

Bhuvadvasu (S) (M) bestowing wealth.

Bhuvadvata (S) (M) **1.** bestowing prosperity. **3.** another name for the ādityas.

Bhūvallabha (S) (M) liked by the universe; universally adored.

Bhuvana (S) (M) **1.** being; the earth; abode. **2.** living creature; human. **3.** a rudra (*V. Purāṇa*); a sage (*M. Bh.*).

Bhuvanaćandra (S) (M) moon of the earth.

Bhuvanādhīśa (S) (M) master of the earth.

Bhuvanadīpa (S) (M) light of the earth.

Bhuvanamohana (S) (M) **1.** attractive to the 3 worlds; universally attractive. **3.** a name of Kṛṣṇa, kept by Rukmiṇī.

Bhuvanāṇḍaka (S) (M) **1.** the cosmic egg. **2.** the universe.

Bhuvanapatī (S) (M) lord of the earth.

Bhuvanarāja (S) (M) king of the earth.

Bhuvanasvara (S) (M) **1.** voice of the earth. **3.** a rudra (*Ṛg Veda*).

Bhuvanatraya (S) (M) **1.** the 3 worlds. **3.** on the basis of knowledge, the 3 worlds are earth, atmosphere and heaven, and on the basis of *karmaphala,* or the fruit of Karma, the 3 worlds are hell, earth and heaven.

Bhuvaneśa (S) (M) lord of the earth.

Bhuvaneśvara (S) (M) lord of the earth.

Bhuvaneśvarī (S) (M) mistress of the earth.

Bhuvanyu (S) (M) **1.** possessing the earth. **3.** another name for the sun, fire and moon.

Bhuvapati (S) (M) lord of the atmosphere.

Bhuvas (S) (M) **1.** air; atmosphere; heaven. **2.** second of the 14 worlds; a mind-born son of Brahmā (*Bhā. Purāṇa*).

Bibhatsu (S) (M) **1.** averse to loathsome acts. **3.** another name for Arjuna who desisted from performing or participating in loathsome deeds (*M. Bh.*).

Biḍaujas (S) (M) **1.** light of the people; powerful sovereign. **3.** another name for Indra.

Bidūla (S) (M) **1.** spotted; variegated. **2.** one with an unusual, attractive body. **3.** the Kachnār tree (*Bauhinia Variegata*).

Bidyut (S) (M) **1.** lightning; electricity; full of knowledge. **2.** effulgent; illumined; enlightened.

Bījanātha (S) (M) **1.** lord of the seed. **2.** lord of the elements. **3.** another name for Śiva and the sun.

Bījavāhana (S) (M) **1.** carrier of seed. **2.** creator. **3.** another name for Śiva.

Bījin (S) (M) **1.** cosmic creator; the owner and giver of seed; progenitor. **3.** another name for the sun.

Bikāsa (S) (M) development; expansion.

Bila (S) (M) **1.** hole. **2.** hollow; opening; cave. **3.** another name for Indra's horse Uććaihśravas.

Billa (S) (M) **1.** hole. **2.** reservoir.

Bilvaḍaṇḍin (S) (M) **1.** one who holds a staff made of bilva wood (*Aegle marmelos*) (the fruit, leaves and wood of the Bilva tree are offered to Śiva and therefore considered sacred). **3.** another name for Śiva.

Bilvaka (S) (M) **1.** living in a hole; living in a cave. **3.** a serpent son of Kaśyapa and Kadru (*M. Bh.*).

Bilvamaṅgala (S) (M) **1.** the auspicious bilva tree (*Aegle marmelos*). **3.** a friend of Kṛṣṇa (*Bhā. Purāṇa*).

Bilvanātha (S) (M) **1.** lord of the bilva tree; lord of serpents. **3.** another name for Śiva.

Bilvapāṇḍura (S) (M) **1.** yellow serpent. **3.** a serpent son of Kaśyapa (*M. Bh.*).

Bilvatejas (S) (M) **1.** energetic serpent. **3.** a serpent son of Takṣaka (*M. Bh.*).

Biman (S) (M) honoured; respected from the heart.

Bimbaka (S) (M) the disc of the sun or the moon; round-faced; mirror.

Bimbeśvara (S) (M) **1.** lord of the sun and the moon; lord of images. **2.** a preceptor. **3.** a temple founded by princess Bimbā (*R. Taraṅgiṇī*).

Bimbisāra (S) (M) **1.** the essence of the Absolute. **3.** a king of Magadha who was a patron of Gautama Buddha (*B. Ćarita*).

Bimbita (S) (M) reflected.

Bindeṣvara (S) (M) **1.** lord of creation. **2.** the Supreme Lord.

Bindu (S) (M) **1.** drop; dot; globule; spot. **2.** a dot worn on the forehead between the eyebrows. **3.** the dot in the alphabet that represents the Anuśvāra which is connected with Śiva and is of mystical importance.

Bindudeva (S) (M) **1.** lord of the Bindu; lord of alphabets. **3.** a Buddhist deity (*B. Literature*); another name for Śiva.

Binduhṛada (S) (M) **1.** knower of truth. **2.** attained salvation or mokṣa. **3.** a lake said to have been formed by the drops of the Gaṅgā shaken from Śiva's locks (*V. Purāṇa*).

Bindumādhava (S) (M) **1.** thinker of the Absolute; lord of the alphabet. **2.** well read; wise; illumined; enlightened. **3.** a form of Viṣṇu (*V. Purāṇa*).

Bindumat (S) (M) **1.** has pearls; knows the truth; knows the alphabet. **2.** wealthy; well-read; wise; enlightened; has attained mokṣa or salvation. **3.** a son of Marīći (*Bhā. Purāṇa*).

Bindunātha (S) (M) **1.** lord of the Bindu; lord of alphabets; lord of truth. **2.** wise; illuminated; enlightened; has attained mokṣa or salvation. **3.** another name for Śiva.

Binduphala (S) (M) a pearl.

Bindusāra (S) (M) **1.** an excellent pearl; essence of truth. **3.** the son of Ćandragupta Maurya and the father of Emperor Aśoka (*H. Parvan*).

Bindusāras (S) (M) **1.** concentrated; pious lake; an ocean of alphabets. **2.** well read; wise; venerated; enlightened. **3.** a sacred lake (*M. Bh.*).

Binota (S) (M) happy.

Binoy (S) (M) humility; humble; request.

Bipin (S) (M) **1.** forest. **2.** free; magnificent; providing shelter.

Bipinćandra (S) (M) **1.** moon of the forest. **3.** another name for Kṛṣṇa.

Biplab (S) (M) **1.** revolution. **2.** revolutionary; progressive.

Bipula (S) (M) **1.** plenty; much; many. **2.** strong; manifold.

Bīrbala (S) (M) a powerful warrior.

Biren (S) (M) **1.** lord of warriors. **2.** great warrior.

Bīrendra (S) (M) **1.** lord of warriors. **2.** a great warrior.

Bīreśvara (S) (M) lord of warriors.

Bīrju (S) (M) powerful.

Biśambharnātha (S) (M) saviour of the universe; lord of the universe.

Bisvājita (S) (M) victorious in the world.

Bittu (S) (M) **1.** seed. **2.** fecund; life-giving.

Boddhavāsara (S) (M) **1.** the day of enlightenment. **3.** the 11th day of the light half of the Kārttika month when Viṣṇu awakens from his sleep (*S. Māhātmya*).

Boddhidharma (S) (M) **1.** follower of Buddhist doctrine; follower of the enlightened path. **3.** a Buddhist patriarch (*B. Literature*).

Boddhṛ (S) (M) **1.** who comprehends; who knows. **2.** a preceptor; a seer.

Bodha (S) (M) **1.** knowledge; awakening. **2.** thought; intelligence; understanding; enlightenment. **3.** knowledge personified as a son of Buddhi.

Bodhadīśana (S) (M) **1.** whose intellect is knowledge. **2.** profoundly wise; a seer.

Bodhamaya (S) (M) **1.** consisting of pure knowledge; pervaded with knowledge. **2.** learned; wise; enlightened.

Bodhana (S) (M) **1.** inspiration; awakening. **2.** prudent; clever; wise; enlightened. **3.** another name for Bṛhaspati.

Bodhāna (S) (M) **1.** arousing; enlightening. **2.** clever; exciting; prudent; wise; enlightening. **3.** another name for Bṛhaspati.

Bodhendra (S) (M) lord of intelligence; lord of enlightenment.

Bodhinmanas (S) (M) **1.** an enlightened mind. **2.** awake; attentive; watchful; wise.

Bodhisattva (S) (M) **1.** whose essence is perfect knowledge. **3.** a term used to denote one who has only one stage to cover before the attaining of Buddha or spiritual enlightenment.

Bogli (S) (M) the pond-heron.

Bolin (S) (M) speaker.

Bora (S) (M) brave.

Bradhna (S) (M) **1.** pale red; yellowish; mighty; ruddy; horse; the world of the sun; great. **2.** fecund; life-giving; strong; illuminating; enlightening; sacred. **3.** a son of Manu Bhautya (*H. Purāṇa*); another name for the sun.

Bradhnāśva (S) (M) **1.** as powerful as a horse. **3.** a king.

Brahmā (S) (M) **1.** creator of the universe. **2.** growth; evolution; prayer. **3.** the one universal spirit represented as the creator and first of the divine Hindu trinity (the other two being Viṣṇu — the sustainer and Śiva — the destroyer), the husband of Sarasvatī, born from the navel of Viṣṇu and creator of the 7 sages or the Saptarṣis who are considered the prajāpatis or lords of creation and from whom originate all the movables and immovables of the universe and the abode of whom is Mount Mahāmeru (*Bhā. Purāṇa*).

Brahmabhuti (S) (M) **1.** created by the absolute; twilight. **2.** soothing and perfect.

Brahmabīja (S) (M) **1.** the seed of the Vedas. **3.** the sacred syllable Om.

Brahmaćāri (S) (M) **1.** devotee of the Absolute; bachelor. **3.** a gandharva who was the son of Kaśyapa and Prādhā (*M. Bh.*); another name for Śiva and Skanda.

Brahmadaṇḍa (S) (M) **1.** the staff of Brahmā. **2.** as just and fair as Brahmā.

Brahmadatta (S) (M) **1.** given by Brahmā. **2.** perfect; held sacred. **3.** a prince of the Pāñćālas (*M. Bh.*); the 12th ćakravartin (*A. Koṣa*); the father of Kṛṣṇadatta; a king of Kāmpila who married the hundred daughters of King Kuśanābha of Kānyakubja (*M. Bh.*); a famous Solar dynasty king of Kāmpilya who was the son of Anūha and Kṛtvī (*Rāmāyaṇa*); the king of Śālva and the father of Hansa and Dībhaka (*H. Purāṇa*); a king of Kāśi (*K. Sāgara*).

Brahmadeva (S) (M) **1.** the god Brahmā; the Absolute. **3.** a warrior on the side of the Pāṇḍavās (*M. Bh.*).

Brahmadhara (S) (M) **1.** possessing sacred knowledge. **2.** has attained salvation or mokṣa.

Brahmadhvaja (S) (M) **1.** a banner of Brahmā; banner of the Absolute. **2.** meritorious; virtuous; venerated; divine; all perfect. **3.** a Buddha (*B. Literature*).

Brahmadṛśa (S) (M) **1.** Brahmā's mirror. **2.** preceptor of the Absolute; illuminated; enlightened; attained spiritual bliss and is a vehicle for the attainment of salvation.

Brahmādya (S) (M) **1.** beginning with Brahmā. **2.** absolute; the beginning.

Brahmagandha (S) (M) **1.** the fragrance of Brahmā. **2.** the fragrance of sacred knowledge.

Brahmaghoṣa (S) (M) **1.** the sacred word. **2.** the sacred syllable Om.

Brahmagiri (S) (M) the mountain of Brahmā.

Brahmagupta (S) (M) **1.** protected by Brahmā. **3.** a son of Brahmā by the wife of the vidyādhara Bhīma; a son of Jiṣṇu.

Brahmajīta (S) (M) **1.** winner of Brahmā; controller of self. **2.** perfect; enlightened. **3.** a son of Kālanemi (*B. Purāṇa*).

Brahmakṛta (S) (M) **1.** offering prayers; caused by Brahmā, caused by the Absolute. **2.** performed by divinity; perfect.

Brahmakuṇḍa (S) (M) a sacred pool; a pool of Brahmā.

Brahmamūrti (S) (M) with the form of Brahmā.

Brahmanābha (S) (M) **1.** with Brahmā as the navel. **2.** in whose navel the Absolute rests; the Supreme Self. **3.** another name for Viṣṇu.

Brahmānanda (S) (M) **1.** bliss; absolute pleasure; joy in Brahmā. **2.** illumined; spiritually enlightened.

Brahmāṇḍa (S) (M) **1.** Brahmā's egg; the Absolute shell. **2.** the universe. **3.** a Purāṇa.

Brahmanīḍa (S) (M) **1.** the resting place of Brahmā. **2.** the nest of the Absolute; in whom all the virtues are found.

Brahmapattra (S) (M) **1.** Brahmā's leaf. **3.** a leaf of the flame of the forest **tree** (*Butea frondosa*) which is considered to have originated from the feet of Brahmā.

Brahmapitṛ (S) (M) **1.** Brahmā's father. **3.** Viṣṇu from whose navel Brahmā is considered to have originated.

Brahmaprabhā (S) (M) **1.** the light of Brahmā. **2.** glory of the Absolute.

Brahmaprakāśa (S) (M) **1.** the light of Brahmā. **2.** light of the Absolute.

Brahmapri (S) (M) **1.** devotee of Brahmā; knower of the Absolute. **2.** delighting in prayer; a preceptor.

Brahmāputra (S) (M) **1.** son of Brahmā. **3.** a river in Assam.

Brahmarasa (S) (M) **1.** the essence of Brahmā; the Supreme Essence.

Brahmarāta (S) (M) **1.** given by Brahmā; absorbed in the Absolute. **3.** the father of Yājñavalkya (*M. Bh.*); another name for Śuka.

Brahmārgha (S) (M) **1.** worthy of Brahmā. **2.** as worthy as the Absolute.

Brahmarūpa (S) (M) **1.** incarnation of the Absolute. **2.** the Absolute in its manifest form. **3.** another name for Viṣṇu.

Brahmasambhava (S) (M) **1.** sprung from Brahmā. **2.** meritorious; virtuous; venerated; divine. **3.** the 2nd Black Vasudeva (*H. Purāṇa*).

Brahmasaras (S) (M) **1.** the lake of Brahmā. **2.** sacred; venerated; divine.

Brahmasatī (S) (M) **1.** granted by Brahmā. **3.** another name for the river Sarasvatī who is considered to be Brahmā's daughter.

Brahmasāvarṇa (S) (M) **1.** resembles Brahmā. **3.** the 10th Manu (*V. Purāṇa*).

Brahmaśiras (S) (M) **1.** the head of Brahmā; with an Absolute mind. **2.** knowing all. **3.** a mythical weapon (*M. Bh.*).

Brahmasū (S) (M) **1.** son of Brahmā. **3.** another name for Kāma and Aniruddha.

Brahmasūnu (S) (M) **1.** son of the Absolute. **3.** the 12th king of Bhārata.

Brahmatejas (S) (M) **1.** the glory of Brahmā. **2.** venerated; illuminating; enlightened; divine. **3.** a Buddha (*L. Vistara*).

Brahmavarman (S) (M) Brahmā's armour.

Brahmāvarta (S) (M) **1.** the holy land; the land of the Absolute; surrounded by the Absolute. **3.** a son of Ṛṣabha (*Bhāgavata*).

Brahmayāna (S) (M) **1.** chariot of Brahmā. **3.** another name for Nārāyaṇa who is paired with Nara.

Brahmayaśas (S) (M) as famous as Brahmā.

Brahmayuj (S) (M) **1.** harnessed by prayer; attached to the Absolute. **2.** pious; devout; blessed.

Brahmāyuṣ (S) (M) lives as long as Brahmā.

Brahmeśaya (S) (M) **1.** dwelling in Brahmā. **3.** another name for Kārttikeya who is depicted as the commander of the divine army.

Brāhmibhūta (S) (M) **1.** essence of Brahmā. **3.** another name for Śaṁkarāćārya.

Brahmottara (S) (M) **1.** treating principally with Brahmā. **3.** a Jaina deity (*D. Śastra*).

Bṛajamaṇi (S) (M) **1.** brilliant jewel. **2.** beautiful; precious; rare; held dear; illuminating.

Bṛbaduktha (S) (M) **1.** highly praiseworthy. **3.** another name for Indra.

Bṛbutṣka (S) (M) **1.** liberal; praiseworthy. **2.** generous; meritorious; virtuous. **3.** a Vedic king known for his generosity and interest in architecture (*Ṛg Veda*).

Bṛgala (S) (M) **1.** fragment. **2.** piece; morsel; analytical.

Bṛhaćchloka (S) (M) **1.** loudly praised. **3.** a son of Urukrama (*Bh. Purāṇa*).

Bṛhadagni (S) (M) **1.** mighty fire. **2.** sacred and all consuming. **3.** a ṛṣi (*H. Purāṇa*).

Bṛhadaśva (S) (M) **1.** possesses mighty horses. **2.** strong, wealthy and fleet-footed. **3.** hermit who taught Yudhiṣṭhira important spells (*M. Bh.*); a king of the Ikṣvāku dynasty who was the son of Śrāvasta and the father of Kuvalayāśva (*M. Bh.*); a gandharva (*M. Bh.*).

Bṛhadātma (S) (M) **1.** has a great soul. **2.** wise; illumined; enlightened. **3.** a king of the Aṅga dynasty (*M. Bh.*).

Bṛhadbala (S) (M) **1.** very strong; with immense power. **3.** the son of King Subala of Gāndhāra (*M. Bh.*); a king of Kosala (*H. Purāṇa*).

Bṛhadbhānu (S) (M) **1.** the great sun. **2.** brilliant; glorious; illuminating; enlightening; shining brightly. **3.** a son of Sattrāyaṇa considered to be a manifestation of Viṣṇu (*Bhāgavata*); a son of Kṛṣṇa (*Bhāgavata*); a hermit who was very learned in the Vedas (*M. Bh.*); Ceylon Leadwort (*Plumbago zeylanica*); another name for Agni.

Bṛhadbhās (S) (M) **1.** has great splendour. **3.** a grandson of Brahmā (*M. Bh.*).

Bṛhadbhaya (S) (M) **1.** feared by many; instilling much fear. **3.** a son of the 9th Manu (*Mā. Purāṇa*).

Bṛhadbrāhmaṇa (S) (M) **1.** great ascetic. **2.** illuminating; enlightened; has attained salvation or *mokṣa*. **3.** a grandson of Brahmā (*M. Bh.*).

Bṛhaddanta (S) (M) **1.** has large teeth. **3.** a king of Ulūka who fought on the side of the Pāṇḍavas (*M. Bh.*); the brother of King Kśemadhurti who fought on the side of the Pāṇḍavās (*M. Bh.*).

Bṛhaddhala (S) (M) **1.** has a mighty shield. **2.** well protected. **3.** the son of King Subala of Gāndhāra (*M. Bh.*); a Yādava king who was the son of Devabhaga and the brother of Vasudeva (*Bhāgavata*).

Bṛhaddharman (S) (M) strong supporter.

Bṛhaddhvaja (S) (M) **1.** with a mighty banner. **2.** mighty; powerful; a ruler of kingdoms. **3.** a rākṣasa who attained the world of Viṣṇu (*Sk. Purāṇa*).

Bṛhadguru (S) (M) **1.** great master. **3.** an ancient king (*M. Bh.*).

Bṛhadīkṣu (S) (M) **1.** broadminded; with great insight. **3.** a king of the family of Bharata (*Bhāgavata*).

Bṛhadiṣṭha (S) (M) **1.** much loved. **3.** a king of the Purū dynasty (*A. Purāṇa*).

Bṛhadkāya (S) (M) large bodied.

Bṛhadketu (S) (M) **1.** with a very bright banner. **2.** bright; glorious; renowned; illuminating. **3.** another name for Agni.

Bṛhadkīrti (S) (M) **1.** far-famed. **3.** a grandson of Brahmā (*M. Bh.*).

Bṛhadphala (S) (M) **1.** with a large fruit. **2.** yielding very high profit. **3.** a class of Buddhist gods (*B. Literature*).

Bṛhadrāja (S) (M) **1.** a mighty king. **3.** a king (*Pur*).

Brhadratha (S) (M) **1.** with a mighty chariot. **2.** a mighty, powerful, heroic warrior. **3.** a king of the Aṅga family who was the son of Jayadratha and father of Viśvajīta (*M. Bh.*); a Purū king who was the son of Girīka and the father of Kusāgra (*A. Purāṇa*); the son of King Uparićara of Ćedi and the father of Jarāsandha of Magadha (*M. Bh.*); an agni who was the son of Vasiṣṭha and the father of Pranīti (*M. Bh.*); another name for Indra.

Bṛhadsena (S) (M) **1.** a mighty leader; has a large army. **2.** a commander. **3.** a son of Kṛṣṇa (*Bhāgavata*); a son of Sunakṣatra (*Bhāgavata*).

Bṛhadtejas (S) (M) **1.** very glorious. **3.** another name for the planet Jupiter.

Bṛhaduktha (S) (M) **1.** loudly praised; extremely famous; originator of many tales. **2.** speaks very much; much spoken of. **3.** an agni who was the son of Tapas (*M. Bh.*); a son of Devarāta (*V. Purāṇa*); the son of the sage Pāñćajanya who was transformed to a god who is remembered at the beginning of a sacrifice (*M. Bh.*).

Bṛhadviṣa (S) (M) **1.** extremely poisonous. **3.** a king of the line of Bharata.

Bṛhajjana (S) (M) an illustrious man.

Bṛhajjyoti (S) (M) **1.** very glorious. **3.** the son of Aṅgiras and Śubhā (*M. Bh.*).

Bṛhajjyotiṣ (S) (M) **1.** very bright. **2.** shining; glorious; famous; illuminating; enlightening. **3.** a grandson of Brahmā (*Bhā. Purāṇa*).

Bṛhaka (S) (M) **1.** fully grown. **2.** massive; mighty adult; mature; evolved. **3.** a deva gandharva (*M. Bh.*).

Bṛhanmanas (S) (M) **1.** broadminded. **3.** a grandson of Brahmā (*M. Bh.*); one of the 7 sons of Aṅgiras and Sumanā (*M. Bh.*); a king (*H. Purāṇa*).

Bṛhanmedhas (S) (M) **1.** highly intelligent. **3.** a Yādava king who was the son of Vapuṣmān and the father of Śrīdeva (*Kū. Purāṇa*).

Bṛhannala (S) (M) **1.** a large reed; an important person. **2.** arm. **3.** name assumed by Arjuna at the court of King Virāṭa (*M. Bh.*).

Bṛhanta (S) (M) **1.** destroyer of the powerful. **2.** large; great. **3.** a king who fought on the side of the Pāṇḍavās (*M. Bh.*); a Kaurava warrior who was the brother of Kśemadhurti (*M. Bh.*).

Bṛhaspati (S) (M) **1.** lord of prayer. **2.** lord of devotion; lord of the powerful. **3.** a deity who is the chief offerer of sacrifices and the god of wisdom and eloquence, regarded as the grandson of Brahmā, the son of Aṅgiras and Vasudā, the husband of Tārā, the father of Romaṣa, Kaća, Kuśadhvaja and the 6 agnis, of Bharadvāja from his elder brother Utathya's wife Mamatā, grandfather of Devavatī who was reborn as Sītā, the regent of the planet Jupiter and the preceptor of the gods (*Ṛg Veda*); the great grandson of Aśoka (*B. Literature*); a king of Kāśmira (*R. Taraṅgiṇī*).

Bṛhat (S) (M) **1.** lofty; tall; large; vast; abundant. **2.** strong; mighty; clear; loud. **3.** a son of Suhotra and father of Ajamīdha (*H. Purāṇa*); a marut (*H. Purāṇa*).

Bṛhata (S) (M) **1.** large; great. **3.** a son of the 9th Manu (*H. Purāṇa*).

Bṛhatka (S) (M) **1.** lofty; massive; mighty; abundant. **3.** a king and son of the asura Kelaya (*M. Bh.*).

Bṛhatkarman (S) (M) **1.** performs mighty deeds. **3.** a king of Aṅga (*M. Bh.*).

Bṛhatkāya (S) (M) **1.** huge bodied. **3.** a king of Bharata family (*M. Bh.*).

Bṛhatketu (S) (M) **1.** has a mighty banner; with great brightness. **2.** king among kings. **3.** another name for Agni.

Bṛhatkīrti (S) (M) **1.** with infinite fame. **2.** renowned. **3.** a son of Aṅgiras; an asura.

Bṛhatkṣatra (S) (M) **1.** with great power; with huge dominion. **3.** father of Suhotra (*H. Purāṇa*).

Bṛhatphala (S) (M) **1.** bringing large rewards. **3.** a class of Buddhist deities.

Bṛhatputra (S) (M) **1.** son of the great. **2.** the great son. **3.** a king of the Purū dynasty who was the son of Suhotra and the father of Ajamīdha, Dvimīdha and Pūrumīdha (*A. Purāṇa*).

Bṛhatsama (S) (M) **1.** considers all as equal. **3.** a teacher of the Aṅgiras family; a hymn (*Ṛg Veda*).

Bṛhatśāstra (S) (M) **1.** knower of many treatises. **2.** well-read; learned; wise. **3.** a king of the family of Bhagīratha (*V. Rāmāyaṇa*); a Kekaya king who fought on the side of the Pāṇḍavas (*M. Bh.*); a Niṣādha king who fought on the side of the Kauravas (*M. Bh.*).

Bṛhatsena (S) (M) **1.** has a huge army. **3.** a king of the family of Bharata (*Bhāgavata*); an asura who was a partial incarnation of Krodhavaśa and whose daughter married Kṛṣṇa (*Bhāgavata*); a sage and disciple of Nārada (*M. Bh.*).

Bṛhita (S) (M) **1.** strengthened. **2.** nourished; cherished. **3.** an attendant in Skanda's retinue (*Sk. Purāṇa*).

Bṛjābhūṣaṇa (S) (M) **1.** ornament of nature. **2.** the ornament of Bṛja. **3.** another name for Kṛṣṇa who spent his childhood in Bṛja, a place near Mathura.

Bṛjamohana (S) (M) **1.** attracts nature; universally attractive. **3.** another name for Kṛṣṇa.

Bṛjanandana (S) (M) **1.** the son of Bṛja. **3.** another name for Kṛṣṇa.

Bṛjarāja (S) (M) **1.** lord of Bṛja. **3.** another name for Kṛṣṇa.

Brjanārāyaṇa (S) (M) **1.** lord of Bṛja. **3.** another name for Viṣṇu/Kṛṣṇa.

Bṛjeśa (S) (M) **1.** lord of nature. **2.** lord of Bṛja. **3.** another name for Kṛṣṇa.

Bubhutsu (S) (M) **1.** desirous to know all. **2.** curious.

Buddha (S) (M) **1.** enlightened; awakened. **3.** the title 'Buddha' was first used for prince Gautama (later known as Śākyāmuni and considered by some to be an incarnation of Viṣṇu), the founder of the Buddhist religion born in Kapilavastu of King Śuddodana and Māyādevī of the Śākya tribe, this title is used to denote successive teachers past and future of this religion (*V. Purāṇa*).

Buduhaćakṣus (S) (M) **1.** the enlightened eye. **2.** eye of the Buddha. **3.** one of the 5 sorts of vision.

Buddhadatta (S) (M) **1.** obtained from enlightenment. **2.** given by the Buddha. **3.** a minister of Ćaṇḍamahāsena (*K. Sāgara*).

Buddhadeva (S) (M) **1.** lord of the wise. **2.** enlightened, honorific of a king.

Buddhaghoṣa (S) (M) **1.** voice of knowledge; speech of the enlightened; village of the enlightened. **3.** Sanskṛt poet (4th century A.D.).

Buddhagupta (S) (M) protected by the Buddha; protected by the wise.

Buddhaguru (S) (M) preceptor of the wise; a Buddhist spiritual teacher.

Buddhajñāna (S) (M) **1.** with the Buddha's knowledge. **2.** with intellectual knowledge; who has attained enlightenment.

Buddhamitra (S) (M) **1.** friend of the wise. **2.** friend of the Buddha. **3.** the 9th Buddhist patriarch (*B. Literature*).

Buddhānandi (S) (M) **1.** one who enjoys knowledge. **2.** well-read; wise; enlightened. **3.** the 8th Buddhist patriarch.

Buddhapāla (S) (M) defender of the wise; defender of the Buddha.

Buddhapālita (S) (M) **1.** protected by the wise; protected by the Buddha. **3.** a disciple of Nāgārjuna (*B. Literature*).

Buddharāja (S) (M) lord of the wise.

Buddhasena (S) (M) leader of the wise.

Buddhasinha (S) (M) lion among the wise.

Buddhiprabha (S) (M) light of reason.

Buddhirāja (S) (M) lord of intellect.

Buddhiśrīgarbha (S) (M) **1.** the womb of divine wisdom. **3.** a bodhisattva (*B. Literature*).

Budha (S) (M) **1.** intelligent; wise. **3.** a descendant of Soma and father of Purūravas, and identified with the planet Mercury (*M. Bh.*); a descendant of Atri and author of *Ṛg Veda* (v); a son of Vegavat and father of Tṛṇabindu (*Purāṇas*); the son of Ćandra and Tārā the wife of Bṛhaspati (*Ṛg Veda*).

Budhana (S) (M) **1.** awaking. **2.** wise; knowing; sage; spiritual guide.

Budharatna (S) (M) **1.** jewel among the wise. **3.** jewel of the planet Mercury; the emerald.

Budhasuta (S) (M) **1.** son of Budha; son of the wise. **3.** another name for Purūravas.

Budhila (S) (M) wise; learned.

Budrasena (S) (M) **1.** with an army of the enlightened; commander of the wise. **3.** a Hehaya king (*H. Purāṇa*).

Budrika (S) (M) learned; enlightened; a king of the 5th lunar dynasty of Magadha (*M. Bh.*).

Bukkā (S) (M) **1.** the heart. **2.** sentimental; loving; sincere.

Bunda (S) (M) **1.** arrow. **2.** which pierces; reaches its aim unfailingly.

C

Ćāchari (S) (M) **1.** moving quickly. **3.** a westler (*R. Taraṅgiṇī*).

Ćāha (S) (M) **1.** desire. **2.** desired; desirable; charming; loving. **3.** the Pintail Snipe (*Gallinago sthenura*).

Ćaidya (S) (M) **1.** intelligent. **2.** administrator. **3.** king of Ćedi; honorifics of Dhṛṣṭaketu and Śiśupāla (*M. Bh.*).

Ćaitanya (S) (M) **1.** consciousness. **2.** intelligence; mind; spirit; soul. **3.** the founder of one of the 4 principal Vaiṣṇava sects, was born in 1485 in Nadia, Bengal and is believed by his followers to have been a reincarnation of Kṛṣṇa.

Ćailra (S) (M) **1.** absorbed in pleasure; as pleasant as the spring. **3.** the 2nd spring month (*J. Śāstra*); a son of Budha and grandfather of Suratha (*Brah. Purāṇa*); Buddhist and Jaina mendicants (*He. Koṣa*).

Ćaitraratha (S) (M) **1.** the chariot of intelligence. **2.** the sun. **3.** a son of King Kuru and Vāhinī (*M. Bh.*); the grove of Kubera situated on Mount Meru (*H. Purāṇa*).

Ćaitrasakhā (S) (M) **1.** a friend of spring. **2.** inciting a feeling of love. **3.** another name for Kāma and Kṛṣṇa.

Ćaitya (S) (M) **1.** pertaining to the mind; the individual soul. **3.** a stupa built in Jaina or Buddhist places of worship.

Ćaityaka (S) (M) **1.** abode of conciousness. **2.** a temple; a monument; a stupa. **3.** a mountain near Magadha worshipped as being sacred and divine (*P. Smṛti*).

Ćaka (S) (M) **1.** to be content; to shine. **3.** a priest at Janamejaya's snake sacrifice (*Tā. Brāhmaṇa*).

Ćakora (S) (M) **1.** shining; content. **3.** the Greek partridge (*Perdis rufa*) fabled to subsist on moonbeams; the Chukor partridge (*Alectoris chukar chukar*).

Ćakra (S) (M) **1.** wheel; disc; circle. **2.** a symbol of the sun. **3.** the son of Vāsuki (*M. Bh.*); an attendant given to Skanda by Tvaṣṭṛ (*M. Bh.*); the weapon of Mahāviṣṇu (*M. Bh.*).

Ćakrabandhana (S) (M) **1.** bound in the form of a circle. **2.** bearer of a wheel or discus; an emperor; one in authority; a great warrior. **3.** another name for Viṣṇu; musk; Jasminum pubescens.

Ćakrabāndhava (S) (M) **1.** friend of the Ćakra birds. **3.** another name for the sun.

Ćakrahandhu (S) (M) **1.** with a disc. **3.** another name for the sun.

Ćakrabhṛt (S) (M) **1.** discus bearer. **3.** another name for Viṣṇu.

Ćakrabhuj (S) (M) **1.** holding a disc. **3.** another name for Viṣṇu.

Ćakraćāra (S) (M) **1.** going in a circle. **3.** a class of superhuman beings.

Ćakradeva (S) (M) **1.** lord of the discus. **2.** with a warchariot for his deity. **3.** a warrior of the Vṛṣṇi dynasty (*M. Bh.*); another name for Viṣṇu.

Ćakradhanuṣ (S) (M) **1.** armed with a bow and a disc. **3.** another name for sage Kapila.

Ćakradhara (S) (M) **1.** bearing a discus. **2.** an emperor. **3.** another name for Viṣṇu.

Ćakradhāri (S) (M) **1.** holding the discus. **3.** another name for Kṛṣṇa.

Ćakradharma (S) (M) **1.** the path of the disc. **2.** righteous and virtuous. **3.** the chief of the vidyādharas who lived in the court of Kubera (*M. Bh.*).

Ćakradṛśa (S) (M) **1.** round eyed. **3.** an asura (*Bhāgavata*).

Ćakradvāra (S) (M) **1.** the way to the sun. **3.** a great mountain on which Agni performed a sacrifice (*M. Bh.*).

Ćakragadābhṛt (S) (M) **1.** holding disc and mace. **3.** another name for Kṛṣṇa (*M. Bh.*).

Ćakragadādhara (S) (M) **1.** holding disc and mace. **3.** another name for Kṛṣṇa (*M. Bh.*).

Ćakragadāpāṇi (S) (M) **1.** holding disc and mace. **3.** another name for Kṛṣṇa.

Ćakraka (S) (M) **1.** circular. **2.** resembling a wheel. **3.** a son of Viśvāmitra (*M. Bh.*).

Ćakrakī (S) (M) **1.** possessing the disc. **3.** another name for Viṣṇu.

Ćakramanda (S) (M) **1.** one who worships the discus; a slow moving wheel. **2.** one who sides with power. **3.** a serpent lord who was entrusted by Ananta, the serpent king, to lead the soul of Balarāma to Pātāla (*M. Bh.*).

Ćakramauli (S) (M) **1.** with a round diadem. **3.** a rākṣasa (*V. Rāmāyaṇa*).

Ćakrapālita (S) (M) **1.** lord of the discus. **3.** another name for Viṣṇu.

Ćakrapāṇi (S) (M) **1.** discus holder. **3.** another name for Viṣṇu.

Ćakrasaṁvara (S) (M) **1.** choosing the disc. **3.** a Buddha.

Ćakrasena (S) (M) **1.** commander of the army. **2.** leader; warrior. **3.** a son of Tārāćandra and father of Siṁha (*K. Sāgara*).

Ćakravāka (S) (M) **1.** has a round mouth; the Ruddy Shelduck (*Anas casarca*). **3.** likened to the aśvins in the *Ṛg Veda.*

Ćakravāla (S) (M) **1.** circle; mass; assemblage; surrounded by people as a circle by spokes; a leader. **3.** one of the mythical range of mountains which encircle the earth and are the limits of light with Mount Meru as the central mountain (*M. Bh.*).

Ćakravāna (S) (M) **1.** possesser of the Ćakra. **2.** worshipper of Viṣṇu. **3.** a mountain frequently extolled in the Purāṇas and on which Viśvakarma made the Sudarśana Ćakra (*V. Rāmāyaṇa*).

Ćakravarman (S) (M) **1.** armoured with the Ćakra. **3.** a king of Kāśmira (*R. Taraṅgiṇī*).

Ćakravartin (S) (M) **1.** whose chariot rolls everywhere. **2.** powerful; renowned; emperor. **3.** another name for the 12 emperors, beginning with Bharata.

Ćakravat (S) (M) **1.** with a discus. **2.** an emperor. **3.** another name for Viṣṇu.

Ćakravāta (S) (M) **1.** fierce; forceful. **2.** whirlwind.

Ćakrayodhin (S) (M) **1.** discus fighter. **3.** a dānava (*V. Purāṇa*).

Ćakrāyudha (S) (M) **1.** fighting with a discus. **3.** another name for Viṣṇu.

Ćakreśa (S) (M) **1.** lord of the discus. **3.** another name for Viṣṇu.

Ćakreśvara (S) (M) **1.** lord of the discus. **3.** another name for Viṣṇu.

Ćakrika (S) (M) discus bearer.

Ćakrin (S) (M) **1.** with a discus. **2.** a king. **3.** another name for Kṛṣṇa and Śiva.

Ćakroddhata (S) (M) **1.** moving the disc upwards. **2.** the Supreme Being. **3.** a king in the dynasty of Yayāti (*Bhāgavata*).

Ćakṣaṇa (S) (M) soothing to the eyes; appearance; aspect.

Ćakṣas (S) (M) **1.** look; sight. **2.** radiance; a teacher. **3.** another name for Bṛhaspati, the teacher of the gods.

Ćākṣīśvara (S) (M) **1.** lord of the eye. **2.** all seeing; all knowing; all pervading; divine. **3.** another name for Viṣṇu.

Ćakṣu (S) (M) **1.** eye. **3.** another name for the sun god Sūrya who sees beyond the sky, earth, waters, and is the eye of all that exists; a prince (*M. Bh.*); the river now called Oxus (*V. Purāṇa*).

Ćakṣus (S) (M) **1.** eyes. **3.** a tributary of the Gaṅgā which falls on the peak of Mount Mālyavāna, and flows through Ketumālā into the western sea (*D. Bhāgavata*); a king born in the lunar dynasty and the son of king Anudruhyu (*Bhāgavata*); a marut; another name for the sun.

Ćakṣuṣa (S) (M) **1.** preceptor. **2.** seer. **3.** a marut (*Ṛg Veda*); a sage and author of *Ṛg Veda*; a son of Anu (Bhā. Purāṇa); a river of ancient India (*Bhā. Purāṇa*); a son of Ṛpu and Bṛhatī (*V. Purāṇa*); a son of Viśvakarmā and Ākritī (*Bh. Purāṇa*); a son of Kakṣeyu; a son of Khanitra (*Bh. Purāṇa*); another name for Agni.

Ćākṣuṣamanu (S) (M) **1.** that which is visible. **2.** believer in the perceivable. **3.** the 6th Manu who was the son of

Ćākṣuṣa and Puṣkaraṇī and husband of Nadvalā.

Ćākṣuṣya (S) (M) **1.** pleasing to the eyes. **2.** beautiful; harmonious; *Pandanus odoratissimus cassia absus.*

Ćala (S) (M) **1.** ever moving. **3.** another name for the Supreme Being.

Ćālaka (S) (M) **1.** directing and driving. **3.** another name for the Supreme Soul.

Ćalāmeśvara (S) (M) **1.** lord of Ćalamā. **3.** another name for Śiva.

Ćalāpati (S) (M) **1.** lord of the moving. **3.** Viṣṇu as consort of Lakṣmī.

Ćāmar (S) (M) **1.** rod with a large tuft of hair; fibre or feathers at the end; animal hair; an army; yak's tail. **2.** this rod was a symbol of authority and was used by kings and Brāhmins in ancient India.

Ćāmarāja (S) (M) leader of an army; lord of the ćāmara.

Ćāmarvāla (S) (M) **1.** with hair as fine as a yak's tail. **3.** a prince (*M. Bh.*).

Ćamasa (S) (M) **1.** a cup; a vessel used for drinking Soma at sacrifices (*Ṛg Veda*); a kind of cake (*A. Koṣa*). **3.** the younger brother of Bharata (*M. Bh.*); a king born in the dynasty of Priyavrata (*Bhāgavata*); a son of Manu (*Bhāgavata*); a son of Ṛṣabha (*Bhāgavata*); a sage (*M. Bh.*).

Ćamasodbheda (S) (M) **1.** priest who is in charge of the drinking vessel for Soma at sacrifices. **3.** holy place in Saurāṣṭra which forms a part of the Hindu sacred places (*M. Bh.*).

Ćamīkara (S) (M) gold.

Ćampa (S) (M) **1.** that which soothes. **3.** a king of the Aṅga dynasty (*M. Bh.*).

Ćampaka (S) (M) **1.** Ćampaka tree (*Michelia champaka*). **3.** a vidyādhara and husband of Madālasā (*K. Sāgara*); the foster father of Ekavīra (*R. Taraṅginī*).

Ćampakaprabhu (S) (M) **1.** eternally blooming; lord of the Ćampaka tree (*Michelia champaka*). **3.** Kalhaṇa's father (*R. Taraṅgiṇī*).

Ćampat (S) (M) fallen from glory.

Ćampeśa (S) (M) **1.** lord of Ćampā a town in Aṅga. **3.** another name for Karṇa.

Ćampeya (S) (M) **1.** fruit of the Kovidāra tree (*Bauhinia vareigala*). **3.** a son of Viśvāmitra (*M. Bh.*).

Ćampū (S) (M) an elaborate and literary form of presenting a story in verse and prose.

Ćamūhara (S) (M) **1.** receptacle; vessel. **2.** heaven and earth as the two receptacles of all living beings. **3.** a viśvādeva (*M. Bh.*).

Ćāmuṇḍarāya (S) (M) **1.** lord of Ćāmuṇḍā. **3.** a scholar of Sanskṛt and Kannaḍa who had the statue of Bāhubali built; another name for Śiva.

Ćāmuṇḍī (S) (M) **1.** slayer of Ćaṇḍa and Muṇḍa. **3.** the terrible form of Durgā as one of the 7 mothers who destroyed the demons Ćaṇḍa and Muṇḍa.

Ćaṇaka (S) (M) Ćhickpea (*Cicer arietinum*); the father of Ćāṇakya (*A. Koṣa*).

Ćāṇakya (S) (M) **1.** son of Ćaṇaka. **3.** a renowned writer on civil polity, the author of the *Arthaśāstra* and a minister of Ćandragupta Maurya (320 B.C.).

Ćañćala (S) (M) **1.** playful; fickle; that which moves. **2.** wind; lover. **3.** an asura.

Ćañću (S) (M) **1.** renowned; famous; a bird's beak. **3.** a son of Harita (*H. Purāṇa*).

Ćānd (S) (M) **1.** to shine; to gladden. **3.** the moon.

Ćaṇḍa (S) (M) **1.** fierce; violent; glowing with passion. **3.** an attendant of Yama and Śiva (*A. Koṣa*); one of the 7 clouds enveloping the earth (*M. Purāṇa*); a river (*H. Koṣa*); an asura who was the brother of Muṇḍa and was killed by Durgā (*D. Bhāgavata*).

Ćaṇḍabala (S) (M) **1.** fiercely strong. **3.** a prominent monkey of Rāma's army (*M. Bh.*).

Ćaṇḍabhārgava (S) (M) **1.** Śiva, the fierce. **3.** a sage in the dynasty of

Ćyavana who was deeply versed in the Vedas (*M. Bh.*).

Ćandaharta (S) (M) **1.** destroyer of the disc. **3.** a son of Kaśyapa and Simhikā (*M. Bh.*).

Ćandaka (S) (M) **1.** the shining one; pleasing. **2.** the moon; moonlight.

Ćaṇḍākauśika (S) (M) **1.** passionate love. **3.** a son of Kakśīvat.

Ćaṇḍakauśika (S) (M) **1.** receptacle of glory. **3.** place where the idol of Ćaṇḍī is installed; a sage and son of akṣivāna who lived in Magadha as the preceptor of the kings (*M. Bh.*).

Ćaṇḍakiraṇa (S) (M) fierce rayed.

Ćaṇḍamahāsena (S) (M) **1.** fierce commander of an army. **3.** a prominent king of Ujjayinī who was the husband of Aṅgāravatī and father of āsavadattā who became the wife of Udayana the emperor of the vidyādharas (*K. Sāgara*).

Ćandana (S) (M) **1.** sandalwood (*Pterocarpus santalinus*). **2.** fragrant; cool; soothing; auspicious and dear to the gods.

Ćandanin (S) (M) **1.** anointed with sandalwood. **3.** another name for Śiva.

Ćaṇḍalāṅśu (S) (M) **1.** hot rayed. **3.** another name for the sun.

Ćandasa (S) (M) moon like.

Caṇḍaśakti (S) (M) **1.** of impetuous valour. **3.** a daitya.

Ćaṇḍatuṇḍaka (S) (M) **1.** has a powerful beak. **3.** a son of Garuḍa (*M. Bh.*).

Ćaṇḍavega (S) (M) **1.** moves with a fierce speed. **2.** very swift; hot, passionate current. **3.** a gandharva (*Bhāgavata*).

Caṇḍavikrama (S) (M) **1.** of impetuous valour. **3.** a prince (*K. Sāgara*).

Ćaṇḍavīra (S) (M) **1.** passionately brave. **2.** extremely brave. **3.** a Buddhist deity.

Ćaṇḍeśvara (S) (M) **1.** lord of Ćaṇḍa. **3.** a Tīrtha; an attendant of Śiva; another name for Śiva.

Ćāndī (S) (M) **1.** silver. **2.** fair; precious; cooling.

Ćaṇḍidāsa (S) (M) **1.** devotee of the fierce. **3.** the devotee of Durgā.

Ćaṇḍila (S) (M) **1.** passionate; angry; hot. **3.** another name for Rudra.

Ćaṇḍīpati (S) (M) **1.** lord of Ćaṇḍi. **3.** another name for Śiva.

Ćandprādyotam (S) (M) **1.** act of lighting. **3.** king of Malva and follower of Mahāvīra (*J. Literature*).

Ćandra (S) (M) **1.** bright; shining; radiant; the moon. **2.** glittering; beautiful; fair; water; a red pearl; eye of a peacock's tail; gold; silver; number one. **3.** the moon personified as the deity Ćandra created from the Ocean of Milk and the king of Soma (*Ś. Brāhmaṇa*); a prominent asura who was born as Ćandravarman the king of Kamboja (*M. Bh.*); a king of the solar dynasty who was the son of Viśvagandhi and the father of Yuvanāśva (*R. Taraṅgiṇī*); the moon as a child of Atri and Anasūyā who lived with Tārā the consort of Bṛhaspati, had 27 of Dakṣa's daughters as his wives which are the 27 lunar ansions, and is considered to be the king of the stars and medicines (*Brah. Purāṇa*); the herb *Bryonopsis laciniosa.*

Ćandrabāhū (S) (M) **1.** as mighty as the moon. **3.** an asura (*H. Purāṇa*).

Ćandrabala (S) (M) power of the moon.

Ćandrabali (S) (M) warrior of the moon; as brave as the moon.

Ćandrabha (S) (M) **1.** as luminous as the moon. **3.** an attendant of Skanda (*M. Bh.*).

Ćandrabhāla (S) (M) **1.** one who bears the moon on his forehead. **3.** another name for Śiva.

Ćandrabhāna (S) (M) as lustrous as the moon.

Ćandrabhānu (S) (M) **1.** radiant moon; sun and moon conjoined. **2.** illuminating; enlightening; renowned; venerated. **3.** a son of Kṛṣṇa (*Bhāgavata*).

Ćandrabhāsa (S) (M) **1.** as brilliant as the moon. **2.** a sword.

Ćandrabhūti (S) (M) **1.** born of the moon. **2.** silver.

Ćandrācārya (S) (M) **1.** moon among teachers. **3.** a Jaina teacher.

Ćandraćūḍa (S) (M) **1.** moon crested. **3.** a Yādava king of a state in Sauraṣṭra; a form of Bhairava (*M. Bh.*); another name for Śiva.

Ćandradatta (S) (M) **1.** moon given. **2.** fair; cool; soothing; tranquil.

Ćandradeva (S) (M) the moon personified as a deity.

Ćandradhara (S) (M) **1.** holding the moon. **3.** another name for Śiva.

Ćandradīpa (Ś) (M) moonlight.

Ćandradūta (S) (M) messenger of the moon.

Ćandradyuti (S) (M) **1.** as bright as the moon. **3.** sandalwood.

Ćandragarbha (S) (M) **1.** one who has the moon as his navel. **2.** tranquil; poised; of a cool-temperament. **3.** a Buddha (*B. Literature*).

Ćandragomin (S) (M) **1.** possessor of moon-like cows. **2.** cows which are fair beautiful and quiet. **3.** a grammarian (*G. Mahodadhi*).

Ćandragupta (S) (M) **1.** moon protected. **3.** a son of Rāvaṇa (*K. Rāmāyaṇa*); a minister of Kārtavīryārjuna (*Bhāgavata*); a king of the Maurya dynasty who reigned in Pāṭaliputra (315 B.C.) (*K. Sāgara*).

Ćandrahantṛ (S) (M) **1.** destroyer of the moon. **3.** an asura who was reborn as King Śunaka (*M. Bh.*).

Ćandrahāsa (S) (M) **1.** smile of the moon; laughter of the moon. **2.** moonlight; a pleasing smile; a glittering sword. **3.** a powerful Kerala king and son of King Sudhārmika who was a friend of Kṛṣṇa (*Bhāgavata*); Rāvaṇa's sword given to him by Śiva (*Rāmāyaṇa*); the king of Ćandanāvatī (*J. Aśvamedha*); the bow of Śiva (*Ś. Purāṇa*).

Ćandraja (S) (M) **1.** born of the moon. **3.** another name for the planet Mercury.

Ćandrajanaka (S) (M) **1.** father of the moon. **3.** another name for the ocean.

Ćandrajīta (S) (M) **1.** conqueror of the moon. **2.** surpassing the moon.

Ćandraka (S) (M) **1.** the crescent moon. **2.** the eye on the tail of a peacock; the red mark on the forehead. **3.** another name for the moon.

Ćandrakānta (S) (M) **1.** as lovely as the moon; loved by the moon. **3.** the White Water lily (*Nymphaea alba*); sandalwood (*Pterocarpus santalinus*).

Ćandrakeśa (S) (M) fair haired.

Ćandraketu (S) (M) **1.** whose banner is the moon. **2.** whose fame and glory is renowned and spotless. **3.** the son of Śatrughna and Śrutaka (*U. Rāmayaṇa*); a vidyādhara king (*K. Sāgara*); a son of Lakṣmaṇa (*Rāmāyaṇa*).

Ćandrākin (S) (M) **1.** wearing the moon. **3.** the peacock who has moonlike eyes on its tail.

Ćandrakiraṇa (S) (M) moonbeam.

Ćandrakīrti (S) (M) **1.** as famous as the moon. **3.** a Buddhist saint; a prince of Ujjayinī (*B. Ćarita*); a teacher of the Mādhyamika-Prasangikā school of Buddhism at Nālandā (600-650A.D.); a Sūri of the Jainas (*J.S. Koṣa*).

Ćandrākṛti (S) (M) **1.** moon shaped. **2.** as beautiful as the moon.

Ćandrakuṭa (S) (M) **1.** a peak as luminous as the moon. **3.** a mountain in Assam (*M. Bh.*).

Ćandralocana (S) (M) **1.** mooneyed. **3.** a dānava.

Ćandramādhava (S) (M) **1.** honey of the moon. **2.** the moonbeam.

Ćandramanas (S) (M) **1.** sprung from the moon. **3.** one of the 10 horses of the moon (*A. Koṣa*).

Ćandramāṇek (S) (M) **1.** jewel of the moon. **2.** the pearl.

Ćandramaṇī (S) (M) moonstone.

Ćandramāsa (S) (M) **1.** lunar month. **2.** gem of the moon. **3.** the deity of the moon (*J. Śāstra*); a sage and advisor of Jaṭāyu (*V. Rāmāyaṇa*); a vasu.

Ćandramauli (S) (M) **1.** moon crested. **3.** another name for Siva.

Ćandramohan (S) (M) as attractive as the moon.

Ćandrāmṛta (S) (M) **1.** essence of the moon's nectar. **2.** nectar like; life giving.

Ćandramukuṭa (S) (M) **1.** moon crested. **3.** another name for Śiva.

Ćandranābha (S) (M) **1.** moon navelled. **3.** a dānava.

Ćandrānana (S) (M) **1.** moon faced. **3.** a son of King Janamejaya (*M. Bh.*); a king of Kāśmira and brother of Tārāpīda (*R. Taraṅgiṇī*); a prince of Kānyakubja (*M. Bh.*); a Jina (*V. Ćarita*); another name for Kārttikeya.

Ćandranātha (S) (M) **1.** lord of the moon. **3.** another name for Siva.

Ćandrāṅgada (S) (M) **1.** wearing moon as a bracelet. **2.** wearing bright shining bracelets. **3.** the grandson of Nala and husband of Sīmantinī (*Nalopākhyāna*); the son of King Indrasena (*Sk. Purāṇa*).

Ćandranibha (S) (M) **1.** moonlike. **2.** bright; handsome.

Ćandrāṅśu (S) (M) **1.** moonbeam. **2.** with the lustre of the moon. **3.** another name for Viṣṇu.

Ćandrapāda (S) (M) **1.** the feet of the moon. **2.** moonbeam.

Ćandraparvata (S) (M) **1.** moon mountain. **2.** lofty; beautiful.

Ćandrāpīḍa (S) (M) **1.** eclipsing the moon; torturing the moon. **3.** a son of Janamejaya and Vapustamā and the father of a 100 brave sons (*H. Purāṇa*); a king of Kāśmira.

Ćandraprabha (S) (M) **1.** moonlight. **2.** as glorious as the moon. **3.** the 7th Jaina Tīrthaṅkara whose emblem was a crescent moon (*J. S. Koṣa*); an Arhat of the present Avasarpiṇī; a Bodhisattva; a yakṣa; *Psoralea corylifolia.*

Ćandraprabhāva (S) (M) the effect of the moon; as glorious as the moon.

Ćandraprakāśa (S) (M) moonlight.

Ćandrapramardana (S) (M) **1.** enemy of the moon. **3.** a brother of Rāhu (*M. Bh.*).

Ćandraprava (S) (M) **1.** belonging to the moon. 3. 8th Jaina Tīrthaṅkara who was the son of King Mahāsena and Queen Lakṣmaṇā of Ćandrapura and whose emblem is the moon.

Ćandraratna (S) (M) **1.** jewel of the moon. **2.** pearl.

Ćandrasaćiva (S) (M) **1.** friend of the moon. **3.** another name for Kāma.

Ćandrasena (S) (M) **1.** moon among the warriors; commander of a glorious army. **2.** an excellent warrior or leader. **3.** a king of Śrī Laṅkā and the father of Mandodarī and Indumatī by his wife Guṇavatī (*V. Ćarita*); a king of Ujjayanī and a great devotee of Śiva (*Ś. Purāṇa*); a son of King Samudrasena of Bengal who fought on the side of the Pāṇḍavas (*M. Bh.*); a warrior on the side of the Kauravas who was killed by Yudhiṣṭhira (*M. Bh.*).

Ćandraśarman (S) (M) **1.** protected and sheltered by the moon. **3.** a Brāhmin of the Agni Gotra and son-in-law of Devaśarman, later reborn as Akrūra (*P. Purāṇa*).

Ćandraśekhara (S) (M) **1.** one who wears the moon as his crest jewel. **3.** a king who was the son of Pauṣya and the husband of Tārāvatī; another name for Śiva.

Ćandraśman (S) (M) **1.** moonstone. **2.** cool; sedate; soothing; tranquil.

Ćandrāśva (S) (M) **1.** horse of the moon. **2.** the moonlight which precedes the moon. **3.** the son of King Kuvalayāśva of the Ikṣvāku dynasty (*M. Bh.*); the son of king Dhundhumāra (*Bhāgavata*).

Ćandrasūrya (S) (M) **1.** sun and moon conjoined. **3.** a Buddha (*L. Vistara*).

Ćandrasūryākṣa (S) (M) **1.** one who has the sun and the moon as eyes. **2.** boundless; omnipresent; omniscient; all pervading; divine. **3.** another name for Viṣṇu.

Ćandrasuta (S) (M) **1.** son of the moon. **2.** fair; handsome; soothing; tranquil. **3.** another name for Mercury.

Ćandrasvāmī (S) (M) **1.** lord of the moon; **3.** a Brāhmin who was the husband of Devamatī and who was brought back to life by worshipping Sūrya (*K. Sāgara*).

Ćandrata (S) (M) **1.** nectar of the moon. **2.** fair; handsome; tranquil;

nectar-like. **3.** a physician of ancient India (*A. Veda*).

Ćandravallabha (S) (M) **1.** beloved of the moon. **3.** Indian Redwood tree (*Soymida febrifuge*).

Ćandrāvaloka (S) (M) **1.** light of the moon; resembling the moon. **3.** a king of Ćitrakūṭanagara and husband of Inīvaraprabhā, the daughter of ṛṣi Kaṇva and apsarā Menakā (*K. Sāgara*).

Ćandravarman (S) (M) **1.** moon; warrior; protector of the moon. **2.** having brilliant armour. **3.** the king of Kamboja who was as handsome as Ćandra (the moon) and who fought on the side of the Kauravas (*M. Bh.*).

Ćandravijaya (S) (M) **1.** conqueror of the moon. **2.** surpassing the moon in all its qualities.

Ćandravimala (S) (M) as pure as the moon.

Ćandravīnśana (S) (M) **1.** destroyer of the moon. **3.** an asura who was reborn as King Jānakī (*M. Bh.*).

Ćandreśa (S) (M) **1.** lord of the moon. **3.** another name for Śiva.

Ćandreṣṭa (S) (M) **1.** beloved of the moon. **3.** the Kumudinī or the night lotus (*Nelumbium speciosum*) which flowers only at night.

Ćandrila (S) (M) **1.** possessing the moon. **3.** another name for Śiva.

Ćandrin (S) (M) golden.

Ćandrodaya (S) (M) **1.** moonrise. **2.** inspiring love. **3.** a brother of the king of Virāṭa (*M. Bh.*).

Ćandurī (S) (M) **1.** belonging to the moon. **2.** like the moon.

Ćaṅga (S) (M) understanding; wise; handsome.

Ćaṅgadāsa (S) (M) **1.** a wise devotee. **3.** a grammarian.

Ćanna (S) (M) **1.** renowned; famous. **3.** the charioteer of Gautama Buddha (*B. Ćarita*).

Ćāṇūra (S) (M) **1.** with thin thighs. **3.** Kṣatriya king who served Yudhiṣṭhira (*M. Bh.*); an asura and attendant of Kaṁsa who was killed by Kṛṣṇa (*Bhāgavata*).

Ćapala (S) (M) **1.** unsteady; moving; fickle; swift. **2.** the wind; lightning; quicksilver. **3.** a king of ancient India (*M. Bh.*).

Ćāpdhara (S) (M) **1.** owns a bow. **2.** an archer. **3.** another name for the zodiac sign of Sagittarius.

Ćāpin (S) (M) **1.** armed with a bow. **2.** an archer. **3.** another name for the zodiac sign of Sagittarius.

Ćaraka (S) (M) **1.** wanderer. **2.** a wandering religious student. **3.** the incarnation of Śeṣa who came to the earth to alleviate sickness and is supposed to have been the author of *Ćaraka Samhitā*, a medical work (*B. Prakāśa*); the court physician of King Kaniṣka.

Ćāraṇa (S) (M) **1.** chanter of praises. **3.** Ćāranas were the wandering minstrels employed by the royal court to sing the king's praises; a class of bird deities (*M. Smṛti*).

Ćaraṇa (S) (M) **1.** foot; support. **2.** a pillar; behaviour; good or moral conduct.

Ćaraṇadāsa (S) (M) **1.** devotee of the feet. **2.** respectful; servant of god. **3.** an author and philosophical poet of ancient India (*Nalopākhyāna*).

Ćāriman (S) (M) beauty; movable.

Ćariṣṇu (S) (M) **1.** moving; wandering. **3.** a son of Manu Sāvarṇa; a son of Kirtimat and Dhenukā (*Vā. Purāṇa*).

Ćaritra (S) (M) **1.** character; nature; disposition; behaviour. **3.** Tamarind tree (*Tamarindus indica*).

Ćarmavān (S) (M) **1.** covered with hides. **2.** protected; sheltered. **3.** a son of King Subala and the brother of Śakuni (*M. Bh.*).

Ćarmin (S) (M) **1.** covered with hides. **3.** an attendant of Śiva; Musa Sapientum.

Ćāru (S) (M) **1.** agreeable. **2.** charming; beautiful; beloved; esteemed. **3.** a son of Kṛṣṇa (*H. Purāṇa*); a son of Dhṛtarāṣṭra (*M. Bh.*); another name for Bṛhaspati; saffron (*Crocus sativus*); Himalayan cherry (*Prunus cersoides*).

Ćārubāhu (S) (M) 1. beautiful arms. 3. a son of Kṛṣṇa and Rukmiṇī (*H. Purāṇa*).

Ćārubhadra (S) (M) 1. an auspicious person; a handsome gentleman. 2. fortunate. 3. a son of Kṛṣṇa and Rukmiṇī (*H. Purāṇa*).

Ćarućandra (S) (M) 1. beautiful moon. 3. a son of Kṛṣṇa and Rukmiṇī (*H. Purāṇa*).

Ćarūćitra (S) (M) 1. beautiful picture; one with a beautiful form. 3. a son of Dhṛtarāṣṭrā (*M. Bh.*).

Ćārudarśana (S) (M) beautiful in appearance.

Ćārudatta (S) (M) 1. born of beauty. 2. extremely handsome. 3. a hero in a Sanskṛta drama (*M. Kaṭikam*).

Ćārudeha (S) (M) 1. with a beautiful form. 3. a son of Kṛṣṇa and Rukmiṇī (*Bhāgavata*).

Ćārudeṣṇa (S) (M) 1. beautiful gift. 3. a son of Kṛṣṇa and Rukmiṇī (*M. Bh./L. Purāṇa*); the father of Gaṇḍūṣa (*H. Purāṇa*).

Ćarūdhiṣṇya (S) (M) 1. the altar of beauty. 3. a ṛṣi of the 11th Manvantara (*H. Purāṇa*).

Ćarūgarbha (S) (M) 1. a vessel of beauty. 3. a son of Kṛṣṇa and Rukmiṇī (*H. Purāṇa*).

Ćārugupta (S) (M) 1. protected by beauty. 3. a son of Kṛṣṇa and Rukmiṇī (*H. Purāṇa*).

Ćāruhāsan (S) (M) with a beautiful smile.

Ćārukesara (S) (M) 1. of golden beauty. 3. *Crysanthemum Indicum*; *Rosa Alba.*

Ćārumat (S) (M) 1. intelligent. 3. a Ćakravartin.

Ćārumatsya (S) (M) 1. beautiful fish. 3. a son of sage Viśvāmitra (*M. Bh.*).

Ćārumoda (S) (M) 1. pleasing; joy; gladness. 3. *Jasminum Officianale.*

Ćārupāda (S) (M) 1. with beautiful feet. 3. a son of Namasyu.

Ćāruśravas (S) (M) 1. with a beautiful voice. 3. a son of Kṛṣṇa and Rukmiṇī.

Ćārusāra (S) (M) 1. the essence of all that is lovely. 2. gold.

Ćāruśīrṣa (S) (M) 1. with a beautiful head. 3. a sage of Ālambagotra who was a friend of Indra (*M. Bh.*).

Ćāruvaktra (S) (M) 1. beautiful faced. 3. an attendant of Skanda who was devoted to Brāhmins (*M. Bh.*).

Ćāruvardhana (S) (M) who enhances beauty.

Ćāruveṣa (S) (M) 1. beautifully attired. 3. a son of Kṛṣṇa and Rukmiṇī (*L. Purāṇa*).

Ćāruvinda (S) (M) 1. striving for beauty; attaining charm. 3. a son of Kṛṣṇa and Rukmiṇī (*H. Purāṇa*).

Ćāruyaśas (S) (M) 1. with charming fame. 3. a son of Kṛṣṇa and Rukmiṇī (*H. Purāṇa*).

Ćārvāka (S) (M) 1. sweet tongued. 3. a rākṣasa friend of Duryodhana (*M. Bh.*); a philosopher of ancient India who was an atheist (*R. Taraṅgiṇī*).

Ćāṣa (S) (M) the Blue Jay (*Coracias benghalensis*).

Ćāṣavaktra (S) (M) 1. jay faced. 3. an attendant of Skanda (*M. Bh.*).

Ćātaka (S) (M) 1. a mythical Indian bird considered to live on raindrops. 3. a poet; Pied Crested Cuckoo (*Clamator jacobinus serratus*).

Ćatuhsana (S) (M) containing the 4 sons, Sanaka, Sananda, Sanātana, Sanatkumāra of Brahmā.

Ćatura (S) (M) 1. clever; skilful. 2. quick; swift; beautiful; charming; agreeable.

Ćaturaṅga (S) (M) 1. 4 limbed; horse. 2. with beautiful limbs. 3. a king of the Aṅga dynasty who was the son of Hemapāda and the father of Pṛthulākṣa (*A. Purāṇa*); a son of Lomapāda (*M. Purāṇa*).

Ćaturānana (S) (M) 1. 4 faced. 3. another name for Brahmā.

Ćaturānīka (S) (M) 1. 4 faced. 3. another name for Varuṇa.

Ćaturaśva (S) (M) 1. one who owns 4 horses. 3. a sage who was the member of Yama's court (*H. Purāṇa*).

Ćaturāsya (S) (M) **1.** quadrangular abode. **2.** living in a quadrangular abode. **3.** a heroic asura who loved the apsarā Rambhā (*K. Rāmāyaṇa*).

Ćaturbāhu (S) (M).**1.** 4 armed. **3.** another name for Viṣṇu and Śiva.

Ćaturbhuja (S) (M) **1.** 4 armed. **3.** another name for Viṣṇu, Kṛṣṇa, Gaṇeśa and Śiva.

Ćaturdanṣṭra (S) (M) **1.** 4 tusked. **3.** an attendant of Skanda (*M. Bh.*); another name for Viṣṇu.

Ćaturdanta (S) (M) **1.** 4 tusked. **3.** another name for Indra's elephant, Airāvata.

Ćaturgati (S) (M) **1.** 4 legged. **2.** has 4 kinds of speed; moving in all the 4 directions at the same time. **3.** another name for the tortoise and the Supreme Soul.

Ćaturmukha (S) (M) **1.** 4 faced. **3.** another name for Brahmā, Viṣṇu and Śiva.

Ćaturmūrti (S) (M) **1.** having 4 appearances. **2.** with 4 forms; versatile. **3.** another name for Brahmā, Viṣṇu, Skanda.

Ćaturvaktra (S) (M) **1.** 4 faced. **3.** a dānava (*H. Purāṇa*); an attendant of Durgā; another name for Brahmā.

Ćaturveda (S) (M) **1.** the 4 Vedas conjoined; the 4 fold knowledge. **3.** the knowledge of Dharma, Artha, Kāma and Mokṣa.

Ćatuṣpāṇī (S) (M) **1.** 4 armed. **3.** another name for Viṣṇu.

Ćaudrāyaṇa (S) (M) **1.** a prince who inspires. **3.** a prince of Daśapura (*H. Purāṇa*).

Ćedi (S) (M) **1.** intelligent. **2.** pleasant; likeable. **3.** a king of the Yaduvanśa and son of Uśika who founded the Ćedi dynasty; a people of Bundelkhand (*Bhāgavata*).

Ćedija (S) (M) **1.** son of Ćedi. **3.** another name for Dhṛṣṭaketu.

Ćedipati (S) (M) **1.** king of the Ćedis; master of bliss. **3.** honorific of Śiśupāla.

Ćedipuṅgava (S) (M) **1.** bull of the Ćedis; chief of the Ćedis. **3.** another name for Dhṛṣṭaketu.

Ćedirāja (S) (M) **1.** king of Ćedi. **3.** another name for Śiśupāla son of Damaghoṣa.

Ćekitāna (S) (M) **1.** intelligent. **3.** an archer of the Vṛṣṇi dynasty who fought on the side of the Pāṇḍavas in the war of Mahābhārata (*M. Bh.*); another name for Śiva.

Ćenćanna (S) (M) vivacious.

Ćetaka (S) (M) **1.** thoughtful **3.** Rānā Pratāp's horse; a Liććhavī prince of Vaiśālī and the uncle of Jaina Tīrthaṅkara Mahāvīra (*M. Ćarita*); *Jasminum grandiflorum*.

Ćetana (S) (M) **1.** conscious; animated; visible; conspicuous; distinguished; elegant; sentient. **2.** soul; mind; man.

Ćetas (S) (M) **1.** intelligence; consciousness; splendour. **2.** soul; heart; mind.

Ćetrāma (S) (M) pervading the conciousness.

Ćhabīlā (S) (M) **1.** charming; picturesque. **2.** beautiful; splendid; brilliant.

Ćhāga (S) (M) **1.** moisture; born of moisture. **3.** the goat which is supposed to have originated from the moisture present on the shell of the cosmic egg (*Y. Veda*).

Ćhaga (S) (M) **1.** he goat. **2.** the Zodiac sign of Aries. **3.** an attendant of Śiva.

Ćhagala (S) (M) **1.** goat. **3.** a sage (*Vā. Purāṇa*).

Ćhagumukha (S) (M) **1.** with the face of a goat. **3.** another name for Subrahmaṇya (*M. Bh.*).

Ćhagavaktra (S) (M) **1.** goat faced. **3.** a companion of Skanda (*Sk. Purāṇa*).

Ćhaggan (S) (M) **1.** intelligence; mind; spirit; soul; goat. **2.** the Zodiac sign of Aries.

Ćhailā (S) (M) a handsome youth.

Ćhajju (S) (M) **1.** shade. **2.** cool; soothing; provides shelter.

Ćhandaka (S) (M) **1.** charming; hymn like; poetic. **3.** Śākyamuni's charioteer (*Divyāvadāna*).

Ćhandakā (S) (M) **1.** assuming any shape at will. **3.** another name for Viṣṇu.

Ćhandodeva (S) (M) **1.** lord of the hymns; invoker of deities with hymns. **3.** another name for sage Mataṅga.

Ćhattra (S) (M) **1.** parasol; umbrella. **2.** with the white parasol symbolizing royal or delegated power. **3.** according to the Hindu scriptures, the universe in divided into 7, arranged one above the other like a number of parasols.

Ćhattradhāra (S) (M) bearer of the royal umbrella.

Ćhatraketu (S) (M) **1.** a bright umbrella banner. **2.** chief; head. **3.** a son of Lakṣmaṇa and Ūrmilā who became the king of Ćandramatī (*U. Rāmāyaṇa*).

Ćhatrapati (S) (M) **1.** lord of the umbrella. **2.** whose kingdom shelters the people like an umbrella; an emperor.

Ćhatravatī (S) (M) possessing the umbrella of power.

Ćhatreśa (S) (M) **1.** lord of the umbrella. **3.** another name for Śiva.

Ćhaturhotri (S) (M) **1.** a litany recited at the new moon. **3.** another name for Kṛṣṇa.

Ćhavillākara (S) (M) **1.** of handsome appearance. **3.** a historian of Kāśmira (*R. Taraṅgiṇī*).

Ćhāyana (S) (M) moon.

Ćhāyānātha (S) (M) **1.** lord of Ćhāyā. **3.** another name for Sūrya.

Ćhāyāṅka (S) (M) **1.** marked with the hare. **2.** one who is like the moon. **3.** another name for the moon.

Ćhedi (S) (M) **1.** which cuts and breaks. **3.** the thunderbolt of Indra.

Ćidākāśa (S) (M) **1.** universal soul. **3.** Absolute Brahmā.

Ćidambara (S) (M) **1.** with a heart as vast as the sky. **3.** a Sanskṛta poet who stayed at the court of Emperor Veṅkaṭa of Vijayanagara and whose greatest work is the *Rāghavayādavapāṇḍavīya* (16th century A.D.); a pilgrimage centre in Tamil Nādu.

Ćidānanda (S) (M) ultimate bliss.

Ćidātma (S) (M) **1.** pure intelligence. **3.** Supreme Spirit.

Ćidātmata (S) (M) consisting of pure thought.

Ćiddhātu (S) (M) Original Soul.

Ćidghana (S) (M) **1.** full of knowledge. **3.** another name for Brahmā.

Ćidrūpa (S) (M) knowledge incarnate.

Ćidullāsa (S) (M) **1.** thoughts that radiate. **2.** has radiant thoughts; wise; spiritually enlightened.

Ćidvilāsa (S) (M) **1.** one who sports in the knowledge of illusion. **3.** a disciple of Śaṅkarāćārya (*Ś. Vijaya*).

Ćidvilasinī (S) (M) **1.** one who sports in the knowledge of illusion. **2.** enlightened and enjoying the thoughts of enlightenment; in a state of eternal bliss.

Ćihir (S) (M) the bird Chummum (*Cheer phasianus wallichi*).

Ćikita (S) (M) **1.** experienced. **2.** well read; wise; enlightened.

Ćikka (S) (M) a small mouse.

Ćikṣura (S) (M) **1.** inflicter of pain. **3.** the war minister of Mahiṣāsura (*D. Bhāgavata*).

Ćikura (S) (M) **1.** mountain; hair on the head. **3.** the son of Āryaka the serpent king and father of Sumukha (*M. Bh.*).

Ćitta (S) (M) **1.** knowledge; consciousness. **3.** another name for Brahmā.

Ćiman (S) (M) curious.

Ćinmaya (S) (M) **1.** consisting of pure intelligence. **3.** the Supreme Spirit.

Ćintāmaṇi (S) (M) **1.** gem of thought; gem that fulfils desires. **3.** a diamond produced from the Ocean of Milk which is considered to grant all desires (*H. Purāṇa*); a Buddha (*B. Literature*); another name for Brahmā.

Ćintāmukta (S) (M) free from worry.

Ćintan (S) (M) **1.** thought; perception. **2.** meditation; mind; intellect.

Ćintāratna (S) (M) **1.** gem of thought. **3.** a fabulous gem considered to grant all desires (*S. Dvatrinśikā*).

Ćintya (S) (M) worthy of thought; worthy of being conceived.

Ćintyadyota (S) (M) **1.** of brightness conceivable only by imagination. **3.** a class of deities.

Ćirajuşa (S) (M) favoured with a long life.

Ćirakāri (S) (M) **1.** making slow progress. **3.** a son of Gautama Maharşi (*M. Bh.*).

Ćirañjīvan (S) (M) **1.** long lived. **2.** infinite. **3.** another name for Vişņu and Kāma.

Ćirantaka (S) (M) **1.** eternal. **3.** a son of Garuḍa (*M. Bh.*).

Ćiravāsas (S) (M) **1.** long lived. **2.** master of one's own death; one who can die as and when he chooses to. **3.** a Kśatriya king born as a reincarnation of the asura Krodhavaśa (*M. Bh.*); a yakşa in the court of Kubera (*M. Bh.*).

Ćirāyu (S) (M) long lived.

Ćirāyus (S) (M) **1.** long lived. **3.** a king of **Ćirāyu** who was the husband of Dhanapārā and the father of Jīvahara, he had the secret elixir of long life and lived a 1000 years (*K. Sāgara*).

Ćīriņī (S) (M) **1.** clothed in bark or rags. **3.** a river on the banks of which Vaivasvata Manu performed his penance (*M. Bh.*).

Ćiriñjīvin (S) (M) **1.** long lived. **3.** another name for Vişņu; Red Silkcotton tree (*Bombax celba*).

Ćirjīvaka (S) (M) **1.** long lived. **3.** another name for Mārkaņḍeya, Bali, Vyāsa, Hanumat, Vibhīşana, Paraśurāma, Kŗpa, Aśvatthāman, Vişņu and crow.

Ćirlabdha (S) (M) obtained after a long time.

Ćitadhana (S) (M) **1.** the conscious. **3.** another name for Brahmā.

Ćitaka (S) (M) ornament of the neck; necklace.

Ćitapati (S) (M) lord of intellect; lord of thought.

Ćitāyu (S) (M) **1.** descended from thought; born of intellect. **3.** a Purū king who was the son of Bhadrāśva (*Agni Purāņa*).

Ćitra (S) (M) **1.** picture; conspicuous. **2.** excellent; distinguished; various; bright. **3.** son of Dhŗtarāşţra (*M. Bh.*); a king of elephants with whom Subrahmaņya played (*M. Bh.*); warriors of the Kauravas (*M. Bh.*); a hero of the Ćedi kingdom who fought on the side of the Pāņḍavas (*M. Bh.*); a gandharva; a Dravida king (*P. Purāņa*); the herb *Cucumis trigonus*; Ceylon Leadwort (*Plumbago zeylanica*); Aśoka tree (*Saraca indica*).

Ćitrabāhu (S) (M) **1.** with a speckled arm. **3.** a son of Dhŗtarāşţra (*M. Bh.*); a gandharva.

Ćitrabāņa (S) (M) **1.** owner of variegated arrows. **3.** a son of Dhŗtarāşţra (*M. Bh.*).

Ćitrabarha (S) (M) **1.** with a variegated tail. **3.** a son of Garuḍa (*M. Bh.*).

Ćitrabarhin (S) (M) **1.** with a variegated tail. **2.** a peacock. **3.** a son of Garuḍa (*M. Bh.*).

Ćitrabhānu (S) (M) **1.** of variegated lustre; the beautiful sun. **2.** multicoloured; shining; lit. **3.** another name for Agni, Bhairava, Śiva, the aśvins and the sun.

Ćitrabhūta (S) (M) painted; decorated.

Ćitraćāpa (S) (M) **1.** owner of a variegated bow. **3.** a son of Dhŗtarāşţra (*M. Bh.*).

Ćitradarśī (S) (M) **1.** seeing clearly; with bright observation. **3.** a sage who was the son of Kuśika.

Ćitradeva (S) (M) **1.** a strange deity. **3.** an attendant of Subrahmaņya who loved Brāhmins (*M. Bh.*).

Ćitradharman (S) (M) **1.** follower of various customs; follower of strange customs. **2.** one of various customs; an arrangement of various hues. **3.** reincarnation of the asura Virūpākşa who was invited by the Pāņḍavas to help them in the Mahābhārata war (*M. Bh.*).

Ćitragu (S) (M) **1.** owner of brindled cows; knower of the wonderful. **3.** a son of Kŗşņa (*Bhāgavata*).

Ćitragupta (S) (M) **1.** secret picture; protected by the wonderful. **3.** the scribe of the gods who was born from the body of Brahmā (*Tithyāditya*); one of Yama's attendants who records the doings of men (*M. Bh.*); the 16th Arhat of the future Utsarpiṇī (*J. S. Koṣa*).

Ćitraka (S) (M) **1.** painted; spotted. **2.** tiger; leopard; bright; beautiful; brave; powerful. **3.** a son of Dhṛtarāṣṭra (*M. Bh.*); a son of Vṛṣṇi (*Vā. Putrāṇa*); a nāga.

Ćitrakaṇṭha (S) (M) **1.** with a speckled throat. **2.** pigeon. **3.** the horse of King Vikramāditya known for his bravery.

Ćitrakarman (S) (M) performer of extraordinary acts.

Ćitraketu (S) (M) **1.** owner of a beautiful banner. **3.** a gandharva who was reborn as the asura Vṛtrāsura (*Bhāgavata*); a son of Garuḍa (*M. Bh.*); a Pāñćāla prince who fought on the side of the Pāṇḍavas (*M. Bh.*); a son of Śiśupāla (*Bhāgavata*); the king of the Śūrasenas and a devotee of Viṣṇu and Śiva (*Bhā. Purāṇa*); another name for Lakṣmaṇa, Kṛṣṇa, Vasiṣṭha, Devabhāga.

Ćitrākṣa (S) (M) **1.** speckle eyed. **2.** with strange eyes; with beautiful eyes. **3.** a son of Dhṛtarāṣṭra (*M. Bh.*); a serpent lord (*M. Bh.*); a Draviḍa king.

Ćitrakuṇḍala (S) (M) **1.** owns radiant earrings. **3.** a son of Dhṛtarāṣṭra (*M. Bh.*).

Ćitrakūṭa (S) (M) **1.** wonderful peak. **3.** a mountain of a district where Rāma and Lakṣmaṇa first spent their exile (*V. Rāmāyaṇa*).

Ćitramanas (S) (M) **1.** with a bright intellect. **3.** a horse of the moon (*Va. Purāṇa*).

Ćitramukha (S) (M) **1.** bright-faced. **3.** a Vaiśya sage who became a Brāhmin by his penances (*M. Bh.*).

Ćitranātha (S) (M) **1.** excellent lord. **3.** a son of Dhṛṣṭa (*M. Purāṇa*).

Ćitrāṅga (S) (M) **1.** with a multicoloured body. **2.** antelope; vermilion. **3.** a warrior killed by Śatrughna during Rāma's Aśvamedha Yajña (*Rāmāyaṇa*); a son of Dhṛtarāṣṭra (*M. Bh.*); Ceylon Leadwort (*Plumbago zeylanica*).

Ćitrāṅgada (S) (M) **1.** decorated with wonderful bracelets. **2.** with bejewelled arms. **3.** a son of King Śāntanu and Satyavatī (*M. Bh.*); a gandharva (*K. Sāgara*); a king of Kaliṅga (*M. Bh.*); a king of Daśārṇa who was killed by Arjuna (*M. Bh.*); a deer in the *Pañćatantra*; a vidyādhara; a divine recorder of men's deeds.

Ćitrāṅgadāsuta (S) (M) **1.** son of Ćitrāngadā. **3.** another name for Babhruvāhana.

Ćitrapakṣa (S) (M) **1.** with speckled wings. **3.** the Northern Painted Partridge (*Francolinus pictus pallidus*).

Ćitraraśmi (S) (M) **1.** with variegated rays. **3.** a marut (*H. Purāṇa*).

Ćitraratha (S) (M) **1.** with a bright chariot. **3.** a gandharva who was the son of sage Kaśyapa and a friend of the Pāṇḍavas (*M. Bh.*); a minister of Daśaratha who belonged to the Sūta dynasty (*V. Rāmāyaṇa*); a king of Śālva (*Br. Purāṇa*); a king of the dynasty of Bharata who was the son of King Gaya (*Bhāgavata*); a prince of Pāñćāla who fought on the side of the Pāṇḍavas (*M. Bh.*); an Aṅga king and the husband of Prabhāvatī (*M. Bh.*); a yādava king who was the son of Uśaṅkhu and father of Śūra (*M. Bh.*); the son of Vīrabāhu and a friend of Rāma who married Hemā the daughter of Kuśa (*Rāmāyaṇa*); river of Purāṇic fame (*M. Bh.*); the king of the gandharvas (*A. Veda*); a descendant of Aṅga and son of Dharmaratha (*H. Purāṇa*); a son of Kṛṣṇa (*Bhāgavata*); a vidyādhara (*A. Koṣa*); another name for the Polar Star and the sun; a son of Uṣadgu.

Ćitrarepha (S) (M) **1.** bright passion. **2.** fire; heat; splendour. **3.** a son of Medhātithi (*Bhāgavata*).

Ćitrarūpa (S) (M) **1.** with a variegated form. **3.** an attendant of Śiva (*D. Bhāgavata*).

Ćitraśarāsana (S) (M) **1.** wearer of a variegated armour. **3.** a son of Dhṛtarāṣṭra (*M. Bh.*).

Ćitrasena (S) (M) **1.** with a bright spear. **2.** commander of a wonderful army. **3.** a gandharva who was the son of Viśvāvasu and husband of Sandhyāvalī and Ratnāvalī and who became a friend of the Pāṇḍavas and instructed Arjuna in music and dancing (*M. Bh.*); a son of Dhṛtarāṣṭra who was with Duryodhana in the game of dice (*M. Bh.*); a son of the 13th Manu; a son of Gada; a divine recorder of the deeds of men; a Purū prince who was the son of Parīkṣit and grandson of Avīkṣita (*M. Bh.*); a minister of Jarāsandha (*M. Bh.*); a king of Abhisāra who fought on the side of the Kauravas (*M. Bh.*); a brother of Suśarmā the king of Tṛgārta (*M. Bh.*); a warrior of Pāñćāla (*M. Bh.*); a son of Karṇa killed by Nakula (*M. Bh.*); a brother of Karṇa killed by Yudhāmanyu (*M. Bh.*); a serpent who helped Arjuna (*M. Bh.*); a king of the dynasty of Vaivasvata Manu (*Bhā. Purāṇa*); the 13th Manu (*H. Purāṇa*); another name for Parīkṣit.

Ćitraśikhaṇḍī (S) (M) **1.** bright crested. **3.** the son of Aṅgiras (*M. Bh.*); another name for the Saptṛṣis, Viśvāmitra and the planet Jupiter.

Ćitrāśvā (S) (M) **1.** a painted horse. **2.** with wonderful horses. **3.** another name for Satyavān (*M. Bh.*).

Ćitrasiras (S) (M) **1.** with a bright head. **3.** a gandharva (*H. Purāṇa*).

Ćitrasvana (S) (M) **1.** clear voiced. **3.** a rākṣasa (*Bhāgavata*).

Ćitravāhana (S) (M) **1.** with decorated vehicles. **3.** a king of Maṇipura and the father of Ćitrāṅgada (*M. Bh.*).

Ćitravāja (S) (M) **1.** owning wonderful riches. **3.** another name for the maruts.

Ćitravarmā (S) (M) **1.** with painted armour. **3.** a son of Dhṛtarāṣṭra (*M. Bh.*); a Pāñćāla prince who was the son of Sućitra who fought on the side of the Pāṇḍavas (*M. Bh.*); the father of Sīmantinī (*Sk. Purāṇa*).

Ćitravasu (S) (M) with many treasures; rich in shining stars.

Ćitravegika (S) (M) **1.** moving with an unusual velocity. **3.** a serpent of the family of Dhṛtarāṣṭra (*M. Bh.*).

Ćitrayodhin (S) (M) **1.** fighting in many ways. **3.** another name for Arjuna.

Ćitrāyudha (S) (M) **1.** various weapons. **3.** a son of Dhṛtarāṣṭra (*M. Bh.*); a king of Siṁhapuri who was defeated by Arjuna (*M. Bh.*); a warrior of Ćedi who fought on the side of the Pāṇḍavas (*M. Bh.*).

Ćitreśa (S) (M) **1.** lord of Ćitrā. **2.** wonderful lord. **3.** the moon.

Ćitrīśa (S) (M) **1.** lord of Ćitra; wonderful lord. **3.** another name for the moon.

Ćitropaćitra (S) (M) **1.** brightly coloured. **2.** variegated. **3.** a son of Dhṛtarāṣṭra (*M. Bh.*).

Ćitrotpala (S) (M) **1.** with various lotus flowers. **3.** a river of Purāṇic fame (*M. Bh.*).

Ćitrūpa (S) (M) **1.** of the form of consciousness. **2.** wise; intelligent; goodhearted. **3.** another name for the Supreme Spirit.

Ćitta (S) (M) **1.** thought; mind. **2.** intellect; reason.

Ćittabhoga (S) (M) **1.** fully conscious; enjoyer of mind. **2.** wise; intelligent; thoughtful.

Ćittahārin (S) (M) one who captures the heart.

Ćittaja (S) (M) **1.** born of the heart. **3.** another name for Kāma, the lord of love.

Ćittanātha (S) (M) **1.** lord of the soul. **3.** the Supreme Being.

Ćittapara (S) (M) **1.** beyond reason. **3.** the Supreme Spirit.

Ćittaprabha (S) (M) the light of the soul.

Ćittaprasāda (S) (M) **1.** gift of mind. **2.** gladdening the mind; pleases the heart; charming.

Ćittaprasādana (S) (M) **1.** gladdening the mind. **2.** pleasing the heart; charming.

Ćittaprasanna (S) (M) **1.** mentally happy. **2.** cheerful; making others happy.

Ćittarañjana (S) (M) **1.** pleasing the mind. **2.** charming; loving.

Ćittavata (S) (M) **1.** with a heart. **2.** understanding; kindhearted.

Ćittāyu (S) (M) **1.** the son of the heart. **2.** born of the mind. **3.** a king of the Purū dynasty who was the son of Bhadrāśva (*A. Purāṇa*).

Ćittin (S) (M) **1.** thinker. **2.** intelligent; wise.

Ćitvana (S) (M) **1.** glance. **2.** a look.

Ćitvata (S) (M) **1.** endowed with mind. **2.** wise; reasonable; logical.

Ćīvarin (S) (M) **1.** wearing rags. **2.** lives austerely in accordance with the guidelines of religion. **3.** another name for Buddhist and Jaina monks.

Ćokṣa (S) (M) pure; clean; agreeable; pleasant.

Ćola (S) (M) **1.** a long robe. **3.** a righteous ruler of Kanśipura who gave his name to the kingdom and dynasty (*P. Purāṇa*).

Ćūḍākaraṇa (S) (M) **1.** crest ceremony. **2.** a particular ceremony in which ascetics and kings tie a lock of hair into a crest.

Ćūḍāmaṇī (S) (M) **1.** jewel worn on the crest. **2.** excellent; best; Rosary Pea (*Abrus precatorius*).

Ćūḍāratna (S) (M) **1.** jewel of the crest. **2.** excellent; best.

Ćūlin (S) (M) **1.** wearing an ornament on the crown. **3.** a sage and spiritual father of Brahmadatta by the apsarā Somadā (*V. Rāmāyaṇa*).

Ćummum (S) (M) **1.** adorable. **3.** the bird *Cheer phasianus wallichi.*

Ćunanda (S) (M) **1.** perception. **2.** learning. **3.** a Buddhist mendicant (*L. Vistara*).

Ćunću (S) (M) **1.** renowned. **3.** a Hehaya king who was the grandson of Rohitāśva, the son of Harita and the father of King Vijaya (*Br. Purāṇa*).

Ćuṇḍa (S) (M) **1.** perceptor. **2.** to perceive; learn; understand. **3.** a pupil of Śākyamuni (*M. Bh.*).

Ćupka (S) (M) the Wooded Sandpiper (*Tringa glareola*).

Ćyavana (S) (M) **1.** moving. **2.** active; agile. **3.** a celebrated sage of the Bhārgava dynasty who was the son of Bhṛgu and Pulomā and the husband of Sukanyā the daughter of King Śaryāti and was restored to youth and beauty by the aśvins (*A. Brāhmaṇa*); a son of Suhotra (*Bhāgavata*); a sage of the 2nd Manvantara (*H. Purāṇa*).

D

Dabhīti (S) (M) **1.** injurer. **3.** a hermit praised in the *Ṛg Veda.*

Dadhīća (S) (M) **1.** sprinkling milk or curd. **3.** a ṛṣi son of Bhṛgu, made of the essences of the world and having a huge body (*Ku. Purāṇa*); the father of Sārasvata by the river Sarasvatī (*Vā. Purāṇa*) who discarded his life so that Indra could make a thunderbolt out of his bones to kill Vṛtrāsura (*M. Bh.*).

Dadhikṛā (S) (M) **1.** born from the Ocean of Milk. **2.** fast in motion. **3.** a divine horse who personifies the morning sun.

Dadhimukha (S) (M) **1.** milk-faced. **3.** a nāga son of Kaśyapa and Kadru (*M. Bh.*); a yakṣa (*M. Bh.*); the brother-in-law of the monkey Sugrīva and general of his army (*V. Rāmāyaṇa*).

Dadhipūraṇa (S) (M) **1.** living on milk. **2.** full of milk. **3.** a nāga (*M. Bh.*).

Dadhivāhana (S) (M) **1.** with a chariot of milk. **2.** curd-carrier. **3.** a king of Bhāratā (*M. Bh.*); a prince who was the son of Aṅga and father of Divaratha (*M. Bh.*); a king of Ćampā (*M. Bh.*).

Dadhivaktra (S) (M) **1.** milk faced. **3.** the uncle of Sugrīva (*Rāmāyaṇa*).

Dadhyān (S) (M) **1.** milk vendor. **2.** bringer of milk. **3.** a hermit to whom Indra taught the art of preparing rice in a particular manner for oblation (*Ṛg Veda*).

Dagdharatha (S) (M) **1.** with a burnt chariot. **3.** a gandharva (*M. Bh.*).

Daha (S) (M) **1.** blazing. **2.** very bright. **3.** one of the 11 rudras, the son of Sthāṇu and grandson of Brahmā (*M. Bh.*); an attendant given to Skanda by the god Anśa (*M. Bh.*).

Dahana (S) (M) **1.** burning; destroying. **3.** a rudra; an attendant of Skanda (*Sk. Purāṇa*); another name for Agni, the lord of fire.

Dahati (S) (M) **1.** one who burns. **2.** destroyer. **3.** an attendant of Skanda given by the god Anśa (*M. Bh.*).

Dahragni (S) (M) **1.** small fire. **3.** Agastya in a former birth.

Daitya (S) (M) **1.** demon. **3.** a class of demons who are sons of Kaśyapa and Diti (*M. Smṛti*); *Caesaria esculenta.*

Daityadvīpa (S) (M) **1.** refuge of daityas. **3.** a son of Garuḍa (*M. Bh.*).

Daityahan (S) (M) **1.** slayer of daityas. **3.** another name for Śiva.

Daityanāśana (S) (M) **1.** destroyer of daityas. **3.** another name for Viṣṇu.

Daityaniṣudana (S) (M) **1.** destroyer of daityas. **3.** another name for Indra.

Daityapati (S) (M) **1.** lord of the daityas. **3.** another name for Vṛtra.

Daityāri (S) (M) **1.** enemy of the daityas. **3.** another name for Kṛṣṇa.

Daityendra (S) (M) **1.** lord of the daityas. **3.** another name for Vṛtra.

Daivarāti (S) (M) **1.** of Devarata. **3.** another name for Janaka.

Daivya (S) (M) **1.** divine; glorious. **3.** a messenger of the asuras (*T. Samhitā*).

Dakṣa (S) (M) **1.** able; talented. **2.** fit; energetic; perfect; fire; gold. **3.** an aditya identified with Prajāpati and the father of Kṛttikā (*T. Samhitā*); a prajāpati born of the right thumb of Brahmā, the husband of Aśikni, the father of Satī who married Śiva, and was killed by Śiva (*D. Purāṇa*), to be later reborn as the mindborn son of the 10 Praćetases and Marīśa, the father of 24 daughters by Prasūti, as also of 60 daughters by Aśikni who became the lunar mansions and the mothers of gods, demons, men and animals (*V. Purāṇa*); a son of Garuḍa (*M. Bh.*); the bull of Śiva (*A. Koṣa*).

Dakṣaketu (S) (M) **1.** with a golden banner. **3.** a son of Manu Dakṣasāvarṇa (*H. Purāṇa*).

Dakṣakratuhara (S) (M) **1.** able minded Śiva. **3.** another name for Śiva.

Dakṣānila (S) (M) a perfect breeze; a cold southern breeze.

Dakṣapatī (S) (M) lord of the perfect; lord of the faculties.

Dakṣāri (S) (M) **1.** Dakṣa's foe. **2.** enemy of the perfect. **3.** another name for Śiva.

Dakṣasāvarṇi (S) (M) **1.** resembling gold; golden coloured. **2.** with a perfect nature. **3.** the 9th Manu (*V. Purāṇa*).

Dakṣayana (S) (M) coming from Dakṣa.

Dakṣayaṇinya (S) (M) **1.** obtained from Dakṣa. **2.** gold; golden ornament. **3.** another name for the sun.

Dakṣeśa (S) (M) **1.** lord of Dakṣa. **3.** another name for Śiva.

Dākṣi (S) (M) son of Dakṣa; golden son; son of a perfect being.

Dakṣiṇa (S) (M) right; the sense of direction; clever; fit; able; towards the south; candid; sincere.

Dakṣinam (S) (M) **1.** right fire. **3.** a son of Agni.

Dakṣināmūrti (S) (M) **1.** the idol of the south. **3.** a tāntric form of Śiva (*T. Śastra*); a copyist (17th century).

Dala (S) (M) **1.** petal. **2.** fragment; group. **3.** the son of the Ikṣvāku King Parīkṣita and Suśobhanā (*M. Bh.*).

Daladhīśvara (S) (M) lord of petals; leader of the group.

Dalajita (S) (M) winning over a group.

Dalakamala (S) (M) lotus (*Nelumbo speciosum*).

Dalamodaka (S) (M) petal honey.

Dalapati (S) (M) **1.** leader of a group. **2.** master of petals. **3.** a prince.

Dalbha (S) (M) **1.** wheel. **3.** a ṛṣi (*M. Bh.*).

Dalbhaghoṣa (S) (M) **1.** sound of the wheel; ascetic; a person living in a grass hut. **3.** a sage (*M. Bh.*).

Dalbhya (S) (M) **1.** belonging to wheels. **2.** an ascetic. **3.** a sage of Naimisaraṇya who was a member of Yudhiṣṭhira's court (*M. Bh.*).

Dalmi (S) (M) **1.** tearing. **3.** Indra's thunderbolt; another name for Indra.

Dama (S) (M) **1.** wealth; house; home; self-restraint. **3.** a brother of Damayantī (*Nalopākhyāna*); a son of Dakṣa (*Bhā. Purāṇa*); a son of Marutta (*V. Purāṇa*); a mahāṛṣi (*M. Bh.*).

Damaćandra (S) (M) **1.** suppressing moon. **3.** a mighty king who was a friend of Yudhiṣṭhira (*M. Bh.*).

Damaghoṣa (S) (M) **1.** with a restrained voice. **3.** a Ćedi prince and the father of Śiśupala (*M. Bh.*).

Dāmagranthi (S) (M) **1.** tied by a rope. **3.** name assumed by Nakula in the court of Virāṭa (*M. Bh.*).

Dāman (S) (M) **1.** rope; girdle; chaplet; wreath. **3.** a friend of Kṛṣṇa.

Damana (S) (M) **1.** subduing; taming. **2.** over-powering; self controlled. **3.** a son of Vasudeva and Rohiṇī (*H. Purāṇa*); a son of Bharadvāja (*Sk. Purāṇa*); a brother of Damayantī and son of King Bhīma; the son of King Paurava who fought on the side of the Kauravas (*M. Bh.*); a hermit who blessed King Bhīma to have children (*M. Bh.*); *Artemisia sieversiana*.

Damanaka (S) (M) **1.** subduer; brave; powerful; four periods of time; six short syllables. **2.** conqueror; a victor. **3.** *Artemisia indica*; a daitya killed by Viṣṇu in his Matsya incarnation (*Sk. Purāṇa*).

Damati (S) (M) subduer; conqueror.

Damāya (S) (M) **1.** to control oneself. **3.** a son of Marutta.

Damayitri (S) (M) **1.** tamer or subduer. **3.** another name for Viṣṇu and Śiva.

Dambara (S) (M) **1.** self restrained. **3.** an attendant given to Skanda by Brahmā (*M. Bh.*).

Dambha (S) (M) **1.** pride. **2.** deceit; ego. **3.** an asura son of Vipraćitti and the father of Śaṅkhaćuḍa (*D. Bh. Purāṇa*).

Dambhodbhava (S) (M) **1.** born of deceit; son of pride. **3.** a mighty emperor of the world subdued by Nara and Nārāyaṇa (*M. Bh.*).

Dambholi (S) (M) **1.** weapon of the proud; a subduing weapon; Indra's thunderbolt. **3.** a ṛṣi of the 1st Manvantara (*H. Purāṇa*).

Dambholipāṇi (S) (M) **1.** holds a thunderbolt in his hand. **3.** another name for Indra.

Damin (S) (M) self controlled.

Dāmodara (S) (M) **1.** with a rope around the waist. **3.** the 9th Arhat of the past Utsarpiṇī (*J. Literature*); a king of Kāśmira (*R. Taraṅgiṇī*); a river held sacred by the Śāntāls (*A. Koṣa*); another name for Kṛṣṇa.

Damoṣ (S) (M) **1.** bound. **2.** wealthy; fortunate. **3.** a sage in the assembly of Yudhiṣṭhira (*M. Bh.*).

Damoṣṇīṣa (S) (M) **1.** desirous of wealth. **3.** an ancient sage (*M. Bh.*).

Damunas (S) (M) **1.** subduer; head of the family. **3.** another name for Agni.

Damya (S) (M) tamable.

Damyasārathī (S) (M) **1.** guide of those who can restrain themselves. **3.** a Buddha (*B. Literature*).

Dānapati (S) (M) **1.** lord of generosity; munificent. **3.** a daitya (*H. Purāṇa*); another name for Akrūra.

Dānasāgara (S) (M) ocean of generosity.

Dānaśūra (S) (M) **1.** hero among the donors. **3.** a bodhisattva (*K. Sāgara*).

Dānava (S) (M) **1.** of Danu; valiant; victor; conqueror. **3.** dānavas are a class of demons described as the children of Kaśyapa and Danu and often identified with the daityas (*M. Bh.*).

Dānavapati (S) (M) **1.** king of the dānavas. **3.** another name for Indra.

Dānavendra (S) (M) **1.** lord of the danavas. **3.** another name for Vṛtra.

Dānavīra (S) (M) hero among the donors; an extremely generous man.

Daṇḍa (S) (M) **1.** stick; staff; club. **3.** punishment personified as the son of Dharma and Kriyā; a son of Ikṣvāku who was a partial incarnation of the asura Krodhahanta; the son of King Vidaṇḍa and brother of King Daṇḍadhara of Magadha (*M. Bh.*); an attendant of the sun (*M. Bh.*); a Ćedi warrior on the side of the Pāṇḍavas (*M. Bh.*); a rākṣasa son of Sumāli and Ketumatī (*U. Rāmāyaṇa*); another name for Yama, Śiva and Viṣṇu.

Daṇḍabāhu (S) (M) **1.** one who takes law in his own hands. **2.** punishing with his arms; just; a judge; an executioner. **3.** a warrior of Skanda (*M. Bh.*).

Daṇḍadhāra (S) (M) **1.** carrying a staff; punisher. **3.** a Magadha king who was a partial incarnation of the asura Krodhavardhana (*M. Bh.*); a son of Dhṛtarāṣṭra (*M. Bh.*); a Pāñćāla warrior on the side of the Pāṇḍavas (*M. Bh.*); another name for Yama.

Daṇḍaka (S) (M) **1.** a small staff; a pole; handle; beam; staff of a banner. **3.** a son of Ikṣvāku (*H. Purāṇa*).

Dāṇḍakidakya (S) (M) **1.** one who uses the staff amicably; good administrator. **2.** a stern ruler. **3.** a prince of the Tṛgarta tribe (*V. Purāṇa*).

Daṇḍamukha (S) (M) **1.** leader of a column. **2.** punishing by word of mouth; leader of an army; a general.

Daṇḍanāyaka (S) (M) **1.** chief justice. **2.** hero among the rod wielders; a judge. **3.** an attendant of the sun (*V's B. Samhitā*).

Daṇḍapāṇi (S) (M) **1.** staff handed. **2.** holding a staff in his hands. **3.** the leader of Śiva's troops (*Sk. Purāṇa*); the father of Buddha's wife Gopā (*L. Vistara*); the grandfather of Kṣemaka (*Bhāgavata*); a King who was the son of Vibhīnara and the father of Nimi (*Bhāgavata*); the son of King Paundraka of Kāśi (*P. Purāṇa*).

Daṇḍasena (S) (M) **1.** with an army of staffs. **2.** whose army wields staffs; a commander of executioners. **3.** a son of Viṣvakṣeṇa (*H. Purāṇa*).

Daṇḍaśrī (S) (M) **1.** best among the staffs. **2.** best judge; best administrator.

Daṇḍavata (S) (M) carrying a staff; with a large army; prostrating the body in a straight line; one who does not bow before anyone; full of self-respect; a leader; a commander.

Daṇḍavīrya (S) (M) power of the staff; possessed with ruling power; the general of an army.

Daṇḍin (S) (M) **1.** carrying a staff. **2.** a class of sannyāsins who carry a staff in their hands. **3.** an order of ascetics founded by Sankarāćārya (*Ś. Vijaya*); a son of Dhṛtarāṣṭra (*M. Bh.*); a god worshipped as an attendant of the sun (*A. Purāṇa*); a Sanskṛta critic of the Gupta reign

(6th century A.D.) (*A. Koṣa*); another name for Yama and Manjuśrī.

Daṅśa (S) (M) **1.** sting; bite. **2.** wrathful; jealous; doesn't forgive and forget enemies. **3.** a rākṣasa who was turned into a beetle (*M. Bh.*).

Daṅṣṭranivāsin (S) (M) **1.** teeth dweller; surrounded by teeth. **2.** the tongue. **3.** a yakṣa.

Daṅṣṭrin (S) (M) **1.** bearer of teeth; tusked. **3.** another name for Śiva.

Dānta (S) (M) **1.** subdued; tamed; tooth. **2.** mild; patient. **3.** the Indian fig tree (*Ficus indica*); the son of King Bhīma of Vidarbha (*M. Bh.*).

Dantadhvaja (S) (M) **1.** tusk-bannered. **3.** a son of Manu Tāmasa (*Vām. Purāṇa*).

Dantamukha (S) (M) **1.** with a tooth on the face; tusked. **3.** an asura killed by Skanda (*Sk. Purāṇa*).

Dantapattraka (S) (M) **1.** with teeth like petals. **2.** the Jasmine flower.

Dantavaktra (S) (M) **1.** tusked; tooth protruding out of mouth. **2.** fierce; terrible. **3.** a Karūṣa king who was an incarnation of Viṣṇu's doorkeeper Vijaya who was killed by Kṛṣṇa and returned to Vaikuṇṭha; another name for Gaṇeśa.

Dantin (S) (M) **1.** tusked. **3.** another name for Gaṇeśa.

Dantivaktra (S) (M) **1.** elephant faced. **3.** another name for Gaṇeśa.

Danu (S) (M) **1.** noisy; high-pitched; one who shouts. **3.** a son of Śrī who was changed into a monster by Indra (*Rāmāyaṇa*); a king who was the father of Rambha and Karambha (*M. Purāṇa*).

Dānu (S) (M) **1.** liberal; courageous. **2.** prosperity; contentment. **3.** air; wind.

Danuja (S) (M) born of Danu; a dānava.

Danujadviṣa (S) (M) **1.** enemy of the dānava. **3.** another name for Indra.

Dāraka (S) (M) **1.** breaking; splitting. **3.** Kṛṣṇa's charioteer.

Darbha (S) (M) sacrificial grass used in oblations (*Saccharum cylindricum*).

Darbhi (S) (M) **1.** with sacrificial grass. **2.** an ascetic. **3.** a hermit who is supposed to have brought the 4 oceans to his bath in Kurukṣetra (*M. Bh.*).

Dardura (S) (M) **1.** big; terrible; with caves. **3.** a mountain personified by a deity in the court of Kubera (*M. Bh.*).

Dari (S) (M) **1.** splitting; opening. **2.** moving slowly. **3.** a nāga born in the family of Dhṛtarāṣṭra (*M. Bh.*).

Daridra (S) (M) **1.** roving; strolling; poor. **3.** a Yayāti king who was the son of Dundubhi and father of Vasu (*Bhāgavata*).

Darpa (S) (M) **1.** pride; arrogance. **3.** pride personified as the son of Adharmā and Śrī (*M. Bh.*); a Yayāti king (*Bhāgavata*).

Darpada (S) (M) **1.** pride inducer; creator of pride. **3.** another name for Śiva.

Darpahan (S) (M) **1.** destroyer of ego. **3.** another name for Śiva.

Darpahara (S) (M) **1.** eliminator of ego. **3.** another name for Śiva.

Darpaka (S) (M) **1.** pride. **3.** another name for Kāma.

Darpaṇa (S) (M) **1.** inducing vanity. **2.** a mirror.

Darpanārāyaṇa (S) (M) **1.** shielding men from vanity. **3.** a king (*Kathārṇava*).

Darśa (S) (M) **1.** looking at; worth looking at. **3.** the day of the new moon personified as the son of Dhātṛ (*Bhāgavata*); another name for Kṛṣṇa.

Darśana (S) (M) seeing; philosophy; showing; observing; discernment; vision; audience.

Darśanapāla (S) (M) protector of vision; a philosopher; a scholar of philosophy.

Darśanīya (S) (M) **1.** worth seeing. **2.** visible; beautiful; worthy of being seen.

Darśata (S) (M) **1.** making things visible. **2.** glowing; visible; conspicuous; beautiful. **3.** another name for the sun and the moon.

Dāru (S) (M) liberal.

Dāruka (S) (M) **1.** a small piece of wood. **2.** breaking; splitting. **3.** an incarnation of Śiva (*Ś. Purāṇa*); the charioteer of Mahiṣāsura (*D. Bh. Purāṇa*); a son of Garuḍa (*M. Bh.*); the charioteer of Kṛṣṇa (*M. Bh.*);

Dāruki (S) (M) **1.** a small piece of wood; breaking; splitting. **3.** Pradyumna's charioteer (*Bhā. Purāṇa*).

Dāruṇa (S) (M) as hard as wood.

Dārvan (S) (M) **1.** the hood of a snake. **3.** a son of Uśinara (*Bhā. Purāṇa*).

Dārvanda (S) (M) a peacock.

Darvarīka (S) (M) **1.** wind. **3.** another name for Indra.

Darvi (S) (M) **1.** wooden ladle. **2.** the hood of a snake. **3.** a son of Uśinara (*V. Purāṇa*).

Daśabāhu (S) (M) **1.** 10 armed. **3.** that form of Śiva in which he performs the tāṇḍava or the cosmic dance.

Daśabala (S) (M) **1.** possessing 10 powers. **3.** a Buddha (*B. Literature*).

Daśadhanuṣ (S) (M) **1.** 10 bowed. **2.** owner; 10 bows; a perfect archer. **3.** an ancestor of Śākyamuni (*D. Śastra*).

Daśadyn (S) (M) **1.** equivalent to 10 heavens; very powerful. **3.** a hermit (*Ṛg Veda*).

Daśagrīva (S) (M) **1.** 10 necked. **3.** a rākṣasa (*M. Bh.*); a son of Damaghoṣa (*G. Purāṇa*).

Daśajyoti (S) (M) **1.** 10 flamed. **2.** whose glory spreads in 10 directions. **3.** a son of Suhṛt (*M. Bh.*); a son of Subhrāj (*M. Bh.*).

Daśakandhara (S) (M) **1.** 10 necked. **3.** another name for Rāvaṇa.

Daśakaṇṭha (S) (M) **1.** 10 necked. **3.** another name for Rāvaṇa.

Daśakaṇṭhajita (S) (M) **1.** conquering the 10 necked one. **3.** Rāma, who conquered the 10 headed Rāvaṇa.

Daśaketu (S) (M) with 10 banners.

Daśamukha (S) (M) **1.** 10 faced. **3.** another name for Rāvaṇa.

Daśamukharipu (S) (M) **1.** enemy of the 10 faced one. **2.** enemy of Rāvaṇa. **3.** another name for Rāma.

Daśānana (S) (M) **1.** 10 faced. **3.** another name for Rāvaṇa.

Daśarāja (S) (M) **1.** master of the 10 directions. **2.** master of the universe. **3.** the foster father of Śāntanu's wife Satyavatī (*M. Bh.*).

Daśaratha (S) (M) **1.** with 10 chariots. **3.** the Ikṣvāku king of Ayodhyā and the son of Aja and Indumatī or Ilabilā, husband of Kauśalyā, Kaikeyī and Sumitrā, and father of Śāntā, Rāma, Bharata, Lakṣmaṇa and Śatrughna (*V. Rāmāyaṇa*); a son of Navaratha (*Bhā. Purāṇa*); son of Suyaśas (*H. Purāṇa*).

Dāśarathi (S) (M) **1.** of Daśaratha. **3.** patronymic of Rāma and Lakṣmaṇa (*V. Rāmāyaṇa*); the 8th black Jaina Vasudeva (*J. S. Koṣa*).

Daṣardhabāṇa (S) (M) **1.** 5 arrowed. **3.** another name for Kāma.

Daśārha (S) (M) **1.** destroyer of 10, eliminator of 10. **2.** taking away 10 sins. **3.** a warrior tribe and its Yadu dynasty king (*Bhāgavata*); another name for Kṛṣṇa.

Dāśarhābhartā (S) (M) **1.** chief of the Dāśarhās. **3.** another name for Kṛṣṇa.

Daśarhādhipa (S) (M) **1.** lord of the Daśarha tribe. **3.** another name for Kṛṣṇa.

Daśarhakulavardhana (S) (M) **1.** increasing the Daśarha tribe. **3.** another name for Kṛṣṇa.

Daśarhanandana (S) (M) **1.** son of the Daśarha tribe. **3.** another name for Kṛṣṇa.

Daśarhanātha (S) (M) **1.** lord of the Daśarha tribe. **3.** another name for Kṛṣṇa.

Daśarhasiṁha (S) (M) **1.** lion of the Daśarha tribe. **3.** another name for Kṛṣṇa.

Daśarhavīra (S) (M) **1.** hero of the Daśarha tribe. **3.** another name for Kṛṣṇa.

Daśārṇa (S) (M) **1.** 10 lakes. **3.** a country and its king (*M. Bh.*).

Daśārṇeyu (S) (M) **1.** master of 10 lakes. **3.** a son of Raudrāśva (*H. Purāṇa*).

Daśarūpa (S) (M) **1.** the 10 forms. **3.** the 10 forms of Viṣṇu.

Daśaśarman (S) (M) protecting 10; with 10 joys.

Daśāśva (S) (M) **1.** with 10 horses. **3.** a son of Ikṣvāku (*M. Bh.*).

Daśāsva (S) (M) **1.** ten mouthed. **3.** another name for Rāvaṇa.

Daśāsyajit (S) (M) **1.** conqueror of Rāvaṇa. **3.** another name for Rāma.

Daśavājin (S) (M) **1.** with 10 horses. **3.** another name for the moon.

Daśavara (S) (M) **1.** with 10 faces. **3.** an asura attendant of Varuṇa (*M. Bh.*).

Dasmata (S) (M) desirable; acceptable.

Dasmaya (S) (M) beautiful.

Dasra (S) (M) **1.** accomplishing wonderful deeds; giving marvellous aid. **3.** one of the twins known as the Aśvinikumāras who were the divine physicians (*A. Veda*).

Dāśu (S) (M) worshipping; sacrificing.

Dāśūra (S) (M) holy; pious.

Dāśūrī (S) (M) devout; pious.

Dasyu (S) (M) **1.** outcast. **3.** a class of demons slain by Indra.

Datta (S) (M) **1.** given; granted. **2.** presented. **3.** a sage in the 2nd Manvantara (*H. Purāṇa*); the 7th Jaina Vasudeva (*H. Koṣa*); the 8th Tīrthaṅkara of the past Utsarpiṇī.

Dattātman (S) (M) **1.** given the soul. **2.** with total concentration of the mind; performing his duty sincerely. **3.** a viśvadeva (*M. Bh.*).

Dattādatta (S) (M) **1.** given and received; transaction. **2.** a businessman.

Dattāmitra (S) (M) **1.** given to a friend. **3.** the Sauvira prince Sumitra (*Bhā. Purāṇa*).

Dattātreya (S) (M) **1.** given by Atri. **3.** a famous Purāṇic hermit, and the son of Atri and Anasūyā, considered an incarnation of Mahāviṣṇu, his penance caused Brahmā, Viṣṇu and Śiva to partially incarnate themselves as his sons Soma, Datta and Durvāsas (*M. Bh./H. Purāṇa/V. Purāṇa*); another name for the 3 headed divinity of Viṣṇu, Śiva and Brahmā.

Dattoli (S) (M) **1.** given the heart. **2.** fully engrossed. **3.** a son of Pulastya and Prīti (*V. Purāṇa*).

Dattra (S) (M) Indra's gift.

Dattravat (S) (M) rich in gifts.

Dāva (S) (M) **1.** wild fire. **3.** another name for Agni.

Dāyāda (S) (M) to whom the transaction is made; son; inheritor.

Dayākara (S) (M) **1.** showing compassion. **2.** compassionate. **3.** another name for Śiva.

Dayākūrča (S) (M) **1.** store of compassion. **3.** another name for Buddha.

Dayāla (S) (M) compassionate; tender; merciful.

Dayānidhi (S) (M) treasure house of mercy.

Dayanīta (S) (M) compassionate conduct.

Dayārāma (S) (M) pervaded with mercy.

Dayāsāgara (S) (M) ocean of compassion.

Dayāśaṅkara (S) (M) Śiva the compassionate.

Dayāvīra (S) (M) heroically compassionate.

Dayita (S) (M) worthy of compassion; cherished; beloved; dear.

Dehabhṛt (S) (M) **1.** of the body; bearer of a body. **2.** corporeal. **3.** another name for Śiva.

Dehabhuj (S) (M) **1.** possessing a body. **3.** another name for Śiva.

Dehaja (S) (M) **1.** born of a body. **2.** child. **3.** another name for Kāma.

Deheśvara (S) (M) **1.** lord of the body. **2.** the soul.

Deśaka (S) (M) one who directs; ruler; guide; preceptor.

Deśākhya (S) (M) **1.** famous in land. **2.** internal. **3.** a rāga.

Deśarāj (S) (M) king of a country; produced in the right country; of genuine descent.

Deśarāja (S) (M) king of a country.

Deva (S) (M) **1.** light; divine; deity; playing divinely; a god. **3.** a class of gods which includes the maruts, apsarās, vidyādharas, tuśitas, gandharvas, nāgas, kinnaras, guhyakas, anilas, aśvins, rudras, ādityas, vasus, viśvadevas, etc. there are 33 crore, devas presided over by 33 presiding spirits with Indra as the chief (*Vedas/Purāṇas*); the 22nd Jaina Arhat of the future Utsarpiṇī (*J. S. Koṣa*); a title of honour; the Kadamba tree (*Anthocephalus cadamba*); *Momordica balsamina.*

Devabāhu (S) (M) **1.** the arm of the gods. **3.** a son of Hṛdika (*Bhāgavala*); a ṛṣi (*H. Purāṇa*).

Devabala (S) (M) with the strength of the gods.

Devabali (S) (M) oblation to the gods.

Devabandhu (S) (M) **1.** a friend of the gods. **2.** belonging to the gods. **3.** a Yayāti king (*Bhā. Purāṇa*); a son of Śūra and brother of Vasudeva (*Bhāgavata*); a ṛṣi who was the son of Śruta (*K. Sāgara*).

Devabhakta (S) (M) devotee of the gods.

Devabhāga (S) (M) **1.** a portion of the gods. **3.** a brother of Vasudeva (*Bh. Purāṇa*).

Devabhrāja (S) (M) **1.** luminous like a god. **3.** a son of Mahya and grandson of Vivasvata (*M. Bh.*).

Devabhrātā (S) (M) **1.** brother of the gods. **3.** an effulgent devata who was the son of Ravi and father of Subhrāta (*M. Bh.*).

Devabhūti (S) (M) **1.** an image of the gods. **3.** the last prince of the Śuṅga dynasty (*V. Purāṇa*).

Devabodha (S) (M) with divine knowledge.

Devabodhi (S) (M) inspired by god.

Devaćandra (S) (M) moon among the gods.

Devaććanda (S) (M) divine necklace; a bright necklace; a necklace of pearls.

Devaćitta (S) (M) the will of the gods.

Devadarśa (S) (M) **1.** preceptor of the divine. **2.** preceptor of heaven; observer of the gods. **3.** a teacher in the line of Vyāsa who was the disciple of Kabandha (*M. Bh.*).

Devadarśana (S) (M) **1.** familiar with the gods. **3.** another name for sage Nārada.

Devadāsa (S) (M) slave of the gods.

Devadatta (S) (M) **1.** god given. **3.** one of the 5 vital airs; a cousin of Gautama Buddha (*B. Literature*); a son of Uruśravas and father of Agniveśya (*Bh. Purāṇa*); a son of King Jayadatta (*K. Sāgara*); a son of Haridatta (*K. Sāgara*); the father of Utathya (*M. Bh.*); the conchshell of Arjuna (*M. Bh.*); a nāga (*Bhāgavata*).

Devadeva (S) (M) **1.** lord of the gods. **3.** another name for Kṛṣṇa.

Devadeveśvara (S) (M) **1.** lord of the gods. **3.** another name for Kṛṣṇa.

Devadharman (S) (M) performing heavenly deeds.

Devādhipa (S) (M) **1.** lord of the gods. **2.** a king identified with the asura Nikumbha (*M. Bh.*); another name for Indra.

Devādhipati (S) (M) **1.** lord of the gods. **3.** another name for Śiva.

Devadīpa (S) (M) lamp of the gods; the eye.

Devadundubhi (S) (M) **1.** drum of the gods. **3.** the sacred basil with red flowers (*Ocimum sanctum*); another name for Indra.

Devadūta (S) (M) messenger of the gods.

Devadyumna (S) (M) **1.** glory of the gods. **3.** a king of the Bharata dynasty who was the son of Devatajita and the father of Parameṣṭhin (*Bhā. Purāṇa*).

Devadyuti (S) (M) **1.** with heavenly lustre. **3.** a ṛṣi (*P. Purāṇa*).

Devagaṇeśvara (S) (M) **1.** lord of the divine people. **2.** lord of the gaṇas. **3.** another name for Indra.

Devagarbha (S) (M) **1.** the womb of the gods. **2.** divine child. **3.** a ṛṣi (*P. Purāṇa*).

Devagāyana (S) (M) a divine song; celestial songster; a gandharva.

Devaghoṣa (S) (M) voice of the gods; village of the gods; the abode of godly virtues.

Devagopa (S) (M) shepherd of the gods; guarded by the gods.

Devaguhya (S) (M) **1.** hidden by the gods. **3.** father of Sārvabhauma (*Bhāgavata*).

Devagupta (S) (M) guarded by the gods.

Devaguru (S) (M) **1.** preceptor of the gods. **2.** father of the gods. **3.** another name for Kaśyapa and Bṛhaspati.

Devahans (S) (M) **1.** divine duct. **3.** the White-winged Wood Duck (*Cairina scutulata*).

Devahavis (S) (M) oblation to the gods.

Devahavya (S) (M) **1.** sacrificing to the gods. **3.** a sage who is a member of Indra's assembly (*M. Bh.*).

Devahotra (S) (M) **1.** making oblations to the gods. **3.** a mahaṛṣi who was the father of Yogeśvara and considered a partial incarnation of Viṣṇu (*H. Purāṇa*).

Devahṛada (S) (M) divine heart; divine pool.

Devahū (S) (M) invoking the gods.

Devaja (S) (M) **1.** born of the gods. **3.** a son of Saṅyama (*Ṛg Veda*).

Devajapa (S) (M) **1.** meditating on the gods. **3.** a vidyādhara (*K. Sāgara*).

Devajuṣṭa (S) (M) agreeable to the gods.

Devajūta (S) (M) attached to the gods; inspired by the gods.

Devajūti (S) (M) **1.** attached to the gods. **3.** an āditya (*T. Samhitā*).

Devaka (S) (M) **2.** heavenly; godly; celestial. **3.** a Yayāti king who was the son of Ugrasena's brother Āhuka and the father of Kṛṣṇa's mother Devakī (*M. Bh.*); a king whose daughter married Vidura (*M. Bh.*); a son of Yudhiṣṭhira and Pauravī (*M. Bh.*); a son of Akrūra (*Bha. Purāṇa*).

Devakalaśa (S) (M) receptacle of the gods.

Devakalpa (S) (M) god like.

Devakāma (S) (M) striving for divinity; loving the gods; pious.

Devakānta (S) (M) beloved of the gods.

Devakīnandana (S) (M) **1.** son of Devakī. **3.** another name for Kṛṣṇa.

Devakīputra (S) (M) **1.** son of Devakī. **3.** another name for Kṛṣṇa.

Devakīrti (S) (M) with heavenly fame.

Devakīsūnu (S) (M) **1.** son of Devakī. **3.** another name for Kṛṣṇa.

Devakoṣa (S) (M) receptacle of the gods.

Devakṣatra (S) (M) **1.** domain of the gods. **3.** a Yayāti king who was the son of Devarāta (*H. Purāṇa*).

Devakṣema (S) (M) assistant of the gods.

Devakumāra (S) (M) son of a deva.

Devala (S) (M) **1.** attached to the gods. **2.** an attendant to an idol. **3.** a descendant of Kaśyapa and an author of *Ṛg Veda* (ix); a son of Muni Asita and the husband of Ekaparṇā (*M. Bh.*); a ṛṣi who was the son of Pratyūṣa (*H. Purāṇa*); an elder brother of ṛṣi Dhaumya and the father of Suvarćalā who married Śvetaketu (*M. Bh.*); the father of Sannatī (*H. Purāṇa*); a son of Viśvāmitra (*H. Purāṇa*); a son of Kṛṣtāśva and Dhīṣaṇā (*Bhāgavata*).

Devamadana (S) (M) gladdening or inspiring the gods.

Devamadhu (S) (M) divine honey; nectar.

Devamāṇaka (S) (M) **1.** jewel of the gods. **3.** the jewel on Viṣṇu's breast (*A. Koṣa*).

Devamaṇi (S) (M) **1.** jewel among the gods. **3.** another name for Śiva.

Devamañjara (S) (M) **1.** divine jewel. **3.** the jewel on Viṣṇu's breast (*A. Koṣa*).

Devamata (S) (M) **1.** approved by the gods. **3.** a ṛṣi (*M. Bh*).

Devamaya (S) (M) consisting of the gods; the abode of all virtues.

Devamidha (S) (M) **1.** god begotten. **3.** the grandfather of Vasudeva (*M. Bh.*); a descendant of Nimi and Janaka (*Rāmāyaṇa*).

Devamīdhusa (S) (M). **1.** bestowed by the gods; divinely liberal. **3.** son of Śūra.

Devamiśra (S) (M) a godly mixture; connected with the gods.

Devamitra (S) (M) **1.** a friend of the gods. **3.** the father of Viṣṇumitra (*M. Bh.*).

Devamuni (S) (M) **1.** divine sage. **3.** a son of Iraṇmadā and the part author of *Ṛg Veda* (x).

Devanābha (S) (M) celestial navel; the origin of celestial beings; the supreme god.

Devanaman (S) (M) bowing before the gods.

Devānanda (S) (M) joy of the gods.

Devanandin (S) (M) **1.** amusing the gods. **3.** Indra's doorkeeper (*A. Koṣa*).

Devanātha (S) (M) **1.** lord of the gods. **3.** another name for Śiva.

Devanāyaka (S) (M) leader of the gods.

Devānīka (S) (M) **1.** an army of gods. **3.** a king belonging to the solar dynasty of Rāma, who was the son of Kṣhemadhanvan and the father of Ṛkṣa (*Rāmāyaṇa*); the son of the 11th Manu (*H. Purāṇa*).

Devanirmita (S) (M) **1.** made by god. **2.** perfect; god's creation.

Devānna (S) (M) food offered to the gods; sacred; auspicious.

Devāṅśa (S) (M) a partial incarnation of the gods.

Devanta (S) (M) **1.** killer of the gods. **3.** a son of Hṛdika (*Bhā. Purāṇa*).

Devāntaka (S) (M) **1.** killer of the gods. **3.** a rākṣasa who was the son of Rudraketu and was slain by Gaṇapati (*P. Purāṇa*).

Devajanman (S) (M) **1.** born of the gods. **2.** the child of the gods. **3.** another name for Yudhiṣṭhira (*M. Bh.*).

Devānućara (S) (M) follower of the gods.

Devapāda (S) (M) the feet of the god.

Devapāla (S) (M) **1.** defender of the gods. **3.** a mountain (*Bh. Purāṇa*).

Devapālita (S) (M) protected by the gods.

Devapaṇḍita (S) (M) scholar of heavenly rites; a divine scholar.

Devapāṇi (S) (M) **1.** god handed; hand of the gods. **2.** assisting the gods; helpful to the gods. **3.** a class of asuras (*M. Smṛti*).

Devapatha (S) (M) **1.** the path of the gods. **3.** another name for the Milky Way or the Ākāśa Gaṅgā.

Devāpi (S) (M) **1.** friend of the gods. **3.** a lunar dynasty king who became a sage, was the son of King Pratīpa and is supposed to be still alive (*M. Bh.*); a Ćedi warrior on the side of the Pāṇḍavas (*M. Bh.*).

Devaprabha (S) (M) **1.** with divine splendour. **3.** a gandharvī (*K. Sāgara*).

Devaprasāda (S) (M) given by the gods.

Devapratha (S) (M) **1.** custom of the gods. **2.** follower of the customs of the gods; virtuous; meritorious; venerated. **3.** a Yayāti dynasty king (*Bhāgavata*).

Devapriya (S) (M) **1.** dear to the gods. **3.** another name for Śiva; and for Kārttikeya as the consort of Devasena; *Wedelia calendulacea.*

Devapūjita (S) (M) **1.** worshipped by the gods. **3.** another name for Kṛṣṇa and Bṛhaspati.

Devapūjya (S) (M) **1.** honoured by the gods. **3.** another name for Bṛhaspati the preceptor of the gods and the planet Jupiter.

Devapuṣpa (S) (M) flower of the gods.

Devarāja (S) (M) **1.** king of the gods. **3.** a king in the assembly of Yama (*M. Bh.*); a Buddha; another name for Indra.

Devarāma (S) (M) **1.** absorbed in divine deeds. **2.** meritorious; virtuous; venerated.

Devāraṇya (S) (M) the garden of the gods.

Devarāta (S) (M) **1.** delighting in the gods; attached to the gods. **2.** pious;

religious; god given. 3. a Mithilā king Śunahśepa after coming into the family of Viśvāmitra (*A. Brāhmaṇa*); a king who was the son of Suketu and descendant of Nimi (*Rāmāyaṇa*); the son of Karambhi (*Purāṇas*); the father of Yājñavalkya (*Bhā. Purāṇa*).

Devaratha (S) (M) vehicle of the gods.

Devārćaka (S) (M) devotee of the gods.

Devārha (S) (M) worthy of the gods.

Devarṣabha (S) (M) 1. a bull among the gods. 2. a powerful god. 3. a son of Dharma and Bhānu (*Bhā. Purāṇa*).

Devārpaṇa (S) (M) offering to the gods.

Devarṣi (S) (M) 1. a ṛṣi among the gods. 3. another name for Nārada.

Devarya (S) (M) 1. divine belief. 3. the last Jaina Arhat of the present Avasarpinī.

Devasakha (S) (M) friend of the gods.

Devaśakti (S) (M) with divine strength.

Devasarasa (S) (M) pool of the gods.

Devaśarman (S) (M) 1. with the gods as refuge. 3. a minister of King Jayapīḍa of Kāśmira (*R. Taraṅgiṇī*); a muni who was the husband of Rući and father of Vipula (*M. Bh.*); an Arhat (*J. S. Koṣa*).

Devasattva (S) (M) with a godly nature.

Devasāvarṇi (S) (M) 1. god like. 3. the 13th Manu (*Bhā. Purāṇa*).

Devaśekhara (S) (M) 1. divine diadem. 3. *Artemisia sieversiana*.

Devasena (S) (M) 1. with an army of gods. 3. a king of Śrāvastī (*K. Sāgara*); the husband of Kīrtisenā (*M. Bh.*); a Buddhist Arhat; another name for Skanda.

Devasiddhi (S) (M) a divine achievement; as perfect as the gods.

Devaśilpa (S) (M) a divine work of art.

Devaśilpin (S) (M) 1. divine artist. 3. another name for Tvaṣṭṛ.

Devasinha (S) (M) 1. god-lion. 3. another name for Śiva.

Devāśīśa (S) (M) blessing of the gods.

Devāśiṣṭa (S) (M) 1. taught by the gods; follows the ways of gods. 2. pious; divine.

Devaśiśu (S) (M) divine child.

Devasoma (S) (M) the drink of the gods.

Devaśravas (S) (M) 1. with divine reknown. 3. a son of Yama (*Ṛg Veda*); a son of Viśvāmitra (*M. Bh.*); a Yayāti king who was the son of Śūra and brother of Vasudeva (*Bhāgavata*).

Devaśreṣṭha (S) (M) 1. best among the gods. 3. a son of the 12th Manu (*H. Purāṇa*).

Devaśrīgarbha (S) (M) 1. creator of the gods and glory. 3. a bodhisattva (*B. Ćarita*).

Devaśrū (S) (M) known to the gods.

Devaśruta (S) (M) 1. with divine knowledge. 3. the 6th Jaina Arhat of the future Utasarpinī (*J. S. Koṣa*); another name for Nārada.

Devasthali (S) (M) the abode of the gods; the temple of the gods.

Devasthāna (S) (M) 1. the abode of the gods. 3. a ṛṣi who was a friend of the Pāṇḍavas (*M. Bh.*).

Devaśūra (S) (M) divine hero.

Devaśūri (S) (M) connected with the gods and demons.

Devāśva (S) (M) 1. divine horse. 3. another name for Uccaiśravas.

Devasvāmin (S) (M) 1. lord of the gods. 3. a Brahmin (*K. Sāgara*).

Devatājita (S) (M) 1. conquering the god. 3. a son of Sumati and grandson of Bharata (*M. Bh.*).

Devatāras (S) (M) released by the gods; godlike.

Devatarū (S) (M) 1. tree of the gods. 3. the 5 sacred trees of paradise (*Bhā. Purāṇa*).

Devatātman (S) (M) 1. with a divine soul. 3. another name for Śiva; *Ficus religiosa*.

Devātideva (S) (M) 1. surpassing all the gods. 3. another name for Śiva, Viṣṇu and Śākyamuni.

Devātithi (S) (M) 1. guest of the gods. 3. a ṛṣi and part author of *Ṛg Veda* (viii); a Purū king who was the son of Akrodhana and Karambhā and the husband of Maryādā (*M. Bh.*).

Devātman (S) (M) **1.** divine soul. **3.** the Bodhi tree (*Ficus religiosa*).

Devavadha (S) (M) weapon of the gods.

Devavāha (S) (M) **1.** with a divine chariot. **3.** a Yayāti king (*Bhāgavata*).

Devavaktra (S) (M) **1.** the mouth of the gods. **3.** another name for Agni, the lord of fire considered to receive oblations on behalf of the gods.

Devavallabha (S) (M) **1.** beloved of the gods. **3.** the tree *Ochrocarpus longifolius*.

Devavardhakī (S) (M) **1.** divine architect. **3.** another name for Viśvakarman.

Devavardhana (S) (M) **1.** supported by the gods. **3.** a son of Devaka (*V. Purāṇa*).

Devavarman (S) (M) **1.** with the armour of the gods. **2.** extremely powerful; protected by the gods.

Devavarṣa (S) (M) divine year.

Devavarya (S) (M) **1.** best of the gods. **3.** another name for Śiva.

Devavata (S) (M) **1.** surrounded by the gods. **2.** guarded by the gods. **3.** another name for Akrūra (*V. Purāṇa*); the 12th Manu (*H. Purāṇa*).

Devavāyu (S) (M) **1.** heavenly wind. **2.** life giving; swift. **3.** the 12th Manu (*H. Purāṇa*).

Devaveśman (S) (M) home of the gods; a temple.

Devavī (S) (M) **1.** gratifying the gods. **2.** a priest; devotee; a worshipper of the gods.

Devavid (S) (M) knowing the gods.

Devavrata (S) (M) **1.** the favourite food of the gods; a religious vow. **2.** follower of the religious path. **3.** a Brāhmin born as a bamboo from which Kṛṣṇa made his flute (*P. Purāṇa*); another name for Bhīṣma and Skanda.

Devāvṛdha (S) (M) **1.** as old as the gods. **3.** the father of Babhru (*M. Bh./H.Purāṇa*); a warrior on the side of the Kauravas (*M. Bh.*).

Devayaji (S) (M) **1.** worshipper of the gods. **3.** a warrior of Skanda (*M. Bh.*).

Devayājin (S) (M) **1.** sacrificing to the gods. **2.** one invested with god like qualities. **3.** a dānava (*H. Purāṇa*); an attendant of Skanda (*M. Bh.*).

Devayāna (S) (M) leading to the gods; the vehicle of a god.

Devayaśas (S) (M) divine glory.

Devāyudha (S) (M) **1.** weapon of the gods. **3.** another name for Indra.

Devāyukta (S) (M) attached to the gods; yoked by the gods; a devotee; a worshipper of the gods.

Devejya (S) (M) **1.** teacher of the gods. **3.** another name for Bṛhaspati.

Devendra (S) (M) **1.** chief of the gods. **3.** another name for Indra.

Deveśita (S) (M) sent by the gods.

Deveṣṭha (S) (M) **1.** best among the gods. **3.** the tree *Commiphora mukul*.

Deveśu (S) (M) divine arrow.

Deveśvara (S) (M) **1.** lord of the gods. **3.** a pupil of Śaṅkarāćārya; another name for Śiva.

Devīdāsa (S) (M) slave of the goddess.

Devīdatta (S) (M) given by the goddess.

Devila (S) (M) **1.** attached to the gods. **2.** righteous; pious; venerated.

Devin (S) (M) resembling a god.

Deviprasāda (S) (M) gift of the goddess.

Devīśa (S) (M) **1.** chief of the gods. **2.** another name for Brahmā, Viṣṇu, Śiva and Indra.

Devya (S) (M) divine power.

Dhāma (S) (M) **1.** ray; strength; splendour; majesty. **2.** light; house; place of pilgrimage. **3.** a ṛṣi who protected Gaṅgā Mahādvāra (*M. Bh.*).

Dhāmādhipa (S) (M) **1.** lord of rays. **3.** another name for Sūrya.

Dhāmakeśin (S) (M) **1.** ray haired. **3.** another name for Sūrya.

Dhāman (S) (M) **1.** ray; light; abode. **2.** majesty; glory; splendour; strength; house. **3.** a ṛṣi of the 4th Manvantara (*H. Purāṇa*).

Dhāmanidhi (S) (M) **1.** treasure of splendour. **3.** another name for Sūrya.

Dhāmavat (S) (M) owner of a house; powerful; strong.

Dhanada (S) (M) 1. wealth bestowing. 3. another name for Kubera.

Dhanadeśvara (S) (M) 1. wealth giving lord. 3. another name for Kubera.

Dhanādhipa (S) (M) 1. lord of wealth. 3. another name for Kubera.

Dhanādhipati (S) (M) 1. wealth giving lord. 3. another name for Kubera.

Dhanādhyakṣa (S) (M) 1. lord of wealth. 3. another name for Kubera.

Dhanagopta (S) (M) 1. guarding treasure. 3. another name for Kubera.

Dhanajita (S) (M) wealth; winner.

Dhanaka (S) (M) 1. avarice. 3. a son of Durmada.

Dhanaṅjaya (S) (M) 1. fire. 2. *Plumbago zeylanica*; *Terminalia arjuna*. 3. a nāga (*M. Bh.*); a king of Kaliṅga; another name for Arjuna and Agni.

Dhanañjaya (S) (M). 1. conqueror of wealth. 2. victorious. 3. a king of Kaliṅga (*Kathārṇava*); a nāga who was the son of Kaśyapa and Kadru and a member of Varuṇa's court (*M. Bh.*); the army given to Skanda by Śiva (*M. Bh.*); a Sanskṛt critic in the court of King Muñja (11th century); a Brāhmin devotee of Viṣṇu (*P. Purāṇa*); another name for Arjuna and Kuṇḍalini.

Dhanaṅjayasuta (S) (M) 1. son of Arjuna. 3. another name for Babhruvāhana.

Dhanapāla (S) (M) guardian of wealth; king.

Dhanapati (S) (M) 1. lord of wealth. 3. another name for Kubera.

Dhanavanta (S) (M) possessing wealth.

Dhanavardhana (S) (M) increasing wealth.

Dhanavat (S) (M) 1. containing wealth. 2. the sea.

Dhanāyuṣ (S) (M) 1. with a rich life. 3. a son of Purūravas (*M. Bh.*).

Dhaneśa (S) (M) 1. lord of wealth. 3. another name for Kubera.

Dhaneśvara (S) (M) 1. lord of wealth. 3. another name for Kubera.

Dhanin (S) (M) 1. wealthy. 3. a messenger of the asuras (*M. Bh.*); another name for Kubera.

Dhanīrāma (S) (M) 1. with Rāma as one's wealth. 2. one who is deeply religious.

Dhanu (S) (M) 1. bow. 3. the zodiac sign of Sagittarius.

Dhanurgraha (S) (M) 1. holding a bow. 3. a son of Dhṛtarāṣṭra (*M. Bh.*).

Dhanurāja (S) (M) 1. king of archers. 3. an ancestor of Śākyamuni (*M. Bh.*).

Dhanurdhara (S) (M) 1. bearer of a bow. 3. the zodiac sign of Sagittarius; a son of Dhṛtarāṣṭra (*M. Bh.*); another name for Śiva.

Dhanurvaktra (S) (M) 1. bow mouthed. 3. an attendant of Skanda (*M. Bh.*).

Dhanurvedin (S) (M) 1. knower of the bow. 2. well versed in archery. 3. another name for Śiva.

Dhanuṣa (S) (M) 1. bow. 3. a ṛṣi (*M. Bh.*).

Dhanuṣākṣa (S) (M) 1. bow eyed. 3. a sage (*M. Bh.*).

Dhanva (S) (M) 1. with a bow. 3. a king of Kāśi who was the father of Dhanvantari (*M. Bh.*).

Dhanvantari (S) (M) 1. moving in a curve. 3. the physician of the gods; founder of Āyurveda produced at the churning of the ocean, later incarnated as King Divodāsa of Benaras.

Dhanvin (S) (M) 1. armed with a bow. 3. a son of Manu Tāmasa (*H. Purāṇa*); another name for Śiva, Arjuna and Viṣṇu.

Dhanyarāja (S) (M) 1. king of grain. 3. Barley (*Hordeum vulgare*).

Dhara (S) (M) 1. bearing; supporting. 3. the king of the tortoises (*A. Koṣa*); the father of Padmapāṇi (*H. Koṣa*); a vasu son of Dharma and Dhūmrā (*M. Bh.*); a king who was a friend of Yudhiṣṭhira (*M. Bh.*).

Dharābhuja (S) (M) earth enjoyer; a king.

Dhāraṇa (S) (M) **1.** bearing. **2.** holding; keeping; resembling. **3.** a king in the family of Ćandravatsa (*M. Bh.*); a serpent son of Kaśyapa (*M. Bh.*); another name for Śiva.

Dharanīdhara (S) (M) **1.** supporting the earth. **2.** tortoise; a king. **3.** one of the 10 elephants that support the earth (*M. Bh.*); the father of Śaśidhara (*R. Taraṅgiṇī*); a Bodhisattva (*B. Ćarita*); the father of Vāsudeva (*Bhagavata*); another name for Viṣṇu, Kṛṣṇa and Śeṣa.

Dharaṇija (S) (M) born of the earth.

Dharāpati (S) (M) **1.** lord of the earth. **3.** another name for Viṣṇu.

Dharbaka (S) (M) **1.** superficial. **3.** a son of Ajātaśatru (*V. Purāṇa*).

Dharendra (S) (M) **1.** king of the earth. **3.** another name for the Himalayas.

Dharma (S) (M) **1.** path of life; religion. **2.** established; law; justice; practice; duty; observance; right. **3.** justice personified as born from the right breast of Yama (*M. Bh.*); the father of Sāma, Kāma, Harṣa, Yudhiṣṭhira and Vidura (*M. Bh.*); as a prajāpati, the husband of 13 daughters of Dakṣa apart from 10 other wives each of whom originated a family of ṛṣis, and the father of, among others Hari, Kṛṣṇa and Nārāyaṇa — the last being an incarnation of Mahaviṣṇu (*H. Purāṇa*); the 15th arhat of the present Avasarpiṇī (*J. S. Koṣa*); a son of Aṇu and father of Ghṛtas (*H. Purāṇa*); a son of Gandhara and father of Dhrita (*V. Purāṇa*); a son of Hehaya and father of Netra (*Bhāgavata*); a son of Pṛthuśravas.

Dharmabhṛt (S) (M) **1.** bearer of religion, supports and practises religion; virtuous. **3.** a ṛṣi (*V. Rāmāyaṇa*).

Dharmaćandra (S) (M) **1.** moon of Dharma. **2.** deeply religious; virtuous; venerated.

Dharmaćara (S) (M) observer of Dharma.

Dharmaćārin (S) (M) **1.** observing Dharma. **2.** virtuous; moral. **3.** the deity in the Bodhi tree (*Ficus religiosa*); another name for Śiva.

Dharmada (S) (M) **1.** bestower of Dharma. **3.** a follower of Skanda (*M. Bh.*).

Dharmadatta (S) (M) **1.** given by Dharma. **3.** the previous incarnation of King Daśaratha as a Brāhmin of Karavīra (*Sk. Purāṇa*).

Dharmadeva (S) (M) god of justice.

Dharmadhara (S) (M) **1.** supporter of Dharma. **3.** a bodhisattva (*B. Literature*).

Dharmadhātu (S) (M) **1.** made of the different metals of law. **3.** a Buddhist deity.

Dharmadhṛt (S) (M) **1.** one who makes Dharma realized; carrier of Dharma. **2.** a judge; a preacher. **3.** a son of Śvaphalka (*H. Purāṇa*).

Dharmadhvaja (S) (M) **1.** Dharma bannered. **2.** extremely virtuous; religious; venerated. **3.** a king of Mithilā who was the son of Kuśadhvaja (*V. Purāṇa*); another name for the sun.

Dharmāditya (S) (M) **1.** sun of Dharma. **2.** extremely virtuous; religious; venerated. **3.** a Buddhist king.

Dharmaghoṣa (S) (M) the voice of Dharma.

Dharmagopa (S) (M) protector of Dharma.

Dharmaja (S) (M) **1.** son of Dharma. **3.** another name for Yudhiṣṭhira.

Dharmākara (S) (M) **1.** mine of Dharma. **3.** the 99th Buddha.

Dharmakāya (S) (M) **1.** law body. **3.** a god of the Bodhi tree; a Buddhist or Jaina Saint.

Dharmaketu (S) (M) **1.** justice bannered. **3.** a Bhārgava king who was the son of Suketu and father of Satyaketu (*H. Purāṇa*); a Buddha (*L. Vistara*); a Jaina saint (*J. S. Koṣa*).

Dharmamatī (S) (M) **1.** with a religious mind. **3.** a god of the Bodhi tree (*Ficus religiosa*) (*L. Vistara*).

Dharmamitra (S) (M) a friend of Dharma.

Dharmāmṛta (S) (M) nectar of Dharma.

Dharman (S) (M) **1.** bearer of Dharma, supporter of Dharma. **3.** a son of Bṛhadraja and father of Kṛtañjaya (*V. Purāṇa*).

Dharmanābha (S) (M) **1.** the centre of Dharma. **3.** another name for Viṣṇu.

Dharmanandana (S) (M) **1.** son of Dharma. **3.** a Bhārgava king (*Bhāgavata*); another name for Yudhiṣṭhira.

Dharmanātha (S) (M) lord of Dharma.

Dharmandhū (S) (M) **1.** well of Dharma. **2.** deeply religious; venerated.

Dharmanetra (S) (M) **1.** Dharma eyed. **3.** a son of Tanṣu and father of Duṣamanta (*H. Purāṇa*); a son of Suvrata (*Bhāgavata*); a son of Dhṛtarāṣṭra (*M. Bh.*); a Hehaya king who was the son of Hehaya and the father of Kṛti (*Br. Purāṇa*); a son of Suvrata (*Bh. Purāṇa*).

Dharmāṅga (S) (M) **1.** whose body is Dharma; receptacle of Dharma. **3.** another name for Viṣṇu.

Dharmāṅgada (S) (M) **1.** ornamented by Dharma. **3.** a king who was the son of Priyaṅkara (*Purāṇas*).

Dharmanitya (S) (M) constant in Dharma.

Dharmapāla (S) (M) **1.** guardian of Dharma. **3.** a minister of King Daśaratha (*A. Purāṇa*).

Dharmaprabhāsa (S) (M) light of Dharma; extremely virtuous; religious; venerated.

Dharmaprabhava (S) (M) **1.** speaking the truth. **3.** another name for Yudhiṣṭhira.

Dharmaprakāśa (S) (M) light of Dharma.

Dharmapriya (S) (M) **1.** loving Dharma. **3.** a gandharva prince (*K. Vyuha*).

Dharmaputra (S) (M) **1.** son of Dharma. **3.** son of the 11th Manu; another name for Yudhiṣṭhira who was the son of Dharma and Kuntī.

Dharmarāja (S) (M) **1.** lord of Dharma. **3.** a Buddha; a king of Gauḍadeśa who revived the Vedic rites (*Bh. Purāṇa*); a king of herons; another name for Yama and Yudhiṣṭhira.

Dharmarājan (S) (M) **1.** Dharma, the king. **2.** a virtuous king. **3.** another name for Yudhiṣṭhira.

Dharmāraṇya (S) (M) **1.** grove of Dharma. **3.** a Brāhmin devotee of the sun (*M. Bh.*).

Dharmaratha (S) (M) **1.** the chariot of Dharma. **3.** an Aṅga king who was the great-grandfather of Lomapāda and the son of Diviratha (*A. Purāṇa*); a son of Sagara.

Dharmasakhā (S) (M) **1.** friend of Dharma. **3.** a Kekaya king (*Sk. Purāṇa*).

Dharmasārathi (S) (M) **1.** charioteer of Dharma. **3.** a son of Tṛkakuda (*Bhāgavata*).

Dharmasāvarṇi (S) (M) **1.** resembling Dharma. **3.** the 11th Manu (*V. Purāṇa*).

Dharmasetu (S) (M) **1.** barrier of Dharma. **3.** a son of Āryaka (*Bhāgavata*).

Dharmaśila (S) (M) follower of Dharma.

Dharmasindhu (S) (M) ocean of Dharma.

Dharmasiṁha (S) (M) lion of Dharma; one who guards; protects and practices Dharma deeply.

Dharmāśoka (S) (M) **1.** Aśoka the dutiful. **3.** another name for Emperor Aśoka.

Dharmasthavira (S) (M) stable in Dharma; one who practises his dharma firmly.

Dharmasuta (S) (M) **1.** son of Dharmā. **3.** another name for Yudhiṣṭhira.

Dharmavāhana (S) (M) **1.** vehicle of Dharma. **3.** another name for Śiva.

Dharmavardhana (S) (M) **1.** increasing Dharma. **3.** another name for Śiva.

Dharmavarman (S) (M) **1.** warrior for Dharma; shield of justice. **3.** another name for Kṛṣṇa.

Dharmavarṇa (S) (M) **1.** colour of Dharma. **2.** clad in Dharma; extremely virtuous; religious.

Dharmavatī (S) (M) **1.** possessing Dharma. **3.** a wife of Dharmadeva and the mother of Dharmavratā who married Marīći (*K. Sāgara*).

Dharmavīra (S) (M) hero of Dharma; a champion of Dharma; one who fights for religious causes.

Dharmavivardhana (S) (M) **1.** promoter of Dharma. **3.** a son of Aśoka.

Dharmayaśas (S) (M) glory of Dharma.

Dharmayoni (S) (M) **1.** the source of Dharma. **3.** another name for Viṣṇu.

Dharmayu (S) (M) **1.** one who lives for Dharma. **3.** a Purū king who was the son of Raudrāśva and Miśrakeśi (*M. Bh.*).

Dharmayūpa (S) (M) a pillar of Dharma.

Dharmendra (S) (M) **1.** lord of Dharma. **3.** another name for Yama and Yudhiṣṭhira.

Dharmeśa (S) (M) **1.** lord of Dharma. **3.** another name for Yama.

Dharmeśvara (S) (M) god of Dharma.

Dharmiṣṭha (S) (M) staying in Dharma; very virtuous and righteous.

Dharmottara (S) (M) entirely devoted to Dharma.

Dharśanātman (S) (M) **1.** with a violent nature. **3.** another name for Śiva.

Dhārtarāṣṭra (S) (M) **1.** son of Dhṛtarāṣṭra. **3.** another name for Duryodhana.

Dharuṇa (S) (M) **1.** bearing; supporting; holding. **3.** another name for Brahmā.

Dhātā (S) (M) **1.** establisher. **2.** creator; founder; supporter. **3.** one of the 12 ādityas (*M. Bh.*); a son of Bhṛgu and Khyāti and the husband of Āyati (*V. Purāṇa*); another name for Brahmā.

Dhātaki (S) (M) **1.** resembling the creator. **3.** a son of Vītihotra (*M. Bh.*).

Dhātṛ (S) (M) **1.** establisher. **2.** creator; founder; supporter. **3.** a divine being who per-sonifies these functions and was later identified with Brahmā or Prajāpati (*M. Bh.*); one of the 12 ādityas and brother of Vidhatṛ (*M. Bh.*); a son of Brahmā (*M. Bh.*); a son of Bhṛgu and Khyāti (*V. Purāṇa*); fate in a per-sonified form (*K. Prakāśa*); one of the 49 winds (*Vah. Purāṇa*); a ṛṣi in the 4th Manvantara (*H. Purāṇa*).

Dhātṛputra (S) (M) **1.** Dhatṛ's son. **3.** Sanatkumāra, the son of the creator or Brahmā.

Dhaumra (S) (M) **1.** grey; smoke; spring; well; a rivulet. **3.** an ancient ṛṣi (*M. Bh.*).

Dhaumya (S) (M) **1.** smoky; grey. **3.** a ṛṣi who was the brother of Upamanyu (*M. Bh.*); a son of Vyāghrapāda (*M. Bh.*); a brother of Devala and family priest of the Pāṇḍavas (*M. Bh.*); a pupil of Vālmīki (*V. Rāmāyaṇa*).

Dhāvak (S) (M) **1.** runner. **2.** quick; swift; flowing. **3.** a poet who composed Ratnāvali for King Śrīharṣa.

Dhavala (S) (M) **1.** dazzling white. **2.** handsome; beautiful. **3.** rāga; one of the elephants of the quarters (*V. Rāmāyaṇa*).

Dhavalaćandra (S) (M) white moon.

Dhavalapakṣa (S) (M) **1.** white winged. **2.** the light half of the mouth.

Dhāvita (S) (M) whitish; washed; purified; clean.

Dhenuka (S) (M) **1.** calf. **2.** a coital posture mentioned in the *Kāmasūtra*. **3.** an asura slain by Balarāma (*Bhāgavata*); a son of Durdama (*V. Purāṇa*).

Dhenukārī (S) (M) **1.** enemy of Dhenuka. **3.** another name for Balarāma.

Dhīmān (S) (M) **1.** possessed with wisdom; wise. **3.** a son of Purūravas (*M. Bh.*).

Dhīmant (S) (M) **1.** possessed with wisdom. **2.** one who is wise; intelligent; learned. **3.** another name for Bṛhaspati.

Dhīmat (S) (M) **1.** possessed with wisdom. **2.** one who is intelligent; wise; learned; sensible. **3.** a son of Virāj (*V. Purāṇa*); a ṛṣi of the 4th Manvantara (*V. Purāṇa*); a son of

Purūravas (*M. Bh.*); another name for Bṛhaspati; a bodhisattva.

Dhīra (S) (M) **1.** patient; tolerant; intelligent; wise; skilful. **3.** a saffron (*Crocus sativus*); South Indian Redwood (*Dalbergia sissoo*); *Luvunya scandens*; *Tinospora cordifolia.*

Dhīradhi (S) (M) **1.** a mine of tolerance. **3.** a Brāhmin devotee of Śiva (*P. Purāṇa*).

Dhīraja (S) (M) **1.** treasure of tolerance; born of tolerance; creator of tolerance. **3.** an attendant of Śiva (*A. Koṣa*).

Dhiraṇa (S) (M) delighting in devotion.

Dhīrćetas (S) (M) a patient mind; one who is strongminded; courageous.

Dhīreśa (S) (M) lord of tolerance.

Dhīrosnin (S) (M) **1.** fiery and brave. **3.** a viśvadeva (*M. Bh.*).

Dhiṣaṇa (S) (M) **1.** wise. **3.** another name for Bṛhaspati.

Dhītika (S) (M) **1.** thoughtful; wise. **3.** a Buddhist patriarchal saint (*L. Vistara*).

Dhīyāmpati (S) (M) **1.** lord of the thoughts. **2.** the soul. **3.** another name for Manjughoṣa.

Dhṛṣaj (S) (M) bold; a hero.

Dhṛṣamān (S) (M) **1.** confident; bold. **3.** a king of the Bharata dynasty.

Dhṛṣita (S) (M) bold; brave; daring.

Dhṛṣṇi (S) (M) a ray of light.

Dhṛṣṇu (S) (M) **1.** fierce; violent. **2.** bold; courageous; strong. **3.** a son of Manu Vaivasvata (*M. Bh./H. Purāṇa*); a son of Manu Sāvarṇa (*H. Purāṇa*).

Dhṛṣṭa (S) (M) **1.** bold; brave; confident; audacious. **3.** a son of Manu Vaivasvata (*Bhāgavata*); a son of Kunti; a son of Bhajamana (*H. Purāṇa*).

Dhṛṣṭadyumna (S) (M) **1.** glorified by bravery. **3.** a son of King Drupada and brother of Draupadī who after death became a part of the fire god (*H. Purāṇa*).

Dhṛṣtaka (S) (M) bold; brave; audacious.

Dhṛṣṭakarma (S) (M) **1.** one who performs brave deeds. **3.** a Yayāti king (*Bhāgavata*).

Dhṛṣṭaketu (S) (M) **1.** marked by boldness. **3.** a king of Ćedi who was the son of Śiśupāla and the reincarnation of Anuhlāda the son of Hiraṇyakaśipu (*M. Bh.*); a king of Mithilā and son of Sudhṛti (*V. Purāṇa*); a son of Sukumāra (*H. Purāṇa*); a son of Dhṛṣṭadyumna (*H. Purāṇa*); a Kekaya king (*Bhāgavata*); a son of Manu (*H. Purāṇa*); a Yayāti king (*Bhāgavata*).

Dhṛṣṭaśartman (S) (M) **1.** protector of the brave; one who performs. **3.** a son of Śvaphalka (*H. Purāṇa*).

Dhṛṣṭi (S) (M) **1.** bold. **3.** a son of Hiraṇyakaśipu (*V. Purāṇa*); a minister of King Daśaratha (*V. Rāmāyaṇa*).

Dhṛṣṭokta (S) (M) **1.** one whose bravery is much spoken of; one who is stubborn in speech. **3.** a son of Arjuna Kārtavīrya.

Dhṛta (S) (M) **1.** held; borne. **2.** maintained; fixed upon; pledged. **3.** a son of the 13th Manu (*H. Purāṇa*); a descendant of Druhyu son of Dharma (*V. Purāṇa*).

Dhṛtadakṣa (S) (M) of calm and constant mind.

Dhṛtadhiti (S) (M) **1.** constant in splendour. **2.** fire.

Dhṛtaka (S) (M) **1.** bearer of constancy. **3.** a Buddhist patriarch (*B. Literature*); Vṛka (*V. Purāṇa*).

Dhṛtaketu (S) (M) **1.** constant flagbearer. **3.** a son of the 9th Manu; a king of the Bhṛgu family (*Bhāgavata*).

Dhṛtarājan (S) (M) ornament bearer.

Dhṛtarāṣṭra (S) (M) **1.** powerful king. **3.** a nāga (*A. Veda*); a king of the gandharvas; a son of the daitya Bali (*H. Purāṇa*); a king of Kāśī; the eldest son of Vyāsa who was the husband of Gāndhārī and the father of the hundred Kauravas (*M. Bh.*); a son of Janamejaya.

Dhṛtarāṣṭraja (S) (M) **1.** son of Dhṛtarāṣṭra. **3.** another name for Duryodhana.

Dhṛtārćis (S) (M) **1.** of constant splendour. **3.** another name for Viṣṇu.

Dhṛtasaṇdhi (S) (M) **1.** supporter of alliance. **2.** keeping faith. **3.** a son of Susandhi and father of Bharata (*M. Bh.*).

Dhṛtasena (S) (M) **1.** supporter of the army; one who holds the army; a commander. **3.** a king on steady mind; the side of the Kauravas (*M. Bh.*).

Dhṛtātman (S) (M) steady mind; steady, calm; firm.

Dhṛtavarman (S) (M) **1.** wearing armour. **3.** the brother of King Suvarṇa of Tṛgartta and a Kaurava warrior (*M. Bh.*).

Dhṛtavrata (S) (M) **1.** maintaining law. **2.** devoted; attached; faithful. **3.** a son of Dhṛti; a Yayāti king (*Bhāgavata*); another name for Rudra.

Dhṛti (S) (M) **1.** patience. **2.** virtue; resolution. **3.** the son of Vijaya and father of Dhṛtavrata (*H. Purāṇa*); a son of king Vītahavya of Videha and the father of Bahulāśva (*M. Bh.*); a son of Babhru (*M. Bh.*); a viśvadeva (*M. Bh.*).

Dhṛtimat (S) (M) **1.** steadfast; resolute. **2.** one who is calm; patient. **3.** a form of Agni (*M. Bh.*); a son of Manu Raivata (*H. Purāṇa*); a ṛṣi in the 13th Maṇvantara (*H. Purāṇa*); a son of Yavīnara (*H. Purāṇa*); a grandson of Aṅgiras.

Dhṛtvan (S) (M) **1.** resolute; steadfast. **2.** the sky; the sea; clever; virtuous. **3.** another name for Viṣṇu and Brahmā.

Dhruva (S) (M) **1.** firm; fixed; constant; permanent; eternal. **3.** the polar star personified as the son of Uttānapāda and Sunītī and the grandson of Manu (*G. Sutra*); a son of Vasudeva and Rohiṇī (*Bhāgavata*); a son of Nahuṣa and brother of Yayāti (*M. Bh.*); a son of Dharma and Dhūmrā, who is also one of the 8 vasus (*M. Bh.*); a son of Rantinara (*V. Purāṇa*); a Kaurava warrior (*M. Bh.*); the serpent holding the earth (*T. Ārāṇyaka*); the syllable Om (*Rā. Upaniṣad*); another name for Brahmā, Viṣṇu and Śiva.

Dhruvaka (S) (M) **1.** stable; firm. **2.** that which is unchangeable; a post; a stake. **3.** an attendant of Skanda (*M. Bh.*).

Dhruvākṣara (S) (M) **1.** the eternal syllable. **3.** Om as Viṣṇu.

Dhruvasaṁdhi (S) (M) **1.** one who is firm in alliance. **3.** a king of Kosala; the son of Susaṇdhi, the husband of Manoramā and Lilāvatī and the father of Sudarśana and Śatrujita; a son of Puṣya.

Dhruvāśva (S) (M) with firm horses.

Dhruvi (S) (M) firmly fixed.

Dhūmaketu (S) (M) **1.** smoke-bannered. **2.** fire; a comet. **3.** a yakṣa (*K. Sāgara*); another name for the sun.

Dhumala (S) (M) **1.** brownish-red; purple; smoke coloured. **3.** *Alpinia galanga.*

Dhūmavarṇa (S) (M) **1.** smoke coloured. **2.** grey or dark complexioned. **3.** the father of the 5 daughters married to Yadu (*Bhāgavata*); a nāga chief (*H. Purāṇa*).

Dhūmin (S) (M) **1.** smoking. **2.** steaming. **3.** one of the 7 tongues of Agni (*G. Sutra*).

Dhūmra (S) (M) **1.** smoky. **2.** grey; purple; dim. **3.** an attendant of Skanda (*M. Bh.*); a dānava (*H. Purāṇa*); a hermit in the court of Indra (*M. Bh.*); another name for Śiva; *Attingia elcelsa.*

Dhūmrakeśa (S) (M) **1.** dark haired. **3.** a son of Pṛthu and Arćis (*Bhāgavata*); a son of Bharata and Pānćajanī (*Bhāgavata*); a dānava (*Bhāgavata*).

Dhūmraketu (S) (M) **1.** grey bannered. **3.** a son of Bharata (*M. Bh.*); a rākṣasa; a son of Tṛṇabindu (*Bhā. Purāṇa*); a son of Pṛthu and Arćis (*Bh. Purāṇa*).

Dhūmrākṣa (S) (M) **1.** grey eyed. **2.** dark eyed. **3.** a son of Hemaćandra and the grandson of Tṛṇabindu (*Bhā. Purāṇa*); a rākṣasa who was the son of Sumāli and Ketumatī and a minister of Rāvaṇa (*V. Rāmāyaṇa*); a Niṣāda king (*Sk. Purāṇa*); an Ikṣvāku king (*M. Bh.*).

Dhūmralocana (S) (M) **1.** grey eyed. **3.** a general of the asura Śumbha (*Mā. Purāṇa*).

Dhūmraśikha (S) (M) **1.** with a smoky plait of hair. **3.** a rākṣasa (*K. Sāgara*).

Dhūmrāśva (S) (M) **1.** with grey horses. **3.** a son of Sućandra, the grandson of Hemaćandra, and the father of Sṛñjaya (*V. Rāmāyaṇa*).

Dhūmravarṇa (S) (M) **1.** smoke coloured. **3.** a son of Ajamīḍha and Dhūminī (*H. Purāṇa*).

Dhuna (S) (M) obsession; tune; ruling passion.

Dhundhī (S) (M) **1.** hazy. **2.** obscure; sought after.

Dhundhu (S) (M) **1.** roaring. **2.** boisterous; obsessed. **3.** an asura son of Madhu and Kaitabhā who was slain by Kuvalaśva (*M. Bh.*).

Dhundhumāra (S) (M) **1.** slayer of Dhundhu. **3.** a son of Triśaṅku and father of Yuvanāśva (*Rāmāyaṇa*); another name for Kuvalayāśva.

Dhundhumat (S) (M) **1.** roaring. **2.** boastful. **3.** an asura killed by Gaṇeśa (*G. Purāṇa*).

Dhundirāja (S) (M) **1.** king of the obscure. **3.** Gaṇeśa who is considered to be complex in character and therefore difficult to understand.

Dhuni (S) (M) **1.** roaring. **2.** loud sounding; boisterous. **3.** a son of the vasu Āpa (*Bhāgavata*); a demon slain by Indra (*Ṛg Veda*).

Dhuninātha (S) (M) **1.** lord of the roaring. **2.** lord of the rivers; the ocean.

Dhūpa (S) (M) sun; perfume; incense; frankincensce.

Dhūpāla (S) (M) fragrant.

Dhūpanravan (S) (M) fragrant; shining; prince.

Dhūrai (S) (M) chief; yoke; head; leader; one charged with important duties.

Dhurandhara (S) (M) **1.** bearing a yoke. **2.** chief; leader, **3.** a rākṣasa (*Rāmāyaṇa*); another name for Śiva.

Dhūri (S) (M) **1.** axis; yoke; pivot. **3.** the son of the vasu Āpa *Bhāgavata*).

Dhūrjaṭi (S) (M) **1.** the pivotal ascetic. **3.** another name for Śiva.

Dhūtaka (S) (M) **1.** agitator. **2.** stirrer; destroyer. **3.** a serpent in the Kaurava family (*M. Bh.*).

Dhūti (S) (M) **1.** agitator. **2.** shaker. **3.** an āditya (*V. Purāṇa*).

Dhvana (S) (M) **1.** making a sound. **3.** a wind (*T. Āraṇyaka*).

Dhvanamodin (S) (M) delighting by its sound.

Dhvani (S) (M) **1.** sound. **2.** thunder; noise; tune; voice. **3.** a son of the vasu Āpa (*V. Purāṇa*); a viśvadava (*V. Purāṇa*).

Dhvanya (S) (M) **1.** suggested meaning. **3.** a son of Lakṣmaṇa (*Rāmāyaṇa*).

Dhvaṣanti (S) (M) **1.** brightened. **3.** a Ṛg Vedic hermit (*Ṛg Veda*)

Dhyāna (S) (M) meditation; reflection; contemplation; discernment; intuition.

Dhyānayogi (S) (M) one who is proficient in meditation.

Dhyāneśa (S) (M) lord of meditation.

Dhyānibuddha (S) (M) a spiritual Buddha.

Dībhaka (S) (M) **1.** destroyer. **3.** a son of King Brahmadatta of Śālva who was killed by Balarāma (*Bh. Purāṇa*).

Dīdhitimat (S) (M) shining; brilliant; the sun.

Didyotiṣu (S) (M) wishing to shine.

Didyu (S) (M) weapon; arrow; missile.

Digadhīpa (S) (M) **1.** lord of a direction. **3.** regent of a quarter of the sky (*M. Bh.*).

Digambara (S) (M) **1.** sky clad. **3.** another name for Śiva and Skanda; a Jaina and Buddhist sect (*B. Literature*).

Digambari (S) (M) **1.** consort of Digambara. **2.** sky clad. **3.** another name for Durgā.

Digbhrāja (S) (M) **1.** fire of the sky. **2.** the sun. **3.** father of Aṇu.

Digīśa (S) (M) **1.** lord of a direction. **3.** the regent of a quarter of the sky (*M. Bh.*).

Digīśvara (S) (M) **1.** god of a direction. **3.** the regent of a quarter of the sky (*M. Bh.*).

Digjaya (S) (M) the conqueror of all directions; wearing the sky as a garment.

Digvāsas (S) (M) **1.** sky clad. **3.** another name for Śiva.

Digvastra (S) (M) **1.** sky clad. **2.** bearing the sky as a garment. **3.** another name for Śiva.

Digvijaya (S) (M) **1.** victorious in all directions; victory over several countries. **3.** a chapter in the *Mahābhārata* describing the victories of Yudhiṣṭhira.

Dikkārin (S) (M) **1.** elephant of the quarter. **3.** a mythical elephant that supports a quarter of the earth (*Bh. Purāṇa*).

Dikpāla (S) (M) **1.** protector of a direction. **3.** regent of a quarter of the sky (*R. Taraṅginī*).

Dīkṣapāla (S) (M) **1.** guardian of initiation. **3.** another name for Agni and Viṣṇu.

Dīkṣin (S) (M) initiated; consecrated.

Dīkṣita (S) (M) initiated; consecrated.

Dilīpa (S) (M) **1.** one who gives, accepts and protects. **2.** a king who donates generously, receives taxes as revenue and protects his subjects. **3.** an Ikṣvāku king regarded as among the noblest, the son of Anśuman, the husband of Sudakṣinā and the father of Bhagīratha and Raghu (*V. Rāmāyaṇa*); a nāga of the Kaśyapa family (*M. Bh.*).

Dimbha (S) (M) **1.** newborn. **2.** a boy; a young shoot.

Dīnabandhu (S) (M) a friend of the poor; Supreme Spirit.

Dinabandhu (S) (M) **1.** friend of the day. **2.** the sun.

Dinādhinātha (S) (M) **1.** lord of the day. **2.** the sun.

Dinādhīśa (S) (M) **1.** god of the day. **2.** the sun.

Dinajyotiṣ (S) (M) illuminating the day; Sūrya or sunshine.

Dinakara (S) (M) **1.** that which causes the day. **3.** the sun; an āditya (*Rā. Upaniṣad*).

Dinakṣaya (S) (M) **1.** day decline. **2.** the evening.

Dinamaṇi (S) (M) **1.** day jewel. **2.** the sun.

Dinānātha (S) (M) **1.** day lord. **2.** the sun.

Dīnānātha (S) (M) **1.** saviour of the poor. **3.** a king who was a famous Vaiṣṇava (*P. Purāṇa*).

Dinānta (S) (M) **1.** day end. **2.** the evening; dusk.

Dinapatī (S) (M) **1.** day lord. **2.** the sun.

Dinarāja (S) (M) **1.** day lord. **2.** the sun.

Dinārambha (S) (M) **1.** daybreak. **2.** the dawn.

Dinaratna (S) (M) **1.** day jewel. **2.** the sun.

Dīndayāla (S) (M) being kind to the poor.

Dineśa (S) (M) **1.** day lord. **2.** the sun.

Dineśvara (S) (M) **1.** day lord. **2.** the sun.

Dinkaradeva (S) (M) **1.** lord of the sun. **3.** another name for Sūrya.

Diṅnāga (S) (M) **1.** mountain of a direction; elephant of a direction. **3.** one of the 4 mountains that stand for and guard the 4 directions (*M. Bh.*); a Buddhist author (*L. Vistara*).

Dīpa (S) (M) **1.** that which illuminates, enlightens. **2.** light; lamp; lantern.

Dīpaka (S) (M) **1.** lamp. **2.** kindling; inflaming; illuminating. **3.** a rāga; a son of Garuḍa (*M. Bh.*); another name for Kāma; saffron (*Crocus sativus*).

Dīpakarṇī (S) (M) **1.** with shining ears. **2.** one who digests what he hears. **3.** a king who was the husband of Śaktimatī and the father of Sātavāhana (*K. Sāgara*).

Dīpaṅkara (S) (M) **1.** light causer. **3.** a mythical Buddha.

Dīpaṅkura (S) (M) the flame of the lamp.

Dipapuṣpa (S) (M) **1.** with illuminated flowers. **3.** Yellow Champa (*Michelia champaka*).

Dīpen (S) (M) lord of the lamp; the light of the lamp.

Dīpin (S) (M) inflaming; exciting; illuminating.

Dīpita (S) (M) inflamed; illuminated; manifested; excited.

Dīpta (S) (M) **1.** illuminated. **2.** blazing; hot; flaming; shining; bright; brilliant. **3.** the son of the 3rd Manu (*V. Purāṇa*); *Gloriosa superba*.

Dīptāgni (S) (M) **1.** blazing fire. **3.** another name for sage Agastya.

Dīptaketu (S) (M) **1.** bright bannered. **3.** a son of Manu Dakṣasāvarni (*Bhā. Purāṇa*).

Dīptakīrti (S) (M) **1.** bright famed. **3.** the family of Purūravas (*M. Bh.*); another name for Skanda.

Dīptaṅśu (S) (M) **1.** bright rayed. **3.** another name for the sun.

Dīptaroman (S) (M) **1.** bright haired. **3.** a viśvadeva (*M. Bh.*).

Dīptaśakti (S) (M) **1.** bright power; owner of a glittering spear. **3.** another name for Skanda.

Dīptaśikha (S) (M) **1.** bright flamed. **3.** a yakṣa (*K. Sāgara*).

Dīptatapas (S) (M) of glowing piety.

Dīptatejas (S) (M) radiant with glory.

Dīptavarṇa (S) (M) **1.** flame coloured. **3.** another name for Skanda.

Dīptavīrya (S) (M) of fiery strength.

Dīpti (S) (M) **1.** light; splendour; beauty. **3.** a viśvadeva (*M. Bh.*).

Dīptiketu (S) (M) **1.** bright bannered. **3.** a son of Manu Dakṣasāvarni (*Bhāgavata*).

Dīptimān (S) (M) **1.** bright; shining. **3.** a seer of the 8th Manvantara (*H. Purāṇa*); a son of Kṛṣṇa.

Dīptopala (S) (M) **1.** brilliant gem. **3.** the white topaz.

Dīrgha (S) (M) **1.** lofty. **2.** long; high; tall; deep. **3.** a king of Magadha (*M. Bh.*); another name for Śiva.

Dīrghabāhu (S) (M) **1.** long armed. **3.** an attendant of Śiva (*H. Purāṇa*); a dānava (*H. Purāṇa*); the son of Dhṛtarāṣṭra (*M. Bh.*); a son of Dilīpa (*Purāṇas*).

Dīrghabhuja (S) (M) **1.** long armed. **3.** an attendant of Śiva (*Ś. Purāṇa*).

Dīrghadanṣtra (S) (M) **1.** long toothed. **3.** father of Śrutā (*K. Sāgara*).

Dīrghadarśana (S) (M) **1.** far seeing. **2.** provident; sagacious; wise.

Dīrghajaṅgha (S) (M) **1.** with long thighs. **3.** a yakṣa who was the elder brother of Puṣpadatta (*K. Sāgara*); a guhyaka (*Bhāgavata*); a servant of Padmapāṇi (*B. Literature*).

Dīrghajihva (S) (M) **1.** long tongued. **3.** a dānava son of Kaśyapa and Danu (*M. Bh.*).

Dīrghakaṇṭha (S) (M) **1.** long necked. **3.** a dānava (*H. Purāṇa*).

Dīrghaloćana (S) (M) **1.** long eyed. **3.** a son of Dhṛtarāṣṭra (*M. Bh.*).

Dīrghamukha (S) (M) **1.** long faced. **3.** a yakṣa (*T. Āraṇyaka*).

Dīrgharoma (S) (M) **1.** long haired. **3.** a son of Dhṛtarāṣṭra (*M. Bh.*).

Dīrgharoman (S) (M) **1.** long haired. **3.** an attendant of Śiva (*H. Purāṇa*).

Dīrghaṣravas (S) (M) **1.** with far reaching fame. **3.** a son of Dīrghatamas (*Ṛg Veda*).

Dīrghaśruta (S) (M) with far reaching knowledge; renowned; respected.

Dīrghatamas (S) (M) **1.** with a lot of anger. **3.** a ṛṣi who was the son of Bṛhaspati, the father of Kakṣivat; Aṅga, Vaṅga, Kaliṅga, Punḍra and Śuhma by King Bali's wife Sudeṣṇā (*M. Bh.*).

Dīrghatapas (S) (M) **1.** long penance. **2.** absorbed in pious deeds for a long time. **3.** the father of Dhanvantari (*H. Purāṇa*).

Dīrghayajña (S) (M) **1.** performing a long yajña. **3.** a king of Ayodhyā (*M. Bh.*).

Diśaćakṣus (S) (M) **1.** purveyor of the skies. **2.** with an all encompassing view. **3.** a son of Garuḍa (*M. Bh.*).

Diśāpāla (S) (M) **1.** guardian of a direction. **2.** a regent of a quarter of the sky.

Diṣṇu (S) (M) liberal.

Diṣṭa (S) (M) **1.** settled; directed. **2.** appointed; assigned; fixed. **3.** a son of Manu Vaivasvata (*Purāṇas*).

Ditakiraṇa (S) (M) **1.** hot rayed. **3.** another name for the sun.

Ditaujas (S) (M) glowing with energy.

Ditija (S) (M) **1.** son of Diti. **3.** another name for Vṛtra.

Ditijaguru (S) (M) **1.** preceptor of the daityas. **3.** the planet Venus.

Ditijarati (S) (M) **1.** enemy of the daityas. **3.** another name for Viṣṇu.

Ditikara (S) (M) bringing glow; irradiating, illuminating.

Ditimat (S) (M) **1.** possessed with a glow. **2.** bright; splendid; brilliant. **3.** a son of Kṛṣṇa (*Bhāgavata*).

Divākara (S) (M) **1.** day maker. **2.** the sun. **3.** an āditya (*Rā. Upaniṣad*); a rākṣasa (*V. Purāṇa*).

Divāmaṇi (S) (M) **1.** day jewel. **3.** another name for the sun.

Divapati (S) (M) **1.** day lord. **3.** another name for the sun.

Divaratha (S) (M) **1.** chariot of the day. **3.** a Bharata king who was the son of Bhumanya (*M. Bh.*); a king who was the son of Dadhivāhana (*M. Bh.*); another name for the sun.

Divasabhartṛ (S) (M) **1.** day lord. **3.** another name for the sun.

Divasakara (S) (M) **1.** day maker. **3.** another name for the sun.

Divasamukha (S) (M) **1.** day break. **3.** another name for the dawn.

Divasanātha (S) (M) **1.** day lord. **3.** another name for the sun.

Divasapati (S) (M) **1.** day lord. **3.** the Indra of the 13th Manvantara (*H. Purāṇa/Bhāgavata*); another name for Indra, Nahuṣa and Viṣṇu.

Divaseśvara (S) (M) **1.** day lord. **3.** another name for the sun.

Divaspati (S) (M) **1.** lord of the day. **3.** another name for Indra.

Divaukasa (S) (M) **1.** sky dweller. **3.** a yakṣa (*Vā. Purāṇa*).

Divavasu (S) (M) treasure of the sky; the sun.

Divi (S) (M) the Blue Jay (*Coracias benghalensis*).

Divigamana (S) (M) **1.** sky travelling. **2.** a planet; a star.

Divija (S) (M) **1.** born of the sky; heavenborn. **2.** celestial; a god.

Divijāta (S) (M) **1.** born of the sky; born of heaven. **3.** a son of Purūravas (*V. Purāṇa*).

Divikṣaya (S) (M) heaven dwelling.

Diviratha (S) (M) **1.** sky chariot. **2.** the sun. **3.** another name for the vasus, ādityas and rudras.

Diviyaj (S) (M) praying to heaven.

Diviyoni (S) (M) **1.** sky born. **3.** another name for Agni.

Divodāsa (S) (M) **1.** heaven's devotee. **2.** seeking the heavens; religious; pious. **3.** the son of Vadhryaśva (*Ṛg Veda*); the father of Sudāsa (*Ṛg Veda*); a Kāśi king who was the son of Bhīmaratha and the founder of the Indian school of medicine (*M. Bh.*); the father of Pratārdana (*M. Bh.*); a descendant of Bhīma (*K. Sāgara*); another name for sage Bharadvāja (*Ṛg Veda*).

Divoja (S) (M) descended from heaven.

Divyaćakṣus (S) (M) with a divine eye.

Divyadarśana (S) (M) of divine appearance.

Divyadeha (S) (M) with a divine body.

Divyagāyana (S) (M) **1.** divine songster. **2.** a gandharva (*A. Koṣa*).

Divyagovṛṣabhadhvaja (S) (M) **1.** with the banner of the celestial bull. **3.** another name for Śiva.

Divyakarmakṛt (S) (M) **1.** performer of divine deeds. **3.** a viśvadeva (*M. Bh.*).

Divyāṅśu (S) (M) **1.** with divine rays. **2.** the sun.

Divyaprabhāva (S) (M) with celestial power.

Divyaratna (S) (M) **1.** a divine jewel. **2.** a fabulous Ćintāmaṇi gem that grants all the desires of its possessor (the Pārasa stone or the philosopher's stone).

Divyasānu (S) (M) **1.** of divine eminence. **3.** a viśvadeva (*M. Bh.*).

Divyendu (S) (M) moonlight.

Doraisvāmi (S) (M) **1.** lord of celestial grass. **2.** sacred; venerated; dear to the gods.

Doṣa (S) (M) **1.** evening. **3.** personified as one of the 8 vasus and the husband of night (*Br. Purāṇa*).

Doṣahari (S) (M) **1.** enemy of sin. **3.** the Aśoka tree (*Saraca indica*).

Doṣakara (S) (M) **1.** night maker. **2.** the moon.

Doṣaramaṇa (S) (M) **1.** beloved of the night. **2.** the moon.

Drākṣārāmeśvara (S) (M) **1.** the lord of the vineyard. **3.** another name for Śiva.

Dramila (S) (M) **1.** born in Dramila. **3.** another name for Ćāṇakya.

Drāpa (S) (M) **1.** matted hair; mud; heaven; sky. **3.** Śiva with his hair matted.

Drauṇayani (S) (M) **1.** son of Droṇa. **3.** another name for Aśvatthāman.

Drauṇī (S) (M) **1.** son of Droṇa. **3.** another name for Aśvatthāman.

Draupada (S) (M) **1.** son of Drupada. **3.** another name for Dhṛṣṭadyumna.

Draupadeya (S) (M) **1.** belonging to Drupada. **3.** patronymic of the 5 sons of Draupadī —Prativindhya, Sutasoma, Śrutakīrti, Śatānīka and Śrutasena (*M. Bh.*).

Drava (S) (M) **1.** flowing; liquid; property. **2.** practical; wealthy; juice; essence. **3.** a viśvadeva (*M. Bh.*).

Draviḍa (S) (M) **1.** property owner. **2.** a landlord; wealthy. **3.** a king of the family of Priyavrata (*Bhāgavata*); a gandharva who was the father of Kaṅsa and Anśumatī (*M. Bh.*); a son of Kṛṣṇa (*Bh. Pu.*).

Draviṇa (S) (M) **1.** moveable property. **3.** a son of the vasu Dhara (*M. Bh./V. Purāṇa*); a son of Pṛthu (*Bhāgavata*); a mountain (*Bhāgavata*).

Draviṇādhipati (S) (M) **1.** lord of wealth. **3.** another name for Kubera.

Draviṇaka (S) (M) **1.** son of a wealthy person. **3.** a son of Agni (*Bhāgavata*).

Draviṇaratha (S) (M) **1.** with a chariot of wealth. **2.** extremely wealthy. **3.** an Aṅga king who was the son of Dadhivāhana and the father of Dharmaratha (*A. Purāṇa*).

Draviṇeśvara (S) (M) **1.** lord of wealth. **3.** another name for Kubera.

Dṛḍha (S) (M) **1.** hard; strong; solid; massive. **3.** a son of the 13th Manu (*H. Purāṇa*); a son of Dhṛtarāṣṭra (*M. Bh.*).

Dṛḍhabhakti (S) (M) firm in devotion.

Dṛḍhaćyuta (S) (M) **1.** departed from firmness. **2.** adaptive; flexible. **3.** a son of Agastya (*Bhāgavata*).

Dṛḍhadasyu (S) (M) **1.** resolute against enemies. **3.** a son of Dṛḍhaćyuta also called Idhmavāha (*Bhāgavata*).

Dṛḍhadhana (S) (M) **1.** with secure wealth. **3.** another name for Gautama Buddha.

Dṛḍhadhanus (S) (M) **1.** with a strong bow. **3.** an ancestor of Gautama Buddha (*V. Purāṇa*).

Dṛḍhadhanvā (S) (M) **1.** with a strong bow. **3.** a king of the Purū dynasty (*M. Bh.*).

Dṛḍhahanu (S) (M) strong jawed.

Dṛḍhahasta (S) (M) **1.** strong handed. **3.** a son of Dhṛtarāṣṭra (*M. Bh.*).

Dṛḍhākṣa (S) (M) strong eyed.

Dṛḍhakṣatra (S) (M) **1.** having strong prowess. **3.** a son of Dhṛtarāṣṭra.

Dṛḍhanemi (S) (M) **1.** firm in beliefs. **2.** an idealist; a strong follower of morals. **3.** a king of the Purū dynasty who was the son of Satyadhṛti and father of Supārśva (*Bhāgavata*).

Dṛḍhanetra (S) (M) **1.** strong eyed. **2.** sure of vision; observation; conclusion. **3.** a son of Viśvāmitra (*V. Rāmāyaṇa*).

Dṛḍhāṅga (S) (M) **1.** strong bodied; hard. **2.** a diamond.

Dṛḍhapāda (S) (M) **1.** firm footed. **3.** another name for Brahmā.

Dṛḍharatha (S) (M) **1.** with a strong chariot. **3.** a son of Dhṛtarāṣṭra (*M. Bh.*); a son of Jayadratha and the present Avasarpiṇī (*He. Koṣa*); a king who should be remembered at dawn and sunset (*M. Bh.*).

Dṛḍharuči (S) (M) with firm tastes; with unshakeable glory.

Dṛḍhasandha (S) (M) **1.** firm in keeping engagements. **3.** a son of Dhṛtarāṣṭra (*M. Bh.*).

Dṛḍhasenu (S) (M) **1.** with a strong army. **3.** a Yayāti king on the side of the Pāṇḍavas (*M. Bh.*).

Dṛḍhāśva (S) (M) **1.** with strong horses. **3.** a son of Dhundhumāra; a son of Kāśya; an Ikṣvāku king who was a son of Kuvalayāśva (*M. Bh.*).

Dṛḍhasyu (S) (M) **1.** violent against the impious. **3.** a son of Agastya.

Dṛḍhavajra (S) (M) **1.** with a strong thunderbolt. **3.** a king of the asuras (*Purāṇas*).

Dṛḍhavarman (S) (M) **1.** with strong armour; a firm warrior. **3.** a king of Prayāga; a son of Dhṛtarāṣṭra (*M. Bh.*).

Dṛḍhavrata (S) (M) **1.** staunch believer in faith. **3.** a sage of South India (*M. Bh.*).

Dṛḍhāyudha (S) (M) **1.** with strong weapons. **3.** a son of Dhṛtarāṣṭra (*M. Bh.*); another name for Śiva.

Dṛḍheṣudhi (S) (M) with a strong quiver.

Dṛḍheyu (S) (M) **1.** with a strong will. **3.** one of the 7 sages of the west (*M. Bh.*).

Driḍha (S) (M) **1.** firm. **2.** fixed; hard; solid; strong; steady; resolute; persevering. **3.** a son of the 13th Manu (*H. Purāṇa*); a son of Dhṛtarāṣṭra (*M. Bh.*).

Driḍhabuddhi (S) (M) firm minded.

Dṛiḍhāyu (S) (M) **1.** living a stable life. **3.** a son of Purūravas and Urvaśī (*M. Bh.*); one of the 7 sages of the South (*M. Bh.*); a son of the 3rd Manu Sāvarṇa (*Sk. Purāṇa*).

Dṛmbhīka (S) (M) **1.** powerful. **2.** one who makes others afraid. **3.** a demon slain by Indra (*V. Purāṇa*).

Droṇa (S) (M) **1.** a bowl. **2.** wooden vessel; bucket; trough; Soma vessel; altar shaped like a trough; saviour of society. **3.** one of the 8 vasus who was the husband of Abhimatī and father of Harṣa (*Bhāgavata*); the son of Bharadvāja and military preceptor of Pāñčāla and general of the Kaurava army, was the husband of Kṛpi and the father of Aśvatthāman (*M. Bh.*); a son of Mandapāla and Jaritā.

Droṇāčārya (S) (M) Droṇa, the preceptor.

Droṇahanta (S) (M) **1.** destroying Droṇa. **3.** another name for Dhṛṣṭadyumna.

Droṇaputra (S) (M) **1.** son of Droṇa. **3.** another name for Aśvatthāman.

Droṇasūnu (S) (M) **1.** son of Droṇa. **3.** another name for Aśvatthāman.

Droṇodana (S) (M) **1.** donated by Droṇa. **3.** a son of Siṁhahanu and uncle of Buddha (*L. Vistara*).

Dṛṣadvata (S) (M) **1.** stone like. **2.** that which is hard; firm; resolute. **3.** the father of Vāraṅgī (*M. Bh.*).

Dṛṣālu (S) (M) **1.** full of light. **3.** another name for the sun.

Dṛṣāṇa (S) (M) **1.** seer; light, brightness; a spiritual teacher. **3.** a ṛṣi (*K. Upaniṣad*).

Dṛśīka (S) (M) good looking; worthy to be seen; splendid.

Dṛṣṭasāra (S) (M) of tried strength.

Dṛṣṭavīrya (S) (M) of tried strength.

Dṛṣṭiguru (S) (M) **1.** lord of sight. **3.** another name for Śiva.

Druha (S) (M) son.

Druhina (S) (M) **1.** who hurts asuras. **3.** another name for Brahmā, Viṣṇu and Śiva.

Druhyu (S) (M) **1.** one who loves nature. **3.** a son of Yayāti and Devayānī and brother of Yadu; a son of king Matīnara (*M. Bh.*).

Druma (S) (M) **1. a tree. 3.** a king who was the incarnation of the asura Śibi (*M. Bh.*); the leader of the kinnaras who sits in the court of Kubera and sings (*M. Bh.*).

Drumasena (S) (M) **1.** with an army of trees. **2.** ascetic. **3.** a king who was a partial incarnation of the asura Garviṣṭha (*M. Bh.*); a warrior on the side of the Kauravas (*M. Bh.*).

Druminīmila (S) (M) **1.** with eyelashes like trees. **2.** one who is a lover of nature. **3.** a dānava king of Śaubha (*H. Purāṇa*); a son of Ṛṣabha (*Bhāgavata*); the husband of Kalāvatī and father of Nārada (*Brah. Purāṇa*).

Drupada (S) (M) **1.** firm footed. **2.** a wooden pillar, a column. **3.** a king of the Pāñćālas who was the son of Pṛṣata and father of Dhṛṣṭadyumna, Śikhaṇḍin and Draupadī (*M. Bh.*).

Dūdha (S) (M) voice; milk.

Dūdhanātha (S) (M) lord of the voice; lord of milk.

Dukul (S) (M) **1.** resting at a shore. **2.** the Nepal Maroonbacked Imperial pigeon (*Ducula badia insignis*).

Dūlāla (S) (M) loveable youth.

Dulī (S) (M) **1.** happy. **3.** a sage (*A. Koṣa*).

Dulīćandra (S) (M) happy moon.

Duliduha (S) (M) **1.** collector of pleasures. **3.** a king of ancient India (*M. Bh.*).

Dundu (S) (M) **1.** flautist. **2.** a musician. **3.** another name for Vasudeva.

Dundubha (S) (M) **1.** born of kettledrum. **2.** the non-poisonous watersnake. **3.** another name for Śiva.

Dundubhi (S) (M) **1.** a large kettledrum; son of Dundu. **3.** a son of Andhaka and grandson of Aṇu (*Purāṇas*); an asura who was the son of Māyā, the brother of Māyāvi, the brother in law of Rāvana and was killed by Balin (*V. Rāmāyaṇa*); another name for Kṛṣṇa and Varuṇa.

Dundubhīśvara (S) (M) **1.** lord of drums. **3.** a Buddha (*B. Literature*).

Dūra (S) (M) **1.** difficult. **3.** vital breath or Prāṇa regarded as a deity (*Ṛg Veda*).

Durabādhana (S) (M) **1.** without an obstacle. **2.** one who cannot be stopped. **3.** another name for Śiva.

Durādhana (S) (M) **1.** difficult to withstand. **3.** son of Dhṛtarāṣṭra (*M. Bh.*).

Durādhara (S) (M) **1.** difficult to be withstood. **2.** irresistible; invincible. **3.** a son of Dhṛtarāṣṭra (*M. Bh.*).

Durāpa (S) (M) **1.** inaccessible. **3.** a dānava.

Durārihan (S) (M) **1.** slaying wicked enemies. **3.** another name for Viṣṇu.

Durāsada (S) (M) **1.** dangerous to be approached. **2.** difficult to be found; unparalleled. **3.** a son of Bhasmāsura (*G. Purāṇa*); another name for Śiva.

Dūrbā (S) (M) sacred grass; this grass is offered at worship.

Durdama (S) (M) **1.** difficult to subdue. **3.** a son of Vasudeva and Rohiṇī (*H. Purāṇa*); a son of Bhadraśreṇya (*H. Purāṇa*); a son of the gandharva Viśvavasu (*V. Purāṇa*).

Durdamana (S) (M) **1.** difficult to subdue. **3.** a son of Śatānīka (*Bhāgavata*).

Dūrdarśin (S) (M) **1.** farsighted. **2.** seer. **3.** a minister of Ćitravarṇa.

Durdhara (S) (M) **1.** difficult to withstand. **2.** irresistible; unrestrainable; quicksilver. **3.** a son of Dhṛtarāṣṭra (*M. Bh.*); one of Śambara's generals (*H. Purāṇa*).

Durdharṣa (S) (M) **1.** difficult to be assaulted. **2.** inviolable; inaccessible; invincible; dangerous. **3.** a son of Dhṛtarāṣṭra (*M. Bh.*); rākṣasa (*Rāmāyaṇa*); name of a mountain (*M. Bh.*).

Durdharṣakumāra (S) (M) **1.** inviolable youth. **3.** a bodhisattva (*B. Literature*).

Durga (S) (M) **1.** difficult to approach. **2.** impassable, unattainable. **3.** a rākṣasa slain by the goddess Durgā (*Sk. Purāṇa*); *Commiphora mukul.*

Durgādāsa (S) (M) devotee of Durgā.

Durgādatta (S) (M) given by Durgā.

Durgama (S) (M) **1.** difficult to travel over. **2.** unattainable; impassable; difficult to traverse. **3.** a son of Vasudeva and Pauravī (*V. Purāṇa*); an asura born in the dynasty of Hiraṇyākṣa, was the son of Taru and to fight whom the devas prayed to Devi who annihilated him and was consequently called Durgā (*Sk. Purāṇa*).

Durgāvallabha (S) (M) **1.** beloved of Durgā. **3.** another name for Śiva.

Duritākṣaya (S) (M) **1.** one whose sins have been eliminated. **2.** sinless. **3.** a son of King Mahāvīrya (*Bhāgavata*).

Durjaya (S) (M) **1.** difficult to conquer. **2.** invincible; irresistible. **3.** a dānava son of Kaśyapa and Danu (*M. Bh.*); a rākṣasa (*M. Bh.*); a son of Dhṛtarāṣṭra (*M. Bh.*); a son of King Suvira of the Ikṣvāku dynasty (*M. Bh.*); a son of Supratīka (*Va. Purāṇa*); another name for Viṣṇu; a son of Supratīka (*Var. Purāṇa*).

Durlabha (S) (M) **1.** difficult to be obtained. **2.** extraordinary; eminent; dear; rare; *Fagonia cretica.*

Dūrlabhaka (S) (M) **1.** difficult to be obtained. **2.** rare, precious. **3.** a king of Kāśmira (*R. Taraṅgiṇī*).

Durmada (S) (M) **1.** false pride; illusion, unclear conception. 3. a son of Dhṛtarāṣṭra (*M. Bh.*); a son of Dhṛta and the father of Praćetas (*Purāṇas*); a son of Bhadrasena and the father of Dhanaka (*Purāṇas*); a son of Vasudeva and Pauravī; a son of the gandharva King Haṅsa, and Unmadā (*K. Sāgara*); a son of the asura Maya (*Ā. Rāmāyaṇa*).

Durmarṣa (S) (M) **1.** difficult to manage. **2.** unmanageable; insupportable; unforgettable. **3.** an asura (*Bhāgavata*).

Durmarṣaṇa (S) (M) **1.** unmanageable. **3.** a son of Dhṛtarāṣṭra (*M. Bh.*); a son of Śṛnjaya and Rāṣṭrapāli (*Bhāgavata*); another name for Viṣṇu.

Durmukha (S) (M) **1.** with a foul mouth. **2.** abusive. **3.** a Pāñćāla prince (*A. Brāhmaṇa*); a son of Dhṛtarāṣṭra (*M. Bh.*); a nāga; a rākṣasa member of Rāvaṇa's court (*M. Bh.*); a yakṣa (*Br. Purāṇa*); a general of Mahiṣa asura (*D. Bhāgavata*); a king in the assembly of Yudhiṣṭhira (*M. Bh.*); an astronomer (*A. Koṣa*).

Dūrvā (S) (M) **1.** celestial grass (*Panicum dactylon*). **3.** a prince who was the son of Nṛpañjaya and father of Timi (*Bhāgavata*).

Durvāra (S) (M) **1.** irresistible. **3.** a son of King Suratha of Kuṇḍalanagara (*P. Purāṇa*).

Durvāraṇa (S) (M) **1.** destroyer of troubles. **3.** a messenger of Jalandhara (*P. Purāṇa*).

Durvartu (S) (M) irresistible.

Durvāsas (S) (M) **1.** badly clad. **3.** a sage who was the son of sage Atri and Anasūyā and thought to be a partial incarnation of Śiva (*Rāmāyaṇa*).

Durvigāha (S) (M) **1.** cannot be pierced. **2.** unpierceable. **3.** a son of Dhṛtarāṣṭra (*M. Bh.*).

Durvimoćana (M) **1.** difficult to be set free. **3.** a son of Dhṛtarāṣṭra (*M. Bh.*).

Durviroćana (S) (M) **1.** unmanageable. **3.** a son of Dhṛtarāṣṭra (*M. Bh.*).

Durviṣa (S) (M) **1.** cannot be obtained by simple rites. **3.** another name for Śiva.

Durviṣaha (S) (M) **1.** difficult to be supported. **2.** intolerable; irresistible. **3.** a son of Dhrtarāṣṭra (*M. Bh.*); another name for Śiva.

Duryodhana (S) (M) **1.** invincible. **3.** the eldest son of Dhṛtarāṣṭra and Gāndhārī and the leader of the Kauravas (*M. Bh.*); the son of Suvīra, the grandson of Durjaya who was the husband of Narmadā and father of Sudarśanā who married Agnideva (*M. Bh.*).

Dūṣaṇa (S) (M) **1.** full of vices. **3.** a rākṣasa general of Rāvaṇa (*M. Bh.*); a daityā slain by Śiva (*Ś. Purāṇa*).

Dūṣaṇāri (S) (M) **1.** enemy of vice. **3.** another name for Rāma.

Duśćyavana (S) (M) **1.** unshaken. **3.** another name for Indra.

Duśkāla (S) (M) **1.** destroyer of time. **3.** another name for Śiva.

Duṣkarṇu (S) (M) **1.** listening to evil. **3.** a son of Dhṛtarāṣṭra (*M. Bh.*).

Duṣparājaya (S) (M) **1.** difficult to conquer. **3.** a son of Dhṛtarāṣṭra (*M. Bh.*).

Duśpradharṣa (S) (M) **1.** not to be attacked. **2.** cannot be attacked, difficult to fight with. **3.** a son of Dhṛtarāṣṭra (*M. Bh.*).

Duśpradharṣana (S) (M) **1.** difficult to tame. **3.** a son of Dhṛtarāṣṭra (*M. Bh.*).

Duśpraharśa (S) (M) **1.** one who rejoices in evil deeds. **3.** a son of Dhṛtarāṣṭra (*M. Bh.*).

Dusśaha (S) (M) **1.** difficult to tolerate. **3.** a son of Dhṛtarāṣṭra (*M. Bh.*).

Dusśala (S) (M) **1.** difficult to shake. **2.** firm; resolute. **3.** a son of Dhṛtarāṣṭra (*M. Bh.*).

Dusśāsana (S) (M) **1.** difficult to overcome. **3.** a son of Dhṛtarāṣṭra who attempted to disrobe Draupadī afler the Pāṇḍavas lost her to the Kauravas in a game of dice (*M. Bh.*).

Dusṭara (S) (M) difficult to resist; unconquerable; irresistable; excellent.

Duṣyanta (S) (M) **1.** destroyer of evil. **3.** a lunar dynasty emperor who was the son of Śanturodha, the husband of Śakuntalā and the father of Bharata (*M. Bh.*); a son of King Ajamīḍha and Nīlī (*M. Bh.*).

Dvādaśakara (S) (M) **1.** 12 rayed. **3.** another name for Kāttikeya and Bṛhaspati.

Dvādaśabhuja (S) (M) **1.** 12 handed. **3.** a warrior of Skanda (*M. Bh.*).

Dvādaśākṣa (S) (M) **1.** 12 eyed. **3.** a Buddha; another name for Vyāsa and Skanda.

Dvadaśātman (S) (M) **1.** appearing in 12 forms. **3.** another name for Sūrya.

Dvaimātura (S) (M) **1.** with 2 mothers. **2.** another name for Gaṇeśa.

Dvāpara (S) (M) **1.** the dice personified as a god. **3.** the earlier form of Śakuni.

Dvārakādāsa (S) (M) **1.** devotee of Dvārakā. **2.** Kṛṣṇa's devotee since Dvārakā is associated with Kṛṣṇa.

Dvārakānātha (S) (M) **1.** lord of Dvārakā. **3.** another name for Kṛṣṇa.

Dvārakāprasāda (S) (M) **1.** one who makes Dvāraka happy. 3. Kṛṣṇa.

Dvārakeśa (S) (M) **1.** lord of Dvārakā. **3.** another name for Kṛṣṇa.

Dvārika (S) (M) **1.** door-keeper. **3.** one of the 18 attendants of Sūrya (*A. Koṣa*; *H. Koṣa*).

Dvibāhuka (S) (M) **1.** 2 armed. **3.** an attendant of Śiva (*H. Purāṇa*).

Dvidhātu (S) (M) **1.** of 2 parts. **3.** another name for Gaṇeśa who is part human and part elephant.

Dvija (S) (M) twice born; a bird; a Brāhmin.

Dvijapati (S) (M) **1.** lord of the twice born. **3.** Ćandra which was born once from Atri's eye and then from the Ocean of Milk.

Dvijarāja (S) (M) **1.** lord of the twice born. **3.** another name for Ćandra, Garuḍa and Ananta.

Dvijavāhana (S) (M) **1.** having a bird as a mount. **3.** another name for Viṣṇu and Kṛṣṇa.

Dvijeśa (S) (M) **1.** lord of the twice born. **3.** another name for Ćandra or the moon.

Dvijeśvara (S) (M) **1.** lord of the twice born. **2.** a Brāhmin. **3.** another name for Ćandra or the moon and Śiva.

Dvimidha (S) (M) **1.** with 2 kinds of intellect. **2.** one who knows the present as well as the future. **3.** a Purū king who was the son of Hastin, the grandson of Suhotra and the brother of Ajamīḍha and Purūmīḍha (*A. Purāṇa*).

Dvimūrdhan (S) (M) **1.** 2 headed. **3.** a son of Hiranyākṣa (*A. Purāṇa*).

Dvīpendra (S) (M) **1.** lord of the island. **3.** another name for Rudra.

Dvita (S) (M) **1.** existing in 2 forms. **2.** one who practices the life of a sannyāsin or an ascetic while living in a house-hold. **3.** a sage who was the son of Gautama (*V. Rāmāyaṇa*).

Dvivaktra (S) (M) **1.** 2 faced. **3.** a dānava (*H. Purāṇa*).

Dvivida (S) (M) **1.** knower of 2 types of truth. **2.** one who knows the empirical as well as the transcendal reality. **3.** a monkey in the army of Rāma (*M. Bh.*).

Dvividāri (S) (M) **1.** destroyer of Dvivida. **3.** another name for lord Viṣṇu.

Dviyodha (S) (M) **1.** fighting with 2. **2.** a skilled warrior. **3.** Kṛṣṇa's charioteer (*Bhā. Purāṇa*).

Dyau (S) (M) **1.** bright. **2.** heaven; illuminating sky; space. **3.** a vasu also called Āpa (*S. Brāhmaṇa*).

Dyota (S) (M) light; brilliance.

Dyuċara (S) (M) **1.** walking through the heavens. **3.** a vidyādhara (*K. Sāgara*).

Dyudhāman (S) (M) with one's abode in heaven; a god.

Dyujaya (S) (M) conqueror of heaven.

Dyukṣa (S) (M) of heaven; celestial.

Dyumaṇi (S) (M) **1.** sky jewel. **3.** another name for Śiva and the sun.

Dyumat (S) (M) **1.** bright; brilliant. **2.** strong; splendid; excellent. **3.** a son of Vasiṣṭha (*Bhāgavata*); a son of Divodāsa (*Bhāgavata*); a son of Manu Svāroċiṣa (*Bhāgavata*); a Bhārgava king (*Bhāgavata*).

Dyumatsena (S) (M) **1.** with an excellent army. **3.** a king of Śālva and father of Satyavān (*M. Bh.*).

Dyumna (S) (M) **1.** splendour. **2.** inspiration; glory; majesty; power. **3.** a son of Manu and Naḍvalā (*Bhāgavata*).

Dyumni (S) (M) **1.** inspired. **2.** majestic; strong; powerful. **3.** a prince (*V. Purāṇa*).

Dyumnīka (S) (M) **1.** inspired. **2.** majestic; powerful. **3.** a son of Vaśiṣṭha (*Ṛg Veda*).

Dyunīśa (S) (M) day and night; one invested with day like, night-like virtues.

Dyupati (S) (M) **1.** sky lord; a god. **3.** another name for Indra and the sun.

Dyuratna (S) (M) **1.** sky jewel. **3.** another name for the sun.

Dyutana (S) (M) shining; bright.

Dyuti (S) (M) **1.** splendour; brightness; lustre. **2.** majesty. **3.** a son of Manu Tāmasa (*H. Purāṇa*).

Dyutikara (S) (M) **1.** illuminating. **2.** bright; handsome. **3.** another name for the Dhruva star.

Dyutimān/Dyutimat (S) (M) **1.** heavenly; bright. **2.** resplendant; majestic. **3.** a Madra king whose daughter Vijayā married Sahadeva (*M. Bh.*); a son of the Ikṣvāku king Madirāśva and the father of King Suvīra (*M. Bh.*); a hermit of the family of Bhṛgu who was the son of Prāṇa (*V. Purāṇa*); a Śālva prince and father of Ṛċika (*M. Bh.*); a ṛṣi under Manu Dākṣasāvarṇi (*Bhāgavata*); a son of Manu Svāyambhuva (*H. Purāṇa*).

Dyutita (S) (M) illuminated; clear; bright; shining.

E

Edha (S) (M) **1.** a type of wood; sacred; holy. **3.** fuel used for the sacred fire (*Ṛg Veda*).

Edhas (S) (M) **1.** sacred wood; happiness. **3.** wood used for the sacrificial fire.

Edhatu (S) (M) **1.** born of wood; having semen; fire. **2.** man; prosperity; happiness.

Edhita (S) (M) **1.** grown. **2.** increased; progressed; evolved.

Eḍi (S) (M) **1.** healing. **3.** a follower of Skanda (*M. Bh.*); a medicinal plant (*Cassia tora*).

Eha (S) (M) **1.** desirous. **2.** desired. **3.** another name for Viṣṇu.

Ehimāyā (S) (M) **1.** an all pervading intellect. **3.** another name for the viśvādevas.

Eila (S) (M) **1.** son of Ila the earth. **3.** another name for Purūravas.

Eilvila (S) (M) **1.** son of Ilvilā. **3.** another name for Kubera.

Eka (S) (M) **1.** one; only. **2.** peerless; matchless; firm; unique. **3.** another name for Viṣṇu and the Supreme Being.

Ekabaṇdhu (S) (M) one friend.

Ekabhakta (S) (M) one who worships one deity.

Ekaćakra (S) (M) **1.** one wheel. **3.** the chariot of the sun; a demon who was the son of sage Kaśyapa and Danu (*M. Bh.*).

Ekachit (S) (M) with one mind; one with concentration; poise.

Ekaćūḍa (S) (M) **1.** single crested. **3.** a follower of Skanda (*M. Bh.*).

Ekadā (S) (M) the 1st one; giver of one; the seers who guide their pupils to know the only reality, the Absolute.

Ekadanta (S) (M) **1.** single tusked. **3.** another name for Gaṇeśa.

Ekādaśī (S) (M) the 11th day; After a new moon or full moon considered sacred to Viṣṇu.

Ekadeha (S) (M) **1.** with one body. **2.** elegantly formed. **3.** another name for the planet Mercury.

Ekadeva (S) (M) **1.** the only God. **3.** Supreme Being.

Ekadhanā (S) (M) **1.** a portion of wealth, **2.** one who has a portion of wealth.

Ekādhipati (S) (M) sole monarch.

Ekadyū (S) (M) **1.** supreme sky. **3.** a sage mentioned in a hymn of the *Ṛg Veda*.

Ekāgra (S) (M) **1.** concentrated. **2.** calm; stable; attentive; tranquil.

Ekahans (S) (M) **1.** the only swan. **2.** soul.

Ekaja (S) (M) born alone; the only child.

Ekajata (S) (M) **1.** with a single twisted lock of hair. **3.** a warrior of Skanda (*M. Bh.*).

Ekajyotis (S) (M) **1.** the sole light. **3.** another name for Śiva.

Ekāk (S) (M) once; alone.

Ekākṣa (S) (M) **1.** single eyed. **2.** one with an excellent eye. **3.** a soldier of Skanda (*M. Bh.*); another name for Śiva.

Ekākṣara (S) (M) **1.** imperishable; the single syllable. **3.** the letter Om.

Ekakuṇḍala (S) (M) **1.** one earringed. **3.** another name for Balarāma, Kubera and Śeṣa who wore only one earring.

Ekalā (S) (M) solitary.

Ekulavya (S) (M) **1.** one with concentrated knowledge. **3.** the son of Hiraṇyadhanuṣ, a king of foresters, who sacrificed his thumb and skill for his Guru Droṇāćārya and who epitomizes steadfastness and courage (*M. Bh.*); a king who fought on the side of the Pāṇḍavas during the Mahābhārata (*M. Bh.*); a brother of Śatrughna who was abandoned in infancy and later adopted by the Niṣādha tribe of which he became the king (*M. Bh.*).

Ekaliṅga (S) (M) **1.** with one liṅga; the supreme phallus. **3.** another name for Śiva.

Ekama (S) (M) **1.** one. **2.** unique; peerless. **3.** the Absolute.

Ekāmbara (S) (M) **1.** with a single dress. **2.** the sky as his dress. **3.** a Jaina sect (*J. Literature*).

Ekamevādvitīyam (S) (M) **1.** the only one without a second. **3.** the Supreme Being—the one eternally existing entity, having no second.

Ekāmranātha (S) (M) **1.** the only lord of the mango. **2.** bestower of the fruit of one's deeds. **3.** the deity of Śiva at Kāñjivaram.

Ekamukha (S) (M) **1.** single faced; with one mouth. **2.** the best kind of Rudrākṣaphala or the fruit of the Rudrākṣa tree (*Guazuma ulmifolia*) which is considered extremely auspicious.

Ekanai (S) (M) the only leader.

Ekanātha (S) (M) the only master.

Ekanāyaka (S) (M) **1.** sole leader. **3.** another name for Śiva as leader of the gods.

Ekāṅga (S) (M) **1.** single bodied. **2.** unique; rare; the only one. **3.** another name for Viṣṇu and the planets Mercury and Mars.

Ekāṅśa (S) (M) the single part; portionless; whole; one.

Ekantin (S) (M) **1.** devoted to one object. **3.** another name for a follower of Viṣṇu.

Ekapāda (S) (M) **1.** one footed. **3.** another name for Śiva and Viṣṇu.

Ekapāt (S) (M) **1.** with a single garment. **3.** a demon son of sage Kaśyapa and Danu (*M. Bh.*); another name for Viṣṇu.

Ekapiṅga (S) (M) **1.** one eyed. **3.** another name for Kubera.

Ekapuruṣa (S) (M) **1.** the sole being. **3.** Supreme Being.

Ékarāja (S) (M) **1.** sole monarch. **3.** the herb *Eclipta alba*.

Ekarāya (S) (M) sole monarch.

Ekasarga (S) (M) closely attentive; concentrated.

Ekaśṛṅga (S) (M) **1.** one horned. **3.** a Saptpitṛ in Brahmā's court (*M. Bh.*).

Ekata (S) (M) **1.** first; single. **3.** the son of Mahārṣī Gautama and brother of Dvita and Tṛta (*V. Purāṇa*).

Ekatāla (S) (M) **1.** a single beat. **2.** rhythmic; melodious; musical harmony.

Ekātan (S) (M) closely attentive; concentrated.

Ekātma (S) (M) one universal soul.

Ekātvachā (S) (M) **1.** one who keeps repeating the same thing. **2.** parrot. **3.** a follower of Skanda (*M. Bh.*).

Ekavaktra (S) (M) **1.** one faced. **3.** a dānava (*H. Purāṇa*).

Ekavīra (S) (M) **1.** outstandingly brave. **3.** the founder of the Hehaya line of kings (*Ṛg Veda / A. Veda*).

Ekayāna (S) (M) that doctrine following which one can be successful in life i.e. the doctrine of unity; worldly wisdom.

Ekayaṣṭī, Ekyaṣṭikā (S) (M) a single string of pearls.

Ekayāvan (S) (M) the wise one.

Ekdak (S) (M) identical.

Ekendra (S) (M) **1.** the sole lord. **3.** the Supreme Being.

Ekeśa (S) (M) **1.** the sole god. **3.** the Supreme Being.

Ekeśvara (S) (M) **1.** the sole god. **3.** the Supreme Being.

Ekiśa (S) (M) one god; the primal god.

Ekodarā (S) (M) **1.** born of the same womb. **2.** a sister.

Ektā (S) (M) **1.** unity. **2.** union. **3.** the son of Maharṣi Gautama (*V. Samhitā*).

Elāparṇa (S) (M) leaves of the Elā creeper (*Elettaria cardamomum*).

Elāputra (S) (M) **1.** of the cardamom creeper. **3.** a serpent son of Kaśyapa and Kadru (*M. Bh.*).

Ellu (S) (M) sesame seed (*Sesamum indicum*), considered divine as it is said to be born of sage Kaśyapa.

Elu (Malayalam) (M) seven.

Emūṣa (S) (M) **1.** the lifter. **3.** the boar who raised up the earth when it was only one span in breadth (*Ś. Brāhmaṇa*).

Eṇa (S) (M) **1.** doe; marked; spotted. **2.** a black antelope. **3.** another name for the zodiac sign of Capricorn.

Eṇavāda (S) (M) **1.** one who speaks of deer; one with a spotted speech. **2.** eloquent; truthful. **3.** a poet mentioned in the *Ṛg Veda.*

Entilaka (S) (M) **1.** marked. **3.** another name for Ćandra. **3.** a grass which turned into a club when plucked by Kṛṣṇa; a nāga of the Kaurava family (*M. Bh.*).

Eśa (S) (M) **1.** desirable. **3.** another name for Viṣṇu.

Eśaṇa (S) (M) desire; wish; aim.

Eṣikā (S) (M) **1.** one that reaches the aim. **2.** an arrow; a dart.

Eṣitā (S) (M) desired.

Eta (S) (M) **1.** shining; painted; dappled. **2.** kind of spotted deer. **3.** the steed of the maruts (*Ṛg Veda/T. Samhitā*).

Etapātra (S) (M) **1.** dappled leaves. **3.** a nāga king who is depicted in both reptile and human form (*Purāṇas*).

Etaśa (S) (M) **1.** shining; dappled horse. **3.** a horse of the sun (*Ṛg Veda*); a sage extolled in the *Ṛg Veda*; a sage whom Indra helped against Sūrya (*Ṛg Veda*).

Ettan (S) (M) breath.

Evāvāda (S) (M) **1.** truthful. **3.** a singer mentioned in the *Ṛg Veda.*

Evyāmarut (S) (M) **1.** protected by the maruts. **3.** a hymn of the *Ṛg Veda*; a sage (*Ṛg Veda*).

Evyāvān (S) (M) **1.** possessed with swiftness; swift. **2.** granting desires. **3.** another name for Viṣṇu.

G

Gabhastimata (S) (M) **1.** containing light. **3.** another name for Sūrya.

Gadā (S) (M) **1.** mace. **2.** a mate of iron wielded only by the very strong (*M. Bh.*) **3.** a demon son of Kaśyapa and Diti who was killed by Viṣṇu and whose bones were made into a club by Viśvakarman (*H. Purāṇa*).

Gada (S) (M) **1.** sentence. **3.** a brother of Balarāma and the son of Vasudeva and Rohiṇī (*H. Purāṇa*).

Gadābhṛt (S) (M) **1.** one who wields a mace. **3.** another name for Viṣṇu. **3.** Viṣṇu's mace personified as a beautiful woman.

Gadādhara (S) (M) **1.** one who wields a mace. **3.** another name for Viṣṇu.

Gadāgada (S) (M) **1.** Gada and Agada conjoined. **3.** the 2 Aśvins regarded as the physicians of the gods (*A. Koṣa*).

Gadāgraja (S) (M) **1.** holding a mace. **3.** another name for Kṛṣṇa (*M. Bh.*).

Gaḍayitnu (S) (M) **1.** covering. **2.** cloud. **3.** another name for Kāma.

Gādhi (S) (M) **1.** one who seeks knowledge. **2.** one who stands. **3.** the father of sage Viśvāmitra (*M. Bh./Rāmāyaṇa*); the son of Kuṣambha (*Rāmāyaṇa*); the father of sage Jamadāgni and grandfather of sage Paraśurāma (*M. Bh./Rāmāyaṇa*).

Gādhija (S) (M) **1.** son of Gādhi. **3.** another name for sage Viśvāmitra.

Gādhinandana (S) (M) **1.** son of Gādhi. **3.** another name for sage Viśvāmitra.

Gādhirāja (S) (M) **1.** King Gādhi. **3.** another name for Gādhi the king of Kauśambhi who is supposed to have been the incarnation of Indra.

Gadin (S) (M) **1.** armed with a club. **3.** another name for Kṛṣṇa.

Gagana (S) (M) **1.** the moving one. **2.** the sky; the heaven.

Gaganadhvaja (S) (M) **1.** banner of the sky. **2.** the sun.

Gaganaghoṣa (S) (M) **1.** the noise of the sky. **2.** thunder.

Gaganamūrdha (S) (M) **1.** with a sky-like forehead. **2.** one with a large forehead. **3.** a famous asura who was the son of sage Kaśyapa and Danu and who was later reborn as a Kekaya king (*M. Bh./H. Purāṇa*).

Gaganasparśana (S) (M) **1.** touching the sky. **3.** a marut.

Gaganātmaja (S) (M) **1.** descendant of heaven. **3.** another name for Soma or the divine nectar.

Gaganavihārī (S) (M) **1.** wandering in the sky. **3.** another name for Sūrya.

Gaganamaṇi (S) (M) **1.** jewel of the sky. **3.** another name for Sūrya.

Gaganeċara (S) (M) **1.** moving through the air. **2.** birds, planets and heavenly spirits.

Gaganeśvara (S) (M) **1.** lord of the sky. **3.** another name for Garuḍa.

Gahininātha (S) (M) **1.** lord of mysteries. **3.** a saint of the Nātha cult (*D. Śāstra*).

Gaja (S) (M) **1.** the origin and the goal; elephant. **3.** one of the 8 elephants of the quarters; a monkey king who fought on the side of Rāma (*M. Bh.*); a son of Subala and younger brother of Śakuni (*M. Bh.*); an asura; an attendant of the sun.

Gajadanta (S) (M) **1.** with the tusk of an elephant. **3.** another name for Gaṇeśa.

Gajakarṇa (S) (M) **1.** elephant eared. **3.** a yakṣa in Kubera's court (*M. Bh.*); another name for Śiva.

Gajakūrmāśin (S) (M) **1.** one who devours an elephant and a tortoise. **3.** another name for Garuḍa, the mount of Viṣṇu.

Gajamukha (S) (M) **1.** elephant faced. **3.** another name for Gaṇeśa.

Gajānanā (S) (M) **1.** elephant faced. **3.** another name for Gaṇeśa.

Gajapati (S) (M) **1.** lord of elephants. **3.** another name for Airāvata, the elephant of Indra.

Gajarāja (S) (M) **1.** lord of elephants. **3.** another name for Airāvata the elephant of Indra.

Gajāri (S) (M) **1.** enemy of elephants. **2.** lion. **3.** another name for Śiva.

Gajarūpa (S) (M) **1.** in the image of an elephant. **3.** another name for Gaṇeśa.

Gajaśiras (S) (M) **1.** elephant headed. **3.** a warrior of Skanda (*M. Bh.*); a dānava (*H. Purāṇa*).

Gajaskandha (S) (M) **1.** with shoulders like an elephant. **3.** a dānava.

Gajaṣya (S) (M) **1.** elephant faced. **3.** another name for Gaṇeśa.

Gajavadana (S) (M) **1.** elephant faced. **3.** another name for Ganeśa.

Gajendra (S) (M) **1.** lord of elephants. **3.** a Pāṇḍyan king called Indradyumna who was reborn as an elephant (*Bhāgavata*); another name for Airāvata, the elephant of Indra.

Gajeṣṭha (S) (M) **1.** best among elephants. **3.** another name for Airāvata; the creeper *Pueraria tuberosa.*

Gajnan (S) (M) root of a lotus.

Gajodara (S) (M) **1.** elephant bellied. **3.** an attendant of Skanda.

Gālava (S) (M) **1.** to worship. **3.** a celebrated sage who was the son of Viśvāmitra (*Br. Upaniṣad*); a pupil of Viśvāmitra (*Vā. Purāṇa*); a seer of the 8th cycle of creation (*H. Purāṇa*); a grammarian (*Nirukta /Pāṇini*); the tree *Sympolocos crataegoides.*

Gambhīra (S) (M) **1.** deep; serious; considerate; patient; thoughtful; grave; influential. **3.** a son of Manu Bhautya (*V. Purāṇa*).

Gaṇa (S) (M) **1.** troop. **3.** the demi god attendants of Śiva and Sūrya who are invoked to protect children.

Gaṇādhīpati (S) (M) **1.** lord of the gaṇas. **3.** another name for Śiva and Gaṇeśa.

Gaṇādhyakṣa (S) (M) **1.** leader of the gaṇas. **3.** another name for Śiva.

Gaṇaka (S) (M) **1.** one who calculates. **2.** a mathematician; an astrologer. **3.** a collection of 8 stars.

Gaṇanātha (S) (M) **1.** lord of the gaṇas. **3.** another name for Śiva and Gaṇeśa.

Gaṇaparvata (S) (M) **1.** mountain of the ganas. **3.** another name for Mount Kailāśa also called the mountain of silver.

Gaṇapati (S) (M) **1.** leader of the gaṇas. **3.** another name for Gaṇeśa.

Gaṇḍakaṇḍu (S) (M) **1.** scratching the cheek **3.** a yakṣa in the court of Kubera. (*M. Bh.*).

Gandhadhārin (S) (M) **1.** possessing perfumes. **3.** another name for Śiva.

Gandhamāda (S) (M) **1.** delighting with perfume. **3.** a son of Śvaphalka (*Bh. Purāṇa*).

Gandhamādana (S) (M) **1.** intoxicating with fragrance. **3.** one of the 4 mountains enclosing the central region of the world and on which dwell Indra, Kubera and the yakṣas, part of the Rudra Himālayas it is east of Meru on the Kailāśa range and is watered by the river Mandākinī, is also the home of healing herbs including the herb Sañjīvanī which was brought by Hanumān to restore Lakṣmaṇa to life during the war between Rāma and Rāvaṇa (*V. Rāmāyaṇa*); a monkey general who was the ally of Rāma and was the son of Kubera (*V. Rāmāyaṇa*); a king in the assembly of Kubera (*M. Bh.*); the large black bee (*A. Koṣa*). **1.** intoxicating fragrance. **3.** the tree *Caesaria esculenta.*

Gandhamālin (S) (M) **1.** with fragrant garlands. **3.** a nāga.

Gandhapālin (S) (M) **1.** protector of fragrance. **3.** another name for Śiva.

Gāndhāra (S) (M) **1.** fragrance. **2.** a country which is now Kandāhar in Afghanistan. 3rd of the 7 primary notes of music personified as a son Rāga Bhairava (*M. Bh.*); a gem.

Gandharāj (S) (M) **1.** king of fragrance. **2.** the Cape Jasmine (*Gardinia jasminoides*). **3.** another name for Ćitraratha the chief of the gandharvas.

Gāndhārapati (S) (M) **1.** lord of Gāndhāra. **3.** another name for Śakuni.

Gandhārin (S) (M) **1.** fragrant. **3.** another name for Śiva.

Gāndhārīputra (S) (M) **1.** son of Gāndhārī. **3.** another name for Duryodhana.

Gandharva (S) (M) **1.** celestial musician. **3.** gandharvas are the sons of sage Kaśyapa and Ariśthā, who are both musicians and dancers and guardians of the Soma juice (*A. Purāṇa*); a king born in the dynasty of Janamejaya (*Bhāgavata*); a sage of ancient India; the Blackheaded Cuckoo (*Coracina melanoptera*); another name for Sūrya.

Gandhasoma (S) (M) **1.** with perfumed juice. **3.** the White Water lily (*Nymphaea alba*).

Gandheśa (S) (M) lord of fragrance. **3.** another name for Pṛthvī; *Caesaria esculenta.*

Gāṇḍīra (S) (M) **1.** hero. **3.** son of Varutha and father of Gāndhāra; a species of cucumber.

Gāṇḍīva (S) (M) **1.** illuminator of the earth; conquering the earth. **2.** a magical bow which no weapon can damage. **3.** the famous bow of Arjuna made by Brahmā which could fight 100,000 people at the same time (*M. Bh.*).

Gaṇendra (S) (M) **1.** lord of a troop. **3.** a Buddha.

Gaṇeśa (S) (M) **1.** lord of the gaṇas. **3.** the son of Śiva and Pārvatī having the head of an elephant, is the god who removes all obstacles from the paths of men, is worshipped at the commencement of any action, is the leader of the attendants of Śiva and occupies the most prominent place among the gods connected with Śiva, is considered to contain the entire universe in his belly and is the husband of Ṛddhi and Siddhi.

Gaṇeśani/Gaṇeśvara (S) (M) **1.** lord of the gaṇas. **3.** another name for Gaṇeśa, Viṣṇu and Śiva.

Gaṅgābhrit (S) (M) **1.** carrying the Gaṅgā. **3.** another name for Śiva and the ocean.

Gaṅgādāsa (S) (M) **1.** devotee of Gaṅgā. **3.** son of Santoṣā.

Gaṅgādatta (S) (M) **1.** given by Gaṅgā. **3.** the 8th son of Gaṅgā and Śāntanu, also known as Bhīṣma (*M. Bh.*).

Gaṅgādhara (S) (M) **1.** holding the Gaṅgā. **3.** another name for Śiva and the ocean.

Gaṅgaja (S) (M) **1.** son of Gaṅgā, **3.** another name for Bhīṣma and Kārttikeya.

Gaṅgājala (S) (M) water of the Gaṅgā; the water of the Gaṅgā is held sacred by the Hindus because it is considered to wash away all sins.

Gaṅgākṣetra (S) (M) land through which the Gaṇgā flows.

Gaṅgāla, Gaṇgola (M) **1.** of the Gaṅgā. **3.** another name for beryl.

Gaṅganātha (S) (M) **1.** lord of Gaṅgā. **3.** another name for Śiva.

Gaṅgāputra (S) (M) **1.** son of Gaṅgā. **3.** another name for Bhīṣma and Kārttikeya.

Gaṅgāsāgara (S) (M) the sea of Gaṅgā; that point where the river Gaṅgā enters the ocean.

Gaṅgāsuta (S) (M) **1.** son of Gaṅgā. **3.** another name for Bhīṣma.

Gaṅgeśa (S) (M) **1.** lord of Gaṅgā. **3.** another name for Śiva.

Gaṅgeśvara (S) (M) **1.** lord of Gaṅgā. **3.** a liṅga.

Gāṅgikā (S) like the Gaṅgā; one who is as pure, sacred and pious as the Gaṅgā river.

Gaṅgodaka (S) (M) water of the Gaṅgā river.

Gāṅgeya (S) (M) **1.** of Gaṅgā. **3.** another name for Bhīṣma; Nut grass (*Cyperus rotundis*).

Gaṇin (S) (M) who has attendants.

Gaṇita (S) (M) **1.** numbered; regarded; mathematics. **3.** a viśvādeva who records time (*K. Upaniṣad*).

Gañjan (S) (M) surpassing; excelling; conquering.

Gañmānya (S) (M) distinguished; honoured; respected.

Gara (S) (M) **1.** fluid. **3.** a friend of Indra who was the author of a mantra or chant (*P.Brāhmaṇa*).

Garbha (S) (M) **1.** inner womb. **2.** the bed of a river; fire. **3.** a son of King Bharata (*A. Purāṇa*).

Garbhaka (S) (M) a chaplet of flowers worn in the hair.

Gārdabhi (S) (M) **1.** an ass. **2.** dungbeetle; scarab. **3.** a son of Viśvāmitra.

Garga (S) (M) **1.** bull. **3.** a sage who descended from Viṣṇu, became the preceptor of the Yādavas, discovered some principles of astronomy and was the chief astronomer in the court of King Pṛthu (*Ṛg Veda*).

Gārgya (S) (M) **1.** of the family of Garga. **3.** a sage who was a son of Viśvāmitra (*M. Bh./Rāmāyaṇa*).

Gārhapati (S) (M) **1.** one who protects the house. **3.** one of the 3 sacred fires (*A. Veda/V. Samhita/S. Brahmaṇa*); a Saptpitṛ (*M. Bh.*); another name for Agni.

Gārhapatyam (S) (M) **1.** householder's fire. **3.** a son of Agni.

Gariman (S) (M) **1.** heaviness. **3.** one of the 8 siddhis of Śiva.

Gariṣṭha (S) (M) **1.** heaviest; most venerable; greatest. **2.** abode of greatness. **3.** a sage who was a devotee of Indra and sat in his assembly (*M. Bh.*); an asura.

Garteśa (S) (M) **1.** master of a cave. **3.** another name for Manjuśrī.

Garuḍa (S) (M) **1.** bearer of a heavy load. **3.** the king of birds who is the son of Kaśyapa and Vinatā, the brother of Aruṇa and Sumati, the husband of 4 daughters of Dakṣa (*Bhāgavata*), the father of Sampāti, Kapota and Mayūra and the vehicle of Viṣṇu; a son of Kṛṣṇa; an attendant of the 16th Arhat of the present Avasarpinī.

Garuḍadhvaja (S) (M) **1.** with Garuḍa as his banner. **3.** another name for Viṣṇu and Kṛṣṇa (*M. Bh.*).

Garuḍāgraja (S) (M) **1.** brother of Garuḍa. **3.** another name for Aruṇa the charioteer of Sūrya.

Garuiṣṭha (S) (M) **1.** extremely proud. **3.** an asura.

Garula (S) (M) **1.** carrier of the great. **3.** another name for Garuḍa.

Garutmat (S) (M) **1.** winged. **2.** one who protects against poison. **3.** another name for Garuḍa; who is considered to live on snakes.

Gārutmata (S) (M) **1.** sacred to Garuḍa. **2.** emerald.

Garviṣṭha (S) (M) **1.** extremely proud. **3.** an asura.

Gāthā (S) (M) story; song; verse.

Gāthin (S) (M) **1.** story teller; a singer. **3.** the son of Kuśika and the father of Viśvāmitra (*A. Brāhmaṇa*).

Gāthina (S) (M) **1.** son of Gathin. **3.** another name for Viśvāmitra (*A. Brāhmaṇa*).

Gatitālin (S) (M) **1.** with a musical gait. **3.** a warrior of Skanda (*M. Bh.*)

Gātra (S) (M) **1.** body; corporeal. **3.** a seer of the 3rd cycle of creation (*H. Purāṇa*); a sage who was the son of sage Vasiṣṭha (*V. Purāṇa*); the husband of Ūrjjā and the father of seven sages (*A. Purāṇa*).

Gātragupta (S) (M) **1.** with a protected body. **3.** a son of Kṛṣṇa and Lakṣmanā.

Gātravat (S) (M) **1.** with a handsome body. **3.** a son of Kṛṣṇa and Lakṣmanā.

Gātravinda (S) (M) **1.** bodied; acquiring a body. **3.** a son of Kṛṣṇa and Lakṣmanā.

Gātū (S) (M) **1.** song; singer; gandharva. **2.** the Indian Cuckoo (*Cuculus Scolopaceus*). **3.** a descendant of Atri.

Gauhar (S) (M) **1.** cow like. **2.** white; one who has taken the colour of the cow; the pearl.

Gaunārda (S) (M) **1.** celebrated bringer of light; that which is illuminating; enlightening. **3.** another name for Patañjali the author of *Mahābhāṣya*.

Gaura (S) (M) **1.** cow coloured. **2.** that which is fair; beautiful; red or white in visage; a species of ox (*Bos gauras*). **3.** mountain of gold, north of Kailāśa where Bhagiratha performed his austerities (*Bhā. Purāṇa*); another name for Śiva; the Button tree (*Anogeissus latifolia*); saffron (*Crocus sativus*); the Indian Beech tree (*Pongamia glabra*); another name for the moon, Śeṣa, the planet Jupiter, Ćaitanya.

Gauradāsa (S) (M) servant of Śiva.

Gauramukha (S) (M) **1.** moon faced. **2.** son of sage Śamīka (*Bhā. Purāṇa*).

Gaurāṅga (S) (M) **1.** fair; cow coloured. **3.** another name for Viṣṇu, Kṛṣṇa, Śiva and sage Ćaitanya.

Gauraprabhā (S) (M) **1.** moonlight. **3.** Vyāsa's grandson and the son of Śuka and Pīvarī (*D. Bh. Purāṇa*).

Gaurapṛstha (S) (M) **1.** mountain of the moon. **3.** a sage who worships Yama in his court (*M. Bh.*).

Gauraśiras (S) (M) **1.** one with a moon like head. **3.** a sage who worships Indra in his court (*M. Bh.*).

Gaurava (S) (M) glory; dignity; prestige; respect; regard; gravity.

Gauravāhana (S) (M) **1.** vehicle of Gaura; vehicle of the white. **3.** the vehicle of Śiva; a king who was present at the investiture sacrifice of Yudhiṣṭhira (*M. Bh.*).

Gaureśa (S) (M) **1.** lord of Gaurī. **3.** a royal sage who was a member of Yama's assembly (*M. Bh.*); another name for Śiva and Varuṇa.

Gaurīhṛdayavallabha (S) (M) **1.** beloved of Gaurī's heart. **3.** another name for Śiva.

Gaurīja (S) (M) **1.** son of Pārvatī. **3.** another name for Kārttikeya.

Gaurīkānta (S) (M) **1.** beloved of Gaurī. **3.** another name for Śiva.

Gaurīnātha (S) (M) **1.** lord of Gaurī. **3.** another name for Śiva.

Gaurīprasanna (S) (M) **1.** one who pleases Gaurī. **3.** another name for Śiva.

Gaurīputra (S) (M) **1.** son of Gaurī. **3.** another name for Kārttikeya.

Gaurīśa (S) (M) **1.** lord of Gaurī. **3.** a ṛṣi of Yama's assembly (*M. Bh.*); another name for Śiva.

Gaurīśaṅkara (S) (M) **1.** Gaurī and Śiva conjoined. **3.** Mount Everest the tallest peak of the Himālayas (*M. Bh./Rāmāyaṇa*); the Himālayan Pear plant (*Purāṇas*).

Gaurīśikhara (S) (M) **1.** with a yellow crest. **3.** a monkey king who helped Rāma with 60,000 monkeys (*M. Bh.*); the son of Subala and the younger brother of Śakuni (*M. Bh.*).

Gauśra (S) (M) **1.** the time of cattle grazing. **2.** daybreak. **3.** a teacher of the *K. Brāhmaṇa.*

Gautama (S) (M) **1.** remover of darkness. **3.** a sage who was the husband of Ahalyā; a Brāhmin in the court of Yudhiṣṭhira (*M. Bh.*); a sage of great erudition and father of Ekata, Dvita and Trita (*M. Bh.*); another name for Śākyamuni, Droṇa, the historical Buddha.

Gavākṣa (S) (M) **1.** bull's eye. **2.** window. **3.** a monkey king who helped Rāma with 60,000 monkeys (*M. Bh*); a brother of Śakuni (*M. Bh.*).

Gavala (S) (M) Wild buffalo; buffalo horn.

Gavalagaṇa (S) (M) **1.** possessing many buffaloes. **2.** a cowherd. **3.** the father of Sañjaya (*M. Bh.*).

Gavalagaṇī (S) (M) **1.** son of Gavalagaṇa. **3.** another name for Sañjaya.

Gavamṛta (S) (M) nectar of the cow; milk; nectar of light.

Gavasīra (S) (M) **1.** mixed with milk. **3.** another name for Soma or the nectar of the gods.

Gavaṣṭhira (S) (M) **1.** steady light. **2.** a deity which emits light. **3.** a sage who was a descendant of Atri (*Ṛg Veda*).

Gavaya (S) (M) **1.** made of milk. **3.** a monkey chief who helped Rāma (*M. Bh.*).

Gavendra (S) (M) **1.** lord of oxen; bull. **3.** another name for Viṣṇu.

Gaveṣin (S) (M) **1.** seeking. **3.** a son of Ćitraka and brother of Pṛthu.

Gaveṣṭhin (S) (M) **1.** seeking cattle. **3.** a dānava (*H. Purāṇa*); father of Śumbha.

Gavīṣṭha (S) (M) **1.** abode of light. **2.** Sūrya as the emitter of light. **3.** an asura who was incar-nated as King Drumasena (*M. Bh.*).

Gavīṣvara (S) (M) **1.** lord of oxen. **3.** another name for Viṣṇu.

Gaya (S) (M) **1.** worth going to; worth having. **2.** wealth; household; offspring; sky. **3.** a sacred place in Bihar near the Gaya mountains where Buddha is supposed to have performed his penance (*B. Literature*); a king who was the son of Āyus and Svarbhānu and the grandson of Purūravas (*H. Purāṇa*); a king of the Pṛthu line (*H. Purāṇa*); a king who was the descendant of Dhruva (*A. Purāṇa*); a king who was also a royal sage and son of Amūrtarayas (*M. Bh.*); an asura (*M. Bh.*); a son of Ūru and Agneyī; a son of Havirdhāna and Dhīśaṇa; a monkey follower of Rāma; a son of Naklṣa and Druti; a Manu.

Gāyaka (S) (M) **1.** singer. **2.** wealthy; with off-spring. **3.** a warrior of Skanda (*M. Bh.*).

Gayan (S) (M) where objects move; the sky.

Gayand (S) (M) tusker; an elephant.

Gayāparvata (S) (M) the mountain of Gaya, the sacred mountain of Gaya on which is situated Brahmāsaras or the pool of Brahmā.

Gayāplata (S) (M) **1.** able to go. **2.** that which is traversable. **3.** the son of Plati and the composer of 2 hymns of the *A. Brāhmaṇa.*

Gayāprasāda (S) (M) the blessing of Gaya, the blessing of the sacred place of pilgrimage — Gaya.

Gayāśiras (S) (M) the peak of the Gaya mountain.

Geyarājan (S) (M) **1.** king of songs. **3.** a ćakravartin.

Ghanāmbu (S) (M) **1.** cloud water. **3.** another name for rain.

Ghanarām (S) (M) **1.** dependant on clouds; abode of clouds. **2.** a garden.

Ghanaśyāma (S) (M) **1.** as dark as a cloud. **3.** another name for Kṛṣṇa who is of a dark visage.

Ghanaśravas (S) (M) **1.** of pervading fame. **3.** an attendant of Skanda (*M. Bh.*).

Ghanavāhana (S) (M) **1.** with clouds as vehicles. **3.** another name for Śiva and Indra.

Ghansara (S) (M) **1.** fragrant; auspicious; sacred. **2.** camphor (*Cinnamonum comphora*).

Ghaṇṭadhara (S) (M) **1.** one who holds a bell. **3.** an asura who was a member of Varuṇa's court (*M. Bh.*).

Ghaṇṭākarṇa (S) (M) **1.** bell eared. **3.** an attendant of Skanda and Śiva (*Ś. Purāṇa*); a demon who attained salvation through the worship of Viṣṇu (*H. Purāṇa*).

Ghaṇṭeśvara (S) (M) **1.** lord of the bells. **3.** a son of Maṅgala or Mars and Medhā (*Brah. Purāṇa*).

Ghaṇṭin (S) (M) **1.** one who sounds like a bell. **3.** another name for Śiva.

Gharbharaṇ (S) (M) to be embedded in one's heart.

Gharman (S) (M) **1.** cauldron. **2.** the cauldron used for boiling milk for the sacrifice. **3.** a king of the Aṅga dynasty (*M. Bh.*).

Ghaṭaja (S) (M) **1.** born from a pitcher. **3.** another name for sage Agastya who is considered to have been born in a water jar.

Ghaṭajānuka (S) (M) **1.** with potshaped knees. **3.** a sage who was a prominent member of Yudhiṣṭhira's assembly (*M. Bh.*).

Ghaṭakarpara (S) (M) **1.** of pitcher. **2.** a collection of weapons. **3.** one of the 9 great poets of Sanskṛt, said to have been one of the 9 gems of Vikramāditya's court.

Ghaṭin (S) (M) **1.** with a waterjar. **3.** the zodiac sign of Aquarius; another name for Śiva.

Ghaṭodara (S) (M) **1.** pot bellied. **3.** an attendant of Varuṇa; a rākṣasa (*M. Bh.*); another name for Gaṇeśa.

Ghaṭotkaća (S) (M) **1.** pot headed. **3.** the son of Bhīma the Pāṇḍava prince and Hiḍimbā (*M. Bh.*).

Ghṛta (S) (M) **1.** clarified butter. **2.** used for the sacrificial fire. **3.** a king of the Aṅga dynasty who was the son of Gharman and the father of Viduṣa (*M. Bh.*).

Ghṛtapas (S) (M) **1.** one who drinks ghee. **3.** a sage who lived on ghee and was a disciple of Brahmā (*Bhā. Purāṇa*).

Ghṛtapṛṣṭha (S) (M) **1.** whose back is brilliant with clarified butter. **3.** a son of Priyavrata and Barhiṣmatī; another name for Agni.

Gīrapati (S) (M) **1.** lord of speech; consort of Sarasvatī. **3.** another name for Brahmā and Bṛhaspati the preceptor of the gods.

Gīratha (S) (M) **1.** learned. **3.** another name for Bṛhaspati.

Giri (S) (M) **1.** mountain; honorific title given to ṛṣis; number 8; cloud; ball. **3.** a son of Śvaphalka.

Giribālā (S) (M) **1.** daughter of the mountain. **3.** another name for Pārvatī.

Giribāndhava (S) (M) **1.** friend of mountains. **3.** another name for Śiva.

Giridhara/Giridhārī (S) (M) **1.** holder of the mountain. **3.** another name for Kṛṣṇa who in order to save the people of Vrindāvana from the deluge which Indra released in anger, lifted the Govardhana mountain on his finger to serve as an umbrella.

Giridhvaja (S) (M) **1.** with the mountain as its banner. **3.** Indra's thunderbolt.

Girijānātha (S) (M) **1.** lord of Pārvatī. **3.** another name for Śiva.

Girijāpati (S) (M) **1.** lord of Pārvatī. **3.** another name for Śiva.

Girijāprasāda (S) (M) given by the blessing of Pārvatī.

Girijāvallabha (S) (M) **1.** beloved of Pārvatī. **3.** another name for Śiva.

Girijāvara (S) (M) **1.** consort of Pārvatī. **3.** another name for Śiva.

Girijvara (S) (M) **1.** best among the rocks. **3.** Indra's thunderbolt.

Girika (S) (M) **1.** the heart of the gods. **3.** a nāga chief; an attendant of Śiva.

Girīkṣita (S) (M) **1.** living on the mountain. **3.** another name for Śiva.

Girilāla (S) (M) **1.** son of the mountain lord. **3.** another name for Gaṇeśa and Kārttikeya.

Girimāna (S) (M) **1.** like a mountain. **2.** a powerful elephant.

Girinandana (S) (M) **1.** son of the lord of the mountain. **3.** another name for Kārttikeya and Gaṇeśa.

Girinātha (S) (M) **1.** lord of the mountains. **3.** another name for Śiva.

Girīndra (S) (M) **1.** lord of speech. **3.** another name for Śiva.

Girindra (S) (M) **1.** lord of the mountains; the highest mountain. **3.** another name for Śiva.

Giripati (S) (M) **1.** lord of the mountain. **3.** another name for Śiva.

Girirāj (S) (M) **1.** king of the mountains. **3.** another name for Himavān.

Girīśa (S) (M) **1.** lord of speech. **3.** another name for Bṛhaspati.

Giriśa (S) (M) **1.** lord of the mountain. **3.** another name for Rudra/Śiva and Himavān.

Girivara (S) (M) **1.** excellent mountain. **3.** another name for Kṛṣṇa after he held Mount Govardhana.

Gīta (S) (M) song; lyric; poem.

Gītapriya (S) (M) **1.** one who loves music. **3.** an attendant of Skanda (*M. Bh.*); another name for Śiva.

Gitavidyādhara (S) (M) **1.** scholar of the art of music. **3.** a gandharva who was a great musician (*H. Purāṇa*).

Go (S) (M) **1.** cow; bull; ox; bullock. **2.** ray, thunderbolt; moon; sun; heaven. **3.** a wife of sage Pulastya and mother of Vaiśravaṇa (*M. Bh.*); a daughter of Kakutstha and wife of Yayāti; another name for Gaurī.

Gobhānu (S) (M) **1.** king of cattle. **3.** a king who was the grandson of Turvasu of the Purū dynasty (*A. Purāṇa*); another name for Śiva.

Godā (S) (M) **1.** one who gives cows. **3.** a follower of Skanda (*M. Bh.*).

Godila (S) (M) **1.** harbour. **3.** a yakṣa servant of Vaiśravaṇa (*K. Sāgara*).

Godhārin (S) (M) **1.** one who keeps cows; cowherd. **3.** another name for Kṛṣṇa.

Godhvaja (S) (M) **1.** with the moon as his banner. **3.** another name for Śiva.

Gogana (S) (M) a multitude of rays.

Gokanyā (S) (M) **1.** a maiden who looks after cows. **3.** a nymph of Vṛndāvana (*Bhāgavata*).

Gokarṇa (S) (M) **1.** cow eared. **3.** a place in north Kerala sacred to Śiva where Yama practised austerities to become a Lokapāla (*M. Bh.*); an incarnation of Śiva; an attendant of Śiva; a muni; a king of Kāśmira (*R. Taraṅginī*).

Gokarṇeśvara (S) (M) **1.** lord of Gokarṇa. **3.** a king of Kāśmīra (*R. Taraṅgiṇī*); a statue of Śiva.

Gokarṇī (S) (M) **1.** cow eared. 3. a follower of Skanda (*Sk. Purāṇa*) *Clematis triloba.*

Gokula (S) (M) **1.** herd of cows. **3.** the district on the banks of the river Yamunā near Mathurā where Kṛṣṇa spent his boyhood (*Bhāgavata*).

Golakī (S) (M) **1.** globe; ball. **2.** water jar. **3.** a woman who sprang from the face of Brahmā in Kṛta Yuga (*U. Rāmāyaṇa*).

Golap (S) (M) mooing of the cow.

Goloka (S) (M) **1.** cows' world. **3.** the paradise of Kṛṣṇa situated on mountain Meru on which dwells the wish fulfilling cow Surabhī (*Purāṇas*).

Goman (S) (M) rich in herds.

Gomateśvara (S) (M) **1.** lord of the Gomanta mountain. **3.** another name for Kṛṣṇa.

Gomiṇ (S) (M) **1.** owner of cattle. **3.** an attendant of the Buddha (*B. Literature*).

Gomukha (S) (M) **1.** cow faced. **3.** the son of Mātali (*M. Bh.*); an asura (*M. Bh.*); an attendant of Śiva; a son of King Vatsa; an attendant of the 1st Arhat of present Avasarpinī.

Gonanda (S) (M) **1.** son of a cow. **3.** a follower of Skanda (*M. Bh.*).

Gopā (S) (M) **1.** herdsman; guardian; protector of cows. **2.** *Ichnocarpus frutescens.*

Gopāla (S) (M) **1.** protector of cows. **2.** a cowherd. **3.** another name for Kṛṣṇa.

Gopāladāsa (S) (M) a devotee of Kṛṣṇa.

Gopālaka (S) (M) **1.** protector of cows. **3.** son of Angāraka.

Gopānandana (S) (M) **1.** son of a cowherd. **3.** another name for Kṛṣṇa.

Gopati (S) (M) **1.** owner of cows. **2.** leader; chief; sun. **3.** a gandharva who was the son of Kaśyapa and Muni (*M. Bh.*); the son of Emperor Śibi (*M. Bh.*); an asura (*M. Bh.*); another name for Viṣṇu, Śiva, Kṛṣṇa and Varuṇa.

Gopendra (S) (M) **1.** lord of cowherds. **3.** another name for Kṛṣṇa.

Gopeśa (S) (M) **1.** chief of the herdsmen. **3.** another name for Kṛṣṇa.

Gopīcandana (S) (M) sandal of the herdswoman; white clay from Dvārakā used to mark the body before worship.

Gopīcandra (S) (M) **1.** the moon of the Gopīs. **3.** another name for Kṛṣṇa.

Gopījanapriya (S) (M) **1.** beloved of the gopīs. **3.** another name for Kṛṣṇa.

Gopīkṛṣṇa (S) (M) Kṛṣṇa and Rādhā conjoined.

Gopila (S) (M) **1.** protector of cows. **2.** a king.

Gopīnātha (S) (M) **1.** lord of the Gopīs. **3.** another name for Kṛṣṇa.

Gopita (S) (M) hidden; guarded; preserved; the Water Wagtail (*Motacilla indica*) regarded as a bird of augury.

Goputra (S) (M) **1.** son of a cow. **2.** a young bull. **3.** another name for Karṇa.

Gorakhanātha (S) (M) **1.** lord of senses; master of senses; one who has control over his senses; cowherd. **3.** a sage of the Nātha cult where Śiva is the Ādinatha or the supreme source of perfection.

Gorala (S) (M) likeable.

Gośālaka (S) (M) 1. master of the cowherds. 3. a contemporary and competitor of Mahāvīra.

Gośarya (S) (M) 1. dawn. 3. a protégé of the aśvins.

Gostanī (S) (M) 1. a dug of a cow; a cluster of blossoms. 3. a follower of Skanda (*M. Bh.*).

Gosvāmī (S) (M) 1. lord of cows. 3. head of a Vaiṣnava cult; another name for Kṛṣṇa.

Gotama (S) (M) 1. best among the wise. 3. a Vedic ṛṣi who was the son of Rāhugaṇa to whom the finest verses in the *Ṛg Veda* have been attributed (*Ṛg/A. Veda*); the gotra (lineage) to which Buddha belonged.

Gotra (S) (M) 1. herd of cows; lineage. 2. that which moves the earth. 3. a son of Vasiṣtha.

Gotrabhid (S) (M) 1. opening the cowpens of the sky. 3. another name for Indra.

Govardhana (S) (M) 1. increasing cows. 3. a mountain of Gokula believed to be a form of Kṛṣṇa.

Govāsana (S) (M) 1. covered with ox hides. 3. a king of Śibi whose daughter married Yudhiṣṭhira (*M. Bh.*).

Govinda (S) (M) 1. master of the mountain. 3. another name for Kṛṣṇa.

Govindadatta (S) (M) 1. given by Kṛṣṇa. 3. a Brāhmin known for his piety (*K. Sāgara*).

Govraja (S) (M) 1. dust that ensues from the feet of moving cows; sunset; an atom; sundust. 3. a soldier of Skanda (*M. Bh.*).

Govṛṣabhadhvaja (S) (M) 1. bull-bannered. 3. another name for Śiva.

Govṛṣāṅka (S) (M) 1. marked by the bull. 3. another name for Śiva.

Govṛṣottamavāhana (S) (M) 1. with the supreme bull as his vehicle. 3. another name for Śiva.

Graharāja (S) (M) 1. lord of planets. 3. another name for the sun and Jupiter.

Graharājan (S) (M) 1. king of planets. 3. another name for the sun.

Grahin (S) (M) 1. of planets. 3. the woodapple fruit (*Feronia Limonia*).

Grahīśa (S) (M) 1. lord of the planets. 3. another name for the sun and Saturn.

Grāmadevatā (S) (M) tutelary god of the village.

Grāmadruma (S) (M) a village tree; it is regarded as sacred and worshipped by the villagers.

Grāmaghóṣin (S) (M) 1. the sound of the village. 2. the voice of men. 3. another name for Indra.

Grāmakūṭa (S) (M) the village mountain; the noblest man in the village.

Grāmapāla (S) (M) guardian of the village.

Granthika (S) (M) 1. one who ties the knots; composer. 2. an astrologer; narrator. 3. name assumed by Nakula at the Virāta palace (*M. Bh.*).

Gṛdhra (S) (M) 1. desiring eagerly. 3. a son of Kṛṣṇa (*Bh. Purāṇa*); a ṛṣi of the 14th Manvantara; a rākṣasa.

Gṛdhu (S) (M) 1. libidinous. 3. another name for Kāma.

Gṛdhukalākeli (S) (M) 1. desirous of amorous play; frolicsome. 3. another name for Kāma.

Gṛhanāyaka (S) (M) 1. lord of the house. 2. one who seizes. 3. another name for the sun and Saturn.

Gṛhapati (S) (M) 1. lord of the house. 2. lord of the planets. 3. a sage who was the son of Viśvānara and Śuciṣmatī; another name for Sūrya and Agni.

Gṛhīta (S) (M) taken up; understood and accepted.

Gṛtsamada (S) (M) 1. associated with ghee. 2. sacrificial wood. 3. a sage who was the son of Vītahavya; a great friend of Indra and the father of Kuceta (*M. Bh.*); a king of the Bhārgava dynasty and the son of King Suhotra (*Bhāgavata*); a son of Indra by Mukundā (*Bhāgavata*).

Gṛtsapati (S) (M) 1. full of clarified butter. 3. a son of King Kapila of the Purū dynasty (*A. Purāṇa*).

Guggul (S) (M) **1.** fragrant. **3.** the Indian Bdellium (*Commiphora mukul*) which is an aromatic gum resin forming the base of perfumes and medicines.

Guha (S) (M) **1.** secret one. **3.** a king of the Niṣādas and friend of Rāma (*V. Rāmāyaṇa*); another name for Kārttikeya; the creeper *Uraria lagopoides*.

Guhamāyā (S) (M) **1.** secret power; secret illusion. **3.** another name for Kārttikeya.

Guhavāhana (S) (M) **1.** Skanda's vehicle. **3.** the peacock.

Guheśvara (S) (M) **1.** lord of caverns. **2.** the secret one. **3.** an attendant of Śiva; another name for Kārttikeya and Śiva.

Guhyaka (S) (M) **1.** concealed; hidden; secret. **3.** a class of half-man half-horse demigods who are the attendants of Kubera, exercise their powers from caves, and carry Kubera's palace from place to place (*M. Smṛti/H. Parāṇa*); a yakṣa who was present at the marriage of Draupadī (*M. Bh.*).

Guhyakadhipati (S) (M) **1.** lord of the guhyakas. **3.** another name for Kubera.

Guṇadhāra (S) (M) bearer of attributes.

Guṇāḍhya (S) (M) **1.** rich in virtues. **3.** the author of the *Bṛhatkathā*.

Guṇajña (S) (M) knower of virtues.

Guṇākara (S) (M) **1.** a mine of virtues. **3.** another name for Śiva and Śākyamuni.

Guṇākeśī (S) (M) **1.** with tied hair. **3.** the daughter of Mātali who was his equal in bravery (*M. Bh.*).

Guṇaketu (S) (M) **1.** flag of virtue. **3.** a Buddha (*L. Vistara*).

Guṇamaya (S) (M) endowed with virtues.

Guṇamukhyā (S) (M) **1.** superior among the virtuous. **3.** an apsarā who danced for Arjuna (*M. Bh.*).

Guṇanidhi (S) (M) treasure of virtues.

Guṇarāśi (S) (M) **1.** with a great number of virtues. **3.** a Buddha (*L. Vistara*); another name for Śiva.

Guṇaratna (S) (M) **1.** jewel of virtues. **3.** a Jaina writer (15th century).

Guṇasāgara (S) (M) **1.** ocean of virtue. **3.** another name for Brahmā.

Guṇaśarman (S) (M) **1.** abode of qualities. **3.** a character in the Purāṇas who was the son of the Brāhmin Ādityaśarman and well versed in all the arts and sciences.

Guṇaśekhara (S) (M) crested with virtues.

Guṇaśraja (S) (M) virtuous; excellent.

Guṇāvaraṇ (S) (M) **1.** on the path of virtue. **3.** a Buddhist āćarya who travelled to China (*B. Literature*).

Guṇavata (S) (M) virtuous.

Guṇayukta (S) (M) endowed with virtue.

Guṇḍrā (S) (M) Nut grass (*Cyperus rotundis*); *Aglaia odoratissima*.

Guṇḍū (Tamil) (M) plump; round; circle.

Guṇeṣa (S) (M) **1.** lord of virtues. **3.** a mountain.

Guṇeśvara (S) (M) **1.** lord of virtues. **3.** another name for the Supreme Being and the Ćitrakūta mountain.

Guṅgla (S) (M) the Openbilled Stork.

Guṇidatta (S) (M) given by a virtuous man.

Guṇin (S) (M) endowed with virtues.

Gunja (S) (M) **1.** well woven. **3.** a flower worn by Kṛṣṇa in his garland (*Bhāgavata*); a ṛṣi (*K. Sāgara*).

Gunjika (S) (M) **1.** humming; reflection; meditation. **3.** the Rosary Pea (*Abrus precartorius*).

Guṇottama (S) (M) endowed with excellent qualities.

Guptaka (S) (M) **1.** protected. **3.** a king of Sauvīra.

Guru (S) (M) **1.** teacher; master; priest; spiritual guide. **3.** another name for Bṛhaspati and Droṇa; Cowage (*Mucuna prurita*).

Gurućaraṇa (S) (M) at the feet of the guru.

Gurudā (S) (M) given by the guru.

Gurudāṅkar (S) (M) **1.** given by the gods. **3.** another name for Viṣṇu.

Gurudara (S) (M) **1.** intellectual hegemony. **3.** a son of Garuḍa (*V. Purāṇa*).

Gurudāsa (S) (M) servant of the guru.

Gurūdatta (S) (M) **1.** given by the guru. **3.** another name for sage Dattātreya.

Gurudéva (S) (M) the divine guru.

Gurudīpa (S) (M) lamp of the guru.

Gurumel (S) (M) to be one with the guru.

Gurumīta (S) (M) friend of the guru.

Gurumukha (S) (M) face of the preceptor; facing the preceptor; one who follows the guru; in the image of the guru.

Gurumūrtī (S) (M) idol of guru; one who tries to follow the path shown by the guru.

Gurunāma (S) (M) name of the guru.

Gurunātha (S) (M) **1.** lord of the spiritual teachers. **3.** another name for the Supreme Being.

Guruprasāda (S) (M) the blessing of the guru.

Guruputra (S) (M) **1.** son of the teacher. **3.** another name for Aśvatthāman.

Gururāja (S) (M) **1.** lord of the spiritual teachers. **3.** another name for Bṛhaspati.

Gururatna (S) (M) **1.** jewel among teachers; Bṛhaspati's jewel. **3.** topaz.

Guruśaraṇa (S) (M) in the guru's protection.

Gurusimran (S) (M) in remembrance of the guru.

Gurusutā (S) (M) **1.** son of the teacher. **3.** another name for Aśvatthāman.

Guruttama (S) (M) **1.** the best teacher. **3.** another name for Viṣṇu.

Guruvaćana (S) (M) word or promise of the guru.

Guruvīra (S) (M) a warrior of the guru.

Guṣaṇa (S) (M) the eye of a peacock's tail.

Gutsaka (S) (M) a cluster of blossoms.

Gvālipa (S) (M) **1.** proud. **3.** a saint after whom the city of Gwalior is named (8th century).

H

Hāhā (S) (M) **1.** exclamation of surprise. **3.** a gandharva who was the son of Kaśyapa and Prādhā and who lived in Kubera's assembly (*M. Bh.*).

Hāha (S) (M) **1.** water; sky; blood; meditation; auspiciousness; moon; heaven; battle; pride; horse; nowledge. **3.** another name for Viṣṇu and Śiva.

Hāhāgiri (S) (M) **1.** the mountain of heaven. **3.** a Jaina monk (*J.S. Koṣa*); another name for Mount Meru.

Haiḍimba (S) (M) **1.** son of Hiḍimbā. **3.** another name for Ghaṭotkaća.

Haiḍimbi (S) (M) **1.** son of Hiḍimbā. **3.** another name for Ghaṭotkaća.

Haihaya (S) (M) **1.** of the horse. **3.** a king who was the greatgrandson of Yadu, the son of Vatsa and the founder of the Haihaya dynasty (*M. Bh.*); Arjuna Kārtavīrya who had a 1000 arms (*M. Bh./Rāmāyaṇa*).

Haima (S) (M) **1.** snow; frost; dew; golden. **3.** another name for the Himālaya mountains; another name for Śiva; Yellow Jasmine (*Jasminum bignoniaceum*).

Hairaṇyagarbha (S) (M) **1.** relating to Hiraṇyagarbha. **3.** another name for Vasiṣṭha.

Hakeśa (S) (M) lord of sound.

Hala (S) (M) **1.** plough. **3.** another name for King Śālivāhana.

Halabhṛt (S) (M) **1.** carrying a plough. **3.** another name for Kṛṣṇa's brother Balarāma.

Haladhara (S) (M) **1.** holding a plough. **3.** another name for Balarāma.

Haladharānuja (S) (M) **1.** younger brother of the ploughman. **3.** another name for Kṛṣṇa (*M. Bh.*).

Halāyudha (S) (M) **1.** plough weaponed. **3.** a Sanskṛt poet whose major work was *Kavirahasya* (10th century A.D.); another name for Balarāma.

Halika (S) (M) **1.** ploughman. **3.** a serpent of the Kaśyapa dynasty (*M. Bh.*).

Halīkṣaṇa (S) (M) a fast moving animal; a lion.

Halīmaka (S) (M) **1.** poison spewing. **3.** a nāga of the Vāsuki family (*M. Bh.*).

Halin (S) (M) **1.** ploughman. **3.** a ṛṣi; another name for Balarāma.

Hansa (S) (M) **1.** swan; gander; duck; flamingo; goose; the Bar-headed Goose (*Anser indicus*); an ascetic; a pure person; the individual soul; the Supreme Soul. **3.** a reincarnation of Viṣṇu in Kṛta Yuga (*V. Parāṇa*); a gandharva who was a son of Kaśyapa and Ariṣṭā; a minister of Jarāsandha (*M. Bh.*); a son of Vasudeva; a horse of the moon; another name for Sūrya, Kāma, Śiva and Viṣṇu.

Hansaćūḍa **1.** the crest of the swan. **3.** a yakṣa who worships Kubera in his assembly (*M. Bh.*).

Hansadhvaja (S) (M) **1.** with the swan as his banner. **3.** a king of ampānagari who was a great devotee of Viṣṇu (*Bhāgavata*).

Hansaja (S) (M) **1.** son of a swan. **3.** a warrior of Skanda (*M. Bh.*).

Hansakāya (S) (M) **1.** a group of swans. **3.** a Kṣatriya who was present at the investiture yajña of Yudhiṣṭhira (*M. Bh.*).

Hansakūṭa (S) (M) **1.** abode of the swan. **3.** a peak of the Himālaya.

Hansanāḍa (S) (M) **1.** the cry of the swan. **3.** a vidyādhara.

Hansarāja (S) (M) king of swans.

Hansaratha (S) (M) **1.** with the swan as his chariot. **3.** another name for Brahmā.

Hansārūḍha (S) (M) **1.** mounted on a swan. **3.** another name for Brahmā and Varuṇa.

Hansavāhana (S) (M) **1.** with the swan as his vehicle. **3.** another name for Brahmā.

Hansavaktra (S) (M) **1.** the beak of a swan. **3.** a warrior of Skanda (*M. Bh.*).

Hansin (S) (M) **1.** containing the universal soul. **3.** another name for Kṛṣṇa.

Hanspāla (S) (M) **1.** lord of the swan. **3.** another name for Brahmā.

Hanugiri (S) (M) the mountain of Hanumān.

Hanumān/Hanumant/Hanumat/ Hanut (S) (M) **1.** heavy jawed. **3.** son of Vāyu, the maruta god of wind and Añjanā the apsarā, and the leader of Rāma's army (*V. Rāmāyaṇa*).

Hanumeśa (S) (M) **1.** lord of Hanumān. **3.** another name for Rāma.

Hanuṣa (S) (M) **1.** anger; wrath. **3.** a rākṣasa.

Hara (S) (M) **1.** seizer; destroyer; divisor. **3.** a dānava who was the son of Kaśyapa and Danu and was reborn as King Subāhu (*M. Bh.*); a rudra (*Ś. Purāṇa*); another name for Śiva and Agni.

Haraćūḍāmaṇī (S) (M) **1.** the crest gem of Śiva. **3.** another name for Ćandra.

Haradeva (S) (M) **1.** the lord of Śiva. **3.** the asterism Śravana with 3 stars; another name for Kṛṣṇa.

Haradikā (S) (M) **1.** king and soul of love. **2.** Brahmā, the sun and Viṣṇu. **3.** a Kṣatriya king who was the son the of asura Aśvapati (*M. Bh.*); another name for Kṛtavarman as the son of Hṛdikā of the Yadu dynasty.

Haragaurī (S) (M) Śiva and Pārvatī conjoined.

Haragovinda, Hargobinda (S) (M) Śiva and Kṛṣṇa conjoined.

Harahāra (S) (M) **1.** Śiva's necklace. **3.** another name for Śeṣa.

Haraka (S) (M) **1.** one who takes away; a rogue; a divisor; a thief. **3.** another name for Śiva.

Harakalpa (S) (M) **1.** the sacred precept of Śiva. **3.** a son of Vipraćitti and Siṁhī (*Vā. Purāṇa*).

Haramanas (S) (M) the soul of Śiva; the soul of God.

Haramohana (S) (M) attracting Śiva.

Haranārāyaṇa (S) (M) Viṣṇu and Śiva conjoined.

Haranétra (S) (M) **1.** the eye of Śiva. **2.** all seeing; omniscient; ommipresent; the number 3.

Hararūpa (S) (M) with the form of Śiva.

Harasakha (S) (M) **1.** Śiva's friend. **3.** another name for Kubera.

Harasiddha (S) (M) eternal Śiva.

Harasūnu (S) (M) **1.** son of Śiva. **3.** another name for Kārttikeya.

Harasvarūpa (S) (M) in the image of Śiva; in the image of God.

Haratejas (S) (M) **1.** Śiva's energy. **2.** quicksilver.

Harava (S) (M) **1.** painful to Śiva. **2.** causing harm to the Supreme Spirit. **3.** an asura born from the teardrops of Brahmā (*Sk. Purāṇa*).

Haravīra (S) (M) a warrior of god.

Harendra (S) (M) Indra the tawny; Indra and Śiva conjoined.

Hareṇu (S) (M) **1.** a creeper which serves as a village boundary; respectable. **3.** the Garden Pea (*Pisum sativum*); another name for Lankā.

Hareśvara (S) (M) Śiva and Viṣṇu conjoined.

Hari (S) (M) **1.** yellow; tawny; green. **2.** the Zodiac sign of Leo; a parrot; a cuckoo; a peacock; a horse; a horse of Indra; a man; a ray of light; wind; fire; the moon; the sun; Indra; Brahmā; Viṣṇu and Śiva. Vāyu; Yama; Śukra. **3.** a warrior of Skanda (*M. Bh.*); a warrior who fought on the side of the Pāṇḍavas (*M. Bh.*); an asura who was the son of Tārakākṣa who had the boon of being able to revive the dead (*M. Bh.*); a group of attendants of Rāvaṇa (*M. Bh.*); a powerful bird born in the dynasty of Garuḍa (*M. Bh.*); a sect of golden coloured horses (*M. Bh.*); a daughter of Kaśyapa and Krodhavaśā who was the mother of lions and monkeys (*V. Rāmāyaṇa*); a son of Dharma by the daughter of Dakṣa (*D. Bhāgavata*); a group of devas (*Bhāgavata*); the Sanskṛt poet Bhartṛhari; another name for King Akaṁpana who was as powerful and proficient in war as Indra.

Hariakṣa (S) (M) **1.** the pivot of Viṣṇu; the eye of Viṣṇu; the eye of the lion. **3.** another name for the lion; Kubera and Śiva.

Hariakṣva (S) (M) **1.** fair coloured. **3.** another name for Sūrya.

Harial (S) (M) green coloured; the common green pigeon (*Crocopus phoenicopterus*).

Hariaṅka (S) (M) **1.** in the lap of Viṣṇu. **3.** a king of Aṅga who was the son of King Ćampā and father of King Bṛhadratha (*A. Purāṇa*).

Hariaśva (S) (M) **1.** horse of Viṣṇu. **3.** the 5000 sons born to Dakṣa and Asiknī (*Br. Purāṇa*); a king of the solar dynasty of Ayodhyā who married Mādhavī the daughter of Yayāti (*M. Bh.*); the father of King Sudeva of Kāśi (*M. Bh.*).

Haribabhru (S) (M) **1.** Viṣṇu the great. **3.** a sage who was a member of Yudhiṣṭhira's assembly (*M. Bh.*)

Haribhadra (S) (M) **1.** as beautiful, auspicious and praiseworthy as Viṣṇu. **3.** a distinguished Jaina writer who composed critical commentaries in Sanskṛt (*J.S. Koṣa*).

Haribhajana (S) (M) a hymn to Viṣṇu.

Haribhakta (S) (M) a devotee of Viṣṇu.

Harićandana (S) (M) **1.** the sandal of Hari; yellow moonlight. **3.** the yellow sandalwood tree (*Santalum album*) as one of the 5 trees of paradise; saffron (*Crocus sativus*); the filament of a lotus (*Nelumbium speciosum*); moonlight.

Harićāpa (S) (M) **1.** Indra's bow. **2.** the rainbow.

Harićaraṇa (S) (M) at the feet of Viṣṇu.

Haridāsa (S) (M) **1.** servant of Viṣṇu. **3.** a monkey king who was the son of Pulaha and Śvetā (*Br. Purāṇa*).

Haridaśva (S) (M) **1.** the 10 incarnations of Viṣṇu; with fallow horses. **3.** another name for the sun.

Haridatta (S) (M) **1.** the blessing of Viṣṇu; given by Viṣṇu. **3.** a dānava.

Haridhāma (S) (M) **1.** the abode of Viṣṇu. **3.** a sage who chanted the Kṛṣṇamantra and so was reborn as the gopī Raṅgaveṇī (*P. Purāṇa*).

Haridhana (S) (M) the treasure of Viṣṇu.

Haridhrava (S) (M) the Yellow Water Wagtail (*Motacilla indica*).

Haridra (S) (M) **1.** yellow. **3.** turmeric (*Curcuma longa*); *Aconitum ferox*; *Berberis asiatica*; the Yellow Sandal tree; a deity.

Haridrāgaṇapati, Haridrāgaṇeśa (S) (M) Gaṇeśa who is offered turmeric by his devotees.

Hāridraka (S) (M) **1.** timid snake. **3.** a nāga born in Kaśyapa's dynasty (*M. Bh.*).

Haridru (S) (M) **1.** free of the gods. **3.** the Devadāra tree (*Pinus deodara*).

Harihara (S) (M) Viṣṇu and Śiva conjoined.

Harihaya (S) (M) **1.** with golden horses; the horse of Viṣṇu. **3.** another name for Indra, Sūrya, Skanda and Gaṇeśa.

Hārija (S) (M) the horizon.

Harikānta (S) (M) dear to Indra; as beautiful as a lion.

Harikeśa (S) (M) **1.** with yellow hair. **3.** one of the 7 principal rays of the sun; a yakṣa; a son of Śyāmaka; another name for Viṣṇu, Śiva, Savitṛ.

Harikirtana (S) (M) devotional hymns to Viṣṇu.

Harikṛṣṇa (S) (M) Kṛṣṇa and Viṣṇu conjoined.

Harilāla (S) (M) son of Viṣṇu.

Harilīna (S) (M) engrossed and merged in Viṣṇu.

Harimaṇī (S) (M) **1.** Viṣṇu's gem. **2.** the sapphire.

Harimat (S) (M) **1.** with bay horses. **3.** another name for Indra.

Harimbhara (S) (M) bearing the yellow thunderbolt.

Harimedhas (S) (M) **1.** an oblation to Viṣṇu. **3.** a saintly king and father of Dhvajavatī (*M. Bh.*); another name for Viṣṇu-Kṛṣṇa.

Harimitra (S) (M) **1.** with Viṣṇu as his friend. **3.** a Brāhmin who had his āśrama on the banks of the Yamunā (*P. Purāṇa*)

Hariṇa (S) (M) **1.** yellowish white. **2.** deer; antelope; gazelle; goose; wearing a garland of pearls; attractive. **3.** a nāga of Airāvata's family (*M. Bh.*); another name for Viṣṇu, Śiva and the sun.

Hariṇākṣa (S) (M) **1.** doe eyed. **3.** another name for Śiva.

Harināma (S) (M) the name of Viṣṇu.

Hariṇāṅka (S) (M) **1.** marked like a deer; camphor. **3.** another name for Ćandra.

Hariṇeśa (S) (M) **1.** deer-lord. **2.** lion.

Harinetra (S) (M) **1.** the eye of Viṣṇu. **3.** another name for the white lotus (*Nelumbium speciosum*).

Hariom (S) (M) **1.** lord of the Om. **3.** another name for Brahmā.

Haripāla (S) (M) **1.** defending Viṣṇu. **2.** the lion.

Hariprasāda (S) (M) the blessing of Viṣṇu.

Haripr̄ita (S) (M) beloved of Viṣṇu.

Harirāja (S) (M) king of lions.

Harirāma (S) (M) Viṣṇu and Rāma conjoined.

Harirudra (S) (M) Viṣṇu and Śiva conjoined.

Har̄iśa (S) (M) **1.** short form of Śiva and Viṣṇu conjoined. **3.** a monkey king.

Hariśaṅkara (S) (M) Śiva and Viṣṇu conjoined.

Hariśara (S) (M) **1.** with Viṣṇu for an arrow. **3.** another name for Śiva.

Hariśćandra (S) (M) **1.** with golden splendour; merciful as the moonlight; full of patience; Viṣṇu and moon conjoined. **3.** the son of Triśaṅku, a king of a solar race, lord of the 7 islands and known for his adherance to truth (*M. Bh.*); a Sanskṛt poet (9th century A.D.).

Harisena (S) (M) **1.** lion like commander. **3.** a son of the 10th Manu; the 10th Jaina ćakravartin.

Hariśipra (S) (M) **1.** ruddy cheeked. **3.** another name for Śiva.

Hariśmaṇ̄i (S) (M) **1.** green gem; gem of Viṣṇu. **2.** the emerald.

Harisuta (S) (M) **1.** son of Viṣṇu. **3.** another name for Arjuna.

Harita (S) (M) **1.** horse of the sun. **2.** lion; sun; yellow; pale red; green; verdant; tawny; gold. **3.** a king who was the son of Rohita and the grandson of Hariśćandra (*Bhāgayata*); a king of Haritavarṣa in the island of Śālmali who was the son of Vapusman and the grandson of Svāyambhuva Manu (*M. Purāṇa*); a son of Yadu by a nāga woman called Dhūmravarṇā who founded a kingdom in the nāga island (*H. Purāṇa*); a great sage whose discourse on eternal truths in Yudhiṣṭhira's assembly is known as the *Hāritagītā* (*M. Bh.*); a son of Kaśyapa; a son of Yuvanāśva (*Bh. Purāṇa*); an author on codes of conduct (*M. Bh.*); Turmeric (*Curcuma longa*); Couch grass (*Cynodon dactylon*); another name for Viṣṇu.

Hārita (S) (M) **1.** green; descendant of Harita; a moderate wind. **3.** a son of Viśvāmitra.

Haritaka (S) (M) yellow green.

Haritāśva (S) (M) **1.** with tawny horses. **3.** a king born in the solar dynasty whose ability in music was superior to that of all the gods (*K. Rāmāyaṇa*).

Harituraṅgam (S) (M) **1.** a horse like the wind, or of the wind. **3.** another name for Indra.

Harivāhana (S) (M) **1.** vehicle of Viṣṇu; with bay horses. **3.** another name for Garuḍa.

Harivana (S) (M) Indra of the bay horses.

Harivanśa (S) (M) **1.** of the family of Viṣṇu. **3.** a celebrated work by Vyāsa which is a sup-plement to the *Mahābhārata*.

Harivarṇa (S) (M) **1.** of the colour of Viṣṇu. **2.** green. **3.** a sage who wrote a mantra or a chant in the *Pañćaviṁśa Brāhmaṇa*.

Hārivāsa (S) (M) **1.** with the perfume of Hari. **3.** a deity.

Harivatsa (S) (M) **1.** beloved of Viṣṇu. **3.** another name for Arjuna.

Harmut (S) (M) **1.** bearing the unbreakable. **3.** the tortoise that upholds the earth; another name for Sūrya.

Harośit (S) (M) very happy; joyful.

Harṣa (S) (M) **1.** joy; delight. **3.** one of the 3 sons of Dharmā, brother of Śama and Kāma and husband of Nandā (*M. Bh.*); a Sanskṛt poet who wrote one of the 5 main epic poems and was a member of the court of King Jaićanda of Kannauj (12th century A.D.); King Harṣavardhana ruler of north India who is remembered mainly as a Sanskṛt poet and author of *Ratnāvali*; a son of Kṛṣṇa; an asura (7th century A.D.).

Harṣada (S) (M) delighted.

Harsaka (S) (M) **1.** gladdening; delighting. **3.** a son of Ćitragupta.

Harṣala (S) (M) glad; a lover.

Harṣamana (S) (M) full of joy; delighted.

Harṣamaya (S) whose essence is joy.

Harṣana (S) (M) **1.** causing delight. **3.** one of the 5 arrows of Kāma (*Ś. Purāṇa*).

Harṣavardhana (S) (M) one who increases joy.

Harṣendu (S) (M) the moon of joy.

Harṣī (S) (M) happy; joyful.

Harṣitā (S) (M) full of joy.

Harṣoda (S) (M) creating joy.

Harṣula (S) (M) **1.** disposed to be cheerful. **2.** a lover; a deer. **3.** a Buddha.

Haryakṣa (S) (M) **1.** yellow eyed. **2.** lion; the zodiac sign of Leo. **3.** an asura; a son of Pṛthu; another name for Kubera and Śiva.

Haryalā (S) (M) **1.** desired; precious; pleasant. **2.** deer. **3.** a ṛṣi (*Ṛg. Veda*).

Haryaṅga (S) (M) **1.** golden bodied. **3.** a son of Ćampa.

Haryaśva (S) (M) **1.** with bay horses. **3.** a solar dynasty king of Ayodhyā and husband of Mādhavī (*M. Bh.*); father of King Sudeva of Kāśī; another name for Indra and Śiva.

Haryavana (S) (M) **1.** joyful lion; protected by lions. **3.** a son of Kṛta.

Hasamukha (S) (M) smiling.

Hasana (S) (M) **1.** laughing. **3.** an attendant of Skanda (*M. Bh.*).

Hasaratha (S) (M) a chariot that delights.

Hasita (S) (M) **1.** delighting; delighted. **3.** the bow of Kāma (*K. Sāgara*).

Hasta (S) (M) **1.** hand. **3.** a constellation.

Hastāmalaka (S) (M) **1.** seeing the world in its totality. **3.** a disciple of Śrī Śaṅkara (*Ś. Vijaya*).

Hastibhadra (S) (M) **1.** with a superior trunk; with a hood as wide as a palm. **3.** a nāga of the Kaśyapa dynasty (*M. Bh.*).

Hastikarṇa (S) (M) **1.** elephant eared. **3.** an attendant of Śiva; a rākṣasa; a nāga.

Hastikaśyapa (S) (M) **1.** elephant and tortoise conjoined. **3.** a sage who was a contemporary of Kṛṣṇa (*M. Bh.*).

Hastimalla (S) (M) **1.** with strong hands. **3.** another name for Airāvata, Gaṇeśa and Śaṅkha.

Hastimukha (S) (M) **1.** elephant faced. **3.** another name for Gaṇeśa.

Hastin (S) (M) **1.** having hands; elephant. **3.** a lunar dynasty king who was the son of Suhotra and Suvarṇā of the Ikṣvāku dynasty, the husband of Yaśodharā, the father of Vikaṇṭha and the builder of the city of Hastināpura (*M. Bh.*); a son of Dhṛtarāṣṭra; a son of Kuru.

Hastipada (S) (M) **1.** with elephant feet. **3.** a nāga of the Kaśyapa dynasty (*M. Bh.*).

Hāṭākeśa (S) (M) **1.** lord of gold. **3.** another name for Śiva.

Hāṭakeśvara (S) (M) **1.** lord of gold. **3.** another name for Śiva as the prime deity of the Nāgara Brāhmins of Gujarat.

Hatiṣa (S) (M) with no desire.

Hatitoṣa (S) (M) not afraid of troubles.

Havaldār (H) (M) to whom the responsibility is given; a constable.

Havana (S) (M) **1.** calling; invocation; the sacrifice. **3.** one of the 11 rudras (*M. Bh.*); another name for Agni.

Havighna (S) (M) **1.** sacrificial. **3.** an ancient king held and remembered both in the morning and evening (*M. Bh.*).

Havirbhuj (S) (M) **1.** eating the oblation. **3.** another name for Agni and Śiva.

Havirdhāna (S) (M) **1.** one whose wealth is the sacrifice. **3.** a grandson of Emperor Pṛthu and son of Antardhāna and Śikhaṇḍiṇī (*V. Purāṇa*).

Havirgandhā (S) (M) **1.** giving the fragrance. **3.** the sacrifice Śami tree (*Prosopis spicigera*).

Havirvarṣa (S) (M) **1.** an area of sacrifice. **3.** a son of Āgnīdhra.

Haviṣkṛta (S) (M) **1.** preparing the oblation. **3.** a sage who was a descendant of Aṅgiras and the author of a mantra or a chant in the *Pañćaviṁśa Brāhmaṇa.*

Haviṣman (S) (M) **1.** sacrificial. **3.** a sage who was a member of the assembly of Indra (*M. Bh.*).

Haviṣmata (S) (M) **1.** believing in sacrifices. **3.** a sage who was a descendant of Aṅgiras and author of a mantra or chant in the *Pañćaviṁśa Brāhmaṇa*; a seer of the 6th, 10th and 11th cycles of creation (*H. Purāṇa*).

Haviṣravas (S) (M) **1.** sounding like the fire. **3.** a Kuru king of the lunar dynasty (*M. Bh.*).

Havya (S) (M) **1.** to be invoked. **3.** a son of Manu Svāyambhuva (*H. Purāṇa*); a son of Atri (*V. Purāṇa*).

Havyaghna (S) (M) **1.** destroyer of the sacrifice. **3.** another name for Agni.

Havyavāhana (S) (M) **1.** oblation bearer. **3.** a ṛṣi under Manu Sāvarna; another name for Agni.

Hayagrīva (S) (M) **1.** with a horse's neck. **3.** an asura who was the son of Kaśyapa and Danu; a king of the Videha dynasty (*M. Bh.*); an asura who guarded the kingdom of Narakāsura (*M. Bh.*); an incarnation of Viṣṇu as a celestial horse (*V. Purāṇa*); a saintly king (*M. Bh.*); a tāntra deity.

Hayapati (S) (M) **1.** lord of horses. **2.** king.

Hayaśiras (S) (M) **1.** horse's head. **3.** an incarnation of Viṣṇu (*V. Purāṇa*).

Hayavāhana (S) (M) **1.** driving horses. **3.** another name for Revanta, the son of the sun.

Héli (S) (M) **1.** embrace. **3.** the sun as all pervasive.

Hema (S) (M) **1.** gold. **2.** a dark horse. **3.** the father of Sutapas; a Buddha; Ironwood tree (*Mesua ferrea*).

Hemabala (S) (M) power of gold; the pearl.

Hemabhojam (S) (M) golden lotus (*Nymphaea alba*).

Hemaćandra (S) (M) **1.** golden moon. **3.** a celebrated Jaina scholar (*J. S. Koṣa*); the son of King Viśāla and the father of Sućandra (*Bhāgavata*).

Hemadhanvan (S) (M) **1.** with a golden bow. **3.** a son of the 11th Manu.

Hemādri (S) (M) **1.** golden mountain. **3.** another name for the mountain Sumerū.

Hemaguha (S) (M) **1.** golden cave. **3.** a nāga born in the Kaśyapa dynasty (*M. Bh.*).

Hemakānta (S) (M) **1.** bright as gold. **3.** the son of King Kuśaketu of Vaṅga (*Sk. Purāṇa*).

Hemakeli (S) (M) **1.** golden sport. **3.** another name for Agni.

Hemakeśa (S) (M) **1.** with golden hair. **3.** another name for Śiva.

Hemaketakī (S) (M) the Golden Screwpine; the fragrant Ketāki plant (*Pandanus odoratissimus*).

Hemamālī (S) (M) **1.** wearing a golden garland. **3.** a son of King Drupada (*M. Bh.*); gardener of Vaiśravaṇa (*P. Purāṇa*).

Hemamālin (S) (M) **1.** garlanded with gold. **3.** another name for Sūrya.

Heman (S) (M) **1.** golden yellow. **2.** the Jasmine blossom (*Jasminum pubescens*); the Saffron flower (*Crocus sativus*); gold; golden ornament. **3.** another name for the planet Mercury.

Heman (S) (M) made of gold.

Hemanātha (S) (M) **1.** lord of gold. **3.** another name for Śiva.

Hemanetra (S) (M) **1.** golden eyed. **3.** a yakṣa who worships Kubera in his assembly (*M. Bh*).

Hemāṅga (S) (M) **1.** golden bodied. **2.** a Brāhmin; a lion; the Ćampaka tree (*Michelia champaka*). **3.** another name for Garuḍa, Viṣṇu, Brahmā and Mount Meru.

Hemanta (S) (M) winter.

Hemanya (S) (M) gold bodied.

Hemapuṣpam (S) (M) **1.** golden flowered. **3.** Aśoka tree (*Saraca indica*).

Hemarāja (S) (M) lord of gold.

Hemaratha (S) (M) **1.** with a golden chariot. **3.** a king of the solar dynasty and grandson of Ćitraratha, son of Kśema and father of Satyaratha (*Bhāgavata*).

Hemaśaṅkha (S) (M) **1.** with a golden conch shell. **3.** another name for Viṣṇu.

Hemasāvarṇi (S) (M) **1.** golden coloured. **3.** father of Svāyamprabha (*Rāmayaṇa*).

Hemaśikha (S) (M) **1.** gold crested. **3.** Prickly Poppy (*Argemone mexicana*).

Hemavarṇa (S) (M) **1.** golden complexioned. **3.** the son of King Rocamāna who fought on the side of the Pāṇḍavas (*M. Bh.*); a son of Garuḍa; a Buddha.

Hemavatīnandana (S) (M) **1.** son of Pārvatī; son of Hemavatī. **3.** another name for Gaṇeśa and Kārttikeya.

Hemendra (S) (M) **1.** lord of gold. **3.** anolher name for Indra.

Heraka (S) (M) **1.** spy. **3.** an attendant of Śiva.

Heramba (S) (M) **1.** son of wealth. **2.** boastful. **3.** another name for Gaṇeśa.

Heti (S) (M) **1.** flame. **3.** another name for Agni.

Hima (S) (M) **1.** snow. **2.** winter; night. **3.** a year as mentioned in scriptures (*V. Purāṇa*); Nut gram (*cyperus rotundis*); Himalayan Cherry (*Prunus cerasoides*).

Himābja (S) (M) the Blue Lotus (*Nymphaea stellata*).

Himāćala (S) (M) abode of snow; the Himālaya mountain.

Himādri (S) (M) peak of snow; the Himālaya mountain.

Himadyuti (S) (M) **1.** of cool radiance. **2.** the moon.

Himajyotī (S) (M) **1.** with snowlike light. **3.** another name for Ćandra.

Himakara (S) (M) **1.** snow handed; causing cold. **2.** white. **3.** another name for the moon.

Himakiraṇa (S) (M) **1.** cold-rayed. **2.** the moon.

Himāmbū (S) (M) water of snow; dew.

Himāṅśu (S) (M) **1.** cool rayed. **3.** another name for Ćandra.

Himaratī (S) (M) **1.** enemy of snow. **2.** fire. **3.** Ceylon Leadwort (*Plumbago zeylanica*); another name for the sun.

Himaśaila (S) (M) **1.** snow mountain. **3.** another name for the Himālaya.

Himavāllūka (S) (M) ice like in appearance.

Himavāna, Himavata (S) (M) **1.** cold; of white; having snow. **3.** the great mountain range on the northern borders personified as a divine soul called Himavāna who is married to Menā and is the father of Pārvatī; another name for Ćandra.

Himośra (S) (M) **1.** white rayed. **3.** another name for Ćandra.

Hiṁsra (S) (M) **1.** cruel; destructive; savage fierce. **3.** a sage who was the son of Kuśika; another name for Bhīma and Śiva.

Hīnadoṣa (S) (M) without fault.

Hiṅgula (S) (M) **1.** vermilion. **2.** auspicious; sacred.

Hiṅkara (S) (M) **1.** chanting of hymns. **2.** the invocation of a deity.

Hīra (S) (M) quintessence; a diamond; thunderbolt; lion.

Hīraka (S) (M) diamond.

Hīral (S) (M) **1.** bearer of diamonds. **2.** very wealthy.

Hirañćaya (S) (M) **1.** deer footed. **3.** a son of Āgnīdhra.

Hiraṅga (S) (M) **1.** diamond bodied. **2.** as hard as a diamond. **3.** the thunderbolt of Indra.

Hiraṇya (S) (M) **1.** gold. **2.** most precious. **3.** another name for Viṣṇu.

Hiraṇyabāhu (S) (M) **1.** golden armed. **2.** very strong. **3.** a nāga born in Vāsuki's dynasty (*M. Bh.*).

Hiraṇyābja (S) (M) **1.** golden lotus (*Nymphaea alba*).

Hiraṇyadanta (S) (M) **1.** gold toothed. **3.** a teacher mentioned in the *Aitereya Brāhmaṇa*.

Hiraṇyadhanuṣ (S) (M) **1.** with a golden bow. **3.** a king of forest tribes and father of Ekalavya.

Hiraṇyagarbha (S) (M) **1.** the golden womb. **3.** another name for Brahmā and Kṛṣṇa.

Hiraṇyahasta (S) (M) **1.** golden handed. **3.** the son of Princess Vadhṛmatī, given by the aśvins who became a sage and married the daughter of King Madirāśva (*M. Bh.*); another name for Sāvitṛ.

Hiraṇyakaśipu (S) (M) **1.** covered with gold. **3.** a son of Viśvāmitra who was a Brahmavādin (*M. Bh.*); a son of Kaśyapa and Diti, the brother of Hiraṇyākṣa and the father of Prahlāda (*V. Purāṇa/M. Bh./Bhāgavata*).

Hiraṇyakeśa (S) (M) **1.** golden haired. **3.** another name for Viṣṇu.

Hiraṇyākṣa (S) (M) **1.** golden eyed. **3.** a son of Kaśyapa and Diti and brother of Hiraṇyakaśipu (*V. Purāṇa/ Bhāgavata/M. Bh.*).

Hiraṇyamaya (S) (M) **1.** full of gold. **2.** a particular region in the Jambu island to the south of Mount Nīla and the north of Mount Niśādha (*Bhāgavata*).

Hiraṇyanābha (S) (M) **1.** with a golden navel. **3.** a solar dynasty king who was the father of Puṣya (*Bhāgavata*); a son of a child of Śṛñjaya who lived for a 1000 years (*M. Bh.*); a Kośalā prince (*P. Upaniṣad*).

Hiraṇyaretas (S) (M) **1.** having gold as seed. **3.** son of Priyavrata who was king of Kuśa island (*Bhāgavata*); an aditya; another name for Śiva and Agni.

Hiraṇyaroman (S) (M) **1.** with golden hair. **3.** a king of Vidharbha who was suzerain of the southern regions (*H. Purāṇa*); a seer of the 5th cycle of creation (*Bhāgavata/ Mā. Purāṇa*).

Hiraṇyastūpa (S) (M) **1.** golden pillar. **3.** a great sage who was the son of Aṅgiras (*Ṛg Veda*).

Hiraṇyava (S) (M) golden ornament; property of a god.

Hiraṇyavāha (S) (M) **1.** bearing gold. **2.** another name for Śiva and the river Śona.

Hiraṇyavarman (S) (M) **1.** with golden armour. **3.** a king of Daśārṇa whose daughter married Śikhaṇḍī (*M. Bh.*).

Hiraṇyina (S) (M) of gold.

Hīren (S) (M) **1.** lord of gems. **2.** attractive pearls.

Hīreśa (S) (M) king of gems.

Hiriśipra (S) (M) **1.** golden checked. **3.** another name for Agni and Indra.

Hīru (S) (M) as hard as a diamond.

Hita (S) (M) **1.** welfare. **2.** beneficial; good; wholesome; friendly; auspicious; kind.

Hitaīṣi (S) (M) well wisher.

Hitaṣa (S) (M) **1.** the oblation eater. **3.** another name for Agni.

Hiteṣin (S) (M) benevolent. others.

Homa (S) (M) **1.** oblation. **3.** a king of the Bharata dynasty who was the son of Kṛsadratha and the father of Sutapas (*Bhāgavata*); Black Catechu tree (*Acacia catechu*).

Honna (S) (M) to possess.

Hośang (S) (M) to be one's own self.

Hotravāhana (S) (M) **1.** with the chariot of invocation. **3.** a saintly king who was the grandfather of Ambā (*M. Bh.*).

Hrāda (S) (M) **1.** sound; noise; roar; reality. **3.** a son of Hiraṇyakaśipu (*V. Purāṇa*); a nāga who helped carry the body of Balarāma to *Pātāla* (*M. Bh.*).

Hrādodara (S) (M) **1.** lake-bellied. **3.** a daitya (*M. Bh.*).

Hrasvaroman (S) (M). **1.** shorthaired. **3.** a king of Videha and son of Svarṇaroman (*Bh. Purāṇa*).

Hṛććhaya (S) (M) **1.** dwelling in the heart; conscience. **3.** another name for Kāmā.

Hṛdambhoja (S) (M) with a lotus-like heart.

Hṛdaya (S) (M) heart.

Hṛidayaja (S) (M) **1.** born of the heart. **2.** son.

Hṛdayanārāyaṇa (S) (M) **1.** lord of the heart. **3.** another name for Viṣṇu.

Hṛdayaṅgam (S) (M) **1.** entered into the heart. **2.** beautiful; beloved; cherished.

Hṛdayeśa (S) (M) lord of the heart.

Hṛdayeśvara (S) (M) lord of the heart; beloved.

Hṛdi (S) (M) **1.** heart. **3.** a Yādava prince (*Bhāgavata*).

Hṛdīka (S) (M) **1.** of heart. **2.** friendship. **3.** a Yādava who was the father of Kṛtavarman (*M. Bh.*).

Hṛdīkātmaja (S) (M) **1.** son of Hṛdīka. **3.** another name for Kṛtavarman.

Hṛdya (S) (M) **1.** agreeable; desired. **3.** a sage who lives in the assembly of Indra (*M. Bh.*); Caraway (*Carum carvi*).

Hrdyānanda (S) (M) joy of the heart.

Hrdyanātha (S) (M) lord of the heart.

Hreśa (S) (M) to be delighted; to be glad.

Hrim (S) (M) **1.** one who takes away; wealth. **3.** a mantra or a holy chant representing Maya the power of illusion and Bhuvanesvarī, the dispeller of sorrow (*V. Samhitā*).

Hrīmān (S) (M) **1.** dispeller of sorrow; wealthy. **3.** a viśvadeva (*H. Purāṇa*).

Hrīniṣeva (S) (M) **1.** relinquisher of wealth. **3.** a saintly king of the asura dynasty who relin-quished his kingdom (*M. Bh.*).

Hṛṣīkeśa (S) (M) **1.** controlling the senses. **3.** Kṛṣṇa with his senses controlled (*M. Bh.*).

Hṛṣu (S) (M) **1.** glad; happy. **3.** another name for Agni, the sun and moon.

Hūhū (S) (M) **1.** in attentive response. **3.** a gandharva who was the son of Kaśyapa and Prādhā (*H. Purāṇa/M. Bh.*).

Hulās (S) (M) jubilation.

Huṇḍa (S) (M) **1.** giver of pain. **2.** one who tortures; tiger. **3.** an asura son of Vipraćitti who abducted Aśokasundarī the sister of Kārttikeya (*P. Purāṇa*).

Hurditya (S) (M) joyous; happy.

Hutabhu **1.** created by the oblation. **3.** another name for Agni.

Hutabhuj (S) (M) **1.** oblation eater. **3.** another name for Agni.

Hutabhuk (S) (M) **1.** oblation eater. **3.** another name for Agni.

I

Ibhāna (S) (M) **1.** elephant faced. **3.** another name for Gaṇeśa.

Ibhānan (S) (M) **1.** elephant faced. **3.** another name for Gaṇeśa.

Ibhya (S) (M) possessor of many attendants.

Iććhaka (S) (M) **1.** granting desires. **3.** the Citron tree (*Citrus medico*).

Iććhavasu (S) (M) **1.** possessing all wealth wished for. **3.** another name for Kubera.

Iḍā (S) (M) **1.** a stream of praise; a period of time; libation. **3.** one of sage Kardama's sons (*V. Purāṇa*); another name for Agni.

Iḍāspati (S) (M) **1.** lord of refreshment. **3.** another name for Pūṣan, Viṣṇu, and Parjanya, the god of rain.

Iḍavida, Ilavilā (S) (M) **1.** knower of libation; one who has insight. **3.** a son of Daśaratha.

Iddham (S) (M) **1.** shining; glowing; blazing. **2.** sunshine; light; heat.

Iḍenya (S) (M) to be praiseworthy.

Idhabodha (S) (M) of illuminative insight.

Idhma (S) (M) sacrificial fuel; the fuel used for a yajña.

Idhmajīhva (S) (M) **1.** fuel tongued. **2.** one who brings fuel for the sacrifice. **3.** a son of Priyavrata and Surūpā and the grandson of Svāyambhuva Manu (*M. Bhāgavata*).

Idhmavāha (S) (M) **1.** carrier of fuel. **2.** one who carries wood for the sacrifice. **3.** a son of Dṛdacyuta; a son of Lopāmudrā and Agastya who was the equivalent of a 1,000 sons in strength (*V. Rāmāyaṇa*).

Ijya (S) (M) **1.** worthy of worship. **2.** a teacher; deity; god. **3.** another name for Bṛhaspati as the teacher of the gods; another name for the Supreme Being, Viṣṇu and the planet Jupiter.

Ijyaśīla (S) (M) performing the sacrifice repeatedly.

Ikṣaṇa (S) (M) sight.

Ikṣuda (S) (M) that which gives sweetness; sweet tongued.

Ikṣura (S) (M) sugarcane; a fragrant grass called Khas (*Vetiveria zizanioides*); *Polytoca barbata* grass.

Ikṣusamudra (S) (M) **1.** the sea of syrup. **3.** one of the 7 seas of the mythical world (*A. Koṣa*).

Ikṣvāku (S) (M) **1.** one who attracts desire. **2.** one who brings wishes to effect. **3.** the son of Manu Vaivasvata, the grandson of Vivasvāna who founded the solar dynasty and ruled at Ayodhyā and the ancestor of Rāma (*M. Bh./Ṛg Veda/Bhāgavata/H. Purāṇa/ Rāmāyaṇa*).

Ikvāla, Ekvāl (S) (M) prosperity, good fortune.

Ilāćandra (S) (M) moon of the earth.

Ilādhara (S) (M) upholder of the earth; mountain.

Ilānko (S) (M) surface of the earth.

Ilāspada (S) (M) foot of the earth; an ancient bathing ghat considered holy and a dip in which is considered to ward off ill-luck.

Ilāspati (S) (M) lord of the earth.

Ilāvarta (S) (M) **1.** surrounding the earth. **2.** cloud over the earth. **3.** a king in the line of Priyavrata (*Bhāgavata*); a son of Svāyambhuva Manu.

Ilavila (S) (M) **1.** protector of earth. **3.** a son of Daśaratha (*V. Rāmāyaṇa*).

Ilāvṛta (S) (M) protector of speech; one of the 9 divisions of the earth (*M. Bh./ Mā. Purāṇa*); a son of Āgnīdhra.

Ilī (S) (M) a small sword; a knife.

Ilībiśa (S) (M) **1.** one who throws knives at the enemy. **3.** an asura conquered by Indra (*Ṛg Veda*).

Ilila, Ilina (S) (M) **1.** possessing high intelligence. **3.** a sword of Indra (*H. Purāṇa*); a king of the Purū dynasty who was the son of King Taṁsu, husband of Rathāntarī and the father of King Duṣyanta (*M. Bh.*).

Ilūṣa (S) (M) **1.** covering the earth; a wanderer. **3.** the father of Kavaṣa (*H. Purāṇa*).

Ilya (S) (M) a mythical tree of paradise.

Inakānta (S) (M) beloved of the sun; the sunstone.

Iṇan (S) (M) sun; lord; master; king.

Inas (S) (M) **1.** able; strong; bold; wild; glorious; powerful; mighty. **3.** an aditya; another name for Sūrya.

Indambara (S) (M) **1.** with precious clothing. **3.** the Blue Lotus (*Nymphaea stellata*).

Indeśvara (S) (M) **1.** lord of the moon. **3.** a pilgrimage centre.

Indirālaya (S) (M) **1.** abode of Indira. **3.** another name for the Blue Lotus (*Nymphaea stellata*) from which Lakṣmī emerged at the time of creation.

Indīvara (S) (M) **1.** best among the precious. **2.** blessing. **3.** the Blue Lotus (*Nymphaea stellata*); another name for Viṣṇu.

Indīvarākṣa (S) (M) **1.** lotus eyed. **3.** a gandharva who was the son of Nalanābha the chief of the vidyādharas (*M. Purāṇa*).

Indīvarasena (S) (M) **1.** the army of Viṣṇu. **3.** the son of King Parityāgasena of Irāvati (*K. Sāgara*).

Indīya (S) (M) knowledgeable; of the river Narmadā; the planet Mercury.

Indra (S) (M) **1.** god of the atmosphere and sky. **2.** excellent; first; chief; symbol of generous heroism. **3.** the deity who fights the demons and is subordinate to Brahmā, Viṣṇu and Śiva in the pantheon but chief of all the other deities (*Ṛg Veda/A. Veda/M. Smṛti/ M. Bh./Rāmāyaṇa*); the plant *Holarrhena antidysenterica*.

Indrabala (S) (M) with the strength of Indra.

Indrabha (S) (M) **1.** with the glory of Indra. **3.** a son of Dhṛtarāṣṭra (*M. Bh.*).

Indrabhūti (S) (M) **1.** image of Indra. **3.** one of the 11 Gaṇādhipas of the Jainas (*J.S. Koṣa*); the main disciple of Mahāvira (*J. Literature*).

Indraćāpa (S) (M) **1.** bow of Indra. **3.** another name for the rainbow.

Indradamana (S) (M) **1.** conqueror of Indra. **3.** a king known for his generosity towards Brāhmins (*M. Bh.*); an asura.

Indradatta (S) (M) gift of Indra.

Indradhvaja (S) (M) **1.** Indra's banner. **3.** a Tathāgata; a nāga.

Indrādu (S) (M) desired by Indra.

Indradyumna (S) (M) **1.** the light, lustre and splendour of Indra. **3.** a king of the Pāṇḍya country from the Svāyambhuva Manu dynasty (*M. Bh.*); a king who was a contemporary of Kṛṣṇa and killed by him (*M. Bh.*); a sage who blessed Yudhiṣṭhira during his exile (*M. Bh.*); the father of King Janaka of Mithilā (*Rāmāyaṇa*); a king of the Ikṣvāku dynasty (*M. Bh.*); a king of the Kṛta yuga who was a devotee of Viṣṇu (*Sk. Purāṇa*); a lake near Mount Gandhamādana visited by the Pāṇḍavas (*M. Bh.*); the son of Sumati and grandson of King Bharata (*M. Bh.*).

Indraghoṣa (S) (M) **1.** the voice of Indra; one who praises Indra. **3.** a deity.

Indragiri (S) (M) **1.** the mountain of Indra. **3.** another name for the mountain Mahendra.

Indrāgni (S) (M) Indra and Agni conjoined; the Indrāgni deity is the embodiment of heroism.

Indragopa (S) (M) protected by Indra.

Indragupta (S) (M) protected by Indra; Khuskhus grass (*Vetiveria zizanioides*).

Indraguru (S) (M) **1.** teacher of Indra. **3.** another name for sage Kaśyapa.

Indraja (S) (M) **1.** born of Indra. **3.** another name for Vālin.

Indrajāla (S) (M) **1.** the net of Indra. **2.** hypnotism, the science of magic. **3.** the weapon of Arjuna (*M. Bh.*).

Indrajālin (S) (M) **1.** of the net of Indra. **2.** a sorcerer. **3.** a bodhisattva (*L. Vistara*).

Indrajit (S) (M) **1.** conqueror of Indra. **3.** another name for Meghanāda the son of King Rāvaṇa of Laṅkā (*U. Rāmāyaṇa*); a dānava; a king of Kāśmira (*R. Taraṅgiṇī*).

Indrakarman (S) (M) **1.** performing Indra's deeds. **3.** another name for Viṣṇu.

Indrakārmuka (S) (M) rainbow.

Indraketu (S) (M) Indra's banner.

Indrakīla (S) (M) **1.** banner of Indra. **3.** a mountain situated between the Himālayas and the Gandhamādana mountain, the deity of which is a devotee of Kubera (*M. Bh.*).

Indramantrin (S) (M) **1.** advisor of Indra. **3.** another name for sage Bṛhaspati.

Indramedin (S) (M) one whose ally is Indra.

Indranīla (S) (M) **1.** as blue as Indra. **2.** the sapphire.

Indrānuja (S) (M) **1.** younger brother of Indra. **3.** another name for Viṣṇu.

Indrapālita (S) (M) **1.** protected by Indra. **3.** a king (*V. Purāṇa*).

Indrapramati (S) (M) **1.** knowledge of Indra; protected by Indra. **3.** a disciple of sage Vyāsa (*M. Bh.*).

Indrapriya (S) (M) dear to Indra.

Indrapūṣan (S) (M) Indra and Pūṣan conjoined; the Indrapūṣan deity is invoked to give assistance in battle.

Indrarājan (S) (M) Indra, the king; having Indra as king.

Indrāsana (S) (M) throne of Indra.

Indrasārathi (S) (M) **1.** the charioteer of Indra. **3.** another name for Mātali the charioteer of Indra; another name for Vāyu.

Indrasāvarṇi (S) (M) **1.** Indra's complexion. **2.** one with the complexion of Indra. **3.** the 14th Manu (*H. Purāṇa*).

Indrasena (S) (M) **1.** the army of Indra; the best warrior. **3.** a son of King Nala (*M. Bh.*); a son of King Parīkṣit (*M. Bh.*); the charioteer of Yudhiṣṭhira (*M. Bh.*).

Indrasoma (S) (M) **1.** Indra and Soma conjoined. **3.** Indrasoma who discovered the sun, supported the heavens, filled the sea with water and gave milk to the cows and the function of whom is to perform heroic deeds for man and invest him with heroic strength (*M. Bh.*).

Indrasunu (S) (M) **1.** son of Indra. **3.** another name for Jayanta; the White Murdah (*Terminalia citrina*).

Indrāsura (S) (M) Indra the brave.

Indrasuras (S) (M) the tree of Indra; the Arjuna tree (*Terminalia arjuna*).

Indrasuta (S) (M) **1.** son of Indra. **3.** another name for the monkey king, Vālin, Arjuna and Jayanta.

Indrasvat (S) (M) accompanied by Indra.

Indratan (S) (M) as strong as Indra.

Indratāpa (S) (M) **1.** the penance of Indra. **2.** offering sacrifices and penances to Indra. **3.** an asura who was a devotee of Varuṇa (*M. Bh.*).

Indratejas (S) (M) **1.** the strength of Indra. **3.** the thunderbolt of Indra.

Indravadana (S) (M) **1.** the face of Indra. **2.** one with the beauty of Indra.

Indravāhana (S) (M) **1.** the vehicle of Indra. **2.** with Indra as the vehicle; one who is carried by Indra. **3.** another name for King Kakutṣṭha of the Ikṣvāku dynasty who made Indra his vehicle while fighting the asuras.

Indravajra (S) (M) the thunderbolt of Indra.

Indrāvaraja (S) (M) **1.** the younger brother of Indra. **3.** another name for Viṣṇu, Kṛṣṇa and Śiva.

Indravarman (S) (M) **1.** protected by Indra. **3.** a king of Mālava who fought on the side of the Pāṇḍavas (*M. Bh.*).

Indravaruṇa, Indravāruṇī (S) (M) **1.** Indra and Varuṇa conjoined. **3.** the deity Indravaruṇa which represents kingly and heroic power and from which comes the bestowal of protection, prosperity, fame and many horses (*Ṛg Veda*); a wild gourd (*Cucumis colocynthis*) considered the favourite plant of both Indra and Varuṇa; another name for Indra's special wine, Soma.

Indravaṣṇu/Indravisṇu (S) (M) **1.** Indra and Viṣṇu. **3.** the deity in which Viṣṇu in his Vedic solar form conjoined with Indra and which is invoked to provide shelter, bestow wealth and accept sacrifice (*Ṛg Veda*).

Indravāyu (S) (M) Indra and Vāyu conjoined.

Indrāyatana (S) (M) depending on Indra.

Indrayava (S) (M) one whose friend is Indra.

Indrāyudha (S) (M) **1.** weapon of Indra. **2.** the rainbow.

Indrayumna (S) (M) **1.** one who can stop Indra. **3.** a Pāṇḍyan king who was incarnated as the elephant Gajendra.

Indrejya (S) (M) **1.** teacher of Indra; excellent teacher. **3.** another name for Bṛhaspati.

Indresita (S) (M) sent by Indra.

Indreśvara (S) (M) **1.** lord of the senses. **3.** a form of the Śivaliṅga.

Indrīṇika (S) (M) desired by Indra.

Indrota (S) (M) **1.** one who lives near Indra. **2.** promoted by Indra. **3.** a sage who was the son of sage Śuka and also known as Śaunaka (*M. Bh.*); the son of Atithigva mentioned in the *Ṛg Veda* as a bestower of gifts.

Indubha (S) (M) with the light of the moon; the water lily (*Nymphaea alba*); a group of lotuses.

Indubhava (S) (M) **1.** creating the moon. **3.** another name for Śiva.

Indubhṛt (S) (M) **1.** with the crescent on his forehead. **3.** another name for Śiva.

Indubhūṣaṇa (S) (M) **1.** with the moon as an ornament. **2.** whose ornament is the moon. **3.** another name for Śiva.

Indugiri (S) (M) **1.** mountain of the moon. **2.** silver; fair; cool; soothing. **3.** another name for Indra's mountain known as Rajata.

Induja (S) (M) **1.** son of the moon. **3.** another name for Budha or the planet Mercury.

Indujanaka (S) (M) **1.** father of the moon. **3.** another name for the ocean and sage Atri.

Indukamala (S) (M) **1.** moon like lotus. **2.** the White Lotus (*Nelumbium speciosum*).

Indukānta (S) (M) **1.** beloved of the moon. **2.** the moonstone.

Indukara (S) (M) **1.** hand of the moon. **2.** a moonbeam.

Indukarman (S) (M) **1.** act of moon. **2.** performing pious deeds. **3.** another name for Viṣṇu.

Indukārmuka (S) (M) encircling the moon; the rainbow.

Indukesarin (S) (M) **1.** golden moon. **3.** a king (*K. Sāgara*).

Induketu (S) (M) **1.** moon bannered. **3.** the banner of Indra (*L. Vistara*).

Indukirīṭa (S) (M) **1.** moon crested. **3.** another name for Śiva.

Indukṣaya (S) (M) **1.** fall of the moon. **2.** the period just after full moon when the moon wanes.

Indukukṣa (S) (M) the belly of the moon.

Indukūṭa (S) (M) the mountain of the moon.

Indumaṇi (S) (M) **1.** gem of the moon. **2.** moonstone.

Indumat (S) (M) **1.** respected by the moon. **3.** another name for Agni.

Indumauli (S) (M) **1.** moon crested. **3.** another name for Śiva.

Indumitra (S) (M) **1.** friend of the moon. **3.** a grammarian (*A. Koṣa*).

Indumukhī (S) (M) **1.** with a face like the moon. **2.** a face as beautiful as the moon.

Indunandana (S) (M) **1.** son of the moon. **3.** another name for the planet Mercury.

Indupāla (S) (M) **1.** gem of the moon. **2.** the moonstone; ocean.

Induputra (M) **1.** son of the moon. **3.** another name for the planet Mercury.

Induśekhara (S) (M) **1.** moon crested. **3.** a kinnara; another name for Śiva.

Ineśa (S) (M) **1.** a strong king. **3.** another name for Viṣṇu.

Iṅganam (S) (M) knowledge.

Iṅgida (S) (M) **1.** granting knowledge. **3.** a plant used in magic rites to ensure the destruction of enemies (*A. Veda*).

Iṅgur (S) (M) **1.** the sacred colour. **2.** the colour vermilion which is considered auspicious and sacred.

Inodaya (S) (M) sunrise.

Iṇu (S) (M) **1.** charming. **3.** a gandharva (*K. Sāgara*).

Inukānta (S) (M) **1.** beloved of the sun. **2.** the sunstone.

Ira (S)(M) wind.

Iraiśa (S) (M) **1.** lord of the earth. **3.** another name for Varuṇa, Viṣṇu and Gaṇeśa.

Irajā (S) (M) **1.** born of the wind. **3.** another name for Hanumān, the son of the wind god Vāyu.

Irāja (S) (M) **1.** son of the primal waters. **3.** another name for Kāma.

Iranmada (S) (M) **1.** delighting in drink. **2.** lightning. **3.** another name for Agni (*A. Purāṇa*).

Irāputra (S) (M) **1.** born of the wind. **3.** another name for Hanumān, the son of the wind god, Vāyu.

Irāvaja (S) (M) **1.** born of water. **3.** another name for Kāma.

Irāvān (S) (M) **1.** possessing water or milk. **2.** ocean; cloud; king. **3.** the son of Arjuna and Ulūpi (*M. Bh.*).

Irāvata (S) (M) **1.** full of water. **2.** cloud.

Irāvatān (S) (M) **1.** resembling water or milk. **2.** satiating; comforting; refreshing. **3.** the son of Arjuna and Ulūpi (*M. Bh.*).

Iremut (S) (M) full of wind; thunder.

Iri (S) (M) **1.** son of the wind. **3.** a king who worships Yama (*M. Bh.*); another name for Hanumān, son of the wind god, Vāyu.

Irimbiṭhi (S) (M) **1.** the path of the wind. **3.** a sage of the family of Kaṇva (*M. Bh.*).

Irimpu (Malayalam) (M) purifying wind; iron.

Irīśa, Ireśa (S) (M) **1.** lord of the earth. **3.** another name for Viṣṇu, Varuṇa and Ganeśa.

Irith (S) (M) of wind; scent.

Irma (S) (M) **1.** of the nature of wind. **2.** moves constantly; instigates everything. **3.** another name for Sūrya.

Irmaṇḍa (S) (M) **1.** delighting in drinking. **2.** a flash of lightning. **3.** another name for Agni.

Irya (S) (M) **1.** powerful; energetic; active. **3.** another name for Pūṣan and the aśvins.

Īśa (S) (M) **1.** god; lord of the universe. **2.** fertile; performing pious deeds; one who impels; swift; powerful; venerated; all pervading; divine. **3.** one of the 13 principal Upaniṣads; the month of the aśvins (September-October); a sage (*H. Purāṇa*); another name for the viśvadevas or universal gods; a rudra; another name for Śiva.

Īśadatta (S) (M) **1.** acquired through pious deeds. **3.** a son of Atri and Anasuyā (*V. Rāmāyaṇa*).

Īśan (S) (M) bestowing wealth.

Īśāna (S) (M) **1.** sovereign; lord. **3.** a rudra; another name for Śiva, Viṣṇu, Agni, and Sūrya; the Śami tree (*Prosopis spicigera*).

Īśānadeva (S) (M) sovereign; lord; guardian of the north-east.

Īśānam (S) (M) light, splendour.

Īśat (S) (M) superiority; greatness.

Īśayu (S) (M) fresh; strong; powerful.

Īśik (S) (M) desirable; the Silkcotton tree (*Salmalia malabarica*).

Iṣir (S) (M) **1.** powerful; strong; quick; active; refreshing. **3.** another name for Agni.

Iṣita (S) (M) desired.

Iṣma (S) (M) **1.** pervaded with desire; desire provoking; impetuous. **3.** the spring season; another name for Kāma.

Iṣmin (S) (M) **1.** as swift as the spring; speedy; impetuous. **2.** like the wind.

Iśrita (S) (M) owner; master; lord of the universe.

Iṣṭagandha (S) (M) fragrant.

Iṣṭaka/Iṣṭika (S) (M) a brick used in preparing the ceremonial altar.

Iṣṭaraśmi (S) (M) **1.** desiring light. **3.** a king mentioned in the *Ṛg Veda* and known for the number of yajñas or sacrifices he performed.

Iṣṭāśva (S) (M) **1.** a desired horse. **3.** a king mentioned in the *Ṛg Veda* and known for the number of yajñas or sacrifices he performed.

Iṣu (S) (M) **1.** quivering. **2.** an arrow; the number 5; a ray of light.

Iṣuka (S) (M) arrow.

Iṣupa (S) (M) **1.** quiver. **3.** a serpent reborn as King Nagnajita (*M. Bh.*).

Iṣupada (S) (M) **1.** the target of an arrow. **3.** an asura born to Kaśyapa and Danu who was later reborn as the heroic king, Nagnajita (*M. Bh.*).

Iśva (S) (M) spiritual teacher.

Īśvara (S) (M) **1.** capable of mastering; ruler; the Supreme Being. **3.** a rudra; another name for Śiva and Kāma.

Īśvaracandra (S) (M) the moon among gods; the greatest god.

Īśvaraprasāda (S) (M) given by the gods.

Iṣvasa (S) (M) arrow shooter; an archer.

Iṣya (S) (M) effecting wishes; the spring season.

Iṭa (S) (M) **1.** to wander; a kind of reed. **3.** a ṛṣi who was a protégé of Indra (*Ṛg Veda*).

Itanta/Idhanta (M (S) **1.** shining; bright; sharp; clean; wonderful. **3.** a sage (*K. Brāhmaṇa*).

Itar (S) (M) another.

Itiśa (S) (M) such a lord.

Ivīlaka (S) (M) **1.** wealthy son. **3.** the son of Lambodara (*V. Purāṇa*).

Iyam (Malayalam) (M) lead.

Iyenar (Tamil) (M) tutelary village god who is the guardian of the fields and the herds.

J

Jābāli (S) (M) **1.** possessing a herd of goats. **2.** a goatherd. **3.** an ancient sage who was the son of Viśvāmitra, the author of a law book and the priest of Daśaratha (*P. Purāṇa*); the son of sage Ṛtadhvaja (*M. Bh.*); a hermit who performed penance on the Mandara mountain and was a devotee of Kṛṣṇa for which he was reborn as the cowherdess Ćitrāṅgadā (*Bhāgavata*); a hermit who was the sometime consort of the apsarā Rambhā (*Sk. Purāṇa*).

Jabbar (S) (M) barley grower; a peasant.

Jādhava (S) (M) a descendant of Jadu (or Yadu); a yādava.

Jagaćakṣu (S) (M) **1.** eye of the universe. **3.** the Supreme Being.

Jagaćandra (S) (M) **1.** moon of the universe. **3.** a Jaina Sūrī (*J. S. Koṣa*).

Jagaćitra (S) (M) wonder of the universe.

Jagad (S) (M) universe; world.

Jagadānanda (S) (M) **1.** pleasure of the universe. **2.** pleasing and satiating the world.

Jagadātman (S) (M) **1.** soul of the universe. **3.** another name for the Supreme Spirit.

Jagadāya (S) (M) **1.** life of the universe. **2.** the wind.

Jagadāyu (S) (M) **1.** life spring of the universe. **2.** the wind.

Jagadbala (S) (M) strength of the universe.

Jagadeva (S) (M) **1.** lord of the world. **3.** the Supreme Being.

Jagadgurū (S) (M) **1.** guru of the universe; preceptor of the world. **3.** another name for Brahmā, Viṣṇu, Śiva and Rāma.

Jagadhratu (S) (M) **1.** abode of the universe. **2.** the creator of the universe. **3.** another namefor Brahmā.

Jagadīpa (S) (M) **1.** lamp of the universe. **3.** another name for Sūrya.

Jagadīśa (S) (M) **1.** lord of the universe. **3.** another name for Brahmā.

Jagadīśvara (S) (M) **1.** god of the universe. **3.** another name for Śiva and Indra.

Jagajīva (S) (M) living force of the world; soul of the world.

Jagamohana (S) (M) **1.** one who attracts the world. **3.** another name for Kṛṣṇa.

Jagan (S) (M) world; universe.

Jaganmaṇi (S) (M) jewel of the world.

Jagannātha (S) (M) **1.** lord of the world. **3.** an idol of Viṣṇu at Puri; a Sanskṛt critic who is known as Paṇḍitarāja or king of scholars (16th century A.D.) (*R. Gaṅgādhara*); another name for Viṣṇu, Kṛṣṇa and Dattātreya.

Jagannetra (S) (M) **1.** eye of the world. **3.** another name for Sūrya and Ćandra.

Jagannidhi (S) (M) receptacle of the world.

Jagannivāsa (S) (M) **1.** abode of the world; one who pervades the world. **3.** another name for Viṣṇu and Kṛṣṇa.

Jaganu (S) (M) living being; fire.

Jagaprīta (S) (M) beloved of the world.

Jāgara (S) (M) armour.

Jagarūpa (S) (M) form of the world.

Jagat (S) (M) **1.** moving; alive. **2.** the world; people.

Jagatādhāra (S) (M) **1.** the abode of the world. **2.** time; wind; air. **3.** another name for Viṣṇu, Śeṣa and Lakṣmaṇa.

Jagatasvāmī (S) (M) **1.** lord of the universe. **3.** another name for Viṣṇu.

Jagatdīpa (S) (M) **1.** lamp of the universe. **3.** another name for Sūrya.

Jagatguru (S) (M) **1.** preceptor of the world; father of the world. **2.** the Supreme Deity. **3.** another name for Śiva, Nārada, Brahmā and Viṣṇu.

Jagati (S) (M) **1.** bestowed with speed. **3.** one of the 7 horses that draw the chariot of Sūrya (*V. Purāṇa*).

Jagatīdhara (S) (M) **1.** earth-supporter. **2.** mountain. **3.** a bodhisattva.

Jagatīpatī (S) (M) **1.** lord of the earth. **2.** a king.

Jagatjīta (S) (M) victor of the world.

Jagatjīva (S) (M) being of the world; a living being.

Jagatkāraṇa (S) (M) the cause of the universe.

Jagatnārāyaṇa (S) (M) **1.** lord of the universe. **3.** another name for Viṣṇu.

Jagatnātha (S) (M) **1.** lord of the world. **3.** another name for Viṣṇu, Dattātreya and Śiva.

Jagatpatī (S) (M) **1.** master of the universe. **3.** another name for Brahmā, Śiva, Viṣṇu, Agni.

Jagatpitṛ (S) (M) **1.** father of the universe. **3.** another name for Śiva.

Jagatprabhu (S) (M) **1.** cause of the universe. **2.** one through whom the world has been brought into existence. **3.** a Jaina Arhat; another name for Brahmā, Viṣṇu and Śiva.

Jagatprakāśa (S) (M) light of the universe.

Jagatprāṇa (S) (M) **1.** breath of the universe. **2.** the wind. **3.** another name for Rāma.

Jagavanta (S) (M) one to whom the world belongs.

Jageśa (S) (M) **1.** lord of the world. **3.** another name for Viṣṇu.

Jagīśa (S) (M) lord of the world.

Jagmi (S) (M) **1.** pervading the world. **2.** the wind.

Jagnu (S) (M) **1.** carrier of the world. **2.** the fire.

Jāgravi (S) (M) **1.** watchful. **2.** bright. **3.** another name for Agni and the sun.

Jāgṛvi (S) (M) **1.** watchful; attentive; not extinguishable. **2.** fire; Soma; a king.

Jāguri (S) (M) one who wakes others up; one who has risen up; one who leads; conducts.

Jāhnavīputra (S) (M) **1.** son of Gaṅgā. **3.** another name for Bhīṣma.

Jahnu (S) (M) **1.** ear. 2. a good listener. **3.** a king and sage who was the son of Ajamīḍha and Keśinī, ancestor of the Kuśikas and who drank up the waters of the Gaṅgā but on the prayers of Bhagīratha discharged them from his ears because of which the river is regarded as his daughter (*M. Bh.*); a ṛṣi of the 4th Manvantara (*H. Purāṇa*); another name for Viṣṇu.

Jahnukanyā (S) (M) **1.** daughter of Jahnu. **3.** another name for Gaṅgā.

Jahnutanayā (S) (M) **1.** daughter of Jahnu. **3.** another name for Gaṅgā.

Jāhuṣa (S) (M) **1.** leftover; young animal. **3.** a king of the Ṛg Vedic period and protégé of the aśvins (*Ṛg Veda*); a son of Puṣpavat.

Jai (S) (M) **1.** conqueror; victor. **2.** a kind of flute. **3.** an attendant of Viṣṇu (*Bhāgavata*); a son of Aṅgiras (*Ṛg Veda*); a son of Dhṛtarāṣṭra (*M. Bh.*); a son of Yuyudhāna (*H. Purāṇa*); a son of Kṛṣṇa (*Bhāgavata*); a son of Kaṅka (*H. Purāṇa*); a son of Vatsara and Svarvīṭhī (*H. Purāṇa*); a son of Purūravas and Urvaśī (*M. Bh.*); 11th ćakravartin of ancient Bhārat; name of Yudhiṣṭhira at Virāṭa's court (*M. Bh.*); one of the 7 flagsticks of Indra's banner (*Ṛg Veda*); the 3rd, 8th and 13th days of each half-month (*V's. B. Saṁhitā*); Aśoka in a former birth (*Divyāvadana*); a dānava (*M. Bh.*); Yellow Jasmine (*Jasminum humile*); another name for Indra, the sun and Arjuna.

Jaibhūṣaṇa (S) (M) ornament of victory.

Jaićandra (S) (M) **1.** moon among victors. **2.** always victorious. **3.** a king of Kānyakubja (*Rāmāyaṇa*); a king of Gauḍa (*R. Taraṅgiṇī*).

Jaideva (S) (M) **1.** lord of victory. **3.** a king of Gujarat (738 A.D.) (*I. Tantra*); a Sanskṛt poet who was the author of the *Gītagovinda* (13th century A.D.) (*Ćandrāloka*).

Jaidhara (S) (M) **1.** bearer of victory. **3.** Saṁkara's great-grandfather (*M. Bh.*).

Jaidharman (S) (M) **1.** victorious in religion. **2.** one who is ever victorious. **3.** heroes from the Kaurava side (*M. Bh.*).

Jaidhvaja (S) (M) **1.** flag of victory. **3.** a son of Arjuna Kārtavīrya and the father of Talajaṅgha (*V. Purāṇa*).

Jaidhvani (S) (M) a shout of victory.

Jaidvala (S) (M) **1.** powerful. **3.** name assumed by Sahadeva at the court of Virāṭa (*M. Bh.*).

Jaigata (S) (M) victorious.

Jaighoṣa (S) (M) shout of victory.

Jaigiśavyā (S) (M) **1.** victorious lord. **3.** a hermit who was the husband of Ekapātalā (*M. Bh.*).

Jaigopāla (S) (M) **1.** Gopāla, the victor. **3.** another name for Kṛṣṇa.

Jaigupta (S) (M) protected by victory.

Jaikara (S) (M) mine of victory.

Jaikīrti (S) (M) glory of victory.

Jaikṛta (S) (M) causing victory.

Jaimalla (S) (M) victorious fighter.

Jaimaṅgala (S) (M) **1.** auspicious victory; victory and welfare conjoined. **2.** a royal elephant.

Jaimati (S) (M) **1.** victorious mind. **3.** a Bodhisattva (*B. Ćarita*).

Jaimini (S) (M) **1.** desiring victory; striving for victory. **3.** a celebrated sage and philosopher who was a member of the council of Yudhiṣṭhira, a pupil of Vyāsa, founder of the *Pūrva Mimāṅsā*, co-author of the work *Jaya* which is the original of the *Mahābhārata* and the narrator of his work the *Brahmāṇḍa Purāṇa* to Hiraṇyanābha at Naimiṣāraṇya (*M. Bh.*); the priest of King Subāhu of the Ćolas (*P. Purāṇa*).

Jainārāyaṇa (S) (M) Viṣṇu, the victor.

Jainabhakti (S) (M) **1.** devoted to Jainism. **3.** a Jaina Sūrī (*J. S. Koṣa*).

Jainendra (S) (M) lord of the Jainas; a religion which worships the Jinas.

Jaipāla (S) (M) **1.** guardian of victory. **2.** a king. **3.** another name for Brahmā and Viṣṇu; *croton tiglium.*

Jaipīḍa (S) (M) victory and torture combined; one who attains victory by torturing others.

Jaipriya (S) (M) **1.** beloved of victory. **3.** a Pāṇḍava hero (*M. Bh.*).

Jairāja (S) (M) victorious ruler.

Jairāma (S) (M) victorious Rāma.

Jairasa (S) (M) the essence of victory.

Jaiśekhara (S) (M) the crest of victory.

Jaisena (S) (M) **1.** with a victorious army. **3.** a prince of Magadha who was a member of the council of Yudhiṣṭhira (*M. Bh.*); a king of Avantī who was the father of Mitravindā who married Kṛṣṇa (*Bhāgavata*); the father of Ćandamahāsena (*M. Bh.*).

Jaisinha (S) (M) **1.** victorious lion; lion among the victors. **3.** a king of Kāśmira (*R. Taraṅginī*).

Jaisinharāja (S) (M) a king like a victorious lion.

Jaiśīṣa (S) (M) **1.** a cheer of victory; victorious head. **2.** best among the victors.

Jaiskandha (S) (M) **1.** shoulder of victory; with victorious shoulders. **2.** one very strong. **3.** a minister of King Yudhiṣṭhira (*M. Bh.*).

Jaiṣṇava (S) (M) desirous of victory.

Jaistambha (S) (M) column of victory.

Jaitāṅga (S) (M) **1.** victorious over body; who has mastered his senses. **2.** who has overcome worldly attachments.

Jaitra (S) (M) **1.** leading to victory. **3.** a son of Dhṛtarāṣṭra (*M. Bh.*).

Jaitrāma (S) (M) **1.** abode of victory. **3.** the chariot of King Hariśćandra (*M. Bh.*); the conch of Dhṛṣṭadyumna (*M. Bh.*).

Jaivāha (S) (M) carrier of victory.

Jaivala (S) (M) **1.** giving life. **3.** name assumed by Sahadeva at the court of Virāṭa (*M. Bh.*).

Jaivanta (S) (M) long lived.

Jaivata (S) (M) **1.** being victorious. **2.** winning.

Jaivātrika (S) (M) **1.** long lived; one for whom long life is desired. **2.** son. **3.** another name for the moon.

Jaivīra (S) (M) victorious warrior.

Jāja (S) (M) warrior; powerful.

Jājali (S) (M) **1.** with the power of judgement. **3.** a hermit who reared birds on his head (*M. Bh.*).

Jājhara (S) (M) **1.** eliminator of power. **2.** very powerful; a warrior.

Jala (S) (M) **1.** water. **3.** the deity of water who was a luminary in the court of Brahmā (*M. Bh.*).

Jalabhuṣaṇa (S) (M) **1.** ornament of the water. **2.** the lotus (*Nelumbium speciosum*); the wind.

Jalada (S) (M) **1.** giving water. **2.** raincloud; ocean.

Jaladeva (S) (M) **1.** with water as its deity. **3.** the constellation of Āṣāḍha.

Jaladevatā (S) (M) god of water; goddess of water.

Jaladhara (S) (M) **1.** holding water. **2.** ocean; with a voice as musical as thunder. **3.** a Buddha (*S. Puṇḍarīka*); Chariot tree (*Ougeinia oojeinensis*).

Jaladhi (S) (M) **1.** living in water; treasure of water. **2.** a crocodile; the ocean. **3.** the black crocodile born from the ear of Rudra and which is the carrier of Varuṇa (*M. Bh.*).

Jalādhipa (S) (M) **1.** lord of the waters. **3.** another name for Varuṇa.

Jalagambu (S) (M) **1.** essence of water. **3.** a son of Sūrya (*Bhā. Purāṇa*).

Jalaja (S) (M) **1.** born of the water. **2.** a conchshell; the lotus (*Nelumbium speciosum*). **3.** another name for the moon.

Jalakaraṅka (S) (M) **1.** embraced by water; born in water. **2.** a conchshell; lotus (*Nelumbium speciosum*); cloud; wave.

Jalāmbara (S) (M) **1.** water clad. **2.** the ocean. **3.** Rāhulabhadra in a former birth (*S. Prābhāsa*).

Jalamūrti (S) (M) Śiva in the form of water.

Jalāñcala (S) (M) **1.** water clad. **2.** a spring; a fountain.

Jalandhama (S) (M) **1.** water blower. **3.** an attendant of Skanda (*M. Bh.*); a dānava (*Sk. Purāṇa*).

Jalandhara (S) (M) **1.** water bearer. **3.** an asura who was the husband of Vṛndā and was produced by the contact of a flash from Śiva's eye with the ocean (*Bhāgavata*).

Jalanidhi (S) (M) **1.** treasure of water. **2.** ocean.

Jalāntaka (S) (M) **1.** containing water. **3.** a son of Kṛṣṇa (*H. Purāṇa*).

Jalapati (S) (M) **1.** lord of the waters. **3.** another name for Varuṇa.

Jalārka (S) (M) **1.** sun in water. **2.** the image of the sun in water.

Jalasa (S) (M) **1.** water like. **2.** appeasing; healing; happiness.

Jalasandha (S) (M) **1.** confluence of waters. **3.** a son of Dhṛtarāṣṭra.

Jalasandhi (S) (M) **1.** confluence of waters. **2.** a place where 2 rivers meet. **3.** a warrior who fought on the side of the Kauravas (*M. Bh.*); a son of Dhṛtarāṣṭra (*M. Bh.*).

Jalāśaya (S) (M) **1.** reposing on water. **2.** a pond. **3.** another name for Viṣṇu.

Jalaukas (S) (M) **1.** living near water. **3.** a king of Kāśmira (*R. Taraṅgiṇī*).

Jalavāhana (S) (M) **1.** water carrier. **3.** Gautama Buddha in a previous birth (*S. Prābhāsa*).

Jalavīrya (S) (M) **1.** power of water. **3.** a son of Bharata (*M. Bh.*).

Jalendra (S) (M) **1.** lord of the waters. **3.** a Jina; another name for Varuṇa.

Jaleśvara (S) (M) **1.** god of waters. **2.** ocean. **3.** another name for Varuṇa.

Jaleyu (S) (M) **1.** inhabitant of water; living in water. **3.** a son of Raudrāśva and the apsarā Miśrakeśī (*M. Bh.*).

Jalīndra (S) (M) **1.** lord of the waters. **2.** the ocean. **3.** another name for Varuṇa and Mahādeva.

Jalpa (S) (M) **1.** talk; discussion; discourse. **3.** a ṛṣi (*M. Purāṇa*).

Jamadagni (S) (M) **1.** consuming fire. **3.** a sage and descendant of Bhṛgu who was the son of Ṛcīka and Satyavatī, the husband of Reṇukā, the father of Paraśurāma, a luminary of the court of Brahmā and is considered the embodiment of Kṣatriya majesty (*Ṛg Veda/A. Veda/V. Samhitā*).

Jamagha (S) (M) **1.** consumer of sins; destroyer of sins. **3.** a king of the family of Yayāti (*Bhāgavata*).

Jamālin (S) (M) **1.** connoisseur. **3.** Mahāvira's son-in-law and the founder of schism I of the Jaina church (*J.S. Koṣa*).

Jaman (S) (M) connoisseur.

Jambakā (S) (M) **1.** possessor of water. **3.** another name for Varuṇa.

Jāmbavat (S) (M) **1.** possessing the Jambu fruit; the fruit of the Roseapple tree (*Eugenia jambolana*). **3.** a monkey chief of extraordinary might born from the yawn of Brahmā and who witnessed all the incarnations of Viṣṇu from Matsya to Kṛṣṇa (*Rāmāyaṇa*); the son of Pitāmaha, the father of Jāmbavatī and a minister of Sugrīva.

Jāmbavatī (S) (M) **1.** daughter of Jāmbavala. **3.** a wife of Kṛṣṇa and mother of Sāmba (*D. Bh. Purāṇa*).

Jambha (S) (M) **1.** tooth; tusk; jaws; yawn. **3.** several demons conquered by Kṛṣṇa (*Bhā. Purāṇa*); a son of Hiraṇyakaśipu (*Bhāgavata*); the father-in-law of Hiraṇyakaśipu (*Bhāgavata*); a daitya who snatched the Amṛta from the hands of Dhanvantari (*A. Purāṇa*); Indra's thunderbolt (*M. Bh.*); the Bergamot tree (*Citrus bergamia*).

Jambhabhedin (S) (M) **1.** destroyer of Jambha. **3.** another name for Indra.

Jambhaka (S) (M) **1.** yawning; crushing; devouring. **3.** an attendant of Śiva (***H. Purāṇa***); a king conquered by Kṛṣṇa (*M. Bh.*).

Jambhārati (S) (M) **1.** enemy of Jambha. **3.** another name for Indra.

Jambudhvaja (S) (M) **1.** having the Jambu tree as a flag. **3.** a nāga (*A. Koṣa*); another name for Mount Meru.

Jambūka (S) (M) **1.** jackal. **3.** an attendant of Skanda (*M. Bh.*); the Screwpine (*Pandanus tectorius*); another name for Varuṇa.

Jambūkésvara (S) (M) **1.** lord of the jackals. **3.** a liṅga or idol of Śiva in Mysore.

Jambuki (S) (M) **1.** jambu coloured. **2.** purple; indigo; the amethyst.

Jambumālikā (S) (M) **1.** garlanded with jambu fruit. **3.** a Śudra sage (*U. Rāmāyaṇa*).

Jambumālin (S) (M) **1.** garlanded with jambu fruit. **3.** a rākṣasa who was the son of Prahasta (*V. Rāmāyaṇa*).

Jambumaṇi (S) (M) jambu coloured jewel; the sapphire.

Jambūnada (S) (M) **1.** coming from the Jambu river; gold. **3.** a golden mountain in Uśīrabīja (*M. Bh.*); a son of Janamejaya (*M. Bh.*).

Jāmbūnadaprabhā (S) (M) **1.** of golden splendour. **3.** a Buddha (*S. Puṇḍarīka*).

Jamburudra (S) (M) **1.** lord of the Jambu tree. **3.** a nāga (*Ś. Purāṇa*).

Jambūsvāmin (S) (M) **1.** lord of the Jambu tree. **3.** the pupil of Mahāvira's pupil Sudharman (*J.S. Koṣa*).

Janaćakṣus (S) (M) **1.** eye of all creatures. **2.** the sun.

Janaćandra (S) (M) moon among people.

Janadeva (S) (M) **1.** god of men. **3.** a Janaka king who ruled over Mithilā (*M. Bh.*).

Janādhinātha (S) (M) **1.** lord of men. **2.** a king. **3.** another name for Viṣṇu and Yama.

Janādhipa (S) (M) lord of men.

Jānaka (S) (M) **1.** knower. **3.** a Buddha.

Janaka (S) (M) **1.** producing; causing; progenitor; father. **3.** a king of Mithilā whose actual name was Śiradhvaja and who was a descendant of Viṣṇu, the father of Sītā and the personification of all virtues (*V. Rāmāyaṇa*); a king of Videha or Mithilā who was the son of Mithi and the father of Udāvasu (*Ś. Brāhmaṇa*).

Janaki (S) (M) **1.** causing; producing. **3.** a Kṣatriya king who was in previous birth, an asura called Ćandravināśa.

Jānakīnātha (S) (M) **1.** lord of Jānakī. **3.** another name for Rāmā.

Janamejaya (S) (M) **1.** causing men to tremble; victorious from birth. **3.** a king of the solar dynasty who was the son of Parīkṣit and Madrāvatī, the great-grandson of Rāma, the husband of Vapustamā and Kāśyā, the father of Śatānīka, Śaṅkukarṇa, Ćandrāpīḍa and Sūryapīḍa, conductor of the Sarpasatra or snake sacrifice which was stopped at the intervention of Āstika and to whom the *Mahābhārata* was related by Vyāsa (*M. Bh.*); a prominent member of Yama's assembly who conquered the world in 3 days and was then defeated by Māndhātā (*M. Bh.*); a king who was the incarnation of the asura Krodhavaśa (*M. Bh.*); a son of King Kuru and Vāhinī (*M. Bh.*); a son of King Kuru and Kauśalyā (*M. Bh.*); a serpent in the council of Varuṇa (*M. Bh.*); a king and son of King Durmukha who helped Yudhiṣṭhira in the great battle of Mahābhārata (*M. Bh.*).

Janasaha (S) (M) **1.** subduing men. **3.** another name for Indra.

Jananātha (S) (M) lord of men; a king.

Jananī (S) (M) **1.** mother; tenderness; compassion. **3.** Indian Madder (*Rubia cordifolia*).

Janapadin (S) (M) country ruler; a king.

Janapālaka (S) (M) protector of men.

Janapati (S) (M) lord of men.

Janapriya (S) (M) **1.** dear to men. **3.** the Drumstick tree (*Moringa oleifera*); another name for Śiva.

Janarājan (S) (M) king of men.

Janārdana (S) (M) **1.** exciting people. **2.** one who makes the asuras tremble. **3.** another name for Viṣṇu and Kṛṣṇa.

Janārdhana (S) (M) **1.** exciting people. **3.** another name for Viṣṇu and Kṛṣṇa.

Janaśruta (S) (M) famous among people.

Janatapa (S) (M) **1.** inflaming men. **3.** father of Atyarīti.

Janāv (S) (M) protecting men.

Jaṇḍakara (S) (M) **1.** bestower of light. **3.** one of the 18 Vināyakas who stays near the sun and carries out the orders of Yama (*Śukasaptati*).

Janendra (S) (M) lord of men.

Janeśa (S) (M) lord of men.

Janeśvara (S) (M) god of men.

Jangari (S) (M) **1.** fast; swift. **3.** a son of Viśvāmitra (*M. Bh.*).

Janghabandhu (S) (M) **1.** strong thighed; speedy. **3.** a sage who was a member of Yudhiṣṭhira's assembly (*M. Bh.*).

Jangi (S) (M) warrior.

Janiṣṭha (S) (M) desired by people.

Janita (S) (M) born.

Janmādhipa (S) (M) **1.** lord of birth. **3.** another name for Śiva.

Janmajyeṣṭha (S) (M) the 1st born.

Janmakīla (S) (M) **1.** birth pillar. **3.** another name for Viṣṇu.

Janmavīra (S) (M) **1.** a warrior by birth. **3.** another name for Abhimanyu the son of Arjuna.

Jantu (S) (M) **1.** born. **2.** a living being. **3.** a king of the Purū dynasty who was the son of King Somaka and father of Vṛṣatanu (*M. Bh./H. Purāṇa*).

Janu (S) (M) the soul.

Jānujaṅgha (S) (M) **1.** knee and thigh conjoined. **3.** a king who should be remembered every morning and evening (*M. Bh.*).

Janya (S) (M) born.

Janyu (S) (M) **1.** born. **2.** creature; fire. **3.** another name for Brahmā.

Jāpaka (S) (M) **1.** reciter. **2.** meditator. **3.** a sage who is constantly engaged in the Gāyatrī mantra (*M. Bh.*).

Japana (S) (M) **1.** muttering prayers. **3.** a brother of Śunaśśepha.

Japendra (S) (M) **1.** lord of reciters. **3.** another name for Śiva.

Japeśa (S) (M) **1.** lord of reciters. **3.** another name for Śiva.

Jara (S) (M) **1.** old age. **3.** a son of Vasudeva and Tūrī; the hunter who accidently killed Kṛṣṇa (*H. Purāṇa*).

Jarābhiru (S) (M) **1.** afraid of old age. **3.** another name for Kāma.

Jarāsandha (S) (M) **1.** born in halves but joined by Jarā. **3.** a king of Magadha and Ćedi, the son of Bṛhadratha and a rākṣasī called Jarā, the father-in-law of Kaṁsa and enemy of Kṛṣṇa, and was killed by Bhīma (*M. Bh.*); a son of Dhṛtarāṣṭra (*M. Bh.*); the father of King Jayatsena who fought on the side of the Kauravas (*M. Bh.*).

Jaratkaru (S) (M) **1.** wearing out the body. **3.** a Purāṇic sage who was born in the Yāyāvara dynasty, married the sister of Vāsuki and was the father of Āstika (*Brahma Purāṇa*).

Jaritāri (S) (M) **1.** enemy of old age. **3.** Mandapāla and Jaritā's eldest son.

Jaritṛi (S) (M) a singer of hymns; a worshipper; an invoker.

Jarṇu (S) (M) **1.** waning. **3.** another name for the moon.

Jarūtha (S) (M) **1.** making old. **3.** a demon conquered by Agni (*Ṛg Veda*).

Jasalinā (S) (M) abode of fame.

Jasamita (S) (M) immensely famous.

Jasapāla (S) (M) protected by fame.

Jasaprīta (S) (M) desiring fame.

Jasarāja (S) (M) lord of fame.

Jasavanta (S) (M) having fame.

Jasavīra (S) (M) famous warrior.

Jasundhi (S) (M) the Aśoka tree (*Jonesia aśoka*).

Jasuri (S) (M) **1.** starved. **3.** Indra's thunderbolt (*Ṛg Veda*).

Jaṭā (S) (M) matted hair; twisted hair; uncombed hair.

Jaṭāćīra (S) (M) wearing a plait of hair as a garment.

Jaṭādhara (S) (M) **1.** bearer of twisted locks. **2.** an ascetic. **3.** an attendant of Skanda (*M. Bh.*); a Buddha; another name for Śiva.

Jaṭādhārin (S) (M) **1.** wearing twisted hair. **3.** another name for Śiva.

Jaṭākara (S) (M) **1.** sprung from twisted hair. **2.** spring; fountain.

Jaṭāsana (S) (M) **1.** sitting on matted hair. **3.** another name for Brahmā.

Jaṭāśaya (S) (M) **1.** network of roots. **2.** the ocean.

Jaṭāśaṅkara (S) (M) Śiva, with matted hair.

Jaṭāśila (S) (M) a stone of matted hair; a massive stone.

Jaṭāsura (S) (M) **1.** demon with twisted locks of hair. **3.** a king who was a member of Yudhiṣṭhira's assembly (*M. Bh.*); a rākṣasa killed by Bhīma (*M. Bh.*); another rākṣasa who was the father of Alambuṣa (*M. Bh.*).

Jātaveda (S) (M) **1.** all-possessor; knowing all created beings. **3.** the son of Purūravas born from the fire (*Bhāgavata*); another name for Agni.

Jātavedas (S) (M) **1.** with tufts of twisted hair. **3.** another name for Agni.

Jaṭāyu (S) (M) **1.** full of twisted hair. **2.** fibrous; a bird. **3.** the king of vultures, the son of Aruṇa and Śyenī and the younger brother of Sampāti, was mortally wounded by Rāvaṇa while trying to rescue Sītā (*V. Rāmāyaṇa*); a Purāṇic bird descended from Viṣṇu; *Commiphora Mukul.*

Jāṭhara (S) (M) **1.** hard; firm; womb; child. **3.** a warrior of Skanda (*M. Bh.*); an erudite Brāhmin scholar of Vedic lore (*M. Bh.*); a mountain on the eastern side of Mahāmeru.

Jaṭi (S) (M) **1.** ascetic. **3.** a warrior of Skanda (*M. Bh.*); another name for Śiva.

Jatikayāna (S) (M) **1.** vehicle of ascetics. **3.** a sage and part author of the *Atharva Veda* (vi).

Jaṭila (S) (M) **1.** complex; having uncombed hair. **2.** a lion. **3.** name assumed by Śiva when disguised as a Brahmaćārin or ascetic (*M. Bh.*); Sweet Flag (*Acorus calamus*).

Jatin (S) (M) **1.** wearing twisted hair. **2.** an ascetic. **3.** an attendant of Skanda (*M. Bh.*); another name for Śiva.

Jatindhara (S) (M) **1.** a true state; bearing the lineage. **3.** physician of Śuddhodana in a previous birth.

Jatūkarṇa (S) (M) **1.** with patient ears. **3.** a sage who was a member of the council of Yudhiṣṭhira (*M. Bh.*); a sage who was one of the 28 transmitters of the Vedas (*V. Purāṇa*); another name for Śiva.

Jātusthira (S) (M) ever solid; never yielding.

Jātya (S) (M) of a noble family; pleasing; beautiful; best.

Javāhara (S) (M) jewel.

Javana (S) (M) **1.** swift. **3.** one of Skanda's attendants (*M. Bh.*).

Javānila (S) (M) swift wind; a hurricane.

Javin (S) (M) swift; a horse; a deer.

Javiṣṭha (S) (M) quickest.

Jaya (S) (M) **1.** victory; victorious. **3.** a son of Dhṛtarāṣṭra (*M. Bh.*); a king in the court of Yama (*M. Bh.*); name assumed by Yudhiṣṭhira in the court of Virāṭa (*M. Bh.*); a nāga born in the family of Kaśyapa (*M. Bh.*); a warrior who fought on the side of the Kauravas (*M. Bh.*); a warrior of Pāñćāla who fought on the side of the Pāṇḍavas (*M. Bh.*); an attendant of Skanda given to him by Vāsuki (*M. Bh.*); gatekeeper of Vaikuṇṭha — Viṣṇu's palace — who was reborn as Hiraṇyākṣa (*Bhāgavata*); the father of the rākṣasa Virādha who was killed by Rāma (*V. Rāmāyaṇa*); the original *Mahābhārata*; Black Myrobalan (*terminalia chebula*); Couch grass (*Cynodon dactylon*); another name for Mahāviṣṇu, Bhīma and the sun.

Jayadā (S) (M) **1.** causing victory. **3.** a tutelary deity of Vāmadeva's family (*Br. Purāṇa*).

Jayadatta (S) (M) **1.** given by victory. **3.** a son of Indra (*A. Koṣa*); a tutelary deity of Vāmadeva's family (*Br. Purāṇa*); a king (*K. Sāgara*); a Bodhisattva; a son of Indra.

Jayadbala (S) (M) **1.** of victorious power. **3.** name assumed by Sahadeva at the Virāṭa court (*M. Bh.*).

Jayadratha (S) (M) **1.** with victorious chariots. **3.** a Sindhu-Sauvīra king who was the son of Bṛhatkāya, the husband of Duśśala, a suitor for the hand of Draupadī who being rejected fought on the Kaurava side (*M. Bh.*); a son of Bṛhanmanas (*H. Purāṇa*); a king in the court of Yama (*V. Purāṇa*); the 10th Manu (*H. Purāṇa*).

Jayānīka (S) (M) **1.** an army of victors. **3.** a grandson of Drupada (*M. Bh.*); a brother of the king of Virāṭa (*M. Bh.*).

Jayanta (S) (M) **1.** victorious in the end. **2.** the moon. **3.** a son of Indra and Śaćī (*H. Purāṇa*); a rudra (*M. Bh.*); a son of Dharma (*Bhāgavata*); the father of Akrūra (*M. Purāṇa*); a gandharva (*K. Sāgara*); name assumed by Bhīma at Virāṭa's court (*M. Bh.*); a minister of Daśaratha (*V. Rāmāyaṇa*); the father of Vikramāditya (*K. Sāgara*); one of the 12 adityas (*M. Bh.*); name of Kṛṣṇa's birthright (*H. Purāṇa*); a mountain (*H. Purāṇa*); another name for Mahāviṣṇu, Śiva and Skanda.

Jayāpīda (S) (M) **1.** garland or chaplet of victory. **3.** husband of Kamalā (*R. Taraṅgiṇī*).

Jayarata (S) (M) **1.** absorbed in victory. **3.** a prince of Kalinga who fought on the side of the Kauravas (*M. Bh.*); Sanskṛta poet of Kāśmira (12th century)(*R. Taraṅgiṇī*).

Jayaratha (S) (M) a chariot of victory.

Jayasena (S) (M) **1.** a victorious army. **3.** the father of Ćaṇḍamahāsena (*M. Bh.*); a prince of Magadha who was a member of the council of Yudhiṣṭhira (*M. Bh.*); a king of Avantī who was the father of Mitravindā who became a wife of Kṛṣṇa (*Bhāgavata*).

Jayāṣṇava (S) (M) one who has tasted victory.

Jayāsva (S) (M) **1.** horse of victory. **3.** a son of King Drupada (*M. Bh.*); a brother of the king of Virāṭa (*M. Bh.*).

Jayāsvāmin (S) (M) the master of victory; lord of Lakṣmī.

Jayātmaja (S) (M) **1.** son of the victorious; son of Arjuna. **3.** another name for Abhimanyu.

Jayatsena (S) (M) **1.** conqueror of the army. **2.** with victorious armies. **3.** a king of Magadha who was the son of Jarāsandha and a friend of the Pāṇḍavas (*M. Bh.*); a king of the Purū dynasty, the son of King Sarvabhauma and Sunandā, the husband of Suśravas and the father of Arvāćīna (*H. Purāṇa*); name assumed by Nakula in the court of Virāṭa (*M. Bh.*); a son of Dhṛtarāṣṭra (*M. Bh.*); an attendant of Skanda (*M. Bh.*).

Jayendra (S) (M) **1.** lord of victory. **3.** a king of Kāśmira (*R. Taraṅgiṇī*); another name for Indra.

Jayeśvara (S) (M) **1.** lord of victors. **3.** a form of Śiva.

Jayin (S) (M) conqueror.

Jayiṣṇu (S) (M) desiring victory.

Jehila (S) (M) **1.** follower. **3.** a Jaina Sūri.

Jeman (S) (M) having victory; one who is victorious.

Jenya (S) (M) of noble origin; true.

Jetṛ (S) (M) **1.** victorious. **3.** a son of Madhuććandas (*Ṛg Veda*); a prince who had a grove near Śrāvastī (*B. Literature*).

Jetva (S) (M) to be gained.

Jhājha (S) (M) **1.** noisy. **3.** the father of asura Sunda and grandfather of Marīća (*V. Rāmāyaṇa*); a musical instrument.

Jharjhara (S) (M) **1.** flow. **2.** making a sound like that of filling water. **3.** a son of Hiraṇyākṣa (*Bhāgavata*).

Jhilli (S) (M) **1.** worm. **3.** a Yādava of the house of Vṛṣṇi who was a minister of Kṛṣṇa in Dvārakā; a warrior of the Vṛṣṇis who fought bravely in the great battle.

Jhilmit (S) (M) partially visible.

Jhinka (S) (M) moth.

Jigīṣu (S) (M) striving to conquer.

Jīmūta (S) (M) **1.** cloud. **2.** nourisher; the sun; mountain; sustainer; enjoyer. **3.** a king of the vidyādharas and hero of the play *Nāgānanda* (*K. Sāgara*); a king of the family of Yayāti (*Bhāgavata*); a wrestler at the court of Virāṭa (*M. Bh.*); a hermit who received treasure from the Himālayas; the horse of King Vasumanas; an ancient sage (*M. Bh.*); another name for Indra.

Jīmūtaketu (S) (M) **1.** cloud flag. **3.** a vidyādhara prince (*K. Sāgara*); another name for Śiva.

Jīmūtavāhana (S) (M) **1.** with a chariot of clouds. **3.** a vidyādhara who was the son of Jīmūtaketu, the husband of Malayavatī and the emperor of the vidyādharas (*K. Sāgara*); son of Śālivāhana (*K. Sāgara*); another name for Indra.

Jina (S) (M) **1.** victor. **3.** a Buddha; an Arhat or the chief saint of the Jainas (*J. Literature*), a son of Yadu (*Ku. Purāṇa*); another name for Viṣṇu.

Jinabhadra (S) (M) **1.** rightly victorious. **3.** a famous Jaina author (*J. S. Koṣa*); a Jaina Sūri (*J. S. Koṣa*).

Jinabhakti (S) (M) **1.** worshipping victory. **3.** a Jaina Sūri (*H. Koṣa*).

Jinaćandra (S) (M) **1.** moon among victors. **3.** 8 Jaina Sūris (*S. Veda*).

Jinadatta (S) (M) **1.** giving victory. **3.** a Jaina Sūri (*H. Koṣa*).

Jinadeva (S) (M) **1.** lord of victory. **3.** an Arhat (*P. Ćhatraprabandha*).

Jinadhāra (S) (M) **1.** bearing victory. **3.** a Bodhisattva (*L. Vistara*).

Jinahansa (S) (M) **1.** the swan of victory. **3.** a Jaina Sūri.

Jinaharṣa (S) (M) **1.** pleasure of victory. **3.** a Jaina Sūri (*V. Samgraha*).

Jinakīrti (S) (M) **1.** the fame of victory. **3.** a Jaina Sūri (*M. Stava*).

Jinakuśala (S) (M) **1.** perfectly victorious. **3.** a Jaina Sūri (*Ć. Vandana*).

Jinalabdhi (S) (M) **1.** receiver of victory. **3.** a Jaina Sūri (*J. Literature*).

Jinalābha (S) (M) **1.** finder of victory. **3.** a Jaina Sūri (*A. Prabodha*).

Jinamāṇikya (S) (M) **1.** jewel of victory. **3.** a Jaina Sūri (*Su. Purāṇa*).

Jinandhara (S) (M) **1.** abode of victory. **3.** a Bodhisattva (*H. Koṣa*).

Jinānkura (S) (M) **1.** seed of victory. **3.** a Bodhisattva (*H. Koṣa*).

Jinapadma (S) (M) **1.** lotus of victory. **3.** a Jaina Sūri (*He. Koṣa*).

Jinapati (S) (M) **1.** master of victory. **3.** a Jaina Sūri (*J. Literature*).

Jinaprabha (S) (M) **1.** light of victory. **3.** a Jaina Sūri (*J. S. Koṣa*).

Jinaprabodha (S) (M) **1.** inspiring of victory. **3.** a Jaina Sūri (*P. Prabodha*).

Jinaputra (S) (M) **1.** son of a victor. **3.** a Bodhisattva (*H. Koṣa*).

Jinarāja (S) (M) **1.** king of the victors. **3.** a Jaina Sūri (1591-1643).

Jinaratna (S) (M) **1.** jewel of victory. **3.** a Jaina Sūri.

Jinasamudra (S) (M) **1.** ocean of victory. **3.** a Jaina Sūri (*J. Literature*).

Jinasaukhya (S) (M) **1.** pleasure of victory. **3.** a Jaina Sūri (*J. S. Koṣa*).

Jinaśekhara (S) (M) **1.** best among the victors. **3.** the founder of the 2nd subdivision of the Kharataragaććā of the Jaina community (*K. gaććha*).

Jinasinha (S) (M) **1.** lion among victors. **3.** the founder of the 3rd subdivision of the Kharataragaćća of the Jaina community (*J. S. Koṣa*); a Jaina Sūri (*J. S. Koṣa*).

Jinavaktra (S) (M) **1.** with a victorious face. **3.** a Buddha (*L. Vistara*).

Jinavallabha (S) (M) **1.** beloved of victors. **3.** a Jaina author (*J. S. Koṣa*).

Jinavardhana (S) (M) **1.** promoter of victory. **3.** the founder of the 5th subdivision of the Kharataragaćća of the Jaina community (*K. gaććha*).

Jindurāja (S) (M) conquering old age.

Jinendra (S) (M) **1.** lord of victors. **3.** a Buddha (*H. Koṣa*); Jaina saint (*P. Ćaritra*).

Jineśa (S) (M) **1.** lord of victors (*K. Stotra*) **3.** an Arhat of the Jainas (*K. Stotra*); 2 Jaina Sūris (*P. Ćhatraprabandha*).

Jinodaya (S) (M) **1.** victorious. **3.** a Jaina Sūri (*H. Koṣa*).

Jinorasa (S) (M) **1.** essence of victory. **3.** a Bodhisattva (*H. Koṣa*).

Jinottama (S) (M) **1.** best among victors. **3.** a Jaina Sūri.

Jiṣṇu (S) (M) **1.** victorious. **3.** a Ćedi warrior who fought on the side of the Pāṇḍavas (*M. Bh.*); the son of Manu Bhautya (*H. Purāṇa*); another name for Viṣṇu, Kṛṣṇa, Indra, Arjuna and the sun.

Jita (S) (M) conquered.

Jitamanyu (S) (M) **1.** one who has subdued anger. **3.** another name for Viṣṇu.

Jitamitra (S) (M) **1.** one who has conquered his enemies. **3.** another name for Viṣṇu.

Jitāri (S) (M) **1.** one who has conquered his enemies. **3.** the father of the Arhat Sambhava; a son of Avīkṣit and the grandson of King Kuru (*M. Bh.*).

Jitaśatru (S) (M) **1.** conqueror of enemies. **3.** the father of the Arhat Ajita (*He. Koṣa*); a Buddha (*L. Vistara*).

Jitātmā (S) (M) **1.** conqueror of the soul. **3.** a viśvadeva (*M. Bh.*).

Jitātmanu (S) (M) **1.** conqueror of the self. **3.** a viśvadeva (*M. Bh.*).

Jitavrata (S) (M) **1.** winning by vows. **3.** a son of Havirdhāna (*Bh. Purāṇa*).

Jitendra (S) (M) conqueror of the senses.

Jittana (S) (M) **1.** conqueror of body. **2.** the zodiac sign of Gemini.

Jituma (S) (M) **1.** full of victory. **2.** the zodiac sign of Gemini.

Jitvan (S) (M) victorious.

Jīva (S) (M) **1.** a living being; alive. **2.** the principle of life; the personal soul. **3.** the Puṣya constellation; one of the 8 maruts, another name for Bṛhaspati, Karṇa and the earth; *Dendrobium fimbriatum.*

Jīvabhūta (S) (M) endowed with life.

Jīvadeva (S) (M) lord of the soul.

Jīvaja (S) (M) born alive.

Jīvala (S) (M) **1.** inspiring; animating; full of life; carries victory. **3.** the tree *Lannea grandis*; a charioteer of King Ṛtuparṇa of Ayodhyā and a friend of Nala (*Nalopākhyāna*).

Jīvana (S) (M) **1.** life; giving life; wind; son. **3.** another name for Śiva and the sun.

Jīvanātha (S) (M) lord of life.

Jīvanadhara (S) (M) bearer of life.

Jīvanikāya (S) (M) the system of life; one who is endowed with life.

Jīvanta (S) (M) **1.** long lived. **2.** *Prosopis spicigera.*

Jīvapriya (S) (M) **1.** beloved of living beings. **3.** Black Myrobalan (*Terminalia chebula*).

Jīvarāja (S) (M) **1.** lord of life. **3.** a Jaina Tīrthaṅkara (*J. S. Koṣa*).

Jīvaratna (S) (M) jewel of life.

Jīvatha (S) (M) **1.** long lived; virtuous. **2.** life; breath; tortoise; peacock; cloud.

Jīvavijaya (S) (M) conqueror of life.

Jīvinī (S) (M) **1.** one who lives really. **2.** the sun; a Brāhmin; praise.

Jīviteśa (S) (M) **1.** lord of the living. **3.** Yama; the sun; the moon.

Jīviteśvara (S) (M) **1.** god of the living. **3.** another name for Śiva.

Jñāna (S) (M) knowledge.

Jñānaćakṣus (S) (M) eye of knowledge; intellectual vision.

Jñānaćandra (S) (M) moon of knowledge.

Jñānadarpaṇa (S) (M) **1.** mirror of knowledge. **3.** a Bodhisattva.

Jñānadarśana (S) (M) **1.** supreme knowledge. **3.** a Bodhisattva.

Jñānadarśana (S) (M) **1.** supreme knowledge. **3.** a Bodhisattva.

Jñānadatta (S) (M) given by knowledge.

Jñānadeva (S) (M) lord of knowledge.

Jñānadīpa (S) (M) lamp of knowledge.

Jñānāgamya (S) (M) **1.** attainable by understanding. **3.** another name for Śiva.

Jñānagarbha (S) (M) **1.** filled with knowledge. **3.** a bodhisattva.

Jñānākara (S) (M) **1.** mine of knowledge. **3.** a Buddha.

Jñānaketu (S) (M) with the marks of intelligence.

Jñānakīrti (S) (M) **1.** with famed knowledge. **3.** a Buddhist teacher.

Jñānamaya (S) (M) **1.** full of knowledge. **3.** another name for Śiva.

Jñānamūrti (S) (M) knowledge personified.

Jñānamūrti (S) (M) a symbol of knowledge.

Jñānaṅghanāćārya (S) (M) teacher of pure intellect.

Jñānapāraga (S) (M) **1.** with celebrated knowledge. **3.** a sage who was the son of Kuśika.

Jñānapāvana (S) (M) **1.** purifying knowledge. **3.** a Tīrtha.

Jñānaprabha (S) (M) **1.** brilliant with knowledge. **3.** a bodhisattva.

Jñānaprakāśa (S) (M) light of knowledge.

Jñānarāja (S) (M) lord of knowledge.

Jñānasāgara (S) (M) **1.** ocean of knowledge. **3.** a Jaina Sūri.

Jñānavajra (S) (M) **1.** thunderbolt of knowledge. **3.** a Buddhist author.

Jñānavata (S) (M) **1.** endowed with knowledge. **3.** a bodhisattva.

Jñānavibhūtigarbha (S) (M) **1.** filled with superhuman knowledge. **3.** a bodhisattva.

Jñānabhāskara (S) (M) sun of knowledge.

Jñāneśa (S) (M) lord of knowledge.

Jñāneśvara (S) (M) lord of knowledge.

Jñānin (S) (M) endowed with knowledge.

Jñānolka (S) (M) meteor of knowledge.

Jñānottama (S) (M) with supreme knowledge.

Jñānaśrī (S) (M) **1.** with divine knowledge. **3.** a Buddhist author.

Jñāta (S) (M) **1.** known; comprehended; understood. **3.** a sage who was the son of Kuśika; family of Mahāvīra.

Jñātaputra (S) (M) **1.** son of the Jñāta family. **3.** another name for Mahāvīra.

Jñātanandana (S) (M) **1.** son of the Jñāta family. **3.** another name for Mahāvīra.

Jvalana (S) (M) **1.** flaming. **3.** another name for Agni.

Joganātha (S) (M) **1.** lord of yoga. **3.** another name for Śiva.

Jogarāja (S) (M) **1.** lord of ascetics. **3.** another name for Śiva.

Jogendra (S) (M) **1.** king of yogis. **3.** another name for Śiva.

Jogeśa (S) (M) **1.** lord of yogis. **3.** another name for Śiva.

Jogiā (S) (M) **1.** the colour worn by ascetics. **2.** the colour saffron. **3.** a rāga.

Jośa (S) (M) approval; pleasure; satisfaction; a bud.

Jośita (S) (M) pleased.

Jotiṅga (S) (M) **1.** absorbed in penance. **2.** an ascetic who subjects himself to severe penan-ces. **3.** another name for Śiva.

Jugala (S) (M) pair.

Jugalakiśora (S) (M) **1.** a pair of adolescents. **3.** a form of Kṛṣṇa with adolescent Rādhā and Kṛṣṇa conjoined.

Jugnu (S) (M) glow worm; firefly; ornament.

Juhū (S) (M) **1.** a tongue. **2.** a flame. **3.** a king of the family of Yayāti (*Bhāgavata*); another name for Brahmā and the sun.

Juśka (S) (M) **1.** lover; worshipper; meritorious. **3.** one of the 3 Kāśmiri Turuśka Kings (*R. Taraṅgiṇī*).

Juṣṭa (S) (M) loved; pleased; welcomed; propitious; served; worshipped.

Jūvas (S) (M) quickness.

Jvāla (S) (M) flame; blaze; light; torchglow; shine.

Jvālājihvā (S) (M) **1.** tongue of fire. **3.** an attendant given to Skanda by Agni; a warrior of Skanda (*M. Bh.*); a dānava (*H. Purāṇa*).

Jvālāliṅga (S) (M) **1.** flame marked with a blazing phallus. **3.** a sanctuary of Śiva.

Jvālanmaṇī (S) (M) a burning jewel; a highly glittering jewel.

Jvālāprasāda (S) (M) gift of fire; passionate; sacred; all consuming.

Jvālāvaktra (S) (M) **1.** flame mouthed. **3.** an attendant of Śiva (*Brahma Purāṇa*).

Jvālin (S) (M) **1.** flaming. **3.** another name for Śiva.

Jvalkā (S) (M) a large flame.

Jyāmagha (S) (M) **1.** great; superior; winning battles. **3.** a king born in the Ikṣvāku dynasty, the husband of Śaibya and the father of Vidarbha (*M. Bh.*).

Jyāyas (S) (M) superior; greater; stronger.

Jyeṣṭha (S) (M) **1.** eldest. **2.** pre-eminent; best; greatest; chief. **3.** the 16th lunar mansion sacred to Indra (*A. Veda*); the middle finger (*A. Koṣa*); a hermit versed in the *Sāma Veda* (*M. Bh.*).

Jyeṣṭhaghnī (S) (M) **1.** the oldest fire. **2.** slaying the eldest. **3.** a lunar mansion (*A. Veda/T. Brāhmaṇa*).

Jyoti (S) (M) **1.** flame. **2.** brilliant; passionate; sacred; all consuming. **3.** a son of the vasu named Aha (*M. Bh.*); one of the 2 attendants given to Skanda by Agni (*M. Bh.*).

Jyotika (S) (M) **1.** with a flame. **2.** brilliant. **3.** a famous serpent who was the son of Kaśyapa and Kadru (*M. Bh.*).

Jyotīndra (S) (M) lord of light.

Jyotiprakāśa (S) (M) the light of the flame.

Jyotirasa (S) (M) **1.** the essence of light. **2.** a gem.

Jyotiratha (S) (M) **1.** chariot of light. **2.** the Pole Star. **3.** a river that joins the river Śoṇa (*M. Bh.*); a nāga (*B. Literature*).

Jyotirbhāga (S) (M) womb of light; possessing light.

Jyotirbhāsin (S) (M) brilliant with light.

Jyotirmaya (S) (M) **1.** consisting of light. **3.** another name for Viṣṇu and Śiva.

Jyotirmukha (S) (M) **1.** bright faced. **3.** one of Rāma's monkey followers (*V. Rāmāyaṇa*).

Jyotirvasu (S) (M) **1.** the deity of light. **3.** a king born in the family of Purūravas who was the son of Sumati and the father of Pratīka (*Bhāgavata*).

Jyotiṣa (S) (M) **1.** full of light; luminous. **2.** fire; the sun; astrology as the study of the luminous objects of the sky i.e. stars and planets. **3.** a son of Manu Svāroćiṣa (*H. Purāṇa*); a marut (*H. Purāṇa*).

Jyotiṣka (S) (M) **1.** luminous. **3.** a luminous weapon of Arjuna (*M. Bh.*); a bright peak of Meru (*M. Bh.*); a serpent son of Kaśyapa and

Kadru (*M. Bh.*); a class of deities of light including the sun, moon, planets, stars and constellations; Intellect tree (*Celastrus paniculata*).

Jyotiṣmān (S) (M) **1.** possessor of light. 3. a king of Kuśadvīpa (*M. Bh.*).

Jyotiṣmat (S) (M) **1.** possessing light. 3. a son of Manu Svāyambhuva (*H. Purāṇa*); a son of Manu Sāvarṇa (*V. Purāṇa*); the 3rd foot of Brahmā (*Ć. Upaniṣad*); a mountain (*Bhāgavata*).

Jyotiṣprabha (S) (M) **1.** brilliant with light. **3.** a Buddha (*B. Literature*); a Bodhisattva (*B. Literature*).

Jyotsnāpriya (S) (M) **1.** beloved of moonlight; one who loves the moonlight. 2. the Ćakora bird (*Alectoris chukar chukar*).

Jyotsneśa (S) (M) **1.** lord of moonlight. 3. the moon.

K

Kā (S) (M) **1.** creator. **2.** prajāpati. **3.** a dakṣa (*M. Bh.*); another name for Viṣṇu.

Kabandha (S) (M) **1.** cloud; comet; water; belly; barrel. **3.** a disciple of Sumanta the earliest teacher of the *Atharva Veda*; a demon who was an incarnation of a gandharva called Viśvavasu, who attacked Rāma and Lakṣmana and was released from his curse by them (*V. Rāmāyaṇa*); another name for Śiva who presides over the cosmic sacrifice; another name for Rāhu.

Kabandhin (S) (M) **1.** bearing vessels of water. **2.** the clouds. **3.** another name for the maruts.

Kabilabarhiṣa (S) (M) **1.** brown lion. **3.** a king of Vṛṣṇivaṅśa (*M. Bh.*).

Kaća(S) (M) **1.** hair; beauty; brilliance; cloud. **3.** the eldest son of Bṛhaspati known for his beauty (*M. Bh./ Bhāgavata/R. Taraṅgiṇī*).

Kaćaṅgala (S) (M) **1.** from whose body the clouds emerge. **2.** the ocean.

Kaćapa (S) (M) **1.** cloud drinker. **2.** leaf.

Kaććhanīra (S) (M) **1.** water near the banks. **3.** a serpent (*M. Bh.*).

Kaććhapa (S) (M) **1.** inhabiting a marsh; tortoise. **3.** one of the 9 treasures of Kubera (*A. Koṣa*).

Kaćeśvara (S) (M) **1.** deity of beauty. **3.** a temple.

Kāćima (S) (M) **1.** abode of clouds; where clouds rest. **2.** a tree; a sacred tree that grows near a temple.

Kadalika (S) (M) made of banana skin; banner; flag.

Kadalīvana (S) (M) **1.** garden of plantain trees. **3.** Hanumān's garden on the banks of the Kuberapuṣkariṇī river (*Rāmāyaṇa*).

Kādambā (S) (M) group; cloud; a particular kind of flower (*Adina cordifolia*).

Kadambānila (S) (M) **1.** fragrant breeze; accompanied by fragrant breezes. **2.** the rainy season.

Kadambavāyu (S) (M) breeze flowing through the Kadambā tree (*Adina cordifolia*); a fragrant breeze; scented with the blossoms of the Kadambā tree.

Kadhmor (S) (M) **1.** killing enemies. **3.** a saintly king who should be remembered in the morning (*M. Bh.*).

Kudītula (S) (M) sword; scimitar.

Kāgni (S) (M) a little fire.

Kāhali (S) (M) **1.** mischievous. **3.** another name for Śiva.

Kāhodara (S) (M) **1.** making a sound in water. **3.** a sage who was the son of Uddālaka and the father of Aṣṭāvakra.

Kāhola (S) (M) bringing water; drinking water.

Kailāsa (S) (M) **1.** a mountain placed in the Himālaya range; a type of temple. **3.** a serpent belonging to the Kaśyapa family (*M. Bh.*); a mountain where Mahāviṣṇu performed penance to please Śiva; the mountain where Śiva and Kubera reside.

Kailāsanātha (S) (M) **1.** lord of Mount Kailāśa. **3.** another name for Śiva and Kubera.

Kailāsanilaya (S) (M) **1.** residing on Kailāsa. **3.** another name for Kubera.

Kailāsapati (S) (M) **1.** master of Mount Kailāśa. **3.** another name for Śiva.

Kairava (S) (M) water born; the White Lotus (*Nelumbium speciosum*).

Kaiśika (S) (M) **1.** hairlike; fine as a hair; love; passion. **3.** a rāga; a son of Vidarbha and brother of Kratha.

Kaiṭabha (S) (M) **1.** water born. **2.** lightning; thunder. **3.** an asura who was killed by Viṣṇu (*D. Bh. Purāṇa/Bhāgavata*).

Kaiṭabhajit (S) (M) **1.** conqueror of Kaiṭabha. **3.** another name for Viṣṇu.

Kaitaka (S) (M) **1.** coming from the Kevra tree (*Pandanus odoratissimus*). **3.** another name for Ulūka.

Kaitava (S) (M) **1.** gambler. **2.** deceitful. **3.** another name for Ulūka the son of Śakuni (*M. Bh.*).

Kaivalya (S) (M) emancipation; bliss.

Kajjala (S) (M) cloud; collyrium.

Kāka (S) (M) **1.** crow; Adam's apple; neck. **3.** a son of Kaṅsa (*Bhāgavata*).

Kakanda (S) (M) gold.

Kākavaktra (S) (M) **1.** crow faced. **3.** a Buddhist goddess.

Kākavarṇa (S) (M) **1.** formed like a crow; crow coloured; with the nature of a crow. **3.** a king and son of Śiśunāga (*V. Purāṇa*).

Kākila (S) (M) worn around the neck; a jewel.

Kakkula (S) (M) **1.** Bakula tree (*Mimusops elengi*). **3.** a Buddhist bhikṣu (*L. Vistara*).

Kākodara (S) (M) **1.** eaten by a crow. **2.** serpent.

Kakṣaka (S) (M) **1.** living in the forest. **3.** a serpent born in the family of Vāsuki (*M. Bh*).

Kakṣapa (S) (M) **1.** water drinker. **2.** tortoise **3.** one of the 9 treasures of Kubera (*A. Koṣa*).

Kakṣasena (S) (M) **1.** warrior of the forest. **3.** the son of Parīkṣit and a member in the court of Yama (*M. Bh.*).

Kakṣeyu (S) (M) **1.** held in the armpit. **2.** overpowered; embraced. **3.** the son of Raudrāśva born of a nymph called Miśrakeśī (*V. Purāṇa*/*H. Purāṇa*).

Kakṣīvān (S) (M) **1.** furnished with a girth. **2.** one with large arms; a king. **3.** a keeper of the forest (*M. Bh.*); a ṛṣi who was the son of Dīrghatamas and Uśīja and the husband of the 10 daughters of Rājasvaṇaja (*Ṛg Veda*); the son of Maharṣi Gautama (*Purāṇas*).

Kakṣīvant (S) (M) **1.** furnished with a girth. **3.** a ṛṣi mentioned frequently in the *Ṛg Veda* who was the son of Uśīja and Dirghatamas and the husband of Vṛćayā (*Ṛg Veda*).

Kakubjaya (S) (M) victorious over the quarters.

Kakudman (S) (M) possessor of peak; high; lofty.

Kakudmin (S) (M) **1.** peaked; mountain. **2.** humped. **3.** a king of the Ānartas (*H. Purāṇa*); another name for Viṣṇu.

Kakuha (S) (M) **1.** reached the peak. **2.** the seat of a chariot; chief; preeminent; lofty; high. **3.** a Yādava prince (*Bhāgavata*).

Kakuṇḍa (S) (M) **1.** peak. **2.** chief; symbol of royalty.

Kakuñjala (S) (M) striving for water; the Ćātaka bird (*Clamator jacobinus serratus*); a bud of the Ćampaka tree (*Michelia champaka*).

Kakutstha (S) (M) **1.** residing on the mountain peak. **3.** the son of King Saṣāda of the Ikṣvāku dynasty (*M. Bh.*); Rāma as he was born in the dynasty of Kakutstha.

Kāla (S) (M) **1.** time; fate; dark blue; black; death; the Supreme Spirit as a destroyer; the Indian cuckoo. **3.** a son of Hṛāda (*H. Purāṇa*); a brother of King Prasenajit (*B. Ćarita*); a future Buddha; a serpent lord; a mountain (*V. Rāmāyaṇa*); a rakṣasa (*Rāmāyaṇa*); another name for Śiva, Rudra, Yama and Saturn.

Kālabandhaka (S) (M) **1.** conqueror of time. **2.** death. **3.** an adviser of Mahiṣāsura (*D. Bhāgavata*).

Kalabhāṣin (S) (M) with a pleasing voice.

Kālabhīti (S) (M) **1.** of whom death is afraid. **2.** immortal; long lived. **3.** a devotee of Śiva and son of Māmti, who performed penance for a 1000 years for the sake of a son (*Ś. Purāṇa*).

Kalābhṛt (S) (M) **1.** bearing digits. **3.** another name for the moon.

Kālabrāhmaṇa (S) (M) **1.** a Brāhmaṇ who is beyond time and death. **3.** a Brāhmin who defeated time and death with his penance (*Sk. Purāṇa*).

Kāladantaka (S) (M) **1.** black toothed. **3.** a serpent born in the dynasty of Vāsuki (*M. Bh.*).

Kalādhara (S) (M) **1.** with digits. **3.** another name for the moon and Śiva.

Kaladhūta (S) (M) silver.

Kāladvija (S) (M) **1.** victor of death. **3.** a serpent (*Sk. Purāṇa*).

Kālaghaṭa (S) (M) **1.** present time; pitcher of time. **3.** a Brāhmin scholar in the Vedas who was a member of the assembly of the serpent yajña (*M. Bh.*).

Kalāguru (S) (M) **1.** lord of the digits. **3.** another name for the moon.

Kalahansa (S) (M) **1.** the black swan; an excellent king; the Supreme Spirit; a rare breed of swan. **3.** a type of hans; another name for Brahmā.

Kalahapriya (S) (M) **1.** quarrelsome. **3.** another name for Nārada.

Kālahara (S) (M) **1.** destroyer of death. **3.** another name for Kṛṣṇa.

Kālakākṣa (S) (M) **1.** black eyed. **3.** an asura killed by Garuḍa (*M. Bh.*); a warrior of Skanda (*M. Bh.*).

Kālakāmukha (S) (M) **1.** dark faced. **2.** inauspicious faced; a species of ape. **3.** a rākṣasa brother of Prahasta, and Rāvaṇa's minister (*V. Rāmāyaṇa*).

Kālakāñja (S) (M) a galaxy of time bearers; the galaxy of stars.

Kālakavi (S) (M) **1.** physician of death; poet of death. **3.** another name for Agni.

Kālakavṛkṣīya (S) (M) **1.** tree of time. **3.** a sage in the assembly of Indra (*M. Bh.*).

Kalakeli (S) (M) **1.** frolicsome. **3.** another name for Kāma.

Kālakendra (S) (M) **1.** lord of the black ones. **3.** a prince of the dānavas (*Rāmāyaṇa*).

Kālaketu (S) (M) **1.** comet of death. **3.** an asura emperor and son of Kaśyapa and Danu (*M. Bh.*).

Kālakeya (S) (M) **1.** of Kālakā. **3.** an asura (*H. Purāṇa*); a dānava race (*M. Bh.*).

Kālakīrti (S) (M) **1.** with timeless fame; with deathless fame. **3.** a Kṣatriya king who was born from the limb of Suparṇa the younger brother of the asura Mayūra (*M. Bh.*).

Kālakuñja (S) (M) **1.** abode of time. **3.** another name for Viṣṇu.

Kālakūṭa (S) (M) **1.** potion of death. **3.** the virulent poison that came up during the churning of the ocean of milk and which was swallowed by Śiva upon the request of Brahmā and retained in his throat (*M. Bh.*).

Kalāl (S) (M) wine seller.

Kalamesi (S) (M) **1.** dark fleeced. **2.** Caraway (*Curum carvi*); *Psoratea corylifolia*; Garden Cress (*Lepidum sativum*).

Kālamūrti (S) (M) time personified.

Kālanābha (S) (M) **1.** black navelled. **3.** a rākṣasa (*H. Purāṇa*); a son of Hiraṇyākṣa (*Bhāgavata*); a son of Vipraćitti and Siṁhikā (*H. Purāṇa/V. Purāṇa*).

Kalānaka (S) (M) **1.** a digit of the moon. **3.** attendants of Śiva (*Ś. Purāṇa*).

Kālanara (S) (M) **1.** dark hero. **3.** a son of Sabhānara (*Bh. Purāṇa*).

Kālanātha (S) (M) **1.** lord of time. **3.** another name for Śiva.

Kalānātha (S) (M) **1.** lord of the digits. **3.** another name for the moon.

Kālanemi (S) (M) **1.** felly of the wheel of time. **3.** a great asura, who in later years was born as Kaṁsa, son of King Ugrasena; a son of Yajñasena of Mālava (*K. Sāgara*); a rākṣasa who was killed by Hanumān (*Ā. Rāmāyaṇa*).

Kalānidhi (S) (M) **1.** with a treasure of digits; treasure of arts or skills. **3.** another name for the moon.

Kālañjagiri (S) (M) **1.** the black mountain; a mountain where saints live. **3.** a mountain at Medhāvika tīrtha.

Kālañjara (S) (M) **1.** destroyer(s) of death; an assembly of sages. **3.** a mountain in Bundelkhand.

Kālañjaya (S) (M) **1.** conqueror of time or death. **3.** another name for Kṛṣṇa.

Kālāṅkura (S) (M) the bud of time; scion of the family.

Kalāpa (S) (M) **1.** intelligent; a quiver of arrows; a peacock's tail; totality; ornament. **3.** a sage who was worshipped by Yudhiṣṭhira at the end of the Rājasūya yajña (*M. Bh.*); another name for the moon.

Kalāpaka (S) (M) **1.** one who has many feathers; possessed with skills; a band; a bundle; an ornament; a single string of pearls; bearing a quiver of arrows; a peacock. **3.** a sage (*M. Bh.*); another name for the moon.

Kālaparvata (S) (M) **1.** the mountain of time. **3.** a mountain beside the sea near Laṅkā (*M. Bh.*); a mountain seen by Arjuna on his way to Śiva with Kṛṣṇa during their dream journey (*M. Bh.*).

Kālapatha (S) (M) **1.** the course of time. **3.** a son of Viśvāmitra (*M. Bh.*).

Kalāpin (S) (M) peacock (*Pavo cristatus*); Indian cuckoo (*Cuculus scolopaceus*).

Kālapraṣṭha (S) (M) **1.** black backed. **3.** a serpent (*M. Bh.*).

Kalāpriya (S) (M) lover of art.

Kalāpūrṇa (S) (M) **1.** perfect in arts; the totality of the digits. **3.** another name for the moon.

Kālarāja (S) (M) lord of death.

Kālāri (S) (M) **1.** enemy of death. **3.** another name for Kṛṣṇa.

Kalaśa (S) (M) **1.** a pitcher; a churn; the pinnacle of a temple. **3.** a serpent born of the family of Kaśyapa (*M. Bh.*).

Kalaśabhū (S) (M) **1.** pitcher born. **3.** another name for Agastya.

Kālaśaila (S) (M) **1.** dark mountain. **3.** a range of mountains in the Uttarākhaṇḍa in ancient India (*M. Bh.*).

Kālaśapotaka (S) (M) **1.** destroyer of peacocks. **3.** a serpent (*M. Bh.*).

Kālaśinha (S) (M) **1.** black lion; lion of time. **3.** a Prākṛt poet.

Kalaśodara (S) (M) **1.** pot bellied. **3.** an attendant of Skanda's retinue (*M. Bh.*); a daitya.

Kalatra (S) (M) **1.** a royal citadel. **3.** the 7th lunar mansion.

Kalāvaka (S) (M) sparrow.

Kalāvata (S) (M) **1.** with digits. **3.** another name for the moon.

Kālavega (S) (M) **1.** speed of time. **3.** a serpent born in the Vāsuki dynasty (*M. Bh.*).

Kālayavana (S) (M) **1.** as horrible as death. **2.** horrible for time and religion. **3.** the king of the Yavana tribe (*H. Purāṇa*); an asura born out of the effulgence of Gargāćārya who was killed by Kṛṣṇa (*V. Purāṇa*); a prince of the Yavanas (*V. Purāṇa*).

Kālayogi (S) (M) **1.** reigning over time. **3.** another name for Śiva.

Kaldhūta (S) (M) completely white; silver.

Kalendu (S) (M) **1.** digit of the moon. **3.** the moon on the 2nd day of the month (*V's B. Samhitā*).

Kalhaṇa (S) (M) **1.** knower of meaning. **2.** knowing; alliteration; sound; reader. **3.** a historian of Kāśmira and author of *Rāja Taraṅgiṇī*.

Kalhara (S) (M) water lily (*Nymphaea alba*).

Kali (S) (M) **1.** the period of sin. **3.** the son of Kaśyapa and Munī (*A. Veda*); the lord of Kalīyuga — a period where sin predominates, considered to thrive on gambling, drinking, gold, women and murder (*A. Brāhmaṇa*); another name for Śiva and Sūrya.

Kālīćaraṇa (S) (M) devotee of Kālī.

Kālīdāsa (S) (M) **1.** servant of Kāli. **3.** a famous dramatist who was one of the 9 gems of the court of King Vikramāditya of Ujjainī (4th century A.D.) (*K. Granthāvali*).

Kalijan (S) (M) men of art; skilled men. blessed; happy; fortunate; excellent; auspicious; beautiful.

Kālika (S) (M) **1.** beyond death. **2.** long lived. **3.** an attendant given to Skanda by Pūṣaṇ (*M. Bh.*); a species of heron (*Ardea jaculator*).

Kalila (S) (M) unpierceable; deep.

Kalimuttu (S) (M) **1.** remover of sins. **2.** pious; faultless.

Kalinda (S) (M) **1.** bestower of arts and skills. **2.** giving blossoms; the sun. **3.** the mountain from which the river Yamunā begins its journey (*M. Bh.*); an attendant of Skanda (*M. Bh.*); Bedda Nut (*Terminalia belerica*).

Kaliṅga (S) (M) **1.** one who knows the arts and the skills. **2.** one who pervades the blossom. **3.** a warrior of Skanda (*M. Bh.*); a daitya who conquered heaven and was finally killed by Devī (*H. Purāṇa*); another name for Śrutāyus, the king of Kaliṅga and a member of Yudhiṣṭhira's court; Sizzling tree (*Albizzla lebbeck*); *Holarrhena antidysenterica.*

Kalita (S) (M) known; understood.

Kāliya (S) (M) **1.** of time; of death. **3.** a 1000 headed serpent son of Kaśyapa and Kadru who was killed by Kṛṣṇa (*Bhāgavata*).

Kalki (S) (M) **1.** destroyer of sins. **3.** the 10th incarnation of Viṣṇu portrayed as mounted on a white horse with a drawn sword as the liberator of the world and destroyer of the wicked.

Kālkṛta (S) (M) **1.** decided by time; fixed; peacock. **3.** another name for the Supreme Spirit and the sun.

Kallola (S) (M) **1.** joy; a huge wave. **2.** surge; billow; happiness; pleasure.

Kalmali (S) (M) **1.** dispelling darkness. **2.** splendour; brightness.

Kalmāṣa (S) (M) **1.** speckled with black. **2.** variegated. **3.** a rākṣasa (*A. Koṣa*); a form of Agni (*H. Purāṇa*); an attendant of the sun (*A. Koṣa*); Sākyamuni in a previous birth (*M.Bh./Rāmāyaṇa*); a nāga (*M. Bh.*).

Kalmāṣakaṇṭha (S) (M) **1.** with a speckled neck. **3.** Śiva whose neck turned black when he drank up the Kālakuta or the poison obtained from the churning of the Ocean of Milk.

Kalmāṣapāda (S) (M) **1.** black footed. **2.** with speckled feet. **3.** another name for Mitrasaha, a famous king of the Ikṣvāku dynasty and son of Sudāsa.

Kalpa (S) (M) **1.** fit; proper; able; competent; perfect. **2.** the 1st astrological mansion; a day in the life of Brahmā equivalent to 4,320,000,000 years; grants wishes; ritual; determination; opinion. **3.** a son of Dhruva and Brāhmī; another name for Śiva.

Kalpaka (S) (M) **1.** of a certain standard. **2.** rite; ceremony. **3.** Śiva's garden (*Ś. Purāṇa*).

Kalpanātha (S) (M) lord of perfection; lord of time.

Kalpavata (S) (M) **1.** as perfect as time. **2.** perfect. **3.** a son of Vasudeva (*Bhāgavata*).

Kalpavṛkṣa (S) (M) **1.** tree of life; a wish granting tree. **3.** a tree in Devaloka (*M. Bh.*).

Kalpeśa (S) (M) lord of perfection.

Kalpita (S) (M) imagined; fit; proper.

Kālskandha (S) (M) the shoulder of death.

Kālu (S) (M) **1.** black complexioned. **3.** the father of the 1st Sikh Guru, Guru Nānak.

Kalvik (S) (M) sparrow.

Kālya (S) (M) timely; pleasant; agreeable; auspicious.

Kalyāṇa (S) (M) **1.** welfare; benefit; virtue; good fortune; beautiful; agreeable; excellent; happy; beneficial; prosperous; propitious. **3.** a sage (*P. Brāhmaṇa*); a rāga which forms the basis for all the other rāgas; a gandharva (*A. Koṣa*).

Kalyāṇamitra (S) (M) **1.** a friend of virtue. **3.** another name for Buddha.

Kalyāṇaśarman (S) (M) **1.** master of virtue. **3.** a commentator on Varāhamihira's *Bṛhat Samhitā.*

Kalyāṇavarman (S) (M) soldier of virtue; a virtuous soldier.

Kalyāṇavata (S) (M) full of virtue.

Kalyāṇin (S) (M) beneficial; happy; lucky; auspicious; prosperous; virtuous; illustrious.

Kāma (S) (M) **1.** desire; wish; longing; love; affection; enjoyment; pleasure. **3.** the god of love (*A. Veda*); the husband of Rati (*H. Purāṇa*); reincarnated as Pradyumna the son of Kṛṣṇa and Rukmiṇī and the father of Aniruddha (*M. Bh.*).

Kāmabāṇa (S) (M) **1.** an arrow of the god of love. **2.** Arabian jasmine (*Jasminum sambac*).

Kāmada (S) (M) **1.** granting desires. **3.** another name for the sun and Skanda.

Kāmadeva (S) (M) **1.** Kāma, the god. **3.** the god of love Kāma, who is said to have been the son of Sahiṣṇu and Yaśodharā (*V. Purāṇa*).

Kāmaja (S) (M) **1.** born of love; son of Kāma. **3.** another name for Aniruddha.

Kāmajit (S) (M) **1.** conqueror of desire. **3.** another name for Śiva and Kārttikeya.

Kamala (S) (M) **1.** lotus (*Nelumbo speciosum*). **2.** pale red; rose coloured. **3.** a pupil of Vaiśampāyana; an asura (*G. Purāṇa*); another name for Brahmā; *Nymphaea rubra*; *Nelumbo nucifera.*

Kamalabhava (S) (M) **1.** sprung from the lotus. **3.** another name for Brahmā.

Kamalabhū (S) (M) **1.** born of the lotus. **3.** another name for Brahmā.

Kamalabuddhi (S) (M) **1.** with lotus like intelligence. **3.** a philosopher who was a student of Buddhapālita of the Madhyamika philosophy (*L.Vistara*).

Kamaladeva (S) (M) **1.** lord of the lotus. **3.** another name for Viṣṇu.

Kamalagarbha (S) (M) **1.** offspring of a lotus. **3.** another name for Brahmā.

Kamalāhāsa (S) (M) smiling like a lotus.

Kamalaja (S) (M) **1.** born of the lotus. **3.** another name for Brahmā and the lunar asterism of Rohiṇī.

Kamalākānta (S) (M) **1.** beloved of Kamalā. **3.** another name for Viṣṇu.

Kamalākara (S) (M) a mass of lotuses.

Kamalākṣa (S) (M) **1.** lotus eyed. **3.** a great warrior who fought against the Pāṇḍavas (*M. Bh.*); a son of Tarakāsura (*M. Purāṇa*).

Kamalamaya (S) (M) consisting of lotus flowers.

Kamalanābha (S) (M) **1.** lotus navelled. **3.** another name for Viṣṇu.

Kamalanayana (S) (M) lotus eyed.

Kamalanetra (S) (M) lotus eyed.

Kamalāpati (S) (M) **1.** husband of Kamalā. **3.** another name for Viṣṇu.

Kamalāsana (S) (M) **1.** with a lotus flower as a seat. **3.** another name for Brahmā; Bastard Teak (*Butea monospenna*).

Kamaleśa (S) (M) **1.** lord of Kamalā. **3.** another name for Viṣṇu.

Kamaleśvara (S) (M) **1.** lord of Kamalā. **3.** another name for Viṣṇu.

Kamalodaya (S) (M) the rising of a lotus; the unfurling of a lotus.

Kamalottama (S) (M) **1.** the best flower. **2.** Wild Saffron (*Carthamus tinctorius*).

Kāmamālin (S) (M) **1.** the gardener of desires. **3.** another name for Gaṇeśa.

Kamana (S) (M) **1.** one who is desirous. **2.** desired; beautiful. **3.** another name for Kāma and Brahmā; *Saraca indica.*

Kāmāndaka (S) (M) **1.** with bound desires. **3.** a sage who was the preceptor of King Aṅgiras (*M. Bh.*).

Kāmāṅga (S) (M) **1.** love bodied. **2.** Mango tree (*Mangifera indica*).

Kāmāṅganāśana (S) (M) **1.** destroying the body of Kāma. **3.** another name for Śiva.

Kāmapāla (S) (M) **1.** gratifier of human desires. **3.** a Yādava dependant on Kṛṣṇa (*Bhāgavata*); another name for Viṣṇu, Śiva and Balarāma (*V. Purāṇa*).

Kāmarāja (S) (M) lord of desire.

Kāmarūpa (S) (M) **1.** of the form of love. **2.** beautiful; pleasing.

Kāmasakha (S) (M) **1.** friend of Kāma. **2.** the season of spring which is considered to inflame passions.

Kāmāśrama (S) (M) the abode of love.

Kāmata (S) (M) **1.** following one's desires. **2.** unrestrained. **3.** a king of Kamboja and member of the court of Yudhiṣṭhira (*M. Bh.*); a serpent born in Dhṛtarāṣṭra's family (*M. Bh.*).

Kamatha (S) (M) **1.** tortoise; water-jar; porcupine; bamboo. **3.** a sage (*M. Bh.*); an asura (*G. Purāṇa*); Spiny Bamboo (*Bambusa arundinacea*).

Kāmavallabha (S) (M) **1.** love's favourite. **3.** another name for moonlight, the season of spring, the Mango tree (*Mangifera indica*) and the Cinnamon tree (*Cinnamomum tamala*).

Kāmavīrya (S) (M) **1.** displaying heroism at will. **3.** another name for Garuḍa.

Kāmāyuṣ (S) (M) **1.** one who lives as long as he desires. **3.** another name for Garuḍa.

Kambala (S) (M) **1.** a small worm. **3.** a serpent of the Kaśyapa family (*M. Bh.*).

Kambara (S) (M) **1.** of variegated colour. **3.** a Tamil poet.

Kamboja (S) (M) **1.** shell; elephant. **3.** a country and its inhabitants (*M. Bh.*).

Kambu (S) (M) conchshell; variegated; elephant; bracelet made of shell.

Kambugrīva (S) (M) **1.** conchshell necked. **2.** according to the *Sāmudrika Śāstra,* a neck marked with 3 lines like that on a shell is considered to be a sign of great fortune. **3.** a son of the King Sudhanvā of Madra (*K. Sāgara/ M. Bh.*).

Kāmeṣṭha (S) (M) **1.** desired by Kāma. **2.** Mango tree (*Mangifera indica*).

Kāmeśvara (S) (M) **1.** lord of desire. **3.** another name for the Supreme Being, Śiva, Kāma and Kubera.

Kāmika (S) (M) desired; wished for.

Kāminīśa (S) (M) **1.** ruling the god of love. **2.** Drumstick tree (*Moringa oleifera*).

Kāmoda (S) (M) **1.** one who grants wishes. **3.** a rāga.

Kampa (S) (M) **1.** tremor. **2.** earthquake. **3.** a Vṛṣṇi prince who became a viśvadeva after his death (*M. Bh.*).

Kampana (S) (M) **1.** trembling. **2.** unsteady. **3.** a king and member of the court of Yudhiṣṭhira (*M. Bh.*); a kind of weapon (*M. Bh.*).

Kāmuka (S) (M) passionate.

Kaṇabhakṣa (S) (M) **1.** atom destroyer. **3.** another name for the sage Kaṇāda.

Kāṇabhuti (S) (M) **1.** with one eye. **3.** a yakṣa (*K. Sāgara*).

Kaṇāda (S) (M) **1.** inventor of the atom. **3.** a son of Dhīmaraṇa (*P. Candrodaya*); a famous sage of ancient India who was also called Kaṇabhakṣa and Pippalāda (*S. Samgraha*); a rāgiṇī.

Kanadeva (S) (M) **1.** youthful god. **3.** a Buddhist patriarch (*B. Literature*).

Kanaka (S) (M) **1.** gold; sandalwood; the ironwood tree (*Mesua ferreo*); Flame of the Forest tree (*Butea frondosa*); the Variegated Bauhinia (*Bauhinia variegata*); the Thornapple (*Datura stramonium*). **3.** a forest near the southern base of Mahāmeru where Hanumān was born (*M. Bh.*).

Kanakadatta (S) (M) **1.** given by gold; a golden gift. **2.** very precious.

Kanakadhvaja (S) (M) **1.** with a golden banner. **3.** a son of Dhṛtarāṣṭra (*M. Bh.*).

Kanakādri (S) (M) **1.** golden mountain. **3.** another name for the Mount Meru.

Kanakakānta (S) (M) one who loves gold.

Kanakākṣa (S) (M) **1.** golden eyed. **3.** a soldier of Skanda (*M. Bh.*).

Kanakamaya (S) (M) consisting of gold; golden.

Kanakāmbujam (S) (M) golden lotus.

Kanakāṅgada (S) (M) **1.** a golden bracelet. **3.** a son of Dhṛtarāṣṭra (*M. Bh.*); a gandharva (*B. Rāmāyaṇa*).

Kanakaparvata (S) (M) **1.** golden mountain. **3.** another name for Mount Meru.

Kanakapīḍa (S) (M) **1.** one who wins gold. **3.** an attendant of Skanda (*M. Bh.*).

Kaṇakarāja (S) (M) **1.** lord of Sītā. **2.** Rāma.

Kanakarasa (S) (M) fluid gold; essence of gold; composed of the essence of gold; person with a golden heart and mind; a golden stream.

Kanakaśakti (S) (M) **1.** with golden power. **2.** the golden speared one. **3.** another name for Kārttikeya.

Kanakavarṇa (S) (M) **1.** of golden colour. **3.** a king supposed to have been the former incarnation of Śākyamuni (*M. Bh.*).

Kanakavarṣa (S) (M) **1.** shower of gold. **3.** the king of Kanakapurī (*R. Taraṅgiṇī*).

Kanakāyus (S) (M) **1.** a golden life. **3.** a son of King Dhṛtarāṣṭra (*M. Bh.*).

Kanakendu (S) (M) golden moon.

Kanala (S) (M) shining; bright.

Kañća (S) (M) shining.

Kāñćana (S) (M) **1.** that which shines. **2.** gold; money; wealth; the filament of a lotus (*Nelumbium speciosum*); the Iron wood tree (*Mesua ferrea*); Yellow Ćampaka (*Michelia champaka*); *Ficus glomerata*; *Bauhinia variegata*. **3.** one of the 2 warriors given byMahāmeru to Skanda (*M. Bh.*); a Purū king (*M. Bh.*); a son of Nārāyaṇa (*V. Purāṇa*); the 5th Buddha.

Kāñćanādri (S) (M) **1.** golden mountain. **3.** another name for Mount Meru.

Kāñćanagiri (S) (M) **1.** golden mountain. **3.** another name for Mount Meru.

Kāñćanaka (S) (M) golden; the variegated Bauhinia (*Bauhinia variegata*).

Kāñćanākṣa (S) (M) **1.** golden eyed. **3.** a warrior of Skanda (*M. Bh.*); a dānava (*H. Purāṇa*).

Kāñćanaprabha (S) (M) **1.** as bright as gold. **3.** a son of Bhīma and the father of Suhotra (*H. Purāṇa*).

Kāñćanavega (S) (M) **1.** with golden passion. **3.** a vidyādhara (*K. Sāgara*).

Kañćāra (S) (M) **1.** shining. **3.** another name for the sun.

Kañćuka (S) (M) armour.

Kañćukita (S) (M) furnished with armour.

Kandala (S) (M) gold; war; battle; a new shoot; a sprig.

Kandalāyana (S) (M) **1.** one who brings forth in abundance. **3.** an ancient sage.

Kandalī (S) (M) *Rhizophora mucronata*; a sweet sound; deer; lotus (*Nelumbo speciosum*); plantain tree.

Kandalin (S) (M) covered with Kandalī flowers (*Rhizophora mucronata*).

Kandan (S) (M) knower; cloud; garlic; radish; camphor.

Kandarpa (S) (M) **1.** inflamer. **3.** another name for Kāma.

Kandarpaketu (S) (M) a banner of passion.

Kaṇḍu (S) (M) **1.** itching. **3.** a sage who was the husband of apsarā Pramloćā and the father of Māriṣā (*M. Bh.*).

Kaṅganīla (S) (M) **1.** resembling a bracelet. **3.** a nāga (*V. Purāṇa*).

Kānhā (S) (M) **1.** the adolescent. **3.** another name for Kṛṣṇa.

Kanhaiya (S) (M) **1.** the adolescent. **3.** another name for Kṛṣṇa.

Kaṇika (S) (M) **1.** a grain; an atom; an ear of corn; heart of wheat. **3.** a minister of Dhṛtarāṣṭra (*M. Bh.*).

Kaṇikarāja (S) (M) lord of the atom.

Kānīna (S) (M) **1.** born of a young wife. **3.** another name for Meghanāda, Vyāsa and Karṇa.

Kanīnaka (S) (M) youth; the pupil of the eye; a boy.

Kaniṣka (S) (M) **1.** small. **3.** a king who supported Buddhism (1st century A.D.) (*B. Literature*).

Kaniṣṭha (S) (M) **1.** the youngest. **3.** a class of deities of the 14th Manvantara (*V. Purāṇa*).

Kañja (S) (M) **1.** produced from water; produced from the head. **2.** a lotus; hair. **3.** another name for Brahmā.

Kañjabāhu (S) (M) **1.** lotus armed; with hairy arms. **3.** an asura (*H. Purāṇa*).

Kañjaka (S) (M) **1.** water and earth born. **2.** Eastern Hill Mynah (*Gracula religiosa*).

Kañjam (S) (M) lotus; ambrosia; nectar.

Kañjana (S) (M) **1.** produced from water. **3.** another name for Kāma.

Kañjanābha (S) (M) **1.** lotus navelled. **3.** another name for Viṣṇu.

Kañjāra (S) (M) **1.** the sun; a hermit; belly; peacock; elephant. **3.** another name for Brahmā.

Kañjasū (S) (M) **1.** from a lotus. **3.** another name for Kāma.

Kañjavadana (S) (M) lotus faced.

Kañji (S) (M) crooked.

Kaṅka (S) (M) **1.** scent of the lotus; heron. **3.** one of the 7 famous archers of the Vṛṣṇi dynasty (*M. Bh.*); name assumed by Yudhiṣṭhira in the palace of the king of Virāṭa (*M. Bh.*); a son of Surasa; a bird; another name for Yama; a son of Ugrasena (*M. Bh.*).

Kaṅkāla (S) (M) skeleton; a collection of bones.

Kaṅkālin (S) (M) **1.** with a necklace of bones. **3.** a yakṣa.

Kaṅkaṇīkā (S) (M) **1.** an ornament of bells. **3.** a serpent (*V. Purāṇa*).

Kāṅkṣitā (S) (M) wished; desired; longed for.

Kaṇsa (S) (M) **1.** vessel of bell-metal. **2.** with a metal like body. **3.** the son of King Ugrasena of Mathurā and maternal uncle of Kṛṣṇa (*M. Bh./Bhāgavata/V. Purāṇa*).

Kaṅsakeśinisūdana (S) (M) **1.** destroyer of Kaṅsa and Keśin. **3.** another name for Kṛṣṇa.

Kaṅsanisūdana (S) (M) **1.** destroyer of Kaṅsa. **3.** another name for Kṛṣṇa.

Kaṅsārāti (S) (M) **1.** slayer of Kaṇsa. **3.** another name for Kṛṣṇa.

Kānta (S) (M) **1.** beloved. **2.** the spring; a jewel. **3.** a son of Dharmanetra; another name for Kṛṣṇa, Kārttikeya and the moon; *Aglaia odoratissima*; *Amomum subulatum*; *Mimordica balsamina.*

Kaṇṭaka (S) (M) **1.** thorn. **3.** the horse of Śākyamuni (*L. Vistara*); another name for Makara, the symbol of Kāma.

Kaṇṭakin (S) (M) **1.** thorny; prickly; *acacia catechu*; bamboo; *Zizyphus jujuba*; Amaranth (*amaranthus tricolor rubra*). **3.** a mother of Skanda's retinue (*M. Bh.*).

Kaṇṭakinī (S) (M) **1.** full of thorn. **2.** a porcupine (*Solanum jacquini*). **3.** a follower of Skanda (*M. Bh.*).

Kaṇṭārikā (S) (M) **1.** thorn like; Prickly Pear (*Opuntia dillenii*). **3.** an ancient sage and founder of a gotra in which the pre-eminent Brahmadatta was born (*K. Sāgara*).

Kaṇṭhaka (S) (M) **1.** of neck. **2.** an ornament for the neck; a one-stringed necklace. **3.** the horse of Śākyamuni (*L. Vistara*).

Kaṇṭhamaṇi (S) (M) a jewel of the neck; a jewel worn on the throat; a dear object.

Kaṇṭhekāla (S) (M) **1.** black necked. **3.** another name for Śiva.

Kāntida (S) (M) giving beauty; adorning.

Kāntimān (S) (M) **1.** lovely. **3.** another name for Kāma and the moon.

Kantu (S) (M) **1.** love. **2.** mind; heart; a granary. **3.** another name for Kāma.

Kaṇva (S) (M) **1.** talented; praised. **2.** honoured; intelligent. **3.** a sage of the Kaśyapa family; the son of Medhātithi, father of Indīvaraprabhā by the apsara Menakā, the foster father of Śakuntalā and one of the 24 ṛṣis associated with the Gāyatrī mantra (*Ṛg Veda*); a king of the Purū dynasty who was the son of Prītiratha and the father of Medhātithi (*A. Purāṇa*).

Kaṇvaka (S) (M) **1.** son of a talented person. **3.** a son of Śūra (*H. Purāṇa*).

Kaṇvala (S) (M) a lotus.

Kaṇvalajita (S) (M) **1.** winner of the lotus. **3.** another name for Viṣṇu.

Kanvar (S) (M) a prince.

Kapālabhṛt (S) (M) **1.** bearing a skull. **3.** another name for Śiva.

Kapālaketu (S) (M) **1.** with a skull for a banner. **3.** another name for a comet.

Kapālamālin (S) (M) **1.** with a garland of skulls. **3.** another name for Śiva.

Kapālaśiras (S) (M) **1.** skull headed. **3.** another name for Śiva.

Kāpālī (S) (M) **1.** skull carrier. **2.** one with a skull. **3.** one of the 11 rudras who was the son of Sthāṇu and the grandson of Brahmā (*M. Bh.*); a son of Kṛṣṇa and Yaudhiṣṭhirī (*H. Purāṇa*); another name for Śiva.

Kāpālika (S) (M) **1.** one who eats in a skull. **3.** a member of a Śaivā sect.

Kāpardi (S) (M) **1.** shell (conch). **2.** as white as a conch shell; fair in visage. **3.** another name for Śiva.

Kapardin (S) (M) **1.** cowrie shell. **3.** Śiva whose hair is braided like a cowrie shell; one of the 11 rudras (*A. Purāṇa*); a yakṣa; another name for Rudra and Pūṣaṇ.

Kapaṭa (S) (M) **1.** deceit. **3.** a demon who was the son of Kaśyapa and Danu (*M. Bh.*).

Kapi (S) (M) **1.** monkey. **2.** the sun; *Emblica officinalis.* **3.** another name for Viṣṇu and Kṛṣṇa.

Kapidhvaja (S) (M) **1.** with a monkey banner. **3.** another name for Arjuna.

Kapiketana (S) (M) **1.** with a monkey as a symbol. **3.** another name for Arjuna.

Kapilā 1. monkey coloured. **2.** a brown cow; perfume; tawny. **3.** a fabulous cow of Indra celebrated in the Purāṇas (*M. Bh.*); a daughter of Dakṣa and wife of Kaśyapa (*M. Bh.*); the mother of Panćāśikha (*M. Bh.*); the consort of Puṇḍarīka an elephant of a quarter (*A. Koṣa*); a holy place of Kurukṣetrā (*M. Bh.*); a river of ancient India (*M. Bh.*); the Śīśam tree (*Dalbergia sissoo*).

Kapila (S) (M) **1.** monkey coloured. **2.** brown; tawny; reddish; the sun. **3.** a sage who was the son of Kardama and Devahutī, an incarnation of Viṣṇu, a great exponent of the Sāṅkhya philosophy and on whose teachings the entire *Yoga Śāstra* is based (*D. Bhāgavata*); son of an agni named Bhānu who is supposed to be an incarnation of sage Kapila (*M. Bh.*); a sage who was the father of Śālihotra (*M. Bh.*); one of the 7 serpent kings who are said to hold the earth in place (*M. Bh.*); a son of Viśvāmitra (*M. Bh.*); Viṣṇu in his 5th incarnation as the lord of all Siddhis (*M. Bh./Bhāgavata*); a form of Agni (*M. Bh.*); a serpent lord (*M. Bh.*); a mountain (*M. Bh.*); *Aloe vera*; another name for Viṣṇu, Śiva and Sūrya.

Kapilākṣa (S) (M) **1.** sun eyed. **2.** whose eyes glow; with piercing and bright eyes. **3.** *Cucumis trigonus*; another name for Indra.

Kapilāñjana (S) (M) **1.** using a brown collyrium. **3.** another name for Śiva.

Kapilapati (S) (M) **1.** lord of the brown. **2.** lord of the brown coloured i.e. Indian. **3.** another name for Drupada (*M. Bh.*).

Kapilāśva (S) (M) **1.** with brown horses. **3.** the son of King Kuvalāśva (*M. Bh.*); another name for Indra.

Kapileya (S) (M) **1.** brown coloured. **3.** a son of Viśvāmitra (*A. Brahmāṇa*).

Kapīndra (S) (M) **1.** lord of monkeys. **3.** another name for Viṣṇu, Jāmbavata, Sugrīva and Hanumān.

Kapiñjala (S) (M) **1.** with brown water. **2.** Baluchistan Grey Partridge (*Francolinus pondicerianus mecranensis*); the Pied Crested Cuckoo which is supposed to drink water only from the clouds. **3.** a son of ṛṣi Śvetaketu (*M. Bh.*); a vidyādhara (*K. Sāgara*).

Kapipati (S) (M) **1.** lord of apes. **3.** another name for Hanumān.

Kapiprabhu (S) (M) **1.** master of monkeys. **3.** another name for Rāma.

Kapiśa (S) (M) **1.** lord of monkeys. **2.** brown; reddish brown; incense. **3.** another name for Śiva and the sun; *Altingia excelsa.*

Kapiśāñjana (S) (M) **1.** using a brown collyrium. **3.** another name for Śiva.

Kapiskandha (S) (M) **1.** monkey shouldered. **2.** a soldier who leaps like a monkey. **3.** a soldier of Skanda (*M. Bh.*); a dānava (*H. Purāṇa*).

Kapīśvara (S) (M) **1.** lord of monkeys. **3.** another name for Sugrīva.

Kapivaktra (S) (M) **1.** monkey faced. **3.** another name for Nārada.

Kapota (S) (M) **1.** Indian Ring Dore (*Columba risoria*); Blue Rock Pigeon (*Columba neglecta*). **3.** a sage who was the husband of Ćitrāṅgadā and the father of Tumburu and Suvarćas (*K. Purāṇa*); a son of Garuḍa (*M. Bh.*).

Kapotaroman (S) (M) **1.** having hair like feathers of a pigeon. **2.** a blond. **3.** the son of Emperor Śibi and a member of Varuṇa's court (*M. Bh.*).

Kapṛtha (S) (M) **1.** increasing pleasure. **3.** another name for Indra.

Kapūri (S) (M) camphor.

Karabha (S) (M) **1.** trunk of an elephant. **2.** anything useful. **3.** a king who was a dependant of Emperor Jarāsandha (*M. Bh.*).

Karabhājana (S) (M) **1.** one born like an elephant. **2.** an elephant. **3.** a son of Ṛṣabhadeva who was a yogī of divine wisdom (*Bhāgavata*).

Karabhin (S) (M) **1.** with a trunk; elephant. **3.** the son of Śakuni (*M. Purāṇa*).

Karaćūra (S) (M) gold.

Karajāla (S) (M) a stream of light.

Karakaṣa (S) (M) **1.** harsh. **2.** hard; firm; a sword. **3.** a soldier who fought on the side of the Kauravas (*M. Bh.*).

Karakaṣaka (S) (M) **1.** harsh. **2.** hard; firm; a sword. **3.** a brother of the king of Ćedi who fought on the side of the Pāṇḍavas (*M. Bh.*).

Karakāyu (S) (M) **1.** having a hard life. **3.** a son of Dhṛtarāṣṭra (*M. Bh.*).

Karāla (S) (M) **1.** terrible; wide; opening; tearing. **2.** great; large; lofty; uneven. **3.** a gandharva (*M. Bh.*); a rākṣasa (*D. Bh. Purāṇa*); another name for Janaka.

Karāladanta (S) (M) **1.** with large teeth. **3.** a great sage who was a member of Indra's court (*M. Bh.*).

Karālajanaka (S) (M) **1.** Janaka the great. **3.** another name for King Janaka of Mithilā whose preceptor was sage Vasiṣṭha (*M. Bh.*).

Karālākṣa (S) (M) **1.** with frightening eyes. **3.** a soldier of Skanda (*M. Bh.*).

Karambha (S) (M) **1.** mixture. **2.** coarsely ground oats; gruel. **3.** sacrificial offering to Pūṣan made of barley and sesame (*Ṛg Veda*); a son of Śakuni and the father of Devarāṭa (*H. Purāṇa*); the father of the asura, Mahiṣa (*Rāmāyaṇa*); a brother of Rambha (*H. Purāṇa*).

Karandhama (S) (M) **1.** clapping of hands. **3.** a king of the Ikṣvāku dynasty and the father of Avīkṣit who was a prominent member of Yama's court (*M. Bh.*).

Karañja (S) (M) **1.** born of hand; the tree (*Pongamia glabra*). **2.** obtained by toil; difficult to obtain; precious.

Karapagam (S) (M) hands and feet.

Karaṭa (S) (M) **1.** with the temple of an elephant. **3.** another name for Gaṇeśa.

Karatoya (S) (M) **1.** with flowing water. **3.** a holy river that started at the time of Pārvatī's marriage to Śiva and which worships Varuṅa (*M. Bh.*).

Karavinda (S) (M) **1.** possessed by hand. **2.** doing; causing; creator.

Karavira (S) (M) **1.** strong armed. **2.** sword; scimitar; thumb. **3.** a daitya (*A. Koṣa*); a serpent (*M. Bh.*); a mountain on the south of Mahāmeru (*Bhāgavata*); a forest near Dvārakā (*H. Purāṇa*); the Oleander tree (*Nerium odorum*).

Karavīrākṣa (S) (M) **1.** the tip of the sword. **3.** a demon who fought against Rāma (*V. Rāmāyaṇa*).

Karbura (S) (M) **1.** variegated. **2.** gold; a venomous leech. **3.** a rākṣasa (*A. Koṣa*).

Kardama (S) (M) **1.** covered with mud. **2.** slime; dirt: clay; filth; shade. **3.** a prajāpati son of Brahmā born from his shadow, reborn as the son of Pulaha and Kṣamā and the grandson of Brahmā, was the husband of Devahūti the daughter of Svāyambhuva Manu, and the father of sage Kapila and 9 daughters who married Marīći (*Bhāgavata*); a sage who sits in the court of Brahmā (*M. Bh.*); a sage who was the grandson of Virāja and the father of Anaṅga (*M. Bh.*); a serpent (*M. Bh.*); a kind of rice produced in the marsh.

Kareṇu (S) (M) elephant.

Karikṛṣṇa (S) (M) black elephant.

Karimukha (S) (M) **1.** elephant faced. **3.** another name for Gaṇeśa.

Kārin (S) (M) doing; accomplishing; rejoicing; praising; jubiliant.

Karīndra (S) (M) **1.** lord of elephants. **2.** war elephant; the largest elephant. **3.** the elephant of Indra.

Karīṣa (S) (M) **1.** dry cow dung. **3.** a son of Viśvāmitra (*M. Bh.*).

Karīṣa (S) (M) **1.** lord of elephants. **3.** another name for Airavata.

Kariṣini (S) (M) **1.** abounding in dung. **3.** a river (*M. Bh.*).

Kariṣṇu (S) (M) doing; accomplishing.

Karka (S) (M) **1.** white; crab; good; excellent; fire; mirror; water-jar; beauty. **3.** the zodiac sign of Cancer.

Karkandhu (S) (M) **1.** crab like; whitish; the jujube tree (*Zizyphus jujuba*). **3.** a protégé of the aśvins (*V. Saṁhitā/Ś. Brāhmaṇa*); a saintly king mentioned in the *Ṛg Veda*.

Karkara (S) (M) **1.** harsh. **2.** hard; firm; a bone; hammer; mirror. **3.** a prominent serpent (*M. Bh.*).

Karkaśa (S) (M) **1.** harsh. **2.** hard; firm; rough; sword; scimitar.

Karki (S) (M) **1.** of crab. **3.** the zodiac sign of Cancer; the son of sage Āpastamba and Akasūtrā (*V. Saṁhitā*).

Karkoṭa (S) (M) **1.** abode of sword. **2.** the sugarcane plant. **3.** a principal serpent of Pātāla (*V. Purāṇa*); helper of Nala (*R. Taraṅgiṇī*).

Karma (S) (M) **1.** fate; destiny; duty; action. **2.** the purple Moorhen (*Porphyrio porphyrio*).

Karmaćandra (S) (M) **1.** moon of destiny. **2.** attaining destiny; successful.

Karmajit (S) (M) **1.** victorious over his destiny. **3.** a king of the family of Arjuna who was the son of Bṛhatsena and the father of Śrutañjaya (*Bhāgavata*).

Karmakara (S) (M) **1.** servant. **3.** another name for Yama.

Karmaṇya (S) (M) **1.** clever in work. **2.** skilful; diligent.

Karmaśa (S) (M) **1.** one who does his duty. **3.** a son of Pulaha (*V. Purāṇa*).

Karmaśīla (S) (M) dutiful.

Karmaśreṣṭha (S) (M) **1.** excellent in work. **3.** a son of Pulaha and Gati (*V. Purāṇa/Bhāgavata*).

Karmaśūra (S) (M) brave in action; assiduous.

Karmātman (S) (M) one whose character is action.

Karmasākṣī (S) (M) **1.** witnessing the performance of duty; standing as a witness to duty. **3.** another name for Sūrya.

Karmavajra (S) (M) one whose power lies in work.

Karmavira (S) (M) brave in action.

Karmendra (S) (M) lord of action.

Kārmuka (S) (M) **1.** bow. **2.** rainbow. **3.** the zodiac sign of Sagittarius; *Acacia ferruginea.*

Karṇa (S) (M) **1.** ear. **2.** skilful; clever; the rudder of a ship; handle of a vessel; an instrument of action; document; field. **3.** the eldest son of Kuntī and Sūrya, the adopted son of the charioteer Adhiratha and Rādhā, who joined sides with the Kauravas and became the king of Aṅga and is the epitome of valour and generosity (*M. Bh.*); a son of Dhṛtarāṣṭra (*M. Bh.*); the younger brother of Ghaṇṭā (*M. Bh.*); another name for the Supreme Being.

Karṇadhāra (S) (M) **1.** one who holds others by the ear. **2.** a leader; pilot; helmsman; sailor.

Karṇādi (S) (M) **1.** of ear. **2.** performing according to the scriptures. **3.** a gaṇa (*Pāṇinī*).

Karṇajit (S) (M) **1.** conqueror of Karṇa. **3.** another name for Arjuna.

Karṇaka (S) (M) **1.** belonging to the ear. **2.** prominence on the side (as in case of the ear); listening carefully.

Karṇamukha (S) (M) having Karṇa as the leader.

Karṇanirvaha (S) (M) **1.** dependant on the ears. **2.** one who listens religiously. **3.** a sage (*M. Bh.*).

Karṇānuja (S) (M) **1.** Karṇa's younger brother. **3.** another name for Yudhiṣṭhira.

Karṇaprayāga (S) (M) **1.** ear shaped confluence. **3.** the confluence of the rivers Gaṅgā and Piṇḍur.

Karṇapuṣpa (S) (M) **1.** flower of the ear. **2.** an earring; the Blue Amaranth (*Amaranthus caudatus*).

Karṇāri (S) (M) **1.** enemy of Karṇa. **3.** another name for Arjuna.

Karṇaśravas (S) (M) **1.** heard by the ears. **2.** famous. **3.** a sage of the Aṇgiras family and seer of mantras or chants (*P. Brāhmaṇa*); a sage who was a member of the court of Yudhiṣṭhira (*M. Bh.*).

Karṇasū (S) (M) **1.** father of Karṇa. **3.** another name for Sūrya.

Karṇāṭa (S) (M) **1.** name of a people. **3.** a rāga; a kind of Mimosa.

Karṇāveṣṭa (S) (M) **1.** an earring. **3.** a Kśatriya king who was the incarnation of the asura Krodhavaśa (*M. Bh.*).

Karṇavīra (S) (M) **1.** whose glory has come to be heard. **2.** a well known warrior.

Karṇi (S) (M) arrow.

Karṇikācala (S) (M) **1.** the central mountain. **3.** another name for Mount Meru.

Karṇikāra (S) (M) **1.** the pericarp of a lotus. **2.** as soft as a lotus; very soft.

Karṇiki (S) (M) judge; examiner; elephant.

Karṇini (S) (M) **1.** arrow; missile; steersman. **3.** one of the 7 principal ranges of mountains dividing the universe (*A. Koṣa/He. Koṣa*).

Karṇotpala (S) (M) **1.** ear-lotus. **2.** a lotus flower that ornaments the ears.

Karpūra (S) (M) camphor.

Karpūratilaka (S) (M) **1.** one who applies camphor on the forehead. **2.** with a white spot on forehead. **3.** an elephant (*Hitopadeśa*).

Karṣin (S) (M) **1.** one who attracts. **3.** another name for Kāma.

Karṣṇi (S) (M) **1.** black. **3.** a gandharva (*M. Bh.*); another name for Kāma and Abhimanyu; *Asparagus racemosus*.

Kārta (S) (M) **1.** to encompass; to spin; to cut; to destroy. **3.** a viśvadeva (*M. Bh.*); a son of Dharmanetra (*H. Purāṇa*).

Kartāra (S) (M) lord of all creation.

Kārtaśvara (S) (M) **1.** gold. **3.** an asura who once became the emperor of the world (*M. Bh.*).

Kārtavīrya (S) (M) **1.** of destructive ability. **2.** of great valour. **3.** son of Kṛtavīrya; the 1000 armed Arjuna who was the king of the Hehayas, father of a 100 sons, ruled at Mahiṣmatī for 86,000 years, was one of the emperors of the world in Bhāratavarṣa and was killed by Paraśurāma (*Br.Purāṇa*).

Kārtik (S) (M) **1.** one who bestows courage and happiness. **3.** which belongs to the month of Kārttika.

Kartṛ (S) (M) **1.** doer. **2.** maker; creator; author. **3.** another name for Brahmā, Viṣṇu and Śiva.

Kārttika (S) (M) **1.** one who gives courage and happiness. **3.** the month of October-November when the full moon is near the Pleiades.

Kārttikeya (S) (M) **1.** one who bestows courage. **2.** brave; vital; energetic. **3.** the son of Śiva and Pārvatī known as the god of war because he led the army of gaṇas against the demons, the foster son of Gaṅgā and the 6 Kṛttikās or Pleiades, also known as Skanda, Subrahmaṇya and Kumāra (*M. Bh.*); the planet Mars.

Kāru (S) (M) poet.

Karuṇa (S) (M) **1.** compassionate. **2.** tender; a Jaina ascetic. **3.** another name for the Supreme Being.

Karuṇākara (S) (M) mine of compassion.

Karuṇāmaya (S) (M) consisting of compassion.

Karuṇānidhi (S) (M) store of compassion.

Karuṇāśaṅkara (S) (M) Śiva, the compassionate.

Karundhaka (S) (M) **1.** one who guides society. **2.** a leader. **3.** a son of Śūra and a brother of Vasudeva (*V. Purāṇa*).

Karuṇeśa (S) (M) **1.** lord of mercy. **3.** another name for the moon.

Karuṇeśvara (S) (M) **1.** god of mercy. **3.** a liṅga.

Karūṣa (S) (M) **1.** dry. **2.** hard. **3.** a tribe; a son of Manu Vaivasvata who was the founder of a tribe which is named after him (*M. Bh*); a yakṣa who became a lord of a Manvantara (*D. Bhāgavata*).

Karutthāma (S) (M) **1.** perfect in duty. **2.** master. **3.** a son of Duṣyanta and father of Ākrīda (*H. Parāṇa*).

Karvara (S) (M) **1.** variegated. **2.** tiger. **3.** a rākṣasa (*A. Koṣa*).

Kāśa (S) (M) **1.** appearance. **2.** *Saccharum spontaneum*. **3.** a son of

Suhotra and father of Kāśirāja; an attendant of Yama.

Kāśageśa (S) (M) sugarcane; a sweet grass (*Saccharum spontaneum*).

Kaşaku (S) (M) **1.** fire. **3.** another name for the sun.

Kāsāra (S) (M) pond.

Kaşāya (S) (M) **1.** saffron colour. **2.** the garment of an ascetic; Button tree (*Anogeissus latifolia*).

Kāşāyin (S) (M) **1.** wearing a saffron garment. **3.** a sage (*Br. Upanişad*); a Buddhist monk.

Kaśeruka (S) (M) **1.** backbone; spine. **3.** a yakşa who was a member of Kubera's assembly (*M. Bh.*).

Kaśerumata (S) (M) **1.** a backbone. **2.** straight; upright. **3.** an asura who was killed by Kŗşņa (*M. Bh.*); a Yavana king (*Bhāgavata*).

Kāśika (S) (M) **1.** the shining one. **3.** the city of Benaras; a famous charioteer on the Pāņḍava side (*M. Bh.*).

Kāśin (S) (M) **1.** shining. **2.** appearing like a conqueror.

Kāśīnātha (S) (M) **1.** lord of Kāśī. **3.** another name for Śiva.

Kāśīpati (S) (M) **1.** lord of Kāśī **3.** another name for Divodāsa Dhanvantari a king of Benaras, the author of certain medical works and the teacher of Ayurveda.

Kāśirāja (S) (M) **1.** king of Kāśī. **3.** the king of Kāśī and the father of Ambā, Ambikā and Ambālikā (*M. Bh.*).

Kāśirāma (S) (M) **1.** abode of Kāśī; living at Kāśī. **2.** seeking deliverance at Kāśī.

Kāśīśa (S) (M) **1.** lord of Kāśī. **3.** another name for Śiva and Divodāsa.

Kāśīśņu (S) (M) shining; brilliant.

Kāśīviśvanātha (S) (M) **1.** universal lord of Kāśī; the idol of Kāśī. **3.** another name for Śiva.

Kāśmari (S) (M) the Coomb tree (*Gmelina arborea*).

Kāśmīra (S) (M) grape; coming from Kāśmir; *Costus speciosus*.

Kāşţha (S) (M) **1.** a piece of wood. **3.** an attendant of Kubera (*M. Bh.*).

Kastūra (S) (M) musk; the Malabar whistling thrush (*Myophonus horsfieldii*).

Kaśu (S) (M) **1.** an iron spear. **3.** a Ćedi prince mentioned in the *Ŗg Veda* for his liberality.

Kāśya (S) (M) **1.** hard grass (*Saccharum spontaneum*); dried grass. **3.** a kind of grass belonging to the Kāśīs; the king of Kāśī (*Ś. Brāhmaņa*); the father of Kaśyapa and ancestor of Kāśirāja Dhanvantari (*H. Purāņa*); the son of Suhotra (*Bhāgavata*); the son of Senājita (*Bhāgavata*); a king of Kāśī who was the father of Ambā, Ambikā and Ambālikā (*M. Bh.*); a sage (*M. Bh.*).

Kāśyapa (S) (M) **1.** son of Kaśyapa. **3.** a priest of Vasudeva and a friend of the Pāņḍavas (*M. Bh.*); a son of Kaśyapa who was a member of Indra's assembly (*M. Bh.*); one of the 5 agnis (*M. Bh.*).

Kaśyapa (S) (M) **1.** one who drinks water; one with black teeth; a tortoise. **3.** chief of the prajāpatis, the son of Marīći, the grandson of Brahmā, husband of 21 wives and the father of all living beings in the world (*Ś. Brāhmaņa*); a serpent who was present at Arjuna's birth (*M. Bh*); a class of semi divine beings; that regulate the course of the sun (*V. Purāņa*); the Water Lily (*Nymphaea esculenta*).

Kaśyapeya (S) (M) **1.** belonging to Kaśyapa. **3.** a patronymic of the 12 ādityas, Garuḍa and Aruņa the Sun.

Kaţaka (S) (M) a bracelet of gold; the ring ornamenting an elephant's tusk.

Katama (S) (M) best; excessively handsome.

Katamarāja (S) (M) **1.** best king. **2.** king among the best.

Kataprū (S) (M) **1.** gambler. **3.** a vidyadhara; a rakşasa; another name for Śiva.

Kaţha (S) (M) **1.** distress. **3.** a sage who was a founder of a branch of *Yajur Veda* which is named after him.

Kathaka (S) (M) **1.** reciting; narrating. **3.** a soldier of Skanda (*M. Bh.*).

Kaṭhamarda (S) (M) **1.** dispelling distress. **3.** another name for Śiva.

Kathita (S) (M) **1.** well recited; one about whom much is said. **2.** praised by all.

Kati (S) (M) **1.** how many? **2.** one possessed with many qualities. **3.** a sage who was the son of Viśvāmitra and the ancestor of Katyāyana (*Ṛg Veda*).

Kātumbi (S) (M) water purifier.

Kātuṅga (S) (M) **1.** seeker of the highest position. **3.** another name for King Dilīpa.

Kaṭvaku (S) (M) **1.** distressing speech. **2.** one who speaks of sad things. **3.** a son of Vaivasvata Manu who constructed Ayodhyā and was an ancestor of Ikṣvāku (*H. Purāṇa*).

Kātyāyana (S) (M) **1.** one who desires. **3.** a descendant of Kati; a grammarian who wrote a commentary on Pāṇini's work; a sage who lived in Indra's assembly (*M. Bh.*).

Kaulīna (S) (M) from a noble family.

Kaumodaki (S) (M) **1.** festive; moon like; made of lilies. **3.** the club of Kṛṣṇa given to him by Varuṇa (*H. Purāṇa/Bhāgavata/M. Bh.*).

Kauṇakutsya (S) (M) **1.** despised due to drinking blood. **3.** a noble Brāhmin (*M. Bh.*).

Kauṇapā (S) (M) **1.** feeding on corpses. **3.** a serpent of the family of Vāsuki (*M. Bh.*).

Kauṇapāśana (S) (M) **1.** feeding on corpses. **3.** a serpent born in the Kaurava family (*M. Bh.*).

Kauṇḍinya (S) (M) **1.** one who lives by priest-hood. **3.** a hermit who lived in the palace of Yudhiṣṭhira (*M. Bh.*).

Kaunteya (S) (M) **1.** son of Kuntī. **3.** another name for the Paṇḍavas; White Murdah (*Terminatia citrina*).

Kaupodaki (S) (M) **1.** made of lilies. **3.** the mace of Kṛṣṇa (*H. Purāṇa*).

Kauravanandana (S) (M) **1.** son of the Kurus. **3.** another name for Bhīsma, Yudhiṣṭhira and Duryodhana.

Kauravanātha (S) (M) **1.** lord of the Kauravas. **3.** another name for Yudhiṣṭhira and Dhṛtarāṣṭra.

Kauravarāja (S) (M) **1.** king of the Kauravas. **3.** another name for Dhṛtarāṣṭra.

Kauravaśārdula (S) (M) **1.** tiger of the Kurus; noblest of the kurus. **3.** another name for Bhīṣma and Yudhiṣṭhira.

Kauravaśreṣṭha (S) (M) **1.** best of the Kauravas. **3.** another name for Yudhiṣṭhira and Dhṛtarāṣṭra.

Kauravendra (S) (M) **1.** lord of the Kauravas. **3.** another name for Dhṛtarāṣṭra, Janamejaya and Duryodhana.

Kauraveya (S) (M) **1.** of the Kauravas. **3.** another name for Bhūriśravas, Yudhiṣṭhira and Duryodhana.

Kauravya (S) (M) **1.** of the Kuru clan. **3.** a noble serpent born of Airāvata who was the father of Ulūpi (*M. Bh.*); another name for Bhīṣma.

Kauśa (S) (M) silken; skill.

Kauśala (S) (M) **1.** welfare. **2.** well being; happiness; prosperity. **3.** Skanda in his goat faced incarnation (*M. Bh.*).

Kausalyānandavardhana (S) (M) **1.** increasing joy and prosperity. **3.** another name for Pāṇḍu.

Kauśika (S) (M) **1.** knower of hidden treasure; a son of Kuśīka; owl; sheathed; one who catches snakes; the sentiment of love. **3.** a hermit who lived in the palace of Yudhiṣṭhira (*M. Bh.*); a son of Vasudeva; a rāga; an asura; a minister of Jarāsandha (*M. Bh.*); a king of the Purū dynasty who was the son of Kapila and the brother of Gṛtsapati who designed the 4 castes (*A. Purāṇa*); another name for Indra, Śiva and Viśvāmitra; *Commiphora mukui*; Indian Dammer tree (*Shorea robustea*); Arabian Jasmine (*Jasminum sambac*).

Kauśikāćārya (S) (M) **1.** master of secrets. **3.** another name for King Ākṛti who ruled over Saurāśtra (*M. Bh.*).

Kaustubha (S) (M) **1.** a heavenly jewel. **2.** a diamond; a pearl. **3.** a precious stone mentioned in the *Agni Purāṇa* as having originated from the Ocean of Milk and worn on the breast by Viṣṇu (*M. Bh.*).

Kaustubhabhūṣaṇa (S) (M) **1.** wearing the Kaustubha jewel. **3.** another name for Kṛṣṇa.

Kauṭilya (S) (M) **1.** crooked thinker. **3.** writer of a renowned work on civil polity called the *Arthaśāstra* and an advisor to King Ćandragupta.

Kautsa (S) (M) **1.** of the family of Kutsa. **2.** that which is crooked; a hymn composed by Kutsa. **3.** a sage and disciple of Varatantu who was given 14 crore gold coins by Emperor Raghu (*Raghuvaṁśa*).

Kavaća (S) (M) **1.** armour. **3.** a sage in the court of Indra (*M. Bh.*).

Kavaćin (S) (M) **1.** covered with armour. **3.** a son of Dhṛtarāṣṭra (*M. Bh.*); another name for Śiva.

Kavana (S) (M) water.

Kavaṣa (S) (M) **1.** shield. **3.** a sage who was the son of Ilūṣa and the author of several hymns of the *Ṛg Veda* (*A. Brāhmaṇa*); an author of a *Dharmaśāstra.*

Kavela (S) (M) **1.** water born. **2.** a lotus flower.

Kavi (S) (M) **1.** omniscient; knows medicine; a poet. **2.** clever; wise; skilful; sensible; a physician; a surgeon; a singer. **3.** a brother of Bhṛgu and Aṅgiras and the adopted son of Brahmā (*M. Bh.*); an agni who is the 5th son of Bṛhaspati (*Ṛg Veda*); a sage and son of Manu (*M. Bh.*); the youngest son of Śraddhādeva Manu and Śraddhā (*H. Purāṇa*); a son of Vaivasvata Manu (*V. Purāṇa*); another name for Brahmā, Śukra, the sun and sage Vālmīki.

Kavibhūṣaṇa (S) (M) jewel among poets.

Kavijyeṣṭha (S) (M) **1.** oldest of poets. **3.** another name for Vālmīki.

Kavikratu (S) (M) of a poet's wisdom; wise.

Kavīndra (S) (M) prince among poets.

Kavīndu (S) (M) **1.** moon among poets. **3.** another name for Vālmīki.

Kavirāja (S) (M) **1.** chief of physicians; chief of poets. **2.** wise; intelligent. **3.** a Sanskṛt poet (12th century).

Kaviratha (S) (M) **1.** with an excellent chariot. **3.** a son of Ćitraratha.

Kavīśa (S) (M) **1.** lord of poets; best physician. **3.** a sage (*V. Rāmāyaṇa*); another name for Śukra.

Kavīśvara (S) (M) lord among poets.

Kavitara (S) (M) **1.** the great poet. **3.** another name for Varuṇa who is supposed to be the god of oceans and oceans are forever singing songs by way of their tides.

Kavitva (S) (M) poetic ability; intelligence.

Kāvya (S) (M) **1.** poem; intelligence; wisdom; prophetic inspiration. **2.** endowed with the qualities of a sage or poet; descended from a sage; prophetic; inspired. **3.** a son of Kavi Prajāpati (*M. Bh.*).

Kāyanavarman (S) (M) **1.** protector of duty. **3.** a king of Kāmarūpa and husband of Gandharvavatī (*R. Taraṅgiṇī*).

Kedāra (S) (M) **1.** field; meadow. **3.** peak of the Himālaya mountain (*M. Bh.*); a sacred place in Kurukṣetra and one of the 12 liṅga centres (*A. Koṣa*); a constellation (*V's. B. Saṁhitā*); a rāga; another name for Śiva.

Kedārāja (S) (M) **1.** lord of the mountain. **3.** Himalayan Cherry (*Prunus cerasoides*).

Kedāranātha (S) (M) **1.** lord of meadows; lord of fields; lord of Mount Kedāra. **3.** another name for Śiva.

Kedāreśa (S) (M) **1.** lord of Mount Kedāra. **3.** the statue of Śiva in Kāśī.

Kedāreśvara (S) (M) **1.** lord of Mount Kedāra. **3.** the statue of Śiva in Kāśī.

Kekāralohita (S) (M) **1.** with fragrant red hair. **3.** a great serpent (*K. Sāgara*).

Kekārava (S) (M) **1.** cry of a peacock. **3.** an asura (*M. Bh.*).

Kekāvala (S) (M) peacock.

Kekaya (S) (M) **1.** full of water. **2.** a place where there are many rivers, ponds and springs. 3. a king of the solar dynasty and father of Sudeṣṇa, Kīćaka and Upakīćaka (*M. Bh.*); a king who was the son of Śibi and the founder of the Kekaya dynasty (*Bhāgavata*); another name for Dhṛṣṭaketu.

Kelasa (S) (M) crystal.

Kelika (S) (M) 1. sporting; sportive. 2. Asoka tree (*Saraca indica*).

Kerkhi (S) (M) a gold necklace.

Kesara (S) (M) a hair of the brow; mane; saffron; the filament of any flower; Saffron (*Crocus sativus*); Ironwood tree (*Mesua ferrea*); *Mimusops elengi.*

Kesarāj (S) (M) 1. lord of hair. 3. *Eclipta alba*; *Wedelia calendulacea.*

Kesarin (S) (M) 1. lion; having a mane; of yellow complexion. 3. a forest king of the Mahāmeru mountain and the husband of Keśinī the mother of Hanumān (*V. Rāmāyaṇa*); the tree *Ochrocarpus longifolius.*

Keśaṭa (S) (M) 1. being richly endowed; an arrow of Kāma. 3. another name for Viṣṇu.

Keśava (S) (M) 1. long haired; slayer of Keśi. 3. the father of Brahmā and uncle of Maheśvara; another name for Viṣṇu and Kṛṣṇa.

Keśavara (S) (M) 1. having beautiful hair. 2. saffron (*Crocus sativus*); *Ochrocarpus longifolius.*

Keśayanti (S) (M) 1. long haired. 3. an attendant of Skanda (*M. Bh.*).

Keśihā (S) (M) 1. destroying Keśi 3. another name for Kṛṣṇa.

Keśihan (S) (M) 1. slayer of Keśin. 3. another name for Kṛṣṇa.

Keśihantā (S) (M) 1. slayer of Keśin. 3. another name for Kṛṣṇa.

Keśin (S) (M) 1. long haired. 2. lion. 3. an asura who was the son of Kaśyapa and Danu (*M. Bh.*); an asura who fought Kṛṣṇa and was killed by him (*Bhā. Purāṇa*); a son of Vasudeva and Kauśalyā (*Bhā. Purāṇa*); Bombay Hemp (*Hibiscus cannabinus*); Common Indigo (*Indigofera tinctoria*); another name for Rudra.

Keśinivadan (S) (M) 1. destroyer of Keśin. 3. another name for Kṛṣṇa.

Keśisūdana (S) (M) 1. slayer of Keśin. 3. another name for Kṛṣṇa.

Keśto, Keśut (S) (M) 1. son of Kesari. 3. another name for Hanumān.

Ketaka (S) (M) banner; flag; gold ornament worn in the hair; the Ketaki flower (*Pandanus odoratissimus*).

Ketana (S) (M) 1. house; flag; banner. 2. sign; symbol; invitation.

Ketita (S) (M) called; summoned.

Ketu (S) (M) 1. brightness; comet; the 9th planet; meteor; lamp; flame; form; intellect; flag; banner; leader. 3. a dānava son of Kaśyapa and Danu who became a planet (*M. Bh.*); *a* king of Bharata's dynasty (*Bhāgavata*); the son of Ṛṣabha (*Bhā. Purāṇa*); a son of Agni (*R. Anukramaṇika*); the 4th Manu (*A. Veda*); a sage (*M. Bh.*); another name for Śiva.

Ketubha (S) (M) cloud.

Ketubhūta (S) (M) 1. having a symbol. 2. a banner.

Ketumāla (S) (M) 1. a garland of light. 3. the grandson of Priyavrata (*M. Bh.*); a son of Āgnidhra (*V. Purāṇa*); a holy place in Jambūdvīpa where the people are equal to gods (*M. Bh.*).

Ketumālin (S) (M) 1. garlanded with light. 3. a dānava (*H. Purāṇa*).

Ketumat (S) (M) 1. bright. 2. splendid; with intellect. 3. a king who fought on the side of the Paṇḍavas and was known for his valour (*M. Bh.*); the son of Dhanvantari and the father of Bhīmaratha (*Bhā. Purāṇa*); the son of Ekalavya who fought on the side of the Kauravas (*M. Bh.*); a son of Kṣema and father of Suketu (*H. Purāṇa*); a king who fought on the side of the Kauravas (*M. Bh.*); the regent of the western part of the world (*A. Purāṇa*); a king of the Purū dynasty (*M. Bh.*); a yakṣa (*A. Koṣa*); a mountain; the palace of Sudattā, one of Kṛṣṇa's wives (*H. Purāṇa*).

Keturatna (S) (M) a bright jewel; Rahu's favourite; beryl; Lapis lazuli.

Ketuśṛṅga (S) (M) 1. horn bannered; with shining horns. 3. a king of ancient India (*M. Bh.*).

Ketutārā (S) (M) comet.

Ketuvarman (S) (M) **1.** flag shooter. **2.** one whose flag flies everywhere. **3.** a ćakravartin; a prince of Trigarta (*M. Bh.*).

Ketuvīrya (S) (M) **1.** with the strength of a leader. **3.** a king of Magadha; a dānava (*H. Purāṇa*).

Kevala (S) (M) **1.** alone; absolute; exclusive. **2.** pure; whole; perfect.

Kevalin (S) (M) seeker of the absolute.

Keya (S) (M) speed.

Keyūra (S) (M) armlet.

Keyūraka (S) (M) **1.** one who wears an armlet. **3.** a gandharva (*Kādambarī*).

Khaḍga (S) (M) **1.** sword. **2.** scimitar; a rhino horn. **3.** a warrior of Skanda (*M. Bh.*).

Khaḍgin (S) (M) **1.** armed with a sword. **3.** another name for Śiva.

Khādi (S) (M) brooch or ring worn by the maruts.

Khadira (S) (M) **1.** heavenly; celestial; Black Catechu tree (*Acacia catechu*). **3.** another name for Indra and the moon.

Khadyota (S) (M) **1.** light of the sky; firefly. **3.** another name for the sun.

Khaga (S) (M) **1.** moving in the air. **2.** sun; planet; air; wind; bird. **3.** a serpent born in the family of Kaśyapa (*M. Bh.*); another name for Śiva.

Khagādhirāja (S) (M) **1.** lord of the birds. **3.** another name for Garuḍa.

Khagaṇa (S) (M) **1.** moving through space. **3.** a king born in the family of Rāma who was the son of Vajranābha and the father of Vidhṛti (*V. Purāṇa*).

Khagañja (S) (M) **1.** best among birds. **3.** the father of Gokarneśvara (*Bhā. Purāṇa*).

Khagāsana (S) (M) **1.** seat of the sun. **3.** the mountain Udaya (*M. Bh.*); Viṣṇu whose seat is a bird.

Khagendra (S) (M) **1.** lord of birds. **3.** another name for Garuḍa.

Khageśa (S) (M) **1.** lord of birds. **3.** another name for Garuḍa.

Khageśvara (S) (M) **1.** lord of birds. **3.** another name for Garuḍa.

Khajit (S) (M) **1.** conquering heaven. **3.** a Buddha (*B. Literature*).

Khalin (S) (M) **1.** one who possesses threshing floors. **3.** another name for Mahāviṣṇu and Śiva.

Khamūrti (S) (M) a celestial person.

Khanaka (S) (M) **1.** miner; digger. **3.** a messenger sent by Vidura to the Pāṇḍavas to save them from the burning house (*M. Bh.*).

Khanḍaparaśu (S) (M) **1.** cutting one's foes with an axe. **3.** the weapons of Śiva and Viṣṇu (*M. Bh.*); another name for Śiva and Rāhu.

Khāṇḍava (S) (M) **1.** sugar candy; sweetmeat. **3.** a forest in Kurukṣetra sacred to Indra.

Khāndikya (S) (M) **1.** that which cuts. **3.** a Kśatriya king (*H. Purāṇa*); another name for Janaka.

Khanīnetra (S) (M) **1.** with eyes like a mine of jewels. **3.** the eldest son of King Vivinśa of the solar dynasty (*M. Bh.*).

Khañjana (S) (M) bird; a dimple.

Khapūra (S) (M) full of space; filler of the skies; the betel nut tree.

Khara (S) (M) **1.** an ass; hard; harsh; rough; sharp; solid; dense; cutting; thorny. **3.** a rākṣasa who was a son of Viśravas and Rāka (*V. Rāmāyaṇa*).

Kharag (S) (M) sword.

Kharāṅsu (S) (M) **1.** sharp rayed. **3.** another name for the sun.

Khararoman (S) (M) **1.** with rough hair. **3.** a nāga chief.

Kharu (S) (M) **1.** white; horse; pride. **3.** another name for Kāma and Śiva.

Khasama (S) (M) **1.** resting in the air. **3.** a Buddha.

Khasarpaṇa (S) (M) **1.** gliding through the air. **3.** a Buddha.

Khaśaya (S) (M) **1.** resting in the air. **3.** a Jina.

Khatilaka (S) (M) **1.** ornament of the sky. **3.** another name for the sun.

Khaṭvāṅga (S) (M) **1.** leg of the cot; with a skull headed club. **3.** a weapon of Śiva (*G's Dharmaśāstra*); another name for the Ikṣvāku dynasty King

Dilīpa (*Bhā. Purāṇa*); an attendant of Devī.

Khaṭvāṅgādhari (S) (M) **1.** bearing the Khaṭvānga club. **3.** another name for Śiva.

Khayāli (S) (M) one who moves in the sky.

Khela (S) (M) **1.** sport. **3.** another name for Vivasvata in whose honour games were held.

Khevanarāja (S) (M) the best rower.

Khila (S) (M) **1.** wasteland. **2.** desert; bare soil; a hymn added to the collection. **3.** another name for Vāyu, Śiva and Brahmā.

Khilāvan (S) (M) **1.** one who plays in the sky; an arrow. **3.** another name for the sun.

Khokhun (S) (M) boy.

Kholka (S) (M) sky meteor.

Khullana (S) (M) small; little.

Khuśila (H) (M) happy; pleasant.

Khuśirāma (H) (M) one who lives happily.

Khuśmana (H) (M) with a happy mind.

Khuśvanta (H) (M) bearer of happiness.

Khyāna (S) (M) perception; knowledge.

Khyāta (S) (M) **1.** pervading the sky; celebrated; named; called. **3.** an attendant of Skanda (*M. Bh.*).

Kīkaṭa (S) (M) **1.** horse. **3.** a king born in the dynasty of Priyavrata who was a son of King Bharata (*Bhāgavata*); a son of Ṛṣabha (*Bhā. Purāṇa*); a son of Śaṅkāta (*M. Bh.*); a tribe (*Bhā. Purāṇa*).

Kīla (S) (M) **1.** flame. **3.** another name for Agni.

Kilāta (S) (M) **1.** dwarf. **3.** an asura priest (*A. Koṣa*).

Kilkita (S) (M) Pied Kingfisher (*Ceryle rudis leucomelanura*).

Kiṁćaṇaka (S) (M) **1.** very small. **3.** a nāga.

Kiṁdatta (S) (M) **1.** given what?; one who has been given very little. **3.** a sacred well of the *Mahābhārata*.

Kiṁkara (S) (M) **1.** what to do?; servant. **3.** one of Śiva's attendants (*K. Sāgara*); Kāla's stick which strikes down living beings (*M. Bh.*); a race of Ćakṣasas who built Indraprastha for the Pāṇḍavas (*M. Bh.*).

Kiṁnara (S) (M) **1.** what sort of man? **2.** unmanly; a singer. **3.** a sect of demigods and celebrated musicians attached to Kubera, portrayed as horse headed with rest of their bodies in human shape, holding vīṇās in their hands (*A. Purāṇa*); the attendant of the 15th Arhat of the present Avasarpiṇī; the son of Vibhīṣaṇa (*V. Rāmāyaṇa*).

Kiṁpuruṣa (S) (M) **1.** what man? **2.** a very small man; a dwarf. **3.** one of the 9 sons of Āgnidhra (*V. Purāṇa*).

Kīnāśa (S) (M) **1.** cultivator of the soil. **2.** ploughman. **3.** a rākṣasa (*Ṛg Veda*); another name for Yama.

Kindama (S) (M) **1.** conqueror of the proud. **3.** a sage who was killed while in the form of a deer by King Pāṇḍu (*M. Bh.*).

Kiñjalka (S) (M) blossom of a lotus; Iron-wood tree (*Mesua ferrea*).

Kiñjata (S) (M) blossom.

Kiṅkana (S) (M) **1.** lotus bud; bell. **3.** a king of the lunar dynasty and the son of King Mahābhoja (*Bhāgavata*).

Kinkiṇa (S) (M) **1.** small drum. **3.** son of Bhajamāna (*Bh. Purāṇa*).

Kiṅkira (S) (M) **1.** horse; Indian cuckoo (*Cuculus scolopaceus*); black bee. **3.** another name for Kāma.

Kiṅkirāta (S) (M) **1.** parrot; Indian cuckoo (*Cuculus scolopaceus*). **3.** another name for Kāma.

Kiraṇa (S) (M) **1.** dust; very minute particle of dust. **2.** ray or beam of light; a sun or moon beam.

Kiraṇamālin (S) (M) **1.** garlanded with rays. **2.** bright; illuminating; enlightening. **3.** another name for the sun.

Kiraṇamaya (S) (M) **1.** full of rays; consisting of rays. **2.** radiant; brilliant; enlightening. **3.** another name for the sun.

Kiraṇapāṇi (S) (M) **1.** ray handed. **3.** another name for the sun.

Kiraṇapati (S) (M) **1.** lord of rays. **3.** another name for the sun.

Kirāta (S) (M) **1.** cave dwellers. **3.** hunters of a mountain tribe; Śiva in his form as a warrior of the Kirāta tribe (*M. Bh.*).

Kirika (S) (M) sparkling; beaming.

Kīriṇ (S) (M) **1.** one who praises. **2.** a poet; a writer; a speaker.

Kirīṭa (S) (M) **1.** crown; diadem. **2.** crest; tiara.

Kirīṭabhṛt (S) (M) **1.** wearing a diadem. **3.** another name for Arjuna.

Kirīṭin (S) (M) **1.** one who wears a crown. **3.** a warrior of Skanda (*M. Bh.*); another name for Arjuna and Indra; White Murdah (*Terminalia citrina*).

Kirīṭitanayātmaja (S) (M) **1.** grandson of Arjuna. **3.** another name for Parīkṣit.

Kirmīra (S) (M) **1.** of variegated colour. **3.** a rākṣasa who was a friend of Hiḍimba (*M. Bh*).

Kīrtana (S) (M) praise; praising; repeating.

Kīrtenya (S) (M) worthy of praise.

Kīrtibhāj (S) (M) **1.** famous. **3.** another name for Droṇāćārya.

Kīrtibhuṣaṇa (S) (M) one whose ornament is fame.

Kīrtideva (S) (M) lord of light; lord of fame.

Kīrtidhara (S) (M) bearer of fame; famous.

Kīrtidharmā (S) (M) **1.** one to whom fame comes naturally. **3.** a Kṣatriya who fought on the side of the Pāṇḍavas (*M. Bh.*).

Kīrtimān (S) (M) **1.** famous. **3.** the 1st son of Vasudeva and Devakī (*Bhā. Purāṇa*); a son of Vīrajas the mindborn son of Brahmā and the father of Kardama (*M. Bh.*); the son of Uttānapāda and Sūnṛtā (*H. Purāṇa*); a son of Aṅgiras (*V. Purāṇa*); a viśvadeva (*M. Bh.*).

Kīrtimanta (S) (M) **1.** famous. **3.** the eldest son of Vasudeva and Devaki (*V. Purāṇa*).

Kīrtimaya (S) (M) **1.** consisting of fame. **2.** famous.

Kīrtimukha (S) (M) **1.** with a famous face. **3.** a gaṇa born from the hair of Śiva (*Ś. Purāṇa*).

Kīrtiratha (S) (M) **1.** one who has fame as a chariot. **2.** one who travels in the chariot of fame. **3.** a prince of Videha and son of Prasiddhaka (*V. Rāmāyaṇa*).

Kīrtisena (S) (M) **1.** with a glorious army. **3.** a nephew of Vāsuki and the husband of Śrutārtha (*K. Sāgara*).

Kīrtita (S) (M) famous; celebrated.

Kisalaya (S) (M) **1.** sprout. **2.** a young shoot.

Kiṣeṇrāj (S) (M) the Hairchested Drongo (*Corvus hottentottus*).

Kiṣku (S) (M) the forearm; handle of an axe.

Kiśni (S) (M) **1.** killer of enemies. **2.** a good administrator.

Kiśora (S) (M) **1.** adolescent; colt. **2.** youth. **3.** another name for Kṛṣṇa and the sun.

Kiśorīlāla (S) (M) **1.** beloved of maidens. **3.** another name for Kṛṣṇa.

Kiśtikumāra (S) (M) prince of saviours.

Kīṭaka (S) (M) **1.** worm like. **3.** a king born from an aspect of the asura Krodhavaśa (*M. Bh.*).

Kitava (S) (M) **1.** gambler. **3.** another name for Śakuni.

Kiyedha (S) (M) **1.** abounding in; containing much. **3.** another name for Indra.

Kodaṇḍin (S) (M) **1.** armed with a bow. **3.** another name for Śiva.

Koel (S) (M) the Indian cuckoo (*Cuculus scolopaceus*).

Kohala (S) (M) **1.** spirituous barley. **2.** one that intoxicates. **3.** a musical instrument (*A. Koṣa*); a Brahmin scholar (*Va. Purāṇa*); a sage who invented drama (*M. Bh.*).

Kohi (S) (M) Shahin falcon (*Falco peregrinator*).

Kokā (S) (M) **1.** cuckoo; Ruddy Shelduck (*Anas casarca*); Wild Date tree (*Phoenix sylvestris*). **3.** an attendant of Skanda (*M. Bh.*); the earlier name of the river Śoṇa (*Ś. Brāhmaṇa*); another name for Viṣṇu.

Kokabandhu (S) (M) **1.** friend of the Ruddy Shelduck. **3.** another name for the sun.

Kokanada (S) (M) **1.** the voice of the cuckoo; the red water lily (*Nymphaea rubra*); reed of a flower. **3.** a Kṣatriya king who was a minor ally of Arjuna (*M. Bh.*); a warrior of Skanda (*M. Bh.*).

Kokila (S) (M) Indian cuckoo (*Cuculus Scolopaceus*); firebrand.

Kokilaka (S) (M) **1.** Indian cuckoo (*Cuculus scolopaceus*). **3.** a warrior of Skanda (*M. Bh.*).

Kola (S) (M) **1.** hog; embrace; a weapon. **3.** a son of Ākrīḍa; another name for Śiva and the Planet Saturn.

Kolāhala (S) (M) **1.** loud noise; chaos. **3.** a rāga.

Komala (S) (M) **1.** tender; soft; delicate. **2.** sweet; handsome; beautiful.

Komri (S) (M) the Grey Junglefowl (*Gallus sonnerati*).

Kooñj (S) (M) Demoiselle Crane (*Ardea virgo*).

Kopana (S) (M) **1.** angry; passionate. **3.** an asura (*H. Purāṇa*).

Kopavega (S) (M) **1.** impetuosity of passion; passionate; full of anger. **3.** a hermit who served Yudhiṣṭhira (*M. Bh.*).

Koṣṭhakoṭi (S) (M) **1.** store house consisting of 10 million rooms. **3.** an attendant of Śiva (*A. Koṣa*).

Koṣṭhavān (S) (M) **1.** store house; a vessel of grain. **3.** a mountain which is the overlord of many mountains (*M. Bh.*).

Koṭaraka (S) (M) **1.** hollow of a tree. **2.** one who lives in the hollow of a tree. **3.** a serpent from the Kaśyapa family (*M. Bh.*).

Kotavī (S) (M) **1.** naked woman. **2.** a form of Durgā; the tutelary deity of the dailyas.

Koṭijit (S) (M) **1.** conquering millions. **3.** another name for Kālidāsa.

Koṭikāśya (S) (M) **1.** abode of millions. **3.** a king of Tṛgarta and son of Suratha who was a follower of Jayadratha (*M. Bh.*).

Kotira (S) (M) **1.** horned. **3.** another name for Indra.

Koṭīśa (S) (M) **1.** pointed harrow; lord of millions. **3.** a serpent born in the family of Vāsuki (*M. Bh.*).

Koṭīśvara (S) (M) lord of millions.

Koṭṭa (S) (M) fort.

Kovida (S) (M) knowledgeable; wise.

Krakaċa (S) (M) **1.** a saw. **3.** a priest (*Ś. Vijaya*).

Krama (S) (M) **1.** order. **2.** sequence; course; custom; succession.

Kramajit (S) (M) **1.** In succession; succeeding. **3.** a Kṣatriya king and constant follower of Yudhiṣṭhira (*M. Bh.*).

Kramaṇa (S) (M) **1.** a step; the foot; a horse. **3.** a son of Bhajamāna (*H. Purāṇa*).

Kramapa (S) (M) **1.** step by step. **3.** a son of Pulaha and Kṣamā (*A. Purāṇa*).

Kramu (S) (M) **1.** going; proceeding. **2.** the Betel-nut tree (*Areca catechu*). **3.** a river in Plakṣadvīpa (*V. Purāṇa*).

Krāntivīra (S) (M) brave warrior.

Kratha (S) (M) **1.** suffocated; to hurt; to injure. **3.** a Kṣatriya king who was an incarnation of Krodhavaśa (*M. Bh.*); a king defeated by Bhīma (*M. Bh.*); a son of Vidarbha and brother of Kaiśika (*M. Bh.*); a warrior on the side of the Kauravas (*M. Bh.*); a warrior of Skanda (*M. Bh.*); a yakṣa who fought with Garuḍa (*M. Bh.*); a demon reborn as King Sūryākṣa (*H. Purāṇa*); a son of Dhṛtarāṣṭra (*M. Bh.*); a hermit (*M. Bh.*).

Krathana (S) (M) **1.** one who is in danger of suffocation. **3.** a nāga son of Dhṛtarāṣṭra (*M. Bh.*); an asura (*H. Purāṇa*).

Kratu (S) (M) **1.** plan; resolution; power; intention; wisdom; sacrifice. **2.** intelligence; ability; determination; will; purpose; design; desire; enlightenment; worship; the month of Āṣāḍha. **3.** one of the 6 mindborn sons of Brahmā and a prajāpati (*M. Smṛti*); a viśvadeva (*V. Purāṇa*); a son of Kṛṣṇa (*Bh. Purāṇa*); a son of Ūru and Āgneyī (*H. Purāṇa*); another name for Viṣṇu.

Kratubhuj (S) (M) **1.** one who eats the sacrificial oblation. **2.** a god; a deity.

Kratudhvaṅsī (S) (M) **1.** destroyer of Dakṣa's sacrifice. **3.** another name for Śiva.

Kratukaraṇa (S) (M) **1.** perfect in oblation. **3.** a sacrificial offering (*Ā. Śrauta Sūtra*).

Kratumata (S) (M) **1.** wise; having power. **2.** intelligent; prudent; vigorous. **3.** a son of Viśvāmitra (*Bhā. Purāṇa*).

Kratumaya (S) (M) endowed with wisdom.

Kratupati (S) (M) lord of sacrifice; lord of wisdom.

Kratvāmagha (S) (M) **1.** gift of wisdom. **2.** constituting a reward gained through intelligence.

Kratvaṅga (S) (M) **1.** pot of sacrifice. **2.** a utensil used in sacrifices.

Krauḍa (S) (M) **1.** belonging to a hog; coming from a hog. **3.** the incarnation of Viṣṇu as a boar.

Krauñća (S) (M) **1.** curlew; osprey; snipe; heron. **3.** the emblem of the 5th Arhat of the present Avasarpiṇī (*He. Koṣa*); a mountain range in North Assam said to have been split by Kārttikeya (*V. Purāṇa*); an asura killed by Kārttikeya (*Vām. Purāṇa*).

Krīḍana (S) (M) **1.** playing. **3.** another name for the wind.

Kriya (S) (M) literary composition; energy; ability; accomplishment; act; instruction; knowledge; worship; the zodiac sign of Aries.

Kriyāvidhi (S) (M) **1.** a rule of action; method of doing. **2.** accomplished person method.

Kṛkaneyu (S) (M) **1.** one who shouts repeatedly; one who wins again and again. **2.** a cock. **3.** a son of Raudrāśva (*M. Bh.*).

Kṛkavākudhvaja (S) (M) **1.** with a cock for his banner. **3.** another name for Kārttikeya.

Kṛmi (S) (M) **1.** silkworm; ant; lac-insect. **3.** a king of the dynasty of Aṅga and the son of King Uśīnara (*A. Purāṇa*); the brother of Rāvaṇa (*V. Rāmāyaṇa*); a serpent lord.

Kṛmilāśva (S) (M) **1.** with worms; having snakes. **3.** a king of the Purū dynasty who was the son of King Bāhyāśvana (*M. Bh.*).

Kṛmīśa (S) (M) **1.** lord of serpents. **3.** a yakṣa (*Divyāvadāna*); hell (*V. Purāṇa*).

Kroḍāṅka (S) (M) a tortoise.

Krodha (S) (M) **1.** anger. **3.** an asura born to Kaśyapa and Kalā (*M. Bh.*); a son of Brahmā born from his eyebrow (*V. Samhitā*).

Krodhana (S) (M) **1.** bad tempered. **3.** an important hermit in the palace of Indra (*M. Bh.*); a son of Kauśika and pupil of Garga (*H. Purāṇa*); a son of Ayuta and father of Devātithi (*Bhā. Purāṇa*); an attendent of Skanda (*M. Bh.*).

Krodhavaśa (S) (M) **1.** the power of anger. **3.** a follower of Indrajit (*M. Bh.*); a rākṣasa (*M. Bh.*).

Kroṣṭa (S) (M) **1.** crying; calling out. **3.** a son of Yadu (*H. Purāṇa*).

Kroṣṭu (S) (M) **1.** one who cries; jackal. **3.** a son of Yadu and father of Vṛjinīvata (*Bhā. Purāṇa*).

Kṛpa (S) (M) **1.** beauty; splendour; appearance; pity; tenderness; compassion; kindness; favour. **3.** a powerful king of ancient India who practiced strict vegetarianism (*M. Bh.*); the son of sage Śaradvata and Janapadī, the twin brother of Kṛpi, brought up by King Śāntanu, a member of the Hastināpura council, a master of archery and the preceptor of the Kauravas and Pāṇḍavas (*M. Bh.*); one of the 10 Ćirañjīvīs or immortals (*M. Bh.*); a friend of Indra (*Ṛg Veda*); a river (*M. Bh.*).

Kṛpādvaita (S) (M) **1.** unrivalled in compassion. **3.** a Buddha (*B. Ćarita*).

Kṛpāla (S) (M) kind; gentle.

Kṛpāṇa (S) (M) sword; dagger; scimitar.

Kṛpāṇaka (S) (M) sword; dagger; scimitar.

Kṛpānanda (S) (M) one who pleases with his kindness; one who takes delight in kindness.

Kṛpānīla (S) (M) **1.** dwelling in splendour. **3.** another name for Agni (*Ṛg Veda*).

Kṛpāsāgara (S) (M) ocean of compassion.

Kṛpāśaṅkarā (S) (M) Śiva, the merciful.

Kṛpīṭayoni (S) (M) **1.** wood born. **3.** another name for Agni.

Kṛśa (S) (M) **1.** lean. **3.** a hermit and friend of sage Śṛṅgi (*M.Bh./Ṛg Veda*); a serpent of the family of Airāvata (*M. Bh.*); a sage endowed with divine powers (*M. Bh.*).

Kṛṣadratha (S) (M) **1.** one who pulls the chariot. **3.** the son of Titīkṣa and nephew of Emperor Śibi (*Bhāgavata*).

Kṛṣaka (S) (M) **1.** farmer. **3.** a sage who stood guard over Soma (*A. Veda*).

Kṛśāuretas (S) (M) **1.** with thin seed. **3.** another name for Śiva.

Kṛśaṇ (S) (M) **1.** mother of pearl. **2.** pearl; gold; form; yielding pearls.

Kṛśaṇćandra (S) (M) **1.** moon and pearl conjoined. **3.** another name of Vasudeva.

Kṛśāṅga (S) (M) **1.** thin. **3.** another name for Śiva.

Kṛśaṇin (S) (M) decorated with pearls.

Kṛśānu (S) (M) **1.** archer. **3.** a divine being identified with Rudra; a sage (*Ṛg Veda*); a gandharva; another name for Viṣṇu and Agni.

Kṛśāśva (S) (M) **1.** with lean horses. **3.** a prajāpati who married Jayā and Suprabhā the daughters of Dakṣa and had a 100 sons in the form of a 100 arrows that Viśvāmitra gave Rāma and Lakṣmaṇa (*V. Rāmāyaṇa*); a king of the solar dynasty (*Bhāgavata*); a king who served Yama in his court (*M. Bh.*).

Kṛśeyu (S) (M) **1.** striving to be slender. **2.** one who is body conscious. **3.** a king of the Purū dynasty (*M. Bh.*).

Kṛṣivala (S) (M) **1.** farmer; tiller. **3.** a sage who lived in Indra's court (*M. Bh.*).

Kṛṣṇa (S) (M) **1.** black; dark blue. **2.** the dark half of the lunar month. **3.** the 9th incarnation of Viṣṇu as a great hero and teacher, the son of Vasudeva and Devakī of the Yādava clan, born on the Aṣṭami day in the month of Sinha (Leo), and was fostered by a herdsman named Nanda and his wife Yaśodā in Gokula and Vṛndāvana (*H. Purāṇa*); the Buddhist chief of the black demons — the enemies of Buddha and the white demons (*B. Literature*); an attendant in Skanda's retinue (*M. Bh*); a king of the nāgas (*M. Bh.*); the father of Dāmodara and uncle of Malhaṇa (*V. Purāṇa*); a son of Śuka and Pīvarī (*V. Purāṇa*); an adopted son of Asamañjas (*V. Purāṇa*); a son of Arjuna (*M. Bh.*); an asura (*H. Purāṇa*); Caraway (*Carumcarvi*); Common Graperine (*Vitis vinifera*); *Luffa acutangula*; *Ichnocarpus frutescens*.

Kṛṣṇāćala (S) (M) **1.** black mountain. **3.** one of the 9 principal ranges that separate the 9 divisions of the world (*A. Koṣa*).

Kṛṣṇadvaipāyana (S) (M) **1.** loved by Kṛṣṇa; black islander. **3.** another name for Vyāsa.

Kṛṣṇagupta (S) (M) **1.** protected by Kṛṣṇa. **3.** another name for Pradyumna.

Kṛṣṇakānta (S) (M) beloved of Kṛṣṇa.

Kṛṣṇakeśa (S) (M) **1.** black haired. **3.** an attendant in Skanda's retinue (*M. Bh.*).

Kṛṣṇamitra (S) (M) friend of Kṛṣṇa; friend of the night.

Kṛṣṇanada (S) (M) **1.** black river. **3.** a Sanskṛt poet who wrote on the theme of Nala (13th century A.D.); author of *Sahṛdayanana Kavya*.

Kṛṣṇanetra (S) (M) **1.** black eyed. **3.** another name for Śiva.

Kṛṣṇāntara (S) (M) the lodestone.

Kṛṣṇānubhautika (S) (M) **1.** one who has realized Kṛṣṇa; one with dark experiences. **3.** a sage (*M. Bh.*).

Kṛṣṇaparvata (S) (M) **1.** black mountain. **3.** a mountain in Kuśa island very dear to Viṣṇu (*M. Bh.*).

Kṛṣṇasārathi (S) (M) **1.** with Kṛṣṇa as a charioteer. **3.** another name for Arjuna; White Murdah (*Terminalia citrina*).

Kṛṣṇātreya (S) (M) **1.** the dark Atreya; the dark complexioned Brāhmin of the Atreya family. **3.** a sage who grasped the whole of Ayurveda (*M. Bh.*).

Kṛṣṇāvartamāna (S) (M) **1.** surrounded by blue flames. **3.** another name for Agni.

Kṛṣṇika (S) (M) related to Kṛṣṇa; of blackness. 3. Black Mustard (*Brassica nigra*).

Kṛṣṇīya (S) (M) **1.** black. **3.** a man protected by the 2 aśvins (*A. Veda*).

Kṛta (S) (M) **1.** accomplished; proper; good. **3.** a king of Janaka's dynasty who was the son of Vijaya and the father of Śunaka (*Bhāgavata*); one of the 7 sons of Vasudeva (*Bhā. Purāṇa*); one of the 4 ages (*M. Smṛti*); a viśvadeva (*M. Bh.*).

Kṛtabhuj (S) (M). **1.** accomplished. **2.** done; made; obtained; gained. **3.** a son of Saṁnati and a pupil of Hiraṇyanābha (*Bhā. Purāṇa*); a son of Kṛtaratha and the father of Vibudha (*V. Purāṇa*); a son of Jaya and father of Haryavana (*Bhā. Purāṇa*); a son of Ćyavana and father of Uparićara (*Vā. Purāṇa*); a viśvadeva (*M. Bh.*); a son of Vasudeva (*Bhā. Purāṇa*).

Kṛtaćetas (S) (M) **1.** with an accomplished intelligence. **3.** a sage (*M. Bh.*).

Kṛtadhvaja (S) (M) **1.** with the flag of achievement. **3.** a king of Janaka's dynasty (*Bhā. Purāṇa*); a son of Dharmadhvaja (*Bhā. Purāṇa*).

Kṛtāgni (S) (M) **1.** possessing fire. **3.** a king of the Yadu dynasty who was the brother of Kṛtavīrya (*M. Bh.*); a son of Kanaka.

Kṛtahasta (S) (M) **1.** with accomplished hands. **2.** dextrous.

Kṛtaka (S) (M) **1.** made. **2.** artificial; adopted. **3.** a son of Vasudeva (*Bhā. Purāṇa*); a son of Ćyavana (*Bhā. Purāṇa*).

Kṛtakāma (S) (M) **1.** accomplisher of desires. **2.** one whose desires are satisfied.

Kṛtakarman (S) (M) **1.** accomplisher of acts. **2.** skilful; clever; the Supreme Spirit.

Kṛtakṣaṇa (S) (M) **1.** one who makes time; one who utilizes lime; successful. **3.** a king of Videha who was a member of Yudhiṣṭhira's court (*M. Bh.*).

Kṛtalakṣaṇa (S) (M) with the mark of accomplishment.

Kṛtamukha (S) (M) with a well made face; skilled; clever.

Kṛtāñjali (S) (M) one who stands in a reverent posture.

Kṛtānta (S) (M) **1.** the end of action. **3.** another name for Yama, the lord of death.

Kṛtaparva (S) (M) **1.** the golden age of the world; one who enjoys festivals. **3.** a king of the Yadu dynasty (*Bhā. Purāṇa*).

Kṛtāratha (S) (M) **1.** with ready chariots. **3.** a grandson of Maru.

Kṛtāśrama (S) (M) **1.** painstaking; laborious. **2.** one who has led his life in accordance with the kind prescribed in the Hindu scriptures. **3.** a sage in the assembly of Yudhiṣṭhira (*M. Bh.*).

Kṛtāśva (S) (M) **1.** accomplished of horses. **2.** one who has many horses, a good rider. **3.** a sage who married 2 of Dakṣa's daughters (*D. Bhāgavata*).

Kṛtavāka (S) (M) **1.** accomplished in speech. **3.** a sage and admirer of Yudhiṣṭhira (*M. Bh.*).

Kṛtavarman (S) (M) **1.** successful warrior. **3.** a king of the Vṛṣṇi dynasty who was the son of Dhānaka and the brother of Kṛṣṇa's grandfather (*M. Bh.*); father of the 13th Arhat of the present Avasarpinī (*He. Koṣa*); son of Hṛdīka (*H. Purāṇa*); a son of Kanaka (*M. Bh.*).

Kṛtavega (S) (M) **1.** that which moves fast. **3.** a sage in the court of Yama (*M. Bh.*).

Kṛtavīrya (S) (M) **1.** accomplished warrior. **2.** strong; powerful. **3.** the son of Kanaka, father of Kārtavīrya and a member of the court of Yama (*M. Bh.*); the father-in-law of solar King Ahaṁyati and the father of Bhānumatī (*M. Bh.*).

Kṛtāyuṣa (S) (M) **1.** master of age. **2.** one who lives as long as one wishes. **3.** a brother of Kṛtāgni (*H. Purāṇa*).

Kṛteyu (S) (M) **1.** controller of an age. **2.** master of an era; one who lives long; immortal. **3.** a king of the Aṅga dynasty (*M. Bh.*); a son of Raudrāśva (*V. Purāṇa*).

Kṛti (S) (M) **1.** creation. **3.** a sage who belonged to the order of Vedavyāsa (*V. Purāṇa*); a pupil of Hiraṇyanābha (*Vā. Purāṇa*); a king of Śūkradeśa who gave a 100 elephants to Yudhiṣṭhira (*M. Bh.*); a son of Nahuṣa (*H. Purāṇa*); a king in the court of Yama (*M. Bh.*); a viśvadeva (*M. Bh.*); another name for Viṣṇu.

Kṛtikara (S) (M) **1.** practising magic. **3.** another name for Rāvaṇa.

Kṛtimān (S) (M) **1.** creator; sculptor. **3.** a son of Yavīnara.

Kṛtin (S) (M) **1.** active; skilful; expert; clever; pure; pious; satisfied; happy; successful; lucky; wise; learned; virtuous; blessed. **3.** a son of Ćyavana and father of Uparićara (*Bhā. Purāṇa*); a son of Saṇnatimat (*Bhā. Purāṇa*).

Kṛtirāta (S) (M) **1.** creating; presenting actions. **3.** a prince (*Bh. Purāṇa*).

Kṛtnu (S) (M) **1.** working well. **2.** an accomplished worker; one who performs one's duty nicely; skilful; clever; mechanic; artist. **3.** a ṛṣi (*Ṛ Ankuramaṇika*).

Kṛtsna (S) (M) entire; whole.

Kṛtsnavid (S) (M) omnicient.

Kṛttivāsas (S) (M) **1.** covered with a skin. **3.** another name for Rudra-Śiva.

Kṛtya (S) (M) action; achievement.

Kṛvi (S) (M) **1.** cloud. **3.** another name for Rudra.

Krūradṛśa (S) (M) **1.** with a cruel aspect. **3.** another name for the planet Saturn.

Krūrākṛti (S) (M) **1.** with a cruel appearance. **3.** another name for Rāvaṇa.

Krūrākṣa (S) (M) **1.** evil eyed. **3.** a minister of the owl King Arimardana (*Pañćatantra*).

Kṣama (S) (M) **1.** of earth. **2.** patient; enduring; bearing; submissive; adequate; fit.

Kṣamābhuj (S) (M) **1.** one who enjoys the earth. **2.** patient; prince; a king.

Kṣamaka (S) (M) **1.** merciful. **3.** a king of the Purū dynasty (*A. Purāṇa*).

Kṣamākara (S) (M) **1.** patient; indulgent. **3.** a yakṣa (*K. Sāgara*).

Kṣamāmitra (S) (M) **1.** friend of the earth. **2.** patient; forgiving; capable.

Kṣaman (S) (M) earth; soil; ground.

Kṣamāpati (S) (M) **1.** lord of the earth; lord of mercy. **2.** a king.

Kṣamātanaya (S) (M) **1.** son of the earth. **3.** the planet Mars (*V's B. Samhitā*).

Kṣamāvarta (S) (M) **1.** surrounded by patience. **3.** a son of Devala (*V. Purāṇa*).

Kṣantu (S) (M) patient; enduring.

Kṣapāćara (S) (M) **1.** one who wanders at night. **3.** another name for the moon.

Kṣapākara (S) (M) **1.** that which causes night. **2.** the moon.

Kṣapākarasekhara (S) (M) **1.** wearing the moon on his head. **3.** another name for Śiva.

Kṣapaṇa (S) (M) **1.** fasting. **2.** a religious mendicant; a Jaina or Buddhist mendicant.

Kṣapaṇaka (S) (M) **1.** fasting. **2.** a religious mendicant; especially a Jaina mendicant who wears no garments. **3.** an author supposed to have lived at the court of King Vikramāditya (*K. Granthāvali*).

Kṣapānātha (S) (M) **1.** lord of the night. **3.** another name for the moon.

Kṣapāramaṇa (S) (M) **1.** night lover. **3.** another name for the moon.

Kṣāpāvāna (S) (M) earth protector.

Kṣapendra (S) (M) **1.** king of the night. **3.** another name for the moon.

Kṣapeśa (S) (M) **1.** lord of the night. **3.** another name for the moon.

Kṣāra (S) (M) **1.** ashes. **3.** another name for Agni.

Kṣaragna (S) (M) supreme soul.

Kṣatradeva (S) (M) **1.** lord of warriors. **3.** the son of Śikhaṇḍi who was a famous archer (*M. Bh.*).

Kṣātradharman (S) (M) **1.** religious warrior. **3.** a son of Dhṛṣṭhadyumna (*M. Bh.*).

Kṣatrañjaya (S) (M) **1.** conqueror of warriors. **3.** a son of Dhṛṣṭhadyumna (*M. Bh.*).

Kṣaya (S) (M) dwelling; dominion.

Kṣayadvīra (S) (M) **1.** ruling. **2.** governing men; granting heroic sons. **3.** another name for Indra, Rudra and Pūṣan.

Kṣayana (S) (M) a place of tranquil water; a dwelling.

Kṣayata (S) (M) to possess; to have power over to rule; to govern; to be the master.

Kṣema (S) (M) **1.** safely; security; welfare; peace. **2.** tranquillity; bliss; final emancipation. **3.** a king who was an incarnation of Krodhavaśa and fought on the side of the Pāṇḍavas (*M. Bh.*); a son of Śući and father of Suvrata (*Bhā. Purāṇa*); a son of Dharma and Śānti (*V. Purāṇa*); a son of Titikṣā (*Bhā. Purāṇa*).

Kṣemadarśi (S) (M) **1.** seer of security. **3.** a king of Koṣala (*M. Bh.*).

Kṣemadhanvan (S) (M) **1.** with the bow of prosperity. **3.** a famous archer who fought on the side of the Kauravas (*M. Bh.*); a son of Manu Sāvarṇa (*H. Purāṇa*); a son of Punḍarīka (*Bhā. Purāṇa*).

Kṣemadhṛti (S) (M) **1.** bearer of security. **3.** a Kṣatriya king who was an incarnation of Krodhavaśa and fought on the side of the Kauravas (*M. Bh.*).

Kṣemaka (S) (M) **1.** one who brings security. **2.** a kind of perfume. **3.** last descendant of Parīkṣit in the Kaliyuga (*V. Purāṇa*); a rākṣasa who was killed before Kāśī was built by King Divodāsa (*H. Purāṇa*); a serpent son of Kaśyapa and Kadru (*M. Bh.*); a king in the court of Yudhiṣṭhira (*M. Bh.*); an attendant of Śiva (*A. Koṣa*); a son of Niramitra (*M. Purāṇa*); a nāga (*M. Bh.*).

Kṣemakara (S) (M) **1.** conferring peace and prosperity. **3.** a mythical Buddha (*B. Literature*).

Kṣemamaya (S) (M) full of peace and or prosperity.

Kṣemamūrti (S) (M) **1.** symbol of peace and prosperity. **3.** a son of Dhṛtarāṣṭra (*M. Bh.*).

Kṣemaṅkara (S) (M) **1.** conferring peace, security, happiness. **3.** a king of Trigarta (*M. Bh.*); a mythical Buddha; a son of Brahmadatta.

Kṣemaśarma (S) (M) **1.** warrior of peace. **3.** a warrior who fought on the side of the Kauravas (*M. Bh.*).

Kṣemavāha (S) (M) **1.** carrier of prosperity. **3.** a warrior of Skanda (*M. Bh.*).

Kṣemavṛddhi (S) (M) **1.** increasing peace and prosperity. **3.** a minister of King Sālva (*M. Bh.*).

Kṣemendra (S) (M) **1.** lord of peace. **3.** a celebrated Kāśmīra poet (11th century).

Kṣemya (S) (M) **1.** resting; at ease; giving peace. **2.** healthy; prosperous; auspicious. **3.** a father of Ketumat; a son of Ugrāyudha and father of Suvīra (*H. Purāṇa*); another name for Śiva.

Kṣetrapāla (S) (M) **1.** protector of the fields. **3.** a 3-eyed deity presumed to be a portion of Śiva, the protector of villages and cities and each eye of which represents Sāttva, Rajasa and Tamasa (*Mā. Purāṇa*); the guardian of the Śaiva temples of South India.

Kṣetrin (S) (M) **1.** owning land. **3.** the soul.

Kṣipaṇu (S) (M) **1.** thrown; moving. **2.** archer; missile; air; wind.

Kṣipra (S) (M) **1.** springing; elastic; quick; speedy. **3.** a son of Kṛṣṇa.

Kṣiprahasta (S) (M) **1.** swift handed. **3.** a rākṣasa; another name for Agni.

Kṣipreṣu (S) (M) **1.** with quick arrows. **3.** another name for Rudra.

Kṣīraja (S) (M) **1.** born of milk. **2.** nectar; pearl. **3.** another name for Śeṣa and the moon.

Kṣīrapāna (S) (M) **1.** to drink milk. **2.** vessel out of which milk is drunk;

milk drinkers. **3.** another name for the Uśīnaras (*Pāṇini*).

Kṣīraśukla (S) (M) as fair as milk.

Kṣitendra (S) (M) **1.** lord of the earth. **2.** a ruler; a king.

Kṣitibhuj (S) (M) **1.** enjoyer of the earth. **2.** a king; a ruler.

Kṣitideva (S) (M) **1.** god of the earth. **3.** another name for Brahmā.

Kṣitigarbha (S) (M) **1.** produced in the earth. **3.** a bodhisattva.

Kṣitija (S) (M) **1.** son of the earth. **2.** tree; earthworm; the horizon; snail. **3.** another name for the demon Naraka and the planet Mars.

Kṣitikampana (S) (M) **1.** an earthquake. **3.** a captain of the army of Skanda (*M. Bh.*).

Kṣitikṣita (S) (M) **1.** ruler of the earth. **2.** a king.

Kṣitilavabhuj (S) (M) **1.** possessing only a small tract of the earth. **2.** a petty prince.

Kṣitinātha (S) (M) lord of the earth.

Kṣitīndra (S) (M) lord of the earth.

Kṣitipati (S) (M) master of the earth.

Kṣitipuruhūta (S) (M) **1.** the Indra of the earth. **2.** a king.

Kṣitiputra (S) (M) **1.** son of the earth. **3.** the demon Naraka (*Kā. Purāṇa*).

Kṣitīśa (S) (M) lord of the earth.

Kṣitīśvara (S) (M) **1.** god of the earth. **2.** a king. **3.** a king of Kānyakubja.

Kṣobhaka (S) (M) **1.** that which shakes; that which agitates. **3.** a mountain in Kāmākhyā sacred to Durgā (*Kā. Purāṇa*); one of the 5 arrows of Kāma; another name for Śiva and Viṣṇu.

Kṣoṇideva (S) (M) earth god.

Kṣudhi (S) (M) **1.** hungry. **3.** a son of Kṛṣṇa (*Bh. Purāṇa*).

Kṣupa (S) (M) **1.** shrub; bush. **3.** a king who was the son of Prasaṇdhi, the grandson of Vaivasvata Manu and the father of Ikṣvāku (*M. Bh.*); a son of Kṛṣṇa and Satyabhāmā (*H. Purāṇa*); a prajāpati born from the sneeze of Brahmā (*Br. Purāṇa*).

Kṣurakarṇī (S) (M) **1.** with sharp ears. **3.** an attendant of Skanda (*M. Bh.*).

Kubera (S) (M) **1.** slow; lazy. **3.** the chief of evil beings with the patronymic Vaiśravaṇa, Kubera who performed penance in Laṅkā to be a Lokapāla and the custodian of wealth—both of which were granted to him by Brahmā, is the son of Viśravas and Īlibilā, the husband of Bhadrā, the father of Nalakūbara, the lord of the oceans which yield him extreme wealth, the lord of the yakṣas, the regent of the Northern Quarters, a special friend of Śiva, considered to live on Mount Gandhamādana with his capital as Alakā and among the Jainas considered the attendant of the 19th Arhat of the present Avasarpiṇī (*J. S. Koṣa*); the great grandfather of the author Bāṇabhatta (*Kādambarī*); a prince of Devarāṣṭra.

Kuberabandhu (S) (M) **1.** friend of Kubera. **2.** one who is wealthy.

Kubha (S) (M) **1.** zigzag; jar. **3.** a river mentioned in the *Ṛg Veda* which is now the Kabul river.

Kućandana (S) (M) the fragrance of the earth.

Kućelu (S) (M) **1.** one who wears dirty clothes. **3.** another name for Sudāmā a classmate of Kṛṣṇa (*Bhāgavata*).

Kudhara (S) (M) **1.** that which supports the earth. **2.** a mountain.

Kuha (S) (M) **1.** deceiver. **3.** a prince of Sauvīra (*M. Bh.*); another name for Kubera.

Kuhara (S) (M) **1.** cavity; hollow; ear; throat. **3.** a king of Kaliṅga who was an incarnation of the asura Krodhavaśa (*M. Bh.*).

Kuhupāla (S) (M) **1.** lord of the moon. **3.** the king of turtles who is supposed to uphold the world; another name for Śiva.

Kuja (S) (M) **1.** born from the earth. **2.** tree. **3.** the gaṇa who wears the rudrākṣa māla (*Ś. Purāṇa*); another name for the daitya Naraka conquered by Kṛṣṇa (*Bhā. Purāṇa*); another name for the planet Mars.

Kujambha (S) (M) **1.** destroyer. **3.** a son of Prahlāda.

Kujapa (S) (M) one whose protector is Mars.

Kujṛmbha (S) (M) **1.** with a wide yawn. **2.** lazy. **3.** an asura (*Mā. Purāṇa*).

Kuka (S) (M) crow pheasant.

Kukīla (S) (M) **1.** a bolt of the earth. **2.** a mountain.

Kukṣi (S) (M) **1.** the abdomen; the interior; a bay; a gulf; the sheath of a sword. **3.** a son of Priyavrata and Kāmyā (*A. Purāṇa*); a son of Ikṣvāku and father of Vikukṣi (*Bhā. Purāṇa*); an asura who was reborn as King Pārvatīya (*M. Bh.*); another name for Bali (*V. Rāmāyaṇa*).

Kukudmi (S) (M) **1.** mountain; humped bull. **3.** the father of Revatī (*D. Bh. Purāṇa*); the son of King Anarta (*D. Purāṇa*).

Kukura (S) (M) **1.** dog; a species of deer. **3.** a king of the lunar dynasty and the founder of the Kukura dynasty (*M. Bh.*); a sage at the court of Yudhiṣṭhra(*M. Bh.*); a son of Andhaka (*M. Bh.*).

Kulabhūṣaṇa (S) (M) ornament of the family.

Kuladeva (S) (M) the deity of the family.

Kuladīpa (S) (M) light of the family.

Kuladīpaka (S) (M) lamp of the family.

Kulaja (S) (M) well born; of a noble family.

Kulamaṇi (S) (M) the jewel of the family.

Kulānanda (S) (M) joy of the family.

Kulapati (S) (M) head of the family.

Kulatilaka (S) (M) **1.** glory of the family. **2.** one who brings honour to his family.

Kulavīra (S) (M) one who fights for the honour of his family.

Kulika (S) (M) **1.** well born. **3.** a serpent of the Kadru family (*M. Bh.*); one of the 8 chiefs of the nāgas having a half moon on his face and of a dusky brown visage (*M. Bh.*).

Kulīn (S) (M) highborn; of a good family.

Kulīra (S) (M) crab; the zodiac sign of Cancer.

Kuliśa (S) (M) **1.** axe. **2.** the thunderbolt of Indra. **3.** a river supposed to be in the middle region of the sky (*Ṛg Veda*); another name for a diamond.

Kuliśāsana (S) (M) **1.** one who commands with his axe. **3.** another name for Śākyamuni.

Kuliśaya (S) (M) that which is as hard as thunderbolt.

Kulīśvara (S) (M) **1.** family god. **3.** another name for Śiva.

Kullūka (S) (M) **1.** land covered with high mountains. **3.** a celebrated commentator on Manu (*D. Śāstra*).

Kulya (S) (M) **1.** well born. **2.** respectable; canal. **3.** a sage who was a disciple of Vyāsa (*Bhā. Purāṇa*).

Kumāra (S) (M) **1.** child; boy; youth; prince. **3.** a son of Agni who is the author of some Ṛg Vedic hymns; the attendant of the 12th Arhat of the present Avasarpiṇī (*J.S. Koṣa*); one of the 9 names of Agni (*R. Aṅkura-maṇikā*); a king who fought on the side of the Pāṇḍavas (*M. Bh.*); a son of Garuḍa (*Gar. Purāṇa*); a prajāpati (*Vā. Purāṇa*); a son of Bhavya; *Crataeva nurvala*; Yellow Champaka (*Michelia champaka*); another name for the Sindhu river; another name for Skanda.

Kumāradarśana (S) (M) **1.** he who sees Skanda. **3.** a prince of the gandharvas (*H. Purāṇa*).

Kumāradāsa (S) (M) **1.** devotee of Skanda. **3.** Sanskṛt poet who wrote *Jānakīharaṇam* (7th century A.D.).

Kumāradatta (S) (M) **1.** given by Kārttikeya. **3.** a son of Nidhipati (*K. Sāgara*).

Kumāradhara (S) (M) **1.** bearer of children; borne of Skanda. **3.** a river with its source in the Brahmarasas, considered to bestow intelligence and wealth upon those who bathe in it (*M. Bh.*).

Kumāragupta (S) (M) protected by Skanda.

Kumāraka (S) (M) **1.** youth; the pupil of the eye. **3.** a serpent of the Kauravya dynasty (*M. Bh.*).

Kumārapāla (S) (M) **1.** protected by Skanda; protector of children. **3.** a king of Gujarat who made Jainism the state religion.

Kumārapita (S) (M) **1.** father of Skanda. **3.** another name for Śiva.

Kumārasū (S) (M) **1.** father of Skanda. **3.** another name for Agni.

Kumāreśa (S) (M) **1.** lord of youths. **3.** another name for Kārttikeya.

Kumārila (S) (M) **1.** intelligent youth. **3.** a renowned teacher of the Mimāmsā philosophy.

Kumbha (S) (M) **1.** jar; pitcher; the zodiac sign of Aquarius. **3.** the father of the 19th Arhat of the present Avasarpinī, one of the 34 rebirths of Śākyamuni; one of the 3 sons of Prahlāda (*M. Bh.*); son of Kumbhakarṇa and Vajrajvālā (*V. Rāmāyaṇa*); a mantra pronounced over a weapon (*V. Rāmāyaṇa*); *Commiphora mukul.*

Kumbhadhara (S) (M) pitcher; the zodiac sign of Aquarius.

Kumbhaja (S) (M) **1.** son of a pitcher. **3.** another name for Agastya.

Kumbhaka (S) (M) **1.** pot; pitcher; the protuberance on an elephant's forehead. **3.** a warrior of Skanda (*M. Bh.*).

Kumbhakarṇa (S) (M) **1.** pot eared. **3.** a son of Viśravas and Puṣpotkaṭā and the brother of Rāvaṇa (*V. Rāmāyaṇa*).

Kumbhaketu (S) (M) **1.** pot-bannered. **3.** a son of Śambara.

Kumbhanābha (S) (M) **1.** pot navelled. **3.** a son of Bali (*V. Rāmāyaṇa*).

Kumbhāṇḍa (S) (M) **1.** one for whom the earth is as light as a pot. **3.** a minister of Bāṇāsura and the father of Ćitralekhā (*Bhā. Purāṇa*).

Kumbhāṇḍakodara (S) (M) **1.** pot bellied. **3.** a warrior of Skanda (*M. Bh.*).

Kumbhahanu (S) (M) **1.** with a pot shaped chin. **3.** a rākṣasa (*V. Rāmāyaṇa*).

Kumbharetas (S) (M) **1.** born in a pot. **2.** a flame in a pot. **3.** an agni who was the son of Bharadvāja and Vīrā (*M. Bh.*).

Kumbhasambhava (S) (M) **1.** born of a pot. **3.** another name for Agastya and Nārāyaṇa.

Kumbhaśravas (S) (M) **1.** pot eared. **3.** an attendant of Skanda (*M. Bh.*).

Kumbhavaktra (S) (M) **1.** pot faced. **3.** an attendant of Skanda (*M. Bh.*).

Kumbhayoni (S) (M) **1.** pot born. **3.** another name for Agastya, Droṇa, Vasiṣṭha.

Kumbhināśa (S) (M) **1.** jar-nosed; poisonous snake. **3.** an asura (*M. Bh.*).

Kumbhīra (S) (M) **1.** crocodile of the Gaṅgā **3.** a yakṣa (*M. Bh.*).

Kumbhodara (S) (M) **1.** pot bellied. **3.** an attendant of Śiva (*K. Granthāvali*).

Kumkum (S) (M) saffron (*Crocus sativus*); red; pollen; red sandalwood paste applied on the forehead.

Kumuda (S) (M) **1.** pleasure of the earth; the white water lily (*Nymphaea alba*); the red lotus (*Nymphaea rubra*); camphor. **3.** one of the 15 attendants given by Brahmā to Skanda (*M. Bh.*); one of the 4 mountains surrounding the Mahāmeru (*V. Purāṇa*); a great elephant born in the dynasty of Supratīka (*M. Bh.*); a monkey attendant of Sugrīva (*M. Bh.*); a warrior who fought with Skanda (*M. Bh.*); a son of Garuḍa (*M. Bh.*); an attendant of Skanda (*M. Bh.*); the elephant of the South West Quarter (*A. Koṣa*); a particular comet (*V's B. Samhitā*); a serpent (*M. Bh.*); a daitya; a son of Gada and Bṛhatī (*H. Purāṇa*); another name for Viṣṇu.

Kumudadi (S) (M) **1.** given by the pleasure of earth; one who gives the white water lily. **3.** a Vedic scholar of the line of Vyāsa's disciples (*V. Purāṇa*); another name for Viṣṇu.

Kumudaka (S) (M) **1.** one who gives the white water lily. **3.** another name for Viṣṇu.

Kumudākṣa (S) (M) **1.** lotus eyed; red eyed. **3.** an attendant of Viṣṇu (*M. Bh.*); a serpent (*M. Bh.*).

Kumudamaṇi (S) (M) **1.** jewel among water lilies. **3.** one of the 4 attendants given by Brahmā to Skanda (*M. Bh.*).

Kumudanātha (S) (M) **1.** lord of the white water lily. **3.** another name for the moon.

Kumudapati (S) (M) **1.** lord of the white water lily. **3.** another name for the moon.

Kumudeśa (S) (M) **1.** lord of the white water lily. **3.** another name for the moon.

Kunābhi (S) (M) **1.** having the earth for a navel. **3.** the collective treasures of Kubera (*M. Bh.*).

Kunadika (S) (M) **1.** one who pleases the earth. **2.** pleaser of the earth. **3.** a warrior of Skanda (*M. Bh.*).

Kuṇāla (S) (M) **1.** lotus; the Painted Snipe bird. **3.** a son of Emperor Aśoka named after the eyes of a Himālayan bird.

Kunda (S) (M) **1.** musk; jasmine (*Jasminum pubescens*); Oleander (*Nerium odorum*); the number 9. **3.** one of Kubera's 9 treasures; another name for Viṣṇu.

Kuṇḍa (S) (M) **1.** bowl; pot; spring; well. **3.** one of the 5 attendants given by Dhātā to Skanda (*M. Bh.*); a son of Dhṛtarāṣṭra (*M. Bh.*); a Brāhmin known for his learning (*M. Bh.*); one of Kubera's 9 treasures; a nāga (*M. Bh.*); a guhyaka; another name for Viṣṇu and Śiva.

Kuṇḍabhedin (S) (M) **1.** pot breaker. **3.** a son of Dhṛtarāṣṭra (*M. Bh.*).

Kundadanta (S) (M) **1.** with jasmine like teeth. **3.** a Videha Brāhmin who studied with sage Vasiṛṭha (*Yogavāśiṣṭha*).

Kuṇḍadhārā (S) (M) **1.** pot bearer. **3.** a nāga (*M. Bh.*); a son of Dhṛtarāṣṭra.

Kuṇḍaja (S) (M) **1.** pot born. **3.** a son of Dhṛtarāṣṭra (*M. Bh.*).

Kuṇḍaka (S) (M) **1.** a pot. **3.** a son of Dhṛtarāṣṭra (*M. Bh.*).

Kuṇḍala (S) (M) **1.** earring. **3.** a serpent of the Kaurava dynasty (*M. Bh.*).

Kuṇḍalīn (S) (M) **1.** decorated with earrings. **3.** another name for Śiva and Varuṇa.

Kuṇḍam (S) (M) altar; grinding stone.

Kundan (S) (M) pure; sparkling; fine; purified; glittering; gold.

Kuṇḍapāyin (S) (M) drinking out of pitchers.

Kuṇḍareśvara (S) (M) **1.** lord of vegetation. **3.** a Liṅga (*Sk. Purāṇa*).

Kuṇḍaśāyin (S) (M) **1.** resting in a pot. **3.** a son of Dhṛtarāṣṭra.

Kuṇḍaśin (S) (M) **1.** panderer. **3.** a son of Dhṛtarāṣṭra.

Kuṇḍika (S) (M) **1.** round pot. **3.** a son of Dhṛtarāṣṭra (*M. Bh.*).

Kuṇḍina (S) (M) **1.** furnished with a pitcher; born of a pitcher. **3.** a son of Dhṛtarāṣṭra (*M. Bh.*); another name for Śiva.

Kuṇḍira (S) (M) strong; powerful.

Kuṇḍodara (S) (M) **1.** pot bellied. **3.** a son of Dhṛtarāṣṭra (*M. Bh.*); a son of King Janamejaya (*M. Bh.*); a serpent (*M. Bh.*).

Kuñjabihāri (S) (M) **1.** living in the woods. **3.** another name for Kṛṣṇa.

Kuni (S) (M) **1.** with a crooked arm; whitlow. **3.** a sage and father of ṛṣī (*Vā. Purāṇa*); father of Jaya (*Bh. Purāṇa*).

Kuṇi (S) (M) **1.** with a withered arm. **3.** a son of Jaya (*Bhā. Purāṇa*); a ṛṣi (*Vā. Purāṇa*); another name for Garga (*M. Bh.*).

Kuṇigarga (S) (M) **1.** saint with a withered arm. **3.** a sage (*Vā. Purāṇa*).

Kūṇika (S) (M) **1.** horn. **3.** a prince of Ćampā (*H. Purāṇa*).

Kuninda (S) (M) **1.** administrator. **3.** a sage who possessed a divine conch (*M. Bh.*).

Kuñja (S) (M) **1.** bower; living in a bush, shrub or jungle. **3.** a sage

(*V. Purāṇa*); Indian Lotus (*Nelumbo nucifera*).

Kuñjakiśore (S) (M) **1.** youth of the woods. **3.** another name for Kṛṣṇa (*Bhā. Purāṇa*).

Kuñjala (S) (M) **1.** living in shrubs. **2.** koel or Indian cuckoo (*Cuculus scolopaceus*); sour gruel. **3.** an attendant of Skanda.

Kuñjara (S) (M) **1.** dwelling in forests. **2.** an elephant; the number 8. **3.** a monkey who was the father of Añjanā (*V. Rāmāyaṇa*); a prince of Sauvīra and follower of Jayadratha (*M. Bh.*); a serpent (*M. Bh.*); *Ficus religiosa.*

Kuñjavihārī (S) (M) **1.** one who sports in the forest. **3.** another name for Kṛṣṇa.

Kuñjeśvara (S) (M) **1.** lord of the forest. **3.** another name for Kṛṣṇa.

Kuñjita (S) (M) hidden in the forest.

Kunśa (S) (M) to shine; to speak.

Kuntaka (S) (M) necklace.

Kuntanātha (S) (M) **1.** lord of vegetation. **3.** the 17th Jaina Tīrathaṅkara whose emblem was a goat (*J.S. Koṣa*).

Kunteśa (S) (M) **1.** master of Kuntī. **3.** another name for Pāṇḍu.

Kunthu (S) (M) **1.** one who hurts. **3.** the 6th Jaina ćakravartin or emperor in Bhāratavarṣa (*J.S. Koṣa*); the 17th Arhat of the present Avasarpinī (*J.S. Koṣa*).

Kunti (S) (M) **1.** spear; lance. **3.** a son of Vidarbha and father of Dhṛṣṭa (*H. Purāṇa*); a son of Supārśva and grandson of Sampāti (*Mā. Purāṇa*); a son of Kṛṣṇa (*Bhā. Purāṇa*); a son of Dharmanetra (*V. Purāṇa*); a grandson of Dharma (*Bh. Purāṇa*); a people; *Commiphora mukul.*

Kuntibhoja (S) (M) **1.** bearer of spears. **3.** a king of the Yadu dynasty and fosterfather of Kuntī (*M. Bh.*).

Kuntīnandana (S) (M) **1.** son of Kuntī. **3.** another name for Yudhiṣṭhira.

Kuntīsuta (S) (M) **1.** son of Kuntī. **3.** another name for Karṇa.

Kupata (S) (M) excellent.

Kupatha (S) (M) **1.** follower of a bad path. **3.** an asura son of Kaśyapa and Danu (*M. Bh.*).

Kupati (S) (M) lord of the earth.

Kupendra (S) (M) **1.** lord of anger. **3.** another name for Śiva.

Kuppusvāmi (S) (M) **1.** lord of anger. **3.** another name for Śiva.

Kurannu (**Malayalam**) (M) **1.** monkey. **3.** the children of Harī the daughter of Kaśyapa and Marīći (*V. Rāmāyaṇa*).

Kuraparvata (S) (M) **1.** spotted mountains. **3.** a mountain that encirles Mahāmeru (*D. Bhāgavata*).

Kūrćāmukha (S) (M) **1.** with a brush like face. **2.** one who has a beard. **3.** a son of Viśvāmitra (*M. Bh.*).

Kurćika (S) (M) a painter's brush.

Kurīrin (S) (M) crested; a peacock.

Kūrma (S) (M) **1.** tortoise; turtle. **2.** the earth considered as a tortoise swimming on water. **3.** the 2nd incarnation of Viṣṇu as a tortoise (*N. Purāṇa*); the son of Gṛtsamada (*R. Ankuramanikā*); a serpent son of Kadru (*M. Bh.*).

Kūrmapṛṣṭha (S) (M) **1.** tortoise shell. **3.** a yakṣa (*Brahma Purāṇa*).

Kūrmāvatāra (S) (M) **1.** the tortoise incarnation. **3.** the 2nd incarnation of Viṣṇu as a tortoise (*N. Purāṇa*).

Kuru (S) (M) **1.** attached. **3.** a king of Dhruva's dynasty who was the grandfather of Veṇa and the great grandfather of Emperor Pṛthu (*V. Purāṇa*); a famous king of the Purū dynasty who was the son of Saṁvarana and Tapatī, the husband of Saudāminī and after whom the Kaurava dynasty was named (*M. Bh.*); a people and a country considered to be the ancient home of the Aryans; a son of Āgnidhra and grandson of Priyavrata (*V. Purāṇa*); a king and brother of Rantideva; a king of the Uttānapāda dynasty (*V. Purāṇa*); a sage; Nut Grass (*Cyperus rotundis*).

Kurūdvaha (S) (M) **1.** elevating the Kurus. **3.** another name for Dhṛtarāṣṭra, Bhīṣma and Yudhiṣṭhira.

Kurujita (S) (M) **1.** conquering the Kurus. **3.** a king of Janaka's dynasty and the son of Aja (*Bhā. Purāṇa*).

Kurukuladhāma (S) (M) **1.** delight of the Kuru family. **3.** another name for Duryodhana.

Kurukulaśreṣṭha (S) (M) **1.** preeminent in the Kuru family. **3.** another name for Bhīṣma and Yudhiṣṭhira.

Kurukullā (S) (M) **1.** belonging to the Kuru race. **3.** a Buddhist deity (*B. Literature*).

Kurukulodvara (S) (M) **1.** elevating the Kuru family. **3.** another name for Bhīṣma and Yudhiṣṭhira.

Kurumukhya (S) (M) **1.** leader of the Kurus. **3.** another name for Bhīṣma, Duryodhana and Yudhiṣṭhira.

Kurumuni (Tamil) (M) **1.** short hermit. **3.** another name for Agastya.

Kurunandana (S) (M) **1.** son of the Kurus. **3.** another name for Bhīṣma, Dhṛtarāṣṭra, Duryodhana and Yudhiṣṭhira.

Kuruṇḍi (S) (M) **1.** resident of the land of Kurus. **3.** a ṛṣi in the 3rd Manvantara (*V. Purāṇa*).

Kuruntika (S) (M) resident of the land of the Kurus.

Kurupāṅḍavāgrya (S) (M) **1.** first of the Kurus and Pāṇḍavas. **3.** another name for Yudhiṣṭhira.

Kurupati (S) (M) **1.** leader of the Kurus. **3.** another name for Bhīṣma and Yudhiṣṭhira.

Kurupravīra (S) (M) **1.** hero of the Kurus. **3.** another name for Yudhiṣṭhira, Janamejaya and Duryodhana.

Kurupṛthānāpati (S) (M) **1.** son of Pṛthā of the Kurus. **3.** another name for Karṇa.

Kurupuṅgava (S) (M) **1.** bull of the Kurus; chief of the Kurus. **3.** another name for Yudhiṣṭhira and Duryodhana.

Kururāja (S) (M) **1.** lord of the Kurus. **3.** another name for Yudhiṣṭhira and Dhṛtarāṣṭra.

Kurusattama (S) (M) **1.** best of the Kurus. **3.** another name for Yudhiṣṭhira, Janamejaya and Duryodhana.

Kurusiṁha (S) (M) **1.** lion of the Kurus. **3.** another name for Duryodhana.

Kuruśreṣṭha (S) (M) **1.** best among the Kurus. **3.** another name for Bhīṣma, Arjuna, and Dhṛtarāṣṭtra.

Kuruttama (S) (M) **1.** best of the Kurus. **3.** another name for Yudhiṣṭhira and Duryodhana.

Kuruvaṅśavardhana (S) (M) **1.** increasing the line of the Kurus. **3.** another name for Dhṛtarāṣṭra.

Kuruvardhana (S) (M) **1.** increasing the Kurus. **3.** another name for Yudhiṣṭhira.

Kuruvatsa (S) (M) **1.** power of the Kurus. **3.** a son of Anavaratha.

Kuruvīra (S) (M) **1.** hero of the Kurus. **3.** another name for Yudhiṣṭhira and Karṇa.

Kuruvṛddha (S) (M) **1.** eldest of the Kurus. **3.** another name for Dhṛtarāṣṭra.

Kuruvṛṣabha (S) (M) **1.** bull of the Kurus. **3.** another name for Yudhiṣṭhira.

Kuruyodha (S) (M) **1.** warrior of the Kurus. **3.** another name for Karṇa.

Kuśa (S) (M) **1.** the sacred grass *Poa cynosuroides* or *Desmostachhupa bipinnata.* **2.** this grass is primarily used in sacred ceremonies. **3.** a sage who was the son of Brahmā, the husband of Vaidarbhī and the father of Kuśāmbha, Kuśanābha, Asurtarajasa and Vasu (*H. Purāṇa*); a king of the Kuru dynasty who was the son of Suhotra and Girīkā (*A. Purāṇa*); a son of Rāma and the king of Kuśāvatī (*V. Rāmāyaṇa*); a sage who was an ancestor of Viśvāmitra (*V. Rāmāyaṇa*); a son of Lava the king of Kāśmira (*R. Taraṅgiṇī*); a son of Vidarbha (*K. Granthāvali*); a great division of the world (*Bhā. Purāṇa*); a son of vasu Uparićara (*H. Purāṇa*); the founder of Kuśasthali (*Sk. Purāṇa*).

Kuśadhvaja (S) (M) **1.** grass flag. **3.** a Brāhmin and son of Bṛhaspati

(*U. Rāmāyaṇa*); a brother of King Janaka (*V. Rāmāyaṇa*); a prince and son of Hrasvaroman (*Brahma Purāṇa*).

Kuśāgra (S) (M) **1.** the sharp edge of a blade of Kuśa grass. **2.** sharp; shrewd. **3.** a son of Bṛhadratha (*H. Purāṇa*).

Kuśaketu (S) (M) **1.** grass bannered. **3.** another name for Brahmā.

Kuśākṣa (S) (M) sharp eyed.

Kuśala (S) (M) **1.** one who brings the sacred grass; skilled; efficient; right; good; happy; clever; auspicious; proficient; skill; strategy; efficiency. **3.** another name for Śiva.

Kuśalin (S) (M) healthy; clever; prosperous; auspicious.

Kuśāmbha (S) (M) **1.** son of Kuśa. **3.** a son of sage Kuśa, the father of Śakra and Gādhi, the grandfather of Viśvāmitra and the builder of Kauśāmbhi (*Br. Purāṇa*); a son of Uparićaravasu (*H. Purāṇa*).

Kuśanābha (S) (M) **1.** with Kuśā grass in his navel. **2.** chaste. **3.** a son of sage Kuśa and Vaidharbhī, husband of Ghṛtāćī and the father of a 100 daughters (*V. Rāmāyaṇa*).

Kuśanetra (S) (M) **1.** grass eyed. **3.** a daitya (*M. Bh.*).

Kuśaśārdula (S) (M) **1.** tiger in the sacrificial grass. **3.** another name for Bhīma.

Kuśāśva (S) (M) **1.** fast horse. **3.** an Ikṣvāku king who was the son of King Sahadeva and the father of Somadatta (*V. Rāmāyaṇa*).

Kuśāvarta (S) (M) **1.** surrounded by kuśā grass; passage of the Gaṅgā. **2.** pious. **3.** a son of King Ṛṣabha (*Bh. Purāṇa*); another name for Śiva.

Kuśeśaya (S) (M) **1.** one who rests on the kuśā grass. **3.** one of the 6 great mountains of the Kuśa island (*M. Bh.*).

Kuṣidin (S) (M) **1.** moneylender. **3.** a sage of the order of Vyāsa's disciples (*Bhāgavata*).

Kuśika (S) (M) **1.** with squint eyes. **3.** a monarch of the Purū dynasty who was the father of Gādhi and the grandfather of Viśvāmitra (*M. Bh./Ṛg Veda*); a sage (*M. Bh.*); Indian Dammer Tree (*Shorea robusta*); Bedda Nut (*Terminalia belerica*).

Kuśīlava (S) (M) **1.** bard. **3.** another name for Vālmīki.

Kuśin (S) (M) **1.** furnished with kuśa grass. **3.** another name for Vālmīki.

Kuṣmāṇḍaka (S) (M) **1.** pumpkin gourd (*Beninkasa cerifera*). **3.** an attendant of Śiva (*M. Bh.*); a serpent (*M. Bh.*).

Kuṣṭha (S) (M) **1.** found on earth; dwelling on earth. **3.** a herb (*Costus speciosus*) which grew along with Soma on the peaks of the Himālayas and was described as the best and all healing (*A. Veda*).

Kustubha (S) (M) **1.** sea; ocean. **3.** another name for Viṣṇu.

Kustumbaru (S) (M) **1.** the coriander plant (*Coriandrum sativum*). **3.** one of Kubera's rākṣasa attendants (*M. Bh.*); a rākṣasa in Kubera's court (*M. Bh.*).

Kusuma (S) (M) **1.** flower. **2.** a form of fire. **3.** an attendant of the 6th Arhat of the present Avasarpinī; one of the 5 attendants given by Dhātā to Skanda (*M. Bh.*).

Kusumabāṇa (S) (M) **1.** flower arrowed. **3.** another name for Kāma.

Kusumākara (S) (M) **1.** treasure of flowers. **2.** a garden; nosegay; the spring season.

Kusumaketu (S) (M) **1.** flower bannered. **3.** a kiṇnara.

Kusumalakṣmaṇa (S) (M) **1.** with flowers as a symbol. **3.** another name for Pradyumna.

Kusumanaga (S) (M) **1.** flower mountain. **3.** a mountain.

Kusumaśekhara (S) (M) **1.** best among flowers. **2.** a chaplet of flowers.

Kusumaśreṣṭha (S) (M) the best flower.

Kusumāyudha (S) (M) **1.** one who has flowers as his weapons. **3.** another name for Kāma.

Kusumbha (S) (M) outward affection; water pot of a sage; gold; Safflower (*Carthamus tinctorius*); Saffron (*Crocus sativus*).

Kusumbbaparvata (S) (M) **1.** golden mountain. **3.** a mountain surrounding Mahāmeru (*D. Bhāgavata*).

Kusumeśa (S) (M) **1.** lord of flowers. **3.** another name for Kāma.

Kusumeśu (S) (M) **1.** with an arrow of flowers. **3.** the bow of Kāma.

Kusumoda (S) (M) sea of flowers.

Kusumojjvala (S) (M) brilliant with blossoms.

Kusumujvala (S) (M) brilliant with blossoms.

Kūṭa (S) (M) **1.** the bone on the forehead; highest; most excellent; heap. **3.** a constellation (*V's B. Samhitā*); another name for Agastya.

Kuta (S) (M) **1.** to spread. **3.** one of the 18 attendants of the sun.

Kūtamohana (S) (M) **1.** bewildering cheats. **3.** another name for Skanda.

Kutanu (S) (M) **1.** deformed. **3.** a form of Kubera with 3 legs.

Kutha (S) (M) **1.** a painted cloth; sacrificial grass (*Poa cynosuroides*); wealth. **3.** Śākyāmuni in one of his 34 births.

Kuṭhāra (S) (M) **1.** spade; axe. **3.** a serpent of Dhṛtarāṣṭra's family who was among those that received Balarāma when he went into the sea (*M. Bh.*).

Kuthumi (S) (M) **1.** dressed in sacrificial grass (*Poa cynosuroides*). **3.** a teacher and author of a law book.

Kuṭilageśa (S) (M) **1.** lord of rivers. **2.** the ocean.

Kuṭimukha (S) (M) **1.** curved face. **3.** an attendant of Kubera (*M. Bh.*).

Kutsa (S) (M) **1.** from where? why? lightning; thunderbolt. **3.** a ṛṣī who was the author of several hymns of the *Ṛg Veda* and a sometime friend of Indra who helped him to defeat the demon Śuṣṇa and win the sun (*Ṛg Veda*); a descendant of Aṅgiras (*Ṛg Veda*).

Kuvala (S) (M) **1.** one who enriches knowledge. **2.** water lily (*Nymphaea alba*); pearl; water.

Kuvalaya (S) (M) **1.** the Blue Lotus (*Nymphaea stellata*). **2.** the orb.

Kuvalayāditya (S) (M) **1.** lord of the Blue Lotus (*Nymphaea stellata*). **3.** a prince (*R. Taraṅgiṇī*); another name for the sun.

Kuvalayapīḍa (S) (M) **1.** gentle as the lotus. **3.** a daitya who changed into an elephant and became the vehicle of Kaṅsa; a king (*R. Taraṅgiṇī*).

Kuvalayāśva (S) (M) **1.** with blue horses. **3.** the prince Dhundhumāra (*V. Purāṇa*); the prince Pratardana (*M. Purāṇa*).

Kuvalayeśa (S) (M) lord of the earth; ruler of waters; lord of the water lilies.

Kuvaleśaya (S) (M) **1.** one who rests in the Blue Lotus (*Nymphaea stellata*). **3.** another name for Viṣṇu.

Kuvam (S) (M) **1.** producer of the earth. **3.** another name for the sun.

Kuvara (S) (M) **1.** astringent in flavour. **2.** fragrant. **3.** a gandharva.

Kuvaya (S) (M) **1.** the Barn Owl. **2.** causing a bad harvest. **3.** a rākṣasa slain by Indra; an asura mentioned in the *Ṛg Veda*.

Kvaṇa (S) (M) **1.** to sound; to tinkle; to hum. **2.** to sound as a musical instrument; to blow a flute.

L

Labdha (S) (M) acquired; obtained.

Labdhakīrti (S) (M) one who has acquired fame.

Labdhasiddhi (S) (M) one who has attained perfection.

Labdhavarṇa (S) (M) **1.** one who has gained a knowledge of letters. **2.** learned; wise; famous; celebrated.

Labdhodaya (S) (M) one who has attained prosperity.

Labdhudaya (S) (M) **1.** one who has attained prosperity. **2.** born; sprung.

Lābha (S) (M) **1.** profit; perception. **2.** advantage; gain.

Lagadāćārya (S) (M) **1.** most beautiful; most handsome. **3.** an astronomer.

Laghat (S) (M) the wind.

Laghiman (S) (M) **1.** lightness. **3.** a siddhi in which one can assume lightness at will.

Laghu (S) (M) **1.** light; small; subtle; swift; soft; low; gentle; lovely, pure; young. **3.** the Nakṣatrās or the constellations Hasta, Puṣya and Aśvinī.

Laghuga (S) (M) **1.** moving quickly. **3.** another name for Vāyu.

Lajjinī (S) (M) shy; modest; the touch-me-not plant (*Mimosa pudica*).

Lakhan/Lakka/Lakke (H) (M) **1.** one who accomplishes the target; one with auspicious marks. **3.** colloquial short forms of Lakṣmaṇa.

Lakhpati (S) (M) **1.** a millionaire. **3.** consort of Lakṣmī and the lord of lakhs; another name for Viṣṇu.

Lakṣa (S) (M) mark; aim; target; 100,000.

Lakṣaka (S) (M) ray of beauty.

Lakṣaṇa (S) (M) with an auspicious mark.

Lakṣaṇā (S) (M) **1.** aim; object; view. **3.** the daughter of Duryodhana and wife of Śamba (*M. Bh.*); an apsarā who danced for Arjuna (*M. Bh.*); the daughter of King Bṛhatsena of Madra and mother of 10 sons (*Bhā. Purāṇa*).

Lakṣaṇya (S) (M) **1.** serving as a mark with auspicious marks; accomplisher of aim. **2.** one who is successful.

Lakṣaprasādan (S) (M) **1.** accomplisher of target. **2.** one who is successful; a diviner.

Lakṣin (S) (M) with auspicious marks.

Lakṣmaṇa (S) (M) **1.** with auspicious marks; accomplisher of target. **2.** lucky; fortunate. **3.** the son of King Daśaratha and Sumitrā of Ayodhyā, half-brother of Rāma, husband of Sītā's sister Ūrmilā, the father of Aṅgada and Ćandraketu, accompanied Rāma into exile and is considered the embodiment of loyalty (*V. Rāmāyaṇa*); a son of Duryodhana who was a great archer (*M. Bh.*); the Sārasa crane (*Ardea Sibirica*).

Lakṣmaṇya (S) (M) **1.** son of Lakṣmaṇa; visible far and wide. **3.** another name for Dhvanya.

Lakṣmīćandra (S) (M) **1.** the moon of Lakṣmī. **3.** another name for Viṣṇu.

Lakṣmīdāsa (S) (M) **1.** devotee of Lakṣmī. **3.** another name for Viṣṇu.

Lakṣmīdeva (S) (M) **1.** lord of Lakṣmī. **3.** another name for Viṣṇu.

Lakṣmīdhara (S) (M) **1.** possessor of Lakṣmī. **3.** another name for Viṣṇu.

Lakṣmīkānta (S) (M) **1.** beloved of Lakṣmī. **3.** another name for Viṣṇu.

Lakṣmīlāla (S) (M) **1.** beloved of Lakṣmī. **3.** another name for Viṣṇu.

Lakṣmīnārāyaṇa (S) (M) Viṣṇu and Lakṣmī conjoined.

Lakṣmīnātha (S) (M) **1.** lord of Lakṣmī. **3.** another name for Viṣṇu.

Lakṣmīndra (S) (M) **1.** lord of Lakṣmī. **3.** another name for Viṣṇu.

Lakṣmīprasāda (S) (M) **1.** given by Lakṣmī. **2.** the ruby.

Lakṣmīpuṣpa (S) (M) **1.** flower of Lakṣmī. **2.** clove; ruby.

Lakṣmīputra (S) (M) **1.** the son of Lakṣmī. **3.** another name for Lava, Kuśa and Kāma.

Lakṣmīramaṇa (S) (M) **1.** beloved of Lakṣmī. **3.** another name for Viṣṇu.

Lakşmīśa (S) (M) 1. lord of Lakşmī. 2. prosperous; the mango tree (*Mangifera indica*). 3. another name for Vişņu.

Lakşmīsahaja (S) (M) 1. brother of Lakşmī. 3. a horse of Indra; another name for the moon.

Lakşmīśaja (S) (M) 1. produced with Lakşmī. 3. another name for the moon.

Lakşmīsakha (S) (M) 1. companion of Lakşmī. 3. another name for Vişņu.

Lakşmīśaṅkara (S) (M) pacifier of Lakşmī; Śiva and Lakşmī conjoined.

Lakşmīvata (S) (M) fortunate; wealthy; handsome; beautiful; the Breadfruit tree.

Lakşmīvinaya (S) (M) good fortune; modest conduct.

Lāla (H) (M) red; heart; son.

Lalāţa (S) (M) the forehead.

Lalāţākşa (S) (M) 1. with an eye in the forehead. 3. another name for Śiva.

Lālavihārī (S) (M) 1. bearer of a red mark; one who dwells in the hearts. 3. another name for Kŗşņa.

Lālila (S) (M) 1. beautiful; looked after with affection. 3. another name for Agni.

Lalita (S) (M) 1. lovely; desirable; pleasing; soft; gentle; graceful; wanton; voluptuous; sporting. 3. a rāga.

Lalitaćandra (S) (M) beautiful moon.

Lalitāditya (S) (M) 1. beautiful sun. 3. an ancient Kāśmira king (*R. Taraṁginī*).

Lalitaka (S) (M) beautiful; favourite.

Lalitakiśor (S) (M) 1. beautiful youth; lovely youth. 3. another name for Kŗşņa.

Lalitakumāra (S) (M) 1. beautiful youth. 3. another name for Kŗşņa.

Lalitamohana (S) (M) 1. handsome; attractive. 3. another name for Kŗşņa.

Lalitāṅga (S) (M) with a beautiful body.

Lālitya (S) (M) loveliness; charm; beauty; grace.

Lallan (S) (M) 1. child. 3. the Śala (*Shorea robusta*) and Piyāla (*Buchanania latifolia*) trees.

Lamaka (S) (M) lover; a gallant.

Lambākşa (S) (M) 1. long eyed. 3. a sage.

Lambana (S) (M) 1. great; large; spacious; tall; pendulous; a long necklace. 3. a son of Jyotişmat (*V. Purāņa*); another name for Śiva.

Lambhit (S) (M) procured; cherished.

Lambodara (S) (M) 1. big bellied. 2. large; great; a glutton. 3. another name for Gaņeśa.

Lāṅgala (S) (M) 1. a plough. 2. the Coconut tree (*Cocos nucifera*). 3. a son of Suddhoda and grandson of Śākya (*Bh. Purāņa*).

Lāṅgalin (S) (M) 1. one who carries a plough. 3. another name for Balarāma.

Laņiban (S) (M) 1. the phlegmatic humour. 3. another name for Śiva.

Laṅkānātha (S) (M) 1. lord of Laṅkā. 3. another name for Rāvaņa and Vibhīşaņa.

Laṅkāpati (S) (M) 1. master of Laṅkā. 3. another name for Rāvaņa and Vibhīşaņa.

Laṅkāri (S) (M) 1. enemy of Laṅkā. 3. another name for Rāma.

Laṅkeśa (S) (M) 1. lord of Laṅkā. 3. another name for Rāvaņa and Vibhīşaņa.

Lasadanśu (S) (M) 1. with flashing rays. 2. the sun.

Lāsaka (S) (M) 1. a dancer; a peacock; one who frolics. 3. another name for Śiva.

Laşita (S) (M) wished; desired.

Lastakin (S) (M) a bow.

Latābāņa (S) (M) 1. creeper arrowed. 3. another name for Kama.

Laţākara (S) (M) a collection of pearls.

Latāparņa (S) (M) 1. the leaf of the vine. 3. another name for Vişņu.

Latāveşţa (S) (M) 1. surrounded by creepers. 3. a 5 coloured mountain on the southern side of Dvārakā (*H. Purāņa*).

Laţkan (S) (M) an ornament of the hair; lace; the Lorikeet bird (*Loriculus vernalis*).

Lauhi (S) (M) **1.** made of metal. **3.** a son of Aṣṭaka.

Lauhita (S) (M) **1.** made of metal; red. **3.** the trident of Śiva.

Lauhitya (S) (M) **1.** red. **3.** a sacred place constructed by Rāma, bathing in the pond of which one turns golden (*M. Bh.*).

Lava (S) (M) **1.** a particle. **2.** a piece; tiny. **3.** a twin son of Rāma and Sītā and the brother of Kuśa (*V. Rāmāyaṇa*).

Lavama (S) (M) **1.** clove. **2.** small. **3.** one of the 7 oceans which surrounded the dvīpas or the islands in concentric belts.

Lavaṇa (S) (M) **1.** handsome; lovely; salt; saline. **3.** a son of a demon called Madhu who was killed by Śatrughna (*D. Bhāgavata*); a king of the Hariśćandra dynasty who conducted the Rajasūya yajña; a demon who lived on the island of Ramaṇīyaka (*M. Bh.*); a grandson of Hariśćandra(*V. Purāṇa*); Intellect tree (*Celastrus paniculata*).

Lavanākara (S) (M) **1.** salt mine. **2.** treasure of grace and beauty.

Lavaṇāśva (S) (M) **1.** horse of salt. **3.** the ocean; a sage who blessed Yudhiśṭhira (*M. Bh.*).

Lavaṇātaka (S) (M) **1.** destroyer of the demon Lavaṇa. **3.** another name for Śatrughna.

Lavaṅika (S) (M) handsome; beautiful; salty.

Lavaṇīśa (S) (M) **1.** lord of the sea. **3.** another name for Varuṇa.

Lavaṇodaka (S) (M) **1.** containing salt water. **3.** another name for the ocean.

Lāvaṇya (S) (M) beauty; lustre.

Lavaṇyālaya (S) (M) **1.** Sea of salt; sea of beauty; abode of beauty. **3.** another name for the ocean.

Lāvaṇyamaya (S) (M) **1.** consisting of salt water. **2.** handsome; beautiful; charming.

Lāvaṇyavata (S) (M) **1.** bearing charm. **2.** handsome; beautiful; charming.

Lavarāja (S) (M) **1.** king of the moment. **3.** a sage (*R. Taraṅginī*).

Lavitra (S) (M) **1.** the subtle one; plucking; wool; hair. **3.** another name for Śiva.

Laya (S) (M) **1.** deep concentration; fusion; rest. **3.** a Purāṇic king who was a member of the court of Yama (*M. Bh.*); another name for the Supreme Being.

Lekha (S) (M) **1.** document. **2.** a deity; god. **3.** a set of 8 celestial beings of the Raivatā Manvantara (*Purāṇas*).

Lekhābhra (S) (M) **1.** as bright as light. **2.** shining.

Lekharāja (S) (M) **1.** lord of the gods. **3.** another name for the Supreme Being.

Lekhaṛṣabha (S) (M) **1.** bull of the gods; best of gods. **3.** another name for Indra.

Lelihāna (S) (M) **1.** darting out the tongue. **2.** a serpent. **3.** another name for Śiva.

Leśa (S) (M) **1.** a small portion. **2.** a small song. **3.** a son of King Suhotra.

Likhita (S) (M) **1.** drawn; fainted; delineated. **3.** a sage whose hands were cut off by King Sudyumna but which grew back due to his penance (*M. Bh.*); a sage and author of works of law (*M. Bh.*).

Līlādhara (S) (M) **1.** playful. **3.** the consort of Lilāvatī; another name for Viṣṇu.

Līlādhya (S) (M) **1.** the abode of pleasure. **3.** a son of Viśvāmitra (*M. Bh.*).

Lilāmbuja (S) (M) lovely lotus.

Līlāvatāra (S) (M) **1.** pleasure incarnate. **3.** the earthly descent of Viṣṇu as Kṛṣṇa.

Limpa (S) (M) **1.** smearing; anointing. **3.** one of Śiva's attendants.

Liṅga (S) (M) mark; sign; symbol; badge; the genital organ of Śiva worshipped in the form of a phallic idol.

Lipsita (S) (M) desired.

Lobha (S) (M) **1.** greed; cupidity. **3.** avarice personified as a son of Dambha and Māyā; a spiritual son of Brahmā born from his lip (*M. Purāṇa*).

Loćamastaka (S) (M) **1.** with a flexible head. **2.** humble; well mannered.

Loćanānanda (S) (M) delight of the eye.

Loha (S) (M) **1.** red; iron. **3.** an asura who attacked the Pāṇḍavas and was blinded (*Sk. Purāṇa*).

Lohajavaktra (S) (M) **1.** with the face of a goat. **3.** another name for Skanda.

Lohajit (S) (M) **1.** that which conquers iron. **2.** a diamond.

Lohamekhala (S) (M) **1.** an iron ornament for the waist. **3.** a follower of Skanda (*M. Bh.*).

Lohamukha (S) (M) **1.** with an iron mouth. **3.** a follower of Skanda (*M. Bh.*).

Lohita (S) (M) **1.** red; copper; the planet Mars. **3.** a king who was conquered by Arjuna (*M. Bh.*); a serpent who is a member of the court of Varuṇa (*M. Bh.*); another name for the river Brahmaputra.

Lohitaćandana (S) (M) red powder; saffron; red sandalwood.

Lohitagātra (S) (M) **1.** red limbed. **3.** another name for Skanda.

Lohitagrīva (S) (M) **1.** red necked. **3.** another name for Agni (*M. Bh.*).

Lohitākṣa (S) (M) **1.** red eyed. **3.** a sage who took part in the Sarpāṣatra yajña of King Janamejaya (*M. Bh.*); an attendant of Skanda given to him by Brahmā (*M. Bh.*); the Indian Cuckoo (*Cuculus varius*) (*A. Koṣa*); another name for Viṣṇu.

Lohitāṅga (S) (M) **1.** red bodied. **3.** the trident of Śiva (*S. Purāṇa*); another name for Mars.

Lohitāśva (S) (M) **1.** with red horses. **3.** another name for Agni and Śiva.

Lohottama (S) (M) **1.** the best metal. **2.** gold.

Loka (S) (M) heaven; world; people.

Lokabandhu (S) (M) **1.** friend of the world. **3.** another name for Śiva and the sun.

Lokaćakṣus (S) (M) **1.** the eye of the world. **3.** another name for the sun.

Lokāćara (S) (M) **1.** one who roams in all the 3 worlds. **2.** one who acts in accordance to the customs of the world.

Lokādhipa (S) (M) lord of the world.

Lokādhipati (S) (M) master of the world.

Lokādhyakṣa (S) (M) president of the world.

Lokādi (S) (M) **1.** creator of the world. **3.** another name for Brahmā.

Lokadvāra (S) (M) the gateway of heaven.

Lokajita (S) (M) **1.** one who conquers the world; winning heaven. **3.** another name for Buddha.

Lokajyeṣṭha (S) (M) **1.** most distinguished among men. **3.** another name for Buddha.

Lokakāra (S) (M) **1.** creator of the world. **3.** another name for Śiva.

Lokākṣi (S) (M) **1.** eye of the world. **3.** a sage.

Lokamaheśvara (S) (M) **1.** lord of the world. **3.** another name for Kṛṣṇa.

Lokanādu (S) (M) master of the world.

Lokanātha (S) (M) **1.** lord of the 3 worlds. **3.** a Buddha; another name for Brahmā, Viṣṇu, Śiva and the sun.

Lokanetra (S) (M) **1.** eye of the world. **2.** one who surveys, checks and guides the world. **3.** another name for Śiva.

Lokapāla (S) (M) **1.** guardian of the world; the guardian of the 8 directions of the world. **3.** title of Indra, Agni, Yama Sūrya, Pavana, Kubera, Soma and Varuṇa.

Lokapati (S) (M) **1.** master of the world. **2.** lord of the 3 worlds. **3.** another name for Brahmā and Viṣṇu.

Lokapitāmaha (S) (M) **1.** progenitor of the world. **3.** another name for Brahmā.

Lokapradipa (S) (M) **1.** light of the world. **3.** a Buddha.

Lokarakṣa (S) (M) **1.** protector of the people. **2.** a king.

Lokarāma (S) (M) one who delights the world.

Lokarañjana (S) (M) delight of the people.

Lokasvāmī (S) (M) **1.** lord of the people. **2.** lord of the 3 worlds.

Lokātman (S) (M) the soul of the universe.

Lokavidhi (S) (M) **1.** creator of the world. **3.** another name for Brahmā.

Lokavya (S) (M) one who deserves heaven.

Lokāyana (S) (M) **1.** father of the world. **3.** another name for Viṣṇu.

Lokendra (S) (M) lord of the 3 worlds.

Lokeśa (S) (M) **1.** lord of the world. **3.** a Buddha; another name for Brahmā.

Lokeśvara (S) (M) **1.** lord of the world. **3.** a Buddha; another name for Brahmā.

Lokin (S) (M) one who has conquered the next world; one who possesses a world.

Lokasādhaka (S) (M) one who creates worlds.

Lomaharṣaṇa (S) (M) **1.** hair raising; thrilling. **3.** the father of Sūta who related the Purāṇic tales and a member of the court of Yudhiṣṭhira (*M. Bh.*).

Lomapāda (S) (M) **1.** with hairy feet. **3.** the king of Aṅga who adopted the daughter of King Daśaratha (*K. Rāmāyaṇa*); a Yadu king who was the son of Vidarbha and the ancestor of the Ćedi dynasty (*P. Purāṇa*).

Lomaśa (S) (M) **1.** hairy. **3.** a great sage and storyteller whose tales form episodes in the Purāṇas; Sweet Flag (*Acorns calamus*).

Lomaśā (S) (M) **1.** hairy. **3.** an attendant of Durgā.

Lubdhaka (S) (M) **1.** hunter. **3.** the star Sirius.

Lūṇadoṣa (S) (M) **1.** sinless. **3.** an attendant of Śiva (*A. Koṣa*).

Lūnaduṣkṛta (S) (M) one whose sins have been destroyed.

Lūṇakarṇa (S) (M) with pierced ears.

Luśa (S) (M) **1.** saffron. **3.** a hermit and worshipper of Indra who composed hymns for the *Ṛg Veda*.

M

Mabala (S) (M) **1.** pondering over troubles before solving them; boastful; deceiver. **3.** another name for Śiva.

Maćakruka (S) (M) **1.** churner; agitator. **3.** a yakṣa guardian of the sacred spot which lies at the entrance to Kurukṣetra.

Mada (S) (M) **1.** rapture; excitement; intoxication; passion; pride; hilarity; musk; wine; honey. **3.** a son of Brahmā born of his pride (*V. Purāṇa*); a dānava (*H. Purāṇa*); a servant of Śiva (*Bhā. Purāṇa*); intoxication personified as a beast created by Ćyavana (*M. Bh.*); the 7th lunar mansion; another name for Kāma and Soma.

Madālambe **1.** dependant upon intoxication. **2.** excited; inspired; arrogant. **3.** the mother of Bāsava the bull.

Madana (S) (M) **1.** passion; love; intoxicating; exhilarating; delighting; spring; Common Emetic Nut (*Randia dumetorum*); the *Vangueria spinosa* tree. **3.** another name for Kāma.

Madanabāṇa (S) (M) **1.** arrow of Kāma. **3.** one of the 5 arrows of Kāma.

Madanāditya (S) (M) the sun of passion; Kāma or the god of love.

Madanadviṣa (S) (M) **1.** enemy of Kāma. **3.** another name for Śiva.

Madanagopāla (S) (M) **1.** herdsman of love. **2.** the attractive cowherd. **3.** another name for Kṛṣṇa.

Madanam (S) (M) delighting; intoxicating.

Madanamohana (S) (M) **1.** one who attracts; love. **3.** another name for Kṛṣṇa and Kāma (*Bha. Purāṇa*).

Madanapāla (S) (M) lord of love.

Madanavega (S) (M) **1.** with the speed of love. **2.** sexual arousal. **3.** the king of the vidyādharas (*K. Sāgara*).

Madapati (S) (M) **1.** lord of the soma. **3.** another name for Viṣṇu and Indra.

Madaprada (S) (M) intoxicating.

Madarāga (S) (M) **1.** intoxicated with passion. **3.** another name for Kāma.

Madavallabha (S) (M) **1.** passionate. **3.** a gandharva.

Mādayiṣṇu (S) (M) delighting; intoxicating.

Mādayitnu (S) (M) **1.** intoxicating. **3.** another name for Kāma.

Maderu (S) (M) **1.** very intoxicating. **2.** worthy of praise.

Madeśa (S) (M) **1.** lord of intoxication. **3.** another name for Śiva.

Mādhava (S) (M) **1.** vernal; relating to the spring; that which belongs to the descendants of Madhu i.e. the Yadavas. **3.** a son of the 3rd Manu (*P. Purāṇa*); a ṛṣi under Manu Bhautya (*T. Samhitā*); son of King Vikrama of Tāladhvaja (*P. Purāṇa*); a son of Yadu and Dhūmravarṇā (*Bhā. Purāṇa*); the 2nd month of spring; Butter tree (*Bassia latifolia*); another name for Kṛṣṇa, Śiva and Indra.

Mādhavabhaṭṭa (S) (M) **1.** learned Madhava. **3.** real name of Kavirāja.

Mādhavaćandra (S) (M) **1.** the moon of the Mādhavas. **3.** another name for Kṛṣṇa.

Mādhavāćārya (S) (M) **1.** the learned Mādhava. **3.** a celebrated scholar and brother of Sāyaṇa.

Mādhavadāsa (S) (M) devotee of Kṛṣṇa.

Mādhavadeva (S) (M) divine Kṛṣṇa.

Mādhavanandana (S) (M) **1.** son of the Mādhavas. **3.** another name for Kṛṣṇa.

Mādhavarāja (S) (M) **1.** lord of the Mādhavas. **3.** another name for Kṛṣṇa.

Mādhavika (S) (M) **1.** one who collects honey. **2.** a creeper (*Gaertnera racemosa*); *Hiptage madoblata.*

Madhu (S) (M) **1.** sweet. **2.** delicious; charming; delightful; honey; nectar; sugar; wine. **3.** the 2 asuras killed by Viṣṇu and Śatrughna (*M. Bh.*); a sage under Manu Ćākṣuṣa (*Mā. Purāṇa*); a son of the 3rd Manu (*H. Purāṇa*); a son of Vṛṣa; a son of Arjuna Kārttavīrya (*H. Purāṇa*); a son of Bindumat (*H. Purāṇa*); a son of Devakṣatra (*H. Purāṇa*); a king in the court of Yama (*M. Bh.*); the Aśoka tree (*Saraca indica*); another name for the

1st month of the year known in the Indian calendar as Ćaitra, in the English calendar as the months of March-April and is the season of spring; Butter tree (*Bassia latifolia*).

Madhubhadra (S) (M) a sweet gentleman; softspoken; handsome.

Madhućandra (S) (M) sweet moon.

Madhuććandasa (S) (M) **1.** one who speaks sweetly. **3.** the 51st of Viśvāmitra's 101 sons (*A. Brāhmaṇa*).

Madhudhvaja (S) (M) **1.** honey bannered. **3.** a king (*V. Purāṇa*).

Madhudīpa **1.** lamp of spring. **3.** another name for Kāma.

Madhudviṣa (S) (M) **1.** foe of Madhu. **3.** another name for Viṣṇu (*Bhā. Purāṇa*).

Madhuhana (S) (M) **1.** destroyer of Madhu. **3.** another name for Viṣṇu.

Madhuja (S) (M) **1.** made of honey. **2.** sugar.

Madhujit (S) (M) **1.** conqueror of Madhu. **3.** another name for Viṣṇu and Kṛṣṇa.

Madhuka (S) (M) **1.** honey coloured; sweet; mellifluous; melodious. **2.** the Aśoka tree (*Saraca indica*).

Madhukaṇṭha (S) (M) sweet voiced; the Indian Cuckoo (*Cuculus scolopaceus*) (*Ś. Brāhmaṇa*).

Madhukara (S) (M) **1.** honey maker. **2.** the bee; the Mango tree (*Mangifera indica*).

Madhukṛta (S) (M) **1.** maker of honey. **2.** the bee.

Madhukṣa (S) (M) **1.** maker of honey. **2.** the bee.

Madhukūṭa (S) (M) mountain of sweetness.

Madhula (S) (M) sweet; an intoxicating drink.

Madhumakṣika (S) (M) **1.** honey fly; the honey bee. **2.** beautiful; the sweet jasmine.

Madhumatha (S) (M) **1.** destroyer of Madhu. **3.** another name for Viṣṇu.

Madhumaya (S) (M) consisting of honey.

Madhumiśra (S) (M) mixed with honey.

Madhunandī (S) (M) **1.** enjoyer of spring. **3.** a king (*V. Purāṇa*).

Madhupa (S) (M) **1.** drinking sweetness. **2.** a bee.

Madhuparka (S) (M) **1.** a mixture of honey and milk. **3.** a son of Garuḍa (*M. Bh.*).

Madhupati (S) (M) **1.** master of spring; chief of the race of Madhu. **3.** another name for Kṛṣṇa (*Bh. Purāṇa*).

Madhupriya (S) (M) **1.** fond of honey or nectar. **3.** another name for Balarāma.

Madhupuṣpa (S) (M) **1.** a spring flower; with sweet flowers. **2.** the Aśoka tree; Sizzling tree (*Albizzia lebbeck*); the Bakula tree (*Mimusops elengi*); the Śirīṣa tree (*Albizzia stipulata*).

Madhura (S) (M) **1.** sweet. **2.** pleasant; charming; delightful; melodious. **3.** a tutelary deity of the race of Vandhula; an attendant of Skanda (*M. Bh.*); a gandharva (*S. Puṇḍarikā*); *Asparagus racemosus*; *Luvunya scandens.*

Madhuranātha (S) (M) **1.** lord of all that is sweet. **3.** another name for Kṛṣṇa.

Madhurapriyadarśana (S) (M) **1.** of sweet and friendly aspect. **3.** another name for Śiva.

Madhurasvara (S) (M) **1.** sweet voiced. **3.** a gandharva (*S. Puṇḍarika*).

Madhuriman (S) (M) sweetness; charm.

Madhuripu (S) (M) **1.** enemy of Madhu. **3.** another name for Viṣṇu.

Madhuruha (S) (M) **1.** with a sweet body. **3.** a son of Ghṛtapṛṣṭha (*Bhā. Purāṇa*).

Mādhurya (S) (M) sweetness; tender affection; charm; exquisite beauty.

Madhusakha (S) (M) **1.** friend of spring. **3.** another name for Kāma.

Madhuśakta (S) (M) **1.** lover of honey. **3.** an asura.

Madhusārathi (S) (M) **1.** with spring for a charioteer. **3.** another name for Kāma.

Madhusūdana (S) (M) **1.** destroyer of Madhu. **3.** another name for Viṣṇu.

Madhusyanda (S) (M) **1.** the sweet offspring. **3.** a son of Viśvāmitra (*V. Rāmāyaṇa*).

Madhutana (S) (M) **1.** with an exotic body. **2.** intoxicating; sweet.

Madhutraya (S) (M) mixture of 3 sweet things.

Madhuvalli (S) (M) sweet citron (*Citrusa urantium*); kind of grape.

Madhuvaraṣa (S) (M) **1.** intoxicated. **2.** a bull.

Madhuvarṇa (S) (M) **1.** honey coloured. **3.** a soldier of Skanda (*M. Bh.*).

Mādhva (S) (M) **1.** born of the spring; born of honey. **2.** beautiful; intoxicating. **3.** the founder of a sect of Vaiṣṇavas in south India believing in the Dvaita doctrine.

Mādhvāćārya 1. preceptor of the Mādhva doctrine. **3.** the author of *Sarvadar-śanasamgraha* and founder of a Vaiṣṇava sect.

Madhvakṣa (S) (M) **1.** with honey coloured eyes. **3.** another name for Agni.

Madhyamdina (S) (M) **1.** midday. **2.** the time near noon personified as a son of Puṣpārṇa and Prabhā (*Bhā. Purāṇa*).

Madin (S) (M) **1.** intoxicating; exhilarating. **2.** lovely; delightful.

Madirāja (S) (M) **1.** lord of the intoxicated; lord of the proud. **3.** the father of Bāsava, the bull.

Madirākṣa (S) (M) **1.** with intoxicating eyes. **3.** a king of the Ikṣvāku dynasty who was the son of King Daśāśva and the father of Dyutimān and Sumadhyā (*M. Bh.*); a brother of King Virāṭa of Matsya (*Bhā. Purāṇa*); a brother of Śatānīka (*M. Bh.*).

Madirāśva (S) (M) **1.** an intoxicated horse. **3.** a king who was the son of Daśāśva and the grandson of Ikṣvāku (*Bhā. Purāṇa*).

Madra (S) (M) **1.** name of a people. **3.** the country northwest of Hindustan and the name of its king (*Ś. Brāhmaṇa*); a son of Śibi.

Madrādhipa (S) (M) **1.** lord of Madra. **3.** another name for Śalya.

Madraja (S) (M) **1.** son of Madra. **3.** another name for Śalya.

Madraka (S) (M) **1.** belonging to the Madra dynasty. **3.** a Kṣatriya king who was a partial incarnation of the demon Krodhavaśa (*M. Bh.*).

Mādraka (S) (M) **1.** of Madra. **3.** another name for Śatya.

Mādreya (S) (M) **1.** son of Mādrī. **3.** another name for Sahadeva.

Mādrinandana (S) (M) **1.** son of Mādrī. **3.** another name for Nakula and Sahadeva.

Mādrīputra (S) (M) **1.** son of Mādrī. **3.** another name for Sahadeva.

Madura (S) (M) a bird.

Madvan (S) (M) **1.** intoxicating. **2.** gladdening. **3.** another name for Śiva.

Māgadha (S) (M) **1.** of Magadha. **3.** a sage of the 14th manvantara (*H. Purāṇa*); a son of Yadu (*H. Purāṇa*).

Magan (S) (M) absorbed; engrossed.

Magaran (S) (M) **1.** following a path. **2.** the wind.

Magha (S) (M) **1.** gift; reward; wealth; power. **3.** another name for Indra.

Māgha (S) (M) **1.** rewarding. **2.** the month of December/January. **3.** the author of *Siśupālavadha* (7th century A.D.)

Maghavan (S) (M) **1.** bountiful; liberal. **3.** the 3rd ćakravartin in Bhārata; a dānava; another name for Indra.

Māghavat (S) (M) belonging to Indra.

Mahābāhu (S) (M) **1.** long armed. **3.** a son of Dhṛtarāṣṭra (*M. Bh.*); a dānava (*H. Purāṇa*); a rākṣasa (*V. Rāmāyaṇa*); another name for Viṣṇu (*M. Bh.*).

Mahābala (S) (M) **1.** exceedingly strong. **2.** wind. **3.** a Buddha; one of the 10 gods of anger (*D. Śāstra*); a follower of Skanda (*M. Bh.*); Indra in the 4th Manvantara (*M. Purāṇa*); a nāga; Gamboge tree (*Garcinia morella*); Common Indigo (*Indigofera tinctoria*); Jelly Leaf (*Sida rhombofolia*).

Mahabaleśvara (S) (M) **1.** lord of the strong ones. **3.** another name for Śiva; a liṅga.

Mahābalī (S) (M) **1.** extremely powerful. **3.** the giant Bali; another name for Śiva.

Mahābhāgin (S) (M) exceedingly fortunate.

Mahābhairava (S) (M) **1.** extremely angry. **3.** a form of Śiva (*Ś. Purāṇa*).

Mahābhāsura (S) (M) **1.** extremely brilliant. **3.** another name for Viṣṇu.

Mahābhaṭa (S) (M) **1.** great warrior. **3.** a dānava (*K. Sāgara*).

Mahābhauma (S) (M) **1.** the great son of the earth. **2.** the great Mars. **3.** a king of the Purū dynasty who was the son of Ariha, the husband of Suyajñā and the father of Ayutanāyi (*M. Bh.*).

Mahābhaya (S) (M) **1.** very dreadful. **3.** a rākṣasa who was the son of Adharma and Nirṛti (*M. Bh.*).

Mahābhijana (S) (M) of noble birth.

Mahābhikṣu (S) (M) **1.** great monk. **3.** another name for Gautama Buddha.

Mahābhīma (S) (M) **1.** very powerful. **3.** one of Śiva's attendants (*A. Koṣa*); another name for Śāntanu (*A. Koṣa*).

Mahābhiṣa (S) (M) **1.** very frightening. **3.** a king of the race of Ikṣvāku (*Bhā. Purāṇa*).

Mahābhīṣma (S) (M) **1.** very dreadful. **3.** a king of the Ikṣvāku dynasty also known as Śāntanu (*K. Sāgara*).

Mahābhiśu (S) (M) very brilliant.

Mahābhoja (S) (M) **1.** great monarch. **3.** Yādava king (*Bhā. Purāṇa*).

Mahābhūṣaṇa (S) (M) costly ornament.

Mahābīja (S) (M) **1.** with much seed. **3.** another name for Śiva (*M. Bh.*).

Mahāćaṇḍa (S) (M) **1.** extremely violent; passionate. **3.** one of Yama's 2 servants (*A. Koṣa*); one of Śiva's attendants.

Mahāćandra (S) (M) great moon.

Mahāćārya (S) (M) **1.** great preceptor. **3.** another name for Śiva.

Mahādaitya (S) (M) **1.** the great daitya. **3.** the grandfather of Ćandragupta II.

Mahādaṅṣṭra (S) (M) **1.** large toothed. **2.** tiger. **3.** a vidyādhara (*K. Sāgara*).

Mahādāyudha (S) (M) a great weapon.

Mahādeva (S) (M) **1.** the great deity. **3.** one of the 8 forms of Rudra or Śiva (*M. Bh.*); a mountain (*K. Sāgara*); another name for Rudra or Śiva.

Mahadguṇa (S) (M) possessing the qualities of the great.

Mahādharma (S) (M) **1.** follower of a great religion. **3.** a prince of the kinnaras.

Mahādhātu (S) (M) **1.** the great metal. **3.** another name for gold and Śiva (*M. Bh.*).

Mahādhipati (S) (M) **1.** lord of understanding. **3.** a tāntric deity.

Mahādhṛti (S) (M) **1.** very patient; very compassionate. **3.** a king of the solar dynasty (*Bhā. Purāṇa*).

Mahādhvani (S) (M) **1.** making a loud noise. **3.** a dānava (*H. Purāṇa*).

Mahādruma (S) (M) **1.** a great tree. **2.** *Ficus religiosa*. **3.** a son of Bhavya (*V. Purāṇa*).

Mahādyuti (S) (M) **1.** of great splendour. **3.** a son of the yakṣa Maṇibhadra and Puṇyajanī (*M. Bh.*); a king of ancient India (*M. Bh.*).

Mahādyutikara (S) (M) **1.** extremely glorious. **3.** another name for the sun.

Mahāgaja (S) (M) **1.** great elephant. **3.** an elephant that supports the earth.

Mahāgaṇapati (S) (M) **1.** great leader of the gaṇas. **3.** another name for Śiva.

Mahāgarta (S) (M) **1.** the great pit. **3.** another name for Śiva.

Mahāghasa (S) (M) **1.** great eater. **3.** one of Śiva's attendants (*A. Koṣa*).

Mahāghoṣa (S) (M) **1.** loud sounding. **3.** a bodhisattva.

Mahāghoṣeśvara (S) (M) **1.** lord of the loud sounding ones. **3.** a king of the yakṣas (*B. Literature*).

Mahāgiri (S) (M) **1.** a large mountain. **3.** a dānava (*H. Purāṇa*).

Mahāgīta (S) (M) **1.** overtly praised. **2.** a great singer. **3.** another name for Śiva.

Mahāgrīva (S) (M) **1.** long necked. **3.** one of Śiva's attendants (*H. Purāṇa*); another name for Śiva.

Mahāguṇa (S) (M) with excellent qualities.

Mahāhansa (S) (M) **1.** the great hansa. **3.** another name for Viṣṇu.

Mahāhanu (S) (M) **1.** large jawed. **3.** an attendant of Śiva (*H. Purāṇa*); a nāga of the family of Takṣaka (*M. Bh.*); a dānava (*H. Purāṇa*).

Mahāhanus (S) (M) **1.** large jawed. **3.** a son of Vasudeva and Rohiṇī (*M. Purāṇa*).

Mahāhaya (S) (M) **1.** with a great horse; a horse of the sun; a great horse. **3.** a king of the Yayāti dynasty (*Bhā. Purāṇa*).

Mahaja (S) (M) **1.** highborn. **2.** of noble descent.

Mahājambha (S) (M) **1.** a great yawn. **2.** having a big yawn. **3.** an attendant of Śiva.

Mahājānu (S) (M) **1.** large kneed. **3.** one of Śiva's attendants (*A. Koṣa*).

Mahājaṭa (S) (M) **1.** a long braid. **2.** wearing long braid. **3.** another name for Śiva.

Mahājaya (S) (M) **1.** extremely victorious. **3.** one of the 2 attendants given to Skanda by Vāsuki (*M. Bh.*); a nāga (*M. Bh.*).

Mahājihva (S) (M) **1.** long tongued. **3.** a daitya (*H. Purāṇa*); another name for Śiva.

Mahājñānin (S) (M) **1.** great preceptor. **3.** another name for Śiva.

Mahājuna (S) (M) **1.** great victor. **3.** a descendant of Parīkṣit and king of the lunar dynasty of Indraprastha (*M. Bh.*).

Mahājvāla (S) (M) **1.** a big flame; blazing greatly. **3.** another name for Śiva.

Mahājyotiṣ (S) (M) **1.** great splendour. **3.** another name for Śiva.

Mahaka (S) (M) **1.** eminent; a tortoise. **3.** another name for Viṣṇu.

Mahākaććha (S) (M) **1.** with vast shores. **2.** the sea. **3.** another name for Varuṇa.

Mahākāla (S) (M) **1.** lord of death; lord of time. **3.** a form of Śiva in his destructive aspect (*M. Bh.*); one of Śiva's attendants (*H. Purāṇa*); one of the 9 treasures of the Jainas (*J.S. Koṣa*); a mythical mountain (*K. Vyūha*); a liṅga in Ujjayinī (*K. Sāgara*); another name for Viṣṇu.

Mahākambu (S) (M) **1.** stark naked. **3.** another name for Śiva.

Mahākānta (S) (M) **1.** very pleasing. **3.** another name for Śiva.

Mahākāntiki (S) (M) with great splendour; the full moon in the month of Kārttika.

Mahākapāla (S) (M) **1.** large headed. **3.** a minister of the rākṣasa Dūṣaṇa (*V. Rāmāyaṇa*); an attendant of Śiva (*A. Koṣa*).

Mahākāpi (S) (M) **1.** great ape. **3.** an attendant of Śiva; one of the 34 incarnations of Buddha (*B. Jātakas*).

Mahākapota (S) (M) **1.** great cheeked. **3.** an attendant of Śiva.

Mahākara (S) (M) **1.** with large hands; having great rays. **3.** a Buddha (*L. Vistara*).

Mahākarman (S) (M) accomplishing great works.

Mahākarṇa (S) (M) **1.** large eared. **3.** a nāga (*H. Purāṇa*); another name for Śiva.

Mahākātyāyana (S) (M) **1.** the great sage. **3.** a disciple of the Buddha.

Mahākavi (S) (M) **1.** great poet. **3.** another name for Śukra.

Mahākāya (S) (M) **1.** great bodied. **2.** very tall; an elephant. **3.** a follower of Skanda (*M. Bh.*); an attendant of Śiva (*M. Bh.*); a king of the Garuḍas; another name for Viṣṇu and Śiva.

Mahākāyika (S) (M) **1.** great bodied; omnipresent. **3.** another name for Viṣṇu.

Mahākeśa (S) (M) **1.** with strong hair. **3.** another name for Śiva.

Mahāketu (S) (M) **1.** with a great banner. **3.** another name for Śiva.

Mahākhyāta (S) (M) greatly renowned.

Mahākīrti (S) (M) highly renowned.

Mahākoṣa (S) (M) **1.** the great treasure. **2.** the great phallus. **3.** another name for Śiva.

Mahākrama (S) (M) **1.** wide striding. **3.** another name for Viṣṇu.

Mahākrodha (S) (M) **1.** with great wrath. **3.** another name for Śiva.

Mahākṣa (S) (M) **1.** large eyed. **3.** another name for Śiva.

Mahākulīna (S) (M) highly noble; highly born.

Mahākumāra (S) (M) the heir apparent.

Mahākuṇḍa (S) (M) **1.** great pond. **3.** an attendant of Śiva.

Mahākūrma (S) (M) **1.** great tortoise. **3.** another name for Viṣṇu.

Mahākuśa (S) (M) **1.** great grass; of sharp intellect. **3.** a ćakravartin.

Mahāmaitra (S) (M) **1.** great friend; friend of many. **3.** a Buddha.

Mahāmāli (S) (M) **1.** protector of many; great gardener. **3.** a hero of Rāvaṇa's army (*V. Rāmāyaṇa*).

Mahāmalla (S) (M) **1.** great wrestler. **3.** another name for Kṛṣṇa.

Mahāmanas (S) (M) **1.** high minded; with a great mind. **2.** noble; virtuous. **3.** a grandson of King Janamejaya of the Aṅga dynasty and father of Uśīnara (*A. Purāṇa*).

Mahāmaṇi (S) (M) **1.** a precious gem. **3.** another name for Śiva.

Mahāmaṇićūḍa (S) (M) **1.** crested with a precious gem. **3.** a nāga.

Mahāmaṇidhara (S) (M) **1.** great bearer of jewels. **2.** the ocean. **3.** a bodhisattva.

Mahamaṇiratna (S) (M) **1.** best among jewels. **3.** a fabulous mountain (*K. Vyuha*).

Mahāmarakata (S) (M) a great emerald.

Mahāmati (S) (M) **1.** great minded. **2.** extremely intelligent; very clever. **3.** the planet Jupiter; a king of the yakṣas; a bodhisattva; a son of Sumati (*K. Sāgara*); a son of sage Aṅgiras (*M. Bh.*).

Mahāmāya (S) (M) **1.** the great illusion. **3.** an asura (*K. Sāgara*); a vidyādhara; another name for Viṣṇu and Śiva.

Mahāmayī (S) (M) **1.** the consort of Mahāmāyā. **3.** a wife of Śuddhodana; another name for Durgā.

Mahāmegha (S) (M) **1.** a dense cloud. **3.** another name for Śiva.

Mahāmeru (S) (M) Meru, the great.

Mahāmukha (S) (M) **1.** large mouthed. **3.** a warrior of King Jayadratha (*M. Bh.*); a Jina (*J.S. Koṣa*); another name for Śiva.

Mahāmūlya (S) (M) very costly; a ruby.

Mahāmuni (S) (M) **1.** great sage. **3.** a ṛṣi of the 5th Manvantara (*V. Purāṇa*); another name for Vyāsa and Agastya; another name for a Buddha or a Jina.

Mahāmūrti (S) (M) **1.** large bodied. **3.** another name for Viṣṇu.

Mahān (S) (M) **1.** great. **2.** mighty; powerful; abundant. **3.** a king of the Purū dynasty who was the son of Matināra (*M. Bh.*); the son of Agni Bhārata who was a prajāpati (*M. Bh.*).

Mahānāda (S) (M) **1.** loud sounding. **2.** a great drum; lion; elephant; camel. **3.** a rākṣasa and uncle of Rāvaṇa (*V. Rāmāyaṇa*); another name for Śiva.

Mahānāga (S) (M) **1.** great serpent; great elephant. **3.** one of the elephants that support the earth.

Mahānanda (S) (M) **1.** great bliss. **2.** mokṣa or the final emancipation. **3.** a disciple of Buddha; a king of Madra (*Mā. Purāṇa*).

Mahānandin (S) (M) **1.** very pleasing. **3.** a Magadha king who was the son of Nandivardhana (*M. Purāṇa*).

Mahānārāyaṇa (S) (M) **1.** the great Nārāyaṇa. **3.** another name for Viṣṇu.

Mahānaṭa (S) (M) **1.** great dancer. **3.** another name for Śiva.

Mahānāyaka (S) (M) **1.** great chief. **2.** a great gem in the centre of a string of pearls.

Mahānetra (S) (M) **1.** large eyed. **3.** another name for Śiva.

Mahānidhi (S) (M) a great treasure house.

Mahānīla (S) (M) **1.** dark blue; sapphire. **3.** a mountain (*H. Purāṇa*); a nāga (*H. Purāṇa*); a tāntra (*K. Sāgara*).

Mahāninăda (S) (M) **1.** loud sounding. **3.** a nāga (*B. Literature*).

Mahānṛtya (S) (M) **1.** great dancer. **3.** another name for Śiva.

Mahānta (S) (M) great.

Mahānurāga (S) (M) great love.

Mahāpāda (S) (M) **1.** with large feet. **3.** another name for Śiva.

Mahāpadma (S) (M) **1.** the great lotus; the Indian Lotus (*Nelumbium nucifera*). **3.** the founder king of the Nanda dynasty who was the son of Mahānandī; an elephant in Ghaṭotkaća's army (*M. Bh.*); one of the 8 elephant guardians of the world (*M. Bh.*); one of the 9 cobras worn by Śiva; a son of Nanda; a dānava (*H. Purāṇa*); a kinnara; one of the 9 treasures of Kubera; another name for Nārada.

Mahāpāla (S) (M) **1.** great protector; protector of many. **2.** a king.

Mahāpāriṣadeśvara (S) (M) **1.** great leader of a community. **3.** a follower of Skanda (*M. Bh.*).

Mahāpārśva (S) (M) **1.** with thick sides. **3.** a heroic warrior of Rāvaṇa (*A. Purāṇa*); a mountain (*M. Bh.*).

Mahāpāśa (S) (M) **1.** having a large noose. **3.** an officer of Yama; a nāga.

Mahāpaurava (S) (M) **1.** the great citizen. **3.** a king (*V. Purāṇa*).

Mahāpavitra (S) (M) **1.** greatly purifying. **3.** another name for Viṣṇu.

Mahāprabhu (S) (M) **1.** great lord. **3.** another name for Viṣṇu, Śiva and Indra.

Mahāpraṇāda (S) (M) **1.** great giver of life. **3.** a ćakravartin.

Mahāpratāpa (S) (M) very dignified; majestic.

Mahāpratibhāna (S) (M) **1.** very learned; with great intellect. **3.** a Bodhisattva (*B. Literature*).

Mahāpūrṇa (S) (M) **1.** absolutely complete. **2.** perfect; whole; satisfied. **3.** a king of the Garuḍas (*Gar. Purāṇa*).

Mahāpūta (S) (M) exceedingly pure.

Mahārāja (S) (M) **1.** great king. **3.** a particular class of Buddhist divine beings who are the guardians of the earth and the heavens against the demons; a Jina (*J.S. Koṣa*); another name for Viṣṇu, Kubera and the moon.

Mahārajana (S) (M) **1.** of great splendour. **2.** Safflower; gold.

Mahārajat (S) (M) **1.** better than silver. **2.** gold.

Mahārajika (S) (M) **1.** the princely one. **3.** another name for Viṣṇu.

Mahārāma (S) (M) great Rāma.

Mahāratha (S) (M) **1.** great warrior; great charioteer. **3.** a rākṣasa; a son of Viśvamitra.

Mahāratna (S) (M) most precious of all jewels.

Mahāraudra (S) (M) **1.** very terrible. **3.** a rākṣasa who was a friend of Ghaṭotkaća (*M. Bh.*).

Mahārava (S) (M) **1.** very noisy. **3.** a king of the Yadu dynasty (*Bhā. Purāṇa*); a daitya (*H. Purāṇa*).

Mahārṇava (S) (M) **1.** the great ocean. **3.** another name for Śiva.

Mahāroman (S) (M) **1.** with many branches; very hairy. **3.** a king of the solar dynasty who was the son of Kṛtirāta and father of Svarṇaroman (*Bhāgavata*); a son of Ikṣvāku; another name for the ocean.

Maharṣi (S) (M) **1.** a great saint. **3.** another name for Śiva.

Mahāṛta (S) (M) **1.** very truthful. **3.** a rāṇā of Mewar.

Mahārūpa (S) (M) **1.** great in form. **3.** another name for Śiva.

Mahaśa (S) (M) **1.** one who does not smile. **3.** a son of Kṛṣṇa (*Bhā. Purāṇa*).

Mahāśakti (S) (M) **1.** very powerful. **3.** a son of Kṛṣṇa (*Bh. Purāṇa*); another name for Śiva and Kārttikeya.

Mahāśakuni (S) (M) **1.** great owl; very intelligent. **3.** a ćakravartin.

Mahāśāla (S) (M) **1.** great householder; possessor of a large house. **2.** very strong; very wealthy. **3.** a king of the Aṅga dynasty who was the son of Janamejaya and the father of Mahāmanas (*H. Purāṇa*).

Mahāsammata (S) (M) **1.** highly honoured. **3.** according to the Buddhists, the name of the 1st king of the present age of the world.

Mahāśaṅkha (S) (M) **1.** great conch. **3.** a crocodile celebrated in the Purāṇas, the husband of Saṅkhinī who was the mother of the maruts in the Svāroćiṣa Manvantara; a nāga who revolves with the sun in the month of Mārgaśīrṣa (*Bhā. Purāṇa*).

Mahāsārathi (S) (M) **1.** great charioteer. **3.** another name for Aruna.

Mahāsatya (S) (M) **1.** the great truth. **3.** another name for Yama.

Mahāsena (S) (M) **1.** with a large army. **3.** the father of the 8th Arhat of the present Avasarpiṇī; a prince of Ujjayinī; another name for Śiva and Skanda.

Mahāsenareśvara (S) (M) **1.** lord of those possessing a large army. **2.** the commander of commanders. **3.** the father of the 8th Arhat of the present Avasarpiṇī.

Mahāśila (S) (M) **1.** great rock. **3.** a son of Janamejaya.

Mahāsiṅha (S) (M) **1.** a great lion; with the bearing of a lion. **3.** another name for Yudhiṣṭhira.

Mahāsiṅhatejas (S) (M) **1.** with the glory of a great lion. **3.** a Buddha.

Mahāśiras (S) (M) **1.** large headed. **3.** a sage in the assembly of Yudhiṣṭhira (*M. Bh.*); the 6th Black Vasudeva (*A. Koṣa*); a nāga in the court of Varuṇa; a dānava (*M. Bh.*).

Mahāśīrśa (S) (M) **1.** big headed. **3.** one of Śiva's attendants (*A. Koṣa*)

Mahāsoṇa (S) (M) **1.** very golden. **3.** the king of Ćandrapuri and the father of the 17th Jaina Tīrthaṅkara Ćandraprabha (*J.S. Koṣa*).

Mahāśruti (S) (M) **1.** the great Vedic scholar; very learned. **3.** a gandharva (*H. Purāṇa*).

Mahāśubhra (S) (M) extremely white; silver.

Mahāśukta (S) (M) **1.** the great pearl. **3.** the composer of the hymns of the 10th maṇḍala of the *Ṛg Veda.*

Mahāsura (S) (M) **1.** great demon. **3.** an asura who fought against Skanda (*Sk. Purāṇa*).

Mahāśva (S) (M) **1.** great horse. **3.** a king in Yama's assembly (*M. Bh.*).

Mahāśvana (S) (M) **1.** great dog. **3.** a follower of Skanda (*M. Bh.*).

Mahasvat (S) (M) glorious; giving pleasure; gladdening; great; splendid.

Mahasvin (S) (M) glorious; brilliant; splendid.

Mahātapas (S) (M) **1.** very austere; great penance. **3.** a sage (*Vār. Purāṇa*); another name for Viṣṇu and Śiva.

Mahātejas (S) (M) **1.** of great splendour; hero; fire. **3.** a king of the Garuḍas; a warrior of Skanda (*M. Bh.*); another name for Skanda.

Mahāthilya (S) (M) **1.** extremely skilful. **2.** absolutely still. **3.** a disciple of Buddha.

Mahātman (S) (M) **1.** great soul. **2.** meritorious; virtuous; noble; wise; eminent; powerful. **3.** a son of Dhīmat (*V. Purāṇa*); the Supreme Spirit.

Mahatpati (S) (M) **1.** great lord. **3.** another name for Viṣṇu.

Mahatrū (S) (M) **1.** greatest of the great. **3.** another name for Śiva.

Mahattara (S) (M) **1.** oldest; mightiest; strongest. **2.** great star; chief. **3.** a son of Agni Pāñćajanya (*M. Bh.*); a son of Kaśyapa (*M. Bh.*).

Mahātuṣita (S) (M) **1.** greatly satisfied; very pleased. **3.** another name for Viṣṇu.

Mahātyāgin (S) (M) **1.** extremely generous. **2.** great renouncer. **3.** another name for Śiva.

Mahāugha (S) (M) **1.** with a strong current. **3.** a son of Tvaṣṭṛ.

Mahaujas (S) (M) **1.** very powerful. **3.** a king invited by the Pāṇḍavas to take part in the great war of Mahābhāratā (*M. Bh.*); another name for Skanda.

Mahāvādi (S) (M) **1.** great disputant. **3.** another name for the poet Aśvaghoṣa.

Mahāvakṣas (S) (M) **1.** broad chested. **3.** another name for Śiva.

Mahāvali (S) (M) **1.** very brave; a great warrior. **3.** a king of the 3rd lunar dynasty of Indraprastha (*M. Bh.*).

Mahāvarāha (S) (M) **1.** great boar. **3.** Viṣṇu in his boar incarnation.

Mahāvāyu (S) (M) **1.** great wind. **2.** gale.

Mahāvega (S) (M) **1.** moving swiftly. **3.** another name for Garuḍa.

Mahāvikrama (S) (M) **1.** very valorous. **2.** lion. **3.** a nāga.

Mahāvikramin (S) (M) **1.** very brave. **3.** a Bodhisattva.

Mahāvila (S) (M) **1.** great veil. **2.** the sky.

Mahāvīra (S) (M) **1.** great hero; sacrificial fire. **2.** warrior; archer; lion; white horse; the Indian cuckoo. **3.** a son of Priyavrata and Surūpā (*D. Bhāgavata*); a king who was an incarnation of the asura Krodhavaśa (*M. Bh.*); the thunderbolts of Indra, Viṣṇu and Hanumān; another name for Vardhamāna the 24th and last Tīrthaṅkara of the present Avasarpiṇī and the most celebrated Jaina teacher of the present age who is supposed to have flourished in Bihar (6th century A.D.); another name for Hanumān and Garuḍa.

Mahāvīrya (S) (M) **1.** of great strength. **3.** Indra in the 4th Manvantara (*M. Purāṇa*); a Buddha; a Jina (*J.S. Koṣa*); Bulb bearing Yam (*Dioscorea bulbifera*); another name for Brahmā.

Mahāviṣṇu (S) (M) the great Viṣṇu.

Mahāvīta (S) (M) **1.** completely detached. **3.** a son of Savana (*V. Purāṇa*).

Mahāyakṣa (S) (M) **1.** the great yakṣa. **3.** a servant of the 2nd Arhat of the present Avasarpinī; a class of Buddhist deities.

Mahāyaśas (S) (M) **1.** very famous. **2.** very glorious; renowned. **3.** the 4th Arhat of the past Utsarpiṇī (*J.S. Koṣa*); a mother attending on Skanda (*M. Bh.*).

Mahāyati (S) (M) a great ascetic.

Mahāyogin (S) (M) **1.** great ascetic. **3.** Viṣṇu or Śiva when worshipped by Buddhists (*B. Literature*).

Mahayya (S) (M) to be gladdened; to be delighted.

Mahendra (S) (M) **1.** Indra, the great; an Indra among kings. **3.** the father of princess Pātalī; the younger brother of Aśoka; a holy mountain of great Purāṇic importance; a range of mountains (*Bhā. Purāṇa*).

Mahendragupta (S) (M) protected by Indra.

Mahendrapāla (S) (M) protected by Indra.

Mahendravarman (S) (M) armoured by Indra.

Maheśa (S) (M) **1.** great lord. **2.** god. **3.** an incarnation of Śiva (*S. Samhitā*); a Buddhist deity.

Maheṣu (S) (M) a great arrow.

Maheśvara (S) (M) **1.** great lord. **2.** chief. **3.** titles of the 4 Lokapālas (*A. Koṣa*); another name for Śiva, Kṛṣṇa and Indra.

Maheśvāsa (S) (M) **1.** great archer. **3.** another name for Śiva.

Mahībhuj (S) (M) **1.** earth enjoyer. **3.** a king.

Mahīcandra (S) (M) moon of the earth.

Mahīdāsa (S) (M) **1.** devotee of the earth. **3.** a preceptor who is believed to be the author of *Aitareya Brāhmaṇa*; a son of Itarā (*T. Āraṇyaka*).

Mahīdhara (S) (M) **1.** supporting the earth. **2.** mountain. **3.** the number 7; a commentator on Vedas; another name for Viṣṇu.

Mahīja (S) (M) **1.** son of the earth. **3.** another name for the planet Mars.

Mahījit (S) (M) **1.** conqueror of the earth. **3.** a king of Mahiṣmatī (*P. Purāṇa*).

Mahikāṅśu (S) (M) **1.** with frosty rays. **3.** another name for the moon.

Mahīkṣatra (S) (M) possessing great power.

Mahīksita (S) (M) **1.** earth ruler. **2.** a king.

Mahimabhaṭṭa (S) (M) **1.** warrior of glory. **3.** a Sanskṛt critic and scholar of logic (11th century A.D.).

Mahiman (S) (M) **1.** greatness. **2.** power; might; dignity. **3.** an āditya who was the son of Bhaga and Siddhi (*Bhā. Purāṇa*).

Mahimati (S) (M) **1.** high minded. **3.** another name for Indra.

Māhin (S) (M) **1.** giving delight. **2.** joyous; great; exalted; mighty.

Mahināśa (S) (M) **1.** destroyer of the great demon. **3.** a form of Śiva or Rudra (*Bh. Purāṇa*).

Mahīnātha (S) (M) lord of the earth.

Mahīndra (S) (M) great Indra of the earth.

Mahīpa (S) (M) **1.** protector of the earth. **3.** a king.

Mahīpāla (S) (M) **1.** protector of the earth. **2.** a king.

Mahīpati (S) (M) **1.** lord of the earth. **2.** a king.

Mahīputra (S) (M) **1.** son of the earth. **2.** the planet Mars.

Mahir (S) (M) expert; proficient.

Mahira (S) (M) **1.** proficient. **3.** another name for Indra and the sun.

Mahiradhvaja (S) (M) **1.** mark of the earth. **2.** banner; flag.

Mahīraṇa (S) (M) **1.** warrior of the earth. **3.** a viśvadeva and the son of Dharma (*H. Purāṇa*).

Mahīratha (S) (M) **1.** chariot of the earth. **3.** a king and follower of sage Kaśyapa (*P. Purāṇa*).

Mahiṣa (S) (M) **1.** mighty; buffalo. **2.** great; powerful; lord of the earth. **3.** the king of the asuras and sometime emperor of the world who was killed by Devī (*D. Bhāgavata*); another name for the sun.

Mahiṣadhvaja (S) (M) **1.** with a buffalo emblem. **3.** another name for Yama.

Mahiṣaga (S) (M) **1.** riding on a buffalo. **3.** another name for Yama.

Mahiṣaghna (S) (M) **1.** destroyer of Mahiṣa. **3.** another name for Śiva.

Mahiṣākṣa (S) (M) **1.** with the eyes of a bull. **3.** an asura (*Sk. Purāṇa*).

Mahiṣārdana (S) (M) Kārttikeya as the destroyer of the demon Mahiṣa.

Mahiṣāsura (S) (M) **1.** the asura Mahiṣa. **3.** the demon Mahiṣa from whom Mysore is said to take its name (*Vam. Purāṇa*).

Mahiṣavāhana (S) (M) **1.** buffalo vehicled. **3.** another name for Yama.

Mahiṣayamana (S) (M) **1.** tamer of buffaloes. **3.** another name for Yama.

Mahiṣmān (S) (M) **1.** rich in buffaloes. **3.** a king of the Hehaya family who built the city Māhiṣmatī (*Br. Purāṇa*); a king of the Vṛṣṇi dynasty who was the son of Kuṇti (*Bhā. Purāṇa*).

Mahiṣmat (S) (M) **1.** rich in buffaloes. **3.** a king of the Hehaya family (*Br. Purāṇa*); a king of the Vṛṣṇi dynasty (*Bhāgavata*).

Mahīsuta (S) (M) **1.** son of the earth. **2.** the planet Mars.

Mahita (S) (M) **1.** honoured; celebrated. **3.** the trident of Śiva (*Ś. Purāṇa*).

Mahīyu (S) (M) **1.** happy. **2.** joyous.

Mahodara (S) (M) **1.** big bellied. **3.** a son of Viśvāmitra (*V. Rāmāyaṇa*); a nāga son of Kaśyapa and Kadru (*M. Bh.*); a son of Dhṛtarāṣṭra (*M. Bh.*); an army chief of Rāvaṇa (*U. Rāmāyaṇa*); a friend of Ghaṭotkaća (*Sk. Purāṇa*); a son of Rāvaṇa (*V. Rāmāyaṇa*); a minister of Rāvaṇa's grandfather Sumālin (*V. Rāmāyaṇa*); a son of Viśravas and Puṣpotkaṭā (*V. Rāmāyaṇa*); a rākṣasa (*V. Rāmāyaṇa*).

Mahodarya (S) (M) **1.** liberal; meritorious. **3.** a king worthy of being remembered every morning (*M. Bh.*).

Mahodaya (S) (M) **1.** greatly risen. **2.** respected; eminent. **3.** a son of Vasiṣṭha (*V. Rāmāyaṇa*).

Mahoka/Mahaka (S) (M) **1.** eminent. **3.** another name for Viṣṇu.

Mahotsāha (S) (M) **1.** with great energy. **3.** another name for Śiva.

Mahottama (S) (M) **1.** best among the great. **2.** perfume.

Mahu (S) (M) **1.** diver-bird; cormorant; a galley or vessel of war. **3.** a son of Śvaphalka (*Bhāgavata*).

Mahya (S) (M) **1.** highly honoured. **3.** a tribe.

Maināka (S) (M) **1.** son of Menā. **3.** a mountain situated north of Kailāsa where Bhagīratha offered penance to bring Gaṅgā to the earth, personified as the son of Himavān and Menā and the father of Krauñca.

Mainda (S) (M) **1.** giver of art. **3.** a monkey who was the son of Avinīdevas and a leader of Rāma's army (*M. Bh.*); a monkey demon killed by Kṛṣṇa (*M. Bh.*).

Mairava (S) (M) belonging to Mount Meru.

Maithila (S) (M) **1.** of Mithilā. **3.** another name for Janaka.

Maitra (S) (M) **1.** friendly. **2.** amicable; kind. **3.** a preceptor (*A. Koṣa*).

Maitrāvaruṇa (S) (M) **1.** Varuṇa, the friend. **3.** another name for the sages Vasiṣṭha and Agastya when they were reborn as sons of Mitra and Varuṇa (*D. Bhāgavata*).

Maitrāyaṇa (S) (M) **1.** of Mitra; friendly. **3.** another name for Agni.

Maitreya (S) (M) **1.** friendly; benevolent. **3.** a sage of great brilliance who was the son of Divodāsa and the father of Somapa (*Bhāgavata*); a Bodhisattva and the future Buddha.

Maitribala (S) (M) **1.** one whose strength is benevolence; popular; supported by many; a Buddha. **3.** a king regarded an an incarnation of Gautama Buddha.

Majjala (S) (M) **1.** bathing; immersing; sinking. **3.** a soldier of Skanda (*M. Bh.*).

Majjara (S) (M) my love.

Majman (S) (M) greatness; majesty.

Mākali (S) (M) **1.** the moon. **3.** the charioteer of lndra (*Ṛg Veda*).

Mākanda (S) (M) **1.** the Mango tree (*Mangifera indica*); Yellow Sandalwood (*Santalum album*). **3.** a city beside the Gaṅgā.

Makara (S) (M) **1.** a kind of sea creature sometimes confused with crocodile, shark, dolphin, regarded as the emblem of Kāma. **3.** one of the 9 treasures of Kubera; the zodiac sign of Capricorn.

Makaradhvaja (S) (M) **1.** makara bannered. **3.** a son of Hanumān and a crocodile (*A. Rāmāyaṇa*); a son of Dhṛtarāṣṭra (*M. Bh.*); another name for Kāma.

Makarākṣa (S) (M) **1.** with the eyes of the makara. **3.** a rākṣasa who was the son of Khara (*V. Rāmāyaṇa*).

Makarānana (S) (M) **1.** makara faced. **3.** an attendant of Śiva (*A. Koṣa*).

Makaranda (S) (M) honey; nectar; Jasmine (*Jasminum pubescens*); the Indian cuckoo (*Cuculus scolopaceus*); the filament of a lotus; a fragrant species of mango; a pleasure garden; bee; pollen; fragrance.

Makarandapāla (S) (M) **1.** protector of nectar. **3.** the father of Trivikrama (*A. Koṣa*).

Makarāṅka (S) (M) **1.** with the makara for a symbol. **2.** the ocean. **3.** another name for Kāma.

Makaraketana (S) (M) **1.** crocodile bannered. **3.** another name for Kāma.

Makaraketu (S) (M) **1.** with a makara as his banner. **3.** another name for Kāma.

Makaravāhana (S) (M) **1.** with a makara for his vehicle. **3.** another name for Varuṇa.

Makha (S) (M) cheerful; active; a feat; a festival; a sacrificial oblation.

Makhaghna (S) (M) **1.** destroying Dakṣa's sacrifice. **3.** another name for Śiva.

Mākhan (S) (M) an oblation; butter.

Makhasvāmin (S) (M) lord of sacrifice.

Makhatrātṛ (S) (M) **1.** protector of oblation. **3.** the protector of Visvāmitra's sacrifice; another name for King Rāma.

Makheśa (S) (M) **1.** lord of sacrifice. **3.** another name for Viṣṇu.

Makṣarin (S) (M) **1.** ascetic. **2.** a religious mendicant. **3.** another name for the moon.

Makṣopeta (S) (M) **1.** surrounded by bees. **3.** a daitya who whirls around with an āditya known as Viṣṇu in the month of Kārttika (*Bhā. Purāṇa*).

Maksūdana (S) (M) one who performs the sacrifice.

Makula (S) (M) a bud.

Makura (S) (M) mirror; a bud; the Indian Medlar (*Mimosops elengi*); Arabian Jasmine (*Jasminum sambac*).

Mālādhara (S) (M) **1.** wearing a garland. **2.** crowned.

Malākara (S) (M) **1.** garland maker; gardener; florist. **3.** a son of Viśvakarman by Ghṛtāćī (*Brahma Purāṇa*).

Mālāmantra (S) (M) **1.** the garland hymn. **2.** sacred text written in the form of a garland.

Mālāṅka (S) (M) **1.** garlanded. **3.** a king (*A. Koṣa*).

Mālatīmādhava (S) (M) **1.** lord of Jasmine. **3.** a celebrated drama by Bhavabhūti.

Mālava (S) (M) **1.** horse keeper. **3.** a country in central India and its people; a rāga.

Malaya (S) (M) **1.** fragrant; Sandalwood tree (*Santalum album*); rich in sandalwood trees. **3.** a mountain in South India, personified by a deity in Kubera's assembly and considered one of the 7 chief mountains of India (*M. Bh.*); a mountain range on the west coast abounding in sandalwood; a mountain just above Kailāsa (*M. Bh.*); the garden of Indra (*M. Bh.*); a son of Garuḍa (*M. Bh.*); a son of Ṛṣabha (*Bhā. Purāṇa*); a son of King Ṛṣabhadeva (*Bhā. Purāṇa*); Himālayan Cherry (*Prunus cerasoides*).

Malayadhvaja (S) (M) **1.** with a sandalwood tree; banner. **3.** a Pāṇḍya king who fought on the side of the Pāṇḍavas (*M. Bh.*); a son of Merudhvaja (*K. Sāgara*).

Malayagiri (S) (M) the Malaya mountains (*V.D. Ćaritam*).

Malayaketu (S) (M) with the banner/glory of the sandalwood tree.

Malayānila (S) (M) **1.** fragrant breeze. **2.** sandalwood scented breeze.

Malayaprabha (S) (M) **1.** with the glory of the sandalwood tree. **3.** a king of Kurukṣetra (*K. Sāgara*).

Malhāra (S) (M) **1.** that which gives rain. **3.** a classical music rāga of the monsoons.

Mālī (S) (M) **1.** fragrant. **3.** a demon who was the son of Sukeśa and Devavatī, the husband of Vasudhā and the father of Anila, Anala, Hara and Sampāti (*V. Rāmāyaṇa*).

Mālīdeva (S) (M) god of fragrance.

Mālin (S) (M) **1.** garlanded; gardener. **2.** crowned; florist. **3.** a son of the rākṣasa Sukeśa (*V. Rāmāyaṇa*).

Mālkausa (S) (M) **1.** garland bearer. **3.** a rāga.

Mālkirata (S) (M) connoisseur of Jasmine.

Malla (S) (M) **1.** wrestler. **3.** the 21st Arhat of the future Utsarpiṇī (*J.S. Koṣa*); an asura.

Mallaga (S) (M) **1.** interested in wrestling. **3.** a son of Dyutimat (*M. Bh.*).

Mallapa (S) (M) **1.** the father of wrestlers. **3.** another name for Viṣṇu.

Mallapriya (S) (M) **1.** beloved of wrestlers. **2.** one who is fond of wrestling. **3.** another name for Kṛṣṇa.

Mallāri (S) (M) **1.** enemy of the asura Malla. **3.** another name for Kṛṣṇa.

Mallārjuna (S) (M) **1.** handsome wrestler. **3.** a king (*Bhā. Purāṇa*).

Malleśa (S) (M) **1.** lord of wrestlers. **3.** another name for Śiva.

Malli (S) (M) **1.** having; holding; possessing. **3.** the 19th Arhat of the present Avasarpinī; *Jasminum sambac*.

Mallikārjuna (S) (M) **1.** white spotted; as white as jasmine. **3.** a form of Śiva; a liṅga consecrated to Śiva at Śriśaila (*Ś. Purāṇa*); the guru of Venkaṭa.

Mallinātha (S) (M) **1.** lord of possession. **3.** a poet and commentator who was the father of Kumārasvāmin and Viśveśvara (14th century); the 19th Jaina Tīrthaṅkara whose emblem is the water jar.

Mālyapiṇḍaka (S) (M) **1.** resembling a garland. **3.** a serpent born in the family of Kaśyapa (*M. Bh.*).

Mālyavān (S) (M) **1.** garland bearer. **2.** one who is wreathed; crowned. **3.** an attendant of Śiva (*V. Rāmāyaṇa*); the son of the demon Sukeśa and brother of Māli and Sumālin (*Rāmāyaṇa*); a golden mountain situated between Meru and Mandāra (*M. Bh.*); a mountain situated in Kiṣkindhā where the fight of Bāli and Sugrīva took place (*M. Bh.*).

Mālyavat (S) (M) **1.** crowned with garlands. **3.** a son of Sukeśa; one of Śiva's attendants; a mountain.

Māmarāja (S) (M) self praised.

Mammaṭa (S) (M) **1.** theoritician. **3.** the author of *Kāvyaprakāśa*.

Māmti (S) (M) **1.** affectionate; loving. **3.** the disciple of Gautama and the guru of Ātreya (*Br. Upaniṣad*); a devotee of Śiva who was the father of Kālabhīti (*Sk. Purāṇa*).

Mana (S) (M) **1.** Indian Spikenard (*Nardostachys jatamansi*). **3.** a son of Śambara (*H. Purāṇa*).

Māna (S) (M) **1.** opinion; dwelling; measure; likeness; resemblance; notion; idea; purpose; pride; respect; honour. **3.** the father of Agastya.

Manabhava (S) (M) **1.** mind born. **3.** another name for Kāma.

Manadatta (S) (M) given by thought; absorbed in thought.

Manahar (S) (M) **1.** wooing the heart. **2.** attractive; fascinating; charming.

Manaharaṇ (S) (M) **1.** one who woos the heart. **2.** lovely; attractive.

Manaja (S) (M) **1.** born of the mind. **3.** another name for Kāma.

Manajit (S) (M) **1.** one who has conquered thought; one who has won the mind. **3.** Indian Madder (*Rubia cordifolia*).

Manakānta (S) (M) dear to the mind.

Manakara (S) (M) fulfiller of wishes.

Manal (S) (M) a bird; the Himālayan Monal Pheasant (*Lopophorus impeyanus*).

Maṇikarṇika (S) (M) **1.** jewelled earring. **3.** one of the 5 pilgrimage centres in Benaras.

Manmatha (S) (M) **1.** churning the mind. **2.** passion; desire. **3.** another name for Kāma.

Manmathakara (S) (M) **1.** causing love. **3.** an attendant of Skanda (*M. Bh.*).

Manamathānanda (S) (M) love's joy.

Manamohana (S) (M) **1.** winning the heart. **3.** another name for Kṛṣṇa.

Manana (S) (M) meditation; reflection; thought; intelligence; understanding.

Manāṅka (S) (M) **1.** marked with heart. **2.** one who is affectionate; compassionate.

Manāpa (S) (M) **1.** gaining the heart. **2.** attracting; beautiful.

Manapati (S) (M) **1.** lord of the heart. **3.** another name for Viṣṇu.

Manaprīta (S) (M) **1.** dear to the heart. **2.** joy; delight; mental satisfaction.

Manapriya (S) (M) **1.** dear to the heart. **2.** joy; delight; mental satisfaction.

Manaratha (S) (M) **1.** wish; desire. **3.** a king.

Manarūpa (S) (M) according to the mind.

Manas (S) (M) **1.** intellect; intelligence; perception. **3.** father-in-law of Āśā (*H. Purāṇa*).

Mānasa (S) (M) **1.** conceived in the mind. **2.** soul; mental powers; spiritual mind; heat. **3.** a form of Viṣṇu (*P. Purāṇa*); a serpent of the family of Vāsuki (*M. Bh.*); a serpent of the family of Dhṛtarāṣṭra (*M. Bh.*); a lake on the peak of Mount Kailāśa frequented by the devotees of Śiva (*M. Bh.*); a son of Vapuṣmat (*M. Bh.*); a sacred lake on Mount Kailāsa.

Mānasāra (S) (M) **1.** ocean of pride. **2.** extremely proud. **3.** a king of Mālava.

Manasārāma (S) (M) absorbed in meditation.

Mānasavega (S) (M) swift as thought.

Manasi (S) (M) with a sound mind.

Manasija (S) (M) **1.** born of the heart. **2.** love. **3.** another name for Kāma and the moon.

Manaskānta (S) (M) dear to the heart.

Manastāla (S) (M) **1.** deep thinker. **3.** the lion which is the vehicle of Durgā.

Manasukha (S) (M) agreeable to the heart.

Manasvin (S) (M) **1.** one who controls the mind. **2.** intelligent; clever; wise. **3.** a son of Devala (*V. Purāṇa*); a nāga.

Manasyu (S) (M) **1.** wishing; desiring. **3.** a Purū king who was the son of Pravīra and Śūrasenī and the husband of Sauvīrī (*M. Bh.*); a son of Mahānta (*V. Purāṇa*).

Manatoṣa (S) (M) mental satisfaction.

Māṇava (S) (M) **1.** youth; lad; a pearl ornament of 16 strings. **3.** one of the 9 treasures of the Jainas.

Mānavāćārya (S) (M) **1.** father of mankind. **3.** another name for Manu.

Mānavadeva (S) (M) god among men.

Mānavapati (S) (M) **1.** lord of men. **2.** a prince.

Mānavasu (S) (M) rich in devotion; loyal; faithful.

Mānavendra (S) (M) **1.** lord of men. **3.** another name for Indra.

Manāyu (S) (M) **1.** zealous. **2.** devoted.

Mandagā (S) (M) **1.** moving slowly. **3.** a son of Dyutimat (*V. Purāṇa*); another name for the planet Saturn.

Mandaka (S) (M) **1.** speed breaker. **3.** a son of the yakṣa Maṇibhadra and Puṇyajanī (*H. Purāṇa*).

Mandakānti (S) (M) **1.** with a soft lustre. **3.** another name for the moon.

Māṅdakarṇi (S) (M) **1.** performing slowly; hearing slowly. **2.** hard of hearing. **3.** a sage who lived only on air for 10,000 years (*V. Rāmāyaṇa*).

Mandālaka (S) (M) **1.** with loving eyes **3.** a serpent of the family of Takṣaka (*M. Bh.*).

Maṇḍana (S) (M) adorning; ornament; decoration.

Mandānila (S) (M) gentle breeze; zephyr.

Maṇḍanmiśra (S) (M) **1.** honourable ornament. **3.** husband of Sarasavāṇi.

Mandanum (S) (M) praise.

Mandapāla (S) (M) **1.** protector of praise. **3.** a sage (*M. Bh.*).

Mandāra (S) (M) **1.** large; thick; firm; slow. **2.** a pearl chain of 8 strings. **3.** the eldest son of Hiraṇyakaśipu (*M. Bh.*); a son of the sage Dhaumya and the husband of Śamīkā (*G. Purāṇa*); a sage extolled in the *Śiva Purāṇa*; a sacred mountain which served as a stick for churning the Ocean of Milk (*M. Bh.*); a vidyādhara (*K. Sāgara*); one of the 5 trees of Paradise; Indian Coral tree (*Erythrina indica*).

Mandāradeva (S) (M) **1.** lord of the Indian Coral tree (*Erythrina indica*); coming from Mount Mandāra. **3.** a king of the vidyādharas; another name for Śiva.

Mandaramāli (S) (M) **1.** garlanded with pearl chains. **3.** a daitya.

Mandayu (S) (M) gay, cheerful; happy.

Māndhana (S) (M) rich in honour.

Māndhara (S) (M) honourable.

Māndhātā (S) (M) **1.** respected; honoured; revered. **3.** an eminent Ikṣvāku king who was the son of Yuvanāśva (*M. Bh.*).

Māndhātṛ (S) (M) **1.** bearer of respect; thoughtful; pious. **3.** a royal ṛṣi of the solar dynasty who was the son of Yuvanāśva and the husband of Bindumatī (*D. Bh. Purāṇa*); a king and son of Madanapāla the patron of Viśveśvara.

Mandin (S) (M) **1.** delighting; exhilarating. **3.** another name for Soma.

Mandiramaṇi (S) (M) **1.** jewel of the temple. **3.** another name for Śiva.

Mandiṣṭha (S) (M) most exhilarating.

Maṇḍita (S) (M) adorned; decorated.

Mandodaka (S) (M) **1.** slow flowing water. **3.** the mythical lake situated on

Mount Kailāśa and said to be the source of the Gaṅgā — the counterpart of the celestial river Mandākinī (*D. Ćarita*).

Mandu (S) (M) **1.** pleased. **2.** joyful; cheerful.

Māṇḍūkeya (S) (M) **1.** son of a frog. **3.** a ṛṣi.

Māṇḍūkya (S) (M) **1.** son of a frog. **3.** one of the 13 principal Upaniṣads.

Manendra (S) (M) lord of the mind.

Maṅgala (S) (M) **1.** happiness; felicity; welfare; bliss; auspiciousness. **3.** a king belonging to the race of Manu; a chief of the Ćālukyas; a Buddha (*B. Literature*); another name for Agni and the planet Mars.

Mangalapāṇi (S) (M) with auspicious hands.

Mangalāvrata (S) (M) **1.** devoted to Mangalā; devoted to Umā. 3. another name for Śiva.

Maṅgalya (S) (M) **1.** pious; pure; beautiful; bringing luck. **2.** gold; sandalwood. **3.** a nāga.

Maṅhana (S) (M) gift; present.

Manhayu (S) (M) liberal.

Manhiṣṭha (S) (M) **1.** granting according to the wishes; granting abundantly. **2.** generous; liberal.

Maṇi (S) (M) **1.** jewel; gem; ornament; crystal; pearl; magnet. **3.** a son of Yuyudhāna (*M. Bh.*); the king of the kinnaras (*K. Vyūha*); a serpent of the family of Dhṛtarāṣṭra (*M. Bh.*); a sage and member of Brahmā's court (*M. Bh.*); an attendant given to Skanda by Ćandra (*M. Bh.*); a nāga son of Kaśyapa and Kadru (*Br. Purāṇa*).

Maṇibandhana (S) (M) ornament of pearls.

Maṇibhadra (S) (M) **1.** jewelled person; jewel among people. **2.** gem of a person. **3.** a brother of Kubera; the king of the yakṣas, the tutelary deity of merchants and travellers and worshipped in the temple of Tāmralipti (*M. Bh.*); a lunar dynasty king who was the husband of Kavikā and whose 7 sons were freed from their curse by Rāma (*K. Rāmāyaṇa*); an attendant of Śiva (*Ś. Purāṇa*).

Maṇibhava (S) (M) **1.** born of a jewel. **3.** one of the 5 Dhyāni Buddhas.

Maṇibīja (S) (M) **1.** with jewelled seeds. **2.** the Pomegranate tree (*Punica granatum*).

Manīća (S) (M) hand; pearl; flower.

Maṇićara (S) (M) **1.** jewel eater. **2.** eater of pomegranate seeds. **3.** a prince of the yakṣas (*V. Rāmāyaṇa*).

Maṇićūḍa (S) (M) **1.** jewel crested. **3.** a vidyādhara; a nāga.

Maṇidara (S) (M) **1.** living in a jewelled cave. **3.** a chief of the yakṣas (*K. Sāgara*).

Maṇidhanu (S) (M) **1.** jewelled bow. **2.** the rainbow.

Maṇidīpa (S) (M) a jewelled lamp; a jewel that shines.

Maṇidvīpa (S) (M) **1.** the island of jewels. **3.** the abode of Devī far beyond Kailāsa (*D. Bhāgavata*).

Maṇigaṇa (S) (M) a group of jewels; pearls.

Maṇigrīva (S) (M) **1.** jewel necked. **3.** a son of Kubera and the brother of Nalakūbara (*Ṛg Veda*).

Maṇihāra (S) (M) a string of jewels.

Mānika (S) (M) highly honoured and esteemed.

Maṇika (S) (M) jewel; gem.

Maṇikam (S) (M) collyrium.

Maṇikaṇṭha (S) (M) **1.** jewel necked. 2. the Blue Jay (*Coracias benghalensis*). **3.** a nāga.

Maṇikāra (S) (M) jeweller; lapidary.

Maṇikarṇa (S) (M) jewel eared.

Maṇiketu (S) (M) **1.** with a jewelled banner. **3.** a comet (*Var. Purāṇa*).

Maṇikusuma (S) (M) **1.** jewelled flower. **3.** a Jina (*J.S. Koṣa*).

Māṇikya (S) (M) ruby.

Māṇikyaćandra (S) (M) moon among rubies.

Māṇikyāditya (S) (M) sun among rubies.

Māṇikyādri (S) (M) **1.** mountain of rubies. 3. a mountain (*M. Bh.*).

Māṇikyamaya (S) (M) made of rubies.

Māṇikyavācakara (S) (M) **1.** with a ruby like speech. **2.** a great orator. **3.** poet and devotee of Śiva from Tamil Nadu who became a minister of the Pāṇḍya king (8th century) (*M. Bh.*).

Maṇilāla (S) (M) jewel of a son.

Maṇimān (S) (M) **1.** jewelled. **3.** a king who was a partial incarnation of the asura Vṛtra and who fought on the side of the Pāṇḍavas (*M. Bh.*); a serpent of the court of Varuna (*M. Bh.*); a yakṣa friend of Kubera (*M. Bh.*); an attendant of Śiva (*Bhā. Purāṇa*); a mountain (*M. Bh.*); another name for the sun.

Maṇimaṇḍita (S) (M) adorned with jewels.

Maṇimat (S) (M) **1.** adorned with jewels. **3.** a servant of Śiva (*Bh. Purāṇa*); a rākṣasa (*M. Bh.*); a nāga (*M. Bh.*); a yakṣa (*M. Bh.*); another name for the sun.

Maṇimaya (S) (M) **1.** made of jewels. **3.** the father of Devavatī and father-in-law of Sukeśa (*U. Rāmāyaṇa*).

Maṇināga (S) (M) **1.** jewelled serpent; jewelled elephant; jewelled mountain. **3.** a serpent son of Kaśyapa and Kadru (*M. Bh.*); a sacred bathing place (*M. Bh.*).

Maṇinanda (S) (M) born of the jewel.

Maṇīndra (S) (M) **1.** chief of jewels. **2.** the diamond.

Maṇipadma (S) (M) **1.** jewelled lotus. **3.** a Bodhisattva.

Maṇipurapati (S) (M) **1.** lord of Maṇipura. **3.** another name for Babhruvāhana.

Maṇipureśvara (S) (M) **1.** lord of Maṇipura. **3.** another name for Babhruvāhana.

Maṇipuṣpaka (S) (M) **1.** jewel and flower conjoined. **3.** the conch of Sahadeva (*M. Bh.*).

Maṇipuṣpeśvara (S) (M) **1.** lord of jewels and flowers. **3.** an attendant of Śiva (*K. Sāgara*).

Maṇirāga (S) (M) with the colour of a jewel.

Maṇirāja (S) (M) **1.** king of jewels. **2.** the diamond.

Maṇirāma (S) (M) existing in jewels.

Manīṣa (S) (M) **1.** lord of the mind. **2.** profound thinker; wise.

Maṇiśaṅkara (S) (M) the jewelled Śiva.

Maṇisānu (S) (M) **1.** jewel ridged. **3.** another name for Mount Meru.

Manisara (S) (M) string of jewels; a necklace.

Manīṣin (S) (M) **1.** thoughtful. **2.** intelligent; wise; prudent; devout; sagacious.

Manīṣita (S) (M) desired; wished; wish.

Maṇiskandha (S) (M) **1.** with jewelled shoulders. **3.** a serpent of the family of Dhṛtarāṣṭra (*M. Bh.*).

Maṇiśṛṅga (S) (M) **1.** jewel horned. **3.** another name for Sūrya.

Maṇīśvara (S) (M) lord of jewels.

Manita (S) (M) honoured; respected; known; understood.

Manīvaka (S) (M) **1.** jewel tongued. **3.** a son of Bhavya (*V. Purāṇa*).

Maṇīvaka (S) (M) **1.** with pearl like words; with flowery speech. **3.** a son of Bhavya and grandson of Priyavrata (*V. Purāṇa*).

Maṇivakra (S) (M) **1.** jewel faced. **3.** a son of the vasu Āpa.

Maṇivara (S) (M) **1.** best jewel. **2.** the diamond. **3.** a yakṣa who was the son of Rajatanātha and the father of the guhyakas (*Br. Purāṇa*).

Maṇivarman (S) (M) a jewelled talisman.

Mañjava (S) (M) swift as thought.

Mañjira (S) (M) a cymbal; an anklet.

Mañjudeva (S) (M) lord of beauty.

Mañjughoṣa (S) (M) **1.** with a sweet voice. **2.** the dove (*Streptopelia chinensis*).

Mañjukeśin (S) (M) **1.** with beautiful hair. **3.** another name for Kṛṣṇa.

Mañjumaṇi (S) (M) **1.** beautiful gem. **2.** the topaz.

Mañjunātha (S) (M) **1.** lord of beauty; lord of ice. **3.** another name for Śiva.

Mañjuprāṇa (S) (M) **1.** beautiful soul. **3.** another name for Brahmā.

Mañjūṣaka (S) (M) celestial flower.

Mañjuśrī (S) (M) **1.** divine beauty. **3.** a celebrated bodhisattva considered the epitome of wisdom.

Mankaṇa (S) (M) **1.** a part of the mind. **3.** a sage who was the son of Vāyubhagavān and Sukanyā, the father of 7 sons by Sarasvatī Devī and a daughter named Kadalīgarbhā by the apsara Menakā.

Maṅkaṇaka (S) (M) **1.** partially thoughtful. **3.** a ṛṣi (*M. Bh.*); a yakṣa (*M. Bh.*).

Maṅki (S) (M) **1.** governed by thought. **3.** a Vaiṣṇavite sage who was the son of Kauṣtikī and the husband of Surupā and Virupā (*P. Purāṇa*); a great sage (*M. Bh.*).

Maṅkṣa (S) (M) **1.** longing. **2.** to long for; to desire.

Maṅkura (S) (M) **1.** that which reflects the mind. **2.** a mirror.

Manmandira (S) (M) **1.** a temple of ego. **2.** arrogance. **3.** another name for Rāvaṇa.

Mannata (S) (M) **1.** with a devoted mind. **2.** a vow to a deity.

Mannītha (S) (M) **1.** heart. **2.** chosen.

Manobhirāma (S) (M) **1.** pleasing to the mind. **2.** delightful; charming; beautiful.

Manobhū (S) (M) **1.** born of the mind. **2.** love. **3.** another name for Kāma.

Manodāhin (S) (M) **1.** influencing the heart. **3.** another name for Kāma.

Manodatta (S) (M) given by the mind.

Manodhara (S) (M) one who bears the mind.

Manohara (S) (M) **1.** winning the heart. **2.** that which steals the heart; *Jasminum pubescens*. **3.** another name for Kṛṣṇa.

Manoja (S) (M) **1.** born of the mind. **2.** love. **3.** another name for Kāma.

Manojāta (S) (M) born of the mind.

Manojava (S) (M) **1.** with the speed of thought; born of the mind. **3.** son of the vasu Anila and his wife Śiva (*M. Bh.*); Indra during the Manvantara of Manu Ćākṣusa (*V. Purāṇa*); a follower of Skanda (*M. Bh.*); a son of the rudra Īśāna; a son of Medhātithi (*Bhā. Purāṇa*).

Manojñasvara (S) (M) **1.** with a pleasing voice. **3.** a gandharva (*S. Puṇḍarīka*).

Manojū (S) (M) as swift as thought.

Manojyotis (S) (M) **1.** whose light is the intellect. **2.** extremely intelligent.

Manomātrā (S) (M) **1.** one who can change forms according to will. **3.** another name for Śiva and Viṣṇu.

Manonīta (S) (M) **1.** carried by the mind. **2.** chosen; approved.

Manorāga (S) (M) **1.** the colour of the heart. **2.** affection; passion.

Manorañjana (S) (M) pleasing to the mind.

Manoratha (S) (M) **1.** chariot of the mind. **2.** wish; cherished desire. **3.** a calf created by Kṛṣṇa.

Manota (S) (M) **1.** born of the mind. **3.** the hymn of *Ṛg Veda* (vi) and the deity to whom it is dedicated.

Manotṛ (S) (M) **1.** one who possesses the mind. **2.** an inventor; a discoverer.

Manoyoni (S) (M) **1.** born of the mind. **3.** another name for Kāma.

Manta (S) (M) **1.** thought. **3.** one of the 12 methods of realization.

Mantha (S) (M) **1.** churning; agitating. **3.** another name for the sun.

Manthāna (S) (M) **1.** that which shakes. **3.** Śiva as one who shakes the universe; an asura in the army of Tārakāsura (*M. Purāṇa*).

Mantra (S) (M) **1.** instrument of thought. **2.** vedic hymn; sacred verse; spell; charm. **3.** the 5th lunar mansion; another name for Viṣṇu and Śiva.

Mantramūrti (S) (M) **1.** lord of spells. **3.** another name for Śiva.

Mantrapāla (S) (M) **1.** protector of hymns. **3.** a minister of King Daśaratha (*V. Rāmāyaṇa*).

Mantreśvara (S) (M) **1.** lord of spells. **3.** another name for Śiva.

Mantrin (S) (M) **1.** the knower of hymns. **2.** wise; eloquent; clever in counsel; minister.

Mantu (S) (M) **1.** advisor. **2.** ruler; arbiter; man; mankind.

Mantuṅga (S) (M) high in honour.

Manu (S) (M) **1.** thinking; wise; intelligent. **3.** the man par excellence or the representative man and father of the human race (*Ṛg Veda*), the name Manu is applied to 13 successive mythical progenitors and sovereigns of the earth, each of whom headed a period of time or Antara known as Manvantara, the 1st Manu was Svāyambhuva or 'self-existent' who produced 10 prajāpatis, the 1st being Marīći or light, the next 6 Svāroćiṣa, Auttami, Tāmasa, Raivata, Ćākṣuṣa and Vaivasvata or sunborn, the last is regarded as the progenitor of the human race and the 8th Manu (*V. Purāṇa*); Sāvarṇi as the 1st of the future Manus; a rudra; an agni (*M. Bh.*); the number 14; the son of the agni Pāñćajanya (*M. Bh.*).

Manuga (S) (M) **1.** follower of wishes. **3.** a son of Dyutimat (*Bhā. Purāṇa*).

Manuja (S) (M) **1.** son of Manu. **2.** man.

Manujanātha (S) (M) lord of man.

Manujendra (S) (M) **1.** lord of men. **2.** a king.

Manujeśvara (S) (M) **1.** lord of men. **2.** a king.

Manujottama (S) (M) best among men.

Manujyeṣṭha (S) (M) best of men; eldest among men; a sword.

Manupati (S) (M) **1.** master of man. **2.** a king.

Manurāj (S) (M) **1.** king of men. **3.** another name for Kubera.

Manuṣkulāditya (S) (M) the sun of the family of Manu.

Manuśreṣṭha (S) (M) **1.** best among men. **3.** another name for Viṣṇu.

Manyu (S) (M) **1.** mind; spirit; mood; temper; zeal; passion; rage; anger. **3.** anger personified as a rudra; a king of the Purū dynasty and the son of Bharadvāja (*M. Bh.*); the author of some of the hymns of *Ṛg Veda* (x); a Vedic god produced from the 3rd eye of Śiva (*M. Bh.*); a king and son of Vitatha (*Bhā. Purāṇa*); another name for Agni (*ṚgVeda*).

Manyumān (S) (M) **1.** spiritual; thoughtful; zealous; passionate; angry. **3.** the son of the agni Bhānu (*M. Bh.*).

Manyumata (S) (M) spirited; ardent; passionate; vehement.

Māpatya (S) (M) **1.** not a child. **2.** an adult. **3.** another name for Kāma.

Māra (S) (M) **1.** destroyer; passion. **3.** a form of Śiva (*S. Purāṇa*); an enemy of Buddha and Buddhism; another name for Kāma.

Mārābhibhu (S) (M) **1.** overthrower of Māra. **3.** a Buddha (*H. Koṣa*).

Māraćitta (S) (M) **1.** destroyer of desires. **3.** a Buddhist deity (*B. Literature*).

Mārajit (S) (M) **1.** conqueror of Māra. **3.** the Buddha who overcame Māra, the chief enemy of Buddhists; another name for Śiva.

Marakata (S) (M) the emerald; with properties of an emerald.

Marāla (S) (M) soft; mild; tender.

Maranda (S) (M) nectar.

Marandaka (S) (M) **1.** the abode of nectar. **2.** flower.

Mārāṅka (S) (M) marked by love.

Marasurāma (S) (M) **1.** that which consists of love. **3.** the festival of Vaisakha.

Māravat (S) (M) full of love.

Marāyin (S) (M) destroying enemies.

Mardana (S) (M) **1.** crushing; grinding. **3.** a chief of the vidyadharas.

Mārḍīka (S) (M) mercy; pity; compassion.

Mārgamarṣi (S) (M) **1.** preceptor of the path. **3.** a son of Viśvāmitra (*M. Bh.*).

Mārgin (S) (M) showing the way; pioneer.

Mārgita (S) (M) sought; desired; required.

Mārīća (S) (M) **1.** glowing; the pepper plant. **3.** the son of Śunda and Tāṭakā, the brother of Subāhu and the uncle of Rāvaṇa who transformed himself into a golden deer to lure Rāma away from

Sītā in order to let Rāvaṇa abduct her (*V. Rāmāyaṇa*); a dānava (*U. Rāmāyaṇa*).

Marīci (S) (M) **1.** a ray of light. **3.** a mindborn son of Brahmā and Prājāpati, regarded as the 1st of the 10 lords of creation, as the husband of Kalā he was the father of Kaśyapa and Pūrṇiman, as the husband of Ūrṇā he fathered sons reborn as the 6 elder brothers of Kṛṣṇa and as the husband of Sambhūtī he was the father of Paurṇamāsa; a king who was the son of Samrāj and the father of Bindumat; a son of the Tīrthaṅkara Ṛṣabha (*J. Literature*); a son of Śaṅkarāćārya; a star in the Great Bear constellation; Kṛṣṇa as a marut (*Bhā. Purāṇa*); a daitya (*V. Rāmāyaṇa*); a maharṣi (*V. Purāṇa*).

Marīćimat (S) (M) **1.** with rays; radiant; shining. **3.** another name for the sun.

Māriṣa (S) (M) respectable; worthy.

Mārīya (S) (M) belonging to Kāma.

Mārjāra (S) (M) **1.** cleaning itself; a cat. **3.** a son of Jāmbavān (*V. Rāmāyaṇa*).

Mārjāri (S) (M) **1.** cat; peacock. 3. a son of Sahadeva (*M. Bh.*).

Marka (S) (M) **1.** the mind; eclipse; the vital breath. **3.** a son of Śukra, the purohita of the asuras (*M. Bh.*); a yakṣa; another name for Vāyu.

Mārkaṇḍeya (S) (M) **1.** winning over death. **3.** a sage and descendant of the line of Bhṛgu, the son of Mṛkaṇḍu and Vedaśiras, the husband of Dhūmorṇā and a great devotee of Śiva (*M. Bh.*); a sage and son of the author of *Mārkaṇḍeya Purāṇa* (*M. Bh.*).

Markatamaṇi (S) (M) the emerald.

Mārmika (S) (M) **1.** having a deep insight into; knowing the essence. **2.** very intelligent; perceptive.

Marmit (S) (M) **1.** the vanquisher of Kāma. **3.** another name for Śiva.

Marṣa (S) (M) patience; endurance.

Marṣaṇa (S) (M) **1.** enduring. **2.** patient; for-giving.

Mārṣaka (S) (M) honourable; respectable.

Mārtaṇḍa (S) (M) **1.** sprung from an egg. **2.** bird; bird in the sky. **3.** an āditya; another name for the sun or the god of the sun.

Maru (S) (M) **1.** desert; mountain; rock. **3.** an Ikṣvāku king who was the son of Śīghra, the father of Prasūśruta who became immortal by his yogic power (*Bhā. Purāṇa*); a Videha king of the Nimi dynasty (*Bhā. Parāṇa*); a warrior of Narakāsura killed by Kṛṣṇa (*M. Bh.*); a son of Haryaśva (*V. Rāmāyaṇa*); a vasu (*H. Purāṇa*).

Marudeva (S) (M) **1.** lord of the desert. **3.** the father of the Arhat Ṛṣabha (*J. Literature*).

Marudhanvan (S) (M) **1.** with a bow of rock. **2.** an invincible bow; one who is ever victorious. **3.** the father-in-law of the vidyādhara Indīvara (*M. Purāṇa*).

Marudvartmana (S) (M) **1.** the path of the clouds. **2.** the sky.

Maruga (S) (M) **1.** living in a desert; a peacock; a deer, an antelope. **3.** another name for Kārttikeya.

Marūka (S) (M) from wilderness; a peacock; deer; antelope.

Marula (S) (M) **1.** rock born; born due to blessings of Śiva; a kind of duck. **3.** one of the 5 ascetics who were said to have sprung from the 5 heads of Śiva and who founded the Vara-Śaiva sect (*K. Sāgara*).

Marupati (S) (M) **1.** lord of the desert. **3.** another name for Indra.

Marur (S) (M) **1.** killer; a tiger. **3.** another name for Rāhu.

Marut (S) (M) **1.** the flashing or shining one; wind; air; breeze; breath. **3.** maruts are the storm gods and the companions of Indra, in the Vedas they are depicted as the sons of Rudra and Pṛṣṇi, in later literature they are the sons of Diti and are led by Mātariśvan (*Ṛg Veda*); the god of wind, the father of Hanumān and the regent of the northwest quarter (*M. Bh.*).

Māruta (S) (M) **1.** breath; wind; air; belonging to the maruts; belonging to the wind; a son of the maruts. **3.** another name for Viṣṇu and Rudra.

Mārutantavya (S) (M) **1.** pervading in the wind. **2.** one who is very popular. **3.** a son of Viśvāmitra (*M. Bh.*).

Marutapāla (S) (M) **1.** protector of the maruts. **3.** another name for Indra.

Marutapati (S) (M) **1.** lord of maruts. **3.** another name for Indra.

Marutaputra (S) (M) **1.** son of the wind god. **3.** another name for Bhīma and Hanumān.

Mārutāśana (S) (M) **1.** feeding on the wind alone. **2.** one who does not consume anything; everfasting. **3.** one of Skanda's attendants (*Brah. Parāṇa*); a dānava (*H. Purāṇa*).

Mārutātmaja (S) (M) **1.** son of the wind. **3.** another name for Agni, Bhīma and Hanumān.

Māruti (S) (M) **1.** son of the wind. **3.** another name for Hanumān, Bhīma and Dyutāna.

Marutta (S) (M) **1.** wind; gale. **3.** a king who was the son of Karandhama, a member of Yama's assembly and considered one of the 5 great emperors (*M. Bh.*); a sage of ancient India (*M. Bh.*).

Maruttama (S) (M) as swift as the maruts.

Marutvān **1.** lord of the winds. **3.** another name for Indra.

Marutvat (S) (M) **1.** attended by the maruts; a cloud. **3.** a son of Dharma by Marutvatī (*Bhā. Purāṇa*); another name for Indra and Hanumān.

Maśāl (S) (M) torch.

Masāra (S) (M) sapphire; emerald.

Maskarin (S) (M) one who moves; a wanderer; a vagabond; a religious mendicant; the moon.

Masṛṇita (S) (M) softened; smoothed.

Mastaka (S) (M) **1.** head; skull; top; summit. **3.** a form of Śiva (*S. Samgraha*).

Mata (S) (M) **1.** thought; understood; honoured; desired; liked. **3.** a son of Śambara (*H. Purāṇa*).

Mātali (S) (M) **1.** charioteer. **3.** Indra's charioteer who was the son of Śamīka and Tapasvinī (*K. Granthīvali*).

Mātalisārathi (S) (M) **1.** with Mātali as his charioteer. **3.** another name for Indra.

Mātaṅga (S) (M) **1.** roaming at will; a cloud. **2.** the chief or best of its kind; an elephant; the Bodhi tree (*Ficus religiosa*). **3.** the servant of the 7th and 24th Arhat of the present Avasarpiṇī (*H. Koṣa*); a preceptor who was the guru of Śabarī (*V. Rāmāyaṇa*); a sage (*V. Rāmāyaṇa*); a nāga (*M. Bh.*); a dānava (*H. Purāṇa*).

Mātariśvan (S) (M) **1.** growing in the firestick. **3.** Agni or a divine messenger of Vivasvata who brought down the hidden fire to the Bhṛgus and is identified with Vāyu (*Ṛg Veda*); a son of Garuḍa (*Ṛg Veda*); a ṛṣi; another name for Śiva.

Māṭhara (S) (M) **1.** traveller; churner. **3.** a demigod deputed by Indra to serve Sūrya (*Bh. Purāṇa*).

Mathin (S) (M) **1.** churning stick. **2.** wind; thunderbolt.

Mathita (S) (M) **1.** produced by churning. **3.** a decendant of Yama and the author of *Ṛg Veda* (x).

Māthura (S) (M) **1.** coming from Mathurā. **3.** a son of Ćitragupta.

Mathurānātha (S) (M) **1.** lord of the city of Mathurā. **3.** another name for Kṛṣṇa.

Mathureśa (S) (M) **1.** lord of Mathurā. **3.** another name for Kṛṣṇa.

Matigarbha (S) (M) **1.** filled with intelligence. **2.** extremely intelligent.

Matila (S) (M) **1.** intelligent. **3.** a king (*M. Bh.*).

Matimat (S) (M) **1.** wise. **3.** a son of Janamejaya (*M. Bh.*).

Matināra (S) (M) **1.** possessing intellect. **3.** a Purū king who was the son of Kṛteyu, the father of Santurodha and Pratiratha and the grandfather of Duṣyanta (*M. Bh.*).

Matīśvara (S) (M) **1.** lord of the mind. **2.** wisest of all. **3.** another name for Viśvakarman.

Mātṛćeta (S) (M) one who knows and honours the mother.

Mātṛdatta (S) (M) **1.** given by the Mātṛs. **2.** given by the divine mothers.

Mātṛnandana (S) (M) **1.** joy of the Mātṛs; son of Mātṛs. **3.** another name for Skanda.

Matṛviṣṇu (S) (M) Lakṣmī and Viṣṇu conjoined.

Matsya (S) (M) **1.** fish; the zodiac sign of Pisces. **3.** a pupil of Devamitra; the 1st incarnation of Mahāviṣṇu (*V. Purāṇa*); another name for Virāṭa who was found with his sister Satyavatī or Matsyā in the body of a fish.

Matsyakāla (S) (M) **1.** destroyer of fish; fish eater. **3.** a Purū king born to Girikā (*M. Bh.*).

Matsyapati (S) (M) **1.** king of Matsya. **3.** another name for Virāta.

Matsyarāja (S) (M) **1.** lord of Matsya. **3.** another name for Virāta.

Matsyāvatāra (S) (M) **1.** fish incarnation. **3.** the 1st incarnation of Viṣṇu (*V. Rāmāyaṇa*).

Matsyendranātha (S) (M) **1.** lord of the fish. **3.** the founder of the Nātha order of yogins and whose 2 sons were the founders of Jainism (*J.S. Koṣa*).

Matta (S) (M) **1.** intoxicated. **2.** excited; proud. **3.** a demon who was the son of Mālyavān and Sundarī (*A. Purāṇa*).

Matthara (S) (M) **1.** traveller; a churner; a Brāhmin. **3.** a disciple of Paraśurāma; an attendant of the sun (*M. Bh.*); another name for Vyāsa.

Maudgalya (S) (M) **1.** of Mudgala; with pleasant speech. **3.** a mahāṛṣi who cursed Rāvaṇa (*K. Rāmāyaṇa*).

Mauli (S) (M) **1.** the head; chief. **2.** foremost; best; diadem; crown.

Maulimaṇi (S) (M) crest gem.

Mauliratna (S) (M) crest gem.

Mauñjāyana (S) (M) **1.** winner of the sacred thread. **2.** chaste; pious. **3.** a mahāṛṣi in the court of Yudhiṣṭhira (*M. Bh.*).

Māvella (S) (M) **1.** a good speaker. **3.** a son of Uparićaravasu of Ćedi (*M. Bh.*).

Maya (S) (M) **1.** illusion; architect. **2.** a builder. **3.** a dānava who served the devas and the asuras, as their architect and builder, the son of Kaśyapa and Danu, the husband of the apsarā Hemā, the father of Māyāvi and Dundubhi and the father of Mandodarī and Somaprabhā and Svayamprabhā (*Bhā. Purāṇa*).

Mayabaṭṭu (S) (M) **1.** possessed of illusory wind. **2.** with a false pride. **3.** a king of the Śabaras (*K. Sāgara*).

Māyādhara (S) (M) **1.** possessing illusion; possessing wealth. **3.** a king of the asuras killed by Purūravas (*K. Sāgara*).

Māyāmṛga (S) (M) **1.** illusory deer. **3.** the golden deer which was a form of Mārīća (*V. Rāmāyaṇa*).

Māyaṇa (S) (M) **1.** detached from wealth. **3.** the father of Mādhava and Sāyaṇa.

Mayanka (S) (M) **1.** deer marked. **3.** another name for the moon.

Māyāpati (S) (M) **1.** lord of illusion. **3.** another name for Viṣṇu.

Mayas (S) (M) refreshment; enjoyment; pleasure; delight.

Mayāsura (S) (M) the asura Maya.

Māyāvāṇi (S) (M) **1.** with a magical voice. **3.** a vidyādhara (*B. Rāmāyaṇa*).

Māyāvin (S) (M) **1.** lord of illusion. **3.** an asura who was the son of Maya and Hemā (*K. Rāmāyaṇa*).

Mayeśvara (S) (M) **1.** lord of illusion. **3.** another name for the asura Maya.

Mayil (Malayalam) (M) peacock.

Māyin (S) (M) **1.** illusionary; skilled in the art of enchantment. **3.** the Supreme Being as the illusionist who created the universe (*Ṛg Veda*); another name for Brahmā, Śiva, Agni and Kāma.

Māyu (S) (M) lowing; roaring; bellowing; magician; celestial musician; a deer.

Mayūkha (S) (M) **1.** ray of light. **2.** brightness; lustre; a flame.

Mayūkhamālin (S) (M) **1.** wreathed with rays. **3.** another name for the sun.

Mayūkheśa (S) (M) **1.** lord of rays. **3.** another name for the sun.

Mayūkhin (S) (M) radiant; brilliant.

Mayūra (S) (M) **1.** peacock. **3.** an asura who fought against Skanda (*Sk. Purāṇa*); Celery (*Apium graveolen*).

Mayūradhvaja (S) (M) **1.** peacock bannered. **3.** a king of Ratnanagara who was blessed by Kṛṣṇa (*Bhā. Purāṇa*); another name for Kārttikeya.

Mayūraja (S) (M) **1.** born of a peacock. **3.** the king of the kinnaras (*H. Purāṇa*); another name for Kubera.

Māyurāja (S) (M) **1.** lord of sorcery. **3.** a son of Kubera.

Mayūraketu (S) (M) **1.** peacock bannered. **3.** another name for Kārttikeya.

Mayūrākṣa (S) (M) peacock eyed.

Mayūraratha (S) (M) **1.** with a peacock as a vehicle. **3.** another name for Skanda.

Mayūravarman (S) (M) protector of peacocks.

Māyus (S) (M) **1.** detached from life. **2.** a good warrior. **3.** a son of Purūravas (*M. Bh.*).

Mećaka (S) (M) **1.** the eye of the peacock's tail. **2.** a gem; a cloud; the colour deep blue.

Mećakagala (S) (M) **1.** blue necked. **2.** peacock. **3.** another name for Śiva.

Meda (S) (M) **1.** fat; the *Sphaeranthus indicus* herb; a mixed caste. **3.** a serpent of the clan of Airāvata (*M. Bh.*).

Medhāćakra (S) (M) the circle of wisdom; yoga.

Medhādhṛti (S) (M) **1.** bearer of wisdom. **3.** a ṛṣi of the 9th Manvantara.

Medhājit (S) (M) **1.** victor of intelligence. **3.** another name for sage Kātyāyana.

Medhas (S) (M) **1.** sacrifice; sacrificial animal; broth. **3.** a ṛṣi (*V. Samhitā*); a son of Priyavrata (*Bhā. Purāṇa*); a son of Manu Svāyambhuva (*H. Purāṇa*).

Medhātithi (S) (M) **1.** the guest of wisdom; the host of wisdom. **2.** very wise. **3.** one of the 7 sages under Manu Sāvarṇa (*H. Purāṇa*); a son of Priyavrata and Surūpā and the king of Plakṣadvīpa (*Purāṇas*); a sage who was the son of Kaṇva and the father of Duṣyanta and Pravīra (*M. Bh.*); a sage who was the father of Arundhatī and the father-in-law of Vasiṣṭha (*K. Purāṇa*); a river which is the birthplace of Agni (*M. Bh.*); the father of Kaṇva (*M. Bh.*); a son of Manu Svāyambhuva (*H. Purāṇa*).

Medhāvat (S) (M) intelligent; wise.

Medhāvi (S) (M) **1.** intelligent; wise. **3.** a sage who was the son of Bāladhi (*M. Bh.*).

Medhāvin (S) (M) **1.** learned man. **3.** a king who was the son of Sutapas and the father of Nṛpañjaya (*V. Purāṇa*); a son of Bhavya (*M. Purāṇa*).

Medhira (S) (M) wise; intelligent.

Medhyātithi (S) (M) **1.** host of intelligence. **3.** a ṛṣi and part author of *Ṛg Veda* (viii).

Medinīja (S) (M) **1.** son of the earth. **3.** another name for Mars.

Medinīpati (S) (M) **1.** master of the earth. **2.** a king.

Medinīśa (S) (M) **1.** lord of the earth. **2.** a king.

Megha (S) (M) **1.** sprinkler. **2.** cloud; mass. **3.** a rāga; a rākṣasa; the father of the 5th Arhat of the present Avasarpinī.

Meghabhūti (S) (M) **1.** cloud born. **2.** a thunderbolt.

Meghaćintaka (S) (M) **1.** anxious for rain clouds. **3.** another name for the Ćataka or the Pied Crested Cuckoo (*Clamator jacobinus scrratus*).

Meghadahunna (S) (M) **1.** music of the clouds; sound of the clouds. **3.** a king of the solar race who was a descendant of Lava; a rāga.

Meghaḍambara (S) (M) **1.** cloud drum. **2.** the thunder.

Meghadīpa (S) (M) **1.** light of the cloud. **2.** the lightning.

Meghadūta (S) (M) **1.** cloud messenger. **3.** a poem by Kālidāsa.

Meghadvāra (S) (M) **1.** cloud gate. **2.** heaven; sky.

Meghahāsa (S) (M) **1.** laugh of the clouds. **2.** one who laughs loudly. **3.** a son of Rāhu (*Br. Purāṇa*).

Meghajanaka (S) (M) father of the clouds.

Meghajyoti (S) (M) **1.** light of the clouds. **2.** a flash of lightning.

Meghamāla (S) (M) **1.** crowned with clouds. **3.** a rākṣasa captain of the army of Khara (*V.Rāmāyaṇa*); one of the 2 attendants given to Skanda by Mahāmeru (*M. Bh.*); a son of Kalki (*K. Purāṇa*); a mountain.

Meghamālin (S) (M) **1.** cloud wreathed. **3.** an attendant of Skanda (*M. Bh.*); an asura (*S. Mahātmya*).

Meghanāda (S) (M) **1.** noise of the clouds. **2.** the thunder. **3.** a son of Rāvaṇa and Mandodarī also called Indrajit (*V. Rāmāyaṇa*); one of Skanda's attendants (*M. Bh.*); a daitya (*V. Rāmāyaṇa*); another name for Varuṇa.

Meghanādajita (S) (M) **1.** conqueror of Meghanāda. **3.** another name for Lakṣmaṇa.

Meghānanda (S) (M) rejoicing in clouds; a peacock.

Meghanīla (S) (M) **1.** a blue cloud. **3.** a gaṇa of Śiva (*H. Purāṇa*).

Meghapravāha (S) (M) **1.** flowing like the clouds. **3.** an attendant of Skanda (*H. Purāṇa*).

Meghapṛṣtha (S) (M) **1.** supported by the clouds. **2.** very powerful. **3.** the son of Ghṛtapṛṣṭha (*Bhā. Purāṇa*).

Meghapuṣpa (S) (M) **1.** cloud flower. **2.** the rainwater. **3.** one of the 4 horses of Viṣṇu-Kṛṣṇa (*M. Bh.*).

Megharāga (S) (M) **1.** the essence of clouds. **3.** a rāga.

Megharāja (S) (M) **1.** lord of the clouds. **3.** a Buddha (*L. Vistara*); another name for Viṣṇu.

Megharatha (S) (M) **1.** with a cloud chariot. **3.** a vidyādhara (*H. Purāṇa*).

Meghasandhi (S) (M) **1.** confluence of clouds. **3.** a prince of Magadha and the grandson of Jarāsandha (*M. Bh.*).

Meghaśarman (S) (M) **1.** best among the clouds. **3.** a Brāhmin and devotee of Sūrya in the court of Śantanu (*Bh. Purāṇa*).

Meghasvara (S) (M) **1.** one who sounds like the clouds. **2.** the thunder. **3.** a Buddha (*B. Literature*).

Meghasvararāja (S) (M) **1.** lord of thunder. **3.** a Buddha.

Meghasvāti (S) (M) **1.** conjoined of clouds and the star arcturus. **3.** a king (*Purāṇas*).

Meghavāhana (S) (M) **1.** cloud vehicled. **3.** a king and dependant of Jarāsandha (*M. Bh.*); another name for Śiva and Indra.

Meghavahni (S) (M) **1.** cloud fire. **2.** the lightning.

Meghavarṇa (S) (M) **1.** cloud coloured. **2.** dark complexioned. **3.** a son of Ghaṭotkaća (*M. Bh.*); Black Plum (*Eugenia jambolana*).

Meghavāśas (S) (M) **1.** clad in clouds. **3.** an asura in Varuṇa's court (*M. Bh.*).

Meghavega (S) (M) **1.** with the speed of clouds. **2.** very swift; agile. **3.** a brave warrior in the Kaurava army (*M. Bh.*).

Meghayāti (S) (M) **1.** cloud bearer. **3.** a king (*V. Purāṇa*).

Mehula (S) (M) rain.

Mekala (S) (M) **1.** knower of the self. **3.** a ṛṣi and father of the river Narmadā (*V. Purāṇa*); another name for the mountain Amarakaṇṭaka in the Vindhyas which is the source of the Narmadā.

Mekhalāla (S) (M) **1.** wearing a girdle. **3.** another name for Śiva-Rudra (*H. Purāṇa*).

Mekhalin (S) (M) **1.** wearing a girdle; wearing a sacred thread; a brahmaćārin. **3.** another name for Śiva.

Mena (S) (M) **1.** one who knows. **3.** Vṛṣṇāśva who was the father of Menā or Menakā (*Shadvinsa Brāhmaṇa*).

Menādhava (S) (M) **1.** lover of intellect; the husband of Menā. **3.** another name for Himavān.

Mendha (S) (M) **1.** wise; learned. **3.** a Sanskṛt poet and the author of *Hastipāka* (5th century A.D.).

Meru (S) (M) **1.** high; principle; union. **2.** the central bead in a rosary, the main gem of a necklace. **3.** a fabulous mountain regarded as the Olympus of Hindu mythology, all the planets revolve around it, the Gaṅgā falls from heaven on its summit, the whole mountain is covered with gems, its summit is the residence of Brahmā and its 4 quarters are guarded by the regents, it is a place of meeting for all the divine beings (*Purāṇas*).

Merudhāman (S) (M) **1.** dweller of the mountain Meru. **3.** another name for Śiva (*M. Bh.*).

Merudhvaja (S) (M) **1.** having a high flag. **2.** a renowned ruler. **3.** a ćakravartin (*K. Sāgara*).

Meruka (S) (M) incense.

Merukuta (S) (M) **1.** the summit of Meru. **3.** a Buddha.

Merunanda (S) (M) **1.** one who pleases the mountain. **2.** pleaser of mountains; pleaser of the masses; a son of Svāroćiṣa (*M. Purāṇa*).

Merusāvarṇi (S) (M) **1.** with high thoughts; like the Meru. **3.** the 11th Manu and father of Svayamprabhā (*V. Rāmāyaṇa*).

Meruśrīgarbha (S) (M) **1.** as high in glory as the Meru. **3.** a Boddhisattva (*B. Literature*).

Meṣa (S) (M) **1.** goat; ram; sheep. **3.** Indra in his form as a goat which he assumed to drink the Soma of sage Medhātithi (*Ṛg Veda*); a soldier of Skanda (*M. Bh.*); the zodiac sign of Aries.

Meṣahṛt (S) (M) **1.** sheep thief. **3.** a son of Garuḍa (*M. Bh.*).

Meva (S) (M) to worship; praise.

Mevalāla (S) (M) a praiseworthy son; a devoted son.

Mīdhuṣa (S) (M) **1.** bountiful. **3.** a son of Indra and Paulomī (*Ṛg Veda*).

Mīdhuṣṭama (S) (M) **1.** most liberal. **3.** another name for the sun.

Mīdhvān (S) (M) **1.** bestowing richly; bountiful; liberal. **3.** another name for Śiva.

Mihikānśu (S) (M) **1.** mist rayed. **2.** the moon.

Mihira (S) (M) **1.** causing heat, light and rain. **2.** the sun; the moon; cloud; wind; air; a sage.

Mihirakula (S) (M) **1.** born in the solar dynasty. **3.** a king (*R. Taraṅginī*).

Mihirāṇa (S) (M) **1.** born of the sun; having sun as one of the testicles. **3.** another name for Śiva.

Milana (S) (M) union; meeting; contract.

Milāp (S) (M) embrace.

Milinda (S) (M) **1.** wanting an encounter. **2.** the bee which looks for an encounter with the flowers. **3.** the King Menander (*B. Literature*).

Mīnaketana (S) (M) **1.** fish bannered. **3.** another name for Kāma.

Mīnaratha (S) (M) **1.** with a fish shaped chariot. **3.** a king (*V. Purāṇa*).

Mīneśvara (S) (M) **1.** lord of the fish. **3.** another name for Śiva.

Minna (S) (M) fat.

Mirata (S) (M) a mirror.

Miśraka (S) (M) **1.** mixed; various; manifold. **3.** Indra's garden of paradise (*M. Bh.*).

Misri (S) (M) **1.** mixed; sweet. **3.** a serpent who was among those that carried Balarāma's soul to Pātāla (*M. Bh.*).

Mita (S) (M) **1.** one who has been measured; which is frugal; little; short; brief; firm; founded; established. **2.** a friend. **3.** a ṛṣi of the 3rd Manvantara (*V. Purāṇa*).

Mitadhvaja (S) (M) **1.** with a strong flag. **3.** a king of Videha and son of Dharmadhvaja Janaka (*Bhā. Purāṇa*).

Mithi (S) (M) **1.** knowledged; truthful. **3.** the son of King Nimi, considered to be the epitome of perfection and the founder of Mithilā (*V. Rāmāyaṇa*).

Mithilādhipa (S) (M) **1.** lord of Mithilā. **3.** another name for Janaka.

Mithileśa (S) (M) lord of Mithilā.

Mithileśvara (S) (M) **1.** lord of Mithilā. **3.** another name for Janaka.

Mithu (S) (M) **1.** falsely; wrongly. **3.** a dānava (*Brahma Purāṇa*).

Mithuna (S) (M) forming a pair; a small statue at the entrance of a temple; the zodiac sign of Gemini; honey and clarified butter.

Miti (S) (M) correct perception.

Mitra (S) (M) **1.** friend; companion; associate. **3.** an āditya and one of the 12 Suryās born of Kaśyapa and Aditi, the father of Utsarga, a member of the court of Indra, the deity of the constellation Anurādhā, generally evoked with Varuṇa and Aryaman and described in the *Ṛg Veda* as the sustainer of the earth and the sky and the beholder of all with an unblinking eye; a follower of Lākuliṣa who founded the Paśupata cult; a son of Vasiṣṭha (*Purāṇas*); a marut (*H. Purāṇa*).

Mitrabāhu (S) (M) **1.** helped by friends. **3.** a son of the 12th Manu (*H. Purāṇa*); a son of Kṛṣṇa (*H. Purāṇa*).

Mitradeva (S) (M) **1.** lord of friends. **3.** the brother of King Suśarmā of Trigarta (*M. Bh.*); a son of the 12th Manu (*H. Purāṇa*); another name for the sun.

Mitradharman (S) (M) **1.** with faith in friends. **3.** a rākṣasa (*V. Rāmāyaṇa*); a son of Divodāsa (*V. Purāṇa*); a son of Agni Pāñćajanya.

Mitraghna (S) (M) **1.** killer of friends. **3.** a rākṣasa (*V. Rāmāyaṇa*); a son of Divodāsa (*V. Purāṇa*).

Mitragupta (S) (M) protected by friends.

Mitrajña (S) (M) **1.** knower of friends; knower of the sun. **3.** a son of the agni Pāñćajanya (*M. Bh.*).

Mitrajit (S) (M) **1.** winning friends. **3.** a son of Suvarṇa (*V. Purāṇa*).

Mitrakṛt (S) (M) **1.** friend maker. **3.** a son of the 12th Manu (*H. Purāṇa*).

Mitrasāha (S) (M) **1.** indulgent towards friends. **3.** a king (*M. Bh.*).

Mitrasakhā (S) (M) **1.** a friend of friends; a friend of the sun. **3.** a king of the solar race also known as Kalmāṣapāda (*M. Bh.*).

Mitrasena (S) (M) **1.** with an army of friends; with an army as glorious as the sun. **3.** a king in the army of the Kauravas (*M. Bh.*); a gandharva (*H. Purāṇa*); a son of the 12th Manu (*H. Purāṇa*); a grandson of Kṛṣṇa (*H. Purāṇa*); a king of the Draviḍa country (*H. Purāṇa*); a Buddhist monk.

Mitravāha (S) (M) **1.** attracting friends. **2.** sun charioted. **3.** a son of the 12th Manu (*H. Purāṇa*).

Mitravān (S) (M) **1.** having friends. **2.** one who knows the sun. **3.** a son of the agni Pāñćajanya (*M. Bh.*); an ascetic and devotee of Śiva (*P. Purāṇa*).

Mitravardhana (S) (M) **1.** cherished by friends. **3.** a son of the agni Pāñćajanya (*M. Bh.*).

Mitravarman (S) (M) warrior among friends; as protective as the sun.

Mitrāvaruṇa (S) (M) **1.** Mitra and Varuṇa conjoined. **3.** together Mitra and Varuṇa are the lords of truth and light upholding religious rites and the rules of the world, conjoined they become the deity bestowing plentiful rain (*Ṛg Veda*).

Mitravat (S) (M) **1.** having friends. **3.** a son of the 12th Manu (*M. Purāṇa*); a son of Kṛṣṇa (*H. Purāṇa*).

Mitravinda (S) (M) **1.** possessor of friends. **3.** a son of the 12th Manu (*H. Purāṇa*); a son of Kṛṣṇa (*H. Purāṇa*); a deva (*M. Bh.*); an agni (*M. Bh.*).

Mitrayu (S) (M) **1.** friendly. **2.** attractive; prudent. **3.** a son of Divodāsa and the father of Ćyavana (*H. Purāṇa*).

Mitrodaya (S) (M) sunrise.

Mitula (S) (M) **1.** measured. **2.** limited; moderate.

Moda (S) (M) **1.** pleasure; enjoyment; joy; fragrance. **3.** a serpent of the clan of Airāvata (*M. Bh.*); a rākṣasa (*M. Bh.*).

Modaka (S) (M) **1.** pleasing; delighting. **2.** a sweetmeat.

Modakara (S) (M) **1.** one who accomplishes joy; full of joy, delighted. **3.** a ṛṣi (*V. Rāmāyaṇa*).

Moha (S) (M) **1.** infatuation; confusion ignorance. **3.** a son of Brahmā born of his lustre (*Bhā. Purāṇa*).

Mohaka (S) (M) **1.** causing infatuation. **2.** attractive. **3.** a son of Suratha (*P. Purāṇa*).

Mohana (S) (M) **1.** infatuating. **2.** confusing; bewildering. **3.** one of the 5 arrows of Kāma (*K. Sāgara*); another name for Śiva and Kṛṣṇa.

Mohanadāsa (S) (M) devotee of Kṛṣṇa.

Mohanalāla (S) (M) the youthful Kṛṣṇa.

Mohantara (S) (M) very infatuating.

Mohī (S) (M) **1.** deluded. **3.** another name for Kāma.

Mohin (S) (M) **1.** deluding; fascinating. **2.** confusing; perplexing; illusive.

Mohita (S) (M) **1.** infatuated. **2.** bewitched; intoxicated by love.

Mokṣa (S) (M) **1.** salvation; final emancipation. **3.** another name for Mount Meru.

Mokṣadvāra (S) (M) **1.** gate of emancipation. **3.** another name for the sun.

Mokṣin (S) (M) free; liberated.

Mokṣita (S) (M) set free; liberated.

Moṇa (S) (M) dry fruit; a kind of fly; a snake-carrying basket.

Monal (S) (M) bird.

Mora (S) (M) peacock.

Morara (S) (M) peacock.

Motī (S) (M) pearl.

Motiā (S) (M) jasmine.

Mṛḍa (S) (M) **1.** compassionate; gracious. **3.** another name for Śiva.

Mṛdākara (S) (M) a thunderbolt.

Mṛdaṅgaketu (S) (M) **1.** drum-bannered. **3.** another name for Yudhiṣṭhira.

Mṛḍanīśvara (S) (M) **1.** lord of Pārvatī. **3.** another name for Śiva.

Mṛdūbhāva (S) (M) softness; mildness.

Mṛdugāmin (S) (M) with a gentle gait.

Mṛdugir (S) (M) soft voiced.

Mṛdula (S) (M) **1.** soft; tender; mild. **2.** water.

Mṛdura (S) (M) **1.** water born; an aquatic animal. **3.** a son of Śvaphalka (*H. Purāṇa*).

Mṛdūtpāla (S) (M) the Soft Lotus (*Nymphaea cyanea*).

Mṛduvāta (S) (M) a gentle breeze.

Mṛduvid (S) (M) **1.** gentle. **3.** a son of Śvaphalka (*H. Purāṇa*).

Mṛgad (S) (M) **1.** animal devourer. **2.** a tiger.

Mṛgadhara (S) (M) **1.** with deer like marks. **2.** the moon.

Mṛgādhipa (S) (M) **1.** lord of animals. **2.** the lion.

Mṛgādhirāja (S) (M) **1.** lord of animals. **2.** the lion.

Mṛgadṛśa (S) (M) **1.** fawn eyed. **2.** the zodiac sign of Capricorn.

Mṛgaja (S) (M) **1.** son of the moon. **3.** another name for Mercury.

Mṛgalakṣaṇa (S) (M) deer marked; the moon.

Mṛgalāñĉana (S) (M) **1.** son of the moon. **3.** another name for the planet Mercury.

Mṛgaloĉana (S) (M) doe eyed; the moon.

Mṛganetra (S) (M) **1.** fawn eyed. **2.** born under the constellation Mṛga or Capricorn.

Mṛgāṅka (S) (M) **1.** deer marked. **2.** the moon; the wind; camphor.

Mṛgāṅkabandhu (S) (M) **1.** friend of the moon. **3.** another name for Kāma.

Mṛgāṅkamauli (S) (M) **1.** moon crested. **3.** another name for Śiva.

Mṛgapiplu (S) (M) **1.** deer marked. **2.** the moon.

Mṛgaprabhu (S) (M) **1.** lord of beasts. **2.** the lion.

Mṛgāra (S) (M) **1.** knower of animals. **2.** knower of the zodiac sign of Capricorn; an astrologer. **3.** a sage and author of *Atharva Veda* (iv); a minister of Prasenajit (*M. Bh.*).

Mṛgarāja (S) (M) **1.** king of beasts. **2.** the lion; the zodiac sign of Leo. **3.** another name for the moon.

Mṛgaratha (S) (M) **1.** with a chariot drawn by deer. **3.** a king of Ayodhyā and the father of the Jaina Tīrathankara Sumatinātha.

Mṛgāri (S) (M) enemy of deer; the lion.

Mṛgaripu (S) (M) **1.** enemy of deer. **2.** the lion; the zodiac sign of Leo.

Mṛgāśana (S) (M) **1.** one who eats deer. **3.** the lion.

Mṛgaśīrṣa (S) (M) **1.** born under the constellation Mṛgaśiras. **3.** a nāga (*K. Vyūha*).

Mṛgasya (S) (M) **1.** the zodiac sign of Capricorn. **3.** another name for Śiva.

Mṛgaṭaṅka (S) (M) **1.** deer marked. **3.** another name for the moon.

Mṛgavadhū (S) (M) fawn; doe.

Mṛgavāhana (S) (M) **1.** deer vehicled. **3.** another name for Vāyu.

Mṛgavyādha (S) (M) **1.** deer hunter. **3.** name assumed by Śiva when he went to test Paraśurāma's devotion; one of the 11 rudras (*M. Bh.*); a marut (*M. Bh.*); the dog star Sirius.

Mṛgayu (S) (M) **1.** living on hunting. **2.** a hunter. **3.** another name for Brahmā.

Mṛgendra (S) (M) **1.** king of beasts. **2.** the lion; the zodiac sign of Leo.

Mṛgīndra (S) (M) **1.** lord of animals. **2.** the lion; the tiger; the zodiac sign of Leo; the moon.

Mṛkaṇḍu (S) (M) **1.** conqueror of death.

Mṛṇāla (S) (M) **1.** liable to be crushed. **2.** the root of a lotus; the lotus fibre.

Mṛṇālin (S) (M) **1.** a lotus. **2.** fragrant; tender; sacred; venerated; dear to the gods.

Mṛṇmaya (S) (M) made of the earth.

Mṛtaṇḍa (S) (M) **1.** illuminating; glorious; enlightening. **3.** the father of the sun (*A. Koṣa*).

Mṛtyu (S) (M) **1.** death. **3.** death personified as a son of Adharma by Nirṛti, sometimes reckoned as a son of Brahmā or Kālī and one of the 11 rudras.

Mṛtyuṁjaya (S) (M) **1.** overcoming death. **3.** another name for Śiva.

Mṛtyuvañćana (S) (M) **1.** one who cheats death. **3.** another name for Śiva.

Mućilinda (S) (M) **1.** the tree *Pterospermum suberifotium.* **3.** a nāga who sheltered the Buddha in a storm; a ćakravartin; a mountain.

Mućira (S) (M) **1.** generous. **2.** liberal; virtuous; the wind; a deity.

Mućukunda (S) (M) **1.** *Pterospermum suberifolium*; cloud. **3.** a king of the solar dynasty who was the son of Māndhātṛ and is listed among those kings who should be remembered morning and evening (*M. Bh.*); a son of Yadu (*H. Purāṇa*); a daitya.

Mudābhāja (S) (M) **1.** desirer of happiness. **3.** a son of Prajāti (*V's B. Samhitā*).

Mudānvita (S) (M) **1.** pleased; delighted. **2.** filled with joy.

Mudāvarta (S) (M) **1.** surrounded by happiness. **3.** a Hehaya king (*M. Bh.*).

Muddayā (S) (M) to be happy; to delight.

Mudgala (S) (M) **1.** ever happy; enchanting; a bean eater; a species of grass; a hammer. **3.** a serpent of the family of Takṣaka (*M. Bh.*); a sage Purāṇic fame who was known for never being provoked into anger (*M. Bh.*); a ṛṣi and an author of *Ṛg Veda* (x); a disciple of Śākalya (*V. Purāṇa*); a son of Viśvāmitra (*M. Bh.*).

Mudgara (S) (M) **1.** hammer. **3.** a nāga (*M. Bh.*).

Mudgarapiṇḍaka (S) (M) **1.** with hammer like knobs. **3.** a serpent born to Kaśyapa and Kadru (*M. Bh.*).

Mudra (S) (M) joyous; glad.

Mugdhamaya (S) (M) full of happiness.

Mugdhānana (S) (M) with a lovely face.

Mugdhendu (S) (M) the lovely moon; the new moon.

Muhira (S) (M) **1.** bewilderer. **3.** another name for Kāma.

Muhūrta (S) (M) **1.** moment; instant. **3.** a period of 48 minutes personified as the children of Muhūrtā and Dharma or Manu (*H. Purāṇa*).

Mūka (S) (M) **1.** silent. **3.** a serpent of the family of Takṣaka (*M. Bh.*); an asura killed by Arjuna (*M. Bh.*).

Mūkakarṇi (S) (M) **1.** deaf. **3.** a follower of Skanda (*M. Bh.*).

Mukeśa (S) (M) **1.** lord of liberation. **2.** another name for Śiva.

Mukhaćandra (S) (M) **1.** moon face. **2.** with a face like the moon.

Mukhaja (S) (M) **1.** born of the mouth. **2.** a Brāhmin who is considered to have been born from the mouth of Brahmā.

Mukhakamala (S) (M) **1.** lotus face. **2.** with a face like a lotus.

Mukhara (S) (M) **1.** talkative; verbose. **3.** a serpent of the family of Kaśyapa (*M. Bh.*).

Mukhendu (S) (M) **1.** moon like face. **2.** with a face as lovely as the moon.

Mukta (S) (M) **1.** freed; emancipated; delivered; opened; a pearl. **3.** a sage under Manu Bhautya (*M. Bh.*); a river (*V. Purāṇa*).

Muktaćetas (S) (M) with a liberated soul.

Muktaguṇa (S) (M) qualities of a pearl.

Muktānanda (S) (M) the joy of liberation.

Muktāphala (S) (M) **1.** the fruit of the Lavali plant; Custard Apple (*Annona reticulata*). **2.** camphor; a pearl. **3.** a king of the Śabaras (*K. Sāgara*).

Muktāphalaketu (S) (M) **1.** with a banner of pearls. **3.** a king of the vidyādharas (*K. Sāgara*).

Muktapīḍa (S) (M) **1.** crowned with pearls. **3.** a king (*R. Taraṅgiṇī*).

Muktapuṣpa (S) (M) pearl flower; *Jasminum multiflorum.*

Muktāratna (S) (M) pearl gem.

Muktāsena (S) (M) **1.** with a free army. **3.** a king of the vidyādharas (*K. Sāgara*).

Muktāsraj (S) (M) a chaplet of pearls.

Mukteśa (S) (M) lord of emancipation.

Mukula (S) (M) **1.** bud. **2.** covered; body; soul; closed; hidden. **3.** a king of the Purū dynasty who was a son of King Bāhyāśva and the father of Pañćāśva (*A. Purāṇa*); *Mimusops elengi.*

Mukulita (S) (M) full of blossoms.

Mukunda (S) (M) **1.** precious stone; one who liberates. **3.** one of the 9 treasures of Kubera (*Mā. Purāṇa*); another name for Viṣṇu-Kṛṣṇa.

Mukundapriya (S) (M) **1.** one who enjoys gems; a devotee of Viṣṇu. **3.** the son of Gadādhara and father of Rāmānanda.

Mukura (S) (M) **1.** mirror; bud. **2.** a bud; a blossom; Indian Medlar tree (*Mimusops elengi*); the double Jasmine (*Jasminum sambac*).

Mukuṭa (S) (M) diadem; crown; crest; point.

Mukuṭeśvara (S) (M) **1.** lord of the crown. **3.** a king (*M. Bh.*).

Mukuṭeśvarī (S) (M) **1.** queen of the crowns. **3.** the Dākṣāyāṇī in Mukuṭa (*M. Bh.*).

Mukuṭopala (S) (M) **1.** jewel of the crown. **2.** the crest gem.

Mūlaka (S) (M) **1.** rooted in; springing from. **3.** a son of Kumbhakarṇa killed by Sītā (*Ā. Rāmāyaṇa*); a prince and son of Aśmaka (*M. Bh.*).

Mūlakarāja (S) (M) the original king.

Mūlarāja (S) (M) lord of creation; the original root.

Mumuću (S) (M) **1.** striving to be free. **3.** a sage of South India (*M. Bh.*).

Muṇḍa (S) (M) **1.** bald; blunt; head; thinker. **3.** a daitya (*H. Purāṇa*); an asura (*D. Bh. Purāṇa*); another name for Rāhu.

Muṇḍaka (S) (M) **1.** born of the head; dwelling on the head. **3.** one of the 18 principal Upaniṣads (*M. Upaniṣad*).

Muṇḍavedāṅga (S) (M) **1.** one whose head knows everything. **3.** a serpent of the family of Dhṛtarāṣṭra (*M. Bh.*).

Mūṅgā (S) (M) the coral gem.

Muni (S) (M) **1.** sage; ascetic; moved by impulse. **2.** seer; monk; devotee; one who is inspired. **3.** the son of a vasu named Ahar (*M. Bh.*); a son of Kuru and Vāhinī (*M. Bh.*); a son of King Dyutimat (*Mā. Purāṇa*); the 7 stars of the Ursa Major (*M. Bh.*); a Buddha or Arhat (*J.S. Koṣa*); another name for Vyāsa, Agastya and Bharata; *Artemisia sieversiana.*

Muniċandra (S) (M) moon among ascetics.

Munikumāra (S) (M) a young ascetic.

Muniratna (S) (M) **1.** jewel among sages. **2.** chaste; pious; enlightened.

Munīndra (S) (M) **1.** chief of munis. **2.** a Buddha; a Jina. **3.** another name for Śiva, Śākyamuni and Bharata.

Muniputra (S) (M) son of a muni; *Artemesia indica.*

Munīśa (S) (M) **1.** chief of the munis. **2.** a Buddha or a Jina. **3.** another name for Vālmīki.

Munisuvrata (S) (M) **1.** a fasting ascetic. **3.** the 12th Arhat of the past and 20th Tīrthaṅkara of the present Avasarpiṇī (*H. Koṣa*).

Munīśvara (S) (M) **1.** lord of ascetics. **3.** another name for Viṣṇu and Buddha.

Munivara (S) (M) **1.** best among munis. **3.** another name for Vasiṣṭha as one of the stars of the Great Bear.

Munivīrya (S) (M) **1.** power of asceticism. **3.** a viśvadeva (*K. Sāgara*).

Muñja (S) (M) **1.** a species of grass (*Saccharum sara*). **3.** a sage in the court of Yudhiṣṭhira (*M. Bh.*); a king of Dhārā; the girdle of a Brāhmin.

Muñjakeśa (S) (M) **1.** with grass like hair. **3.** a king who was an incarnation of an asura called Niċandra (*M. Bh.*); another name for Viṣṇu and Śiva.

Muñjaketu (S) (M) **1.** grass bannered. **3.** a king and member of Yudhiṣṭhira's court (*M. Bh.*).

Muñjasūnu (S) (M) **1.** son of Muñja. **3.** another name for Dāśaśarman.

Munnu (S) (M) three.

Mupanāra (S) (M) **1.** not a small being. **2.** a great person.

Mura (S) (M) **1.** merciless. **2.** terrible; horrible; destroyer. **3.** an asura born of Kaśyapa and Diti and killed by Kṛṣṇa (*Bhā. Purāṇa*); an asura born of a part of Brahmā and killed by Ekādaśī — a form of Devī (*P. Purāṇa*); the son of Talajaṅgha (*P. Purāṇa*); a Yādava king whose daughter married Ghaṭotkaċa (*M. Bh.*).

Murada (S) (M) **1.** destroyer of Mura. **3.** the discus of Viṣṇu; another name for Kṛṣṇa.

Murajaka (S) (M) **1.** a drum. **3.** one of Śiva's attendants (*K. Sāgara*).

Murajit (S) (M) **1.** conqueror of Mura. **3.** another name for Kṛṣṇa.

Muralīdhara (S) (M) **1.** flute bearer. **3.** another name for Kṛṣṇa.

Muramathana (S) (M) **1.** slayer of Mura. **3.** another name for Kṛṣṇa.

Murārī (S) (M) **1.** enemy of Mura. **3.** another name for Kṛṣṇa.

Mūrċana (S) (M) **1.** stupifying. **3.** one of the 5 arrows of Kāma.

Mūrdhagata (S) (M) **1.** going up. **2.** one who grows, ascends, progresses and rules over people. **3.** a ċakravartin (*Divyāvadāna*).

Mūrdhaja (S) (M) **1.** born of the head. **3.** a ċakravartin (*Divyāvadāna*).

Mūrdhana (S) (M) forehead; head; summit; chief.

Mūrdhanavata (S) (M) **1.** dweller of the summit. **2.** top; headed; chief. **3.** a gandharva (*T. Āranyaka*).

Mūrdheśvara (S) (M) the highest god.

Murita (S) (M) **1.** slayed; bound; encompassed; entwined. **3.** a son of Yadu and a king of the lunar race.

Murmura (S) (M) **1.** an ember. **3.** a horse of the sun (*M. Bh.*); another name for Kāma.

Mūrtaya (S) (M) **1.** substantial; material; incarnate; embodied. **3.** a son of Kuśa (*V. Rāmāyaṇa*).

Mūrti (S) (M) **1.** statue; idol. **2.** embodiment; incarnation. **3.** a ṛṣi in the 10th Manvantara (*Bhā. Purāṇa*); a son of Vasiṣṭha (*V. Purāṇa*).

Muru (S) (M) **1.** detached. **3.** a Yādava king whose daughter married Ghaṭotkaċa (*M. Bh.*); a daitya (*M. Bh.*); another name for Vasiṣṭha.

Murugesa (S) (M) **1.** lord of the detached; lord of the peacocks. **3.** another name for Kārttikeya.

Mūṣakāda (S) (M) **1.** eater of rats. **3.** a serpent son of Kaśyapa and Kadru and member of Varuṇa's court (*M. Bh.*).

Mūṣakaratha (S) (M) **1.** rat vehicled. **3.** another name for Gaṇeśa.

Musala (S) (M) **1.** iron rod; pestle. **2.** mace; club. **3.** a son of Viśvāmitra (*M. Bh.*).

Musalapāṇi (S) (M) **1.** club handed. **3.** another name for Balarāma.

Musalāyudha (S) (M) **1.** club armed. **3.** another name for Balarāma.

Musalin (S) (M) **1.** armed with a club. **3.** another name for Balarāma.

Muṣṭika (S) (M) **1.** handful; with a fist. **3.** an asura who was a servant of Kaṁsa and killed by Balarāma (*M. Bh.*).

Muthu (S) (M) nice; gentle.

Mutya (S) (M) a pearl.

N

Nābha (S) (M) **1.** nave; navel; central point; king. **3.** a son of Śruta and the father of Sindhudvīpa (*Bhā. Purāṇa*); a son of Manu Vaivasvata and an author of *Ṛg Veda* (x) (*T. Saṃhitā*); another name for Śiva.

Nabha (S) (M) **1.** expanding; the sky; atmosphere; the month Srāvaṇa. **3.** the son of Manu Svāroćiṣa; a sage of the 6th Manvantara (*H. Purāṇa*); a demon who was the son of Vipraćitti and Sinhikā; a son of Nala and the father of Puṇḍarīka (*Bhā. Purāṇa*); the city of the sun.

Nabhadana (S) (M) **1.** donated by the heavens. **2.** heavenly; celestial. **3.** a descendant of Virūpa and the author of *Ṛg Veda* (x).

Nābhāga (S) (M) **1.** moving in the sky. **2.** a bird. **3.** a son of Manu Vaivasvata and father of Ambarīṣa; a son of Yayāti and the father of Aja (*Bhā. Purāṇa*); a brother of Ikṣvāku (*M. Bh.*).

Nābhāgāriṣṭa (S) (M) **1.** dweller of the sky. **3.** a son of Manu Vaivasvata (*M. Bh.*).

Nābhāka (S) (M) **1.** belonging to the sky. **3.** a ṛṣi of the Kaṇva family and an author of *Ṛg Veda* (viii).

Nabhakānti (S) (M) splendour of the sky.

Nabhaketana (S) (M) **1.** sky banner. **3.** another name for the sun.

Nabhanyu (S) (M) **1.** springing forth from the heavens. **2.** ethereal; celestial; heavenly.

Nabhapāntha (S) (M) **1.** walking the skies. **3.** another name for the sun.

Nabhaprāṇa (S) (M) **1.** the breath of the sky. **2.** the wind.

Nabhas (S) (M) **1.** sky; mist; clouds; vapour. **2.** sun; sky; the month of the rainy season; a rope of lotus fibre.

Nābhasa (S) (M) **1.** vapoury; misty; of sky. **2.** sky; celestial; heavenly; divine; the ocean. **3.** a ṛṣi of the 10th Manvantara; a dānava (*H. Purāṇa*).

Nabhasad (S) (M) **1.** sky dweller. **2.** ethereal; celestial; heavenly; divine; a god; planet.

Nabhasadīpa (S) (M) **1.** light of the sky. **3.** another name for the moon.

Nabhasaras (S) (M) **1.** sky lake. **2.** the clouds.

Nabhaśćakṣus (S) (M) **1.** eye of the sky. **3.** another name for the sun.

Nabhaśćamasa (S) (M) **1.** goblet of the sky. **3.** another name for the moon.

Nabhaśćyuta (S) (M) fallen from the sky.

Nabhasthala (S) (M) **1.** residing in the sky. **3.** another name for Śiva.

Nabhasvān (S) (M) **1.** bearer of the sky. **3.** a son of Narakāsura (*Bhā. Purāṇa*).

Nabhasvat (S) (M) **1.** bearer of the sky; young. **2.** the wind. **3.** a son of Naraka Bhauma (*Bhāgavata*).

Nabhaśvata (S) (M) **1.** born of the sky. **2.** young; wind; air.

Nabhasya (S) (M) **1.** of the sky. **2.** vapour; misty; the ocean; the rainy season. **3.** a ṛṣi of the 10th Manvantara (*H. Purāṇa*); a son of Manu Svāroćiṣa; another name for Śiva.

Nābhi (S) (M) **1.** nave; navel; central point. **2.** sovereign; lord. **3.** a grandson of Priyavrata and father of Ṛṣabha (*J.S. Koṣa*); the father of the 1st Arhat of the present Avasarpiṇī (*J. S. Koṣa*).

Nābhigupta (S) (M) **1.** hidden in the navel. **3.** a son of Hiraṇyaretas.

Nābhija (S) (M) **1.** navel born. **3.** another name for Brahmā.

Nābhijanmā (S) (M) **1.** born of the navel. **3.** another name for Brahmā.

Nabhīta (S) (M) fearless.

Nabhoda (S) (M) **1.** one who has arisen from the sky. **2.** a cloud. **3.** a viśvadeva (*M. Bh.*).

Nabhodhvaja (S) (M) **1.** banner of the sky. **2.** a cloud.

Nabhoga (S) (M) **1.** travelling in the sky. **2.** a planet.

Nabhogaja (S) (M) **1.** elephant of the sky. **2.** a cloud.

Nabhoja (S) (M) born of the sky.

Nabhomaṇī (S) (M) 1. jewel of the sky. 3. another name for the sun.

Nabhorūpa (S) (M) 1. form of the sky. 2. beyond any shape; ethereal. 3. a mythical being (*V. Samhitā*).

Nabhovīthī (S) (M) the path of the sun.

Nabhoyoni (S) (M) 1. skyborn. 3. another name for Śiva.

Nābhya (S) (M) 1. central; of the navel. 3. another name for Śiva.

Nāćika (S) (M) 1. not experienced. 3. a son of Viśvāmitra (*M. Bh.*).

Nāćiketa (S) (M) 1. not conscious. 2. fire. 3. an ancient sage who was the son of Uddālaka (*Kau. Upaniṣad*).

Naḍa (S) (M) 1. a brook; a river; a stream; a species of Reed (*Arundo tibialis*). 3. a nāga.

Naḍāgiri (S) (M) 1. grass mountain. 3. an elephant endowed with the powers of discrimination (*K. Sāgara*).

Nadal (S) (M) 1. of a river. 2. fortunate.

Nadanu (S) (M) 1. noisy. 2. battle; cloud; lion.

Nadīdhara (S) (M) 1. bearer of the river. 3. another name for Śiva.

Nadīja (S) (M) 1. from a river. 3. a king (*M. Bh.*); Kadamba tree (*Anthocephalus cadamba*); another name for Bhīṣma.

Nādījaṅgha (S) (M) 1. hollow-thighed. 3. a kite who was a friend of Brahmā; a stork who lives eternally.

Nadīkānta (S) (M) 1. loving rivers. 2. the ocean.

Nadīna (S) (M) 1. lord of rivers. 3. a son of Sahadeva and father of Jagatsena (*H. Purāṇa*); another name for Varuṇa.

Naga (S) (M) 1. not moving. 2. mountain; the number 7.

Nāga (S) (M) serpent; elephant.

Nāgabala (S) (M) 1. with the strength of elephants. 3. another name for Bhīma; *Plectronia parviflora.*

Nāgabhuṣaṇa (S) (M) 1. decorated with snakes. 3. another name for Śiva.

Nāgaćūḍa (S) (M) 1. serpent crested. 3. another name for Śiva.

Nāgadatta (S) (M) 1. given by serpents. 3. a son of Dhṛtarāṣṭra (*M. Bh.*); a king of Āryavarta.

Nāgadeva (S) (M) 1. lord of snakes. 3. another name for Vāsuki.

Nagadhipa (S) (M) 1. lord of mountains. 3. another name for Mount Kailāsa and Śiva.

Nāgadhipa (S) (M) 1. lord of snakes. 3. another name for Śiva.

Nagaja (S) (M) mountain born.

Nāgakumāra (S) (M) 1. prince of the serpents. 3. a class of deities guarding Kubera's treasures.

Nagamūrdhana (S) (M) 1. peak of a mountain. 2. the mountain crest.

Naganaćaraya (S) (M) 1. preceptor of mountains. 2. minstrel.

Nāgānanda (S) (M) joy of the serpents.

Nāgantaka (S) (M) 1. destroyer of serpents. 3. another name for Garuḍa.

Nāgapāla (S) (M) protector of serpents.

Nagapati (S) (M) 1. lord of the mountains. 3. another name for the Himālaya.

Nāgapurādhipa (S) (M) 1. lord of Nāgapura (*Hāstinapura*). 3. another name for Paṇḍu.

Nāgapurasiṁha (S) (M) 1. lion of Nāgapura. 3. another name for Paṇḍu.

Nāgarāja (S) (M) lord of serpents; a large elephant.

Nāgāri (S) (M) 1. enemy of serpents. 3. a prominent child of Garuḍa (*Bhā. Purāṇa*); another name for Garuḍa.

Nagarin (S) (M) lord of a town.

Nāgaripu (S) (M) 1. enemy of serpents. 3. another name for Garuḍa.

Nāgārjuna (S) (M) 1. best among the snakes; a white snake. 3. an ancient Buddhist teacher of the rank of a Bodhisattva; a minister of King Ćirāyuṣ.

Nagasata (S) (M) 1. mountain of truth. 2. a holy mountain. 3. the mountain where King Pāṇḍu performed his penance (*M. Bh.*).

Nāgasena (S) (M) **1.** with an army of elephants; the ruler of the nāgas. **3.** a great Buddhist philosopher; a king of Āryāvarta.

Nāgāśraya (S) (M) living in mountains.

Nagavāhana (S) (M) **1.** bearer of mountains. **3.** another name for Śiva.

Nāgavārika (S) (M) **1.** feeding on snakes; a better elephant. **2.** a peacock; the royal elephant; hierarchically the chief person in a royal court. **3.** another name for Garuḍa.

Nagendra (S) (M) **1.** mountain lord. **3.** another name for the Himālaya.

Nāgendra (S) (M) **1.** lord of serpents. **3.** another name for Vāsuki.

Nageṣa (S) (M) **1.** lord of the mountains. **3.** another name for Mount Kailāsa and Śiva.

Nāgeśa (S) (M) **1.** lord of the serpents; lord of the elephants. **2.** a large and noble elephant. **3.** another name for Patañjali.

Nāgeśvarī (S) (M) **1.** goddess of the serpents; goddess of the mountains; goddess of the elephants. **3.** another name for Manasā.

Nagna (S) (M) **1.** naked; bare; new. **2.** a mendicant. **3.** another name for Śiva.

Nagnajit (S) (M) **1.** conqueror of mendicants. **3.** a Kṣatriya king of Gāndhāra who was born from a part of the asura Iśupāda (*M. Bh.*); an asura disciple of Prahlāda (*Bhā. Purāṇa*); a prince of the Gāndhāras and the father of one of Kṛṣṇa's wives (*M. Bh.*).

Nāgrāndhakara (S) (M) **1.** destroyer of serpents. **2.** a peacock. **3.** another name for Kārttikeya.

Nahnābhai (H) (M) **1.** younger brother. **3.** another name for Rāmakṛṣṇa the son of Dāmodara.

Nahuṣa (S) (M) **1.** fellow creature; man. **3.** a lunar dynasty king the son of Āyuṣ and Indumatī, the husband of Aśokasundarī the daughter of Śiva and the father of Yayāti (*P. Purāṇa*); a serpent demon who was the son of Kaśyapa and Kadru (*M. Bh.*); a marut (*Vām. Purāṇa*); a son of Manu and part author of *Ṛg Veda* (ix); another name for Viṣṇu and Kṛṣṇa.

Naidhruva (S) (M) **1.** near perfection. **3.** the grandson of Kaśyapa and the son of sage Avatsara (*Vā. Purāṇa*).

Naigameya (S) (M) **1.** goat faced. **3.** a form of Skanda also considered his son and playfellow (*V. Purāṇa*).

Naiguta (S) (M) destroyer of enemies.

Naikadriṣ (M) **1.** many eyed. **3.** a son of Viśvamitra.

Naikarupa (S) (M) taking many forms.

Naimiṣa (S) (M) **1.** momentary; transient. **3.** a sacred pilgrimage spot and forest where an army of asuras was destroyed in a trice (*V. Rāmāyaṇa*).

Naināhhirāma (S) (M) **1.** pleasing to the eye. **2.** beautiful.

Naināra (S) (M) **1.** preceptor; observer. **3.** an author.

Nainasukha (S) (M) delightful to the eye.

Nairañjana (S) (M) **1.** pure; pleasing; spotless. **3.** a river that falls into the Gaṅgā in Magadha (*Ś. Purāṇa*).

Nairṛti (S) (M) **1.** lord of the southwest. **3.** a rākṣasa who was one of the ancient guards of the world (*M. Bh.*).

Naiṣadha (S) (M) **1.** king of the Niṣadhas. **3.** another name for Nala.

Nāk (S) (M) night.

Nāka (S) (M) **1.** where there is no pain. **2.** vault of heaven; sky; firmament; the sun. **3.** a mythical weapon of Arjuna (*M. Bh.*).

Nākanātha (S) (M) **1.** lord of the sky. **3.** another name for Indra.

Nākanāyaka (S) (M) **1.** leader of the sky. **3.** another name for Indra.

Nākapāla (S) (M) guardian of the sky.

Nākapati (S) (M) **1.** lord of the sky. **3.** another name for Indra.

Nākeśa (S) (M) **1.** lord of the sky. **3.** another name for Indra.

Nakhaka (S) (M) **1.** shaped like a talon. **2.** curved. **3.** a serpent lord (*R. Taraṅginī*).

Nākin (S) (M) **1.** dwelling in the sky. **2.** a god.

Nakra (S) (M) **1.** crocodile. **3.** the zodiac sign of Capricorn.

Nakraketana (S) (M) **1.** crocodile bannered. **3.** another name for Kāma.

Nakṣa (S) (M) **1.** to come near; to arrive at; to attain. **3.** the son of Pṛthusena and Ākūti, the husband of Druti and the father of Gaya (*Bhā. Purāṇa*).

Nakṣatra (S) (M) **1.** heavenly body; a constellation; a lunar mansion; a pearl. **3.** in the Vedas the Nakṣatras are considered the abode of the gods and in the later Hindu scriptures, they are depicted as the daughters of Dakṣa and the wives of the moon (*M. Bh.*).

Nakṣatraja (S) (M) **1.** born of the stars; the son of the stars. **3.** another name for the planet Mercury.

Nakṣatranandana (S) (M) **1.** son of the stars. **3.** another name for planet Mercury.

Nakṣatranātha (S) (M) **1.** lord of the constellations. **3.** another name for the moon.

Nakṣatranemi (S) (M) **1.** the axis of the constellations; the centre of the constellations; the pole star. **3.** another name for Viṣṇu and the moon.

Nakṣatrarāja (S) (M) **1.** lord of the constellations. **3.** a Bodhisattva; another name for the moon.

Nakṣatrin (S) (M) **1.** holding the stars. **2.** fortunate; lucky. **3.** another name for Viṣṇu.

Nakta (S) (M) **1.** night. **3.** a son of Pṛthuśena and Ākūti (*Bhā. Purāṇa*); a son of Pṛthu (*V. Purāṇa*).

Nākuja (S) (M) **1.** born of an anthill. **3.** another name for Vālmiki.

Nakula (S) (M) **1.** of the colour of an Ichneumon. **2.** a son; a musical instrument; the Bengal Mongoose (*Viverra ichneumon*) **3.** a son of the aśvins and Mādrī, the brother of Sahadeva and the 4th of the Pāṇḍu princes known for his beauty (*M. Bh.*); another name for Śiva.

Nakulānuja (S) (M) **1.** younger brother of Nakula. **3.** another name for Sahadeva.

Nākuli (S) (M) **1.** son of Nakula. **3.** another name for Śatanīka.

Nala (S) (M) **1.** stem; any hollow pipe; stem of a flower; lotus; nectar; a species of Reed (*Amphidonax karka*). **3.** a divine being mentioned with Yama; a king of the Niṣadhas who was the son of Vīrasena and the husband of Damayantī (*M. Bh.*); a son of Niṣadha and the father of Nabha (*H. Purāṇa*); a son of Sudhanvan and father of Uktha; a son of Yadu (*V. Purāṇa*); a monkey chief who was the son of Tvaṣṭṛ (*V. Rāmāyaṇa*); a hermit who lived in the court of Indra (*M. Bh.*); a daitya (*Br. Purāṇa*).

Nālāgiri (S) (M) **1.** lotus plucker. **2.** an elephant. **3.** an elephant associated with Gautama Buddha; the elephant of Pradyota.

Nalakūbara (S) (M) **1.** with a carriage of reeds; beautiful; fragrant; agreeable. **3.** a son of Kubera and the husband of Rambhā and Somaprabhā (*M. Bh.*).

Nalandā (S) (M) nectar of a flower.

Nalasetu (S) (M) **1.** reed bridge. **3.** the bridge constructed by the monkey Nala for Rāma to Laṅkā (*V. Rāmāyaṇa*).

Nalatantu (S) (M) **1.** made of lotus threads. **3.** a son of Viśvāmitra (*M. Bh.*).

Naleśa (S) (M) king of flowers.

Nālīka (S) (M) arrow; spear; limb; Lotus flower (*Nelumbium nucifera*).

Nalina (S) (M) the Lotus (*Nelumbium speciosum*); the Water Lily (*Nymphaea alba*); the Indian crane; the Indigo plant (*Indigofera tinctoria*); water.

Nalinanābha (S) (M) **1.** lotus navelled. **3.** another name for Viṣṇu.

Nalināsana (S) (M) **1.** lotus throned. **3.** another name for Brahmā.

Nalinīnandana (S) (M) **1.** a lotus bud. **3.** a garden of Kubera (*V. Rāmāyaṇa*).

Nalinīruha (S) (M) **1.** born of a lotus. **3.** another name for Brahmā.

Nāman (S) (M) name; form; mark; renowned; of a great name.

Namana (S) (M) **1.** bending; bowing. **2.** offering homage.

Namasita (S) (M) **1.** revered. **2.** virtuous; auspicious; sacred.

Namasyu (S) (M) **1.** bowing. **2.** worshipping; deferential. **3.** a king of Yayāti's family (*Bhā. Purāṇa*); a son of Pravīra (*Bhā. Purāṇa*).

Namata (S) (M) **1.** bending; bowing. **2.** paying homage.

Nameśa (S) (M) **1.** lord of obeisance. **2.** worshipped; a divine being.

Nāmgiri (S) (M) sacred mountain.

Nāmi (S) (M) **1.** of great renown. **3.** another name for Viṣṇu.

Naminātha (S) (M) **1.** bowing before the master. **2.** a devotee. **3.** the 21st Jaina Tirthaṅkara whose emblem is a lotus (*J. S. Koṣa*).

Namita (S) (M) **1.** bowed; bent down. **2.** one who worships; a devotee; humble; modest; submissive.

Namrāṅga (S) (M) **1.** bowed posture. **2.** humble; modest; submissive.

Namuća (S) (M) **1.** not loose. **2.** taut; firm; fixed. **3.** a sage of ancient India (*M. Bh.*).

Namūći (S) (M) **1.** not loose. **2.** taut; firm; fixed. **3.** a rākṣasa son of Kaśyapa and Danu, killed by Indra and the aśvins (*Ṛg Veda*); an army captain of Hiraṇyākṣa (*P. Purāṇa*); another name for Kāma.

Namūćighna (S) (M) **1.** slayer of Namućī. **3.** another name for Indra.

Namūćisudana (S) (M) **1.** conqueror of Namūći. **3.** another name for Indra.

Nāmvara (S) (M) renowned.

Namya (S) (M) to be bowed to; venerable.

Nanagābhu (S) (M) **1.** born of light. **3.** a king of the family of Yayāti (*Bhā. Purāṇa*).

Nānaka (S) (M) **1.** without darkness. **2.** grief-less; fearless; happy; a coin; anything stamped with an impression. **3.** the founder of Sikhism and the 1st of the 10 Gurus.

Nāṇaka (S) (M) coin; anything with an impression.

Nanda (S) (M) **1.** joy; delight; happiness; a flute; a son; number 9. **3.** one of Yudhiṣṭhira's drums (*M. Bh.*); one of Kubera's 9 gems (*A. Koṣa*); one of Skanda's attendants (*A. Koṣa*); a nāga born in the family of Kaśyapa (*A. Koṣa*); an attendant of Dakṣa (*Bhā. Purāṇa*); a son of Dhṛtarāṣṭra (*M. Bh.*); a stepbrother and disciple of Gautama Buddha (*B. Literature*); a son of Vasudeva (*M. Bh.*); the foster father of Kṛṣṇa (*M. Bh.*); a leader of the Sātvatas (*Bhā. Purāṇa*); a king of Pāṭaliputra; an ancestor of Durgā (*M. Bh.*); a devotee and attendant of Viṣṇu (*M. Bh.*); a Buddhist deity; another name for Viṣṇu (*M. Bh.*); Indian Mahogany (*cedrela Toona*); Couchgrass (*Cynodon dactylon*); Malay Apple (*Eugenia jambos*).

Nandabhadra (S) (M) **1.** delightful person. **3.** a devotee of Kapileśvara (*Ś. Purāṇa*).

Nandagopa (S) (M) **1.** cowherd Nanda. **3.** another name for the cowherd Nanda.

Nandaka (S) (M) delighting; rejoicing; gladdening; the deity of weapons (*M. Bh.*); Kṛṣṇa's sword (*M. Bh.*).

Nandakin (S) (M) **1.** possessor of the Nandaka sword. **3.** another name for Kṛṣṇa.

Nandakiśora (S) (M) **1.** son of Nanda. **3.** another name for Kṛṣṇa.

Nandakumāra (S) (M) **1.** son of Nanda. **3.** another name for Kṛṣṇa.

Nandalāla (S) (M) **1.** son of Nanda. **3.** another name for Kṛṣṇa.

Nandana (S) (M) **1.** rejoicing; gladdening. **2.** a son; a type of temple. **3.** an attendant of Skanda given to him by the aśvins (*M. Bh.*); a son of Hiraṇyakaśipu who became a gaṇa of Śiva (*Ś. Purāṇa*); a Buddhist (*L. Vistara*); another name for Viṣṇu and Śiva.

Nandanta (S) (M) **1.** rejoicing; gladdening. **2.** a son; a friend; a king.

Nandapāla (S) (M) **1.** guardian of the Nanda. **2.** guardian of one of Kubera's 9 gems called 'Nanda'. **3.** another name for Varuṇa.

Nandathu (S) (M) joy; delight; happiness.

Nandi (S) (M) **1.** the happy one. **3.** the chief of the attendants of Śiva (*Vām. Purāṇa*); a gandharva (*M. Bh.*); Indian Mahogany (*Cedrela toona*); Wax Flower (*Ervatamia coronaria*); Portia tree (*Thespesia populnea*); another name for Viṣṇu and Śiva.

Nandighoṣa **1.** the music of joy. **3.** Arjuna's chariot (*M. Bh.*).

Nandigupta (S) (M) **1.** protected by happiness. **3.** a king of Kāśmira (*R. Taraṅgiṇī*).

Nandika (S) (M) **1.** pleasure giving. **3.** one of Śiva's attendants; a pupil of Gautama Buddha; the tree *Cedrela toona.*

Nandikara (S) (M) **1.** causing joy. **3.** another name for Śiva.

Nandikeśvara (S) (M) **1.** one who pleases the god. **3.** the chief of Śiva's gaṇas or attendants and his bull (*Vām. Purāṇa*).

Nandil (S) (M) delighted; glad.

Nandin (S) (M) **1.** son; delightful. **3.** one of the 9 north Indian kings whose empire was an-nexed by Samudragupta; one of Kubera's attendants (*M. Bh.*); a place held sacred by the Jainas; an attendant of Śiva (*Ś. Purāṇa*); Śiva's bull (*Ś. Purāṇa*).

Nandirudra (S) (M) Śiva in a joyful or serene form.

Nandīśa (S) (M) **1.** lord of pleasure; lord of the bulls. **3.** the chief attendant of Śiva (*Vām. Purāṇa*); another name for Śiva.

Nandisena (S) (M) **1.** with an army of bulls. **3.** one of the 4 attendants of Skanda given to him by Brahmā (*M. Bh.*).

Nandīśvara (S) (M) **1.** lord of happiness; lord of the bulls. **3.** the chief attendant of Śiva; an attendant of Kubera.

Nandivardhana (S) (M) **1.** enhancing pleasure; a son; a friend; the day of the full moon. **3.** a king of the solar dynasty, the son of Vīrada and the father of Suketu (*Bhā. Purāṇa*); a prince who was the son of Udāvasu (*V. Purāṇa*); a son of Janaka (*V. Purāṇa*); a son of Udayāśva; a son of Rājaka (*Bh. Purāṇa*); a brother of Mahāvira; the conch of Sātyaki (*M. Bh.*); another name for Śiva.

Nandivega (S) (M) **1.** with the speed of Nandi. **2.** with the speed of Śiva's bull Nandin. **3.** a Kṣatriya family into which King Sama was born (*M. Bh.*).

Naṅhasa (S) (M) a god who is kind to his worshipper.

Naṅja (S) (M) **1.** consumer of poison. **3.** another name for Śiva.

Naṅṣa (S) (M) acquisition.

Nāntra (S) (M) **1.** praise; eulogy. **3.** a sage; another name for Śiva.

Naoraṅga (S) (M) the Indian Pitta (*Corvus brachyurus*).

Naparājit (S) (M) **1.** not yielding. **3.** another name for Śiva.

Naparājita (S) (M) **1.** not yielding. **3.** another name for Śiva.

Napāt (S) (M) **1.** descendant. **2.** son off-spring; path of the gods. **3.** a viśvadevā (*V. Purāṇa*).

Naptā (S) (M) **1.** unfulfilled; unsatisfied. **3.** a viśvadeva concerned with offerings to the manes or ancestors (*M. Bh.*).

Nara (S) (M) **1.** man; male; eternal spirit pervading the universe. **3.** always associated with Nārāyaṇa, in poetry they are the sons of Dharma and Mūrti or Ahinsa and the emanations of Viṣṇu who became great hermits and lived in Badarikāśrama performing penance to Brahmā for a 1000 years and were later reborn as Arjuna and Kṛṣṇa (*M. Bh.*); a class of mythical beings like the gandharvas and the kinnaras (*M. Bh.*); a son of Manu Tāmasa (*Bhā. Purāṇa*); a son of Viśvāmitra (*H. Purāṇa*); a son of Gaya and the father of Virāj (*V. Purāṇa*); a son of Sudhṛti and father of Kevala (*V. Purāṇa*); one of the 10 horses of the moon (*A. Koṣa*); a gandharva who stayed in the palace of Kubera (*M. Bh.*); 2 kings of Kāśmira (*R. Taraṅginī*); another name for Arjuna.

Narabhu (S) (M) **1.** father of man; born of man. **3.** another name for Indra.

Naraćandra (S) (M) moon among men.

Nārada (S) (M) **1.** one who gives knowledge to men. **2.** a messenger. **3.** a ṛṣi son of Brahmā born from his lap, one of the 10 prajāpatis, considered a messenger between the gods and men, in later mythology depicted as a friend of Kṛṣṇa and regarded as the inventor of the Vīṇā or the lute; a son of Viśvāmitra (*M. Bh.*).

Naradeva (S) (M) the god of men.

Narādhipa (S) (M) lord of men.

Nāradin (S) (M) **1.** telling tales. **2.** providing knowledge through tales. **3.** a son of Viśvāmitra (*M. Bh.*).

Narahari (S) (M) **1.** man lion. **3.** another name for Viṣṇu.

Naraka (S) (M) **1.** hell. **3.** hell personified as a son of Anṛta and Nirṛti (*M. Bh.*); a demon son of Hiraṇyākṣa and Bhūmi who was slain by Kṛṣṇa (*V. Purāṇa*); a rākṣasa son of Kaśyapa and Danu, slain by Indra, upon being reborn, stayed in the palace of Varuṇa (*Bhā. Purāṇa*).

Narakajit (S) (M) **1.** conqueror of Naraka. **3.** a son of Vipraćitti (*V. Purāṇa*); another name for Viṣṇu and Kṛṣṇa.

Narakāntaka (S) (M) **1.** destroyer of Naraka. **3.** another name for Viṣṇu.

Narakesarin (S) (M) **1.** lion among men. **3.** Viṣṇu in his 4th incarnation as the man lion.

Nāram (S) (M) **1.** of Nara. **2.** water.

Naran (S) (M) **1.** belongs to men. **2.** that which is human.

Naranārāyaṇa (S) (M) **1.** Nara and Nārāyaṇa conjoined. **3.** another name for Kṛṣṇa and Arjuna conjoined.

Naranātha (S) (M) **1.** lord of men; controller of men. **2.** a king.

Naranāyaka (S) (M) leader of men.

Nāraṅga (S) (M) **1.** orange coloured; having a human form; a living being; a twin. **2.** an orange tree (*Citrus aurantium*).

Narānta (S) (M) **1.** destroyer of men. **3.** a son of Hṛdika (*H. Purāṇa*).

Narāntaka (S) (M) **1.** killer of men. **3.** a captain in the army of Rāvaṇa (*V. Rāmāyaṇa*); the son of the asura Rudraketu who was killed by Gaṇapati (*G. Purāṇa*).

Narapāla (S) (M) protector of men; king.

Nararāja (S) (M) **1.** king of men. **3.** another name for Kubera.

Narāśaṅsa (S) (M) **1.** the desire of men. **3.** another name for Agni.

Naraśārdūla (S) (M) **1.** lion among men. **2.** very powerful; courageous; brave; a great warrior; a leader among men.

Narasiṁha (S) (M) **1.** lion among men. **2.** extremely powerful; courageous; brave; a great warrior; a leader among men. **3.** Viṣṇu in his 4th incarnation (*Purāṇas*); the father of King Bhairava.

Naravāhana (S) (M) **1.** with men as the vehicle. **2.** that which is drawn or borne by men. **3.** the successor of Śālivāhana; a minister of King Kṣemagupta (*R. Taraṅginī*); another name for Kubera.

Naravāhanadatta (S) (M) **1.** given by Kubera. **3.** a vidyādhara emperor who was the son of King Udayana and Vāsavadattā and the husband of Madanamañćukā and Alaṅkārāvatī.

Naravarman (S) (M) **1.** protector of men. **3.** a Mālava prince (12th century) (*R. Taraṅginī*).

Naravīra (S) (M) hero among men.

Nārāyaṇa (S) (M) **1.** the son of the original man. **3.** the incarnation of Viṣṇu, regarded as a Kaśyapa, the son of Dharma, the brother of Nara with whom he performed a penance for 1000 years, reborn as Kṛṣṇa and in the Jaina scriptures depicted as the 8th of the 9 Black Vasudevas; a son of prince Bhūmitra of the Kāṇvayānas; son of Narahari; a son of Ajāmila (*Bhā. Purāṇa*).

Nārāyaṇadāsa (S) (M) a devotee of Nārāyaṇa.

Nārāyaṇi (S) (M) 1. belonging to Viṣṇu or Kṛṣṇa. 3. a son of Viśvāmitra (*M. Bh.*).

Narbadeśvara (S) (M) 1. lord of the Narmadā river. 3. another name for Śiva.

Nardana (S) (M) 1. roarer. 2. celebrating; praising aloud. 3. a serpent lord.

Narendra (S) (M) lord of men.

Narendradeva (S) (M) divine lord of men.

Narendrāditya (S) (M) 1. sun among the lords of men. 2. with qualities that shine forth even among the lords of men. 3. 2 kings of Kāśmira (*R. Taraṅginī*).

Narendranātha (S) (M) 1. king among lords of men. 2. king of kings.

Nareśa (S) (M) king of men.

Nārikavaća (S) (M) 1. women as armour; protected by women. 3. the solar dynasty king Mūlaka who was the son of Aśmaka (*Purāṇas*).

Nārikera (S) (M) the Coconut tree (*Cocos nucifera*).

Nāriratna (S) (M) 1. a jewel of a woman. 2. beautiful; meritorious; virtuous.

Nariṣyanta (S) (M) 1. detached from women. 3. a king who was the son of Marutta, the husband of Indrasenā and the father of Dama (*Mā. Purāṇa*); the son of Manu Vaivasvata and the brother of Ikṣvāku (*Bhā. Purāṇa*).

Narmadeśvara (S) (M) 1. lord of Narmadā. 3. another name for Śiva.

Narman (S) (M) joke; wit; humour; jest; play; sport.

Narmaṭa (S) (M) 1. a potsherd. 2. a broken piece of earthenware. 3. another name for the sun.

Narottama (S) (M) 1. best among men. 3. another name for Viṣṇu and the Buddha.

Naruṇa (S) (M) 1. leader of men. 3. another name for Pūṣan.

Narya (S) (M) manly; strong; powerful; heroic.

Nāsatya (S) (M) 1. helpful; of the nose. 2. kind; friendly; breath. 3. an aśvin (*M. Bh.*).

Nasīka (S) (M) 1. perishable. 3. the grandson of Lomapāda (*Bhā. Purāṇa*).

Nāśīra (S) (M) 1. at the head; at the top. 2. a champion who advances at the head of the army.

Naṭanārāyaṇa (S) (M) 1. the dance of Viṣṇu. 3. a rāga.

Naṭarāja (S) (M) 1. lord of the cosmic dance. 3. another name for Śiva.

Natāri (S) (M) 1. subduing enemies. 3. another name for Kṛṣṇa.

Naṭavara (S) (M) 1. best among dancers. 3. another name for Kṛṣṇa.

Naṭeśa (S) (M) 1. lord of the Naṭas or dancers. 3. another name for Śiva.

Naṭeśvara (S) (M) 1. lord of the Naṭas or dancers. 3. another name for Śiva.

Nāthan (S) (M) 1. controller; protector; patron lord. 2. one who protects. 3. another name for Kṛṣṇa.

Nathin (S) (M) protected.

Naubandhana (S) (M) 1. ship anchorage. 3. the highest peak of the Himālayas to which Manu moored his ship during the great deluge (*M. Bh.*).

Naudīśvara (S) (M) 1. pleasing to the god. 2. victor. 3. another name for Śiva.

Naunihāl (S) (M) 1. new crop. 2. child.

Nava (S) (M) 1. new; fresh; young; praised; celebrated. 3. a son of Uśinara and Navā (*H. Purāṇa*); a son of Viloman (*V. Purāṇa*).

Navajā (S) (M) 1. recently born. 2. new moon.

Navajāta (M) fresh; new.

Navajyota (S) (M) 1. new light. 2. the fresh light; 1st light of day.

Navala (S) (M) new; novel.

Navana (S) (M) 1. the act of praising. 2. laudation.

Navanidhi (S) (M) 1. the 9 treasures. 3. another name for the 9 fabled treasures of Kubera.

Navanīta (S) (M) 1. new butter. 2. fresh butter; mild; soft; gentle. 3. one of the 6 aspects of Gaṇeśa.

Navānna (S) (M) new fruits; the 1st fruit.

Navapallava (S) (M) new shoot.

Navaraṅga (S) (M) of a new design; novel.

Navaratha (S) (M) **1.** with 9 chariots. **3.** the son of Bhīmaratha and father of Daśaratha (*V. Rāmāyaṇa*).

Navaratna (S) (M) 9 gems (pearl, ruby, topaz, diamond, emerald, lapiz lazuli, coral, sapphire and Gomedha).

Navaśakti (S) (M) **1.** with 9 faculties. **3.** another name for Viṣṇu and Śiva.

Navasara (S) (M) a pearl ornament.

Navateja (S) (M) new energy.

Navatidhanuṣa (S) (M) **1.** with 90 bows. **3.** an ancestor of Gautama Buddha.

Navavrata (S) (M) **1.** new duties. **2.** taking up new duties.

Navendra (S) (M) **1.** the new Indra. **2.** the young Indra.

Navīna (S) (M) new; novel.

Navīnaćandra (S) (M) new moon.

Naviṣṭha (S) (M) newest; youngest.

Navodita (S) (M) **1.** newly risen. **2.** new born. **3.** another name for the sun.

Navya (S) (M) **1.** worth praising. **2.** laudable.

Naya (S) (M) **1.** wisdom; doctrine. **2.** conduct; behaviour; good; management; prudence; maxim. **3.** a son of Dharma and Kriyā (*Purāṇas*); a son of the 13th Manu (*H. Purāṇa*).

Nayaćakṣuṣ (S) (M) the eye of prudence.

Nāyaka (S) (M) **1.** leader. **2.** lord; principal; the central gem of a necklace. **3.** another name for Gautama Buddha.

Nayana (S) (M) leading; directing; an eye; prudent conduct; polity.

Nayanādhyakṣa (S) (M) lord of the eye.

Nayanadīpa (S) (M) light of the eye.

Nayanotsava (S) (M) **1.** festival to the eye. **2.** a lovely sight; a lamp.

Nayat (S) (M) leading; guiding.

Nayiṣṭha (S) (M) **1.** leading in the best way. **3.** a son of Manu Vaivasvata (*V. Purāṇa*).

Nediṣṭha (S) (M) **1.** nearest. **3.** a son of Manu Vaivasvata (*V. Purāṇa*).

Neka (S) (M) good; virtuous.

Nekaćandra (S) (M) **1.** the moon of virtuosity. **2.** a highly virtuous person.

Nekarāma (H) (M) the gentle lord.

Nemaćandra (S) (M) half moon.

Nemi (S) (M) **1.** the felly of a wheel; edge; rim. **2.** with many edges; a thunderbolt. **3.** the 22nd Arhat of the present Utsarpiṇī (*J.S. Koṣa*); the real name of Daśaratha (*V. Rāmāyaṇa*); a ćakravartin; Chariot tree (*Ougenia oojeninensis*).

Nemićakra (S) (M) **1.** felly of the wheel. **3.** a prince who was a descendant of Parīkṣit and the ruler of Hastināpura (*Bhā. Purāṇa*).

Nemināthа (S) (M) **1.** lord of the thunderbolt. **3.** the 22nd Tīrthaṅkara whose emblem is a conchshell (*J.S. Koṣa*).

Netṛ (S) (M) **1.** leader. **2.** leading; guiding; bringer; offerer; leader of an army; hero of a drama. **3.** another name for Viṣṇu.

Netra (S) (M) **1.** eye. **2.** leader; guide. **3.** a son of Dharma and the father of Kuntī (*Bhā. Purāṇa*); a son of Sumati (*M. Purāṇa*).

Netrakoṣa (S) (M) **1.** treasure of the eye. **2.** the eyeball; the bud of a flower.

Netrāmuṣa (S) (M) **1.** capturing the eye. **2.** beautiful; unusual.

Netrayoni (S) (M) **1.** of the eye. **3.** the moon because it was produced from the eye of Atri.

Niagha (S) (M) **1.** sinless. **2.** flawless; virtuous; divine.

Nibāraṇa (S) (M) removal.

Nibhṛta (S) (M) **1.** firm. **2.** immovable; fixed; quiet; modest; mild; gentle.

Nićandra (S) (M) **1.** leading moon. **2.** foremost among the moons; a moon like leader. **3.** a rākṣasa (*M. Bh.*).

Nićāya (S) (M) to honour; worship; observe; perceive.

Nićūla (S) (M) **1.** overcoat; the tree *Barringtonia acutangula*; Chairbottom cane (*Calamus rotang*). **3.** a poet and contem-porary of Kālidāsa (*K. Granthāvali*).

Nidāgha (S) (M) **1.** scorching heat. **2.** summer. **3.** a sage and son of Pulastya (*V. Purāṇa*).

Nidarśin (S) (M) seeing; pleasing; familiar.

Nidhāna (S) (M) abode of treasure.

Nidhinātha (S) (M) **1.** guardian of treasure. **3.** another name for Kubera.

Nidhipa (S) (M) **1.** lord of treasure. **3.** another name for Kubera.

Nidhipati (S) (M) **1.** master of treasure. **3.** another name for Kubera.

Nidhiprabhu (S) (M) **1.** lord of treasure. **3.** another name for Kubera.

Nidhīśvara (S) (M) **1.** god of treasure. **3.** another name for Kubera.

Nīdhra (S) (M) **1.** the circumference of a wheel. **3.** another name for the moon; the lunar mansion Revatī.

Nidhṛti (S) (M) **1.** established; appointed. **3.** a son of Vṛṣni (*Agni Purāṇa*).

Nidhruva (S) (M) **1.** constant. **2.** persevering; faithful. **3.** a sage of the Kaśyapa dynasty, the son of sage Vatsāra, the husband of Sumedhas, the father of Kuṇḍapāyin and part author of *Ṛg Veda* (ix).

Nidrālu (S) (M) **1.** sleepy; drowsy. **3.** another name for Viṣṇu.

Nighna (S) (M) **1.** docile; obedient. **3.** a king of Ayodhyā, the son of Anāraṇya and the father of Anamitra and Raghuttama (*P. Purāṇa*).

Nigu (S) (M) pleasing; charming.

Nihāl (S) (M) **1.** satisfied. **2.** contented; happy.

Nīhāra (S) (M) **1.** mist. **2.** fog; dew.

Nihārarañjana (S) (M) **1.** delighting in dew. **3.** another name for the moon.

Nikāma (S) (M) **1.** desire; wish; pleasure. **3.** an agni (*Ṛg Veda*).

Nikara (S) (M) **1.** collection. **2.** mass; gift; treasure; the best of anything. **3.** a treasure of Kubera (*M. Bh.*).

Nikaṣa (S) (M) touchstone.

Nikaṣā (S) (M) **1.** tried on a touchstone. **2.** the streak of gold made on the touchstone. **3.** the mother of Rāvaṇa (*Rāmāyaṇa*).

Nīkāśa (S) (M) appearance; look.

Nikāśa (S) (M) horizon.

Nikaṣāya (S) (M) to serve as a touchstone.

Nikharvata (S) (M) **1.** possessing treasure. **3.** a rākṣasa in Rāvaṇa's camp (*V. Rāmāyaṇa*).

Nikhila (S) (M) complete; all; whole; entire.

Nikṣa (S) (M) kiss.

Nikumbha (S) (M) **1.** pot like. **2.** resembles a pot. **3.** a dānava of the Hiraṇyakaśipu dynasty and father of Sunda and Upasunda (*M. Bh.*); the son of Haryaśva and father of Saṁhatāśva (*H. Purāṇa*); a son of Kumbhakarṇa and Vajramālā (*V. Rāmāyaṇa*); an attendant of Śiva (*H. Purāṇa*); a viśvādeva (*A. Koṣa*); a warrior on the side of the Kauravas (*M. Bh.*); a form of Gaṇapati (*A. Koṣa*).

Nikumbhila (S) (M) **1.** a place where oblations are offered. **3.** a form of Bhadrakālī (*V. Rāmāyaṇa*).

Nikunja (S) (M) **1.** an abode; a bush. **2.** the abode of love; beautiful; enchanting; hidden in a bush; secretive; mysterious; enchanting.

Nīla (S) (M) **1.** dark blue; indigo; sapphire; the Ceylon Hill Mynah (*Gracula ptilogenys*); the Indian Fig tree (*Ficus indica*). **3.** one of the 9 treasures of Kubera; a prince of Mahiṣmatī; a son of Yadu (*H. Purāṇa*); a son of Ajamīḍha; a monkey chief attending on Rāma said to be the son of Agni (*M. Bh.*); a serpent of the family of Kaśyapa and Kadru (*M. Bh.*); a king of the Hehaya dynasty who was a partial rebirth of the asura Krodhavaśa and who fought on the side of the Kauravas (*M. Bh.*); the king of Anūpadeśa who fought on the Pāṇḍava side (*M. Bh.*); a mountain.

Nīlābha (S) (M) **1.** of bluish hue. **3.** another name for moon.

Nīlābja (S) (M) Blue Lotus (*Nymphaea stellata*).

Nīlaćandra (S) (M) blue moon.

Nīlaććhada (S) (M) **1.** blue winged. **3.** another name for Garuḍa.

Nīlāda (S) (M) **1.** bestower of blue; bestower of water. **2.** cloud. **3.** a yakṣa.

Nīladaṇḍa (S) (M) **1.** with a dark blue staff. **3.** one of the 10 Buddhist gods of anger.

Nīladhvaja (S) (M) **1.** blue bannered. **2.** with a blue banner. **3.** a prince of Mahiṣmatī.

Nīlādri (S) (M) blue peak.

Nīlagala (S) (M) **1.** blue necked. **3.** another name for Śiva.

Nīlagrīva (S) (M) **1.** blue necked. **3.** another name for Śiva.

Nīlaja (S) (M) **1.** produced in the blue mountains. **2.** blue steel.

Nīlakamala (S) (M) Blue Water lily (*Nympaea stellata*).

Nīlakaṇṭha (S) (M) **1.** blue necked; a peacock; the Indian Roller (*Coracias benghalensis*). **3.** another name for Śiva.

Nīlākṣa (S) (M) blue eyed.

Nīlalohita (S) (M) **1.** red and blue. **3.** another name for Śiva and Kārttikeya.

Nīlama (S) (M) of dark blue colour; emerald; sapphire; indigo; blue topaz.

Nīlamādhava (S) (M) blue Kṛṣṇa.

Nīlāmbara (S) (M) **1.** dressed in blue. **3.** another name for the planet Saturn and Balarāma.

Nīlapadma (S) (M) Blue Lotus (*Nymphaea stellata*) or Blue Water lily (*Nymphaea alba*).

Nīlapakṣman (S) (M) with black eyelashes.

Nīlaratna (S) (M) **1.** blue gem. **2.** sapphire.

Nīlāruṇa (S) (M) the first light of dawn.

Nīlāśoka (S) (M) the blue blossomed Aśoka tree.

Nīlavajra (S) (M) **1.** with a blue thunderbolt. **3.** an attendant of Śiva (*H. Purāṇa*).

Nīlavastra (S) (M) **1.** blue clad. **3.** another name for Balarāma.

Nilaya (S) (M) place of refuge.

Nīlībha (S) (M) **1.** with a blue hue. **2.** moon; cloud; bee.

Nilimpa (S) (M) **1.** to anoint; to become invisible; a yakṣa. **3.** a class of supernatural beings; a troop of maruts (*T. Āranyaka*).

Nīloda (S) (M) **1.** with blue water. **2.** river.

Nīlopala (S) (M) sapphire.

Nīlotpala (S) (M) Blue Lotus (*Nymphaea stellata*).

Nīluppala (S) (M) **1.** blue gem. **2.** Lapiz lazuli.

Nimala (S) (M) spotless; clean; pure; bright.

Nīmāy (S) (M) **1.** adjusted; ascetic. **3.** the childhood name of sage Ćaitanya.

Nimbū (S) (M) lemon; the Common Lime (*Citrus acida*).

Nimeṣa (S) (M) **1.** moment; eye wink. **3.** a son of Garuḍa (*M. Bh.*).

Nimeya (S) (M) **1.** to be measured; measurable. **2.** one whose character is known.

Nimī (S) (M) **1.** the winking of an eye. **2.** a moment. **3.** a son of sage Dattātreya (*M. Bh.*); a son of Ikṣvāku (*Bh. Purāṇa*); the 21st Jaina Arhat of the present Avasarpiṇī (*J.S. Koṣa*); son of Bhajamāna (*V. Purāṇa*); a son of Daṇḍapāṇi (*Bh. Purāṇa*); a king of Vidarbha whose daughter married sage Agastya (*M. Bh.*); a dānava (*H. Parāṇa*).

Nimiṣa (S) (M) **1.** twinkling of an eye. **3.** a son of Garuḍa (*M. Bh.*); another name for Viṣṇu.

Nimīśvara (S) (M) **1.** lord of the moment. **3.** the 16th Arhat of the past Utsarpinī (*J. S. Koṣa*).

Nimita (S) (M) fixed; erected; raised.

Nimitta (S) (M) token; omen; mark; sign; cause.

Nimittaka (S) (M) kissing; a kiss.

Nimrući (S) (M) **1.** sunset. **3.** a king of the Yādava dynasty who was the son of Bhoja and the father of Kiṅkaṇa and Vṛṣṇi.

Nināda (S) (M) gentle murmur; humming; sound.

Ninādita (S) (M) full of sound; resonant.

Niṅga (S) (M) knower of secrets; a mark; a symbol; the Śivaliṅga (*Ś. Purāṇa*).

Nīpa (S) (M) **1.** situated; low; deep. **3.** a Puru king who was the husband of Kirtimat (*M. Bh.*); a son of Kṛtin and father of Ugrāyudha (*Bh. Purāṇa*).

Nipāka (S) (M) intelligent; wise; chief.

Nīpātithi (S) (M) **1.** arriving at the foot of the mountains. **3.** a descendant of Kaṇva and the author of *Ṛg Veda* (viii).

Nipuṇa (S) (M) adept; proficient; skilful; kindly; complete; perfect; clever; adroit; sharp; efficient.

Nirabhilāṣa (S) (M) without any desire; above all desires.

Nirabhimāna (S) (M) without pride; free from pride.

Nirabhra (S) (M) free from clouds.

Nīrada (S) (M) **1.** water giver. **2.** cloud.

Niradāna (S) (M) **1.** accepting; missing. **3.** a Buddha (*B. Literature*).

Nīradhauta (S) (M) washed with water; polished; purified; bright; clean.

Nirādhi (S) (M) free from anxiety.

Nīradindu (S) (M) clouded moon.

Nirāga (S) (M) free from passion.

Niragha (S) (M) **1.** free from sins. **2.** innocent; sinless.

Nīrāj (S) (M) to illuminate; irradiate.

Niraja (S) (M) **1.** free from dust; free from passion. **3.** another name for Śiva.

Nīrājana (S) (M) **1.** offering of light. **2.** act of offering light to the deity.

Nirālā (S) (M) unique.

Nirāmayā (S) (M) **1.** free from illness. **2.** healthy; wholesome; pure. **3.** an ancient river (*M. Bh.*).

Nirāmiṣa (S) (M) free from convetuousness.

Niramitra (S) (M) **1.** free from enemies. **3.** a son of Nakula and Kareṇumatī (*M. Bh.*); a son of the king of Trigarta (*M. Bh.*); a son of Ayutāyuṣ (*M. Bh.*); a sage considered as Śiva's son (*M. Bh.*).

Nirañjana (S) (M) **1.** without collyrium; without a blackspot. **2.** spotless; pure; unpainted; devoid of passion. **3.** an attendant of Śiva; another name for Śiva.

Nirāntaka (S) (M) free from end; free from all that brings the end; free from fear and pain; another name for Śiva.

Nirantara (S) (M) without any gap; perpetual.

Nirāpada (S) (M) without difficulties.

Nirapāya (S) (M) imperishable.

Nirargala (S) (M) unimpeded; free, irresisted.

Nirasa (S) (M) without anger.

Nirāśaṅka (S) (M) without any doubt; free from any doubt; fearless.

Nirata (S) (M) engrossed; absorbed; pleased; satisfied.

Niratyaya (S) (M) secure; free from danger.

Nīrava (S) (M) free from sound; quiet; silent; still.

Niravadya (S) (M) flawlessness; excellence.

Niravaśeṣa (S) (M) **1.** without a remainder. **2.** whole; complete.

Niravinda (S) (M) **1.** without shine; not glowing; dull. **2.** smoky; dusky. **3.** a mountain (*M. Bh.*).

Niravyalīka (S) (M) not causing pain; harmless; sincere.

Niraya (S) (M) hell personified as a son of Bhaya and Mṛtyu (*Bh. Purāṇa*).

Nirbhaya (S) (M) **1.** fearless. **3.** a son of the 13th Manu (*H. Purāṇa*).

Nirbhī (S) (M) fearless.

Nirbhīka (S) (M) fearless.

Nireka (S) (M) without an equal; superior; pre-eminent.

Nirgahana (S) (M) knowing no difficulties.

Niriṅga (S) (M) immovable; not flickering; still.

Nirjara (S) (M) young; fresh; not becoming old; immortal; gold; a gold.

Nirjaya (S) (M) conquest; complete victory.

Nirjetṛ (S) (M) conqueror.

Nirjhara (S) (M) **1.** cascade. **2.** mountain; torrent; waterfall; elephant. **3.** a horse of the sun.

Nirjita (S) (M) conquered; subdued; gained; won.

Nirjvara (S) (M) healthy.

Nirlepa (S) (M) **1.** unsmeared. **2.** stainless; sinless. **3.** another name for Śiva.

Nirlipta (S) (M) **1.** undefiled. **3.** another name for Kṛṣṇa.

Nirlobha (S) (M) free from greed.

Nirmada (S) (M) without intoxication; sober; quiet; humble; modest.

Nirmala (S) (M) **1.** not dirty; spotless; clean; pure; bright; shining; sinless. **3.** another name for Skanda.

Nirmalendu (S) (M) full moon; bright moon.

Nirmama (S) (M) **1.** unselfish. **3.** the 25th Arhat of the future Utsarpiṇī; another name for Śiva.

Nirmantu (S) (M) faultless; innocent.

Nirmanyu (S) (M) free from anger.

Nirmatsara (S) (M) without envy; unselfish.

Nirmita (S) (M) created; built; fashioned.

Nirmoha (S) (M) **1.** free from illusion. **3.** a son of the 5th Manu (*H. Purāṇa*); a ṛṣi of the 13th Manvantara; another name for Śiva (*P. Purāṇa*).

Nirmoka (S) (M) **1.** setting free. **2.** sky. **3.** a son of the 8th Manu (*Bh. Purāṇa*); a ṛṣi under the 13th Manu (*Bh. Purāṇa*).

Nirmokṣa (S) (M) liberation.

Nirmuta (S) (M) **1.** ever rising; ever growing. **2.** a tree; the sun.

Nirodha (S) (M) restraint; constraint; control.

Niroṣa (S) (M) without anger.

Nirṛti (S) (M) **1.** death; destruction. **3.** a deva who is the guardian of the southwestern quarter and the son of Śthāṇu (*A. Purāṇa*); a rudra (*M. Bh.*); one of the 8 vasus (*H. Purāṇa*).

Niruja (S) (M) healthy; wholesome.

Nīrulatā (S) (M) a water vine; a vine that grows in water.

Nirunmāda (S) (M) free from pride; humble.

Nīrūpa (S) (M) formless; air; wind; ether; a god.

Nirupadhi (S) (M) guileless; honest; secure.

Nirupama (S) (M) unparalled; fearless; unequalled; incomparable.

Nirūpita (S) (M) seen; considered; appointed; elected; chosen.

Nīruppala (S) (M) **1.** water stone; a stone as clear as water. **2.** a crystal.

Nirutsuka (S) (M) **1.** without curiosity; not curious; tranquil. **3.** a son of Manu Raivata; a ṛṣi of the 13th Manvantara (*H. Purāṇa*).

Niruttara (S) (M) without an answer; having no superior.

Nirvala (S) (M) **1.** guide less; sacred; pious. **2.** the sacred Barna tree.

Nirvāṇin (S) (M) **1.** one who has attained nirvāna or final emancipation. **3.** the 2nd Arhat of the past Utsarpiṇī (*J.S. Koṣa*).

Nirvara (S) (M) without a superior; unique; excellent.

Nirvāta (S) (M) sheltered; calm.

Nirvighna (S) (M) unobstructed.

Nirvikāra (S) (M) unchangeable.

Nirviśaṅka (S) (M) fearless; doubtless.

Nirvṛta (S) (M) emancipated; contented; satisfied; happy; tranquil; at rest.

Nirvṛti (S) (M) **1.** complete happiness; bliss; emancipation. **3.** a son of Vṛṣṇi.

Nirvyagra (S) (M) unconfused; calm.

Nirvyāja (S) (M) free from deceit; pure.

Nirvyaṅga (S) (M) without any deformity.

Nirvyūha (S) (M) without formation; turret, a crest ornament.

Niśāćarapati (S) (M) **1.** lord of the wanderer of the night.

2. lord of the moon. 3. another name for Śiva.

Niṣāda (S) (M) 1. to sit. 2. a low caste; the last note of the musical gamut. 3. a king said to have sprung from the thigh of Vena.

Niṣādanareśa (S) (M) 1. king of the Niṣādas or forest hunters. 3. a king who was an incarnation of the daityas Kālakeya and Krodhahanta (*M. Bh.*); another name for Nala.

Niṣadha (S) (M) 1. hunter. 2. place where hunting is done. 3. a mountain range north of the Himālaya; the grandson of Kuśa and son of Aditi; a king of Bharata's dynasty who was the son of Janamejaya (*M. Bh.*).

Niṣadhāśva (S) (M) 1. one with mountain horses. 3. a son of Kuru (*Bh. Purāṇa*).

Niśāhāsa (S) (M) 1. smiling in the night. 2. the White Water Lily flower (*Nymphaea alba*).

Niśākānta (S) (M) 1. beloved of night. 3. another name for the moon (*K. Sāgara*).

Niśākara (S) (M) 1. one who makes the night. 3. a ṛṣi who foretold the future for Sampāti (*V. Rāmāyaṇa*); another name for the moon.

Niśalya (S) (M) free from pain; happy; painless; one who doesn't cause pain to others.

Niśāmaṇi (S) (M) 1. jewel of night. 3. another name for the moon.

Niśamanya (S) (M) uncommon; extraordinary.

Niśāmukha (S) (M) 1. the face of the night. 2. twilight.

Niśānātha (S) (M) lord of night; another name for the moon.

Nisaṅga (S) (M) absence of attachment; moving freely; unselfish.

Niṣangin (S) (M) 1. having a sword or quiver. 3. a son of Dhṛtarāṣṭra (*M. Bh.*).

Niśanka (S) (M) free from fear or risk.

Niśankara (S) (M) 1. creator of night. 3. another name for the moon.

Niśānta (S) (M) 1. night close. 2. daybreak; tranquil; calm; quiet.

Niśāpati (S) (M) 1. lord of night. 3. another name for the moon.

Niśaṭha (S) (M) 1. not false. 2. honest. 3. the son of Balarāma and Revatī who became a viśvadeva after his death (*M. Bh.*); a king in the court of Yama (*M. Bh.*).

Niśatru (S) (M) free from enemies.

Niścala (S) (M) 1. immovable; fixed; steady; calm. 3. *Desmodium gangeticum*.

Niścara (S) (M) 1. to come forth; appear; rise. 3. a ṛṣi of the 2nd Manvantara (*H. Purāṇa*).

Niścint (S) (M) without anxiety, worry, care; carefree.

Niścinta (S) (M) free from anxiety, worry and care.

Niścyavana (S) (M) 1. imperishable. 2. fire. 3. a ṛṣi of the 2nd Manvantara; (*H. Purāṇa*) the 2nd son of Bṛhaspati (*M. Bh.*); a ṛṣi of the 2nd Manvantara (*H. Purāṇa*).

Niśeṣa (S) (M) 1. lord of night. 2. another name for the moon.

Nisīman (S) (M) unbounded; infinite; grand.

Nisita (S) (M) sharpened; sharp; excited; eager; prepared; iron; steel.

Niśitha (S) (M) 1. born of night; one of the 3 sons of Doshā or night (*Bh. Purāṇa*). 3. a king of Dhruva's dynasty who was the son of Puṣpārṇa and Prabhā (*Bhāgavata*).

Niṣkaitava (S) (M) undeceitful; honest; pure.

Niṣkaivalya (S) (M) pure; emancipation; absolute; release.

Niṣkalaṅka (S) (M) 1. flawless; immaculate. 3. another name for Śiva.

Niṣkāma (S) (M) selfless.

Niṣkāmuka (S) (M) free from worldly desires.

Niṣkaṇṭaka (S) (M) 1. free from thorns; unhurt; secure. 3. another name for Śiva.

Niṣkarūṣa (S) (M) free from dirt.

Niṣkaṣāya (S) (M) 1. free from dirt. 3. the 13th Arhat of the future Utsarpiṇī.

Niṣkleśa (S) (M) free from pain; free from quarrel.

Niṣkṛti (S) (M) **1.** restoration; atonement; complete development; cure. **3.** an agni who was the son of Bṛhaspati (*M. Bh.*).

Niṣkupita (S) (M) **1.** without anger. **3.** a marut (*V. Purāṇa*).

Niṣkumbha (S) (M) **1.** *Croton polyandrum*. **2.** a visvādeva.

Niśoka (S) (M) free from sorrow.

Niṣpāra (S) (M) boundless; unlimited.

Niṣpatti (S) (M) to originate from; to issue from.

Niṣpraćāra (S) (M) not spread; concentrated.

Niṣprakampa (S) (M) **1.** without quiver. **2.** immovable. **3.** a ṛṣi of the 13th Manvantara (*H. Purāṇa*).

Niṣpratīpa (S) (M) unopposed.

Niṣpulāka (S) (M) **1.** free from chaff. **2.** tree of all impurity; pure. **3.** the 14th Arhat of the future Utsarpiṇī (*J.S. Koṣa*).

Niśreṇī (S) (M) **1.** ladder. **3.** the wild date tree (*Phoenix sylvestris*).

Niśreyasa (S) (M) **1.** having no better. **2.** best; ultimate bliss. **3.** another name for Śiva.

Nissaṅgha (S) (M) without attachment; absolute concentration; detached from worldly things.

Niṣṭhānaka (S) (M) **1.** speaking loud; roar. **3.** a nāga who was the son of Kaśyapa and Kadru (*M. Bh.*).

Niṣṭhurika (S) (M) **1.** cruel; severe; hard; rough. **3.** a nāga who was born in the Kaśyapa dynasty (*M. Bh.*).

Nistula (S) (M) matchless; incomparable.

Nistuṣa (S) (M) free from chaff; pure.

Niśumbha (S) (M) **1.** killing; slaughter. **3.** an asura who was the son of Kaśyapa and Diti and the brother of Śumbha (*H. Purāṇa*).

Nisūna (S) (M) **1.** son of the bright ones. **3.** an asura killed by Kṛṣṇa (*M. Bh.*).

Nisvana (S) (M) **1.** sound; voice; soundless; noiseless. **3.** another name for Agni.

Niṭalākṣa (S) (M) **1.** with an eye in the forehead. **3.** another name for Śiva.

Nitambhū (S) (M) **1.** carrying the earth; remover of the darkness of earth; suffocating the earth. **3.** a great sage (*M. Bh.*).

Nītha (S) (M) **1.** leader. **3.** a king of the Vṛṣṇi dynasty (*M. Bh.*).

Nīti (S) (M) policy; moral code; guidance; management; conduct; prudence.

Nītigotra (S) (M) **1.** knower of policy; knower of moral code. **2.** managing a dynasty; politician; preceptor. **3.** a king of the Bhṛgu dynasty (*Bhāgavata*).

Nītila (S) (M) bearer of moral code; the forehead.

Nītilākṣa (S) (M) **1.** with an eye of Nīti. **3.** Śiva with the 3rd eye.

Nītin (S) (M) having knowledge of law; moralist; policy maker.

Nītīndra (S) (M) lord of policy; king.

Nitya (S) (M) **1.** perpetual; eternal; invariable. **2.** sea; ocean.

Nityagati (S) (M) **1.** moving constantly. **2.** wind. **3.** another name for Vāyu.

Nityamaya (S) (M) consisting of eternity; eternal.

Nityānanda (S) (M) eternal happiness.

Nityanātha (S) (M) **1.** eternal lord. **3.** another name for Śiva.

Nityapāda (S) (M) lord of Nityā.

Nityapriya (S) (M) **1.** eternally pleasing. **3.** another name for Śiva.

Nityasiddha (S) (M) ever perfect.

Nityayūj (S) (M) ever attached; with the mind always concentrated.

Nityayukta (S) (M) **1.** always active; always energetic. **3.** a bodhisattva.

Nivaha (S) (M) **1.** bringing; multitude; heap; killing. **3.** one of the 7 winds and one of the 7 tongues of fire.

Nivān (S) (M) **1.** reigned; bound. **2.** reined horse. **3.** one of the 10 horses of the moon.

Nivāta (S) (M) **1.** unhurt; compact; safe; secure. **2.** sheltered from the wind; an impenetrable coat of mail.

Nivātakavaća (S) (M) **1.** with impenetrable armour. **3.** the grandson of Hiraṇyakaśipu (*Bhā. Purāṇa*).

Nivatha (S) (M) calm; sheltered; safe.

Nivedana (S) (M) announcement; dedication; offering.

Nivedin (S) (M) **1.** requesting; announcing; proclaiming; offering; delivering. **3.** another name for Śiva.

Nivida (S) (M) instruction; information; invocation.

Nivīta (S) (M) **1.** adorned with. **3.** the sacred thread worn as a garland round Brahmā's neck.

Nivrāṅśu (S) (M) rays of the moon.

Niyama (S) (M) fasten; restrain; grant; govern; control; determine.

Niyantraṇa (S) (M) control; restraint; definition.

Niyatāyu (S) (M) **1.** with a limited age. **3.** the son of Śrutāyu (*M. Bh.*).

Niyudha (S) (M) warrior.

Nodhas (S) (M) **1.** seer of 9 fold devotion. **3.** a ṛṣi of the *Ṛg Veda* (*Ṛg Veda*).

Nṛćakṣus (S) (M) **1.** the eye of men. **3.** a king of the Yayāti dynasty (*M. Bh.*).

Nṛdeva (S) (M) king of men.

Nṛga (S) (M) **1.** originating from men. **3.** a king of the dynasty of Vaivasvata Manu who was the son of Kṣupa and the younger brother of Ikṛvaku (*M. Bh.*); a grandson of Oghavat; a son of Uśīnara; a son of Manu (*M. Bh.*); the father of Sumati (*M. Bh.*).

Nṛgaćandra (S) (M) **1.** moon among men. **3.** the son of Rantinara (*M. Bh.*).

Nṛgadeva (S) (M) god among men.

Nṛgajit (S) (M) conqueror of men.

Nṛgamanas (S) (M) king to men.

Nṛgamaṇi (S) (M) jewel among men.

Nṛgamithuna (S) (M) **1.** pair of men. **2.** twin. **3.** zodiac sign of Gemini.

Nṛgapāla (S) (M) protector of men.

Nṛgapati (S) (M) king of men.

Nṛgaṣada (S) (M) **1.** dwelling among men. **3.** father of Kaṇva.

Nṛgasinha (S) (M) **1.** lion among men. 3. Viṣṇu and his 4th incarnation (*H. Purāṇa*).

Nṛgasoma (S) (M) moon among men.

Nṛgātama (S) (M) most manly; strongest among men.

Nṛgavara (S) (M) best among men; sovereign; chief.

Nṛkesarin (S) (M) **1.** lion among men. **3.** great men; manlion; Viṣṇu in his 4th incarnation.

Nṛpa (S) (M) protector of men; king.

Nṛpadīpa (S) (M) a lamp among kings; a king as radiant and illuminating as the glow of lamp.

Nṛpamana (S) (M) saluted by men.

Nṛpañjaya (S) (M) **1.** conqueror of men. **3.** a son of Suvīra (*H. Purāṇa*); a son of Medhāvin (*Bh. Purāṇa*).

Nṛpavallabha (S) (M) dear to a king.

Nṛśad (S) (M) **1.** using man as vehicle; hounting on men; worshipped by men. **3.** a sage who was the father of Kaṇva (*Ṛg Veda*).

Nṛsoma (S) (M) moon among men; illustrious; great.

Nṛt (S) (M) truth; the sacred thread round the neck.

Nṛtu (S) (M) **1.** dancing. **2.** lively; active. **3.** another name for Indra and the maruts.

Nṛtyapriyā (S) (M) **1.** fond of dancing. **2.** peacock. **3.** a Mātṛ attending Skanda (*Sk. Purāṇa*).

Nu (S) (M) praise; eulogium; weapon; time.

Nūtana (S) (M) young; fresh; new; curious; strange; modern.

Nyagrodha (S) (M) **1.** growing downward. **2.** Banyan tree (*Ficus indica*). **3.** a son of Ugrasena who was killed by Balarāma (*Bhā. Purāṇa*); a son of Kṛṣṇa (*Bh. Purāṇa*).

Nyāma (S) (M) restraining; controlling.

Nyāṅku (S) (M) **1.** antelope. **3.** a ćakravartin (*M. Bh.*).

Nyāyāćaryā (S) (M) teacher of the moral law; teacher of syllogism; the correct.

Nyāyavid (S) (M) knowing the law; knowing the logic; logician; attaining truth through syllogism.

O

Ob/Obal (S) (M) **1.** phallus. **3.** the Śivaliṅga or the male organ which represents Śiva.

Obaleśa (S) (M) **1.** lord of the liṅga. **3.** another name for Śiva.

Obaleśvara (S) (M) **1.** lord of the liṅga. **3.** another name for Śiva.

Obbana (**Tamil**) (M) **1.** lord of the liṅga. **3.** another name for Śiva.

Odana (S) (M) food; boiled rice; grain cooked with milk; cloud.

Ogaṇa (S) (M) wave; assembled; united.

Ogha (S) (M) **1.** stream; current; swift; flood. **2.** uninterrupted tradition. **3.** a musical concert.

Ogharatha (S) (M) **1.** with a swift chariot. **3.** the son of Oghavāna (*M. Bh.*).

Oghavāna (S) (M) **1.** conqueror of the current. **3.** a grandson of King Nṛga and father of Ogharatha and Oghavatī (*M. Bh.*); a warrior who fought on the side of the Kauravas in the Mahābhārata (*M. Bh.*).

Oha (S) (M) vehicle; bringing near; excellence; true knowledge; meditation.

Ohabrahman (S) (M) a true Brāhmin; having knowledge; meditating.

Ohas (S) (M) vehicle; praise; idea; true notion.

Oja (S) (M) to increase; virility; to grow in lustre and vigour.

Ojal (S) (M) having splendour; vision.

Ojas (S) (M) **1.** virility; energy; power; strength; splendour. **2.** water; light; appearance. **3.** a son of Kṛṣṇa (*Bh. Purāṇa*); a yakṣa (*Bh. Purāṇa*).

Ojasīn (S) (M) strong; powerful.

Ojasvī (S) (M) brave; bright; splendid.

Ojasvin (S) (M) **1.** brave; bright; energetic; vigorous; shining; powerful. **3.** a son of Manu Bhautya (*V. Purāṇa*).

Ojasyā (S) (M) possessing virility; strong; powerful.

Ojāyita (S) (M) made virile; on whom courage has been bestowed; courageous.

Ojiṣṭha (S) (M) **1.** residing in virility; best among the powerful. **2.** powerful; vigorous; strongest. **3.** a sage (*Bhā. Purāṇa*).

Ojodā (S) (M) one who gives strength.

Ojopati (S) (M) **1.** master of power. **3.** a deity of the Bodhi tree.

Okāb (H) (M) Tawny Eagle (*Aquila rapax*).

Okas (S) (M) house; shelter; refuge.

Okithak (S) (M) **1.** speaker; preacher. **3.** a Brāhman who studies the prayers of the *Sāma Veda* (*S. Veda*).

Om (S) (M) creation; development and destruction; essence of life; the sacred syll-able which is the seed of all mantras; assent; so be it; the sound is a combination of 'A' which signifies Viṣṇu, 'U' for Śiva and 'M' signifying Brahmā, the sound is called 'Praṇava' (essence of life) or 'Brahman' (ultimate essence).

Oma (S) (M) life giving; friend; helper; protector.

Oman (S) (M) life giving; protection; favour; friend; protector.

Omasvata (S) (M) friendly; favourable.

Omeśa (S) (M) lord of the Om.

Omeśvara (S) (M) **1.** lord of the sacred word. **2.** Om. **3.** another name for Śiva.

Omkāra (S) (M) **1.** the syllable Om. **3.** a liṅga.

Omkaranātha (S) (M) **1.** lord of the Om. **3.** the deity at Māndhātā; another name for Śiva.

Ompati (S) (M) master of the Om.

Ompatu (**Malayālam**) (M) master of the Om; 9.

Omprakāśa (S) (M) the light from of Om; the sacred light; the light spread by the sacred syllable Om.

Oṇi (S) (M) **1.** protection; shelter. **2.** heaven and earth conjoined. **3.** a vessel used in distilling Soma (*Ṛg Veda*).

Opaśa (S) (M) support; pillar; ornament of the head.

Oṣadhinātha (S) (M) **1.** lord of herbs. **3.** another name for the moon.

Oṣadhipati (S) (M) **1.** lord of herbs. **3.** another name for the moon.

P

Paćata (S) (M) **1.** cooked; boiled. **3.** another name for sun, fire and Indra.

Padāti (S) (M) **1.** pedestrian; foot soldier. **3.** a son of Janamejaya (*Bhā. Purāṇa*).

Padma (S) (M) **1.** Lotus (*Nelumbium speciosum*); a thousand billion. **3.** the sacred lotus flower said to have arisen from the navel of Viṣṇu, it supports Brahmā and represents creation; one of the 9 treasures of Kubera (*M. Bh.*); the 9th Jaina ćakravartin of Bhārata; one of the 8 serpents worn by Śiva and who is a son of Kaśyapa and Kadru (*M. Bh.*); a king in the court of Yama (*M. Bh.*); a king of Kāśmira; a soldier of Skanda (*M. Bh.*); an attendant of Skanda (*M. Bh.*); a mythical Buddha; an elephant (*Rāmāyaṇa*); a nāga (*M. Bh.*).

Padmabandhu (S) (M) **1.** friend of the lotus. **3.** another name for the sun.

Padmabhāsa (S) (M) **1.** with the brilliance of the lotus. **3.** another name for Viṣṇu.

Padmabhava (S) (M) born of the lotus.

Padmabhū (S) (M) born of the lotus.

Padmabhūta (S) (M) **1.** of the lotus. **3.** another name for Brahmā.

Padmadhara (S) (M) lotus bearer.

Padmādhīśa (S) (M) **1.** lord of the lotus. **3.** another name for Viṣṇu.

Padmagandha (S) (M) smelling like a lotus; fragrant.

Padmagarbha (S) (M) **1.** the calyx of a lotus. **2.** one who is born from a lotus; sprung from a lotus. **3.** a Buddha (*L. Vistara*); a bodhisattva; another name for Brahmā, Viṣṇu, Śiva and the sun.

Padmahāsan (S) (M) **1.** lotus smile. **3.** another name for Viṣṇu.

Padmaja (S) (M) **1.** born of a lotus. **3.** another name for Brahmā.

Padmakara (S) (M) **1.** with a lotus in hand. **3.** another name for the sun.

Padmakesara (S) (M) filament of a lotus.

Padmaketana (S) (M) **1.** lotus bannered. **3.** a son of Garuḍa (*M. Bh.*).

Padmākṣa (S) (M) **1.** lotus eyed. **3.** the son of Ćandrahāsa and Ćampakamālinī (*A. Koṣa*); another name for Viṣṇu; Himālayan Cherry (*Prunus cerasoides*).

Padmalāñćana (S) (M) **1.** lotus marked; a king. **3.** another name for Brahmā, Kubera and the sun.

Padmālaya (S) (M) **1.** dwelling in a lotus. **3.** another name for Brahmā.

Padmaloćana (S) (M) lotus eyed.

Padmamālin (S) (M) **1.** garlanded with a lotus. **3.** a rākṣasa (*Rāmāyaṇa*).

Padmamihira (S) (M) **1.** lotus sun. **2.** the sun, that makes the lotus bloom; one who delights the nobles. **3.** a historian of Kāśmira (*R. Taraṅgiṇī*).

Padmanābha (S) (M) **1.** lotus navelled. **3.** a son of Dhṛtarāṣṭra (*M. Bh.*); the 1st Arhat of the future Utsarpiṇī; a nāga of Naimiśāraṇya (*M. Bh.*); another name for Viṣṇu.

Padmanābhi (S) (M) **1.** lotus navelled. **3.** another name for Viṣṇu.

Padmānana (S) (M) lotus faced.

Padmanandana (S) (M) **1.** arisen from a lotus. **3.** another name for Brahmā.

Padmanandin (S) (M) rejoicing in the lotus.

Padmanetra (S) (M) **1.** lotus eyed. **3.** a future Buddha.

Padmanidhi (S) (M) **1.** abounding in lotuses. **2.** a treasure worth a 1000 billion. **3.** one of the 9 treasures of Kubera (*Pañćatantra*).

Padmapāṇi (S) (M) **1.** lotus handed. **3.** another name for Brahmā, Viṣṇu and the bodhisattva Avalokiteśvara.

Padmaprabha (S) (M) **1.** with the light of the lotus. **2.** lotus coloured; shining like a lotus. **3.** the 6th Arhat of the present Avasarpiṇī (*J.S. Koṣa*); a future Buddha (*L. Vistara*).

Padmarāga (S) (M) **1.** lotus hued. **2.** a ruby.

Padmaratha (S) (M) **1.** with a lotus chariot. **3.** another name for Rāma.

Padmaratna (S) (M) **1.** lotus jewelled. **3.** a Buddhist patriarch.

Padmaśekhara (S) (M) **1.** lotus crested. **3.** a king of the gandharvas (*K. Sāgara*).

Padmavarṇa (S) (M) **1.** lotus coloured. **3.** a son of Yadu (*H. Purāṇa*).

Padmaveśa (S) (M) **1.** dressed in lotus petals. **3.** a king of the vidyādharas.

Padmayoni (S) (M) **1.** lotus born. **3.** a Buddha (*L. Vistara*); another name for Brahmā.

Padmeśa (S) (M) **1.** lord of the lotus. **3.** another name for Brahmā and Viṣṇu.

Padmeśaya (S) (M) **1.** sleeping in a lotus. **3.** another name for Viṣṇu.

Padmin (S) (M) lotus like; one who plucks the lotus; one who likes the lotus; elephant.

Padminīkantā (S) (M) **1.** beloved of lotuses. **3.** another name for the sun.

Padminīśa (S) (M) **1.** lord of lotuses. **3.** another name for the sun.

Padmodbhava (S) (M) **1.** sprung from a lotus. **3.** another name for Brahmā.

Padmottara (S) (M) **1.** the best lotus. **2.** beyond comparison; the best. **3.** a Buddha; wild saffron (*Carthamus tinctorius*).

Padvāya (S) (M) leader; guide.

Paila (S) (M) **1.** son of Pīlā. **3.** a disciple of Vyāsa; a teacher of the *Ṛg Veda*.

Paināka (S) (M) **1.** belonging to Pināka. **3.** belonging to Rudra-Śiva (*V. Rāmāyaṇa*).

Paiṭhaka (S) (M) **1.** one who does not leave his seat. **3.** an asura killed by Kṛṣṇa (*M. Bh.*).

Pājas (S) (M) **1.** firmness; vigour; strength; glitter; sheen; brightness. **2.** heaven and earth.

Pajrahoṣin (S) (M) **1.** with rich or fat oblations. **2.** to whom many oblations are offered; divine. **3.** another name for Indra and Agni.

Pajriya (S) (M) **1.** fat; stout; strong. **3.** another name for Kakṣīvat.

Pāka (S) (M) **1.** simple; ignorant; young; child. **3.** a daitya slain by Indra (*M. Bh.*).

Pākadviṣ (S) (M) **1.** destroyer of Pāka. **3.** another name for Indra.

Pakal (Malayalam) (M) day.

Pākaśāsana (S) (M) **1.** punisher of Pāka. **2.** instructor of the ignorant. **3.** another name for Indra.

Pākaśāsani (S) (M) **1.** son of Indra. **3.** another name for Jayanta and Arjuna (*M. Bh.*).

Pakṣacchid (S) (M) **1.** cutter of wings. **3.** another name for Indra.

Pakṣaja (S) (M) **1.** produced in half a month. **3.** another name for the moon.

Pakṣālu (S) (M) **1.** feathered. **2.** a bird.

Pakṣarāja (S) (M) **1.** lord of birds. **3.** another name for Garuḍa and Jatāyu.

Pakṣila (S) (M) **1.** full of feathers; full of examples; full of logic. **3.** another name for the sage Vātsyāyana.

Pakṣīndra (S) (M) **1.** king of birds. **3.** another name for Garuḍa and Jaṭāyu.

Pakṣman (S) (M) eyelashes; filament of a flower; leaf; wing.

Paktha (S) (M) **1.** cook. **3.** a king who was a protégé of the aśvins (*Ṛg Veda*).

Pāla (S) (M) **1.** guardian; protector; keeper; herdsman; king. **3.** a nāga belonging to Vāsuki's race (*M. Bh.*).

Pālaka (S) (M) **1.** protector; prince; sovereign. **3.** a son of Aṅgāraka.

Pālakāpya (S) (M) **1.** involved in the work of protection. **3.** an ancient sage.

Palakṣa (S) (M) white.

Palāśa (S) (M) **1.** leaf; petal; foliage. **2.** green. **3.** the Bastard Teak (*Butea monosperma*).

Palāśapattra (S) (M) **1.** a leaf of the *Butea frondosa*. **3.** a nāga.

Palāśarañjana (S) (M) **1.** liking green. **2.** the spring.

Palījaka (S) (M) **1.** disturber. **3.** a demon (*A. Veda*).

Pālin (S) (M) **1.** protecting; guarding; keeping. **2.** a son of Pṛthu (*H. Purāṇa*).

Pālita (S) (M) **1.** grey; aged. **2.** mouse. **3.** a king (*H. Purāṇa*).

Pallava (S) (M) sprout; shoot; spray; bud; blossom.

Pallavāstra (S) (M) **1.** with blossoms for weapons. **3.** another name for Kāma.

Panasa (S) (M) **1.** resident of a tree; Breadfruit tree (*Artocarpus integrifolia*). **2.** monkey. **3.** a commander of Rāma's monkey army (*Rāmāyaṇa*).

Panasyu (S) (M) worthy of admiration; glorious.

Paṇava (S) (M) **1.** a small drum; a cymbal. **3.** a prince (*V. Purāṇa*).

Paṇavin (S) (M) **1.** possessing a small drum. **3.** another name for Ś.iva.

Panāyya (S) (M) praiseworthy.

Pañćabāhu (S) (M) **1.** 5 armed. **3.** an attendant of Śiva (*H. Purāṇa*).

Pañćabāṇa (S) (M) **1.** 5 arrowed. **3.** another name for Kāma.

Panćaćakṣus (S) (M) **1.** five eyed. **3.** a buddha.

Pañćaćīra (S) (M) **1.** one who wears 5 sacred clothes. **3.** another name of the Buddhist saint Mañjuśṛī.

Pañćadhanuṣ (S) (M) **1.** 5 bowed. **3.** a Purū king who was the son of Sṛñjaya and the father of Somadatta (*A. Purāṇa*).

Pañćahasta (S) (M) **1.** 5 handed. **3.** a son of Manu (*V. Purāṇa*).

Pañćahāva (S) (M) **1.** performer of 5 sacrifices. **3.** a son of Manu Rohita (*H. Purāṇa*).

Pañćaja (S) (M) **1.** born of 5. **3.** an asura who lived in a conch and was killed by Kṛṣṇa; this conch later came to be known as Kṛṣṇa's Panćajanya conch (*Bhāgavata*); another name for Asamañjas who was the son of Sagara and Keśinī.

Pañćajana (S) (M) **1.** the 5 classes of beings. **2.** the 5 classifications are men, gods, apsarās, gandharvas and manes; king; prince. **3.** a demon slain by Kṛṣṇa (*M. Bh.*); a son of Saṁhrāda and Kṛti (*Bhā. Purāṇa*); a prajāpati whose daughter Aśiknī married Dakṣa (*Bhāgavata*); a son of Sagara and Keśinī (*H. Purāṇa*); the son of Sṛñjaya and father of Somadatta (*H. Purāṇa*).

Pañćajanendra (S) (M) lord of men; king; prince.

Pāñćajanya (S) (M) **1.** born of 5. **2.** containing the 5 races of men. **3.** an agni born of the parts of 5 sages (*M. Bh.*); the conch of Śiva; the conch of Kṛṣṇa.

Pañćajñāna (S) (M) **1.** possessing 5 fold knowledge. **3.** a Buddha.

Pañćaka (S) (M) **1.** consisting of 5 elements. **3.** an attendant of Skanda given to him by Indra (*M. Bh.*); a son of Nahuṣa; one of the first 5 disciples of Gautama Buddha (*B. Literature*).

Pañćākṣa (S) (M) **1.** 5 eyed. **3.** an attendant of Śiva (*Ś. Purāṇa*).

Pañćāla (S) (M) consisting of 5; surrounded by 5 rivers; a style of singing; a warrior tribe of the north; a ṛṣi (*M. Bh.*); a nāga; another name for Śiva.

Pāñćāla (S) (M) **1.** of the Pāñćālas. **3.** another name for Dhṛṣṭadyumna and Drupada.

Pāñćāladāyāda (S) (M) **1.** possessing Pāñćāla. **3.** another name for Dhṛṣṭadyumna.

Pāñćālakulavardhana (S) (M) **1.** increasing the Pāñćāla family. **3.** another name for Dhṛṣṭadyumna.

Pāñćālamukhya (S) (M) **1.** leader of the Pāñćālas. **3.** another name for Dhṛṣṭadyumna.

Pāñćālaputra (S) (M) **1.** son of Pāñćāla. **3.** another name for Dhṛṣṭadyumna.

Pāñćālarāja (S) (M) **1.** lord of Pāñćāla. **3.** another name for Dhṛṣṭadyumna and Drupada.

Pañćālika (S) (M) **1.** spices; pepper; dry ginger. **3.** belonging to a yakṣa son of Kubera worshipped as a vigour giving deity in some parts of India.

Pāñćālya (S) (M) **1.** of Pāñćāla. **3.** another name for Dhṛṣṭadyumna and Drupada.

Pañćama (S) (M) the 5th note of classical music; dextrous; clever; beautiful; brilliant.

Pañćamara (S) (M) **1.** 5th among the mortals; slayer of 5. **2.** the 5th spoke in the wheel of time. **3.** a son of Balarāma (*Bhā. Purāṇa*).

Pañćamukha (S) (M) **1.** 5 faced. **3.** another name for Śiva.

Pañćamūla (S) (M) **1.** 5 rooted. **3.** an attendant of Durgā.

Pañćānana (S) (M) **1.** 5 faced. **2.** very fierce; lion. **3.** another name for Śiva.

Pañćanātha (S) (M) lord of the 5; the 5 elements of existence.

Pañćārćis (S) (M) **1.** with 5 rays. **3.** another name for Mercury.

Pañćaśara (S) (M) **1.** 5 arrowed. **3.** another name for Kāma.

Pañćaśikha (S) (M) **1.** 5 crested. **3.** an attendant of Śiva (*K. Sāgara*); a ṛṣi in the court of Janaka (*M. Bh.*); a gandharva.

Pañćāśva (S) (M) **1.** with 5 horses. **3.** a Purū king.

Pañćāsya (S) (M) **1.** 5 faced; lion. **3.** a form of Śiva.

Pañćavaktra (S) (M) **1.** 5 faced. **3.** an attendant of Skanda (*M. Bh.*); another name for Śiva.

Pañćavīra (S) (M) **1.** with 5 warriors. **3.** a viśvadeva (*M. Bh.*).

Pañćayāma (S) (M) **1.** with 5 courses. **3.** a son of Ātapa and grandson of Vibhāvasu and Uṣā (*Bh. Purāṇa*).

Pañćāyatana (S) (M) **1.** one whc makes 5 kinds of effort; one who performs 5 kinds of penance. **3.** an idol of Śiva in Kāśi also called Omkāra.

Pāñćika (S) (M) **1.** with the length of 5; with 5 essences. **2.** the 5 essences of existence. **3.** the leader of the yakṣas.

Pāṇḍa (S) (M) **1.** white; yellow. **3.** a son of Kaṇva and Āryavatī who married Sarasvatīputrī and became the father of 17 sons who will be the future originators of races (*Bh. Purāṇa*).

Paṇḍaka (S) (M) **1.** weakling. **3.** a son of Manu Sāvarṇa (*H. Purāṇa*).

Pāṇḍara (S) (M) **1.** pale. **2.** white; white-yellow. **3.** a nāga of of Airāvata's race (*M. Bh.*).

Pāṇḍava (S) (M) **1.** son of Paṇḍu. **3.** a mountain (*L. Vistara*); another name for Yudhiṣṭhira, Bhīma, Arjuna, Nakula, Sahadeva; White Murdah (*Terminalia citrina*).

Pāṇḍavabhīla (S) (M) **1.** protector of the Pāṇḍavas (*M. Bh.*). **3.** another name for Kṛṣṇa.

Pāṇḍavanandana (S) (M) **1.** son of the Pāṇḍavas. **3.** another name for Yudhiṣṭhira and Janamejaya.

Pāṇḍavānīka (S) (M) the army of the Pāṇḍavās.

Pāṇḍavaśreṣṭha (S) (M) **1.** first of the Pāṇḍavas. **3.** another name for Yudhiṣṭhira.

Pāṇḍaveya (S) (M) **1.** of the Pāṇḍavas. **3.** another name for Yudhiṣṭhira and Janamejaya.

Paṇḍhārinātha (S) (M) **1.** the lord of Pandharpura. **3.** another name for Vithoba (*Bhā. Purāṇa*).

Paṇḍitaka (S) (M) **1.** wise; learned. **2.** pedantic. **3.** a son of Dhṛtarāṣṭra (*M. Bh.*).

Paṇḍitarāja (S) (M) king of learned men.

Paṇḍu (S) (M) **1.** pale. **2.** white. **3.** a son of Vyāsa by the wife of Vićitravīrya, he was the brother of Dhṛtarāṣṭra and Vidura and the husband of Kunti and Mādri; he fathered the 5 Pāṇḍavas (*M. Bh.*); a son of Dhātṛ by Āyatī (*V. Purāṇa*); an attendant of Śiva; the 2nd son of Janamejaya (*M. Bh.*); a serpent lord.

Pāṇḍuka (S) (M) **1.** pale; yellow white. **3.** one of the 9 treasures of the Jainas (*J.S. Koṣa*); a son of Janamejaya (*M. Bh.*).

Pāṇḍuputra (S) (M) son of Paṇḍu; any one of the Pāṇḍava princes (*M. Bh.*).

Pāṇḍura (S) (M) **1.** pale; white; yellow white. **3.** an attendant of Skanda (*M. Bh.*); Button tree (*Anogeissus latifolia*); *Holarrhena antidysentcrica.*

Pāṇḍya (S) (M) **1.** born of Paṇḍu. **3.** a people and country in South India (*M. Bh.*); a son of Akriḍa; a king of Vidarbha (*M. Bh.*).

Pāṇika (S) (M) **1.** the hand. **3.** an attendant of Skanda (*M. Bh.*).

Pāṇikarṇa (S) (M) **1.** hands and ears conjoined. **2.** one who believes in action and is a good listener. 3. another name for Śiva.

Pāṇikūrććas (S) (M) 1. knower of hands. 2. one who understands hand signs; one who understands gestures. 3. an attendant of Skanda (*M. Bh.*).

Pāṇimān (S) (M) 1. with hands. 2. skilled. 3. a nāga at Varuṇa's court (*M. Bh.*).

Pāṇinī (S) (M) 1. with beautiful hands. 2. skilled. 3. the most eminent of all Sanskṛt grammarians, he was the grandson of Devala and the son of Dākṣī.

Pāṇipraṇayin (S) (M) loved; resting in the hand.

Paniṣṭha (S) (M) very wonderful.

Panita (S) (M) admired; praised.

Pāṇitaka (S) (M) 1. one who walks on his hands. 3. one of Skanda's attendants given to him by a deva named Pūṣan (*M. Bh.*).

Pānīya (S) (M) to be commended; to be defended or cherished.

Paṅkaja (S) (M) 1. born of mud; lotus (*Nelumbium nucifera*). 3. another name for Brahmā.

Paṅkajamālin (S) (M) 1. wearing a lotus crown. 3. another name for Viṣṇu.

Paṅkajit (S) (M) 1. destroying sin. 3. a son of Garuḍa (*M. Bh.*).

Paṅkti (S) (M) 1. row; line; numbers 5 and 10. 3. a horse that draws the chariot of Sūrya (*V. Purāṇa*).

Paṅktigrīva (S) (M) 1. 10 necked. 3. another name for Rāvaṇa.

Paṅktiratha (S) (M) 1. with 10 chariots. 3. another name for Daśaratha.

Pannaga (S) (M) 1. serpent. 3. another name for Vāsuki.

Pannagāśana (S) (M) 1. destroying serpents. 3. another name for Garuḍa.

Pannageśa (S) (M) 1. lord of the creeping ones; lord of serpents. 3. another name for Śiva.

Pānśućandana (S) (M) 1. with a yellow mark on the forehead; sandalwood mark on the forehead. 3. another name for Śiva.

Pānśujālika (S) (M) 1. one who rubs dust on the body. 3. another name for Viṣṇu.

Pānśula (S) (M) 1. covered with sandalwood dust. 2. dusty; sandy. 3. Śiva's staff; another name for Śiva; Screwpine (*Pandanus tectorius*).

Pāpabhakṣaṇa (S) (M) 1. devouring the evil. 3. another name for Kālabhairava, a son of Śiva.

Pāpamoćana (S) (M) liberating from sin.

Papī (S) (M) 1. drinker. 3. another name for the sun and the moon.

Papīhā (S) (M) Common Hawk-Cuckoo (*Eudynamys scolopacea*).

Papu (S) (M) protector.

Papuri (S) (M) bountiful; liberal; abundant.

Para (S) (M) 1. far; remote; another; adversary. 3. a son of Viśvāmitra (*M. Bh.*); a king of Kosala; the Supreme Being.

Pāra (S) (M) 1. bringing across; fulfilling; beyond. 3. a son of Pṛthuśena and father of Nīpa (*H. Purāṇa*); a son of Samara and father of Pṛthu (*H. Purāṇa*); a son of Aṅga and father of Diviratha (*H. Purāṇa*); a sage (*Ma. Purāṇa*).

Parabrahman (S) (M) 1. beyond the absolute. 2. the Supreme Spirit.

Parāga (S) (M) the pollen of a flower; fragrant; powder; fame; celebrity.

Pāragata (S) (M) 1. one who has crossed over safely; pure; holy. 3. a Jaina Arhat.

Parahan (S) (M) 1. one who kills others. 2. killer of enemies. 3. an ancient king of Bhārata (*M. Bh.*).

Pāraj (S) (M) gold.

Pāraka (S) (M) carrying over; saving; delivering; satisfying; pleasing.

Parākrama (S) (M) 1. to march forward. 2. to excel; to show courage. 3. a chief of the vidyādharas (*K. Sāgara*); a Kaurava warrior (*M. Bh.*); another name for Viṣṇu.

Paramabhāśvara (S) (M) very radiant.

Paramādvaita (S) (M) **1.** without a second. **2.** the highest beings. **3.** another name for Viṣṇu.

Paramahansa (S) (M) supreme ascetic.

Paramajīta (S) (M) winning perfection; supreme hero.

Paramajñā (S) (M) **1.** holding supreme power. **3.** another name for Indra.

Paramaka (S) (M) highest; best; greatest.

Paramakrodhin (S) (M) **1.** eternally angry; very angry. **3.** a viśvadeva (*M. Bh.*).

Paramākṣara (S) (M) **1.** the supreme syllable. **2.** the sacred syllable Om. **3.** another name for Brahmā.

Paramānanda (S) (M) supreme bliss.

Paramaṇi (S) (M) excellent jewel.

Paramanyu (S) (M) **1.** beyond thought; beyond anger. **3.** a son of Kakśeyu (*M. Bh.*).

Paramaprabha (S) (M) supreme light.

Paramāra (S) (M) **1.** beyond death. **3.** a son of ṛṣi Śaunaka.

Paramarāja (S) (M) supreme monarch.

Paramekṣu (S) (M) **1.** desiring supreme things. **3.** a son of Anu (*V. Purāṇa*).

Parameśa (S) (M) **1.** supreme lord. **3.** another name for Viṣṇu and the Supreme Being.

Parameṣṭhaja (S) (M) **1.** son of Brahmā. **3.** another name for Nārada.

Parameṣṭhin (S) (M) **1.** highest; chief; principal. **3.** another name for Agni, Prajāpati, Brahmā, Śiva, Viṣṇu, Garuḍa and Manu Ćākṣusa; a king of Pānćāla who was the son of Ajamīdha (*M. Bh.*); a son of Indradyumna and the father of Pratīhāra (*V. Purāṇa*).

Parameṣṭhiputra (S) (M) **1.** son of Brahmā. **3.** another name for Nārada.

Parameśvara (S) (M) **1.** supreme god. **2.** king. **3.** another name for Viṣṇu and Indra.

Parāṅgada (S) (M) **1.** giving form to another. **3.** another name for Śiva.

Paraṇtapa (S) (M) **1.** destroying foes. **2.** hero. **3.** a son of Manu Tāmasa (*H. Purāṇa*); a king of Magadha.

Pārapāra (S) (M) **1.** beyond the beyond; the absolute; abode of the ocean. **3.** another name for Viṣṇu.

Parapauravatantava (S) (M) **1.** wearing human clothes. **3.** son of Viśvāmitra.

Parāpurañjaya (S) (M) **1.** winner of the heart of the ocean. **2.** very popular; born in an ocean. **3.** a Hehaya prince.

Pāras (S) (M) the philosopher's stone (a stone supposed to change iron and other such metals into gold by touch).

Parāśa (S) (M) iron.

Parāśara (S) (M) **1.** crusher. **2.** destroyer. **3.** the grandson of Vasiṣṭha and son of Śakti and Adriṣyantī, he was the father of Vyāsa by Satyavatī (*V. Purāṇa*); a son of Kuṭumi (*V. Purāṇa*); a serpent of the family of Dhṛtarāṣṭra (*M. Bh.*).

Pāraśava (S) (M) **1.** made of iron. **3.** a mine in which pearls are found (*V's B. Samhitā*); another name for Vidura (*M. Bh.*).

Pārāśarya (S) (M) **1.** abode of protection; a refuge to enemies. **3.** a sage who was a member of Yudhiṣṭhira's court (*M. Bh.*); the Mādhavi creeper (*Hiptage madoblata*); another name for Vyāsa.

Paraspā (S) (M) protector.

Paraśu (S) (M) made of iron; thunderbolt; hatchet; axe.

Paraśući (S) (M) **1.** very pure; sacred; holy. **3.** a son of Manu Auttama (*M. Purāṇa*).

Paraśudhara (S) (M) **1.** axe holder. **3.** another name for Ganeśa.

Paraśurāma (S) (M) **1.** Rāma with the axe. **3.** the 6th avatāra of Viṣṇu born as the son of Jamadagni and Reṇukā (*Bhā. Purāṇa*).

Paravāṇi (S) (M) **1.** judge. **3.** Kārttikeya's peacock.

Parāvasu (S) (M) **1.** keeping off wealth. **3.** a sage who was the grandson of Viśvāmitra; a son of Raibhya; a gandharva.

Pārāvata (S) (M) **1.** coming from a distance. **2.** pigeon; turtledove. **3.** a nāga of the Airāvata family (*M. Bh.*).

Pārāvatākṣa (S) (M) dove eyed.

Pārāvatasavarṇa (S) (M) **1.** dove coloured. **3.** the horses of Dhṛṣṭadyumna (*M. Bh.*).

Pārayiṣṇu (S) (M) successful; victorious.

Parāyus (S) (M) **1.** reaching the highest age. **3.** another name for Brahmā.

Pāreraka (S) (M) **1.** one that pierces. **2.** sword; scimitar.

Pareśa (S) (M) **1.** highest lord. **3.** another name for Brahmā.

Pareṣṭi (S) (M) with the highest worship.

Paribarha (S) (M) **1.** with many feathers; surroundings; wealth; property; royal insignia. **3.** a son of Garuḍa (*M. Bh.*).

Pāribhadra (S) (M) **1.** the noble coral tree. **2.** as noble as the coral; as auspicious as the Coral Jasmine tree (*Nyctantes arbor tristis*). **3.** a son of Yajñabāhu (*Bh. Purāṇa*).

Paribhrāj (S) (M) to shed brilliance all around.

Paribodha (S) (M) reason.

Paribṛdha (S) (M) firm; strong; solid; superior; lord.

Paridhi (S) (M) circumference; boundary; enclosure; fence; the ocean; the halo around the sun and moon; the circumference of a circle.

Paridvīpa (S) (M) **1.** crossing many islands. **2.** one who travels a lot. **3.** a son of Garuḍa (*Bhā. Purāṇa*).

Parigha (S) (M) **1.** iron rod. **2.** chain used to close doors; a line of clouds crossing the sun at sunrise or sunset. **3.** an attendant of Skanda given to him by the deva Anṣa (*M. Bh.*).

Parigīta (S) (M) sung; celebrated; declared.

Pārijāta (S) (M) **1.** born; the Coral Jasmine (*Nyctantes arbor tristis*). **3.** one of the 5 trees of paradise produced at the churning of the ocean (*M. Bh.*); a serpent cf the family of Airāvata (*M. Bh.*); a ṛṣi (*M. Bh.*).

Parijātaka (S) (M) **1.** of the Coral Jasmine tree. **3.** a sage who was a member of the court of Yudhiṣṭhira (*M. Bh.*).

Parijetṛ (S) (M) victor; conqueror.

Parijman (S) (M) **1.** surrounding; omnipresent. **2.** fire; the moon.

Parijñana (S) (M) perception; knowledge; experience; discrimination.

Parijvāl (S) (M) surround by flames; to burn brightly; to blaze.

Parijvān (S) (M) **1.** fully incited; surrounded by invocations. **3.** another name for the moon, fire and Indra.

Parīkṣit (S) (M) **1.** well examined; fully perceived; tested; dwelling; surrounding; extending. **3.** a celebrated king of the lunar race who was the son of Abhimanyu and Uttarā and father of Janamejaya (*M. Bh.*); a son of Avīkṣit of the Kuru dynasty (*M. Bh.*); a son of Anaśvan and Amṛtā of the Kuru race and the father of Bhīmasena by Suvaśā (*M. Bh.*); an Ikṣvāku king who was the husband of Suśobhanā and the father of Śala, Bala and Dala (*M. Bh.*); a king of Ayodhyā (*M. Bh.*); a son of Kuru (*H. Purāṇa*); another name for Agni, heaven and earth.

Pārīkṣit (S) (M) **1.** son of Parīkṣit. **3.** another name for Janamejaya.

Parikūṭa (S) (M) **1.** barrier; trench. **3.** a nāga (*M. Bh.*).

Parimala (S) (M) fragrance; perfume.

Parīmaṇa (S) (M) quality; bounty; plenty.

Parimantrita (S) (M) well advised; surrounded by praises; charmed; enchanted; consecrated.

Parimita (S) (M) measured; regulated.

Parimohana (S) (M) extremely fascinating; beguiling; alluring; fascinating.

Pariṇāha (S) (M) **1.** circumference; width. **3.** another name for Śiva.

Parīndana (S) (M) present; gift.

Pārīndra (S) (M) **1.** lord of all around. **2.** lion.

Parinirmita (S) (M) **1.** formed; created. **3.** another name for Viṣṇu.

Pariṇuta (S) (M) praised; celebrated.

Paripati (S) (M) lord of all around.

Pāriplava (S) (M) **1.** moving to and fro. **2.** agitated. **3.** a king of the Bharata race who was the son of Nṛćakṣus and the grandson of Nala and the father of Medhāvi (*Bhāgavata*).

Pariprīta (S) (M) full of love; gratified; delighted.

Parisambhu (S) (M) to arise; spring from; be produced from.

Parisatya (S) (M) the pure truth.

Pariśruta (S) (M) **1.** well heard of. **2.** famous; celebrated. **3.** an attendant of Skanda (*M. Bh.*).

Parisuta (S) (M) impelled to come forth; elicited by the gods.

Pariśvanga (S) (M) **1.** an embrace; touch. **3.** a son of Devaki (*Bh. Purāṇa*).

Paritoṣa (S) (M) delight.

Parivaha (S) (M) **1.** carrying around. **2.** one that carries everything away. **3.** the wind that courses over the Gaṅgā river; a tongue of Agni.

Parivarta (S) (M) **1.** revolving; stirring; an abode; spot; place. **3.** a son of Duhsaha and grandson of Mṛtyu (*M. Purāṇa*); another name for Kūrma the 2nd incarnation of Viṣṇu.

Parīveśa (S) (M) **1.** circumference; situation; surrounding. **2.** circlet; that which surrounds and protects; winding round. **3.** the disc of the sun and moon; the halo around them (*K. Sāgara*).

Parivyādha (S) (M) **1.** surrounded by hunters. **3.** a sage in the west (*M. Bh.*).

Pariyaṇga (S) (M) **1.** with a strong body. **3.** a mahaṛṣi who was the son of Marīći and Ūrṇā (*Bhāgavata*).

Pāriyātra (S) (M) **1.** Western Vindhya range. **3.** a son of Ahīnagu a descendant of Rāma (*Bhāgavata*).

Parjanya (S) (M) **1.** cloud; rain; raincloud. **3.** personified; one of the 12 ādityas (*H. Purāṇa*); a prajāpati who was the father of Hiraṇyaroman; a gandharva (*M. Purāṇa*).

Parmāḍi (S) (M) **1.** the absolute beginning. **3.** a prince of Karṇāṭa (*R. Taraṅginī*).

Paramasukha (S) (M) ultimate bliss.

Parṇa (S) (M) **1.** leaf; feather; full of leaves; surrounded by leaves; surrounded by feathers. **2.** Flame of the Forest (*Butea frondosa*); which represents royalty and holiness.

Parnāda (S) (M) **1.** feeding on leaves. **3.** a sage who was a member of the court of Yudhiṣṭhira (*M. Bh.*).

Parṇāmaṇi (S) (M) jewel among the leaves; a kind of musical instrument made of Parnawood.

Parokṣa (S) (M) **1.** beyond observation. **2.** mysterious. **3.** a king of the lunar race (*Bhāgavata*).

Parparīka (S) (M) **1.** braided. **3.** another name for Agni and the sun.

Pārṣada (S) (M) **1.** associate; companion; attendant of a god; spectator. **3.** another name for Dhṛṣṭadyumna.

Pārṣada (S) (M) **1.** son of Pṛṣata. **3.** another name for Drupada.

Pārṣata (S) (M) **1.** son of Pṛṣata. **3.** another name for Drupada.

Parśava (S) (M) bearer of an axe; a warrior armed with an axe.

Pārśṇikṣemnan (S) (M) **1.** the basis of enquiry. **3.** a viśvādeva (*M. Bh.*).

Parśupāṇi (S) (M) **1.** axe holder. **3.** another name for Gaṇeśa.

Pārśva (S) (M) **1.** the rib region; side; flank. **2.** the side horse on a chariot; heaven and earth. **3.** the 23rd Jaina Arhat of the present Avasarpinī and his servant; an ancient Buddhist teacher (*B. Literature*).

Pārśvanātha (S) (M) **1.** lord who is always beside his devotees; lord of the chariot horses. **3.** the 23rd Jaina Tirathankara.

Pārtha (S) (M) **1.** son of Pṛthā; son of the earth; prince; king. **3.** metronymic of the 3 elder Pāṇḍavas specially of Arjuna (*M. Bh.*); a king of Kāśmira (*R. Taraṅginī*); White Murdah (*Terminalia citrina*).

Pārthasārathi (S) (M) **1.** Arjuna's charioteer. **3.** another name for Kṛṣṇa (*V. Purāṇa*).

Pārthiva (S) (M) **1.** of the earth; royal; earthen. **2.** prince; king; warrior; Indian Valerian (*Valeriana wallichii*).

Pārthivendra (S) (M) greatest of lords of the earth; lord of mortals.

Paru (S) (M) limb; member; mountain; ocean; sky; paradise.

Pāru (S) (M) the sun; fire.

Parućchepa (S) (M) **1.** preceptor of practical knowledge. **3.** a ṛṣi who was the son of Divodāsa and part author of *Ṛg. Veda* (i).

Paruṣa (S) (M) **1.** keen; sharp; violent; harsh; an arrow. **3.** a rākṣasa (*V. Rāmāyaṇa*).

Parvadhi **1.** container of time periods. **3.** another name for the moon.

Parvata (S) (M) **1.** rocky; rugged. **2.** mountain; the number 7. **2.** rock; stone. **3.** a ṛṣi who was the nephew of Nārada (*V. Purāṇa*); a son of Paurṇamāsa; (*M. Purāṇa*); a minister of King Purūravas; a vasu (*H. Purāṇa*).

Parvataćyut (S) (M) **1.** shaking mountains. **3.** another name for the maruts.

Parvataja (S) (M) born of the mountains; mountain born.

Parvatarāj (S) (M) king of the mountains; the highest mountain.

Parvateṣṭha (S) (M) **1.** dwelling in the mountains. **3.** another name for Indra (*M. Bh.*).

Parvateśvara (S) (M) **1.** lord of the mountains. **3.** a king of Vindhyā (*P. Purāṇa*).

Parvateya (S) (M) **1.** belonging to the mountains. **3.** a king who was also a ṛṣi (*M. Bh.*).

Pārvatīnandana (S) (M) **1.** son of Pārvatī. **3.** another name for Gaṇeśa and Kārttikeya.

Pārvatīnātha (S) (M) **1.** lord of Pārvatī. **3.** another name for Śiva.

Pārvatīpati (S) (M) **1.** husband of Pārvatī. **3.** another name for Śiva.

Pārvatīya (S) (M) **1.** belonging to the mountains. **3.** a king mentioned in the *Mahābhārata* (*M. Bh.*).

Parvita (S) (M) **1.** surrounded; encompassed. **2.** veiled; covered. **3.** the bow of Brahmā (*Ṛg Veda*).

Paryaṅka (S) (M) **1.** bed. **2.** litter; a particular mode of sitting. **3.** a mountain regarded as the son of Vindhya (*Ṛg Veda*).

Payetṛ (S) (M) subduer; conqueror.

Pāśa (S) (M) **1.** noose; chain; tie; bond. **3.** a divine weapon of Varuṇa unequalled in swift-ness (*M. Bh.*).

Pāśadhara (S) (M) **1.** holding a noose. **3.** another name for Varuṇa.

Pāṣaka (S) (M) an ornament for the feet.

Pāśin (S) (M) **1.** with a noose. **3.** a son of Dhṛtarāṣṭra; another name for Varuṇa and Yama.

Paśubhartā (S) (M) **1.** master of beasts; protecting animals. **3.** another name for Śiva.

Paśunātha (S) (M) **1.** lord of cattle. **3.** another name for Śiva.

Paśupā (S) (M) **1.** herdsman. **3.** another name for Pūṣan.

Pāśupata (S) (M) **1.** sacred to Śiva. **3.** the arrow used on Śiva's bow called Pināka (K. *Granthāvali*).

Paśupati (S) (M) **1.** lord of animals; lord of the soul. **3.** the later incarnation of Rudra-Śiva (*Ś. Purāṇa*).

Paśurāja (S) (M) **1.** king of beasts. **2.** lion.

Paśusakha (S) (M) **1.** friend of animals. **3.** the husband of Gaṇḍā the maid of the Saptaṛṣis (*M. Bh.*).

Paśyat (S) (M) visible; conspicuous.

Pataga (S) (M) **1.** one who flies in the sky. **2.** bird. **3.** another name for the sun.

Patagapati (S) (M) **1.** lord of birds. **3.** another name for Garuḍa.

Patageśvara (S) (M) **1.** lord of birds. **3.** another name for Garuḍa and Jaṭāyu.

Patākin (S) (M) **1.** bearing flags; standard bearer. **3.** a soldier of the Kaurava army (*M.Bh.*).

Pātāla (S) (M) **1.** descent. **3.** one of the 7 regions under the earth and the abode of the nāgas (*M. Bh.*); the attendant of the 14th Arhat of the present Avasarpinī; a monkey of Kiśkdndhā (*P. Purāṇa*).

Pātālaketu (S) (M) **1.** with the flag of the nether regions. **3.** a daitya (*Bhā. Purāṇa*).

Pātālarāvaṇa (S) (M) **1.** making a noise under the earth. **3.** a king of the rākṣasas who was the nephew of Malyavān (*K. Rāmāyaṇa*).

Pāṭalāvatī (S) (M) **1.** of a pale red. **3.** a holy river of North India (*M. Bh.*); another name for Durgā.

Pāṭalopala (S) (M) red gem; ruby.

Patana (S) (M) **1.** fall; descent. **2.** what flies or falls. **3.** a rākṣasa (*M. Bh.*).

Pataṅga (S) (M) **1.** flying. **2.** the sun; kite; butterfly; bee. **3.** one of the 7 suns; a ṛṣi who was part author of *Ṛg Veda* (x); a mountain near Mahāmeru; another name for Kṛṣṇa (*Bhā. Purāṇa*).

Pātaṅgi (S) (M) **1.** son of the sun. **3.** another name for Saturn.

Patañjali (S) (M) **1.** one who should be worshipped. **3.** a celebrated grammarian and author of *Mahābhāṣya*; a philosopher and propounder of yoga.

Patara (S) (M) **1.** with a skin; a ray of sunlight. **3.** the 3rd of the 7 suns; another name for Varuṇa.

Patatri (S) (M) **1.** bird. **3.** a warrior on the side of the Kauravas (*M. Bh.*).

Pāṭava (S) (M) clever; sharp; dextrous.

Paṭavāsaka (S) (M) **1.** scented powder. **3.** a serpent of the family of Dhṛtarāṣṭra (*M. Bh.*).

Pātha (S) (M) path; fire; sun.

Patharvan (S) (M) **1.** horse of the path. **2.** a preceptor who moves from place to place. **3.** a rajaṛṣī well versed in the *Ṛg Veda* (*Ṛg Veda*).

Pāthas (S) (M) spot; place; water; air.

Pāthaspati (S) (M) **1.** lord of water. **3.** another name for Varuṇa.

Pathikṛt (S) (M) **1.** preparing the way. **3.** another name for Agni.

Pāthinātha (S) (M) lord of direction.

Pāthoja (S) (M) **1.** waterborn. **2.** Lotus (*Nelumbo nucifera*).

Pāthonātha (S) (M) **1.** lord of water. **3.** another name for Varuṇa.

Pāthoruha (S) (M) **1.** growing in water; water grown. **2.** lotus.

Pathuṣa (S) (M) **1.** eating everything in the way. **3.** a rākṣasa of the army of Rāvana (*M. Bh.*).

Pāthya (S) (M) **1.** heavenly. **3.** a ṛsi (*Ṛg Veda*).

Pātṛ (S) (M) defender; protector.

Pattrapati (S) (M) **1.** lord of feathers. **3.** another name for Garuda.

Pattrorṇa (S) (M) **1.** with woven silk garments. **3.** a king at the court of Yudhiṣṭhira (*M. Bh.*).

Paṭu (S) (M) sharp; intense; keen; strong; violent; clever; skilful.

Paṛul (S) (M) yellow coloured.

Paṭurūpa (S) (M) very clever.

Paṭuśa (S) (M) **1.** clever. **3.** a rākṣasa (*M. Bh.*).

Paulastya (S) (M) **1.** descended from Pulastya. **3.** another name for Kubera and Rāvaṇa.

Paulastyatanaya (S) (M) **1.** son of Pulastya. **3.** another name for Rāvaṇa.

Paulomīpatī (S) (M) **1.** lord of Paulomī. **3.** another name for Indra.

Pauīomīṣa (S) (M) **1.** lord of Paulomi. **3.** another name for Indra.

Pauṇḍarīka (S) (M) consisting of lotus flowers.

Pauṇḍra (S) (M) **1.** sugarcane of a straw colour. **2.** pale. **3.** the conch shell of Bhīma (*M. Bh.*); a country and its king who is regarded as a son of Vasudeva.

Pauṇḍraka (S) (M) **1.** straw coloured. **3.** a son of Nikumbha (*A. Rāmāyaṇa*); a king of Kārūśa killed by Kṛṣṇa (*Bhāgavata*); Yama's buffalo (*Vam. Purāṇa*).

Paundramatsyaka (S) (M) **1.** yellow fish. **3.** a king who was the son of the rākṣasa Vīra and Danāyus (*M. Bh.*).

Paura (S) (M) **1.** filler; increaser. **3.** a ṛṣi and part author of *Ṛg Veda* (v); another name for Soma, Indra and the aśvins.

Paurava (S) (M) **1.** born of the Purū dynasty. **3.** a king who was a commander of the Kaurava army

(*M. Bh.*); a king of Aṅga (*M. Bh.*); a son of Viśvāmitra (*M. Bh.*).

Paurṇamāsa (S) (M) **1.** the day of full moon. **2.** related to the full moon. **3.** a son of Marīci and Sambhūti and the father of Virajas and Parvata (*V. Purāṇa*).

Pauruṣeya (S) (M) **1.** of men; manly. **2.** strong; powerful. **3.** a rākṣasa who travels with the sun in the month of Jyeṣṭha (*Bhāgavata*).

Pauṣajit (S) (M) **1.** one who has won over cold. **2.** unaffected by cold. **3.** a sage in the line of Vyāsa's disciples (*Bhā. Purāṇa*).

Pauṣpinji (S) (M) **1.** with a cool temperament. **3.** a sage in the line of Vyāsa's disciples (*Bhā. Purāṇa*).

Pauṣya (S) (M) **1.** of the asterism Puṣya. **3.** the king of Karavīrapura who was the son of Pūṣan and the father of Ćandraśekhara (*K. Purāṇa*).

Pava (S) (M) **1.** purification. **2.** air; wind. **3.** a son of Nahuṣa (*M. Bh.*).

Pāvaka (S) (M) **1.** purifier. **2.** pure; clear; bright; shining; fire. **3.** an agni said to be the son of Agni Abhimānin and Svāhā (*M. Bh.*); Ceylon Leadwort (*Plumbago zeylanica*).

Pāvaki (S) (M) **1.** a son of fire. **3.** another name for Skanda, Sudarśana and Viṣṇu.

Pavamāna (S) (M) **1.** purified. **2.** flowing clear; the wind personified. **3.** an agni who was the son of Agni and Svāhā (*V. Purāṇa*); a son of Vijitāśva who was the reincarnation of an agni (*Bhāgavata*); the son of Antardhāna and Śikhaṇḍinī; a mountain near Meru (*D. Bh. Purāṇa*).

Pavana (S) (M) **1.** breeze; air; the number 5. **3.** wind personified as a god; the regent of the north west region; a son of Manu Uttama (*Bh. Purāṇa*).

Pāvana (S) (M) **1.** purifying; holy. **2.** fire; incense. **3.** a son of Kṛṣṇa and Mitravindā (*Bhāgavata*); a viśvādeva (*M. Bh.*); another name for Vyāsa.

Pavanaja (S) (M) **1.** son of the wind. **3.** another name for Hanumān.

Pavanatanaya (S) (M) **1.** son of the wind. **3.** another name for Bhīma.

Pavanātmaja (S) (M) **1.** son of the wind. **3.** another name for Bhīma.

Pāvanta (S) (M) holiness; purity; sanctity.

Pavayitṛ (S) (M) purifier.

Pavi (S) (M) **1.** of fire; lightning; brightness; sheen; arrow; thunderbolt; speech; fire. **3.** the golden tyre on the wheel of the aśvins' chariot (*Ṛg Veda*).

Pavinasa (S) (M) **1.** with a nose like a spear-Bead. **3.** a demon (*A. Veda*).

Pavitṛ (S) (M) purifier.

Pavitra (S) (M) **1.** purifying; filtering. **2.** honey; water; butter; Kusa grass. **3.** another name for Viṣṇu; (*Curcuma longa*; *Prosopis spicigera*; *Desmostachya bipinnata.*).

Pavitrakīrti (S) (M) of flawless renown.

Pavitrapāṇi (S) (M) **1.** holding purity. **2.** holding Darbha grass in the hand. **3.** a ṛṣi(*M. Bh.*).

Pavitrapati (S) (M) lord of purity.

Pavitravāṇi (S) (M) **1.** pure speech. **3.** a sage in the court of both Yudhiṣthira and Indra (*M. Bh.*).

Payas (S) (M) milk; water; rain; juice; power.

Payaspati (S) (M) **1.** lord of milk. **3.** another name for Viṣṇu.

Payasya (S) (M) **1.** made of milk. **3.** a son of Aṅgiras (*M. Bh.*).

Payoda (S) (M) **1.** milk giving; water giving. **2.** cloud. **3.** a son of Yadu (*Bhā. Purāṇa*).

Payodhi (S) (M) **1.** water receptacle. **2.** the ocean.

Pāyu (S) (M) guard; protector.

Pedhāla (S) (M) **1.** one who hides. **3.** the 8th Arhat of the future Utsarpiī (*J.S. Koṣa*).

Pedu (S) (M) **1.** protection. **2.** coverer. **3.** a man protected by the aśvins.

Pehlaj (S) (M) first born.

Peru (S) (M) **1.** drinking; rescuing; swelling. **2.** the sun; fire; ocean.

Peruka (S) (M) **1.** rescuer. **3.** a king who gave refuge to Bharadvāja (*Ṛg Veda*).

Peśala (S) (M) **1.** adorned; decorated; beautiful; charming; soft; tender. **3.** another name for Viṣṇu.

Peśalākṣa (S) (M) with beautiful eyes.

Peṣi (S) (M) **1.** pounding. **2.** thunderbolt.

Pesvara (S) (M) going; moving; splendid.

Phāla (S) (M) **1.** ploughshare. **2.** pointed portion of the plough. **3.** another name for Balarāma and Śiva.

Phalādhyakṣa (S) (M) lord of the fruit.

Phalaka (S) (M) plank; shield; sky; a plank used in the construction of a chariot or in the extraction of the Soma juice; pericarp of the lotus.

Phalakapāṇi (S) (M) armed with a shield.

Phalamaṇi (S) (M) jewel.

Phalārāma (S) (M) consisting of fruits; orchard.

Phalgu (S) (M) **1.** small; red. **2.** spring; a red powder made from wild ginger considered holy by the Hindus; Fig tree (*Ficus oppositifolia*); Wild Champaka (*Bauhinia tomentosa*). **3.** a holy river in Gayā (*M. Bh.*).

Phalguna (S) (M) **1.** red. **2.** of the month of Phālguna; the Hindu month of February-March when the Phālguna constellation is ascendant. **3.** another name for Arjuna who was born during this period; another name for the Arjuna tree (*Terminalia arjuna*); another name for Indra.

Phālgunī (S) (M) **1.** the full moon day of the month of Phālguna. **3.** another name for Abhimanyu.

Phālgunya (S) (M) **1.** moonlight. **3.** another name for the planet Jupiter.

Phalgutantra (S) (M) **1.** to govern well. **3.** another name for the king of Ayodhyā and father of King Sāgara.

Phalin (S) (M) fruitful; bearing fruit.

Phalodaka (S) (M) **1.** fruit juice. **3.** a yakṣa who was a member of the court of Kubera.

Phaṇa (S) (M) hood; ornament; the expanded hood of a serpent.

Phaṇadhara (S) (M) **1.** possessing serpents. **3.** another name for Śiva.

Phaṇādhara (S) (M) **1.** bearing a serpent. **3.** another name for Śiva.

Phaṇamaṇi (S) (M) jewel in the hood of the serpent.

Phāṇḍin (S) (M) **1.** hooded. **3.** a serpent lord.

Phaṇibhuj (S) (M) **1.** eating serpents; living on serpents. **2.** peacock. **3.** another name for Garuḍa.

Phaṇibhūṣana (S) (M) **1.** decorated with serpents. **3.** another name for Śiva.

Phanikesa (S) (M) **1.** lord of the hooded ones. **3.** another name for Viṣṇu who reclines on the coiled form of Śeṣa.

Phaṇin (S) (M) **1.** hooded. **2.** serpent. **3.** another name for Rāhu (the planet Saturn); another name for Patañjali.

Phaṇinātha (S) (M) **1.** lord of the hooded ones. **3.** another name for Śiva.

Phaṇīndra (S) (M) **1.** lord of hoods. **3.** another name for Śeṣa the lord of serpents; another name for Patañjali.

Phaṇipati (S) (M) **1.** hooded. **3.** a huge serpent (*B. Śatakam*); another name for the serpent Śeṣa.

Phaṇīśvara (S) (M) **1.** king of the hooded ones. **3.** another name for Śiva; another name for Vāsuki.

Phāṇita (S) (M) raw sugar; juice of the sugarcane.

Pharendra (S) (M) lord of the scatterers; the Kewra plant (*Pandanus odoratissimus*).

Phena (S) (M) **1.** foam. **3.** a king belonging to the race of Uśīnara and who was the father of Sutapas (*H. Purāṇa*); *Acacia rugata*.

Pheṇapa (S) (M) **1.** one who drinks foam; foam drinking. **3.** a member of the Bhṛgu family who described the greatness of cows to Yudhiṣṭhira and lived on the froth of cows milk alone (*M. Bh.*).

Pheṇavāhin (S) (M) **1.** foam bearing. **2.** the ocean. **3.** Indra's thunderbolt.

Phullendu (S) (M) full moon.

Piććhala (S) (M) **1.** slippery. **3.** a nāga of the Vāsuki family (*M. Bh.*).

Piću (S) (M) **1.** cotton; a grain; a weight; fat; thick; heavy. **3.** one of the 8 faces of Bhairava (*S. Samhitā*); an asura.

Piho (S) (M) the Pheasant tailed Jacana (*Tringa chirurgus*).

Pikānanda (S) (M) **1.** the cuckoo's joy. **3.** another name for spring.

Pīlu (S) (M) **1.** arrow; flower; stem of the plant; atom; insect; elephant. **3.** a rāga; Wild Guava (*Careya arborea*).

Pināka (S) (M) **1.** a staff; a bow. **3.** bow of Rudra-Śiva (*K. Granthāvali*).

Pinākadhṛk (S) (M) **1.** bearer of Pināka. **3.** another name for Śiva.

Pinākagopta (S) (M) **1.** preserver of Pināka. **3.** another name for Śiva.

Pinākahasta (S) (M) **1.** Pināka handed. **3.** another name for Śiva.

Pinākapāṇi (S) (M) **1.** holding the Pināka. **3.** another name for Śiva.

Pinākasena (S) (M) **1.** armed with the Pināka. **3.** another name for Skanda.

Pinākāvasa (S) (M) **1.** controlling the Pināka. **3.** another name for Rudra.

Pinākīn (S) (M) **1.** armed with the Pināka. **3.** one of the 11 rudras who was the son of Sthāṇu and grandson of Brahmā (*M. Bh.*); another name for Rudra-Śiva.

Piṇḍāraka (S) (M) **1.** gatherer; unites; assembles; join. **2.** cowherd; buffalo herdsman. **3.** a nāga of the Kaśyapa family (*M. Bh.*); a son of Vasudeva and Rohiṇī.

Piṇḍasektṛ (S) (M) **1.** a vessel for oblations. **3.** a serpent of the family of Takṣaka (*M. Bh.*).

Piṅgadṛśa (S) (M) **1.** yellow eyed. **3.** another name for Śiva.

Piṅgajaṭa (S) (M) **1.** with yellow braided hair. **3.** another name for Śiva.

Piṅgākṣa (S) (M) **1.** yellow eyed. **3.** rākṣasa; a bird who was the son of Drona (*Mā Purāṇa*); another name for Agni and Śiva.

Piṅgala (S) (M) **1.** of yellow hue; reddish-brown; tawny; yellow; golden. **2.** fire; lion. **3.** a demigod attendant of the sun (*M. Bh.*); a king of the yakṣās and a friend of Śiva (*M. Bh.*); a nāga son of Kaśyapa and Kadrū (*M. Bh.*); an attendant of Śiva (*K. Sāgara*); a sage (*M. Bh.*); a Jaina treasure (*J.S. Koṣa*); a dānava (*K. Sāgara*).

Piṅgalaka (S) (M) **1.** redbrown; tawny. **3.** a yakṣa.

Piṅgalākṣa (S) (M) **1.** tawny eyed; with red-brown eyes. **3.** another name for Śiva.

Pingalarāja (S) (M) **1.** king of the Piṅgala state. **3.** a yakṣa who acts as Śiva's pilot (*M. Bh.*).

Pingalavarman (S) (M) **1.** with yellow armour. **3.** father of Suvarṇaśiras.

Piṅgekṣana (S) (M) **1.** yellow eyed. **3.** another name for Śiva.

Piṅgeśvara (S) (M) **1.** the yellow deity. **3.** an attendant of Pārvatī (*D. Purāṇa*).

Piñjaraka (S) (M) **1.** yellow; golden. **2.** gold. **3.** a son of Kaśyapa and Kadrū (*M. Bh.*).

Pippala (S) (M) **1.** the sacred Fig tree (*Ficus religiosa*). **3.** a son of Mitra and Revatī (*Bh. Purāṇa*); a sage of the Kaśyapa race (*P. Purāṇa*).

Pippalāda (S) (M) **1.** eating the fruit of the Pippala tree. **3.** an ancient teacher of the *Atharva Veda*.

Pippalāyana (S) (M) **1.** living under a Fig tree. **2.** sensual. **3.** a son of Ṛṣabhadeva and Jayantī (*Bhā. Purāṇa*).

Pippalśa (S) (M) lord of the Pippala tree (*Ficus religiosa*).

Pipru (S) (M) **1.** mark; spot; mole. **3.** a demon conquered by Indra (*Ṛg Veda*).

Piśāća (S) (M) **1.** of yellow colour. **2.** corpse like in appearance; a ghost. **3.** a class of yellow demons personified as the children of Krodhā, during the Mahābhārata many of these were reborn as kings.

Piśaṅga (S) (M) **1.** yellow bodied; red brown; tawny. **3.** a serpent of Dhṛtarāṣṭra's family (*M. Bh.*).

Piśaṅgaka (S) (M) **1.** red brown; tawny. **3.** an attendant of Viṣṇu (*Br. Purāṇa*).

Piśuna (S) (M) **1.** slanderous; betrayer. **2.** cotton; crow. **3.** a sage who was the son of Kuśika; another name for Nārada

Pitāmaha (S) (M) **1.** grandfather. **3.** another name for Bhīṣma and Brahmā.

Pītāmbara (S) (M) **1.** dressed in yellow. **3.** another name for Viṣṇu and Kṛṣṇa.

Pītāruṇa (S) (M) yellowish red; mid dawn.

Pītaśam (S) (M) **1.** yellow stone. **2.** topaz.

Pītāśman (S) (M) yellow stone; topaz.

Pītavāsas (S) (M) **1.** dressed in yellow. **3.** another name for Viṣṇu.

Pīṭha (S) (M) **1.** seat; pedestal. **3.** a demon killed by Kṛṣṇa (*M. Bh.*); a minister of Kaṅsa (*H. Purāṇa*).

Piṭhara (S) (M) **1.** pot; boiler; pan used for cooking. **3.** a dailya who was a member of Varuna's court (*M. Bh.*).

Piṭharaka (S) (M) **1.** boiler. **3.** a serpent of the Kaśyapa family (*M. Bh.*).

Pīvara (S) (M) **1.** fat; thick; dense; large. **3.** a ṛṣi under Manu Tāmasa (*Mā. Purāṇa*); a son of Dyutimat (*V. Purāṇa*).

Pīyūṣa (S) (M) **1.** nectar. **2.** the 1st milk of a cow. **3.** nectar produced at the churning of the Ocean of Milk.

Pīyūṣabhānu (S) (M) **1.** nectar rayed. **3.** another name for the moon.

Pīyūṣadyuti (S) (M) **1.** nectar rayed. **3.** another name for the moon.

Plakṣa (S) (M) Fig tree (*Ficus religiosa*); *Fiats infectoria.*

Plavaga (S) (M) **1.** going by leaps and bounds. **3.** the charioteer of the sun; a son of the sun (*Bhā. Purāṇa*).

Poṣita (S) (M) nourished; protected; cherished.

Potaka (S) (M) **1.** a young animal; the site of a house. **3.** a nāga of the family of Kaśyapa (*M. Bh.*).

Poṭalapriyā (S) (M) **1.** fond of the Poṭala mountain. **3.** a Buddha.

Prabāhu (S) (M) **1.** with strong arms. **3.** a warrior of the Kauravas (*M. Bh.*).

Prabala (S) (M) **1.** strong; powerful; mighty. **3.** a son of Kṛṣṇa; an attendant of Viṣṇu (*Bhā. Purāṇa*); a daitya (*K. Sāgara*); *Paederia foetida.*

Prabātaka (S) (M) **1.** powerful; strong. **3.** a yakṣa of the court of Kubera (*M. Bh.*).

Prabhāgaćandra (S) (M) a part of the moon.

Prabhākānta (S) (M) **1.** beloved of light. **3.** another name for the moon.

Prabhākara (S) (M) **1.** one who creates light; light maker. **3.** a sage of the race of Atri who was the husband of the 10 daughters of Ghṛtāćī and Raudrāśva; a serpent of Kaśyapa's race (*M. Bh.*); a son of Jyotiṣmat (*V. Purāṇa*); another name for Śiva, the sun and the moon (*V. Purāṇa*).

Prabhāna (S) (M) light; splendour; radiance.

Prabhañjana (S) (M) **1.** crushing; destroying. **2.** wind; storm; tempest. **3.** a son of King Ćitravāhana of Manipura (*M. Bh.*); a king and father of Putātmā (*Sk. Purāṇa*).

Prabhāñjanasuta (S) (M) **1.** son of the god of wind. **3.** another name for Bhīma.

Prabhāñjani (S) (M) **1.** born of wind. **3.** another name for Hanumān and Bhīma.

Prabhānu (S) (M) **1.** the brightest sun. **2.** the sun at noon, **3.** a son of Kṛṣṇa and Satyabhāmā (*Bhāgavata*).

Prablāpāla (S) (M) **1.** protector of light. **3.** a bodhisattva.

Prabhāsa (S) (M) **1.** splendour. **2.** beauty; radiance. **3.** a vasu son of Dharma and Prabhātā and the husband of the sister of Bṛhaspati (*V. Purāṇa*); an attendant of Skanda.

Prabhāsana (S) (M) **1.** illuminating. **3.** a place of pilgrimage near Dvārakā (*Bhā. Purāṇa*).

Prabhāta (S) (M) **1.** shone forth. **2.** morning; dawn; sunrise. **3.** a son of Sūrya and Prabhā (*V. Purāṇa*).

Prabhāva (S) (M) **1.** cause of existence. **2.** prominent; excelling; distinguished; source; origin; majesty; dignity;

mighty; power; strength; splendour; beauty. **3.** a son of Manu Svāroćiṣa (*M. Purāṇa*).

Prabhāvyuha (S) (M) **1.** circle of light. **2.** origin of light. **3.** a Buddhist deity (*L. Vistara*).

Prabhu (S) (M) **1.** effector; creator. **2.** mighty; powerful; rich; abundant; eternal; master; lord; king; god. **3.** a son of Kardama (*H. Purāṇa*); a son of Śuka and Pīvarī (*M. Purāṇa*); a son of Bhaga and Siddhi (*Bh. Purāṇa*); a soldier of Skanda (*M. Bh.*); another name for God.

Prabhudāsa (S) (M) slave of the gods; a devotee.

Prabhūta (S) (M) come forth; arisen; appeared.

Prabodha (S) (M) awakening; consciousness; knowledge; understanding.

Prabodhaćandra (S) (M) the moon of knowledge.

Prabodhana (S) (M) **1.** awaking; arousing. **3.** a Buddha.

Prabodhika (S) (M) awaking others; one who awakens; dawn; daybreak.

Prabuddha (S) (M) awakened; roused; expanded; come forth; known; understood; enlightened; wise; appeared.

Praćakṣas (S) (M) **1.** one who tells; one who illumines. **3.** another name for Bṛhaspati.

Praćaṇḍa (S) (M) **1.** violent. **2.** furious; passionate; terrible; fiery; fierce. **3.** a son of Vatsaprī and Sunandā (*Mā. Purāṇa*); a dānava (*K. Sāgara*).

Praćetas (S) (M) **1.** with an awakened mind. **2.** wise; clever; happy; delighted. **3.** the 10 sons of Prāćīnabarhis (*M. Bh.*); a son of Durmada (*Bh. Purāṇa*); a son of Duryāman (*V. Purāṇa*); another name for Agni, Varuṇa.

Praćetṛ (S) (M) charioteer.

Prācīna (S) (M) ancient; astern; former; prior; preceding; the ancient fire; Velvet Leaf (*Cissampelos pareira*).

Prāćīnabarhis (S) (M) **1.** eastern bed of Kuśā grass; eastern light. **3.** a prajāpati who was the son of Havirdhāna and Dhīṣaṇa and the husband of Savarṇā; he fathered the 10 Praćetas (*V. Purāṇa*).

Prāćīnvān (S) (M) **1.** gathering; collecting. **3.** a king who was the son of Janamejaya and Anantā and the husband of Aśmakī, he was the father of Saṁyāti and Manasyu (*M. Bh.*).

Prāćīpati (S) (M) **1.** lord of the east. **3.** another name for Indra.

Praćīrṇa (S) (M) to come forth; to appear.

Pradānaśūra (S) (M) **1.** hero in giving. **2.** liberal. **3.** a Bodhisattva.

Pradātṛ (S) (M) **1.** giver; bestower. **3.** a viśvādeva; another name for Indra.

Pradatta (S) (M) **1.** bestowed; given. **3.** a gandharva (*Rāmāyaṇa*).

Pradhi (S) (M) the disc of the moon; felly of a wheel.

Pradīpa (S) (M) **1.** to blaze forth; immensely illuminating. **2.** light; lamp; lantern.

Pradoṣa (S) (M) **1.** deteriorating; the 1st part of the night. **3.** evening personified as a son of Dakṣa or as a son of Doṣā (*M. Bh.*); a son of Puṣpārṇa and Prabhā and grandson of Dhruva (*Bhāgavata*).

Pradoṣaka (S) (M) born in the evening.

Pradyota (S) (M) **1.** light; radiance. **3.** a yakṣa in the court of Kubera (*M. Bh.*); a son of King Śunaka; a king of Magadha (*V. Purāṇa*).

Pradyotana (S) (M) **1.** full of light. **3.** a king of Ujjayinī; another name for the sun.

Pradyumna (S) (M) **1.** extremely mighty; the pre-eminently mighty one. **3.** the god of love reborn as the son of Kṛṣṇa and Rukminī, he was the father of Aniruddha; a son of Manu and Naḍvalā (*Bhā. Purāṇa*).

Pradyuta (S) (M) lighted; to begin to shine.

Prāgahi (S) (M) **1.** beholder of knowledge. **3.** a teacher of yajñas.

Praghoṣa (S) (M) **1.** sound; noise. **3.** a son of Kṛṣṇa (*Bhāgavata*).

Prāghuṇa (S) (M) guest.

Pragīta (S) (M) singing; reciting; wellsung; highly praised; lyric; song.

Prāgītya (S) (M) celebrity; excellence.

Prāgra (S) (M) the highest point; summit.

Praguṇa (S) (M) full of qualities; straight; honest; upright; efficient; right.

Praharaṇa (S) (M) **1.** striking; removing. **2.** the verse spoken while throwing grass into the sacrificial fire. **3.** a son of Kṛṣṇa (*Bhāgavata*).

Prahāsa (S) (M) **1.** laughter. **2.** appearance; display; splendour of colours. **3.** an attendant of Śiva (*M. Bh*); a minister of Varuṇa (*Rāmāyaṇa*); a serpent of the family of Dhrtarāṣṭra (*M. Bh.*); a soldier of Skanda (*M. Bh.*); a rākṣasa (*V. Rāmāyaṇa*); another name for Śiva.

Prahasita (S) (M) **1.** laughing; cheerful. **3.** a king of the kinnaras; a Buddha.

Prahasta (S) (M) **1.** with long hands. **3.** a minister of Rāvaṇa who was the son of Sumālī and Ketumatī (*V. Rāmāyaṇa*).

Praheti (S) (M) **1.** one that strikes. **2.** missile; weapon. **3.** a demon who travels with the sun in the month of Vaiśākha (*Bhāgavata*); the father of the sun; a king of rākṣasas.

Prahlāda (S) (M) **1.** delight; joy; happiness. **3.** the son of Hiraṇyakaśipu and Kayādhu who was a devotee of Viṣṇu (*Bhā. Purāṇa*); the chief of the asuras and crowned emperor of the demons in Pātāla, he was the son of Viroćana (*M. Bh.*); a serpent in the court of Varuṇa (*M. Bh.*); a prajāpati (*M. Bh.*).

Prahvala (S) (M) of magnificent form; a beautiful body.

Praja (S) (M) **1.** propagation; birth; offspring; man. **3.** a son of Ajamīdha.

Prajādhara (S) (M) **1.** supporting creatures. **3.** another name for Viṣṇu.

Prajādhyakṣa (S) (M) **1.** surveyer of creation. **3.** another name for the sun, Kardama and Dakṣa.

Prajāgara (S) (M) **1.** watchman; guardian. **3.** another name for Viṣṇu.

Prajākara (S) (M) creator of people; potent; a symbol.

Prajānātha (S) (M) **1.** lord of creation. **3.** another name for Brahmā, Manu and Dakṣa.

Prajaṅgha (S) (M) **1.** with strong thighs. **3.** a rākṣasa in Rāvaṇa's army (*V. Rāmāyaṇa*).

Prajāpāla (S) (M) **1.** protector of creatures. **2.** king. **3.** another name for Kṛṣṇa.

Prajāpati (S) (M) **1.** lord of creation; father; king. **3.** time personified; the first 10 or 21 lords created by Brahmā; the father of Ūṣas the goddess of dawn and one who encompasses all the 33 crore gods in himself; another name for Viṣṇu, Śiva, Agni, Sāvitṛ, Soma and the sun.

Prajas (S) (M) **1.** born; produced; to produce; to bring forth. **3.** a son of Manu Auttami (*Ṛg Veda*).

Prajāsṛj (S) (M) **1.** creator of beings. **3.** another name for Brahmā and Kaśyapa.

Prajāti (S) (M) **1.** generation; production; delivery. **3.** a prince (*Ma. Purāṇa*).

Prajavīn (S) (M) swift; fleet.

Prajeśa (S) (M) lord of creatures.

Prajeśvara (S) (M) **1.** lord of creatures. **2.** king.

Prajina (S) (M) **1.** moving; swift. **2.** wind; air.

Prajit (S) (M) conquering; defeating.

Prajīvin (S) (M) **1.** exuberant with life; lively. **3.** a minister of Meghavarṇa the king of crows.

Prajñāćakṣuṣa (S) (M) **1.** with an eye of wisdom. **2.** one who possesses inner wisdom; blind. **3.** another name for Dhṛtarāṣṭra.

Prajñāćandra (S) (M) the moon of wisdom.

Prajñadeva (S) (M) god of wisdom.

Prajñāditya (S) (M) sun of wisdom.

Prajñāgupta (S) (M) protected by knowledge; wise.

Prajñākāya (S) (M) 1. with a body of wisdom. 3. another name for Manjuśrī.

Prajñākośa (S) (M) store of wisdom.

Prajñākūṭa (S) (M) 1. mountain of wisdom. 3. a bodhisattva.

Prajñāna (S) (M) intelligent; wise; clever.

Prajñāsagara (S) (M) ocean of wisdom.

Prajñasahāya (S) (M) with wisdom as companion.

Prajñāvarman (S) (M) armoured by knowledge.

Prajñendra (S) (M) lord of wisdom.

Prakālana (S) (M) 1. to urge; to incite; driving on. 3. a serpent of the family of Vāsuki (*M. Bh.*).

Prakāma (S) (M) intense desire; fulfilment of desire; joy; delight.

Prākara (S) (M) 1. doing well; friendship; respect. 3. a son of Dyutimat.

Prakarṣaka (S) (M) 1. harasser. 3. another name for Kāma.

Prakāśa (S) (M) 1. visible; light; clearness; brightness; splendour; lustre; fame; renown; glory; appearance; sunshine. 3. a sage of the family of Bhṛgu who was the son of Tāmasa (*M. Bh.*); the messengers of Viṣṇu; another name for Manu Raivata (*H. Purāṇa*).

Prakāśāditya (S) (M) sun among the enlightened; sunlight.

Prakāśakarman (S) (M) 1. bestowing light. 3. another name for the sun.

Prakāśātman (S) (M) 1. enlightened soul. 2. brilliant in nature. 3. another name for Śiva and the sun.

Prakāśavat (S) (M) 1. possessing light. 2. bright; brilliant; shining. 3. one of Brahmā's feet (*Bhā. Purāṇa*).

Prakaśendra (S) (M) 1. lord of light. 3. the father of Kṣemendra.

Praketa (S) (M) perception; intelligence; knowledge; appearance.

Prakoṣṇā (S) (M) 1. ever prepared. 2. sensuous. 3. an apsarā (*V. Purāṇa*).

Prākṛta (S) (M) 1. original; natural. 3. a yakṣa (*M. Bh.*).

Prakula (S) (M) a handsome or excellent body.

Pralamba (S) (M) 1. hanging down. 2. pendant; garland of flowers round the neck. 3. a daitya slain by Balarāma and Kṛṣṇa (*M. Bh.*); adānava son of Kaśyapa and Danu (*M. Bh.*).

Pralambaghna (S) (M) 1. slayer of Pralamba. 3. another name for Balarāma and Kṛṣṇa.

Pralambahan (S) (M) 1. destroyer of Pralamba. 3. another name for Balarāma and Kṛṣṇa.

Pralambodara (S) (M) 1. with a portruding belly. 3. a king of the kinnaras.

Pralayānśu (S) (M) 1. frosty rayed. 3. another name for the moon.

Pramada (S) (M) 1. joy; delight; pleasure. 3. a son of Vasiṣṭha (*Bh. Purāṇa*); a dānava (*H. Purāṇa*).

Pramagandha (S) (M) 1. with an enticing smell. 3. a king of the Kīkaṭas (*Ṛg Veda*).

Pramahas (S) (M) of great might and splendour.

Pramandhu (S) (M) 1. crusher of thought; crusher of protection. 3. a yakṣa (*Sk. Purāṇa*).

Pramanthu (S) (M) 1. tormentor. 3. a son of Vīravrata and the younger brother of Manthu (*Bhā. Purāṇa*).

Pramardana (S) (M) 1. crushing; devastating. 3. an attendant of Śiva; a vidyādhara (*K. Sāgara*); another name for Viṣṇu.

Pramat (S) (M) wise; prudent.

Pramaṭaka (S) (M) 1. wise; thought out. 3. a sage (*M. Bh.*).

Pramathādhipa (S) (M) 1. head of the Pramathas. 3. another name for Śiva.

Pramathapati (S) (M) 1. lord of the Pramathas. 3. another name for Śiva.

Pramathin (S) (M) 1. harassing; destroying. 3. a brother of Dūṣana who was an associate of Rāvaṇa (*V. Rāmāyaṇa*); a rākṣasa friend of Ghaṭotkaća (*M. Bh.*); a son of Dhṛtarāṣṭra (*M. Bh.*).

Pramati (S) (M) **1.** wise; prudent; intelligent; provider; protector. **3.** a sage who was the son of Ćyavana and Sukanyā and the husband of Pratāpī and the father of Ruru (*M. Bh.*); a minister of Vibhīṣaṇa (*V. Rāmāyaṇa*); a sage in the 10lh Manvantara (*H. Purāṇa*); a son of Janamcjaya (*Rāmāyaṇa*); a son of Prānśu (*Bh. Purāṇa*).

Pramita (S) (M) limited; moderate; measured out.

Pramoda (S) (M) **1.** joy; delight; gladness. **3.** pleasure personified as a child of Brahmā born from his neck (*M. Purāṇa*); a serpent of the family of Airāvata (*M. Bh.*); a soldier of Skanda (*M. Bh.*).

Pramodana (S) (M) **1.** one who delights. **3.** another name for Viṣṇu.

Pramodita (S) (M) **1.** delighted; glad. **3.** another name for Kubera.

Pramući (S) (M) **1.** released; liberated. **3.** a sage of south India (*M. Bh.*).

Prāṇa (S) (M) **1.** the breath of life; spirit; vitality; vigour; energy; power. **3.** a marut; the son of Dhātā and Āyati and the grandson of Bhṛgu (*V. Purāṇa*); a son of the vasu Soma and Manoharā (*M. Bh,*); a ṛṣi in the 2nd Manvantara (*H. Purāṇa*); a son of Vasu Dhara (*H. Purāṇa*); a son of Dhatṛ; a son of Vidhātṛ (*Bh. Purāṇa*); another name for Brahmā and Viṣṇu.

Prāṇada (S) (M) **1.** life giving. **3.** another name for Brahmā and Viṣṇu; Black Myrobalan (*Terminalia chebula*); *Dendrobium fimbriatum.*

Praṇāda (S) (M) **1.** roar. **3.** a Ćakravartin.

Prāṇādhika (S) (M) dearer than life.

Prāṇaka (S) (M) **1.** living being. **2.** one who gives life; giver of breath. **3.** the son of an agni called Prāna (*M. Bh.*).

Prānanārāyaṇa (S) (M) **1.** lord of life. **3.** a king of Kāmarūpa (*A. Koṣa*).

Prāṇanātha (S) (M) **1.** lord of life. **3.** another name for Yama.

Praṇava (S) (M) the mystical syllable Om.

Praṇaya (S) (M) leader; guidance; conduct; affection; love.

Ptraṇayin (S) (M) beloved; dear; intimate; friend; favourite.

Prāṇeśa (S) (M) **1.** lord of life; lord of breath. **3.** a marut (*Bhā. Purāṇa*).

Praṇetṛ (S) (M) leader; guide.

Pranidhi (S) (M) **1.** spy. **3.** the son of an agni called Pāñćajanya (*M. Bh.*).

Praṇidhi (S) (M) **1.** request; solicitation; prayer. **3.** a son of Bṛhadratha (*M. Bh.*).

Praṇīta (S) (M) fire consecrated by prayer; agreeable; pleasing.

Prāñjala (S) (M) straight; upright; honest; sincere.

Praṇoda (S) (M) **1.** driving; directing. **2.** one who drives; directs; leads.

Praṇmaṇi (S) (M) **1.** leading jewel; jewel among the leaders. **3.** another name for Nārāyaṇa and Brahmā.

Prānśu (S) (M) **1.** high; tall; long; strong; intense. **3.** a son of Manu Vaivasvata (*H. Purāṇa*); a son of Vatsaprī (*Purāṇas*).

Prānśunṛga (S) (M) **1.** strongly praised; noblest among men. **3.** a Manu (*D. Bh. Purāṇa*).

Praṇuta (S) (M) praised; celebrated; lauded.

Prapakṣa (S) (M) **1.** extremity of a wing; in an army. **3.** a son of Kṛṣṇa (*V. Purāṇa*).

Prapālin (S) (M) **1.** protector. **3**. another name for Balarāma.

Prapanćikā (S) (M) **1.** multiplying; amplifying; manifestation. **3.** a yoginī.

Praphulla (S) (M) blooming; blossoming; covered with blossoms; shining; cheerful.

Prapitāmaha (S) (M) **1.** paternal grandfather. **3.** another name for Bhīṣma.

Prāpti (S) (M) **1.** achievement; advent; occurrence; arrival; discovery obtainment. **3.** the wife of Śama who was a son of Dharma (*M, Bh.*); a daughter of Jarāsandha (*H. Purāṇa*); a wife of Kansa (*Bhāgavata*).

Prarādhya (S) (M) satisfied.

Praruja (S) (M) **1.** shining forth; likable. **2.** exciting; seductive; handsome; graceful; to break. **3.** a deva who guards the amṛta (*M.Bh.*); a rākṣasa (*M. Bh.*).

Prasāda (S) (M) **1.** clearness; brightness; purity; free gift; calmness; propitiatory offering; food presented to an idol; favour. **3.** kindness personified as a son of Dharma and Maitri (*Bhā. Purāṇa*).

Prasādhikā (S) (M) adorning; beautifying; accomplishing.

Prasāha (S) (M) overpowering; defeating; force; power.

Prasala (S) (M) **1.** cool; tranquil. **2.** the cold season; winter.

Praśama (S) (M) **1.** peaceful; calm; cool; reposed; pacified; healing; tranquillity; autumn. **3.** a son of Ānakadundubhi (*Bh. Purāṇa*).

Praśan (S) (M) successful; winner.

Prasandhi (S) (M) **1.** expert negotiator. **2.** peace maker. **3.** a son of Vaivasvata Manu and the father of Kṣupa (*M. Bh.*).

Prasaṇga (S) (M) adherance; attachment; devotion; union; connection; context.

Prasanna (S) (M) clear; bright; pure; distinct; true; placid; tranquil; soothed; pleased.

Prasannateyu (S) (M) **1.** eternally happy. **3.** a son of Raudraśva (*Ś. Purāṇa*).

Prasanneyu (S) (M) **1.** always pleased. **3.** a son of Raudraśva (*Ś. Purāṇa*).

Praśānta (S) (M) calm; quiet.

Prasatta (S) (M) satisfied; pleased; bright; pure; clean.

Prasena (S) (M) **1.** with an expert army. **3.** a king who was the son of Nighna; a king of Ujjayinī; a son of Karṇa (*M. Bh.*).

Prasenajit (S) (M) **1.** conqueror of an expert army. **2.** a great warrior. **3.** the father of Suyajñā (*M. Bh.*); the father of Reṇukā (*Br. Purāṇa*); a king of Śrāvastī who was a contemporary of Gautama Buddha.

Prasiddhaka (S) (M) **1.** accomplished; celebrated; famous. **3.** a king of Janaka's line who was the son of Maru and father of Kīrttiratha (*Bhā. Purāṇa*).

Praskaṇva (S) (M) **1.** son of Kaṇva. **3.** a king who was the son of Medhātithi (*Bhāgavata*); a son of Kaṇva (*M. Bh.*).

Praśravana (S) (M) **1.** streaming forth; well; spring; spout. **3.** the mouth of the Sarasvatī river.

Praśravas (S) (M) **1.** loud sounding. **3.** the maruts (*Ṛg Veda*).

Praśraya (S) (M) **1.** resting place. **2.** modesty; respect; affection; relaxation. **3.** civility personified as a son of Dharma and Hrī (*M. Bh.*); a king of the family of Manu (*Bhāgavata*).

Praśṛta (S) (M) **1.** modest; well behaved; hidden. **2.** expanded. **3.** a demon killed by Garuḍa (*M. Bh.*); a son of Ānakadundubhi (*Bh. Purāṇa*).

Prastava (S) (M) hymn of praise; chant; song.

Prastha (S) (M) **1.** expanding; expanse; plain. **3.** a monkey (*Rāmāyaṇa*).

Prastharoman (S) (M) **1.** with expanding hair. **3.** son of Svarṇaroman.

Prāśu (S) (M) very quick or speedy.

Prasūna (S) (M) **1.** born; produced. **2.** blossom.

Praśūśruka (S) (M) **1.** knowing the scripture. **3.** a son of Maru (*V. Purāṇa*).

Praśūśruta (S) (M) **1.** knower of scriptures. **3.** a king who was a descendant of Rāma (*Bhāgavata*); a son of Maru (*Rāmāyaṇa*).

Prasūta (S) (M) born; produced; a flower; the primordial essence.

Prasvāra (S) (M) the great syllable; the syllable Om.

Pratāna (S) (M) branching out; a shoot; tendril.

Pratanu (S) (M) of delicate body; delicate; slender; small; minute.

Pratāpa (S) (M) **1.** heat; warmth; splendour; brilliance; majesty; glory;

power; strength; energy. **3.** a Sauvira prince (*M. Bh.*).

Pratapamukha (S) (M) **1.** with a shining face. **3.** king of varanasi (*K. Sāgara*).

Pratāpavat (S) (M) **1.** full of splendour; majestic; glorious. **3.** an attendant of Skanda (*H. Purāṇa*); another name for Śiva.

Prātara (S) (M) **1.** glorious; shining. **3.** the dawn; morning personified as the son of Puṣpārṇa and Prabhā (*Bh. Purāṇa*); a son of the āditya Dhātā and his wife Rākā (*Bhāgavata*).

Pratardana (S) (M) **1.** piercing; destroying. **3.** a Purū king who was the son of Divodāsa and Mādhavī (*M. Bh.*); a rākṣasa (*Rāmāyaṇa*).

Prātaścandra (S) (M) the moon in the morning.

Pratayankara (S) (M) causing a deluge.

Prathita (S) (M) **1.** spread; extended; known; celebrated. **3.** another name for Manu Svārociṣa and Viṣṇu.

Prathu (S) (M) **1.** widespead. **2.** omnipresent. **3.** another name for Viṣṇu.

Prati (S) (M) **1.** near to; in comparison with; towards. **3.** a son of Kuśa (*Bhā. Purāṇa*).

Pratibāhu (S) (M) **1.** with tethered arms. **3.** father of Subahu (*B. Literature*).

Pratibhānakūṭa (S) (M) **1.** mountain of understanding. **3.** a bodhisattva.

Pratibhānu (S) (M) **1.** as glorious as the sun; an image of the sun. **3.** a son of Kṛṣṇa and Satyabhāmā (*Bhāgavata*).

Pratibhāvatī (S) (M) full of understanding; splendid; bright; intelligent; bold; ready witted.

Pratibuddha (S) (M) **1.** awakened; awake; illuminated; enlightened; celebrated; great; prosperous. **2.** the dawn.

Pratidriṣṭa (S) (M) visible; conspicuous; famous; celebrated.

Pratiha (S) (M) **1.** to receive auspicious knowledge; to go towards the sky. **3.** husband of Suvarćalā (*Bh. Purāṇa*).

Pratīhāra (S) (M) **1.** door-keeper. **2.** guardian; watchman. **3.** a king who was the son of Parameṣṭhī and the father of Pratihartṛ (*V. Purāṇa*).

Pratihatṛ (S) (M) **1.** averter; one who draws back. **3.** the son of Pratihāra and Suvarćalā and the husband of Stuti (*Bhāgavata*).

Pratīka (S) (M) **1.** look; appearance; image; symbol; portion. **2.** member; limb. **3.** a son of Vasu and father of Oghavat (*Bhāgavata*); a son of Maru (*V. Purāṇa*)

Pratikāma (S) (M) desired; beloved.

Pratikāmin (S) (M) **1.** messenger; servant. **3.** the charioteer of Duryodhana (Af. *Bh.*).

Pratikṣatra (S) (M) **1.** respected by all warriors. **3.** a king of the family of Paraṣurāma (*Bhā. Purāṇa*); a son of Anenas (*H. Purāṇa*); a son of Śamin (*H. Purāṇa*); a descendant of Atri (*Ṛg Veda*).

Pratimāćandra (S) (M) a reflection of the moon.

Pratimāna (S) (M) model; image; idol; resemblance.

Pratinava (S) (M) ever new; new; young; fresh.

Pratīpa (S) (M) **1.** contrary; opposite; opponent against the stream. **3.** the lunar dynasty king who was the father of Śāntanu and grandfather of Bhīśma (*M. Bh.*).

Pratipāda (S) (M) **1.** demonstration; proof; explanation. **3.** a king of the Bharata race who was the son of Gandhamādana (*Bhāgavata*).

Pratīra (S) (M) **1.** shore; bank. **3.** a son of Manu Bhautya (*Mā. Purāṇa*).

Pratiratha (S) (M) **1.** equal adversary. **3.** a Purū king who was the son of King Antibhāra (*Bhā. Purāṇa*); a son of Matināra and father of Kaṇva (*H. Purāṇa*); a son of Vajra and father of Śućāru (*H. Purāṇa*).

Pratirūpa (S) (M) **1.** image; likeness; agreeable. **3.** an asura who once ruled the world (*M. Bh.*).

Pratiskandha (S) (M) **1.** like a shoulder. **2.** strong. **3.** an attendant of Skanda (*M. Bh.*).

Pratiśravas (S) (M) **1.** incomparable in fame; well heard of. **3.** the son of King Bhīmasena and Kumārī and a descendant of Parīkṣit (*M. Bh.*).

Pratiśruta (S) (M) **1.** promised; accepted; echoing. **3.** a son of Ānakadundubhi (*Bh. Purāṇa*).

Pratiṣṭha (S) (M) **1.** well established. **2.** steadfast; famous. **3.** the father of Supārśva.

Pratīta (S) (M) **1.** recognized; known; appeared; manifest; wise. **3.** a viśvadeva (*M. Bh.*).

Pratithī (S) (M) **1.** born on an auspicious day. **3.** a ṛṣi (*M. Bh.*).

Pratīvāha (S) (M) **1.** leading. **3.** a son of Śvaphalka (*H. Purāṇa*).

Prativedin (S) (M) experienced; knowledgeable.

Prativindhya (S) (M) **1.** near the Vindhya mountains. **2.** ruler of a part of the Vindhyās. **3.** a son of Yudhiṣṭhira and Draupadī (*M. Bh.*).

Pratoṣa (S) (M) **1.** complete satisfaction; gratification. **3.** a son of Manu Svāyambhuva (*Ṛg Veda*).

Pratulya (S) (M) **1.** uncomparable. **2.** unique. **3.** another name for Kārttikeya.

Pratuṣ (S) (M) delighted; to delight in.

Pratvakṣas (S) (M) **1.** energetic; vigorous; strong. **3.** another name for the maruts and Indra.

Pratyagadhāman (S) (M) radiant within; self-illuminating.

Pratyagāsapati (S) (M) **1.** lord of the western quarter. **3.** another name for Varuṇa.

Pratyagraha (S) (M) **1.** fresh; new; young; pure. **3.** a son of Vasu Uparićara and the king of the Ćedis (*M. Bh.*).

Pratyaṅga (S) (M) **1.** secondary parts of the body. **3.** a king of Bhārata (*M. Bh.*).

Pratyātmika (S) (M) of unique soul; original; peculiar.

Pratyūṣa (S) (M) **1.** every morning. **2.** dawn. **3.** a vasu son of Dharma and Prabhātā and father of sage Devala (*M. Bh.*).

Pravaha (S) (M) **1.** bearing along; carrying. **3.** one of the 7 winds around the planets; one of the 7 tongues of fire; a soldier of Skanda (*M. Bh.*).

Pravāhana (S) (M) **1.** bearing down. **3.** a king of Pañćāla (*H. Purāṇa*).

Pravābita (S) (M) **1.** flowing. **3.** a ṛṣi of the 3rd Manvantara (*V. Purāṇa*).

Pravālaka (S) (M) **1.** with shoots; coral like. **2.** as red as coral. **3.** a yakṣa (*M. Bh.*).

Pravan (S) (M) to vanquish; to conquer.

Pravara (S) (M) **1.** chief; best; principal; eldest; eminent; excellent. **3.** a messenger of the gods (*H. Purāṇa*); a dānava (*H. Purāṇa*); a minister of Kṛṣṇa (*V. Purāṇa*).

Pravarasena (S) (M) with the best army.

Pravasara (S) (M) **1.** emancipated; released. **3.** a Buddha (*B. Literature*).

Pravasu (S) (M) **1.** full of wealth; wealthy. **3.** a son of Īlina and Rathantarā (*M. Bh.*).

Praveka (S) (M) most excellent; principal; chief.

Pravepana (S) (M) **1.** tremulous. **3.** a serpent of the Takṣaka family (*M. Bh.*).

Pravilasena (S) (M) **1.** chief of the prominent. **3.** a king (*V. Purana*).

Pravīṇa (S) (M) **1.** skilful; clever. **3.** a son of the 14th Manu (*H. Purāṇa*).

Pravira (S) (M) yellow sandalwood.

Pravīra (S) (M) **1.** surpassing heroes. **2.** prince; hero; chief. **3.** a son of Prāćinvat and grandson of Purū; a son of Haryaśva; a son of Dharmanetra (*H. Purāṇa*); a Purū king who was the son of Santurodha (*A. Purāṇa*); a son of Purū and Pauṣṭī who was the husband of Sūraṣenī and the father of Manasyu (*M. Bh.*).

Pravīrabāhu (S) (M) **1.** strong armed. **3.** a rākṣasa (*V. Rāmāyaṇa*).

Pravīravara (S) (M) **1.** best of heroes. **3.** an asura (*K. Sāgara*).

Pravitṛ (S) (M) protector; patron; friend.

Prayāga (S) (M) **1.** place of sacrifice; confluence; meeting place. **3.** the confluence of the 3 holy rivers Gaṅgā, Jamunā and Sarasvatī (*A. Purāṇa*).

Prayas (S) (M) pleasure; enjoyment; delight.

Prayuj (S) (M) impulse; motive.

Prayuta (S) (M) **1.** conjoined; mingled with. **3.** a gandharva son of Kaśyapa and Muni (*M. Bh.*).

Prayutsu (S) (M) **1.** warrior; ascetic. **2.** ram; air; wind. **3.** another name for Indra.

Prema (S) (M) love; affection.

Premadhara (S) (M) full of love.

Premaja (S) (M) born of love.

Premajita (S) (M) one who wins love.

Premāmṛta (S) (M) the nectar of love.

Preman (S) (M) love; affection; kindness; favour.

Premānanda (S) (M) the joy of love.

Premanidhi (S) (M) pleasure of love.

Premasāgara (S) (M) ocean of love.

Premendra (S) (M) **1.** lord of love. **3.** another name for Kāma.

Premin (S) (M) loving; affectionate.

Pretvan (S) (M) **1.** moving along. **2.** wind; air. **3.** another name for Indra.

Prīaṅka (S) (M) **1.** with a beautiful mark. **2.** deer; bee; saffron.

Prīṇa (S) (M) pleased; satisfied.

Prīṇana (S) (M) pleasing; gratifying; soothing.

Prīṇita (S) (M) pleased; gratified; delighted.

Prīta (S) (M) pleased; delighted; joyful; glad.

Priya (S) (M) beloved; dear.

Priyadarśhna (S) (M) **1.** pleasant to behold. **3.** a prince of the gandharvas (*K. Granthāvali*); a son of Vāsuki (*K. Sāgara*); a soldier of Skanda (*M. Bh.*); a son of King Drupada (*M. Bh.*).

Priyadarśin (S) (M) **1.** pleasant to look at. **2.** looking with kindness. **3.** another name for Aśola.

Priyadhanva (S) (M) **1.** fond of the bow. **3.** another name for Śiva.

Priyaka (S) (M) **1.** loving. **2.** a deer; a bee. **3.** a soldier of Skanda (*M. Bh.*); Indian Kino tree (*Pterocarpus marsupium*); Kadamba tree (*Anthocephalus cadamba*).

Priyam (S) (M) beloved.

Priyamadhu (S) (M) **1.** fond of wine. **3.** another name for Balarāma.

Priyambū (S) (M) **1.** fond of water. **2.** the mango tree.

Priyamedha (S) (M) **1.** with pleasant wisdom. **3.** a ṛṣī and part author of *Ṛg Veda* (viii); a descendant of Ajamīdha (*Bhā. Purāṇa*).

Priyamitra (S) (M) **1.** dear friend. **3.** a mythical Ćakravartin.

Priyamvada (S) (M) **1.** sweet tongued. **3.** a gandharva (*K. Granthāvali*); Spanish Jasmine (*Jasminum grandiflorum*).

Priyaṅkara (S) (M) **1.** showing kindness. **2.** attracting regard; amiable. **3.** a dānava (*K. Sāgara*).

Priyarañjana (S) (M) **1.** good looking. **2.** pleasant; loving.

Priyaśravas (S) (M) **1.** loving glory. **2.** one whose glory is pleasant to the ears. **3.** another name for Kṛṣṇa (*Bhā. Purāṇa*).

Priyatama (S) (M) most beloved; dearest.

Priyatara (S) (M) dearer.

Priyātman (S) (M) **1.** dear to soul. **2.** agreeable; pleasant.

Priyavrata (S) (M) **1.** fond of obedience. **3.** the eldest son of Svāyambhuva Manu and Śatarūpā and the husband of Baṛhismatī and the father of Samrat, Kukṣi and 10 other sons.

Pṛṣad (S) (M) **1.** spotted; variegated. **2.** tiger; antelope.

Pṛṣadaśva (S) (M) **1.** with piebald horses. **3.** a son of Anaranya and father of Haryaṣva (*V. Purāṇa*); a son of Virūpa (*Bh. Purāṇa*); another name for the maruts, Vāyu and Śiva.

Pṛṣadhra (S) (M) **1.** like an antelope. **3.** a warrior on the side of the Pāṇḍavas; a son of Vaivasvata Manu

(*H. Purāṇa*); a son of King Drupada (*M. Bh.*).

Pṛṣata (S) (M) **1.** spotted; vareigated. **2.** speckled; a drop of water; spot. **3.** a Pānćāla king who was the father of Drupada (*M. Bh.*).

Pṛṣatāśva (S) (M) **1.** spotted horse. **2.** wind; air. **3.** a solar dynasty king who was the son of Ambarīṣa (*Bhāgavata*).

Pṛṣatātmaja (S) (M) **1.** son of Pṛṣata. **3.** another name for Drupada.

Pṛśṇi (S) (M) **1.** dappled; speckled; spotted; small; thin. **3.** the father of Śvaphalka (*H. Purāṇa*); a sage (*M. Bh.*).

Pṛśnibhadra (S) (M) **1.** propitious to the earth. **3.** another name for Kṛṣṇa.

Pṛśnidhara (S) (M) **1.** earth bearer. **3.** another name for Kṛṣṇa.

Pṛśnigarbha (S) (M) **1.** the womb of the earth. **3.** another name for Viṣṇu and Kṛṣṇa (*M. Bh.*).

Pṛśnīśṛṅga (S) (M) **1.** with a vareigated crest. **3.** another name for Viṣṇu and Gaṇeśa.

Pṛṣṭhaja (S) (M) **1.** backbone. **3.** a form of Skanda(*M. Bh.*).

Pṛtanāja (S) (M) hero.

Pṛthabhū (S) (M) **1.** son of Pṛthā. **3.** another name for Yudhiṣṭhira.

Pṛthāja (S) (M) **1.** son of Pṛthā. **3.** another name for Arjuna; White Murdah (*Terminalia citrina*).

Pṛthāpati (S) (M) **1.** husband of Pṛthā. **3.** another name for Pāṇḍu.

Pṛthasūnu (S) (M) **1.** son of Pṛtha. **3.** another name for Yudhiṣṭhira (*M. Bh.*).

Pṛthāśva (S) (M) **1.** with large horses. **3.** a king in the court of Yama (*M. Bh.*).

Pṛthavinandana (S) (M) son of the earth.

Pṛthī (S) (M) **1.** of earth; large. **2.** material; ruler of lower animals. **3.** a mythical personage said to have been the 1st anointed sovereign of men, he is enumerated among the ṛṣis; a man protected by the aśvins (*Ṛg Veda*).

Pṛthīśa (S) (M) lord of the world.

Pṛthu (S) (M) **1.** broad; wide; expansive; large; great; important; ample. **2.** fire. **3.** a son of Prastāra; an emperor of great virtue who was the son of Vena and who was a partial incarnation of Mahāviṣṇu his rule is considered a golden period of Bhārata, he was the husband of Arćis and the father of Vijitāśva, Haryakṣa, Dhūmrakeśa, Vṛka and Draviṇa; a son of Anaraṇya and father of Triśaṅkhu; a viś-vadeva (*V. Purāṇa*); a dānava (*H. Purāṇa*); *a* son of Anenas (*M. Bh.*); a son of Ćitraka (*H. Purāṇa*); a son of Ćitraratha (*Bh. Purāṇa*); a son of Pāra (*H. Purāṇa*); a son of Rućaka (*Bh. Purāṇa*); a son of Vaṭeśvara and the father of Viśākhadatta; a Saptarṣi (*H. Purāṇa*); another name for Śiva (*M. Bh.*); Nutmeg flower (*Nigella sativa*).

Pṛthudāna (S) (M) **1.** one who donates a lot. **3.** a son of Śaśabindu (*V. Purāṇa*).

Pṛthūdara (S) (M) **1.** broad bellied. **3.** a yakṣa.

Prithudarbha (S) (M) **1.** large grass. **3.** a king of Aṅga (*A. Purāṇa*).

Pṛthugrīva (S) (M) **1.** broadnecked. **3.** a rākṣasa (*Ṛg Veda*).

Pṛthuhara (S) (M) **1.** annihilator of earthly beings. **3.** another name for Śiva.

Pṛthujaya (S) (M) **1.** victorious far and wide. **3.** a son of Śaśabindu and grandson of Ćitraratha (*V. Parāṇa*).

Pṛthukarman (S) (M) **1.** whose deeds have travelled. **3.** a son of Saśabindu (*V. Purāṇa*).

Pṛihukīrti (S) (M) **1.** one whose fame has reached far. **3.** a son of Śaśabindu (*V. Purāṇa*).

Pṛthula (S) (M) broad; expanded; fat; robust; stout.

Pṛthulākṣa (S) (M) **1.** large eyed. **3.** an Aṅga king who lived in the court of Yama (*M. Bh.*); the son of Ćaturaṅga (*Bhā. Purāṇa*).

Pṛthulāśva (S) (M) **1.** large horse. **2.** one who has strong horses. **3.** an Ikṣvāku king who was the son of Pṛthu and the father of Adra (*Br. Purāṇa*).

Pṛthumat (S) (M) **1.** abounding in importance. **2.** very important.

Pṛthupājas (S) (M) far shining; resplendent.

Pṛthurukma (S) (M) **1.** with a lot of gold. **3.** a son of Parājit (*V. Purāṇa*).

Pṛthuśekhara (S) (M) **1.** broad crested. **2.** mountain.

Pṛthuśeṇa (S) (M) **1.** with an extensive army. **3.** a son of Rućirāśva (*H. Purāṇa*); a son of Vibhu (*Bhā. Purāṇa*).

Pṛthuśravas (S) (M) **1.** one whose fame has reached far and wide. **2.** far famed. **3.** a son of Śaśabindu (*V. Purāṇa*); a son of Raghu (*Bhā. Purāṇa*); a son of the 9th Manu (*M. Purāṇa*); an attendant of Skanda; the elephant of the north quarter; a Ṛg Vedic king protected by Indra; king whose daughter Kāmā married King Ayutanāyī (*M. Bh.*); a sage who was a friend of Yudhiṣṭhira (*M. Bh.*); a soldier of Skanda (*M. Bh.*); a serpent who helped carry the soul of Balarāma (*M. Bh.*).

Pṛthuśrī (S) (M) with great fortune.

Pṛthutama (S) (M) greatest; broadest; widest; largest.

Pṛthutara (S) (M) greater; larger; wider; broader.

Pṛthuvega (S) (M) **1.** with great speed. **3.** a king in the court of Yama (M. *Bh.*).

Pṛthuyaśas (S) (M) **1.** far famed. **3.** a son of Śaśabindu (*V. Purāṇa*).

Prthvīćandra (S) (M) **1.** moon of the earth. **3.** a king of the Trigartas (*R. Taraṅginī*).

Pṛthvīdhara (S) (M) **1.** supporter of the earth. **2.** mountain. **3.** a demon.

Pṛthvīgarbha (S) (M) **1.** centre of the earth; womb of the earth. **3.** a bodhisattva; another name for Gaṇeśa.

Pṛthvīja (S) (M) born of the earth; the planet Mars.

Pṛthvīkṣit (S) (M) **1.** ruling over the earth. **2.** king.

Pṛthvīñjaya (S) (M) **1.** earth conqueror. **3.** a son of Virāṭa (*M. Bh.*); a dānava (*M. Bh.*).

Pṛthvīpāla (S) (M) protector of the earth.

Pṛthvīpati (S) (M) **1.** lord of the earth. **2.** king. **3.** another name for Yama.

Pṛthvīra (S) (M) warrior of the earth.

Pṛthvīrāja (S) (M) lord of the earth.

Pṛthvīśa (S) (M) **1.** lord of the earth. **2.** king.

Pṛthvīvaraloćana (S) (M) **1.** one who has roamed all over the earth. **3.** a bodhisattva (*K. Vyuha*).

Puććhāṇḍaka (S) (M) **1.** carrying eggs on the tail. **3.** a serpent of the Takṣaka family (*M. Bh.*).

Pudgala (S) (M) **1.** anything living; handsome; beautiful. **2.** the body; the soul; the ego. **3.** another name for Śiva.

Pudgalapati (S) (M) **1.** master of the living. **2.** prince; king.

Pukharāja (S) (M) **1.** king of jewels. **2.** topaz.

Pula (S) (M) **1.** extended wide; living being. **3.** an attendant of Śiva (*Ś. Purāṇa*).

Pulaha (S) (M) **1.** creator of living beings; lord of animals. **3.** a prajāpati who was the father of butterflies, lions, tigers, lambs, wolves and kinnaras; a star (*H. Purāṇa*); another name for Śiva.

Pulaka (S) (M) **1.** a thrill of joy. **2.** gem. **3.** a gandharva; a nāga.

Pulakeśin (S) (M) rejoicing; happy; thrilling.

Pulasti (S) (M) of a head wearing the hair straight.

Pulastya (S) (M) **1.** with straight hair. **3.** a prajāpati born from the ear of Brahmā and who was married to Prīti, Havirbhū, Sandhyā and Pratīćyā (*A. Veda*); another name for Śiva.

Pulina (S) (M) the bank of a river; islet.

Pulomajit (S) (M) **1.** conqueror of Puloman. **3.** another name for Indra.

Puloman (S) (M) **1.** thrilled in rapture. **3.** a demon whose daughter married Indra and who was destroyed by him (*M. Bh.*).

Punāna (S) (M) clear; bright; purified.

Puñću (S) (M) 1. of pious form; pentagon. 3. a solar dynasty king who was the son of Harita and the father of Vijaya (*Br. Purāṇa*).

Puṇḍarīka (S) (M) 1. Lotus flower (*Nelumbo nucifera*); white umbrella; a mark on the forehead; tiger; white. 3. the elephant of the south east quarter (*K. Granthāvati*); a Brāhmin worshipped as the god Vithoba; the son of Śvetaketu and Lakṣmī (*K. Vyūha*); a king of the race of Rāma who was the son of Niśādha and the father of Kṣemadhanvā (*Bhā. Purāṇa*); a son of Nabhas (*H. Purāṇa*); a nāga (*M. Bh.*).

Puṇḍarīkākṣa (S) (M) 1. lotus eyed. 3. another name for Viṣṇu/Kṛṣṇa.

Puṇḍarīkamukha (S) (M) 1. lotus faced. 3. an eminent serpent king.

Puṇḍarīkanayana (S) (M) 1. lotus eyed. 3. another name for Viṣṇu/Kṛṣṇa (*M. Bh.*).

Puṇḍarīyaka (S) (M) 1. lotus faced. 3. a viśvadeva (*M. Bh.*).

Puṇḍra (S) (M) 1. mark; sign. 2. a line made with ashes on the forehead. 3. the son of the daitya Bāli (*M. Bh.*); a son of Vasudeva.

Pūnīśa (S) (M) lord of the pious.

Punīta (S) (M) holy; pious; sacred; cleaned; purified.

Puñjarāja (S) (M) lord of a multitude.

Punkhitaśara (S) (M) 1. armed with feathered arrows. 3. another name for Kāma.

Puṇya (S) (M) 1. holy; auspicious; fair; good; right; meritorious; pure; sacred. 3. a son of sage Dīrghatamas.

Puṇyabala (S) (M) 1. the strength of goodness. 3. one of the 10 forces of a bodhisattva.

Puṇyadarśana (S) (M) of virtuous appearance.

Puṇyagandhin (S) (M) 1. of virtuous fragrance. 2. virtuous; famous; sweet scented; fragrant; *Michelia champaka*; Common White Jasmine (*Jasminum officianale*).

Puṇyajana (S) (M) 1. good; honest. 3. a rākṣasa (*V. Purāṇa*); another name for the yakṣas.

Puṇyajaneśvara (S) (M) 1. lord of the yakṣas. 3. another name for Kubera.

Puṇyajita (S) (M) gained by virtue.

Puṇyakīrti (S) (M) 1. famous for virtues. 2. with celebrated virtues. 3. a man whose shape was assumed by Viṣṇu.

Puṇyakṛt (S) (M) 1. doer of meritorious acts. 3. a viśvādeva (*M. Bh.*).

Puṇyalakṣmīka (S) (M) 1. virtuous wealth; with a wealth of virtues. 2. auspicious; prosperous.

Puṇyālaṅkṛta (S) (M) adorned by virtue.

Puṇyamahas (S) (M) of pure glory.

Puṇyamitra (S) (M) 1. a friend of virtue. 3. a Buddhist patriarch.

Puṇyanāman (S) (M) 1. with a pious name. 3. a soldier of Skanda (*M. Bh.*).

Puṇyanātha (S) (M) lord of virtue.

Puṇyanidhi (S) (M) 1. treasure of virtue. 3. a king of the lunar race (*Sk. Purāṇa*).

Puṇyasena (S) (M) 1. commander of virtues. 2. with an army of pious people.

Puṇyaśloka (S) (M) 1. well spoken of. 3. another name for Nala, Yudhiṣṭhira and Kṛṣṇa.

Puṇyaśravas (S) (M) 1. much heard of virtues. 2. famous for virtues. 3. a sage who was reborn as Nanda the cowherd's niece Lavangā (*P. Purāṇa*).

Puṇyaśrīgarbha (S) (M) 1. womb of virtue. 3. a bodhisattva (*B. Literature*).

Puṇyātman (S) (M) pure souled; virtuous.

Puṇyatoya (S) (M) 1. holy water. 3. the river in the stomach of Bālamukunda.

Puṇyavardhana (S) (M) increasing virtue.

Puṇyavarman (S) (M) 1. armoured with virtue. 3. a king of Vidarbha.

Puṇyavrata (S) (M) 1. with a vow to virtue. 2. virtuous.

Puradviṣ (S) (M) **1.** enemy of a city; enemy of a fortress; enemy of the asura Tripura. **3.** another name for Śiva.

Purahan (S) (M) **1.** slayer of Pura. **3.** another name for Śiva.

Purajit (S) (M) **1.** conqueror of fortresses; conqueror of pura. **3.** the son of Aja and father of Ariṣṭanemi; another name for Śiva.

Purandara (S) (M) **1.** destroyer of strongholds. **3.** Indra in the Vaivasvata Manvantara; another name for Indra, Agni and Śiva.

Purañjana (S) (M) **1.** life; soul. **3.** another name for Varuṇa.

Purañjaya (S) (M) **1.** conqueror of the city. **3.** a warrior on the side of the Kurus; a son of Sṛñjaya and father of Janamejaya; a son of Bhajamāna; a son of Śaśada (*V. Purāṇa*); a son of Medhāvin;a son of the elephant Airāvata (*H. Purāṇa*); a king of Ayodhyā.

Purāri (S) (M) **1.** enemy of Pura. **3.** another name for Viṣṇu.

Puraśāsana (S) (M) **1.** chastiser of the asura Tripura. **3.** another name for Śiva.

Purāvasu (S) (M) **1.** 1st treasure. **3.** another name for Bhīṣma.

Pūrayitri (S) (M) **1.** one who fulfils or satisfies. **3.** another name for Viṣṇu and Śiva.

Pūrṇa (S) (M) **1.** complete; entire. **2.** full; abundant; rich; content; strong; capable; auspicious. **3.** a serpent of the family of Vāsuki (*M. Bh.*); a gandharva son of Kaśyapa and Prādhā (*M. Bh.*).

Pūrṇabhadra (S) (M) **1.** perfectly gentle. **3.** the father of the yakṣa Harikeśa (*M. Bh.*); a serpent son of Kaśyapa (*M. Bh.*); the son of the yakṣa Ratnabhadra and the father of an attendant of Śiva.

Pūrṇaćandra (S) (M) **1.** full moon. **3.** a bodhisattva.

Pūrṇamāsa (S) (M) full moon; personified as a son of Dhatṛ and Anumati (*Bh. Purāṇa*); a son of Kṛṣṇa (*V. Purāṇa*).

Pūrṇāmṛta (S) (M) full of nectar.

Pūrṇamukha (S) (M) **1.** with a perfect face. **3.** a serpent of the family of Dhṛtarāṣṭra (*M. Bh.*).

Pūrṇānanda (S) (M) **1.** supremely happy. **3.** the Supreme Being.

Pūrṇāṅgada (S) (M) **1.** perfect bodied. **3.** a serpent of the family of Dhṛtarāṣṭra (*M. Bh.*).

Pūrṇārtha (S) (M) one whose wishes have been realized.

Pūrṇaśrī (S) (M) with fortune.

Pūrṇāyuṣ (S) (M) **1.** with a perfect life. **3.** a gandharva son of Kaśyapa and Prādhā (*M. Bh.*).

Pūrṇendu (S) (M) the full moon.

Pūrṇiman (S) (M) **1.** complete; fully satisfied. **3.** a brother of Kaśyapa and son of Marīći and Kalā (*V. Rāmāyaṇa*).

Pūrṇotsangha (S) (M) **1.** far advanced in pregnancy. **3.** a king (*M. Bh.*).

Purobhū (S) (M) 1st born; excelling; in front; superior.

Purocana (S) (M) **1.** builder of a city. **3.** a minister of Duryodhana.

Purojava (S) (M) **1.** excelling in speed. **3.** a son of Medhātithi; a son of the vasu Prāṇa and Urjjaṣvatī (*Bhāgavata*).

Purojyotiṣ (S) (M) preceded by radiance.

Puroratha (S) (M) **1.** one whose chariot is in front. **2.** preeminent; superior.

Purovasu (S) (M) **1.** preceded by wealth. **2.** very wealthy. **3.** an Aṅga king who was the son of Babhrusetu (*A. Purāṇa*).

Pūrpati (S) (M) lord of a city.

Purū (S) (M) **1.** much; many; people; abundant; every. **2.** the pollen of a flower; heaven; paradise. **3.** a son of Vasudeva and Sahadevā (*Bhā. Purāṇa*)] a son of Madhu (*V. Purāṇa*); a son of Manu Cākṣuṣa and Nadvalā (*H. Purāṇa*); a celebrated king of the Lunar dynasty who was the son of Yayāti and Śarmiṣṭhā and the husband of Pauṣṭi, he was the father of Pravīra or Janamejaya, Īśvara and Raudrāsva

(*M. Bh.*); the charioteer of Arjuna (*M. Bh.*); a son of Jahnu (*Bhā. Purāṇa*); a mountain.

Purućchepa (S) (M) **1.** throwing with great speed. **3.** a sage who was the son of Divodāśa (*Ṛg Veda*).

Purudanśas (S) (M) **1.** abounding in mighty deeds. **2.** protecting all; residing in the hearts of everyone; having many virtues; having the support of many people. **3.** another name for Indra.

Purudaya (S) (M) abounding in compassion.

Purūdvāha (S) (M) **1.** abounding in religion. **2.** very religious. **3.** a son of the 11th Manu.

Puruhotra (S) (M) **1.** abounding in ritual. **3.** a son of Anu (*Bhā. Purāṇa*).

Puruhūta (S) (M) **1.** invoked by many. **3.** another name for Indra.

Puruja (S) (M) **1.** born of Purū. **2.** born in the Purū dynasty. **3.** a son of Suśānti.

Purujit (S) (M) **1.** conquering many. **3.** a brother of Kuntibhoja who fought on the side of the Pāṇḍavas; a son of Rućaka (*Bhā. Purāṇa*); a son of Ānaka (*Bhā. Purāṇa*); another name for Viṣṇu (*Bhā. Purāṇa*).

Purukṛtvan (S) (M) achieving great deeds.

Purukutśa (S) (M) **1.** abused by many. **3.** a son of King Māndhātā and Bindumatī (*H. Purāṇa*); a descendant of Ikṣvāku (*Ś. Brāhmaṇa*).

Purumandra (S) (M) delighting many.

Purumantu (S) (M) full of wisdom.

Purumedha (S) (M) full of wisdom.

Purumīdha (S) (M) **1.** full of wisdom. **3.** a Purū king who was the son of Bṛhatputra and the brother of Ajamīḍha (*Bhā. Purāṇa*).

Purumīlha (S) (M) **1.** met by many. **3.** a son of Suhotra (*M. Bh.*); a son of Hastin (*H. Purāṇa*).

Purumitra (S) (M) **1.** friend of many. **3.** a warrior on the Kuru side (*M. Bh.*); a son of Dhṛtarāṣṭra (*M. Bh.*).

Purūravas (S) (M) **1.** crying loudly. **2.** overtly praised. **3.** a famous king of the lunar race who was the son of Buddha and Īlā and the husband of the apsarā Urvaśī, he was the father of Āyus and the ancestor of Purū, Duṣyanta, Bharata, Kuru, Dhṛtarāṣṭra and Pāṇḍu.

Puruṣa (S) (M) **1.** person. **2.** the pupil of the eye; the conscious principle; man; the Supreme Being; the spirit. **3.** a son of Manu Ćākṣuṣa (*Bh. Purāṇa*); one of the 18 attendants of the sun (*Bhā. Purāṇa*).

Puruṣaćandra (S) (M) moon among men.

Puruṣādya (S) (M) **1.** 1st among men. **3.** another name for Viṣṇu and Ṛṣabha the 1st Arhat.

Puruṣakesarin (S) (M) **1.** lion among men; man-lion. **3.** Viṣṇu's 4th incarnation.

Puruṣanti (S) (M) **1.** large gift. **3.** a sage protected by the aśvins (*Ṛg Veda*).

Puruṣapati (S) (M) **1.** lord of men. **3.** another name for Rāma.

Puruṣapuṇḍarīka (S) (M) **1.** lotus among men. **3.** the 6th Jaina Black Vasudeva.

Puruṣasiṅha (S) (M) **1.** lion among men. **3.** the 5th Jaina Black Vasudeva (*J. Literature*).

Puruṣavara (S) (M) **1.** best among men. **3.** another name for Viṣṇu.

Purusena (S) (M) with a large army; commander of many.

Puruṣendra (S) (M) **1.** lord of men. **2.** king.

Puruṣottama (S) (M) **1.** best among men. **2.** the highest being. **3.** the 4th Jaina Black Vasudeva; another name for Kṛṣṇa and Viṣṇu.

Puruṣṭuta (S) (M) **1.** highly lauded. **3.** another name for Śiva.

Puruvāsa (S) (M) dwelling in all; omnipresent.

Puruviśruta (S) (M) **1.** much renowned. **3.** a son of Vasudeva (*Bhā. Purāṇa*).

Puruyaśas (S) (M) **1.** perfection; much renowned. **2.** very famous. **3.** a king of Pāñćāla who was the son of Bhūriyaśas (*Sk. Purāṇa*).

Pūrvapālin (S) (M) **1.** ancient protector. **3.** another name for Indra.

Pūṣan (S) (M) **1.** nourisher; protector. **3.** a Vedic deity originally connected with the sun and associated with the moon as protector of the universe, he is regarded as the keeper of flocks and bringer of prosperity, in later times he is an āditya and regent of the Nakṣatra Revatī.

Pūṣānuja (S) (M) **1.** son of Puṣān. **3.** another name for Parjañya.

Puṣkala (S) (M) **1.** much; copious; abundant; rich; magnificent; full; complete; powerful; excellent; best; loud; purified. **3.** a son of Varuṇa (*M. Bh.*); an asura; (*H. Purāṇa*); a soldier of Rāvaṇa (*P. Purāṇa*); a son of Bharata and Māṇḍavī and grandson of Daśaratha (*V. Rāmāyaṇa*), he was the husband of Kāntimatī; a ṛṣi (*Bhā. Purāṇa*); a Buddha (*L. Vistara*); another name for Śiva (*M. Bh.*).

Puṣkara (S) (M) **1.** Blue Lotus (*Nelumbium speciosum*). **2.** sky; heaven; sun; a night of new moon falling on Monday, Tuesday or Saturday; arrow; the blade of a sword. **3.** a general of Varuṇa (*M. Bh.*); a son of Kṛṣṇa (*Bhā. Purāṇa*); the brother of Nala; a son of Bharata (*V. Purāṇa*); a son of Vṛka and Dūrvākṣī (*M. Bh.*); a son of Varuṇa and husband of the daughter of Soma (*M. Bh.*); a sage who was the preceptor of Paraśurama (*M. Bh.*); an asura (*H. Purāṇa*); a Buddha (*L. Vistara*); a place of pilgrimage in Rājasthan; another name for Kṛṣṇa and Śiva.

Puṣkaraćūda (S) (M) **1.** lotus crested. **3.** one of the 4 elephants that support the earth (*Bhā. Purāṇa*).

Puṣkarākṣa (S) (M) **1.** lotus eyed. **3.** a king who was the son of King Sućandra (*Br. Purāṇa*); another name for Viṣṇu.

Puṣkaranābha (S) (M) **1.** lotus navelled. **3.** another name for Viṣṇu.

Puṣkarekṣaṇa (S) (M) **1.** lotus eyed. **3.** another name for Viṣṇu.

Puṣpa (S) (M) **1.** flower; blossom. **2.** perfume; topaz. **3.** a son of Śliṣṭi (*H. Purāṇa*); a son of Śaṅkha (*H. Purāṇa*); a serpent of the family of Kaśyapa (*M. Bh.*); the vehicle of Kubera (*A. Koṣa*).

Puṣpabhūti (S) (M) the essence of flowers.

Puṣpadanta (S) (M) **1.** flower toothed; the sun and moon conjoined. **2.** one with shining and hard teeth. **3.** an attendant of Śiva (*M. Bh.*); an attendant of Viṣṇu (*Bhā. Purāṇa*); the 9th Jaina Arhat of the present Avasarpinī (*J.S. Koṣa*); the elephant of the northwest quarter (*Bhā. Purāṇa*); an at-tendant given to Skanda by Pārvatī (*M. Bh.*); a vidyādhara; a nāga (*V. Rāmāyaṇa*); another name for Śiva (*A. Koṣa*).

Puṣpadhanuṣ (S) (M) **1.** with a bow of flowers. **3.** another name for Kāma.

Puṣpadhanvan (S) (M) **1.** armed with a bow of flowers. **3.** another name for Kāma.

Puṣpadhara (S) (M) bearing flowers.

Puṣpadhāraṇa (S) (M) **1.** flower bearer; embellished with flowers. **3.** another name for Kṛṣṇa.

Puṣpahāsa (S) (M) **1.** smiling like flowers. **2.** a flower garden. **3.** another name for Viṣṇu.

Puṣpaja (S) (M) **1.** born from a flower. **2.** nectar.

Puṣpaketana (S) (M) **1.** flower bannered. **2.** one who is characterised by flowers. **3.** another name for Kāma.

Puṣpaketu (S) (M) **1.** flower bannered. **2.** characterized by flowers. **3.** a Buddha.

Puṣpaloćana (S) (M) **1.** flower like eyes. **2.** one whose eyes are as beautiful as a flower.

Puṣpam (S) (M) **1.** topaz eyed. **2.** with eyes as brilliant as a topaz; flower; blossom; topaz.

Puṣpāmbu (S) (M) **1.** water of flowers. **2.** honey; nectar.

Puṣpamitra (S) (M) **1.** friend of flowers. **3.** a king and father of Agnimitra (*Bhā. Purāṇa*).

Puṣpānana (S) (M) **1.** flower faced. **3.** a yakṣa in the court of Kubera (*M. Bh.*).

Puṣpapīḍa (S) (M) **1.** chaplet of flowers. **3.** a gandharva; another name for Kāma.

Puṣparāga (S) (M) flower hued; topaz.

Puṣpārṇa (S) (M) **1.** flower stream. **3.** a king of the family of Dhruva and husband of Prabhā (*Bhāgavata*); a son of Vatsara and Svarvīthi.

Puṣpaśekhara (S) (M) flower crested; a chaplet of flowers.

Puṣpaśrīgarbha (S) (M) **1.** filled with the beauty of flowers. **3.** a Bodhisattva.

Puṣpavāhana (S) (M) carrier of flowers.

Puṣpāvakīrṇa (S) (M) **1.** strewn with flowers. **3.** a prince of the kinnaras (*H. Purāṇa*).

Puṣpavān (S) (M) **1.** possessing flowers. **2.** perfumed; flowering. **3.** a king who once ruled the 3 worlds (*M. Bh.*).

Puṣpavata (S) (M) **1.** possessing flowers. **2.** flowery; blossoming; decorated with flowers. **3.** a daitya (*M. Bh.*).

Puṣpāyudha (S) (M) **1.** flower armed. **3.** another name for Kāma.

Puṣpendra (S) (M) lord of flowers.

Puṣpeśa (S) (M) lord of flowers.

Puṣpeṣu (S) (M) **1.** flower arrow. **3.** another name for Kāma.

Puṣpin (S) (M) **1.** blossoming. **2.** rich in flowers.

Puṣpita (S) (M) **1.** flowered; bearing flowers; blooming. **3.** a Buddha.

Puṣya (S) (M) **1.** nourishment; the blossom. **2.** the best of anything. **3.** one of the 24 mythical Buddhas; an asterism (*Ṛg Veda*).

Puṣyamitra (S) (M) friend of blossoms.

Pūtadakṣa (S) (M) pure minded.

Pūtakratu (S) (M) **1.** pure minded. **3.** another name for Indra.

Pūtamali (S) (M) **1.** pure minded. **3.** another name for Śiva.

Putra (S) (M) **1.** son. **2.** child. **3.** a son of Brahmiṣṭha (*K. Granthāvali*); a son of Priyavrata (*V. Purāṇa*).

Pūtrima (S) (M) purified; pure; clean.

Puttala (S) (M) pure; made of soil; doll.

R

Rā (S) (M) **1.** fire. **2.** strength. **3.** another name for Indra.

Rabhasa (S) (M) **1.** impetuous; shining. **2.** vehemence; passion; zeal; rapid; fierce; wild; strong. **3.** a monkey in Rama's army (*V. Rāmāyaṇa*); a rākṣasa of Rāvaṇa (*V. Rāmāyaṇa*); the son of Rambhā (*Bhā. Purāṇa*).

Rabhoda (S) (M) bestowing strength.

Rābhu (S) (M) messenger.

Rabhya (S) (M) **1.** pleasant; agreeable; a kind of śruti in music. **3.** a king who was known for his justice.

Racita (S) (M) produced; fashioned; prepared.

Rāddhi (S) (M) accomplishment; comple-tion; perfection; success.

Rādhaka (S) (M) liberal; bountiful.

Rādhākānta (S) (M) **1.** beloved of Rādhā. **3.** another name for Kṛṣṇa.

Rādhākṛṣṇa (S) (M) Rādhā and Kṛṣṇa conjoined.

Rādhāramaṇa (S) (M) **1.** beloved of Rādhā. **3.** another name for Kṛṣṇa.

Rādhāsuta (S) (M) **1.** son of Rādhā. **3.** another name for Karṇa.

Rādhātanaya (S) (M) **1.** son of Rādhā. **3.** another name for Karṇa.

Rādheśa (S) (M) **1.** lord of Rādhā. **3.** another name for Kṛṣṇa.

Rādheya (S) (M) **1.** of Radha. **3.** another name for Karṇa.

Rādhika (S) (M) **1.** successful; prosperous. **3.** the son of King Jayasena (*Bhā. Purāṇa*).

Rāga (S) (M) **1.** love; to colour; to tinge with emotion; loveliness; passion; harmony; king; sun; moon. **3.** a musical mode personified and wedded to a rāgiṇī (*R. Taraṅgiṇī*).

Rāgacchana (S) (M) **1.** love covered. **3.** another name for Kāma and Rāma.

Rāgamaya (S) (M) **1.** red; full of passion; full of colour; full of love. **2.** beloved; dear.

Rāgavṛnta (S) (M) **1.** passion stem. **3.** another name for Kāma.

Rāgayuj (S) (M) **1.** attached to; coloured; attached to love. **2.** ruby.

Rāghava (S) (M) **1.** descendant of Raghu. **3.** another name for Rāma.

Rāghavendra (S) (M) **1.** chief of the Raghus. **3.** another name for Rāma.

Rāghaveśvara (S) (M) **1.** chief of the Raghus. **3.** another name for Rāma; a linga of Śiva.

Raghu (S) (M) **1.** fleet; rapid. **2.** light; fleet. **3.** a celebrated king of the solar race who was the son of Dilīpa and Sudakṣiṇā and father of Aja, the great-grandfather of Rāma, described as the ideal monarch, the dynasty was called after his name, it is believed that the Kṣatriyas who praise Raghu will not be defeated in war, he is among the kings to be remembered at dawn and dusk (*M. Bh.*); a son of Gautama Buddha.

Raghukara (S) (M) **1.** inspirer; accelerater. **3.** another name for Kālidāsa the author of *Raghuvaṅśa*.

Raghukumāra (S) (M) **1.** son of Raghu. **3.** another name for Rāma.

Raghumaṇi (S) (M) **1.** jewel of the Raghus. **3.** another name for Rāma.

Raghumanyu (S) (M) quick tempered; eager; zealous.

Raghunandana (S) (M) **1.** descendant of Raghu. **3.** another name for Rāma.

Raghunātha (S) (M) **1.** lord of the Raghus. **3.** another name for Rāma.

Raghunāyaka (S) (M) **1.** chief of the Raghus. **3.** another name for Rāma.

Raghupati (S) (M) **1.** lord of the Raghus. **3.** another name for Rāma.

Raghurāma (S) (M) Rāma of the Raghu clan.

Raghutilaka (S) (M) **1.** ornament of the Raghus. **3.** another name for Rāma.

Raghūttama (S) (M) **1.** the best of the Raghus. **3.** another name for Rāma.

Raghuvaṅśa (S) (M) **1.** of the family of Raghu. **3.** a poem by Kālidāsa.

Raghuvanśi (S) (M) **1.** of the family of Raghu. **3.** another name for Rāma.

Raghuvīra (S) (M) **1.** hero of the Raghus. **3.** another name for Rāma.

Rāgi (S) (M) **1.** full of love; coloured; affectionate; delighting. **3.** a prominent king of the Purū dynasty (*M. Bh.*).

Rāgyula (S) (M) coloured; ruby.

Rahovādī (S) (M) **1.** speaking guardedly. **3.** a king of the Purū dynasty who was the son of Saṁyāti and the father of Bhadrāśva (*A. Purāṇa*).

Rāhu (S) (M) **1.** seizer. **3.** a demon son of Kaśyapa or Vipraćitti and Siṁhikā supposed to devour the sun and moon hence being responsible for their eclipses, he is also a member of the court of Brahmā (*M. Bh.*); a daitya.

Rāhubhedin (S) (M) **1.** severing Rāhu. **3.** another name for Viṣṇu.

Rāhugaṇa (S) (M) **1.** an attendant of Rāhu (*A. Veda*). **3.** the son of Suddhodana (*V. Purāṇa*); son of Gautama Buddha.

Rāhula (S) (M) **1.** able; efficient; given by Rāhu. **2.** fetter. **3.** the son of Śuddhodana (*V. Purāṇa*); a son of Gautama Buddha.

Rāhuśatru (S) (M) **1.** the foe of Rāhu. **3.** another name for Viṣṇu and the moon.

Rāhusuta (S) (M) **1.** son of Rāhu. **2.** comet.

Raibhya (S) (M) **1.** of praisers; praising; ritualistic verses. **3.** a famous hermit of Yudhiṣṭhira's palace who was the son of Aṅgiras and the father of Arvāvasu and Parāvasu (*M. Bh.*); the father of King Duṣyanta and the son of Sumati (*Bhāgavata*); a son of Brahmā (*Var. Purāṇa*).

Raikva (S) (M) **1.** place of wealth. **3.** a king of ancient India who was the son-in-law of King Janaśruti (*Ć. Upaniṣad*).

Raivata (S) (M) **1.** wealthy; descended from a rich family. **3.** one of the 11 rudras; the 5th Manu (*H. Purāṇa*); the son of King Revata of Anarta and a king who should be praised at dawn and dusk; a son of Amṛtodana and Revatī; a mountain (*M. Bh.*); a daitya; another name for Śiva.

Raivataka (S) (M) **1.** abounding in wealth. **2.** very rich. **3.** the son of Priyavrata and Surūpā who became a lord of a Manvantara (*H. Purāṇa*); another name for the Girnār mountain near Junāgarh in Gujarat.

Raja (S) (M) **1.** sand; silvery; shining; pollen; emotion; affection. **3.** a warrior of Skanda (*M. Bh.*); a sage who was the son of Vasiṣṭha and Ūrjā, he and his 6 brothers became the Saptaṛṣis of the 3rd Manvantara; a son of Viraja (*V. Purāṇa*); one of the 2 gatekeepers of Sūrya (*Bh. Purāṇa*).

Rājā (S) (M) king; lord.

Rājabījin (S) (M) of royal descent.

Rājadharman (S) (M) **1.** the duty of a king. **3.** a king of storks who was the son of Kaśyapa and a friend of Brahmā (*M. Bh.*).

Rājadīpa (S) (M) **1.** lamp of kings. **2.** lamp among the kings.

Rājahansa (S) (M) **1.** royal swan. **2.** an excellent king; the Barheaded Goose (*Anser indicus*).

Rājaka (S) (M) illuminating; splendid; king; prince.

Rājakarṇa (S) (M) **1.** with royal ears; an elephant's tusk. **2.** an elephant.

Rājakumāra (S) (M) **1.** son of a king. **2.** prince.

Rājakuñjara (S) (M) **1.** elephant among kings. **2.** powerful monarch.

Rājalakṣmana (S) (M) **1.** with marks of royalty. **3.** another name for Yudhiṣṭhira.

Rajamukha (S) (M) with a king's face.

Rājan (S) (M) **1.** king. **2.** ruler; Kṣatriya. **3.** a yakṣa; one of the 18 attendants of the sun; another name for Yudhiṣṭhira, Indra, the moon and Pṛthu.

Rājana (S) (M) **1.** belonging to a royal family. **3.** the teacher mentioned in the *Yajur Veda* who was the son of Kuṇiya and the father of Ugradeva (*Ṛg Veda*).

Rājanandana (S) (M) **1.** son of a king. **2.** prince.

Rajanīćara (S) (M) **1.** night rover. **3.** another name for the moon and a rakṣasa.

Rajanīkānta (S) (M) **1.** beloved of the night. **3.** another name for the moon.

Rajanīkara (S) (M) **1.** night maker. **3.** another name for the moon.

Rājanīla (S) (M) royal blue; emerald.

Rajanīpati (S) (M) **1.** lord of night. **3.** another name for the moon.

Rajanīramaṇa (S) (M) **1.** beloved of the night. **3.** another name for the moon.

Rajanīśa (S) (M) **1.** lord of the night. **3.** another name for the moon.

Rājanya (S) (M) **1.** kingly. **3.** a Vedic designation of the Kṣatriya class (*M. Bh.*); another name for Agni.

Rājapati (S) (M) **1.** master of kings. **3.** another name for Soma.

Rājaputra (S) (M) **1.** son of a king. **2.** prince, **3.** a noted writer on *Kāma Śāstra*; another name for the planet Mercury.

Rājarāj (S) (M) **1.** king of kings. **3.** another name for the moon and Kubera.

Rājārāma (S) (M) King Rāma.

Rajas (S) (M) **1.** silvery; the region between heaven and earth; vapour; mist; dust; pollen; passion; autumn. **3.** a son of Vasiṣṭha (*V. Purāṇa*).

Rajasānu (S) (M) **1.** of silvery or misty hue. **2.** soul; heart; cloud.

Rājaśekhara (S) (M) **1.** crown of a king. **3.** a Sanskṛt dramatist who was also the preceptor of a king of Kannauj (7th century); a Sanskṛt commentator and author of *Kāvya Mimāṁsa*; a poet who was the son of Durdaka and Śīlāvatī and the tutor of King Mahendrapāla of Kānyakubja (10th century).

Rājasi (S) (M) **1.** passionate. **3.** another name for Durgā.

Rājasiṅha (S) (M) lion among kings.

Rājasūya (S) (M) **1.** the royal oblation. **3.** a Vedic ceremony of royal consecration (*M. Bh.*).

Rājasvāmin (S) (M) **1.** lord of kings. **3.** another name for Yudhiṣṭhira and Viṣṇu.

Rajasvaṇaja (S) (M) **1.** of passionate sound. **3.** the father-in-law of Kakṣivān.

Rajata (S) (M) **1.** silver; pearl bright; pleasing. **2.** mind; pearl; ivory. **3.** a constellation.

Rajatadaṅṣṭra (S) (M) **1.** silver toothed. **3.** a son of King Vajradaṅṣṭra of the vidyādharas (*K. Sāgara*).

Rajatādri (S) (M) **1.** silver mountain. **3.** another name for Mount Kailāsa.

Rajatadyuti (S) (M) **1.** shining like silver. **3.** another name for Hanumān.

Rajatakūṭa (S) (M) **1.** silver mountain. **3.** a peak of the Malaya mountains (*K. Sāgara*).

Rajatanābha (S) (M) **1.** silver navelled. **3.** a yakṣa who was the husband of Maṇivarā and the father of Maṇivara and Maṇibhadra (*Ṛg Veda*).

Rajatanābhī (S) (M) **1.** silver navelled. **2.** very rich. **3.** a descendant of Kubera; another name for Kubera.

Rajataprastha (S) (M) **1.** silver place. **2.** place where silver is found; place with a silvery lustre. **3.** another name for Mount Kailāsa.

Rājavāhana (S) (M) **1.** royal steed. **3.** the vehicle on which Soma is carried; the son of King Rājahaṅsa (*V. D. Ćaritam*).

Rājāvarta (S) (M) **1.** of various colours. **2.** Lapis lazuli.

Rājavata (S) (M) **1.** royal fragrance. **3.** an ascetic of the Bhṛgu dynasty and son of Dyutimān (*V. Purāṇa*).

Rājendra (S) (M) **1.** lord of kings; emperor. **2.** a Ćakravartin.

Rājeśvara (S) (M) lord of kings.

Raji (S) (M) **1.** silvery; shining. **3.** a prominent king of the Purū dynasty and the son of Āyus by Svarbhānu (*M. Bh.*); a demon subdued by Indra.

Rāji (S) (M) **1.** streak; line; stripe. **3.** a son of Āyu (*M. Bh.*).

Rājin (S) (M) **1.** moonlight. **2.** light considered as a horse of the moon.

Rājindu (S) (M) **1.** moon among kings. **2.** an excellent king.

Rajiṣṭha (S) (M) straightest; most honest and upright.

Rajita (S) (M) affected; captivated; allured.

Rājīva (S) (M) **1.** living at a king's expense; streaked; striped. **2.** elephant; deer; Blue Lotus (*Nymphaea slellata*); Indian crane. **3.** a pupil of Viśvanātha (*M. Bh.*).

Rājju (S) (M) **1.** rope like; cord like. **2.** plain; simple. **3.** a son of Vasudeva and Devaki (*Bhā. Purāṇa*).

Rajju (S) (M) **1.** rope; cord. **3.** a constellation (*V's. B. Samhitā*).

Rajjukaṇṭha (S) (M) **1.** rope necked. **2.** one who wears a cord round his neck. **3.** a grammarian who was a sage with great knowledge of the Vedas.

Rajogātra (S) (M) **1.** with an illuminated body. **3.** a son of Vaṣṭha (*M. Bh.*).

Rājyasena (S) (M) **1.** commander of state. **2.** leader of the kingdom. **3.** a king of Nandipura.

Rājyavardhana (S) (M) **1.** enhancer of kingdom. **2.** increasing the glory of the kingdom. **3.** a king of Vaiśālī who could tell the past and future (*Mā. Purāṇa*); the brother of King Harṣavardhana; a son of Dama.

Raka (S) (M) the sun gem; crystal; the Arakan silver pheasant.

Rākāćandra (S) (M) **1.** lord of the Rākā. **3.** another name for the full moon.

Rākānīśa (S) (M) **1.** lord of night. **3.** another name for the full moon.

Rākendra (S) (M) **1.** lord of Rākā. **2.** the full moon.

Rākeśa (S) (M) **1.** lord of the full moon. **3.** another name for Śiva.

Rakṣa (S) (M) **1.** protector. **2.** to guard; protect; ashes.

Rakṣābhūṣaṇa (S) (M) an ornament of protection; an amulet.

Rakṣahpati (S) (M) **1.** lord of rākṣasas. **3.** another name for Rāvaṇa.

Rakṣaka (S) (M) **1.** protector. **2.** guard; amulet; tutelary deity; lac.

Rakṣāmalla (S) (M) **1.** warrior who protects. **3.** a king.

Rakṣamantra (S) (M) **1.** a hymn of protection. **2.** a collection of Vedic hymns chanted to protect one from malefic forces.

Rakṣaṇa (S) (M) **1.** protector. **3.** another name for Viṣṇu.

Rakṣapāla (S) (M) protector; guard.

Rākṣasa (S) (M) **1.** guarding; watching; annihilator of protection; demonical. **3.** a particular set of demons who were the offspring of Kaśyapa and Muni (*A. Purāṇa*), in the *Uttar Rāmāyaṇa* they are the forms that have arisen from the anger of Brahmā or his foot.

Rākṣasādhipa (S) (M) **1.** lord of the rākṣasas. **3.** another name for Ghaṭotkaća and Rāvaṇa.

Rākṣasādhipati (S) (M) **1.** lord of the rākṣasas. **3.** another name for Kubera.

Rākṣasakaṇṭaka (S) (M) **1.** destroyer of rākṣasas. **3.** another name for Bhīma.

Rākṣasamaheśvara (S) (M) **1.** lord of the rākṣasas. **3.** another name for Rāvaṇa.

Rākṣasapuṅgava (S) (M) **1.** bull of the rākṣasas; chief of the rākṣasas. **3.** another name for Ghaṭotkaca.

Rākṣasendra (S) (M) **1.** lord of the rākṣasas. **3.** another name for Ghaṭotkaća.

Rākṣaseśvara (S) (M) **1.** lord of the rākṣasas. **3.** another name for Ghaṭotkaća.

Rākṣeśvara (S) (M) **1.** lord of the rākṣasas. **3.** another name for Kubera.

Rakṣikā (S) (M) guard; protector.

Rakṣohan (S) (M) destroying rakṣasas.

Rakta (S) (M) **1.** blood; painted; reddened; excited; beloved; dear; pleasant; lovely; safflower; lac; vermilion. **3.** the son of Mahiṣāsura and the father of Bala and Atibala; another name for Śiva and Mars.

Raktagandhaka (S) (M) pleasant perfume; myrrh.

Raktagrīva (S) (M) **1.** iron necked. **3.** a rākṣasa.

Raktahaṅsa (S) (M) **1.** red swan. **3.** a rāga.

Raktaja (S) (M) **1.** born red; born of blood. **2.** saffron; copper. **3.** Arjuna in his previous incarnation as a thousand handed being that emerged from the blood of wounded Viṣṇu (*P. Purāṇa*).

Raktakamala (S) (M) Red Lotus (*Nymphea rubra*).

Raktakanda (S) (M) **1.** red root. **2.** coral.

Raktakeśara (S) (M) red saffron; Coral tree.

Raktamaṇḍala (S) (M) **1.** with a red disc. **3.** another name for the moon.

Raktāṅga (S) (M) **1.** red bodied. **2.** the sun and moon on rising. **3.** a nāga of Dhṛtarāṣṭra's dynasty; another name for Mars.

Raktāṅka (S) (M) **1.** red marked. **2.** coral.

Raktapakṣa (S) (M) **1.** red winged. **3.** another name for Garuḍa.

Raktasūryāya (S) (M) to be like the red sun.

Raktavīja/Raktabīja (S) (M) **1.** a seed of blood. **2.** pomegranate tree. **3.** another name for the giant asura Rambhāsura, father of Mahiṣāsura, who fought Ćāmuṇḍa and whose every drop of blood became a warrior.

Rāma (S) (M) **1.** causing rest; enchanting; all pervading; omnipresent; pleasing; charming; lovely; pleasant; pleasure; joy; delight; dark. **3.** the 7th avatara of Viṣṇu, son of sage Jamadagni and Reṇukā; one of the 7 ṛṣis of the 8th Manvantara (*H. Purāṇa*); a king of Mallapura; a king of Śṛṅgavera, a patron of Nāgeśa (*Ṛg Veda*); another name for Balarāma, elder brother of Kṛṣṇa; another name of Rāmachandra, a descendant of Raghu, son of Daśaratha and Kauśalyā, husband of Sītā of Miṭhilā, father of Lava and Kuśa; another name for Varuṇa.

Rāmabhakta (S) (M) devotee of Rāma.

Rāmaćandra (S) (M) Rāma, the excellent one.

Rāmaćaraṇa (S) (M) **1.** the feet of Rāma. **2.** a devotee of Rāma.

Rāmadāsa (S) (M) devotee of Rāma.

Rāmadatta (S) (M) **1.** given by Rāma. **3.** a minister of King Nṛsinha of Mithilā.

Ramādhipa (S) (M) **1.** lord of Ramā. **3.** another name for Viṣṇu.

Rāmadūta (S) (M) **1.** messenger of Rāma. **3.** another name for Hanumān.

Rāmagiri (S) (M) **1.** Rāma's mountain. **3.** the mountain in Ramtek near Nāgpur (*K. Granthāvali*).

Rāmagopāla (S) (M) Rāma and Kṛṣṇa conjoined.

Rāmaharṣaṇa (S) (M) **1.** pleasing to Rāma. **2.** thrilling; inspiring. **3.** a disciple of Vyāsa (*M. Bh.*).

Rāmahṛdaya (S) (M) the heart of Rāma.

Rāmajīvana (S) (M) **1.** one whose life is Rāma. **3.** a king who was the son of Rudrarāya.

Rāmaka (S) (M) **1.** sporting; dallying; lover; delighting; gratifying. **3.** a mountain conquered by Sahadeva (*M. Bh.*).

Ramākānta (S) (M) **1.** beloved of Ramā. **3.** another name for Viṣṇu.

Rāmakavaća (S) (M) Rama's breastplate.

Ramākha (S) (M) **1.** lover of Lakṣmī. **3.** another name for Viṣṇu.

Rāmakiṅkara (S) (M) servant of Rāma.

Rāmakṛṣṇa (S) (M) Rāma and Kṛṣṇa conjoined.

Rāmala (S) (M) **1.** lover. **3.** another name for Kāma.

Rāmaliṅga (S) (M) the mark of Rāma.

Rāmamanohara (S) (M) attracting Rāma.

Rāmamohana (S) (M) attracting Rāma; Rāma and Kṛṣṇa conjoined.

Rāmamūrti (S) (M) **1.** the idol of Rāma. **2.** the sign; the symbol of Rāma.

Ramaṇa (S) (M) **1.** pleasing; delightful; charming. **2.** lover; husband. **3.** the son of the vasu named Soma and Manoharā (*M. Bh.*);

another name for an island near Dvārakā; another name for Aruṇa the charioteer of the sun; another name for Kāma; the Curry Leaf tree (*Murraya koenigii*).

Ramaṇaka (S) (M) **1.** devotee of love. **3.** a son of Yajñabāhu (*Bh. Purāṇa*); a son of Vītihotra and grandson of Priyavrata (*Bhāgavata*).

Rāmānanda (S) (M) **1.** pleasure of Rāma. **3.** a disciple of Rāmānuja and founder of a subdivision of the sect.

Rāmanārāyaṇa (S) (M) Rāma and Viṣṇu conjoined.

Ramānātha (S) (M) **1.** lord of Ramā. **3.** another name for Viṣṇu.

Ramaṇika (S) (M) **1.** worth loving. **2.** pleasing; attractive.

Rāmanivāsa (S) (M) the dwelling of Rāma.

Rāmānuja (S) (M) **1.** younger brother of Rāma. **3.** a celebrated Vaiṣnava reformer and founder of the doctrine of Viśiṣṭādvaita, he lived at Kanchipuram in South India and was thought to be an incarnation of Śeṣa (12th century); another name for Kṛṣṇa and Lakṣmaṇa.

Ramāpati (S) (M) **1.** lord of Ramā. **3.** another name for Viṣṇu.

Rāmaphala (S) (M) **1.** the fruit of Rāma. **2.** given by Rāma.

Rāmaprakāśa (S) (M) the glory of Rāma.

Rāmaprasāda (S) (M) the blessing of Rāma.

Rāmapraveśa (S) (M) one into whom Rāma has access.

Ramāpriya (S) (M) **1.** beloved of Ramā. **3.** another name for Viṣṇu.

Rāmarati (S) (M) the jewel of Rāma; dwelling in Rāma; devotee of Rāma.

Rāmarūpa (S) (M) with the form of Rāma.

Rāmasakha (S) (M) **1.** friend of Rāma. **3.** another name for Sugrīva.

Ramāśankara (S) (M) Lakṣmī and Viṣṇu conjoined.

Rāmaśeṣa (S) (M) Rāma and Śeṣa conjoined.

Rāmasetu (S) (M) **1.** the bridge of Rāma. **3.** the bridge between India and Laṅkā, built by Rāmā's army (*Rāmāyaṇā*).

Rāmasinha (S) (M) **1.** the lion of Rāma; Rāma the lion. **3.** a king who was the son of Jayasinha.

Rāmāśrama (S) (M) the refuge of Rāma.

Ramāśraya (S) (M) **1.** refuge of Ramā. **3.** another name for Viṣṇu.

Rāmasvarupa (S) (M) incarnation of Rāma.

Ramati (S) (M) **1.** lover. **2.** paradise; time. **3.** another name for Kāma.

Rāmavallabha (S) (M) **1.** dear to Rāma. **2.** cinnamon. **3.** an author of a commentary on *Rāmāyaṇa.*

Rāmāvatāra (S) (M) **1.** incarnated as Rāma. **3.** Viṣṇu in his incarnation as Rāma.

Rāmavilāsa (S) (M) the pleasure of Rāma; pleasing Rāma.

Rambha (S) (M) **1.** prop; support; a bamboo. **3.** the father of asura Mahiṣa and brother of Karambha; a nāga (*V. Purāṇa*); son of Āyu (*H. Purāṇa*); a son of Viviṅśati (*Bh. Purāṇa*); a son of Purūravas and brother of Nahuṣa (*Bh. Purāṇa*).

Ramendra (S) (M) **1.** lord of Ramā. **3.** another name for Viṣṇu.

Rameśa (S) (M) **1.** lord of Ramā. **3.** another name for Viṣṇu.

Rāmeśvara (S) (M) **1.** lord Rāma. **3.** a sacred pilgrimage centre in South India where Rāma is supposed to have crossed to Laṅkā and which has the Śiva temple built by Rāma; a sacred island in the Bay of Bengal.

Rāmī (S) (M) right.

Rāmila (S) (M) **1.** lover. **3.** another name for Kāma.

Ramita (S) (M) loved; gladdened; delighted.

Ramra (S) (M) **1.** beauty; splendour. **3.** another name for Aruṇa.

Ramya (S) (M) **1.** enjoyable. **2.** pleasing; delightful; beautiful. **3.** a son of Agnīdhra (*V. Purāṇa*).

Ramyaka (S) (M) **1.** lover. **3.** the son of Āgnidhra who was the king of Ramyaka Varṣa near the Nīlgiris and the husband of Pūrvacitti (*Bhāgavata*); Persian Lilac (*Melia azedarach*).

Ramyaśrī (S) (M) **1.** most desired. **3.** another name for Viṣṇu.

Raṇa (S) (M) **1.** delight; pleasure; joy; battle; sound; the joy of battle; mother. **3.** a rākṣasa (*P. Purāṇa*).

Raṇaćhoḍa (S) (M) **1.** one who leaves the battlefields. **3.** another name for Kṛṣṇa, who left the battlefield in the war with Jarāsandha, so as to save his army from massacre and went to Dvārakā.

Raṇadeva (S) (M) lord of battle.

Raṇadhīra (S) (M) **1.** patient in battle. **2.** one who does not lose control in a battle; steady warrior.

Raṇādya (S) (M) **1.** beginning of a battle; beginning of a sound. **2.** delightful. **3.** another name for Dāmodara.

Raṇahastin (S) (M) best warrior.

Raṇajīt (S) (M) victorious in battle.

Raṇaka (S) (M) warrior; king.

Raṇakauśala (S) (M) master of battle.

Raṇañjaya (S) (M) victor in war.

Raṇapriya (S) (M) warlike; interested in war; falcon.

Raṇaśūra (S) (M) hero of war.

Raṇasvāmin (S) (M) **1.** lord of water. **3.** an idol of Śiva as lord of the battlefield.

Raṇavijaya (S) (M) victor in war.

Raṇavikrama (S) (M) victorious warrior.

Raṇavīra (S) (M) hero of the battle; warrior.

Rāṇāyanī (S) (M) **1.** knowing the art of battle. **3.** a preceptor in the line of disciples of Vyāsa.

Randhra (S) (M) **1.** opening; aperture. **3.** the 8th astrological mansion; a son of Manu Bhautya.

Raṇećara (S) (M) **1.** moving in the field of battle. **3.** another name for Viṣṇu.

Raṇeśa (S) (M) **1.** lord of battle. **3.** another name for Śiva.

Raṅga (S) (M) **1.** colour; love; music; amusement; arena; a field of battle. **3.** another name for Viṣṇu and Kṛṣṇa.

Raṅgadāsa (S) (M) **1.** devotee of Kṛṣṇa. **3.** a great scholar and devotee of Viṣṇu who built temples around Venkatāćala (*Sk. Purāṇa*).

Raṅgadeva (S) (M) **1.** god of happiness. **3.** a tutelary god supposed to preside over sport, diversion and pleasure.

Raṅgadhara (S) (M) bearer of love; devotee of Viṣṇu; musician.

Raṅgalāla (S) (M) beloved of Viṣṇu; lover of music.

Raṅgaṇa (S) (M) loving; dancing; merrymaking.

Raṅganātha (S) (M) **1.** lord of love. **3.** Viṣṇu on the serpent.

Raṅgarāja (S) (M) Viṣṇu on his serpent; royal Kṛṣṇa.

Raṅgavatī (S) (M) **1.** full of colour; full of love; loving; happy. **3.** the wife of Rantideva.

Raṅgavidyādhara (S) (M) **1.** knowing music. **2.** knowing music; dance; drama and art. **3.** a gandharva (*H. Purāṇa*).

Raṅgavihārī (S) (M) **1.** abode of happiness; pervading in pleasure. **3.** another name for Kṛṣṇa.

Raṅgeśa (S) (M) **1.** hero of the play. **3.** a king who was the patron of Pārāśarabhaṭṭa.

Raṅgita (S) (M) **1.** well coloured. **2.** handsome.

Rañjana (S) (M) colouring; pleasing; entertaining; delighting; contenting.

Rāñjhā (S) (M) lover.

Rañjideva (S) (M) **1.** lord of entertainers. **3.** a king of the lunar race who was a descendant of King Bharata.

Rañjula (S) (M) **1.** bestower of entertainment. **2.** charming; handsome.

Raṇotkaṭa (S) (M) **1.** furious in battle. **3.** a warrior of Skanda (*M. Bh.*); a daitya (*H. Purāṇa*).

Ransu (S) (M) cheerful; delighting.

Rantideva (S) (M) **1.** lord of pleasure; best warrior; best fighter; lord of devotion. **3.** a king of the lunar race who was a son of Saṁkṛti (*M. Bh.*); the kindest and most liberal king of ancient India who was a descendant of Viṣṇu and the son of Nara, he is one of the kings to be remembered at dawn and dusk (*M. Bh.*); another name for Viṣṇu.

Rantināra (S) (M) **1.** warrior. **3.** father of Apratiratha (*V. Purāṇa*).

Rantu (Malayalam) (M) two.

Raṇvita (S) (M) pleasant; lovely; joyous; gay.

Raphenaka (S) (M) **1.** tormentor. **2.** injurer; wretched. **3.** a nāga of the Takṣaka dynasty (*M. Bh.*).

Rāsamaṇī (S) (M) **1.** jewel of the Rāsa. **3.** another name for Kṛṣṇa.

Rasanāyaka (S) (M) **1.** lord of feelings. **3.** another name for Kāma and Śiva.

Rasasirā (S) (M) **1.** stream of nectar. **3.** another name for Soma.

Rāsavihāri (S) (M) **1.** immersed in the Rāsa. **3.** another name for Kṛṣṇa.

Rasāyana (S) (M) **1.** the vehicle of essence. **3.** another name for Garuḍa.

Raseśa (S) (M) **1.** lord of the Rāsa; lord of sentiments. **3.** another name for Kṛṣṇa.

Rāseśvara (S) (M) **1.** lord of the Rāsa. **3.** another name for Kṛṣṇa.

Rāśi (S) (M) wealth; quantity; number; zodiac sign.

Rasika (S) (M) passionate; one who appreciates the sentiment; graceful; elegant; beautiful; discriminating; delighting; humourous; tasteful.

Rasikeśvara (S) (M) **1.** lord of a passionate wife. **3.** another name for Kṛṣṇa.

Rasilā (S) (M) with taste; covered with gold; gilded.

Rasindra (S) (M) lord of chemicals; mercury; the philosopher's stone.

Raśmiketu (S) (M) **1.** beam bannered. **3.** a comet; a rākṣasa who fought on the side of Rāvaṇa (*Rāmāyaṇa*); another name for the sun.

Raśmimālin (S) (M) **1.** garlanded with rays. **3.** another name for the sun.

Raśmin (S) (M) **1.** bearer of rays. **3.** another name for the sun and moon.

Raśmiprabhāsa (S) (M) **1.** illuminated by rays. **3.** a Buddha.

Raśmivān (S) (M) **1.** bearer of rays. **3.** a viśvadeva (*M. Bh.*); another name for the sun and moon.

Rāṣṭra (S) (M) **1.** realm; kingdom. **3.** a son of Kāśī (*Bh. Purāṇa*).

Rāṣṭrabhṛt (S) (M) **1.** holding sway. **3.** a son of Bharata (*Bh. Purāṇa*).

Rāṣṭrapāla (S) (M) **1.** guardian of the kingdom. **3.** a son of Ugrasena (*H. Purāṇa*).

Raṣṭravardhana (S) (M) **1.** increasing the kingdom. **3.** a minister of Daśaratha (*A. Purāṇa*).

Rathabhṛt (S) (M) **1.** possessing a chariot. **3.** a yakṣa (*V. Purāṇa*).

Rathaćitra (S) (M) **1.** with a multicoloured chariot. **3.** a yakṣa (*V. Purāṇa*).

Rathadhvaja (S) (M) **1.** chariot bannered. **3.** the father of King Kuśadhvaja of Videha and the grandfather of Vedavatī (*Bhā. Purāṇa*).

Rathadhvana (S) (M) **1.** making the sound of the chariot. **3.** another name for Vīrāgni the son of Śaṁyu.

Rathāgraṇī (S) (M) **1.** one who makes the sound of the chariot. **3.** a warrior who accompanied Śatrughna during Rāma's Aśvamedha Yajña (*P. Purāṇa*).

Rathajit (S) (M) **1.** conquering chariots. **2.** winning affection; charming; level. **3.** a yakṣa.

Rathakṛććhra (S) (M) **1.** wheel of a chariot; designer of a chariot. **3.** a yakṣa (*V. Purāṇa*).

Rathakṛta (S) (M) **1.** chariot maker. **3.** a yakṣa (*V. Purāṇa*).

Rathākṣa (S) (M) **1.** the axle of the chariot. **3.** a warrior of Skanda (*M. Bh.*).

Rathamaṇi (S) (M) **1.** with a jewelled chariot. **3.** another name for the moon.

Rathamitra (S) (M) **1.** protector of the chariot; friend of the warrior. **3.** a yakṣa.

Rathāṅgin (S) (M) **1.** possessing a discus. **3.** another name for Viṣṇu.

Rathantara (S) (M) **1.** dweller of the chariot. **3.** son of the agni called Pāñćajanya (*M. Bh.*).

Rathaprabhu (S) (M) **1.** lord of the chariot. **3.** another name for Vīrāgni the son of Śaṁyu (*M. Bh.*).

Ratharāja (S) (M) **1.** lord of the chariot. **2.** king of warriors. **3.** an ancestor of Gautama Buddha.

Ratharvi (S) (M) **1.** moving like a chariot. **3.** a nāga mentioned in the *Atharva Veda*.

Rathasena (S) (M) **1.** warrior on the chariot. **3.** a warrior who fought on the side of the Pāṇḍavas (*M. Bh.*).

Rathaspati (S) (M) **1.** lord of chariots. **3.** a deity presiding over pleasure and enjoyment.

Rathasthā (S) (M) **1.** on the chariot. **3.** one of the 7 tributaries of the Gaṅgā (*M. Bh.*).

Rathastha (S) (M) **1.** on the chariot. **3.** a yakṣa (*Bhāgavata*).

Rathavāhana (S) (M) **1.** one who draws the chariot. **2.** horse. **3.** the brother of the king of Virāta who fought against the Pāṇḍavas (*M. Bh.*).

Rathavara (S) (M) **1.** best chariot; best warrior. **3.** a king (*V. Purāṇa*).

Rathāvarta (S) (M) **1.** harness of the chariot. **3.** a holy place that grants salvation to those who visit it (M. *Bh.*).

Rathavīthī (S) (M) **1.** path of a chariot. **2.** highway. **3.** a sage (*Ṛg Veda*).

Rathika (S) (M) one who rides a chariot.

Rathin (S) (M) one who moves in a chariot.

Rathīndra (S) (M) lord of the chariot.

Rathītara (S) (M) **1.** good charioteer. **3.** a sage of the Bhṛhadevata; a king of the solar dynasty who was the son of Pṛṣatāśva (*Bhāgavata*).

Rāti (S) (M) **1.** generous; favourable. **3.** the giver personified as a deity.

Ratiguṇa (S) (M) **1.** with a passionate disposition. **2.** loving; desirous. **3.** a gandharva who was the son of Kaśyapa and Prādhā (*M. Bh.*).

Ratik (S) (M) satisfied; joyful; delighted; loved.

Ratināyaka (S) (M) **1.** lord of Rati. **3.** another name for Kāma.

Ratipati (S) (M) **1.** lord of Rati. **3.** another name for Kāma.

Ratiramaṇa (S) (M) **1.** beloved of Rati. **3.** another name for Kāma.

Ratīśa (S) (M) **1.** lord of Rati. **3.** another name for Kāma.

Rativara (S) (M) **1.** consort of Rati. **3.** another name for Kāma.

Rativardhana (S) (M) increasing love.

Ratna (S) (M) gift; present; wealth; desirable; jewel; the best of its kind; magnet.

Ratnabāhu (S) (M) **1.** with jewelled arms. **3.** another name for Viṣṇu.

Ratnaćandra (S) (M) **1.** moon among jewels. **2.** the best jewel. **3.** a tutelary deity who is the guardian of jewel mines; a bodhisattva; a son of Bimbisāra.

Ratnaććhattra (S) (M) **1.** jewelled umbrella. **3.** a Buddha.

Ratnaćūḍa (S) (M) **1.** jewelled forehead. **3.** a Bodhisattva.

Ratnadhā (S) (M) possessing jewels; distributing riches.

Ratnadhara (S) (M) possessing jewels.

Ratnādhipati (S) (M) **1.** supreme lord of jewels. **2.** guardian of treasures. **3.** another name for sage Agastya.

Ratnadhvaja (S) (M) **1.** jewelled banner. **3.** a Bodhisattva.

Ratnadīpa (S) (M) jewelled lamp; a jewel that illuminates.

Ratnagarbha (S) (M) **1.** womb of jewels. **2.** filled with jewels. **3.** a bodhisattva; another name for Kubera and the ocean.

Ratnagrīva (S) (M) **1.** jewel necked. **3.** a king of Kāñcananagarī who was a great devotee of Viṣṇu (*P. Purāṇa*); another name for the earth, Kubera and the sea.

Ratnahasta (S) (M) **1.** possessing jewels. **3.** another name for Kubera.

Ratnākara (S) (M) **1.** jewel mine. **2.** the ocean. **3.** a Buddha; a bodhisattva; another name for Kubera.

Ratnaketu (S) (M) **1.** jewel bannered. **3.** name common to 2000 future Buddhas; a bodhisattva.

Ratnakirīṭin (S) (M) **1.** with a jewelled crown; with jewel like fame. **3.** a king of the kinnaras (*K. Vyūha*).

Ratnakīrti (S) (M) **1.** with jewel like glory. **3.** a Buddha.

Ratnakūṭa (S) (M) **1.** jewelled peak. **3.** a mountain; a bodhisattva; the future Buddha.

Ratnam (S) (M) jewel; precious object.

Ratnamatī (S) (M) **1.** jewelled intellect; jewel among intellectuals. **3.** a Sanskṛta grammarian.

Ratnamukhya (S) (M) **1.** chief of jewels. **2.** diamond.

Ratnamukuṭa (S) (M) **1.** jewelled crown. **3.** a bodhisattva.

Ratnanābha (S) (M) **1.** with a jewelled navel. **3.** another name for Viṣṇu.

Ratnanātha (S) (M) lord of jewels; a diamond.

Ratnāṅga (S) (M) coral.

Ratnanidhī (S) (M) **1.** treasure of jewels; treasure of pearls. **3.** another name for Viṣṇu, Mount Meru and the ocean.

Ratnāṅka (S) (M) vehicle of Viṣṇu.

Ratnapāṇi (S) (M) **1.** holding jewels. **3.** a Bodhisattva (*B. Literature*).

Ratnapāra (S) (M) **1.** one who is beyond jewels. **3.** a bodhisattva.

Ratnaparvata (S) (M) **1.** jewelled mountain. **3.** another name for the mountain Meru.

Ratnarāj (S) (M) **1.** king of jewels. **2.** the ruby.

Ratnārćis (S) (M) **1.** shining like a jewel. **3.** a Buddha.

Ratnasambhava (S) (M) **1.** born of jewels. **3.** one of the 5 Dhyāni Buddhas; a bodhisattva (*L. Vistara*).

Ratnasānu (S) (M) **1.** mountain of jewels. **3.** another name for Mountain Meru.

Ratnaśekhara (S) (M) **1.** jewelled crown. **3.** a Jaina author (15th century) (*J. S. Koṣa*).

Ratnaśikhaṇḍa (S) (M) **1.** jewel crested. **3.** a mythical bird considered to be a companion of Jaṭāyu (*V. Rāmāyaṇa*).

Ratnaśikhara (S) (M) **1.** jewelled peak. **3.** a bodhisattva.

Ratnaśikhin (S) (M) **1.** with a jewelled plait. **3.** a Buddha.

Ratnavardhana (S) (M) increasing jewels; bestower of wealth.

Ratnayaṣṭi (S) (M) **1.** jewelled pillar. **3.** a Buddha.

Ratnendra (S) (M) chief of jewels.

Ratneśa (S) (M) **1.** lord of jewels. **2.** the diamond.

Ratneśvara (S) (M) **1.** lord of jewels. **2.** the diamond.

Ratnin (S) (M) possessing or receiving gifts.

Ratnojjvala (S) (M) shining with pearls.

Ratnottama (S) (M) **1.** best jewel. **3.** a Buddha.

Rātrihāsa (S) (M) **1.** laughing night; the white lotus opening at night. **2.** another name for the moon.

Rātrija (S) (M) **1.** born at night. **2.** star.

Rātrinātha (S) (M) **1.** lord of the night. **3.** the moon.

Ratujit (S) (M) conqueror of truth.

Rātula (S) (M) **1.** truth seeking. **2.** interested; desiring. **3.** the son of Śuddhodana (*V. Purāṇa*).

Raubhya (S) (M) **1.** misty; foggy. **3.** a sage (*U. Rāmāyaṇa*).

Raućya (S) (M) **1.** a staff of Bilva wood (*Aegle marmelos*). **3.** the 13th Manu.

Raudra (S) (M) wild; impetuous; fierce; coming from Rudra or Śiva.

Raudrakarman (S) (M) **1.** fierce in action. **2.** a magic rite performed for a terrible purpose. **3.** a son of Dhṛtarāṣṭra (*M. Bh.*).

Raudraśa (S) (M) **1.** violent; impetuous; fierce; wild. **3.** the constellation Ārdrā when it passes through Rudra; another name for Kārttikeya and Yama.

Raudrāśva (S) (M) **1.** abode of Rudra. **3.** a son of Emperor Pṛthu and Pauṣṭī and the husband of the apsarā Miśrakeśī.

Rauhiṇa (S) (M) **1.** red; born under the constellation of Rohiṇī. **3.** a demon who was Indra's enemy (*Ṛg Veda*).

Rauhita (S) (M) **1.** coming from Manu Rohita. **3.** a son of Kṛṣṇa (*H. Purāṇa*).

Raumya (S) (M) **1.** salty. **3.** attendants of Śiva.

Raurava (S) (M) **1.** unsteady; dishonest. **3.** a hell personified as a husband of Vedanā and father of Duhkha (*Ma. Purāṇa*).

Rauśadaśva (S) (M) **1.** angry horse. **3.** another name for Vasśumanas, part author of *Ṛg Veda* (x).

Rava (S) (M) sound; noise; roar; song; hum.

Rāvaṇa (S) (M) **1.** making a noise; making others weep. **3.** the rākṣasa king of Laṅkā who was the son of Viśravas and Kaīkaśi or Keśinī and the half-brother of Kubera (*K.Rāmāyaṇa*), he was killed by the Ayodhyā prince Rāma who was the 7th avatāra of Viṣṇu (*Rāmāyaṇa*).

Rāvaṇī (S) (M) **1.** son of Rāvaṇa. **3.** another name for Indrajit.

Ravatha (S) (M) **1.** humming; calling out. **3.** the Indian cuckoo (*Cuculus varius*).

Ravi (S) (M) **1.** sun. **2.** Arka plant; the number 12. **3.** a prince of Sauvīra (*M. Bh.*); a son of Dhṛtarāṣṭra (*M. Bh.*); a mountain.

Ravicandra (S) (M) **1.** the sun and moon conjoined. **3.** an author of a commentary on the *Amaru Śatākā*.

Ravidāsa (S) (M) **1.** devotee of the sun. **3.** a poet.

Ravideva (S) (M) **1.** lord of the sun. **3.** another name for Sūrya.

Ravidhvaja (S) (M) **1.** sun bannered. **2.** the day.

Ravidīpta (S) (M) lit by the sun.

Ravija (S) (M) **1.** born of the sun. **3.** another name for Karṇa, Yama and the planet Saturn.

Ravikānta (S) (M) **1.** beloved of the sun. **2.** sunstone *(A. Koṣa)*.

Ravikiraṇa (S) (M) ray of the sun.

Ravikīrti (S) (M) **1.** with fame as bright as the sun. **2.** renowned. **3.** a Sanskṛt poet (7th century).

Ravilocana (S) (M) **1.** with eyes as bright as the sun. **2.** with fiery eyes. **3.** another name for Śiva.

Ravinandana (S) (M) **1.** son of the sun. **3.** another name for Karṇa, Sugrīva and Manu Vaivasvata.

Ravinātha (S) (M) **1.** whose lord is the sun. **2.** Lotus (*Nelumbo speciosum*).

Ravīndra (S) (M) **1.** lord of the sun; sun and Indra conjoined. **3.** another name for Sūrya.

Ravinetra (S) (M) **1.** with eyes as bright as the sun. **3.** another name for Viṣṇu.

Raviputra (S) (M) **1.** son of the sun. **3.** another name for the planet Saturn.

Ravirāja (S) (M) king of the sun.

Raviratha (S) (M) chariot of the sun.

Raviratna (S) (M) **1.** jewel of the sun. **2.** ruby.

Ravīsa (S) (M) **1.** one who desires the sun. **3.** another name for Kāma.

Raviśaṅkara (S) (M) **1.** lord of the sun. **3.** another name for Sūrya.

Ravisārathi (S) (M) **1.** charioteer of the sun. **3.** another name for Aruṇa.

Raviśekhara (S) (M) one whose crest is the sun; with sun as the crest; sun crested.

Ravīśu (S) (M) **1.** desired by the sun; as inflammatory as the sun. **3.** another name for Kāma.

Ravisūnu (S) (M) **1.** son of the sun. **3.** another name for Karṇa.

Ravisuta (S) (M) **1.** son of the sun. **3.** another name for Sugrīva and Saturn.

Ravitanaya (S) (M) **1.** son of the sun. **3.** another name for Karṇa and Yama and Saturn.

Raya (S) (M) **1.** flow of a river; zeal; ardour; quickness; force; velocity. **2.** king; prince. **3.** a king of the Lunar dynasty who was the son of Purūravas and Urvaśī (*Bhāgavata*).

Rāyāṇa (S) (M) **1.** ever moving. **2.** forceful. **3.** a brother of Yaśoda.

Rayidā (S) (M) bestowing wealth.

Rayipati (S) (M) lord of wealth.

Rayiṣṭha (S) (M) **1.** very swift. **3.** another name for Agni, Kubera and Brahmā.

Ṛbhava (S) (M) skilled; an intensely glowing ray of the sun.

Ṛbhu (S) (M) **1.** skilful; prudent. **3.** one of the 3 sons of Sudhanvān who obtained divinity through good deeds; a sage who was the son of Brahmā and a brilliant scholar (*V.Purāṇa*), the god who is worshipped by other gods; another name for Agni, Indra and the ādityas.

Ṛbhukṣa (S) (M) **1.** most prudent. **3.** another name for Indra's heaven; heaven; the thunderbolt of Indra.

Ṛbhvan (S) (M) **1.** clever; skilful; wise. **3.** another name for Indra, Tvaṣṭṛ and Agni.

Ṛćaka (S) (M) effected by a hymn; desire; wish.

Ṛćeyu (S) (M) **1.** knower of the hymns. **3.** a king of the Purū dynasty who was the son of Raudrāśva (*H. Purāṇa*).

Ṛćīka (S) (M) **1.** knower of hymns; praiser. **3.** a sage who was the father of Jamadagni and the grandfather of Paraśurāma, one of the 12 ādityas (*A. Veda*); a king who was the grandson of Emperor Bharata and the son of Dyumanyu (*M. Bh.*).

Ṛćīkaputra (S) (M) **1.** son of Ṛćīka. **3.** another name for Jamadagni.

Ṛddhinātha (S) (M) **1.** lord of prosperity. **3.** another name for Śiva and Gaṇeśa.

Ṛddhimān (S) (M) **1.** prosperous; successful. **3.** a great serpent which was killed by Garuḍa (*M. Bh.*).

Rebha (S) (M) **1.** singer of praise. **3.** a protégé of the aśvins.

Reneśa (S) (M) **1.** lord of love. **3.** another name for Kāma.

Reṇu (S) (M) **1.** dust; sand; pollen; an atom. **3.** a sage who was the son of Viśvāmitra and the author of a Ṛg Vedic Sūkta (*A. Brāhmaṇa*); a king of the Ikṣvāku dynasty, who was the father of Reṇukā the wife of sage Jamadagni (*M. Bh.*); a son of Vikukṣi (*V. Rāmāyaṇa*).

Reṇuka (S) (M) **1.** born of dust. **3.** a formula recited over weapons (*V. Rāmāyaṇa*); a yakṣa; a mythical elephant (*M. Bh.*).

Reṇumat (S) (M) **1.** full of sand; sandy. **3.** a son of Viśvāmitra and Reṇu (*H. Purāṇa*).

Repha (S) (M) **1.** having low thoughts; cruel. **3.** a Ṛg Vedic hermit.

Reṣman (S) (M) storm; whirlwind.

Retasvat (S) (M) **1.** possessed of seed. **2.** prolific. **3.** another name for Agni.

Reva (S) (M) to go; to move.

Revanta (S) (M) **1.** killer of speed. **2.** speedbreaker; retarder. **3.** a son of Sūrya and Saṁjñā who is the lord of guhyakas or forest spirits and is considered the ideal horseman (*V. Purāṇa*).

Revata (S) (M) **1.** wealthy; rich. **2.** prosperous; brilliant, splendid, beautiful. **3.** a son of king Ānarta and the father of Revatī (*Bhāgavata*).

Revatīramaṇa (S) (M) **1.** beloved of Revatī. **3.** another name for Balarāma and Viṣṇu.

Ṛgmin (S) (M) jubilant with praise.

Ricatka (S) (M) **1.** removing armour. **3.** father of Śara.

Ripu (S) (M) **1.** foe; enemy. **2.** deceiver. **3.** a grandson of Dhruva and son of Śliṣṭi and Sućchāyā (*H. Purāṇa*); a son of Yadu and Bābhru (*Bhā. Purāṇa*).

Ripughna (S) (M) **1.** one who destroys his enemies. **3.** another name for Gaṇeśa.

Ripuñjaya (S) (M) **1.** vanquisher of foes. **3.** a son of Suratha lord of Kuṇḍala city (*P. Purāṇa*); a Brāhmin who was reborn as King Divodāsa of Kāśi (*Sk. Purāṇa*).

Ripusūdana (S) (M) destroyer of enemies.

Ripuvarjita (S) (M) free from enemies.

Riṣṭa (S) (M) **1.** one that cuts; pushed; thrust. **2.** a sword. **3.** a king who worshipped Yama in his assembly (*M. Bh.*); a daitya; a son of Manu (*Mā. Purāṇa*).

Ṛjīṣa (S) (M) **1.** expeller of enemies. **3.** another name for Indra.

Ṛjrāśva (S) (M) **1.** with quick horses; with red horses. **3.** a celebrated sage of the *Ṛg Veda* who was an ally of Indra (*V. Purāṇa*).

Ṛju (S) (M) **1.** straight; honest; sincere. **3.** a son of Vasudeva (*Bh. Purāṇa*).

Ṛjuda (S) (M) bestowed by truth; honesty; sincerity, righteousness.

Ṛjukratu (S) (M) **1.** whose works are right. **3.** another name for Indra.

Ṛjula (S) (M) simple; honest; innocent.

Ṛjuta (S) (M) simplicity; honesty.

Ṛkṣa (S) (M) **1.** bear; ape; the best; the most excellent; the Pleiades. **3.** a king of the Purū dynasty and the father of Saṁvaraṇa (*M. Bh.*); the son of King Ariha and Sudevā and the husband of Jvālā and father of Matināra (*H. Purāṇa*).

Ṛkṣadeva (S) (M) **1.** lord of the stars; the Great Bear; ape. **3.** a son of Śikhaṇḍī (*M. Bh.*); another name for the moon.

Ṛkṣanātha (S) (M) **1.** lord of the stars. **3.** another name for the moon.

Ṛkṣaputra (S) (M) **1.** son of Ṛkṣa. **3.** another name for Saṁvarana.

Ṛkṣarāja (S) (M) **1.** lord of the stars; lord of the bears; lord of the apes. **3.** the king of Kiṣkindhā and foster father of Bāli and Sugrīva (*V. Rāmāyaṇa*).

Ṛkṣavala (S) (M) **1.** forest of the apes; forest of the bears. **3.** one of the 7 mountains of India (*M. Bh.*).

Ṛkta (S) (M) **1.** of true nature. **2.** simple; innocent; truthful.

Ṛkthan (S) (M) heir; gold.

Ṛkvan (S) (M) jubilant with praise.

Ṛmā (S) (M) emancipated; released.

Roća (S) (M) one who enlightens; shining; radiant.

Roćaka (S) (M) brightening; enlightening; of taste; agreeable.

Roćamāna (S) (M) **1.** shining; bright. **3.** a Kṣatriya king of Aśvamedha who fought on the side of the Pāṇḍavas (*M. Bh.*).

Roćana (S) (M) **1.** shining; radiant; giving pleasure; agreeable; charming. **3.** an arrow of Kāma (*A. Koṣa*); a son of Viṣṇu and Dakṣiṇā; (*Bhā. Purāṇa*); a viśvadeva (*V. Purāṇa*); a son of Vasudeva (*V. Purāṇa*); Indra under Manu Svāroćiṣa (*Bh. Purāṇa*).

Roćanāmukha (S) (M) **1.** red faced. **3.** an asura of the *Mahābhārata*.

Roćiṣa (S) (M) **1.** light; brightness; splendour. **3.** a son of Vibhāvasu (*Bhā. Purāṇa*).

Roćiṣmat (S) (M) **1.** possessing light. **3.** a son of Manu Svāroćiṣa (*Bh. Purāṇa*).

Roćita (S) (M) glorious; delighting.

Rodas (S) (M) heaven and earth.

Rohaka (S) (M) rising.

Rohaṇa (S) (M) **1.** ascending; climbing. **2.** blossom. **3.** a mountain (Adam's Peak in Śri Laṅkā); Indian Redwood tree (*Soymida febrifuga*); another name for Mount Sumerū and Viṣṇu.

Rohanta (S) (M) ascending; tree.

Rohil (S) (M) risen; ascended.

Rohiṇ (S) (M) **1.** rising; ascending. **2.** born under the asterism Rohiṇī; Banyan tree (*Ficus indica*) and the Sandalwood tree. **3.** another name for Viṣṇu.

Rohiṇībhava (S) (M) **1.** son of Rohiṇī. **3.** another name for planet Mercury.

Rohiṇīkānta (S) (M) **1.** beloved of Rohinī. **3.** another name for the moon.

Rohiṇīramaṇa (S) (M) **1.** beloved of Rohiṇī. **3.** another name for the moon.

Rohiṇīśa (S) (M) **1.** lord of Rohiṇī. **3.** another name for the moon.

Rohita (S) (M) **1.** red. **2.** the sun; an ornament made of precious stones; a rainbow; blood; Saffron (*Crocus sativus*). **3.** a son of King Hariśćandra (*Bhā. Purāṇa*); a son of Kṛṣṇa (*Bhā. Purāṇa*); a son of King Vapuṣmat of Śālmala (*V. Purāṇa*); a class of gandharvas (*V. Rāmāyaṇa*); a river; a Manu (*H. Purāṇa*) another name for Sūrya and Agni.

Rohitaka (S) (M) **1.** of red hue. **3.** a mountain mentioned in the Purāṇas.

Rohitāśva (S) (M) **1.** red horse; one who possesses red horses. **3.** a son of Hariśćandra (*V. Purāṇa*); another name for Agni.

Rohtākṣa (S) (M) **1.** red eyed. **3.** another name for the sun.

Rola (S) (M) painting.

Roladeva (S) (M) lord of painting.

Roma (S) (M) hair.

Romaharṣa (S) (M) **1.** goose flesh. **3.** the father of Ugrāśrava; the father of Sūta (*Bhā. Purāṇa*).

Romaharṣaṇa (S) (M) **1.** causing goose flesh. **2.** causing the hair to stand erect. **3.** a famous disciple of Vyāsa (*Bhā. Purāṇa*).

Romika (S) (M) salt; magnet.

Romir (S) (M) causing goose flesh; interesting; pleasant.

Rośāna (S) (M) passionate; touchstone; quicksilver.

Roṣāroha (S) (M) **1.** diminisher of anger. **3.** a warrior on the side of the gods against the asuras.

Ṛpin (S) (M) deceitful; injurer.

Ṛṣabha (S) (M) **1.** bull. **2.** most excellent; the 2nd note of the musical septet. **3.** a king of the Lunar dynasty who was the grandson of Uparićaravasu; a sage who was the grandson of King Agnīdhra and the husband of Jayantī; a nāga of the family of Dhṛtarāṣṭra (*M. Bh.*); an asura (*M. Bh.*).

Ṛṣabhadeva (S) (M) **1.** god of bulls; the best god. **2.** best; most excellent. **3.** the 8th incarnation of Viṣṇu as the son of King Nābhi and Merudevī, he was the husband of Jayantī and the father of Bharata; the husband of Devananda and the father of Mahāvīra *(J.S. Koṣa)*.

Ṛṣabhaketu (S) (M) **1.** bull bannered. **3.** another name for Śiva.

Ṛṣal (S) (M) angry; injured.

Ṛṣi (S) (M) singer of sacred hymns; seer; sage; author of the Vedic hymns; circle of; light.

Ṛṣigiri (S) (M) **1.** mountain of the ṛṣis. **3.** a mountain near Girivraja (*M. Bh.*).

Ṛṣika (S) (M) **1.** belonging to seers. **2.** holy; sacred. **3.** a sage who was the reincarnation of Arkka the asura (*M. Bh.*).

Ṛṣirāja (S) (M) lord of the ṛṣis.

Ṛṣṭāśva (S) (M) **1.** with moving horses. **3.** husband of Bhadrā (*M. Bh.*).

Ṛṣu (S) (M) great; powerful; wise; a ray of the sun; strong; a ṛṣi; firebrand; glowing fire.

Ṛṣvanjas (S) (M) **1.** with sublime power. **3.** another name for Indra.

Ṛṣyaketu (S) (M) **1.** flag of the hermits; best among the ascetics. **3.** another name for Aniruddha and Kāma.

Ṛṣyaśṛṅga (S) (M) **1.** deer horned. **3.** the son of the hermit Vibhāndaka and husband of Śāntā, daughter of King Daśaratha, he is the sage who performed the sacrifice by which Daśaratha begot his 4 sons (*V. Rāmāyaṇa*).

Ṛṭa (S) (M) **1.** truth. **3.** a rudra (*M. Bh.*).

Ṛta (S) (M) **1.** proper; right; respected; luminous; fit; promise; truth. **3.** one of the 11 rudras

(*M. Bh.*); a son of Manu Cākṣuṣa (*Bh. Purāṇa*).

Ṛtadhāma (S) (M) **1.** house of truth. **2.** ray of light. **3.** a Manu (*V.Purāṇa*); Indra in the 12th Manvantara (*Bh. Purāṇa*); another name for Kṛṣṇa.

Ṛtadhvaja (S) (M) **1.** having the banner of truth. **2.** upholding the values of truth. **3.** a king of the Ikṣvāku dynasty who was the son of Adri; a sage who was the father of Jābāli; a rudra (*Bh. Purāṇa*); another name for Śiva.

Ṛtajit (S) (M) **1.** gaining truth. **3.** a yakṣa (*V. Purāṇa*).

Ṛtam (S) (M) **1.** truth like. **2.** fixed; settled; law; sacred action; divine truth; right; duty; custom personified as an object of worship. **3.** a son of Dharma.

Ṛtambhara (S) (M) **1.** bearing the truth in oneself. **3.** another name for Viṣṇu.

Ṛtapa (S) (M) guarding divine truth.

Ṛtapsu (S) (M) **1.** whose appearance is truth. **3.** another name for the aśvins.

Ṛtasena (S) (M) **1.** leader of truth. **3.** a gandharva (*Bh. Purāṇa*).

Ṛtaspati (S) (M) **1.** lord of pious works. **3.** another name for Vāyu.

Ṛtastubha (S) (M) **1.** propounder of truth. **3.** a ṛṣi (*Ṛg Veda*).

Ṛtavasu (S) (M) whose wealth is piety.

Ṛtayu (S) (M) **1.** truthful. **3.** a king of the Lunar dynasty; a sage who was Varuṇa's priest (*M. Bh.*).

Ṛtayus (S) (M) **1.** observing the sacred law. **3.** son of Purūravas.

Ṛteśa (S) (M) lord of truth.

Ṛtīṣā (S) (M) subduing enemies.

Ṛtodaya (S) (M) true speech.

Ṛtunātha (S) (M) **1.** lord of the seasons. **3.** spring.

Ṛtuñjaya (S) (M) one who conquers the seasons; one who conquers truth.

Ṛtuparṇa (S) (M) **1.** fertile; fruitful; truthwinged. **3.** a king of the Ikṣvāku dynasty who was the son of Ayutāyus, he provided shelter to King Nala; a king of Ayodhyā (*M. Bh.*).

Ṛtupati (S) (M) **1.** lord of the seasons. **2.** spring. **3.** another name for Agni.

Ṛturāja (S) (M) **1.** king of the seasons. **3.** another name for spring.

Ṛtva (S) (M) **1.** belonging to season. **3.** a gandharva (*M. Bh.*).

Ṛvik (S) (M) **1.** sacrificing at the proper time. **2.** present.

Ruća (S) (M) bright; brilliant; radiant; good; beautiful.

Rućaka (S) (M) **1.** large; agreeable; golden; ornamental. **2.** any object that brings good luck; dove; a sweet voice. **3.** a son of Uśanas; a mountain; a son of Dharma.

Rućeru (S) (M) pleasing; beautiful; charming.

Rućeyu (S) (M) **1.** delightful; shining. **3.** a son of Yayāti (*M. Bh.*).

Rući (S) (M) **1.** beauty; lustre; light; desire; zest; pleasure. **3.** a prajāpati; a son of Viśvāmitra (*M. Bh.*); a son of Brahmā who married Ākūti and was the father of a reincarnation of Viṣṇu called Yajña and a daughter named Dakṣiṇā who was an incarnation of Mahālakṣmī.

Rućidhāman (S) (M) abode of light.

Rućikara (S) (M) causing desire.

Rućiparva (S) (M) **1.** festival of lights; filled with beauty. **3.** the son of King Ākṛti who fought on the side of the Pāṇḍavas and was killed while trying to save Bhīma (*M. Bh.*).

Rućipati (S) (M) lord of light; master of desires.

Rućiprabha (S) (M) **1.** lustrous; shining. **3.** a daitya (*M. Bh.*).

Rućira (S) (M). **1.** bright; brilliant; radiant; splendid; beautiful; golden; agreeable. **2.** handsome; shining. **3.** a son of Senajit (*H. Purāṇa*); Garden Radish (*Raphamus sativus*); Saffron (*Crocus sativus*).

Rućiraketu (S) (M) **1.** with a golden banner. **3.** a Bodhisattva.

Rućiraśrīgarbha (S) (M) **1.** the womb of light. **2.** the origin of illumination; enlightenment; origin of light. **3.** a bodhisattva.

Rućirāśva (S) (M) **1.** shining horse. **3.** a king of the Lunar dynasty (*Bhāgavata*); a son of Senajit.

Rućita (S) (M) delighted; bright; shining; pleasant; sweet; dainty.

Rućya (S) (M) bright; radiant; of taste; desirable; beautiful; pleasing; a lover.

Rucyavāhana (S) (M) **1.** carrying glory; happiness. **3.** one of the 7 ṛṣis under Manu Rohita (*H. Purāṇa*).

Rudhikrā (S) (M) **1.** rising; ascending; famous. **3.** an asura conquered by Indra (*Ṛg Veda*).

Rudhira (S) (M) **1.** red; blood. **2.** the planet Mars.

Rudita (S) (M) crying.

Rudra (S) (M) **1.** crying; howling; roaring; terrific; roarer. **2.** angry; thunder and lightning; red and flashing. **3.** a form of Śiva considered to have originated from the eyebrows of Brahmā when they curved with fury, Rudra divided himself into 11 male parts and 11 female parts who became the wives (*V. Purāṇa*); Vedic god of the tempest and father of the rudras or maruts he is identified with Indra and Agni and later with Śiva in his terrible aspect.

Rudradaman (S) (M) **1.** conquering Rudra; subduing passion. **3.** a Vallabhi king of Saurāṣṭra.

Rudradeva (S) (M) **1.** the divine Rudra. **3.** one of the 9 kings of Āryāvarta.

Rudragarbha (S) (M) **1.** offspring of Rudra. **3.** another name for Agni.

Rudraja (S) (M) **1.** produced from Rudra. **2.** quicksilver; mercury.

Rudraka (S) (M) **1.** a small rudra. **2.** horrible; terrible. **3.** a Brāhmin teacher of Buddha (B. *Literature*).

Rudraketu (S) (M) **1.** fierce bannered. **3.** an asura who was the husband of Śāradā and the father of Devāntaka and Narāntaka who were killed by Gaṇeśa (*G. Purāṇa*).

Rudrākṣa (S) (M) **1.** fierce eyed. **3.** the fruit of the tree *Elaeocarpus ganitrus* which is said to have originated from the tears of Rudra and is used to make rosaries.

Rudramārga (S) (M) **1.** fearful path. **3.** a holy place at which if one fasts for a day and a night one attains the kingdom of Indra (*M. Bh.*).

Rudrapatnī (S) (M) **1.** wife of Rudra. **3.** another name for Pārvatī.

Rudraprayāga (S) (M) **1.** confluence of sound. **3.** the sacred place where the Mandākinī river joins the Gaṅgā (*Bhā. Purāṇa*).

Rudraputra (S) (M) **1.** son of Rudra. **3.** another name for the 12th Manu.

Rudrāri (S) (M) **1.** the enemy of Rudra. **3.** another name for Kāma.

Rudrarodana (S) (M) **1.** the tears of Rudra. **3.** another name for gold.

Rudraroman (S) (M) **1.** with frightful hair. **3.** an attendant of Skanda (*M. Bh.*).

Rudrasakha (S) (M) **1.** friend of Rudra. **3.** another name for Kubera.

Rudrasāvarṇī (S) (M) **1.** resembling Rudra. **3.** a Manu (*Bhā. Purāṇa*).

Rudrasena (S) (M) **1.** with a terrifying army. **3.** a king who was a helper of Yudhiṣṭhira (*M. Bh.*).

Rudrasuta (S) (M) **1.** son of Rudra. **3.** another name for Skanda.

Rudraṭa (S) (M) **1.** roaring; howling. **3.** a Sanskṛta critic of Kāśmira who wrote *Kāvyālaṅkāra* (9th century).

Rudratanaya (S) (M) **1.** son of Rudra personified as punishment. **3.** the 3rd Jaina Black Vasudeva (*Bhā. Purāṇa*).

Rudrāyaṇa (S) (M) **1.** in favour of Rudra. **3.** a king of Roruka.

Ruhānī (S) (M) of higher values; spiritual.

Rukma (S) (M) **1.** radiant; gold; sun; ornament. **3.** a son of Rućaka (*Bh. Purāṇa*).

Rukmabāhu (S) (M) **1.** golden armed. **3.** a son of Bhīṣmaka (*M. Bh.*).

Rukmābha (S) (M) shining like gold.

Rukmadhara (S) (M) **1.** possessing gold. **3.** a king (*V. Purāṇa*).

Rukmakavaća (S) (M) **1.** with golden armour. **3.** a grandson of Uśanas (*H. Purāṇa*).

Rukmakeśa (S) (M) **1.** golden haired. **3.** the youngest son of King Bhīṣmaka of Vidarbha (*Bhāgavata*).

Rukmamālin (S) (M) **1.** garlanded with gold. **3.** a son of Bhīṣmaka.

Rukmāṅgada (S) (M) **1.** golden ornament. **3.** son of King Śalya of Madra (*M. Bh.*).

Rukmaratha (S) (M) **1.** golden chariot. **3.** the chariot of Droṇāćārya; a son of King Śalya of Madra (*M. Bh.*); another name for Droṇāćarya (*M. Bh.*).

Rukmaśukra (S) (M) **1.** with golden power; with golden virility. **3.** a son of Priyavrata (*D. Bh. Purāṇa*).

Rukmat (S) (M) **1.** bright; shining. **3.** another name for Agni.

Rukmavat (S) (M) **1.** possessing gold. **3.** the eldest son of King Bhīṣmaka (*H. Purāṇa*).

Rukmeṣu (S) (M) golden arrowed.

Rukmidarpa (S) (M) **1.** one who overcame Rukmin. **3.** another name for Balarāma.

Rukmin (S) (M) **1.** wearing golden ornaments. **3.** the eldest son of King Bhīṣmaka of Vidarbha.

Rukmiṇeśa (S) (M) **1.** lord of Rukmiṇī. **3.** another name for Kṛṣṇa.

Rumāṅgada (S) (M) **1.** born of the salt lake. **3.** the incarnation of Indra as a king on earth.

Rumāṇvata (S) (M) **1.** possessing salt. **3.** the son of Supratīpa a captain of Udayana's army; the eldest son of sage Jamadagni and Renukā (*M. Bh.*).

Rumata (S) (M) **1.** salt like. **2.** bitter; biting; bright; shining. **3.** another name for Agni.

Rumra (S) (M) tawny; beautiful.

Rūpa (S) (M) form; shape; figure; beauty; mark.

Rūpadhara (S) (M) shapely; slender; handsome.

Rūpaka (S) (M) form; sign; figure.

Rūpala (S) (M) made of silver.

Rūpam (S) (M) beauty; form.

Rūpanārāyaṇa (S) (M) with the form of Viṣṇu.

Rūpaṅga (S) (M) with a beautiful body.

Rūpapati (S) (M) **1.** lord of forms. **3.** another name for Tvaṣṭṛ.

Rūpasena (S) (M) **1.** handsome leader. **3.** a vidyādhara (*K. Sāgara*).

Rūpāśraya (S) (M) a receptacle of beauty.

Rūpāstra (S) (M) **1.** having beauty as a weapon. **3.** another name for Kāma.

Rūpaśvin (S) (M) handsome; beautiful.

Rūpavāna (S) (M) possessed with beauty; handsome.

Rūpāvata (S) (M) possessed with beauty; handsome.

Rūpendra (S) (M) **1.** lord of form. **3.** another name for the eye.

Rūpeśa (S) (M) lord of form.

Rūpeśvara (S) (M) lord of form.

Rūpiṇa (S) (M) **1.** having a beautiful form. **3.** the son of Emperor Ajamīdha and Keśinī and brother of Jahnu and Praja (*M. Bh.*).

Rūpyāćala (S) (M) **1.** silver mountain. **3.** another name for Mount Kailāsa.

Ruru (S) (M) **1.** antelope. **3.** a famous sage of the Bhṛgu dynasty who was the son of sage Pramati and Pratāpi or Ghṛtāćī and the husband of Pramadvarā the daughter of Menakā by Viśvavasu (*D. Bhāgavata*); an asura who was killed by the devī (*P. Purāṇa*); a son of Ahīnagu (*V. Purāṇa*); a son of one of the viśvadevas; one of the 7 ṛṣis under Manu Sāvarṇi; a daitya slain by Durgā (*K. Sagara*).

Ruruka (S) (M) **1.** deer like; wild. **3.** a king of the Ikṣvāku dynasty who was a scholar of economics and administration (*H. Purāṇa*).

Ruṣadratha (S) (M) **1.** with a white chariot. **3.** a king of the Aṅga family who was the son of Titikṣu and the father of Paila (*A. Purāṇa*).

Ruṣadru (S) (M) **1.** remover of anger; one who eliminates anger. **3.** a king of ancient India who stayed in the palace of Yama (*M. Bh.*).

Ruśaṅgu (S) (M) **1.** with white cattle. **3.** a hermit called Viśvāmitra obtained salvation by doing penances in his āśvama (*M. Bh.*).

Ruśat (S) (M) brilliant; shining; white; bright.

Ruśeku (S) (M) **1.** with a bright chariot. **3.** a son of Śvahi and father of Ćitraratha.

Rutva (S) (M) **1.** speech; intensity. **3.** a gandharva.

S

Sabala (S) (M) **1.** accompanied by strength. **2.** full of strength; strong. **3.** a son of Manu Bhautya; a son of Vasiṣṭha; one of the 7 ṛṣīs under Manu Rohita (*V. Purāṇa*); son of Bhṛgu; fire (*M. Bh.*).

Śabalā (S) (M) **1.** spotted; variegated. **3.** a nāga son of Kaśyapa and Kadru (*M. Bh.*); another name for Kāmadhenu.

Śabalākṣa (S) (M) **1.** with variegated eyes. **3.** a divine mahāṛṣi (*M. Bh.*).

Śabalāśva (S) (M) **1.** with a dappled horse. **3.** a son of Avīkṣit (*M. Bh.*); a child of Dakṣa and Vairaṇī (*H. Purāṇa*).

Śabalodara (S) (M) **1.** having a spotted belly. **3.** a demon.

Sabar (S) (M) milk; nectar.

Śabasta (S) (M) **1.** born with armour. **3.** a son of Yuvanāśva.

Śabdabhedin (S) (M). **1.** aiming an arrow by listening to the sound. **3.** another name for Arjuna.

Śabdarāśimaheśvara (S) (M) **1.** great lord of the alphabet. **3.** another name for Śiva.

Śabdavedhin (S) (M) **1.** piercer of sound. **2.** aiming an arrow by listening to the sound. **3.** another name for Arjuna.

Sabhājit (S) (M) honoured; praised; celebrated.

Sabhānara (S) (M) **1.** man of the council. **2.** chairman of the senate. **3.** a king of the Bharata dynasty who was the son of Anudruhyu and father of Kālanara (*Bhāgavata*); a son of Kakṣeyu (*H. Purāṇa*).

Sabhāpati (S) (M) **1.** master of the assembly; president of the assembly. **3.** a prince on the Kaurava side (*M. Bh.*).

Sabhāsinha (S) (M) **1.** lion of the assembly. **3.** a king of Bundelkhand.

Sabhāvana (S) (M) **1.** effecting welfare. **3.** another name for Śiva.

Sabhya (S) (M) **1.** fit for an assembly. **2.** politej courteous; refined; of honourable parentage. **3.** one of the 5 sacred fires.

Saćana (S) (M) ready to befriend; kindly disposed.

Sāćāra (S) (M) well conducted; well behaved.

Saćāru (S) (M) very beautiful.

Saććidānanda (S) (M) **1.** consisting of existence and thought and joy. **3.** a conjoining of Brahmā and Viṣṇu.

Saććīla (S) (M) consisting of good character; virtuous.

Saććinmaya (S) (M) consisting of existence and thought.

Saććit (S) (M) **1.** pure existence and thought. **3.** another name for Brahmā.

Sāći (S) (M) **1.** following; accompanying. **3.** another name for Agni.

Śāćigu (S) (M) with strong rays.

Saćin (S) (M) **1.** pure existence; affectionate. **3.** another name for Śiva.

Śaćinandana (S) (M) **1.** son of Śaći. **3.** another name for Viṣṇu.

Śaćinara (S) (M) **1.** like Indrāṇī. **3.** a king of Kāśmīra (*R. Taraṅgiṇī*).

Saćinta (S) (M) thoughtful.

Śaćīpati (S) (M) **1.** lord of might and aid; husband of Śaćī. **3.** another name for Indra.

Śaćīramaṇa (S) (M) **1.** beloved of Śaćī. **3.** another name for Indra.

Śaćīśa (S) (M) **1.** lord of Śaćī. **3.** another name for Indra.

Śaćiṣṭha (S) (M) most powerful; helpful.

Saćita (S) (M) wise.

Saćitta (S) (M) endowed with reason.

Sadā (S) (M) always; ever.

Sada (S) (M) **1.** fruit. **3.** a son of Dhṛtarāṣṭra (*M. Bh.*).

Sadābhū (S) (M) fellow; companion; friend.

Ṣaḍabindu (S) (M) **1.** with 6 drops, with 6 spots. **3.** another name for Viṣṇu.

Sadāćandra (S) (M) the eternal moon.

Sadācaraṇa (S) (M) good moral conduct.

Sadācārin (S) (M) with pure and good conduct.

Sadācārya (S) (M) good teacher.

Sadādīna (S) (M) always liberal.

Sadāgati (S) (M) **1.** always in motion. **3.** another name for the sun and Vāyu; the universal spirit.

Sadājit (S) (M) **1.** eternally victorious. **3.** a Bharata dynasty king who was the son of Kuntī and the father of Māhiṣmān (*Bhā. Purāṇa*).

Sadala (S) (M) **1.** with petals. **2.** a flower.

Ṣaḍānana (S) (M) **1.** 6 faced. **3.** another name for Skanda.

Sadānanda (S) (M) **1.** perpetual bliss. **3.** another name for Śiva.

Sadānīrā (S) (M) **1.** always full of water. **3.** a river of Purāṇic India (*M. Bh.*).

Sadāparibhūta (S) (M) **1.** always in fear. **3.** a bodhisattva.

Sadāpriṇa (S) (M) **1.** always munificent. **3.** a ṛṣi and part author of *Ṛg Veda* (v).

Sadara (S) (M) **1.** fearful. **3.** an asura (*H. Purāṇa*).

Sādara (S) (M) showing respect; considerate; attentive; devoted.

Sadāśiva (S) (M) eternal Śiva; always kind, happy and prosperous.

Sadaspati (S) (M) **1.** lords of the sacrificial assembly. **3.** Indra and Agni conjoined (*ṚgVeda*).

Sadaśva (S) (M) **1.** possessing good horses. **3.** a son of Samara (*H. Purāṇa*); a king in Yama's court (*M. Bh.*).

Sadasyormi (S) (M) **1.** member of an assembly. **3.** a king in Yama's court (*M. Bh.*).

Sadātanaja (S) (M) **1.** always young. **3.** another name for Viṣṇu.

Ṣaḍavaktra (S) (M) **1.** 6 faced. **3.** another name for Skanda.

Sadāvīra (S) (M) eternally brave.

Sadāyogin (S) (M) **1.** always practicing yoga. **3.** another name for Viṣṇu.

Saddhan (S) (M) **1.** with money; prosperous. **3.** a gandharva (*M. Bh.*).

Saddhī (S) (M) wise; a sage.

Sadguṇa (S) (M) good qualities; virtuous.

Sadguru (S) (M) good teacher.

Sadhan (S) (M) possessing money; rich.

Sadhanī (S) (M) companion; comrade.

Sadhī (S) (M) endowed with reason.

Sādhilā (S) (M) accomplished; perfected; mastered; subdued.

Sadhīman (S) (M) full of intelligence.

Sādhiman (S) (M) goodness; perfection; excellence.

Sādhin (S) (M) accomplishing; performing.

Sadhri (S) (M) **1.** with the same goal. **3.** ṛṣi and part author of *Ṛg Veda* (x); another name for Agni.

Sādhu (S) (M) **1.** straight; right. **2.** unerring; peaceful; excellent; good; virtuous; classical; pure; noble; sage; seer. **3.** an incarnation of Śiva (*Br. Purāṇa*).

Sādhuja (S) (M) wellborn; good conduct.

Sādhupuṣpa (S) (M) **1.** beautiful flower. **2.** *Hibiscus mutabilis.*

Sadhvaṅsa (S) (M) **1.** destroyer. **3.** a ṛṣi and part author of *Ṛg Veda* (viii).

Sādhya (S) (M) **1.** conquerable; achievable; feasible. **3.** demigods and attendants of Śiva who are celestial beings of the middle region between the sun and earth (*Ṛg Veda*).

Sādi (S) (M) having a beginning.

Sadiva (S) (M) eternal like the truth.

Sadman (S) (M) abode; temple.

Śadri (S) (M) **1.** cloud. **2.** hovering over the enemies like a thundercloud. **3.** another name for Arjuna.

Śadru (S) (M) **1.** falling. **3.** another name for Viṣṇu.

Sādyanta (S) (M) **1.** from beginning to end. **2.** complete; entire.

Sadyojāta (S) (M) **1.** a newly born calf. **3.** a form of Śiva.

Sagaṇa (S) (M) **1.** with troops; attended by followers. **2.** a leader; a chieftain. **3.** another name for Śiva.

Sagara (S) (M) **1.** full of moisture; accompanied by praise; containing poison. **2.** atmosphere; air. **3.** a solar dynasty king of Ayodhyā who was the son of Bāhuka and Yādavī and the husband of Sumati and Keśmī, he fathered Asamañjasa and 60,000 other sons, he is an auspicious king who should be remembered at dawn and dusk (*M. Bh.*).

Sāgara (S) (M) **1.** of Sagara. **2.** ocean. **3.** a nāga; the 3rd Arhat of the past Utsarpiṇī.

Sāgaradatta (S) (M) **1.** given by the ocean. **3.** a king of the gandharvas (*K. Sāgara*).

Sāgaragāsuta (S) (M) **1.** son of the river. **3.** another name for Bhīṣma.

Sāgarālaya (S) (M) **1.** living in the ocean. **3.** another name for Varuṇa.

Sāgaramati (S) (M) **1.** with an ocean of knowledge. **3.** a bodhisattva; a nāga king.

Sāgarapāla (S) (M) **1.** guardian of the ocean. **3.** a nāga king.

Sāgaraśaya (S) (M) **1.** resting on the ocean. **3.** another name for Viṣṇu.

Sāgarasūnu (S) (M) **1.** son of the ocean. **3.** another name for the moon.

Sāgaravīra (S) (M) hero of the ocean.

Sāgaravyūhagarbha (S) (M) **1.** carrying the body of the ocean. **3.** a bodhisattva.

Śagmā (S) (M) **1.** powerful; mighty. **2.** elephant; mountain; strong; effective, kind, friendly.

Sāgni (S) (M) maintaining a sacred fire, connected with fire.

Śagun (S) (M) auspicious; a lucky omen; a prognostic.

Saguṇa (S) (M) **1.** complete with virtues. **2.** virtuous.

Sāguṇya (S) (M) excellence; superiority.

Śāgurikā (S) (M) capable; energetic.

Saha (S) (M) **1.** tolerant; powerful; mighty; defying; causing; equal to. **3.** a son of Manu (*H. Purāṇa*); a son of Prāṇa and Ūrjasvatī (*Bh. Purāṇa*); a son of Dhṛtarāṣṭa (*M. Bh.*); a son of Kṛṣṇa and Mādrī (*Bh. Purāṇa*); an Agni (*M. Bh.*).

Sahadeva (S) (M) **1.** with the gods; protected by the gods; mighty god. **3.** the 5th Pāṇḍava brother who was the son of Pāṇḍu and Mādrī and the twin brother of Nakula, he was the father of Śrutasena by Pāñćālī and of Suhotra by Vijayā (*M.Bh.*); a mahaṛṣi in the court of Indra (*M. Bh.*); a king in the court of Yama (*M. Bh.*); a son of Jarāsandha who fought on the side of the Pāṇḍavas (*M. Bh.*); a rākṣasa son of Dhumrākṣa and father of Kṛśāśva (*Bhāgavata*); a solar dynasty king who was the son of Dharmanandana and father of Jayatsena (*Bhāgavata*); a solar dynasty king who was the son of Sudāsa and father of Somaka (*Bhāgavata*); a son of Haryaśvat (*H. Purāṇa*); a son of Harṣavardhana (*V. Purāṇa*); a son of Somadatta (*H. Parāṇa*); a son of Divākara (*V. Purāṇa*); a son of Devapi (*Bhāgavata*); an uncle of Gautama Buddha (*B. Literature*); Jelly Leaf (*Sida rhombofolia*); Ash Coloured Heabane (*Vemonia cinerea*).

Sahaja (S) (M) **1.** simple innate; hereditary; original; natural. **3.** a Ćedi king (*M. Bh.*).

Sahajānanda (S) (M) **1.** getting happiness easily. **3.** founder of a Vaiṣnava sect.

Sahajanya (S) (M) **1.** produced together. **3.** a yakṣa.

Śāhaji (S) (M) **1.** king. **3.** the father of Śivāji.

Sahajit (S) (M) **1.** victorious at once. **3.** a Bharata dynasty king and son of Mahābhoja (*Bhā. Purāṇa*).

Sahamāna (S) (M) conquering; victorious.

Sahāmpati (S) (M) **1.** always uttering the sacred sound. **3.** a bodhisattva; a serpent demon; another name for Brahmā.

Sāhañja (S) (M) **1.** easily won. **3.** a king (*H. Purāṇa*).

Sahānya (S) (M) mighty mountain.

Sahāpati (S) (M) **1.** lord of the world of man. **3.** another name for Brahmā.

Sahara (S) (M) **1.** like Hara; Śiva like. **3.** another name for Śiva; a dānava (*H. Purāṇa*).

Sahari (S) (M) **1.** like Hari. **2.** a bull; a lion. **3.** another name for the sun.

Saharṣa (S) (M) joyful; glad.

Sahasāna (S) (M) powerful; mighty; a sacrifice; peacock.

Sahasānu (S) (M) patient; enduring.

Sahasin (S) (M) powerful; mighty.

Sahaskṛt (S) (M) bestowing strength or power.

Sahaskṛta (S) (M) **1.** produced by strength. **3.** another name for Agni.

Sahasrabāhu (S) (M) **1.** 1,000 armed. **3.** an attendant of Skanda (*M. Bh.*); another name for Śiva and Arjuna Kārtavīrya and Bāṇa.

Sahasrabhānu (S) (M) **1.** 1000 rayed. **3.** another name for the Sun.

Sahasrabhuja (S) (M) **1.** 1000 armed. **3.** a gandharva; another name for Viṣṇu (*M. Bh.*).

Sahasraĉakṣus (S) (M) **1.** 1000 eyed. **3.** another name for Indra.

Sahasraĉaraṇa (S) (M) **1.** 1000 footed. **3.** another name for Viṣṇu.

Sahasraĉitya (S) (M) **1.** making a 1000 cremation grounds. **3.** a Kekaya king who was the grandfather of King Śatayūpa (*M. Bh.*).

Sahasrada (S) (M) **1.** giver of a 1000 cows. **3.** another name for Śiva.

Sahasradhāman (S) (M) **1.** with a 1000 fold splendour. **3.** another name for the Sun.

Sahasradīdhiti (S) (M) **1.** 1000 rayed. **3.** another name for the Sun.

Sahasradoṣ (S) (M) **1.** having a 1000 arms. **3.** another name for Arjuna Kārtavīrya.

Sahasradṛśa (S) (M) **1.** 1000 eyed. **3.** another name for Indra and Viṣṇu.

Sahasragu (S) (M) **1.** possessing a 1000 cows; 1000 rayed; 1000 eyed. **3.** another name for the sun and Indra.

Sahasrahasta (S) (M) **1.** 1000 handed. **3.** another name for Śiva.

Sahasrajit (S) (M) **1.** conqueror of the thousands. **3.** a Bharata dynasty king who was a son of Mahābhoja (*Bhāgavata*); a son of Bhajamana; a son of Kṛṣṇa (*Bh. Purāṇa*); another name for Viṣṇu.

Sahasrajyoti (S) (M) **1.** with a 1000 flames. **2.** very glorious. **3.** a son of King Samrāt who had a million sons (*M. Bh.*).

Sahasrajyotis (S) (M) **1.** with a 1000 stars. **2.** a galaxy of stars. **3.** a son of Śubhrāja (*M. Bh.*).

Sahasrakara (S) (M) **1.** thousand rayed. **3.** another name for the Sun.

Sahasrākṣa (S) (M) **1.** 1000 eyed. **3.** another name for Indra, Viṣṇu and Śiva.

Sahasrākṣajit (S) (M) **1.** conqueror of Indra. **3.** a son of Rāvaṇa.

Sahasraloĉana (S) (M) **1.** 1000 eyed. **3.** another name for Indra and Viṣṇu.

Sahasramauli (S) (M) **1.** 1000 crested. **3.** another name for Viṣṇu.

Sahasramukharāvaṇa (S) (M) **1.** 1000 headed demon king. **3.** a daitya king of Trilokapuri island who possessed a 1000 heads, he was the husband of Indumukhī and the father of Vajrabāhu, he was killed by Sītā (*K. Rāmāyaṇa*).

Sahasramūrdhan (S) (M) **1.** 1000 headed. **3.** another name for Viṣṇu and Śiva.

Sahasrānana (S) (M) **1.** 1000 faced. **3.** another name for Viṣṇu.

Sahasranayana (S) (M) **1.** 1000 eyed. **3.** another name for Indra and Viṣṇu.

Sahasranetra (S) (M) **1.** 1000 eyed. **3.** another name for Indra and Viṣṇu.

Sahasrānīka (S) (M) **1.** with an army of thousands. **3.** a lunar king who was the father of Udayana (*K. Sāgara*).

Sahasrāṅśu (S) (M) **1.** 1000 rayed. **3.** another name for the Sun.

Sahasrāṅśuja (S) (M) **1.** son of the Sun. **3.** another name for Saturn.

Sahasrapāda (S) (M) **1.** 1000 footed. **3.** a maharṣi (*M. Bh.*); another name for Puruṣa, Viṣṇu, Śiva and Brahmā.

Sahasrārĉis (S) (M) **1.** 1000 rayed. **3.** another name for the Sun.

Sahasrāsya (S) (M) **1.** 1000 headed. **3.** another name for Ananta.

Sahasravāk (S) (M) **1.** with a 1000 mouths. **2.** very knowledgeable. **3.** a son of Dhṛtarāṣṭra (*M. Bh.*).

Sahasravīra (S) (M) with the strength of a 1000 men.

Sahasrāyu (S) (M) living a 1000 years.

Sahasvat (S) (M) **1.** full of valour. **2.** powerful; mighty, victorious.

Sahasya (S) (M) **1.** mighty; strong. **3.** the month of Pauṣa (December/January).

Sahasyaćandra (S) (M) the winter moon.

Sahat (S) (M) mighty; strong.

Sahaujas (S) (M) endowed with strength or power.

Sahāvan (S) (M) possessing strength; mighty.

Sahāya (S) (M) **1.** one who goes along with. **2.** companion; helper. **3.** another name for Śiva.

Sahendra (S) (M) **1.** with Indra. **2.** Indra like; resembling Indra in power.

Sahira (S) (M) mountain.

Sahiṣṇu (S) (M) **1.** patient; forebearing; enduring. **3.** a ṛṣi under the 6th Manu; a son of Prajāpati Pulaha and Kṣamā (*V. Purāṇa*); another name for Viṣṇu.

Sahiṣṭha (S) (M) strongest; most powerful.

Sāhlāda (S) (M) having joy; cheerful.

Sahodara (S) (M) **1.** born from the same womb. **2.** brother.

Sahoja (S) (M) full of strength; produced by strength.

Sahojit (S) (M) victorious by strength.

Sahora (S) (M) good; excellent; pious; a saint.

Sahovan (S) (M) mighty; superior.

Śahughātin (S) (M) **1.** killing enemies. **3.** a son of Śatrughna (*Rāmāyaṇa*).

Sahuri (S) (M) **1.** full of heat; mighty; strong; victorious. **3.** another name for the sun.

Sahvan (S) (M) powerful; mighty.

Sahya (S) (M) **1.** able to bear; powerful; strong; agreeable. **3.** one of the principal ranges of mountains in India; a son of Vivasvat.

Sahyu (S) (M) conquering; victorious.

Śaibya (S) (M) **1.** belonging to the Śibis; belonging to Śiva. **3.** a king who was the father of Sṛñjaya (*M. Bh.*); a Śibi king who was the grandson of Uśīnara and a father-in-law of Yudhiṣṭhira (*M. Bh.*); a horse of Kṛṣṇa (*M.Bh.*); a Vṛṣṇi hero in Yudhisthira's court (*M. Bh.*); a warrior of the Kauravas (*M. Bh.*); a Sauvīra king and father of Ratnā who married Akrūra (*M. Purāṇa*); one of the 4 horses of Viṣṇu.

Śaikhāvatya (S) (M) **1.** has plaited hair. **2.** an ascetic; king of the Sailehavatas. **3.** a ṛṣi who gave refuge to Ambā (*M. Bh.*).

Śailabāhu (S) (M) **1.** strong armed. **3.** a nāga.

Śailābha (S) (M) **1.** like a mountain. **2.** massive; stout; tall; highly esteemed; as high as a mountain. **3.** a viśvadeva (*M. Bh.*).

Śailadhara (S) (M) **1.** mountain holder. **3.** another name for Kṛṣṇa.

Śailādhipa (S) (M) **1.** king of mountains. **3.** the Himālaya.

Śailakampin (S) (M) **1.** shaking mountains. **2.** very powerful. **3.** an attendant of Skanda (*M. Bh.*); a dānava (*H. Purāṇa*).

Śailālaya (S) (M) **1.** abode of rocks. **2.** mountain. **3.** a king who was the grandfather of Bhagadatta (*M. Bh.*).

Śailapati (S) (M) **1.** lord of mountains. **3.** another name for Himavān.

Śailarāja (S) (M) lord of mountains.

Śailendra (S) (M) **1.** lord of the mountain. **3.** another name for Śiva and Himavān.

Śaileśa (S) (M) **1.** lord of the mountains. **3.** another name for the Himālaya.

Śailūṣa (S) (M) **1.** actor; dancer. **3.** a gandharva who serves Kubera in his assembly (*M. Bh.*); Bengal Quince (*Aegle marmelos*).

Saindhava (S) (M) **1.** lord of the Sindhus. **3.** another name for Jayadratha.

Saindhavaka (S) (M) **1.** lord of the Sindhus. **3.** another name for Jayadratha.

Saindhavāyana (S) (M) **1.** from the sea. **3.** a son of Viśvāmitra (*M. Bh.*).

Sainhika (S) (M) leonine.

Sainika (S) (M) **1.** soldier; martial. **3.** a son of Śambara (*H. Purāṇa*).

Śaiśirāyaṇa (S) (M) **1.** belonging to winter. **2.** cold; of a cool temper. **3.** a mahaṛṣi who was the husband of Gopālī and the father of Kālayavana (*H. Purāṇa*).

Śaiśireya (S) (M) **1.** related to winter. **2.** cold; of a cool temper. **3.** a disciple of Śākalya and author of the authoritative *Śākalya* treatise.

Śaiśupāla (S) (M) **1.** son of Śiśupāla. **3.** another name for Dhṛṣṭaketu.

Śaiva (S) (M) **1.** sacred to Śiva; follower of Śiva. **3.** a sect of the Hindus; the 5th Jaina Black Vasudeva (*J. Literature*).

Śaivala (S) (M) **1.** *Blyxa octandra.* **3.** a nāga.

Śaivasutā (S) (M) **1.** daughter of Śiva. **3.** another name for Gaṅgā.

Śaivya (S) (M) the cult of Śiva; prosperous; auspicious.

Śaivyasugrīvavāhana (S) (M) **1.** with Śaivya and Sugrīva as horses. **3.** another name for Kṛṣṇa.

Sajiṣṇu (S) (M) accompanied by Arjuna.

Sajitvan (S) (M) victorious; superior.

Sajīva (S) (M) full of life; living; alive.

Sajjambhava (S) (M) **1.** ready. **3.** the author of *Daśavaikālika Sutra,* he succeeded Prabhava as the head of the Jaina church (*J. S. Koṣa*).

Sajjana (S) (M) wellborn; respectable; nobleman; gentleman; guard; sentry.

Sajvara (S) (M) **1.** heat. **3.** another name for Agni.

Śaka (S) power; might; help; aid; herb; vegetation.

Śakadala (S) (M) fragment of power.

Śakāditya (S) (M) **1.** sun of the Śakas. **3.** another name for King Śālivāhana.

Sakala (S) (M) **1.** all; whole; complete; full. **2.** perfect; universe.

Śakalā (S) (M) **1.** cart. **3.** the 5 stars forming the asterism Rohiṇī; a demon slain by child Kṛṣṇa.

Sakalādhāra (S) (M) **1.** receptacle of all. **3.** another name for Śiva.

Sakaladīpa (S) (M) illuminator of all.

Sakalendu (S) (M) the full moon.

Śakalendu (S) (M) the half moon.

Sakaleśvara (S) (M) lord of all.

Śākalya (S) (M) **1.** an amulet of woodchips. **3.** a mahaṛṣi who systematized the *Veda Samhitās.*

Śakara (S) (M) piece; bit; fragment; chip.

Sākāra (S) (M) having form; beautiful.

Sākāśa (S) (M) with the light shining on.

Śakaṭa (S) (M) **1.** cart; weapon. **3.** a demon slain by child Kṛṣṇa.

Śakaṭāri (S) (M) **1.** enemy of Śakaṭa. **3.** another name for Kṛṣṇa.

Śākaṭāyana (S) (M) **1.** belonging to the cart. **3.** a grammarian and author of *Uṇādisūtrapāṭha.*

Śākavaktra (S) (M) **1.** vegetable faced. **3.** a soldier of Skanda (*M. Bh.*).

Śākayanya (S) (M) **1.** belonging to vegetables or herbs; a mendicant. **3.** a mahaṛṣi.

Sāketa (S) (M) **1.** city of people. **3.** another name for Ayodhyā.

Saketa (S) (M) **1.** with the same intention. **3.** an āditya.

Śākha (S) (M) **1.** branch of a tree. **3.** the son of Subrahmaṇya born from his face (*K. Sāgara*), also regarded as Subrahmaṇya's younger brother and the son of the vasu Anala (*M. Bh.*).

Śākin (S) (M) helpful; powerful.

Śākin (S) (M) **1.** of herbs. **2.** god of herbs.

Śākman (S) (M) **1.** capability; power; strength; capacity. **3.** another name for Indra.

Śakra (S) (M) **1.** strong; powerful; mighty. **3.** an āditya; the number 14; another name for Indra; *Terminalia arjuna.*

Śakradeva (S) (M) **1.** lord Indra. **3.** a Kaliṅga king who fought on the Kaurava side (*M. Bh.*); a son of Śṛgāla.

Śakrāditya (S) (M) **1.** sun among the strong; sun and Indra conjoined. **2.** as powerful as sun and Indra conjoined; most capable; as radiant as the sun. **3.** another name for India.

Śakradyumna (S) (M) **1.** with powerful splendour. **3.** a king of Rāma's dynasty.

Śakraja (S) (M) son of Indra.

Śakrajit (S) (M) **1.** conqueror of Indra. **3.** another name for Meghanāda.

Śakraketu (S) (M) Indra's banner.

Śakranandana (S) (M) **1.** son of Indra. **3.** another name for Arjuna.

Śakrāri (S) (M) **1.** Indra's enemy. **3.** another name for Kṛṣṇa.

Śakrasārathi (S) (M) **1.** Indra's charioteer. **3.** another name for Mātali.

Śakrasuta (S) (M) **1.** son of Indra. **3.** another name for Vālin and Arjuna.

Śakrātmaja (S) (M) **1.** son of Indra. **3.** another name for Arjuna.

Śakravāpin (S) (M) **1.** pond of the powerful; living in Indra's pond. **3.** a nāga (*M. Bh.*).

Śakri (S) (M) cloud; thunderbolt; elephant; mountain.

Sakṣam (S) (M) able; powerful.

Sakṣaṇi (S) (M) conquering; vanquishing; comrade; companion.

Śakta (S) (M) **1.** competent; capable. **3.** a son of Manasyu (*M. Bh.*); the son of Manasvī and Sauvirī of the Purū dynasty (*M. Bh.*).

Sakti (S) (M) **1.** help; assistance; the force of a magic formula. **2.** sword; spear; gift. **3.** the son of Vasiṣṭha and Arundhatī he was the husband of Adṛśyantī and the father of Parāśaramuni (*V. Purāṇa*); the weapon of Skanda made by Viśvakarman (*V. Purāṇa*).

Śaktibhadra (S) (M) **1.** holding a spear. **3.** Sanskṛt dramatist of Kerala (7th century A.D.)

Śaktibhṛt (S) (M) **1.** spearholder. **2.** powerful. **3.** another name for Skanda.

Śaktidhara (S) (M) **1.** holding a spear. **2.** powerful. **3.** another name for Skanda.

Śaktika (S) (M) **1.** powerful; mighty. **3.** another name for Kārttikeya.

Śaktinātha (S) (M) **1.** lord of Śakti; lord of power. **3.** another name for Śiva.

Śaktipāṇi (S) (M) **1.** spear handed. **3.** another name for Skanda.

Śaktirakṣita (S) (M) **1.** protected by power. **3.** a king of the Kirātas (*K. Sāgara*).

Śaktisena (S) (M) with a powerful spear carrying army.

Śaktivega (S) (M) **1.** power motivated; speedy and energetic. **3.** a vidyādhara (*K. Sāgara*).

Śakuni (S) (M) **1.** large bird. **2.** peacock. **3.** a son of Duhsaha (*Mā. Purāṇa*); an asura who was the son of Hiraṇyākṣa and father of Vṛka (*H. Purāṇa*); a son of Vikukṣi and grandson of Ikṣvāku (*H. Purāṇa*); a son of Daśaratha (*Bhā. Purāṇa*); the great grandfather of Aśoka (*R. Taraṅgiṇī*); a serpent of Dhṛtarāṣṭra dynasty (*M. Bh.*); a king of the Bharata dynasty who was the son of Bhīmaratha and father of Urudbhī (*Bhāgavata*); a son of Ikṣvāku; a maharṣi (*P. Purāṇa*); the son of King Subala of Gāndhāra and brother of Gāndhāri who was supposed to be the incarnation of Dvāpara (*M. Bh.*).

Śakunīśvara (S) (M) **1.** lord of birds. **3.** another name for Garuḍa.

Śakunta (S) (M) **1.** bird; blue jay. **3.** a son of Viśvāmitra (*M. Bh.*).

Śākvara (S) (M) might; powerful; strong.

Śakvarī (S) (M) **1.** a finger; girdle. **3.** a river.

Śakya (S) (M) possible; within reach.

Śākyaketu (S) (M) **1.** banner of the Śākyas. **3.** another name for Gautama Buddha.

Śakyakīrti (S) (M) **1.** glory of the Śakas; a tribe from Kapilavastu. **3.** another name for Gautama Buddha.

Śakyamitra (S) (M) friend of the Śākya tribe.

Śākyamunī (S) (M) 1. Śākya sage. 3. another name for Gautama Buddha.

Śākyapuṅgava (S) (M) 1. bull among the Śākyas. 3. another name for Gautama Buddha.

Śākyasinha (S) (M) 1. lion of the Śākyas. 3. another name for Gautama Buddha.

Śākyavardhana (S) (M) 1. accomplisher of the possible. 3. a temple (*Divyāvadāna*).

Sāl (S) (M) 1. water; dog; moving. 3. the king of Pṛṣṭaćampa who was the follower of Mahāvīra.

Śāla (S) (M) 1. rampart; wall; fence; the tree *Vatica robusta*. 3. a son of Vṛka.

Śala (S) (M) 1. dart; spear; staff. 3. an attendant of Śiva; a son of Śunahotra (*H. Purāṇa*); a wrestler of Kaṅsa killed by Kṛṣṇa (*Bhāgavata*); a serpent of the Vāsuki dynasty (*M. Bh.*); a son of Dhṛtarāṣṭra (*M. Bh.*); a son of King Somadatta of the Kuru dynasty who fought on the side of the Kauravas (*M. Bh.*); a son of King Parīkṣit and Suśobhanā (*M. Bh.*); a son of Śunahotra.

Śalabha (S) (M) 1. grasshopper. 3. locust fabled to be the children of Pulastya or of Tārkṣya and Yāminī; a gandharva (*M. Bh.*); a warrior of the Pāṇḍavas (*M. Bh.*); an asura son of Kaśyapa and Danu (*M. Bh.*).

Sālaćandra (S) (M) moon of the house.

Śalāgraja (S) (M) 1. elder brother of Śala. 3. another name for Bhūriśravas.

Śālagrāma (S) (M) 1. the fence around a village; the protector; belonging to a village near Sāl trees. 3. an ammonite stone worshipped by the Vaiṣṇavas as being pervaded by Viṣṇu, it is found in the Sālagrāma village on the Gaṇḍakī river (*Purāṇas*); another name for Viṣṇu.

Śalakara (S) (M) 1. staff handed. 3. a nāga of the Takṣaka dynasty (*M. Bh.*).

Śālakāṭaṅka (S) (M) 1. the thorn of the Śāl tree. 3. a rākṣasa.

Śalālu (S) (M) perfume.

Śalaṅga (S) (M) king.

Sālaṅkāyana (S) (M) 1. with a large quantity, 3. a son of Viśvāmitra (*M. Bh.*).

Śālankāyana (S) (M) 1. tree marked. 2. living in the woods; an ascetic. 3. a ṛṣi and son of Viśvāmitra (*M. Bh.*); an attendant of Śiva.

Śalendrarāja (S) (M) 1. lord of the Śal trees. 3. a Buddha.

Śālihotra (S) (M) 1. receiving oblations of rice. 3. a muni whose āśrama was visited by the Pāṇḍavas (*M. Bh.*).

Śālika (S) (M) 1. rice flour. 3. a divine maharṣi (*M. Bh.*).

Salila (S) (M) 1. flowing. 2. water.

Salīla (S) (M) playing; sporting; sportive.

Salilapati (S) (M) 1. lord of water. 2. the ocean. 3. another name for Varuṇa (*V's B. Samhitā*).

Salilarāja (S) (M) 1. lord of water. 3. another name for Varuṇa.

Salileśa (S) (M) 1. lord of the waters. 3. another name for Varuṇa.

Salileśvara (S) (M) 1. lord of water. 3. another name for Varuṇa.

Śālin (S) (M) 1. possessing a house; praiseworthy. 2. rice; civet cat. 3. a yakṣa; a maharṣi (*Vā. Purāṇa*).

Śālipiṇḍa (S) (M) 1. rice serpent. 3. a nāga son of Kaśyapa and Kadru (*M. Bh.*).

Śāliśiras (S) (M) 1. with a tree like head; with high intellect; confident. 3. a gandharva son of Kaśyapa and Muni (*M. Bh.*).

Śālivāhana (S) (M) 1. with a chariot made of Sāla wood. 3. a celebrated sovereign of India who instituted the Śāka era and whose capital was Pratiṣṭhāna on the Godāvarī (*S. Dvatrinśikā*).

Śālmali (S) (M) 1. the Semul tree (*Bombax ceiba*) 3. a lunar king who was the son of Avīkṣit and grandson of Kuru (*M. Bh.*).

Śālmalin (S) (M) 1. living in the Śālmali tree. 3. Garuḍa.

Śālu (S) (M) frog; perfume; lotus root.

Sālva (S) (M) 1. dynamic people. 3. the ruler of Śubha who was the beloved of princess Ambā of Kāśī and is considered a partial incarnation of Ajaka (*M. Bh.*).

Śalvāyana (S) (M) 1. belonging to the Śālvas. 3. a king of ancient India who escaped to South India in fear of Jarāsandha (*M. Bh.*).

Śalya (S) (M) 1. dart; javelin; spear; arrow. 2. porcupine; fence; boundary. 3. an asura (*H. Purāṇa*); a king of Madra and brother of Madrī the wife of Paṇḍu, he fought on the side of the Kauravas (*M. Bh.*).

Śayāri (S) (M) 1. enemy of Śalya. 3. another name for Yudhiṣṭhira.

Sama (S) (M) 1. equal. 2. even; smooth; flat; honest; just; peace. 3. a son of Dharma (*V. Purāṇa*); a son of Dhṛtarāṣṭra (*M. Bh.*).

Śāma (S) (M) 1. equanimity; calmness. 3. the dog that followed Yudhiṣṭhira and was a son of Saramā (*Br. Purāṇa*).

Śama (S) (M) 1. tranquillity; calmness; quietude; equanimity. 3. peace personified as a son of Dharma and husband of Prāpti (*M. Bh.*); a son of Andhaka (*H. Purāṇa*); the son of the vasu Aah (*M. Bh.*).

Samabuddhi (S) (M) 1. esteeming all things alike. 3. a muni.

Samādara (S) (M) great respect; veneration.

Samadyuti (S) (M) equal in radiance.

Sāmagarbha (S) (M) 1. destroying sin. 3. another name for Viṣṇu.

Samagrendu (S) (M) full moon.

Samaja (S) (M) 1. forest; multitude. 3. another name for Indra.

Śamaka (S) (M) peacemaker; pacifier.

Samakarṇa (S) (M) 1. with equal ears. 3. another name for Buddha and Śiva.

Samālya (S) (M) garlanded; crowned.

Sāman (S) (M) calming; tranquillizing; destroying sin; a song of praise; chanted hymn.

Samāna (S) (M) 1. similar; equal; identical; possessing honour. 3. one of the 5 vital airs of the body personified as a son of Sādhya (*A. Veda*).

Samana (S) quiet; calm; rich; affluent; abundant; universal.

Samaṅga (S) (M) 1. with balanced features. 3. a cowherd of Duryodhana (*M. Bh.*); a hermit (*M. Bh.*); Sensitive Plant (*Mimosa pudica*).

Samaṅgala (S) (M) full of happiness; auspicious.

Samañjasa (S) (M) 1. proper; right; fit; correct; sound; good; excellent. 3. another name for Śiva.

Sāmanta (S) (M) 1. bordering; limiting; chief of a district. 2. leader; general; champion.

Samanta (S) (M) contiguous; being on every side; universal; whole; entire.

Samantabhadra (S) (M) 1. wholly auspicious. 3. a Bodhisattva.

Samantabhuj (S) (M) 1. all devouring. 3. another name for Agni.

Samantaćaritamati (S) (M) 1. with an even mind. 3. a bodhisattva.

Samantadarśin (S) (M) 1. seeing all. 3. a Buddha.

Samantaka (S) (M) 1. destroyer of tranquillity. 3. another name for Kāma.

Samantanetra (S) (M) 1. universal eye. 3. a bodhisattva.

Samantaprabha (S) (M) 1. universal light. 3. a bodhisattva.

Samantaprabhāsa (S) (M) 1. universal illumination. 3. a Buddha.

Samantaprasādika (S) (M) 1. offering help on all sides. 3. a bodhisattva.

Samantaraśmi (S) (M) 1. composed of rays of light; all-illuminating. 3. a bodhisattva.

Samantra (S) (M) accompanied by sacred verseṣ.

Samanyu (S) (M) 1. wrathful. 3. another name for Śiva.

Samara (S) (M) 1. concourse; confluence. 3. a king of the vidyādharas (*K. Sāgara*); a king of Kāmpīlya (*H. Purāṇa*); a brother of King Avantivarman (*R. Taraṅgiṇī*); a son of King Pṛthuśena of the Bharata dynasty (*Bhāgavata*).

Sāmara (S) (M) with the immortals; accompanied by the gods.

Samarajit (S) (M) victorious in war.

Samaramardana (S) (M) **1.** destroying in battle. **3.** another name for Śiva.

Samarañjaya (S) (M) victorious in a battle.

Samarasinha (S) (M) lion in battle.

Samaratha (S) (M) **1.** with a smooth chariot. **3.** a brother of King Virāṭa who fought on the side of the Pāṇḍavas (*M. Bh.*).

Samaravijaya (S) (M) victorious in battle.

Samaravīra (S) (M) **1.** hero of the battle. **3.** the father of Yaśodā.

Samarćaka (S) (M) worshipping.

Samarćita (S) (M) worshipped; adored.

Samardhana (S) (M) causing to prosper.

Samarendra (S) (M) lord of war.

Samasaurabha (S) (M) **1.** with an even fragrance. **2.** with a delightful fragrance. **3.** a Brāhmin who was a guest of Janamejaya (*M. Bh.*).

Śamatha (S) (M) **1.** residing in peace; tranquil; calm. **3.** a Brāhmin at Yudhiṣṭhira's court (*M. Bh.*).

Śamavāna (S) (M) **1.** tranquil; calm. **3.** a son of Viśvāmitra (*M. Bh.*).

Samāvarta (S) (M) **1.** turning back; returning. **3.** another name for Viṣṇu.

Samavartin (S) (M) **1.** of fair and impartial disposition. **3.** another name for Yama.

Sāmavat (S) (M) **1.** connected with a Sāma. **3.** a son of Sārasvata.

Samaya (S) (M) **1.** coming together. **2.** covenant; understanding; rule; order; direction; time; season; limit; speech; end of trouble. **3.** a son of Dharma (*V. Purāṇa*).

Samayānanda (S) (M) happy time.

Sāmba (S) (M) **1.** with the mother. **3.** the son of Kṛṣṇa and Jāmbavatī (*M. Bh.*).

Śambara (S) (M) **1.** made of iron; war; fight; cloud; best; excellent. **3.** a demon who was slain by Indra (*Ṛg Veda*); and in the Mahabhārāta by Kāma (*Ṛg Veda*); a leader of the asuras who was the son of Kaśyapa and Danu and was killed by Śiva; a son of Hiraṇyākṣa and the husband of Māyāvatī; a Jīna (*L. Vistara*); Ceylon Leadwort (*Plumbago zeylanica*); California Cinchona (*Symplocos racemosa*); White Murdah (*Terminalia citrina*).

Śambarāghna (S) (M) **1.** Śambara slayer. **3.** another name for Kāma.

Śambarāri (S) (M) **1.** enemy of Śambara. **3.** another name of Kāma.

Sāmbaśiva (S) (M) **1.** with Pārvatī. **3.** another name for Śiva.

Sambhā (S) (M) to shine fully; to be visible; to be very bright.

Sambhara (S) (M) supporter; bestower; bringing together.

Śambhava (S) (M) **1.** peacefully born. **3.** the 3rd Arhat of the present Avasarpiṇī.

Śāmbhava (S) (M) coming from Śiva; sacred to Śiva.

Sambhava (S) (M) **1.** meeting; union; birth; origin; ability intimacy, manifestation, creation. **3.** a Purū king who was the son of Ūrja and father of Jarāsandha (*A. Purāṇa*).

Sambhavanātha (S) (M) **1.** lord of creation. **3.** the 3rd Jaina Tīrthaṅkara who was the son of King Jitāri and queen Senā of Śrāvastī.

Sambhāvya (S) (M) **1.** honoured; respected; well treated; suited; fit. **3.** a son of Manu Raivata (*V. Purāṇa*).

Sambhrama (S) (M) **1.** whirling round; agitation; activity, zeal; awe; respect. **3.** a class of beings attendant on Śiva.

Śambhu (S) (M) **1.** causing happiness. **2.** existing for welfare and happiness; helpful; benevolent; kind. **3.** a son of Viṣṇu (*M. Bh.*); Indra in the 10th Manvantara (*Bhā. Purāṇa*); one of the 11 rudras (*M. B'h.*); a king of the daityas (*Rāmāyaṇa*); an Arhat; a son of Śuka (*H. Purāṇa*); a son of

Viśvarūpa and the grandson of Tvaṣṭā (*A. Purāṇa*); a son of Ambarīṣa (*Bhāgavata*); a rākṣasa son of Vidyujjīhva and Śūrpaṅakhā (*K. Rāmāyaṇa*); a son of Kṛṣṇa and Rukmiṇī (*M. Bh.*); a Bharata dynasty king who was a son of Ugrasena (*Bhāgavata*); another name for Śiva, Brahmā and Viṣṇu.

Śambhubhairava (S) (M) 1. Śiva the terrible. 3. a form of Śiva.

Śambhukumāra (S) (M) 1. son of the daitya Śambhu. 3. a son of Śūrpaṇakhā.

Śambhunandana (S) (M) 1. son of Śiva. 3. another name for Skanda and Gaṇeśa.

Śambhunātha (S) (M) 1. lord Śiva. 3. a temple of Śiva in Nepāl.

Sambhūta (S) (M) 1. born; originated; manifested; capable; equal. 3. a king who was the son of Trasadasyu and the father of Anaraṇya (*Vā. Purāṇa*).

Śambhutanaya (S) (M) 1. son of Śiva. 3. another name for Skanda and Gaṇeśa.

Sambhūti (S) (M) 1. born; manifested. 3. a son of Duhsaha (*V. Purāṇa*); a brother of Trasadasyu (*V. Purāṇa*).

Sambhūtivijaya (S) (M) 1. victorious over birth. 2. one who has achieved bliss and shall therefore not be reborn. 3. the monk who succeeded Yaśobhadra as the head of the Jaina church (*J. Literature*).

Śambhuvallabha (S) (M) beloved of Śiva; the white lotus (*Nelumbium speciosum*).

Sambodha (S) (M) perfect knowledge.

Sambuddha (S) (M) wide awake; clever; wise; prudent.

Sambuddha (S) (M) eternally wise.

Śambūka (S) (M) 1. small conchshell. 3. a Śūdra muni (*K. Rāmāyaṇa*).

Samedha (S) (M) full of strength.

Śamen (S) (M) happy; prosperous; blessing; protection.

Samendra (S) (M) lord of equality; like the god.

Śamendu (S) (M) Viṣṇu as conferring happiness.

Sameśa (S) (M) lord of equality; like the gods.

Saṁgharṣaṇa (S) (M) 1. rubbing together. 2. ointment. 3. another name for Balarāma.

Śamī (S) (M) 1. toil; work; effort. 2. legume; the Śami tree supposed to contain fire (*Prosopis spicigera*). 3. a son of Andhaka (*H. Purāṇa*); a king who was the son of Uśīnara (*Bhāgavata*).

Sarmīċa (S) (M) the ocean; sea.

Samiddha (S) (M) perfect; full; complete; inflamed; ignited.

Samīka (S) (M) 1. vanquisher of peace. 2. conflict; fight. 3. a son of Śurā; a ṛṣi (*M. Bh.*).

Śamīka (S) (M) 1. peaceful. 2. self restrained. 3. a muni who was the father of Sṛṅgi; a great warrior of the Vṛṣṇi dynasty (*M. Bh.*); a son of Śūra and brother of Vasudeva.

Samin (S) (M) 1. accomplisher of peace; tranquil; pacific. 2. consoler. 3. a son of Rājādhideva (*H. Purāṇa*).

Śamin (S) (M) 1. tranquil; pacific. 2. one who has subdued his passions; self-controlled. 3. a son of Rājādhideva (*H. Purāṇa*); a son of Śūra (*V. Purāṇa*); a son of Andhaka (*V. Purāṇa*).

Samīra (S) (M) 1. set in motion; to create; to urge on. 2. wind; air. 3. another name for Vāyu and Śiva; *Prosopis spicigera*.

Samīraṇsuta (S) (M) 1. son of the wind. 3. another name for Bhīma.

Samitiñjaya (S) (M) 1. victorious in battle; eminent in an assembly. 3. one of the 7 great heroes of the Yādava clan (*M. Bh.*); another name for Yama and Viṣṇu.

Śamitṛ (S) (M) one who keeps his mind calm.

Śammad (S) (M) 1. one who has conquered his ego. 3. an aṅgiras.

Sammada (S) (M) 1. joy; happiness; exhilaration. 3. a king of the fish (*V. Purāṇa*).

Sammardana (S) (M) 1. crushing; rubbing; trampling. 3. a king of the vidyādharas (*K. Sāgara*); a son of Vasudeva and Devakī (*Bhāgavata*).

Sammata (S) (M) **1.** agreed; consented; thought highly of; highly honoured. **3.** a son of Manu Sāvarna (*H. Purāṇa*).

Sammiśla (S) (M) **1.** universal mingler. **3.** another name for Indra.

Sammita (S) (M) **1.** symmetrical; measured. **3.** a son of Vasiṣṭha.

Sammiteyu (S) (M) **1.** with balanced thoughts. **3.** a Purū king who was a son of Bhadrāśva (*A. Purāṇa*).

Sammoda (S) (M) fragrance.

Sammohana (S) (M) **1.** bewildering; bewitching. **3.** one of the 5 arrows of Kāma.

Sammud (S) (M) joy; delight.

Sāmoda (S) (M) full of joy; joyful; pleased; fragrant.

Sampadin (S) (M) **1.** perfect; accomplisher. **3.** a grandson of Aśoka.

Sampadvasan (S) (M) **1.** perfectly dressed. **3.** one of the 7 principal rays of the sun.

Sampadvasu (S) (M) **1.** god of success. **3.** one of the 7 principal rays of the sun.

Śampaka (S) (M) **1.** created by thunderbolts. **2.** shining as lightning. **3.** a pious Brāhmin (*M. Bh.*).

Sampāra (S) (M) **1.** conveyed to the other side; accomplished; fulfilled. **3.** a king and son of Samara and brother of Pāra (*V. Purāṇa*).

Sampata (S) (M) fortune; wealth; prosperity; welfare.

Sampāti (S) (M) **1.** flying; confluence; encounter. **3.** the eldest son of Garuḍa and brother of Jaṭāyu (*M. Bh.*); a son of Bahugava and father of Ahaṁyati (*H. Purāṇa*); a rākṣasa who was the son of Kumbhīnādī (*Rāmāyaṇa*); a Kaurava warriors (*M. Bh.*).

Sampatkumāra (S) (M) **1.** son of wealth; prosperous youth. **3.** a form of Viṣṇu.

Sampāvana (S) (M) perfect purification.

Sampraṇīta (S) (M) brought together; composed as poetry.

Samprati (S) (M) **1.** in the right way; righteous; now; just at present. **3.** a grandson of Aśoka who helped in spreading Buddhism; the 24th Arhat of the past Utsarpinī.

Samprīta (S) (M) completely satisfied; pleased; delighted.

Sampūjan (S) (M) treating with great respect.

Sampūrṇa (S) (M) **1.** complete; full; whole; entire; fulfilled; accomplished. **3.** one of the 4 wagtails employed for augury.

Samrāj (S) (M) **1.** universal ruler. **3.** the son of Citraratha and Ūrṇā and the husband of Utkalā, he was the father of Marīći (*Bhā. Purāṇa*); a grandson of Kāmya (*H. Purāṇa*).

Sararāṭ (S) (M) universal; supreme ruler.

Samṛddha (S) (M) **1.** accomplished; perfect; complete; whole; abundant; rich. **3.** a nāga of Dhṛtarāṣṭra's family (*M. Bh.*).

Sāmṛta (S) (M) provided with nectar.

Saṁsāraguru (S) (M) **1.** lord of the universe. **3.** another name fo Kāma.

Samud (S) (M) **1.** full of joy. **2.** joyful; glad.

Samudra (S) (M) **1.** full of water. **2.** ocean; sea; the number 4.

Samudradeva (S) (M) **1.** lord of the waters. **3.** another name for Varuṇa.

Samudragupta (S) (M) **1.** hidden ocean. **3.** a king (345-380 A.D.).

Samudrasāra (S) (M) **1.** essence of the sea. **2.** pearl.

Samudrasena (S) (M) **1.** leader of the waters. **3.** a king who was a rebirth of the asura Kāleya (*M. Bh.*).

Samudravega (S) (M) **1.** with the passion or speed of the sea. **3.** a warrior of Skanda (*M. Bh.*).

Samudravijaya (S) (M) **1.** conqueror of the ocean. **3.** the king of Dvārakā and the father of Neminātha Jaina Tīrthaṅkara.

Samudronmādana (S) (M) **1.** with the passion of the ocean. **3.** an attendant of Skanda (*M. Bh.*).

Samūha (S) (M) **1.** collection; sum; essence; group; assembly. **3.** a viśvadeva (*M. Bh.*).

Samunnada (S) (M) **1.** roaring; shouting. **3.** a rākṣasa (*Rāmāyaṇa*).

Samvara (S) (M) **1.** satisfied; contended; fulfilled. **2.** best in every aspect. **3.** a king of Ayodhyā and father of Abhinandana Jaina Tīrthaṅkara (*J. Literature*).

Śamvat (S) (M) auspicious; prosperous.

Sana (S) (M) **1.** lasting long; old. **3.** one of the 4 spiritual sons of Brahmā.

Sanadvāja (S) (M) **1.** bestowing wealth. **3.** a son of Śuċi (*Bh. Purāṇa*).

Sānaga (S) (M) **1.** beautiful mountain. **3.** a preceptor.

Śanaisċara (S) (M) **1.** moving slowly. **3.** another name for Saturn.

Sanaj (S) (M) ancient.

Sanaka (S) (M) **1.** former; old; ancient. **3.** a ṛṣi who was a mindborn son of Brahmā and described as one of the counsellers of Viṣṇu along with Sana, Sanatkumāra and Sanandana (*M. Bh.*).

Śanaka (S) (M) **1.** slow walker. **3.** a son of Śambara.

Sānala (S) (M) **1.** containing fire. **2.** fiery; vigorous; powerful.

Sanana (S) (M) gaining; acquiring.

Sānanda (S) (M) **1.** full of pleasure. **2.** joyful; glad; delighted. **3.** an attendant of Rādhā.

Sanandana (S) (M) **1.** joyful. **3.** a son of Brahmā who was born of his mind (*M. Bh.*); a disciple of Śaṅkarāċārya.

Sanasa (S) (M) laughing; smiling.

Sānasi (S) (M) bringing wealth or blessings.

Sanaśruta (S) (M) famous of old.

Sanat (S) (M) **1.** eternal. **2.** always; ever. **3.** another name for Brahmā.

Sanātana (S) (M) **1.** eternal; perpetual; permanent; ancient. **3.** a hermit in the court of Yudhiṣṭhira (*M. Bh.*); another name for Brahmā, Viṣṇu and Śiva.

Sanātha (S) (M) with a protector.

Sanatkumāra (S) (M) **1.** eternal youth; son of Brahmā. **3.** one of the 4 sons of Brahmā said to be the oldest of the progenitors of mankind, with Jainas he is one of the 12 ċakravartins.

Sanatsujāta (S) (M) **1.** always beautiful. **3.** one of the 7 mindborn sons of Brahmā; another name for Sanatkumāra.

Śaṇavāsika (S) (M) **1.** wearing flax/hemp. **3.** an Arhat (*L. Vistara*).

Sanċāraka (S) (M) **1.** one who delivers. **2.** leader; guide; messenger. **3.** a warrior of Skanda (*M. Bh.*).

Sanċārin (S) (M) **1.** transitory. **2.** the smoke rising from burnt incense.

Sanċitta (S) (M) evenminded; equable.

Śāṇḍa (S) (M) **1.** son of the collector. **3.** the father of Lakṣmīdhara.

Śaṇḍa (S) (M) **1.** curd. **3.** an asura priest who was the son of Śukra; a yakṣa.

Ṣaṇḍa (S) (M) **1.** neuter; impotent. **3.** a son of Dhṛtarāṣṭra.

Saṅdarśana (S) (M) gazing; sight; vision; manifestation; appearance.

Saṅdeśa (S) (M) message; gift.

Saṅdhā (S) (M) compact; promise; ultimate union.

Saṅdhātṛ (S) (M) **1.** one who joins. **3.** Śiva and Viṣṇu conjoined.

Saṅdhyābali (S) (M) **1.** twilight oblation. **3.** the bull of Śiva.

Saṅdhyānāṭin (S) (M) **1.** dancing at twilight. **3.** another name for Śiva.

Saṅdhyānśu (S) (M) twilight ray.

Saṅdhyārama (S) (M) **1.** delighting in the Saṅdhyā. **3.** another name for Brahmā.

Śāṇḍilya (S) (M) **1.** son of Śāṇḍilī, derived from fire. **3.** a sage and author of a law book and doctrine of *Bhaktisūtra*; a mahaṛṣi who was a member of Yudhiṣṭhira's court (*M. Bh.*); a mahaṛṣi in the dynasty of Kaśyapa (*M. Bh.*); another name for Agni; Bengal Quince (*Aegle marmelos*).

Saṅdīpa (S) (M) blazing; burning; glowing.

Saṅdīpana (S) (M) **1.** inflaming; exciting; arousing. **3.** one of Kāma's 5 arrows.

Sāndīpanī (S) (M) **1.** illuminator. **2.** preceptor. **3.** the preceptor of Kṛṣṇa and Balabhadrarāma.

Sanemi (S) (M) **1.** with a felly. **2.** complete; perfect.

Saṅgal (S) (M) ductile; melting together.

Saṅgamana (S) (M) **1.** gatherer. **3.** another name for Yama.

Saṅgata (S) (M) **1.** come together; proper; fit; suitable; consistent; compatible. **3.** a Maurya dynasty king who was the son of King Suyaśas and the father of Śāliśūraka (*Bhāgavata*).

Saṅgava (S) (M) **1.** afternoon. **3.** the supervisor of Duryodhana's cattleshed (*M. Bh.*).

Saṅghamitra (S) (M) sun of the assembly; friend of society.

Saṅghānanda (S) (M) delighting people; delight of the society.

Saṅgīta (S) (M) chorus; concert; symphony.

Saṅgoda (S) (M) **1.** with water. **2.** pond; lake; ocean.

Saṅgraha (S) (M) **1.** holding together; collecting; check; control; protection. **2.** guardian; ruler. **3.** an attendant given to Skanda by the sea (*M. Bh.*); another name for Śiva.

Saṅgrāma (S) (M) host; troop; army; battle; war; combat.

Saṅgrāmaćandra (S) (M) **1.** the moon of battle. **2.** one who excels in battle.

Saṅgrāmadeva (S) (M) god of battle.

Saṅgrāmajit (S) (M) **1.** victorious in battle. **3.** a son of Kṛṣṇa and Bhadrā (*M. Bh.*).

Saṅgrāmapāla (S) (M) protector in battle.

Saṅgrāmasinha (S) (M) **1.** lion in battle. **2.** a fierce and courageous warrior.

Saṅgupta (S) (M) perfectly hidden.

Sanhadana (S) (M) **1.** chariot. **3.** Yudhiṣṭhira's chariot.

Sanhanana (S) (M) **1.** compact; firm; solid. **3.** a son of Manasyu (*M. Bh.*).

Sanhara (S) (M) **1.** drawing together; destroying. **3.** an asura (*H. Purāṇa*).

Sanhārabhairava (S) (M) **1.** Bhairava as world destroyer. **3.** one of the 8 forms of Bhairava.

Sanhāta (S) (M) **1.** conciseness. **3.** an attendant of Śiva.

Saṅhatāśva (S) (M) **1.** with closely joined horses. **3.** a Purū king who was the son of Nikumbha and grandson of Haryāśva (*Br. Purāṇa*).

Saṅhitāśva (S) (M) **1.** with horses; close together. **3.** a Bhṛgu dynasty king who was the son of Nikumbha (*Br. Purāṇa*).

Saṅhlāda (S) (M) **1.** shouter. **3.** a rākṣasa son of Sumāli and Ketumatī (*U. Rāmāyaṇa*); a son of Hiraṇyakaśipu (*M. Bh.*).

Saṅhrāda (S) (M) **1.** shouter. **3.** an asura son of Hiranyakaśipu (*M. Bh.*).

Sani (S) (M) gain; gift; reward; a quarter of the sky.

Śani (S) (M) **1.** slow moving. **3.** Saturn and its regent fabled as the offspring of Sūrya and Ćhāyā; a son of Atri.

Sanīhāra (S) (M) bestowing gifts; liberal.

Sanil (S) (M) gifted; rewarded.

Śanipriya (S) (M) **1.** dear to Śani. **2.** emerald; sapphire.

Saniṣṭha (S) (M) gaining most.

Sāniya (S) (M) beyond comparison.

Saṅja (S) (M) **1.** universal creator. **3.** another name for Brahmā and Śiva.

Sañjana (S) (M) one who joins; creator.

Sañjaya (S) (M) **1.** completely victorious. **2.** triumphant. **3.** a chief of the yakṣas; a minister of Dhṛtarāṣṭra who was the son of Sūta and a partial incarnation of Gavalgaṇa and was blessed with divine sight through which he was able to witness in great detail the battle of Mahābhārata without actually being present at Kurukṣetra (*M. Bh.*); a Sauvīra prince (*M. Bh.*); a son of Dhṛtarāṣṭra (*M. Bh.*); a son of Supārśva (*V. Purāṇa*); a son of Raṇañjaya (*Bh. Purāṇa*).

Sañjit (S) (M) perfectly victorious.

Sañjīva (S) (M) possessed with life; living; existing.

Sañjīvin (S) (M) **1.** rendering alive; enlivening. **3.** a minister of Meghavarṇa the king of crows.

Saṅjvala (S) (M) well-lit; blazing brightly.

Saṅkalpa (S) (M) **1.** conception; notion; conviction; vow. **3.** will personified as a son of Sankalpā and Brahmā or Dharma (*Bhāgavata*).

Saṅkalpaja (S) (M) **1.** born of resolution; mindborn; heartborn; love. **3.** another name for Kāma.

Śankana (S) (M) causing awe.

Śaṅkara (S) (M) **1.** causer of tranquillity; causing prosperity; auspicious. **3.** a son of Kaśyapa and Danu (*V. Purāṇa*); a nāga; another name for Śiva and Rudra.

Śankarabharaṇa (S) (M) **1.** pleasing Śankara. **3.** a rāga.

Śankarāćārya (S) (M) **1.** Śiva the teacher; preceptor of the auspicious. **3.** a celebrated teacher of the Vedānta and reviver of Brāhmaṇism, might have lived between A.D. 788 and 820, according to tradition he lived in 200 B.C., was the son of Śivaguru and Āryāmbā was born in the village of Kalāti and also supposed to have lived 32 years, considered an incarnation of Śiva.

Śankaradāsa (S) (M) servant of Śiva.

Śankaradeva (S) (M) **1.** lord Śiva. **3.** a form of Śiva.

Śankaragaṇa (S) (M) servant of Śiva.

Śankarānanda (S) (M) **1.** pleasing Śankara. **3.** a philosopher and guru of Sāyaṇa; a commentator on the Upaniṣads.

Śankaranārāyaṇa (S) (M) Śiva and Viṣṇu conjoined.

Śankarapriya (S) (M) **1.** dear to Śiva. **2.** Francoline Partridge.

Saṅkarṣaṇānuja (S) (M) **1.** younger brother of Śiva. **3.** another name for Kṛṣṇa.

Śankarāsvāmin (S) (M) **1.** auspicious lord. **3.** the father of Upavarṣa.

Śankaravardhana (S) (M) increasing prosperity.

Sankarṣaṇa (S) (M) **1.** one who ploughs. **2.** ploughing; making rows. **3.** the father of Nilāsura; another name for Balarāma.

Sāṅkāsin (S) (M) full visibility or appearance.

Sāṅkāsya (S) (M) **1.** unstable. **3.** a king in Yama's court (*M. Bh.*).

Sankaṭa (S) (M) **1.** brought together; dense; impassable; dangerous, critical. **3.** a son of Kakubh (*Bh. Purāṇa*).

Sankaṭanāśana (S) (M) one who removes difficulties and eliminates dangers.

Sankaṭanātha (S) (M) lord of dangers; lord who removes dangers.

Śaṅkha (S) (M) **1.** conch shell. **2.** the bone of the forehead. **3.** one of the Kubera's treasures and its guardian (*M. Bh.*); one of the 8 chiefs of the nāgas (*M. Bh.*); a daitya conquered by Vṣṇu (*H. Purāṇa*); a son of Vajranābha (*H. Purāṇa*); the son of King Virāṭa and brother of Uttarā (*M. Bh.*); a maharṣi who was the elder brother of Likhita maharṣi; a Kekaya prince on the side of the Pāṇḍavas (*M. Bh.*); a nāga son of Kaśyapa and Kadru (*M. Bh.*).

Śaṅkhabhṛt (S) (M) **1.** conch bearer. **3.** another name for Viṣṇu.

Śaṅkhaćakragadādhara (S) (M) **1.** holding the conch, disc and mace. **3.** another name for Kṛṣṇa.

Śaṅkhaćakragadāhasta (S) (M) **1.** holding the conch, disc and mace. **3.** another name for Kṛṣṇa.

Śaṅkhaćakragadāpāṇi (S) (M) **1.** holding the conch, disc and mace. **3.** another name for Kṛṣṇa.

Śaṅkhaćakrāsipāni (S) (M) **1.** holding the conch and disc. **3.** another name for Kṛṣṇa.

Śaṅkhaćari (S) (M) a sandalwood mark of the shape of a conch shell, on the forehead.

Śaṅkhaćūḍa (S) (M) **1.** crested with a conchshell. **3.** a gandharva; an attendant of Kubera (*Bh. Purāṇa*); a nāga (*Bhā. Purāṇa*); an asura who was an incarnation of Sudāmā.

Śaṅkhadhara (S) (M) **1.** bearer of a conchshell. **3.** another name for Kṛṣṇa.

Śaṅkhakarṇa (S) (M) **1.** shell eared. **3.** an attedant of Śiva.

Śaṅkhamaṇi (S) (M) jewel among conches.

Śaṅkhamekhala (S) (M) **1.** girdled with shells. **3.** a maharṣi (*M. Bh.*).

Śaṅkhana (S) (M) **1.** with a conchshell. **3.** father of Sudarṣaṇa.

Śaṅkhanābha (S) (M) **1.** shell navelled. **3.** a son of Vajranābha (*V. Purāṇa*).

Śaṅkhanakha (S) (M) **1.** with nails of conch. **3.** a nāga in the court of Varuṇa (*M. Bh.*).

Śaṅkhapā (S) (M) **1.** one who drinks from a conchshell. **3.** a son of Kardama (*V. Purāṇa*).

Śaṅkhapada (S) (M) **1.** with feet of shells. **3.** a viśvadeva (*H. Purāṇa*); a son of Kardama; a son of Manu Svārocisa and the father of Suvarṇābha (*M. Bh.*).

Śaṅkhapāla (S) (M) **1.** protector of the conch. **3.** a son of Kardama (*V. Purāṇa*); a nāga (*H. Purāṇa*).

Śaṅkhapāṇi (S) (M) **1.** with a shell in the hand. **3.** another name for Viṣṇu.

Śaṅkhapiṇḍa (S) (M) **1.** made of shell. **3.** a nāga son of Kaśyapa and Kādru (*M. Bh.*).

Śaṅkhaśiras (S) (M) **1.** shell headed. **3.** a nāga son of Kaśyapa and Kadru (*M. Bh.*).

Śaṅkhaśīrṣa (S) (M) **1.** shell headed. **3.** a nāga son of Kaśyapa and Kadru (*M. Bh.*).

Śaṅkhāvatī (S) (M) **1.** full of shells. **3.** a river (*Mā. Purāṇa*).

Śaṅkhāyana (S) (M) **1.** belonging to a conchshell. **3.** a teacher and author of a Brāhmaṇa and 2 sūtras.

Śaṅkhin (S) (M) **1.** possessor of a conch; possessor of pearls; bearer of shells. **3.** another name for the ocean and Viṣṇu.

Śaṅkhukarṇanaga (S) (M) **1.** peaked mountain. **3.** a son of Janamejaya.

Sānkhyāyana (S) (M) **1.** calculating; reasoning. **3.** a preceptor who was a prominent disciple of Sanatkumāra (*Bhāgavata*).

Saṅkila (S) (M) **1.** possessed with fire. **2.** a burning torch; a firebrand.

Saṅkoca (S) (M) **1.** contraction; withdrawal. **3.** a rākṣasa who ruled the earth in ancient days (*M. Bh.*).

Saṅkrama (S) (M) **1.** progress; transition. **2.** bridge; a shooting star. **3.** a son of Vasu and king of the vidyādharas (*M. Bh.*); an attendant of Skanda given to him by Viṣṇu (*M. Bh.*).

Saṅkrandana (S) (M) **1.** calling; shouting; roaring. **3.** a king who was the father of Vapuṣmat (*Mā. Purāṇa*); a son of Manu Bhautya (*H. Purāṇa*); another name for Indra.

Saṅkṛti (S) (M) **1.** arranger. **3.** a king in the court of Yama (*M. Bh.*); a muni of the Atri dynasty (*M. Bh.*); a son of Viśvāmitra; a king of the Bharata dynasty who was the son of King Naraka and father of Rantideva (*Bhāgavata*).

Śanku (S) (M) **1.** arrow; dart; spear; spike; javelin; weapon. **3.** a son of Hiraṇyākṣa (*A. Purāṇa*); a Yādava king (*M. Bh.*); a gandharva attendant of Śiva; a nāga; a son of Kṛṣṇa (*H. Purāṇa*); a son of Ugrasena (*M. Bh.*); another name for Śiva and Kāma.

Śaṅku (S) (M) **1.** sharp. **3.** a son of Hiraṇyākṣa (*A. Purāṇa*); a Yādava king (*M. Bh.*).

Śaṅkuka (S) (M) **1.** a small nail. **3.** a son of Mayūra (*R. Taraṅgiṇī*).

Śaṅkukarṇa (S) (M) **1.** with pointed ears. **3.** a muni mentioned in *Padma Purāṇa*; a nāga in Dhṛtarāṣṭra's dynasty (*M. Bh.*); an attendant of Śiva (*M. Bh.*); an attendant given to Skanda by Pārvatī (*M. Bh.*); a dānava (*H. Purāṇa*); a son of Janamejaya (*M. Bh.*); a rākṣasa (*Rāmāyaṇa*).

Śaṅkukarṇeśvara (S) (M) **1.** lord with the pointed ears. **3.** a form of Śiva (*M. Bh.*).

Śaṅkura (S) (M) **1.** frightful; formidable. **3.** a dānava (*V. Purāṇa*).

Sāṅkura (S) (M) budding; possessing shoots.

Śankura (S) (M) **1.** causing fear. **3.** a dānava (*V. Purāṇa*).

Śaṅkuroma (S) (M) **1.** with needlelike hair. **3.** a nāga son of Kaśyapa and Kadru (*M. Purāṇa*).

Śaṅkuśiras (S) (M) **1.** spear headed. **3.** an asura (*H. Purāṇa*).

Saṅmaṇi (S) (M) genuine jewel.

Ṣaṇmātura (S) (M) **1.** having 6 mothers. **3.** another name for Kārttikeya.

Ṣaṇmukha (S) (M) **1.** 6 faced. **3.** a Bodhisattva; another name for Skanda.

Ṣaṇmukhapriya (S) (M) **1.** beloved of Kārttikeya. **3.** another name for Śiva; a rāga.

Saṅnateyu (S) (M) **1.** bowing evenly. **2.** respectful. **3.** a son of Raudrāśva and Miśrakeśī (*M. Bh.*).

Saṅnati (S) (M) **1.** sound; noise; humility. **3.** a son of Sumati (*H. Purāṇa*); a son of Alarka (*H. Purāṇa*).

Sannihita (S) (M) **1.** pervading. **2.** absorbed; hidden. **3.** an agni who was the 3rd son of Manu (*M. Bh.*).

Sannimitta (S) (M) a good omen.

Sannivāsa (S) (M) **1.** staying with the good; dwelling in truth. **3.** another name for Viṣṇu.

Saṅniveśa (S) (M) **1.** seat; abode; appearance; form; composition; construction. **3.** personified as a son of Tvaṣṭṛ and Raćanā (*Bhāgavata*).

Sanrādhya (S) (M) acquired by perfect meditation.

Saṅrāga (S) (M) **1.** redness; passion. **2.** vehemence.

Sanrāj (S) (M) to reign universally.

Sanrañjana (S) (M) **1.** full of charm. **2.** gratifying; charming; pleasant.

Śānśapāyana (S) (M) **1.** who removes all doubts. **3.** an ancient teacher.

Saṅsāra (S) (M) **1.** course; passage. **2.** the world.

Sanskṛti (S) (M) **1.** making ready; preparation; perfection; consecration; determination. **3.** another name for Kṛṣṇa.

Sanśraya (S) (M) **1.** connection; association; aim; alliance; asylum; shelter. **3.** a prajapati (*Rāmāyaṇa*).

Saṅśrutya (S) (M) **1.** hearsay; thoroughly heard. **3.** a son of Viśvāmitra (*M. Bh.*).

Sanstubh (S) (M) a shout of joy.

Sanśubh (S) (M) radiant; beautiful.

Santa (S) (M) **1.** calm. **2.** ascetic; hermit. **3.** a son of Satya of the family of King Vītahavya aad the father of Śravas (*M. Bh.*).

Śānta (S) (M) **1.** tranquil; calm; free from passions; mild; gentle; friendly. **3.** a son of day (*M. Bh.*); son of Manu Tāmasa (*Mā. Purāṇa*); son of Sambara (*H. Purāṇa*); son of Idhmajīhva (*Bhā. Purāṇa*); son of the vasu Āpa (*V. Purāṇa*); a king who was the son of Priyavrata (*Bhāgavata*).

Śāntabhaya (S) (M) **1.** fearless. **3.** a son of Medhātithi (*V. Purāṇa*).

Śantāćī (S) (M) beneficient; auspicious.

Śāntahaya (S) (M) **1.** calm horse. **3.** a son of Manu Tāmasa (*V. Purāṇa*).

Śaṅtama (S) (M) most beneficient.

Śāntamati (S) (M) composed in mind.

Santāna (S) (M) **1.** continued succession; connection. **3.** one of the 5 trees of Indra's heaven; a son of Rudra (*Mā. Purāṇa*).

Saṅtanagaṇapatī (S) (M) **1.** ever spreading lord of people; omnipresent lord of people. **3.** a form of Gaṇeśa as the giver of progeny.

Saṅtānaka (S) (M) **1.** stretching; spreading. **2.** that which stretches. **3.** one of the 5 trees of Indra's heaven; the Kalpa tree.

Śāntanava (S) (M) **1.** patronymic of Bhīṣma. **3.** a son of Medhātithi (*V. Purāṇa*); a grammarian and author of *Phit Sūtra*.

Śāntānika (S) (M) **1.** auspicious. **3.** a king of Vatsya and follower of Mahāvīra.

Saṅtanitanu (S) (M) **1.** a body of music. **3.** a youth attending on Rādhā.

Śāntāntakara (S) (M) **1.** destroyer of peace. **3.** a son of Śambara (*H. Purāṇa*).

Śantanu (S) (M) **1.** wholesome. **3.** the Lunar dynasty Kuru king who was the son of King Pratīpa and Sunandā, he was the father of Bhīṣma by Gaṅgā and of Vićitravīrya and Ćitrāṅgada by Satyavatī, he is one of the kings who should be remembered at dawn and dusk (*M. Bh.*).

Śantanuja (S) (M) **1.** son of Śantanu. **3.** another name for Bhīṣma.

Śantanuputra (S) (M) **1.** son of Śantanu. **3.** another name for Bhīṣma.

Śantanusuta (S) (M) **1.** son of Śantanu. **3.** another name for Bhīṣma.

Santāpa (S) (M) **1.** heat. **3.** another name for Agni.

Saṅtāpana (S) (M) **1.** one that heats. **2.** increasing passion; burning. **3.** an attendant of Śiva; an arrow of Kāma.

Śantarajas (S) (M) **1.** without anger; one whose desires have been quenched. **3.** a king of Kāśī who was the son of King Trikakalpava and father of King Raji (*Bhāgavata*).

Santarakṣita (S) (M) **1.** protected by the saints. **3.** a teacher of the Madhyamika-Svātantrika school of Buddhism in Nālandā (705-762 A.D.)

Śāntaraya (S) (M) **1.** slackened in speed. **3.** a son of Dharmasārathi (*Bhā. Purāṇa*).

Saṅtardana (S) (M) **1.** connecting; fastening together. **3.** a son of Kekaya King Dhṛṣṭaketu (*Bhāgavata*).

Saṅtarjana (S) (M) **1.** threatening. **3.** a warrior of Skanda (*M. Bh.*).

Śāntasena (S) (M) **1.** with a tranquil army. **3.** a son of Subāhu.

Saṅtateya (S) (M) continuous; extended.

Saṅtati (S) (M) **1.** continuous line; multitude; lineage; race. **3.** a son of Alarka (*Bh. Purāṇa*).

Santavīra (S) (M) courageous saint; a saintly warrior.

Santhānam (S) (M) to spread.

Śānti (S) (M) **1.** peace; tranquillity. **3.** a Bharata dynasty king who was the son of Nīla and father of Suśānti (*V. Purāṇa*); the Indra of the 4th Manvantara (*M. Bh.*); a son of Aṅgiras (*M. Bh*); a son of Indra (*M. Bh.*); Indra in the 10th Manvantara (*Purāṇas*); a son of Viṣṇu and Dakṣiṇā; a son of Kṛṣṇa and Kālindī; a ṛṣi (*M. Bh.*); a Jaina Arhat and Ćakravartin.

Śāntideva (S) (M) **1.** lord of peace. **3.** a teacher of the Mādhyamika-Prāsaṅgika school of Buddhism at Nālandā (691-743 A.D.).

Śāntinātha (S) (M) **1.** lord of peace. **3.** the 16th Jaina Tirthankara and the son of Viśvasena and Aćirā of Hastināpur (*J. Literature*).

Śāntiva (S) (M) **1.** bearer of piece. **2.** beneficient; friendly; kind.

Santoṣa (S) (M) **1.** satisfaction. **3.** satisfaction personified as a son of Dharma and Tuṣṭi and considered to be a Tuṣita.

Śantṛ (S) (M) reciter; praiser.

Santurodha (S) (M) **1.** with obstacle; waves pressing together. **3.** a Purū king who was the son of Matināra (*A. Purāṇa*).

Santya (S) (M) bestowing gifts; bountiful; kind.

Sānuga (S) (M) having attendants; with followers.

Sānurāga (S) (M) affectionate; feeling passion.

Saṅvaha (S) (M) **1.** carrying along. **2.** bearing. **3.** one of the 7 tongues of fire; one of the 7 winds.

Saṅvara (S) (M) **1.** stopping. **2.** dam; bridge. **3.** 2 Jaina Arhats (*J. Literature*).

Saṅvaraṇa (S) (M) **1.** covering; enclosing. **2.** resisting; containing. **3.** a lunar dynasty king who was the son of Ṛkṣa and husband of Tapatī, and father of Kuru and is one of those kings who should be remembered at dawn and dusk.

Saṅvarta (S) (M) **1.** meeting; destruction; a rain cloud. **3.** a son of Aṅgiras (*M. Bh.*).

Saṅvartaka (S) (M) **1.** rolling up; the end of the world; a submarine fire. **3.** a nāga son of Kaśyapa and Kadru (*M. Bh.*); an eternal fire on Mount Mālyavān (*M. Bh.*); another name for Balarāma.

Saṅvatsara (S) (M) **1.** the year personified. **3.** another name for Śiva.

Saṅvṛta (S) (M) **1.** happened; occurred. **3.** a nāga of the Kaśyapa dynasty (*M. Bh.*); another name for Varuṇa.

Saṅyadvara (S) (M) **1.** chief in battle. **2.** a king.

Sanyadvasu (S) (M) **1.** with continuous wealth; god of wealth. **3.** one of the 7 rays of the sun.

Saṅyama (S) (M) **1.** effort; control; self restraint. **3.** the son of the rākṣasa Śataśṛṅga (*M. Bh.*); a son of Dhūmrākṣa and father of Kṛśāśva (*Bh. Purāṇa*).

Saṅyamana (S) (M) **1.** effort; self restraint. **3.** a king of Kāśī (*M. Bh.*); the city of Yama (*Bh. Purāṇa*).

Saṅyāti (S) (M) **1.** coming; following. **3.** a son of Nahuṣa (*M. Bh.*); a Purū king who was the son of Praćinvān and Aśmakī and the husband of Vārāṅgī, he was the father of Ahaṅyāti (*M. Bh.*).

Sanyodhakaṇṭaka (S) (M) **1.** a thorn in batlie. **3.** a yakṣa attendant of Kubera (*V. Rāmāyaṇa*).

Śanyu (S) (M) **1.** benevolent; beneficient. **2.** happy; fortunate. **3.** eldest son of Bṛhaspati and the husband of Satyā (*M. Bh.*).

Saparyu (S) (M) honouring; devoted; faithful.

Sapatnajit (S) (M) **1.** conquering rivals. **3.** a son of Kṛṣṇa and Sudattā.

Sapatniśa (S) (M) **1.** lord of cowives. **3.** another name for Śiva.

Saprabha (S) (M) possessing splendour; brilliant.

Saprathas (S) (M) **1.** extensive; wide; effective. **3.** another name for Viṣṇu.

Saptadhiti (S) (M) **1.** with 7 rays of light. **3.** another name for Agni.

Saptagu (S) (M) **1.** with 7 cows. **3.** an aṅgiras ṛṣi and part author of *Ṛg Veda* (x).

Saptajihva (S) (M) **1.** 7 tongued. **3.** another name for Agni.

Saptakṛt (S) (M) **1.** one who performs 7 deeds; created by the 7. **3.** a viśvadeva (*M. Bh.*).

Saptamarīći (S) (M) **1.** 7 rayed. **3.** another name for Agni.

Saptānśu (S) (M) **1.** 7 rayed. **2.** fire.

Saptapattra (S) (M) **1.** 7 leaved; drawn by 7 horses. **2.** the Devil's tree (*Alstonia scholaris*); Jasmine. **3.** another name for the sun.

Saptaraśmi (S) (M) **1.** 7 rayed. **3.** another name for Agni.

Saptarāva (S) (M) **1.** one who makes 7 sounds; singer of 7 notes. **3.** a son of Garuḍa (*M. Bh.*).

Saptarćis (S) (M) **1.** 7 rayed. **3.** another name for Saturn and Agni.

Saptaṛṣi (S) (M) the 7 ṛṣis; the 7 stars of the constellation Ursa Major; Ceylon Leadwort (*Plumbago zeylanica*).

Saptarući (S) (M) 7 rayed; Agni.

Saptaśīrṣa (S) (M) **1.** 7 headed. **3.** another name for Viṣṇu.

Saptāśva (S) (M) **1.** with 7 horses. **3.** another name for the sun.

Saptātman (S) (M) **1.** with 7 essences. **3.** another name for Brahman.

Saptavāra (S) (M) **1.** 7 days of the week. **3.** a son of Garuḍa.

Sapti (S) (M) **1.** horse; steed. **3.** a ṛṣi and part author of *Ṛg Veda* (x).

Śara (S) (M) **1.** arrow; reed; the number 5. **3.** a son of Rićatka (*Ṛg Veda*); an asura.

Sarā (S) (M) wandering about; brook; cascade; waterfall.

Śarabendra (S) (M) **1.** lord of animals. **2.** lion.

Śarabha (S) (M) **1.** an animal; a kind of fabulous animal; a deer said to be stronger than a lion or elephant. **3.** an asura; a son of Śiśupāla (*M. Bh.*); a brother of Śakuni (*M. Bh.*); a monkey in Rāma's army (*Rāmāyaṇa*); a king of the Aśmakas; a nāga of the Takṣaka dynasty (*M. Bh.*); a nāga of the Airāvata dynasty (*M. Bh.*); a son of Kaśyapa and Danu (*M. Bh.*); a mahaṛṣi in Yama's court (*M. Bh.*); the brother of King Dhṛṣṭaketu of Ćedi who fought on the Pāṇḍava side (*M. Bh.*); a brother of Śakuni (*M. Bh.*); an incarnation of Vīrabhadra (*Ś. Purāṇa*); another name for Viṣṇu.

Śarabhaṅga (S) (M) **1.** an arrow breaker; destroyer of reeds. **3.** a maharṣi in the Daṇḍaka forest (*V. Rāmāyaṇa*).

Śarabhava (S) (M) **1.** bowman; born of arrows. **3.** another name for Kārttikeya.

Śarabhoji (S) (M) **1.** reed eater. **3.** a king of Tanjore and a writer (1798-1833).

Śarabhū (S) (M) **1.** the bowman. **3.** another name for Kārttikeya.

Śarada (S) (M) autumn.

Śaradaćandra (S) (M) the autumnal moon.

Śaradajyoti (S) (M) autumn moonlight.

Śāradambā (S) (M) **1.** lute handed mother. **3.** another name for Sarasvatī.

Śāradandāyani (S) (M) a Kekaya king whose wife was the younger sister of Kuṅtī (*M. Bh.*).

Śaradapadma (S) (M) an autumnal lotus; white lotus (*Nelumbium speciosum*).

Śaradavasu (S) (M) **1.** autumn treasure. **3.** a muni.

Sāradhātṛ (S) (M) **1.** bestower of strength. **3.** another name for Śiva.

Śaradija (S) (M) produced in autumn.

Śaradindu (S) (M) moon of the autumn season.

Śaradvān (S) (M) **1.** full of years. **2.** old. **3.** a muni who was the son of Gautama and the father of Kṛpa and Kṛpī by the apsarā Janapadī.

Śaradvat (S) (M) **1.** full of years. **2.** aged. **3.** a descendant of Gotama (*M. Bh.*).

Śāradvata (S) (M) **1.** autumn like; cool. **3.** another name for Kṛpa.

Sarāga (S) (M) having colour; impassioned; passionate.

Sāragandha (S) (M) **1.** with perfection of scent. **2.** sandalwood.

Sāragrīva (S) (M) **1.** strong necked. **3.** another name for Śiva.

Śaragulma (S) (M) **1.** collection of arrows. **3.** a monkey in Rāma's army (*V. Rāmāyaṇa*).

Saraja (S) (M) **1.** born in water. **2.** lotus (*Nelumbo speciosum*).

Sarajanmā (S) (M) **1.** born in water. **3.** another name for Kārttikeya.

Śarajanman (S) (M) **1.** reed born. **3.** another name for Kārttikeya.

Śaraka (S) (M) **1.** born in reeds. **3.** a son of King Kuśāmba (*Br. Purāṇa*).

Śaraloman (S) (M) **1.** reed haired. **3.** a maharṣi who was the father of Dāśūra.

Sāramaya (S) (M) exceedingly firm; the best of anything.

Sārameya (S) (M) **1.** the fleet one. **2.** dog. **3.** a Bharata dynasty king who was the son of Śvaphalka (*Bhāgavata*).

Sāramiti (S) (M) measure of all truth.

Śarana (S) (M) **1.** injuring. **3.** an arrow of Kāmadeva.

Sāraṇa (S) (M) **1.** cracked; split. **2.** the autumn wind. **3.** a son of Vasudeva and Devakī and brother of Kṛṣṇa (*M. Bh.*); a minister of Rāvaṇa (*Rāmāyaṇa*).

Śaraṇa (S) (M) **1.** protecting; guarding; defending. **3.** a nāga of the Vāsuki dynasty (*M. Bh.*).

Sarana (S) (M) moving; running.

Śaraṇāgata (S) (M) seeking refuge.

Sāraṅga (S) (M) **1.** dappled. **2.** musical instrunent; ornament; jewel; a bow; sandalwood; gold; the earth; light; night; a peacock; a Rājahans; a bee; a spotted antelope; swan. **3.** a rāga; another name for Śiva and Kāma.

Śāraṅgin (S) (M) **1.** bowman; archer. **3.** another name for Viṣṇu-Kṛṣṇa.

Sarañjita (S) (M) protected.

Śaranmegha (S) (M) autumn cloud.

Śaraṇya (S) (M) **1.** affording shelter. **2.** yielding help. **3.** another name for Śiva.

Śaraṇyu (S) (M) **1.** protector; defender. **2.** wind; cloud.

Saraṇyu (S) (M) **1.** moving fast; quick; nimble; fleet footed. **2.** wind; cloud; water; spring.

Śarāri (S) (M) **1.** destroying forests; an enemy of arrows. **3.** a monkey who accompanied Hanumān (*V. Rāmāyaṇa*).

Sārasa (S) (M) **1.** coming from a lake. **2.** the Indian Crane (*Ardea sibirica*); the moon. **3.** a son of Garuḍa (*M. Bh.*); a son of Yadu (*H. Purāṇa*).

Sārasam (S) (M) lotus (*Nelumbo speciosum*).

Śarāsana (S) (M) **1.** shooting arrows. **3.** a son of Dhṛtarāṣṭra (*M. Bh.*).

Sarasāpati (S) (M) **1.** lord of lakes; a buffalo. **3.** another name for Brahmā.

Sarasija (S) (M) **1.** that which originates in water. **2.** lotus (*Nelumbo speciosum*).

Sarasijanman (S) (M) **1.** lotus born. **3.** another name for Brahmā.

Saraśmi (S) (M) with rays; radiant.

Sarasvat (S) (M) **1.** abounding in lakes. **2.** connected with water; juicy; sapid. **3.** a deity considered as the offspring of the water and which acts as guardian of the waters and bestower of fertility.

Sārasvata (S) (M) **1.** blessed by Sarasvati; eloquent; learned. **3.** an ancient hermit who was the son of Dadhīća and the river Sarasvatī (*M. Bh.*); a son of sage Atri (*M. Bh.*).

Śarat (S) (M) autumn; wind; cloud.

Śaratakāntimaya (S) (M) as lovely as autumn.

Śaratpadma (S) (M) autumn lotus; white lotus (*Nelumbium speciosum*).

Śaravaṇa (S) (M) a clump of reeds.

Śaravāni (S) (M) archer; foot soldier.

Śarāvara (S) (M) quiver; shield.

Śaravindu (S) (M) **1.** genius. **3.** a king of the Bharata dynasty who was the son of Ćitraratha (*Bhāgavata*).

Śaravṛṣṭi (S) (M) **1.** a shower of arrows. **3.** a marutvat.

Sārći (S) (M) flaming; burning.

Sarddvīpa (S) (M) **1.** island in the river. **3.** a son of Garuḍa (*M. Bh.*).

Śardhanīti (S) (M) acting boldly; leading the host of maruts.

Śardhat (S) (M) defiant; bold; daring.

Śardhya (S) (M) bold; strong.

Sārdūla (S) (M) **1.** lion; tiger. **2.** best; eminent. **3.** a spy of Rāvaṇa (*V. Rāmāyaṇa*).

Śārdula (S) (M) **1.** tiger. **3.** another name for Bhūriśravas.

Sārdūlakarṇa (S) (M) **1.** tiger eared. **3.** a son of Triśaṅku.

Śareṣṭa (S) (M) **1.** desired by arrows. **2.** the mango tree.

Sargam (S) (M) **1.** going smoothly. **2.** notes of music.

Sarvāmbha (S) (M) **1.** omnipresent; liked by all. **3.** another name for Kārttikeya.

Sariddvīpa (S) (M) **1.** island in the river. **3.** a son of Garuḍa (*M. Bh.*).

Sārika (S) (M) **1.** the Mynah bird (*Turdus salica*). **3.** a hermit in Yudhiṣṭhira's court (*M. Bh.*).

Sarikānātha (S) (M) lord of Durgā.

Sarila (S) (M) **1.** one that brings essence. **2.** water.

Sāriman (S) (M) **1.** going. **2.** wind.

Sārimejaya (S) (M) **1.** together with. **3.** an ancient king (*M. Bh.*).

Sarīn (S) (M) **1.** approaching. **2.** helpful. **3.** another name for Balarāma.

Sarinnātha (S) (M) **1.** river lord. **2.** the ocean.

Śāriputra (S) (M) **1.** son of a bird. **3.** the 1st disciple of Gautama Buddha.

Śariraja (S) (M) **1.** produced from the body. **2.** a son. **3.** another name for Kāma.

Saritpati (S) (M) **1.** lord of rivers. **2.** the ocean.

Saritsuta (S) (M) **1.** son of the river. **3.** another name for Bhīṣma.

Sarjū (S) (M) **1.** going; following. **2.** a neck. lace; a merchant.

Sarjura (S) (M) a day.

Śarka (S) (M) **1.** creeping. **3.** a son of King Kuśāmba (*Br. Parāṇa*).

Sarka (S) (M) **1.** wind, air, mind. **3.** another name for Prajāpati.

Śarmada (S) (M) conferring happiness; making prosperous; propitious.

Śannakāma (S) (M) desirous of happiness.

Śarman (S) (M) **1.** shelter; protection. **2.** joy; bliss; delight; happiness.

Śarmaṇya (S) (M) **1.** giving shelter. **2.** a protector.

Śarmin (S) (M) **1.** lucky; auspicious; possessing happiness. **3.** a ṛṣi (*M. Bh.*).

Śārṅga (S) (M) **1.** made of horn; bow. **3.** the bow of Kṛṣṇa made by Brahmā (*M. Bh.*).

Śārṅgadhanurdhara (S) (M) **1.** holding the bow. **3.** another name for Kṛṣṇa.

Śārṅgadhanuṣ (S) (M) **1.** armed with a bow. **3.** another name for Viṣṇu and Kṛṣṇa.

Śārṅgadhanvā (S) (M) **1.** armed with a bow. **3.** another name for Kṛṣṇa.

Śārṅgagadāpāṇi (S) (M) **1.** holding the bow and mace. **3.** another name for Kṛṣṇa.

Śārṅgagasipāṇi (S) (M) **1.** holding the bow. **3.** another name for Kṛṣṇa.

Śārṅgapāṇi (S) (M) **1.** holding the Śāraṅga bow. **3.** another name for ViṣṇuKṛṣṇa.

Sāraṅgapāṇi (S) (M) holding a musical intrument.

Śāraṅgarava (S) (M) **1.** making a noise like a deer. **3.** a ṛṣi (*M. Bh.*).

Śārṅgāyudha (S) (M) armed with a bow.

Śārṅgi (S) (M) **1.** bowman; archer. **3.** another name for Kṛṣṇa.

Sārñjaya (S) (M) **1.** most powerful. **3.** a son of Sahadeva; a *Ṛg Veda* king.

Saroja (S) (M) **1.** produced or found in lakes. **2.** lotus (*Nelumbo speciosum*).

Sarojin (S) (M) **1.** abounding in lotuses; living in a lotus. **3.** another name for Brahmā.

Saroṣa (S) (M) **1.** with anger. **2.** angry.

Śarottama (S) (M) the best arrow.

Sarpa (S) (M) **1.** creepy. **2.** a snake; serpent; nāga. **3.** one of the 11 rudras; a son of Tvaṣṭā (*A. Purāṇa*); a son of Sthāṇu (*M. Bh.*).

Sarpamālin (S) (M) **1.** garlanded with snakes. **3.** a maharṣi in Yudhiṣṭhira's court (*M. Bh.*); another name for Śiva.

Sarpānta (S) (M) **1.** destroyer of serpents. **3.** a child of Garuḍa (*M. Bh.*).

Sarparāja (S) (M) **1.** lord of snakes. **3.** another name for Vasuki (*Rāmāyaṇa*).

Sarpārāti (S) (M) **1.** enemy of snakes. **3.** another name for Garuḍa.

Sarpāri (S) (M) **1.** enemy of serpents. **2.** peacock. **3.** another name for Garuḍa.

Sarparṣi (S) (M) **1.** the sage among serpents. **3.** another name for Arbuda (*A. Brāhmaṇa*).

Sarpāsya (S) (M) **1.** snake faced. **2.** serpent eater. **3.** a rākṣasa who was the commander-in-chief of Khara's army (*Rāmāyaṇa*).

Sarpeśvara (S) (M) **1.** the king of snakes. **2.** snake king. **3.** another name for Vāsuki.

Sārthaka (S) (M) having meaning; important; significant.

Sārthavāha (S) (M) **1.** leader of caravans. **3.** a son of Māra; a Bodhisattva.

Śaru (S) (M) **1.** missile; dart arrow. **2.** passion; a partridge. **3.** a gandharva (*M. Bh.*); a son of Vasudeva; another name for Viṣṇu.

Saruċi (S) (M) possessing splendour; splendid.

Saruha (S) (M) attainer; achiever; prosperous.

Sarūpa (S) (M) uniform; similar; embodied; beautiful; handsome.

Sarura (S) (M) **1.** heart of the pond. **2.** lotus (*Nelumbo speciosum*).

Śarva (S) (M) **1.** killing with an arrow. **3.** a god who is mentioned with Bhava and Rudra-Śiva; one of the 11 Rudras (*Bhāgavata*); a son of Dhanuṣa; another name for Śiva.

Sarva (S) (M) **1.** whole entire; various manifold. **3.** another name for Kṛṣṇa and Śiva (*M. Bh.*).

Sārvabhauma (S) (M) **1.** universal; monarch; emperor. **3.** a king of the Bharata dynasty who was the son of Vidūratha and the father of Jayatsena (*Bhāgavata*); a lunar dynasty king who was the son of King Ahaṅyāti and Bhānumatī and the husband of

Sunandā (*M. Bh.*); an incarnation of Sāvarṇi Manu as the son of Devaguhya and Sarasvatī (*Bhāgavata*); the elephant of Kubera (*Rāmāyaṇa*).

Sarvabhāvakara (S) (M) **1.** causer of all being. **3.** another name for Śiva.

Sarvabhāvana (S) (M) **1.** all creating. **3.** another name for Śiva.

Sarvabhibhū (S) (M) **1.** enlightening all. **3.** a Buddha.

Sarvaćakra (S) (M) **1.** possessing all the facets of yoga. **3.** a tāntra deity (*B. Literature*).

Sarvaćārin (S) (M) **1.** all pervading. **3.** another name for Śiva.

Sarvada (S) (M) **1.** all bestowing. **3.** another name for Śiva.

Sarvadamana (S) (M) **1.** all subduing. **3.** an asura (*K. Sāgara*); another name for Bharata the son of Śakuntalā (*M. Bh.*).

Sarvadarśi (S) (M) **1.** seeing everywhere; seen everywhere. **3.** a sage who was the son of Kuśika.

Sarvadāśārhaharta (S) (M) **1.** universal bearer of the Dāśārhas. **3.** another name for Kṛṣṇa.

Sarvadeva (S) (M) **1.** god of all. **3.** another name for Śiva.

Sarvadhā (S) (M) all pleasing; all containing; all yielding.

Sarvadhārin (S) (M) **1.** holding all. **3.** another name for Śiva.

Sarvādhikārin (S) (M) master of all; all administering.

Sarvaga (S) (M) **2.** all pervading; omnipresent. **2.** spirit; soul. **3.** a son of Paurṇamāsa (*V. Purāṇa*); a son of Manu Dharma-Sāvarṇika (*V. Purāṇa*); a son of Bhīmasena and Balandharā (*M. Bh.*); another name for Śiva.

Sarvagata (S) (M) **1.** all that exists. **3.** a son of Bhīmasena (*Bh. Purāṇa*).

Sarvaguṇin (S) (M) possessing all excellences.

Sarvahara (S) (M) **1.** appropriating all; all destroying. **3.** another name for Yama.

Sarvahita (S) (M) **1.** useful to all. **3.** another name for Sākyamunī.

Sarvajit (S) (M) all conquering.

Sarvajña (S) (M) **1.** all knowing. **3.** another name for Siva.

Sarvaka (S) (M) all; whole; universal.

Sarvakāma (S) (M) **1.** whose desires are fulfilled. **2.** possessing everything wished for. **3.** a son of Ṛtuparṇa (*Bhāgavata*); an Arhat; another name for Śiva.

Sarvakara (S) (M) **1.** maker of all. **3.** another name for Śiva.

Sarvakarmā (S) (M) **1.** performer of all acts. **3.** a son of King Saudāsa (*M. Bh.*).

Sarvakarman (S) (M) **1.** one who performs all acts. **3.** a son of Kalmāsapāda (*M. Bh.*); another name for Śiva.

Sarvalakṣaṇa (S) (M) **1.** with all auspicious marks. **3.** another name for Śiva.

Sarvalālasa (S) (M) **1.** desired by all. **3.** another name for Śiva.

Sarvaloćana (S) (M) the all seeing eye.

Sarvalokeśvara (S) (M) **1.** lord of all the worlds. **3.** another name for Brahmā.

Sarvāmbha (S) (M) **1.** omnipresent; liked by all. **3.** another name for Kārttikeya.

Sarvamitra (S) (M) friend of all.

Sarvamohana (S) (M) attracting all.

Sarvamūrti (S) (M) the idol of all; possessed with infinite forms.

Sarvanāgaripudhvaja (S) (M) **1.** universal banner of Garuḍa. **3.** another name for Kṛṣṇa.

Sarvānanda (S) (M) making all happy.

Sarvaṅdama (S) (M) **1.** all subduing. **3.** another name for Shakuntalā's son Bharata.

Sarvaṅga (S) (M) **1.** perfect in limb; complete. **3.** another name for Śiva.

Śarvāṇīramaṇa (S) (M) **1.** Śarvāṇī's husband. **3.** another name for Śiva.

Sarvanivaraṇaviṣkambhin (S) (M) **1.** doing away with all that is poisonous; destroyer of pains and troubles. **2.** possessed with an enlightenment. **3.** a bodhisattva.

Sarvānubhuti (S) (M) **1.** all perceiving. **3.** 2 Jaina Arhats.

Sarvapati (S) (M) lord of all.

Sarvapāvana (S) (M) **1.** all purifying. **3.** another name for Śiva.

Sarvapayañjaha (S) (M) **1.** remover of all miseries. **3.** a boddhisatva.

Sarvaprabhu (S) (M) lord of all.

Sarvaprada (S) (M) all bestowing.

Sarvapriya (S) (M) beloved of all.

Sarvapūjita (S) (M) **1.** worshipped by all. **3.** another name for Śiva.

Sarvapuṇya (S) (M) full of all merits; perfectly beautiful.

Sarvapūta (S) (M) perfectly pure.

Śarvara (S) (M) **1.** variegated. **3.** another name for Kāma.

Sarvarājendra (S) (M) chief of all kings.

Sarvaratna (S) (M) **1.** having all gems; a gem among all. **3.** a minister of Yudhiṣṭhira.

Sarvaratnaka (S) (M) **1.** complete with jewels. **3.** one of the 9 Jaina treasures and the deity who guards it.

Śarvarīpati (S) (M) **1.** lord of night. **3.** another name for the moon and Śiva.

Śarvarīśa (S) (M) **1.** lord of night. **3.** another name for the moon.

Śarvarīśvara (S) (M) **1.** lord of the night. **3.** another name for the moon.

Sarvasādhana (S) (M) **1.** accomplishing all. **3.** another name for Śiva.

Sarvasākṣin (S) (M) **1.** witness of all. **3.** wind; fire. **3.** the Supreme Being.

Sarvasāraṅga (S) (M) **1.** spotted all over. **3.** a nāga of Dhṛtarāṣṭra's dynasty (*M. Bh.*).

Sarvasattvapriyadarśana (S) (M) **1.** with the most beautiful face. **3.** a Buddha; a bodhisattva.

Sarvaśaya (S) (M) **1.** refuge of all. **3.** another name for Śiva.

Sarvasena (S) (M) **1.** leader of all armies. **3.** a king of Kāśi whose daughter Sunandā married Emperor Bharata (*M. Bh.*).

Sarvaśokatamonirghātamatī (S) (M) **1.** destroyer of all grief and darkness. **3.** a bodhisattva.

Sarvaśubhaṅkara (S) (M) **1.** auspicious to all. **3.** another name for Śiva.

Śarvata (S) (M) bearer of arrows.

Sarvatāpana (S) (M) **1.** all inflaming. **3.** another name for Kāma.

Sarvatejas (S) (M) **1.** universal splendour; universally powerful; omnipresent. **3.** a king in Dhruva's dynasty who was the son of Vyuṣṭa (*Bhāgavata*).

Sarvātman (S) (M) **1.** the whole person; the universal soul. **3.** another name for Śiva.

Sarvatomukha (S) (M) **1.** facing in all directions; complete; unlimited. **2.** soul; spirit. **3.** another name for Brahmā, Śiva and Agni.

Sarvatraga (S) (M) **1.** all pervading; omnipresent. **2.** wind; air. **3.** a son of a Manu (*H. Purāṇa*); a son of Bhīmasena (*V. Purāṇa*).

Sarvavādin (S) (M) **1.** spokesman of all; knower of all the doctrines. **3.** another name for Śiva.

Sarvavāsa (S) (M) **1.** all abiding. **3.** another name for Śiva.

Sarvayādavanandana (S) (M) **1.** universal son of the Yādavas. **3.** another name for Kṛṣṇa.

Sarvayogeśvareśvara (S) (M) **1.** lord of all lords of ascetics. **3.** another name for Śiva.

Sarvayogin (S) (M) **1.** the sage among all. **3.** another name for Śiva.

Sarvendra (S) (M) universal deity; lord of all.

Sarveśa (S) (M) lord of all.

Sarveśvara (S) (M) **1.** lord of all. **3.** another name for Śiva.

Sarvavīra (S) (M) all heroic; accompanied by heroes.

Sarvayudha (S) (M) **1.** armed with every weapon. **3.** another name for Śiva.

Sarvodaya (S) (M) upliftment of everyone.

Sarvottama (S) (M) best among all; supreme; the best.

Śaryāti (S) (M) **1.** an arrow shooter. **3.** a son of Vaivasvata Manu and the father of Ānarta and Sukanyā (*M. Bh.*); a Purū king who was the son of Prāćīnvān and father of Aharṁyāti; a son of Nahuṣa.

Śaśabhṛt (S) (M) **1.** hare bearer. **3.** another name for the moon.

Śaśabindu (S) (M) **1.** hare spotted. **3.** a king who was the son of Ćitraratha; another name for the moon.

Śaśāda (S) (M) **1.** hare eater. **3.** a son of King Vikukṣi of Ayodhyā and father of Purañjaya (*Br. Purāṇa*); a son of Ikṣvāku.

Śaśadhara (S) (M) **1.** bearer of hare marks. **3.** another name for the moon.

Śaśalakṣaṇa (S) (M) **1.** hare marked. **3.** another name for the moon.

Śaśalakṣmāṇa (S) (M) **1.** hare marked. **3.** another name for the moon.

Śaśaloman (S) (M) **1.** with hare's hair. **3.** a Purāṇicking.

Sasaṅga (S) (M) adhering; attached.

Śaśāṅka (S) (M) **1.** hare marked. **3.** another name for the moon.

Śaśāṅkaja (S) (M) **1.** son of the moon. **3.** another name for Mercury.

Śaśāṅkamukuta (S) (M) **1.** moon crested. **3.** another name for Śiva.

Śaśāṅkaśatru (S) (M) **1.** foe of the moon. **3.** another name for Rāhu.

Śaśāṅkaśekhara (S) (M) **1.** moon crested. **3.** another name for Śiva.

Śaśāṅkopala (S) (M) moonstone.

Sasāra (S) (M) possessing strength and energy.

Sasatya (S) (M) accompanied by truth.

Sasena (S) (M) commanding an army.

Sāsi (S) (M) armed with a sword.

Śaśibhūṣaṇa (S) (M) **1.** moon decorated. **3.** another name for Śiva.

Śaśideva (S) (M) lord of the moon.

Śaśidhāman (S) (M) the moon's splendour.

Śaśidhvaja (S) (M) **1.** moon bannered. **3.** an asura (*H. Purāṇa*).

Śaśikānta (S) (M) moon loved; moonstone.

Śaśikara (S) (M) moonbeam.

Śaśikhaṇḍa (S) (M) **1.** crescent moon. **3.** a vidyādhara.

Śaśikiraṇa (S) (M) moonbeam.

Śaśin (S) (M) **1.** hare marked. **3.** the moon.

Śaśimaṇi (S) (M) moonstone.

Śaśimauli (S) (M) **1.** having the moon as a diadem. **3.** another name for Śiva.

Sāsipāṇi (S) (M) with sword in hand.

Śaśiprabhā (S) (M) **1.** as radiant as the moon. **2.** the White Water Lily (*Nymphaea alba*); a pearl; moonlight.

Śaśipriya (S) (M) **1.** beloved of the moon. **2.** pearl.

Śaśirekhā (S) (M) **1.** moon crowned. **3.** another name for Buddha and Śiva.

Śaśīśa (S) (M) **1.** lord of the moon. **3.** another name for Śiva.

Śaśiśekhara (S) (M) **1.** moon crested. **3.** a Buddha; another name for Śiva.

Śaśitanaya (S) (M) **1.** son of the moon. **3.** another name for Mercury.

Śaśitejas (S) (M) **1.** power of the moon. **3.** a vidyādhara.

Śasman (S) (M) invocation; praise.

Śaśmān (S) (M) exerting oneself; zealous.

Sasmita (S) (M) accompanied with smiles; smiling.

Śāstā (S) (M) **1.** one who rules. **2.** a ruler; punisher; chastiser. **3.** the idol of the Sabarimala temple which is considered the offspring of Śiva and Mahāviṣṇu in his form as Mohini; Śāstā was the husband of Pūrṇa and Puṣkalā and father of Sātyaka.

Ṣaṣṭhipriya (S) (M) **1.** beloved of Durgā. **3.** another name for Skanda.

Ṣaṣṭibhāga (S) (M) **1.** 60 parts. **3.** another name for Śiva.

Śāstri (S) (M) chastiser; punisher; ruler; teacher; the sword personified.

Saśūka (S) (M) a believer in the existence of god.

Sasura (S) (M) with the gods.

Sāśva (S) (M) **1.** with horses. **3.** a king in the court of Yama (*M. Bh.*).

Śaśvat (S) (M) perpetual; endless; numerous.

Śāśvata (S) (M) **1.** eternal; constant; perpetual. **3.** a son of Śruta and father of Sudhanvan (*V. Purāṇa*); another name for Śiva and Vyāsa.

Śāśvatānanda (S) (M) eternal bliss.

Sasyahan (S) (M) **1.** destroying crops. **3.** son of Duhsaha (*Mā. Purāṇa*).

Sasyaka (S) (M) **1.** possessed of good qualities; perfect. **2.** sword; precious stone.

Sata (S) (M) lasting; enduring; being; existing; real; a truth; good; honest; a sage.

Sāta (S) (M) **1.** pleasure; delight; handsome; bright. **3.** a yakṣa friend of Vaiśravaṇa.

Śaṭa (S) (M) **1.** sour. **2.** astringent. **3.** a son of Vasudeva (*H. Purāṇa*).

Śatabāhu (S) (M) **1.** 100 armed. **3.** an asura (*Bhā. Purāṇa*).

Śatabali (S) (M) **1.** as strong as 100. **2.** very strong; a kind of fish. **3.** a monkey in the army of Sugrīva (*V. Rāmāyaṇa*).

Śatābdi (S) (M) centenary; century.

Śatabhīru (S) (M) **1.** extremely shy. **3.** Arabian Jasmine (*Jasminum sambac*).

Śataćandra (S) (M) **1.** as beautiful as a 100 moons; adorned with a hundred moons. **3.** a brother of Śakuni (*M. Bh.*).

Sataćita (S) (M) **1.** existence and thought. **3.** another name for Brahmā.

Satadeva (S) (M) the true god; god of existence.

Śatadhāman (S) (M) **1.** with a 100 forms. **3.** another name for Viṣṇu.

Śatadhanuṣ (S) (M) **1.** with a 100 bows. **3.** a Yādava king.

Śatadhanvan (S) (M) **1.** with a hundred bows. **3.** father of Avidānta; father of Bhīṣaj.

Śatadhṛti (S) (M) **1.** with a 100 sacrifices. **3.** another name for Indra and Brahmā.

Śatadrū (S) (M) **1.** flowing in 100 branches. **3.** the Purāṇic name of the river now called Sutlej (*H. Purāṇa*).

Śatadyumna (S) (M) **1.** with the glory of 100's. **3.** a son of Manu Ćākṣusa and Nadvalā (*V. Purāṇa*).

Śataghnī (S) (M) **1.** a deadly weapon. **3.** another name for Śiva.

Śatahaya (S) (M) **1.** with a 100 horses. **3.** a son of Manu Tāmasa (*V. Purāṇa*).

Śatahrada (S) (M) **1.** thunderbolt. **3.** an asura.

Śatajīhva (S) (M) **1.** 100 tongued. **3.** another name for Śiva.

Śatajit (S) (M) **1.** vanquisher of 100. **3.** a Yādava king who was the son of Sahasrajit and the father of Mahāhaya, Veṇuhaya and Hehaya (*Bhāgavata*); a son of Kṛṣṇa and Jāmbavatī (*Bhāgavata*); a son of Viraja (*Purāṇas*); a son of Bhajamāna (*Bhā. Purāṇa*); a yakṣa (*Bhā. Purāṇa*).

Śatajyoti (S) (M) **1.** with a 100 flames. **2.** the moon. **3.** a son of King Subhrāj (*M. Bh.*).

Śatakapāleśa (S) (M) **1.** lord of a 100 skulls. **3.** another name for Siva.

Śātakarṇi (S) (M) **1.** with sharp ears. **3.** a son of King Pūrṇotsaṅgha (*M. Purāṇa*).

Śatakīrti (S) (M) **1.** with the fame of 100s. **3.** the 10th Arhat of the future Utsarpinī.

Śatakratu (S) (M) **1.** with a 100 fold power. **3.** another name for Indra.

Śātakumbha (S) (M) gold.

Śataloćana (S) (M) **1.** 100 eyed. **3.** an asura (*H. Purāṇa*); a warrior of Skanda (*M. Bh.*).

Śatāmagha (S) (M) **1.** distributing a 100 rewards. **3.** another name for Indra.

Śatamakha (S) (M) **1.** with a 100 sacrifices. **3.** another name for Indra.

Śatamanyu (S) (M) **1.** with a 100 fold wrath. **3.** another name for Indra.

Śatamukha (S) (M) **1.** with a 100 mouths. **3.** a king of the kinnaras; the father-in-law of Sahasramukha Rāvaṇa; an asura devotee of Śiva (*M. Bh.*).

Satanāma (S) (M) the name of truth.

Ṣatānana (S) (M) **1.** 6 faced. **3.** another name for Skanda.

Śatānanda (S) (M) **1.** delighting 100s. **3.** the vehicle of Viṣṇu; the family priest of Janaka who was a son of Gautama and Ahalyā (*Bhāgavata*); another name for Viṣṇu and Kṛṣṇa.

Śatānīka (S) (M) **1.** with an army of hundreds. **3.** a king of the Yayāti dynasty who was the son of Bṛhadratha and the father of Durdama (*Bhāgavata*); the son of Nakula and Draupadī (*M. Bh.*); a son of Janamejaya and Vapuṣṭamā and the father of Aśvamedhadatta and Sahasrānīka (*M. Bh.*); a royal ṛṣi of the Kuru dynasty after whom Nakula named his son (*M. Bh.*); a brother of King Virāṭa of Matsya (*M. Bh.*).

Satapāla (S) (M) good protector.

Śataratha (S) (M) **1.** with 100s of chariots. **3.** a king in Yama's court (*M. Bh.*).

Śatarati (S) (M) **1.** loved by a 100; attached to 100s. **3.** another name for Indra, Brahmā and heaven.

Satarūpa (S) (M) with true beauty; really beautiful.

Śataśīrṣa (S) (M) **1.** 100 headed. **3.** a king of the nāgas.

Śataśṛṅga (S) (M) **1.** with a 100 horns. **3.** the muni who cursed Pāṇḍu; a rākṣasa and father of Saṅyama, Viyama and Suyama (*M. Bh.*); a mountain (*M. Bh.*).

Sātavāha (S) (M) **1.** with 7 chariots. **3.** a king.

Śatavāhana (S) (M) **1.** with a 100 chariots. **3.** a king of whom Guṇāḍhya was a minister.

Śatavāṇi (S) (M) **1.** knowing 100s of arts and sciences. **3.** a royal ṛṣi (*Ṛg Veda*).

Satavānt (S) (M) **1.** possessed with truth. **2.** true; faithful; pious; sacred.

Śatavapuṣ (S) (M) **1.** with a 100 bodies. **3.** a son of Uṣanas.

Śatāvarta (S) (M) **1.** with a 100 curls on the bead. **3.** another name for Śiva and Viṣṇu.

Śatavartin (S) (M) **1.** 100 locked. **3.** another name for Viṣṇu.

Satavīra (S) (M) a true warrior.

Śatavīra (S) (M) **1.** warrior among 100s. **3.** another name for Viṣṇu.

Śatāyudha (S) (M) wielding a 100 weapons.

Śatayūpa (S) (M) **1.** with a 100 pillars; well equipped with every type of weapon. **3.** a Kekaya royal sage (*M. Bh.*).

Śatayuṣ (S) (M) **1.** a 100 years old. **2.** elderly. **3.** a son of Purūravas and Urvaśī (*M. Bh.*).

Śatāyus (S) (M) **1.** fighting 100 battles. **3.** a son of Purūravas and Urvaśī (*M. Bh.*); a Kaurava warrior (*M. Bh.*).

Satejas (S) (M) full of power; full of splendour.

Śateśa (S) (M) lord of 100s.

Śaṭha (S) (M) **1.** dishonest; depraved; wicked. **3.** an asura son of Kaśyapa and Danu (*M. Bh.*); a son of Vasudeva (*H. Purāṇa*).

Satīna (S) (M) real; essential.

Satīnātha (S) (M) **1.** husband of Satī. **3.** another name for Śiva.

Satīndra (S) (M) **1.** lord of Satī. **3.** another name for Śiva.

Satīśa (S) (M) **1.** lord of Satī. **3.** another name for Śiva.

Sātiśaya (S) (M) superior; better; best; eminent.

Satkāra (S) (M) **1.** a virtuous deed. **2.** honour; respect.

Satkārī (S) (M) respectful; doer of virtuous deeds.

Satkarman (S) (M) **1.** a virtuous act; doing virtuous deeds. **3.** a son of Dhṛtavrata (*Bh. Purāṇa*).

Satkartṛ (S) (M) **1.** doing good. **2.** a benefactor. **3.** another name for Viṛṇu.

Satkṛta (S) (M) **1.** doer of virtuous deeds; honoured; respected; adored. **3.** another name for Śiva.

Satkṛti (S) (M) **1.** doing good. **2.** virtuous. **3.** a solar dynasty king who was the son of Jayatsena (*Bhāgavata*).

Sātman (S) (M) with a soul; united with the Supreme Spirit.

Śatodara (S) (M) **1.** with a 100 bellies. **3.** an attendant of Śiva.

Satpati (S) (M) **1.** a true lord; leader; champion; a good lord. **3.** another name for Indra.

Śatrajit (S) (M) **1.** always victorious. **3.** a Yādava king who was the son of Nimna and the brother of Prasena, he fathered Satyabhāmā who married Kṛṣṇa (*Bhāgavata*).

Satrasaha (S) (M) irresistible.

Sātrāsāha (A) (M) **1.** all subduing. **3.** a nāga (*A. Veda*).

Śatrudamana (S) (M) subduing enemies.

Śatruddha (S) (M) making enemies run away.

Śatrugha (S) (M) slaying enemies.

Śatrughna (S) (M) **1.** destroying enemies. **3.** a son of Daśaratha and Sumitrā and twin brother of Lakṣmaṇa and the husband of Śrutakīrtī (*Rāmāyaṇa*); a son of Devaśravas (*H. Purāṇa*).

Śatruhan (S) (M) **1.** destroyer of enemies. **3.** a son of Śvaphalka (*H. Purāṇa*).

Śatrujaya (S) (M) conquering an enemy.

Śatrujit (S) (M) **1.** conquering enemies. **3.** a son of Rājādhideva (*H. Purāṇa*); the father of Kuvalayāsva (*Purāṇas*); a son of Dhruvasandhi and Līlāvatī; another name for Śiva.

Śatrumardana (S) (M) **1.** crushing enemies. **3.** a son of Daśaratha; a son of Kuvalayāśva (*Mā. Purāṇa*); a king of Videha; a son of King Ṛtadhvaja and Madālasā (*Mā. Purāṇa*).

Śatruñjaya (S) (M) **1.** enemy conquering. **3.** a son of Dhṛtarāṣṭra (*M. Bh.*); a brother of Karṇa (*M. Bh.*); a son of Drupada (*M. Bh.*); a king of Sauvīra (*M. Bh.*).

Śatruntapa (S) (M) **1.** tormentor of enemies. **3.** a king in Duryodhana's army (*M. Bh.*).

Śatrusaha (S) (M) **1.** tolerating enemies. **3.** a son of Dhṛtarāṣṭra (*M. Bh.*).

Śatrutāpana (S) (M) **1.** tormentor of enemies. **3.** an asura son of Kaśyapa and Danu (*M. Bh.*); another name for Śiva.

Śatruvināśana (S) (M) **1.** destroying enemies. **3.** another name for Śiva.

Satsahāya (S) (M) good companion; with virtuous friends.

Sattrāyaṇa (S) (M) **1.** course of sacrifices; follower of truth; moving in the Soma sac. **3.** the father of Bṛhadbhānu (*Bh. Purāṇa*).

Sattva (S) (M) **1.** being; existence; reality; true essence; life; resolute; energy; courage. **3.** a tāntra deity (*B. Literature*); a son of Dhṛtarāṣṭra.

Sattvapati (S) (M) lord of creatures.

Satvadanta (S) (M) **1.** having a wisdom tooth. **2.** very wise. **3.** a son of Vasudeva and Bhadrā (*Vā. Purāṇa*).

Satvat (S) (M) **1.** truthful. **2.** faithful. **3.** a son of Madhu (*H. Purāṇa*); a son of Mādhava and Anśa (*V. Purāṇa*); another name for Kṛṣṇa.

Sātvata (S) (M) **1.** full of truth. **2.** delighted; pleasant; sacred to Kṛṣṇa. **3.** a Yadu king who was the son of Devakśatra (*M. Bh.*); a son of Āyu (*Purāṇas*).

Sātvika (S) (M) real; virtuous; essential; good.

Satvindra (S) (M) lord of virtue.

Satya (S) (M) **1.** true; real; pure; virtuous. **3.** a viśvadeva; a son of Havirdhāna; a hermit in [he court of Yudhiṣṭhira (*M. Bh.*); an agni who was the son of Agni Niśćyavana and the father of Svana (*M. Bh.*); a warrior of Kalinga (*M. Bh.*); a son of Vitatya and the father of Sānta; another name for Viṣṇu, Kṛṣṇa and the Aśvattha tree.

Satyadarśin (S) (M) **1.** seer of truth. **3.** a ṛṣi in the 13th Manvantara (*H. Purāṇa*).

Satyadeva (S) (M) **1.** lord of truth. **3.** a Kaliṅga warrior (*M. Bh.*).

Satyadhara (S) (M) **1.** bearer of truth. **2.** truthful; honest; virtuous.

Satyadharma (S) (M) **1.** moral law; abiding by the moral law. **2.** the law of eternal truth. **3.** a son of the 13th Manu (*Bh. Purāṇa*); a lunar dynasty king (*M. Bh.*); a brother of King Suśarman of Trigarta (*M. Bh.*); Bengal Quince (*Aegle marmelos*).

Satyadhṛta (S) (M) **1.** abode of truth. **3.** a son of Puṣpavata (*V. Purāṇa*).

Satyadhṛti (S) (M) **1.** bearer of truth. **3.** a son of Satānanda (*A. Purāṇa*); a prominent warrior on the side of the Pāṇḍavas (*M. Bh.*); a son of King Kṣemaka who fought on the side of Pāṇḍavas (*M. Bh.*).

Satyadhvaja (S) (M) **1.** true fire. **2.** eternal fire. **3.** another name for Agastya.

Satyahita (S) (M) **1.** eternal welfare. **3.** a Purū dynasty king who was the son of Ṛṣabha and the father of Sudhanvā (*A. Purāṇa*).

Satyaja (S) (M) **1.** born of truth. **2.** of a true nature.

Satyajit (S) (M) **1.** conquering by truth. **3.** a dānava (*H. Purāṇa*); Indra in the 3rd Manvantara; the son of Bṛhaddharman; the son of Kṛṣṇa; the son of Anaka; the son of Amitrajit (*H. Purāṇa*); a yakṣa; a Yayāti dynasty king who was the son of Sunītha and the father of Kṣema (*Bhāgavata*); a brother of Drupada of Pāñćāla.

Satyajyota (S) (M) **1.** lamp of truth. **2.** leading others on to the path of truth.

Satyajyoti (S) (M) having real splendour; having a real beauty.

Satyaka (S) (M) **1.** ratification of a bargain. **3.** a son of Śini (*M. Bh.*); a son of Manu Raivata (*Mā. Purāṇa*); a son of Kṛṣṇa and Bhadrā (*Bh. Purāṇa*); a Yādava king who was the father of Sātyakī.

Satyakāma (S) (M) **1.** desirer of truth. **2.** seeker of truth. **3.** a noble hermit (*Ć. Upaniṣad*).

Satyakarman (S) (M) **1.** a true act. **2.** doer of truthful acts; doing pious deeds. **3.** a Bharata dynasty king who was the son of Dhṛtavrata and the father of Aṇuvrata (*Bhāgavata*); a brother of King Śuśarmā of Trigarta (*M. Bh.*).

Satyakarṇa (S) (M) **1.** listener of truth. **3.** a son of Ćandrapīḍa (*H. Purāṇa*).

Satyaketu (S) (M) **1.** one whose banner is truth. **2.** standing by the values of truth. **3.** a Pāñćāla king (*Br. Purāṇa*); a Purū dynasty king who was the son of Śukumāra (*A. Purāṇa*); a solar dynasty king who was the son of Dharmaketu and father of Dhṛṣṭaketu (*Bhāgavala*); a son of Akrūra; a Buddha (*L. Vistara*).

Sātyakī (S) (M) **1.** truthful; faithful. **3.** a Yādava warrior of the Vṛṣṇi dynasty who was the son of Satyaka and a great friend of Kṛṣṇa, he is supposed to have been a partial incarnation of the maruts (*M. Bh.*).

Satyam (S) (M) **1.** the truth. **2.** truthful; honest; virtuous.

Satyamedhas (S) (M) **1.** with true intelligence. **3.** another name for Viṣṇu.

Satyamoti (S) (M) **1.** pearl of truth. **2.** jewel among the truthful.

Satyamūrti (S) (M) symbol of truth.

Satyānanda (S) (M) true bliss.

Satyanārāyaṇa (S) (M) **1.** controller of truth. **3.** a divinity called Satyapīr in Bengal; another name for Viṣṇu.

Satyanetra (S) (M) **1.** truth eyed. **2.** seer of truth. **3.** a son of Atri.

Satyapāla (S) (M) **1.** protector of truth. **3.** a hermit in the court of Yudhiṣṭhira (*M. Bh.*).

Satyapriya (S) (M) lover of truth; one who likes truthful people.

Satyarata (S) (M) **1.** devoted to truth. **3.** a son of Satyavrata (*M. Purāṇa*); another name for Vyāsa.

Satyaratha (S) (M) **1.** with a chariot of truth. a brother of King Suśarma of Trigarta (*M. Bh.*); a king of Vidarbha; a son of Mīnaratha (*V. Purāṇa*).

Satyasāgara (S) (M) **1.** ocean of truth. **2.** best among the truthful.

Satyasāhas (S) (M) **1.** with true courage. **2.** truly courageous. **3.** the father of Svadhāman.

Satyasandha (S) (M) **1.** true in promise. **2.** keeping one's promise.

3. a son of Dhṛtarāṣṭra (*M. Bh.*); an attendant given to Skanda by the god Mitra (*M. Bh.*); another name for Rāma, Bharata, Bhīsma and Janamejaya.

Satyasaṅgara (S) (M) **1.** true to a promise. **3.** another name for Kubera.

Satyasāra (S) (M) the essence of truth.

Satyasena (S) (M) **1.** with a virtuous army. **3.** a brother of King Suśarmā of Trigarta (*M. Bh.*); a son of Karṇa (*M. Bh.*).

Satyaśīla (S) (M) **1.** of a virtuous disposition. **2.** very virtuous; pious.

Satyaśravas (S) (M) **1.** listener of truth; truly famous. **3.** a warrior on the Kaurava side (*M. Bh.*); a son of sage Mārkaṇḍeya (*M. Bh.*).

Satyaśrī (S) (M) **1.** glory of truth; best among the truthful. **3.** a son of Satyahita.

Satyatapas (S) (M) the true sage; practising true austerity; following the true path of penance.

Satyātman (S) (M) **1.** true soul. **2.** with a truthful soul; virtuous.

Satyavāća (S) (M) **1.** speaking the truth. **3.** a gandharva (*M. Bh.*); a son of Manu Ćākṣuṣa (*H. Purāṇa*); a son of Manu Sāvarṇa (*Mā. Purāṇa*).

Satyavāha (S) (M) **1.** carrying the truth. **3.** teacher of Aṅgiras.

Satyavāka (S) (M) **1.** truth speaking. **3.** a son of Manu Ćākṣuṣa and Nadvalā (*A. Purāṇa*); a gandharva son of Kaśyapa and Muni (*M. Bh.*).

Satyavara (S) (M) adopter of truth; best among the truthful.

Satyavarmā (S) (M) **1.** warrior of truth; wearing the armour of truth. **3.** a brother of King Suśarmā of Trigarta (*M. Bh.*).

Satyavarman (S) (M) wearing the armour of truth.

Satyavat (S) (M) **1.** truthful. **2.** veracious. **3.** a son of Manu Raivata (*H. Purāṇa*); a son of Manu Ćākṣuṣa (*Bhā. Purāṇa*); a son of Dyumatsena of Śālva and husband of Sāvitrī.

Satyavrata (S) (M) **1.** devotee to the vow of truth. **3.** a son of Dhṛtarāṣṭra (*M. Bh.*); a son of Devadatta; a son of Trayyāruṇa (*H. Purāṇa*); a brother of King Suśarmā of Trigarta (*M. Bh.*).

Satyāyu (S) (M) **1.** with a true life. **2.** one who has had a pious life. **3.** a son of Purūravas and Urvaśī (*Bhāgavata*).

Satyendra (S) (M) best among the truthful.

Satyeṣu (S) (M) **1.** desirer of truth. **2.** seeker of truth. **3.** a brother of King Suśarmā of Trigarta (*M. Bh.*); a rākṣasa who ruled the earth in ancient times (*M. Bh.*).

Satyeyu (S) (M) **1.** striving for truth. **3.** a Purū dynasty king who was a son of Raudrāśva and Ghṛtāćī (*Bhāgavata*).

Saubala (S) (M) **1.** full of power. **2.** very powerful. **3.** the father of Saubalī who married Dhṛtarāṣṭra (*M. Bh.*); another name for Śakuni.

Saubalā (S) (M) **1.** belonging to Subala. **3.** patronymic of Gāndhārī.

Saubhadra (S) (M) **1.** of Subhadrā. **3.** matronymic of Abhimanyu.

Saubhaga (S) (M) **1.** full of fortunes. **2.** auspicious.

Saubhāgya (S) (M) welfare; success; luck; happiness; beauty; grace; affection.

Saubhara (S) (M) **1.** born of vitality; son of vigour. **3.** an agni born from a portion of Varćas (*M. Bh.*); Saffron (*Crocus sativus*).

Saubhari (S) (M) **1.** born of vigour. **3.** a hermit who married the 50 daughters of Māndhātā (*Bhāgavata*).

Saubhīki (S) (M) **1.** surrounded by people of the Saubha city. **3.** another name for Drupada.

Śaućin (S) (M) pure.

Saućuka (S) (M) **1.** made of sacred threads; sharp witted. **3.** the father of Bhutīrāja.

Saudāsa (S) (M) **1.** son of a great devotee; son of Sudāsa. **3.** an Ikṣvāku king and son of Sudāsa (*T. Samhitā*).

Saudeva (S) (M) **1.** of Sudeva. **3.** another name for Divodāsa.

Saudevatanaya (S) (M) **1.** descendant of Sudeva. **3.** another name for Divodāsa.

Saudhākara (S) (M) belonging to the moon.

Saugandhaka (S) (M) **1.** fragrant. **2.** blue waterlily.

Saugata (S) (M) **1.** gone into everything; knowing everything; an enlightened person. **2.** a Buddhist. **3.** a son of Dhṛtarāṣṭra (*M. Bh.*).

Sauharda (S) (M) goodheartedness; affection.

Saujas (S) (M) full of energy; strong; powerful.

Śaulkāyani (S) (M) **1.** with a spearlike body. **3.** a hermit disciple of Vyāsa.

Saumaki (S) (M) **1.** of Somaka. **3.** another name for Drupada.

Sauman (S) (M) flower; blossom.

Saumanasa (S) (M) **1.** made of flowers. **2.** comfort; benevolence; satisfaction; pleasure. **3.** one of the 8 elephants supporting the globe.

Saumanasya (S) (M) **1.** causing gladness. **3.** a son of Yajñabahu (*Bh. Purāṇa*).

Saumendra (S) (M) belonging to Soma and Indra.

Saumila (S) (M) easily available; substance.

Saumitra (S) (M) **1.** son of Sumitrā. **3.** another name for Lakṣmaṇa.

Saumedhika (S) (M) **1.** possessed with supernatural wisdom. **2.** a sage.

Saumya (S) (M) **1.** related to the moon. **2.** handsome; pleasing; gentle; soft; mild; auspicious; brilliant. **3.** a division of the earth; *Desmodium gangelicum*; *Hedychium specatum*; Couch grass (*Cynodon dactylon*).

Śaunaka (S) (M) **1.** of Śunaka. **3.** a celebrated grammarian and teacher of Kātyāyana; according to the *Viṣṇu Purāṇa* he was the son of Gṛtsamada and created the 4 castes; a renowned āćarya of the Bhṛgu family who was the son of Śunaka (*M. Bh.*); a Brāhmin who went to the forest with Yudhiṣṭhira (*M. Bh.*).

Saunanda (S) (M) **1.** born of a good milkman. **3.** the club of Balarāma.

Saunandin (S) (M) **1.** possessing Saunanda. **3.** another name for Balarāma.

Saura (S) (M) **1.** sacred to the sun; celestial; divine. **3.** another name for the planet Saturn.

Saurabha (S) (M) fragrant; *Zanlhoxylum alalum*.

Saurama (S) (M) the Vedic mantra of Sūrya.

Saurava (S) (M) sweet sounding.

Śaurava (S) (M) belonging to the brave.

Śauri (S) (M) **1.** heroic; of the brave. **3.** patronymic of Vasudeva the son of Śurasena (*Bhā. Purāṇa*); another name for the sun, Balarāma and Viṣṇu-Kṛṣṇa.

Sauri (S) (M) **1.** son of the Sun. **3.** another name for Saturn.

Saurika (S) (M) **1.** heavenly; celestial. **3.** another name for Saturn.

Sauriratna (S) (M) **1.** Saturn stone. **2.** sapphire.

Śaurya (S) (M) heroism; might; prowess; valour.

Śausā (S) (M) praise; wish; eulogium; desire.

Sauśruti (S) (M) **1.** born of scriptures. **2.** pious. **3.** the brother of King Suśarmā of Trigarta (*M. Bh.*).

Sauṣṭhava (S) (M) excellence; superior goodness; cleverness.

Sauti (S) (M) **1.** son of a charioteer. **3.** the son of sage Romaharṣana and the arranger of the Mahābhārata; another name for Karṇa (*M. Bh.*).

Śauṭīra (S) (M) liberal; munificent; hero; ascetic; proud.

Sautraman (S) (M) belonging to Indra.

Sauvāna (S) (M) **1.** celestial; heavenly. **3.** the grandson of Buddha and son of Rāhula.

Sauvīra (S) (M) **1.** of Sauvīra. **3.** another name for Jayadratha.

Sauvīraja (S) (M) **1.** son of Sauvīra. **3.** another name for Jayadratha.

Sauvīrarāja (S) (M) **1.** lord of Sauvīra. **3.** another name for Jayadratha.

Savai (S) (M) an instigator; stimulator.

Śavakrit (S) (M) **1.** corpse maker. **3.** another name for Kṛṣṇa.

Sāvana (S) (M) **1.** institutor of a sacrifice. **3.** another name for Varuṇa.

Savana (S) (M) **1.** fire. **3.** a son of Vasiṣṭha (*V. Purāṇa*); a son of Manu Svāyambhuva (*H. Purāṇa*); a son of Priyavrata and Surūpā and the husband of Suvedā (*D. Bhāgavata*); a son of Bhṛgu Muni (*M. Bh.*).

Sāvanta (S) (M) **1.** employer. **3.** a king in the Pṛthu dynasty who was the son of Yuvanāśva and father of Bṛhadaśva (*D. Bhāgavata*).

Sāvarṇa (S) (M) **1.** belonging to the same colour, tribe or caste. **3.** the 8th Manu who was the son of Sūrya and Suvarṇā; a hermit in the court of Yudhiṣṭhira (*M. Bh.*).

Sāvarṇi (S) (M) **1.** of the same colour. **3.** a hermit in the council of Indra (*M. Bh.*); the 8th Manu.

Śavas (S) (M) strength; power; might; prowess; valour; heroism.

Savāsa (S) (M) scented; perfumed.

Śavasāna (S) (M) **1.** strong; vigorous; powerful. 2. road.

Śavasī (S) (M) **1.** the strong one. 3. Indra's mother.

Savibhāsa (S) (M) **1.** having great lustre. **3.** one of the 7 suns (*V. Purāṇa*).

Savīra (S) (M) **1.** possessed with many warriors; having followers. **2.** a leader.

Śāvirī (S) (M) **1.** moving, motivating. 3. a rāga.

Savīrya (S) (M) full of strength; powerful; mighty.

Savitā (S) (M) **1.** the sun. **3.** a son of Kaśyapa and Aditi who is an āditya and the husband of Pṛṣṇī, he is the father of the 3 great sacrifices Agnihotra, Paśusoma and Ćāturmāsya (*V. Purāṇa*).

Savitara (S) (M) resembling the sun.

Savitṛ (S) (M) **1.** rouser; stimulator. **3.** a sun deity personified in the Vedas as the vivifying power of the sun, also reckoned as one among the ādityas and worshipped as lord of all creatures delivering his votaries from sin, he is the husband of Pṛṣṇi (*M. Bh.*).

Sāvitra (S) (M) **1.** belonging to the sun. **2.** fire; oblation; embryo. **3.** one of the 11 rudras (*M. Bh.*); one of the 8 Vasus (*M. Bh.*); a peak of Mount Sumeru adorned with gems (*M. Bh.*); another name for Karṇa.

Savya (S) (M) **1.** left handed. **3.** Indra incarnated as a son of Aṅgiras (*Ṛg Veda*); another name for Viṣṇu.

Savyasāćin (S) (M) **1.** able to aim with the left hand; ambidextrous. **3.** another name for Arjuna (*M. Bh.*); White Murdah (*Terminalia citrina*).

Savyasīvya (S) (M) **1.** stitching with the left hand. **3.** an asura son of Vipraćitti and Siṅhikā (*Br. Purāṇa*).

Sāya (S) (M) **1.** close of the day. **3.** evening personified as the son of Puṣpārṇa and Doṣā or a son of Dhātṛ and Kuhū (*Bh. Purāṇa*).

Sāyaka (S) (M) **1.** fit to be hurled. **2.** missile; arrow; *5 saccharum sara,* the latitude of the sky.

Sayana (S) (M) **1.** binding. **3.** a son of Viśvāmitra (*M. Bh.*).

Sāyaṇa (S) (M) **1.** possessing arrows. **2.** companion. **3.** a commentator of the Vedas in the court of Bukka I of Vijayanagara (14th century A.D.).

Sayanti (S) (M) controlling.

Sāyasūrya (S) (M) **1.** brought by the evening sun. **2.** guest.

Śayu (S) (M) **1.** sleeping; resting. **3.** a person protected by the aśvins; a ṛṣi (*Ṛg Veda*).

Sayuj (S) (M) **1.** united. **2.** companion; comrade.

Sećaka (S) (M) **1.** sprinkler. **2.** cloud. **3.** a nāga of the family of Dhṛtarāṣṭra (*M. Bh.*).

Seduka (S) (M) **1.** existent. **3.** a king of ancient India (*M. Bh.*).

Śekhara (S) (M) crown of the head; diadem; crest; chaplet; peak; best; chief.

Śelvamaṇi (S) (M) beautiful jewel.

Śelvarāj (S) (M) most handsome.

Sena (S) (M) **1.** army. **2.** leader; body. **3.** the son of King Ṛṣabha (*Bhāgavata*).

Senābindu (S) (M) **1.** pivot of the army. **3.** a Kṣatriya king who was a partial incarnation of the asura Tuhuṇḍa (*M. Bh.*); a warrior of the Pāṇḍavas (*M. Bh.*).

Senaćitta (S) (M) **1.** war minded. **3.** a Bharata dynasty king who was the son of Viśada and the father of Rućirāśva (*Bhāgavata*).

Senāhan (S) (M) **1.** destroying armies. **3.** a son of Śambara (*H. Purāṇa*).

Senajit (S) (M) **1.** vanquishing armies. **3.** a son of Kṛśāśva (*Bh. Purāṇa*); a son of Kṛṣṇa (*H. Purāṇa*); a son of Viśvajit (*V. Purāṇa*); a son of Bṛhatkarman (*V. Purāṇa*); a son of Kṛṣāśva (*Bhā. Purāṇa*); a son of Viśāda (*Bh. Purāṇa*).

Senaka (S) (M) **1.** soldier. **3.** a son of Śambara (*H. Purāṇa*).

Senānī (S) (M) **1.** leader; general; chief. **3.** a rudra (*H. Purāṇa*); a son of Śambara (*H. Purāṇa*); a son of Dhṛtarāṣṭra (*M. Bh.*); another name for Kārttikeya.

Senapāla (S) (M) protector of the army.

Senāpati (S) (M) **1.** leader of an army. **3.** a son of Dhṛtarāṣṭra; another name for Kārttikeya and Śiva.

Senāskandha (S) (M) **1.** company of an army; a battalion. **3.** a son of Śambara (*H. Purāṇa*).

Senika (S) (M) soldier.

Sephalendu (S) (M) moon among the brave.

Śephara (S) (M) charming; delightful.

Śeṣa (S) (M) **1.** remainder. **2.** the rest. **3.** a 1000 headed serpent regarded as the emblem of eternity and represented as forming the couch of Viṣṇu, also known as Ananta, he was partially incarnated as Balabhadrarāma; a prajāpati (*Rāmāyaṇa*); one of the mythical elephants that support the earth.

Śeṣabhūṣaṇa (S) (M) **1.** having Śeṣa as an ornament. **3.** another name for Viṣṇu.

Śeṣadeva (S) (M) lord of serpents; the god Śeṣa.

Śesādri (S) (M) the mountain of Śeṣa.

Śeṣagiri (S) (M) the mountain of Śeṣa.

Śeṣaka (S) (M) Śeṣa.

Śeṣānanda (S) (M) **1.** delighting Śeṣa. **3.** another name for Viṣṇu.

Śeṣānanta (S) (M) Śeṣa, the lord of serpents.

Śeṣanārāyaṇa (S) (M) Viṣṇu and Śeṣa conjoined.

Seśvara (S) (M) believing in god; attaining the favour of gods; theist.

Setu (S) (M) **1.** bond; dam; mound; dike. **2.** Rāma's bridge; an established institution; the sacred symbol Om. **3.** a son of Druhyu and brother of Babhru (*H. Purāṇa*); a Bharata dynasty king who was the son of Babhru and the father of Anārabdha (*Bhāgavata*).

Setuprada (S) (M) **1.** one who binds. **2.** bridge builder. **3.** another name for Kṛṣṇa.

Śevadhi (S) (M) **1.** treasure receptacle; wealth; jewel. **3.** one of the 9 treasures of Kubera.

Śevāra (S) (M) treasury.

Seya (S) (M) **1.** obtaining; achieving. **3.** a son of Viśvāmitra (*M. Bh.*).

Seyana (S) (M) **1.** obtainer; achiever. **3.** a son of Viśvāmitra (*M. Bh.*).

Śībhara (S) (M) fine rain.

Śībhya (S) (M) **1.** moving quickly. **2.** bull. **3.** another name for Śiva.

Śibi (S) (M) **1.** palanquin. **3.** a country; a ṛṣi and part author of *Ṛg Veda* (x); a king renowned for his liberality (*M. Bh.*); a son of Indra (*M. Bh.*); Indra in the 4th Manvantara (*V. Purāṇa*); a son of Manu Ćākṣuṣa (*Bhā. Purāṇa*); a daitya who was the son of Sanhrāda and grandson of Hiraṇyakaśipu (*A. Purāṇa*); a king in the Uśīnara dynasty who was the father of Bhadra, Suvīra, Kekaya and Vṛṣadarbha (*Bhāgavata*); an ancient rājarṣi who was the son of Uśīnara and Mādhavī and the father of Kapotaroma.

Siddha (S) (M) **1.** accomplished; successful; perfected; sacred; divine;

effective; pure; one who has attained power in penance. **3.** semi-divine beings who occupy the sky north of the sun (*V.Purāṇa*); a gandharva son of Kaśyapa and Prādhā (*M. Bh.*); another name for Śiva; *Altingia excelsa.*

Siddhadeva (S) (M) **1.** perfected deity. **3.** another name for Śiva.

Siddhaheman (S) (M) perfected gold.

Siddhānanda (S) (M) one who has achieved happiness.

Siddhanātha (S) (M) lord of power.

Siddhānta (S) (M) **1.** established end. **2.** principle; moral; doctrine.

Siddhapati (S) (M) lord of perfection; lord of power.

Siddhapātra (S) (M) **1.** accomplished devotee. **3.** a warrior of Skanda (*M. Bh.*).

Siddharāja (S) (M) lord of perfection; lord of power.

Siddhārtha (S) (M) **1.** one who has accomplished his aim. **3.** a king who was a partial incarnation of the asura Krodhavaśa (*M. Bh.*); a warrior of Skanda (*M. Bh.*); a minister of Daśaratha (*V. Rāmāyaṇa*); Gautama Buddha in his childhood; the father of the 24th Arhat of the present Avasarpiṇī (*K. Sāgara*); Wild Turnip (*Brassica campestris*).

Siddhasena (S) (M) **1.** with a divine army. **3.** another name for Kārttikeya.

Siddhasevita (S) (M) **1.** honoured by Siddhas. **3.** a form of Bhairava.

Siddhavīrya (S) (M) possessing perfect strength.

Siddhayogin (S) (M) **1.** the perfect yogi. **3.** another name for Śiva.

Siddheśa (S) (M) lord of the blessed.

Siddheśvara (S) (M) **1.** lord of the blessed. **3.** another name for Śiva; Peacock flower (*Caesalpinia pulcherrima*).

Siddhi (S) (M) **1.** accomplishment; power; performance; prosperity. **3.** the son of the agni Vīra and Sarayū (*M. Bh.*); another name for Śiva (*M. Bh.*).

Siddhida (S) (M) **1.** conferring felicity. **3.** another name for Śiva.

Siddhiśvara (S) (M) **1.** lord of magical power. **3.** another name for Śiva.

Sidhra (S) (M) perfect; good; successful; efficacious.

Sidhya (S) (M) auspicious.

Śīghra (S) (M) **1.** quick; speedy; swift. **3.** a son of Agnivarṇa; a solar dynasty king who was the son of Agnipūrṇa and the father of Maru (*Bhāgavata*); another name for Vāyu.

Śīghraga (S) (M) **1.** moving quickly. **3.** a son of Agnivarṇa (*Rāmayaṇa*); another name for the sun; a son of Sampāti (*M. Purāṇa*).

Śīghrīya (S) (M) **1.** quick; fleet. **3.** another name for Viṣṇu and Śiva.

Sikata (S) (M) **1.** sand; gravel. **3.** an ancient hermit (*M. Bh.*).

Śikha (S) (M) **1.** crest; pinnacle; peak. **3.** a serpent demon.

Śikhādhara (S) (M) **1.** with a topknot. **2.** peacock. **3.** another name for Manjuśrī.

Śikhāmaṇi (S) (M) **1.** crest jewel. **2.** chief; best.

Śikhaṇḍiketu (S) (M) **1.** with a peacock emblem. **3.** another name for Skanda.

Śikhaṇḍin (S) (M) **1.** tufted; crested; peacock; arrow. **2.** attaining a certain degree of emancipation. Rosary Pea (*Abrus precatorius*); Yellow Jasmine (*Jasminum bignoniaceum*); a ṛṣi who is one of the stars of the Great Bear; a son of Drupada born as a female but changed into a male who was the reincarnation of Ambā (*M. Bh.*); another name for Viṣṇu-Kṛṣṇa.

Śikharin (S) (M) **1.** pointed; peaked; crested. **2.** resembling the buds of the Arabian Jasmine; mountain.

Śikharīndra (S) (M) the chief of mountains.

Śikhāvān (S) (M) **1.** with a topknot of hair; crested. **3.** a maharṣi in the court of Yudhiṣṭhira (*M. Bh.*); another name for Agni.

Śikhāvarta (S) (M) **1.** surrounded by peaks. **3.** a yakṣa in the court of Kubera (*M. Bh.*).

Śikhidhvaja (S) (M) **1.** peacock marked. **3.** a king of Mālavā and husband of Ćūḍālā; another name for Kārttikeya.

Śikhin (S) (M) **1.** crested; reaching the summit of knowledge; the number 3. **2.** peacock; arrow; a religious mendicant. **3.** a nāga of the Kaśyapa dynasty (*M. Bh.*); Indra under Manu Tāmasa (*Mā. Purāṇa*); the 2nd Buddha (*L. Vistara*); another name for Kāma.

Śikhivāhana (S) (M) **1.** with a peacock as vehicle. **3.** another name for Kārttikeya.

Sikkarī (S) (M) **1.** sprinkler. **2.** the peacock.

Śikṣā (S) (M) **1.** education; knowledge. **2.** training **3.** a king of the gandharvas (*Rāmāyaṇa*).

Śikṣaka (S) (M) **1.** one who bestows knowledge; teacher; preceptor. **3.** a warrior of Skanda (*M. Bh.*).

Śikṣākara (S) (M) **1.** instruction causing. **2.** teacher. **3.** another name for Vyāsa.

Śikṣitā (S) (M) docile; skilfull; clever; modest; studied.

Śikṣu (S) (M) helpful; liberal.

Śikvas (S) (M) mighty; powerful; able.

Śila (S) (M) **1.** gathering corn. **3.** a son of Pāryātra.

Śīla (S) (M) moral conduct; disposition; custom; character; piety; virtue.

Śīlabhadra (S) (M) eminent in virtue.

Śīladhara (S) (M) virtuous; honourable.

Śilādhara (S) (M) **1.** carrying stone. **3.** the chamberlain of Himavata.

Śīladhārin (S) (M) **1.** virtue possessor. **3.** another name for Śiva.

Śīlāditya (S) (M) sun of virtue.

Śīlakīrti (S) (M) glory of virtue.

Śīlaṅga (S) (M) with virtuous features.

Śīlanidhi (S) (M) treasury of virtue.

Śilaukas (S) (M) **1.** dwelling in rock. **3.** another name for Garuḍa.

Śīlavān (S) (M) **1.** virtuous; moral. **3.** a divine maharṣi (*M. Bh.*).

Śilāyūpa (S) (M) **1.** high mountain. **3.** a son of Viśvāmitra (*M. Bh.*).

Śilin (S) (M) **1.** rocky; mountain like. **3.** a nāga in the Takṣaka dynasty (*M. Bh.*).

Śīlin (S) (M) **1.** virtuous. **2.** moral; honest.

Śilīśa (S) (M) lord of the mountain; with a rocklike will.

Śilparāja (S) (M) **1.** king of artisans. **3.** another name for Viśvakarman.

Śilūṣa (S) (M) **1.** *Aegle marmelos.* **3.** ṛṣi who was an early teacher of dancing.

Sīmanta (S) (M) **1.** boundary; limit; parting of the hair. **3.** a son of King Bhadrasena.

Śimyu (S) (M) vigorous; aggressive.

Sindhu (S) (M) **1.** river; ocean; sea. **2.** number 4. **3.** a rāga; a king of the gandharvas (*Rāmāyaṇa*); another name for Varuṇa and Viṣṇu.

Sindhudvīpa (S) (M) **1.** island in the ocean. **3.** a solar dynasty king who was the son of Jahnu and the father of Balākaṣva (*M. Bh.*).

Sindhuka (S) (M) **1.** marine. **3.** a king (*V. Purāṇa*).

Sindhula (S) (M) **1.** procurer of ocean; one who brings the streams. **3.** the father of Bhoja.

Sindhunandana (S) (M) **1.** son of the ocean. **3.** another name for the moon.

Sindhunātha (S) (M) **1.** lord of rivers. **2.** the ocean.

Sindhupati (S) (M) **1.** lord of the waters. **3.** another name for Jayadratha.

Sindhuputra (S) (M) **1.** son of the ocean. **3.** another name for the moon.

Sindhurāja (S) (M) **1.** king of rivers. **2.** the ocean. **3.** another name for Jayadratha.

Sindhusauvīrabhartā (S) (M) **1.** chief of Sindhu-Sauvīra. **3.** another name for Jayadratha.

Sindhuvīrya (S) (M) **1.** warrior of the Sindhus. **3.** a king of the Madras (*Mā. Purāṇa*).

Sindhuvṛṣa (S) (M) **1.** drinking the ocean. **3.** another name for Viṣṇu.

Śineyu (S) (M) **1.** white coloured. **2.** shining. **3.** a son of Uśat (*H. Purāṇa*).

Siṅha (S) (M) **1.** the powerful one. **2.** lion; the zodiac sign of Leo; hero; chief. **3.** a son of Kṛṣṇa (*Bhā. Purāṇa*); a king of the vidyādharas (*K. Sāgara*).

Siṅhabāhu (S) (M) **1.** with the arms of a lion. **2.** very powerful. **3.** the father of Vijaya the founder of the first Buddhist dynasty in Sri Laṅka (*B. Literature*).

Siṅhabala (S) (M) with the strength of a lion.

Siṅhaćandra (S) (M) **1.** moon amongst the lions. **2.** most courageous. **3.** a king who helped Yudhiṣṭhira (*M. Bh.*).

Siṅhadaṅṣṭra (S) (M) **1.** lion toothed. **2.** an arrow. **3.** another name for Śiva.

Siṅhadatta (S) (M) **1.** lion given. **3.** an asura (*K. Sāgara*).

Siṅhadhvaja (S) (M) **1.** lion bannered. **3.** a Buddha.

Siṅhaga (S) (M) **1.** going like a lion. **3.** another name for Śiva.

Siṅhaghoṣa (S) (M) **1.** the roar of a lion. **3.** a Buddha.

Siṅhagiri (S) (M) **1.** the lion mountain; an elevated lion. **3.** the monk who succeeded Dinna as the head of the Jaina church (*J. Literature*).

Siṅhagupta (S) (M) **1.** lion guarded. **3.** the father of Vāgabhaṭa.

Siṅhahanu (S) (M) lion jawed.

Siṅhakarman (S) (M) **1.** behaving like a lion. **2.** achieving lion like deeds.

Siṅhakeli (S) (M) **1.** sporting like a lion. **3.** a bodhisattva.

Sinhaketu (S) (M) **1.** lion bannered. **3.** a warrior of the Pāṇḍava army (*M. Bh.*); a Bodhisattva.

Siṅhamukha (S) (M) **1.** lion faced. **3.** an attendant of Śiva (*H. Purāṇa*).

Siṅhanāda (S) (M) **1.** lion roar. **3.** an asura (*K. Śagara*); a son of Rāvaṇa (*B. Rāmāyaṇa*); a king of Malaya; another name for Śiva.

Siṅhasena (S) (M) **1.** with an army of lions. **3.** a commander of the army of kartavīryārjuna (*Br. Purāṇa*); a Pāñćāla warrior (*M. Bh.*); a king of Ayodhyā and father of Jaina Tīrthaṅkara Anantanātha (*J. Literature*).

Siṅhavāhana (S) (M) **1.** drawn by lions. **3.** another name for Śiva.

Siṅhavakra (S) (M) **1.** lion faced. **3.** a rākṣasa (*Rāmāyaṇa*).

Sinhavikrama (S) (M) **1.** horse. **3.** a king of the vidyādharas (*K. Sāgara*).

Siṅhendra (S) (M) mighty lion.

Siṅhīya (S) (M) small lion.

Śini (S) (M) **1.** bright. **2.** of the race of bright people. **3.** a king of the Yādava dynasty (*M. Bh.*); a son of Sumitra (*M. Bh.*); a son of Garga (*H. Purāṇa*); the father of Sātyaka (*Purāṇas*).

Sinivāk (S) (M) **1.** illustrious preacher. **3.** a hermit in the council of Yudhiṣṭhira (*M. Bh.*).

Sinīvālī (S) (M) **1.** the first day of the new moon. **3.** a goddess presiding over fecundity who in later Vedic texts is the presiding deity of the first day of the new moon; daughter of Aṅgiras (*M. Bh.*); the wife of Dhātṛ and mother of Darṣa (*Bh. Purāṇa*).

Śipi (S) (M) a ray of light.

Śipiviṣṭa (S) (M) **1.** pervaded by rays of light. **3.** another name for RudraŚiva and Viṣṇu.

Śipraka (S) (M) **1.** full cheeked. **3.** the 1st king of the Āndhrakas.

Sīradhvaja (S) (M) **1.** plough bannered. **3.** a son of Hrasvaroman (*V. Purāṇa*); another name for Janaka and Balarāma.

Sīraka (S) (M) **1.** plough. **2.** the sun.

Sīrapāṇi (S) (M) **1.** plough handed. **3.** another name for Balarāma.

Sīrāyudha (S) (M) **1.** plough handed. **3.** another name for Balarāma.

Sīrin (S) (M) **1.** holding a plough. **3.** another name for Balarāma.

Śīrin (S) (M) Kuśa grass.

Śirīṣa (S) (M) Sizzling tree (*Albizzia lebbeck*).

Śiriṣaka (S) (M) **1.** a serpent residing in the *Acacia sirissa*. **3.** a nāga of the Kaśyapa dynasty (*M. Bh.*).

Śiriśeṣa (S) (M) **1.** with only the head left. **3.** another name for Rāhu.

Śirīṣin (S) (M) **1.** *Acacia sirissa*. **3.** a son of Viśvāmitra (*M. Bh.*).

Śīṇapāda (S) (M) **1.** with shrivelled feet. **3.** another name for Yama.

Śirobhūṣana (S) (M) head ornament.

Śirohārin (S) (M) **1.** wearing a garland of heads. **3.** another name for Śiva.

Śiromālin (S) (M) **1.** garlanded with skulls. **3.** another name for Śiva.

Śiromaṇi (S) (M) crest jewel.

Śiromauli (S) (M) crest jewel; eminent; best.

Śiroratna (S) (M) crest jewel.

Sīsara (S) (M) **1.** flown from a straight line. **3.** husband of Saramā the dog.

Śiśaya (S) (M) liberal; munificent.

Śiśira (S) (M) **1.** cool; cold; frost; dew; the cold season. **3.** a mountain; son of Dhara and Manoharā (*M. Bh.*); son of Medhātithi (*Mā. Purāṇa*); son of the vasu Soma and Manoharā (*M. Bh.*); Velvet Leaf (*Cissampelos pareira*).

Śiśiraghna (S) (M) **1.** cold destroying. **3.** another name for Agni.

Śiśirakara (S) (M) **1.** cold rayed. **3.** another name for the moon.

Śiśirānśu (S) (M) **1.** having cold rays. **3.** another name for the moon.

Siṣnu (S) (M) ready to give.

Śiṣṭha (S) (M) **1.** polite; modest; taught; commanded; disciplined; cultured; eminent. **3.** son of Dhruva and Dhānyā, husband of Sucćhāyā and father of Kṛpa, Ripuñjaya, Vṛtta and Vṛka (*M. Purāṇa*).

Śiṣṭi (S) (M) **1.** direction; order; command; punishment. **3.** a son of Dhruva and Śambhu (*V. Purāṇa*).

Śiśu (S) (M) **1.** child; infant. **3.** a son of Sāraṇa (*V. Purāṇa*); a son born to the Saptamātṛs due to the blessing of Subrahmaṇya (*M. Bh.*); a descendant of Aṅgiras; another name for Skanda.

Śiśubhūpati (S) (M) young prince.

Śiśukumāra (S) (M) **1.** young prince. **3.** a ṛṣi who lived in the form of a crocodile (*P. Brāhmaṇa*); a constellation said to be a starry form of Viṣṇu (*V. Purāṇa*).

Śiśula (S) (M) infant; child.

Śiśumāra (S) (M) **1.** porpoise (*Delphinus gangelicus*); child killer. **3.** a collection of stars supposed to represent a dolphin and personified as a son of Doṣa and Śarvarī or as father of Brāhmī the wife of Dhruva (*M. Bh.*).

Śiśunāga (S) (M) **1.** young snake; young elephant. **3.** the first king of the Śiśunāga dynasty and the father of Kākavarṇa (*Vā. Purāṇa*); a king of Magadha (*Bhā. Purāṇa*).

Śiśunandi (S) (M) young bull.

Śiśupāla (S) (M) **1.** child protector. **3.** the king of Ćedi who was an incarnation of Jaya, the gatekeeper of Viṣṇu, born as the son of King Damaghoṣa and Śrutaśravas, he was killed by Kṛṣṇa (*Bhāgavata*).

Śiśupalātmaja (S) (M) **1.** son of Śiśupala. **3.** another name for Dhṛṣṭaketu.

Śiśupriya (S) (M) **1.** dear to children. **2.** treacle; the White Waterlily (*Nymphaea alba*).

Śiśuroman (S) (M) **1.** having hair like that of a child. **3.** a nāga in the family of Takṣaka (*M. Bh.*).

Śita (S) (M) **1.** good natured. **3.** a son of Viśvāmitra (*M. Bh.*).

Sita (S) (M) **1.** bright; white; candid; pure. **3.** an attendant of Skanda (*M. Bh.*); another name for the planet Venus.

Śītabhānu (S) (M) **1.** cool rayed. **3.** another name for the moon.

Sitābja (S) (M) White Lotus (*Nelumbium speciosum*).

Sitakamala (S) (M) White Lotus (*Nelumbium speciosum*).

Śītakara (S) (M) **1.** cool rayed. **3.** another name for the moon.

Sitakara (S) (M) **1.** white rayed. **3.** another name for the moon.

Sitakarman (S) (M) pure in deed.

Sitakeśa (S) (M) **1.** whitehaired. **3.** a dānava (*H. Purāṇa*).

Śītakiraṇa (S) (M) **1.** cool rayed. **3.** another name for the moon.

Śītala (S) (M) **1.** cool; cold. **2.** calm; gentle; free from passion; the wind. **3.** *Michelia champaka*; the 10th Arhat of the present Avasarpinī; another name for the moon.

Śītalanātha (S) (M) **1.** lord of the gentle. **3.** the 10th Jaina Tīrthaṅkara, he was the son of King Dṛḍharatha and Sunandā of Bhādilpura (*J. Literature*).

Śītalaprasāda (S) (M) given in the cold season.

Sitamanas (S) (M) pure hearted.

Sitamaṇi (S) (M) crystal.

Sitāmbara (S) (M) **1.** clothed in white. **2.** one of the 2 divisions of Jaina monks.

Sitāmbuja (S) (M) White Lotus (*Nelumbium speciosum*).

Sitānana (S) (M) **1.** white faced. **3.** an attendant of Śiva; another name for Garuḍa.

Sītānātha (S) (M) **1.** lord of Sītā. **3.** another name for Rāma.

Sitānṣu (S) (M) **1.** white rayed. **3.** another name for the moon.

Śītanśu (S) (M) **1.** cool rayed. **3.** another name for the moon.

Śītapāṇi (S) (M) **1.** cold handed; cool rayed. **3.** another name for the moon.

Sītāpati (S) (M) **1.** lord of Sītā. **3.** another name for Rāma.

Sitaprabha (S) (M) white crystal.

Sītārāma (S) (M) Sītā and Rāma conjoined.

Sitarañjana (S) (M) yellow.

Sitaraśmi (S) (M) **1.** white rayed. **3.** another name for the moon.

Sitaruċi (S) (M) **1.** bright. **3.** another name for the moon.

Śītaśman (S) (M) moonstone.

Sitāśva (S) (M) **1.** with white horses. **3.** another name for Arjuna.

Sitaturaga (S) (M) **1.** white horsed. **3.** another name for Arjuna.

Sitavājin (S) (M) **1.** with white horses. **3.** another name for Arjuna.

Sītāvallabha (S) (M) **1.** beloved of Sītā. **3.** another name for Rāma.

Sitavarman (S) (M) armoured in purity.

Sīteśa (S) (M) **1.** lord of Sītā. **3.** another name for Rāma.

Śitikaṇṭha (S) (M) **1.** white necked; blue necked. **3.** a nāga (*M. Bh.*); another name for Śiva.

Sitikanṭha (S) (M) **1.** dark throated. **3.** another name for Śiva.

Śitikeśa (S) (M) **1.** white haired. **3.** a warrior of Skanda (*M. Bh.*).

Śitīkṣu (S) (M) **1.** striving for the earth. **3.** a son of Uśanas (*V. Purāṇa*).

Sitiman (S) (M) whiteness.

Śitipṛṣṭha (S) (M) **1.** white backed. **3.** a serpent priest.

Śitiratna (S) (M) **1.** blue gem. **2.** sapphire.

Sitivāsas (S) (M) **1.** dark clothed. **3.** another name for Balarāma.

Sitodara (S) (M) **1.** white bellied. **3.** another name for Kubera.

Śiva (S) (M) **1.** in whom all things lie; auspicious; propitious; gracious; favourable; benign; kind; friendly; dear. **2.** the auspicious one. **3.** the destroying and reproducing deity who constitutes the 3rd god of the triad, in his destructive character he is Kāla often identified with time, as reproducer his symbol is the phallus or liṅga, he has three eyes, the middle one in the forehead bears the crescent moon; his thickly matted and coiled hair bears the Gaṅgā, his throat is dark blue, around his neck are garlands of snakes and skulls and in his hand he holds a trident, his consort is Durgā or Pārvatī, Umā, Gaurī, Kālī and his sons are Gaṇeśa and Kārttikeya, his heaven is Kailāsa mountain in the Himālayas, his ferocious form is Rudra, he is considered the father of the 11 rudras; a son of Medhātithi (*Mā. Purāṇa*); a son of Idhmajīhva (*Bhā. Purāṇa*); *Commiphorra mukul*; *Curcuma longa*; Couch Grass (*Cynodon dactylon*); Prosopis spicigera; Black Myrobalan (*Terminalia chebula*).

Śivabhadra (S) (M) an auspicious person; servant of Śiva.

Śivabhāskara (S) (M) Śiva compared to the sun.

Śivadāsa (S) (M) servant of Śiva.

Śivadatta (S) (M) given by Śiva.

Śivadeva (S) (M) lord of grace; prosperity and welfare.

Śivadīna (S) (M) devotee of Śiva.

Śivagāmi (S) (M) follower of Śiva.

Śivagaṇa (S) (M) attendant of Śiva.

Śivagati (S) (M) **1.** auspicious; happy; prosperous. **3.** a Jaina Arhat of the past Utsarpinī.

Śivaguru (S) (M) **1.** Śiva the preceptor. **3.** the son of Vidyādhirāja and father of Śankarāćārya.

Śivājī (S) (M) **1.** the auspicious one. **3.** a Marāṭhā king.

Śivakara (S) (M) **1.** causing happiness; auspicious. **3.** a Jaina Arhat of past Utsarpinī.

Śivakeśava (S) (M) Śiva and Kṛṣṇa conjoined.

Śivakiṅkara (S) (M) servant of Śiva.

Śivakīrtana (S) (M) **1.** Śiva praiser. **3.** another name for Viṣṇu.

Śivakumāra (S) (M) son of Śiva.

Śivalāla (S) (M) son of Śiva.

Śivam (S) (M) **1.** of Śiva. **2.** prosperous; auspicious; graceful.

Śivamūrti (S) (M) idol of Śiva.

Śivānanda (S) (M) Śiva's joy.

Śivanārāyaṇa (S) (M) Śiva and Viṣṇu conjoined.

Śivanātha (S) (M) lord Śiva.

Śivāṅka (S) (M) mark of Śiva.

Śivaṅkara (S) (M) **1.** punishment personified as an attendant of Śiva. **3.** a demon causing illness (*H. Purāṇa*).

Śivapattra (S) (M) **1.** leaf of prosperity. **2.** Red Lotus flower (*Nymphaea rubra*).

Śivaprakāśa (S) (M) light of prosperity; light of Śiva.

Śivaprasāda (S) (M) **1.** given by Śiva. **3.** the father of Gaṅgādhara.

Śivaputra (S) (M) **1.** son of Śiva. **3.** another name for Gaṇeśa.

Śivarāja (S) (M) Śiva the lord.

Śivarāma (S) (M) pervaded by Śiva; Śiva and Rāma conjoined.

Śivaratha (S) (M) the chariot of Śiva.

Śivarūpa (S) (M) the form or image of Śiva.

Śivasahāya (S) (M) companion of Śiva.

Śivaśakti (S) (M) Śiva and his Śakti conjoined.

Śivaśaṅkara (S) (M) Śiva the prosperous.

Śivaśaraṇa (S) (M) protected by Śiva.

Śivaśekhara (S) (M) **1.** Śiva's crest. **3.** another name for the moon.

Śivasiṅha (S) (M) **1.** lion of prosperity and grace. **3.** a king of Mithilā.

Śivaśrī (S) (M) glory of Śiva.

Śivasūnu (S) (M) **1.** son of Śiva. **3.** another name for Gaṇeśa and Kārttikeya.

Śivasvāmin (S) (M) **1.** considering Śiva as master; benign lord. **3.** a Sanskṛt poet in the court of the King of Kāśmīra, King Avantivarman (854-888 A.D.).

Śivatama (S) (M) most fortunate.

Śivavarman (S) (M) prosperous protector; protected by Śiva.

Śivendra (S) (M) Śiva and Indra conjoined.

Śiveśvara (S) (M) god of welfare.

Skambha (S) (M) **1.** support; prop. **3.** the fulcrum of the universe identified with the Supreme Being.

Skanda (S) (M) **1.** hopper; attacker. **2.** king; clever; quicksilver. **3.** Kārttikeya as the god of war (*M. Bh.*); another name for Śiva.

Skandaguru (S) (M) **1.** father of Skanda. **3.** another name for Śiva.

Skandajit (S) (M) **1.** conqueror of Skanda. **3.** another name for Viṣṇu.

Skandha (S) (M) **1.** shoulder. **3.** a nāga of the family of Dhṛtarāṣṭra (*M. Bh.*).

Skandhākṣa (S) (M) **1.** with eyes like quicksilver. **3.** a warrior of Skanda (*M. Bh.*).

Śliṣṭhi (S) (M) **1.** adherence; connection; embrace. **3.** a son of Dhruva and Śambhu and the husband of Sućchāyā and the father of Ripu, Ripuñjaya, Puṇya, Vṛkala and Vṛkatejas (*H. Purāṇa*).

Smadibha (S) (M) having followers.

Smarabhū (S) (M) arisen from love.

Smaraguru (S) (M) **1.** love preceptor. **3.** another name for Viṣṇu.

Smarahara (S) (M) **1.** destroying Kāma. **3.** another name for Śiva.

Smarasakha (S) (M) **1.** love's friend. **2.** the spring; the moon.

Smarodgitha (S) (M) **1.** love song. **3.** a son of Devakī (*Bh. Purāṇa*).

Śmaśānavāsī (S) (M) **1.** residing in burning grounds. **3.** another name for Śiva.

Smayana (S) (M) smile; gentle laughter.

Smita (S) (M) smiling; blossomed.

Smṛta (S) (M) recorded; regarded; remembered.

Sneha (S) (M) oiliness; affection; tenderness; love.

Snehakānta (S) (M) lord of love; beloved of love.

Snehana (S) (M) **1.** anointing; lubricating; affectionate; a friend. **3.** another name for the moon and Śiva.

Snehaprabha (S) (M) light of love.

Snehu (S) (M) **1.** moist. **3.** another name for the moon.

Śobhaka (S) (M) brilliant; beautiful.

Śobhana (S) (M) **1.** handsome; excellent. **3.** the son-in-law of Mućukuṇḍa; another name for Śiva and Agni; *Curcuma longa*.

Śobhin (S) (M) brilliant; splendid; beautiful.

Śobhita (S) (M) splendid; beautiful; adorned; embellished.

Šoćiṣkeśa (S) (M) flame haired; another name for Agni and the sun.

Šoćiṣṭha (S) (M) most brilliant.

Sohan (H) (M) handsome.

Śoka (S) (M) **1.** flame; glow; heat; sorrow. **3.** sorrow personified as the son of death or of Droṇa and Abhimatī (*Purāṇas*)

Sollasa (S) (M) rejoicing; delighted.

Soma (S) (M) **1.** juice. **2.** juice of the Soma plant offered in libations to the gods. **3.** personified as an important Vedic god identified with Ćandra, the moon and ray of light; water; a son of Agni Bhānu and Niṣā (*M. Bh.*); one of the 8 vasus (*V. Purāṇa*); a son of Jarāsandha (*Bhāgavata*); another name for Kubera, Śiva, Yama and Sugrīva.

Somabandhu (S) (M) friend of the moon; the white esculent Water Lily (*Nymphaea alba*).

Somābhojana (S) (M) **1.** eating Soma. **3.** a son of Garuḍa (*M. Bh.*).

Somabhu (S) (M) **1.** Somaborn; belonging to the family of the moon. **3.** the 4th Jaina Vasudeva; another name for Mercury.

Somaćandra (S) (M) the tranquil moon.

Somadatta (S) (M) **1.** given by the moon. **3.** an Ikṣvāku dynasty king of Pāñćāla who was the son of Kṛśāśva and the grandson of Sahadeva (*V. Rāmāyaṇa*); a Kuru dynasty king who was the son of Bālhīka and the father of Bhūri, Bhūriśavas, and Śala.

Somadeva (S) (M) **1.** god of the moon. **3.** the author of the *Kathāsaritsāgara*.

Somadhara (S) (M) moon bearing; the sky; heaven.

Somāditya (S) (M) the sun and moon conjoined.

Somagarbha (S) (M) **1.** creator of nectar. **3.** another name for Viṣṇu.

Somaja (S) (M) **1.** son of the moon. **3.** another name for the planet Mercury.

Somaka (S) (M) **1.** little moon. **3.** a Pāñcāla king who was the son of Sahadeva and the grandson of Subhāsa (*M. Bh.*); a ṛṣi (*V. Samhitā*); a son of Kṛṣṇa (*Bhā. Purāṇa*).

Somakānta (S) (M) as lovely as the moon; beloved of the moon; the moonstone.

Somākhya (S) (M) **1.** as virtuous as the moon. **2.** the Red Lotus (*Nymphaea rubra*).

Somakīrti (S) (M) **1.** as famous as the moon. **3.** a son of Dhṛtarāṣṭra (*M. Bh.*).

Somāla (S) (M) soft; placid.

Somalaka (S) (M) topaz.

Somāli (S) (M) **1.** soft; bland. **3.** father of Anuśrutaśravas (*V. Purāṇa*).

Soman (S) (M) **1.** Soma sacrificer. **3.** the moon.

Somanandin (S) (M) **1.** delighted by the moon. **3.** an attendant of Śiva.

Somanātha (S) (M) **1.** lord of the moon. **3.** a liṅga of Śiva.

Somānśu (S) (M) moonbeam; a shoot of the Soma plant.

Somapa (S) (M) **1.** one who drinks Soma juice; Soma sacrificer. **3.** a viśvadeva (*M. Bh.*); an attendant of Skanda (*M. Bh.*); an asura (*H. Purāṇa*); one of the 7 Pitṛs who dwells in the palace of Brahmā.

Somapāla (S) (M) **1.** guardian of the Soma. **3.** another name for the gandharvas.

Somapati (S) (M) **1.** lord of Soma. **3.** another name for Indra.

Somapi (S) (M) **1.** drinker of Soma. **3.** a son of Sahadeva.

Somaputra (S) (M) **1.** son of the moon. **3.** another name for the planet Mercury.

Somarāga (S) (M) **1.** nectar rāga. **3.** a rāga.

Somarāja (S) (M) **1.** lord of Soma. **3.** another name for the moon.

Somaraśmi (S) (M) **1.** moonlight. **3.** a gandharvā.

Somaśekhara (S) (M) **1.** moon crested. **3.** another name for Śiva.

Somasena (S) (M) **1.** with an army of moons; lord of the moon. **3.** a son of Śambara (*H. Purāṇa*).

Somasindhu (S) (M) **1.** ocean of Soma. **3.** another name for Viṣṇu.

Somaśravas (S) (M) **1.** as famous as the moon. **3.** a hermit who was the son of Śrutaśravas.

Somasundara (S) (M) beautiful moon.

Somavarćas (S) (M) **1.** with the splendour of the moon. **3.** a viśvadeva (*M. Bh.*); a gandharva (*H. Purāṇa*).

Somavat (S) (M) like the moon; containing Soma.

Somendra (S) (M) **1.** belonging to Soma and Indra; lord of Soma. **3.** another name for the moon.

Somendu (S) (M) the moon.

Someśa (S) (M) **1.** lord of Soma. **3.** another name for the moon.

Someśvara (S) (M) **1.** lord of the moon. **3.** a liṅga of Śiva set up by Soma; another name for Kṛṣṇa.

Somin (S) (M) **1.** lord of Soma; possessing Soma. **3.** another name for the moon.

Somodbhava (S) (M) **1.** sprung from the moon; moon producer. **3.** another name for Kṛṣṇa.

Śoṇa (S) (M) **1.** redness; fire. **3.** a Pāñćāla prince (*Ś. Brāhmaṇa*); a river.

Śonāhaya (S) (M) **1.** with red horses. **3.** another name for Droṇa.

Sonala (H) (M) golden.

Sonam (H) (M) **1.** gold-like. **2.** beautiful; lucky.

Śoṇapadma (S) (M) red lotus (*Nymphaea rubra*).

Śoṇaratna (S) (M) **1.** red gem. **2.** ruby.

Śoṇaśman (S) (M) ruby.

Śoṇāśva (S) (M) **1.** with red horses. **3.** a son of Rājādhideva (*H. Purāṇa*); another name for Droṇa.

Śonāśvavāha (S) (M) **1.** borne by red horses. **3.** another name for Droṇa.

Śoṇitoda (S) (M) **1.** blood and water. **3.** a yakṣa in Kubera's assembly (*M. Bh.*).

Śoṇopala (S) (M) ruby.

Śoṣana (S) (M) **1.** absorption; drying up; draining; parching. **3.** an arrow of Kāma.

Soṣman (S) (M) having heat; warm; hot.

Sotpala (S) (M) possessing lotuses.

Sotṛ (S) (M) **1.** generating. **2.** one who extracts Soma.

Sovala (S) (M) powerful.

Soven (S) (M) beautiful.

Sphaṭikayaśas (S) (M) **1.** crystal-like flame. **3.** a vidyadhara (*K. Sāgara*).

Sphuliṅga (S) (M) **1.** sparks. **3.** another name for Agni.

Sraja (S) (M) **1.** garland. **3.** a viśvadeva (*M. Bh.*).

Śrama (S) (M) **1.** labour. **2.** toll; exertion; weariness. **3.** a son of the vasu Āpa (*V. Purāṇa*); a son of Vasudeva (*Bh. Purāṇa*).

Śrānta (S) (M) **1.** tired; calmed; tranquil. **3.** a son of Āpa (*V. Purāṇa*).

Śrāntha (S) (M) **1.** tying; binding; stringing together. **3.** another name for Viṣṇu.

Śrāva (S) (M) **1.** hearing; listening. **3.** a son of King Yuvanāśva and the father of King Śrāvasta (*M. Bh.*).

Śravā (S) (M) **1.** loud praise; glory; fame; renown. **3.** a son of maharṣi Santa and the father of Tāmasa (*M. Bh.*).

Śravaṇa (S) (M) **1.** ear; to hear; lame. **3.** a nakṣatra presided over by Viṣṇu and which contains 3 stars; a son of Naraka (*Bh. Purāṇa*); a son of Murāsura (*Bhāgavata*); *Sphaeranthus indicus*.

Śrāvaṇa (S) (M) **1.** the rainy season of July/August. **3.** son of Murāsura (*Bhāgavata*); one of the 27 constellations (*M. Bh.*).

Śravaṇīya (S) (M) worthy to listen.

Śrāvasta (S) (M) **1.** much heard; famous. **3.** the son of King Srāva (*M. Bh.*).

Śraviṣṭha (S) (M) most famous.

Śraviṣṭhāramaṇa (S) (M) **1.** lover of Śravisthā. **3.** another name for the moon.

Śravojit (S) (M) winning renown; glorious.

Śreṇi (S) (M) line; row; troop; necklace; garland; chain.

Śreṇika (S) (M) **1.** front tooth. **3.** a king of Magadha and follower of Mahāvīra.

Śreṇiniān (S) (M) **1.** having followers. **3.** a rājarṣi who fought on the side of the Pāṇḍavas (*M. Bh.*).

Śreṣṭha (S) (M) **1.** excellent; best; chief; foremost. **3.** another name for Viṣṇu and Kubera.

Śreṣṭhapāla (S) (M) the best guardian.

Śreyānśanātha (S) (M) **1.** lord of fortune; lord of bliss; master of welfare. **3.** the 11th Jaina Tīrthaṅkara and the son of King Viṣṇu and Queen Viṣṇu of Sinhapur.

Śreyas (S) (M) **1.** best; most beautiful; excellent; auspicious; fortunate. **3.** the deity of the Bodhi tree (*L. Vistara*).

Śṛgāla (S) (M) **1.** jackal. **3.** a king (*M. Bh.*).

Sṛgalavadana (S) (M) **1.** jackal-faced. **3.** an asura (*H. Purāṇa*).

Śrī (S) (M) **1.** diffusing light. **2.** adorning; sacred; holy. **3.** a rāga.

Śrībandhu (S) (M) **1.** brother of Lakṣmī. **3.** another name for the moon.

Śrībhadra (S) (M) **1.** best among men. **3.** a nāga.

Śrībhānu (S) (M) **1.** divine sun. **3.** a son of Kṛṣṇa and Satyabhāmā (*Bhā. Purāṇa*).

Śrībhartṛ (S) (M) **1.** husband of Śrī. **3.** another name for Viṣṇu.

Śrībinda (S) (M) **1.** knower of fortune. **3.** a demon slain by Indra.

Śrībindu (S) (M) mark of fortune.

Śrīćanda (S) (M) divine moon.

Śrīćandra (S) (M) divine moon.

Śrīda (S) (M) **1.** bestowing prosperity. **3.** another name for Kubera.

Śrīdāman (S) (M) **1.** tied by fortune. **3.** a playmate of Kṛṣṇa.

Śrīdatta (S) (M) **1.** fortune giver. **3.** a son Kālanemi (*K. Sāgara*).

Śrīdayita (S) (M) **1.** Śrī's husband. **3.** another name for Viṣṇu.

Śrīdhara (S) (M) **1.** possessor of fortune. **3.** a form of Viṣṇu (*M. Bh.*); the 7th Arhat of the past Utsarpiṇī.

Śrīgaṇeśa (S) (M) divine Gaṇeśa; divine master of the horde.

Śrīgarbha (S) (M) **1.** having welfare as the inner nature. **3.** a Bodhisattva; another name for Viṣṇu.

Śrīgupta (S) (M) **1.** possessing a hidden treasure; possessed with an inner glory. **3.** a teacher of the Mādhyamika-Svātantrika school of Buddhism at Nālandā (8th century).

Śrīhari (S) (M) **1.** lion of prosperity. **3.** another name for Viṣṇu.

Śrīharṣa (S) (M) **1.** delighting in prosperity. **3.** author of *Naiṣadhaćarita* (12th century A. D.).

Śrīja (S) (M) **1.** born of Śrī. **3.** another name for Kāma.

Śrīkānta (S) (M) **1.** beloved of Śrī. **3.** another name for Viṣṇu.

Śrīkaṇṭha (S) (M) **1.** beautiful throated. **3.** another name for Śiva.

Śrīkaṇṭhasakha (S) (M) **1.** friend of Śiva. **3.** another name for Kubera.

Śrīkara (S) (M) **1.** causing prosperity. **3.** another name for Viṣṇu.

Śrīkeśava (S) (M) the divine Kṛṣṇa.

Śrīkīrtana (S) (M) chanting for prosperity.

Śrīkṛṣṇa (S) (M) divine Kṛṣṇa.

Śrīmālā (S) (M) blossom of the Parijāta tree (*Nyctantes arbor tristis*).

Śrīman (S) (M) **1.** bearer of prosperity, beauty and grace. **2.** fortunate. **3.** a son of Nimi and grandson of Dattātreya.

Śrīmanta (S) (M) pleasant; charming; glorious; royal; wealthy.

Śrīmat (S) (M) **1.** bearer of prosperity. **2.** beautiful; charming; pleasant; glorious; auspicious; royal; wealthy. **3.** a son of Nimi (*M. Bh.*); another name for Viṣṇu, Kubera and Śākyamitra.

Śrīmohana (S) (M) **1.** seducer of grace; lover of Lakṣml or Rādhā. **3.** divine Kṛṣṇa.

Śrīmukha (S) (M) a beautiful face.

Śrīmūrti (S) (M) divine image; idol.

Śrīnanda (S) (M) **1.** delighting Śrī. **3.** another name for Viṣṇu.

Śrīnandana (S) (M) **1.** son of Śrī. **3.** another name for Kāma and Rāma.

Śrīnātha (S) (M) **1.** lord of Śrī. **3.** another name for Viṣṇu.

Śrīnidhi (S) (M) **1.** receptacle of beauty. **3.** another name for Viṣṇu.

Śrīniketa (S) (M) **1.** abode of beauty; abode of Śrī. **2.** lotus flower (*Nelumbo speciosum*).

Śrīniketana (S) (M) **1.** dwelling with Śrī. **3.** another name for Viṣṇu.

Śrīnivāsa (S) (M) abode of Śrī.

Śrīpāda (S) (M) divine feet.

Śrīpadma (S) (M) **1.** divine lotus. **3.** another name for Kṛṣṇa.

Śrīpāla (S) (M) **1.** protector of prosperity. **3.** another name for Viṣṇu.

Śrīpati (S) (M) **1.** lord of Śrī; lord of fortune. **3.** another name for Viṣṇu-Kṛṣṇa as worshipped on the hill Venkaṭa.

Śrīputra (S) (M) **1.** son of Śrī. **3.** another name for Kāma.

Śrīrāma (S) (M) the divine Rāmaćandra.

Śrīrāmakṛṣṇa (S) (M) a great Hindu philospher born in 1836 who was the son of Khudīrāma Ćaṭṭopādhyāya and Ćandrādevī.

Śrīraṅga (S) (M) **1.** divine Viṣṇu. **3.** a Vaiṣṇava temple near Tricinopoly.

Śrīraṅgam (S) (M) divine Kṛṣṇa.

Śrīraṅgeśa (S) (M) **1.** lord of Śrīranga. **3.** another name for Viṣṇu.

Śrīraṅgeśvarī (S) (M) consort of Śrīraṅga.

Śrīrañjana (S) (M) **1.** amusing Lakṣmī. **3.** another name for Viṣṇu.

Srīrūpā (S) (M) **1.** with the form of Lakṣmī. **3.** another name for Rādhā.

Śrīśa (S) (M) **1.** lord of fortune; lord of Śrī. **3.** another name for Viṣṇu and Rāma.

Śrīsahodara (S) (M) **1.** brother of Śrī. **3.** another name for the moon.

Śrīśaila (S) (M) divine rock.

Śrīsvāmin (S) (M) **1.** lord of Śrī. **3.** the father of Bhaṭṭi.

Śrīsvarūpa (S) (M) **1.** with the form of Śrī. **3.** a disciple of Ćaitanya.

Śrīsvarūpiṇī (S) (M) **1.** with the form of Śrī. **3.** another name for Rādhā.

Śrītejas (S) (M) **1.** extremely glorious. **3.** a Buddha (*L. Vistara*).

Śrīvaha (S) (M) **1.** bringing fortune. **3.** a nāga son of Kaśyapa and Kadru (*M. Bh.*).

Śrīvallabha (S) (M) favourite of fortune.

Śrīvarāha (S) (M) **1.** divine boar. **3.** another name for Viṣṇu.

Śrīvardhana (S) (M) **1.** increaser of fortune. **3.** another name for Śiva and Viṣṇu.

Śrīvāsa (S) (M) **1.** abode of Śrī. **3.** another name for Viṣṇu.

Śrīvatsa (S) (M) **1.** favourite of Srī. **3.** a mole on Viṣṇu's chest (*M. Bh.*); another name for Viṣṇu.

Śrīvatsalāñćana (S) (M) **1.** marked by a white curl of hair on the chest. **3.** another name for Kṛṣṇa.

Śriyāditya (S) (M) divine sun.

Śriyaśas (S) (M) desirous of splendour and glory.

Sṛjavāna (S) (M) **1.** wearing a garland. **3.** a son of Dyutimat (*V. Purāṇa*).

Śṛmala (S) (M) **1.** wrestler. **3.** an asura.

Śṛṅga (S) (M) **1.** horn; peak; summit of a mountain; highest point; perfection. **3.** a muni who is worshipped in some parts of India in times of drought; the musical instrument of Śiva (*M. Bh.*).

Śṛṅgapriya (S) (M) **1.** fond of hornblowing. **3.** another name for Śiva.

Śṛṅgāra (S) (M) **1.** horned one. **2.** love; passion; elegant dress; dainty; gold; powder.

Śṛṅgārajanman (S) (M) **1.** born from desire. **3.** another name for Kāma.

Śṛṅgavān (S) (M) **1.** with horns. **3.** a sage who was the son of Gālava (*M. Bh.*).

Śṛṅgavera (S) (M) **1.** full of horns; dried ginger. **3.** a nāga of the Kaurava family (*M. Bh.*).

Śṛṅgaviśa (S) (M) **1.** one who stays on a peak. **3.** a sage from whose stomach Indra was born (*Ṛg Veda*).

Śṛṅgeśa (S) (M) **1.** lord of peaks. **3.** another name for Śiva.

Śṛṅgi (S) (M) **1.** horned; crested peaked. **2.** bull; mountain. **3.** a mythical mountain chain encirling the earth; the sage who cursed Parīkṣit (*M. Bh.*).

Śṛñjaya (S) (M) **1.** giving victory. **3.** an Ikṣvāku king who was the son of Śviti and also the father of Sućismitā and Suvarṇaṣṭhīvī (*M. Bh.*); a royal hermit who was the grandfather of Ambā of Kāśī (*M. Bh.*); a son of Devavata (*Ṛg Veda*).

Srotasya (S) (M) **1.** flowing in streams. **2.** a thief. **3.** another name for Śiva.

Sṛṣṭa (S) (M) **1.** creator. **3.** another name for Brahmā.

Sṛtañjaya (S) (M) **1.** conquering the running one. **3.** a son of Karamjit (*Bh. Purāṇa*).

Śruṣṭhigu (S) (M) **1.** obedient. **3.** a ṛṣi.

Śruta (S) (M) **1.** heard; known; famous; celebrated; knowledge; scriptures. **3.** a son of Bhagīratha (*H. Purāṇa*); a son of Kṛṣṇa and Kālindī (*Bhā. Purāṇa*); a son of Upagu (*V. Purāṇa*); a son of Bhīmasena (*A. Purāṇa*); a solar dynasty king who was the son of Subhāṣaṇa and father of Jaya (*Bhāgavata*); a Bharata dynasty king who was the son of Dharmanetra and father of Dṛḍhasena (*Bhāgavata*).

Śrutabandhu (S) (M) **1.** companion of knowledge. **3.** a ṛṣi.

Śrutadeva (S) (M) **1.** the well known god; with god like knowledge. **3.** a son of Kṛṣṇa; a servant of Kṛṣṇa.

Śrutadharman (S) (M) **1.** follower of scriptures. **3.** a son of Udāpi (*H. Purāṇa*).

Śrutadhī (S) (M) receptacle of knowledge.

Śrutadhvaja (S) (M) **1.** characterized by knowledge. **3.** a brother of King Virāṭa (*M. Bh.*).

Śrutāhva (S) (M) **1.** known to be firm. **3.** a king on the side of the Pāṇḍavas (*M. Bh.*).

Śrutakakṣa (S) (M) **1.** abode of scriptures. **3.** a ṛṣi.

Śrutakarman (S) (M) **1.** according to the scriptures. **3.** a son of Sahadeva (*M. Bh.*); a son of Arjuna (*M. Bh.*); a son of Somapi (*V. Purāṇa*).

Śrutakīrti (S) (M) **1.** one whose fame is heard about. **3.** a son of Arjuna and Draupadī (*M. Bh.*).

Śrutanābha (S) (M) **1.** centre of the scriptures. **3.** a solar dynasty king who was the son of Bhagīratha and father of Sindhudvīpa (*Bhāgavata*).

Śrutānīka (S) (M) **1.** with a celebrated army. **3.** a brother of King Virāṭa (*M. Bh.*)

Śrutañjaya (S) (M) **1.** with celebrated victory. **3.** a brother of King Suśarmā of Trigarta (*M. Bh.*); a son of Senajit (*V. Purāṇa*); a son of Satyāyu (*Bhā. Purāṇa*); a son of Karmajit.

Śrutānta (S) (M) **1.** the limit of fame. **2.** most famous. **3.** a son of Dhṛtarāṣṭra (*M. Bh.*).

Śrutapāla (S) (M) guardian of knowledge.

Śrutārva (S) (M) **1.** with known resistance. **3.** a son of Dhṛtarāṣṭra (*M. Bh.*)

Śrutārya (S) (M) **1.** knower of the scriptures; learned; famous. **3.** a hermit mentioned in the *Ṛg Veda*.

Śrutaśarman (S) (M) **1.** celebrated protector; protector of knowledge; armoured with knowledge. **3.** a son of Udāyus (*V. Purāṇa*); a prince of the vidyādharas (*K. Sāgara*).

Śrutasena (S) (M) **1.** with a famous army. **3.** a brother of King Janamejaya (*Ś. Brāhmaṇa*); the younger brother of the serpent Takṣaka (*M. Bh.*); an asura; a warrior on the Kaurava side (*M. Bh.*); a son of Sahadeva (*M. Bh.*); a son of Parīkṣit (*M. Bh.*); a son of Śatrughna (*Bh. Purāṇa*); a son of Bhīma (*Bhā. Purāṇa*); a son of Śambara (*H. Purāṇa*); a prince of Gokarṇa (*K. Sāgara*).

Śrutasoma (S) (M) **1.** moon. **3.** a son of Bhīma (*V. Purāṇa*).

Śrutaśravas (S) (M) **1.** listener of scriptures. **3.** a king of Magadha (*Bhāgavata*); a maharṣi who was the father of Somaśravas and a priest of Janamejaya (*M. Bh.*); a rājarṣi in the palace of Yama (*M. Bh.*).

Śrutaśrī (S) (M) **1.** with wellknown wealth. **3.** an asura (*M. Bh.*).

Śrutavat (S) (M) **1.** learned; pious. **3.** a son of Somapi (*Bhā. Purāṇa*).

Śrutayajña (S) (M) **1.** acting according to the scriptures. **3.** a Bharata dynasty king who was the son of Karmajit and grandson of Vivanava (*Bhāgavata*).

Śrutāyudha (S) (M) **1.** possessor of famous weapons. **3.** a king of Kaliṅga who was the son of Varuṇa by Parṇāśā (*M. Bh.*).

Śrutāyus (S) (M) **1.** with a celebrated life. **3.** a son of Purūravas (*M. Bh.*); a Kṣatriya king who was a partial incarnation of the daitya Krodhavaśa (*M. Bh.*); a brother of Ayutāyus who fought on the Kaurava side (*M. Bh.*); a Solar dynasty king and descendant of Kuśa.

Śruti (S) (M) **1.** knowledge of scriptures. **3.** a king of ancient India (*M. Bh.*).

Śrutirañjana (S) (M) delighting in knowledge.

Śrutya (S) (M) to be famous; glorious.

Stambamitra (S) (M) **1.** friend of grass. **3.** a bird child of sage Mandapāla and Jaritā (*M. Bh.*).

Stambha (S) (M) **1.** pillar. **2.** mountain; shrub. **3.** one of the 7 sages of the Manu Svāroćiṣa age (*V. Purāṇa*).

Stambhaka (S) (M) **1.** post; pillar. **3.** an attendant of Śiva (*K. Sāgara*).

Stanayitnu (S) (M) thunder personified as a child of Vidyota or lightning.

Stava (S) (M) praise; eulogy.

Staveyya (S) (M) **1.** who can be stolen. **3.** another name for Indra.

Stavitṛ (S) (M) praiser; singer.

Sthāga (S) (M) **1.** dead body. **3.** an attendant of Śiva.

Sthala (S) (M) **1.** place; spot. **2.** chapter. **3.** son of Bala.

Sthaleyu (S) (M) **1.** terrestrial. **3.** a son of Raudrāśva (*H. Purāṇa*).

Sthāman (S) (M) strength; power.

Sthaṇḍileya (S) (M) **1.** belonging to a sacrificial ground. **3.** son of Raudrāśva and Miśrakeśī (*M. Bh.*).

Sthāṇu (S) (M) **1.** immobile; firm; fixed. **2.** a trunk of a tree. **3.** a prajāpati (*Rāmāyaṇa*); a nāga; a rākṣasa; Śiva as the son of Brahmā and the father of the 11 rudras (*M. Bh.*); one of the 11 rudras (*M. Bh.*); a hermit in the palace of Indra (*M. Bh.*).

Sthapati (S) (M) **1.** place lord. **2.** best; eminent; chief; king; architect; guard. **3.** another name for Kubera and Bṛhaspati.

Sthavira (S) (M) **1.** broad; thick; solid; old; venerable. **3.** another name for Brahmā.

Sthira (S) (M) **1.** sure; immovable; permanent; certain; fixed. **3.** an attendant given to Skanda by Meru (*M. Bh.*).

Sthirabuddhi (S) (M) **1.** noble; steadfast. **3.** an asura (*K. Sāgara*).

Sthitivarman (S) (M) **1.** living in armour. **3.** a king.

Sthūla (S) (M) **1.** dense; large; thick; massive; big. **3.** an attendant of Śiva.

Sthūlabhadra (S) (M) **1.** a strong opponent; a stout person. **3.** a son of Śakadala and Laććhadevī he succeeded Bhadrabāhu as the head of the Jaina church (*J. Literature*).

Sthūlabhuja (S) (M) **1.** strong armed. **3.** a vidyādhara (*K. Sāgara*).

Sthūlakarna (S) (M) **1.** large eared. **3.** a ṛṣi (*M. Bh.*).

Sthūlakeśa (S) (M) **1.** with thick hair. **3.** a hermit who was the foster father of Pramadvarā (*M. Bh.*).

Sthūlākṣa (S) (M) **1.** large eyed. **3.** a rākṣasa (*V. Rāmāyaṇa*); a hermit (*M. Bh.*).

Sthūlaśiras (S) (M) **1.** strong headed. **3.** a hermit in the court of Yudhiṣṭhira (*M. Bh.*); a rākṣasa (*K. Sāgara*).

Sthūna (S) (M) **1.** post; pillar. **2.** beam of a house. **3.** a son of Viśvāmitra (*M. Bh.*); a yakṣa (*M. Bh.*).

Sthūṇakarṇa (S) (M) **1.** with marked ears. **2.** cattle. **3.** a hermit in the court of Yudhiṣṭhira (*M. Bh.*); a yakṣa who helped Śikhaṇḍī (*M. Bh.*).

Stīrṇa (S) (M) **1.** spread; strewn. **3.** an attendant of Śiva (*Ś. Purāṇa*).

Stotra (S) (M) praise; hymn of praise.

Stotri (S) (M) **1.** praising. **3.** another name for Viṣṇu.

Stubha (S) (M) **1.** uttering a joyful sound; humming; chanting hymns. **2.** goat. **3.** a son of Agni Bhānu (*M. Bh.*).

Stutyavrata (S) (M) **1.** one who praises; a devotee. **3.** a son of Hiraṇyaretas (*Bhā. Purāṇa*).

Stuvat (S) (M) praiser; worshipper.

Stuvi (S) (M) praiser; worshipper.

Subāhu (S) (M) **1.** with strong arms. **3.** a nāga son of Kaśyapa and Kadru (*M. Bh.*); a Kṣatriya king who was the incarnation of the asura Hara (*M. Bh.*); a Kṣatriya king who was the partial incarnation of the asura Krodhavaśa (*M. Bh.*); a son of Dhṛtarāṣṭra (*M. Bh.*); a king of Kāśi and father of Śaśikalā (*M. Bh.*); a rākṣasa who was a son of Tāṭaka (*M. Bh.*); a king of Ćedi who was a son of Vīrabāhu (*M. Bh.*); a Kulinda king who fought on the side of the Pāṇḍavas (*M. Bh.*); a warrior of the Kauravas (*M. Bh.*); a warrior of Skanda (*M. Bh.*); the father of Sagara of the Solar dynasty (*H. Purāṇa*); a Ćola king and worshipper of Viṣṇu (*P. Purāṇa*); a dānava (*H. Purāṇa*); a yakṣa (*V. Purāṇa*); a son of Matināra (*H. Purāṇa*); a king of Videhā (*B. Literature*); a son of Ćitraka (*H. Purāṇa*); a son of Kṛṣṇa (*Bhā. Purāṇa*); son of Śatrughna (*Rāmāyaṇa*); a son of Kuvalayāśva (*Mā. Purāṇa*); a son of Pratibāhu (*B. Literature*); a brother of Alarka (*Mā. Purāṇa*); a Bodhisattva.

Subāhuka (S) (M) **1.** possessing strong arms. **3.** a yakṣa (*V. Purāṇa*).

Subala (S) (M) **1.** very powerful. **3.** a mythical bird who was the son of Vainateya (*M. Bh.*); a son of Manu Bhautya; a son of Sumati (*V. Purāṇa*); a Gāndhārā king who was the father of Śakuni and Gāndhārī (*M. Bh.*); an Ikṣvāku king (*M. Bh.*); a son of Garuḍa (*M. Bh.*); another name for Śiva.

Subāla (S) (M) **1.** good boy. **2.** a god.

Subalaja (S) (M) **1.** son of Subala. **3.** another name for Śakuni.

Śubana (S) (M) shining brightly; brilliant.

Subandhu (S) (M) **1.** good friend. **3.** the author of the *Vāsavadattā* (7th century A.D.); the main priest of King Asamāti (*Ṛg Veda*).

Subarmā (S) (M) strong warrior.

Subbārao (S) (M) **1.** divine leader. **3.** another name for Kārttikeya.

Subbāratna (S) (M) **1.** auspicious jewel. **2.** the white jewel of Kārttikeya.

Śubha (S) (M) **1.** splendid; bright; beautiful; auspicious; prosperous; good; virtuous. **3.** a son of Dharma (*Bhā. Purāṇa*); Himalayan Cherry (*Prunus cerasoides*).

Subhadra (S) (M) **1.** glorious; splendid; fortunate; auspicious. **3.** a son of Kṛṣṇa (*Bh. Purāṇa*); a son of Vasudeva (*Bhā. Purāṇa*); a son of Idhmajihva (*Bh. Purāṇa*); the last man converted by Gautama Buddha (*S. Puṇḍarikā*); another name for Viṣṇu; Neem tree (*Azadirachta indica*).

Subhāga (S) (M) fortunate; rich; wealthy.

Subhaga (S) (M) **1.** very fortunate; lucky; prosperous; blessed; lovely; charming; beloved; dear. **3.** a son of Subala and brother of Śakuni (*M. Bh.*); another name for Śiva; *Michelia champaka*; *Saraca indica*; red amaranth.

Subhagarbha (S) (M) **1.** centre of virtue and prosperity. **3.** a Bodhisattva.

Śubhakarman (S) (M) **1.** acting nobly. **3.** an attendant of Skanda (*M. Bh.*).

Śubhākṣa (S) (M) **1.** auspicious eyed. **3.** another name for Śiva.

Śubhalakṣaṇa (S) (M) with auspicious marks.

Śubhalocana (S) (M) fair eyed.

Śubhamaya (S) (M) full of splendour; splendid; beautiful.

Śubhamitra (S) (M) auspicious friend.

Śubhāna (S) (M) shining; bright; brilliant.

Śubhānana (S) (M) **1.** with a beautiful face. **2.** handsome; good looking.

Śubhāṅga (S) (M) **1.** handsome limbed. **3.** another name for Śiva.

Śubhāṅgada (S) (M) **1.** of beautiful form; handsome. **3.** a king at Draupadī's svayamvara (*M. Bh.*).

Śubhāñjana (S) (M) decorated with beauty.

Śubhaṅkara (S) (M) **1.** doer of good deeds; virtuous. **3.** an asura (*K. Sāgara*); another name for Śiva.

Subhānu (S) (M) **1.** shining brightly. **3.** a son of Kṛṣṇa and Satyabhāmā (*Bhāgavata*).

Subhāsa (S) (M) **1.** shining beautifully. **3.** a dānava (*K. Sāgara*); a son of Sudhanvan (*V. Purāṇa*).

Subhāṣa (S) (M) well spoken; eloquent.

Subhāṣacandra (S) (M) moon among the eloquent.

Subhāṣana (S) (M) **1.** speaking well. **3.** a solar dynasty king who was the son of Yuyudhāna and father of Śruta (*Bhāgavata*).

Śubhāṣaṇa (S) (M) good speaker.

Śubhaśīla (S) (M) with a good disposition.

Śubhāśiṣa (S) (M) blessings.

Śubhaspati (S) (M) **1.** lord of splendour. **3.** another name for the 2 aśvins.

Subhāsvara (S) (M) radiant; splendid.

Subhaṭa (S) (M) great soldier; champion.

Subhaṭṭa (S) (M) learned; wise.

Subhavimalagarbha (S) (M) **1.** with pure and bright garment. **2.** centre of splendour and cleanliness. **3.** a Bodhisattva.

Śubhāya (S) (M) to be bright and beautiful; to become a blessing.

Śubhendra (S) (M) lord of virtue.

Subhīma (S) (M) **1.** terrible; dreadful; bewildering. **3.** a son of the agni Tapa (*M. Bh.*).

Subhojita (S) (M) well fed.

Śubhra (S) (M) **1.** radiant; shining; beautiful; clear; white. **2.** heaven; sandal. **3.** the husband of Vikuṇṭhā and father of Vaikuṇṭha (*Bhā. Purāṇa*).

Śubhrabhānu (S) (M) **1.** white rayed. **3.** another name for the moon.

Subhrāja (S) (M) **1.** shining brightly. **3.** a son of Devabhrāja (*M. Bh.*); an attendant given to Skanda by Sūrya (*M. Bh.*).

Śubhraraśmi (S) (M) **1.** white rayed. **3.** another name for the moon.

Subhrata (S) (M) a good brother.

Śubhri (S) (M) **1.** bright; beautiful; shining. **2.** a Brāhmin. **3.** the sun.

Śubhū (S) (M) of an excellent nature; good; strong; powerful.

Subhūma (S) (M) **1.** possessed with good land. **2.** a king. **3.** another name for Kārtavirya as the 8th Jaina Ćakravartin.

Subhūmi (S) (M) **1.** a good place. **3.** a son of Ugrasena; the 9th Jaina Tīrthaṅkara and the son of King Sugrīva and Queen Ramā of Kakanādī (*J. Literature*).

Subirāja (S) (M) well decorated.

Subodha (S) (M) right intelligence.

Subrahmaṇya (S) (M) **1.** good hermit. **2.** good devotee; kind to hermits. **3.** the son of Śiva and Pārvatī born to destroy the demon Tārakāsura, delivered by Gaṅgā from Agni and fostered by the 6 kṛttikās, he has 6 faces and is known by the names Kārttikeya, Kumāra, Skanda, Guha, Mahāsena and Śravāna according to his various parents, he is the husband of Devasenā.

Subrāṅgsu (S) (M) having beautiful limbs; born of a beautiful person.

Śubrānśu (S) (M) **1.** with white rays. **3.** another name for the moon.

Sućakra (S) (M) **1.** a good chariot. **3.** an attendant of Skanda (*M. Bh.*); a son of Vatsaprī and Sunandā (*Mā. Purāṇa*).

Sućakṣus (S) (M) **1.** with beautiful eyes. **3.** one of the 7 tributaries of the Gaṅgā; another name for Śiva.

Sućandra (S) (M) **1.** beautiful moon. **3.** a gandharva (*M. Bh.*); an Ikṣvāku king and the son of Hemaćandra and the father of Dhūmrāśva (*V. Rāmāyaṇa*); an asura son of Siṅhikā (*M. Bh*); a gandharva son of Kaśyapa and Prādhā (*M. Bh.*); a king of Vaiśālī; a bodhisattva.

Śućanti (S) (M) **1.** in continuous grief. **3.** a person under the protection of the aśvins (*Ṛg Veda*).

Sućāru (S) (M) **1.** very lovely; handsome; pleasing; delightful. **3.** a son of Viśvakṣena (*H. Purāṇa*); a son of Pratiratha; a son of Bāhu (*V. Purāṇa*); a son of Dhṛtarāṣṭra (*M. Bh.*); a son of Kṛṣṇa and Rukmiṇī (*M. Bh.*).

Sućendra (S) (M) lord of piousness.

Sućetana (S) (M) very concious; very notable; distinguished.

Sućetas (S) (M) **1.** extremely wise; intelligent; benevolent. **3.** a son of Praćetas (*H. Purāṇa*); a son of Gṛtsamada and father of Varćas (*M. Bh.*).

Sūći (S) (M) **1.** needle; magnet. **2.** a military array; sight. **3.** a son of Niṣāda.

Śući (S) (M) **1.** shining; radiant; pure; bright; clean; holy; innocent; honest; virtuous. **2.** a ray of light; a true friend. **3.** a fire personified as the son of Agni Abhimānin and Svāhā (*V. Purāṇa*) or as a son of Antardhāna and Śikhaṇḍinī and brother of Pavamāna and Pāvaka (*Purāṇas*); a son of Bhṛgu (*M. Bh.*); a son of Gada (*H. Purāṇa*); a son of the 3rd Manu; Indra in the 14th Manvantara (*Purāṇas*); a son of Śatadyumna (*M. Bh.*); a son of Andhaka; a son of Vipra; a son of Manu Ćākṣuṣa and Nadvalā (*V. Purāṇa*); a solar dynasty king who was the son of Śakradyumna and father of Vanadvāja (*Bhāgavata*); a king in Yama's assembly (*M. Bh.*); a son of Viśvāmitra (*M. Bh.*); a son of sage Bhṛgu (*M. Bh.*); a maharṣi of Aṅgiras' family who was reborn as the son of King Vijitāśva (*Bhāgavata*); the son of Śuddha and the father of Trikālpava (*Bhāgavata*); a son of Kaśyapa and Tāmrā; another name for the sun, the moon, wind, Śiva and the planet Venus.

Śućikāma (S) (M) of pure desires; one who loves purily.

Śućikarṇika (S) (M) White Lotus (*Nelumbium speciosum*).

Śućimaṇi (S) (M) 1. pure jewel. 2. crystal.

Śućīndra (S) (M) lord of purity.

Śućipati (S) (M) 1. lord of purity. 2. fire.

Sućira (S) (M) 1. of long duration. 2. eternity.

Śućiratha (S) (M) 1. with a virtuous chariot. 3. a king of the Bharata dynasty who was a son of Ćitraratha and Dhṛṣaman's father (*Bhāgavata*).

Śućirocis (S) (M) 1. white rayed. 3. another name for the moon.

Sućiroṣita (S) (M) 1. long lived. 3. a minister of Daśaratha (*V. Rāmāyaṇa*).

Śućiṣmat (S) (M) 1. shining; radiant. 3. a son of Kardama.

Śućiśravas (S) (M) 1. with bright renown. 3. a prajāpati (*V. Purāṇa*); another name for Viṣṇu.

Sućitra (S) (M) 1. well marked; having auspicious marks. 2. distinguished; manifold; variegated. 3. a nāga in the family of Dhṛtarāṣṭra (*M. Bh.*); the father of King Sukumāra of Pulinda; a son of Dhṛtarāṣṭra (*M. Bh.*); a king on the side of the Pāṇḍavas (*M. Bh.*).

Śućivaktra (S) (M) 1. with a needle like mouth. 3. a warrior of Skanda (*M. Bh.*); an asura (*H. Purāṇa*).

Śućivarćas (S) (M) having pure splendour.

Śućivrata (S) (M) 1. pious; follower of purity. 3. an ancient Indian king (*M. Bh.*).

Sūdā (S) (M) munificent.

Sudakṣiṇa (S) (M) 1. with an excellent right hand. 2. dextrous; courteous; polite; sincere; liberal. 3. the son of King Pauṇḍraka (*Bhāgavata*); a king of Kāmboja who fought on the side of the Kauravas (*M. Bh.*); a warrior on the side of the Pāṇḍavas (*M. Bh.*).

Sudāman (S) (M) 1. bountiful. 2. cloud; mountain. 3. a King Daśarṇa whose daughters married Bhīma of Vidarbha and Vīrabāhu of Ćedi (*M. Bh.*); a minister of King Janaka (V. *Rāmāyaṇa*); an attendant of Skanda (*M. Bh.*); a cowherd reborn as an asura because of the curse of Rādhā; a warrior on the side of the Pāṇḍavas (*M. Bh.*); the keeper of the garden of Kaṅsa (*Bhāgavata*); a childhood friend of Kṛṣṇa; a gandharva (*Rāmāyaṇa*); another name for Airāvata.

Sudāmana (S) (M) 1. good donor. 2. mythical weapon. 3. a councillor of Janaka (*Rāmāyaṇa*).

Sudaṅṣṭra (S) (M) 1. with beautiful teeth. 3. a rākṣasa (*Rāmāyaṇa*); a son of Kṛṣṇa (*H. Purāṇa*): a son of Śambara (*H. Purāṇa*); a son of Asamañjasa.

Sudānu (S) (M) bounteous; munificent.

Sudarśa (S) (M) 1. lovely in appearance; pleasing to eyes. 2. easily seen; conspicuous; beautiful; lovely.

Sudarśana (S) (M) 1. lovely in appearance; pleasing to eyes; easily seen; keen sighted. 3. the discus of Viṣṇu (*M. Bh.*); a king rescued by Kṛṣṇa (*M. Bh.*); a king on the side of the Kauravas (*M. Bh.*); a Mālava king on the side of the Pāṇḍavas (*M. Bh.*); a son of Dhṛtarāṣṭra (*M. Bh.*); *a* son of King Dhruvasaṅdhi and Manoramā of Kosala; a son of Bharata and Pañćajanī (*Bhāgavata*); the son of Agni and Sudarśanā and the husband of Oghavatī: a vidyādhara (*Bhāgavata*); a son of Dīrghabāhu (*Bh. Purāṇa*); the chariot of Indra (*M. Bh.*); a Buddha (*L. Vistara*); a nāga; a ćiakravartin; a king of Ujjayinī; a son of Śaṅkhana (*Rāmāyaṇa*); a son of Arthasiddhi (*H. Purāṇa*); a son of Dadhīći; a son of Ajamīḍha (*H. Purāṇa*); a son-in-law of Pratīka (*Bh. Purāṇa*); a king of Hastināpur and father of Tīrthaṅkara Aranātha; a son of Śaṅkhana (*Rāmāyaṇa*).

Sudarśi (S) (M) 1. easily seen; conspicuous. 3. a sage who was the son of Kuśika.

Sudāsa (S) (M) 1. a good servant. 2. worshipping the gods well. 3. a king of the Tṛtsus and son of Divodāsa; a king of Kosala who is among those that should be remembered at dawn and dusk

(*M. Bh.*); a king of Ayodhyā who was the son of Sarvakāma and the father of Kalmāṣapāda (*Bhāgavata*); the grandson of Ṛtuparṇa (*H. Purāṇa*); a son of Ćyavana; a son of Bṛhadratha (*H. Purāṇa*); the father of Mitrasaha.

Sudatta (S) (M) **1.** well given. **3.** a son of Śatadhanvan (*H. Purāṇa*).

Sudāvan (S) (M) bounteous; munificent.

Sudāya (S) (M) good and auspicious gift.

Śuddha (S) (M) **1.** clean; clear; pure; bright; white; blameless; right; correct; genuine; true. **3.** one of the 7 sages under the 14th Manu (*Bhā. Purāṇa*); a Bhṛgu dynasty king who was the son of Anenas and father of Sūći (*Bhāgavata*); another name for Śiva.

Śuddhābha (S) (M) consisting of pure light.

Śuddhabhairava (S) (M) **1.** pure. **3.** a rāga.

Śuddhakarman (S) (M) pure; honest.

Śuddhakīrti (S) (M) having pure renown.

Śuddhamati (S) (M) **1.** pure minded. **3.** the 21st Arhat of the past Utsarpinī.

Śuddhānanda (S) (M) pure joy.

Śuddhātman (S) (M) **1.** pure minded. **3.** another name for Śiva.

Śuddhodana (S) (M) **1.** having pure food. **3.** a king of Kapilavastu and father of Gautama Buddha (*B. Literature*).

Sudeśa (S) (M) good place.

Sudeṣṇa (S) (M) **1.** born in a good place. **3.** a son of Kṛṣṇa and Rukmiṇī (*H. Purāṇa*); a son of Asamañjas.

Sudeva (S) (M) **1.** a real god. **3.** a captain of the army of King Ambarīṣa (*M. Bh.*); a son of King Haryaśva of Kāśī (*M. Bh.*); a king whose daughter married Nābhāga; a son of Akrūra (*H. Purāṇa*); a son of Ćañcu (*H. Purāṇa*); a son of Devaka (*V. Purāṇa*); a son of Viṣṇu (*Bh. Purāṇa*).

Sudhābhuja (S) (M) **1.** eating nectar. **2.** a deity.

Sudhaāhāra (S) (M) **1.** nectar receptacle. **3.** another name for the moon.

Sudhākara (S) (M) **1.** receptacle of nectar. **3.** another name for the moon.

Sudhāman (S) (M) **1.** a holy place; belonging to a holy place; living in a sacred house. **3.** a son of King Ghṛtapṛṣṭha (*Bhāgavata*); a mountain.

Sudhāmṛta (S) (M) nectar and honey conjoined.

Sudhana (S) (M) very rich.

Sudhāṅga (S) (M) **1.** nectar bodied. **3.** another name for the moon.

Sudhānidhi (S) (M) **1.** treasure of nectar. **3.** another name for the moon.

Sudhānśu (S) (M) **1.** nectar rayed. **3.** another name for the moon.

Sudhanuṣ (S) (M) **1.** good archer. **2.** with a good bow. **3.** a Purū king who was the son of King Kuru (*A. Purāṇa*); the father of Suhotra (*Bhāgavata*); a Pānćāla warrior who was the son of King Drupada and the brother of Viraketu and who fought on the side of the Pāṇḍavas (*M. Bh.*); an ancestor of Gautama Buddha.

Sudhanvan (S) (M) **1.** with an excellent bow. **3.** a son of Vairāja (*H. Purāṇa*); a son of Sambhūta (*H. Purāṇa*); a son of Ahīnagu; a son of Kuru (*H. Purāṇa*); a son of Śāśvata (*V. Purāṇa*); a son of Satyadhṛta; the guard at the end of the eastern quarter of the world (*A. Purāṇa*); son of sage Aṅgiras and the father of Ṛbhū, Vibhvan and Vāja (*Ṛg Veda*); a warrior on the side of the Kauravas (*M. Bh.*); king of Saṅkāśya (*V. Rāmāyaṇa*); another name for Viṣṇu, Ananta and Tvaṣṭṛi.

Sudhanya (S) (M) overtly blessed; good archer; much praised.

Sudhapāṇi (S) (M) **1.** bearing nectar in his hands. **3.** another name for Dhanvantari.

Sudhara (S) (M) **1.** abode of the good. **3.** an Arhat.

Sudharma (S) (M) **1.** maintaining law or justice. **3.** one of the 10 disciples of Mahāvira; a king of the kinnaras; a Vṛṣṇi prince who was a member of

Yudhiṣṭhira's assembly (*M. Bh.*); a king of Dāśārṇa (*M. Bh.*); a Kaurava army warrior (*M. Bh.*); the son of Dhammilla and Bhaddalā, he became the head of the Jaina church after Mahāvira's death (*J. Literature*).

Sudharman (S) (M) **1.** of right path; the maintainer of a family. **3.** a viśvadeva (*H. Purāṇa*); a son of Dṛḍhanemi (*H. Purāṇa*); a son of Ćitraka (*H. Purāṇa*).

Sudharmiṣṭha (S) (M) most virtuous.

Sudhāsū (S) (M) **1.** nectar producer. **3.** another name for the moon.

Sudhāsūti (S) (M) **1.** producing nectar. **2.** a lotus flower (*Nelumbo speciosum*). **3.** another name for the moon.

Sudhavāsa (S) (M) **1.** abode of nectar. **3.** another name for the moon.

Sudhendra (S) (M) **1.** lord of nectar. **3.** another name for the moon.

Sudhendu (S) (M) nectar and moon conjoined.

Sudhibhūṣaṇa (S) (M) with knowledge as his ornament.

Sudhīra (S) (M) very considerate or wise; firm; resolute.

Sudhita (S) (M) well disposed; kind; benevolent; nectarlike.

Sudhṛti (S) (M) **1.** very patient; very tolerant. **3.** a king of Videha who was the son of Mahāvīrya and the father of Dhṛṣṭaketu (*Bhāgavata*).

Sudīpa (S) (M) very bright.

Sudīpta (S) (M) shining brightly.

Sudiva (S) (M) shining brightly.

Śūdraka (S) (M) **1.** of the 4th caste. **3.** Sanskṛt dramatist and author of *Mrcćhākaṭikū* (2nd century A.D.).

Sudṛś (S) (M) **1.** pleasing to the eye. **2.** handsome; with beautiful eyes.

Sudurjaya (S) (M) **1.** very difficult to overcome. **3.** a son of Suvīra (*M. Bh.*); one of the 13 stages of a Bodhisattva.

Sudya (S) (M) **1.** shining brightly; very well illuminated. **3.** a Yayāti dynasty king who was the son of Ćārupāda and the father of Bahugava (*Bhāgavata*).

Sudyotman (S) (M) shining brightly.

Sudyumna (S) (M) **1.** very glorious. **2.** with an illuminating beauty. **3.** a son of Manu Ćākṣuṣa and Nadvalā (*V.Parāṇa*); a son of Manu Vaivasvata (*M. Bh.*); a son of Abhayada (*H. Purāṇa*).

Sudyut (S) (M) shining beautifully.

Sugandha (S) (M) **1.** fragrance. **3.** a rākṣasa killed by Agni (*P. Purāṇa*).

Sugandhi (S) (M) **1.** sweet smelling. **2.** fragrance; lion; virtuous; pious. **3.** Supreme Being.

Sugandhimukha (S) (M) **1.** one who has a fragrant mouth. **3.** a Bodhisattva.

Sugata (S) (M) **1.** going well; well bestowed. **3.** a Buddha.

Sugati (S) (M) **1.** welfare; bliss; happiness. **3.** a Bharata dynasty king who was the son of Gaya (*M. Bh.*); an Arhat.

Sugātra (S) (M) fair limbed; graceful.

Sugātu (S) (M) welfare; prosperity.

Sugavi (S) (M) **1.** with a beautiful; gait; possessing good cattle. **3.** a son of Prasuśruta (*V. Purāṇa*).

Sughosa (S) (M) **1.** making a pleasant sound. **3.** the conch of Nakula (*M. Bh.*); a Buddha (*L. Vistara*).

Sugopta (S) (M) **1.** well protected. **3.** a viśvadeva (*M. Bh.*).

Sugrīva (S) (M) **1.** handsome necked. **2.** hero; swan; a type of weapon. **3.** the father of the 9th Arhat of the present Avasarpiṇī; a conch; the monkey son of Sūrya and Aruṇī and the brother of Bāli and king of Kiṣkindhā after Rāma killed Bāli (*Rāmāyaṇa*); an asura minister of Śumbha (*D. Bhāgavata*); a horse of Kṛṣṇa (*M. Bh.*).

Sugrīveśa (S) (M) **1.** lord of Sugrīva. **3.** another name for Rāma.

Suguṇa (S) (M) with good qualities.

Suhala (S) (M) with an excellent plough.

Suhanu (S) (M) **1.** with beautiful jaws. **3.** an asura in Varuṇa's assembly (*M. Bh.*).

Suhara (S) (M) **1.** seizing well. **3.** an asura (*M. Bh.*).

Suhāsa (S) (M) with a beautiful smile.

Suhasta (S) (M) **1.** with beautiful hands. **2.** skilled; dextrous. **3.** a son of Dhṛtarāṣṭra (*M. Bh.*).

Suhastin (S) (M) **1.** a good elephant. **3.** the successor of Mahāgiri as the head of the Jaina church (*J. Literature*).

Suhastya (S) (M) **1.** with beautiful hands; possessing nice elephants. **3.** a muni extolled in the *Ṛg Veda* who was the son of Ghoṣā.

Suhava (S) (M) **1.** invoking well. **2.** performer of rites; devout; pious; performing oblation.

Suhavis (S) (M) **1.** offering many oblations. **2.** devout. **3.** a Bharata dynasty king who was the son of Bhūmanyu and Puṣkariṇī (*M. Bh.*).

Suhita (S) (M) **1.** beneficial. **2.** very fit; suitable.

Suhma (S) (M) **1.** measuring happiness. **3.** a son of Dīrghatamas and Sudeṣṇā.

Suhotṛ (S) (M) **1.** sacrificer. **3.** a son of Bhumanyu (*M. Bh.*); a son of Vitatha (*H. Purāṇa*).

Suhotra (S) (M) **1.** good priest. **3.** a son of Bhumanyu (*M. Bh.*); a son of Kañćanaprabha (*H. Purāṇa*); a son of Bṛhatkṣatra (*H. Purāṇa*); a son of Bṛhadīkṣu (*H. Purāṇa*); a son of Sudhanus; a daitya; sage Jamadagni and Reṇukā (*Br. Purāṇa*); a Ćandra dynasty king who was a grandson of Emperor Bharata and the husband of Suvarnā and the father of Ajamīḍha, Sumīdha and Purumīdha (*M. Bh.*); a son of Sahadeva and Vijayā (*M. Bh.*); a Kuru dynasty king; a rākṣasa who once ruled the world (*M. Bh.*).

Suhṛda (S) (M) **1.** kind hearted. **2.** friend; another name for Śiva.

Suhu (S) (M) **1.** invoking. **3.** a Yādava king who was a son of Ugrasena (*Bhāgavata*).

Suhva (S) (M) **1.** cordially invited. **3.** a king of the Bharata dynasty who was a son of Bali's wife and the sage Dīrghatamas (*Bhāgavata*).

Sujala (S) (M) **1.** of good water. **2.** the Indian Lotus (*Nelumbium nucifera*).

Sujana (S) (M) **1.** a nice person; good; virtuous; kind; benevolent; a gentlemen. **3.** another name for Indra's charioteer.

Sujantu (S) (M) **1.** good animal. **3.** a son of Jahnu (*V. Purāṇa*).

Sujānu (S) (M) **1.** with beautiful knees. **3.** a hermit (*M. Bh.*).

Sujāta (S) (M) **1.** well-born; noble; fine; beautiful. **3.** a son of Dhṛtarāṣṭra (*M. Bh.*); a monkey king who was the son of Pulaha and Śvetā (*Br. Purāṇa*); a son of Bharata (*V. Purāṇa*).

Sujāti (S) (M) **1.** of good tribe. **3.** a son of Vitihotra.

Sujaya (S) (M) a great triumph.

Sujita (S) (M) great conqueror.

Sujīthava (S) (M) related to a great triumph.

Sujyeṣṭha (S) (M) **1.** great noble. **3.** a king who was the son of Agnimitra and the father of Vasumitra (*Bhāgavata*).

Suka (S) (M) **1.** arrow; air; wind; lotus (*Nelumbo speciosum*) **3.** a son of Hrāda (*H. Purāṇa*).

Śuka (S) (M) **1.** the bright one. **2.** parrot. **3.** a son of sage Vyāsa and apsarā Ghṛtāćī and husband of Pīvarī and father of Kṛṣṇa, Gauraprabhā, Bhūri and Devaśruta and a daughter named Kīrtī (*Bhāgavata*); a messenger of Rāvaṇa (*V. Rāmāyaṇa*); a lunar dynasty king (*Bhāgavata*); a king of the Śaryāti dynasty who was the son of Pṛṣata (*M. Bh.*); a son of King Subala of Gāndhāra (*M. Bh*); a son of the monkey Śarabha and the husband of Vyāghrī and father of Ṛkṣa (*Br. Purāṇa*); an asura (*H. Purāṇa*); a king of the gandharvas (*Rāmāyaṇa*); a minister of Rāvaṇa (*Rāmāyaṇa*).

Śukadeva (S) (M) **1.** lord of parrots. **3.** a son of Vyāsa; a son of Harihara; another name for Kṛṣṇa.

Sukakṣa (S) (M) **1.** abode of good. **3.** a ṛṣi and author of *Ṛg Veda* (viii).

Sukalya (S) (M) perfectly sound.

Sukāma (S) (M) having good desires; much desired; lovely.

Sukamala (S) (M) **1.** beautiful lotus flower. **3.** a yakṣa who was the son of Manivara and Devajanī (*Br. Purāṇa*).

Śukanābha (S) (M) **1.** parrot navelled. **3.** a rākṣasa in the army of Rāvaṇa (*V. Rāmāyaṇa*).

Sukānta (S) (M) very handsome.

Sukanṭha (S) (M) sweet voiced.

Sukānti (S) (M) full of glory; very handsome.

Sukarmā (S) (M) **1.** doer of good; virtuous. **3.** an attendant given to Skanda by Vidhātā (*M. Bh.*); a teacher of the Sāma Veda.

Sukarman (S) (M) **1.** doer of good; virtuous; good; good architect. **3.** another name for Viśvakarman; a class of deities.

Sukarṇa (S) (M) **1.** beautiful eared. **3.** a rākṣasa (*Rāmāyaṇa*).

Śukasangīti (S) (M) **1.** singing like a parrot. **3.** a gandharva.

Śukāyana (S) (M) **1.** resembling a parrot. **2.** with a bright path. **3.** an Arhat (*B. Literature*).

Sukendu (S) (M) the Tāmala tree; like the moon.

Sukeśa (S) (M) **1.** with beautiful hair. **3.** a rākṣasa son of Vidyutkeśa and Śālakaṭaṅkā who married Devavatī and the father of Māli, Sumāli and Mālyavān (*U. Rāmāyaṇa*).

Sukesara (S) (M) of saffron colour; beautiful orange; the Citron tree (*Citrus medico*).

Suketa (S) (M) **1.** having good intentions; benevolent. **3.** an āditya.

Suketana (S) (M) **1.** with a good banner. **3.** a Bhṛgu dynasty king who was the son of Sunīthā and father of Dharmaketu (*Bhāgavata*).

Suketu (S) (M) **1.** very bright. **3.** a king of the yakṣas; a solar dynasty king who was the son of Nandivardhana and father of Devarāta (*Bhāgavata*); a Purū dynasty king who was a son of Bharata (*A. Purāṇa*); a son of Śiśupāla (*M. Bh.*); a king on the side of the Pāṇḍavas who was the son of Ćitraketu (*M. Bh.*); the son of the Gandharva king, Surākṣaka and the father of Tāṭakā (*K. Rāmāyaṇa*); another name for Viṣṇu.

Sukha (S) (M) happiness personified as the son of Dharma and Siddhi.

Sukhadarśina (S) (M) seer of happiness.

Sukhadeva (S) (M) lord of happiness.

Sukhadīpa (S) (M) lamp of happiness.

Sukhagandha (S) (M) sweet smelling; fragrant.

Sukhājāta (S) (M) **1.** happy. **3.** another name for Śiva.

Sukhajīt (S) (M) conquering happiness.

Sukhakara (S) (M) **1.** causing happiness. **3.** another name for Rāma.

Sukhaleśa (S) (M) a little pleasure.

Sukhamaṇi (S) (M) jewel of happiness.

Sukhamaya (S) (M) filled with happiness.

Sukhamitra (S) (M) friend of happiness.

Sukhamukha (S) (M) **1.** happy faced. **3.** a yakṣa.

Sukhānanda (S) (M) the joy of happiness.

Sukhanātha (S) (M) **1.** lord of happiness. **3.** a deity worshipped in Mathurā.

Sukhaṅkara (S) (M) giving pleasure.

Sukhapāla (S) (M) protecting happiness.

Sukhaprada (S) (M) giving happiness.

Sukharāja (S) (M) lord of happiness.

Sukharañjana (S) (M) delighting in happiness; coloured with pleasure.

Sukharūpa (S) (M) with a pleasant appearance.

Sukhasāgara (S) (M) ocean of happiness.

Sukhāśakta (S) (M) **1.** devoted to happiness. **3.** another name for Śiva.

Sukhavanta (S) (M) happy.

Sukhavarman (S) (M) warrior of happiness.

Sukhayitrī (S) (M) one who gladdens.

Sukheśa (S) (M) lord of happiness.

Sukheśin (S) (M) desirer of happiness; desiring others happiness; wishing well.

Sukheṣṭha (S) (M) **1.** living in joy. **3.** another name for Śiva.

Sukhin (S) (M) **1.** happy; glad; joyful. **2.** a religious ascetic.

Sukhīnala (S) (M) **1.** carrier of joy. **3.** a son of Sućakṣus (*Bhā. Purāṇa*).

Sukhodaya (S) (M) **1.** resulting in happiness; the realization of pleasure. **3.** an intoxicating honey drink. **3.** a son of Medhātithi (*Mā. Purāṇa*).

Sukhsam (S) (M) delicate.

Sukhyāta (S) (M) very renowned.

Sukīrti (S) (M) **1.** well praised. **3.** a ṛṣi and author of *Ṛg Veda* (x).

Śukla (S) (M) **1.** white; bright; light; pure; unsullied. **3.** a Pānćāla warrior on the side of the Pāṇḍavas (*M. Bh.*); the month Vaiśākha; a son of Havirdhāna (*H. Purāṇa*); another name for Śiva and Viṣṇu.

Śuklāćāra (S) (M) pure in conduct.

Śuklodana (S) (M) **1.** pure water. **3.** a brother of Śuddhodana.

Śukra (S) (M) **1.** bright; resplendent; clear; pure; white; spotless. **3.** the month of Jyeṣṭha (May/June), personified as the guardian of Kubera's treasure (*M. Bh.*); a marutvat (*H. Purāṇa*); the 3rd Manu (*H. Purāṇa*); one of the 7 sages under Manu Bhautya (*Mā. Purāṇa*); a son of Bhava (*V. Purāṇa*); the planet Venus and its regent regarded as the preceptor of the asuras who was a son of Bhṛgu and Pulomā, he married Jayantī the daughter of Indra, Ūrjāsvatī and Sataparvā and was the father of Devayānī, Arā, Devī and 4 sons (*M. Bh.*); a son of Vasiṣṭha and Ūrjjā and a saptarṣi of the 3rd Manvantara (*V. Purāṇa*); a king of the Pṛthu dynasty who was a son of Havirdhāna and Dhīṣaṇā (*V. Purāṇa*); another name for Agni (*Rāmāyaṇa*).

Śukrāćārya (S) (M) **1.** preceptor of purity. **3.** the regent of the planet Venus and the preceptor of the daityas.

Sukratu (S) (M) **1.** one who does virtuous deeds. **2.** benevolent; virtuous; pious. **3.** another name for Agni, Śiva, Indra, Mitra, Varuṇa, Sūrya, and Soma.

Śukriman (S) (M) brightness; purity.

Sukṛṣa (S) (M) **1.** very thin. **3.** a hermit (*Mā. Purāṇa*).

Sukṛta (S) (M) **1.** a pious deed; doing good; virtuous; pious; wise; benevolent. **2.** lucky; well made. **3.** another name for Tvaṣṭṛ and fire; a prajāpati (*V. Purāṇa*); a son of Pṛthu (*H. Purāṇa*).

Sukṛtin (S) (M) **1.** righteous; virtuous. **3.** a son of Manu Svāroćiṣa (*H. Purāṇa*); a ṛṣi in the 10th Manvantara (*Bhā. Purāṇa*).

Sukṣatra (S) (M) **1.** great warrior; ruling well; powerful. **3.** a son of the king of Kosala who fought on the side of the Pāṇḍavas (*M. Bh.*); a son of Niramitra (*V. Purāṇa*).

Sukṣetra (S) (M) **1.** sprung from a good womb. **2.** noble. **3.** a son of the 10th Manu (*Mā. Purāṇa*).

Sūkṣma (S) (M) **1.** thin; subtle. **3.** a dānava son of Kaśyapa and Danu and who was reborn as King Jayadratha (*M. Bh.*).

Sūkṣmanābha (S) (M) **1.** mystical navelled. **3.** another name for Viṣṇu.

Sūktā (S) (M) **1.** well recited. **2.** the Sārika bird.

Śukta (S) (M) **1.** astringent; sour. **3.** a son of Vasiṣṭha (*Mā. Purāṇa*).

Śuktikarṇa (S) (M) **1.** shell eared. **3.** a serpent demon (*H. Purāṇa*).

Sukula (S) (M) sprung from a noble family.

Sukumāra (S) (M) **1.** very tender; very delicate. **2.** the wild Ćampaka flower (*Michelia champaka*). **3.** a Pulinda king who was the son of King Sumitra (*M. Bh.*); a nāga in the family of Takṣaka (*M. Bh.*); a Purū dynasty king who was a son of Vibhu and the father of Satyaketu (*A. Purāṇa*); a son of King Bhavya of Sāka island (*M. Bh.*); banana (*Musa sapientum*); Blackeye Pea (*Vigna catiang*); Yellow Ćampa (*Michelia champaka*).

Sukumāraka (S) (M) **1.** very tender. **3.** a son of Jāmbavat (*V. Purāṇa*).

Sukuṇḍala (S) (M) **1.** with beautiful earrings. **3.** a son of Dhṛtarāṣṭra (*M. Bh.*).

Śūlabhṛt (S) (M) **1.** bearing a spear. **3.** another name for Śiva and Kṛṣṇa.

Śūladhara (S) (M) **1.** bearing a spear. **3.** another name for Rudra-Śiva.

Śūladhṛk (S) (M) **1.** bearing a spear. **3.** another name for Śiva.

Śūlahasta (S) (M) **1.** holding a spear. **3.** another name for Śiva.

Sulakṣa (S) (M) **1.** having auspicious marks. **2.** fortunate.

Śūlānka (S) (M) **1.** marked by a spear. **3.** another name for Śiva.

Śūlapāṇi (S) (M) **1.** with a spear in hand. **3.** another name for Rudra-Śiva.

Suleka (S) (M) **1.** the sun. **3.** the ādilya having beautiful rays.

Śūlī (S) (M) **1.** spear carrier. **3.** another name for Kṛṣṇa.

Śūlin (S) (M) **1.** armed with a spear. **3.** another name for Rudra-Śiva.

Suločana (S) (M) **1.** having beautiful eyes. **2.** deer. **3.** a son of Dhṛtarāṣṭra (*M. Bh.*); the father of Rukmiṇī; a Buddha (*L. Vistara*).

Suma (S) (M) the moon; the sky; camphor; flower.

Sūma (S) (M) milk; water.

Sumada (S) (M) **1.** joyful; delighting. **3.** a ṛṣi.

Sumadhura (S) (M) sweet speech.

Sumaha (S) (M) **1.** glorious. **3.** the charioteer of Paraśurāma (*M. Bh.*).

Sumahasvana (S) (M) **1.** very loud sounding. **3.** another name for Śiva.

Sumahu (S) (M) with glory.

Sumāla (S) (M) nice garland.

Sumālin (S) (M) **1.** well garlanded. **3.** a rākṣasa who was the son of Sukeśa; a son of Patālarāvaṇa (*K. Rāmāyaṇa*); an asura son of Praheti (*Br. Purāṇa*).

Sumālya (S) (M) **1.** wearing a nice garland. **3.** a son of Nanda.

Sumana (S) (M) **1.** of nice disposition; of a great heart; extremely thoughtful; charming; handsome. **3.** a nāga.

Sumanas (S) (M) **1.** of high intellect; pure-hearted. **2.** benevolent; gracious; favourable; agreeable; cheerful; easy; a god. **3.** a son of Ūru and Āgneyī; a dānava (*H. Purāṇa*); a son of Ulmuka (*Bhā. Purāṇa*); a son of Haryaśva (*V. Purāṇa*); a king in Yudhiṣṭhira's court (*M. Bh.*); a king in Yama's court (*M. Bh.*); a son of Purū and Atrī (*A. Purāṇa*).

Sumanda (S) (M) **1.** well decorated; watchful; very slow. **3.** son of Santurodha and brother of King Duṣyanta (*A. Purāṇa*).

Sumaṇḍala (S) (M) **1.** charmed circle; halo round the moon or sun. **3.** a king.

Sumaṅgala (S) (M) auspicious.

Sumaṇi (S) (M) **1.** adorned with jewels; a nice jewel. **3.** an attendant given to Skanda by the moon (*M. Bh.*).

Sumanomukha (S) (M) **1.** with a nice face and heart. **3.** a nāga in the Kaśyapa dynasty (*M. Bh.*).

Sumanta (S) (M) easily known; a friendly sentiment.

Sumantra (S) (M) **1.** good advisor; following good advice. **3.** a minister and charioteer of Daśaratha (*V. Rāmāyaṇa*); a son of Antarīkṣa (*V. Purāṇa*).

Sumantraka (S) (M) **1.** following good advice. **3.** an elder brother of Kalki (*K. Purāṇa*).

Sumantu (S) (M) **1.** well known. **2.** invocation. **3.** a son of Jahnu (*V. Purāṇa*); a disciple of Vyāsa (*M. Bh.*).

Surnanyu (S) (M) **1.** liberal. **3.** a gandharva (*M. Bh.*).

Sumat (S) (M) **1.** of a good nature; highly intellectual. **2.** benevolent; wise.

Sumati (S) (M) **1.** good mind; benevolence; kindness; devotion. **3.** a daitya (*M. Bh.*); a ṛṣi under Manu Sāvarṇa (*M. Bh.*); a son of

Bharata (*Bh. Purāṇa*); a son of Somadatta (*Bh. Purāṇa*); a son of Janamejaya (*V. Purāṇa*); a son of Nṛga (*Bh. Purāṇa*); a son of Ṛteyu; a son of Viduratha.

Sumatinātha (S) (M) **1.** lord of wisdom. **2.** master of a better intellect. **3.** the 5th Jaina Tīrthaṅkara who was the son of King Megharatha and Queen Maṅgalā of Ayodhyā.

Sumāya (S) (M) **1.** with excellent plans; very wise. **3.** a king of the asuras (*K. Sāgara*); a vidyādhara (*K. Sāgara*).

Śumbha (S) (M) **1.** killer; tormentor. **3.** an asura who was the son of Gaveṣṭhin and grandson of Prahlāda and who was slain by Durgā (*H. Purāṇa*).

Sumbha (S) (M) **1.** killer; destroyer; attacker. **3.** an asura who was the son of Kaśyapa and Danu and the brother of Niśumbha.

Śumbhana (S) (M) purifying.

Sumedhas (S) (M) **1.** of high intellect. **2.** sensible; intelligent; wise. **3.** a ṛṣi under Manu Ćākṣuṣa; a son of Vedamitra.

Sumeru (S) (M) **1.** very exalted. **2.** excellent. **3.** a mountain; a vidyādhara (*K. Sāgara*); another name for Śiva.

Sumeṣa (S) (M) good ram.

Sumīdha (S) (M) **1.** good sacrificer. **3.** a son of King Suhotra and Aikṣvākī of the Solar dynasty (*M. Bh.*).

Sumīndra (S) (M) lord of nectar.

Sumita (S) (M) well measured.

Sumitra (S) (M) **1.** a nice friend; having many friends. **3.** a king of the Sauvīras (*M. Bh.*); a king of Mithilā (*B. Literature*); a son of Gada (*H. Purāṇa*); a son of Śyāma (*H. Purāṇa*); son of Śamīka (*Bhā. Purāṇa*); son of Vṛṣṇi (*Bh. Purāṇa*); son of Agnimitra; a Yādava king who was the son of Vṛṣṇi and the brother of Yudhajit (*Bhāgavata*); a Sauvīra king who was a partial incarnation of the asura Krodhavaśa and a supporter of the Pāṇḍavas (*M. Bh.*); a maharṣi who was a member of Yudhiṣṭhira's court (*M. Bh.*); a son of Kālindanagara who was the father of Sukumāra (*M. Bh.*); a son of the agni Tapa (*M. Bh.*); a charioteer of Abhimanyu (*M. Bh.*); a Hehaya dynasty king (*M. Bh.*); a son of King Suratha and the last king of the Ikṣvāku dynasty (*Bhāgavata*); a son of Kṛṣṇa and Jāmbavatī (*Bhāgavata*); a king of Rājagṛha and father of Munisuvrata Jaina Tīrthaṅkara (*J. Literature*); a son of Kṛṣṇa (*Bh. Purāṇa*).

Sumitrābhū (S) (M) **1.** born of Sumitrā. **3.** the 20th Arhat of the present era; Sāgara as a Ćakravartin.

Sumukha (S) (M) **1.** bright faced. **2.** fair; handsome. **3.** a son of Droṇa (*Mā. Purāṇa*); a king of the kinnaras (*K. Vyuha*); an asura (*H. Purāṇa*); a ṛṣi (*M. Bh.*); a nāga son of Kaśyapa and Kadru who married Guṇakeśi (*M. Bh.*); a son of Garuḍa (*M. Bh*); another name for Śiva and Gaṇeśa.

Śuna (S) (M) **1.** the auspicious one. **3.** another name for Vāyu and Indra.

Sunābha (S) (M) **1.** having deep navel. **2.** with a stable centre. **3.** a son of Dhṛtarāṣṭra (*M. Bh.*); a minister of Varuṇa (*M. Bh.*); a dānava who was the brother of Vajranābha and the father of Ćandrāvatī and Guṇavatī (*H. Purāṇa*); a son of Garuḍa; a mountain (*M. Bh.*).

Sunaha (S) (M) **1.** well dressed. **3.** a son of Jahnu.

Śunahotra (S) (M) **1.** offering auspicious sacrifices. **3.** a son of Bharadvāja.

Śunahśepa (S) (M) **1.** dog tailed. **3.** a vedic ṛṣi son of Ajīgarta (*A. Brāhmaṇa*).

Śunaka (S) (M) **1.** young dog. **3.** a solar dynasty king who is the son of Kṛta and the father of Vītihotra (*Bhāgavata*); a rājarṣi who is a partial incarnation of the asura Ćandrahantā (*M. Bh.*); a maharṣi who was the son of King Ruru and Pramadvarā (*M. Bh.*); a son of Ṛćīka (*Rāmāyaṇa*); a son of Ṛta (*Bhā. Purāṇa*); a son of Gṛtsamadā (*H. Purāṇa*); the father of Pradyota (*Bhā. Purāṇa*).

Sunakṣatra (S) (M) **1.** born under an auspicious nakṣatra. **3.** the son of Marudeva (*Bhā. Purāṇa*); a Bharata dynasty king who was the son of Niramitra and father of Bṛhatsena (*Bhāgavata*).

Sunāman (S) (M) **1.** well named. **3.** the son of King Suketu (*M. Bh.*); a son of King Ugrasena and brother of Kansa (*M. Bh.*); a son of Garuḍa (*M. Bh.*); a warrior of Skanda (*M. Bh.*); a daitya; a son of Suketu (*M. Bh*); a son of Vainateya (*M. Bh.*).

Sunanda (S) (M) **1.** pleasing; delighting. **3.** a son of Pradyota (*Bhā. Purāṇa*).

Śunaṅkari (S) (M) **1.** causing growth and prosperity. **3.** a rural deity.

Sūnara (S) (M) glad; joyous; merry; delightful.

Sunartaka (S) (M) **1.** good dancer. **3.** name assumed by Śiva.

Sūnaśara (S) (M) **1.** flower arrowed. **3.** another name for Kāma.

Śunāsīra (S) (M) **1.** share and plough. **3.** 2 rural deities favourable to the growth of grain identified with Indra and Vāyu.

Śunasśepha (S) (M) **1.** dogtailed. **3.** a vedic ṛṣi who was the son of Ajīgarta.

Śunassakha (S) (M) **1.** with a dog. **3.** another name for Indra.

Sunaya (S) (M) **1.** very just; well conducted. **3.** a king who was the son of the king of Pāriplava and the father of Medhāvi (*Bhāgavata*); a son of Ṛta (*Purāṇas*); a son of Khaninetra.

Sunayaka (S) (M) wise leader.

Sunda (S) (M) **1.** one who shines. **3.** a daitya who was the son of Niśumbha; the brother of Upasunda and son of Nisunda (*M. Bh.*); another name for Viṣṇu.

Sundara (S) (M) **1.** beautiful; handsome; charming; agreeable; noble. **3.** a son of Pravilasena (*V. Purāṇa*); a gandharva son of Virabāhu (*Sk. Purāṇa*); an Āndhra monarch who was the son of Pulindasena and the father of King Śātakarṇi (*V. Purāṇa*); another name for Kṛṣṇa and Kāma.

Sundareśvara (S) (M) **1.** lord of beauty. **3.** a form of Śiva.

Śundhyu (S) (M) **1.** pure; bright; radiant; beautiful; purified. **3.** another name for Agni.

Śuṇḍu (S) (M) **1.** elephant. **3.** a Purū king who was the son of Vīlabhaya and the father of Bahuvidha (*A. Purāṇa*).

Sunetra (S) (M) **1.** fair eyed; a good leader. **3.** a son of Vainateya (*M. Bh.*); a son of the 13th Manu (*H. Purāṇa*); a son of Dhṛtarāṣṭra (*M. Bh.*); a son of Garuḍa (*M. Bh.*).

Śuṅgī (S) (M) **1.** *Ficus infectoria*; the sheath of a bud. **3.** the mother of Garuḍa.

Śuni (S) (M) **1.** dog. **3.** a Solar dynasty king who was the son of Vivanava and father of Śruta (*Bhāgavata*).

Sunīla (S) (M) **1.** very blue; dark. **2.** the pomegranate tree (*Punica granatum*); sapphire; Common Flax (*Linum Usitatissimum*); Blue grass (*Cymbopogon jwarancusa*).

Sunīta (S) (M) **1.** well conducted. **2.** prudent. **3.** a son of Subala (*V. Purāṇa*).

Sunītha (S) (M) **1.** well disposed; righteous; virtuous; moral. **2.** a good leader; well conducted; righteous. **3.** a maharṣi in the court of Indra (*M. Bh.*); a king in the court of Yama (*M. Bh.*); a Vṛṣṇi dynasty king (*M. Bh.*); a Bharata dynasty king who was the son of Suṣeṇa and father of Nṛkṣuṣ (*M. Bh.*); a son of Kṛṣṇa (*H. Purāṇa*); a son of Saṁtati (*H. Purāṇa*); a son of Subala (*H. Purāṇa*).

Suniti (S) (M) **1.** guiding well. **3.** a son of Vidūratha (*Mā. Piirāṇa*); another name for Śiva.

Śunolāṅgūla (S) (M) **1.** dog tailed. **3.** a son of Ṛcīka (*A. Brāhmaṇa*).

Sunṛta (S) (M) **1.** one who dances very well. **3.** a constellation.

Śuṇṭhacārya (S) (M) **1.** small white bull. **2.** teacher. **3.** a great Śaiva sage.

Sūnu (S) (M) **1.** son; child; offspring; inciter. **3.** another name for the sun.

Sunvat (S) (M) **1.** offerer of the Soma sacrifice. **3.** son of sage Sumantu (*Bh. Purāṇa*).

Śūnyabandhu (S) (M) **1.** with no friend; friend of dogs. **3.** a son of Tṛṇabindu.

Śūnyapāla (S) (M) **1.** preceptor of the cypher. **3.** a divine maharṣi (*M. Bh.*).

Supadma (S) (M) as lovely as a lotus; having beautiful lotuses.

Suparṇa (S) (M) **1.** with beautiful wings; with beautiful leaves. **2.** a ray of the sun. **3.** a gandharva son of Kaśyapa and Muni (*M. Bh.*); a gandharva son of Kaśyapa and Prādhā (*M. Bh.*); an asura who was the brother of Mayūra and was reborn as King Kālakīrti (*M. Bh.*); a mythical bird often identified with Garuḍa (*Ṛg Veda*); the sun and moon as having beautiful rays; a son of Antarīkṣa (*V. Purāṇa*); another name for Mahāviṣṇu.

Suparṇaketu (S) (M) **1.** bird bannered. **3.** another name for Viṣṇu.

Suparṇi (S) (M) **1.** with beautiful wings. **2.** personification of the mother of metres. **3.** one of the 7 tongues of fire.

Supārśva (S) (M) **1.** with beautiful sides. **2.** good looking. **3.** the son of Sampāti and elder brother of Jatāyu (*V. Rāmāyaṇa*); a son of Rukmaratha (*H. Purāṇa*); a son of Śrutāyu (*V. Piirāṇa*); the 7th Arhat of the present Avasarpinī; a mountain (*M. Bh.*); a king who was an incarnation of the asura Kapaṭa (*M. Bh.*); a king in the Yayāti dynasty who was a son of Dṛdhanemi and father of Sumati (*Bhāgavata*); a rākṣasa brother of Prahasta (*Rāmāyaṇa*).

Supārśvaka (S) (M) **1.** with beautiful sides. **2.** good looking. **3.** a Yādava king who was the son of Akrūra and Aśvinī (*M. Purāṇa*); a son of Vasudeva and Rohiṇī (*Vā. Purāṇa*); a son of Ćitraka (*H. Purāṇa*); a son of Śrutāyu (*Bhā. Purāṇa*); the 3rd Arhat of the future Utsarpinī.

Supārśvanātha (S) (M) **1.** the neighbouring god. **2.** the guardian angel. **3.** the 7th Jaina Tīrthaṅkara and son of King Pratiṣṭha and Queen Prithvī of Benāras.

Suparvan (S) (M) **1.** with beautiful sections. **2.** arrow; a god; a deity. **3.** a viśvadeva (*H. Purāṇa*); son of the 10th Manu (*Mā. Purāṇa*); a son of Antarīkṣa (*V. Purāṇa*).

Supāśa (S) (M) **1.** with a good noose. **3.** another name for Gaṇeśa.

Supeśas (S) (M) **1.** well adorned. **2.** beautiful; handsome.

Suphala (S) (M) good result; good fruit.

Supiś (S) (M) with fine ornaments; graceful.

Supoṣa (S) (M) prosperous.

Suprabuddha (S) (M) **1.** completely enlightened. **3.** a king of the Śākyas.

Suprakāśa (S) (M) well illuminated.

Supraketa (S) (M) very bright; conspicuous; notable; wise.

Suprasāda (S) (M) **1.** auspicious; gracious. **3.** an asura (*H. Purāṇa*); an attendant of Skanda (*M. Bh.*); another name for Śiva.

Suprasanna (S) (M) **1.** very clear; gracious; serene; very happy. **3.** another name for Kubera.

Suprāta (S) (M) beautiful dawn.

Supratardana (S) (M) **1.** deity of the beautiful dawn. **3.** an ancient king and companion of Indra (*M. Bh.*).

Supratīka (S) (M) **1.** with a beautiful form. **2.** handsome; lovely. **3.** one of the 8 elephants that support the earth and ancestor of Airāvata (*M. Bh.*); a yakṣa (*K. Sāgara*); a sage and brother of Vibhāvasu; another name for Śiva and Kāma.

Supratima (S) (M) **1.** beautiful idol. **3.** a king referred to as chief among those in ancient India (*M. Bh.*).

Supratiṣṭha (S) (M) **1.** standing firm; well established. **2.** famous; glorious. **3.** a king of Benaras and father of Supārśvanātha Jaina Tīrthaṅkara (*J. Literature*).

Supravṛddha (S) (M) **1.** well extended; full grown. **3.** a Sauvīra prince (*M. Bh.*).

Suprīta (S) (M) **1.** very dear. **2.** lovely; cherished; kind; friendly.

Suprītikara (S) (M) **1.** causing great joy or delight. **3.** a king of the kinnaras (*B. Literature*).

Supritīkara (S) (M) **1.** causing delight. **3.** a king of the kinnaras.

Suptāghna (S) (M) **1.** killer of sleeping persons. **3.** a son of the rākṣasa Mālyavat and Sundarī (*Rāmāyaṇa*).

Supuñjika (S) (M) **1.** well knit. **3.** a son of Vipraćitti and Siṅhikā (*Br. Purāṇa*).

Supuṣya (S) (M) **1.** blossom. **3.** a Buddha (*L. Vislara*).

Sura (S) (M) **1.** god; divinity; idol; sage. **2.** the sun.

Sūra (S) (M) **1.** wise; learned. **2.** the sun. **3.** father of the 17th Arhat of the present Avasarpinī.

Śūra (S) (M) **1.** powerful; brave; valiant. **2.** lion; tiger; a warrior. **3.** a lunar dynasty king who was the son of Vidūratha and father of Śini (*Bhāgavata*); a son of Kārtavīrya (*Br. Purāṇa*); a son of King Ilina and Rathāntarī (*M. Bh.*); a Sauvira prince (*M. Bh.*); a Yādava king who was the husband of Māriṣā and father of Vasudeva (*Vā. Purāṇa*); the father of Daśaratha's wife Sumitrā (*V. Rāmāyaṇa*); a son of Devamīdhuṣa (*H. Purāṇa*); son of Bhajamāna (*H. Purāṇa*); a son of Vasudeva (*Bh. Purāṇa*); a son of Vatsaprī (*Mā. Purāṇa*).

Surabhibāṇa (S) (M) **1.** with fragrant arrows. **3.** another name for Kāma.

Surabhimān (S) (M) **1.** virtuous; fragrant. 3. an agni (*M. Bh.*).

Surabhivatsa (S) (M) **1.** a calf. **3.** a vidyādhara (*K. Sāgara*).

Surabhūṣaṇa (S) (M) ornament of the gods.

Surāćārya (S) (M) **1.** preceptor of the gods. **3.** another name for Bṛhaspati.

Sūradāsa (S) (M) **1.** devotee of the sun. **3.** a commentator on *Harivamśa Purāṇa*.

Śūradeva (S) (M) **1.** lord of heroes. **3.** a son of King Vīradeva; the 2nd Arhat of the future Utsarpinī.

Suradhāman (S) (M) a piece of the gods.

Suradhas (S) (M) **1.** liberal; bountiful. **3.** a ṛṣi and part author of *Ṛg Veda* (i).

Surādhipa (S) (M) **1.** lord of the gods. **3.** another name for Indra.

Surādhipati (S) (M) **1.** lord of the gods. **3.** another name for Nahuṣa.

Surādhīśa (S) (M) **1.** lord of the gods. **3.** another name for Indra.

Suradhunī (S) (M) **1.** river of the gods. **3.** another name for the Gaṅgā.

Suradhvaja (S) (M) banner of the gods.

Suragarṇa (S) (M) **1.** with servants of god. **3.** another name for Śiva.

Suragiri (S) (M) the mountain of the gods.

Suragrāmaṇi (S) (M) **1.** chief of the gods. **3.** another name for Brahmā.

Suraguru (S) (M) **1.** preceptor of the gods. **3.** another name for Bṛhaspati.

Surahanta (S) (M) **1.** destroyer of gods. **3.** a son of the agni Tapa (*M. Bh.*).

Śūraja (S) (M) son of a hero.

Surājan (S) (M) well illuminated; divine; a good king.

Surajana (S) (M) the race of gods.

Sūrajaprakāśa (S) (M) the light of the sun.

Surajit (S) (M) victorious over the gods.

Surājīva (S) **1.** livelihood of the gods. **3.** another name for Viṣṇu.

Surajyeṣṭha (S) (M) **1.** oldest of the gods. **3.** another name for Brahmā.

Surakāru (S) (M) **1.** artificer of the gods. **3.** another name for Viśvakarman.

Suraketu (S) (M) the banner of the gods.

Surakṛt (S) (M) **1.** act of god. **3.** a son of Viśvāmitra (*M. Bh.*).

Sūrakṛta (S) (M) procured by the sun.

Sūrakṣaka (S) (M) **1.** protecting well; protector; defender. **3.** a gandharva king who was the grandfather of Tāṭaka.

Suralokasundarī (S) (M) **1.** celestial woman. **3.** an apsarā; another name for Durgā.

Śurama (S) (M) a great warrior.

Suramitra (S) (M) friend of the gods.

Suramukha (S) (M) with a divine face.

Suraṇa (S) (M) joyous; gay; a pleasing sound.

Suranāyaka (S) (M) **1.** leader of the gods. **3.** another name for Indra.

Suraṅga (S) (M) **1.** good colour; vermilion. **2.** Sweet Orange (*Citrus aurantium*).

Suraṅgama (S) (M) **1.** with a beautiful body; according to the rhythm. **2.** musical; rhyming with music. **3.** a Bodhisattva.

Suranimnagā (S) (M) **1.** river of the gods. **3.** another name for Gaṅgā.

Surañjana (S) (M) delighting greatly; Arccanut Palm (*Areca catechu*).

Śūrapadma (S) (M) **1.** lotus among heroes. **3.** an asura (*Sk. Parāṇa*).

Surapānsulā (S) (M) **1.** covered with celestial dust. **3.** an apsarā..

Surapati (S) (M) **1.** leader of the gods. **3.** another name for Indra.

Surapravīra (S) (M) **1.** best among the gods. **3.** a son of the agni Tapa (M. Bh.).

Surapriya (S) (M) **1.** beloved of the gods. **3.** another name for Indra and Bṛhaspati.

Surapuṣpa (S) (M) celestial flower.

Surarāja (S) (M) **1.** king of the gods. **3.** another name for Indra.

Surāri (S) (M) **1.** enemy of the gods. **3.** an ancient king (*M. Bh.*).

Surārihan (S) (M) **1.** destroyer of the enemy of the gods. **3.** another name for Śiva.

Surarṣi (S) (M) **1.** ṛṣi of the gods. **3.** another name for Nārada.

Surasakha (S) (M) friend of the gods.

Surasena (S) (M) with an army of gods.

Śūrasena (S) (M) **1.** with a heroic army. **3.** a king of Mathurā (*M. Bh.*); a son of Śatrughna (*V. Purāṇa*); a Yadu king and father of Vasudeva; son of Kārtavīrya (*H. Purāṇa*); a king who fought on the Kaurava side (*M. Bh.*).

Suraskandha (S) (M) **1.** divine shoulder. **3.** a demon.

Suraśreṣṭha (S) (M) **1.** best of the gods. **3.** another name for Viṣṇu, Śiva, Indra, Brahmā, Dharma and Gaṇeśa.

Surasū (S) (M) father of gods.

Śūrasūinu (S) (M) **1.** son of Śūra. **3.** another name for Vasudeva.

Sūrasūta (S) (M) **1.** charioteer of the sun. **3.** another name for Aruṇa.

Surata (S) (M) well disposed; tender; tranquil; calm.

Śūratara (S) (M) **1.** better warrior. **3.** a king on the Pāṇḍava side (*M. Bh.*).

Suratha (S) (M) **1.** having a good chariot. **3.** son of Sudeva (*Rāmāyaṇa*); a son of Ādiratha; son of Kuṇḍaka; a son of Raṇaka (*Bh. Purāṇa*); son of Ćaitra; a Purū dynasty king who was a son of Jahnu (*V. Purāṇa*); a son of Janamejaya and father of Vidūratha (*H. Purāṇa*); husband of Ćitrāṅgadā the daughter of Viśvakarmā; a king who was a partial incarnation of the asura Krodhavaśa (*M. Bh.*); father of King Koṭikāśya of Śibi (*M. Bh.*); a king of Trigarta (*M. Bh.*); a warrior on the Kaurava side (*M. Bh.*); a son of Drupada (*M. Bh.*); a son of Jayadratha and Duśśalā (*M. Bh.*); a king of Kundalānagari (*P. Purāṇa*).

Suratna (S) (M) possessing rich jewels.

Surāvān (S) (M) **1.** intoxicater. **3.** a horse of Agastya'ṣ chariot.

Suravarćas (S) (M) **1.** glory of the gods. **3.** an agni who was the son of Tapas (*M. Bh.*).

Suravarman (S) (M) armoured by the gods.

Surāvi (S) (M) divine sun.

Surebha (S) (M) fine voiced.

Surejya (S) (M) **1.** preceptor of the gods. **3.** another name for Bṛhaspati.

Surendra (S) (M) **1.** chief of the gods. **3.** another name for Indra.

Surendrajit (S) (M) **1.** conqueror of Indra. **3.** another name for Garuḍa.

Sureśa (S) (M) **1.** lord of the gods. **3.** a viśvadeva (*M. Bh.*); a son of the agni Tapa (*M. Bh.*); another name for Indra and Śiva.

Sureṣṭa (S) (M) beloved of the gods.

Sureśvara (S) (M) **1.** lord of the gods. **3.** one of the 11 rudras (*M. Bh.*); another name for Brahmā, Śiva and Indra.

Surgati (S) (M) being born as a god.

Sūri (S) (M) **1.** learned man. **2.** worshipper. **3.** another name for the Sun and Kṛṣṇa.

Suri (S) (M) **1.** sage. **3.** another name for Bṛhaspati.

Sūrin (S) (M) **1.** wise; learned. **2.** scholar.

Surīndra (S) (M) Indra the god.

Sūrmya (S) (M) **1.** channelled. **3.** a wife of Anuhrāda (*Bh. Purāṇa*).

Surośis (S) (M) **1.** much liked. **3.** son of Vasiṣṭha and Arundhatī (*Bhāgavata*).

Surodha (S) (M) **1.** good growth; well-stopped. **3.** a son of Tanṣu (*H. Purāṇa*).

Suroman (S) (M) **1.** with beautiful hair. **3.** a nāga of the Takṣaka dynasty (*M. Bh.*).

Surottama (S) (M) chief of the gods.

Śūrpaka (S) (M) **1.** with a winnowing fan. **3.** a gandharva; a demon enemy of Kāma.

Suru (S) (M) excellent; with fine tastes.

Suruća (S) (M) **1.** fine taste. **2.** glorious; taking great delight. **3.** son of Garuḍa (*M. Bh.*).

Surući (S) (M) **1.** with fine tastes; taking great delight in. **3.** a gandharva king (*H. Purāṇa*); a yakṣa (*Bhā. Purāṇa*).

Surudha (S) (M) very prominent.

Surūpa (S) (M) **1.** well formed. **2.** handsome; wise; learned. **3.** another name for Śiva.

Surūṣa (S) (M) shining.

Suruttama (S) (M) **1.** best among the gods. **3.** another name for Viṣṇu, the Sun and Indra.

Sūrya (S) (M) **1.** the sun. **3.** the sun is said to be born of sage Kaśyapa and Aditi as an āditya, is regarded as part of the original Vedic triad with Agni and Indra, in later mythology identified with Savitṛ as one of the 12 ādityas, also called Vivasvān and founder of the solar race through his son Vaivasvata Manu, married Sanjñā and Ćhāyā and was the father of Manu, Yama, Yamī, the Aśvinīkumāras, Revanta, Sanaścara and Tapatī, on other occasions he became the father of Sugrīva, Kālindī and Karṇa (*Ṛg Veda*); a king of Ayodhyā and father of Tīrthaṅkara Kuntanātha.

Sūryabali (S) (M) as powerful as the sun.

Sūryabhānu (S) (M) **1.** with the heat and light of the sun; reflector of the sun; as bright as the sun. **3.** gatekeeper of Kubera's city Alakapuri (*V. Rāmāyaṇa*): a Yakśa (*Rāmāyaṇa*).

Sūryabhrāj (S) (M) radiant as the sun.

Sūryaćakṣus (S) (M) **1.** the eye of the sun. **3.** a rākṣasa (*Rāmāyaṇa*).

Sūryaćandra (S) (M) the sun and moon conjoined.

Sūryadāsa (S) (M) devotee of the sun.

Sūryadatta (S) (M) **1.** given by the sun. **3.** a brother of King Virāṭa (*M. Bh.*).

Sūryadeva (S) (M) the god Sūrya.

Sūryadhvaja (S) (M) **1.** sun bannered. **3.** a ling of ancient India (*M. Bh.*).

Sūryāditya (S) (M) Surya, the son of Aditi.

Sūryagarbha (S) (M) **1.** the band of the sun; having sun as the navel; sun centred. **3.** a boddhisattva (*K. Vyuha*).

Sūryahasta (S) (M) **1.** the hands of the sun. **2.** ray of the sun.

Sūryaja (S) (M) **1.** sun born. **3.** another name for Sugrīva, the planet Saturn and Karṇa.

Sūryakamala (S) (M) the sunflower (*Helianthus anuus*); heliotrope.

Sūryakānta (S) (M) **1.** sun loved. **2.** the sun stone; sun crystal.

Sūryaketu (S) (M) **1.** having the sun for a banner. **3.** a daitya killed by King Purañjaya (*K. Rāmāyaṇa*).

Sūryakīrti (S) (M) sunlight; the Sesamum flower (*Sesamum indicum*).

Sūryākṣa (S) (M) **1.** the eye of the sun; sun eyed. **3.** a king who was an incarnation of King Kratha (*M. Bh.*).

Sūryamālā (S) (M) **1.** garlanded by the sun. **3.** another name for Śiva.

Sūrvamaṇi (S) (M) sunstone.

Sūryamāsa (S) (M) **1.** the solar month. **3.** warrior of the Kauravas (*M. Bh.*).

Sūryanābha (S) (M) **1.** sun navelled. **3.** a dānava (*H. Parāṇa*).

Sūryānana (S) (M) sun faced.

Sūryanandana (S) (M) **1.** son of the sun. **3.** another name for Saturn.

Sūryanārāyaṇa (S) (M) the lord of the sun; thc sun and Viṣṇu conjoined.

Sūryanetra (S) (M) **1.** sun eyed. **3.** son of Garuḍa (*M. Bh.*).

Sūryanśu (S) (M) sunbeam.

Sūryapati (S) (M) the god Sūrya.

Sūryapīḍa (S) (M) **1.** tormentor of the sun. **3.** a son of Parīkṣit.

Sūryaprabha (S) (M) **1.** bright as the sun. **3.** a nāga; a Bodhisattva.

Sūryaprakāśa (S) (M) light of the sun.

Sūryaputra (S) (M) **1.** son of the sun. **3.** patronymic of the aśvins, Yama, the planet Saturn, Varuṇa, Karṇa and Sugrīva.

Sūryaraśmi (S) (M) sunbeam.

Sūryasambhava (S) (M) **1.** son of the sun. **3.** another name for Karṇa.

Sūryasārathi (S) (M) **1.** charioteer of the sun. **2.** dawn.

Sūryasāvitra (S) (M) **1.** sun, the pious; Sūirya and Sāvitra conjoined. **3.** a viśvadeva (*M. Bh.*).

Sūryasnāta (S) (M) devotee of the sun; the sun worshipper.

Sūryaśrī (S) (M) **1.** divine sun. **3.** a viśvadeva.

Sūryatapas (S) (M) **1.** heat of the sun. **3.** a muni (*K. Sāgara*).

Sūryatejas (S) (M) **1.** with the power of the sun. **3.** sunshine.

Sūryavarćas (S) (M) **1.** as splendid as the sun. **3.** a gandharva son of Kaśyapa (*M. Bh.*).

Sūryavarma (S) (M) **1.** as powerful as the sun. **3.** a king of Trigarta (*M. Bh.*).

Sūryavarman (S) (M) **1.** protected or armoured by the sun. **3.** a king of Trigarta.

Sūryavighna (S) (M) **1.** destroyer of the sun. **3.** another name for Viṣṇu.

Sūryodaya (S) (M) sunrise.

Suṣāḍha (S) (M) **1.** 6 good faces. **3.** another name for Śiva.

Susaha (S) (M) **1.** bearing well. **3.** another name for Siva.

Suṣama (S) (M) very beautiful; very cven.

Susāman (S) (M) **1.** a beautiful song. **3.** a Brāhmin in Yudhiṣṭhira's court (*M. Bh.*).

Susambhāvya (S) (M) **1.** knower of the sacred texts; singer of *Sāma Veda* hymns. **3.** son of Manu Raivata (*V. Purāṇa*).

Susandhi (S) (M) **1.** fully reconciled; a good treaty. **3.** a son of Māndhātṛ (*Rāmāyaṇa*); a son of Prasuśruta (*V. Purāṇa*).

Suśansa (S) (M) saying good things; blessing.

Suśānta (S) (M) very calm; placid.

Suśānti (S) (M) **1.** perfect calm. **3.** Indra under the 3rd Manu; a son of Ajamīḍha; a son of Śānti (*V. Purāṇa*).

Suśaraṇya (S) (M) **1.** offering secure protection. **3.** another name for Śiva.

Suśarman (S) (M) **1.** granting secure refuge. **3.** a king of Trigarta who was the son of Vṛddhakṣema (*M. Bh.*); a Pānćāla warrior of the Pāṇḍavas (*M. Bh.*); the last king of the Kanva dynasty (*Bhāgavata*).

Suṣeṇa (S) (M) **1.** with a good missile. **3.** a nāga of the Dhṛtarāṣṭra family (*M. Bh.*); a son of Dhṛtarāṣṭra (*M. Bh.*); a Purū dynasty king who was son of Parīkṣit (*M. Bh.*); a son of sage Jamadagni (*M. Bh.*); son of

Varuṇa and father-in-law of the monkey king, Bāli and father of Tārā (*V. Rāmāyaṇa*); a son of Karṇa (*M. Bh.*); a Bharata dynasty king who was the son of Dhṛṣa and father of Sunītha (*Bhāgavala*); a king who married Rambhā the apsarā; a gandharva; a yakṣa (*V. Purāṇa*); a son of the 2nd Manu (*H. Purāṇa*); a son of Kṛṣṇa; a son of Śūrasena; a son of Viśvagarbha (*H. Purāṇa*); son of Vasudeva (*Bh. Purāṇa*); a son of Śambara (*H. Purāṇa*); a son of Vṛṣṇimat (*V. Purāṇa*); a vidyādhara (*K. Sāgara*); another name for Viṣṇu and Śiva; Chair bottom Cane (*Calamus rotang*).

Suśenta (S) (M) ray of the sun.

Suśeva (S) (M) very dear; auspicious; kind; favourable.

Suṣinandi (S) (M) **1.** good pleasure. **3.** a king (*V. Purāṇa*).

Suśira (S) (M) with a good head.

Suśita (S) (M) very bright; white.

Suśīla (S) (M) **1.** good tempered; amiable. **3.** a gandharva.

Śuśila (S) (M) air; wind.

Suśīma (S) (M) **1.** cold. **2.** moonstone.

Susīma (S) (M) **1.** with the hair well parted. **3.** a son of Bindusāra.

Suśivendra (S) (M) **1.** lord of divine welfare. **3.** Siva and Indra conjoined.

Śuṣka (S) (M) **1.** dry. **3.** a mahaṛṣi of the Gokarṇa temple.

Suska (S) (M) **1.** dry. **3.** a mahārṣi of Gokarṇa.

Śuṣma (S) (M) **1.** hissing; roaring; fragrant; strength; vigour; courage; valour; fire; flame. **3.** another name for the sun.

Śuṣmi (S) (M) **1.** wind. **3.** another name for Vāyu.

Śuṣmiṇa (S) (M) **1.** strong; fiery; courageous; bold. **3.** a king of the Śibis.

Susmita (S) (M) with a pleasant smile.

Śuṣṇa (S) (M) **1.** hisser. **2.** the sun; fire. **3.** a demon slain by Indra (*Ṛg Veda*).

Suśoka (S) (M) shining beautifully.

Suśona (S) (M) dark red.

Suśrama (S) (M) **1.** hard work. **3.** a son of Dharma (*V. Purāṇa*).

Suśravas (S) (M) **1.** much heard of. **2.** abounding in fame and glory. **3.** a prajāpati (*V. Purāṇa*); a nāga (*R. Taraṅginī*); a spy of the gods.

Suśruta (S) (M) **1.** much heard of; very famous. **3.** the grandson of King Gādhi and son of Viśvāmitra and the reputed master of the science of surgery (*M. Bh.*); a son of Subhāṣa (*V. Purāṇa*); a son of Padmodbhava.

Susthīla (S) (M) **1.** fortunate. **2.** well off; firm; unshaken. **3.** the monk who succeeded Suhasti as the head of the Jaina church (*J. Literature*).

Sustuta (S) (M) **1.** overtly praised. **3.** a son of Supārśva.

Śuśukvāna (S) (M) shining; resplendent; brilliant.

Suṣumna (S) (M) **1.** very gracious; kind. **3.** one of the 7 main rays of the sun (*V. Purāṇa*).

Susvara (S) (M) **1.** a beautiful voice. **3.** a son of Garuḍa (*M. Bh.*).

Sūta (S) (M) **1.** charioteer. **3.** a hermit son of sage Lomaharṣa and pupil of Vyāsa (*Bhāgavata*); a son of Viśvāmitra (*M. Bh.*).

Suta (S) (M) **1.** begotten. **2.** son. **3.** son of the 10th Manu (*H. Purāṇa*).

Sutama (S) (M) best among the virtuous.

Sutambhara (S) (M) **1.** carrying away Soma. **3.** a ṛṣi and part author of *Ṛg Veda* (V).

Sūtanandana (S) (M) **1.** son of a charioteer. **3.** another name for Karṇa.

Sutanjaya (S) (M) **1.** winning. **2.** son.

Sutantu (S) (M) **1.** with fair offspring. **3.** a dānava (*K. Sāgara*); another name for Śiva and Viṣṇu.

Sutanu (S) (M) **1.** with a beautiful body. **3.** a gandharva (*Rāmāyaṇa*); a son of Ugrasena (*H. Purāṇa*).

Sutapa (S) (M) **1.** drinking Soma juice. **3.** a class of deities.

Sutapas (S) (M) **1.** one who has done a lot of penance; very hot. **2.** ascetic. **3.** a Bharata dynasty king who was the son of Homa and father of Bala (*Bhāgavata*); a prajāpati and the husband of Pṛṣṇi and the father of Pṛṣṇigarbha who was supposed to be a partial incarnation of Mahāviṣṇu; a son of Vasiṣṭha; father of the hermit Upamanyu (*Br. Purāṇa*); a hermit of the Bhṛgu family; a sage of the Bharadvāja family whose wife became the mother of Aśvinīsuta by the sun.

Sūtaputra (S) (M) **1.** son of a charioteer. **3.** another name for Karṇa.

Sutārā (S) (M) divine star.

Sutasoma (S) (M) **1.** offerer of Soma. **3.** a son of Bhīmasena and Draupadī (*M. Bh.*).

Sutasravas (S) (M) born of fame.

Sūtasūnu (S) (M) **1.** son of a charioteer. **3.** another name for Karṇa.

Sūtasuta (S) (M) **1.** son of a charioteer. **3.** another name for Karṇa.

Sūtatanaya (S) (M) **1.** son of a charioteer. **3.** another name for Karṇa.

Sutejana (S) (M) **1.** well pointed; a sharpened arrow. **3.** a king who was a friend of Yudhiṣṭhira (*M. Bh.*).

Sutejas (S) (M) **1.** very bright. **2.** splendid; mighty; a worshipper of the sun. **3.** the 10th Arhat of the past Utsarpiṇī; a son of Gṛhatsamada (*M. Bh.*); *Cleome viscosa.*

Sutīkṣṇa (S) (M) **1.** very sharp. **3.** a hermit who was a brother of Agastya (*V. Rāmāyaṇa*).

Śutīra (S) (M) a hero.

Sutīrtha (S) (M) **1.** a good preceptor. **3.** another name for Śiva.

Sutrāman (S) (M) **1.** protecting well. **3.** another name for Indra.

Sutrāvan (S) (M) guarding well.

Sutṛpta (S) (M) fully satisfied.

Suvāća (S) (M) **1.** praiseworthy; sounding good; keeper of the Soma. **3.** a son of Dhṛtarāṣṭra.

Suvah (S) (M) patient; enduring.

Suvaha (S) (M) **1.** carrying well; bearing well. **2.** lute.

Suvāha (S) (M) **1.** easily carried away. **2.** a good stallion. **3.** a warrior of Skanda (*M. Bh*).

Suvāk (S) (M) **1.** soft spoken; with a sweet voice; very learned. **3.** a maharṣi (*M. Bh.*).

Suvaktra (S) (M) **1.** handsome faced. **3.** a son of Dantavaktra (*H. Purāṇa*); a warrior of Skanda (*M. Bh.*).

Suvana (S) (M) the sun; fire; the moon.

Suvanśa (S) (M) **1.** with a good pedigree. **3.** a son of Vasudcva (*Bh. Purāṇa*).

Suvapus (S) **1.** with a handsome body. **3.** an apsarā (*V. Purāṇa*).

Suvara (S) (M) the sun; light; heaven.

Suvarćas (S) (M) **1.** full of life; fiery; very glorious; splendid. **3.** a son of the 10th Manu; a brother of Bhūti (*Mā. Parāṇa*); a son of Dhṛtarāṣṭra (*M. Bh.*); a son of Suketu (*M. Bh.*); a son of the agni Tapa (*M. Bh.*); a son of Garuḍa (*M. Bh.*); an attendant given to Skanda by Himavān (*M. Bh.*); a son of King Khanīnetra (*M. Bh.*); another name for Śiva.

Suvarman (S) (M) **1.** having good armour. **2.** a great warrior. **3.** a son of Dhṛtarāṣṭra (*M. Bh.*).

Suvarṇa (S) (M) **1.** of beautiful colour; gold. **2.** famous; of noble birth. **3.** a gandharva (*M. Bh.*); a minister of Daśaratha; a son of Antarīkṣa (*V. Purāṇa*); a king of Kāśmīra (*R. Taraṅgiṇī*); another name for Śiva.

Suvarṇābha (S) (M) **1.** having a golden shine. **3.** a king who was a grandson of Manu Svāroćiṣa and son of Śaṅkhapāda (*M. Bh.*).

Suvarṇabindu (S) (M) **1.** golden spot. **3.** another name for Viṣṇu.

Suvarṇaćūḍā (S) (M) **1.** gold crested. **3.** a son of Garuḍa (*M. Bh.*).

Suvarṇagarbha (S) (M) **1.** golden womb. **2.** bringing forth gold. **3.** a Bodhisattva.

Suvarṇaka (S) (M) golden.

Suvarṇakeśa (S) (M) **1.** golden haired. **3.** a nāga.

Suvarṇākṣa (S) (M) **1.** golden eyed. **3.** another name for Śiva.

Suvarṇapadma (S) (M) golden lotus.

Suvarṇaprabhāsa (S) (M) **1.** with golden radiance. **3.** a yakṣa.

Suvarṇaretas (S) (M) **1.** with golden semen. **3.** another name for Śiva.

Suvarṇaroman (S) (M) **1.** golden haired. **3.** a son of Mahāroman (*V. Purāṇa*).

Suvarṇaśiras (S) (M) **1.** golden headed. **3.** a sage who was the son of Piṅgalavarman (*M. Bh.*).

Suvarṇasthīvī (S) (M) **1.** residing in gold. **3.** son of King Śṛñjaya (*M. Bh.*).

Suvarṇavarman (S) (M) **1.** golden warrior. **3.** a king of Kāśi whose daughter Vapustamā married Janamejaya.

Suvasa (S) (M) **1.** perfume. **3.** another name for Śiva.

Suvāsa (S) (M) **1.** well clad. **3.** another name for Śiva.

Suvāsaraka (S) (M) **1.** well clad; very fragrant. **3.** a son of Kaśyapa.

Suvāstuka (S) (M) **1.** an efficient architect. **3.** a king in ancient India (*M. Bh.*).

Suvavrata (S) (M) acting for welfare.

Suvela (S) (M) tranquil; still; quiet.

Suvibhu (S) (M) **1.** very bright. **3.** a son of Vibhu (*H. Purāṇa*).

Suvidha (S) (M) of a kind nature.

Suvidhinātha (S) (M) **1.** lord of the right manner. **3.** the 8th Jaina Tīrthaṅkara.

Suvidyut (S) (M) **1.** with the brilliance of lightning. **3.** an asura.

Suvikrama (S) (M) **1.** great valour. **3.** a son of Vatsaprī (*Mā. Purāṇa*).

Suvimala (S) (M) perfectly pure.

Suvipra (S) (M) very learned.

Suvīra (S) (M) **1.** very brave; hero. **3.** a king who was a partial incarnation of the asura Krodhavaśa (*M. Bh.*); a son of King Dyutimān (*M. Bh.*); a son of Kṣemya (*H. Purāṇa*); a son of Śibi (*H. Purāṇa*); a son of Devaśravas (*Bh. Purāṇa*); another name for Śiva and Jayadratha.

Suviraja (S) (M) free from all passion.

Suvīrya (S) (M) **1.** with heroic strength; chivalrous. **2.** White Emetic Nut (*Gardenia lucida*).

Suviśāla (S) (M) **1.** very large. **3.** an asura (*K. Sāgara*).

Suvita (S) (M) easy to traverse; a good path; welfare; prosperity; good luck.

Suvrata (S) (M) **1.** ruling well; very religious. **3.** a Bharata dynasty king who was the son of Kṣema and father of Viśvajit (*Bhāgavata*); an Aṅga king who was the son of King Uṣīnara and Daśa (*A. Purāṇa*); a famous muni (*M. Bh.*); an attendant given to Skanda by Mitra (*M. Bh.*); an attendant given to Skanda by Vidhātā (*M. Bh.*); a prajāpati (*Rāmāyaṇa*); a son of Manu Raućya (*Mā. Purāṇa*); a son of Nābhāga (*Rāmāyaṇa*); a son of Priyavrata; the 20th Arhat of the present Avasarpinī.

Suvṛddha (S) (M) **1.** very ancient. **3.** an elephant of the southern quarter.

Suvṛtta (S) (M) **1.** well behaved. **2.** virtuous; good.

Suyajña (S) (M) **1.** a good sacrifice. **3.** a son of Rući and Ākūti who is considered an incarnation of Viṣṇu (*Bhā. Purāṇa*); a son of Vasiṣṭha (*Rāmāyaṇa*); a son of Antara (*H. Purāṇa*); a king of the Uśīnaras (*Bhā. Purāṇa*).

Suyajus (S) (M) **1.** worshipping well. **3.** a son of Bhūmanyu (*M. Bh.*).

Suyama (S) (M) **1.** easily controlled. **3.** son of the rākṣasa Śataśṛṅga (*M. Bh.*).

Suyāmuna (S) (M) **1.** a palace. **2.** belonging to a mountain; a kind of cloud. **3.** another name for Viṣṇu.

Suyaśas (S) (M) **1.** glorious fame; very famous. **3.** a son of Aśokavardhana (*Purāṇas*).

Suyaṣṭavya (S) (M) a son of Raivata.

Suyati (S) (M) **1.** one who has controlled his passion. **3.** a son of Nahuṣa; another name for Viṣṇu.

Suyodhana (S) (M) **1.** good warrior. **3.** another name for Duryodhana.

Svābhāsa (S) (M) very illustrious.

Svabhīla (S) (M) very formidable.

Svabhirāma (S) (M) very delightful.

Śvabhra (S) (M) **1.** chasm; hole. **3.** a son of Vasudeva (*H. Purāṇa*); a king of Kampana (*R. Taraṅginī*).

Svabhū (S) (M) **1.** self born. **3.** another name for Brahmā, Śiva and Viṣṇu.

Svabhūmi (S) (M) **1.** one's proper place; own land. **3.** a son of Ugrasena (*V. Purāṇa*).

Svadhādhipa (S) (M) **1.** lord of the Svadhā. **3.** another name for Agni.

Svadhāman (S) (M) **1.** self radiant. **3.** a son of Satyasahas and Sūnṛtā (*Bh. Purāṇa*).

Svādhīna (S) (M) self willed; free.

Svadhita (S) (M) firm; solid.

Svadhīta (S) (M) well read.

Svāditya (S) (M) befriended by the ādityas.

Svādman (S) (M) sweetness.

Svāgata (S) (M) **1.** welcome. **3.** a Buddha (*L. Vistara*).

Svāhi (S) (M) **1.** sacrificer. **3.** the son of Vṛjinīvat (*H. Purāṇa*).

Śvaitreya (S) (M) **1.** son of white; brilliancy of lightning; fiery. **3.** the son of Śvitra (*Ṛg Veda*).

Svaketu (S) (M) **1.** self bannered. **3.** a king (*V. Purāṇa*).

Svakṣa (S) (M) handsome eyed.

Svalīna (S) (M) **1.** absorbed in oneself. **3.** a dānava.

Svāmikumāra (S) (M) **1.** son of the lord. **2.** young prince. **3.** another name for Kārttikeya.

Svāmin (S) (M) **1.** owner; master; lord; chief. **3.** the 11th Arhat of the past Utsarpini; another name for Viṣṇu, Śiva, Garuḍa and Skanda.

Svāminātha (S) (M) **1.** lord of lords. **2.** lord of ascetics. **3.** another name for Gaṇeśa.

Svana (S) (M) **1.** sound; noise. **3.** the son of the agni Satya (*M. Bh.*).

Svanaya (S) (M) **1.** self carried; self judgement. **3.** a son of King Bhāvayavya whose daughter married sage Kakṣivān.

Svaṅga (S) (M) with a handsome body.

Svani (S) (M) **1.** noisy; turbulent. **3.** son of Āpa.

Svanīka (S) (M) with a radiant countenance.

Śvānta (S) (M) tranquil; placid.

Śvaphalka (S) (M) **1.** fruit of a citron tree. **3.** the son of Vṛṣṇi and husband of Gandīnī and father of Akrūra (*H. Purāṇa*).

Svāpi (S) (M) good friend.

Svapna (S) (M) dream; sleep.

Svapnas (S) (M) wealthy; rich.

Svara (S) (M) **1.** sound; a musical note. **3.** one of the 7 rays of the sun; another name for Viṣṇu.

Svaradhīta (S) (M) **1.** reaching heaven. **3.** another name for Mount Meru.

Svārāj (S) (M) **1.** king of heaven. **3.** another name for Indra.

Svarāja (S) (M) **1.** self rule. **3.** one of the 7 rays of the sun (*V. Purāṇa*); another name for the Supreme Being, Brahmā, Viṣṇu and Indra.

Svārājya (S) (M) sovereignly; union with Brahmā; self effulgence.

Svarapurañjaya (S) (M) **1.** victor of music. **3.** a son of Śeṣa (*V. Purāṇa*).

Svarbhānu (S) (M) **1.** light of heaven. **2.** the divine sun. **3.** a dānava son of Kaśyapa and Danu who was reborn as Ugrasena the father of Kaṅsa (*M. Bh.*); a son of Kṛṣṇa and Satyabhāmā (*Bhāgavata*); a demon supposed to eclipse the sun and moon, later identified with Rāhu (*Ṛg Veda*).

Svarćanas (S) (M) pleasing to heaven; as lovely as light.

Svarćis (S) (M) flashing beautifully.

Svardā (S) (M) bestowing heaven.

Svardhāman (S) (M) abiding in light.

Svarga (S) (M) **1.** leading to light or heaven; heaven. **3.** Indra's paradise; son of the rudra Bhīma (*V. Purāṇa*).

Svargapati (S) (M) **1.** lord of heaven. **3.** another name for Indra.

Svargiri (S) (M) **1.** the mountain of light. **3.** another name for Sumeru.

Svarhat (S) (M) very honourable.

Svarjit (S) (M) winning heaven.

Svarmaṇi (S) (M) **1.** sky jewel. **3.** another name for the sun.

Svarṇa (S) (M) **1.** gold. **3.** a form of Gaṇapati the lord of the ganas.

Svarṇabindu (S) (M) **1.** golden spot. **3.** a warrior of Skanda (*M. Bh.*); another name for Viṣṇu.

Svarṇaćūḍa (S) (M) gold crested; the blue jay.

Svarṇagaṇapati (S) (M) **1.** golden lord of the ganas. **3.** a form of Gaṇeśa.

Svarṇagrīva (S) (M) **1.** golden necked. **3.** an attendant of Skanda (*M. Bh.*).

Svarṇajit (S) (M) gold winner.

Svarṇakalā (S) (M) a piece of gold.

Svarṇakāya (S) (M) **1.** gold bodied. **3.** another name for Garuḍa.

Svarṇaprabha (S) (M) shining like gold.

Svarṇapuṣpa (S) (M) **1.** golden flower. **2.** the Ćampaka tree (*Michelia champaka*); *Cassia fistula.*

Svarṇaroman (S) (M) **1.** golden haired. **3.** a solar dynasty king who was the son of Mahāromā and the father of Prastharomā.

Svarnetṛ (S) (M) guide to heaven.

Svarnīta (S) (M) led to heaven.

Svaroćas (S) (M) self shining.

Svaroćis (S) (M) **1.** self shining. **3.** a son of King Dyutimān and Varūthinī who married Manoramās, Vibhāvā and Kalāvatī and was the father of Śvāroćiṣa who became an emperor (*Mā. Purāṇa*); the son of the apsarā Varūthinī (*Mā. Purāṇa*).

Svāroćiṣa (S) (M) **1.** self shining. **3.** Manu as the son of Svāyambhuva's daughter Ākūti.

Svarpati (S) (M) lord of light.

Svarūpa (S) (M) **1.** having one's own form. **2.** pleasing; handsome; wise. **3.** a son of Sunandā (*Mā. Purāṇa*); a daitya (*M. Bh.*); an asura in the palace of Varuṇa (*M. Bh.*).

Svaryu (S) (M) desirous of light or splendour.

Svāsa (S) (M) the breath.

Śvasana (S) (M) **1.** breathing; panting; blowing; hissing. **2.** air; wind. **3.** a vasu and son of Śvāsā (*M. Bh.*); a nāga.

Svastibhāva (S) (M) **1.** god of fortune. **3.** another name for Śiva.

Svastika (S) (M) **1.** any lucky or auspicious object or mark; a mystical cross. **3.** a dānava (*H. Purāṇa*); a nāga in the palace of Varuṇa (*M. Bh.*); a warrior of Skanda (*M. Bh.*).

Svastikṛt (S) (M) **1.** causing prosperity. **3.** another name for Śiva.

Svastimatī (S) (M) **1.** auspicious. **3.** an attendant of Skanda (*M. Bh.*).

Svastyātreya (S) (M) **1.** auspicious ascetic. **3.** an ancient hermit of South India (*M. Bh.*).

Svāśū (S) (M) very swift.

Svaśva (S) (M) **1.** with excellent horses; goodrider. **3.** a king praised in the *Ṛg Veda.*

Śvāśva (S) (M) **1.** with a dog as steed. **3.** another name for Bhairava.

Svāti (S) (M) **1.** born under the Svāti star. **3.** a son of Meghasvāti; a grandson of Ćākṣuṣa Manu and son of Ūru and Āgneyi (*A. Purāṇa*).

Svaujas (S) (M) having natural energy.

Svayambhoja (S) (M) **1.** self made. **3.** son of Pratikṣatra (*H. Purāṇa*); a son of Śini (*Bhā. Purāṇa*).

Svāyambhū (S) (M) **1.** self existent. **3.** another name for Brahmā, Śiva, Viṣṇu, Buddha, Kāla and Kāma; the Jaina 3rd Black Vasudeva.

Svāyambhūta (S) (M) **1.** self created. **3.** another name for Śiva.

Svāyambhuva Manu (S) (M) **1.** selfborn Manu. **3.** the 1st Manu and son of Brahmā and husband of Śātarūpa and father of Priyavrata and Uttānapāda, he is considered the ancestor of human beings.

Svāyamīśvara (S) (M) one's own lord; absolute sovereign.

Svayamprabha (S) (M) **1.** self shining. **3.** the Jaina 4th Arhat of the future Utsarpini.

Svāyus (S) (M) full vigour.

Svedaja (S) (M) **1.** born of sweat. **3.** an asura.

Śveta (S) (M) **1.** white; white horse; white shell; white cloud. **3.** an ancient king who is considered among those who should be remembered at dawn and dusk (*M. Bh.*); a son of King [illegible]āṭa and Surathā (*M. Bh.*); a warrior of Skanda (*M. Bh.*); the elder brother of King Sudeva; a nāga; a daitya and son of Vipraćitti (*H. Purāṇa*); an incarnation of Śiva; a pupil of Śiva; a manifestation of Viṣṇu in his Varāha incarnation; a son of King Sudeva (*Rāmāyaṇa*); a son of Vapuṣmat (*Mā. Purāṇa*); a mythical elephant (*M. Bh.*); another name for the planet Venus.

Śvetābha (S) (M) white shine.

Śvetabhadra (S) (M) **1.** white gentleman; having a fair complexion. **3.** a guardian of Kubera's treasury.

Śvetabhānu (S) (M) **1.** white rayed. **3.** the moon.

Śvetadvipa (S) (M) **1.** white elephant. **3.** another name for Airāvata.

Śvetaka (S) (M) **1.** white. **2.** cowry; silver. **3.** a nāga.

Śvetakamala (S) (M) white lotus (*Nelumbium speciosum*).

Śvetakarṇa (S) (M) **1.** white eared. **3.** a son of Satyakarṇa (*H. Purāṇa*).

Śvetaketu (S) (M) **1.** white bannered. **3.** a comet; a son of Senajit (*H. Purāṇa*); Gautama Buddha as a Bodhisattva (*L. Vistara*); another name for maharṣi Auddālaki who was the son of sage Āruṇi.

Śvetakī (S) (M) **1.** fair complexioned. **3.** a king who spent his whole life performing yajñas (*M. Bh.*).

Śvetāmbara (S) (M) **1.** clad in white. **3.** the 2nd great Jaina seet (*J. Literature*); a form of Śiva.

Śvetāṅka (S) (M) **1.** having a white mark. **2.** bright.

Śvetānśu (S) (M) **1.** white rayed. **3.** another name for the moon.

Śvetapāda (S) (M) **1.** white footed. **3.** an attendant of Śiva.

Śvetapadma (S) (M) white lotus (*Nelumbium speciosum*).

Śvetaparṇa (S) (M) **1.** of white leaves; of white glory; glorious; famous. **3.** the king of Bhadrāvatī (*M. Bh.*).

Śvetapiṅgala (S) (M) **1.** pale yellow; tawny. **2.** lion. **3.** another name for Śiva.

Śvetaraśmi (S) (M) **1.** white rayed. **3.** the white elephant of King Ratnādhipa (*K. Sāgara*); a gandharva (*K. Sāgara*); another name for the moon.

Śvetārćis (S) (M) **1.** white rayed. **3.** another name for the moon.

Śvetarohita (S) (M) **1.** white and red. **3.** another name for Garuḍa.

Śvetasiddha (S) (M) **1.** with bright accomplishments. **3.** a warrior of Skanda (*M. Bh.*).

Śvetaśīrṣa (S) (M) **1.** white headed. **3.** a daitya (*H. Purāṇa*).

Śvetavāha (S) (M) **1.** borne by white horses. **3.** another name for Indra.

Śvetavāhana (S) (M) **1.** with a white chariot. **3.** a son of Rājādhideva (*H. Purāṇa*); a son of Śūra (*V. Purāṇa*); another name for the moon, Śiva and Arjuna.

Śvetavāhin (S) (M) **1.** borne by white horses. **3.** another name for Arjuna.

Śvetavājin (S) (M) **1.** with white horses. **3.** another name for the moon and Arjuna.

Śvetavaktra (S) (M) **1.** white faced. **3.** a warrior of Skanda (*M. Bh.*).

Sviṣṭakṛt (S) (M) **1.** offering a correct sacrifice. **3.** a son of Bṛhaspati (*M. Bh.*).

Śvojas (S) (M) very strong or powerful.

Śyāma (S) (M) **1.** black; dark blue; dark complexioned; cloud; the kokila bird. **3.** a rāga; a son of Śūra and brother of Vasudeva (*H. Purāṇa*); a sacred figtree at Prayāga (*Rāmāyaṇa*); another name for Kṛṣṇa.

Śyāmaka (S) (M) **1.** dark. **3.** a brother of Vasudeva and a son of Śūra and Māriṣā (*Bhāgavata*).

Śyāmakaṇṭha (S) (M) **1.** black throated. **3.** another name for Śiva.

Śyāmala (S) (M) dark; Black Plum (*Eugenia Jambolana*).

Śyāmāṅga (S) (M) dark bodied; the planet Mercury.

Syamantaka (S) (M) **1.** destroyer of dangers. **3.** the celebrated jewel worn by Kṛṣṇa on his wrist described as yielding gold and preserving from all danger (*H. Purāṇa*).

Śyāmasundara (S) (M) **1.** dark and beautiful. **3.** another name for Kṛṣṇa.

Śyāmavihāri (S) (M) Kṛṣṇa the wanderer.

Śyāmāyana (S) (M) **1.** very dark coloured or darkness personified. **3.** a son of Viśvamitra.

Syandana (S) (M) **1.** moving on swiftly. **2.** chariot; air; wind. **3.** the 23rd Arhat of the past Utsarpinī.

Śyavaka (S) (M) **1.** brown. **3.** the horses of the sun.

Śyāvāśva (S) (M) **1.** dark house. **3.** the son of sage Arćanānas.

Śyena (S) (M) **1.** eagle; falcon; hawk. **3.** a sage in Indra's assembly (*M. Bh.*).

Śyenagāmī (S) (M) **1.** moving like an eagle. **2.** as fast as an eagle. **3.** a commander of Khara's army (*V. Rāmāyaṇa*).

Śyenajit (S) (M) **1.** conqueror of the falcon. **3.** a son of the Ikṣvāku king, Dala (*M. Bh.*); the uncle of Bhīmasena (*M. Bh.*).

Syona (S) (M) **1.** mild; soft; gentle; pleasing; auspicious. **2.** ray of light; the sun.

Syūma (S) (M) ray of light; happiness; water.

Syūmaraśmi (S) (M) **1.** ray of light. **3.** an ancient hermit.

Syūnā (S) (M) a ray of light.

T

Taittiri (S) (M) **1.** sprung from a partridge. **3.** a sage and elder brother of Vaiśampāyana (*M. Bh.*); a son of Kapotaroman (*H. Purāṇa*).

Takṣa (S) (M) **1.** cutting through. **3.** a son of Bharata and Māṇḍavī (*Vā. Purāṇa*).

Takṣaka (S) (M) **1.** cutter; carpenter. **3.** the architect of the gods; a son of Prasenajit (*Bhā. Purāṇa*); a deity worshipped in Bengal as the bestower of rain; a serpent lord who is the son of Kaśyapa and Kadru and is one of the 8 snakes worn by Śiva, he lives in the court of Varuṇa; the son of Lakṣmaṇa and Ūrmilā and the king of Agati (*U. Rāmāyaṇa*).

Tāladhvaja (S) (M) **1.** palm bannered. **3.** the husband of Nārada when the latter became the woman Saubhāgyasundarī; a mountain; another name for Balarāma and Bhīṣma.

Tālajaṅgha (S) (M) **1.** with legs as long as a palm tree. **3.** a descendant of Śaryāti; a son of Jayadhvaja and grandson of Kārtavīrya (*Br. Purāṇa*); a rākṣasa (*Rāmāyaṇa*); a tribe (*M. Bh.*).

Tālaketu (S) (M) **1.** palm bannered. **3.** a dānava killed by Kṛṣṇa (*M. Bh.*); another name for Bhīṣma and Balarāma.

Tālanka (S) (M) **1.** endowed with every auspicious sign. **3.** another name for Balarāma and Śiva.

Talava (S) (M) musician.

Tālin (S) (M) **1.** furnished with cymbals. **3.** another name for Śiva.

Tālīṣa (S) (M) **1.** lord of the earth. **2.** mountain.

Tallaja (S) (M) excellent.

Taluna (S) (M) young; youth; wind.

Tālūra (S) (M) whirlpool.

Tama (S) (M) **1.** darkness. **3.** a king who was the son of Śravā of the race of Ghṛtasamada (*M. Bh.*).

Tamāla (S) (M) **1.** dark barked; mark on the forehead. **2.** *Xanthochymos piciorius.*

Tamas (S) (M) **1.** darkness; gloom. **3.** a son of Pṛthuśravas (*V. Purāṇa*); a son of Dakṣa.

Tāmasa (S) (M) **1.** dark; malignant. **3.** the 4th Manu who was the son of Priyavrata and Barhiśmatī (*Bh. Purāṇa*); an attendant of Śiva.

Tamisrahā (S) (M) **1.** destroying darkness. **3.** another name for Sūrya.

Tamīśvara (S) (M) **1.** lord of the darkness. **3.** another name for the moon.

Tamoghna (S) (M) **1.** destroying darkness. **3.** another name for the sun, the moon, Agni, Viṣṇu, Śiva and Buddha.

Tamohara (S) (M) **1.** one who removes darkness. **3.** another name for the moon.

Tamontakṛt (S) (M) **1.** exterminating darkness. **3.** an attendant of Skanda.

Tamonud (S) (M) **1.** dispersing darkness. **2.** fire; lamp; the sun and moon.

Tamori (S) (M) **1.** enemy of darkness. **3.** another name for the sun.

Tāmra (S) (M) **1.** of a coppery red colour; made of copper. **3.** a son of the demon Murāsura and the minister of Mahiṣāsura who was killed by Kṛṣṇa (*D. Bh. Purāṇa*); a son of Naraka Bhauma (*Bh. Purāṇa*).

Tāmrajākṣa (S) (M) **1.** copper eyed. **3.** a son of Kṛṣṇa and Satyabhāmā (*H. Purāṇa*).

Tāmraka (S) (M) **1.** copper. **3.** a gandharva; Redwood (*Adenanthera pavonina*).

Tāmrākhya (S) (M) a red pearl.

Tāmralipta (S) (M) **1.** surrounded by copper. **3.** an ancient king who was crowned by Sahadeva (*M. Bh.*).

Tāmrapakṣa (S) (M) **1.** copperclad. **3.** a son of Kṛṣṇa.

Tāmrasa (S) (M) day lotus; gold; copper.

Tāmratapta (S) (M) **1.** redhot like copper. **3.** a son of Kṛṣṇa (*Bhā. Purāṇa*).

Tāmroṣṭha (S) (M) **1.** red lipped. **3.** a yakṣa in the court of Kubera (*M. Bh.*).

Tana (S) (M) offspring.

Tanaka (S) (M) a reward.

Tanamaya (S) (M) embodied.

Tanas (S) (M) offspring.

Tanavīra (S) (M) strong; robust.

Tanaya (S) (M) **1.** belonging to one's family. **2.** son.

Tanayuta (S) (M) wind; night; thunderbolt.

Tāṅḍa (S) (M) **1.** dance. **3.** an attendant of Śiva skilled in dance and inventor of the Taṇḍava nṛtya.

Tāṇḍavapriya (S) (M) **1.** fond of the Tāṇḍava dance. **3.** another name for Śiva.

Tāṅḍi (S) (M) **1.** the art of dancing. **3.** a celebrated sage who repeated to Brahmā the 1000 names of Śiva (*M. Bh.*).

Tāṅḍya (S) (M) **1.** of dance. **3.** a sage and friend of Indra (*M. Bh.*).

Taniṣṭha (S) (M) smallest.

Tañjala (S) (M) the Ćataka bird.

Taṅkā (S) (M) **1.** leg. **3.** a rāgiṇī.

Taṅsu (S) (M) **1.** decorative. **3.** a Purū dynasty king who was the son of Matīnāra and the father of Īlina (*M. Bh.*).

Tāntava (S) (M) **1.** made of threads. **2.** a son.

Tantipāla (S) (M) **1.** guardian of the cows. **3.** name assumed by Sahadeva at Virāta's court (*M. Bh.*).

Tantrāyin (S) (M) **1.** drawing out threads of light. **3.** another name for the sun.

Tantripāla (S) (M) **1.** guardian of the calves. **3.** another name for Sahadeva.

Tantu (S) (M) **1.** thread. **2.** propogator of the family. **3.** a son of Viśvāmitra (*M. Bh.*).

Tantuvardhana (S) (M) **1.** procreator; propagator; increaser of the race. **3.** another name for Viṣṇu and Śiva.

Tanu (S) (M) **1.** slender; little; minute; delicate. **3.** a sage in the court of King Vīradyumna (*M. Bh.*).

Tanūbhava (S) (M) son.

Tanūja (S) (M) **1.** born of the body. **2.** son.

Tanūna (S) (M) **1.** bodiless. **3.** the wind.

Tanūnapāt (S) (M) **1.** self generated. **2.** the sacred name of fire (*Ṛg Veda*). **3.** another name for Śiva.

Tanūrja (S) (M) **1.** with heat in the body. **3.** a son of the 3rd Manu (*H. Purāṇa*).

Tanūvaśin (S) (M) **1.** having power over the person; ruling. **3.** another name for Agni and Indra.

Tanvin (S) (M) **1.** possessed of a body. **3.** a son of Manu Tāmasa (*H. Purāṇa*).

Tapa (S) (M) **1.** consuming by heat; warming; burning; shining. **2.** the sun. **3.** a deva with fire like splendour who was born of the penance of 5 sages and is therefore also known as Pāñćajanya; an attendant of Śiva; a fire that generated the 7 mothers of Skanda (*M. Bh.*).

Tapana (S) (M) **1.** illuminating; burning. **2.** the sun; the hot season; the sunstone. **3.** one of Kāma's arrows; a Pāñćala soldier in the Mahābhārata battle (*M. Bh.*); a rākṣasa (*Rāmāyaṇa*); a yakṣa (*M. Bh.*); another name for Agastya; Common Marking Nut tree (*Semecarpus anacardium*).

Tapanaććhada (S) (M) **1.** to please the sun. **2.** sunflower.

Tapanadyuti (S) (M) as brilliant as the sun.

Tapanakara (S) (M) sunbeam; the ray of the sun.

Tapanamaṇi (S) (M) **1.** gem of the sun. **2.** the sunstone.

Tapanāśman (S) (M) sunstone.

Tapanatanaya (S) (M) **1.** son of the sun. **3.** another name for Karṇa.

Tapanīyaka (S) (M) **1.** purified through fire. **2.** gold.

Tapanopala (S) (M) sunstone.

Tapas (S) (M) **1.** penance; warmth; heat; fire; meditation; merit; bird;

ascetic; potential power. **3.** the 9th lunar mansion; another name for the sun, Agni and the moon.

Tāpasanidhi (S) (M) **1.** store of ascetism. **3.** the Supreme Spirit.

Tapasarāja (S) (M) **1.** lord of ascetics. **3.** another name for the moon.

Tapasomūrti (S) (M) **1.** an example of austerity. **3.** a ṛṣi of the 12th Manvantara (*H. Purāṇa*).

Tapasvat (S) (M) hot; ascetic; devout; pious.

Tapasvin (S) (M) **1.** hermit; ascetic. **3.** a son of Manu Ćākṣusa and Nadvalā (*V. Purāṇa*); seer of the 12th Manvantara (*Bhā. Purāṇa*); another name for Nārada; Indian Beech (*Pongamia glabra*).

Tāpasya (S) (M) **1.** produced by heat; belonging to austerity. **2.** the Phālguna season. **3.** a son of Manu Tāmasa (*H. Purāṇa*); the flower *Jasminum multiflorum*; another name for Arjuna.

Tapeśa (S) (M) **1.** lord of penances. **3.** another name for the divine trinity (Brahmā, Viṣṇu and Śiva) and the sun.

Tapeśvara (S) (M) **1.** lord of penances. **3.** another name for Śiva and the sun.

Tāpīja (S) (M) a gem found near the Tāpatī river.

Tapiṣṇu (S) (M) warming; burning.

Tapiṣṇudeva (S) (M) **1.** lord of heat. **3.** another name for the sun.

Tapita (S) (M) refined gold.

Tapodhana (S) (M) **1.** rich in religious austerities. **3.** son of Manu Tāmasa (*V. Purāṇa*); a ṛṣi of the 12th Manvantara (*V. Purāṇa*).

Tapodharma (S) (M) **1.** religious ascetic. **3.** a son of the 13th Manu (*H. Purāṇa*).

Tapodhika (S) (M) **1.** menacing the sun. **3.** a sage who was the son of Kuśika.

Tapodhriti (S) (M) **1.** observing religious austerities. **3.** a son of the 12th Manu.

Tapodyuti (S) (M) **1.** brilliant with religious merit. **3.** the ṛṣi of the 12th Manvantara (*V. Purāṇa*).

Tapoja (S) (M) **1.** born from heat. **2.** to become a saint through religious austerities.

Tapomūla (S) (M) **1.** founded on austerities. **3.** a son of Manu Tāmasa (*H. Purāṇa*).

Tapomūrti (S) (M) an incarnation of religious austerities.

Taponidhi (S) (M) **1.** a treasure of austerities. **3.** a seer of the 12th Manvantara.

Taporāja (S) (M) **1.** lord of austerities. **3.** another name for the moon.

Taporati (S) (M) **1.** rejoicing in religious austerities. **3.** a son of Manu Tāmasa (*H. Purāṇa*); a seer of the 12th Manvantara.

Taporavi (S) (M) **1.** the sun of ascetics. **3.** a ṛṣī of the 12th Manvantara (*H. Purāṇa*).

Taposana (S) (M) **1.** one whose food is austerity. **3.** a ṛṣi of the 12th Manvantara (*H. Purāṇa*); a son of Manu Tāmasa.

Tapurmūrdhan (S) (M) **1.** fire headed. **3.** the son of Bṛhaspati and part author of *Ṛg Veda* (x); another name for Agni.

Tāra (S) (M) **1.** carrying across. **2.** saviour; protector; shining; radiant; good; excellent; silver; star. **3.** one of Rāma's monkey generals who was the son of Bṛhaspati and the husband of Tārā; a daitya (*H. Purāṇa*).

Tārāćandra (S) (M) the stars and moon conjoined.

Tārādhipati (S) (M) **1.** lord of the stars. **3.** another name for the moon.

Tārādhīśa (S) (M) **1.** lord of the stars. **3.** another name for the moon.

Tārahemābha (S) (M) shining like silver and gold.

Tāraka (S) (M) **1.** rescuing; liberating; saving; helmsman. **2.** belonging to the stars. **3.** an asura chief who fathered Tārakākṣa, Kamalākṣa and Vidyunmālikā and was killed by Skanda (*M. Bh.*); a minister of King Bhadrasena of Kāśmira and a great devotee of Śiva (*Ś. Purāṇa*).

Tārakajit (S) (M) **1.** conqueror of Tāraka. **3.** another name for Skanda.

Tārakākṣa (S) (M) **1.** star eyed. **3.** a son of Tārakāsura and lord of the golden city of Tripura (*M. Bh.*).

Tārakānātha (S) (M) **1.** lord of the stars. **3.** another name for the moon.

Tārakārāja (S) (M) **1.** lord of the stars. **3.** another name for the moon.

Tārakeśvara (S) (M) **1.** lord of the stars. **3.** another name for the moon.

Tārakita (S) (M) star spangled.

Tārākṣa (S) (M) **1.** star eyed. **3.** a king of the Niṣadhas; a mountain.

Tārakṣya (S) (M) the sun as a white horse.

Tarala (S) (M) **1.** tremulous; glittering. **2.** the central gem of a necklace; a wave; ruby; iron.

Taraṅga (S) (M) **1.** goes across. **2.** wave; billow.

Taraṅgabhīru (S) (M) **1.** afraid of the waves. **3.** a son of the 14th Manu (*H. Purāṇa*).

Taraṇi (S) (M) **1.** moving forward; quick; untired; energetic; helping. **3.** another name for the sun.

Taraṇiratna (S) (M) **1.** jewel of the sun. **2.** ruby.

Taranta (S) (M) the ocean.

Tarantuka (S) (M) **1.** boat. **3.** a yakṣa installed on the boundary of Kurukṣetra (*M. Bh.*).

Tārāpati (S) (M) **1.** lord of Tārā. **3.** another name for Bṛhaspati, Śiva and the monkey Bālin.

Tārāramaṇa (S) (M) **1.** beloved of the stars. **3.** another name for the moon.

Tārāśaṅkara (S) (M) the stars and Śiva conjoined.

Tarasvat (S) (M) **1.** quick; violent; energetic; bold. **3.** a son of the 14th Manu (*H. Purāṇa*).

Tarasvin (S) (M) **1.** quick; energetic; violent; bold. **2.** courier; hero; falcon; the wind. **3.** another name for Śiva and Garuda.

Tārendra (S) (M) star prince; the prince of stars.

Tāreya (S) (M) **1.** son of Tārā. **3.** another name for Aṅgada.

Tāriṇićaraṇa (S) (M) **1.** the feet that enable one to cross over. **3.** another name for Viṣṇu.

Tarīśa (S) (M) **1.** raft; boat. **2.** a competent person; the ocean.

Tarit (S) (M) one who has crossed over.

Tārkṣya (S) (M) **1.** amulet; creeper; bird. **3.** a mythical bird who was the son of Kaśyapa and Vinatā and who with Garuḍa formed a class of demigods (*M. Bh.*); a sage and member of Indra's court (*M. Bh.*); another name for Garuḍa; another name for Śiva.

Tārkṣyadhvaja (S) (M) **1.** Garuḍa symboled. **3.** another name for Viṣṇu.

Tārkṣyarakṣaṇa (S) (M) **1.** protecting Garuda. **3.** another name for Kṛṣṇa.

Tarpaṇa (S) (M) satiating; refreshing; gladdening.

Tarṣa (S) (M) **1.** with a fine shape. **2.** raft; ocean; sun.

Taru (S) (M) **1.** quick; protecting; a tree. **3.** a son of Manu Ćākṣuṣa (*M. Purāṇa*).

Taruṇa (S) (M) **1.** young; tender; fresh; new. **3.** a ṛṣī of the 11th Manvantara (*H. Purāṇa*).

Taruṇaka (S) (M) **1.** youthful. **3.** a serpent of the family of Dhṛtarāṣṭra (*M. Bh.*).

Taruṇapat (S) (M) **1.** with new attire. **3.** another name for Agni.

Taruṇendu (S) (M) the waxing moon; the new moon.

Taruṣa (S) (M) conqueror.

Tarutṛ (S) (M) conqueror.

Tarutra (S) (M) triumphant; conquering; superior.

Tāspandra (S) (M) **1.** one who discloses secrets. **3.** a ṛṣī.

Tāṭaṅka (S) (M) **1.** earring. **3.** King Sinhadhvaja in his previous incarnation.

Tathāgata (S) (M) **1.** being such; he who goes and comes in the same way (as the Buddhas before him). **3.** another name for Gautama Buddha.

Tathavādin (S) (M) telling the exact truth.

Tattvadarśin (S) (M) **1.** knower of substance; perceiving truth. **3.** a seer of the 13th Manvantara; a son of Manu Raivata (*H. Purāṇa*).

Taturi (S) (M) conquering.

Taṭya (S) (M) **1.** living on slopes. **3.** another name for Śiva.

Taukṣika (S) (M) **1.** balance. **2.** the zodiac sign of Libra.

Taulika (S) (M) painter.

Tauṭeśa (S) (M) **1.** guardian of the banks; guard of the banks. **3.** a kṣetrapāla.

Tautika (S) (M) the pearl oyster; pearl.

Tavalīna (S) (M) **1.** absorbed in god. **2.** one with god in meditation.

Tavaṣya (S) (M) strength.

Taviṣa (S) (M) **1.** strong; energetic; courageous. **2.** the ocean; heaven; gold.

Tāvura (S) (M) the zodiac sign of Taurus.

Tāyin (S) (M) protector.

Teja (S) (M) lustre; glow; effulgence; sharpness; protection.

Tejala (S) (M) **1.** bringing light. **2.** the Francoline Partridge.

Tejapāla (S) (M) controller of power.

Tejas (S) (M) fiery energy; spiritual and moral power; glory; majesty; authority; the sharp edge of a knife; the point of a flame; splendour; brilliance; light; clearness of the eyes; energy; power; spirit; essence; gold; marrow; dignity.

Tejasāmrāśi (S) (M) **1.** a heap of splendour. **3.** another name for Sūrya.

Tejasćaṇḍa (S) (M) **1.** very bright; sharp and powerful. **3.** a deity who adorns the god Sūrya with a garland daily.

Tejasiṁha (S) (M) **1.** lion of power. **3.** a son of Raṇadāra.

Tejasvat (S) (M) sharp edged; splendid; bright; glorious; beautiful; energetic; spirited.

Tejasvin (S) (M) **1.** brilliant; bright; strong; heroic; dignified; famous; sharp; powerful; splendid; energetic; noble; inspiring respect. **3.** a son of Indra (*M. Bh.*); one of the 5 Indras.

Tejeyu (S) (M) **1.** one who is possessed with splendour. **3.** a son of Raudrāśva and Miśrakeśī (*M. Bh.*).

Tejindra (S) (M) glorious chief.

Tejiṣṭha (S) (M) very sharp; very hot; very bright.

Tejita (S) (M) sharpened; whetted.

Tejomūrti (S) (M) consisting totally of light.

Tejonidhi (S) (M) abounding in glory.

Tejorāśi (S) (M) **1.** mass of splendour. **3.** another name for Mount Meru.

Tejorūpa (S) (M) **1.** consisting of splendour. **3.** another name for Brahmā.

Tevana (S) (M) sport; a pleasure garden.

Thanavelu (Tamil) (M) the youthful Balarāma.

Thangam (Tamil) (M) full of joy; gold.

Thirumāla (S) (M) the hills of Tirupati.

Tidiri (S) (M) the Shoveller bird.

Tigma (S) (M) **1.** sharp; pointed; hot; scorching; violent; intense; weapon; fame; ray of light. **3.** Indra's thunderbolt.

Tigmaketu (S) (M) **1.** flame bannered. **3.** a son of Vatsara and Svarvīthi (*Bh. Purāṇa*).

Tigmamanyu (S) (M) **1.** of violent wrath. **3.** another name for Śiva.

Tigmāṅśu (S) (M) **1.** hot rayed. **2.** fire.

Tigmaraśmi (S) (M) **1.** hot rayed. **3.** the sun.

Tijila (S) (M) the moon.

Tīkam (S) (M) moving.

Tīkamćandra (S) (M) the moving moon.

Tīkṣṇāṅṣu (S) (M) **1.** sharp rayed. **3.** another name for the sun.

Tilaka (S) (M) **1.** a freckle compared to a sesamum seed. **2.** a mark on the forehead made either as an ornament or as a distinction; the ornament of anything; California Cinchona (*Symplocos racemosa*).

Tilakarāja (S) (M) the best king; an ornament to kings.

Tilakāśraya (S) (M) **1.** one that receives the tilaka. **2.** the forehead.

Tilakottara (S) (M) **1.** the supreme tilaka. **3.** a vidyādhara.

Timī (S) (M) **1.** a whale or mythical fish of an enormous size. **3.** a son of Dūrva and father of Bṛhadratha (*Bhā. Purāṇa*); the zodiac sign of Pisces.

Timidhvaja (S) (M) **1.** whale bannered. **3.** a son of asura Śambara who made King Daśaratha faint, the latter was helped by Kaikeyī and promised her 2 boons (*Rāmāyaṇa*).

Timikoṣa (S) (M) **1.** receptacle of Timi. **2.** the ocean.

Timiṁgila (S) (M) **1.** a large fabulous fish. **3.** a king defeated by Sahadeva (*M. Bh.*).

Timirānud (S) (M) **1.** darkness destroyer. **3.** another name for the sun.

Timirāri (S) (M) **1.** enemy of darkness. **3.** another name for the sun.

Timirāripu (S) (M) **1.** the enemy of darkness; darkness destroyer. **3.** another name for the sun.

Timita (S) (M) calm; tranquil; steady; quiet; fixed.

Tiraśćī (S) (M) **1.** striped across. **3.** a ṛṣi who was a descendant of Aṅgiras (*Ṛg Veda*).

Tīrthadeva (S) (M) **1.** lord of the pilgrimage. **3.** another name for Śiva.

Tīrthaka (S) (M) sanctified.

Tīrthakara (S) (M) **1.** creating a passage through life. **2.** a term used to denote the head of a sect. **3.** another name for Viṣṇu and Śiva.

Tīrthakīrti (S) (M) one whose fame carries on through life.

Tīrthaṅkara (S) (M) **1.** creating a passage; ascetic. **2.** a term used to denote a sanctified teacher and saint of the Jainas. **3.** another name for Viṣṇu.

Tīrthapad (S) (M) **1.** with sanctifying feet. **3.** another name for Kṛṣṇa.

Tīrtharāma (S) (M) resting in a holy place.

Tīrthatama (S) (M) an object of the highest sanctity.

Tīrtheśvara (S) (M) **1.** maker of the passage. **3.** a Jaina Arhat.

Tīrujnānasambandha (S) (M) **1.** connoisseur of learning. **3.** one of the 4 southern Śaivaite teachers who was born in Thanjāvūr and is supposed to have merged with the Śiva statue at the Ćidambara temple (7th century).

Tirunavukkarasa (S) (M) **1.** knower of the divine. **3.** Śaivaite and a disciple of Tirujñanasambandha who acquired divine knowledge.

Tiryagīśa (S) (M) **1.** lord of the animals. **3.** another name for Kṛṣṇa.

Tiṣya (S) (M) **1.** auspicious; fortunate. **3.** a heavenly archer; the 8th Nakṣatra, the month Pauṣa.

Tiṣyagupta (S) (M) **1.** auspicious; fortunate; protected by the Tiṣya Nakṣatra. **3.** the founder of schism 2 of the Jaina community.

Tiṣyaketu (S) (M) **1.** with the banner of fortune. **3.** another name for Śiva.

Titha (S) (M) **1.** fire; love; time; autumn. **3.** another name for Kāma.

Titikṣu (S) (M) **1.** enduring patiently. **3.** a king who was the son of Uśīnara and the father of Ruṣadratha (*A. Purāṇa*); a son of Mahāmanas.

Tittiri (S) (M) **1.** partridge. **3.** a sage who was a member of the council of Yudhiṣṭhira (*M. Bh.*); a nāga (*M. Bh.*); a pupil of Yāska.

Tīvradyuti (S) (M) **1.** hot rayed. **3.** another name for the sun.

Tīvrānanda (S) (M) **1.** eternally intense and sharp. **3.** another name for Śiva.

Toḍara (S) (M) **1.** removing fear. **3.** a minister of Akbar who was one of his Navratnas.

Tola (S) (Malayalam) (M) **1.** with a deer skin belt. **3.** a Sanskṛt scholar who was a great satirical poet of Malayālam literature and a minister of King Bhāskara Ravi Varmā of Kerala (11th century).

Tomara (S) (M) lance; javelin.

Tomaradhara (S) (M) **1.** lance bearer. **2.** fire.

Torāmana (S) (M) a Hūṇ king and father of Mihirākula.

Toraṇa (S) (M) **1.** arch; a triangle supporting a large balance. **3.** another name for Śiva.

Toṣa (S) (M) **1.** satisfaction; contentment; pleasure; joy. **3.** the son of Bhāgavata and one of the 12 tuśitas (*Bhā. Purāṇa*).

Toṣin (S) (M) satisfied.

Toṣita (S) (M) satisfied; pleased.

Toyadhī (S) (M) **1.** containing water; water receptacle. **2.** the ocean.

Toyarāj (S) (M) **1.** the king of waters. **2.** the ocean.

Toyeśa (S) (M) **1.** lord of water. **3.** another name for Varuṇa.

Trailokyabandhu (S) (M) **1.** friend of the 3 worlds. **3.** another name for the sun.

Trailokyanātha (S) (M) **1.** lord of the 3 worlds. **3.** another name for Rāma and Kṛṣṇa.

Trailokyavikramin (S) (M) **1.** striding through the 3 worlds. **3.** a Bodhisattva.

Traiṣāṇi (S) (M) **1.** desirer of the trinity of gods. **3.** a king of the family of Turvasu who was the father of Karaṁdhāma.

Traivali (S) (M) **1.** with 3 lines on the stomach. **3.** a sage at the court of Yudhiṣṭhira (*M. Bh.*).

Trāman (S) (M) protection.

Trāṇana (S) (M) protecting.

Trasadasyu (S) (M) **1.** before whom the dasyus tremble; tormentor of the demons. **3.** a king of the Ikṣvāku dynasty who was the son of Purukutsa and is one of the kings who should be remembered in the morning (*M. Bh.*).

Trāta (S) (M) protected.

Trātṛ (S) (M) **1.** protector; defender. **3.** another name for Indra.

Trayitanu (S) (M) **1.** with the 3 vedas for a body. **3.** another name for Sūrya.

Trayyāruṇa (S) (M) **1.** the sun as depicted in the 3 Vedas. **3.** a king of the solar dynasty who was the son of Tridhanvan and the father of Triśanku (*Br. Purāṇa*).

Trayyāruṇi (S) (M) **1.** knowing the sun of the 3 Vedas. **3.** a sage in the line of disciples of Vyāsa.

Tṛbhi (S) (M) a ray.

Triakṣa (S) (M) **1.** 3 eyed. **3.** another name for Śiva.

Triambaka (S) (M) **1.** 3 eyed. **3.** a rudra; another name for Śiva.

Tribandhana (S) (M) **1.** the 3 bonds. **2.** bonded 3 ways to the parents and the preceptor. **3.** a son of Aruṇa (*Bh. Purāṇa*)

Tribandhu (S) (M) **1.** a friend of the 3 worlds. **3.** another name for Indra.

Tribhānu (S) (M) **1.** the sun of the 3 Vedas; the sun of the morning, noon and evening. **3.** a descendant of Yayāti and father of Karaṁdhama (*Bhāgavata*).

Tribhuvana (S) (M) the 3 worlds.

Tribhuvaneśvara (S) (M) **1.** lord of the 3 worlds. **3.** another name for Indra.

Tribhuvaneśvarī (S) (M) **1.** wife of Tribhuvaneśvara. **3.** another name for Pārvatī.

Tricakṣus (S) (M) **1.** 3 eyed. **3.** another name for Śiva.

Tridaśendra (S) (M) **1.** chief of the gods. **3.** another name for Indra.

Tridaśeśvara (S) (M) **1.** lord of the gods. **3.** another name for Śiva, Indra, Agni, Varuṇa and Yama.

Tridasyu (S) (M) **1.** with the qualities of 3 dasyus. **3.** a sage who was the son of Agastya and Lopāmudrā.

Trideśvara (S) (M) **1.** lord of heaven. **2.** a god.

Tridhāma (S) (M) **1.** shining in the 3 worlds. **3.** the 10th incarnation of Śiva.

Tridhāman (S) (M) **1.** shining in the 3 worlds. **3.** another name for Viṣṇu, Brahmā, Śiva and Agni.

Tridhanvan (S) (M) **1.** with the 3 bows (Sāma, Dāma, Daṇḍa) of power. **3.** a king of the solar dynasty who was the grandfather of Triśanku (*Bh. Purāṇa*).

Tridharman (S) (M) **1.** follower of 3 paths. **3.** another name for Śiva.

Tridhātu (S) (M) **1.** consisting of 3 parts. **3.** another name for Gaṇeśa.

Tridīpa (S) (M) with 3 lights (Jñāna, Karma, Bhakti).

Trigarta (S) (M) **1.** king of Trigarta. **3.** another name for Suśarman.

Trijaṭa (S) (M) **1.** with 3 locks of hair (i.e. having desire, anger and lust). **3.** a son of Viśvāmitra who was a poor sage and was granted cattle by Rāma (*V. Rāmāyaṇa*); another name for Śiva.

Trijña (S) (M) **1.** omniscient; seer; deity. **3.** a Buddha.

Trikakalpava (S) (M) **1.** of the 3rd Kalpa. **3.** a king (*Bhāgavata*).

Trikakubdhāmā (S) (M) **1.** abode of the 3 worlds. **3.** another name for Mahāviṣṇu.

Trikakubha (S) (M) **1.** triply pronged; triply distinguished. **3.** Indra's thunderbolt.

Trikakud (S) (M) **1.** having 3 peaks. **2.** thrice excelling one's equals. **3.** a mountain (*Ś. Brāhmaṇa*); a prince (*Bhā. Purāṇa*).

Trikakup (S) (M) **1.** 3 peaked. **3.** son of Āyus and Svarbhānu.

Trikālajña (S) (M) **1.** knower of 3 times (past, present and future). **2.** omniscient. **3.** a Buddha.

Trikālavid (S) (M) **1.** omniscient. **3.** a Buddha; an Arhat of the Jainas.

Trikāya (S) (M) **1.** with 3 bodies. **3.** a Buddha.

Trikha (S) (M) **1.** sharp. **2.** nutmeg.

Trikṣā (S) (M) **1.** destroying in 3 ways. **3.** another name for Kaśyapa.

Trilocana (S) (M) **1.** 3 eyed. **3.** another name for Śiva.

Trilocanapāla (S) (M) defender of Śiva.

Trilokacandra (S) (M) **1.** the moon of the 3 worlds; providing light to the 3 worlds. **3.** another name for the moon.

Trilokanātha (S) (M) **1.** lord of the 3 worlds. **3.** another name for Indra and Śiva.

Trilokātman (S) (M) **1.** soul of the 3 worlds. **3.** another name for Śiva.

Trilokavīra (S) (M) **1.** hero of the 3 worlds. **3.** a Buddhist deity.

Trilokeśa (S) (M) **1.** lord of the 3 worlds. **3.** another name for Śiva, Viṣṇu and the sun.

Trilokījit (S) (M) conquering the 3 worlds.

Trilokīnātha (S) (M) **1.** lord of the 3 worlds. **3.** another name for Viṣṇu.

Trimadhura (S) (M) made of sugar, ghee and honey.

Trimukha (S) (M) **1.** 3 faced. **3.** the 3rd Arhat of the present Avasarpinī.

Trimūrti (S) (M) **1.** with 3 forms. **3.** Brahmā, Viṣṇu and Śiva conjoined; a Buddha; one of the 8 Vidyeśvaras.

Trinābha (S) (M) **1.** one whose navel supports the 3 worlds. **3.** another name for Viṣṇu.

Trinayana (S) (M) **1.** 3 eyed. **3.** another name for Śiva.

Trinetra (S) (M) **1.** 3 eyed (the eyes represent the sun, moon and fire). **3.** a minister of Mahiṣāsura (*Bh. Purāṇa*); another name for Śiva; Bulb bearing Yam (*Dioscorea bulbifera*).

Tripād (S) (M) **1.** 3 footed. **3.** a rākṣasa slain by Skanda (*M. Bh.*).

Tripan (S) (M) pleasing; refreshing.

Tripanna (S) (M) **1.** follower of 3 types of knowledge; thrice worthy of admiration. **3.** a horse of the moon.

Tripat (S) (M) **1.** with pleasure; to one's satisfaction. **3.** another name for the moon.

Tripṛṣṭha (S) (M) **1.** with 3 spines; 3 backed. **3.** the 1st Black Vasudeva of the Jainas; another name for Viṣṇu.

Tripuraghātī (S) (M) **1.** destroyer of Tripurā. **3.** another name for Śiva.

Tripuraghna (S) (M) **1.** destroyer of Tripurā. **3.** another name for Śiva.

Tripurahartā (S) (M) **1.** destroyer of Tripurā. **3.** another name for Śiva.

Tripurajīt (S) (M) **1.** conqueror of Tripurā. **2.** conqueror of the city Tripurā of the asuras. **3.** another name for Śiva.

Tripuranāśana (S) (M) **1.** destroyer of Tripurā. **3.** another name for Śiva.

Tripurāntaka (S) (M) **1.** destroyer of Tripurā. **3.** another name for Śiva.

Tripurāntakara (S) (M) **1.** destroyer of Tripurā. **3.** another name for Śiva.

Tripurāri (S) (M) **1.** enemy of the city Tripurā. **3.** another name for Śiva.

Tripurmardana (S) (M) **1.** destroyer of Tripura. **3.** another name for Śiva.

Tripuṣkara (S) (M) decorated with 3 lotus flowers

Trirāva (S) (M) **1.** making 3 types of sound. **3.** a son of Garuḍa.

Triśaṅku (S) (M) **1.** sacrificing for the 3 (Dharma, Artha, Kāma). **3.** an Ayodhya king of the dynasty of Māndhātā who was the son of Tribandhana and the father of Hariśćandra (*Bhā. Purāṇa*); a famous Solar dynasty king who was the son of Trayyāruṇa and who remains suspended in mid air between heaven and earth forming the southern cross constellation (*Ṛg Veda*); a son of Pṛthu (*H. Purāṇa*); a mythical river.

Trisara (S) (M) a triple pearl string.

Triṣavana (S) (M) **1.** connected with 3 Soma libations. **3.** a sage (*M. Bh.*).

Triśikha (S) (M) **1.** trident; 3 pointed. **3.** Indra in Manu Tāmasa's Manvantara (*Bh. Purāṇa*); Bengal Quince (*Aegle marmelos*).

Triśiras (S) (M) **1.** 3 headed. **3.** a rākṣasa who was a friend of Rāvaṇa; a son of the prajāpati Tvaṣṭā who was killed by Indra and from each of whose heads birds were born; another name for Kubera.

Triṣṇāri (S) (M) **1.** removing thirst. **2.** satisfying; fulfilling. **3.** Fine leaved Fumitory (*Fumaria parvifloria*).

Triśoka (S) (M) **1.** 3 types of grief. **2.** physical, emotional and spiritual grief. **3.** a sage who was the son of Kaṇva (*Ṛg Veda*).

Trisrotā (S) (M) **1.** with 3 streams. **3.** another name for Gaṅgā.

Triṣṭup (S) (M) **1.** stopping 3 times. **3.** a Vedic metre; a horse of the sun (*V. Purāṇa*).

Triśukra (S) (M) triply pure.

Triśūla (S) (M) **1.** 3 pronged. **3.** Śiva's trident. (*H. Purāṇa*).

Triśūlahasta (S) (M) **1.** holding the Triśūla. **3.** another name for Śiva.

Triśūlāṅka (S) (M) **1.** marked by the Triśula. **3.** another name for Śiva.

Triśūlapāṇi (S) (M) **1.** holding the Trisula. **3.** another name for Śiva.

Triśulin (S) (M) **1.** bearing the Triśula. **3.** another name for Śiva.

Trisuvarćaka (S) (M) triply splendid.

Trita (S) (M) **1.** 3rd. **3.** an inferior Vedic deity associated with the maruts, Vāyu and Indra who conquered the demons with the help of Indra, he is also the keeper of nectar. In the epics Ekata, Dvita and Trita are the sons of Gautama or Prajāpati or Brahmā, he is also described as one of the 12 sons of Manu Ćākṣuṣa and Nadvalā.

Trivarćaka (S) (M) **1.** shining in 3 ways. **3.** a sage who was the son of Aṅgiras and who joined with 4 others to produce Pāñćajanya.

Trivāstapa (S) (M) **1.** the sky as the abode of the 3 worlds. **3.** another name for Dyaus the god of the sky.

Trividyā (S) (M) a Brāhmin versed in 3 Vedas.

Trivikrama (S) (M) the 3 steps of Viṣṇu; possessed with 3 types of power.

Trivṛṣan (S) (M) **1.** with 3 bulls. **3.** a father of Trayyaruṇa.

Triyuga (S) (M) **1.** appearing in the first 3 yugas. **3.** another name for Kṛṣṇa.

Tṛṇabindu (S) (M) **1.** water drops on grass; pieces of grass; a mortal. **3.** a sage who was the father of Mānini and grandfather of Viśravas (*U. Rāmāyaṇa*).

Tṛṇaka (S) (M) **1.** a blade of grass; mortal. **3.** a king in the court of Yama (*M. Bh.*).

Tṛṇamaṇi (S) (M) **1.** a jewel that attracts grass when rubbed. **2.** sapphire; amber.

Tṛṇaṅku (S) (M) **1.** fragrant grass. **3.** a sage (*Ṛg Veda*).

Tṛṇapa (S) (M) **1.** grass swallower. **3.** a gandharva (*M. Bh.*).

Tṛṇapāṇi (S) (M) **1.** holding grass in his hand. **3.** a ṛṣī.

Tṛṇasomāṅgiras (S) (M) **1.** accepting nectar made from grass. **3.** a sage who lived in South India (*M. Bh.*).

Tṛṇāvarta (S) (M) **1.** surrounded by straw. **2.** tornado. **3.** the son of Tārakāsura who was killed by Kṛṣṇa (*Bhāgavata*).

Tṛpta (S) (M) satiated; satisfied with.

Tṛptātman (S) (M) with a contented soul.

Tryaksa (S) (M) **1.** 3 eyed. **3.** an asura; another name for Śiva.

Tryambaka (S) (M) **1.** born of 3 mothers; 3 eyed. **3.** one of the 11 rudras; another name for Rudra.

Tugra (S) (M) **1.** water. **3.** a king and father of Bhujyu who was once saved by the aśvins (*Ṛg Veda*); an enemy of Indra.

Tuhara (S) (M) **1.** remover of darkness. **3.** a soldier of Skanda (*M. Bh.*).

Tuhina (S) (M) **1.** frost; cold; mist; dew. **3.** moonlight; camphor.

Tuhinakara (S) (M) **1.** cold rayed. **3.** another name for the moon.

Tuhināṅśu (S) (M) **1.** cold rayed. **3.** another name for the moon.

Tuhuṇḍa (S) (M) **1.** destroyer of darkness; causing pain. **2.** an iron rod that keeps darkness away. **3.** a dānava who was the son of Kaśyapa and Danu (*M. Bh.*); a son of Dhṛtarāṣṭra (*M. Bh.*).

Tuka (S) (M) **1.** young; youthful; boy. **3.** an astronomer.

Tukarāma (S) (M) **1.** youthful Rama. **3.** a saint and poet (17th century).

Tula (S) (M) **1.** balance; scale. **2.** the zodiac sign of Libra.

Tuladhara (S) (M) **1.** scale holder. **2.** the zodiac sign of Libra.

Tulaka (S) (M) ponderer.

Tulakući (S) (M) **1.** balanced. **2.** with a good heart. **3.** a prince and son of Śalin.

Tulāpurusa (S) (M) **1.** a gift of gold equivalent to a man's weight. **3.** another name for Viṣṇu/Kṛṣṇa.

Tulasidāsa (S) (M) **1.** devotee of Tulasī. **3.** the author of *Rāmaćaritamānas*.

Tulya (S) (M) equal to; of the same kind.

Tulyabala (S) (M) compare; equal in strength.

Tulyatejas (S) (M) equal in splendour.

Tulyavīrya (S) (M) of equal strength.

Tumbavīṇā (S) (M) **1.** having the gourd for a lute. **3.** another name for Śiva.

Tumburu (S) (M) **1.** fruit of the Tumba gourd (*Lagenaria vulgaris*). **3.** a pupil of Kalāpin; the attendant of the 5th Arhat of the present Avasarpinī; the best musician of the gandharvas who was the son of Kaśyapa and Prādhā and a member of Kubera's court (*M. Bh.*); a sage (*U. Rāmāyaṇa*).

Tūṇava (S) (M) a flute.

Tuṇḍa (S) (M) **1.** mouth; trunk; the point of an arrow. **3.** a king invited by the Pāṇḍavas to take part in the Mahābhārata (*M. Bh.*); a rākṣasa who fought on the side of Rāvaṇa (*M. Bh.*); another name for Śiva.

Tundi (S) (M) **1.** with a prominent navel. **3.** a gandharva.

Tuṇḍin (S) (M) the bull of Śiva.

Tuṅga (S) (M) **1.** prominent; erect; lofty; high; chief; strong; peak. **2.** *Prosopis spicigera.*

Tuṅgabala (S) (M) very strong.

Tuṅgadhanvan (S) (M) **1.** with a lofty bow. **3.** a king of Suhmā.

Tuṅganātha (S) (M) lord of height; lord of mountains.

Tuṅgaśaila (S) (M) **1.** with high words; rocks. **3.** a mountain with a temple of Śiva.

Tuṅgaśekhara (S) (M) **1.** high peaked. **2.** mountain.

Tuṅgeśvara (S) (M) **1.** lord of mountains. **3.** a temple of Śiva.

Tuṅgīpati (S) (M) **1.** lord of the night. **3.** another name for the moon.

Tuṅgīśa (S) (M) **1.** lord of the night. **3.** another name for Śiva, Kṛṣṇa, the sun and the moon.

Tuṅgīśvara (S) (M) **1.** lord of the night. **3.** another name for Śiva.

Tūṇi (S) (M) **1.** quiver bearer. **3.** Yugandhara's father.

Turaga (S) (M) **1.** moving swiftly; going quickly. **2.** the mind; horse; thought; the number 7. **3.** the white horse that emerged from the churning of the ocean and was claimed by Sūrya (*M. Bh.*).

Turaṇya (S) (M) **1.** to be swift. **3.** a horse of the moon.

Turaṇyu (S) (M) swift; zealous.

Turāṣāt (S) (M) **1.** overpowering the mighty. **3.** another name for Indra.

Tūrṇi (S) (M) **1.** quick; clever; zealous; expeditious. **2.** the mind.

Turṣārasuvra (S) (M) as white as snow.

Turvaṇi (S) (M) victorious.

Turvaśa (S) (M) **1.** overpowering; victorious. **3.** a hero king extolled in the *Ṛg Veda* and ancestor of the Āryan race.

Turvasu (S) (M) **1.** victorious. **3.** a son of Yayāti by Devayānī and the brother of Yadu (*M. Bh.*).

Tūrvayāṇa (S) (M) **1.** overpowering. **3.** a king extolled in the *Ṛg Veda.*

Tūrvi (S) (M) superior.

Turvīti (S) (M) **1.** superior; overpowering; fast moving. **3.** a sage protected by Indra.

Tuṣāra (S) (M) cold; frost; snow; mist; dew.

Tuṣāradyuti (S) (M) **1.** cold rayed. **3.** another name for the moon.

Tuṣāragiri (S) (M) **1.** snow mountain. **3.** another name for the Himālaya.

Tuṣātakānti (S) (M) **1.** beloved of the snow mountains. **3.** another name for Śiva.

Tuṣārakara (S) (M) **1.** cold rayed. **3.** another name for the moon.

Tuṣārakiraṇa (S) (M) **1.** cold rayed. **3.** another name for the moon.

Tuṣārānśu (S) (M) **1.** cold rayed. **3.** another name for the moon.

Tuṣāraraśmi (S) (M) **1.** cold rayed. **3.** another name for the moon.

Tuṣita (S) (M) **1.** satisfied; contented. **3.** Viṣṇu in the 3rd Manvantara; another name for 12 devas in the Ćākṣuṣa Manvantara.

Tuṣṭa (S) (M) satisfied; pleased.

Tuṣṭimān (S) (M) **1.** satisfied. **3.** a king of the Yayāti dynasty (*Bhāgavata*).

Tuṣya (S) (M) **1.** satisfied. **3.** another name for Śiva.

Tuvideṣṇa (S) (M) **1.** giving much. **3.** another name for Indra.

Tuvidyumna (S) (M) **1.** very glorious; powerful. **3.** another name for Indra, the maruts and Agni.

Tuvigra (S) (M) **1.** swallowing much. **3.** another name for Agni.

Tuvijāta (S) (M) **1.** of powerful nature. **3.** another name for Indra and Varuṇa.

Tuvikṣa (S) (M) **1.** powerful. **3.** Indra's bow.

Tuvikūrmi (S) (M) **1.** powerful in working. **3.** another name for Indra.

Tuvimanyu (S) (M) **1.** very zealous. **3.** another name for the maruts.

Tuviśravas (S) (M) **1.** highly renowned. **3.** another name for Agni.

Tuviṣṭama (S) (M) strongest.

Tuviśuṣma (S) (M) **1.** high spirited. **3.** Indra and Varuṇa conjoined.

Tūyam (S) (M) **1.** strong; quick. **2.** water.

Tvakṣas (S) (M) energy; vigour.

Tvaṣṭṛ, Tvaṣṭā (S) (M) **1.** carpenter; maker of carriages; creator of living beings; heavenly builder. **3.** a prajāpati who was the maker of divine implements including Indra's thunderbolt, teacher of the Ṛbhus, supposed author of the *Ṛg Veda*, the father of Śaraṇyū, Triśiras or Viśvarūpa by Rećana and the grandfather of Yama, Yamī and the aśvins; a king of the Bharata dynasty who was the son of Bhauvana and father of Viraja; one of the ādityas (*M. Bh.*); a son of Manasyu; a rudra (*Bh. Purāṇa*); another name for Viśvakarman.

Tvaṣṭādhara (S) (M) **1.** abode of creation. **3.** one of the 2 sons of Śukrāćārya.

Tveṣin (S) (M) impetuous.

Tviṣāmpati (S) (M) **1.** lord of light. **3.** another name for Sūrya.

Tyāgarāja (S) (M) **1.** lord of renunciation. **3.** the deity at Tiruvarun (*Thaurajana*) temple; a Bhakti saint of a high order and a great composer of Carnatic music.

Tyāgin (S) (M) ascetic; sacrificing; donor; liberal; hero.

U

Ućatha (S) (M) verse; praise.

Ućathya (S) (M) **1.** deserving praise. **3.** a muni and disciple of Vyāsa (*Bhāgavata*) and the father of Śibi and Veṇa by Mādhavī; a king of the Yādavas.

Uććadeva (S) (M) **1.** superior god. **3.** another name for Viṣṇu and Kṛṣṇa.

Uććadhvaja (S) (M) **1.** with a lofty banner. **2.** highly eminent. **3.** another name for Śākyāmuni.

Uććaghana (S) (M) laughter in the mind.

Uććaihśravas (S) (M) **1.** having lifted ears. **2.** long eared; neighing loudly. **3.** Indra's horse who emerged from the churning of the Ocean of Milk (*M. Bh.*); a king of the Purū dynasty who was the son of Avīkṣit (*M. Bh.*).

Uććairdhāman (S) (M) with intense rays.

Uććairmanyu (S) (M) highly placed.

Uććaka (S) (M) **1.** to look fearlessly. **2.** a king. **3.** a king of the Solar dynasty (*Bhāgavata*).

Uććala (S) (M) going up; the mind; understanding.

Uććalalāṭa (S) (M) with a high forehead; proud; lucky.

Uććaṇḍa (S) (M) rising fervour; very passionate; violent; terrible; mighty.

Uććandras (S) (M) **1.** the high moon; the moon that has gone high i.e. moon that has gone beyond vision. **2.** the moonless period of the night; the last watch of the night.

Uććārya (S) (M) to be spoken; to be pronounced; having spoken; uttered.

Uććāryamāna (S) (M) being uttered or pronounced.

Uććāṭana (S) (M) **1.** ruining. **3.** one of the 5 arrows of Kāma (S. *Purāṇa*).

Uććataru (S) (M) lofty tree; the Coconut tree (*Cocos nucifera*).

Uććedin (S) (M) resolving difficulties.

Uććharāyin (S) (M) high; raised; lofty.

Uććhikha (S) (M) **1.** with an upright comb. **2.** flaming; blazing; radiant; high crested. **3.** a serpent of the family of Takṣaka (*M. Bh.*); another name for Nārada.

Uććhikhaṇḍa (S) (M) **1.** high crested. **3.** another name for Nārada.

Uććhiras (S) (M) **1.** high headed. **2.** with the head held high. **3.** a mountain.

Uććhirayata (S) (M) **1.** rising up. **2.** standing erect; ambitious. **3.** a rākṣasa who was the son of Mālyavān (*V. Rāmāyaṇa*).

Uććhiṣṭabhojana (S) (M) **1.** eating remains of someone else's food. **3.** the attendant upon an idol (whose food is the leavings of offerings).

Uććhiṣṭagaṇapati (S) (M) Gaṇeśa as worshipped by the Uććhiṣṭas (or men who leave the remains of food in their mouth during prayer); a form of tāntric worship for early success.

Uććhrayopeta (S) (M) possessing height; high; lofty; elevated.

Uććhreya (S) (M) high; lofty.

Uććhṛta (S) (M) raised; lifted up; erect; arising; growing powerful.

Uććhuṣma (S) (M) **1.** with rising heat. **2.** one whose crackling becomes manifest. **3.** a deity (*B. Literature*); another name for Agni.

Uććṛṅga (S) (M) **1.** with erect horns. **3.** one of the 2 attendants given to Skanda by Vindhya (*M. Bh.*).

Uććūda (S) (M) the rising cloth; the flag or pennon of a banner; an ornament tied on top of a banner.

Ućita (S) (M) delightful; pleasurable; agreeable; proper; fit; right.

Udadhi (S) (M) **1.** receptacle of water. **2.** cloud; river; sea; ocean.

Udadhirāja (S) (M) **1.** lord of the ocean. **3.** another name for Varuṇa (*V. Rāmāyaṇa*).

Udaja (S) (M) **1.** born in water. **2.** lotus (*Nelumbo speciosum*).

Udakapati (S) (M) **1.** lord of water. **3.** another name for Varuṇa.

Udamaya (S) (M) **1.** made of water. **3.** a ṛṣi (*A. Brāhmaṇa*).

Udanćita (S) (M) raised up; worshipped.

Udanta (S) (M) good; virtuous; end of work; rest; news; message; folktale.

Udanvata (S) (M) **1.** abounding in water. **2.** the ocean. **3.** a ṛṣi.

Udāpekṣī (S) (M) **1.** requiring water. **3.** a son of Viśvāmitra.

Udāpi (S) (M) **1.** one who attains. **2.** successful. **3.** a son of Sahadeva (*M. Bh.*).

Udāra (S) (M) high; lofty; exalted; great; best; noble; generous; liberal; gentle; munificent; dignified; illustrious; splendid; kind; distinguished.

Udāradhī (S) (M) with an exalted intellect; wise; sagacious.

Udāraka (S) (M) **1.** excellent person. **3.** a minister of Mahiṣāsura.

Udārākṣa (S) (M) **1.** with generous eyes; merciful. **3.** a warrior of Skanda (*M. Bh.*).

Udāraśāṇḍilya (S) (M) **1.** benevolent fire. **3.** a hermit of the court of Indra (*M. Bh.*).

Udārathi (S) (M) **1.** rising; arising. **3.** another name for Viṣṇu.

Udarćiṣ (S) (M) **1.** shining upwards. **2.** flaming; brilliant; resplendent. **3.** another name for Śiva.

Udarśa (S) (M) overflowing.

Udātta (S) (M) **1.** lofty; elevated; high; great; illustrious; dear; beloved; gift; ornament; generous; gentle. **2.** the raised tone of the Vedic chant.

Udāvasu (S) (M) **1.** treasure of nobility. **3.** a son of King Janaka of Videha (*V. Rāmāyaṇa*).

Udaya (S) (M) **1.** ascending; prosperity; accomplishment. **2.** splendour; the rising of the sun; the mountains of the east behind which the sun is supposed to rise; coming forth; appearance; development; production; creation; success. **3.** the 1st lunar mansion (*V. Rāmāyaṇa*).

Udayāditya (S) (M) sunrise.

Udayagiri (S) (M) mountain of ascent; mountain of sunrise; the eastern mountain from behind which the sun rises.

Udayajit (S) (M) conqueror of the rising sun.

Udayana (S) (M) **1.** rising up. **2.** rising of the sun; result; conclusion. **3.** a renowned king of the lunar dynasty of Vatsa who was the son of Sahasrānīka and Mṛgāvatī and the husband of princess Vāsavadattā of Ujjayanī and Padmāvatī and the father of Naravāhanadatta who became king of the vidyādharas; another name for King Vatsa of Kausambhi and sage Agastya.

Udayanta (S) (M) risen; end of sunrise.

Udayāśva (S) (M) **1.** horse of development; progressing horse. **2.** fast and progressing; strong and swift. **3.** a grandson of Ajātaśatru (*V. Purāṇa*).

Udayatuṅga (S) (M) **1.** lofty among the mountains. **2.** lord of the mountains. **3.** a king (*Ś. Brāhmaṇa*).

Udayavīra (S) (M) emerging as a hero.

Udāyin (S) (M) **1.** rising; ascending; coming forward. **2.** prosperous; flourishing. **3.** a grandson of Ajātaśatru (*A. Brāhmaṇa*); another name for Viṣṇu.

Udāyus (S) (M) **1.** to stir up. **3.** father of Śrutaśarman.

Udbala (S) (M) highly strong; powerful.

Udbhāṣa (S) (M) radiance; splendour.

Udbhāsita (S) (M) come forth; lit up; splendid; ornamented; beautiful.

Udbhāsura (S) (M) highly shining; radiant.

Udbhaṭa (S) (M) high gentry; excellent; eminent; exalted; magnanimous; passionate; extraordinary; invincible.

Udbhava (S) (M) **1.** originate from. **2.** existence; origin; birth. **3.** a son of Nahuṣa (*Bhā. Parāṇa*).

Udbhida (S) (M) **1.** sprouting; germinating. **3.** a son of Jyotiṣmat (*V. Purāṇa*).

Udbhrama (S) (M) **1.** whirling. **2.** excitement; intoxication. **3.** a class of deities attendant on Śiva.

Uddālaka (S) (M) **1.** burnt open; a kind of honey. **3.** son of sage Aruṇa and a prominent teacher of the Vedas (*Ṛg Veda*); *Bauhinia vareigata.*

Uddāma (S) (M) **1.** flaring up. **2.** unrestrained; free; extraordinary; unlimited; large; great; violent; impetuous. **3.** another name for Yama and Varuṇa.

Uddāmara (S) (M) excellent; respectable; of high rank

Uḍḍāmarīn (S) (M) making an extraordinary noise.

Uddaṇḍaśāstrī (S) (M) **1.** extraordinary scholar. **3.** one of the 18 famous poets of Kerala.

Uddānta (S) (M) humble; energetic; elevated; pure; virtuous.

Uddarśana (S) (M) **1.** with clear vision. **3.** a king of the nāgas

Uddarśita (S) (M) made visible; appearing; come forth.

Uddātta (S) (M) high; lofty; noble; exalted; generous; famous; beloved.

Uddeśa (S) (M) exemplification; illustration.

Uddhara (S) (M) **1.** freed from burdens. **2.** wild; lively; cheerful; unrestrained.

Uddharaṇa (S) (M) **1.** rescuing; final emancipation; raising; delivering. **3.** the father of King Śantanu (*M. Bh.*).

Uddharṣa (S) (M) courage to undertake anything.

Uddhas (S) (M) **1.** to break into laughter. **2.** lightning.

Uddhava (S) (M) **1.** lifting up; lifting up the spirits of others. **2.** sacrificial fire; festival; joy; pleasure. **3.** a Yādava who was a friend and minister of Kṛṣṇa and a disciple of Bṛhaspati (*Bhā. Purāṇa*).

Uḍḍīnam (S) (M) flying up; soaring.

Uddīpa (S) (M) inflaming; lighting up; illuminating.

Uddīpaka (S) (M) stimulating; inflaming.

Uddīrṇa (S) (M) **1.** created; formed; blossomed; progressed; secret. **3.** another name for Viṣṇu.

Uḍḍīśa (S) (M) **1.** lord of the flying ones. **2.** lord of divine beings. **3.** a tāntra work (containing charms and incantations); another name for Śiva.

Uḍḍīyakavi (S) (M) a lofty poet.

Uḍḍīyamāna (S) (M) one who soars; flying up; soaring.

Uḍḍīyana (S) (M) soaring; flying up.

Uddṛṣṭa (S) (M) **1.** seen properly. **2.** the appearance of the moon.

Uddyota (S) (M) shining; flashing.

Udgama (S) (M) the rising of a star; the elevation of a mountain.

Udgandhi (S) (M) giving forth perfume; fragrant.

Udgata (S) (M) **1.** risen; ascended; coming forth. **2.** leader; priest; preceptor. **3.** one of the 7 chief priests of the Vedas (*Ṛg Veda*).

Udgātṛ (S) (M) **1.** chanter. **2.** priest.

Udgītha (S) (M) **1.** chanting of the *Sāma Veda.* **3.** the syllable Om; a son of Bhuva (*V. Purāṇa*).

Udīcya (S) (M) **1.** living in the north. **3.** a disciple of Vyāsa (*Bhāgavata*).

Udīṣita (S) (M) risen; elevated.

Udita (S) (M) **1.** risen; ascended; high; lofty; tall; born; produced; apparent; visible. **2.** the sunrise.

Uditvara (S) (M) risen; surpassed; extraordinary.

Udojas (S) (M) exceedingly powerful; effective.

Udraka (S) (M) **1.** of the water. **3.** a ṛṣi (*Ṛg Veda*).

Udrapāraka (S) (M) **1.** helping to cross the water. **3.** a serpent of the family of Dhṛtarāṣṭra (*M. Bh.*).

Udreka (S) (M) blossoming of a thought; passion; preponderance; superiority; predominance.

Udrodhana (S) (M) rising; growing.

Uḍugaṇādhīpa (S) (M) **1.** the lord of the stars. **3.** another name for the moon and the Nakṣatra Mṛgaśiras.

Udumbala (S) (M) of wide reaching power.

Udumbara (S) (M) **1.** the ultimate tree; the essence of all trees. **3.** *Ficus glomerata.*

Uḍunātha (S) (M) **1.** lord of the stars. **3.** another name for the moon.

Uḍūpa (S) (M) protecting from water; drinking water; a raft or float; a kind of drinking vessel covered with leather.

Uḍupas (S) (M) **1.** boat shaped. **2.** the crescent moon.

Uḍupatha (S) (M) the path of the stars; firmament; the ether.

Uḍupati (S) (M) **1.** lord of the stars. **3.** another name for the moon and Soma.

Uḍurāj (S) (M) **1.** king of the stars. **3.** another name for the moon.

Udvaha (S) (M) **1.** carrying up; continuing. **2.** eminent; best; son. **3.** the 4th of the 7 winds or courses of air and the one that supports the lunar constellations (*H. Purāṇa*); one of the 7 tongues of fire; a Kṣatriya king born of the family of the asura Krodhavaśa (*M. Bh.*).

Udvanśa (S) (M) of noble descent.

Udyat (S) (M) **1.** rising. **2.** astar.

Udyota (S) (M) shining forth; light; lustre.

Udyotana (S) (M) to enlighten; to make manifest; illuminated.

Ugāgra (S) (M) high peak.

Ugam (S) (M) rising upwards.

Ugaṇa (S) (M) **1.** consisting of extended troops. **2.** an army.

Ugra (S) (M) **1.** powerful; violent; mighty; impetuous; strong; huge; formidable; terrible; high; noble; cruel; fierce; ferocious; savage; angry; passionate; wrathful; hot; sharp; pungent; acrid; rude. **3.** a military captain of Sūrapadmāsura the chief of asuras (*H. Purāṇa*); a son of Dhṛtarāṣṭra (*M. Bh.*); a Yādava prince (*M. Bh.*); the son of Prajāpati Kavi (*M. Bh.*); another name for Rudra (*M. Bh.*).

Ugrabāhu (S) (M) one whose arms are large or powerful.

Ugrabhairava (S) (M) **1.** powerful and fierce. **2.** terrible; frightful; horrible. **3.** a Kāpālika (*K. Sāgara*).

Ugrabhata (S) (M) **1.** powerful soldier. **2.** mighty soldier. **3.** a king (*K. Sāgara*).

Ugraćārin (S) (M) **1.** moving impetuously. **3.** another name for the moon.

Ugrāćārya (S) (M) **1.** powerful teacher. **3.** an author.

Ugraćaya (S) (M) strong desire.

Ugradaṇḍa (S) (M) stern in punishment; stern sceptred; holding a terrible rod.

Ugradeva (S) (M) **1.** mighty deity. **2.** worshiping mighty deities. **3.** a ṛṣi (*Ṛg Veda*).

Ugradhanvan (S) (M) **1.** with a powerful bow. **3.** another name for Indra.

Ugragandha (S) (M) **1.** strong smelling. **2.** garlic; *Michelia champaca*; Wild Turnip (*Brassica campestris*).

Ugraka (S) (M) **1.** brave; powerful. **3.** a serpent (*M. Bh.*).

Ugrakarman (S) (M) **1.** fierce in action. **2.** violent; one who does cruel deeds. **3.** a king of Śālva (*M. Bh.*); the military chief of the Kekaya prince Viśoka (*M. Bh.*).

Ugrakarṇikā (S) (M) with large earrings.

Ugramaya (S) (M) **1.** with a violent image. **3.** a demon causing diseases (*H. Purāṇa*).

Ugranarasiṁha (S) (M) **1.** ferocious manlion. **3.** Viṣṇu in his lion incarnation (*Bhā. Purāṇa*).

Ugraputra (S) (M) **1.** son of the ferocious; son of Śiva; son of a powerful man; having mighty sons. **3.** another name for Kārttikeya.

Ugraravas (S) (M) **1.** speaking violently. **3.** a muni.

Ugraretas (S) (M) **1.** possessor of a horrible weapon. **3.** a form of Rudra (*Bhā. Purāṇa*).

Ugraśakti (S) (M) **1.** of terrible might. **3.** a son of King Amaraśakti.

Ugraśāsana (S) (M) severe in command; strict in orders.

Ugrasena (S) (M) **1.** formidable leader. **2.** fierce; high; noble; powerful. **3.** the Yādava king of Mathurāpuri who was the son of Āhuka and the father of

Kaṇsa (*Bhā. Purāṇa*); a brother of King Janamejaya (*M. Bh.*); a son of Kaśyapa and Muni (*M. Bh.*); a king who was the incarnation of the asura Svarbhānu; a son of Dhṛtarāṣṭra (*M. Bh.*); a son of King Parīkṣit (*M. Bh.*).

Ugrasenānī (S) (M) **1.** the mighty warrior; with a mighty army. **3.** another name for Kṛṣṇa.

Ugraśravas (S) (M) **1.** with enormous fame. **2.** very famous. **3.** the son of ṛṣi Lomaharṣa (*M. Bh.*); a son of Dhṛtarāṣṭra (*M. Bh.*); the husband of Śīlāvatī.

Ugratapas (S) (M) **1.** mighty ascetic. **2.** doing terrible penances. **3.** the son of ṛṣi Sutapas of the Bhṛgu dynasty who was reborn as a gopi (*P. Purāṇa*).

Ugratejas (S) (M) **1.** with violent energy. **2.** fiercely worthy; noble and passionate. **3.** a serpent (*M. Bh.*); a Buddha (*L. Vistara*); another name for Śiva.

Ugratīrtha (S) (M) **1.** visiting places of violence. **3.** a Kṣatriya king who was an incarnation of the asura Krodhavaśa (*M. Bh.*).

Ugratyās (S) (M) terribly energetic; endowed with great or terrible energy.

Ugravega (S) (M) with terrible velocity; very fast; very active; very swift.

Ugravīra (S) (M) violent hero.

Ugravīrya (S) (M) terrible in might.

Ugravyaghra (S) (M) **1.** violent tiger. **3.** a dānava (*H. Purāṇa*).

Ugrāyudha (S) (M) **1.** with terrible weapons. **3.** a son of Dhṛtarāṣṭra (*M. Bh.*); a Pāñcala king who fought on the side of the Pāṇḍavas (*M. Bh.*); a warrior of the Kauravas (*M. Bh.*); an emperor killed by Bhīṣma (*M. Bh.*).

Ugreśa (S) (M) **1.** the mighty or terrible lord. 3. another name for Śiva (*A. Veda*).

Ujāsa (S) (M) light before dawn.

Ujjāgara (S) (M) excited.

Ujjaya (S) (M) **1.** archer whose bow string is open; archer ever ready to win. **3.** a son of Viśvāmitra (*M. Bh.*).

Ujjayana (S) (M) conqueror.

Ujjayanta (S) (M) **1.** having conquered. **3.** a mountain (*M. Bh.*).

Ujjendra (S) (M) victor.

Ujjeṣa (S) (M) victorious.

Ujjeṣin (S) (M) **1.** victorious. **3.** one of the 7 maruts.

Ujjhaka (S) (M) cloud; devotee.

Ujji (S) (M) to win; to conquer.

Ujjīvin (S) (M) **1.** revival. **2.** one who has revived; having the power of correcting one's self. **3.** a counsellor of Meghavarṇa the king of crows (*Pañcatantra*).

Ujjūṭitā (S) (M) with upgoing hair; wearing the hair twisted together and coiled upwards.

Ujjvala (S) (M) highly inflamed; bright; illuminated; splendid; light; burning; clean; clear; lovely; beautiful; sunshine; the sentiment of love.

Ujjvaladatta (S) (M) **1.** bestowed with brightness. **2.** bright; intelligent. **3.** the author of a commentary on the *Unadi Sūtras* (*K. Sāgara*).

Ujjvalanam (S) (M) **1.** burning; shining; lighting up. **2.** fire; gold.

Ujjvalas (S) (M) inflamed; love; passion.

Ukha (S) (M) **1.** boiler; cauldron; vessel; a part of the upper leg. **3.** a pupil of Tittiri (*P. Ratra*).

Ukhya (S) (M) **1.** being in a cauldron. **3.** a grammarian (*Ṛg Veda*).

Ukṣaṇ (S) (M) **1.** sprinkling; consecrating. **2.** an ox or bull as impregnating the flock. **3.** in the Vedas the ox or bull draw the chariot of the dawn; another name for Soma, the maruts, the sun and Agni.

Ukṣasena (S) (M) **1.** having an army of bulls; commander of bulls; one who possesses bulls; chief of the bulls. **3.** a king (*M. Upaniṣad*).

Ukṣatara (S) (M) a young bull; a strong bull.

Ukṣita (S) (M) sprinkled; moistened; strong; of full growth.

Ukta (S) (M) uttered; said; spoken.

Uktapratyukta (S) speech and reply; discourse; conversation; a kind of anthem or alternate song.

Uktatva (S) (M) spoken speech.

Uktavākya (S) (M) spoken sentence; one who has given an opinion; a dictum; decree.

Uktavat (S) (M) one who has spoken.

Uktha (S) (M) **1.** saying; sentence; verse; eulogy; praise; hymn; ritual recitation. **2.** Sāman verses which are sung or muttered as sacrificial formula; treasure; a special beat. **3.** an agni and the father of Parāvāṇī (*M. Bh.*); another name for the sun, *Sāma Veda, Yajur Veda* and Brāhmā.

Ukthabhṛt (S) (M) offering verses.

Ukthāmada (S) praise and rejoicing conjoined.

Ukthamukha (S) (M) preface of the recitation; the beginning of an Uktha recitation.

Ukthapātra (S) (M) **1.** vessel of praise. **2.** vessels of libation offered during the recitation of an Uktha.

Ukthapattra (S) (M) having verses as wings; one who flies with praise.

Ukthaśansin (S) (M) reciter of hymns; praising; uttering the Ukthas.

Ukthaśāstra (S) (M) discipline of recital; recitation and praise according to the Śāstras.

Ukthasuṣma (S) (M) beauty of the hymn; loudly resonant with verses; moving on with the sound of verses (as with the roaring of waters); accompanied by sound of verses; one whose strength is praise.

Ukthavardhana (S) (M) **1.** having hymns as a cause of refreshment. **2.** one who is refreshed or delighted by praise.

Ukthāvī (S) (M) fond of hymns.

Ukthavid (S) (M) knower of hymns; conversant with hymns of praise.

Ukthavidha (S) (M) verse like; knower of the verse.

Ukthavīrya (S) power of the verse; a particular part of Śāstra, conversant in speech.

Ukthāyu (S) (M) eager for praise.

Uktopaniṣatka (S) (M) one to whom the Upaniṣads have been spoken; one who has been taught the Upaniṣads.

Ulanda (S) (M) **1.** throwing out. **3.** a king (*P. Ratra*).

Ulapa (S) (M) **1.** spreading. **2.** a species of soft grass; a spreading vine. **3.** a pupil of Kalāpin.

Ulapya (S) (M) **1.** abiding in or belonging to the Ulapa grass. **3.** a rudra (*M. Samhitā*).

Ulbaṇa (S) (M) **1.** abundant; excessive; immense; strong; powerful. **3.** a son of Vasiṣṭha (*Bh. Purāṇa*).

Ulkāmukha (S) (M) **1.** with a fiery mouth. **3.** a son of Agni (*A. Koṣa*); a rākṣasa (*Rāmāyana*).

Ullāgha (S) (M) **1.** to be able. **2.** dextrous; clever; pure; happy.

Ullāsa (S) (M) light; splendour; appearance; joy; delight; increase; growth.

Ullāsin (S) (M) playing; sporting; dancing.

Ullāsit (S) (M) shining; brilliant; splendid; happy.

Ulmuka (S) (M) **1.** firebrand. **3.** a son of Balarāma (*M. Bh.*); a son of Manu Ćakṣuṣa; a king of the Vṛṣṇi dynasty (*V. Purāṇa*).

Ulūka (S) (M) **1.** owl; tip of a needle; a kind of grass. **3.** another name for Indra; a muni (*V. Purāṇa*); a naga (*M. Bh.*); the son of Sakuni (*M. Bh.*); a yakṣa (*M. Bh.*); a son of Viśvāmitra (*M. Bh.*).

Ulūkajit (S) (M) **1.** conqueror of Indra. **3.** another name for Indrajit (*V. Purāṇa*).

Ulūpya (S) (M) **1.** with a charming face. **3.** another name for Rudra.

Ūma (S) (M) helper; friend; companion.

Umāguru (S) (M) **1.** father of Umā. **3.** another name for Himavat.

Umākānta (S) (M) **1.** beloved of Umā. **2.** lord of night; moonlight. **3.** another name for Śiva and the moon.

Umāmaṇi (S) (M) **1.** gem of Umā; gem of fame. **2.** a special kind of gem that attracts men.

Umānātha (S) (M) **1.** lord of Umā. **3.** another name for Śiva.

Umāpati (S) (M) **1.** lord of Umā. **3.** another name for Śiva.

Umāprasāda (S) (M) given by Umā; gift of Umā; gift of splendour; light; fame.

Umāśahāya (S) (M) **1.** companion of Umā. **3.** another name for Śiva.

Umāśaṅkara (S) (M) Parvatī and Śiva conjoined.

Umāsuta (S) (M) **1.** son of Umā. **3.** another name for Skanda.

Umbara (S) (M) **1.** lintel of a door. **3.** a gandharva (*H. Purāṇa*).

Umeśa (S) (M) **1.** lord of Umā. **3.** Umā and Śiva conjoined; another name for Śiva.

Umeśvara (S) (M) **1.** lord of Umā. **3.** another name for Śiva.

Unćādi (S) (M) **1.** gathering grains. **3.** a gaṇa (*Ś. Purāṇa*).

Ūṇi (S) (M) a Soma vessel.

Uṅkara (S) (M) **1.** bestower of pleasure. **3.** companion of Viṣṇu (*Ṛg Veda*).

Unma (S) (M) joy.

Unmādana (S) (M) **1.** intoxicating; causing madness. **3.** one of the 5 arrows of Kāma (*Ś. Purāṇa*).

Unmaj (S) (M) rising upwards; emerging; progressing.

Unmanda (S) (M) cheerful; delighted; amused.

Unmaṇi (S) (M) superior gem; a gem lying on the surface.

Unmātha (S) (M) **1.** shaking; killing. **2.** a trap. **3.** an attendant given to Skanda by Yama (*M. Bh.*); an attendant given to Skanda by Pārvatī (*M. Bh.*).

Unmatta (S) (M) **1.** disordered; furious; frantic. **3.** a rākṣasa (*Rāmāyaṇa*); one of the 8 forms of Bhairava (*V. Rāmāyaṇa*).

Unmayūkha (S) (M) shining forth; radiant.

Unmeṣa (S) (M) opening the eyes; flashing; blossoming of a flower; coming forth; visible.

Unmīla (S) (M) becoming visible; to appear.

Unnābha (S) (M) **1.** as high as the sky. **3.** a king (*Bhā. Purāṇa*).

Unnāda (S) (M) **1.** crying out. **2.** clamour. **3.** a son of Kṛṣṇa (*Bhā. Purāṇa*).

Unnamana (S) (M) raising; lifting up; increase; prosperity.

Unnata (S) (M) **1.** elevated. **2.** raised; high; tall; prominent; great; noble. **3.** a Buddha (*L. Vistara*); a ṛṣi in the Manu Ćakṣuṣa Manvantara (*V. Purāṇa*); a mountain (*V. Purāṇa*).

Unnatīśa (S) (M) **1.** lord of progress; desiring prosperity; lord of Unnati. **3.** another name for Garuḍa.

Unnī (S) (M) to lead up; help; rescue; free; redeem; set up; promote; raise.

Unnidra (S) (M) beyond sleep; sleepless; awake; blossomed; shining as the rising sun or the moon.

Upabarhaṇa (S) (M) **1.** cushion; pillow. **3.** another name for the gandharvā Nārada.

Upaćārumat (S) (M) **1.** civil; polite. **3.** father of Bhadra.

Upaćitra (S) (M) **1.** variegated; coloured. **3.** a son of Dhṛtarāṣṭra (*M. Bh.*).

Upāćyutam (S) (M) near Kṛṣṇa.

Upadeśa (S) (M) sermon; teaching; advice.

Upadeva (S) (M) **1.** a secondary deity. **3.** a king of the Purū dynasty (*Bhā. Purāṇa*).

Upadevaka (S) (M) **1.** minor god. **3.** son of Akrūra.

Upādeya (S) (M) useful; to be chosen; excellent; admirable; not to be refused.

Upādhyāya (S) (M) **1.** nearing knowledge. **2.** teacher; preceptor.

Upadiśa (S) (M) **1.** suggested; pointing out; showing. **2.** teacher. **3.** a son of Vasudeva (*Bhā. Purāṇa*).

Upādya (S) (M) 2nd.

Upagahana (S) (M) **1.** nearing a forest or cave. **2.** a person with a depth of character; serious person. **3.** a ṛṣi (*M. Bh.*).

Upagraha (S) (M) **1.** a secondary planet. **2.** satellite; comet; meteor. **3.** a son of Viśvāmitra (*M. Bh.*).

Upagu (S) (M) **1.** near a teacher; assistant teacher. **3.** a king.

Upagupta (S) (M) **1.** secret; hidden. **3.** a king of the lunar dynasty.

Upaguru (S) (M) **1.** assistant teacher; near teachers. **3.** a king (*Bhā. Purāṇa*).

Upahāra (S) (M) offering; gift; oblation to a deity.

Upahūta (S) (M) called; invited; summoned; invoked.

Upajas (S) (M) **1.** produced; coming from. **3.** a deity.

Upajaya (S) (M) **1.** to help; to support. **3.** a hermit who performed the sacrifice for King Drupada to bear children (*M. Bh.*).

Upajīka (S) (M) **1.** living near water plants. **3.** a Vedic water deity (*A. Veda*).

Upajit (S) (M) to acquire by victory.

Upakāla (S) (M) **1.** almost black. **2.** dark. **3.** a king of nāgas.

Upakāra (H) (M) favour; kindness; ornament; decoration; embellishment.

Upakāśa (S) (M) wearing the sky; aurora; dawn.

Upakṛṣṇaka (S) (M) **1.** almost black. **3.** a warrior of Skanda (*M. Bh.*).

Upakṣatra (S) (M) **1.** with a small domain. **3.** a king (*V. Purāṇa*).

Upakṣaya (S) (M) **1.** secondary destruction. **3.** the destroyer of the world; another name for Śiva.

Upakuśa (S) (M) **1.** near Kuśa. **3.** son of Kuśa (*V. Rāmāyaṇa*).

Upāli (S) (M) **1.** friend of a friend. **3.** one of Buddha's most eminent pupils and the 1st propounder of Buddhist law (*B. Literature*).

Upama (S) (M) highest; best; nearest; 1st.

Upamanyu (S) (M) **1.** striving for knowledge. **2.** zealous; knowing; intelligent. **3.** a hermit son of Sutapas (*Br. Purāṇa*); the son of Vyāsa; a Śaiva sage whose hermitage in the Himālayas became a sanctuary for all the animals; a ṛṣi who received the Ocean of Milk from Śiva (*L. Purāṇa*).

Upamaśravas (S) (M) **1.** highly renowned. **3.** a son of Kuruśravana and grandson of Mitratithi.

Upamātiṣ (S) (M) **1.** granting wealth. **3.** another name for Agni.

Upananda (S) (M) **1.** approaching happiness; pleasant; mythical. **3.** a son of Dhṛtarāṣṭra (*M. Bh.*); a serpent (*M. Bh.*); a warrior of Skanda (*M. Bh.*).

Upanandaka (S) (M) **1.** giving or nearing pleasure. **3.** a son of Dhṛtarāṣṭra (*M. Bh.*).

Upanandana (S) (M) **1.** like a son. **3.** a form of Śiva (*A. Koṣa*).

Upanara (S) (M) offering; present; gift.

Upanāya (S) (M) leader.

Upanetṛ (S) (M) **1.** bringing near. **2.** spiritual preceptor.

Upāṅga (S) (M) **1.** the act of anointing; secondary part of the body; additional work; mark of sandalwood on the forehead. **3.** the secondary Vedas.

Upanibha (S) (M) similar; equal.

Upanidhi (S) (M) **1.** a deposit. **2.** pledge; a ray of light. **3.** a son of Vasudeva (*V. Purāṇa*).

Upāriśu (S) (M) a prayer uttered in a low voice.

Upapati (S) (M) gallant.

Uparatna (S) (M) a secondary gem.

Upariċaravasu (S) (M) **1.** a deity who travels above. **2.** guardian angel. **3.** a descendant of Viṣṇu he was the son of Kṛti and the father of Bṛhadratha, Kuśāmbha, Mavella, Yadu and Rājanya (*M. Bh.*).

Upaśloka (S) (M) **1.** secondary verse. **3.** the father of the 10th Manu (*Bh. Purāṇa*); a son of Kṛṣṇa and Sairindrī.

Upaśobhin (S) (M) acquiring beauty; beautiful; brilliant; bright.

Upastava (S) (M) praise.

Upastu (S) (M) to invoke; celebrate in song; praise.

Upastuta (S) (M) **1.** invoked; praised. **3.** a ṛṣi (*Ṛg Veda*).

Upaśubha (S) (M) nearing auspiciousness; to be beautiful and brilliant.

Upasunda (S) (M) **1.** younger brother of Sunda. **3.** a daityā (*M. Bh.*).

Upatiṣyam (S) (M) **1.** near the asterism Tiṣya. **2.** asterisms called Āśleṣā and Punarvasu (*T. Brahmaṇa*).

Upavarṣa (S) (M) **1.** acquiring knowledge. **2.** possessed of extraordinary knowledge. **3.** the younger brother of Varṣa and son of Śankarasvāmin, author of the Mimānsā philosophy.

Upavata (S) (M) **1.** similar to the Vata tree. **2.** pious; sacred; *Buchnania latifolia.*

Upāvī (S) (M) cherishing; pleasing.

Upavīta (S) (M) invested with the sacred thread; the sacred thread worn over the left shoulder.

Upayāma (S) (M) **1.** with restraint; a ladle used in the Soma sacrifice. **3.** a deity (*V. Samhitā*).

Upayuta (S) (M) **1.** performing sacrifices. **3.** a king (*V. Purāṇa*).

Upekṣa (S) (M) **1.** to wait on patiently; to expect; to neglect; to connive. **3.** a son of Śvaphalka.

Upendra (S) (M) **1.** younger brother of Indra. **3.** another name for Viṣṇu/ Kṛṣṇa born after Indra in his dwarf incarnation.

Upendrabala (S) (M) **1.** with Viṣṇu's power. **3.** the son of a minister of King Śrīdatta (*V. Purāṇa*).

Upodayam (S) (M) at the time of sunrise.

Upoditi (S) (M) **1.** advancing. **3.** a ṛṣi (*T. Samhitā*).

Uppala (S) (M) precious stone; jewel; cloud; lotus (*Nelumbo speciosum*).

Uragabhūṣaṇa (S) (M) **1.** decorated or ornamented with serpents. **3.** another name for Śiva.

Uragarāja (S) (M) **1.** king of snakes. **3.** another name for Vāsuki.

Uragāri (S) (M) **1.** enemy of snakes. **3.** another name for Garuḍa.

Uragīndra (S) (M) **1.** lord of serpents. **3.** another name for Vāsuki and Seṣa.

Urasila (S) (M) broadchested.

Ūrdhvabāhu (S) (M) **1.** with lifted hands. **2.** devotee. **3.** a son of Vasiṣṭha and Ūrjā (*A. Purāṇa*).

Urdhvabhāk (S) (M) **1.** going up. **3.** the agni who was the 5th son of Bṛhaspati (*M. Bh.*).

Ūrdhvabhās (S) (M) rising splendour; one whose splendour rises.

Ūrdhvadeva (S) (M) **1.** upper god. **2.** god of the upper regions. **3.** another name for Viṣṇu.

Ūrdhvaga (S) (M) **1.** ascending. **3.** a son of Kṛṣṇa (*Bh. Purāṇa*).

Urdhvāsana (S) (M) sitting high; high superior; victorious.

Ūrjamedha (S) (M) strong intelligence; very wise.

Ūrjasani (S) (M) **1.** granting strength. **3.** another name for Agni.

Ūrjastambha (S) (M) **1.** pillar of strength. **3.** a ṛṣi of the 2nd Manvantara (*Bhā. Purāṇa*).

Ūrjasvala (S) (M) **1.** powerful; strong; mighty. **3.** a ṛṣi in the 2nd Manvantara (*V. Purāṇa*).

Ūrjaśvin (S) (M) powerful; strong; mighty.

Ūrjayoni (S) (M) **1.** originator of energy. **3.** a son of Viśvāmitra (*M. Bh.*).

Ūrjita (S) (M) possessed with power; powerful; distinguished; excellent; beautiful; noble; strong; mighty; great; important; gallant.

Ūrjitśraya (S) (M) **1.** abode of strength. **2.** a hero.

Ūrjja (S) (M) **1.** powerful. **3.** a king of the Hehaya dynasty who was the grandfather of Jarāsandha (*A. Purāṇa*); a ṛṣi of the Svārociṣa Manvantara (*V. Purāṇa*).

Ūrjjaketu (S) (M) **1.** with a strong (victorious) flag. **3.** a king of the dynasty of King Janaka (*Bhāgavata*).

Ūrṇa (S) (M) **1.** wool. **3.** a yakṣa (*Bhā. Purāṇa*).

Ūrṇanābha (S) (M) **1.** with a woolly navel. **2.** spider; a particular position of the hands. **3.** a son of Dhṛtarāṣṭra (*M. Bh.*); a dānava.

Ūrṇāyu (S) (M) **1.** wool carder. **3.** a gandharva who fell in love with Menakā (*M. Bh.*).

Ūru (S) (M) **1.** wide; broad; spacious; great; excellent; large; thigh. **3.** a son of the 14th Manu (*Bh. Purāṇa.*); the son of Manu Ćākṣusa and Nadvalā and the husband of Ātreyī (*A. Veda*).

Urućakri (S) (M) **1.** doing great work; the circle of evolution. **3.** a descendant of Atri (*Ṛg Veda*).

Urućakṣas (S) (M) **1.** far seeing. **3.** another name for Varuna, Sūrya and the ādityas.

Urūći (S) (M) far reaching; capacious; extending far.

Urudbhī (S) (M) **1.** terrifying in many ways. **3.** son of Śakuni.

Urudhiṣṇya (S) (M) **1.** exceedingly thoughtful. **3.** a sage of the 11th Manvantara.

Urugāya (S) (M) **1.** wide striding; much praised. **3.** another name for Indra, Viṣṇu, Kṛṣṇa, Soma and the aśvins.

Ūruja (S) (M) **1.** born from the thigh. **3.** another name for the ṛṣi Aurva.

Urukrama (S) (M) **1.** far stepping; with wide strides. **3.** another name for Vāmana.

Urukṣaya (S) (M) **1.** occupying spacious dwellings. **3.** another name for Varuṇa and the maruts.

Uruloka (S) (M) ample; vast.

Uruśanṣa (S) (M) **1.** of far reaching praise; praised by many. **3.** another name for Varuṇa; Pūṣan, Indra, the Soma and the ādityas.

Urusattva (S) (M) of a generous or noble nature.

Uruśravas (S) (M) of wide reaching fame; an ardent listener.

Uruvalka (S) (M) **1.** well dressed. **3.** a son of Vasudeva (*Bhā. Purāṇa*).

Ūrva (S) (M) **1.** of the thigh. **3.** a renowned hermit of the Bhṛgu family who was the son of Ćyavana and the father of Ṛćīka (*V. Samhitā*).

Ūrvāṅga (S) (M) **1.** large bodied. **2.** a mountain; ocean.

Urvarāpati (S) (M) **1.** lord of the cultivated soil. **3.** another name for Indra.

Urvarīyān (S) (M) **1.** fertile. **3.** the son of Prajāpati Pulaha and Kṣamā (*V. Purāṇa*).

Urvībhuj (S) (M) **1.** earth enjoyer. **2.** king.

Urvīdhara (S) (M) **1.** earth bearer. **2.** king.

Urvīpati (S) (M) **1.** master of the earth. **2.** king.

Urvīśa (S) (M) **1.** lord of the earth. **2.** king.

Urvīśvara (S) (M) **1.** god of the earth. **2.** king.

Uṣadgu (S) (M) **1.** remover of darkness. **3.** a son of Svāhi (*V. Purāṇa*).

Uṣadratha (S) (M) **1.** chariot of the sun. **3.** a son of Titikṣu (*V. Purāṇa*).

Uṣākara (S) (M) **1.** night maker. **3.** another name for the moon.

Uṣakiraṇa (S) (M) the 1st ray of dawn.

Uśanas (S) (M) **1.** with desire. **3.** a sage later identified with Śukra the son of Bhṛgu and the regent of the planet Venus (*Ṛg Veda*); a Vedic ṛṣi who was associated with the fire ritual in the *Ṛg Veda*; a son of Kavi, he was the friend of Indra.

Uṣaṇgava (S) (M) **1.** one who rises at dawn. **2.** early riser. **3.** a king in the court of Yama (*M. Bh.*).

Uṣaṅgu (S) (M) **1.** one who gets up at dawn. **2.** early riser. **3.** a hermit (*M. Bh.*); a king of the Yadu family who was the son of Vṛjinivān and the father of Ćitraratha (*M. Bh.*); a sacred cow; another name for Śiva.

Uṣāpati (S) (M) **1.** master of Uṣā. **3.** another name for Aniruddha and the moon.

Uṣāramaṇa (S) (M) **1.** beloved of Uṣā. **3.** another name for Aniruddha.

Uṣarbhudha (S) (M) **1.** waking with the morning light. **3.** another name for Agni.

Uṣasti (S) (M) **1.** true dawn. **3.** a ṛṣi who was the husband of Ātikī.

Uśenya (S) (M) to be wished for; desirable.

Uṣeśa (S) (M) **1.** lord of Uṣā. **3.** another name for the moon.

Uśija (S) (M) **1.** desire born; wishing; desiring; zealous; amiable; desirable; fire; ghee. **3.** the father of Kakṣīvat; a son of Ūru (*V. Purāṇa*).

Uṣika (S) (M) **1.** dawn worshipper; early riser. **3.** a hermit mentioned in the *Ṛg Veda*.

Uśīnara (S) (M) **1.** most desired. **3.** a famous king of the lunar dynasty who was the son of Śṛṇjaya and the husband of Mādhavī and father of Śibi and Veṇa; a Yādava king (*M. Bh.*).

Ūṣmā (S) (M) **1.** heat. **2.** spring; passion; anger; ardour; the hot season. **3.** a son of the agni Pāñćajanya (*M. Bh.*).

Ūṣman (S) (M) heat; glow; ardour.

Uṣṇa (S) (M) hot; passionate; ardent; sharp; active.

Uṣṇagu (S) (M) **1.** hot rayed. **3.** another name for the sun.

Uṣṇakara (S) (M) **1.** hot rayed; creator of heat. **3.** another name for the sun.

Uṣnaraṣmi (S) (M) **1.** hotrayed. **3.** another name for Sūrya.

Uṣṇih (S) (M) **1.** attached. **2.** metre of poetry. **3.** one of the 7 horses of the sun (*V. Purāṇa*).

Uṣṇinābha (S) (M) **1.** fire navelled. **3.** a viśvadeva (*M. Bh.*).

Uṣnīṣa (S) (M) anything worn on the head; turban; diadem; crown.

Uṣnīṣin (S) (M) **1.** wearing a crown. **3.** another name for Śiva.

Uṣojala (S) (M) **1.** water of dawn; the dawn's tears. **2.** dew.

Uṣorāga (S) (M) morning light; the dawn.

Usra (S) (M) morning light; sun; bright; shining; morning; dawn; the 2 aśvins; flame; bull.

Uśrāyus (S) (M) **1.** with a bright life. **3.** a son of Purūravas (*Ṛg Veda*).

Uṣṭrajihva (S) (M) **1.** buffalo tongued. **3.** an attendant of Skanda (*M. Bh.*).

Utaṅka (S) (M) **1.** stretching out. **3.** a ṛṣi (*M. Bh.*).

Utathya (S) (M) **1.** deliberation. **2.** intensity. **3.** elder brother of Bṛhaspati (*V. Purāṇa*); Viṣṇu born as the son of Aṅgiras and Śraddhā who married Soma's daughter Bhadrā and was the advisor to King Māndhāta (*M. Bh.*).

Utathyānuja (S) (M) **1.** Utathya's younger brother. **3.** another name for Bṛhaspati (*M. Bh.*).

Utkala (S) (M) **1.** glorious. **2.** glorious country; a porter; carrying a burden or load; a fowler; a bird catcher. **3.** a son of Dhruva (*Bhā. Purāṇa*); the son of Vaivasvata Manu (*Br. Purāṇa*); a country now called Orissa; another name for Sudyumna.

Utkarṣa (S) (M) superior; eminent; much; excessive; attractive; pulling upwards; drawing; elevation; increase; prosperity; rising to something better; excellence; eminence; progress; development.

Utkāśa (S) (M) to shine forth; flash; coming forth.

Utkaṭa (S) (M) exceeding the usual measure; immense; gigantic; richly endowed with; abounding in; superior; high; uneven; difficult.

Utkhalin (S) (M) **1.** perfumed. **3.** a Buddhist deity.

Utkīla (S) (M) **1.** excited. **2.** opened. **3.** ṛṣi (*Ṛg Veda*).

Utkroṣa (S) (M) **1.** loud speaker. **3.** one of the 2 attendants given to Skanda by Indra (*M. Bh.*).

Utkṛṣṭa (S) (M) excellent; eminent; superior; best.

Utkumuda (S) (M) with lotus flowers on the surface.

Utpaksha (S) (M) **1.** with up turned wings. **3.** a son of Śvaphalka (*H. Purāṇa*).

Utpala (S) (M) **1.** to burst open. **2.** the blossom of the Blue Lotus (*Nymphaea stellata*).

Utpalābha (S) (M) glory of a lotus; lotus like; soft; tender; precious.

Utpalāćārya (S) (M) **1.** master of the Blue Lotus. **3.** a pupil of Somanada who wrote the *Iśvara-Pralyabijña-Kārikā.*

Utpalākṣa (S) (M) **1.** lotus eyed. **3.** another name for Viṣṇu.

Utpalaśrīgarbha (S) (M) **1.** divine womb of lotus. **3.** a bodhisattva.

Utpalin (S) (M) abounding in lotus flowers.

Utpāra (S) (M) boundless; endless.

Utprabhas (S) (M) flashing forth; bright fire; shining.

Utsāha (S) (M) courage; courageous; powerful; energetic; perseverance; firmness; determination; happiness.

Utsarga (S) (M) **1.** emission; setting free; delivering; gift; donation; oblation. **3.** excretion personified as a son of Mitra and Revatī.

Utsmaya (S) (M) **1.** open; blooming. **2.** a smile.

Uttāla (S) (M) great; strong; roaring; formidable; swift; excellent; tall; high; abundant.

Uttama (S) (M) **1.** best; excellent; greatest. **2.** highest; chief. **3.** a son of Uttānapāda and Surući and brother of Dhruva (*V. Purāṇa*); a son of Priyavrata and Barhismatī (*Bhā. Purāṇa*).

Uttamabala (S) (M) strongest.

Uttamāha (S) (M) a fine day; a lucky day.

Uttamamaṇi (S) (M) the best gem.

Uttamatejas (S) (M) extremely glorious; of excellent glory.

Uttamaujas (S) (M) **1.** of excellent valour. **3.** a warrior of the Mahābhārata.

Uttamaveśa (S) (M) **1.** excellently dressed; with the best dress. **3.** another name for Śiva.

Uttambha (S) (M) upholding; supporting; propping.

Uttana (S) (M) **1.** to stretch out and upwards. **3.** a deity who is a form of the earth (*A. Brāhmaṇa*).

Uttānabarhis (S) (M) **1.** with a high tail. **2.** peacock. **3.** the son of Śaryāti of the family of Vaivaśvata Manu (*Bhāgavata*).

Uttānahaya (S) (M) **1.** with a flying horse. **2.** fast thinker. **3.** a son of Śatājit.

Uttānapāda (S) (M) **1.** with a high position. **3.** the star called Little Bear personified as the king who was the son of Svāyambhuva Manu and the brother of Priyavrata and the husband of Surućī and Sunītī and father of Dhruva (*V. Purāṇa*).

Uttaṅka (S) (M) **1.** high cloud. **2.** a type of cloud. **3.** a disciple of Āpodadhaumya who prompted the snake sacrifice of Janamejaya (*M. Bh.*).

Uttanśa (S) (M) a crest; chaplet; ornament.

Uttansika (S) (M) **1.** adorned with a crest. **3.** a nāga (*M. Bh.*).

Uttara (S) (M) **1.** north; higher; upper. **2.** superior. **3.** the son of King Virāṭa of Maṭsya (*M. Bh.*); a fire (*M. Bh.*); a king of nāgas; a mountain (*K. Sāgara*); another name for Śiva.

Uttāraka (S) (M) **1.** deliverer. **3.** another name for Śiva.

V

Vabhravāyani (S) (M) **1.** weaver. **3.** a son of Viśvāmitra (*M. Bh.*).

Vaćaknu (S) (M) eloquent.

Vaćana (S) (M) declaration; oath; command; order.

Vāćasāmpati (S) (M) **1.** master of speech. **3.** another name for Bṛhaspati.

Vāćaspati (S) (M) **1.** lord of speech. **3.** another name for Bṛhaspati.

Vaćasya (S) (M) well spoken of; praiseworthy; celebrated.

Vaćchacārya (S) (M) **1.** teacher of children. **3.** the grandfather of Nīlakaṇṭha.

Vāćispati (S) (M) **1.** lord of speech. **3.** another name for Bṛhaspati; an author of *Tattvakāumudi*; the constellation Puṣya.

Vaḍabāsuta (S) (M) **1.** son of a mare; son of Vaḍabā. **3.** another name for the aśvins.

Vadānya (S) (M) **1.** bountiful; liberal; munificent; eloquent. **3.** a ṛṣi (*Ṛg Veda*).

Vadha (S) (M) **1.** murder. **2.** killer; slayer; a deadly weapon. **3.** the son of giant Yātudhāna and the father of Vighna and Śama (*Br. Parāṇa*).

Vadhryaśva (S) (M) **1.** with a castrated horse. **3.** a king in the court of Yama (*M. Bh.*).

Vādīn (S) (M) **1.** speaker; disputant; propounder of a theory. **3.** a son of Emperor Pṛthu (*V. Purāṇa*).

Vādindra (S) (M) excellent disputant.

Vādirāj (S) (M) **1.** king among disputants. **3.** a Baudhya sage; another name for Mañjuśrī.

Vādiśa (S) (M) lord of disputants; one who resolves disputes, peace maker; learned; virtuous; seer; sage.

Vādisiṁha (S) (M) **1.** lion among disputants; resolver of disputes; one who dispels doubts. **3.** another name for Buddha.

Vādīśvara (S) (M) god of disputants; peace maker.

Vāduli (S) (M) **1.** orator; logician. **3.** a son of Viśvāmitra (*V. Rāmāyaṇa*).

Vāgabali (S) (M) possessing the power of speech.

Vāgabhaṭa (S) (M) **1.** scholar of speech. **3.** a Sanskṛt scholar of rhetorical science (12th century).

Vāgadhipa (S) (M) **1.** lord of speech. **3.** another name for Bṛhaspati.

Vāgaduṣṭa (S) (M) **1.** vile in speech; sophistry. **3.** a son of sage Kauśika (*M. Purāṇa*).

Vāgara (S) (M) **1.** ascertainment. **2.** scholar; hero.

Vāghat (S) (M) institutor of a sacrifice.

Vāgindra (S) (M) **1.** lord of speech. **2.** lord of cranes. **3.** the son of King Prakāśaka of the family of Gṛtsamada and the father of King Pramiti (*M. Bh.*).

Vāgīśa (S) (M) **1.** lord of speech; master of language. **3.** another name for Bṛhaspati and Brahmā.

Vāgīśvara (S) (M) **1.** master of language. **2.** a deified sage. **3.** a Jina; another name for Brahmā.

Vāgmin (S) (M) **1.** eloquent. **3.** a son of King Manasyu and Sauvīrī (*M. Bh.*); another name for Bṛhaspati.

Vahati (S) (M) **1.** friend. **2.** wind. **3.** a river.

Vāhi (S) (M) **1.** carrying; bearing. **3.** a devil living in the Vipāśā river (*M. Bh.*).

Vahika (S) (M) vehicle drawn by oxen; one who carries; one who bears along; an inhabitant of Punjab.

Vāhin (S) (M) **1.** driving; bearing; bringing; causing; carrying. **3.** Śiva as one who carries the world.

Vāhinara (S) (M) **1.** drawn by men. **3.** a king in the palace of Yama (*M. Bh.*).

Vahni (S) (M) **1.** conveying. **2.** a draught animal. **3.** an asura who was a lokapāla (*M. Bh.*); a son of Turvasu (*Bh. Purāṇa*); a son of Kṛṣṇa and Mitravindā (*Bhāgavata*).

Vāhni (S) (M) **1.** one who carries; one who conveys or bears along or is borne along. **2.** draught animal; charioteer. **3.** a son of Kukura (*M. Bh.*); an asura who was once a Lokapāla (*M. Bh.*); the son of King Turvasu and the father of Bharga (*Bhāgavata*); a son of Kṛṣṇa and Mitravindā (*Bhāgavata*); another name for Agni, Indra, the maruts and Soma.

Vahnigarbha (S) (M) **1.** with fire in the womb; bamboo. **3.** a gaṇa of Śiva (*Ś. Purāṇa*).

Vahnih (S) (M) **1.** bearing along; carrying oblations. **3.** another name for Agni.

Vahnimitra (S) (M) **1.** friend of fire. **2.** air; wind.

Vahninetra (S) (M) **1.** fiery eyed. **3.** another name for Śiva.

Vāhūka (S) (M) **1.** with strong arms. **3.** name assumed by King Nala (*M. Bh.*).

Vāhuli (S) (M) **1.** leader. **3.** a son of Viśvāmitra (*V. Rāmāyaṇa*).

Vaibhātika (S) (M) of the dawn.

Vaibhava (S) (M) might; power; greatness; grandeur; glory.

Vaibhrāja (S) (M) garden of the gods.

Vaibudha (S) (M) belonging to the gods; divine.

Vaićitravīrya (S) (M) **1.** son of Vićitravīrya. **3.** another name for Dhṛtarāṣṭra.

Vaidarbhi (S) (M) **1.** belonging to Vidarbha. **3.** a king who was the father of Lopāmudrā (*M. Bh.*).

Vaidat (S) (M) knowing.

Vaideha (S) (M) **1.** belonging to the Videhas; with a handsome body. **3.** another name for Janaka.

Vaidehībandhu (S) (M) **1.** consort of Sītā. **3.** another name for Rāma.

Vaidhava (S) (M) **1.** son of the moon. **3.** another name for Mercury.

Vaidhṛta (S) (M) **1.** lying on the same side. **3.** a particular position of the sun and moon; Indra in the 11th Manvantara (*Bhā. Purāna*).

Vaidhyata (S) (M) **1.** supporter of law. **3.** Yama's doorkeeper.

Vaiḍūrya (S) (M) **1.** anything excellent of its kind. **2.** a cat's eye jewel.

Vaiḍūryakānti (S) (M) with the lustre of the cat's eye jewel.

Vaiḍūryamaṇi (S) (M) the cat's eye jewel.

Vaiḍūryaprabhā (S) (M) **1.** with the light of the cat's eye jewel. **3.** a nāga.

Vaidya (S) (M) **1.** versed in medical science; learned; physician. **3.** a ṛṣi (*M. Bh.*); a son of Varuṇa and Suṇādevī and the father of Ghṛṇi and Muni (*Vā. Purāṇa*).

Vaidyalingam (S) (M) knowing the secrets of medicine; emblem of learning.

Vaidyanātha (S) (M) **1.** lord of physicians. **3.** a form of Śiva; another name for Dhanvantari.

Vaidyarāja (S) (M) **1.** king among physicians. **3.** another name for Dhanvantari.

Vaidyuta (S) (M) **1.** coming from lightning. **2.** flashing; brilliant. **3.** a son of Vapuṣmat (*Mā. Purāṇa*).

Vaijayanta (S) (M) **1.** bestower of victory. **2.** banner; flag. **3.** the flag of Indra (*M. Bh.*); a mountain in the Sea of Milk visited daily by Brahmā for meditation (*M. Bh.*); the palace of Indra (*B. Literature*); a Jaina group of deities (*J. S. Koṣa*); another name for Skanda (*M. Bh.*).

Vaijayi (S) (M) **1.** victor. **3.** the 3rd ćakravartin of Bhārata (*M. Bh.*).

Vaijayika (S) (M) conferring victory.

Vaikartana (S) (M) **1.** belonging to the sun. **3.** another name for Karṇa.

Vaikhāna (S) (M) **1.** abode of the absolute. **3.** another name for Viṣṇu.

Vaikuṇṭhanātha (S) (M) **1.** lord of Vaikuṇṭha. **3.** another name for Viṣṇu.

Vainateya (S) (M) **1.** humble; modest. **3.** a son of Garuḍa (*M. Bh.*); another name for Garuḍa.

Vaiṇavīka (S) (M) flautist.

Vaiṇavīn (S) (M) **1.** possessing a flute. **3.** another name for Siva.

Vainya (S) (M) **1.** of Vena. **3.** another name for Emperor Pṛthu.

Vairāga (S) (M) freedom from passions and desires.

Vairāgya (S) (M) **1.** loss of colour. **2.** asceticism. **3.** a son of Bhakti.

Vairāja (S) (M) **1.** divine glory. **2.** belonging to Brahmā. **3.** the father of Ajita (*Bhā. Purāṇa*); one of the Saptapitṛs or 7 manes (*M. Bh.*); another name for the Manus, Puruṣa and sage Ṛsabha.

Vairaṅgika (S) (M) free from passions and desires.

Vairāta (S) (M) **1.** a precious stone; an earthworm. **3.** a son of Dhṛtarāṣṭra (*M. Bh.*).

Vairatha (S) (M) **1.** without chariot. **3.** a son of Jyotiṣmat (*V. Purāṇa*).

Vairinćya (S) (M) **1.** son of the creator. **3.** a son of Brahmā (*Ṛg Veda*).

Vairivīra (S) (M) **1.** triumphing over enemies. **3.** a son of Daśaratha (*V. Purāṇa*).

Vairoćana (S) (M) **1.** belonging to the sun. **3.** a son of the sun; a son of Viṣṇu; a son of Agni; patronymic of Bali (*M. Bh.*); one of the 5 Dhyāni Buddhas; the consort of Loćana and father of Bodhisattva Samantabhadra.

Vaiśampāyana (S) (M) **1.** connoisseur of a cup of nectar. **3.** a sage who was a pupil of Vyāsa and the narrator of the *Mahābhārata* to Janamejaya (*G. Sutra*); a son of Śukanāsa; the compiler of *Yajur Veda* and the preceptor of Yājñavalkya (*M. Bh.*).

Vaiśrambhaka (S) (M) **1.** awakening. **2.** inspiring confidence. **3.** a celestial grove (*Bhā. Purāṇa*).

Vaiśravaṇa (S) (M) **1.** widely known; belonging to Viśravas. **3.** another name for Kubera and Rāvaṇa.

Vaiṣtra (S) (M) the world.

Vaiśvānara (S) (M) **1.** belonging to all men. **2.** omnipresent; worshipped everywhere. **3.** an agni (*Ṛg Veda*); a hermit in the palace of Indra (*M. Bh.*); a son of the agni called Bhānu (*M. Bh.*); a son of Kaśyapa and Manu (*Bhāgavata*).

Vaiśyaputra (S) (M) **1.** son of a Vaiśya woman. 3. another name for Yuyutsu.

Vaitālin (S) (M) **1.** possessed with ghostly power; magician. **3.** a warrior of Skanda (*M. Bh.*).

Vaitaṇḍa (S) (M) **1.** disputatious; captious. **3.** a son of the vasu Āpa (*V. Purāṇa*).

Vaitrāsura (S) (M) **1.** a demon who resides in cane. **2.** reed dweller. **3.** an asura (*Bhā. Purāṇa*).

Vaivasvata (S) (M) **1.** belonging to the sun. **3.** a rudra (*V. Purāṇa*); the 7th Manu also called Satyavrata who was the son of Vivasvān and the husband of Śraddhā (*Ṛg Veda*), their most prominent children were Yama, Yamī, Aśvinīkumaras, Revanta, Ikṣvāku, Nṛga, Sudyumna, Śaryāti, Kavi, Nabhāga Karūṣa and Pṛśadhra (*M. Bh.*).

Vāja (S) (M) **1.** strength; vigour; energy; speed. **2.** contest; battle; booty; gain; reward; wing; feather; wing. **3.** one of the 3 Ṛbhus (*Ṛg Veda*); a son of Laukya; a son of Manu Sāvarṇa; a son of Sudhanvā and grandson of Angīras (*Ṛg Veda*).

Vajaćandra (S) (M) moon among the strong.

Vājajit (S) (M) reward winner; winning the reward in a contest.

Vājapati (S) (M) **1.** the lord of reward. **3.** another name for Agni.

Vājapeya (S) (M) **1.** the drink of strength. **3.** one of the 7 forms of sacrifice offered by kings or Brāhmins (*A. Veda*).

Vājaratna (S) (M) gem of rewards; rich in treasure as the Ṛbhus.

Vājasaneya (S) (M) **1.** steadfast; vigorous; mighty; awarded; honoured. **3.** another name for Yājñavalkya, the author of the *Vajasaneyi Samhitā* or the *Śukla Yajur Veda*.

Vājasani (S) (M) **1.** winning reward; victorious; granting strength. **3.** another name for Viṣṇu.

Vajaśravas (S) (M) **1.** famous for wealth. **3.** a son of Naćiketas (*Br. Upaniṣad*).

Vajin (S) (M) swift; spirited; heroic; war like; strong; manly; hero; the number 7; arrow; steed.

Vājineya (S) (M) son of a hero.

Vājinīvasu (S) (M) giving strength and power.

Vajra (S) (M) **1.** the hard or mighty one; thunderbolt. **2.** lightning; diamond; pillar. **3.** a mountain (*Rāmāyaṇa*); an asura; a son of Manu Sāvarṇa; a son of Bhūti; a son of Viśvāmitra (*M. Bh.*); the son of Aniruddha who was appointed by Kṛṣṇa to be the king of the remaining Yādavas after the Mausala fight; the monk who succeeded Sinhagiri as the head of the Jaina church (*J. S. Koṣa*); Prickly Pear (*Opuntia dillenii*); *Pavonia odorata.*

Vajrabāhu (S) (M) **1.** thunderbolt armed. **2.** with hard arms. **3.** an asura who was the son of the vidyādharī Ćanćalākṣī (*K. Rāmāyaṇa*); another name for Indra, Agni, Rudra.

Vajrābha (S) (M) **1.** diamond like. **2.** opal.

Vajradakṣiṇa (S) (M) **1.** with a thunderbolt in the right hand. **3.** another name for Indra.

Vajradanṣtra (S) (M) **1.** with adamantine teeth. **2.** lion. **3.** an asura captain of Tripurāsura (*G. Purāṇa*); a rākṣasa in Rāvaṇa's army (*V. Rāmāyaṇa*); the king of the vidyādharas (*K. Sāgara*).

Vajradatta (S) (M) **1.** born of a mighty one. **3.** the king of Prāgjyotisapura who was the son of Bhāgadatta (*M. Bh.*); a king of Puṅḍarikinī (*M. Bh.*).

Vajradhara (S) (M) **1.** holding a thunderbolt. **3.** a bodhisattva (*B. Literature*); a primordial monotheistic god of Vajrayāna Buddhism; another name for Indra.

Vajradhridhanetra (S) (M) **1.** with thunderous eyes. **3.** a king of the yakṣas (*Ṛg Veda*).

Vajragarbha (S) (M) **1.** the matrix of the thunderbolt. **3.** a bodhisattva.

Vajraghoṣa (S) (M) sounding like a thunderbolt.

Vajrahasta (S) (M) **1.** thunderbolt handed. **3.** another name for Indra, the maruts, Agni and Śiva.

Vajrajit (S) (M) **1.** conquerer of the thunderbolt. **2.** powerful. **3.** another name for Indra.

Vajrakaṅkata (S) (M) **1.** with adamantine armour. **3.** another name for Hanumān.

Vajrakarṣaṇa (S) (M) **1.** ploughing with the thunderbolt. **3.** another name for Indra.

Vajraketu (S) (M) **1.** thunderbolt bannered. **3.** another name for the demon Naraka.

Vajrakīla (S) (M) hard nail; thunderbolt.

Vajramaṇi (S) (M) **1.** hard jewel. **2.** diamond.

Vajramati (S) (M) **1.** with diamond like intelligence. **3.** a bodhisattva.

Vajramitra (S) (M) friend of Indra.

Vajramukuṭa (S) (M) diamond crowned.

Vajramuṣṭi (S) (M) **1.** grasping a thunderbolt; hard fisted. **3.** a gana of Śiva; a rākṣasa son of Mālyavān and Sundarī (*U. Rāmāyaṇa*); another name for Indra.

Vajranābha (S) (M) **1.** diamond navelled. **3.** Kṛṣṇa's discus; a son of Uktha; a dānava (*H. Purāṇa*); a son of Unnābha (*Bhā. Purāṇa*); a warrior of Skanda (*M. Bh.*); a king of the line of Rāma who was the son of Vinda and the father of Khagaṇa (*Bhāgavata*); an asura whose daughter Prabhāvatī was the wife of Pradyumna (*H. Purāṇa*); a king of Mathurā (*Bhā. Purāṇa*).

Vajranetra (S) (M) **1.** diamond eyes. **3.** a king of the yakṣas.

Vajrāṅga (S) (M) **1.** hard limbed; with a curved body. **3.** an asura son of Kaśyapa and Diti and the husband of Varāngī and the father of Tarakāsura (*M. Bh.*).

Vajrānśu (S) (M) **1.** diamond rayed. **2.** as bright as a diamond. **3.** a son of Kṛṣṇa (*M. Bh.*).

Vajrapāṇi (S) (M) **1.** thunderbolt handed. **3.** a bodhisattva; another name for Indra.

Vajraprabha (S) (M) **1.** as shiny as a diamond. **3.** a vidyādhara (*H. Purāṇa*).

Vajraprabhava (S) (M) **1.** diamond born. **2.** bright as a diamond. **3.** a king of the Karūṣas.

Vajrapuṣpam (S) (M) **1.** diamond flower; valuable flower. **2.** the blossom of the Sesamum plant.

Vajrasamhata (S) (M) **1.** attacking like thunderbolts. **3.** a Buddha (*B. Literature*).

Vajrasāra (S) (M) the essence of a diamond; bright; precious.

Vajrasattva (S) (M) **1.** with an adamantine soul. **3.** another name for a Dhyāni Buddha.

Vajrasena (S) (M) **1.** diamond armied. **3.** a Bodhisattva (*K. Vyuha*); a king of Śrāvastī.

Vajraśīrśa (S) (M) **1.** diamond headed. **3.** a son of Bhṛgu (*M. Bh.*).

Vajrasūrya (S) (M) **1.** thunderbolt and sun conjoined. **3.** a Buddha.

Vajraṭa (S) (M) **1.** severe; hard; impregnable. **3.** the father of Uvata.

Vajraṭīka (S) (M) **1.** diamond like. **3.** a Buddha.

Vajratulya (S) (M) resembling a diamond.

Vajratuṇḍa (S) (M) **1.** hard beaked; hard tusked. **3.** another name for Garuḍa and Gaṇeśa.

Vajravega (S) (M) **1.** as swift as lightning. **3.** a giant brother of Khara and the attendant of Kumbhakarṇa (*M. Bh.*); a vidyādhara (*H. Purāṇa*).

Vajravelu (S) (M) **1.** with a diamond hard plough. **3.** another name for Balarāma.

Vajravīra (S) (M) **1.** strong warrior. **3.** another name for Mahākāla.

Vajraviṣkambha (S) (M) **1.** hurling the thunderbolt; a hard support. **3.** a son of Garuḍa (*M. Bh.*).

Vajrāyudha (S) (M) **1.** thunderbolt armed. **3.** another name for Indra and the weapon of Indra.

Vajrendra (S) (M) **1.** lord of the thunderbolt. **3.** another name for Indra.

Vajrijit (S) (M) **1.** conqueror of Indra. **3.** another name for Garuḍa.

Vajrin (S) (M) **1.** holding a thunderbolt; wielder of the Vajra weapon. **3.** another name for Indra; a viśvadeva (*M. Bh.*).

Vakanakha (S) (M) **1.** with crooked nails. **3.** a son of Viśvāmitra (*M. Bh.*).

Vākapati (S) (M) **1.** lord of speech. **3.** another name for Bṛhaspati.

Vākasiddha (S) (M) perfection in speech.

Vakman (S) (M) utterance; speech; hymn of praise.

Vākmya (S) (M) to be worthy of praise.

Vakra (S) (M) **1.** crooked; curled. **2.** cunning; cruel. **3.** another name for the planets Mars and Saturn, Rudra, the asura Bāṇa.

Vakrabhuja (S) (M) **1.** crooked armed. **3.** another name for Gaṇeśa.

Vakradanta (S) (M) **1.** crooked teeth. **3.** a prince of the Karūṣas (*M. Bh.*).

Vakrapāda (S) (M) **1.** crooked legged. **3.** another name for Gaṇeśa.

Vakratu (S) (M) **1.** crooked. **3.** a deity (*Mā. Purāṇa*).

Vakratuṇḍa (S) (M) **1.** with a curved trunk. **3.** another name for Gaṇeśa.

Vakṣa (S) (M) chest; breast; strength giving; nourishing.

Vakṣana (S) (M) nourishing; strengthening; refreshing; invigorating.

Vakṣogrīva (S) (M) **1.** ox necked. **2.** proud and strong. **3.** a son of Viśvāmitra (*M. Bh.*).

Vakṣomaṇi (S) (M) a jewel worn on the breast.

Vakṣu (S) (M) **1.** refreshing. **3.** the Oxus river.

Vaktṛ (S) (M) speaker; eloquent; learned; wise.

Vaktraja (S) (M) **1.** born of the mouth of Brahmā. **2.** a Brāhmin.

Vaktrāmbuja (S) (M) with a lotus like face.

Vaktrayodhin (S) (M) **1.** fighting with the mouth. **3.** an asura (*H. Purāṇa*).

Vaktrendu (S) (M) with a moonlike face.

Vakula (S) (M) crooked; curved.

Vala (S) (M) **1.** enclosure; cave; beam; pole. **3.** an asura killed by Indra (*P. Purāṇa*).

Valabhi (S) (M) **1.** the pinnacle of a house. **3.** a 7th century king.

Valāka (S) (M) **1.** beam; pole. **3.** a sage under Manu Tāmasa (*Ṛg Veda*).

Valārāti (S) (M) **1.** enemy of Vala. **3.** another name for Indra.

Valāsaka (S) (M) **1.** handsome. **3.** the Koel or Indian Cuckoo (*Cuculus varius*).

Valgu (S) (M) **1.** handsome; beautiful; attractive. **3.** one of the 4 tutelary deities of the Bodhi tree (*L. Vistara*).

Valgujaṅgha (S) (M) **1.** handsome legged. **3.** a son of Viśvāmitra (*M. Bh.*).

Valguka (S) (M) very handsome.

Vālihantri (S) (M) **1.** slayer of Vāli. **3.** another name for Rāma.

Valāmukha (S) (M) **1.** with a wrinkled face. **3.** a monkey in Rāma's army (*V. Rāmāyaṇa*).

Vālin (S) (M) **1.** hairy; tailed. **3.** a monkey who was the son of Indra and elder brother of Sugrīva (*Rāmāyaṇa*).

Vāliśikha (S) (M) **1.** with a crest of hair. **3.** a nāga (*M. Bh.*).

Valkala (S) (M) **1.** the bark of a tree. **3.** a daitya (*M. Bh.*).

Vallabha (S) (M) **1.** beloved. **2.** above all; favourite; desired; cowherd. **3.** a son of Balākāśva and the father of Kuśika (*V. Rāmāyaṇa*).

Vallabhāćārya (S) (M) **1.** beloved teacher. **3.** a celebrated Vaiṣṇava teacher and author of commentaries on the Purāṇas and Vedānta (15th century).

Vallabhānanda (S) (M) rejoicing in being loved.

Vallabhendra (S) (M) Indra among the beloved; best beloved.

Vallabheśvara (S) (M) most beloved; god among the beloved.

Vallava (S) (M) **1.** cowherd. **3.** another name for Bhīma in the court of king Virāta.

Vallikāgra (S) (M) **1.** tip of a vine. **2.** coral.

Vallura (S) (M) arbour; bower; a cluster of blossoms.

Vālmīki (S) (M) **1.** from a white anthill. **3.** a hermit who is 1st among poets and the author of the *Vālmīki Rāmāyaṇa* and is said to have been the 10th son of Varuṇa, from dacoity he turned to religion and built a hermitage in Bānḍā in Bundelkhand where he received Sītā when banished by Rāma, he is now a member of the palace of Indra (*M. Bh.*); a son of Garuḍa (*M. Bh.*).

Vāma (S) (M) **1.** lovely; dear; pleasant; splendid; noble. **3.** a rudra (*Bhā. Purāṇa*); a son of Ṛćika; a son of Kṛṣṇa and Bhadrā; a son of Dharma (*Bhā. Purāṇa*); a horse of the moon (*V. Purāṇa*); an attendant of Skanda (*M. Bh.*); another name for Śiva, Kāma and Varuṇa.

Vāmadatta (S) (M) given by Śiva.

Vāmadeva (S) (M) **1.** noble lord. **3.** one of the 5 faces of Śiva; a hermit who was the son of King Parīkṣit and Suśobhanā (*M. Bh.*); a son of Manu and Śatarūpā who was an incarnation of Śiva (*M. Purāṇa*); a ṛṣi and part author of *Rg Veda* (iv); a minister of Daśaratha; a son of Nārāyaṇa (*Ṛg Veda*); father of Viśvanātha (*H. Purāṇa*); another name for Śiva.

Vāmaka (S) (M) **1.** hard; cruel; rough; left; contrary. **3.** a king of Kāśī (*M. Bh.*); a son of Bhajamāna (*V. Purāṇa*); a ćakravartin.

Vāmana (S) (M) **1.** small; short; dwarf. **3.** the 5th incarnation of Mahāviṣṇu who was born as the dwarf son of Kaśyapa and Aditi to defeat the asura Mahābali (*Bhāgavata*); one of the 8 elephants supporting the universe and the son of Irāvatī (*M. Bh.*); a nāga; a son of Garuḍa (*M. Bh.*); a son of Hiraṇyagarbha (*H. Purāṇa*); one of the 18 attendants of the sun (*H. Purāṇa*); a dānava (*H. Purāṇa*).

Vāmanabhaṭṭabāṇa (S) (M) **1.** the arrow of the noble dwarf. **2.** subtle. **3.** a Sanskṛt poet (15th century).

Vana (S) (M) **1.** forest; cluster of plants; water; fountain; spring; longing; desire. **3.** a son of Uśīnara (*Bhā. Purāṇa*).

Vāna (S) (M) **1.** intelligent. **3.** another name for Yama.

Vanaćampaka (S) (M) the wild Ćampaka tree (*Michelia champaka*).

Vanaćandana (S) (M) the sandalwood of the forest; the Devadāru tree (*Pinus deodora*).

Vanada (S) (M) **1.** bestowing; longing; desire; desirable; rain giving. **2.** a cloud.

Vanadeva (S) (M) forest god.

Vanadvāja (S) (M) **1.** desiring strength and energy. **3.** son of Śući.

Vanahāsa (S) (M) **1.** smile of the forest. **3.** Musk Jasmine (*Jasminum pubescens*).

Vanajan (S) (M) Blue Lotus (*Nymphaea stellata*).

Vanakapīvat (S) (M) **1.** resembling a wild monkey. **3.** a son of Pulaha (*M. Bh.*).

Vanamālin (S) (M) **1.** wearing a garland of wild flowers. **3.** another name for Kṛṣṇa.

Vanana (S) (M) longing; desire.

Vananātha (S) (M) **1.** controller of forest. **2.** a lion.

Vananitya (S) (M) **1.** with an eternal longing. **3.** a son of Raudrāśva (*H. Purāṇa*).

Vanapāla (S) (M) **1.** protector of forest. **3.** a son of Devapāla.

Vanapriya (S) (M) **1.** beloved of forest. **2.** the Indian cuckoo; the Cinnamon tree.

Vanarāja (S) (M) **1.** lord of the forest. **2.** lion; *Bauhinia racemosa.*

Vānaraketu (S) (M) **1.** monkey bannered. **3.** another name for Arjuna.

Vānarendra (S) (M) **1.** lord of monkeys. **3.** another name for Hanumān.

Vanas (S) (M) loveliness; longing; desire.

Vanaspati (S) (M) **1.** king of the forest. **2.** the Indian Fig tree (*Ficus indica*); the Soma plant; wooden beam; ascetic. **3.** a son of King Ghṛtapṛṣṭha (*Bhāgavata*); another name for Kṛṣṇa.

Vanastamba (S) (M) **1.** pillar of the forest. **2.** a bunch of wild flowers; a wild thicket. **3.** a son of Gaḍa (*H. Purāṇa*).

Vanāyu (S) (M) **1.** long lived; like a forest. **3.** a son of Kaśyapa and Dānu (*M. Bh.*); a son of Urvaśī and Purūravas (*M. Bh.*).

Vanćita (S) (M) wished; desired; beloved.

Vanćula (S) (M) **1.** a cow that gives a lot of milk. **3.** a bird whose cry forbodes victory (*V. Rāmāyaṇa*).

Vandana (S) (M) **1.** praise; worship; adoration. **3.** a hermit saved from an asura by the Aśvinikumāras (*Ṛg Veda*).

Vandanavāra (S) (M) a sequence of adorations; a wreath of green leaves hung on auspicious occasions.

Vandāru (S) (M) praising; celebrating; respectful; polite.

Vandatha (S) (M) deserving praise.

Vandin (S) (M) **1.** one who praises. **2.** one who honours; a class of poets and scholars who sing songs of praise in the royal courts. **3.** a scholar in King Janaka's court (*V. Rāmāyaṇa*).

Vandita (S) (M) praised; extolled; celebrated.

Vanditṛ (S) (M) one who praises.

Vandra (S) (M) worshipping.

Vaneyu (S) (M) **1.** residing in the forest. **2.** hermit; ascetic. **3.** a king who was the son of Raudrāśva and Miśrakeśī (*M. Bh.*).

Vaṅga (S) (M) **1.** Bengal. **3.** a king of the lunar race who was a son of Dīrghatamas and who is regarded as the ancestor of the people of Bengal (*M. Bh*); a mountain.

Vāṅgāla (S) (M) **1.** of Vaṅga. **3.** a rāga.

Vāṇija (S) (M) 1. merchant; trader; submarine fire. 3. the zodiac sign of Libra; another name for Śiva.

Vaniṣṭha (S) (M) very munificent; very generous.

Vañita (S) (M) wished for; desired; loved.

Vañjula (S) (M) 1. of the beauty of the forest. 2. the Aśoka tree (*Saraca indica*); *Hibiscus mutabilis*; Chairbottom Cane (*Calamus rotang*); Chariot tree (*Ougeinia oojeinensis*).

Vaṅkālakāćārya (S) (M) 1. crooked teacher. 3. an astronomer who wrote in Prakṛt.

Vaṅmali (S) (M) 1. eloquent. 3. a sacred river.

Vanśaja (S) (M) from a good family.

Vanśakara (S) (M) perpetuating a race; son.

Vanśapota (S) (M) bamboo shoot; offspring of a good family.

Vanśarāja (S) (M) lord of the race.

Vanśavardhana (S) (M) bringing prosperity to the family; son.

Vanśīdhara (S) (M) 1. holding a flute. 3. another name for Kṛṣṇa.

Vanyavid (S) (M) 1. knower of the forest. 3. a ṛṣi. (*M.Bh.*)

Vapodara (S) (M) 1. corpulent. 3. another name for Indra (*Ṛg Veda*).

Vapra (S) (M) 1. rampart; shore; bank; father. 3. a son of the 14th Manu (*H. Purāṇa*).

Vapuna (S) (M) 1. bodyless; formless. 2. a god; knowledge.

Vapunandana (S) (M) son of the body.

Vapurdhara (S) (M) embodied; handsome; with a beautiful form.

Vapuṣa (S) (M) embodied; wonderful; admirable.

Vapuṣmān (S) (M) 1. possessing a body; embodied; possessing a beautiful body. 3. the son of King Sankrandana of Vidarbha (*Mā. Purāṇa*).

Vapuṣmat (S) (M) 1. embodied. 2. handsome. 3. a viśvadeva (*H. Purāṇa*); a son of Priyavrata (*Purāṇas*); a ṛṣi in the 11th Manvantara (*V. Purāṇa*); a king of Kuṇdina (*V. Purāṇa*).

Vapuṣṭama (S) (M) best in form; most beautiful; most wonderful.

Vapusya (S) (M) possessing a form; wonderfully beautiful or handsome.

Vara (S) (M) 1. boon; choice; gift; reward; benefit; blessing. 2. choosing; best; valuable; excellent; royal. 3. a son of Svaphalka (*V. Purāṇa*); *Curcuma longa.*

Varada (S) (M) 1. granting wishes. 3. a ṛṣi in the 4th Manvantara (*V. Purāṇa*); a Dhyāni Buddha (*B. Literature*); a warrior of Skanda (*M. Bh.*); another name for Agni.

Varadarāja (S) (M) 1. lord of boons. 3. another name for Viṣṇu.

Varadhā (S) (M) granter of a boon.

Varadharmin (S) (M) noble; very religious.

Varādi (S) (M) 1. group of excellence; cause of excellence. 3. a rāga.

Varagātra (S) (M) fair limbed; beautiful.

Varaghaṇṭa (S) (M) 1. gift of Śiva. 3. another name for Skanda.

Varāha (S) (M) 1. boar. 2. superiority; preeminence. 3. a hermit in the palace of Yudhiṣṭhira (*M. Bh.*); one of the 10 incarnations of Mahāviṣṇu who was born of the nose of Brahmā to destroy Hiraṇyākṣa and Hiraṇyakaśipu.

Varāhadatta (S) (M) given by Viṣṇu.

Varāhadeva (S) (M) Viṣṇu as the boar.

Varāhaka (S) (M) 1. boar like. 3. a serpent born in the family of Dhṛtarāṣṭra (*M. Bh.*).

Varāhakarṇa (S) (M) 1. boar eared. 3. a yakṣa (*M. Bh.*).

Varāhāmba (S) (M) 1. making others bow down. 3. an asura (*M. Bh.*).

Varāhamihira (S) (M) 1. Viṣṇu and the sun conjoined. 3. an astrologer who was one of the 9 gems at King Vikramādityā's court (*K. Granthāvali*).

Varāhaśṛṅga (S) (M) 1. boar horned. 3. another name for Śiva.

Varajānuka (S) (M) **1.** preceptor of the noble. **2.** disciple of a noble preceptor. **3.** a ṛṣi (*M. Bh.*).

Varakratu (S) (M) **1.** doer of good deeds; granter of boons. **3.** another name for Indra.

Varāli (S) (M) **1.** friend of the noble. **2.** the moon. **3.** a rāga.

Vāranātha (S) (M) **1.** lord of the waters. **2.** ocean; cloud. **3.** another name for Varuṇa.

Varaprabha (S) (M) **1.** of best brightness. **2.** brightest. **3.** a Bodhisattva.

Vārarāja (S) (M) **1.** lord of the waters. **3.** another name for Varuṇa.

Varāraka (S) (M) **1.** magnificent stone. **2.** diamond.

Varāroha (S) (M) **1.** an excellent rider; with fine hips. **3.** another name for Viṣṇu.

Vararući (S) (M) **1.** taking pleasure in boons. **3.** an ancient scholar of astronomy and astrology who is supposed to have been the incarnation of an attendant of Śiva called Puṣpadanta born to Somadatta; a grammarian, poet and author of the *Varttikas,* who is placed among the 9 gems of Vikramāditya (*Panćatantra*).

Vararūpa (S) (M) **1.** with an excellent form. **3.** a Buddha (*L. Vistara*).

Varaśikha (S) (M) **1.** well crested. **3.** an asura (*Ṛg Veda*).

Varatama (S) (M) **1.** best among excellent. **2.** most preferable.

Varatantu (S) (M) **1.** well clad. **3.** the preceptor of the hermit Kautsa (*H. Ć. Ćintāmaṇi*).

Varatanu (S) (M) **1.** with an excellent body. **3.** a Kuru dynasty king.

Varatara (S) (M) most excellent.

Varatri (S) (M) **1.** desiring. **2.** chooser; wooer. **3.** a son of Śuka.

Varavṛddha (S) (M) **1.** eldest among the best. **3.** another name for Śiva.

Varayu (S) (M) **1.** best born. **3.** a king of the family of Mahaujas (*M. Bh.*).

Varćas (S) (M) **1.** vigour; energy; brilliance; lustre; light; colour; form; figure; shape. **3.** the son of the vasu Soma and Manoharā, he was reborn as Abhimanyu; the son of the hermit Sućetas and the father of Vihavya (*M. Bh.*); a son of Sutejas; a rākṣasa.

Varćasvin (S) (M) **1.** vigorous; energetic. **2.** active. **3.** a son of Varćas and grandson of Soma.

Varćāvasu (S) (M) **1.** sunbeam. **3.** a gandharva (*V. Purāṇa*).

Vārddhakṣatrī (S) (M) **1.** descended from Vṛddhakṣhatra. **3.** another name for Jayadratha.

Vārdhakṣemi (S) (M) **1.** looking after elders. **3.** a king of the Vṛṣṇi dynasty who fought on the side of the Pāṇḍavas (*M. Bh.*).

Vardhamāna (S) (M) **1.** striving to prosper; crescent moon; increasing; growing; prosperous. **3.** another name for Viṣṇu (*Bhā. Purāṇa*); the 24th Arhat; one of the 8 elephants that support the world (*J.S. Koṇa*).

Vardhamānamati (S) (M) **1.** with a growing intellect. **3.** a bodhisattva.

Vardhana (S) (M) **1.** increasing; growing. **2.** animator; bestower of prosperity. **3.** a son of Kṛṣṇa and Mitravindā (*Bhā. Purāṇa*); an attendant of Skanda (*M. Bh.*); another name for Śiva (*M. Bh.*).

Vardhanasūrī (S) (M) **1.** prosperous sun. **3.** a Jaina preceptor (*J.S. Koṣa*).

Vardhin (S) (M) increasing; augmenting.

Vardhita (S) (M) **1.** increased. **2.** augmented; strengthened; gladdened.

Varendra (S) (M) **1.** lord of the nobles. **2.** chief; sovereign.

Vareṇya (S) (M) **1.** to be wished for; desirable. **3.** a son of Bhṛgu (*M. Bh.*).

Vareśa (S) (M) presiding over boons.

Vareśvara (S) (M) **1.** god of boons. **2.** able to grant all wishes. **3.** another name for Śiva.

Varīdāsa (S) (M) **1.** devotee of water. **3.** the father of the gandharva Nārada (*K. Sāgara*).

Vāridhi (S) (M) **1.** treasure of water. **2.** ocean.

Varija (S) (M) **1.** born of water. **2.** lotus (*Nelumbo speciosum*).

Varīman (S) (M) best; expanse; width; breadth.

Varin (S) (M) **1.** rich in gifts, **3.** a viśvadeva (*M. Bh.*).

Varīndra (S) (M) lord of the chosen.

Vāripa (S) (M) **1.** lord of water. **3.** another name for Varuṇa.

Vāriśā (S) (M) **1.** sleeping on the ocean. **3.** another name for Viṣṇu.

Varīṣa (S) (M) **1.** lord of the waters. **2.** ocean. **3.** another name for Varuṇa.

Variṣāpriya (S) (M) **1.** friend of the rains. **3.** the Ćātaka bird (*Clamator jacobinus serratus*) (*T. Brāhmaṇa*).

Vārisena (S) (M) **1.** lord of water. **3.** a king in the palace of Yama (*M. Bh.*).

Variṣṭha (S) (M) **1.** most excellent. **2.** best; chief. **3.** a son of Manu Ćākṣuṣa (*H. Purāṇa*).

Variṣu (S) (M) **1.** chooser of the best. **3.** another name for Kāma.

Varītākṣa (S) (M) **1.** with wooing eyes. **3.** an asura (*M. Bh.*).

Varīyas (S) (M) **1.** excellent; best. **3.** a son of Manu Sāvarṇa (*H. Purāṇa*); a son of Pulaha and Gati (*Bh. Purāṇa*); another name for Śiva.

Vārkṣi (S) (M) **1.** relating to trees; arboreous. **3.** the daughter of sage Kanḍu and the wife of the 10 Praćetases she was the mother of Dakṣa (*Bhāgavata*).

Varmaćit (S) (M) **1.** protected by the mind. **3.** a king of the Lunar dynasty (*Bhāgavata*).

Varṇakavi (S) (M) **1.** arranger of verse. **3.** a son of Kubera.

Varṇu (S) (M) **1.** coloured. **2.** the sun.

Varpeyu (S) (M) **1.** master of forms. **2.** designer. **3.** a son of Raudrāśva (*V. Purāṇa*).

Varṣa (S) (M) **1.** year; cloud. **3.** the teacher of Vararući.

Vārṣagaṇya (S) (M) **1.** whose years are counted. **3.** a hermit and preceptor of the gandharva King Viśvāvasu (*M. Bh.*).

Varṣaketu (S) (M) **1.** cloud bannered. **3.** a son of Ketumat (*H. Purāṇa*); a Purū king who was the son of Kṣemaka and the father of Vipu (*A. Purāṇa*).

Varṣāmada (S) (M) **1.** rejoicing in the rain. **2.** peacock.

Varṣandhara (S) (M) **1.** bearer of rain; cloud. **3.** a ṛṣi.

Varṣman (S) (M) **1.** body. **2.** auspicious; handsome; great.

Vārṣṇeya (S) (M) **1.** of the Vṛṣṇi clan. **3.** patronymic of Kṛṣṇa; a charioteer of King Nala; another name for Mahāviṣṇu (*M. Bh.*).

Vārtta (S) (M) **1.** healthy; right; with means of subsistance. **3.** a king in the palace of Yama (*M.Bh.*).

Vartula (S) (M) **1.** round; circular. **2.** a pea. **3.** an attendant of Śiva.

Varuṇa (S) (M) **1.** all enveloping sky. **3.** an āditya who is one of the oldest Vedic gods and was regarded as the supreme deity, he is described as fashioning and upholding heaven and earth and the guardian of immortality (*Ṛg Veda*); one of the 8 guardians of the quarters, he is the guardian of the west, prominent among his wives are Gaurī, Varuṇānī, Ćarṣaṇī, Devī Jyeṣṭhā, among his children are Suṣena, Vandī, Vasiṣṭha, Vāruṇī, the sage Bhṛgu, Vālmīki, Puśkara, Bala, Sūrā, Adharmaka, the name of his city is Śraddhāvatī, in later Vedic literature he is regarded as the god of the waters in the *Mahābhārata,* he is the son of Kardama and father of Puṣkara and is variously represented as a gandharva son of Kaśyapa and Muni, a nāga, as a Lokapāla (*Ṛg Veda*), the Jainas consider him the servant of the the 20th Arhat of the present Avasarpiṇī (*J.S. Koṣa*); *Crataeva nurvala.*

Varuṇaśarman (S) (M) **1.** commander of the waters; commander of the navy. **3.** a warrior of the gods in their battle with the daityās (*K. Sāgara*).

Varuṇeśa (S) (M) with Varuna as the lord.

Vāruṇi (S) (M) **1.** of Varuna. **3.** sage Bhṛgu when reborn as the son of Varuṇa (*M. Bh.*).

Varūtha (S) (M) **1.** protection; defence; abode; shelter. **3.** an Aṅga king (*A. Purāṇa*).

Varūtṛ (S) (M) protector; guardian; deity.

Varya (S) (M) **1.** chosen. **2.** treasure; excellent; eminent; chief. **3.** another name for Kāma (*M. Bh.*).

Vaśa (S) (M) **1.** authority; dominion personified as a god (*A. Veda*). **3.** a hermit praised in the *Ṛg Veda.*

Vāsaka (S) (M) **1.** dweller; populating. **3.** a nāga.

Vasanta (S) (M) **1.** bestower of desires. **3.** brilliant spring personified as a companion of Kama (*K. Granthāvali*); Arabian Manna plant (*Alhagi Camelorum*); Custard Apple (*Annona reticulata*); Musk Jasmine (*Jasminum pubescens*); Bedda Nut (*Terminalia belerica*).

Vasantabandhu (S) (M) **1.** friend of spring. **3.** another name for Kāma.

Vasantadeva (S) (M) **1.** the lord of spring. **3.** another name for Kāma.

Vasantadūta (S) (M) **1.** the messenger of spring; the Indian Cuckoo (*Cuculus varius*); the Mango tree (*Mangifera indica*). **3.** a rāga.

Vasantagandhi (S) (M) **1.** the fragrance of spring. **3.** a Buddha (*L. Vistara*).

Vasantaka (S) (M) spring.

Vasantapuṣpa (S) (M) **1.** spring blossom. **2.** Kadamba flower (*Anthocephalus cadamba*).

Vasantarāja (S) (M) king of spring.

Vasantarañjana (S) (M) delight of spring.

Vasantasahāya (S) (M) **1.** supporter of spring. **3.** another name for Kāma.

Vasantasakha (S) (M) **1.** companion of spring. **3.** the wind blowing from the Malaya mountains (*K. Granthāvali*).

Vasantaśekhara (S) (M) **1.** crested with the spring. **2.** best among the charming. **3.** a kinnara.

Vasantasena (S) (M) with spring as the commander; loving; with the charms of spring.

Vasantatilaka (S) (M) the ornament of spring.

Vasantaviṭṭhala (S) (M) **1.** god of the spring. **3.** a form of Viṣṇu (*Bhā. Purāṇa*).

Vasantayodha (S) (M) **1.** warrior of spring. **2.** spring combatant. **3.** another name for Kāma.

Vāsara (S) (M) **1.** day. **3.** a nāga.

Vāsarādhiśa (S) (M) **1.** lord of the day. **3.** another name for the sun.

Vāsaramaṇi (S) (M) **1.** jewel of the day. **3.** another name for the sun.

Vasātika (S) (M) **1.** as bright as the dawn; belonging to the dawn. **3.** a warrior on the side of the Kauravas (*M. Bh.*).

Vāsava (S) (M) **1.** descended from or relating to the vasus. **3.** a son of King Vasu (*Bhā. Purāṇa*); another name for Indra.

Vāsavadatta (S) (M) **1.** given by Indra. **3.** a king of Bijoypuri and follower of Mahāvīra (*J. S. Koṣa*).

Vāsavaja (S) (M) **1.** son of Indra; son of the omnipresent. **3.** another name for Arjuna.

Vasavāna (S) (M) preserver of wealth.

Vasavānuja (S) (M) **1.** younger brother of Indra. **3.** another name for Upendra.

Vasavartin (S) (M) **1.** having power over gods. **3.** another name for Viṣṇu.

Vāsavavarāja (S) (M) **1.** Indra's younger brother. **3.** another name for Viṣṇu.

Vāsavi (S) (M) **1.** son of Indra. **3.** another name for Arjuna and Vālin.

Vāsavopama (S) (M) resembling Indra.

Vaśāyu (S) (M) **1.** one who controls his age. **3.** a son of Purūravas and Urvaśī (*P. Purāṇa*).

Vaśendriya (S) (M) **1.** controller of senses. **2.** one who controls his senses.

Vāśi (S) (M) **1.** roaring. **3.** another name for Agni.

Vaśin (S) (M) **1.** having will or power. **2.** ruler; lord; master of one's passions. **3.** a son of Kṛti (*Bhā. Purāṇa*).

Vasiṣṭha (S) (M) **1.** most excellent; best; richest; master of every vasu or desirable object. **3.** a celebrated sage who was a mindborn son of Brahmā born of his breath, he was reborn as the son of Mitravarunas, he was the husband of Arundhatī or Ūrjā who was reborn with him as Akṣamālā and the father of 7 sons who became the saptaṛsis in the 1st Manvantara, both are now stars and Vasiṣṭha shines in the assembly of Brahmā, he was the owner of Nandinī or the cow of plenty which granted all desires (*K. Granthāvali*), he is enumerated among the 10 prajāpatis produced by Manu Svāyambhuva, he was the family priest of the Ikṣvāku clan and is also regarded as one of the arrangers of the Vedas (*M. Bh.*); an agni (*M. Bh.*).

Vāstoṣpati (S) (M) **1.** house protector. **3.** a deity who presides over the foundation of a house; another name for Indra and Rudra.

Vastu (S) (M) **1.** site or foundation of a dwelling; a thing; the real; matter; property; whatever exists. **3.** one of the 8 vasus; a rākṣasa (*Bhā. Purāṇa*).

Vāstunara (S) (M) deity who protects the house.

Vāstupāla (S) (M) tutelary deity of a house.

Vāstupati (S) (M) master of the house; a deity who protects the house.

Vāstupuruṣa (S) (M) **1.** lord of architecture. **3.** the deity of all that is built on earth (*A. Purāṇa*).

Vastuvṛtta (S) (M) the actual fact; real matter; beautiful creature.

Vasu (S) (M) **1.** dwelling in all beings; divine; existing; precious; god; gem; gold; water; wealthy; ray of light; excellent; good; beneficient. **3.** a particular class of 8 demigods or ganadevatas who were personifications of natural phenomena who were born of Dharma and Vasu (*M. Bh.*); in some Purāṇas they are the children of Kaśyapa, they are the lords of the elements, the 1st vasu Āpa was reborn as Bhīsma, the others are the first 7 sons of Gaṅgā; a son of Kuśa and Vaidarbhī (*V. Rāmāyaṇa*); a son of Jamadagni and Reṇukā and brother of Paraśurāma (*Br. Purāṇa*); a son of Murāsura (*Bhāgavata*); a mighty king of the Kṛmi dynasty (*M. Bh.*); a son of King Īlina and Rathāntari (*M. Bh.*); a hermit and father of Paila (*M. Bh.*); a king who was the son of Uttānapāda and Sūnṛtā (*M. Purāṇa*); a son of Manu (*H. Purāṇa*); a son of Vasudeva (*Bh. Purāṇa*); a son of Kṛṣṇa (*Bh. Purāṇa*); a son of Vatsara; a son of Hiraṇyaretas; a son of Bhūtajyotis (*Bh. Purāṇa*); a son of Naraka (*Bhā. Purāṇa*); the Supreme Soul of the universe (*Ṛg Veda*); another name for the Sun, Kubera, Śiva, Bhīsma, Viṣṇu and Agni.

Vasubandhu (S) (M) **1.** friend of the gods. **3.** a celebrated Buddhist scholar (*B. Literature*).

Vāsubhadra (S) (M) **1.** best of the deities. **3.** another name for Kṛṣṇa.

Vasubhāga (S) (M) **1.** share of the gods. **2.** offering to the gods.

Vasubhṛdyāna (S) (M) **1.** chariot carried by the gods; led by the gods. **3.** a son of Vasiṣṭha (*V. Rāmāyaṇa*).

Vasubhūta (S) (M) **1.** born of Vasu; embodied wealth. **3.** a gandharva (*H. Purāṇa*).

Vasuċandra (S) (M) **1.** moon among the gods. **2.** most beautiful. **3.** a king who was a supporter of Yudhiṣṭhira and as mighty as Indra (*M. Bh.*).

Vasuda (S) (M) **1.** granting wealth. **3.** another name for Kubera.

Vasudāman (S) (M) **1.** controller of divine beings. **3.** a son of Bṛhadratha.

Vasudāna (S) (M) **1.** gift of the divine. **2.** donor of the earth. **3.** a king of Pānśu who was a member of Yudhiṣṭhira's council (*M. Bh.*); a prince of Panċala who fought for the Pāṇḍavas (*M. Bh.*).

Vasudānaputra (S) (M) **1.** son of the donor of wealth. **3.** a king on the Kaurava side (*M. Bh.*).

Vasudatta (S) (M) gift of the divine.

Vasudeva (S) (M) **1.** lord of living beings; god of wealth; god of earth. **3.** a son of Śurā of the line of Yadu and the brother of Kuntī and the husband of Rohiṇī, Devakī, Upadevī, Saptamīdevī, Vṛkadevī, Jani, Srutandharā, Śraddhādevī and the father of Kṛṣṇa, Subhadrā, Balarāma, he is regarded as an incarnation of sage Kaśyapa and is now a viśvadeva; a king of the Kaṇva dynasty (*M. Bh.*).

Vāsudeva (S) (M) **1.** son of Vasudeva. **3.** another name for Kṛṣṇa; a king of the Puṇḍras (*M. Bh.*).

Vasudevabhaṭṭatiri (S) (M) **1.** worshipper of the omnipresent. **3.** a Sanskṛtapoet of Kerala.

Vasudevaputra (S) (M) **1.** son of Vasudeva. **3.** another name for Kṛṣṇa.

Vasudevya (S) (M) **1.** granting wealth. **3.** 9th day of a fortnight (*Ṛg Veda*).

Vasudhāra (S) (M) **1.** holding treasure. **3.** a mountain.

Vasuhoma (S) (M) **1.** one who sacrifices to the gods. **3.** a king of Aṅga (*M. Bh.*).

Vasujit (S) (M) conqueror of wealth.

Vasujyeṣṭha (S) (M) **1.** the best wealth; 1st among the gods. **3.** a king and son of Puṣyamitra (*M. Purāṇa*).

Vasukarṇa (S) (M) **1.** with divine ears. **3.** a ṛṣi and part author of *Ṛg Veda.*

Vāsuki (S) (M) **1.** one who resides under earth. **3.** the eldest serpent son of Kaśyapa and Kadrū and one of the 7 nāgas that hold up the earth, he is the bracelet of Śiva and in the burning of Tripura acted as his bowstring and the axle of his chariot, he is the king of the nāgas and was used by the gods and demons as a rope for twisting Mount Mandāra to churn the ocean (*Bhā. Purāṇa*).

Vasukra (S) (M) **1.** knower of the gods. **3.** a ṛṣi and a part author of *Ṛg Veda* (x).

Vasukṛt (S) (M) **1.** one who behaves like the gods. **2.** with a pious conduct; act of the gods. **3.** a ṛṣi and an author of *Ṛg Veda* (x).

Vasula (S) (M) a god.

Vasumanas (S) (M) **1.** with a rich mind; knower of all. **3.** an Ikṣvāku king who was the son of Haryaśva and Mādhavī (*M. Bh.*); a king in the council of Yudhiṣṭhira (*M. Bh.*); an agni; a king of the Janaka family (*M. Bh.*); a king of Kosala (*M. Bh.*).

Vasumat (S) (M) **1.** possessing treasure; attended by the Vasus. **3.** a son of Manu Vaivasvata (*Purāṇas*); another name for Kṛṣṇa.

Vasumitra (S) (M) **1.** friend of the gods. **2.** friend of treasure. **3.** a Kṣatriya king who was a partial incarnation of the asura Vikṣara (*M. Bh.*); a Śuṅga dynasty king who was the father of Udaṅka (*Bhāgavata*).

Vasunanda (S) (M) delighting the gods.

Vasunemi (S) (M) **1.** felly of the gods. **3.** a nāga.

Vasunītha (S) (M) bringing wealth.

Vasunīti (S) (M) bringing wealth.

Vasupāla (S) (M) **1.** protector of wealth. **2.** king.

Vasupati (S) (M) **1.** lord of wealth and good things; lord of the vasus. **3.** another name for Kṛṣṇa, Agni, Indra, Kubera.

Vasupātṛ (S) (M) **1.** protector of the vasus. **3.** another name for Kṛṣṇa.

Vasuprabha (S) (M) **1.** with divine glory. **3.** a warrior of Skanda (*M. Bh.*).

Vasuprada (S) (M) **1.** bestowing wealth. **3.** an attendant of Skanda (*M. Bh.*).

Vasuprāṇa (S) (M) **1.** breath of the vasus. **2.** fire.

Vasupūjyarāj (S) (M) **1.** honoured by the gods. **3.** the father of the 12th Arhat of the present Avasarpiṇī (*J.S. Koṣa*).

Vasura (S) (M) **1.** valuable. **2.** rich.

Vasuratha (S) (M) **1.** chariot of the gods. **2.** led by gods.

Vasuretas (S) (M) 1. with divine power. 3. another name for Agni (*Ṛg Veda*).

Vasuruċi (S) (M) 1. with divine glory; having divine tastes. 3. a gandharva (*A. Veda*).

Vasurūpa (S) (M) 1. of a divine form; with the nature of the vasus. 3. another name for Śiva.

Vasuśakti (S) (M) 1. divine power. 2. with the power of the vasus (*P. Ratra*).

Vasusena (S) (M) 1. divine army; divine commander; distributer of wealth. 3. Karna in his boyhood; another name for Viṣṇu (*M. Bh.*).

Vasuśravas (S) (M) famous for wealth; flowing with wealth.

Vasuśreṣṭha (S) (M) 1. best of the vasus. 2. silver; wrought gold. 3. another name for Kṛṣṇa.

Vasuttama (S) (M) 1. best of the vasus. 3. another name for Bhīṣma (*Bh. Purāṇa*).

Vasuvāha (S) (M) 1. bringing wealth; preceptor of the divine. 3. a ṛṣi (*M. Bh.*).

Vasuvāhana (S) (M) bringing wealth.

Vasuvinda (S) (M) gaining wealth.

Vasuvīrya (S) (M) with the power of the vasus.

Vasvānanta (S) (M) 1. infinite wealth; external divinity; eternal wealth. 3. a king of Videha who was the son of Upagupta and the father of Yuyudha (*Bhāgavata*).

Vaśyā (S) (M) 1. dutiful; humble; tamed; obedient. 3. a son of Āgnīdhra (*Mā. Purāṇa*).

Vaṭa (S) (M) 1. the Indian Fig or Banyan tree (*Ficus indica*); cowrie shell (*Cypraea moneta*); pawn in chess. 3. one of the 5 attendants given to Skanda by the god Anśa (*M. Bh.*).

Vāta (S) (M) 1. wind; the god of wind. 3. a rākṣasa (*V. Purāṇa*); a son of Śūra; a Saptaṛṣi of the Manvantara of Manu Svāroċisa (*V. Purāṇa*).

Vāṭadhāna (S) (M) 1. an officer who knows his army. 3. a king who was a partial incarnation of the asura Krodhāvaśa (*M. Bh.*).

Vātādhipa (S) (M) 1. lord of wind. 3. a famous Purāṇic king (*M. Bh.*).

Vātaghna (S) (M) 1. vanquisher of the wind. 3. a son of Viśvāmitra (*M. Bh.*).

Vātajava (S) (M) 1. swift as the wind. 3. a rākṣasa.

Vātāpi (S) (M) 1. with the wind as an ally; swollen by the wind. 3. an asura who was the son of Hrāda (*M. Bh.*); an asura born of Kaśyapa and Danu (*M. Bh.*).

Vātaputra (S) (M) 1. son of the wind. 3. another name for Hanumān and Bhīma.

Vātaskandha (S) (M) 1. the direction from where the wind blows. 3. a hermit in the palace of Indra (*M. Bh.*).

Vatāśraya (S) (M) 1. dwelling in the fig tree. 3. another name for Kubera.

Vātātmaja (S) (M) 1. son of the wind. 3. another name for Hanumān and Bhīma (*M.Bh.*).

Vātavega (S) (M) 1. with the speed of wind. 2. as fast as wind; very swift. 3. a son of Dhṛtarāṣṭra (*M. Bh.*); a son of Garuḍa (*M. Bh.*); another name for Garuḍa.

Vaṭeśa (S) (M) 1. lord of the Banyan tree. 3. the father of Śiśu (*A. Purāṇa*).

Vaṭeśvara (S) (M) 1. lord of the Banyan tree. 3. the father of Pṛthu (*Ṛg Veda*).

Vāti (S) (M) air; wind; sun; moon.

Vātika (S) (M) 1. airy. 2. a talker; the Ċātaka bird. 3. a warrior of Skanda (*M. Bh.*).

Vatsa (S) (M) 1. calf; child; darling; son; boy. 3. a descendant of Kaṇva (*Ṛg Veda*); a son of Senajit (*H. Purāṇa*); a son of Akṣamālā; a son of Urukṣepa (*V. Purāṇa*); the son of King Pratardana of Kāśi (*M. Bh.*); a king of the Śaryāti family who was the father of Tālajangha and Hehaya (*M. Bh.*).

Vatsabālaka (S) (M) 1. loving child. 3. a brother of Vasudeva (*M. Bh.*).

Vatsahanu (S) (M) 1. with a calf-like chin. 3. a son of Senajit (*V. Purāṇa*).

Vatsaka (S) (M) **1.** young calf. **2.** a term of endearment. **3.** a son of Śūra (*Bh. Purāṇa*); an asura (*Bh. Purāṇa*).

Vatsala (S) (M) **1.** child loving; affectionate towards offspring. **3.** a son of Bhūmi.

Vatsanābha (S) (M) **1.** with a loving navel; aconite. **3.** a hermit once saved by Dharma in the form of a she-buffalo (*M. Bh.*).

Vatsapāla (S) (M) **1.** keeper of calves; protector of children. **3.** another name for Kṛṣṇa and Balarāma.

Vatsapati (S) (M) **1.** lord of calves; lord of the Vatsa tribe. **3.** another name for Udayana.

Vatsaprīti (S) (M) **1.** affectionate to children; calf loving. **3.** a hermit and author of *Ṛg Veda* (ix).

Vatsara (S) (M) **1.** a year; the 5th year in a cycle of 5 years. **3.** the year personified as a son of Dhruva and Bhrami who was the husband of Svarvīthi and the father of Puṣpārṇa, Tigmaketu, Iśa, Vasu, Ūrja and Jaya (*Bhāgavata*); another name for Viṣṇu (*M. Bh.*); a son of Kaśyapa (*M. Bh.*).

Vatsavat (S) (M) **1.** having many calves. **2.** rich in cattle. **3.** a son of Śūra (*Bhā. Purāṇa*).

Vatsavṛddha (S) (M) **1.** veterinary physician. **3.** a son of Urukriya (*Bhā. Purāṇa*).

Vatsin (S) (M) **1.** with many children. **3.** another name for Viṣṇu.

Vātsyāyana (S) (M) **1.** loving. **2.** preceptor of the art of love. **3.** a hermit who wrote the famous *Vātsyāyana Sūtra* or Science of Love.

Vavri (S) (M) **1.** a cover; vesture; the body. **3.** a hermit and supposed part author of *Ṛg Veda* (v).

Vayasya (S) (M) **1.** contemporary; friend; companion. **3.** a brother of Bṛhaspati.

Vāyava (S) (M) sacred to the god of wind.

Vāyu (S) (M) **1.** wind. **3.** air personified as a deity of equal rank though not as prominent as Indra, he is one of the 8 guardians of the world being the guardian of the north west, he was born from the breath of Viśvapuruṣa (*Ṛg Veda*), he is the father of Bhīma, Hanumān and Agni and is the father-in-law of Tvaṣṭā, his palace is known as Gandhavatī, he is the messenger of the gods; a vasu (*H. Purāṇa*); a daitya; the king of the gandharvas (*V. Purāṇa*); a marut (*V. Purāṇa*).

Vāyubala (S) (M) **1.** as mighty as the wind. **3.** one of the 7 ṛṣis said to have been the fathers of the maruts (*V. Purāṇa*).

Vāyubhakṣa (S) (M) **1.** one who lives on wind. **3.** a hermit in the palace of Yudhiṣṭhira (*M. Bh.*).

Vāyubhūti (S) (M) **1.** born of wind. **3.** a main disciple of Mahāvira (*V. Rāmāyaṇa*).

Vāyućakra (S) (M) **1.** discus of the wind. **3.** a pot born hermit son of Maṅkanaka (*M. Bh.*); one of the 7 ṛṣis said to have been the fathers of the maruts (*M. Bh.*).

Vāyuhan (S) (M) **1.** friend of wind. **3.** a pot born hermit son of Maṅkanaka (*M. Bh.*); one of the 7 ṛṣis said to have been the fathers of the maruts.

Vayujāta (S) (M) **1.** wind born. **3.** another name for Hanumān.

Vāyujvāla (S) (M) **1.** inflamer of the wind. **2.** cause of the wind. **3.** a pot born hermit son of Maṅkanaka (*M. Bh.*); one of the 7 ṛṣis said to have been the fathers of the maruts (*M. Bh.*).

Vāyukeśa (S) (M) **1.** with windswept hair. **3.** another name for the gandharvas.

Vāyumaṇḍala (S) (M) **1.** atmosphere. **3.** a pot born hermit son of Maṅkanaka (*M. Bh.*); one of the 7 ṛṣis said to have been the father of the maruts.

Vayuna (S) (M) **1.** moving; active; alive; clear. **3.** a son of Kṛṣāśva and Dhīṣaṇā (*Bhā. Purāṇa*).

Vāyuna (S) (M) god; a deity.

Vāyunandana (S) (M) **1.** son of the wind. **3.** another name for Hanumān and Bhīma.

Vāyupatha (S) (M) **1.** the path of the wind. **3.** a king (*K.* Sāgara).

Vāyuputra (S) (M) **1.** son of the wind. **3.** another name for Hanumān and Bhīma.

Vāyuretas (S) (M) **1.** power of wind; as powerful as wind; as subtle as wind; as pervading as wind. **3.** a pot born hermit son of Maṅkanaka (*M. Bh.*); one of the 7 ṛṣis said to have been the father of the maruts.

Vayusakha (S) (M) **1.** friend of the wind; with the wind as ally. **3.** another name for Agni.

Vāyusuta (S) (M) **1.** son of Vāyu. **3.** another name for Bhīma.

Vāyuvāhana (S) (M) **1.** travelling with the wind. **3.** another name for Viṣṇu and Śiva.

Vāyuvega (S) (M) **1.** with the speed of wind. **3.** a pot born hermit son of Maṅkanaka (*M. Bh.*); a king who was a partial incarnation of the asura Krodhavaśa (*M. Bh.*); a son of Dhṛtarāṣṭra; one of the 7 ṛṣis said to have been the fathers of the maruts (*M. Bh.*).

Vayya (S) (M) **1.** friend; companion. **3.** an asura (*Ṛg Veda*).

Veda (S) (M) **1.** knowledge; wealth; obtaining; weaving together; all that is to be known. **3.** four books that constitute the basis for the Hindu religion.

Vedabāhu (S) (M) **1.** armed with the Vedas. **3.** a ṛṣi under Manu Raivata (*H. Purāṇa*); a son of Pulastya (*V. Purāṇa*); a son of Kṛṣṇa (*Bhā. Purāṇa Purana*).

Vedācārya (S) (M) teacher of the Vedas.

Vedadharma (S) (M) **1.** devotee of the sacred text. **3.** a son of Paila (*Ṛg Veda*).

Vedadhideva (S) (M) **1.** deity of the Vedas. **3.** another name for Brahmā.

Vedādhyakṣa (S) (M) **1.** protector of the Vedas. **3.** another name for Kṛṣṇa.

Vedadiṣa (S) (M) **1.** point or precept with the Vedas. **3.** a son of King Bṛhadratha of Ćedi (*Bhāgavata*).

Vedagarbha (S) (M) **1.** womb of the Vedas. **3.** another name for Brahma and Visnu.

Vedagātha (S) (M) **1.** singer of the texts. **3.** a ṛṣi (*H. Purāṇa*).

Vedaghoṣa (S) (M) **1.** the voice of Vedas. **2.** sound caused by the recitation of the Vedas.

Vedāgraṇī (S) (M) **1.** leader of the Vedas. **3.** another name for Sarasvatī.

Vedagupta (S) (M) **1.** preserver of the Vedas. **3.** another name for Kṛṣṇa the son of Parāśara.

Vedakartṛ (S) (M) **1.** author of the Vedas. **3.** another name for the Sun, Śiva and Viṣṇu.

Vedakumbha (S) (M) master of Vedas; pitcher of the Vedas.

Vedamitra (S) (M) **1.** friend of the Vedas. **3.** father of Sumedhas.

Vedamūrti (S) (M) embodiment of the Vedas.

Vedāngarāya (S) (M) **1.** scholar of the Vedic school. **3.** an author who wrote the *Shrāddhudīpikā* for Shahjahān (17th century).

Vedanidhi (S) (M) storehouse of the Vedas.

Vedaprakāśa (S) (M) light of the Vedas.

Vedasāra (S) (M) **1.** essence of the Vedas. **3.** another name for Viṣṇu.

Vedaśarmā (S) (M) **1.** protector of the Vedas. **3.** the son of the hermit Śivaśarmā.

Vedaśiras (S) (M) **1.** head of the Vedas. **3.** a son of Prāṇa; a hermit of the Bhṛgu clan, son of Mārkaṇḍeya and Mūrdhanyā or Dhūmrā and husband of Pīvarī (*Vā. Purāṇa*); a hermit and son of Kṛśāśva and Dhīṣaṇā who learnt the *Viṣṇu Purāṇa* from the nāgas in Pātāla (*V. Purāṇa*).

Vedasparśa (S) (M) **1.** touched by the sacred text. **3.** a disciple of the hermit Kabandha (*Vā. Purāṇa*).

Vedaśravas (S) (M) listener of the scriptures; famous in the scriptures.

Vedaśrī (S) (M) **1.** beauty of the Vedas. **3.** a ṛṣi (*Mā. Purāṇa*).

Vedāśva (S) (M) **1.** horse of the scriptures. **2.** famous carrier. **3.** a river (*M. Bh.*).

Vedātman (S) (M) **1.** soul of the Veda. **3.** another name for Viṣṇu (*Ṛg Veda*).

Vedavṛddha (S) (M) learned in the Vedas.

Vedavyāsa (S) (M) **1.** arranger of the Vedas. **3.** another name for Vyāsa.

Vedeśa (S) (M) lord of the Vedas.

Vedha (S) (M) **1.** breaking through; piercing; pious; faithful. **3.** a son of Ananta (*Vah. Purāṇa*).

Vedhagupta (S) (M) **1.** with an inner penetration; possessing a hidden disturbance. **3.** a rāga.

Vedhas (S) (M) **1.** pious; religious; virtuous; good; brave; arranger; disposer; creator. **3.** the father of Hariśćandra; part of the hand at the root of the thumb considered sacred to Brahmā; a ṛṣi of the family of Aṅgiras (*Ṛg Veda*).

Vedi (S) (M) wise man; teacher.

Vedijā (S) (M) **1.** altar born. **3.** another name for Draupadī.

Vedin (S) (M) **1.** knowing; feeling. **3.** another name for Brahmā.

Vedīśa (S) (M) **1.** lord of the wise. **3.** another name for Brahmā.

Vedodaya (S) (M) **1.** origin of the Vedas. **3.** another name for Sūrya.

Veduka (S) (M) **1.** striving for knowledge. **2.** acquiring; obtaining.

Vedya (S) (M) well known; famous; celebrated.

Vegavān (S) (M) **1.** fast; violent; rapid; swift. **2.** leopard. **3.** a nāga of the family of Dhṛtarāṣṭra (*M. Bh.*); an asura son of Kaśyapa and Danu who was reborn as the prince of Kekaya (*M. Bh.*); a daitya killed by Sāmba the son of Kṛṣṇa (*M. Bh.*); a son of Kṛṣṇa (*Bhā. Purāṇa*); a vidyādhara (*K. Sāgara*); an asura (*M. Bh.*); a king and son of Bandhumat (*Ṛg Veda*).

Vegin (S) (M) **1.** swift. **2.** hawk; falcon. **3.** another name for Vāyu.

Vekata (S) (M) a youth.

Velan (S) (M) **1.** pungent. **3.** a son of Śiva.

Velumaṇi (S) (M) **1.** strong willed. **2.** diamond.

Vemaćitra (S) (M) **1.** woven picture. **3.** an asura king.

Veṇa (S) (M) **1.** yearning; loving; longing; eager. **3.** a notorious king of the Manu Ćākṣuṣa family who was the son of Aṅga and Sunīthā the daughter of Yama and the father of Pṛthu (*Vām. Purāṇa*); a son of Vaivasvata Manu (*M. Bh.*).

Veṇavin (S) (M) **1.** furnished with a flute. **3.** another name for Śiva.

Veṇimādhava (S) (M) **1.** god with braided hair. **3.** a 4 handed idol at Prayāga (*Ma. Purāṇa*).

Veṇin (S) (M) **1.** with a hood like braided hair. **3.** a serpent in the family of Dhṛtarāṣṭra (*M. Bh.*).

Veṇiprasāda (S) (M) gift of braided hair.

Veṇirāma (S) (M) with braided hair.

Veṇiskandha (S) (M) **1.** with braided shoulders. **3.** a serpent of the Kaurava family (*M. Bh.*).

Veṅkaṭa (S) (M) **1.** self born. **2.** naturally manifest; divine. **3.** a sacred hill in the Draviḍa country near Madras, on its summit is a temple dedicted to Viṣṇu/Kṛṣṇa as Lord Veṅkata or Śrīpati or Thirupati; a king of Vijayanagara (*Bhā. Purāṇa*).

Veṅkaṭāćala (S) (M) the Veṅkata mountain.

Veṅkaṭaćaleśa (S) (M) **1.** lord of the Veṅkaṭa mountain. **3.** another name for Viṣṇu.

Veṅkatadhvari (S) (M) **1.** performing sin destroying sacrifices. **3.** a Sanskṛt poet and author of Yādavarāghaviya (*17th century*)

Veṅkaṭagiri (S) (M) the Veṅkaṭa mountain.

Veṅkaṭanātha (S) (M) **1.** lord of the Veṅkaṭa hill. **3.** a poet and philospher venerated now as divine (14th century); another name for Viṣṇu/Kṛṣṇa.

Veṅkaṭarāghavana (S) (M) **1.** Veṅkaṭa, the Rāghava. **3.** Viṣṇu in his incarnation as Rāma (*A. Koṣa*).

Veṅkaṭaraman (S) (M) **1.** Veṅkaṭā, the Rāma. **3.** Viṣṇu in his incarnation as Rāma (*A. Koṣa*).

Veṅkatasvāmin (S) (M) **1.** lord of the Veṅkaṭa mountain. **3.** another name for Viṣṇu/Kṛṣṇa (*V. Koṣa*).

Veṅkatavaradāna (S) (M) the boon of Viṣṇu.

Veṅkateśa (S) (M) **1.** lord of Veṅkata. **3.** another name for Viṣṇu/Kṛṣṇa.

Veṅkaṭeśvara (S) (M) lord of Veṅkaṭa.

Veṇu (S) (M) **1.** bamboo; reed; flute; fife; pipe. **3.** a deity of the Bodhi tree (*L. Vistara*); a king of the Yādavas (*M. Bh.*); a son of Śatajita (*V. Purāṇa*); a mountain (*Mā. Purāṇa*); a river; Solid Bamboo (*Dendrocalamus strictus*).

Veṇudāri (S) (M) **1.** tearing the flute. **3.** a Yādava warrior (*M. Bh.*).

Veṇugopāla (S) (M) **1.** the flute bearing cowherd. **3.** another name for Kṛṣṇa.

Veṇuhaya (S) (M) **1.** resounding like a flute. **3.** a king of the lunar dynasty who was the son of Śatajita and the brother of Mahāhaya and Hehaya (*Bhāgavata*).

Veṇujaṅgha (S) (M) **1.** bamboo thighed. **3.** a hermit in the assembly of Yudhiṣṭhira (*M. Bh.*).

Veṇukā (S) (M) flute; pipe.

Veṇumanta (S) (M) **1.** possessing bamboos. **3.** a white mountain on par, in the Purāṇas, with Mandāra.

Veṇumat (S) (M) **1.** with bamboo. **3.** a mountain (*Bhā. Purāṇa*); a son of Jyotiṣmat (*V. Purāṇa*).

Verācarya (S) (M) **1.** master of the body. **3.** a prince (*B. Literature*).

Vetāla (S) (M) **1.** ghost; spirit; phantom; goblin. **3.** a ghost in Kathāsarit Sāgara (*K. Sāgara*); an attendant of Śiva (*K. Purāṇa*).

Vetrāsura (S) (M) **1.** the reed demon; a large reed. **3.** an asura (*M. Bh.*).

Vetravat (S) (M) **1.** made of reeds. **3.** a son of Pūsan (*K. Sāgara*).

Vettṛ (S) (M) **1.** one who knows. **2.** sage.

Vībhā (S) (M) to become visible; to glitter; shining; bright.

Vibhākara (S) (M) **1.** light maker; creator of brightness. **2.** sun; fire; moon; king; Ceylon Leadwort (*Plumbago zeylanica*).

Vibhāṇḍaka (S) (M) **1.** without any possessions. **3.** a hermit of the Kaśyapa family and father of Ṛṣyaśṛṅga (*M. Bh.*).

Vibhānu (S) (M) shining; beaming; radiant.

Vibhāsa (S) (M) **1.** brightness; splendour. **3.** a rāga; a deity (*Mā. Purāṇa*); one of the 7 suns (*T. Āraṇyaka*).

Vibhāsita (S) (M) illuminated.

Vibhāta (S) (M) **1.** shining forth; appearing. **2.** dawn.

Vibhava (S) (M) power; riches; omnipresence; might; magnanimity; loftiness.

Vibhāva (S) (M) **1.** friend; acquaintaince. **3.** another name for Śiva.

Vibhavarīśa (S) (M) **1.** lord of the night. **3.** another name for the Moon.

Vibhāvasu (S) (M) **1.** abounding in light. **2.** garland. **3.** one of the 8 vasus; a son of Naraka; a dānava (*Bh. Purāṇa*); a gandharva; a hermit and brother of Supratīka (*M. Bh.*); a son of Kaśyapa and Danu; another name for Agni, Soma, Kṛṣṇa, the sun and the moon.

Vibhī (S) (M) fearless.

Vibhīndu (S) (M) **1.** fearless moon; moon among the fearless. **3.** a king famous for his liberality (*Ṛg Veda*).

Vibhrāja (S) (M) **1.** shining; splendid; luminous. **3.** a king who was a descendant of Yayāti the son of Kṛti and the father of Anuha and father-in-law of Kīrtī the daughter of Śuka (*Bhāgavata*).

Vibhu (S) (M) **1.** all pervading; omnipresent; eternal; mighty; powerful; excellent; great; strong; effective. **2.** king; lord. **3.** a god who was the son of Vedaśiras and Tuṣitā (*Bhā. Purāṇa*); a son of Viṣṇu and Dakṣiṇā (*Bhā. Purāṇa*); a son of

Bhaga and Siddhī (*Bhā. Purāṇa*); a son of Śambara (*H. Purāṇa*); a son of Satyaketu and father of Suvibhu; a son of Dharmaketu and father of Sukumāra; a son of Bhṛgu; father of Ānarta (*H. Purāṇa*); a king of the Bharata family who was the son of Prastotā and the father of Pṛthusena (*Bhā. Purāṇa*); Indra in the 5th Manvantara (*Bh. Purāṇa*); the brother of Śakuni (*M. Bh.*); another name for Brahmā, Viṣṇu, Śiva, Buddha, and Kubera.

Vibhudharāja (S) (M) **1.** king of the gods. **3.** another name for Indra.

Vibhumat (S) (M) **1.** omnipresent; extending everywhere; omnipotent; appearing in many forms. **3.** another name for Kṛṣṇa.

Vibhūrasi (S) (M) **1.** highly powerful. **3.** son of the agni called Adbhuta (*M. Bh.*).

Vibhūṣana (S) (M) **1.** ornament; adorning. **3.** another name for Manjuśrī.

Vibhūṣṇu (S) (M) **1.** omnipresent. 3. another name for Śiva.

Vibhūti (S) (M) **1.** pervading. **2.** penetrating; abundant; plentiful; mighty; powerful; ash. **3.** a son of Viśvāmitra (*M. Bh.*).

Vibhūtibhūṣaṇa (S) (M) **1.** full of powers; adorned by ash. **3.** another name for Śiva.

Vibhūvas (S) (M) powerful.

Vibhvan (S) (M) **1.** far-reaching; penetrating; all pervading. **3.** a semi-divine being and son of Sudhanvan a descendant of Aṅgiras who became divine due to his good works; a ṛbhu (*Ṛg Veda*).

Vibodha (S) (M) intelligence; awakening; perception.

Vibuddha (S) (M) awakened; expanded; clever; skilful.

Vibudha (S) (M) **1.** wise; learned. **2.** sage; god; teacher. **3.** the son of Devamīdha (*Rāmāyaṇa*); another name for the moon.

Vibudhāćārya (S) (M) **1.** teacher of the gods; preceptor of the wise. **3.** another name for Bṛhaspati.

Vibudhaguru (S) (M) **1.** teacher of the gods. **3.** another name for Bṛhaspati.

Vibudhapati (S) (M) **1.** king of the gods. **3.** another name for Indra.

Vibudhendra (S) (M) best of the wise.

Vibudheśvara (S) (M) king of the gods.

Vićakṣaṇa (S) (M) conspicuous; visible; sagacious; far-sighted.

Vićakṣṇu (S) (M) **1.** perceiver; observer. **3.** an ancient king and propounder of vegetarianism (*M. Bh.*).

Vićakṣus (S) (M) **1.** eyeless; blind. **3.** a king (*H. Purāṇa*).

Vićāru (S) (M) **1.** thoughtful; charming; handsome; evermoving; traveller. **3.** a son of Kṛṣṇa and Rukmiṇī (*Bhāgavata*).

Vićintana (S) (M) thought.

Vićitra (S) (M) **1.** strange; variegated; motley; brilliant; manifold; various; wonderful; diverse; charming; lovely; beautiful. **3.** a son of Manu Raućya (*H. Purāṇa*); a Kṣatriya king born from a portion of the asura Krodhavaśa (*M. Bh.*); Curcumis trigonus; Aśoka tree (*Saraca indica*).

Vićitrabhūṣaṇa (S) (M) wonderful brilliant ornament.

Vićitravīrya (S) (M) **1.** of marvellous heroism. **3.** the son of Śāntanu and Satyavatī and half-brother of Bhīṣma, he married Ambikā and Ambālikā of Kāśi but died childless (*M. Bh.*).

Vidalla (S) (M) **1.** split; expanded; divided; a fragment; pomegranate bark. **3.** a minister of King Dhruvasandhi (*M. Bh.*).

Vidaṇḍa (S) (M) **1.** doorkeeper; door. **3.** an ancient king (*M. Bh.*).

Viḍaṅga (S) (M) clever; skilful; able.

Vidarbha (S) (M) **1.** without darbhā grass. **3.** a son of Ṛṣabha and brother of Bharata and the father of Nimi (*Bhāgavata*); a son of Jyāmagha; a country and its people (*H. Purāṇa*).

Videha (S) (M) **1.** bodyless. **2.** one who doesn't care for the body; one who is ever involved in the divine pursuits. **3.** another name for the Emperor Nimi and the king of Mithilā (*V. Rāmāyaṇa*).

Vidhaliṅgām (S) (M) the mark of creation.

Vidhātā (S) (M) **1.** disposer; arranger; creator. **3.** a son of Bhṛgu and Khyāti and husband of Niyati and father of Mṛkaṇḍu (*V. Purāṇa*); another name for Brahmā.

Vidhātṛ (S) (M) **1.** disposer; arranger. **2.** creator; maker; author; granter; giver. **3.** the son of Brahmā or Bhṛgu and brother of Dhātṛ; another name for Brahmā, Viṣṇu, Śiva, Kāma and Viśvakarman.

Vidhatru (S) (M) **1.** maker; creator. **3.** another name for Brahmā.

Vidhava (S) (M) resembling the moon.

Vidhi (S) (M) **1.** method; precept; creation; law; system; worshipper. **3.** another name for Brahmā.

Vidhisāra (S) (M) **1.** essence of law. **3.** a king and father of Ajātaśatru (*V. Puṛāṇa*).

Vīdhra (S) (M) **1.** clean; clear; pure. **2.** sunshine; wind; fire.

Vidhṛti (S) (M) **1.** separation; division; partition; arrangement. **3.** father of Hiraṇyanābha (*Bhāgavata*).

Vidhu (S) (M) **1.** solitary; alone. **3.** a rākṣasa; another name for Brahmā, Viṣṇu and the moon.

Vidhūma (S) (M) **1.** smokeless. **3.** a vasu (*K. Sāgara*).

Vidīp (S) (M) shining forth; illuminating.

Vidīpaka (S) (M) **1.** one that illuminates. **2.** lamp.

Vidipta (S) (M) shining; bright.

Vidita (S) (M) known; learnt; understood.

Vidman (S) (M) knowledge; intelligence; wisdom.

Vidojas (S) (M) **1.** with well-known power. **3.** another name for Indra.

Vidrāvana (S) (M) **1.** putting to flight. **3.** a son of Kaśyapa and Danu (*M. Purāṇa*).

Vidruta (S) (M) **1.** with great speed. **3.** a king in the family of Yayāti who is the son of Rućaka (*Bhāgavata*).

Vidu (S) (M) **1.** intelligent; wise. **3.** a deity of the Bodhi tree (*B. Literature*).

Vidura (S) (M) **1.** knowing; wise; intelligent; learned; skilled. **3.** half-brother of Dhṛtarāṣṭra and Pāṇḍu who was advisor to the former and a man of colossal intelligence, known for his righteousness, he was a partial incarnation of Dharma born of Vyāsa and a Śudra woman (*M. Bh.*).

Vidūra (S) (M) **1.** very remote or distant; far removed from. **3.** a Kuru king who was the son of Kuru and Śubhaṅgi and the husband of Saṁpriyā and the father of Anaśvā (*M. Bh.*).

Viduraja (S) (M) **1.** son of the wise. **2.** the cat's-eye jewel.

Vidūrastha (S) (M) **1.** thrown far. **3.** father of Māninī (*Ma. Purāṇa*).

Vidūratha (S) (M) **1.** distant. **3.** a king of the Vṛṣṇi dynasty who became a viśvadeva after death; a Purū king (M. Bh.); a king who was the father of Sunīti, Sumati and Mudāvatī (Mā. Purāṇa); a king of the Bharata family who was the son of Suratha and the father of Sarvabhauma (*Bhāgavata*); the brother of Dantavaktra (*Bhāgavata*); a muni; a son of the 12th Manu; a descendant of Vṛṣṇi; a son of Kuru (*M. Bh.*); a son of Bhajamana and father of Śura; a son of Suratha and father of Ṛkṣa; a son of Ćitraratha (*Bhā. Purāṇa*).

Vidurya (S) (M) **1.** belonging to the wise. **2.** Lapiz lazuli.

Viduṣa (S) (M) **1.** wise. **3.** a king of the Aṅga dynasty who was the son of King Ghṛta and father of Praćetas (*A. Purāṇa*).

Vidvala (S) (M) clever.

Vidvattama (S) (M) **1.** most wise. **3.** another name for Śiva.

Vidvattara (S) (M) very wise.

Vidyābhūṣaṇa (S) (M) ornament of knowledge.

Vidyaćandra (S) (M) **1.** moon of knowledge; most knowledgeable. **3.** a sage who was the son of Kuśika.

Vidyādhara (S) (M) **1.** possessed of science and spells. **3.** attendants of Śiva dwelling in the Himālayas (*H. Purāṇa*).

Vidyādhāra (S) (M) receptacle of knowledge.

Vidyādhipa (S) (M) **1.** lord of knowledge. **3.** another name for Śiva.

Vidyākara (S) (M) mine of learning.

Vidyānanda (S) (M) delight in knowledge.

Vidyānātha (S) (M) **1.** lord of knowledge. **3.** a Sanskṛt writer of rhetoric and the member of the court of Warangal (14th century).

Vidyāpati (S) (M) master of knowledge.

Vidyāraṇya (S) (M) **1.** taking pleasure in knowledge. **3.** an authority on medical diagnosis (14th century A.D.).

Vidyāratna (S) (M) jewel of learning.

Vidyāsāgara (S) (M) **1.** ocean of knowledge. **3.** the father of Bhartṛhari.

Vidyāvatansa (S) (M) **1.** perfect in learning. **3.** a vidyadhara.

Vidyeśa (S) (M) **1.** lord of learning. **3.** another name for Śiva.

Vidyota (S) (M) **1.** shining; glittering. **3.** a son of Dharma and Lambā and the father of Sthanayitnu (*Bhā. Purāṇa*).

Vidyudakṣa (S) (M) **1.** with glittering eyes. **3.** a daitya (*H. Purāṇa*).

Vidyuddhara (S) (M) **1.** bearer of lightning; cloud. **3.** a gandharva.

Vidyuddhvaja (S) (M) **1.** lightning bannered. **3.** an asura (*K. Sāgara*).

Vidyudrūpa (S) (M) **1.** of the form of lightning. **2.** with a shining form. **3.** a yakṣa who was a favourite of Kubera and the husband of Madanikā the daughter of Menakā (*Mā. Purāṇa*).

Vidyudvarćas (S) (M) **1.** flashing like lightning. **3.** a viśvadeva (*M. Bh.*).

Vidyujjihva (S) (M) **1.** with a lightning like tongue. **3.** a rākṣasa who was a friend of Ghaṭotkaća (*M. Bh.*); the husband of Śūrparṇakhā and the father of Śambhukumāra (*K. Rāmāyaṇa*); a rākṣasa follower of Rāvaṇa (*V. Rāmāyaṇa*); a son of Viśravas and Vākā (*Vā. Purāṇa*); a yaksa (*K. Sāgara*).

Vidyunmālin (S) (M) **1.** garlanded with lightning. **3.** a son of Tārakāsura; a rākṣasa friend of Rāvaṇa (*Rāmāyaṇa*); a vidyādhara (*H. Purāṇa*).

Vidyut (S) (M) **1.** flashing; glittering. **3.** an asura; a rākṣasa (*V. Purāṇa*).

Vidyutākṣa (S) (M) **1.** lightning eyed. **2.** with glittering eyes. **3.** a warrior of Skanda (*M. Bh.*).

Vidyutapuñja (S) (M) **1.** heap of lightning. **3.** a vidyādhara.

Vidyutkeśin (S) (M) **1.** with glittering hair. **3.** a rākṣasa king and father of Sukeśa (*M. Bh.*).

Vidyutprabha (S) (M) **1.** flashing like lightning. **3.** a king of the daityas; a hermit (*M. Bh.*); a dānava who was a devotee of Rudradeva (*M. Bh.*).

Vigāhana (S) (M) **1.** plunger; penetrator; diver; obtainer; practiser. **3.** a king of Mukuṭa Vanśa (*M. Bh.*); another name for fire.

Vigataśoka (S) (M) **1.** griefless. **3.** a grandson of Aśoka.

Vigatoddhava (S) (M) **1.** free from levity. **3.** another name for Buddha.

Vighana (S) (M) **1.** cloudless; best attacker. **3.** a rākṣasa on the side of Rāvaṇa (*V. Rāmāyaṇa*).

Vighnahāntṛ (S) (M) **1.** destroyer of obstacles. **3.** another name for Gaṇeśa.

Vighnahārin (S) (M) **1.** vanquisher of obstacles. **3.** another name for Gaṇeśa.

Vighnajit (S) (M) **1.** overcoming obstacles. **3.** another name for Gaṇeśa.

Vighnanāśaka (S) (M) **1.** destroyer of obstacles. **3.** another name for Gaṇeśa.

Vighnanāyaka (S) (M) **1.** lord of obstacles. **2.** one who removes obstacles. **3.** another name for Gaṇeśa.

Vighnapati (S) (M) **1.** master of obstacles. **3.** another name for Gaṇeśa.

Vighnarāja (S) (M) **1.** king of obstacles. **3.** another name for Gaṇeśa.

Vighnavināyaka (S) (M) **1.** vanquisher of obstacles. **3.** another name for Gaṇeśa.

Vighneśvara (S) (M) **1.** god of obstacles. **3.** another name for Gaṇeśa.

Vigraha (S) (M) **1.** separate; independent; idol; image. **3.** one of the 2 attendants given to Skanda by the ocean (*M. Bh.*); another name for Śiva.

Vihān (S) (M) morning; dawn.

Vihaga (S) (M) **1.** sky goer. **2.** arrow; bird. **3.** another name for the sun and moon.

Vihagapati (S) (M) **1.** king of birds. **3.** another name for Garuḍa.

Vihagavega (S) (M) **1.** as swift as a bird. **3.** a vidyādhara (*H. Purāṇa*).

Vihaṅga (S) (M) **1.** flying; sky going. **2.** bird; arrow. **3.** a serpent of the family of Airāvata (*M. Bh.*); another name for the sun and moon.

Vihaṅgama (S) (M) **1.** moving in the sky. **3.** soldier of the army of Khara (*V. Rāmāyaṇa*); another name for the sun, and Garuḍa as the incarnation of Viṣṇu.

Vihārin (S) (M) **1.** wandering. **2.** a wanderer for pleasure. **3.** another name for Kṛṣṇa.

Vihava (S) (M) invocation.

Vihavya (S) (M) **1.** to be invoked; to be desired. **3.** a ṛṣi of the Aṅgiras family (*Ṛg Veda*); the son of Varćas of the Gṛtsamada dynasty and the father of Vitatya (*M. Bh.*).

Vihuṇḍa (S) (M) **1.** not a tiger. **3.** an asura who was the son of Huṇḍa and who was killed by Pārvatī (*P. Purāṇa*).

Vijaya (S) (M) **1.** victory; conquest; triumph. **3.** the hour of Kṛṣṇa's birth; a kind of flute (*Bh. Purāṇa*); a chariot of the gods; a son of Jayanta (*H. Purāṇa*); a son of Vasudeva (*H. Purāṇa*); a son of Kṛṣṇa (*Bh. Purāṇa*); an attendant of Viṣṇu; an attendant of Padmapāṇi; a warrior on the Pāṇḍava side (*M. Bh.*); a son of Svaroćiṣ (*Ma. Purāṇa*); a councillor of Daśaratha (*Rāmāyaṇa*); a son of Jaya (*H. Purāṇa*); a son of Ćanću; a son of Bṛhanmānas (*H. Purāṇa*); a son of Yajñaśrī; the founder of Buddhist civilization in Ceylon (*B. Literature*); the 20th Arhat of the future and the father of the 21st Arhat of the present Avasarpiṇī; an attendant of the 8th Arhat of the present Avasarpinī (*J.S. Koṣa*); a son of Kalki (*K. Purāṇa*); a lance of Rudra; a son of Sanjaya (*V. Purāṇa*); a son of Sudeva (*Bh. Purāṇa*); a gatekeeper of Vaikuṇṭha (*Bh. Purāṇa*); a son of Purūravas and Urvaśī (*Bh. Purāṇa*); a Kosala king (*V. Rāmāyaṇa*); secret name given to Arjuna by Yudhiṣṭhira (*M. Bh.*); a son of Dhṛtarāṣṭra (*M. Bh.*); a king of Vārāṇasī (*Bh. Purāṇa*); the trident of Śiva (*M. Bh.*); a bow of Indra (*M. Bh.*); the divine bow of Karṇa (*M. Bh.*); Sweet Flag (*acorus calamus*); Couch Grass (*Cynodon dactylon*); Common Indigo (*Indigofera tinctoria*); Indian Madder (*Rubia cordifolia*); Black Myrobalan (*Terminalia chebula*); another name for Yama, Arjuna, Śiva and Viṣṇu.

Vijayaćandra (S) (M) moon of victory.

Vijayadatta (S) (M) **1.** bestowed by victory. **3.** the hare in the moon (*P. Ratra*).

Vijayāditya (S) (M) sun of victory.

Vijayakānta (S) (M) beloved of victory.

Vijayaketu (S) (M) **1.** victory bannered. **3.** a vidyādhara (*V. Samhitā*).

Vijayanandana (S) (M) **1.** delighting in victory; son of victory. **3.** a ćakravartin.

Vijayanātha (S) (M) lord of victory.

Vijayānka (S) (M) with a mark of victory.

Vijayanta (S) (M) **1.** victorious in the end. **3.** another name for Indra.

Vijayarāja (S) (M) king of victory.

Vijayarāma (S) (M) victorious Rāma; abode of victory; consisting of victory.

Vijayavega (S) (M) **1.** with a passion for victory. **3.** a vidyādhara (*K. Sāgara*).

Vijayendra (S) (M) lord of victory.

Vijayeśa (S) (M) **1.** lord of victory. **3.** another name for Śiva.

Vijayin (S) (M) victor.

Vijeṣakṛt (S) (M) bestowing victory.

Viji (S) (M) to conquer; win; to excel; to defeat.

Vijita (S) (M) **1.** conquered. **2.** defeated; won.

Vijitāśva (S) (M) **1.** with subdued horses. **3.** a son of Emperor Pṛthu (*Bhāgavata*).

Vijitātman (S) (M) **1.** self subdued. **3.** another name for Śiva.

Vijña (S) (M) knowing; intelligent; wise.

Vijñāna (S) (M) understanding; intelligence; knowledge.

Vijñānaprasāda (S) (M) with the blessing of knowledge; gift of science.

Vijṛmbhaka (S) (M) **1.** blossoming; yawning; expanding. **3.** a vidyādhara (*H. Purāṇa*).

Vijula (S) (M) the Silkcotton tree (*Bombax heptaphyllum*).

Vijvala (S) (M) **1.** blessing of knowledge. **3.** the son of the bird Kunjala and a famous scholar.

Vika (S) (M) bird; wind.

Vikaća (S) (M) **1.** hairless; shining; brilliant; radiant; opened. **3.** a dānava (*H. Purāṇa*).

Vikaćānana (S) (M) with a radiant face.

Vikadru (S) (M) **1.** tawny complexioned. **3.** a Yādava warrior (*M. Bh.*).

Vikala (S) (M) **1.** crippled; imperfect. **3.** a son of Śambara; a son of Lambodara (*Bh. Purāṇa*); a son of Jīmūta (*V. Purāṇa*).

Vikāla (S) (M) twilight.

Vikalaṅka (S) (M) spotless; bright as the moon.

Vikāma (S) (M) free from desire.

Vikarṇa (S) (M) **1.** large eared. **3.** a kind of arrow (*M. Bh.*); a son of Karṇa; a son of Dhṛtarāṣṭra (*M. Bh.*); a hermit and devotee of Śiva (*M. Bh.*).

Vikarṣaṇa (S) (M) **1.** distractor. **3.** an arrow of Kāma.

Vikartaṇa (S) (M) **1.** dividing; cutting as under. **3.** a solar dynasty king (*P. Purāṇa*); another name for the sun.

Vikāsa (S) (M) brightness; light; lustre; budding; cheerfulness; expansion; serenity; to appear; to become visible; to shine forth; radiance; development; growth.

Vikaṭa (S) (M) **1.** huge; large; great; terrible; ugly; dreadful. **3.** an attendant of Skanda (*M. Bh.*); a rākṣasa (*H. Purāṇa*); a brother of Prahasta; a son of Dhṛtarāṣṭra (*M. Bh.*).

Vikaṭābha (S) (M) **1.** of terrible appearance. **3.** an asura (*H. Purāṇa*).

Vikaṭākṣa (S) (M) **1.** with dreadful eyes. **3.** an asura (*H. Purāṇa*).

Vikaṭānana (S) (M) **1.** ugly faced. **3.** a son of Dhṛtarāṣṭra (*K. Sāgara*).

Vikaṭavadana (S) (M) **1.** monstrous faced. **3.** an attendant of Durgā (*M. Bh.*).

Vikheda (S) (M) free from weariness.

Vikoka (S) (M) **1.** detached from sex. **3.** the son of the asura Vṛka and the younger brother of Koka (*K. Purāṇa*).

Vikrama (S) (M) **1.** step; stride; pace; valour; strength; heroism; power. **3.** a son of Vasu (*K. Sāgara*); a son of Vatsaprī; a son of Kanaka (*Mā. Purāṇa*); another name for Viṣṇu.

Vikramaćandra (S) (M) moon among heroes.

Vikramāditya (S) (M) **1.** son of valour. **3.** a mighty emperor of Bhārata who was the king of Ujjayinī and the son of King Mahendrāditya of Ujjayinī and Saumyadarśanā and was considered an incarnation of Mālyavān, he was the founder of the Vikrama era, a great patron of literature, he was supposed to have been killed by King Śālivāhana of the Deccan.

Vikramaka (S) (M) **1.** petty hero. **3.** an attendant of Skanda (*M. Bh.*).

Vikramakesarin (S) (M) **1.** strong like a lion. **3.** a king of Pāṭaliputra (*K. Sāgara*).

Vikramaśīla (S) (M) **1.** strong in character. **3.** a king who was the husband of Kālindī and the father of Durgama (*Mā. Purāṇa*).

Vikrameśa (S) (M) **1.** lord of valour. **3.** a Buddhist saint.

Vikramin (S) (M) **1.** striding; courageous; gallant. **3.** another name for Viṣṇu.

Vikrānta (S) (M) **1.** courageous; bold; taking wide strides; victorious. **3.** a prajāpati (*V. Purāṇa*); a son of Kuvalayāśva and Madālasā (*Mā. Purāṇa*); a king who was the son of Sudhṛti and the father of King Dama (*Vā. Purāṇa*); *Adiantum lunulatum*; *Cleome viscosa*.

Vikrīta (S) (M) **1.** sold. **3.** a prajāpati.

Vikrodha (S) (M) free from anger.

Vikṛta (S) (M) **1.** deformed; altered; strange. **3.** a prajāpati (*V. Rāmāyaṇa*); a demon son of Parivarta (*Mā. Purāṇa*); Kāma in his form as a Brāhmin (*M. Bh.*).

Vikṛtadaṅṣṭra (S) (M) **1.** with strange teeth. **3.** a vidyādhara (*H. Purāṇa*).

Vikṛti (S) (M) **1.** change; alteration. **3.** a king of the Yayāti family who was the son of Jīmūta and the father of Bhīmaratha (*Bhāgavata*).

Vikṣara (S) (M) **1.** to flow out. **3.** an asura son of Kaśyapa and Danu who was reborn as King Vasumitra (*M. Bh.*); another name for Viṣṇu/Kṛṣṇa.

Vikukṣi (S) (M) **1.** with a prominent belly. **3.** a son of Ikṣvāku and the father of Kakutstha (*D. Bhāgavata*).

Vikuṇṭha (S) (M) **1.** not blunt. **2.** sharp; keen; penetrating; irresistible. **3.** another name for Viṣṇu.

Vikuṇṭhāna (S) (M) **1.** sharpening; penetration. **3.** a son of King Hastin of the lunar dynasty and Yaśodharā who was the husband of Sudevā and the father of Ajamīdha (*M. Bh.*).

Vikuṇṭhānana (S) (M) **1.** with an irresistible face. **2.** very attractive. **3.** a son of Hastin (*M. Bh.*).

Vikusra (S) (M) **1.** crying out. **2.** the moon.

Vīlāpana (S) (M) **1.** causing moaning. **3.** an attendant of Śiva.

Vilāsa (S) (M) **1.** shining forth; appearance; grace; beauty, liveliness; play; sport. **3.** a hermit.

Vilāsin (S) (M) **1.** shining; radiant; sportive; playful. **2.** lover. **3.** another name for Kṛṣṇa, Śiva, Kāma, and the moon.

Vilasita (S) (M) gleaming; glittering; shining forth; appearing.

Vilohita (S) (M) **1.** deep red. **3.** a rākṣasa son of Kaśyapa (*Vā. Purāṇa*); another name for Śiva, Rudra and Agni.

Viloman (S) (M) **1.** opposite; inverse; hairless. **3.** a king who is the son of King Vahni (*Bhāgavata*) or Kapotaromā (*V. Purāṇa*).

Vimada (S) (M) **1.** sober; free from intoxication. **3.** a king known for his truthfulness (*Ṛg Veda*).

Vimahat (S) (M) very great; immense.

Vimala (S) (M) **1.** stainless; spotless. **2.** clean; bright; pure; clear; transparent; white. **3.** the brother of Yaśas; an asura (*K. Sāgara*); the 5th Arhat of the past Utsarpiṇī and the 13th in the present Avasarpiṇī (*J.S. Koṣa*); a king of South India who was the son of Sudyumna (*Bhāgavata*); a king of Ratnatāṭa and ally of Śatrughna's (*P. Purāṇa*); one of the 13 stages of a Bodhisattva (*B. Literature*); *Acacia rugata*.

Vimalabhadra (S) (M) spotless person.

Vimalabodha (S) (M) pure intelligence.

Vimalaċandra (S) (M) spotless moon.

Vimaladatta (S) (M) given by purity.

Vimalagarbha (S) (M) **1.** womb of purity. **2.** originator of purity. **3.** a Bodhisattva.

Vimalakīrti (S) (M) of spotless fame.

Vimalanātha (S) (M) **1.** lord of the pure ones. **3.** the 13th Jaina Tīrthaṅkara son of King Kṛtavarmā and Queen Śyāmā of Kāmpilapur (*J.S. Koṣa*).

Vimalanetra (S) (M) **1.** pure eyed. **3.** a Buddha.

Vimalapiṇḍaka (S) (M) **1.** spotless snake. **3.** a nāga son of Kaśyapa and Kadru (*M. Bh.*).

Vimalaprabha (S) (M) **1.** pure light. **3.** a Buddha.

Vimalaśrīgarbha (S) (M) **1.** divine womb of purity. **3.** a Boddhisattva.

Vimalavegaśrī (S) (M) **1.** master of pure emotions. **3.** a gandharva.

Vimaleśa (S) (M) lord of purity.

Vimanyu (S) (M) free from anger.

Vimardana (S) (M) **1.** pressing; squeezing; destroying. **2.** fragrance; perfume. **3.** a rākṣasa (*V. Rāmāyaṇa*); a vidyādhara (*K. Sāgara*).

Vimarśa (S) (M) **1.** deliberation; examination; test; discussion; knowledge; intelligence. **3.** another name for Śiva.

Vimarśana (S) (M) **1.** discussion; discourse. **3.** the king of the Kirātas.

Vimba (S) (M) **1.** an illuminated point. **2.** an intensely glowing ray of the sun.

Vimoćana (S) (M) **1.** unyoking; loosening; delivering. **3.** another name for Śiva.

Vimṛdha (S) (M) **1.** averter of enemies. **3.** another name for Indra.

Vimuća (S) (M) **1.** freed; liberated. **3.** a south Indian hermit (*M. Bh.*).

Vimukha (S) (M) **1.** with the face averted. **3.** a hermit in Indra's court (*M. Bh.*).

Vimuktaćandra (S) (M) **1.** moon among the free. **2.** liberated. **3.** a Bodhisattva.

Vimuktāćārya (S) (M) liberated teacher; preceptor of the liberated.

Vimuktasena (S) (M) **1.** commander of the liberated. **3.** a teacher of the Mādhyamika-Svātantrika school of Buddhism at Nālanda.

Vīṇādatta (S) (M) **1.** bestowed by lute. **2.** musician. **3.** a gandharva (*K. Sāgara*).

Vīṇāhasta (S) (M) **1.** holding a lute. **3.** another name for Śiva.

Vinanda (S) (M) to rejoice.

Vīṇāpāṇi (S) (M) **1.** lute handed. **3.** another name for Nārada.

Vināśana (S) (M) **1.** destroyer; killer; murderer. **3.** an asura born to Kaśyapa and Kālā (*M. Bh.*).

Vinata (S) (M) **1.** inclined; bowing. **2.** humble. **3.** a son of Sudyumna; a son of Śveta and a captain of Rāma's monkey army (*V. Rāmāyaṇa*).

Vinatānandavardhana (S) (M) **1.** increasing the joy of Vinatā. **3.** another name for Garuḍa.

Vinatāsūnu (S) (M) **1.** son of Vinatā. **3.** another name for Garuḍa.

Vinatāsuta (S) (M) **1.** son of Vinatā. **3.** another name for Garuḍa.

Vinatāśva (S) (M) **1.** with modest horses. **3.** a son of Ilā or Sudyumna and grandson of Vaivaśvata Manu (*V. Purāṇa*).

Vinatātmaja (S) (M) **1.** son of Vinatā. **3.** another name for Garuḍa.

Vīṇāvinoda (S) (M) **1.** lute player; amusing with the lute. **3.** a vidyādhara (*B. Rāmāyaṇa*).

Vinaya (S) (M) **1.** taking away; leading; guidance; decency; modesty; control. **3.** mildness personified as the son of Kriyā or Lajjā; a son of Sudyumna (*Mā. Purāṇa*).

Vināyaka (S) (M) **1.** remover; leader; guide; lord of prayer. **3.** a deity of the ganas or attendants of Śiva (*M. Bh.*); another name for Gaṇeśa.

Vinda (S) (M) **1.** finding; getting; gaining. **3.** a son of Dhṛtarāṣṭra (*M. Bh.*); a prince of Avanti who fought on the side of the Kauravas; a Kekaya prince on the side of the Kauravas (*M. Bh.*).

Vindhya (S) (M) **1.** gaining height. **3.** a low range of hills connecting the Western and Eastern Ghats which form the southernmost portion of the middle region of India, they are personified by a deity who elevated himself to bar the progress of the sun and moon and was stopped by Agastya (*M. Bh.*).

Vindhyaketu (S) (M) **1.** mountain bannered. **3.** a king of the Pulindas (*K. Sāgara*).

Vindhyapāra (S) (M) **1.** beyond the Vindhyas; higher than the Vindhyas. **3.** a king of the vidyādharas (*K. Sāgara*).

Vindhyaṭana (S) (M) **1.** conqueror of Vindhya; as high as Vindhya. **2.** a great scholar. **3.** another name for sage Agastya.

Vindu (S) (M) knowing; familiar with; finding; getting; acquiring.

Vindumān (S) (M) **1.** knower; scholar; wise. **3.** a king in the dynasty of Bharata who was the son of Mari and the father of Madhu (*Bhāgavata*).

Vinetṛ (S) (M) leader; guide; teacher.

Vinetra (S) (M) teacher; preceptor.

Vinīla(S) (M) very blue.

Vinimeṣa (S) (M) a twinkle; twinkling of the eye.

Vinirjaya (S) (M) complete victory; conquest.

Viniśćala (S) (M) immovable; firm; steady.

Vinīta (S) (M) **1.** tamed; trained. **2.** well behaved; humble; modest; educated; handsome; neat. **3.** a son of Pulastya (*V. Purāṇa*).

Vinna (S) (M) known; understood.

Vinoda (S) (M) diversion; sport; pastime; pleasure.

Vinśa (S) (M) **1.** the number 20. **3.** the eldest son of Ikṣvāku and the father of Vivinśa (*M. Bh.*).

Vinśabahu (S) (M) **1.** 20 armed. **3.** another name for Rāvaṇa.

Vinu (S) (M) to spread in different directions.

Vipāpman (S) (M) **1.** free from suffering. **3.** a viśvadeva (*M. Bh.*).

Viparṣi (S) (M) **1.** wise sage. **3.** another name for Mārkaṇḍeya.

Vipaśćit (S) (M) **1.** inspired. **2.** wise; learned. **3.** Indra in the Manvantara of Manu Svāroćiṣa; the husband of Pāvarī (*M. Purāṇa*); another name for Buddha.

Vipaśyin (S) (M) **1.** discerning. **2.** seeing in detail. **3.** a Buddha mentioned as the 1st of the 7 Tathāgatas or principal Buddhas (*B. Literature*).

Vipāta (S) (M) **1.** shooting arrows; melting; killing. **3.** a brother of Karṇa killed by Arjuna (*M. Bh.*).

Vipina (S) (M) jungle; wood.

Vipinavihāri (S) (M) **1.** wanderer of the jungle. **2.** one who roams the forest. **3.** another name for Kṛṣṇa.

Vipra (S) (M) **1.** stirred; excited; inspired. **2.** wise; sage; seer. **3.** a son of Śrutañjaya; a son of Dhruva; a king of the family of Dhruva who was the son of Śliṣṭi and Suććhaya (*V. Purāṇa*); another name for the moon.

Vipraćitti (S) (M) **1.** sagacious. **3.** a dānava son of Kaśyapa and Danu and the husband of Simhikā who was reborn as Jarāsandha (*M. Bh.*); a dānava and father of Rāhu (*M. Bh.*).

Vipraćūḍāmaṇi (S) (M) crest jewel among the sages; an excellent Brāhmin.

Viprādhipa (S) (M) **1.** lord of the wise. **3.** another name for the moon.

Vipratama (S) (M) wisest.

Viprayogi (S) (M) **1.** wise ascetic. **3.** another name for Pulastya.

Viprṣṭha (S) (M) **1.** with a solid back. **2.** warrior. **3.** a son of Vasudeva (*Bhā. Purāṇa*).

Viprthu (S) (M) **1.** not fat. **2.** slender; sharp. **3.** a member of the Vṛṣṇi clan who was a member of Yudhiṣṭhira's court (*M. Bh.*); an ancient emperor (*M. Bh.*); a son of Ciṭraka and younger brother of Pṛthu (*M. Bh.*).

Vipula (S) (M) **1.** large; great; wide; thick; abundant. **3.** a prince of the Sauvīras (*M. Bh.*); a pupil of Devaśarman (*M. Bh.*); a mountain; a son of Vasudeva and Rohiṇī and a brother of Balarāma (*Bhā. Purāṇa*).

Vipulamati (S) (M) **1.** abounding in intelligence. **3.** a Bodhisattva.

Vīra (S) (M) **1.** brave; hero. **2.** son. **3.** an asura born of Kaśyapa and Danu (*M. Bh.*); a son of Dhṛtarāṣṭra (*M. Bh.*); an agni born of Bharadvāja and his wife Vīrā who was the husband of Sarayū and the father of Siddhi (*M. Bh.*); a son of the agni called Pānćajanya (*M. Bh.*); a king of the Purū dynasty who was the son of

Girīka (*A. Purāṇa*); a son of Puruṣa and Vairāja and the father of Priyavrata and Uttānapāda (*H. Purāṇa*); a son of Gṛñjima (*H. Purāṇa*); *2* sons of Kṛṣṇa; a son of Kṣupa and father of Vivinṣa; the father of Līlāvatī; the last Arhat of the present Avasarpiṇī (*J.S. Koṣa*); *Aconitum heterophyllum*; *Costus speciosus*; Saffron (*Crocus sativus*).

Vīrabāhu (S) (M) **1.** strong armed. **3.** a son of Dhṛtarāṣṭra; a brother of Subrahmanya (*Sk. Purāṇa*); a Ćedi king who protected Damayanti (*M. Bh.*); another name for Viṣṇu.

Vīrabhadra (S) (M) **1.** distinguished hero. **3.** a form of Śiva said to have emerged from his mouth with a 1000 heads, eyes and feet for the destruction of the sacrifice of Dakṣa and the protection of the devas, after that he became the Mangala planet in the sky and one portion was reborn as Ādiśankara or Śankarāćarya (*P. Purāṇa*); Khuskhus grass (*Vetiveria zizanioides*).

Vīrabhānu (S) (M) brave sun; sun among the brave; best warrior.

Vīrabhūpati (S) (M) **1.** brave king. **2.** king of the brave.

Vīrāćārya (S) (M) preceptor of the brave.

Virādha (S) (M) **1.** thwarter. **3.** a rākṣasa who was an incarnation of the gandharva Tumburu, he was killed by Rāma and Lakṣmaṇa and regained his old form (*V. Rāmāyaṇa*).

Virādhahan (S) (M) **1.** slayer of Virādha. **3.** another name for Indra or Viṣṇu.

Vīradhanvan (S) (M) **1.** brave archer; with a strong bow. **3.** a Trigarta warrior who fought on the side of the Kauravas (*M. Bh.*); a gandharva; another name for Kāma.

Vīradharmā (S) (M) **1.** following the path of bravery. **3.** an ancient king (*M. Bh.*).

Vīradyumna (S) (M) **1.** shining with bravery; with the glory of strength. **3.** a king and father of Bhūṛidyumna (*M. Bh.*).

Virāja (S) (M) **1.** ruling far and wide; shining; brilliant; splendid. **2.** king; excellence; preeminence; dignity; majesty. **3.** the 1st son of Brahmā who then produced the 1st Manu, he is also identified with Prajāpati, Brahmā, Agni, Puruṣa and later Viṣṇu/Kṛṣṇa (*Ṛg Veda*); a son of Priyavrata and Kāmyā (*H. Purāṇa*); a son of Nara (*V. Purāna*); a son of Radha (*V. Purāṇa*); a Kuru king who was the son of Avīkṣit (*M. Bh.*); another name for Agni, the sun and Buddha.

Viraja (S) (M) **1.** free from dust; clean; pure. **3.** a marut, a son of Tvaṣṭṛ (*Bh. Purāṇa*); a son of Purṇiman (*Bhā. Purāṇa*); a nāga son of Kaśyapa and Kadru (*M. Bh.*); a son of Dhṛtarāṣṭra (*M. Bh.*); a son born of the radiance of Mahāviṣṇu who was the father of Kīrtimān (*M. Bh.*); a sage under Manu Ćākṣuṣa (*H. Purāṇa*); a son of Manu Sāvarṇi (*Mā. Purāṇa*); a son of Nārāyaṇa; a son of Kavi; a son of Vasiṣṭha (*Bh. Purāna*); a son of Paurṇamāsa.

Virajaprabha (S) (M) **1.** pure light. **3.** a Buddha.

Virajāśka (S) (M) **1.** clear eyed. **2.** one whose perception is pure and clean. **3.** a son of Manu Sāvarṇī (*Ṛg Veda*).

Virājin (S) (M) splendid; brilliant.

Vīrājit (S) (M) conquering heroes; eminent; illustrious; brilliant; glorious; splendid.

Vīraka (S) (M) **1.** petty warrior. **3.** a king of the Aṅga dynasty who was the son of Śibi (*A. Purāṇa*); the adopted son of Śiva and Pārvatī; a sage under Manu Ćākṣuṣa (*Bh. Purāṇa*).

Vīraketu (S) (M) **1.** with a flag of bravery. **3.** a son of King Drupada of Panćāla (*M. Bh.*); a king of Ayodhyā (*K. Sāgara*).

Virala (S) (M) rare.

Vīramaṇi (S) (M) **1.** jewel among the brave. **3.** a king and husband of Śrutāvatī who was a devotee of Śiva.

Vīraṇa (S) (M) **1.** tuft of Khus grass. **3.** a prajāpati and preceptor of sage Ṛaibhya (*M. Bh.*); and father of Aśikni or Vīraṇī (*M. Bh.*).

Vīraṇaka (S) (M) **1.** made of khus grass. **3.** a nāga born in the family of Dhṛtarāṣṭra (*M. Bh.*).

Vīranārāyaṇa (S) (M) **1.** divine hero. **3.** another name for Viṣṇu.

Vīranātha (S) (M) lord of the brave.

Virañća (S) (M) **1.** heavenly; celestial. **3.** another name for Brahmā.

Vīrandhara (S) (M) peacock; possessor of the brave; the mount of the bravest.

Vīrarāghava (S) (M) Rāma among the warriors; Rāma the hero.

Vīraratha (S) (M) bearer of bravery; with a powerful chariot.

Virasa (S) (M) **1.** tasteless; insipid; essenceless. **3.** a nāga son of Kaśyapa (*M. Bh.*).

Vīraśekhara (S) (M) **1.** best of heroes; best among heroes. **3.** a vidyādhara; a brother of Subrahmanya (*Sk. Purāṇa*); a son of Dhṛtarāṣṭra (*M. Bh.*); a Ćedi king who protected Damayantī (*M. Bh.*).

Vīrasena (S) (M) **1.** having an army of heroes. **3.** a dānava; a Niśāda king who was the father of Nala; a king of Kanyakubjā; a king of Kalinga; a king of Murala; a king of Kosala (*M. Bh.*).

Vīrasiṁha (S) (M) **1.** brave lion; lion among the brave. **3.** a captain of the army of the asura Vyālīmukha who fought with Skanda (*Sk. Purāṇa*); a son of King Vīramani (*M. Bh.*).

Vīrasvāmibhaṭṭa (S) (M) **1.** bravest warrior. **3.** the father of Medhālithi (*Ṛg Veda*).

Vīrasvāmin (S) (M) **1.** lord of the brave. **3.** a dānava.

Virāt (S) (M) **1.** shining; brilliant. **3.** the grandson of Priyavrata and the son of sage Kardama (*A. Purāṇa*); the 1st incarnation of Brahmā (*Ṛg Veda*).

Virāṭa (S) (M) **1.** majestic; magnificent. **3.** the king of Matsya country who sheltered the Pāṇḍavas and was the father-in-law of Arjuna, he is supposed to have been an incarnation of the Marudgaṇas (*M. Bh.*); he was the husband of Suratha and Sudeṣṇā and the father of Śveta, Śaṅkha, Uttarā and Uttara (*D. Purāṇa*).

Vīratara (S) (M) stronger hero.

Virāva (S) (M) **1.** resounding; roaring. **3.** the horse of sage Agastya (*M. Bh.*).

Vīravarman (S) (M) **1.** protector of the brave. **3.** the son of King Tāladhvaja by Nārada in his female form; a son of Sārasvata and Mālinī and the father of Subhāla, Sulabha, Lola, Kuvala and Sarasa.

Viravin (S) (M) **1.** shouting; roaring; resounding. **3.** a son of Dhṛtaraṣṭra (*M. Bh.*).

Vīravrata (S) (M) **1.** keeping to one's purpose. **3.** a king of the family of Bharata who was the son of Madhu and the father of Manthu and Amanthu (*Bhāgavata*).

Vīrendra (S) (M) chief of heroes.

Virepas (S) (M) blameless; faultless.

Vīreśa (S) (M) **1.** lord of heroes. **3.** another name for Śiva and Vīrabhadra.

Vīreśvara (S) (M) **1.** god of heroes. **3.** another name for Śiva and Vīrabhadra.

Vīresvarānanda (S) (M) **1.** delight of the god of heroes; delighting the brave. **2.** victory; success; achievement.

Virinća (S) (M) **1.** illuminating. **3.** another name for Brahmā, Viṣṇu and Śiva.

Viroćana (S) (M) **1.** illuminating; shining upon. **3.** an asura who was the son of Prahlāda and Dhṛti and the husband of Viśālākṣi and Devi and the father of Mahābali, Bala and Yaśodharā; a son of Dhṛtarāṣṭra (*M. Bh.*); another name for Sūrya, the moon and Viṣṇu.

Viroćiṣṇu (S) (M) shining; bright; illuminating.

Viroha (S) (M) **1.** causing to heal. **3.** a nāga (*M. Bh.*).

Virohaṇa (S) (M) **1.** growing out; budding. **3.** a nāga of the family of Takṣaka (*M. Bh.*).

Virohin (S) (M) sprouting; shooting forth.

Viroka (S) (M) shining; gleaming; a ray of light; effulgence.

Virūdhaka (S) (M) **1.** sprouted grain. **3.** the guardian of the south; a son of Ikṣvāku; a son of Prasenajit.

Viruj (S) (M) **1.** healthy; free from disease. **3.** a submarine agni (*Ṛg Veda*).

Virukmat (S) (M) **1.** shining; brilliant; bright. **2.** a bright weapon or ornament.

Virūpa (S) (M) **1.** many coloured; manifold; variegated; altered; changed; different from. **3.** an asura; a son of the demon Parivarta (*Mā. Purāṇa*); a sage of the Āṅgiras family; a solar dynasty king who was the father of Pṛṣadāśva and son of Ambarīṣa (*Ṛg Veda*); a son of Kṛṣṇa (*Bhā. Purāṇa*); a descendant of Manu Vaivaśvata; a son of King Ambarīṣa of the solar dynasty (*Bhāgavata*); Krodha in its human form (*M. Bh.*); an asura killed by Kṛṣṇa (*M. Bh.*); a son of Aṅgiras (*M. Bh.*); *Aconitum heterophyllum*; *Fagonia cretica*.

Virūpaćakṣus (S) (M) **1.** diversely eyed. **3.** another name for Śiva.

Virūpaka (S) (M) **1.** disfigured. **3.** an asura who once ruled the world (*M. Bh.*).

Virūpākṣa (S) (M) **1.** diversely eyed. **3.** an elephant that holds up the earth and who causes earthquakes by the shaking of his head; a rākṣasa son of Mālyavān and Sundarī who was a captain of Rāvaṇa's army; one of the 33 dānavas born to Kaśyapa and Danu who was reborn as King Ćitravarmā (*M. Bh.*); a rākṣasa friend of Ghaṭotkaća (*M. Bh.*); one of the 11 rudras; an asura who was a follower of Narakāsura (*M. Bh.*); the Buddhist guardian of the east (*B. Literature*); one of Śiva's attendants (*K. Sāgara*); a yakṣa (*K. Sāgara*); a nāga (*J.S. Koṣa*); another name for Śiva.

Virūpaśakti (S) (M) **1.** with manifold powers. **3.** a vidyādhara (*K. Sāgara*).

Virūpāśva (S) (M) **1.** with variegated horses. **3.** a king famed for his vegetarianism (*M. Bh.*).

Vīryaćandra (S) (M) **1.** moon among the brave. **3.** the father of Vīrā.

Vīryaja (S) (M) **1.** produced from manliness. **2.** son.

Vīryamitra (S) (M) friend of the brave.

Vīryasaha (S) (M) **1.** famous for bravery. **3.** a son of Saudāsa.

Vīryavat (S) (M) **1.** strong; powerful. **2.** efficacious. **3.** a viśvadeva (*M. Bh.*); a son of the 10th Manu (*H. Purāṇa*).

Viśada (S) (M) **1.** conspicuous. **2.** bright; brilliant; shining; splendid; white; spotless; pure; calm; easy; cheerful; tender. **3.** a son of King Jayadratha and the father of King Senajit (*Bhāgavata*).

Viśadānana (S) (M) radiant faced.

Viśadaprabha (S) (M) shedding pure light.

Viśadātman (S) (M) pure hearted; pure soul.

Viṣadhātrī (S) (M) **1.** venom preserver. **3.** another name for Manasā.

Viṣāgnipā (S) (M) **1.** drinker of burning poison. **3.** another name for Śiva.

Viṣahara (S) (M) **1.** removing venom. **3.** a son of Dhṛtarāṣṭra (*M. Bh.*).

Viṣakaṇṭha (S) (M) **1.** poison necked. **3.** another name for Śiva.

Viśākha (S) (M) **1.** branched. **3.** one of the 3 brothers of Skanda who was born of his body (*H. Purāṇa*); a hermit in the palace of Indra (*M. Bh.*); born under the Viśākhā constellation (*M. Bh.*); a dānavā (*K. Sāgara*); another name for Śiva.

Viśakhadatta (S) (M) **1.** given by Viśākha. **3.** a Sanskṛta playright who was the son of King Bhāskaradatta and the grandson of Vaṭeśvaradatta and the author of *Mudrā Rākṣasa* (5th century A.D.).

Viṣākṣa (S) (M) with venomous eyes.

Viśāla (S) (M) **1.** spacious; extensive; wide; great; important; mighty; illustrious; eminent. **3.** the father of

Takṣaka (*S.G. Sutra*); an asura (*K. Sāgara*); a son of Tṛṇabindu; a son of Ikṣvāku by the apsarā Alambusā and the father of Hemaćandra; a son of Abja.

Viśālaka (S) (M) **1.** *Feronia elephantum.* **3.** a yakṣa (*M. Bh.*); a king whose daughter Bhadrā married Vasudeva; a yakṣa in the palace of Kubera (*M. Bh.*); another name for Garuḍa.

Viśālākṣa (S) (M) **1.** large eyed. **3.** a nāga (*H. Purāṇa*); a son of Dhṛtarāṣṭra (*M. Bh.*); a younger brother of King Virāṭa also known as Madirākṣa (*M. Bh.*); a son of Garuḍa (*M. Bh.*); a king of Mithilā (*Bhāgavata*); another name for Śiva and Garuḍa.

Viśālanetra (S) (M) **1.** large eyed. **3.** a Bodhisattva.

Viṣamākṣa (S) (M) **1.** with an odd number of eyes; 3 eyed. **3.** another name for Śiva.

Viṣamāyudha (S) (M) **1.** with an odd number of arrows; 5 arrowed. **3.** another name for Kāma

Viṣambāṇa (S) (M) **1.** with an odd number of arrows; 5 arrowed. **3.** another name for Kāma.

Viṣamekṣaṇa (S) (M) **1.** with an odd number of eyes; 3 eyed. **3.** another name for Śiva.

Viṣameśu (S) (M) **1.** with an odd number of arrows; 5 arrowed. **3.** another name for Kāma.

Viśampa (S) (M) protecting people.

Viṣamśara (S) (M) **1.** with an odd number of arrows; 5 arrowed. **3.** another name for Kāma.

Viṣamśīla (S) (M) **1.** with an unequable disposition. **2.** rough; difficult; cross tempered. **3.** another name for Vikramāditya.

Viṣāṇa (S) (M) **1.** peak; summit; the best of its kind. **3.** the tuft on Śiva's head.

Viśanka (S) (M) fearless.

Viṣāntaka (S) (M) **1.** poison destroying. **3.** another name for Śiva.

Viṣāpaha (S) (M) **1.** vanquisher of poison. **2.** antidotal. **3.** another name for Garuḍa.

Viṣaparvan (S) (M) **1.** with poison in every part. **3.** a daitya (*K. Sāgara*).

Viśārada (S) (M) **1.** proficient. **2.** *Fagonia cretica*; *Mimusops elengi.*

Viśasta (S) (M) praised; celebrated.

Viśātana (S) (M) **1.** destroying; setting free; delivering. **3.** another name for Viṣṇu.

Visaṭha (S) (M) **1.** holding the stalk of a lotus. **3.** a son of Balarāma and Revatī (*M. Bh.*).

Viśaujas (S) (M) ruling people.

Viṣavidya (S) (M) **1.** knower of poison. **2.** antidote. **3.** a child of Garuḍa.

Viṣayin (S) (M) **1.** sensual; material. **2.** prince; king. **3.** another name for Kāma.

Viśeṣa (S) (M) special; excellent; superior; distinguished.

Viśikha (S) (M) **1.** bald; unfeathered. **2.** arrow. **3.** a king of the birds born of Garuḍa and Śukī.

Viṣita (S) (M) **1.** released. **2.** the sun just before setting.

Viṣkambhin (S) (M) **1.** the bolt of a door. **3.** a Bodhisattva; another name for Śiva.

Viṣkara (S) (M) **1.** bolt of a door. **3.** an asura who once ruled the world (*M. Bh.*).

Vismāpana (S) (M) **1.** conjurer; illusion. **3.** another name for Kāma.

Viṣṇāpu (S) (M) **1.** as pure as Viṣṇu. **3.** a hermit son of Viśvaka helped by the aśvins (*Ṛg Veda*).

Viṣṇu (S) (M) **1.** all pervader. **3.** the preserver in the Hindu triad or Trimurti, he is the sustainer and whenever there is injustice in the world he incarnates himself to restore righteousness, hermits, Manus, devas, sons of Manus, prajāpatis all these are portions of Viṣṇu, of the 21 incarnations the most prominent are of Rāma, Kṛṣṇa and Buddha (*B. Literature*), in the Vedic period he is a personification of light and the sun, later he was given the foremost position among the ādityas (*Ṛg Veda*);

in the epics he rises to supremacy and is described as having 22 incarnations, he is identified with Nārāyaṇa the primeval living spirit, the god Brahmā is described as emerging from his navel, the wives of Viṣṇu are Aditi and Śinivali, later Lakṣmī or Srī, his son is Kāmadeva and his paradise Vaikuṇṭha, he is worshipped under a 1000 names (*Ṛg Veda*); the king of Siṁhapuri and father of Jaina Tīrthaṅkara Śreyansanātha (*J.S. Koṣa*); a son of Manu Sāvarṇa.

Viṣṇućakra (S) (M) discus of Viṣṇu.

Viṣṇućandra (S) (M) **1.** moon and Viṣṇu conjoined. **3.** the calm form of Viṣṇu.

Viṣṇućitta (S) (M) **1.** with an omnipresent mind. **3.** a Vaiṣṇavite devotee of Tamil Nadu who was supposed to have been the incarnation of Garuḍa and was the father of Āṇḍāl.

Viṣṇudāsa (S) (M) **1.** devotee of Viṣṇu. **3.** a Vaiṣṇavite devotee of the Ćola court who was rewarded by Viṣṇu for his devotion (*P. Purāṇa*).

Viṣṇudatta (S) (M) **1.** given by Viṣṇu. **3.** another name for Parīkṣit.

Viṣṇudeva (S) (M) lord of Viṣṇu; the omnipresent god.

Viṣṇudharman (S) (M) **1.** acting like Viṣṇu. **3.** a son of Garuḍa (*M. Bh.*).

Viṣṇugopa (S) (M) **1.** protected by Viṣṇu, the cattle keeper. **3.** a Pallava king of Kāñći; another name for Kṛṣṇa.

Viṣṇugupta (S) (M) **1.** hidden by Viṣṇu. **3.** another name for Vātsyāyana and sage Kaundinya.

Viṣṇumitra (S) (M) **1.** a friend of Viṣṇu. **3.** son of Devamitra (*M. Bh.*).

Viṣṇupada (S) (M) **1.** footmark of Viṣṇu. **2.** lotus (*Nelumbo speciosum*); the sky; the Sea of Milk.

Viṣṇuprasāda (S) (M) gift of Viṣṇu.

Viṣṇuputra (S) (M) son of Viṣṇu.

Viṣṇurāta (S) (M) **1.** given by Viṣṇu. **3.** another name for Parīkṣit (*Bh. Purāṇa*).

Viṣṇuratha (S) (M) **1.** vehicle of Viṣṇu. **3.** another name for Garuḍa.

Viṣṇuvāhana (S) (M) **1.** vehicle of Viṣṇu. **3.** another name for Garuḍa.

Viṣṇuvṛddha (S) (M) **1.** knower of the omnipresent. **3.** a king who was the son of Trasadasyu.

Viṣṇuyaśas (S) (M) **1.** with the fame of Viṣṇu. **3.** another name of Kalki (*M. Bh.*).

Viśodhana (S) (M) **1.** cleansing; purifying; washing away. **3.** the capital of Brahmā (*M. Bh.*); another name for Viṣṇu.

Viśoka (S) (M) **1.** griefless. **3.** the charioteer of Bhīma (*M. Bh.*); a prince of Kekaya on the side of the Pāṇḍavas (*M. Bh.*); a son of Kṛṣṇa and Trivakrā; a spiritual son of Brahmā (*V. Purāṇa*); a ṛṣi (*S. Veda*); a dānava.

Viśpati (S) (M) lord of the house.

Viśrama (S) (M) tranquillity; calm; composure; rest.

Viśrānta (S) (M) reposed; rested.

Viśravaṇa (S) (M) much heard of; very famous.

Viśravas (S) (M) **1.** much heard of. **2.** great fame. **3.** a ṛṣi who was the son of Pulastya and Havirbhū and the father of Rāvaṇa and Kumbhakarṇa by his wife Kaikasī and of Vaiśravaṇa or Kubera by his wife Ilabīla and Khara and Surpaṇakha by his wife Rākā and Vibhīṣaṇa by Mālinī (*M. Bh.*).

Viśruta (S) (M) **1.** much heard of. **2.** famous; celebrated; pleased; delighted; happy. **3.** a son of Vasudeva (*Bhā. Purāṇa*).

Viṣṭap (S) (M) top; summit; highest.

Viṣṭāraśravas (S) (M) **1.** far famed. **3.** another name for Viṣṇu/Kṛṣṇa and Śiva.

Viṣṭārāśva (S) (M) **1.** having a well travelled horse. **3.** a son of Pṛthu.

Viṣṭi (S) (M) **1.** compulsory work. **3.** a ṛṣi in the 11th Manvantara.

Viśuddha (S) (M) clean; clear; pure; virtuous; honest.

Viśuddhīra (S) (M) pure and grave.

Viśuṇḍī (S) (M) **1.** with an excessively long neck. **3.** a nāga of the family of Kaśyapa (*M. Bh.*).

Viṣupa (S) (M) the equinox.

Viśva (S) (M) **1.** whole; entire; all; universe; world. **2.** the number 13. **3.** a king who was a partial incarnation of the asura Mayūra (*M. Bh.*).

Viśvabandhu (S) (M) a friend of the world.

Viśvabhānu (S) (M) all illuminating; sun of the world.

Viśvabhāvana (S) (M) **1.** abode of universe. **3.** a spiritual son of Brahmā; another name for Viṣṇu.

Viśvabhraj (S) (M) all illuminating.

Viśvabhū (S) (M) **1.** creator of the universe. **3.** a Buddha.

Viśvabhuj (S) (M) **1.** all enjoying. **3.** another name for Indra.

Viśvabhuk (S) (M) **1.** one who eats everything. **3.** a son of Bṛhaspati who is the digestor of all food as he sits in the lining of all living things, he is supposed to have been the husband of the river Gomatī (*M. Bh.*).

Viśvabhūta (S) (M) being everything; born of universe.

Viśvabodha (S) (M) **1.** knower of universe. **3.** a Buddha.

Viṣvāċ (S) (M) **1.** universally present. **3.** an asura killed by the aśvins (*Ṛg Veda*).

Viśvaċandra (S) (M) moon of the universe; all radiant; all brilliant; illuminator of the universe.

Viśvāċārya (S) (M) universal teacher.

Viśvaċyvas (S) (M) **1.** moving the universe. **3.** one of the 7 principal rays of the sun.

Viśvadāni (S) (M) all giving; donor of universe.

Viśvadaṅṣṭra (S) (M) **1.** with all eating teeth. **3.** an asura (*M. Bh.*).

Viśvadeva (S) (M) **1.** all divine; god of universe. **3.** a class of deities who are the sons of Dharmā and Viśva who are supposed to be offered to daily—a boon bestowed by Brahmā in return for their austerities (*V. Purāṇa*); *Sida spinosa*; Ash coloured Fleabane (*Vemonia cinerea*).

Viśvadhara (S) (M) **1.** abode of the universe. **2.** preserving all things. **3.** a son of Medhātithi (*Bh. Purāṇa*); another name for Viṣṇu.

Viśvadhārin (S) (M) **1.** abode of the universe. **2.** all maintaining. **3.** another name for Viṣṇu.

Viśvadhriṣṭa (S) (M) seer of the universe; all seeing.

Viśvadīpa (S) (M) light of the universe.

Viśvaga (S) (M) **1.** going everywhere. **3.** a son of Pūrṇiman; another name for Brahmā.

Viśvagandhi (S) (M) **1.** with an all pervading fragrance. **3.** a son of Pṛthu (*Bhā. Purāṇa*).

Viśvagarbha (S) (M) **1.** womb of the universe. **2.** containing all things. **3.** a son of Raivata (*H. Purāṇa*).

Viśvagāśva (S) (M) **1.** one whose horses go everywhere. **3.** a king who was the son of the Emperor Pṛthu and the father of King Adri (*M. Bh.*); a Purū king.

Viśvagopṭṛ (S) (M) **1.** preserver of the universe. **3.** another name for Viṣṇu, Śiva and Indra.

Viśvaguru (S) (M) father of the universe; preceptor of the universe.

Viśvahetu (S) (M) **1.** cause of the universe. **3.** another name for Viṣṇu.

Viśvajayin (S) (M) conquerer of the universe.

Viśvajit (S) (M) **1.** conquerer of the universe. **2.** all conquering. **3.** the noose of Varuṇa; a dānava (*M. Bh.*); a son of Gādhi (*H. Purāṇa*); an Aṅga king who was the son of Jayadratha (*A. Purāṇa*); a king of the Yayāti dynasty who was the son of Suvrata and the father of Ripuñjaya (*Bhāgavata*); a son of Bṛhaspati who has the intelligence of all the living beings of the universe (*M. Bh.*); an asura who was ruler of the world for a short while (*M.Bh.*).

Viśvajyotis (S) (M) **1.** one whose light spreads everywhere; illuminator of universe. **3.** the eldest son of Śatajit.

Viśvaka (S) (M) **1.** all pervading. **2.** all containing. **3.** a hermit who was the father of Viśṇāpū (*Ṛg Veda*).

Viśvakāraka (S) (M) **1.** creator of the universe. **3.** another name for Śiva.

Viśvakarman (S) (M) **1.** creator of the world. **2.** accomplishing or creating everything; all doer. **3.** the divine architect and weapon maker and chariot maker of the devas said to be a son of Brahmā, earlier mythology identified him with Prajāpati (*Ṛg Veda*); later he was identified with Tvaṣṭṛ, he presides over the 64 mechanical arts; variously the son of Bhuvana, the vasu Prabhāsa and Yogasiddhā or Varastrī he was the father of 5 sons -Ajaikapāt, Ahirbudhnya, Tvaṣṭā, Rudra and the monkey Nala, the daughters are Saṁjñā, Ćitrāṅgadā, Surūpā and Barhiṣmatī (*Ṛg Veda*).

Viśvakartṛ (S) (M) creator of the world.

Viśvakāru (S) (M) **1.** architect of the universe. **3.** another name for Viśvakarman (*Ṛg Veda*).

Viśvakārya (S) (M) **1.** architect of the universe; effector of the universe. **3.** one of the 7 principal rays of the sun (*V. Purāṇa*).

Viśvaketu (S) (M) **1.** one whose banner is the universe. **3.** another name for Kāma and Aniruddha.

Viśvakṛt (S) (M) **1.** creator of the universe. **2.** creating all. **3.** a viśvadeva (*M. Bh.*); a son of Gādhi (*H. Purāṇa*); another name for Viśvakarman.

Viśvakṣeṇa (S) (M) **1.** one whose powers go everywhere. **3.** a hermit in the palace of Indra (*M. Bh.*); an attendant of Viṣṇu (*Bhā. Purāṇa*); the 14th Manu (*V. Purāṇa*); a son of Brahmadatta (*H. Purāṇa*); a son of Śambara (*H. Purāṇa*); a ṛṣi (*Bhā. Purāṇa*); *Aglaia odoratissima*; another name for Viṣṇu/Kṛṣṇa and Śiva.

Viśvamahas (S) (M) most powerful in universe; all powerful; all pleasant.

Viśvamahat (S) (M) **1.** great principle of the universe. **3.** a son of Viśvaśarman (*V. Purāṇa*).

Viśvamanas (S) (M) with a universal mind; perceiving all.

Viśvambhara (S) (M) **1.** feeding the universe; all bearing; all sustaining. **2.** Supreme Being; fire; another name for Kṛṣṇa.

Viśvamitra (S) (M) **1.** friend of all. **3.** a celebrated sage of the lunar race who was the son of Gādhi and the father of Śakuntalā by Menakā.

Viśvamūrti (S) (M) idol of the universe; having all forms.

Viśvanābha (S) (M) **1.** navel of the universe. **3.** another name for Viṣṇu.

Viśvananda (S) (M) **1.** delighting the universe. **2.** pleasing all. **3.** a son of Brahmā (*V. Purāṇa*).

Viśvānara (S) (M) **1.** man of the universe. **2.** dear to all men. **3.** a king who was the husband of Śućismitā and the father of Gṛhapati (*Sk. Purāṇa*); the father of Agni.

Viśvanātha (S) (M) **1.** lord of the universe. **3.** the form of Śiva worshipped in Benaras (*Mā. Purāṇa*); a Sanskṛt literary critic of Orissa (14th century).

Viśvāntara (S) (M) **1.** subduing the universe. **2.** all subduing. **3.** the Buddha in a former existence; a son of Suṣadmān (*B. Literature*).

Viśvapā (S) (M) **1.** protector of the universe. **2.** all protecting. **3.** another name for the sun, the moon and fire.

Viśvapāla (S) (M) protector of the universe; all protecting.

Viśvapāṇi (S) (M) **1.** palm of the universe. **3.** a Dhyāni Bodhisattva.

Viśvapati (S) (M) **1.** master of the universe. **3.** a son of the agni called Manu (*M. Bh.*); another name for Mahāpuruṣa and Kṛṣṇa.

Viśvārādhya (S) (M) **1.** granting all. **3.** an ascetic and a founder of the Vara-Śaiva sects.

Viśvarāj (S) (M) universal sovereign.

Viśvarandhi (S) (M) **1.** conqueror of the universe. **3.** the son of King Pṛthu of the solar dynasty who was the father of King Ćandra and the grandfather of Yuvanāśva (*D. Bhāgavata*).

Viśvaratha (S) (M) **1.** with the universe as his chariot; chariot of the universe. **3.** the father of Gādhi (*H. Purāṇa*).

Viśvaretas (S) (M) **1.** seed of the universe. **3.** another name for Brahmā and Viṣṇu.

Viśvarući (S) (M) **1.** all glittering; enjoyer of the universe. **3.** a gandharva king (*M. Bh.*).

Viśvarūpa (S) (M) **1.** with the form of the universe. **2.** many coloured; variegated; the body that fills the universe. **3.** a rākṣasa in the palace of Varuṇa (*M. Bh.*); the son of Tvaṣṭṛ and Raćanā and brother of Sanniveśa (*Ṛg Veda*); another name for Viṣṇu/Kṛṣṇa and Hanumān.

Viśvāsa (S) (M) confidence; trust.

Viśvasāhvan (S) (M) **1.** companion of the world. **3.** a son of Mahasvat (*Bhā. Purāṇa*).

Viśvasakha (S) (M) friend of all.

Viśvaśambhu (S) (M) **1.** benefactor of all. **3.** a submarine fire (*Ṛg Veda*).

Viśvasāra (S) (M) **1.** essence of the universe. **3.** a son of Kṣatraujas.

Viśvaśarman (S) (M) **1.** honoured by all; best in the universe. **3.** the father of Viśvamahat (*V. Purāṇa*).

Viśvasćandra (S) (M) moon of the universe; all glittering.

Viśvaśrī (S) (M) **1.** treasure of the universe. **2.** useful to all. **3.** another name for Agni.

Viśvasvāmin (S) (M) lord of the universe.

Viśvatanu (S) (M) one whose body is the universe; omnipresent.

Viśvātman (S) (M) universal soul.

Viśvatrayarćas (S) (M) **1.** honoured by the 3 worlds namely the earth, the heaven and the netherworld. **3.** one of the 7 principal rays of the sun (*V. Purāṇa*).

Viśvavārya (S) (M) containing all good things.

Viśvāvasu (S) (M) **1.** beneficient to all. **3.** a gandharva regarded as the author of several Ṛg Vedic hymns; a marutvata (*H. Purāṇa*); a son of Purūravas; a prince of the Siddhas; a son of Jamadagni; a brother of Paraśurama (*Br. Purāṇa*); a gandharva king who was the son of Kaśyapa and Prādhā and the father of Pramadvarā by the apsarā Menakā (*M. Bh.*).

Viśvavedi (S) (M) **1.** knower of the universe. **3.** a son of Prajapati and a minister of King Śauri (*Ma. Purana*).

Viśvavṛkṣa (S) (M) **1.** tree of the universe. **3.** another name for Viṣṇu.

Viśvavyaćas (S) (M) **1.** absorbing all things. **3.** another name for Aditi.

Viśvayoni (S) (M) **1.** womb of the universe. **3.** another name for Brahmā and Viṣṇu.

Viśvāyu (S) (M) **1.** universally known. **3.** a son of Purūravas (*M. Bh.*); a viśvadeva (*M. Bh.*).

Viśveśa (S) (M) **1.** lord of the universe; desired by all. **3.** another name for Brahmā, Viṣṇu and Śiva.

Viśveśvara (S) (M) **1.** the lord of the universe. **3.** a form of Śiva worshipped in Benaras (*M. Bh.*).

Viśveśvaraya (S) (M) lord of the universe.

Vītabhaya (S) (M) **1.** fearless. **3.** a Purū king who was the son of King Manasyu and the father of King Śuṇḍu (*A. Purāṇa*); another name for Śiva and Viṣṇu.

Vītabhī (S) (M) fearless.

Vītabhīti (S) (M) **1.** fearless. **3.** an asura (*K. Sāgara*).

Vītabhūta (S) (M) **1.** free from the past; fearless. **3.** an asura in the palace of Varuna (*M. Bh.*).

Vītadhvaja (S) (M) **1.** without a banner. **3.** a king of the Janaka dynasty who was the son of Dharmadhvaja and the father of Khāndikya (*Bhāgavata*).

Vītadru (S) (M) **1.** motionless. **3.** a Yādava king (*M. Bh.*).

Vītahavya (S) (M) **1.** one whose offerings are acceptable. **3.** a son of Śunaka and father of Dhṛti; another name for King Ekavīra and Kṛṣṇa.

Vītamala (S) (M) free from darkness.

Vītamanyu (S) (M) free from anger.

Vitamas (S) (M) free from darkness.

Vitanu (S) (M) **1.** thin; slender; with no essence or reality. **3.** another name for Kāma.

Vītarāga (S) (M) free from passion; calm.

Vitarka (S) (M) **1.** guess; fancy; imagination; conjecture; opinion. **3.** a son of Dhṛtarāṣṭra (*M. Bh.*).

Vītaśanka (S) (M) fearless; without doubt.

Vītaśoka (S) (M) free from sorrow.

Vitatha (S) (M) **1.** false. **3.** another name for the hermit Dīrghatamas who was the foster son of Bharata (*Ṛg Veda*).

Vitatya (S) (M) **1.** to stretch; expand. **3.** the son of the Gṛtsamada dynasty king Vihavya and the father of King Satya (*H. Purāṇa*).

Vītīhotra (S) (M) **1.** invited to a feast. **2.** a god; king. **3.** a son of Priyavrata (*Bhā. Purāṇa*); a son of Indrasena (*Bhā. Purāṇa*); a son of Sukumāra; a son of Tālajaṅgha; the husband of Śabari in her previous life; another name for the sun and Agni (*R. Taraṅgiṇī*).

Vittadha (S) (M) wealth possessing.

Vittagoptā (S) (M) **1.** hiding wealth. **3.** another name for Kubera.

Vittaka (S) (M) very wealthy; very famous.

Vittanātha (S) (M) **1.** lord of wealth. **3.** another name for Kubera.

Vittapa (S) (M) **1.** guarding wealth. **3.** another name for Kubera.

Vittapati (S) (M) **1.** lord of wealth. **3.** another name for Kubera.

Vitteśa (S) (M) **1.** lord of wealth. **3.** another name for Kubera.

Viṭṭhala (S) (M) **1.** fortune giver. **2.** ascetic; homeless; without any desire for shelter. **3.** a god worshipped in Pandharpur stated to be an incarnation of Viṣṇu/Kṛṣṇa who visited the city to reward a pious Brāhmin.

Vitula (S) (M) **1.** large; wide; thick; long; loud. **3.** one of the 7 winds; one of the 7 tongues of fire (*H. Purāṇa*); a Sauvira king (*M. Bh.*).

Vivardhana (S) (M) **1.** augmenting; increasing; promoting. **3.** a king in the assembly of Yudhiṣṭhira (*M. Bh.*).

Vivāsa (S) (M) shining forth; dawning.

Vivāsana (S) (M) illuminating.

Vivasvata (S) (M) **1.** the brilliant one. **2.** shining forth; diffusing light. **3.** the sun born as one of the 12 ādityas of Kaśyapa and Aditi (*V. Purana*); also known as Mārtaṇḍa he was the husband of Saṁjñā and the father of Vaivaśvata Manu from whom the Solar dynasty begins, he was also the father of Yama and Yamī and the Aśvinidevas, Nasatya and Dasra from his wife Ćhāyā he was the father of Manu Sāvarṇi, Śani and Tapatī (*M. Bh.*); an asura killed by Garuḍa (*M. Bh.*); a viśvadeva (*M. Bh.*); the 1st human being who offered sacrifice who is supposed to have been the son of Kaśyapa and Dākṣāyāṇī, the father of Manu and Yama and the ancestor of all the people on earth (*Ṛg Veda*).

Viveka (S) (M) discrimination; distinction; true knowledge.

Vivekānanda (S) (M) rejoicing in knowledge.

Vivekin (S) (M) discriminating; judicious; prudent; discreet; wise.

Vivići (S) (M) **1.** discriminating; discerning. **3.** another name for Agni and Indra.

Vivida (S) (M) **1.** knowing. **3.** an asura follower of Kaṅsa (*Bhāgavata*).

Vivikta (S) (M) **1.** distinguished; solitary; pure; neat; clear; profound. **3.** a king of Kuṣadvīpa who was the son of Hiraṇyaretas (*Bhāgavatd*).

Viviktanāman (S) (M) **1.** sign of discrimination. **3.** one of the sons of Hiraṇyaretas (*Ṛg Veda*).

Vivikvas (S) (M) **1.** discerning; discriminating. **3.** another name for Indra (*Ṛg Veda*).

Vivindhya (S) (M) **1.** frightening. **3.** an asura killed by Ćārudeṣṇa (*M. Bh.*).

Vivinśa (S) (M) **1.** of a group of 20. **3.** the son of King Vinśa of the solar dynasty and the father of Khaninetra and 14 others (*M. Bh.*).

Vivinśati (S) (M) **1.** best of 20. **3.** a king who sat in the dice game of Duryodhana and Yudhiṣṭhira; a son of Dhṛtarāṣṭra (*M. Bh.*).

Vivitsu (S) (M) **1.** desirous of knowledge. **3.** a son of Dhṛtarāṣṭra (*M. Bh.*).

Viyama (S) (M) **1.** to stretch out; to extend. **3.** a son of the hermit Śataśṛṅga (*M. Bh.*).

Viyanmaṇi (S) (M) **1.** sky jewel. **3.** another name for the sun.

Viyāsa (S) (M) **1.** tormentor; divider. **3.** a demon who inflicts torment in Yama's world.

Viyati (S) (M) **1.** stretched out. **3.** a son of Nahuṣa (*Bhāgavata*).

Vopadeva (S) (M) **1.** walking like a demigod. **3.** a grammarian who was the son of Keśava and pupil of Dhaneśvara and who lived at the court of King Hemādri of Devagiri (13th century).

Vraja (S) (M) **1.** cowpen; cattleshed; host; multitude. **3.** the district around Āgra and Mathurā and the abode of young Kṛṣṇa (*Bhā. Purāṇa*); a king of the Manu Svāyambhuva dynasty who was the son of Havirdhāna and Dhīṣaṇā (*A. Purāṇa*).

Vrajabhuṣaṇa (S) (M) **1.** ornament of Vraja. **3.** another name for Kṛṣṇa.

Vrajakiśora (S) (M) **1.** adolescent of Vraja. **3.** another name for Kṛṣṇa.

Vrajalāla (S) (M) **1.** son of Vraja. **3.** another name for Kṛṣṇa.

Vrajamohana (S) (M) **1.** fascinator of Vraja. **3.** another name for Kṛṣṇa.

Vrajana (S) (M) **1.** travelling. **2.** a road. **3.** a son of Ajamīdha and Keśinī and brother of Jahnu (*M. Bh.*).

Vrajanandana (S) (M) **1.** son of Vraja. **3.** another name for Kṛṣṇa

Vrajanātha (S) (M) **1.** lord of Vraja. **3.** another name for Kṛṣṇa.

Vrajarāja (S) (M) **1.** king of Vraja. **3.** another name for Kṛṣṇa.

Vrajaspati (S) (M) **1.** master of the cattle. **3.** another name for Kṛṣṇa.

Vrajavallabha (S) (M) **1.** beloved of Vraja. **3.** another name for Kṛṣṇa.

Vrajavara (S) (M) **1.** best in Vraja. **3.** another name for Kṛṣṇa.

Vrajendra (S) (M) **1.** lord of Vraja. **3.** another name for Kṛṣṇa.

Vrajeśa (S) (M) **1.** lord of Vraja. **3.** another name for Kṛṣṇa.

Vrajeśvara (S) (M) **1.** lord of Vraja. **3.** another name for Kṛṣṇa.

Vrajīravan (S) (M) **1.** the noise of the hard. **3.** a Yadu king who was the son of Kroṣṭu and the father of Kuṣanku (*Bhāgavata*).

Vrata (S) (M) **1.** law; obedience; service; pious austerity; holy practice; vow. **3.** a son of Manu and Naḍvalā.

Vrateśa (S) (M) **1.** lord of observances. **3.** another name for Śiva.

Vrateyu (S) (M) **1.** follower of law; keeper of promises. **3.** a son of Raudrāśva (*Purāṇas*).

Vratin (S) (M) observing vows; worshipping.

Vratya (S) (M) obedient; faithful.

Vrayas (S) (M) with superior power.

Vṛddhakṣatra (S) (M) **1.** eminent warrior. **3.** ancestor of Jayadratha.

Vṛddhakṣema (S) (M) **1.** giving security to elders by the learned. **2.** desiring the welfare of all. **3.** the king of Trigarta and father of Suśarmā (*M. Bh.*).

Vṛddhaśarma (S) (M) **1.** great preceptor. **3.** a son of King Ayus and Svarbhānū (*M. Bh.*).

Vṛddhaśravas (S) (M) **1.** possessed of great swiftness. **3.** another name for Indra.

Vṛja (S) (M) **1.** strength. **3.** a hermit of the family of Emperor Pṛthu who was the son of Havirdhāna and Dhīṣaṇā (*V. Purāṇa*).

Vṛjabala (S) (M) strong.

Vṛjinīvān (S) (M) 1. wicked; deceitful. 3. a son of Kroṣṭa and the father of Uṣaṅgu (*M. Bh.*).

Vṛka (S) (M) 1. tearer. 2. wolf; cow; Kṣatriya; plough; thunderbolt. 3. a son of Bharuka (*H. Purāṇa*); a son of Pṛthu (*Bhā. Purāṇa*); a son of Vatsaka; a son of the Kekaya King Dhṛṣṭaketu and Durvā (*Bhāgavata*); a son of Kṛṣṇa and Mitravindā (*Bhā. Purāṇa*); an asura (*Bhāgavata*); a warrior on the Pāṇḍava's side (*M. Bh.*); a son of Śūra and Māriṣā who was the husband of Dūrvakṣi and the father of Takṣa and Puṣkara (*Bhāgavata*); another name for the moon, the sun.

Vṛkadeva (S) (M) 1. lord of the wolves. 3. a son of Vasudeva (*H. Purāṇa*).

Vṛkadevi (S) (M) 1. goddess of the plough. 3. a daughter of Devaka (*V. Purāṇa*).

Vṛkadīpti (S) (M) 1. shining like lightning. 3. a son of Kṛṣṇa. (*H. Purāṇa*).

Vṛkakarman (S) (M) 1. acting like a wolf; wolf like. 3. an asura.

Vṛkala (S) (M) 1. a garment made of bark. 3. the grandson of Dhruva and the son of Śliṣṭi and Sućchāyā (*V. Purāṇa*).

Vṛkanirvṛti (S) (M) 1. free from thunderbolts. 3. a son of Kṛṣṇa (*H. Purāṇa*).

Vṛkāsya (S) (M) 1. wolfmouthed. 3. a son of Kṛṣṇa.

Vṛkatejas (S) (M) 1. with the power of the thunderbolt. 3. a grandson of Dhruva and the son of Śliṣṭi and Sućchāyā (*V. Purāṇa*).

Vṛkati (S) (M) 1. murderer; one who tears. 3. a son of Kṛṣṇa; a son of Jīmūta (*H. Purāṇa*).

Vṛkodara (S) (M) 1. wolf bellied. 3. a class of attendants of Śiva (*M. Bh.*); another name for Bhīma and Brahmā.

Vṛndāra (S) (M) 1. surrounded by a group. 2. deity; a god.

Vṛndāraka (S) (M) 1. surrounded by a group. 2. chief; head; eminent; most beautiful; a god. 3. a son of Dhṛtarāṣṭra (*M. Bh.*); a warrior on the side of the Kauravas (*M. Bh.*).

Vṛndāvana (S) (M) 1. forest of Vṛnda; forest of Tulasī; forest of Rādhā. 3. the forest near Gokula where Kṛṣṇa spent his early years (*Bhā. Purāṇa*).

Vṛndāvaneśa (S) (M) 1. lord of Rādhā's forest. 3. another name for Kṛṣṇa.

Vṛṣa (S) (M) 1. bull. 2. man; male; the zodiac sign of Taurus; chief; best. 3. justice or virtue personified as Śiva's bull; Indra in the 11th Manvantara; 2 sons of Kṛṣṇa (*Bhā. Purāṇa*); a son of Vṛṣasena and grandson of Karṇa (*H. Purāṇa*); a Yādava and son of Madhu (*H. Purāṇa*); the son of Śṛnjaya (*H. Purāṇa*); one of the 10 horses of the moon; a warrior of Skanda (*M. Bh.*); an asura (*M. Bh.*); a king of the family of Bharata who was the son of Duṣyanta and Śakuntalā (*Bhā. Purāṇa*); the incarnation of Śiva as an ox (*Ś. Purāṇa*); a son of Kārtavīryārjuna (*Br. Purāṇa*); another name for Viṣṇu/Kṛṣṇa, Indra, the sun and Kāma.

Vṛṣabha (S) (M) 1. the bull. 2. manly; mighty; strong; chief; excellent; eminent. 3. an asura killed by Viṣṇu (*H. Purāṇa*); a son of the 10th Manu (*Mā. Purāṇa*); a son of Kuśāgra; a son of Kārtavīrya (*J. S. Koṣa*); the Jaina 1st Arhat of the present Avasarpiṇī; a mountain; the son of King Subala of Gāndhāra and the brother of Śakuni (*M. Bh.*); a Yādava king who was the son of Anāmitra and the husband of Jayantī (*M. Purāṇa*); the zodiac sign of Taurus.

Vṛṣabhadhvaja (S) (M) 1. bull bannered. 3. an attendant of Śiva (*M. Bh.*).

Vṛṣabhagati (S) (M) 1. going on a bull. 3. another name for Śiva.

Vṛṣabhaketu (S) (M) 1. bull bannered. 3. another name for Śiva.

Vṛṣabhāṅka (S) (M) 1. marked by a bull. 3. another name for Śiva.

Vṛṣabhānu (S) (M) **1.** best bull. **3.** a king who was the son of Śūrabhanu and father of Rādhā (*Brah. Purāṇa*).

Vṛṣabhasvāmin (S) (M) **1.** lord of the bulls. **3.** another name for Śiva; a king who was the founder of the family of Īkṣvāku and the father of Draviḍa (*H. Purāṇa*).

Vṛṣabhavāhana (S) (M) **1.** bull vehicled. **3.** another name for Śiva.

Vṛṣabhekṣaṇa (S) (M) **1.** bull eyed. **3.** another name for Viṣṇu/Kṛṣṇa.

Vṛṣadarbha (S) (M) **1.** grass for the bull. **3.** a son of Śibi (*H. Purāṇa*); a saintly king in the palace of Yama (*M. Bh.*); another name of King Uśīnara of Kāṣī.

Vṛṣādarbhi (S) (M) **1.** bull feeder. **3.** a king of Kāśī also known as Yuvanāśva who was the son of Vṛṣadarbha (*M. Bh.*); a son of Śibi (*H. Purāṇa*).

Vṛṣadarpa (S) (M) **1.** as proud as a bull. **3.** a son of Emperor Śibi (*Bhāgavata*).

Vṛṣadhara (S) (M) **1.** bull bearer. **3.** another name for Śiva.

Vṛṣadhvaja (S) (M) **1.** rat bannered. **3.** a king of the line of Pravīra (*M. Bh.*); another name for Gaṇeśa.

Vṛṣaga (S) (M) **1.** going on a bull. **3.** another name for Śiva.

Vṛṣāgir (S) (M) **1.** strong voiced. **3.** a hermit and father of Ṛjrāśva.

Vṛṣaka (S) (M) **1.** poisonous. **3.** a son of King Subala of Gāndhāra (*M. Bh.*); a Kaliṅga prince.

Vṛṣākapi (S) (M) **1.** bull and monkey conjoined. **3.** a semi-divine being; one of the 11 rudras (*A. Purāṇa*); a hermit (*M. Bh.*); another name for Viṣṇu.

Vṛṣaketana (S) (M) **1.** having a bull for a sign. **3.** another name for Śiva.

Vṛṣaketu (S) (M) **1.** bull bannered. **3.** a son of Karṇa; another name for Paraśurāma.

Vṛṣakrātha (S) (M) **1.** killing bulls. **3.** a Kaurava warrior (*M. Bh.*).

Vṛṣakrātu (S) (M) acting like a bull; manly.

Vṛṣalākṣa (S) (M) **1.** horse eyed. **3.** a king in the line of Bharata who was the son of Ćaturaṅga and the grandson of Romapāda (*Bhāgavata*).

Vṛṣāmitra (S) (M) **1.** a friend of bulls. **3.** a hermit and devotee of Yudhiṣṭhira (*M. Bh.*).

Vṛṣaṇa (S) (M) **1.** sprinkling; fertilizing. **3.** a son of Madhu (*H. Purāṇa*); a son of Kārtavīrya; another name for Siva.

Vṛṣaṇāśva (S) (M) **1.** drawn by stallions; fertilized by stallions. **3.** a Ṛg Vedic king who was the father of Indra as the girl Menā (*Ṛg Veda*); a gandharva; another name for Indra.

Vṛṣaṇḍa (S) (M) **1.** bull testicled. **3.** an asura (*M. Bh.*).

Vṛṣaṅgan (S) (M) **1.** not to be doubted. **3.** another name for Śiva.

Vṛṣāṅka (S) (M) **1.** bull marked. **3.** another name for Śiva.

Vṛṣaṅku (S) (M) **1.** without any sin. **3.** a hermit (*U. Rāmāyaṇa*).

Vṛṣaparvan (S) (M) **1.** with joints as strong as that of a bull. **2.** strong jointed. **3.** a son of Kaśyapa and Danu who was reborn as the King Dīrghaprajña and was the father of Śarmiṣṭhā (*M. Bh.*); a hermit; another name for Indra, Viṣṇu and Śiva.

Vṛṣapati (S) (M) **1.** lord of the bull. **3.** another name for Śiva.

Vṛṣasena (S) (M) **1.** with an army of bulls. **3.** a son of the 10th Manu (*H. Purāṇa*); a son of Karna; a great-grandson of Aśoka; another name for Karṇa.

Vṛṣaskandha (S) (M) **1.** bull shouldered. **3.** another name for Śiva.

Vṛṣātmaja (S) (M) **1.** son of the Sun. **3.** another name for Karṇa.

Vrṣavāhana (S) (M) **1.** whose vehicle is a bull. **3.** another name for Śiva.

Vṛśćika (S) (M) **1.** scorpion. **2.** the zodiac sign of Scorpio.

Vṛścikeśa (S) (M) **1.** lord of scorpions. **2.** ruler of the sign of Scorpio. **3.** another name for the planet Mercury.

Vṛṣin (S) (M) **1.** fond of rain. **2.** a peacock.

Vṛṣṇī (S) (M)) **1.** strong; manly; powerful; mighty; passionate; a ram; bull; ray of light; air; wind. **3.** a famous king of the Yadu dynasty who was the son of Madhu and the husband of Mādrī and Gāndhārī, he was the founder of the dynasty and Kṛsṇa was born in it (*M. Bh.*); another name for Śiva, Viṣṇu/Kṛṣṇa, Indra and Agni.

Vṛṣṇigarbha (S) (M) **1.** born in the Vṛṣṇi family. **3.** another name for Kṛṣṇa.

Vṛṣṇijīva (S) (M) **1.** soul of the Vṛṣṇis. **3.** another name for Kṛṣṇa.

Vṛṣṇikulodvaha (S) (M) **1.** elevating the Vṛṣṅi family. **3.** another name for Kṛṣṇa.

Vṛṣṇinandana (S) (M) **1.** son of the Vṛṣṇis. **3.** another name for Kṛṣṇa.

Vṛṣṇipati (S) (M) **1.** lord of the Vṛṣṇis. **3.** another name for Kṛṣṇa.

Vṛṣṇipravara (S) (M) **1.** chief of the Vṛṣṇis. **3.** another name for Kṛṣṇa.

Vṛṣṇipuṅgava (S) (M) **1.** bull of the Vṛṣṇis. **3.** another name for Kṛṣṇa.

Vṛṣṇiśārdula (S) (M) **1.** tiger of the Vṛṣṇis; noblest of the Vṛṣṇis. **3.** another name for Kṛṣṇa.

Vṛṣṇisattama (S) (M) **1.** best of the Vṛṣṇis. **3.** another name for Kṛṣṇa.

Vṛṣṇisiṁha (S) (M) **1.** lion of the Vṛṣṇis. **3.** another name for Kṛṣṇa.

Vṛṣṇiśreṣṭha (S) (M) **1.** first of the Vṛṣṇis. **3.** another name for Kṛṣṇa.

Vṛṣṇivareṇya (S) (M) **1.** best of the Vṛṣṇis. **3.** another name for Kṛṣṇa.

Vṛṣṇyandhakapati (S) (M) **1.** lord of the mighty. **3.** another name for Kṛṣṇa.

Vṛṣṇyandhakottama (S) (M) **1.** best of the mighty. **3.** another name for Kṛṣṇa.

Vṛṣtimat (S) (M) **1.** rainy. **3.** a son of Kaviratha (*Bhā. Purāṇa*).

Vṛtra (S) (M) **1.** coverer; restrainer; enemy; foe. **3.** the Vedic personification of a demon of darkness and drought which takes possession of clouds causing them to keep back the waters; an asura who was an incarnation of the Emperor Ćitraketu created by Kaśyapa (*P. Purāṇa*) or Tvaṣṭa (*D. Purāṇa*) and was killed by Indra.

Vṛtrāghnī (S) (M) **1.** killing enemies; destroyer of Vṛta. **3.** another name for Indra.

Vṛtrahā (S) (M) **1.** killer of Vṛtra. **3.** another name for Indra.

Vṛtta (S) (M) **1.** circle; fixed; firm character; conduct. **3.** a nāga son of Kaśyapa and Kadru (*M. Bh.*).

Vyābhāsa (S) (M) to illuminate beautifully.

Vyadvan (S) (M) **1.** having various paths. **3.** another name for Agni.

Vyāghra (S) (M) **1.** tiger. **3.** the tiger offspring of Śardūlī or Kaśyapa and Danṣṭrā (*A. Veda*).

Vyāghrabala (S) (M) with the strength of the tiger.

Vyāghrabhaṭa (S) (M) **1.** as powerful as the tiger. **3.** an asura (*K. Sāgara*); a minister of King Śṛdatta (*K. Sāgara*).

Vyāghradatta (S) (M) **1.** given by a tiger. **3.** a Magadha prince who fought on the side of the Kauravas (*M. Bh.*).

Vyāghraketu (S) (M) **1.** tiger bannered. **3.** a Pāñcāla warrior on the Paṇḍava side (*M. Bh.*).

Vyāghrākṣa (S) (M) **1.** tiger eyed. **3.** a follower of Skanda (*M. Bh.*); an asura (*H. Purāṇa*).

Vyāghramukha (S) (M) **1.** tiger faced. **3.** a king; a mountain (*Mā. Purāṇa*).

Vyāghrapad (S) (M) **1.** tiger footed. **3.** a hermit and father of Upamanyu (*M. Bh.*).

Vyāghrasena (S) (M) one who fights like a tiger.

Vyāghravaktra (S) (M) **1.** tiger faced. **3.** an attendant of Śiva (*H. Purana*).

Vyakta (S) (M) **1.** manifest; distinguished; wise; adorned; embellished; beautiful. **3.** one of the main disciples of Mahāvira (*J.S. Koṣa*); another name for Viṣṇu.

Vyaktarūpa (S) (M) **1.** with a manifested form. **3.** another name for Viṣṇu.

Vyālimukha (S) (M) **1.** snake faced. **3.** an asura killed by Skanda (*M. Bh.*).

Vyāna (S) (M) **1.** vital air. **2.** one of the 5 vital airs of the body personified as the son of Udāna and the father of Apāna.

Vyanśa (S) (M) **1.** with wide shoulders; broad shouldered. **3.** a son of Vipraćitti; a demon killed by Indra (*Ṛg Veda*).

Vyāsa (S) (M) **1.** separation; division. **2.** distributing; arranging; compiling. **3.** a celebrated sage regarded as the original compiler of the Vedas, he was the son of sage Pārāśara and Satyavatī and half-brother of Vićitravīrya and Bhīṣma, he is also called Bādarāyaṇa and Kṛṣṇa Dvaipayana, he became the father of Dhṛtarāṣṭra and Paṇḍu by Vićitravīrya's widows, he was also the father of Vidura by a servant girl and of Śuka the narrator of the *Bhāgavata Purāṇa,* he was the spiritual preceptor of the Kauravas and Pāṇḍavas; towards the close of his life he dictated the story of the *Mahābharata* to Gaṇapati, he was reborn as Apāntaratamas.

Vyāsamātṛ (S) (M) **1.** mother of Vyāsa. **3.** another name for Satyavatī.

Vyāsamūrti (S) (M) **1.** idol of the compiler. **3.** another name for Śiva.

Vyaśva (S) (M) **1.** horseless. **3.** a ṛsi; a king in the palace of Yama (*M. Bh.*).

Vyavasāya (S) (M) **1.** effort; resolve; purpose; act; strategem. **3.** resolution personified as a son of Dharmā and Vapus; another name for Viṣṇu and Śiva.

Vyomabha (S) (M) **1.** heaven like. **3.** another name for a Buddha.

Vyomadeva (S) (M) **1.** lord of the sky. **3.** another name for Śiva.

Vyomādhipa (S) (M) **1.** lord of the sky. **3.** another name for Śiva.

Vyomakeśa (S) (M) **1.** sky haired. **3.** another name for Śiva.

Vyomamṛga (S) (M) **1.** the animal of the sky. **3.** one of the 10 horses of the moon (*M. Bh.*).

Vyoman (S) (M) **1.** heaven; sky; atmosphere; wind; air. **3.** a temple sacred to the sun (*Bhā. Purāṇa*); the year personified; a king in the dynasty of Bharata who was the son of Dāśārha and father of Jīmūta (*Bhāgavāta*).

Vyomaratna (S) (M) **1.** sky jewel. **3.** another name for the sun.

Vyomāri (S) (M) **1.** shining in the sky. **3.** a viśvadeva (*M. Bh.*).

Vyomasad (S) (M) **1.** dwelling in the sky. **2.** a god; a gandharva (*Ṛg Veda*).

Vyomāsura (S) (M) **1.** demon of the sky. **3.** a son of Māyāsura killed by Kṛṣṇa (*Bhā. Purāṇa*).

Vyomeśa (S) (M) **1.** lord of the sky. **3.** another name for the sun.

Vyomin (S) (M) **1.** travelling in space. **3.** one of the 10 horses of the moon (*A. Koṣa*).

Vyūdhoru (S) (M) **1.** with thick thighs. **3.** a son of Dhṛtarāṣṭra (*M. Bh.*).

Vyūharāja (S) (M) **1.** lord of reason. **3.** a bodhisattva.

Vyuṣa (S) (M) dawn; daybreak.

Vyuśitāśva (S) (M) **1.** with the horses of dawn. **3.** a Purū king and husband of Bhadrā considered the most beautiful woman in India; she was the mother of the 3 Satvas and 4 Madras (*M. Bh.*); a king and descendant of Daśaratha.

Vyuṣṭa (S) (M) **1.** dawned; grown bright and clear. **3.** daybreak personified as a son of Kalpa or as a son of Puṣpārna and Doṣā or as a son of Vibhāvasu and Uṣas (*Bhā. Purāṇa*); a king of the Dhruva dynasty who was the son of King Puṣpārna and Prabhā and the father of Sarvatejas (*Bhāgavata*).

Y

Yādasambharta (S) (M) **1.** chief of marine animals. **3.** another name for Varuṇa.

Yādaspati (S) (M) **1.** lord of marine animals. **3.** another name for Varuṇa.

Yādava (S) (M) **1.** descended from Yadu. **3.** another name for Kṛṣṇa.

Yādavāgrya (S) (M) **1.** First of the Yādavas. **3.** another name for Kṛṣṇa.

Yādavaprakāśa (S) (M) **1.** light of the Yādavas. **3.** another name for Kṛṣṇa.

Yādavaputra (S) (M) **1.** son of Yadu. **3.** another name for Kṛṣṇa.

Yādavarāya (S) (M) **1.** king of the Yādavas. **3.** another name for Kṛṣṇa.

Yādavaśārdūla (S) (M) **1.** tiger or chief of the Yādavas. **3.** another name for Kṛṣṇa.

Yādavaśreṣṭha (S) (M) **1.** first of the Yādavas. **3.** another name for Kṛṣṇa.

Yādavendra (S) (M) **1.** lord of the Yādavas. **3.** another name for Kṛṣṇa.

Yādaveśvara (S) (M) **1.** lord of the Yādavas. **3.** another name for Kṛṣṇa.

Yādīśa (S) (M) lord of marine animals.

Yādonatha (S) (M) **1.** lord of sea animals. **3.** another name for Varuṇa.

Yadu (S) (M) **1.** cowherd. **3.** an ancient hero in the Vedas and the founder of the Yādava Vanśa, he was the son of Yayāti and Devayānī and the brother of Turvasu, he was the father of Sahasrajit, Kroṣṭā, Nala and Ṛpu; a son of Uparićara Vasu who was considered invincible (*M. Bh.*).

Yadūdvaha (S) (M) **1.** supporter of the Yadus. **3.** another name for Kṛṣṇa and Vasudeva.

Yadukumāra (S) (M) **1.** youth of the Yadu tribe. **3.** another name for Kṛṣṇa.

Yadumaṇi (S) (M) **1.** jewel of the Yadus. **3.** the father of Parama.

Yadunandana (S) (M) **1.** son of Yadu. **3.** another name for Akrūra (*V. Purāṇa*).

Yadunātha (S) (M) **1.** lord of the Yadus. **3.** another name for Kṛṣṇa.

Yadupati (S) (M) **1.** lord of the Yadus. **3.** another name for Kṛṣṇa.

Yadupuṅgava (S) (M) **1.** bull of the Yadus; chief of the Yadus. **3.** another name for Kṛṣṇa.

Yadurāj (S) (M) **1.** lord of the Yadus. **3.** another name for Kṛṣṇa.

Yaduśreṣṭha (S) (M) **1.** best of the Yādus. **3.** another name for Kṛṣṇa.

Yadusukhāvaha (S) (M) **1.** bringing pleasure to the Yadus. **3.** another name for Kṛṣṇa.

Yaduttama (S) (M) **1.** best of the Yadus. **3.** another name for Kṛṣṇa.

Yaduvanśavivardhana (S) (M) **1.** dividing the Yadu family. **3.** another name for Kṛṣṇa.

Yaduvīra (S) (M) **1.** hero of the Yadus. **3.** another name for Kṛṣṇa.

Yahu (S) (M) offspring; child; restless; swift; mighty; strong.

Yahva (S) (M) **1.** restless; swift. **2.** active. **3.** another name for Agni, Soma, Indra.

Yāja (S) (M) **1.** sacrificer. **2.** worshipper. **3.** a sage born in the Kaśyapa gotra.

Yajāka (S) (M) worshipping; liberal.

Yajamāna (S) (M) **1.** sacrificing; worshipping. **2.** patron of priests.

Yajana (S) (M) act of sacrificing or worshipping.

Yajanīya (S) (M) to be orshipped.

Yajata (S) (M) **1.** holy; divine; dignified; worthy of worship. **2.** adorable. **3.** another name for Śiva, the moon and the officiating priest of a sacrifice.

Yajatra (S) (M) worthy of worship; deserving adoration.

Yajin (S) (M) worshipper.

Yajiṣṇu (S) (M) worshipping the gods.

Yajña (S) (M) **1.** worship; devotion; oblation; sacrifice; worshipper; sacrificer. **3.** an incarnation of Viṣṇu as the son of Prajāpati Rući and Ākūti and the twin of Dakṣiṇā, they married each other and their 12 children were the demigods known as the Yāmas in the Svāyambhuva Manvantara (*Bhāgavata*); a sage who was an author of *Ṛg Veda* (x).

Yajñabāhu (S) (M) **1.** arm of sacrifice. **2.** fire. **3.** a sage who was the son of Priyavrata and Barhismatī and grandson of Svāyambhuva Manu (*Bhāgavata*).

Yajñadatta (S) (M) **1.** given by sacrifice. **3.** the *Agni Purāṇa* name for the youthful sage otherwise known as Śravaṇa who was shot by Daśaratha.

Yajñodaya (S) (M) risen from the sacred fire.

Yajñadhara (S) (M) **1.** the bearer of the sacrifice. **3.** another name for Viṣṇu.

Yajñahamya (S) (M) **1.** accessible through worship. **3.** another name for Viṣṇu/Kṛṣṇa.

Yajñaguhya (S) (M) **1.** lord of the sacrifice. **3.** another name for Viṣṇu/Kṛṣṇa.

Yajñahotri (S) (M) **1.** a priest at a sacrifice. **3.** a son of Manu Uttama (*Bhā. Purāṇa*).

Yajñakṛt (S) (M) **1.** worshipping; causing sacrifice. **3.** another name for Viṣṇu.

Yajñamaya (S) (M) containing the sacrifice.

Yajñamūrti (S) (M) **1.** the idol of sacrifice. **3.** another name for Viṣṇu.

Yajñanemi (S) (M) **1.** surrounded by sacrifices. 3. another name for Kṛṣṇa.

Yajñapati (S) (M) **1.** lord of sacrifice. **3.** another name for Viṣṇu and Soma.

Yajñapātra (S) (M) a sacrificial vessel.

Yajñaphala (S) (M) the fruit of worship.

Yajñapriya (S) (M) **1.** fond of sacrifice. **3.** another name for Kṛṣṇa.

Yajñapuruṣa (S) (M) **1.** soul of the sacrifice. **3.** another name for Viṣṇu.

Yajñarāj (S) (M) **1.** king of the sacrifice. **3.** another name for the moon.

Yajñāri (S) (M) **1.** enemy of the sacrifice. **3.** another name for Śiva.

Yajñarupa (S) (M) **1.** the form of a sacrifice. **3.** another name for Kṛṣṇa.

Yajñaśarman (S) (M) **1.** protector of the sacrifice. **3.** a Brāhmin made famous in the Purāṇas.

Yajñaśatru (S) (M) **1.** enemy of the sacrifice. **3.** another name for Rāma and Lakṣmaṇa; a rākṣasa (*Rāmāyaṇa*).

Yajñasena (S) (M) **1.** leader of the sacrifice. **3.** a king of Vidarbha; a dānava (*K. Sāgara*); another name for Viṣṇu and Drupada of Pāñćāla (*M. Bh.*).

Yajñaseni (S) (M) **1.** son of Drupada. **3.** another name for Dhṛṣṭadyumna.

Yajñasenisuta (S) (M) **1.** son of Drupada. **3.** another name for Dhṛṣṭadyumna.

Yajñaśīla (S) (M) performing the sacrifice diligently.

Yajñātman (S) (M) **1.** the soul of sacrifice. **3.** another name for Viṣṇu.

Yajñatrātṛ (S) (M) **1.** protector of the sacrifice. **3.** another name for Viṣṇu.

Yajñavāha (S) (M) **1.** conducting the sacrifice to the gods. **3.** an attendant of Skanda; another name for the aśvins.

Yajñavāhana (S) (M) **1.** having sacrifice as a vehicle. **3.** another name for Śiva and Viṣṇu.

Yajñavalkya (S) (M) **1.** clad in oblation. **2.** surrounded or covered by the sacrifice. **3.** an ancient sage and the first teacher of the white *Yajur Veda* said to have been revealed to him by the sun, he was also the author of a code of laws secondary in importance only to Manu and the author of *Vājasaneyī Samhitā,* he was King Janaka's priest (*A. Purāṇa*).

Yajñavarāha (S) (M) **1.** deity of oblation. **3.** Viṣṇu in his boar incarnation.

Yajñavardhana (S) (M) increasing sacrifice.

Yajñavīrya (S) (M) **1.** one whose might is sacrifice. **3.** another name for Viṣṇu.

Yajñayoga (S) (M) **1.** worthy of sacrifice. **3.** another name for Viṣṇu.

Yajñeśa (S) (M) **1.** lord of the sacrificial fire. **3.** another name for Viṣṇu and the sun.

Yajñeśvara (S) (M) **1.** lord of sacrifice. **3.** another name for Viṣṇu, Vāyu and the moon.

Yājñikadeva (S) (M) lord of sacrifices.

Yājñikāśraya (S) (M) **1.** refuge of sacrificers. **3.** another name for Viṣṇu.

Yājñīya (S) (M) **1.** worthy of worship and sacrifice; sacred; godly; divine. **3.** *Ficus glomerata.*

Yajñu (S) (M) worshipping; pious; worthy of worship.

Yaju (S) (M) **1.** a sacrificial prayer. **3.** one of the 10 horses of the moon.

Yajuṣpati (S) (M) **1.** lord of the sacrifice. **3.** another name for Viṣṇu.

Yajvin (S) (M) worshipper.

Yakṣa (S) (M) **1.** protector of forests; quick; speedy; living supernatural being. **3.** a class of semi-divine beings who are attendants of Kubera and sometimes of Viṣṇu, they are variously descibed as the sons of Pulastya, Pulaha, Kaśyapa and Krodha and also produced from the feet of Brahmā, they are generally regarded as beings of a benevolent and inoffensive disposition and they live in trees; a son of Śvaphalka (*V. Puraṇa*); Indra's palace; the attendants of the Jaina Tīrthaṅkaras (*J. Literature*).

Yaksādhipa (S) (M) **1.** lord of the yakṣas. **3.** another name for Kubera.

Yakṣanāyaka (S) (M) **1.** lord of the yakṣas. **3.** the servant of the 4th Arhat of the present Avasarpinī.

Yakṣapati (S) (M) **1.** king of the yakṣas. **3.** another name for Kubera (*H. Purāṇa*).

Yakṣapravara (S) (M) **1.** chief of the yakṣas. **3.** another name for Kubera.

Yakṣarāj (S) (M) **1.** king of the yakṣas. **3.** another name for Kubera and Maṇibhadra.

Yakṣarakṣodhipa (S) (M) **1.** leader of the yakṣas and rākṣasas. **3.** another name for Kubera.

Yakṣarāṭ (S) (M) **1.** giving yakṣas. **3.** another name for Kubera.

Yakṣataru (S) (M) **1.** tree of the yakṣas. **3.** the Indian Fig tree' (*Ficus indica*).

Yakṣendra (S) (M) **1.** lord of the yakṣas. **3.** another name for Kubera.

Yakṣeśa (S) (M) **1.** lord of the yakṣas. **3.** the servants of the 11th and 18th Arhats of the present Avasarpinī.

Yakṣeśvara (S) (M) **1.** lord of the yakṣas. **3.** an incarnation of Siva (*Ś. Purāṇa*); another name for Kubera.

Yakṣin (S) (M) having life; living.

Yama (S) (M) **1.** rein; curb; bridle; restraint; number. **2.** driver; charioteer; twin born. **3.** the god who rules over the spirits of the dead, he is regarded as the first of men and the son of Vivasvat the sun and Śaranyū, his twin sister is Yamī, his abode is a nether region called Yamapura, he is also one of the 8 guardians of the world and the regent of the southern quarter, he is the regent of the constellation Bharaṇī and the supposed author of *Ṛg Veda* (x); one of Skanda's attendants.

Yamadaṅṣṭra (S) (M) **1.** with restraining teeth. **3.** a rākṣasa (*K. Sāgara*); a warrior on the side of the gods.

Yamadevatā (S) (M) **1.** having Yama for one's deity. **3.** another name for the lunar constellation Bharaṇī.

Yamadruma (S) (M) **1.** Yama's tree. **3.** *Bombax heptaphyllum.*

Yamadūta (S) (M) **1.** Yama's messenger sent to bring the departed spirit to the seat of judgement. **3.** a son of Viśvāmitra (*M. Bh.*)

Yamaghna (S) (M) **1.** one who destroys Yama. **3.** another name for Viṣṇu.

Yamaja (S) (M) twin born.

Yamajit (S) (M) **1.** conqueror of Yama. **3.** another name for Siva.

Yāmaka (S) (M) **1.** restraint; a watch on 3 hours or one-eighth of a day. **3.** the constellation Punarvasu.

Yamakīla (S) (M) **1.** self restrained. **3.** another name for Viṣṇu.

Yamala (S) (M) **1.** a twin. **3.** a magic tree identified with the sons of Kubera; the Arjuna tree (*Terminalia arjuna*).

Yāman (S) (M) motion; course; flight; invocation; prayer; march.

Yamaṇa (S) (M) 1. restraining; governing; managing. 3. a rāga; another name for Yama.

Yamanetra (S) (M) having Yama as the leader.

Yamantaka (S) (M) 1. destroyer of Yama. 3. another name for Śiva.

Yamānućara (S) (M) a servant of Yama.

Yamapriya (S) (M) 1. loved by Yama. 3. *Ficus indica.*

Yamarāja (S) (M) King Yama.

Yamāri (S) (M) 1. enemy of Yama. 3. another name for Viṣṇu.

Yamasū (S) (M) 1. bringing forth twins. 3. another name for the sun.

Yamavat (S) (M) one who governs himself; self restrained.

Yameśa (S) (M) 1. having Yama as ruler. 3. another name for the constellation Bharaṇī.

Yamin (S) (M) one who has curbed his passions.

Yaminemi (S) (M) 1. felly of a chariot wheel. 2. bearer of motion. 3. another name for Indra.

Yāmininātha (S) (M) 1. lord of night. 3. another name for the moon.

Yāminīpāti (S) (M) 1. the beloved of night. 3. another name for the moon.

Yāmīra (S) (M) 1. lord of night. 3. another name for the moon.

Yamita (S) (M) restrained; checked.

Yāmuna (S) (M) 1. growing in the Yamuna. 3. a mountain standing between the rivers Gaṅgā and Yamunā (*M. Bh.*).

Yamunāćārya (S) (M) 1. preceptor from the Yamunā. 3. a principal teacher of the Vaiṣṇava cult.

Yamunājanaka (S) (M) 1. father of Yamunā. 3. another name for the sun.

Yamunāpati (S) (M) 1. lord of Yamunā. 3. another name for Viṣṇu.

Yāmya (S) (M) 1. southern; the right hand; belonging to Yama. 3. another name for Śiva, Viṣṇu and Agastya; the Sandalwood tree.

Yantri (S) (M) restraining; establishing; granting; bestowing; charioteer; ruler; governor; guide.

Yantur (S) (M) ruler; guide.

Yaśaćandra (S) (M) as famous as the moon.

Yaśahketu (S) (M) 1. with a famous banner. 3. a king of a city called Śobhāvatī (*K. Sāgara*).

Yaśakāva (S) (M) with a body of fame and glory.

Yaśapāla (S) (M) lord of fame.

Yaśapāṇi (S) (M) 1. holding fame. 2. renowned. 3. a Buddhist king of Benaras.

Yaśas (S) (M) 1. beauty; splendour; worth; glory; fame. 3. renown personified as a son of Kāma and Rati or of Dharma and Kīrti; the father of Kalki the 10th incarnation who will come at the end of time.

Yaśaskāma (S) (M) 1. desiring fame. 3. a Bodhisattva.

Yaśaskara (S) (M) 1. conferring glory; causing renown; glorious. 3. a king of Kāśmira.

Yaśastara (S) (M) more renowned and resplendent.

Yaśasvat (S) (M) glorious; famous; honourable; splendid; magnificent; excellent.

Yāska (S) (M) 1. desiring heat; exerting. 3. a Sanskṛt grammarian of ancient times who composed the Nirukta in 500 B.C. (*M. Bh.*).

Yaśo (S) (M) beauty; fame; splendour; glory; honour.

Yaśobhadra (S) (M) 1. famous for one's gentleness. 3. son of King Manobhadra (*P. Purāṇa*).

Yaśobhagin (S) (M) rich in glory.

Yaśobhāgya (S) (M) one whose destiny is glory.

Yaśobhṛt (S) (M) conferring fame; possessing fame.

Yaśodeva (S) (M) 1. lord of fame and beauty. 3. a son of Ramaćandra.

Yaśodhāman (S) (M) abode of glory.

Yaśodhana (S) (M) one whose wealth is fame.

Yaśodhara (S) (M) **1.** maintaining or preserving glory. **3.** the 18th Jaina Arhat of the preceding and 19th Arhat of the coming Utsarpiṇī; the son of Durmukha who fought on the side of the Pāṇḍavas (*M. Bh.*); a son of Kṛṣṇa and Rukmiṇī (*M. Bh.*).

Yaśomādhava (S) (M) **1.** excellent and famous descendant of Madhu. **3.** a form of Viṣṇu.

Yasomitra (S) (M) a friend of fame.

Yaśonandi (S) (M) with happy fame.

Yaśnidhi (S) (M) one whose wealth is fame.

Yaśorāja (S) (M) lord of fame.

Yaśorāśi (S) (M) a mass of glory.

Yaśovara (S) (M) **1.** reputed. **3.** a son of Kṛṣṇa and Rukmiṇī.

Yaśovarman (S) (M) **1.** armoured by fame. **3.** a king of Kanyākubjā (720 A.D.).

Yaśovat (S) (M) possessing glory and fame.

Yaśoyuta (S) (M) possessing fame; renowned.

Yaṣṭi (S) (M) **1.** anything slender. **2.** support; staff; pillar; rod; mace; stem; sugarcane.

Yaṣṭṛ (S) (M) worshipper.

Yāśu (S) (M) embrace.

Yataćetas (S) (M) with a controlled mind.

Yatagir (S) (M) one who restrains his speech.

Yatakṛta (S) (M) restrained; governed; subdued.

Yatamanyu (S) (M) subduing anger.

Yatamkara (S) (M) subduer; conqueror.

Yatendriya (S) (M) chaste; pure; of controlled passions.

Yathāvāsa (S) (M) **1.** in the manner of perfume. **3.** a sage (*M. Bh.*).

Yati (S) (M) **1.** ascetic; devotee; one who has renounced his possessions. **3.** a son of Brahma; a king who was the eldest son of Nahuṣa and the brother of Yayāti (*M. Bh.*); a son of Viśvāmitra (*M. Bh.*); another name for Śiva.

Yatidharman (S) (M) **1.** follower of an ascetic path. **3.** a son of Śvaphalka.

Yatin (S) (M) ascetic; devotee.

Yatinātha (S) (M) **1.** lord of ascetics. **3.** an incarnation of Śiva as a forest sage.

Yatīndra (S) (M) **1.** lord of the yatis or ascetics. **3.** another name for Indra.

Yatirāja (S) (M) **1.** king of ascetics. **3.** another name for Rāmānuja.

Yatīśa (S) (M) lord of ascetics.

Yatīśvara (S) (M) lord of ascetics.

Yatīyasa (S) (M) silver.

Yatna (S) (M) activity of will; performance; effort; energy; zeal.

Yātnika (S) (M) making efforts.

Yātu (S) (M) **1.** going. **2.** traveller; wind; time.

Yātudhāna (S) (M) **1.** creating obstacles for others. **2.** sorcerer; magician. **3.** a rākṣasa who was the son of Kaśyapa and Surasā.

Yātughna (S) (M) **1.** destroyer of Yatus or evil spirits. **3.** the Balsamodendron plant whose gum is said to protect one from curses; bdellium.

Yātuvid (S) (M) one who knows magic; skilful in sorcery.

Yaudheya (S) (M) **1.** warrior. **3.** a son of Yudhiṣṭhira and Devikādevī (*M. Bh.*); a king who was the son of Prativindhya (*M. Purāṇa*).

Yaudhiṣṭhira (S) (M) **1.** son of Yudhiṣṭhira. **3.** another name for Prativindhya.

Yaugandharāyaṇa (S) (M) **1.** lord of the strong ones. **3.** a minister of Prince Udayana who is celebrated in the Purāṇas.

Yaugāndharī (S) (M) **1.** descendant of Yugandhara. **3.** a king of the Śalvas.

Yauvanobheda (S) (M) **1.** the ardour of youthful passion. **3.** another name for Kāma.

Yauyudhāni (S) (M) **1.** son of a warrior. **3.** son of King Sātyaki of the Yādavas (*M. Purāṇa*).

Yavakṛta (S) (M) **1.** purchased with barley. **3.** a son of Aṅgiras; a son of Bharadvāja who practised austerities to gain the knowledge of the Vedas without studying them and was granted his wish by Indra (*M. Bh.*).

Yavana (S) (M) **1.** quick; swift; a Greek; mixing; mingling; keeping aloof; averting. **2.** wheat (*Triticum aestivum*).

Yavāśira (S) (M) **1.** mixed with barley. **3.** another name for Soma.

Yavayaśa (S) (M) **1.** controller of anger; self restrained. **3.** a son of Idhmajihva and the country ruled by him.

Yavīnara (S) (M) **1.** young. **3.** a king of the Purū dynasty who was the son of Bahyāśva (*A. Purāṇa*); a son of jamīdha (*H. Purāna*).

Yaviṣṭha (S) (M) **1.** youngest; last born. **3.** another name for Agni.

Yavīyas (S) (M) **1.** younger. **3.** a preceptor.

Yavya (S) (M) **1.** a stock of barley and fruit. **3.** a family of ṛṣis.

Yayāti (S) (M) **1.** wanderer; traveller; mover; goer. **3.** a monarch of the lunar race who was the son of Nahuṣa, from his 2 wives came the 2 lines of the lunar race, Yadu the son of Devayānī and Purū of Śarmiṣṭhā, Yayāti is also represented as an author of *Ṛg Veda* (ix) and a member of Yama's court.

Yayin (S) (M) **1.** quick; hastening. **3.** another name for Śiva.

Yayu (S) (M) **1.** going; moving; swift. **3.** a horse of the moon.

Yodhaka (S) (M) fighter; soldier.

Yodheya (S) (M) warrior; combatant.

Yodhin (S) (M) fighter; warrior; soldier; conqueror.

Yoga (S) (M) **1.** the act of harnessing; yoke; application; means; charm; remedy; union; junction; connection; arrangement; fitness; zeal; concentration; meditation; devotion. **2.** abstract meditation; practised as a philosophy taught by Pātañjali. **3.** yoga personified as a son of Dharma and Kriyā or Śraddhā and the grandson of Manu Svāyambhuva (*Bhāgavata*).

Yogaćakṣus (S) (M) **1.** one whose eye is contemplation. **3.** another name for Brahmā.

Yogaćandra (S) (M) moon among zealots.

Yogaćara (S) (M) **1.** one who performs meditation. **3.** another name for Hanumān.

Yogadeva (S) (M) **1.** lord of meditation. **3.** a Jaina author (*J. Literature*).

Yogaja (S) (M) arising from meditation.

Yogāmbara (S) (M) **1.** ever in meditation; clad in meditation. **3.** a Buddhist deity.

Yogānanda (S) (M) delighting in meditation.

Yoganātha (S) (M) **1.** lord of yoga. **3.** another name for Śiva.

Yoganidrālu (S) (M) **1.** in the sleep of meditation. **3.** another name for Visnu.

Yoganilaya (S) (M) **1.** in impenetrable meditation. **3.** another name for Śiva.

Yogapāraṁga (S) (M) **1.** expert in yoga. **3.** another name for Śiva.

Yogapati (S) (M) **1.** lord of yoga. **3.** another name for Viṣṇu.

Yogarāja (S) (M) lord of medicines; lord of meditation.

Yogaraṅga (S) (M) the Sweet Orange tree (*Citrus aurantium*).

Yogātman (S) (M) one whose essence is yoga.

Yogayuj (S) (M) one who has given himself to yoga.

Yogendra (S) (M) **1.** lord of yoga. **3.** another name for Śiva.

Yogeśa (S) (M) **1.** lord of yoga. **3.** the city of Brahmā; another name for Yājñavalkya and Śiva.

Yogeśanandana (S) (M) **1.** son of the lord of yoga. **3.** another name for Kārttikeya.

Yogeśvara (S) (M) **1.** master of yoga. **2.** deity; object of devout contemplation. **3.** a son of Devahotra (*Bh. Purāṇa*); another name for Kṛṣṇa and Yajñavalkya.

Yogī (S) (M) **1.** contemplative saint; devout; ascetic. **3.** a Buddha; another name for Yājñavalkya, Arjuna, Viṣṇu and Śiva.

Yogīśa (S) (M) **1.** lord of yogis. **3.** another name for Kṛṣṇa.

Yojaka (S) (M) **1.** yoker; employer; user; arranger. **3.** another name for Agni.

Yojanabāhu (S) (M) **1.** with long arms like a Yojana. **3.** another name for Rāvaṇa.

Yoktṛ (S) (M) one who excites or rouses; one who yokes; charioteer.

Yūpaketana (S) (M) **1.** flag of victory. **3.** another name for Bhūriśravas.

Yūpaketu (S) (M) **1.** flag of victory. **3.** another name for Bhūriśravas.

Yoṭaka (S) (M) a combination of stars; a constellation.

Yotimastaka (S) (M) **1.** with a bright forehead. **3.** a king who was asked by the Pāṇḍavas to take part in the great war (*M. Bh.*).

Yotu (S) (M) cleaning; purifying.

Yuddha (S) (M) **1.** fought; conquered; subdued. **3.** a son of Ugrasena (*V. Purāṇa*).

Yuddhāćārya (S) (M) one who teaches the art of war.

Yuddhakīrti (S) (M) **1.** famous in war. **3.** a pupil of Śankarāćārya.

Yuddhamuṣṭi (S) (M) **1.** one who fights with his fists. **3.** a son of Ugrasena (*V. Purāna*).

Yuddhānivartin (S) (M) heroic; valiant.

Yuddhapravīṇa (S) (M) skilled in war.

Yuddharaṅga (S) (M) **1.** one whose arena is battle; battlefield. **3.** another name for Kārttikeya.

Yuddhavīra (S) (M) hero; warrior.

Yudhājit (S) (M) **1.** victorious in battle. **3.** a son of Kroṣṭu and Mādrī (*H. Purāṇa*); a son of Vṛṣṇi (*V. Purāṇa*); a king of Ujjayinī; a Kekaya king who was the brother of Kaikeyī, Daśaratha's wife, and the uncle of Bharata (*V. Rāmāyana*); a king of Avantī who was the brother of Śatrujita; a Yādava king who was the son of Pṛthvī and Anamitra (*P. Purāṇa*).

Yudhāmanyu (S) (M) **1.** young warrior. **3.** a Pāñćāla warrior who fought the war on the side of the Pāṇḍavas (*M. Bh.*).

Yudhaśālin (S) (M) warlike; valiant.

Yudhiṣṭhira (S) (M) **1.** firm or steady in battle. **3.** the eldest son of the 5 sons of Paṇḍu, he was actually the child of Kuntī and Dharma, he succeeded Paṇḍu as king, first reigning over Indraprastha and then Hastināpura, he was known for his unswerving dedication to truth (*M. Bh.*); a son of Kṛṣṇa. (*H. Purāṇa*).

Yudhma (S) (M) warrior; hero; battle; arrow; bow.

Yudhvan (S) (M) martial; warrior.

Yugādhyakṣa (S) (M) **1.** superintendant of a yuga or cycle of time. **3.** another name for Śiva.

Yugadikrt (S) (M) **1.** creator of the beginning of the world. **3.** another name for Śiva.

Yugandhara (S) (M) **1.** bearing the yoke; the pole of a carriage; bearer of an era; strongest person of the era. **3.** a warrior who fought on the side of the Pāṇḍavas (*H. Purāna*); a mountain (*M. Bh.*).

Yugapa (S) (M) **1.** best of the era. **3.** a gandharva (*M. Bh.*).

Yugavāha (S) (M) one who directs the age.

Yugavarta (S) (M) one who changes the eras.

Yugma (S) (M) **1.** even; twins. **2.** the zodiac sign of Gemini.

Yujya (S) (M) connected; related; allied; equal in power; proper; capable.

Yukta (S) (M) **1.** yoked; absorbed; attentive; skilful; clever; fit; prosperous. **3.** a son of Manu Raivata (*H. Purāṇa*); a ṛṣi under Manu Bhautya.

Yuktāśva (S) (M) **1.** with yoked horses. **2.** having wealth. **3.** a sage and scholar in the Vedas.

Yuktimat (S) (M) ingenious; clever; inventive.

Yuñjāna (S) (M) uniting; suitable; proper; successful; prosperous.

Yūpākṣa (S) (M) **1.** the eye of victory. **3.** a military commander of Rāvana who was killed by Hanumān; a rākṣasa killed by the monkey Mainda (*V. Rāmāyaṇa*).

Yutajit (S) (M) **1.** accompanied by victory; victorious. **3.** a son of King Bhoja of the Yadu clan (*Bhāgavata*).

Yūthanātha (S) (M) the chief of a troop.

Yuvana (S) (M) **1.** young; strong; healthy. **3.** another name for the moon.

Yuvanāśva (S) (M) **1.** young horse. **3.** a king of the Ikṣvāku dynasty who was the son of Prasenajit and the father of Māndhātā (*M. Bh.*); another king of the Ikṣvāku dynasty who was the son of Adri and the father of King Śrāva; a son of Vṛṣadarbha; an Ikṣvāku king who was the grandson of Māndhātā.

Yuvarāja (S) (M) young king; crown prince.

Yuyudhāna (S) (M) **1.** Kṣatriya; warrior. **3.** a son of Sātyaka and an ally of the Pāṇḍavas (*M. Bh.*); a king of Mithila (*Bh. Purāṇa*); another name for Indra.

Yuyudhi (S) (M) warlike; martial.

Yuyutsu (S) (M) **1.** combative; pugnacious. **3.** a son of Dhṛtarāṣṭra by a Vaiśya woman who joined the Pāṇḍavas, he was an honest and mighty hero; a son of Dhṛtarāṣṭra and Gāndhārī (*M. Bh.*).

List of the Sources

Āśvālayana Gṛhyasūtra	–	*Ā. Gṛhyasūtra*
Āpasthambha Srantasūtra	–	*Ā. Śrantasūtra*
Ātma Prabodha	–	*A. Prabodha*
Āryabhaṭīya	–	*Āryabhṭīya*
Bāla Bhārata	–	*B. Bhārata*
Buddhist Jātakas	–	*B. Jātakas*
Bhartṛhari Śatakam	–	*B. Śatakam*
Devi Bhāgavata	–	*D. Bhāgavata*
Devi Bhāgvata Purāna	–	*D. Bh. Purāna*
Mahādevi Bhāgavata	–	*M. Bhāgavata*
Aitareya Brāhmaṇa	–	*A. Brāhmaṇa*
Kauśītaki Brāhmaṇa	–	*K. Brāhmaṇa*
Pañćavimśa Brāhmaṇa	–	*P. Brāhmaṇa*
Śatapatha Brāhmaṇa	–	*Ś. Brāhmaṇa*
Tāṇḍya Brāhmaṇa	–	*Tā. Brāhmaṇa*
Vanśa Brāhmaṇa	–	*V. Brāhmaṇa*
Bhāva Prakāśa	–	*B. Prakāśa*
Ćaitya Vandana	–	*Ć. Vandana*
Ćandrāloka	–	*Ćandraloka*
Naisadha Ćarita	–	*N. Ćarita*
Mahāvīra Ćarita	–	*M. Ćarita*
Buddha Ćarita	–	*B. Ćarita*
Bhadrabāhu Ćarita	–	*Bha. Ćarita*
Vīra Ćarita	–	*V. Ćarita*
Chandraswamy Ćarita	–	*Ć. Ćarita*
Divyāvadāna	–	*Divyāvadāna*
Datta Ćandrikā	–	*D. Ćandrikā*
Durgāsaptaśati	–	*D. Saptaśati*
Gaṇaratna Mahodadhi	–	*G. Mahodadhi*
Gautama's Dharmaśāstra	–	*G's. Dharmaśāstra*
Gobhila's Śraddhā Kalpa	–	*G's Ś. Kalpa*
Gṛhya Samigraha	–	*G. Samigraha*
Gṛhya Sūtra	–	*G. Sūtra*
Hitopadeśa	–	*Hitopadeśa*
Hemendrīya Ćaturvarga Ćintāmaṇi	–	*H.Ć. Ćintāmaṇi*

Īśa Tantra	–	*Ī. Tantra*
Jaimini Aśvamedha	–	*J. Aśvamedha*
Jaimuni Bhārata	–	*J. Bhārata*
Jātākam	–	*Jātakam*
Jaina Sāhitya	–	*J. Literature*
Kāvya Prakāśa	–	*K. Prakāśa*
Kalpa Sūtra	–	*K. Sūtra*
Kālidasa Granthāvali	–	*K. Granthāvali*
Kaṇvādi	–	*Kaṇvādi*
Kādambari	–	*Kādambari*
Kathārṇava	–	*Kathārṇava*
Kharatara Gaccha	–	*K. Gaccha*
Kathāsaritasāgara	–	*K. Sāgara*
Karaṇḍvyūha	–	*K. Vyūha*
Amar Koṣa	–	*A. Koṣa*
Hatayudha Koṣa	–	*H. Koṣa*
Hemaćandra Koṣa	–	*He. Koṣa*
Jainendra Siddhānta Koṣa	–	*J. S. Koṣa*
Lalita Vistara	–	*L. Vistara*
Buddha Sāhitya	–	*B. Literature*
Maskāra Stava	–	*M. Stava*
Mṛcchakaṭikam	–	*M. Katikam*
Manu Smṛti	–	*M. Smṛti*
Mahābhārata	–	*M. Bh*
Naćiketupākhyana	–	*N. Pākhyāna*
Nirukta	–	*Nirukta*
Nalopākhyāna	–	*Nalopākhyāna*
Nīti Śataka	–	*N. Śataka*
Pañćdaṇḍa Ćatraprabandha	–	*P. Ćatraprabandha*
Agni Purāṇa	–	*A. Purāṇa*
Bhāgvata Purāṇa	–	*Bhā. Purāṇa*
Bhaviṣya Purāṇa	–	*Bh. Purāṇa*
Bhīṣma Purāṇa	–	*Bhī. Purāṇa*
Brahmāṇḍa Purāṇa	–	*Br. Purāṇa*
Brahmavaivarta Purāṇa	–	*Brah. Purāṇa*

Brahma Purāṇa	–	*Brahma Purāṇa*
Devī Purāṇa	–	*D. Purāṇa*
Gaṇeśạ Purāṇa	–	*G. Purāṇa*
Garuḍa Purāṇa	–	*Gar. Purāṇa*
Harivaṁśa Purāṇa	–	*H. Purāṇa*
Harivaṅśa Purāṇa	–	*H. Purāṇa*
Kalkī Purāṇa	–	*K. Purāṇa*
Liṅga Purāṇa	–	*L. Purāṇa*
Matsya Purāṇa	–	*M. Purāṇa*
Mārkaṇḍeya Purāṇa	–	*Mā. Purāṇa*
Nārada Purāṇa	–	*N. Purāṇa*
Nahni Purāṇa	–	*Nah. Purāṇa*
Padma Purāṇa	–	*P. Purāṇa*
Śiva Purāṇa	–	*Ś. Purāṇa*
Skanda Purāṇa	–	*Sk. Purāṇa*
Subāhu Purāṇa	–	*Su. Purāṇa*
Vasiṣṭha Purāṇa	–	*V. Purāṇa*
Viṣṇu Purāṇa	–	*V. Purāṇa*
Vāyu Purāṇa	–	*Vā. Purāṇa*
Vāmana Purāṇa	–	*Vam. Purāṇa*
Ṿarāha Purāṇa	–	*Var. Purāṇa*
Varuṇa Purāṇa	–	*Varuṇa Purāṇa*
Purāṇas	–	*Purāṇas*
Prabhodha Ćandrodaya	–	*P. Ćandrodaya*
Pāṇinī	–	*Pāṇinī.*
Pañćatantra	–	*Pañćatantra*
Pārśavanatha Ćaritra	–	*P. Ćaritra*
Ānanda Rāmāyaṇa	–	*A. Rāmāyaṇa*
Bāla Rāmāyaṇa	–	*B. Rāmāyaṇa*
Kamba Rāmāyaṇa	–	*K. Rāmāyaṇa*
Uttar Rāmāyaṇa	–	*U. Rāmāyaṇa*
Vālmīki Rāmāyaṇa	–	*V. Rāmāyaṇa*
Rāja Taraṅgiṇī	–	*R. Taraṅgiṇī*
Rasa Gaṅgādhara	–	*R. Gaṅgādhara*
Raghuvanśa	–	*Raghuvanśa*
Ṛg Veda Anukramaṇikā	–	*R. Anukramaṇikā*
Āpastamba Samhitā	–	*Ā. Samhitā*
Pārāśara Samhitā	–	*P. Samhitā*
Suśruta Samhita	–	*S. Samhitā*

Taittirīya Samhita	–	*T. Samhitā*
Vājasaneyī Samhita	–	*V. Samhitā*
Varāhamihira's Bṛhat Samhitā	–	*V's B. Samhitā*
Yajurveda Samhitā	–	*Y. Samhitā*
Śiva Rāja Vijaya	–	*Ś R. Vijaya*
Suvarṇa Prābhāsa	–	*S. Prābhāsa*
Saddharma Puṇḍarīkā	–	*S. Puṇḍarīkā*
Sinhāsanadvātrinśikā	–	*S. Dvātrinśikā*
Śatruñjaya Mahātmya	–	*Ś. Mahātmya*
Śaṅkaravijaya	–	*Ś. Vijaya*
Svapna Vāsavadattam	–	*S. Vāsavadattam*
Sarvadarśana Saṁgraha	–	*S. Saṁgraha*
Sānkhyayan Śrauta Sūtra	–	*S. Ś. Sūtra*
Tantra Śāstra	–	*T. Śāstra*
Dharma Śāstra	–	*D. Śāstra*
Jyotiṣa Śāstra	–	*J. Śāstra*
Tīrthyāditya	–	*Tīrthyāditya*
Taittirīya Prātiśākhya	–	*T. Prātiśākhya*
Taittirīya Āraṇyaka	–	*T. Āraṇyaka*
Bṛhadāraṇyaka Upaniṣad	–	*Br. Upaniṣad*
Ćhandogya Upaniṣad	–	*Ć. Upaniṣad*
Kaṭhopaniṣad	–	*K. Upaniṣad*
Kauśitaki Upaniṣad	–	*Kau. Upaniṣad*
Maitreya Upaniṣad	–	*M. Upaniṣad*
Muṇḍaka Upaniṣad	–	*Mu. Upaniṣad*
Rāmatapanīya Upaniṣad	–	*Rā. Upaniṣad*
Vetāla Pañćavinśatikā	–	*V. Pañćavinśatikā*
Vikramorvaśiyam	–	*Vikramorvaśīyam*
Vićārāmṛta Saṁgraha	–	*V. Saṁgraha*
Vikramāṅka Deva Ćaritam	–	*V.D. Ćaritam*
Atharva Veda	–	*A. Veda*
Ṛg Veda	–	*Ṛg. Veda*
Sāma Veda	–	*S. Veda*
Yajur Veda	–	*Y. Veda*
Yogavāsiṣṭha	–	*Yogavāsiṣṭha*